The Psychology of
Interrogations and Confessions

Wiley Series in
The Psychology of Crime, Policing and Law

Series Editors

Graham Davies and **Ray Bull**
University of Leicester, UK   *University of Portsmouth, UK*

The Wiley series in the Psychology of Crime, Policing and Law publishes concise and integrative reviews on important emerging areas of contemporary research. The purpose of the series is not merely to present research findings in a clear and readable form, but also to bring out their implications for both practice and policy. In this way, it is hoped the series will not only be useful to psychologists but also to all those concerned with crime detection and prevention, policing, and the judicial process. Current titles of interest in the series include

Offender Profiling: Theory, Research and Practice
Edited by Janet L. Jackson and Debra A. Bekerian

Psychology, Law and Eyewitness Testimony
Peter B. Ainsworth

Detecting Lies and Deceit: The Psychology of Lying and the Implications for Professional Practice
Aldert Vrij

Children's Testimony: A Handbook of Psychological Research and Forensic Practice
Edited by Helen L. Westcott, Graham M. Davies and Ray H. C. Bull

Stalking and Psychosexual Obsession: Psychological Perspectives for Prevention, Policing and Treatment
Edited by Julian Boon and Lorraine Sheridan

The Psychology of Interrogations and Confessions: A Handbook
Gisli H. Gudjonsson

The Psychology of Interrogations and Confessions

A Handbook

Gisli H. Gudjonsson
Institute of Psychiatry, King's College, London, UK

WILEY

Copyright © 2003 John Wiley & Sons, Ltd,
The Atrium, Southern Gate, Chichester,
West Sussex PO19 8SQ, England

Telephone (+44) 1243 779777

Email (for orders and customer service enquiries): cs-books@wiley.co.uk
Visit our Home Page on www.wileyeurope.com or www.wiley.com

Reprinted August 2003, April 2005

All Rights Reserved. No part of this publication may be reproduced, stored in a retrieval system or transmitted in any form or by any means, electronic, mechanical, photocopying, recording, scanning or otherwise, except under the terms of the Copyright, Designs and Patents Act 1988 or under the terms of a licence issued by the Copyright Licensing Agency Ltd, 90 Tottenham Court Road, London W1T 4LP, UK, without the permission in writing of the Publisher. Requests to the Publisher should be addressed to the Permissions Department, John Wiley & Sons Ltd, The Atrium, Southern Gate, Chichester, West Sussex PO19 8SQ, England, or emailed to permreq@wiley.co.uk, or faxed to (+44) 1243 770571.

This publication is designed to provide accurate and authoritative information in regard to the subject matter covered. It is sold on the understanding that the Publisher is not engaged in rendering professional services. If professional advice or other expert assistance is required, the services of a competent professional should be sought.

Other Wiley Editorial Offices

John Wiley & Sons Inc., 111 River Street, Hoboken, NJ 07030, USA

Jossey-Bass, 989 Market Street, San Francisco, CA 94103-1741, USA

Wiley-VCH Verlag GmbH, Boschstr. 12, D-69469 Weinheim, Germany

John Wiley & Sons Australia Ltd, 33 Park Road, Milton, Queensland 4064, Australia

John Wiley & Sons (Asia) Pte Ltd, 2 Clementi Loop #02-01, Jin Xing Distripark, Singapore 129809

John Wiley & Sons Canada Ltd, 22 Worcester Road, Etobicoke, Ontario, Canada M9W 1L1

Library of Congress Cataloging-in-Publication Data

Gudjonsson, Gisli H.
    The psychology of interrogations and confessions : a handbook / Gisli H. Gudjonsson.
      p. cm.—(Wiley series in the psychology of crime, policing and law)
    Includes bibliographical references and index.
    ISBN 0-471-49136-5—ISBN 0-470-84461-2 (pbk. : alk. paper)
      1. Police questioning—Psychological aspects.   2. Confession (Law)—Psychological aspects.
    3. Confession (Law)—Great Britain.   4. Confession (Law)—United States.   I. Title.   II. Wiley series in psychology of crime, policing, and law.

HV8073 .G889   2003
363.2'54—dc21
                                                2002151145

British Library Cataloguing in Publication Data

A catalogue record for this book is available from the British Library

ISBN 10: 0-471-49136-5 (CB)   ISBN 13: 978-0-471-49136-1

ISBN 10: 0-470-84461-2 (PB)   ISBN 13: 978-0-470-84461-8

Typeset in 10/12pt Century Schoolbook by TechBooks, New Delhi, India
Printed and bound in Great Britain by TJ International Ltd, Padstow, Cornwall
This book is printed on acid-free paper responsibly manufactured from sustainable forestry in which at least two trees are planted for each one used for paper production.

þora Hannesdottir (b. 2.6.1918, d. 6.2.2000).

Contents

About the Author xiii

Series Preface xv

Preface xvii

Acknowledgements ix

   Introduction 1

PART I   INTERROGATIONS AND CONFESSIONS

  1. Interrogation Tactics and Techniques 7
     Police Training Manuals 7
     The Reid Technique 10
     The Format and Recording of the Confession 21
     The Context of the Interrogation 24
     American Research on Interrogation 31
     How Things Can Go Wrong During Interrogation 34
     Conclusions 36

  2. Interrogation in Britain 38
     Irving's Studies 39
     Softley's Study 43
     Walsh's Study 43
     Research at the University of Kent 44
     Baldwin's Study 48
     British Training Manuals 51
     Conclusions 55

  3. Persons at Risk During Interviews in Police Custody: the Royal
     Commission Studies 57
     The 1993 Royal Commission Study by Gudjonsson and Colleagues 58
     Who Confesses? 69
     Detainees' Legal Rights 71

General Conclusions	73
4. The Identification and Measurement of 'Oppressive' Police Interviewing Tactics in Britain.	75
John Pearse and Gisli H. Gudjonsson	
Background to the Research	75
The Cases Analysed	77
Methodology	79
Interview Tactics	80
Suspects' Responses	83
Methodological Issues	85
Statistical Procedures	86
Application of the Framework to Individual Cases	87
The Heron Murder Case	96
The Miller Murder Case	106
Court Outcome	112
Conclusions	114
5. Why do Suspects Confess? Theories	115
Factors Inhibiting Confession	115
Theoretical Models of Confession	117
Conclusions	128
6. Why do Suspects Confess? Empirical Findings	130
How Important are Confessions?	130
How Commonly do Suspects Confess?	133
Factors Associated with Admissions and Denials	140
Self-Report Studies into Why Suspects Confess	151
Conclusions	156
7. Miscarriages of Justice and False Confessions	158
Miscarriages of Justice	158
Studies of Miscarriages of Justice	159
The Leo–Ofshe Study	164
Some Notorious British Cases	166
Conclusions	172
8. The Psychology of False Confession: Research and Theoretical Issues	173
Definitions of False Confession	174
The Frequency of False Confessions	174
False, Retracted and Disputed Confessions	178
The Innocent Pleading Guilty	184
The Broader Context of False Confessions	186
The Causes of False Confessions	193
Theoretical Implications of the Different Types of False Confession	197

The Ofshe–Leo Model of Confessions	203
Differences between True and False Confessions	208
A Proposed Modified Framework	211
Recovered Memory and False Confession	212
Conclusions	215

9. **The Psychology of False Confession: Case Examples** — 217

Voluntary False Confessions	218
Pressured–Compliant False Confessions	224
Pressured–Internalized False Confessions	233
Conclusions	242

PART II LEGAL AND PSYCHOLOGICAL ASPECTS

10. **The English Law on Confessions** — 247

The Admissibility and Reliability of Confession Evidence	248
The Voire Dire	258
Issues Affecting Vulnerable Defendants	259
The Admissibility of Expert Evidence	275
Conclusions	281

11. **The American Law on Confessions** — 283
    Gisli H. Gudjonsson and Lorca Morello

The Basic Law of Confessions	283
Voluntariness and Mentally Vulnerable Suspects	288
Challenging a Confession in Court	293
Differences between English and American Law and Practice	304
Conclusions	306

12. **The Psychological Assessment** — 308

The Assessment Framework	309
Psychological Vulnerabilities	316
Learning Disability as a Vulnerability	320
The Court Report and Oral Evidence	327
Conclusions	330

13. **Suggestibility: Historical and Theoretical Aspects** — 332

Theoretical Approaches	334
Some Characteristics of Suggestion and Suggestibility	335
Brief Historical Background to Suggestibility	336
The Classification of Suggestibility	338
Theories of Suggestibility	340
Reinforcement and Suggestibility	343
Suggestibility: a State or a Trait?	343
Definition of Interrogative Suggestibility	344
The Gudjonsson–Clark Theoretical Model	347
Implications of the Model and Hypotheses	352

External Evaluation of the Model	353
Conclusions	358

14. Interrogative Suggestibility: Empirical Findings — 360

The Gudjonsson Suggestibility Scales	361
Suggestibility and Hypnotic Susceptibility	368
Compliance	370
Acquiescence	376
Correlations between Suggestibility, Compliance and Acquiescence	378
Suggestibility and Gender	379
Suggestibility and Ethnic Background	380
Suggestibility and Age	380
Suggestibility and Intelligence	381
Suggestibility and Memory	384
Suggestibility and Anxiety	385
Suggestibility and Impulsivity	388
Suggestibility and the MMPI-2	389
Suggestibility and Sleep Deprivation	389
Suggestibility: Dissociation and Fantasy Proneness	390
Suggestibility and Instructional Manipulation	391
Suggestibility and the Experimenter Effect	392
Suggestibility and Social Desirability	394
Suggestibility and Coping Strategies	395
Suggestibility and Assertiveness	396
Suggestibility and Self-Esteem	396
Suggestibility and Locus of Control	398
Suggestibility and Field Dependence	399
Suspiciousness and Anger	400
Suggestibility and Test Setting	402
Suggestibility and Previous Convictions	403
Police Interviewing and Suggestibility	403
Resisters and Alleged False Confessors	404
Suggestibility and False Confessions	407
Suggestibility and Eyewitness Testimony	410
Suggestibility and Recovered Memory	411
Conclusions	412

15. The Effects of Drugs and Alcohol Upon the Reliability of Testimony — 415

The Extent of the Problem	416
Theoretical Perspectives	418
The Effects of Intoxication and Withdrawal	421
The Effects of Alcohol Withdrawal on Interrogative Suggestibility	428
False Confessions to Murder by a Heroin Addict	430
Conclusions	432

PART III BRITISH COURT OF APPEAL CASES

16. The Court of Appeal — 437

The Beginning of Expert Psychological Testimony	440
Conclusions	441

17. The 'Guildford Four' and the 'Birmingham Six'. 445
Gisli H. Gudjonsson and J. A. C. MacKeith

The Guildford Four	445
The Birmingham Six	452
Conclusions	456

18. Psychological Vulnerability 458

Engin Raghip—The Beginning: Landmark Decision for Psychology	458
Jacqueline Fletcher—Unidentified Borderline Intelligence	468
Judith Ward—Personality Disorder	470
David MacKenzie—Inability to Distinguish Facts from Fantasy	472
Idris Ali—Pathological Lying	473
George Long—Clinical Depression	476
Patrick Kane—Anxiety and Compliance	479
Andrew Evans—Misdiagnosed Psychogenic Amnesia	482
John Roberts—Abnormal Compliance	492
Ashley King—Abnormal Suggestibility and Compliance	493
Darren Hall—Disorder in the Absence of a Psychiatric Diagnosis	495
Ian Hay Gordon—Exploitation of Sexuality	499
Peter Fell—Poor Self-Esteem	506
Conclusions	512

19. Police Impropriety 514

Stephen Miller	515
Alfred Allen (the 'UDR Four')	517
The Carl Bridgewater Case	519
Derek Bentley	520
Conclusions	522

20. Misleading Special Knowledge 523

Stefan Kiszko	523
The Darvell Brothers	530
Donald Pendleton	533
Conclusions	537

PART IV FOREIGN CASES OF DISPUTED CONFESSIONS

21. Four High Profile American Cases 541

Waneta Hoyt	541
Joe Giarratano	550

Henry Lee Lucas	554
John Wille	563
General Conclusions	572
22. Canadian and Israeli Cases	**573**
A Canadian Case of Non-Custodial Interrogation	573
An Israeli Terrorist Case	582
General Conclusions	589
23. Murder in Norway: a False Belief Leading to a False Confession	**590**
Background to the Case	590
Pre-Trial (1997) Psychological Evaluation	594
The First Trial	595
The Psychological Evaluation Prior to the Appeal	596
Interviews with Informants	602
Mr A's Strengths and Vulnerabilities	605
The Interrogation and Confinement	606
Repression and Psychogenic Amnesia	608
The Appeal	609
Conclusions	611
Conclusions	615
General Comments and Conclusions	615
Interrogation	619
Psychological Vulnerability	621
True Confessions	622
Retracted and False Confessions	623
Appendix	628
References	631
Author Index	663
Subject Index	672

About the Author

Gisli Gudjonsson is a Professor of Forensic Psychology at the Institute of Psychiatry, King's College, London, and Head of the Forensic Psychology Services at the Maudsley Hospital. He is a Fellow of the British Psychological Society and an Honorary Fellow of the Icelandic Psychological Society. In 2001 he was awarded an Honorary Doctorate in Medicine from the University of Iceland in recognition for his research in the field of forensic psychiatry and psychology. Gisli has published extensively in the areas of psychological vulnerability, false confession and police interviewing. He pioneered the empirical measurement of suggestibility and provided expert evaluation in a number of high profile cases, including those of the Guildford Four, the Birmingham Six, the Tottenham Three, the Cardiff Three, Jill Dando murder case, Kenneth Erskine (the 'Stockwell strangler'), Derek Bentley, the UDR Four and 'IRA funeral murders' cases (both in Northern Ireland), Henry Lee Lucas and John Wille (USA), and the Birgitte Tengs and Orderud cases (Norway). He acts as a consultant on cases both for prosecution and defence.

Gisli is the author of *The Psychology of Interrogations, Confessions and Testimony* (John Wiley & Sons, 1992), *The Gudjonsson Suggestibility Scales Manual* (Psychology Press, 1997), *Forensic Psychology: A Guide to Practice* (Routledge, 1998, jointly written with Lionel Haward), and *The Causes and Cures of Criminality* (Plenum Press, 1989, jointly written with Hans Eysenck). He is the co-editor-in-chief of *Personality and Individual Differences*.

Series Preface

The Wiley Series in the Psychology of Crime, Policing and Law publishes single author and edited reviews of emerging areas of contemporary research. The purpose of this series is not merely to present research findings in a clear and readable form, but also to bring out their implications for both practice and policy. The series will be useful not only to psychologists, but also to all those concerned with crime detection and prevention, policing and the judicial process.

The first book in this series was *The Psychology of Interrogations, Confessions and Testimony* by Gisli Gudjonsson, published in 1992. This seminal work was recognized quickly as a modern classic of the forensic psychology literature, translated into a number of foreign languages and frequently cited, in both learned papers and the courts of law. As the title implied, the book dealt broadly with the issues surrounding the interrogation of both witnesses and suspects and the real dangers of false confession. Professor Gudjonsson's new book, *The Psychology of Interrogations and Confessions: A Handbook* deals specifically with the area which is now synonymous with his name; it summarizes much new research and describes many cases of disputed or false confessions with which he has been associated.

Much of the new research has involved the Gudjonsson Suggestibility Scales (GSSs), a measure of suggestibility and compliance, which can be administered to persons where the issue of false confession arises. Equally importantly, expert testimony from Professor Gudjonsson, based on the results of these tests, his observations of the suspect's behaviour and the circumstances leading up to a confession have been admitted as evidence in high-profile criminal cases in the United Kingdom, the United States and continental Europe. The admission of such evidence in the English courts is a major achievement for forensic psychology in general and Professor Gudjonsson in particular. For a long time, the courts have clung to the judgment, enunciated in *R. v. Turner* (1975), that implied that the courts had no reason to listen to expert testimony from psychologists or psychiatrists on such matters as these were well within the common experience of jury members. It was only when judges were confronted with unmistakable instances of apparently normal people who, when confined to a police station for questioning for just a few hours, could confess fulsomely to crimes they could not have committed, that the united front against such expert evidence began to bend and crack. In the process, miscarriages of justice, some of them dating back decades, were finally redressed, thanks in major part to the insights of Professor Gudjonsson.

Professor Gudjonsson's book is divided into four sections. Part I summarizes much research and theory on interrogation and confession and notably in a chapter co-authored with John Pearse, an experienced police officer, illustrates how far the British police have come in their recognition of the impact of oppressive interviewing practices on false and misleading confessions. Part II summarizes much work on the GSS, which has been widely taken up by researchers in several countries, and summarizes the legal position on the admissibility of confession evidence in Britain and the United States. Part III covers appeal court cases in the United Kingdom and reveals an impressive readiness on the part of the courts in recent years to listen to new psychological evidence and to attempt to redress in part the grievances of the falsely convicted. Part IV follows the judicial trail to the United States, Canada and Norway and uncovers striking parallels between the interrogation processes leading to false confessions in the UK and those perpetrated elsewhere. However, there appears to be a disturbing lack of readiness on the part of many of these judiciaries to address these issues and provide legal remedies.

The Psychology of Interrogations and Confessions: A Handbook will be invaluable to all psychologists who work with offenders and the courts and provides an object lesson in how psychologists, through their writings and research, can have a real and profound influence on public policy. It will also be of interest to lawyers and lay persons, who will find, in the striking case material and accessible descriptions of research, reason enough as to how our judicial system can err.

GRAHAM DAVIES
University of Leicester

March 2002

Preface

The Psychology of Interrogations, Confessions and Testimony was published in 1992 and has been reprinted on several occasions. It was extensively reviewed in the legal, psychological, psychiatric, and medical literature. Its publication brought the issue of false confessions from a scientific perspective to the attention of the legal, psychological and psychiatric professions. It provided a much-needed comprehensive and authoritative text for practitioners, researchers and academics. The book had a major impact in Britain and abroad, which can be seen from numerous legal judgments.

Reviewers' comments on the original book provided invaluable information about how the book might be improved and I have taken this seriously into consideration when writing the current book. Ronald Fisher, in *Contemporary Psychology*, pointed out that my attempt at completeness on occasions led me to describe cases and introduce material that was not central to the main focus of the book. Some other reviewers expressed similar views and suggested that I focus more exclusively on disputed confessions, and provide a more extensive analysis of how expert opinion in this area has affected the judicial process. This is what I have attempted to do in the current book. In addition, since the publication of the original book, the number of cases of disputed confessions that I have assessed has more than doubled and I have testified in well over 100 criminal cases where confession evidence was disputed, including many high profile murder cases in the appellant courts in Britain and abroad. All the important cases are reviewed in this book and the psychological contribution and legal implications discussed.

There has been increasing recognition in recent years that false confessions occur and no legal system should ignore the risk of false confession. In order to prevent future miscarriages of justice, complacency, lack of open-mindedness, ignorance, unwillingness to accept mistakes and judicial cover-up must be replaced by a more positive approach to a problem that will not go away unless we actively confront it. There are various steps that can be taken to reduce the risk of false confessions and prevent miscarriages of justice. These steps, including judicial, educational and psychological means, are equally applicable to legal systems of Britain, USA, Australia and on the continent of Europe.

When I planned this book it was originally commissioned by Wiley as a second edition of my previous book. As I began to write however, it became evident that the field had expanded dramatically and this development has continued as the book has developed. As a result, it is largely a new book rather than a second edition of the previous one. Some themes have had to be omitted from the current book to accommodate new material. This includes some of the basic principles and theory of interviewing, child witnesses, psychological techniques for enhancing memory retrieval and evaluating testimony and documents. There are now other books available that make these chapters unnecessary and these will be indicated in the text, as appropriate.

Accompanying new and important court case material, and important legal changes since the original book, there has been considerably more research into police interrogation tactics, psychological vulnerabilities and false confessions. All the material that remains from the original book has been re-written and up-dated to accommodate these new findings. The current book is larger and more substantial than the original and the focus more international.

GISLI H. GUDJONSSON

Acknowledgements

I am grateful to Professor Graham Davies, the Series Editor, and to my wife, Julia, for their continued encouragement and support throughout my writing this book. They both read and commented on drafts of the individual chapters. Other persons who provided helpful comments on one or more of the individual draft chapters are Professor Ursula Bentele, Sir Louis Blom-Cooper Ian Donaldson QC, Richard Joselson, Denny LeBoeuf, Professor Richard Leo, Dr James MacKeith, Paula Montonye, Lorca Morello, Dr John Pearse, Susan Rutter, John Wagstaff and Dr Susan Young. I am grateful to Sarah Medford for her proofreading of the draft manuscript. Thanks also goes to the people who consented to my writing up their cases. Lastly, I am indebted to John Wiley & Sons for allowing me to produce a manuscript that is longer than originally contracted for, so that detailed case illustrations and important recent legal judgments could be provided.

Introduction

On a Saturday morning in the early part of 1987 a 17-year-old youth was arrested and taken to a police station for questioning. A few hours later he had confessed in great detail as to how he had sexually molested and then murdered two elderly women before leaving their house. The following day the youth confessed again to the murders, in the presence of a solicitor. In spite of the lack of forensic evidence to link the youth to the murders, the case against the youth was potentially strong because (a) eye witnesses who knew the youth by sight had placed him near the scene and (b) during interrogation the youth had apparently given the police detailed and specific information about the crime, which the police believed could only have been known by the murderer. On the strength of the available evidence the youth's case was referred to the Crown Court, during which time he was remanded in custody. The case had all the hallmarks of a successful crime detection, which would result in a conviction for two murders and sexual molestation.

Whilst on remand in prison the youth consistently told his solicitor and his family that he was innocent of the crimes he had been charged with. He claimed that his self-incriminating confession was due to persuasive police questioning. Matters had been made worse for the youth by the fact that during early detention in prison he had confessed to the murders to prison officers and to a fellow inmate. The youth clearly had been interviewed quite extensively and persuasively by the police officers, but he was a young man of reasonable education and without any obvious mental illness or handicap. On the face of it, the youth had confessed due to skilful interrogation carried out by experienced police officers who had reason to believe that he had committed the crimes. The murder enquiry was thus successfully conducted except for one important fact. The youth was innocent of the crimes with which he had been charged. While the youth was in prison on remand, the real murderer committed another very serious offence before being apprehended.

This brief case history, which will be discussed in more detail in Chapter 9, is one of many that are used in this book to illustrate some of the processes and mechanisms involved in producing erroneous testimony, including a false confession.

The terms 'interview' and 'interrogation', as applied to the police investigative process, imply some form of questioning, whether of a witness to a crime, a victim, a complainant or a suspect. Both are essentially a way of gathering information for use in further enquiries and perhaps judicial purposes. The term interrogation is more commonly used in the literature, and in police practice, to refer to the questioning of criminal suspects, whereas witnesses and victims are 'interviewed' (Rabon, 1992). Such a distinction is, however, quite an arbitrary one, and the term 'investigative interviewing' has been proposed to cover both the interviewing of witnesses and suspects in England. This term has now been incorporated into police training and its evaluation (Clarke & Milne, 2001; Williamson, 1994).

The purpose of the book is to examine in detail the various aspects of investigative interviewing and to highlight the factors that influence the *accuracy* and *completeness* of the information collected. The emphasis is on the application of psychological knowledge and principles to investigative interviewing and confessions. The major issue addressed is to what extent psychological knowledge and principles can assist the police, psychologists, social workers, probation officers and the legal profession, in the gathering and evaluation of confession evidence.

The book shows that during the past 20 years or so there have been major advances in psychological theory, research relevant to interrogations and confessions, the law pertaining to investigative interviewing and the admissibility of confession evidence, police training and the contribution of expert psychological and psychiatric testimony to criminal court proceedings. My previous book, *The Psychology of Interrogations, Confessions, and Testimony* (Gudjonsson, 1992a), provided a detailed discussion of scientific advances, and their implications, up to 1992. Since then, further psychological and legal developments have taken place and these are comprehensively discussed in this book. As far as children's testimony is concerned, which was discussed at some length in my previous book, the recently edited book by Westcott, Davies and Bull (2002) gives a comprehensive coverage of the recent developments in the area.

In view of the extensive amount of material presented in this book, which comprises 23 individual chapters, it is separated into four main parts. In Part I, entitled 'Interrogations and Confessions', the theoretical, research and practical aspects of interrogation and confessions are reviewed. There are nine chapters in this section of the book. The first four focus on interrogation, its contexts and the tactics used by the police in the USA and Britain. Empirical research findings are presented into interrogation tactics and the psychological vulnerability of detainees. Two chapters enquire into the reasons why suspects confess to crimes they have committed. Both theoretical perspectives and empirical evidence are presented. This part of the book concludes with three chapters where the focus is on miscarriages of justice and false confessions. Relevant research and theoretical aspects of false confessions are discussed and case examples are presented of different types of false confession.

One of the chapters in Part I, 'The identification and measurement of "oppressive" police interviewing tactics in Britain', is co-authored with Dr John Pearse, a senior police officer at New Scotland Yard, with whom I have worked jointly on cases and conducted extensive research over the past 10 years.

Part II, 'Legal and Psychological Aspects', consists of six chapters. It commences with a detailed discussion of the English and American confession law. Differences and similarities between the two legal systems and legal practice are highlighted. The chapter on the American law is co-authored with a New York attorney, Lorca Morello. After discussing the legal issues and practice there is a chapter on psychological assessment. The concepts of interrogative suggestibility, compliance and acquiescence, which have become increasingly important legally in the context of disputed confessions, are discussed in detail within the context of the relevant theoretical and empirical evidence. Part II concludes with a chapter on the effects of drugs and alcohol on the reliability of testimony. In this chapter a double murder case of the false confession of a heroin addict is presented.

In Part III, 'British Court of Appeal Cases', the role of the Court of Appeal is discussed and 22 leading disputed confession cases in England and Northern Ireland are presented and the judgments evaluated. In all but one of the cases the convictions were quashed, often on the basis of fresh psychological or psychiatric testimony. In the one unsuccessful case, the House of Lords later quashed the appellant's conviction and criticized the Court of Appeal's decision to uphold the conviction. The cases demonstrate how the Court of Appeal views confession evidence and expert testimony and how its approach to such cases has developed over the past 12 years. I have carefully traced this development and will show how high court judges have become more sophisticated in the way in which they admit and rely on expert psychological and psychiatric testimony, particularly as it relates to psychological vulnerability. The legal criteria for admitting psychological evidence have broadened considerably. The courts are no longer restricted to admitting evidence where there is mental illness or learning disability. Personality disorder is now judged as a potential psychological vulnerability relevant to the reliability of confession evidence. Furthermore, personality traits, such as suggestibility, compliance and trait anxiety, when falling outside the normal range, are now regularly admitted into evidence to challenge the admissibility and the weight of confession evidence. The impact of psychological research and expert testimony on legal changes, police practice and legal judgments is a development unparalleled in the rest of the world (Gudjonsson, 2001).

The cases of the 'Guildford Four' and the 'Birmingham Six' were the first to have a great impact on the English legal system. They brought the risk of false confession to the attention of the legal establishment and the public. The chapter on these two cases was prepared jointly with my psychiatrist colleague, Dr James MacKeith. We were both commissioned as experts to work on the cases prior to their successful appeal. We review these cases and present some of our medical and psychological findings.

Part IV, 'Foreign Cases of Disputed Confessions', provides a detailed discussion of seven high profile cases from outside Britain. The cases demonstrate how different legal systems—American, Canadian, Israeli and Norwegian—approach, view and evaluate disputed confession evidence and expert testimony. As will be seen from reading these chapters, there is much to be learned from cases in different jurisdictions. The dangers of coercive interrogation techniques, the risk of false confession and miscarriages of justice are of international importance and all judicial systems must take these seriously.

In the final chapter of the book, 'Conclusions', I draw together the main findings from the other chapters and provide a conceptual framework for future work on investigative interviewing and confessions.

This book is aimed primarily at practitioners involved with different aspects of investigative interviewing. This includes clinical psychologists and psychiatrists who have been asked by legal advocates to assist with the evaluation of the likely validity of self-incriminating statements, such as confessions. Detailed assessment techniques will be provided for this purpose, including the assessment of specific and idiosyncratic psychological states and traits. The relevant legal concepts, legal practice, Court of Appeal judgments and detailed case presentations, will be provided to assist expert witnesses in how to assess a wide range of cases of disputed confessions.

Police officers will find many parts of the book directly applicable to their investigative work. The book is not a training manual for police officers on how to interview, but it does provide police officers with a further understanding of the processes involved in producing erroneous and misleading testimony. In addition, it identifies the circumstances under which information can be collected most effectively. At a policy level, the book has major implications for police training.

Social workers and probation officers will find several of the chapters useful as they commonly have to interview and assess groups of individuals who need special care, such as persons with learning disabilities, the mentally ill, children and the sexually abused. The increased role of social workers as 'appropriate adults' during custodial interrogation in England and the criticism they have received in the past about their interviewing techniques of allegedly sexually abused children mean that this book is going to be particularly helpful for them.

The legal profession will learn from the book what kinds of contribution clinical psychologists and psychiatrists can offer to judicial proceedings. Case histories will be used to illustrate specific points throughout the book and these provide an important insight into how the judicial system deals with the problems created by disputed confessions. Many of the findings highlighted in the book provide an important insight into safeguards against false confession.

Finally, the combination of theoretical ideas, empirical findings, case histories and leading Court of Appeal judgments brings together knowledge that will also appeal to researchers and other academics. Hopefully, it will stimulate more research, both theoretical and practical, in an exciting field that is already rapidly expanding.

PART I
INTERROGATIONS AND CONFESSIONS

CHAPTER 1

Interrogation Tactics and Techniques

The purpose of this chapter is to discuss the tactics and techniques advocated by practical interrogation manuals and the context in which interrogations occur. Nearly all published interrogation manuals originate in the USA (for a review see Leo, 1992, 1994). One exception is Walkley's (1987) *Police Interrogation. A Handbook for Investigators*, which was the first manual written for British police officers. It was heavily influenced by traditional American interrogation manuals and never gained national support in Britain.

In this chapter I shall discuss the nature of these techniques, their strengths and merits, and how their use can 'go wrong'. Of course, there are a large number of interrogation manuals regularly published in the USA, with each author claiming special expertise in the field and offering advice to interrogators. It would be unrealistic to try to review all of these manuals. Undoubtedly, the most influential practical manual is the one written by Inbau, Reid and Buckley (1986). This manual has just been revised, up-dated and expanded (Inbau, Reid, Buckley & Jayne, 2001). Hundreds of thousands of investigators have received the training in their technique (Inbau *et al.*, 2001). Their book has also influenced many other authors; thus the main focus of this chapter will be on this approach and its implications. Other relevant publications will be referred to at appropriate points and issues discussed.

POLICE TRAINING MANUALS

Practical interrogation manuals are generally based on the extensive experience of interrogators and offer allegedly effective techniques for breaking down suspects' resistance. The authors of these manuals argue that most criminal suspects are reluctant to confess because of the shame associated with what they have done and the fear of the legal consequences. In their view, a certain amount of pressure, deception, persuasion and manipulation is essential if the 'truth' is to be revealed. Furthermore, they view persuasive interrogation techniques as essential to police work and feel justified in using them. The degree of persuasion recommended varies in different manuals. One of the most crude and extreme forms of persuasion recommended in a modern interrogation manual is in a book by Patrick McDonald (1993) entitled *Make 'Em Talk! Principles of Military Interrogation*, which states on the back cover:

> Every military has its ways of making subjects talk and this book takes you step-by-step through the most common, effective, and notorious methods used, including those favored by the Japanese, Germans, Koreans, Vietnamese, and Iraqis.

McDonald then goes on to describe how he recommends interrogators break down resistance and denials by inducing debilitation and exhaustion:

> If you have subjects under your total physical control, you can wear them down and make them easier to exploit and more compliant. One of the simplest methods to debilitate people physically is to severely limit their food intake or intermittently refuse them food altogether (p. 44).

Most other manuals (e.g. Inbau, Reid & Buckley, 1986; Inbau *et al*., 2001; Macdonald & Michaud, 1992; Rabon, 1992, 1994; Royal & Schutte, 1976; Stubbs & Newberry, 1998; Walkley, 1987) are more psychologically sophisticated than McDonald's coercive guide to interrogators, but they rely to a varying degree on the processes of influence and persuasion. This reliance on persuasion is inevitable in view of the reluctance of many suspects to admit to their crimes or certain aspects of their crimes. There is an extensive literature on the psychology of persuasion, which demonstrates its potentially powerful influence in different contexts (Cialdini, 1993).

Leo (1994) correctly points out that persuasion in the context of interrogation is the process of convincing suspects that their best interests are served by their making a confession. In order to achieve this objective the police may engage in a range of deception strategies. These include the following.

- Police officers concealing their identity while trying to obtain a confession (e.g. pretending to be a fellow prison inmate, befriending a person under false pretences, posing as a criminal). Such undercover operations are practised in some countries, for example, in Canada, the USA, and Britain. In Britain such an undercover operation went seriously wrong in the case of the famous murder of Rachel Nickell in 1992 on Wimbledon Common, South London (Britton, 1997; Fielder, 1994; Gudjonsson & Haward, 1998; Stagg & Kessler, 1999). In Britain, undercover police officers are not allowed legally to entrap people or coerce a confession out of them. In contrast, such undercover operations are commonly used in Canada to coerce confessions out of resistant suspects and they are allowed in evidence because they fall outside the legal framework of custodial interrogation (see Chapter 22).
- During interrogation the police may misrepresent the nature or seriousness of the offence (e.g. in a murder case by lying to the suspect that the victim is still alive and may talk, or implying that the death must have been an accident or unpremeditated).
- Employing trickery is, according to Leo (1994), the most common police deception during interrogation. This typically involves presenting the suspect with false evidence of guilt (e.g. falsely claiming that a co-defendant

has confessed, exaggerating the strength of evidence against the suspect, falsely claiming that the police are in possession of forensic or eyewitness evidence that indicates the suspect's guilt or lying about the results from a polygraph test).

There is a general reluctance among the authors of police interrogation manuals to accept the possibility that their recommended techniques could, in certain instances, make a suspect confess to a crime that he or she had not committed. Indeed, most interrogation manuals completely ignore this possibility. Some authors of interrogation manuals, for example Macdonald and Michaud (1992), at least acknowledge that false confessions do happen on occasions, but their understanding of false confessions is restricted to two main causes: 'A wish for publicity and notoriety' and 'Forceful prolonged questioning with threats of violence' (p. 7). This represents a very restricted view of false confessions. Macdonald and Michaud (1992), unlike Inbau, Reid and Buckley (1986), point to the dangers of using leading questions and recommend that interviewers should not lie to suspects. Their apparently ethical approach falls down when they recommend how suspects should be advised of their legal rights:

> Do not make a big issue of advising the suspect of his rights. Do it quickly, do it briefly, and do not repeat it (p. 17).

Zimbardo (1967) argued, on the basis of his early review of American police training manuals, that the techniques recommended were psychologically sophisticated and 'coercive'. He went as far as to suggest that they were an infringement of the suspect's dignity and fundamental rights, and might result in a false confession. This was an important early acknowledgement that psychologically manipulative and deceptive interrogation techniques have the potential to cause false confessions to occur. This potential risk of false confessions occurring during custodial interrogation was extensively discussed in *The Psychology of Interrogations, Confessions and Testimony* (Gudjonsson, 1992a). Subsequently a number of American scientists have written extensively about the potential dangers of coercive interrogation techniques. These include Kassin (1998), Leo (1998, 2001a), Leo and Ofshe (1998a), McCann (1998), Ofshe and Leo (1997a, 1997b), Underwager and Wakefield (1992), Wakefield and Underwager (1998) and Wrightsman and Kassin (1993).

The opposing views of Zimbardo and the authors of police interrogation manuals are the result of looking at police interrogation from different perspectives. Police interrogation manuals base their techniques on instinctive judgements and experience, whilst psychologists such as Zimbardo view the recommended techniques within the framework of what is known in the literature about the psychology of attitudes, compliance and obedience. The fundamental problem is the lack of scientific research into the police interrogation process and the techniques utilized. Recent research in Britain and America into police interrogation techniques has significantly advanced our knowledge in this very important area. These studies will be discussed in this and subsequent chapters.

THE REID TECHNIQUE

The 'Reid Technique' is described in detail by Inbau, Reid and Buckley (1986) and Inbau *et al.* (2001). The first edition to this manual was published by Inbau and Reid (1962). These authors had previously published similar books on interrogation under a different title (Inbau, 1942, 1948; Inbau & Reid, 1953). There was a second edition of the present book published in 1967 and the third edition, published in 1986 by Inbau, Reid and Buckley. The third edition gave the up-to-date state of the art of interrogation and introduced an important legal section and an appendix on the psychology of interrogation (Jayne, 1986). Important differences existed between the three editions, but the third edition was psychologically most sophisticated (Leo, 1992). It introduced a nine-step method aimed at breaking down the resistance of reluctant suspects and making them confess, referred to as the "Reid Technique". Inbau *et al.* (2001) have recently published a fourth edition of the book, which builds on the previous work of the authors, updates it and introduces new topics, such as false confessions, guidance to court room testimony and responses to defence experts' criticisms of their work.

In the introduction to their new book Inbau and his colleagues set out their working principles and disclaimer:

> To protect ourselves from being misunderstood, we want to make it unmistakably clear that we are unalterably opposed to the so-called third degree, even on suspects whose guilt seems absolutely certain and who remain steadfast in their denials. Moreover, we are opposed to the use of any interrogation tactic or technique that is apt to make an innocent person confess. We are opposed, therefore, to the use of force, threats of force, or promises of leniency. We do approve, however, of psychological tactics and techniques that may involve trickery and deceit; they are not only helpful but frequently indispensable in order to secure incriminating information from the guilty or to obtain investigative leads from otherwise uncooperative witnesses or informants (Inbau *et al.*, 2001, p. xii).

I have two comments to make on the above disclaimer. First, it seems rather half-hearted and defensive with regard to their approval of trickery and deceit. Their use of the word 'may' is misleading, because there is nothing 'may' about it. Their recommended tactics and techniques *do* involve trickery and deceit. It is an essential part of the Reid Technique, as will become evident from reading a description of their recommended techniques. Elsewhere two of the authors (Jayne & Buckley, 1991) go as far as to state that not only are trickery and deceit justified, they are 'absolutely essential in discovering the facts'. Second, the authors' reassurance that they disapprove of 'the use of force, threats of force, or promises of leniency', is not entirely correct when their techniques are carefully scrutinized. Admittedly, they do not recommend physical threats and force, but there is considerable psychological manipulation and pressure applied by the Reid Technique to break down resistance. This is perhaps best illustrated by their article in the *Prosecutor* (Jayne & Buckley, 1991), where the authors are more forthcoming about the nature of their techniques than in the more cautiously worded fourth edition of their book. For example, at one point in the article they imply, if not openly admit, the importance of uses of promises of leniency:

> Because of this, after a suspect confesses—even though he or she acknowledges committing the crime—this suspect is likely to believe that because the crime was somewhat justified, or could have been much worse, he or she should receive some special consideration.

The basic assumptions made by Inbau and his colleagues are the following.

- Many criminal investigations can only be solved by obtaining a confession.
- Unless offenders are caught in the commission of a crime they will ordinarily not give a confession unless they are interrogated over an extended period of time in private, using persuasive techniques comprised of trickery, deceit and psychological manipulation.
- To break down resistance interrogators will need to employ techniques which would in the eyes of the public normally be seen as unethical:

> Of necessity, therefore, investigators must deal with criminal suspects on a somewhat lower moral plane than upon which ethical, law-abiding citizens are expected to conduct their everyday affairs (Inbau *et al.*, 2001, p. xvi).

The Reid Technique is broadly based on two processes.

- Breaking down denials and resistance.
- Increasing the suspect's desire to confess.

Inbau *et al.* recommend that prior to the interrogation proper suspects are interviewed, preferably in a non-custodial setting where they do not have to be informed of their legal rights. The purpose of this non-accusatory interview is for the investigator to establish rapport and trust, trick the suspect into a false sense of security through malingered sincerity, gather detailed information about the suspect and his background, which can be used to break down resistance during subsequent interrogation, determining by observations of verbal and non-verbal signs whether or not the suspect is guilty, and offering the suspect the opportunity of telling the truth without confrontation. Once these objectives have been achieved, and the investigator is 'definite or reasonably certain' about the suspect's guilt, the interrogation proper commences. Inbau *et al.* recommend that the same investigator should ideally conduct both the interview and the interrogation.

During this pre-interrogation interview a polygraph examination may be conducted on the suspect. The results, if unfavourable, are then used to confront the suspect with his apparent lies and this often proves effective in eliciting confessions (Gudjonsson, 1992a).

Since the work of Inbau and his colleagues is very influential and commonly used by police and military interrogators, I shall review the Reid Technique in some detail. The authors appear to have blind faith in their technique in relation to false confessions:

> None of the techniques or tactics presented here would cause an innocent person to confess to a crime (Jayne & Buckley, 1991).

In Chapter 15 of their book, Inbau *et al.* recognize that interrogations have resulted in false confessions, but they do not associate this possibility with their own techniques:

> It must be remembered that none of the steps is apt to make an innocent person confess and that all the steps are legally as well as morally justified (p. 212).

The 'Steps' for Effective Interrogation

Inbau *et al.* (2001) suggest 'nine steps' to effective interrogation of allegedly guilty suspects. These are the types of case where the interrogator feels reasonably certain that the suspect is guilty of the alleged offence. As in the case of the pre-interrogation interview, they repeatedly emphasize the importance of interviewing suspects in private.

The nine steps of interrogation were apparently developed over many years of careful observation of successful interrogations and by interviewing suspects after they had confessed, although it is important to note that Inbau and his colleagues have not published any data or studies on their observations. In other words, they have not collected any empirical data to scientifically validate their theory and techniques. We simply do not know the following:

- How many confessions are obtained by the use of the Reid Technique in contrast to the use of less coercive techniques? In other words, what is the incremental value over other techniques?
- How many suspects falsely confess as a result of the use of the Reid Technique? More specifically, what is the proportion of false over true confessions?

The advantage of interviewing suspects after they have confessed is that the interrogator can learn more about the processes and mechanisms that elicit successful confessions (Gudjonsson & Sigurdsson, 1999). The importance of post-confession interviews is recognized by Inbau and his colleagues and they recommend them to interrogators as a standard practice. Material obtained during post-confession interviews formed the basis for the Reid Technique (see Inbau *et al.*, 2001, p. 392). The nine steps of interrogation are briefly discussed below, whereas the theory behind the development of the nine steps, and why they are effective in eliciting a confession, is discussed in Chapter 5.

Prior to proceeding through the nine steps the interrogator should be thoroughly familiar with all the available facts about the case and the suspect. In other words, he must be well prepared before conducting the interrogation. An ill prepared interrogator will be at a serious disadvantage when trying to elicit a confession from an allegedly guilty suspect, because the tactics and techniques of effective interrogation are dependent upon the interrogator coming across as confident and fully knowledgeable about the case. Another advantage of good preparation, which is implicit in the use of interrogative 'theme development', is that the more the interrogator knows about the suspect and his background the more he can identify the suspect's weaknesses and use them to his advantage when attempting to break down resistance. This is why the authors emphasize the need for an informal non-accusatory interview prior to the interrogation.

The selection of the interrogation strategy in a given case depends largely on the personality of the suspect, the type of offence he or she is accused of, the probable motive for the crime and the suspect's initial reaction to questioning. Suspects are classified into two broad groups: *emotional* versus *non-emotional* offenders. Emotional offenders are considered likely to experience feelings of distress and remorse in relation to the commission of the offence. For emotional offenders a sympathetic approach, appealing to their conscience, is the strategy of choice. Non-emotional offenders are those not likely to experience feelings of remorse for the offence and they do not become emotionally involved in the interrogation process. Here the interrogator uses a factual analysis approach, appealing to the suspect's common sense and reasoning. The two approaches are not mutually exclusive and both may be used with suspects with somewhat different emphasis.

Step 1: 'Direct Positive Confrontation'

This consists of the suspect being told with 'absolute certainty' that he or she committed the alleged offence. The interrogator states confidently that the results of extensive enquiries by the police indicate that the suspect committed the offence. Even if the interrogator has no tangible evidence against the suspect he or she should not give any indication of this to the suspect and if necessary must pretend that there is evidence. After the initial confrontation there is a brief pause, during which the suspect's behavioural reactions are closely observed. The suspect is then confronted with the accusations again. Passive reaction to the accusation is considered to be evidence of deception. The interrogator then proceeds to convince the suspect of the benefit of telling the truth (i.e. the truth as seen by the interrogator), without an obvious promise of leniency, which would invalidate any subsequent confession. This may focus on pointing out the suspect's 'redeeming qualities' to get him to explain his side of the story, explaining that it is all a matter of understanding his character and the circumstances that led to the commission of the offence and pointing out the need to establish the extent of his criminal activity (i.e. the extent of his criminal activity is exaggerated to elicit a reaction from the suspect). The interrogator then proceeds to Step 2.

Step 2: 'Theme Development'

Here it is important that the interrogator displays an understanding and sympathetic attitude in order to gain the suspect's trust. The interrogator suggests various 'themes' to the suspect, which are aimed to either minimize the moral implications of the alleged crime or give the suspect the opportunity of accepting 'moral excuses' for the commission of the crime (i.e. they are face-saving excuses). In this way the suspect can accept physical responsibility for the crime while at the same time minimizing either the seriousness of it or the internal blame for it. Inbau *et al.* point out that this kind of theme development is most effective with emotional offenders, because they experience feelings of shame and guilt. Giving them the opportunity of relieving their guilt by accepting moral excuses for what they have done acts as a powerful confession-inducing factor. It is not clear how useful in practice the distinction is between the emotional and non-emotional offenders, because interrogators may have problems differentiating between the two groups.

The themes suggested by the interrogator are aimed to 'reinforce the guilty suspect's own rationalizations and justifications for committing the crime' (Inbau et al., 2001, p. 232). This has to be presented in such a way as not to jeopardize the validity of the confession when the case goes to court (i.e. any inducements must be implicit and subtle so that they are not construed legally as a promise of leniency).

Themes for emotional suspects. It is recommended that the type of theme utilized by interrogators should take into account the personality of the suspect. The following themes are recommended for the emotional type of suspects.

(a) *Tell the suspect that anyone else being faced with the same situation or circumstance might have committed the same type of offence.* This has the effect of normalizing the criminal behaviour of the suspect and, combined with the comfort from the interrogator's apparent sympathy with the suspect, makes it easier for the latter to confess. As I explained in Gudjonsson (1992a), Inbau, Reid and Buckley (1986) appeared to take theme development far beyond ethical and professional limits when they recommended that,

> In sex cases, it is particularly helpful to indicate to the suspect that the interrogator has indulged, or has been tempted to indulge, in the same kind of conduct as involved in the case under investigation (p. 98).

This amounts to the police officer being encouraged to make a false confession in order to manipulate and trick the suspect into making a confession (Gudjonsson, 1993a). It is therefore not surprising that they do not want the session to be properly recorded.

Interestingly, in the revised edition of their book, Inbau et al. (2001) try to distance themselves from the above statement. It now reads:

> In sex offenses cases, it is particularly helpful to indicate to the suspect that the investigator has a friend or relative who indulged in the same kind of conduct as involved in the case under investigation. In some situations, it may even be appropriate for the investigator himself to acknowledge that he has been tempted to indulge in the same behaviour (p. 243).

(b) *Attempt to reduce the suspect's feelings of guilt for the offence by minimizing its moral seriousness.* This can be achieved, for example, by the interrogator commenting that many other people have committed more shameful acts than that done by the suspect. This has the effect of reducing the suspect's embarrassment over talking about the offence. Inbau et al. (2001) suggest that this theme is particularly effective when suspects are questioned about sex crimes, although it is also effective with many other types of crime. There is some evidence from our own research that such tactics are likely to be effective with sex offenders (see Gudjonsson & Sigurdsson, 2000, and Chapter 6).

(c) *Suggest to the suspect a morally acceptable reason for the offence.* This includes such ploys as telling the suspect that he probably only committed the offence because he was intoxicated or on drugs at the time. Another ploy, in certain types of offence, is to suggest that the suspect never really meant to do any harm, or attributing the offence to some kind of an accident. The purpose is to 'ease' the suspect into some kind of a self-incriminating admission, no matter how small, which makes him more amenable to making a full and detailed confession at a later stage of the interrogation. Being able to provide the suspect with some face-saving explanations for the crime greatly increases the likelihood of a confession being forthcoming.

(d) *Condemnation of others as a way of sympathizing with the suspect.* The rationale for this theme is that it will make it much easier for the suspect to confess if some responsibility for the offence can be attributed to the victim, an accomplice, or somebody else. The interrogator can use this ploy to his advantage by exploiting the readiness of many suspects to attribute partial blame for what they have done to others. Inbau *et al.* suggest that this type of theme can be particularly effective in certain sex crimes, for example, where children and women are the victims.

(e) *Using praise and flattery as a way of manipulating the suspect.* The argument here is that most people enjoy the approval of others and the appropriate use of praise and flattery facilitates rapport between the suspect and the interrogator. This ploy is considered particularly effective with people who are uneducated and dependent upon the approval of others.

(f) *Point out that perhaps the suspect's involvement in the crime has been exaggerated.* The emphasis here is that the interrogator makes the suspect believe that perhaps the victim has exaggerated his involvement in the offence. Pointing out the possibility of exaggeration may make some offenders more willing to make partial admission, which can subsequently be built upon.

(g) *Make the suspect believe that it is not in his interest to continue with criminal activities.* This theme is considered particularly effective with first time offenders and juveniles. It is pointed out to them that it is in their own interest to own up to what they have done in order to prevent serious trouble later in life. In other words, the suspect is told that by confessing he can learn from his mistakes and escape more serious difficulties.

Themes for non-emotional suspects. Inbau *et al.* suggest the following themes for non-emotional suspects.

(a) *Try to catch the suspect telling some incidental lie.* Once a suspect has been caught telling a lie regarding the case under investigation, no matter how small the lie is, he will be at a psychological disadvantage; in fact, from then onwards he has to make serious attempts to convince the interrogator that everything he is saying is now the truth.

Inbau *et al.* (2001) make an important point regarding the use of this technique:

> ...the interrogator should bear in mind that there are times and circumstances when a person may lie about some incidental aspect of the offense without being guilty of its commission (p. 281).

The lesson to be learned for interrogators is that innocent suspects as well as guilty ones may lie during interrogation about some incidental aspect of the offence, such as giving a false alibi because they do not want to reveal where they really were at the time.

(b) *Try to get the suspect to somehow associate himself with the crime.* This ploy may form part of some other theme, but it can be used as an effective theme in its own right. This consists of, for example, trying to get the suspect to agree to having been at or near scene of the crime, or somehow having incidental links with the crime. This should be done early on during the interrogation so that the suspect does not fully realize at the time the implications of agreeing to his presence at the scene of the crime.

(c) *Suggest there was a non-criminal intent behind the act.* Here the interrogator points out to the suspect that the criminal act may have been accidental or committed in self-defence rather than intentional. The idea is to persuade the suspect to accept the physical part of the offence while minimizing the criminal intention. Inbau *et al.* are aware of the potential legal implications of this theme:

> The investigator must appreciate that, unlike other themes presented, suggesting a noncriminal intention behind an act does directly imply that *if* the behavior was accidental or inadvertent the suspect may not suffer negative consequences. This is an attractive escape route for the guilty suspect anxious to avoid facing consequences for his crime. However, a critical question to ask is whether an innocent suspect would be apt to accept physical responsibility for an act he knows he did not commit. Absent a full confession, this is a question a judge or jury will ultimately decide based on the background, experience, and cognitive abilities of the defendant. It is our contention, however, that an innocent suspect operating within normal limits of competency would not accept physical responsibility for an act he did not commit. Furthermore, since this interrogation tactic is merely a stepping stone approach to eventually elicit the complete truth, this approach would not cause an innocent person to provide false evidence concerning his involvement in a crime (p. 286).

The above quote is an excellent illustration of self-justification for a technique that the authors recognize, presumably after being confronted with the issue in the court case they cite (*State v. Christoff* [1997], Fla. Cir. Ct), seriously distorts suspects' perceptions of the negative consequences of their self-incriminating admissions. I am in no doubt that this kind of theme development is potentially very dangerous and on occasions results in a false confession (see case of Mr R in Chapter 9).

(d) *Try to convince the suspect that there is no point in denying his involvement.* Here the interrogator points out to the suspect that all the evidence points to his guilt and that it is futile to attempt to resist telling the truth. The effectiveness of this theme depends upon the ability of the interrogator to persuade the suspect that there is sufficient evidence to convict him, regardless of any forthcoming confession. The suspect is told that the interrogator is only concerned about the suspect being able to tell his side of the story, in case there were any mitigating circumstances.

(e) *Play one co-offender against the other.* When there is more than one person suspected of having committed the offence, then each one will be very concerned about the possibility that the other(s) will confess in an attempt to obtain special consideration when the case goes to court. This fear of mutual distrust can be used to 'play one against the other'. The main ploy is to inform one, usually the assumed leader, that his co-offender has confessed and that there is no point in his continuing to deny his involvement in the commission of the offence. This can be an effective technique with certain offenders (Sigurdsson & Gudjonsson, 1994). However, this kind of tactic has its dangers. For example, in one British case a police officer produced a bogus confession and presented it to a co-defendant, who subsequently confessed and implicated others in one of the worse miscarriages of justice in British history (Foot, 1998).

Step 3: 'Handling Denials'

It is recognized that most offenders are reluctant to give a confession, even after direct confrontation, and their denials need to be handled with great care and expertise:

> Confessions usually are not easily obtained. Indeed, it is a rare occurrence when a guilty person, after being presented with a direct confrontation of guilt, says: 'Okay, you've got me; I did it'. Almost always, the suspect, whether innocent or guilty, will initially make a denial (pp. 303–304).

Repeated denials by the suspect are seen as being very undesirable because they give the suspect a psychological advantage. Therefore, they must be stopped by the interrogator. This means that the interrogator does not allow the suspect to persist with the denials. The suspect's attempts at denial are persistently interrupted by the interrogator, who keeps telling the suspect to listen to what he has got to say.

Inbau *et al.* argue that there are noticeable qualitative differences between the denials of innocent and guilty suspects, and these can be detected from various verbal and non-verbal signs. For example, innocent suspects' denials are said to be spontaneous, forceful, and direct, whereas the denials of guilty suspects are more defensive, qualified, and hesitant. Similarly, innocent suspects more commonly look the interrogator in the eye, and lean forward in the chair in a rather rigid and an assertive posture.

Inbau *et al.* (2001) recommend the use of the 'friendly–unfriendly' technique (when the various attempts at sympathy and understanding have failed). The 'friendly–unfriendly' technique, also known as the 'Mutt and Jeff' technique (Irving & Hilgendorf, 1980), can be applied in various ways. This commonly involves two interrogators working together, one of whom is friendly and sympathetic and the other being unfriendly and critical. A variant of this technique is for the same interrogator to play both roles, at different times during the interrogation.

The purpose of the 'friendly–unfriendly' technique, according to Inbau et al., is to highlight the difference between a friendly and an unfriendly approach, which in the end makes the suspect more responsive to the sympathetic approach. This technique is said to be particularly effective with the quiet and unresponsive suspect.

Step 4: 'Overcoming Objections'

This consists of the interrogator overcoming various objections that the suspect may give as an explanation or reasoning for his innocence. Innocent suspects are said to more commonly continue with plain denials, whereas the guilty suspect will move from plain denials to objections. There are various ways of overcoming these objections, which are said to be an attempt, particularly by guilty suspects, to gain control over the conversation as their denials begin to weaken. Once the suspect feels that the objections are not getting him anywhere he becomes quiet and begins to show signs of withdrawal from active participation in the interrogation. He is now at his lowest point and the interrogator needs to act quickly in order not to lose the psychological advantage he has gained.

Step 5: 'Procurement and Retention of Suspect's Attention'

Once the interrogator notices the suspect's passive signs of withdrawal, he tries to reduce the psychological distance between himself and the suspect and to regain the suspect's full attention. He achieves this, Inbau et al. argue, by moving physically closer to the suspect, leaning forward towards the suspect, touching the suspect gently, mentioning the suspect's first name, and maintaining good eye contact with the suspect. The suspect will look defeated and depressed. As a result of this ploy, a guilty suspect becomes more attentive to the interrogator's suggestions.

Step 6: 'Handling Suspect's Passive Mood'

This is a direct continuation of Step 5. As the suspect appears attentive to the interrogator and displays indications that he is about to give up, the interrogator should focus the suspect's mind on a specific and central theme concerning the reason for the offence. The interrogator exhibits signs of understanding and sympathy and urges the suspect to tell the truth. Attempts are then made to place the suspect in a more remorseful mood by having him become aware of the stress he is placing upon the victim by not confessing. The interrogator appeals to the suspect's sense of decency and honour, and religion if appropriate.

The main emphasis seems to be to play upon the suspect's potential weaknesses in order to break down his remaining resistance. Some suspects cry at this stage and this is reinforced and used to the interrogator's advantage: 'Crying is an emotional outlet that releases tension. It is also good indication that the suspect has given up and is ready to confess' (p. 351). They are no longer resistant to the interrogator's appeal for the truth. A blank stare and complete silence is an indication that the suspect is ready for the alternatives in Step 7.

Step 7: 'Presenting an Alternative Question'

Here the suspect is presented with two possible alternatives for the commission of the crime. Both alternatives are highly incriminating, but they are worded in such a way that one alternative acts as a face-saving device whilst the other implies some repulsive or callous motivation. It represents the culmination of theme development and in addition to a face-saving function, it provides an incentive to confess (i.e. if the suspect does not accept the lesser alternative others may believe the worst case scenario). This is undoubtedly the most important part of the Reid Model and one commonly seen in cases where suspects' resistance has been broken down during interrogation. It is a highly coercive procedure where suspects are pressured to choose between two incriminating alternatives when neither may be applicable. This is a very dangerous technique to apply, particularly among suspects who are of below average intelligence, which applies to a large proportion of suspects detained at police stations for questioning (see Chapter 3).

The psychological reasoning behind the alternative question is:

> A person is more likely to make a decision once he had committed himself, in a small way, toward that decision. This is precisely what the alternative question accomplishes during an interrogation. It offers the guilty suspect the opportunity to start telling the truth by making a single admission (Inbau *et al.*, 2001, p. 353).

In other words, the suspect is given the opportunity to provide an explanation or an excuse for the crime, which makes self-incriminating admission much easier to achieve. The timing of presentation of the alternative question is critical. If presented at the right time it will catch the suspect by surprise and make him more likely to confess.

Inbau *et al.* point out that occasionally suspects will persist with their face-saving excuses, but the interrogator will usually have no problem in obtaining a more incriminating explanation for the crime by pointing out flaws in the excuses given.

The potential impact of the presentation of the alternative question is illustrated by the following comment:

> It is important to note that even the most experienced and skilled investigators achieve a confession rate of about 80%. Of the approximately 20 percent of suspects who do not confess after being offered an alternative question, it might be argued that a small percentage of them could have been innocent (Inbau *et al.*, 2001, p. 364).

It is evident from the above quote that the authors have great faith in the ability of interrogators to detect deception by the use of non-verbal signs:

> ...the vast majority of suspects who have exhibited the previously described behaviours indicative of deception throughout the course of the interrogation are, in fact, guilty of the offense (p. 364).

The above comment makes no reference to the possibility of a false confession. Indeed, the authors are very confident in their technique:

Furthermore, *none of what is recommended is apt to induce an innocent person to offer a confession* (p. 313).

> More to the point, no innocent suspect, with normal intelligence and mental capacity, would, acknowledge committing a crime merely because the investigator contrasted a less desirable circumstance to a more desirable one and encouraged the suspect to accept it (p. 365).

These comments demonstrate a remarkable naivety of these authors and lack of psychological sophistication. It is not just a question of the interrogator merely contrasting two alternative scenarios in isolation; as the authors point out themselves, the alternative question represents the culmination of theme development and may have involved several hours of interrogation. It is the end product of a long and demanding confrontation.

Step 8: 'Having Suspect Orally Relate Various Details of Offense'

This relates to the suspect having accepted one of the alternatives given to him in Step 7 and consequently providing a first self-incriminating admission. In Step 8 the initial admission is developed into a full blown confession which provides details of the circumstances, motive and nature of the criminal act.

Inbau et al. (2001) emphasize that it is important at this point in the interview that the interrogator is alone with the suspect, because the presence of another person may discourage the suspect from talking openly about the offence. Once a full confession has been obtained the interrogator asks somebody to witness the confession. This is done in case the suspect refuses to sign a written statement.

Step 9: 'Converting an Oral Confession into a Written Confession'

This is very important because a signed confession is much stronger legally than an oral one. Furthermore, as a large number of suspects subsequently retract or withdraw their self-incriminating confession it is considered advisable to convert the oral confession into a written statement as soon as practicable. Suspects can easily deny that they ever made an oral confession, whereas it is much more difficult to challenge a written confession that has the suspect's signature on it. The authors warn that delaying taking a written statement may result in the confessor having been able to reflect upon the legal consequences of the confession and retracting it.

Inbau et al. (2001) repeatedly state that interrogators should under no circumstances minimize the legal responsibility for the offence. This is simply not true when one carefully studies their manual. Some of the themes they suggest to interrogators are based on implanting in the suspect's mind the idea that legal responsibility will be reduced or eliminated (e.g. the act was self-defence, an accident, or unintentional). Therefore, irrespective of what these authors claim, the reality is that the themes are very much based on minimizing, in the mind of the suspect, the responsibility for the offence and its perceived legal consequences.

Discussion

Kassin and McNall (1991) argue that the interrogation techniques embodied in the above nine steps approach consist of two main strategies, which they refer to as 'maximization' and 'minimization', respectively. The former strategy, which Inbau *et al*. recommend for non-emotional suspects, involves the interrogator frightening the suspect into a confession by exaggerating the strength of evidence against him or her and the seriousness of the offence. The 'minimization' strategy, by contrast, is recommended for remorseful suspects. Here the interrogator tricks the suspect into a false sense of security and confession by offering sympathy, providing face-saving excuses, partly blaming the victim or circumstances for the alleged offence, and minimizing the seriousness of the charges. Kassin and McNall (1991) provide convincing experimental evidence to show some of the inherent dangers of these so-called 'subtle' interrogation approaches to the perceptions of potential judges and jurors. That is, these interrogation approaches contain implicit ('hidden') messages which have important conviction and sentencing implications, generally against the interest of the defendant. The experiments of Kassin and McNall are important because they show that the techniques advocated by Inbau and his colleagues are inherently coercive in that they communicate implicit threats and promises to suspects. Taken as a whole, these experiments raise serious concerns about the use of 'maximization' and 'minimization' as methods of interrogation and the confessions they produce should be used cautiously as evidence in court.

Inbau *et al*., who cite these experiments in their article, unconvincingly dismiss their relevance to real life interrogation. When criticisms are made of their technique Inbau and his colleagues demand data and ecologically valid empirical support, but their book is full of assertions and generalizations about their technique without supporting empirical evidence.

THE FORMAT AND RECORDING OF THE CONFESSION

Inbau *et al*. (2001) argue that confession statements can be prepared in two different ways. First, the interrogator can obtain a narrative account from the suspect, which gives all the necessary details of the offence itself and its circumstances. Second, a written confession can be prepared in the form of 'questions and answers'; that is, the interrogator asks the specific questions and the suspect provides his answers to the questions asked. Probably the best approach is to combine the two formats as appropriate according to the nature of the case and the ability of the suspect to give a detailed narrative account. Inbau and colleagues point out that the main legal advantage of a question-and-answer format is that parts of the statement can more easily be deleted if considered inadmissible by the trial judge.

Inbau *et al*. recommend that the suspect be initially interrogated without the entire content being formally recorded. Once the confession has been obtained, the interrogator then draws up a concise summary, using the suspect's own words as far as possible. These authors argue strongly against the use of tape and video-recording of interrogation, maintaining that it results in a number of practical problems and would dramatically reduce the number of confessions given by suspects. Similar concerns were raised by some British police officers who were initially resistant to the introduction of tape-recorded interrogations (McConville & Morrell, 1983), but these have proved unfounded. In spite of being against video-recorded interrogations, Inbau and his colleagues can see the advantage in selected recording of confessions, but are concerned about the consequences:

> ...while the videotaping of selected confessions may certainly be beneficial to the prosecution, the practice opens the door for wider sweeping court rulings or standards that could eventually require the videotaping of the entire interrogation along with its subsequent confession for each and every suspect interrogated. In the final analysis, would this be good for the criminal justice system? (Inbau et al., 2001, pp. 395–396).

My answer is definitely yes. The electronic recording of all police interviews and interrogations would be in the interests of justice, and it will come. It would ensure that what happens in private within the walls of the interrogation room becomes open to public scrutiny. This is clearly not what Inbau and his colleagues want. They are undoubtedly right that electronic recording potentially gives the defence useful material for disputing confessions at suppression hearings, although it does of course also protect the police against unfounded allegations.

The failure to record all interrogation sessions makes it difficult, if not impossible, to retrospectively evaluate the entire interrogation process (e.g. what was said and done by the interrogator to break down resistance and obtain a confession).

There is no doubt that tape-recording, or video-recording, of police interviews protects the police against false allegations as well as protecting the suspect against police impropriety. It provides the court with the opportunity of hearing and seeing the whole picture relating to the interrogation. It also has the advantage of making it easy to systematically analyse and evaluate the entire interrogation and confession process (Baldwin, 1993; Pearse & Gudjonsson, 1996a, 1999; Pearse, Gudjonsson, Clare & Rutter, 1998).

In England and Wales contemporaneous recording of statements, which are handwritten by one of the interviewers, was implemented in 1986 as an interim arrangement until tape recorders were introduced and installed at police stations. Contemporaneous recording of statements meant that all questions and answers in interviews had to be recorded. This inevitably slowed down the interview process. Prior to that a taped or handwritten statement was produced at the end of the interrogation session, which represented a summary of what had emerged from the questions and answers. According to McConville and Morrell (1983), 'The main impetus behind the pressure to monitor police interrogations has been a concern to ensure that suspects are fairly treated and that evidence of alleged confessions is based on something more than the bare word of the interrogators' (p. 162).

Since 1991 there has been mandatory tape-recording of any person suspected of an indictable offence who is interviewed under caution (English & Card, 1999; Ord & Shaw, 1999). Prior to that date routine tape-recording of interviews had already commenced at some stations on an experimental basis (Baldwin, 1993).

The early work of Barnes and Webster (1980) showed that a routine system of tape-recording could provide an important means of 'strengthening police interrogation evidence whilst helping to ensure that the rights of suspects are safeguarded' (pp. 47–48). More recently, experience with tape-recordings has shown that it does not interfere unduly with standard interrogation practices (Willis, Macleod & Naish, 1988).

Some police forces in England have already begun to experiment with the use of video-recording of suspect interviews (Baldwin, 1992a) and there is a move in some states in America towards video-recording police interviews (Leo, 1996a). Hopefully in the near future police interrogations in England and America will be video-recorded. An experimental project in Canada with the video-recording of police interrogations produced favourable results (Grant, 1987). Most importantly perhaps, video-recording did not appear to inhibit suspects from making self-incriminating admissions and confessions, and it provided the court with important information for assessing the reliability of the confession. More recently, closed circuit television (CCTV) is being installed in the reception area of the custody suite, in the corridors and designated cells at some English police stations to protect the rights and health of the detainee (Newburn & Hayman, 2002).

Video-taping of interrogations is now commonly used in serious cases in America with many positive results (Geller, 1992). Geller found that law enforcement agencies were generally positive about the use of video-taping and found that it helped to prove the voluntariness of the confession at trial, it had led to improvements in interrogation techniques and it was helpful to use the tapes for training purposes.

However, in spite of the advantages of video-recording police interviews, it is not without certain dangers, such as undue reliance being placed by jurors on non-verbal signs and the fact that even the position of the camera can influence perceptions of coercion (Lassiter & Irvine, 1986).

Another potential problem is that in American cases tapes of crucial interrogations are sometimes 'lost', or that the first interrogation where the suspect's resistance is broken down is not recorded (Shuy, 1998). Not being able to listen to all the interviews may give a misleading picture of what really took place during the interrogation and prove prejudicial against the defendant.

The use of electronic recording of interrogations, whether audio or video recorded, is one of the best protections against wrongful convictions. However, it is not foolproof. No systems or safeguards are. Most importantly, it is potentially open to abuse and misinterpretation. This is particularly likely to happen when interrogations are selectively recorded, which is not uncommon practice in America. In other words, the interrogator only makes an electronic recording of the part of the interrogation that favours the prosecution (i.e. after the suspect has been broken down to confess and provides a post-confession statement). The danger here is that the recording will not give the whole picture of the interrogation process and may seriously mislead the court. It is essential that all interviews are properly recorded so that the court will have the best record possible of what took place during the interrogation. Otherwise it is open to abuse by the police and can mislead the court. Indeed, without a complete record, allegations of police impropriety (e.g. threats, inducements, feeding suspects with pertinent case details) are difficult to prove or disprove. McConville (1992) gives an excellent illustration of two such cases.

The ultimate confession statement may look very convincing when taken out of context. It is typically highly prejudicial against the defendant and without the complete picture of how it came about the court may place too much weight on it. In other words, such statements have the potential of being seriously misleading to the court.

Another potential problem with electronic recording is that if police officers are no longer able to place suspects under pressure during tape-recorded interviews they may shift the pressure outside the formal interview. This may happen by officers informally interviewing suspects prior to their arriving at the police station (Heaton-Armstrong, 1987; Wolchover & Heaton-Armstrong, 1991), or in the police cell prior to or between interviews (Dixon, Bottomley, Cole, Gill & Wall, 1990).

Moston and Stephenson (1993) found evidence that in England interviews are commonly conducted prior to the formal interview, and this practice significantly influenced whether or not the suspect subsequently made a confession during the audio- or video-recorded interview. This demonstrates the great impact that pre-interview conversations can have on the likelihood that the suspect will subsequently confess. No doubt, many police officers will view this as a positive and legitimate way of 'getting to the truth' and will be tempted to resort to such behaviour in spite of the fact that they are in breach of their codes of practice. The problem is that without a proper record of these conversations or informal interviews there is no way of determining the tactics used by the police and how they may have influenced the voluntariness and reliability of the subsequent confession. In most instances no record is kept of these informal interviews, and when a record is kept it is typically unsatisfactory. Moston and Stephenson (1993) conclude:

> Encounters outside the police station are important for understanding why suspects make admissions inside the police station. Interviews inside the police station, either recorded or audio or video taped, contain only one part of the relevant exchanges between the suspect and police workers. The current legislation, by emphasising the importance of interviews inside the police station has resulted in a situation in which evidence gathered outside the station is seemingly of minimal value. It is widely assumed that the use of tape or video recording equipment inside the station gives a complete picture of the interview with a suspect. This assumption appears to be incorrect. The statements made by suspects on tape are the outcome of a series of conversations with police officers. The interview inside the police station is merely the final part of this process (p. 47).

THE CONTEXT OF THE INTERROGATION

The context in which the interrogation takes place and the conditions of detention can vary immensely. In some cases suspects are detained in custody, even incommunicado, for days. They may be physically exhausted, emotionally distraught and mentally confused when interrogated. With improved legal provisions in England and Wales stipulated in the Police and Criminal Evidence Act

(PACE; Home Office, 1985a) and the accompanying Codes of Practice (Home Office, 1985b, 1995) the police are obliged to follow certain stringent guidelines and procedures with regard to detention and interrogation. These are intended as important safeguards against police impropriety, false confessions and wrongful convictions. This includes restricting the length of time during which suspects can be detained without being formally charged and, while in custody, giving suspects sufficient rest between interviews. The physical and mental welfare of suspects is the responsibility of the duty 'Custody Officer'. The Custody Officer is also responsible for keeping a detailed, timed record, known as the 'Custody Record', of all important events surrounding the suspect's detention.

Even with markedly improved legal provisions for detainees, it is difficult to think of any custodial interrogation that is not potentially 'coercive'. Indeed, it is recognized by the United States Supreme Court that all custodial interrogations are 'inherently coercive' to a certain extent (for reviews see Ayling, 1984; Driver, 1968; Inbau, Reid & Buckley, 1986). This is because the interrogator is part of a system that gives him or her certain powers and controls (e.g. powers of arrest and detention, the power to charge the suspect, the power to ask questions and control over the suspect's freedom of movement and access to the outside world). Therefore, it is inevitable that there are certain 'coercive' aspects to any police interrogation. Not only is the inevitable 'coerciveness' associated with the nature and circumstances of the interrogation and confinement, but the characteristics of the detainee affect the extent to which his free will is likely to be overborne (e.g. *Schneckloth v. Bustamonte*, 412 US 218).

In *Miranda v. Arizona* (384 US, 436, 1966), which was decided by the US Supreme Court in 1966, the judges were particularly critical of the psychologically manipulative techniques recommended by the leading interrogation manual of Inbau and Reid (1962), which had substituted physical coercion with psychological coercion as a way of obtaining confessions from reluctant suspects (Leo, 1992).

Anxiety and Fear During Interrogation

Inbau *et al.* (2001) point out that signs of nervousness may be evident during interrogation among both innocent and guilty subjects. They list three reasons why innocent suspects may be nervous when interrogated:

1. they may be worried that they are erroneously assumed to be guilty;
2. they may be worried about what is going to happen to them whilst in custody and during interrogation;
3. they may be concerned that the police may discover some previous transgressions.

Inbau *et al.* speculate that the main difference between the anxiety (they use the word 'nervousness') of innocent and guilty suspects is the *duration* of the anxiety. That is, the anxiety of innocent suspects, unlike that of guilty suspects, diminishes as the interrogation progresses. There is no empirical support for this claim. This will undoubtedly depend on the nature of the interrogation and custodial confinement, as well as on the mental state and personality of the suspect.

In the third edition of the book, Inbau, Reid and Buckley (1986) argued the main difference between guilty and innocent suspects related to the *degree* of anxiety rather than its *duration*. Innocent and guilty suspects both experience and exhibit signs of anxiety when interrogated, but the latter will experience a greater degree of anxiety, because they have committed an offence and really have something to worry about. This seems a reasonable assumption, because the lying of a guilty suspect is likely to generate its own anxiety. However, there is no doubt that for innocent suspects being wrongly accused of a crime, subjected to repeated challenges and not being believed can create severe anxiety of its own, which can be misconstrued as indications of deception.

Irving and Hilgendorf (1980) discuss in considerable detail the types of factor that may cause stress or anxiety in suspects during interrogation, irrespective of whether they are innocent or guilty of the alleged offence. Their work is particularly important because it relates experimental and laboratory findings to stressors that pertain to a police station.

Irving and Hilgendorf describe three general classes of stressors that are relevant to police interrogation situations:

1. stress caused by the physical environment at the police station;
2. stress caused by confinement and isolation from peers;
3. stress caused by the suspect's submission to authority.

Each of these classes of stressors can cause sufficient anxiety, fear and physiological arousal in the suspect to markedly impair his performance during interrogation.

The physical characteristics of the interrogation environment may cause anxiety and fear in some suspects. This is particularly true if the suspect has never been in a police station before so that the environment is unfamiliar to him. The more often a suspect has been in a police station on previous occasions, the greater the opportunity he has had for learning the rules of conduct of the setting. In addition, the more likely he is to know his legal rights (this may not always be the case: see Fenner, Gudjonsson & Clare, 2002). A familiar police environment is likely to be less stress-provoking than an unfamiliar one.

However, having been at a police station before is not always a stress-reducing factor, but this possibility is not discussed by Irving and Hilgendorf. Indeed, a stressful experience at a police station may result in psychiatric disability and could easily exacerbate the suspect's anxieties and fears when interrogated on a subsequent occasion (Gudjonsson & MacKeith, 1982). This happens when suspects have been so traumatized by the previous interrogative experience that their ability to learn constructively from it is adversely affected (Shallice, 1974).

Further types of stressor associated with the physical environment at the police station are *uncertainty* and *lack of control* over the environment. Suspects have little or no control over what is happening. If arrested, they cannot leave the police station until they are told that they are free to go. They cannot move freely within the police station, they are not free to obtain refreshments, make telephone calls, receive visits or use toilet facilities without permission. They have limited opportunity for privacy, and indeed, interrogators may cause stress by positioning themselves very close to the suspect during the interrogation. Such invasion of the suspect's personal space can cause agitation and increased physiological arousal (Sommer, 1969).

As suspects have little or no control over the physical environment at the police station, they are inevitably faced with a number of uncertainties, which include uncertainties about the fulfilment of their basic needs, and not knowing how long they are going to be detained at the police station or what is going to happen to them. The timing and duration of the interrogation, confinement and social isolation from others, are very important factors which are discussed by Irving and Hilgendorf. Uncertainty is something which has been found to be stressful to suspects who are waiting at the police station to be interviewed (Gudjonsson, Clare, Rutter, & Pearse, 1993).

Irving and Hilgendorf (1980) argue that the inevitable subordination of suspects to police officers' authority, when detained at a police station, can cause considerable stress for the suspect. Irving and Hilgendorf point out an important parallel between experimental findings of obedience to authority (Milgram, 1974) and what may happen to suspects who are interrogated by the police:

> ...the parallel lies in the way both Milgram's subjects, and suspects in interrogation, are prone to obey instructions which they would ordinarily dismiss. Under certain conditions, the subject will, against his principles, inflict pain. Likewise, we would argue under similar conditions of obedience to authority, suspects will provide information or even confess, even though normally they would not do so because of the obvious negative consequences (p. 39).

Projects researching the effects of the historic decision in *Miranda v. Arizona* (383 US 436, 1966) indicate that interrogation may be so stressful to most suspects that it impairs their ability to exercise their powers of judgement and legal rights (Griffiths & Ayres, 1967; Leiken, 1970; Leo, 1994, 1996a, 1996b; Wald, Ayres, Hess, Schantz & Whitebread, 1967). Stress was assumed to be mainly caused by the fact that there was a great deal at stake for the suspects. Furthermore, all four studies showed that police interrogation techniques following *Miranda* are very subtle and persuasive and greatly influence the decision of suspects to incriminate themselves. Griffiths and Ayres (1967) give an example of the subtlety of the police questioning:

> Often the pressure consisted of little more than reiteration by a detective of the same question several times alternated with small talk and appropriate urging (p. 313).

More recently, Leo (1996b) has gone even further and construes contemporary police interrogation as a confidence game:

> Although interrogation is fundamentally an information-gathering activity, it closely resembles the process, sequence, and structure of a confidence game (p. 265).

The objective of the confidence game is to use subtle psychological strategies to get suspects to voluntarily waive their *Miranda* warning and then trick them into making a confession. The technique is allegedly so effective that

> Most suspects who confess, however, do not appear to see through the con (p. 280).

Anger During Interrogation

Interrogation manuals generally acknowledge that anger, whether experienced by the suspect or the interrogator, is an undesirable emotion during interrogation as it inhibits constructive communication between the suspect and the interrogator. Rapport, trust and cooperation are generally considered to be essential components for the process of successful interrogation and feelings of anger and suspiciousness interfere with this process. There is some empirical evidence for this view. Gudjonsson (1989a) found that there was a negative relationship between suggestibility and anger and suspiciousness. In other words, people who were angry or suspicious when tested were less susceptible to giving in to leading questions and interrogative pressure.

In his survey of 100 British detectives, Walkley (1987) found that 42% claimed that failure to establish satisfactory rapport with a suspect by a previous interviewer had contributed to the suspect's denial. Once good rapport had been established with another detective the suspects confessed. This study supports the view that good rapport and trust are important components of the confession process.

An expression of anger among suspects during interrogation is often difficult to interpret, but an important difference is assumed to exist between guilty and innocent subjects. Inbau *et al.* (2001) point out that innocent suspects may be genuinely angry, and on occasions outraged, about being accused or suspected of a crime of which they are innocent. However, guilty suspects may on occasions pretend to be angry and their feigned anger may be difficult to differentiate from the genuine anger of innocent suspects. These authors argue that an important difference between the behavioural symptoms of anger among innocent and guilty suspects relates to the persistence and duration of the expressed emotion. Innocent suspects are assumed to persist with their anger over time, whereas guilty suspects will find it difficult to maintain the emotion over long periods of time. In other words, Inbau *et al.* speculate that the feigned anger among guilty suspects will subside more quickly than the genuine anger among innocent suspects. I am not aware of any published scientific study which provides empirical support for such differentiation between innocent and guilty suspects in their anger responses.

Impatience and anger among interrogators are likely to interfere with sound judgement and reasoning, which could result in unprofessional behaviour, such as the use of threats or violence. An arrogant attitude towards the suspect is a psychological characteristic which is considered to be highly undesirable during interrogation (Royal & Schutte, 1976). The reason is that, like anger and suspiciousness, it reduces the suspect's cooperation with the interrogation and makes him less receptive to the suggestions offered by the interrogator.

Desirable Attributes of the Interrogator

Inbau *et al.* (2001) list a number of indispensable attributes that make a good interrogator. They draw a distinction between the required personal qualities of *interviewers* and *interrogators*, but since both are normally conducted by the same investigator the qualities are presented together in this section. In terms of personal qualities, the following are most important in their view.

- Good intelligence.
- Good understanding of human nature.
- Ability to get on well with others.
- Patience and persistence.
- A good listener (this applies particularly to interviewers).
- A good communicator (this applies principally to interrogators, who are less interested in listening and more actively involved with persuasion to break down resistance).
- A high degree of suspicion (i.e. it makes the interrogator actively look for deception).
- Even temperament and good emotional control.
- Good inner confidence in the ability to detect deception.
- Feeling comfortable with using persuasive interrogation techniques, which may be considered morally offensive by other investigators.

In addition, the interrogator should be interested in police interrogation and needs to study the range of tactics and techniques. He or she should be familiar with new developments in the art of interrogation and be aware of the laws and regulations that govern interrogation procedures. An understanding of the psychological principles and theories of interrogation and confessions is considered very important. In particular, a good understanding and insight into signs of deception, including non-verbal cues, is considered essential. This is because the effectiveness of interrogation tactics and techniques is largely based on the ability of the interrogator to detect defensiveness, evasiveness and various forms of deception, and turn these to their advantage in breaking down resistance.

Interestingly, in contrast to what would normally be considered as good interviewing practice, the interrogation techniques advocated by Inbau and his colleagues rely on frequent interruptions by the interrogator as a way of feeding the suspect with themes and breaking down resistance (this of course does not apply to their pre-interrogation interview and only to the interrogation proper). The reason for this is that by this stage the interrogator is not interested in what the suspect has to say unless it agrees with the interrogator's scenario. The interrogator has already decided, on the basis of the pre-interrogation interview, that the suspect is guilty or very probably guilty. What remains is to persuade the suspect to confess and give a written confession. No listening is required until a confession is forthcoming.

Inbau *et al.* make the interesting and valuable point that interrogation is a highly specialized area of police work and the qualities that make a good interrogator may not necessarily be the same qualities as those that make a good investigator. They quote, as an example, that impatience may be an advantage for investigators in completing certain assignments, but it is a handicap when interrogating people. These authors argue that interrogation should be a specialism within police departments, implying that investigators, as a rule, should not interrogate suspects. They argue that increased specialism is likely to increase the number of confessions obtained from criminal suspects, the confessions are more likely to meet the necessary legal requirements and innocent suspects would be more expeditiously and reliably identified.

The Physical Environment of the Interrogation

There are a number of physical features associated with the police interrogation and confinement environment that can have major effects on the way suspects react to police interrogation. Inbau *et al.* (2001) describe various ways in which the physical environment can be deliberately arranged to maximize the likelihood that the suspect will confess. These include isolating the suspect from outside influences, making sure that there are no objects in the interrogation room that can distract the suspect's attention, sitting close to the suspect, and having colleagues surreptitiously observing the interview behind a one-way mirror for suspects' signs of vulnerabilities.

An excellent experimental illustration of the powerful emotional reactions of normal and healthy individuals to custodial confinement is seen in the classic study of Haney, Banks and Zimbardo (1973). Twenty-one Stanford University students were assigned to either a 'guard' or a 'prisoner' condition in a simulated prison environment. The purpose of the study was to analyse closely the behaviour and reactions of the two experimental groups to the respective roles over a two week period. The study had to be terminated after six days because of the severe distress and emotional disturbance of about half of the 'prisoners'. This was in spite of the fact that all the subjects had been carefully selected for the study because of their emotional stability. The typical reactions of the 'prisoners' comprised 'passivity, dependency, depression, helplessness and self-deprecation' (p. 89). The relevant processes that brought about these reactions were described by the authors as:

1. 'loss of personal identity' (i.e. loss of recognition of one's individuality and privacy);
2. 'arbitrary control' (i.e. the arbitrary and often unpredictable exercise of power and control by the 'guards');
3. 'dependency and emasculation' (i.e. being dependent on the 'guards' for exercising basic human activities).

The limitation of this study relates to the fact that the 'guards' were role-playing what they construed as typical prison officers' behaviour, rather than exhibiting behaviour which happens in a real-life 'prison'. Nevertheless, what is interesting was the apparent ease with which even stable individuals become immensely distressed by 'prison' confinement.

Irving (1980), in an observation study, emphasized the importance of the physical environment in influencing the decision-making of suspects. The factors he considered important included unfamiliarity with the physical environment of the police station, the effect of confinement on 'under-arousal', and the absence of control that the suspect has over the physical environment.

The ways in which the physical environment can affect the physiological state of suspects whilst they are in police custody have been discussed in detail by Hinkle (1961) and Shallice (1974). Social isolation, sensory deprivation, fatigue, hunger, the lack of sleep, physical and emotional pain, and threats are all factors that can powerfully influence the decision-making of suspects and the reliability of their statements. According to Hinkle (1961), these factors commonly result in impaired judgement, mental confusion and disorientation, and increased suggestibility. He concludes by stating:

> Most people who are exposed to coercive procedures will talk and usually reveal some information that they might not have revealed otherwise (p. 44).

However,

> ...the personality of a man and his attitude toward the experience that he is undergoing will affect his ability to withstand it (p. 33).

In my own experience of assessing defendants for a pre-trial examination, many complain of having had insufficient sleep prior to the interrogation. They often claim that this seriously impaired their ability to cope with the demands of interrogation. There is considerable evidence that a lack of sleep impairs mental functioning, especially if it continues for two or three days (Hinkle, 1961; Mikulincer, Babkoff & Caspy, 1989). Loss of sleep is associated with increased circadian oscillations (i.e. heart rate irregularity), lack of motivation to initiate and perform tasks, attentional problems, cognitive confusion and slowness of thought (Mikulincer, Babkoff & Caspy, 1989). The peak hours for reported problems occur between four and eight a.m. There is also empirical evidence that people deprived of sleep are significantly more suggestible, as measured by the Gudjonsson Suggestibility Scale, than normal controls (Blagrove, Cole-Morgan & Lambe, 1994). The degree of suggestibility increases with the amount of sleep deprivation (Blagrove, 1996). This indicates that sleep deprivation impairs the person's ability to resist leading questions and interrogative pressure. It explains why sleep deprivation is apparently effective in breaking down suspects' resistance during interrogation.

AMERICAN RESEARCH ON INTERROGATION

In Chapter 2 a number of British studies into interrogation techniques will be reviewed. In fact, most of the observational research into interrogation techniques has been conducted in Britain. In contrast, as noted by Leo (1996a), American researchers have largely failed to directly observe custodial interrogations. Apart from Leo's own research (1992, 1994, 1996a) there have only been two previous American observational studies (Milner, 1971; Wald *et al.*,

1967) into police interrogations. Both studies focused principally on the effects of *Miranda* warnings on confessions, and these will be discussed in Chapter 6. In contrast, Leo's research describes the interrogation techniques used and process of the interrogation. I shall briefly describe this unique American study in this chapter.

Leo (1994, 1996a) describes his analyses of the interrogations of 182 suspects at three police departments. Most of the cases ($N = 122$, 67%) involved Leo sitting in on the interrogations in a major urban police department and contemporaneously observing the interrogation tactics used and the suspects' reactions. Unfortunately, he was excluded from being present in some of the more serious cases, which means that he was not able to select randomly the cases he observed. In order to compensate for this methodological limitation Leo analysed 60 tape-recorded interrogations from two other police departments where he had specifically requested videotapes of interrogations involving serious felony crimes (e.g. homicide, rape, assault). The total sample was comprised of robbery (43%), assault (24%), homicide (12%), burglary (12%) and various other crimes (9%).

The great majority (87%) of the suspects had previous criminal convictions and had therefore had some prior experience with the criminal justice system. As far as the current offence was concerned, Leo estimated that in about one-third of the cases (33%) the strength of the evidence against the suspect was weak (i.e. highly unlikely to lead to a charge). In a further 32% of cases, the evidence was moderately strong (i.e. probably likely to lead to a charge), and in the remaining 35% of cases the evidence against the suspect was strong (i.e. highly likely to lead to a charge).

Leo identified 24 interrogation tactics used by the police. The 12 most commonly used tactics, and the percentage of cases where it was used for each tactic, were as follows.

1. Appeal to the suspect's self-interest (88%).
2. Confront suspect with existing evidence of guilt (85%).
3. Undermine suspect's confidence in denial of guilt (43%).
4. Identify contradictions in suspect's story (42%).
5. Any Behavioural Analysis Interview question (40%).
6. Appeal to the importance of cooperation (37%).
7. Offer moral justifications/psychological excuses (34%).
8. Confront suspect with false evidence of guilt (30%).
9. Use praise or flattery (30%).
10. Appeal to the detective's expertise/authority (29%).
11. Appeal to the suspect's conscience (23%).
12. Minimize the moral seriousness of the offence (22%).

Many of the tactics were used in combination, with several tactics being used during each interrogation. The average number of tactics per interrogation was 5.6. According to Leo, interrogators typically began by confronting the suspect with the evidence against him, followed by implying his guilt and then undermining his denial of involvement in the offence, while identifying contradictions in the suspect's story or alibi, appealing to his self-interest and conscience and providing moral justifications and psychological excuses. This suggests a combination of tactics, which resulted in 41.8% of the suspects making admissions (i.e. admitted at least to some of the elements of the crime), and a further 22.5% provided self-incriminating statements while not directly admitting to the crime. This means that 64% of the suspects provided self-incriminating statements, which could be used against them in court.

Leo concludes that the four most successful interrogation tactics in terms of obtaining a confession were the following (the success rate for each tactic is in parenthesis).

1. Appeal to the suspect's conscience (97%).
2. Identify contradictions in suspect's story (91%).
3. Use praise or flattery (91%).
4. Offer moral justifications/psychological excuses (90%).

The greater the number of tactics used and the longer the duration of the interrogation, the significantly more likely the suspect was to make a confession. Interestingly, most of the interviews (70%) were completed within one hour and only eight per cent lasted more than two hours. As far as coercive interviewing is concerned, Leo found that coercion was present in only four (2%) of the cases. He used ten conditions as possible indicators of coercion, and at least one had to be present for the interrogation to be deemed coercive. These included failure of the police to issue the *Miranda* warning, the use of threats and inducements, unrelenting and hostile questioning, the interrogation lasting more than six hours, and the suspect's will being overborne by some other factor or combination of factors.

In terms of the outcome of cases within the criminal justice system, suspects who gave self-incriminating statements to the police were 20% more likely to be charged than the other suspects, 25% more likely to plea bargain and 26% more likely to be convicted. This gives strong support for the view that self-incriminating statements are important in determining the outcome of the case. Once a confession is made the negative outcome for the suspect is likely to be greatly enhanced.

The main conclusions from this study are that police officers typically employ *some* of the techniques recommended by Inbau, Reid and Buckley (1986), these techniques can be highly effective in obtaining confessions, they rarely amount to coercive questioning as defined by Leo and the self-incriminating statements obtained during interrogation significantly affect the outcome of the case in terms of an increased likelihood of being charged, and convicted. In view of the inherently coercive nature of the Reid Technique of interrogation, the low level of coercion observed by Leo is noteworthy. One would have expected a much higher level of coercion. There could be a number of explanations for this. First, Leo was excluded from observing the most serious cases, where coercion was more likely to be present, and he was not able to select cases at random. Second, Leo's presence during the interrogation may have resulted in less coercive tactics being used by the police than would otherwise have been the case. Third, the 60 video-recorded interrogations may not have been randomly selected by the police. Fourth, Leo's criteria for defining coercion may have been too stringent. The alternative, of course, is that the most coercive components of the Reid Technique are not commonly practised in the police districts where the study took place.

Unfortunately, Leo does not present data on how many of the suspects confessed at the beginning of the interrogation, and what proportion confessed due to persuasive police interrogation after making an initial denial.

HOW THINGS CAN GO WRONG DURING INTERROGATION

The main purpose of interrogation is to gather valid information and factual accounts from suspects in an ethical and legally accepted fashion. The purpose, scope and nature of the interview will depend on the circumstances of the case and who is being interviewed. Often suspects are unforthcoming with the relevant information that the police require and remain deceptive, evasive and defensive. When this is the case the police may need to be persuasive in their questioning in order to obtain a complete and truthful account of events. The extent to which the police can legally use psychological pressure and manipulation varies from country to country, and even within a given country this may vary over time (Gudjonsson, 1995a; Conroy, 2000).

Police interrogation can go 'wrong' in the sense that it results in 'undesirable consequences' for the criminal justice system or the suspect (Gudjonsson, 1994c). There are a number of ways in which this can happen and I shall discuss these briefly below.

1. *False confessions due to coercion*. False confessions can happen when police officers wrongly assume that the suspect is guilty (e.g. by their having blind faith in their ability to detect deception through non-verbal signs) and feel justified in coercing a confession from the suspect. This is not to say that false confessions do not happen without coercion or police impropriety. In fact, it will be shown in later chapters that they do. However, the greater the pressure suspects are placed under during interrogation the greater the likelihood that false confessions will occur. My concern is that some police officers have blind faith in their ability to detect deception, and the interrogation manual by Inbau et al. (2001) encourages such a myth. The empirical evidence clearly shows that non-verbal signs are unreliable indicators of deception (Ekman, 1992; Kassin & Fong, 1999; Vrij, 2000, 2001), although recent research into micro-momentary facial expressions of emotions are looking promising for the future (Frank & Ekman, 1997; Stubbs & Newberry, 1998).
2. *Inadmissible confessions*. When confessions are coerced by the police there is a risk of the evidence being ruled inadmissible when the case goes to court, even if the confession is true. Confessions are commonly disputed in court and if it can be proved that the confession was obtained by police impropriety and or coercion then it is of no evidential value. Obtaining a confession should not be viewed as a substitute for a good criminal investigation.

3. *Coerced confessions resulting in resentment.* There is considerable evidence that coercive and manipulative interrogation techniques, such as those recommended by Inbau et al. (2001), often cause resentment and bitterness among offenders, which may last over many years (Gudjonsson & Bownes, 1992; Gudjonsson & Petursson, 1991; Gudjonsson & Sigurdsson, 1999). Suspects do resent being tricked, deceived and coerced by the police and this may influence how likely they are to dispute the confession when their case goes to court. In contrast, when offenders confess because the other evidence against them is strong and where they have an internal need to confess, they view their confession more favourably (Gudjonsson & Sigurdsson, 1999).
4. *Coercion resulting in post-traumatic stress disorder.* Studies into the psychological effects of torture (e.g. Basoglu et al., 1994; Daly, 1980; Forrest, 1996; Gonsalves, Torres, Fischman, Ross & Vargas, 1993), show that many survivors suffer from post-traumatic stress disorder (PTSD). I am not aware of any similar research being conducted into the psychological effects of police arrest, confinement and interrogation. However, a study of the interrogation techniques of the British police officers in Northern Ireland in the early 1970s indicated that some detainees suffered from PTSD as a result of their ordeal (Shallice, 1974). Similarly, Hinkle (1961) has argued that harsh interrogation techniques can cause serious mental disturbance in some suspects.

Undoubtedly, being arrested, detained and interrogated is a very stressful experience for some suspects. Gudjonsson et al. (1993) found that about 20% of suspects detained for a police interview scored abnormally high on the Spielberger State Anxiety Inventory (Spielberger, 1983). In addition, a clinical interview indicated that about one-third of the suspects were in an abnormal mental state which might have interfered with their ability to cope with the interrogation.

How suspects may be traumatized by being arrested detained and interrogated, and the long-term sequelae of the experience, are unknown. Gudjonsson and MacKeith (1982) discuss two cases where suspects had been traumatized by being arrested by the police and interrogated. In such cases it is difficult to separate the individual effects of the arrest, confinement and interrogation. The humiliation of being arrested and detained may be sufficient to cause post-traumatic stress disorder in vulnerable individuals (Gudjonsson, 1996b). This can be illustrated by two cases seen by the present author. Both individuals, a man and a woman, were perfectionists and their identity was very much associated with being honest and respected. Neither person was charged with any offences by the police, but they were arrested and kept in custody for several hours before their innocence was established. The feeling of shock and humiliation associated with the arrest and confinement resulted in persistent symptoms which were consistent with post-traumatic stress disorder (PTSD). In other cases it was the police interrogation itself which resulted in PTSD. For example, two alibi witnesses to a major crime were pressured and threatened by the police to alter their evidence, which they resisted. Both subsequently experienced major problems with intrusive thoughts and other symptoms of PTSD concerning the police interrogation, which lasted for several years before they sought treatment.

5. *Undermining public confidence*. Leo (1992) suggests that coercive and manipulative police interrogation techniques may undermine the public confidence in the police and encourage police corruption. Indeed, there is evidence that in England a series of miscarriage of justice cases involving coerced confessions have undermined the public faith in the police and the judiciary as a whole (*Royal Commission on Criminal Justice Report*, 1993; Williamson, 1994). Such a situation may make jurors highly sceptical of police and confession evidence and increase the acquittal rate (Robbins, 2001, 2002).

6. *The 'boomerang effect'*. Coercing suspects to confess may sometimes result in the opposite effects intended by the police. Thus, suspects who would have confessed in their own time refuse to confess when they feel they are being rushed or unfairly treated by the police. In other instances, suspects who have already confessed may retract their confession when they feel they are pressured too much to provide further information.

These phenomena can be explained in terms of 'reactance theory' (Brehm, 1966; Brehm & Brehm, 1981). That is, when people perceive that their freedom to choose or act is threatened they may respond by becoming increasingly assertive. In exceptional cases this may result in the so-called 'boomerang' effect. This means that people may not only become less suggestible and compliant when pressurized, but they take the *opposite* view to that communicated by the interrogator (i.e. they react in an extremely resistant way). Gudjonsson (1995b) discusses how this can happen in real life police interrogations when suspects feel they have been pressured too much. The consequences may be devastating for the police when the case goes to court and judges rule the confession statement as being inadmissible.

CONCLUSIONS

The techniques recommended in police interrogation manuals, such as that of Inbau *et al.* (2001), are based on 'psychological principles' that undoubtedly can be immensely effective in influencing the beliefs and decision-making of suspects during interrogation. What we do not know is the rate of *'true'* and *'false'* confessions elicited, respectively, and how these rates compare with less coercive techniques. The basic ingredient of the techniques involves the interrogator being able to 'read' the signs of suspects' lying and 'guilt', which forms the justification for manipulating them into confessing by playing on their vulnerabilities and using trickery and deceit. The main persuasive ingredients involve exaggeration or misrepresentation of the evidence against the suspect ('maximization') and theme development ('minimization'). The interrogator suggests various 'themes' to the suspect which are aimed at minimizing either the seriousness of the crime (e.g. pretending it was an accident, committed in self-defence, or unintentional) or the responsibility for it (e.g. blaming the victim or circumstances). The potentially most dangerous part of the Reid Technique relates to suspects being pressured to choose between two incriminating alternatives, one with obviously very serious consequences and the other with more ambiguous, and by implication, less serious consequences (i.e. that the act was an unintentional, accidental, self-defence).

There are potential problems with these techniques. The first relates to the nature and extent of psychological coercion involved. There is no doubt that these techniques are inherently coercive in the sense that their objective is to overcome the suspects' resistance and will-power not to incriminate themselves. In other words, suspects are manipulated and persuaded to confess when they would otherwise not have done so.

It is, of course, perfectly true that no police interrogation is completely free of coercion, nor will it ever be. Furthermore, a certain amount of persuasion is often needed for effective interrogation. The real issue is about the extent and nature of the manipulation and persuasion used. What is legally allowed varies from country to country, between different jurisdictions, and within jurisdictions over time.

Another problem relates to ethical and professional issues. Many of the tactics and techniques recommended encourage the police officer to employ trickery, deceit and dishonesty. Although such measures are commonly allowed in American courts, they raise very serious questions about the ethical nature of this form of interrogation. Public awareness of this kind of police behaviour must inevitably undermine the public's respect for the professionalism of police officers. Deception and trickery will also cause resentment among suspects and are likely to increase the likelihood that the confession will be disputed at trial.

Innocent suspects may be manipulated to confess falsely, and in view of the subtlety of the techniques utilized innocent suspects may actually come to believe that they are guilty. Inbau *et al.* state that their techniques, when applied in accordance with their recommendations, do not result in a false confession. This is simply not true. There is ample evidence that their advocated techniques do on occasions lead to false confessions. How often this happens we do not know. Their failure to accept the possibility that false confessions can occur shows either a limited insight into the potentially deleterious effects of their techniques, or reluctance to face the reality that their recommended techniques do on occasion result in false confessions.

Finally, all police manuals are based on experience rather than objective and scientific data. Experience is invaluable to police work and its usefulness is illustrated by the effectiveness of the techniques recommended. However, relying solely upon experience in determining procedure may create serious pitfalls (e.g. untested assumptions) and fail to bring to light important facts about human behaviour, such as the susceptibility of some suspects to give erroneous information when placed under interrogative pressure. What is needed is more research into the effectiveness and pitfalls of different interrogation techniques.

CHAPTER 2

Interrogation in Britain

In Chapter 1 the focus was primarily on American interrogation manuals. In contrast to North America, where many interrogation manuals and training courses have been available for several decades, until the early 1990s there was no national training in interrogation being offered to British police officers. Indeed, 20 years ago in their review of current practice for the Royal Commission on Criminal Procedure (1981), Irving and Hilgendorf (1980) cite evidence from the Association of Chief Police Officers of England, Wales and Northern Ireland that

> ...police officers receive no formal training in the art of interrogation. They are given some advice, in addition to instruction on the law, at training school and by colleagues but by and large skills develop through experience (Irving & Hilgendorf, 1980, p. 52).

Irving and Hilgendorf also commented on the absence of published research on police interrogation in England and Wales. However, following their review there have been several major research projects carried out in Britain into interrogation techniques. First, Irving (1980) looked closely at the current practice of interrogation at one police station in England. This study has been replicated twice (Irving & McKenzie, 1989). Second, Softley (1980) carried out an observational study in four English police stations. Third, Walsh (1982) carried out a very limited study into police interrogation practices of suspected terrorists in Northern Ireland. Fourth, researchers at the University of Kent have analysed tape-recordings of real-life police interviews and written extensively about their research (Moston, 1990a; Moston & Engelberg, 1993; Moston & Stephenson, 1992, 1993; Moston, Stephenson & Williamson, 1992, 1993; Sear & Stephenson, 1997; Williamson, 1990, 1993, 1994). Fifth, Baldwin (1993) evaluated the interview techniques used by English police officers at six police stations by analysing 600 tape-recorded interviews. These studies will be reviewed in this chapter. In addition, English training manuals will be briefly discussed as well as current training in police interviewing.

In addition to the above studies, Pearse and Gudjonsson (1996a) analysed the techniques used by police officers at two South London police stations from tape recordings of interviews. They subsequently extended their research to investigate the techniques used by officers to move suspects in serious cases from an initial denial to a full confession (Pearse, 1997; Pearse & Gudjonsson, 1999). These studies will be discussed in detail in Chapters 3 and 4.

IRVING'S STUDIES

Irving (1980) and Irving and McKenzie (1989) carried out observational studies of suspects who were being interviewed by the police in Brighton, which is on the south coast of England. There were three studies in total, carried out in 1979, 1986 and 1987.

The background to these studies is that in 1979 Barrie Irving, at the request of the Royal Commission on Criminal Procedure, undertook a field study of interrogation practice and procedure of an English Criminal Investigation Department (Irving, 1980). The Royal Commission on Criminal Procedure (1981) was appointed in February 1978. Its terms of reference were to study and make recommendations on the process of pre-trial procedures in England and Wales. The main impetus behind the setting up of the Royal Commission on Criminal Procedure was the result of the Confait Inquiry by Sir Henry Fisher (Fisher, 1977). Sir Henry Fisher had expressed serious concerns about the circumstances surrounding the confessions of three psychologically vulnerable suspects and these concerns were taken up by the Royal Commission (see Chapter 7 for a detailed discussion of the Confait case). The nature and fairness of custodial interrogation was at the heart of the Commission's concerns. As a result they commissioned reviews and empirical studies into police interrogation (Irving, 1990). Irving and Hilgendorf (1980) were asked to consider a decision-making model of the interrogation process. Irving (1980) carried out an empirical investigation into current practice of interrogation techniques and psychological vulnerabilities. The main aim was to find out 'What actually goes on in English interview rooms during the interrogation of suspects?' (p. 81).

Irving's First Observational Study

Irving (1980) observed the interviews of suspects and recorded the tactics used by interrogators. Irving also carefully monitored the mental state of the suspects prior to and during the police interviews. Over a six-month period 76 interviews involving 60 suspects were observed. Although interviews in only one police station were observed, the study gave important information about various aspects of the police interview process.

Thirty-three suspects (55%) were interviewed within 3 hours of arriving at the police station and 48 (80%) within 8 hours. Long delays were typically caused by the unfitness of the suspect to be interviewed (e.g. severe intoxication, a psychotic episode). Forty-three (81%) of the suspects were interviewed only once or twice. The average interview lasted 76 minutes (range 5–382 minutes) and the average length in police custody was 12 hours (range 50 minutes to over 26 hours).

According to Irving, the main purpose of the interrogation was to obtain a confession, either as the main evidence in the case or as subsidiary evidence. It was considered in the majority of cases to be central to the police investigation.

Even when there was forensic, documentary or witness statement evidence against the suspect, a confession helped to secure a conviction and often provided evidence about other crimes which could be 'cleared up'. Out of the 60 suspects, 35 (58%) made self-incriminating admissions during the interviews observed. A further four suspects confessed after the interviews were terminated.

Below are the main findings from Irving's observations concerning the impact of custody, the interrogation itself and the suspects' mental state whilst being interrogated.

1. *The effects of custody*. Many suspects showed distress and seemed to be in an abnormal mental state before their interrogation. Part of the distress was, according to Irving, caused by unfamiliarity with the police cells, being confined against their will, being isolated from social contact and being under the physical control of the police.

   The individual reaction of the suspects varied considerably. Those with claustrophobia reacted violently when being locked up. Irving believed that, for most suspects, confinement prior to interrogation causes significant *under-arousal*, which suspects find uncomfortable and motivates them to talk to the police. A particular danger involves the interviewing of suspects who are claustrophobic, because terminating an interview means that they will be placed back in their cell, which is terrifying for them.

   Irving noticed that it was the first-time offenders, and particularly those suspected of sexual crimes, who showed the greatest amount of fear reactions during the interrogation. A confession commonly resulted in almost immediate relief of behaviourally related stress symptoms, which Irving interpreted as being due to reduced uncertainty about the suspects' immediate predicament.

2. *Suspects' mental state*. Out of the 60 suspects, 11 (18%) were judged to be intoxicated or experiencing drug or alcohol withdrawal, five (8%) were rated as mentally ill and only one (2%) was classified as being of low intelligence or possibly mentally handicapped. A further eight suspects (13%) were judged to be mentally disordered. Some other suspects were judged to be in an abnormal mental state due to fear or distress concerning the detention and pending interrogation. All together, about half of the suspects were considered in some way to be mentally disturbed during the police interview.

   To summarize his findings, Irving stated:

   In conclusion, we would argue from these observations that in a substantial proportion of cases interviews are held with individuals who are not in a normal mental state. Abnormalities may result from intoxication, mental handicap, personality problems or from the character of custodial interrogation itself. However, while watching any given suspect being interviewed, the observer found it impossible to judge whether the state of that suspect would have constituted sufficient grounds for excluding the statements which ensued either on the basis of involuntariness or oppression (p. 136).

3. *Interrogation tactics used.* In about two-thirds of cases the police were observed to use persuasive and manipulative interrogation tactics in order to obtain information and admissions. Each tactic was sometimes used more than once with each suspect and more than one type of tactic was commonly used. Irving noted that each detective seemed to have a repertoire of approaches that he tended to use, which were 'not particularly finely tuned to the suspect' (Irving, 1980, p. 148).

Irving classified the tactics used into five different groups according to their type. The most frequently used types involved the following.

a. *Telling suspects that it was futile to deny their involvement* in the crime and they might as well own up to it. This included the use of 'information bluffs' (i.e. the police pretending they had more information to link the suspect with the crime than they had). A variant of this tactic was used with about half of the suspects.
b. *Influencing the suspects' perception of the consequences of confession* was used with 28 suspects (47%). This included minimizing the seriousness of the offence and manipulating the suspects' self-esteem so as to make it easier for them to confess.
c. *Advising suspects that it was in their best interest to confess* was used in one-third of all cases. Here the police implied or suggested to suspects that it was in the suspects' best interest to provide the wanted information, for example, by pointing out the advantages of confessing and disadvantages of persistent denial.
d. *Using custodial conditions, such as confinement and asserting authority.* In this way the police officer may influence the decision-making of the suspect. This tactic was used with 24 suspects (40%).
e. *The offer of promises relating to police discretion*, such as hinting that accomplices would never find out who informed on them and suggesting that unless the suspect cooperated friends and acquaintances would be interviewed. These types of tactic were used with 14 suspects (23%).

Irving (1980) concluded that the police commonly used manipulative and persuasive interrogation techniques, which were in many respects similar to those recommended in American police interrogation manuals. However, the English detectives did not appear to have had any formal training in these tactics and used a personal repertoire of approaches. These were not always related to the suspect's characteristics and vulnerabilities, but were nevertheless, in Irving's view, highly effective in securing admissions.

Irving (1980) recognized the limitations of his study; observations were carried out at one police station only, over a specified period only; by one observer only; serious crimes were over-represented, and juvenile offenders were under-represented. In view of these factors Irving warned that generalizing from the findings might not be justified.

Irving's Subsequent Research

Irving's original research at Brighton Police Station has been replicated twice jointly with his colleague Ian McKenzie (Irving & McKenzie, 1989). In 1986, six months after the implementation of the Police and Criminal Evidence Act 1984 (PACE) (Home Office, 1985a), which has had radical effects on police interrogation procedures, Irving and McKenzie replicated Irving's original study. The interviews of 68 criminal subjects were observed by McKenzie at Brighton Police Station. As certain noticeable changes had been detected with the implementation of PACE, Irving and McKenzie decided to replicate the second study in 1987, again observing the interviews of 68 suspects. The main methodological difference between the 1986 and 1987 studies was that more serious cases were observed in the latter study. One of the main purposes of the replication studies was to look at the effect that the new legislation might have had on police interviewing behaviour.

The 1986 study indicated that there had been a dramatic fall in the number of manipulative and persuasive tactics used by detectives at Brighton Police Station (Irving & McKenzie, 1989). In the 1979 sample of 60 suspects, a total of 165 tactics had been used. In 1986 the number of tactics used had fallen to 42 in 68 cases. This fall in the number of manipulative tactics used by the police was almost certainly due to the implementation of PACE, which is the first Act in England that attempted to provide a comprehensive code of police powers and practices for the investigation of crime (Bevan & Lidstone, 1985).

Between 1986 and 1987 the number of tactics used at Brighton Police Station rose from 42 to 88, which may have been due to the diminishing of initial rigidity in applying the new rules or because suspects were being interviewed about more serious offences. However, the number of tactics observed was still below that observed in 1979. In the 1986 and 1987 samples, the most persuasive tactics were used in the more serious cases. Nevertheless, the rate of admissions for the most serious crimes fell in 1986 and 1987. This left Irving and McKenzie with confusing findings. They concluded 'Either some of the essential power of the tactics used was destroyed by the cumbersome note-taking procedure, or by the general reduction in the potential of custody conditions to produce compliance or by a combination of both. The advent of tape recording will partly resolve these issues because skilled interrogators in serious cases will be able to get back to their previous standard of performance' (Irving & McKenzie, 1989, p. 182).

The main conclusion is that the new Act appears to have markedly reduced the number of manipulative and persuasive techniques that police officers use when interrogating suspects, except perhaps in the most serious cases. Interestingly, there appears to have been no overall effects on the confession rate of suspects (see Chapter 6). The main limitation of the three observational studies was the small number of suspects in each study.

SOFTLEY'S STUDY

In 1979, a team from the Home Office Research Unit, at the request of the Royal Commission on Criminal Procedure, conducted an observational study into police questioning of suspects at four police stations in England (Softley, 1980). The purpose of the study was to provide an objective account, with reference to the general 'run-of-the-mill' cases, of what happens to suspects from the time of their arrival at the police station and until they are put in a police cell after being charged. This included a direct observation of the interrogation of suspects. The study was modelled on a similar American study (Wald et al., 1967). The four police areas selected were from West Yorkshire, Nottinghamshire, Avon and Somerset, and the Metropolitan (London) Police.

Softley and his colleagues observed the interviews of 218 criminal suspects, of which 187 were interviewed at a police station. Since it was impracticable to observe all the cases at the police stations the researchers selected the more serious offences, such as burglary, wounding or assault occasioning actual bodily harm. Forty-eight per cent of the suspects interviewed at a police station made a confession, and a further 13% made a damaging admission that fell short of a full blown confession. Two suspects subsequently retracted their confession, but they were nevertheless convicted. Only 12% of the 187 suspects exercised their right to silence.

The observers noted persuasive interviewing tactics in about 60% of the initial interviews. The most common tactic, reported in 22% of the interviews, involved the police officer pointing to a contradiction or an inconsistency in the suspect's statement. In 13% of cases, the police told suspects firmly about the overwhelming evidence against them. In a further 15% of cases the police appeared to 'bluff or hint that other evidence would be forthcoming' (p. 79). In about 6% of the initial interviews the police minimized the seriousness of the offence or the suspect's part in it. This tactic was commonly used in cases where suspects were unduly ashamed of what they had done or that they appeared to have exaggerated views about the severity of the likely sentence they would receive. In about 7% of the initial interviews the police hinted that unless the subjects cooperated they would be detained for a longer period at the police station.

The researchers concluded that the interrogators were generally fair to the suspect and rarely applied coercive tactics to obtain a confession. Unlike Irving and McKenzie, the researchers in this study did not make a direct observation of the mental state of the suspect. This is an important limitation.

WALSH'S STUDY

Walsh (1982) examined the arrest and interrogation practices under the emergency legislation in Northern Ireland. The Royal Ulster Constabulary (RUC) had refused Walsh access to the records of interrogation so instead he interviewed 60 people who had been subjected to custodial interrogation by the RUC between September 1980 and June 1981, in connection with suspected terrorist activities. Thirty subjects (50%) claimed to have requested access to a solicitor and of these only seven (23%) were allowed access to one, but only after having been in custody for more than 48 hours. This means that none of the subjects were allowed access to a solicitor within 48 hours of arrest. All the subjects were released by the RUC without being charged. Of the total sample, 35% claimed to have been pressured to provide in the future information about the activities of others. Almost half (48%) of the sample alleged that they had been subjected to verbal abuse by the police during their interrogation. Two subjects claimed to have been physically beaten.

In his paper, Walsh quotes some official statistics, which indicate that the great majority of suspects (89%) who were interrogated in 1980 in connection with suspected terrorist activities were released without being charged. According to Walsh, the corresponding figure for England and Wales, for all offences, was between 10 and 20%.

Walsh's main conclusion was that the RUC had failed to implement many of the recommendations of the Bennett Committee, including the absolute right of suspects to have access to a solicitor after having spent 48 hours in custody. The Bennett Committee had been set up in 1978 to carry out an extensive official inquiry into police interrogation in Northern Ireland, following allegations that suspects were being beaten and tortured whilst in police custody. The allegations resulted in international publicity and condemnation. The Bennett Committee offered 64 principal conclusions and recommendations (Bennett Committee, 1979).

There is a fundamental weakness in Walsh's study in that the information of the subjects about their arrest, interrogation and detention could not be verified by either the official record or an independent source. Furthermore, the sample selected was very small and may not have been representative of all those arrested. However, it remains a matter of public record that in the early 1970s the RUC were using interrogation techniques that amounted to torture (Shallice, 1974). Shallice argues that the techniques used in Ulster, which included isolation, sensory deprivation, 'hooding' and other forms of torture, were aimed at completely breaking the suspects' resistance. As a result many suspects suffered long-term mental effects (Shallice, 1974; Wade, 1972). Interestingly, the Israeli General Security Services still use similar techniques as the RUC did in the early 1970s to break down resistance among alleged terrorists (Conroy, 2000; Gudjonsson, 1995a; Human Rights Watch/Middle East, 1994).

RESEARCH AT THE UNIVERSITY OF KENT

Researchers at the University of Kent have carried out a number of projects into police interrogation, which will be reviewed. The part of the work that relates to confessions (Moston, Stephenson & Williamson, 1992, 1993) will be discussed in detail in Chapters 5 and 6. The focus in this chapter is specifically on police interrogation.

With the mandatory use of tape-recorded police interviews in England it has become possible to study more objectively than before police–suspect interactions and behaviour. Moston (1990a) argued that contemporaneous note taking resembles dictation whereas tape-recorded interviews resemble a conversation.

Moston and Engelberg (1993) listened to over 400 taped police interviews which had been conducted by detectives in the Metropolitan Police Force. Of those taped interviews, 118 were analysed in detail in terms of interviewing strategies. It was found that the interviews typically began in one of two ways, which are referred to as 'inquisitorial' (76.3%) and 'accusatorial' (14.7%) strategies respectively.

Inquisitorial strategies are aimed at general information gathering whereas the accusatorial strategy focused on obtaining a confession. The choice of the initial strategy used appeared to relate to the interrogator's skills in interviewing as well as the interrogator's assumptions about the suspect's guilt or innocence.

The purpose of the inquisitorial style of questioning at the beginning of interviews is to establish good rapport with the suspect and to find out more about the suspect's general demeanour and reactions. Asking background questions, which are unrelated to the alleged offence, can be used to achieve these objectives. However, Moston and Engelberg surprisingly found that in only 5% of cases was there initial questioning to establish rapport. The most common type of questioning in the inquisitorial group was 'offence specific information gathering', and this was found in 43.2% of cases.

With confrontational (accusatorial) styles of questioning the emphasis is not to establish what happened, but to obtain a confession. There are three main ways in which the interrogator confronts a suspect. First, there is 'direct accusation', where the interrogator straightforwardly asks the suspect about his guilt or innocence (e.g. 'Did you stab Joe Smith?'). This strategy was found in 13.5% of cases. Second, the evidence against the suspect is presented and an explanation is required, which takes the form of either an admission or a denial (5.1% of cases). Moston and Engelberg refer to this as the 'evidence strategy'. Third, the interrogator combines the evidence strategy with direct confrontation (5.1% of cases). This is referred to as 'supported direct accusation', and is the most persuasive way of obtaining a confession.

Moston and Engelberg suggest that the 'supported direct accusation' strategy can lead to false confession among suggestible or compliant suspects. Furthermore, if details of the crime have been communicated to the suspect at the beginning of the interview, which Moston (1990a) argues is commonly the case, then it becomes virtually impossible to establish whether or not the suspect is simply echoing the information given earlier to him by the police. In other words, it becomes much more difficult to validate the confession because the suspect was not given the opportunity of spontaneously providing information that could be used to corroborate his confession.

In other cases, according to Moston and Engelberg, some interrogators terminated the interview immediately after the suspect had made a confession. This prevented the opportunity of a good post-confession statement being taken to corroborate the validity of the confession.

When suspects choose to exercise their right to silence the police are still entitled to interview them. The most common response to questions of suspects exercising their right of silence is by saying 'No comment' and in only 5%

of interviews do they remain completely silent (Moston, Stephenson & Williamson, 1993). In their study, Moston and Engelberg (1993) found that police officers used five types of strategy to deal with the silences of suspects. These are the following.

1. 'Avoidance' (i.e. stop interviewing the suspect).
2. 'Downgrading' (e.g. shifting the questioning to a less threatening topic).
3. 'Persistence' (i.e. the officer will continue with the interview along the same lines).
4. 'Upgrading' (i.e. exaggerating or emphasizing the seriousness of the offence in the hope that the suspect will begin to challenge the allegations).
5. 'Rationalization' (e.g. telling the suspect that he does not have to follow the solicitor's advice to remain silent, or that this is his opportunity to tell his side of what happened).

The most common strategies used to deal with suspects who exercised their right to silence were Persistence (38.3%) and Upgrading (39.1%).

The study of Moston and Engelberg was completed prior to the right to silence being modified under sections 34–37 of the Criminal Justice and Public Order Act 1994 (England & Wales; see Wasik & Taylor, 1995), which means that a court or a jury may now under certain circumstances draw adverse inferences if suspects fail to answer questions put to them by the police (Home Office, 1995; Morgan & Stephenson, 1994). The modification to the right to silence will undoubtedly place many suspects under pressure to speak when questioned by the police (Gudjonsson, 1994a). Indeed, there is recent evidence that fewer suspects are exercising their right of silence following these amendments (Bucke & Brown, 1997).

A major limitation with the Moston–Engelberg study is that the authors failed to compare the different interview strategies with the outcome of interview (e.g. confession versus denial). This would have been an interesting factor to investigate and the authors presumably had all the necessary data.

Moston and Engelberg conclude that the manipulative police interviewing techniques identified by Irving (1980) ten years previously have largely disappeared. They argue that this has occurred because of legal restrictions which make it more difficult for police officers to offer inducements as well as there being greater awareness about what constitutes psychological coercion.

Moston and Engelberg argue that interrogators commonly lack the necessary skills to cope with suspects who do not readily come forward with a confession. This lack of interviewing skill has also been observed by other researchers (e.g. Baldwin, 1993; Mortimer, 1994; Williamson, 1993). Williamson, a serving senior English police officer, was very concerned about how traditional coercive interrogations had de-skilled interrogators and undermined public confidence in the police:

> Unethical behaviour by interrogators has undermined public confidence and left the police service with a serious skills deficit in its ability to obtain evidence through questioning (Williamson, 1994, p. 107).

The work of Williamson (1990, 1993, 1994) is particularly important in showing the growth of professionalism in the questioning of suspects following the implementation of the Police and Criminal Evidence Act (PACE) 1984, making it inherently less coercive. Williamson (1990) listened to a large number of post-PACE audio-recorded police interviews and in addition made a detailed questionnaire study of 80 police detectives at busy London police stations (see Williamson, 1990, 1993, for a detailed discussion of the questionnaire study).

From listening to the tapes of interviews Williamson (1990, 1993) identified four interrogation styles—'collusive', 'counselling', 'business-like' and 'dominant'. He placed these four styles against two dimensions—'evidence orientated' versus 'confession orientated' (horizontal dimension) and 'cooperative' versus 'confrontational' (vertical dimension). The 'collusive' style was characterized by a cooperative and problem solving approach, aimed at securing a confession. The 'counselling' style was characterized by a cooperative non-judgemental approach, aimed at securing evidence. The 'business-like' style was confrontational and aimed at securing evidence, whereas the 'dominant' style, which was also confrontational, was aimed at securing a confession. Unfortunately, the different interviewing styles were not studied in relation to admissions and denials.

Williamson asked 80 detectives which of the four interviewing styles they identified with. Twenty-one (26%) officers identified with the 'collusive' style, 16 (20%) with the 'counselling' style, 11 (14%) with the 'business-like' style and five (6%) with the 'dominant' style. A third of the officers did not appear to be able to identify with any one particular technique. When asked which style they thought was most unsatisfactory just over half indicated that it was the 'dominant' style.

It would have been interesting to match the officers' self-reported style with those identified from Williamson's own ratings of the tape-recorded interviews. It appears that the officers who completed the questionnaire did not conduct the tape-recorded interviews, which Williamson analysed. We simply do not know whether the officers were accurate in rating their own style of interviewing.

Interestingly, when asked to identify the main purpose of an interview, only 12% of the officers said it was 'to obtain a confession', whereas 38% and 24% said it was 'to get to the truth' and 'to seek an explanation', respectively. When asked to rank order their preferred method of recording an interview 61% said video-recording, 33% preferred audio-recording, 5% preferred making notes after an interview and 1% ranked contemporaneous note-taking. This finding suggests that the great majority of officers prefer electronic recording to manual note-taking, which is reassuring in view of the mandatory use by police in England and Wales of tape-recorded interrogations.

Sear and Stephenson (1997) examined the relationship between the personality of police officers and their interviewing performance. Nineteen police officers completed a personality questionnaire measuring Dominance, Agreeableness, Conscientiousness, Neuroticism and Openness. Four interview tapes were rated for each officer in terms of 13 skill factors considered necessary in a police interview. A multiple regression analysis revealed no significant predictors of personality factors on the interview performance. The authors concluded that personality is not related to interviewing performance in a straightforward way. Problems with this study relate to the very small sample size, the selective nature of the participants and the possible unreliability of the personality measure in this context.

BALDWIN'S STUDY

In 1989 three police forces in England experimented with the use of video-recorders in police interview rooms. Baldwin (1992a, 1993) was commissioned to evaluate the outcome of this experimental use of video-recorders. He analysed 400 video-recorded interviews of suspects, which were conducted at four police stations. In addition, 200 audio-recorded interrogations from two busy police stations in Birmingham were also studied. The main purpose of the study was to assess the interview techniques used by the police officers. The police interviews included in the study were conducted in 1989 and 1990. There were a total of six police stations involved with 100 interviews being studied at each police station (Baldwin, 1993).

The majority of the 600 interviews involved 'run-of-the-mill' cases, typically involving offences of theft, burglary or violence. Almost three-quarters (73%) of the interviews were conducted by officers of the rank of a police constable or detective constable (i.e. the most junior ranks). Typically there were two officers conducting each interview. In only 2.5% of cases was an inspector or officer of higher rank present in the interview. Most (88.5%) of the suspects were interviewed only once. Nearly one-quarter of the interviews were completed within ten minutes, almost three-quarters were concluded within 30 minutes and only 7% lasted for more than one hour. Therefore, the interviews tended to be of very short duration. A legal representative was present in 182 (30%) of the cases.

The Interview Techniques

Baldwin does not appear to have constructed a detailed coding frame for analysing what the officers said in the interviews and no details are given about the number and type of tactics used. However, his research highlights certain problems with the interview tactics used by many of the officers. A summary of these is as follows.

1. Interview formalities, such as introducing the persons present, explaining procedures and reading the police caution were often delivered hurriedly and in a casual manner. In a few cases no caution was delivered at all, and where it was delivered it was sometimes incomprehensible or inaudible. Overall in over 10% of cases the caution was delivered wrongly or unsatisfactorily.
2. Four principal flaws were identified from viewing the interview tapes. These were labelled by Baldwin as *'general ineptitude'* (e.g. lack of planning, no

real structure, officer lacking in skill and confidence), *'assumption of guilt'* (e.g. as evident by leading questions and repetitive questioning), *'poor interviewing technique'* (e.g. interruptions, failure to establish facts) and *'too much pressure having been exerted'* (viewed by Baldwin as unfair and unprofessional). For the four overlapping categories above these were found in 19.5, 15, 13.5 and 9% of the cases, respectively.
3. The interviewers apparently often had little understanding of the legal elements that need to be proved in an offence. Admissions were often left without clarification, because once an admission had been made the officer quickly terminated the interview and failed to obtain a satisfactory post-admission statement (a post-admission statement refers to the details that the suspect is able to provide once he has began to confess to the crime in question).
4. Police officers appeared to find the presence of a solicitor or legal representative in an interview inhibiting, and in some cases apparently intimidating. In spite of this legal representatives often remained quiet during interviews even when intervention appeared to be required.

It seems from Baldwin's research that in an interview situation police officers and lawyers are apprehensive about their respective roles when in the presence of each other. This could impair their ability to function effectively in an interview and satisfactorily fulfill their respective roles. Indeed, both professional groups appeared to exhibit general ineptitude, although in Baldwin's study this was more specifically investigated in relation to the police officers' performance in interview. The apparently inept behaviour of some of the legal advisors was alluded to only briefly. Ede and Shepherd (2000) have produced an important guide for practising solicitors, which should enhance their confidence and effectiveness as legal advisers at police stations. Better training of police officers should improve their skills and confidence in conducting an interview (Ord & Shaw, 1999).

Suspects' Responses

Baldwin observed the predominant attitude of the suspects during the interviews and their responses to questions. Overall, 442 (74%) of the suspects were rated as being either cooperative or submissive during the interview. Only 82 (14%) suspects were found to be awkward or difficult to interview. A small minority (6%) was reported as being remorseful or tearful. A similar number (7%) were described as cocky or self-assured.

Only 13 (2%) suspects exercised their legal rights to remain silent during the police interview. Over one-third (214; 36%) of the suspects gave a full confession at the beginning of the interview. A further 97 (16%) confessed to some part of the allegation from the onset. In 39 cases (6.5%) there was some change in their story from the initial position of a denial, but interestingly in only 20 cases (3%) did suspects completely move from a denial to a full confession. Out of these 20 cases where there had been a dramatic change, in only nine cases did Baldwin attribute the change to the persuasive skills of the interviewer.

The findings suggest that most suspects enter the police interview having already decided whether or not to make a confession or a denial. For this reason most of the interviews tended to be very short. Typically, this involved the interviewer asking the suspect to tell his story and then this was followed up by a few questions to clarify basic details. Where there was a denial very few suspects went from a complete denial to a complete confession. Baldwin concluded:

> In very few taped interviews, then, are suspects persuaded to admit participation in criminal offences. The great majority of suspects stick to their starting position—whether admission, denial, or somewhere in between—regardless of how the interview is conducted. The simple truth is that it is extremely difficult to induce reluctant suspects to confess by methods that would nowadays be regarded acceptable. Yet many police officers and legal commentators continue to view the 'art of persuasion' as being the essence of police interviewing. Much public concern about miscarriages of justice is the product of such 'persuasive interviewing' techniques, however, and it is surely time that such techniques were outlawed. Enough is known about the causes of miscarriages of justice to demonstrate that, if the risk of their occurring is to be minimized, then such tactics have to be eliminated (Baldwin, 1993, p. 333).

These are strong words indeed. The problem is that there is a fine balance between the need for the police do their job effectively, which includes being able to obtain detailed and reliable accounts from suspects, and the protection of the suspect from persuasive questioning and possible involuntary self-incrimination. Relentless and coercive questioning is clearly unacceptable within the legal framework of PACE and obtaining a confession should not be a convenient short-cut to a criminal investigation. However, Baldwin himself clearly highlights the problems involved in determining what is a coercive interview:

> The tapes are, then, of limited utility in they offer no way of examining the social context (or the social 'construction') of interrogation. There is in consequence an almost limitless number of ways of making sense of them. Questioning which a psychologist might regard as overbearing or coercive might well be seen very differently by a lawyer attending an interview or by the police officer conducting the interview. Such assessments cannot be made objectively since there is no consensus about what constitutes a 'good' or an 'effective' interview. Such qualities are largely in the eye of the beholder. What a police interviewer regards as a good or successful interview is not necessarily what a lawyer, or civil libertarian, or researcher, still less a suspect, would see as such (Baldwin, 1993, p. 328).

Finally, since so many of the officers in Baldwin's study were judged as poor and inept interviewers, we do not know whether more skilful interviewers would have been able to change more of the initial denials to a full confession by using legally acceptable interview techniques. Or do suspects only move from a denial to a confession through coercive questioning? This is an important issue, which will be taken up again in later chapters.

BRITISH TRAINING MANUALS

Until the early 1990s there was no systematic or formal national police training in interviewing. However, in 1982 the Metropolitan (London) Police had begun to offer a training course to officers and soon some other police forces developed their own courses (see Mortimer & Shepherd, 1999, for an excellent review of these early developments). The absence of formal training in police interviewing was raised by the Royal Commission on Criminal Procedure (1981). The Royal Commission recommended that police officers should receive proper training in interviewing techniques. This emphasis for the need for national training was taken up again during the subsequent Royal Commission on Criminal Justice (1993), which stated:

> The new national training in basic interviewing skills announced in Home Office Circular 22/1992, as supplemented by Home Office Circular 7/1993 should, so far as practicable, be given to all ranks of police officers (p. 189).

Walkley (1987) produced the first British police interrogation manual. This manual was clearly heavily influenced by the work of Inbau, Reid and Buckley (1986), although there were some differences. First, Walkley's manual was placed within the framework of the Police and Criminal Evidence Act 1984, although some of the persuasive and manipulative tactics recommended for influencing the decision-making of the suspect were probably in breach of the Police Codes of Practice. Furthermore, some of its content goes against the general trend in England to place police interviewing training within the context of a social skills model rather than manipulative procedures (Mortimer & Shepherd, 1999; National Crime Faculty, 1996; Ord & Shaw, 1999). In spite of the introduction of PACE, one police force in England went even further than Walkley's recommendations and largely adopted the Nine Steps of Interrogation of Inbau, Reid and Buckley's (Mortimer & Shepherd, 1999).

The emphasis in Walkley's manual was very much on the interviewer learning to read the correct 'lie' and 'buy' signs and becoming an *'effective persuader'* in order to obtain a confession. Walkley (1987) gives the following example of his recommended strategy:

> The interviewer will first deal with the lie-telling denials which the suspect is making and convince him that they have little or no value to him, possibly even may have certain penalties. He will hint that confession on the other hand has certain advantages. Whenever the suspect takes a step away from lie telling, he will be rewarded by suitable reinforcement ploys (p. 109).

Walkley (1983) had previously completed a Master's thesis where he discovered that over half of the British detectives he interviewed claimed that they were prepared to use force, or the threat of force, when questioning suspects (cited by Williamson, 1994). It may be for this reason that the techniques recommended by Inbau and his colleagues are sometimes resorted to by British detectives in serious cases when confessions are not readily forthcoming (Irving & McKenzie, 1989; Pearse, 1997; Pearse & Gudjonsson, 1999).

Unlike Inbau, Reid and Buckley (1986), Walkley acknowledged that some interrogation techniques can result in a false confession being elicited. He states:

> Perhaps even more powerfully, if an interviewer wrongly assesses the truth teller as a lie teller he may subject that suspect to questioning of a type which induces a false confession. Whilst instances of false confessions may not be as common as some would have us believe, there are well documented cases where they have occurred, and apart from the obvious damage they do to the suspect they also bring the police service and the legitimate practice of interrogation into disrepute (p. 5).

Walkley's comments imply recognition that police officers can misjudge deception (i.e. they are not infallible in reading the 'lie' and 'buy' signs); when this occurs it influences the tactics they use to break down resistance, this in turn increases the likelihood of a false confession occurring, and brings the practice of interrogation into disrepute.

Walkley's interrogation handbook did not meet with much enthusiasm in Britain and it does not appear to have had much impact on police training and interrogation techniques used by police interviewers. There were a number of reasons for this, as follows.

1. Changes in police practice following the introduction of PACE and Codes of Practice for police officers, which reduced the scope for coercive questioning, and the use of deception, trickery and psychological manipulation (Bull, 1999; McKenzie, 1994; Mortimer & Shepherd, 1999; Williamson, 1994).
2. Research into false confessions and psychological vulnerability (Gudjonsson, 1983, 1984a, 1984b, 1992a; Gudjonsson & MacKeith, 1982, 1988, 1990), and the increased recognition by the judiciary that 'wrongful convictions may be occasioned by false confessions and psychological vulnerability' (Corre, 1995, p. 9).
3. The successful appeal of the 'Guildford Four' in October 1989 and 'Birmingham Six' in March 1991 raised public and judicial awareness about wrongful convictions arising from coerced confessions (Gudjonsson, 1992a). This was followed in May 1992 by the successful appeal of Judith Ward (Gudjonsson & MacKeith, 1997; Kennedy, 1992; Ward, 1993). These three cases, dating back to 1974, all involved major terrorist offences and multiple deaths of members of the public. The case of the 'Birmingham Six' led to the setting up of the Royal Commission on Criminal Justice (1993).
4. Increased acceptance by the English Crown Courts of expert psychological evidence in the late 1980s, followed by the successful appeal of the 'Tottenham Three' in December 1991 (*R. v. Raghip*, *The Independent*, Friday 6 December 1991, p. 19; Rose, 1992; see Chapter 18 in this book). For the admissibility of psychological evidence in cases of disputed confessions, and the introduction of the concept of 'interrogative suggestibility', this was the most important and influential judgment and is discussed in Part III along with other more recent judgments.
5. In December 1992 there was an important and influential legal judgment concerning 'oppressive' police interviewing in the case of the 'Cardiff Three'

(*R. v. Paris, Abdullahi & Miller* [1993], 97 Cr.App.R. 99), which was drawn to the attention of the Royal Commission of Criminal Justice by the Lord Chief Justice who presided over the appeal (Williamson, 1994). This concern was followed in November 1993 by another case involving 'oppressive' questioning from Leeds Crown Court (*R. v. Heron*, unreported; see Chapter 4).

As a consequence of the above factors, there was pressure on police forces in England to implement a new approach to interrogation. This new approach to interviewing was first set out in *Home Office Circular* 22/1992, where certain principles were developed through the collaboration between police officers, psychologists and lawyers (Williamson, 1994). This was followed by *Home Office Circular* 7/1993, where a new training package for basic interviewing skills was introduced. Two booklets on interviewing were produced (CPTU, 1992a, 1992b) and were issued to all 127 000 operational police officers in England and Wales (Bull, 1999). One-week training programmes were set up to supplement the booklets (Williamson, 1993, 1994).

The booklets, and the interview theoretical model on which they are based, became nationally agreed guidelines on interviewing for both witnesses and suspects. The mnemonic 'PEACE' was used to describe the five distinct parts of the new interview approach.

1. *'Preparation and Planning'*. Interviewers are taught to properly prepare and plan for the interview and formulate aims and objectives.
2. *'Engage and Explain'*. The purpose of the interview is explained to the interviewee, the persons present are introduced, the caution is administered to the suspect, rapport is established and the officers engage the person in conversation.
3. *'Account'*. Officers are taught two methods of eliciting an account from the interviewee. These are referred to as the 'Cognitive Interview' and 'Conversation Management', respectively. The former is based on the work of Fisher and Geiselman (1992) and can be used with cooperative suspects as well as with witnesses. In contrast, 'Conversation Management', which is based on the work of Eric Shepherd (see Mortimer & Shepherd, 1999), is recommended when the degree of cooperation from the suspect is insufficient for the 'Cognitive Interview' techniques to work satisfactorily.
4. *'Closure'*. Officers are taught how to conclude an interview. This involves the officer summarizing the main points from the interview and providing the suspect with the opportunity to correct or add anything.
5. *'Evaluate'*. Once the interview is finished, there is need for evaluating the information obtained and how it impacts on the investigation. The performance of the interviewers should also be evaluated, but unfortunately the tapes of interviews are very rarely listened to by police officers (Williamson, 1994). The opportunity for constructive feedback is therefore sadly missed. This is something that must be corrected in the future.

According to Williamson (1994), the principles of this new 'investigative interviewing' approach were to provide officers with an ethical foundation for police questioning. Now the focus was on information gathering rather than obtaining a confession *per se* (i.e. reliably establishing the facts), non-coercive interviewing and accurate recording of the interview. Police officers adopting 'oppressive' questioning would be in breach of these national guidelines and would find judges less willing to admit such statements into evidence than they had in the past. Williamson goes even further:

> In future the judges will also be paying particular attention to confessions from those who expert psychological evidence could show were at risk in making false confessions (Gudjonsson 1992a). There has to be greater awareness of these issues by police officers and also a change in questioning style in order to satisfy the legal requirement for the prosecution to show that nothing has been done which could render a confession unreliable (Williamson, 1994, p. 109).

The PEACE model has undergone some minor changes since its introduction in 1992 to take into account changes in legislation (Mortimer & Shepherd, 1999; National Crime Faculty, 1996, Ord & Shaw, 1999). It will be interesting to see in the future whether the enthusiasm for police interview training continues.

A number of studies have attempted to evaluate the effectiveness of the PEACE model. An early review produced favourable results (McGurk, Carr & McGurk, 1993). However, concerns have been expressed about the quality of management and supervision of police interviews (Stockdale, 1993; Williamson, 1994). The most detailed national evaluation of PEACE to date (Clarke & Milne, 2001) has raised concerns about the apparent lack of sufficient effectiveness of the national training in improving officers' interview skills. It is clear that training alone will not assist officers in developing new skills. Many officers appear to fail to put into practice what they have learned on the course, with planning and basic communication skills still remaining relatively poor, although some improvement has been noted since the introduction of the National Training Programme. About 10% of the interviews evaluated in the study were rated as possibly being in breach of the PACE Codes of Practice. Nevertheless, Clarke and Milne remain reasonably positive about the potential value of the National Training Programme. They emphasize that since the introduction of PEACE the approach to interviewing has become more ethical and the findings from their study are more favourable than those reported by Baldwin (1993). Clarke and Milne offer a number of important recommendations for future training.

The Clarke and Milne (2001) study also provides the first large-scale evaluation of interviews with victims and witnesses. These interviews were found to be far more defective than those conducted on suspects and the authors point to the absence of proper guidelines in relation to the taking of witness statements and the lack of audio or video recording of many such interviews.

In 1992 there was also new legislation and procedures introduced in relation to the interviewing of child witnesses and victims in criminal proceedings (Bull & Davies, 1996). Recently various Government agencies have jointly produced important guidance about the interviewing and treatment of vulnerable witnesses and children in criminal proceedings, which will undoubtedly influence future practice (Action for Justice, 2001). Hopefully these will be evaluated in the near future.

The miscarriage of justice cases in the late 1980s and early 1990s, and the accompanying evidence of police impropriety, may have undermined the public confidence in the police and increased the acquittal rate. From the mid-1970s to the end of the 1980s the acquittal rate by juries in England remained at about 32%, but it increased rapidly in the 1990s (Robbins, 2001, 2002). The police now have a great deal of work to do to improve their public image and the conviction rate.

CONCLUSIONS

During the past two decades major changes have taken place in England in relation to police interrogations. This has occurred largely in response to some celebrated cases of miscarriages of justice (i.e. the 'Confait Case', the 'Guildford Four', the 'Birmingham Six', the 'Tottenham Three' and the 'Cardiff Three'). The impact on legal changes, police practice and legal judgments appears to be unparalleled by that seen anywhere else in the world.

The changes began with the Fisher Inquiry (Fisher, 1977), followed by the setting up of the Royal Commission on Criminal Procedure (1981), the research that emerged from the Commission and the changes in legal provisions with the introduction of the Police and Criminal Evidence Act (PACE) 1984 (Home Office, 1985a). This was followed by the Royal Commission on Criminal Justice (1993), which resulted in more research studies being carried out into police interrogation. Scientific findings from psychological research over two decades have been influential in the development of legal concepts, legal judgments and police interview training. What has facilitated the changes has been the willingness of the British Government, the judiciary and the police to accept that serious mistakes have been made and that something needed to be done about it. Many valuable lessons have been learned as a result, which should encourage other nations to review their own practice.

With the implementation of the Police and Criminal Evidence Act in January 1986, and the accompanying Codes of Practice, manipulative tactics appear to have been markedly reduced, except perhaps occasionally in the most serious crimes (see Chapter 4). It seems that the persuasive interrogation style of the past has been replaced by questioning that is less manipulative in nature and is not dependent on lying to suspects. Trickery and deceit, which are so commonly recommended in American interrogation manuals (see Chapter 1), are not tolerated by the English Courts to the same extent (however, in spite of the apparently positive impact of PACE on police interviewing, one study of Crown Court cases suggests that the new Act may have had limited effect upon police behaviour (Bryan, 1997)).

In recent years, accompanying the introduction of new police training manuals and courses on interviewing, there appears to have been a general move away from interviewing primarily for obtaining a confession to obtaining reliable information. This represents a more ethical approach to interviewing and should result in fewer wrongful convictions in the future.

> Underpinning the new approach of investigative interviewing is a firm commitment to apply the lessons learnt from studies of interviewing (Williamson, 1993, p. 98).

Studies on police interviewing carried out prior to the new approach to interviewing indicate a general lack of skills among officers when interviewing suspects. There is some indication from recent research that the National Training Courses improve interviewing skills, although there remain serious problems with transferring the new interviewing skills to police practice. In spite of the new approach to interviewing, it should not be forgotten that obtaining a confession is still an important part of the investigative process and will no doubt continue to be so.

Prior to 1993 only three English studies had investigated the psychological vulnerabilities of persons detained at police stations. The main weakness of these studies is that the evaluation was based on observations only; no formal interview or psychometric testing was conducted. This has now been compensated for and the relevant research will be discussed in Chapter 3.

CHAPTER 3

Persons at Risk During Interviews in Police Custody: the Royal Commission Studies

The British government set up the Royal Commission on Criminal Justice immediately following the successful appeal of the 'Birmingham Six' on 14 March 1991. The terms of reference required the Commission to

> ...examine the criminal justice system from the stage at which the police are investigating an alleged or reported criminal offence right through to the stage at which a defendant who has been found guilty of such an offence has exhausted his or her rights to appeal (Royal Commission on Criminal Justice, 1993, p. 1).

The Commission's report took two years to complete. A total of 22 research studies had been commissioned as a part of the report. A number of these studies are cited in this book. This chapter includes a study by my colleagues and I, which directly examined the psychological vulnerabilities of persons detained at police stations through a clinical interview and psychometric testing. Gudjonsson et al. (1993) investigated empirically, for the first time anywhere in the world, the psychological characteristics and vulnerabilities of persons detained at police stations for questioning. It remains the only study that has gone beyond observational research.

The study was subsequently extended to investigate the relationships between different types of psychological vulnerability (Gudjonsson, Clare & Rutter, 1994; Gudjonsson, Rutter & Clare, 1995), the interview tactics used by the police (Pearse & Gudjonsson, 1996a) and the factors that predicted the likelihood of a confession (Pearse et al., 1998). These studies will be reviewed in this chapter.

In addition, I shall briefly review another study that Isabel Clare and I carried out for the Royal Commission on Criminal Justice, which focused on *Devising and Piloting an Experimental Version of the Notice to Detained Persons* (Clare & Gudjonsson, 1992). This study is important, because it demonstrated how difficult it is for intellectually disadvantaged persons to read and understand written material pertaining to their legal rights.

The structure of this chapter is in three parts. In the first part, the study by Gudjonsson and his colleagues (Gudjonsson *et al.*, 1993) for the Royal Commission on Criminal Justice is reviewed in detail since the comprehensive findings of the study are only available in the original 1993 *HMSO Report*. In the second part, further analyses and additional data from the study are presented. These focus on the relationship between psychological vulnerabilities and confessions made in police interviews. In other words, what are the factors that can successfully predict the likelihood of a confession? In the third part, the work on detainees' understanding of their legal rights and legal documents will be reviewed and the relevant related research cited.

THE 1993 ROYAL COMMISSION STUDY BY GUDJONSSON AND COLLEAGUES

Aims

The broad aim of the study was to extend the work done by Irving (1980) and Irving and McKenzie (1989) by formally assessing the psychological characteristics of detainees while at police stations, prior to their being interviewed by the police. It was expected that the data obtained would provide crucial information about the type and extent of potential vulnerabilities exhibited by suspects detained for interviewing at English police stations. This had never been attempted before and was considered of great importance.

The psychological variables chosen were selected on the basis of relevance to the legal issues concerning admissibility and reliability as discussed in detail by Gudjonsson (1992a). There was a crucial limitation, however, in terms of the comprehensiveness of the assessment. On the basis of discussions with the police it was apparent that the assessment should be limited to a maximum of one hour. This was to avoid the detainee's detention being prolonged beyond that which it would otherwise be. There was an opportunity for testing in that detainees were rarely interviewed immediately after being brought to the custody suite and where a solicitor was requested there was commonly a wait of between one and two hours.

Bearing in mind the time constraints, the following psychological variables were chosen.

- Current mental state.
- Intellectual functioning.
- Reading ability.
- Interrogative suggestibility.
- State and trait anxiety.
- Understanding of legal rights.

Another aim was to investigate how readily detainees' intellectual deficits could be determined by superficial observation prior to formal testing of intelligence. The hypothesis tested was that many intellectually disadvantaged detainees possess intellectual deficits which are not readily detected without formal psychological testing. Gudjonsson (1992a) had found in a number of criminal cases that even experienced clinicians often grossly over-estimated the intellectual abilities of the clients they were interviewing.

Methodology

Two police stations in the South East of England were selected: Peckham for an inner London police station and Orpington for a suburban, outer London, police station. Both police stations were within reasonable reach for the researchers and had the necessary facilities for the psychological assessment to be conducted. The Metropolitan Police fully cooperated with the study and a good working relationship with the custody officers and detectives at the two police stations was established.

Three experienced clinical psychologists regularly visited two police stations over a period of three months. All seven days of the week were included. However, attendance was focused on periods when the police stations were likely to be busy in order to reduce unnecessary waiting time. The criteria used for selecting the participants in the Royal Commission study were as follows.

- The participant was not a juvenile (i.e. was 17 years of age or above). Juveniles are automatically entitled to the presence of an 'appropriate adult' (i.e. responsible adult whose functions are discussed in detail in Chapter 10), irrespective of their mental state or psychological characteristics.
- The participant was detained at the police station for the purpose of an interview in connection with a criminal offence.
- The participant was not so intoxicated, disturbed or violent that it would be unsafe and unwise to conduct the psychological assessment.

All suitable suspects who arrived at the police station whilst one of the psychologists was there were asked to participate in the study.

The Psychological Evaluation

Prior to any psychological testing, the participant was interviewed about his or her occupational, academic, forensic, medical and psychiatric background. This was followed by questions about how the participant had been feeling mentally during the previous seven days. In addition, each participant was asked questions about their understanding of their legal rights and whether or not he or she had had their rights explained to them by the police.

In the final section of the interview protocol the researcher was required to make a clinical judgement about how the detainee seemed behaviourally and mentally during the interview with the researcher (by that time, the researcher had spent about 10–15 minutes with the detainee). The items were only endorsed in the affirmative if there was clear evidence of the behaviour or mental characteristic relevant to the question. For example, the heading 'learning difficulty' was only endorsed if there were strong positive signs that the detainee was likely to be 'mentally handicapped'. The reason for using such stringent criteria was that the researchers were trying to reduce the number of false positive errors to a minimum, although this was at the risk of producing some false negative errors (i.e. not identifying vulnerabilities when they were present).

After the interview schedule was completed a number of psychological tests, including the Gudjonsson Suggestibility Scale (GSS 2; Gudjonsson, 1987a), the Wechsler Adult Intelligence Scale—Revised (WAIS-R; Wechsler, 1981; in view of the time restriction allowed for the overall assessment, only the vocabulary, comprehension and picture completion subtests were administered), the Schonell Graded Word Reading Test (Schonell & Goodacre, 1974) and the State–Trait Anxiety Inventory (STAI; Spielberger, Gorsuch & Lushene, 1970).

The duration of the psychological assessment varied considerably across detainees, but most of the sessions lasted between 45 minutes and 1 hour.

Results

General Background

Out of 197 participants who were approached for their consent to cooperate with the study, 24 (12%) refused to take part, all of whom were male. Therefore, 173 assessments commenced, consisting of 144 (83%) males and 29 (17%) females, with mean ages of 28 and 29 years, respectively. In nine cases the detainee did not complete all the tests or answer all the questions asked. In a further eight cases the detainee was not subsequently interviewed by the police as originally planned. The majority (74%) of the detainees were Caucasian and 25% were Afro-Caribbean. The main offences under investigation were property offences ($N = 102$, 59%), violent offences ($N = 23$, 13%), and drug related offences ($N = 18$, 10%).

At the time of the study, 120 (70%) of the detainees were reported to be unemployed, 121 (71%) had previous criminal convictions, 61 (36%) had served a previous prison sentence, 56 (33%) had consumed alcoholic beverages within 24 hours of arrest and 37 (22%) reported having taken illicit drugs during the previous 24 hours. The alcohol consumption consisted mainly of having had a few beers prior to arrest, whereas the use of illicit drugs consisted mainly of smoking cannabis, or taking heroin or methadone.

Nineteen detainees (12%) said they had suffered from a nervous disorder and/or depression during the previous one year. Few sought treatment for their problem, claiming that their condition was not sufficiently serious to warrant treatment.

Mental State Prior to Arrest

The detainees were asked about their mental state during the seven days prior their arrest. The researchers only endorsed each item if there was clear indication from the detainees' replies that these 'problems' had been present.

Feeling low in mood was the most commonly reported symptom. It was reported in 74 (43%) of cases. The most common explanations given for the low mood were that the detainee had no job, no money and no sense of purpose. Low mood was followed by marked sleep disturbance, which was present in 65 (38%) of cases. It involved having problems getting to sleep, waking up earlier than

Table 3.1. Clinical evaluation of detainees prior to psychological testing ($N = 171$)

No apparent problems	112 (65%)
Problems:	
1. Intoxicated	2 (1%)
2. Drugged	12 (7%)
3. Crying	6 (4%)
4. Highly agitated	21 (12%)
5. Angry/suspicious	5 (3%)
6. Withdrawn	7 (4%)
7. Mentally ill	12 (7%)
8. Mentally handicapped	4 (3%)
9. Major language problems	3 (2%)
10. Stated unable to read	5 (3%)
11. Brain damage	1 (<1%)
12. Claustrophobia	1 (<1%)

From Gudjonsson et al., 1993.

usual or having restless sleep (i.e. waking up frequently throughout the night). Thirty-three (19%) reported feeling paranoid prior to their arrest. In 16 cases (9%) the detainees claimed to have been feeling suicidal during the previous week.

Detainees' Mental State at the Police Station

After the initial interview with the detainee, which took about 10–15 minutes, and prior to any psychological testing, the researchers conducted a clinical evaluation of each detainee on the basis of the mental state examination. The results are shown in Table 3.1.

The results indicate that 59 (35%) of the detainees were considered to have problems that might interfere with their functioning or ability to cope with the police interview(s). Twenty-one detainees (12%) were highly agitated and this made the psychological assessment difficult to conduct. Twelve detainees (7%) were considered to be mentally ill, the primary diagnoses being schizophrenia and severe depression (in exactly equal proportion). Twelve detainees (7%) appeared to be under the influence of drugs during the assessment. Only five detainees (3%) appeared to suffer from learning disability. Interestingly, only one detainee complained of claustrophobia. The police called in a forensic medical examiner (also known as a 'police surgeon') and he was prescribed a sedative. There were many detainees who were technically not claustrophobic, but they expressed distress about being locked up in a police cell and were clearly very anxious to be released from custody.

The Use of an Appropriate Adult

An appropriate adult was only called in seven (4%) of the cases. On the basis of their brief mental state examination, the researchers decided there were good clinical grounds for having an appropriate adult present during the police interview in 25 (15%) of the cases. This figure does not include cases where there were medical problems, such as epilepsy, diabetes and heart problems. Some medical problems can make detainees very agitated and distressed. There were two cases in the present study, one involving epilepsy and the other heart problems, where the detainees were extremely distressed because they did not have their medication with them. Their distress was overcome when the police allowed them access to their medication. There were also some heroin addicts who might have been vulnerable because of their withdrawal symptoms, but they were only included in the figures if they were also suffering from psychiatric problems, such as depression with clear suicidal ideas. The significant effects of drug withdrawal symptoms on the detainees' likelihood to confess to the police are discussed later in this chapter.

The 15% figure recommended by the researchers on the basis of their clinical interview alone is clearly an underestimate if one takes into account all the various medical conditions, drug withdrawal symptoms and low IQ scores obtained on testing. However, in the researchers' view, the police were able to detect the most vulnerable detainees and called in an appropriate adult. Interestingly, there were no cases where the police called in an appropriate adult where the researchers considered that one was not needed. Therefore, the police were able to identify accurately 28% of psychologically vulnerable detainees who were, according to the brief clinical evaluation, in need of an appropriate adult.

The police made frequent use of forensic medical examiners. They were called in 26 (16%) cases. They were typically called in when the police suspected or noted physical problems (e.g. physical injuries, intoxication or drug problems, and headaches), rather than involving cases where psychiatric or psychological problems needed to be evaluated.

Knowledge of Their Legal Rights

The researchers asked the detainees to list the rights to which they were entitled whilst at the police station. A total of 139 (82%) reported that they were entitled to see a solicitor and 113 (67%) knew that they could have somebody informed of their detention. A small minority (17%) reported that they were able to have a look at the Codes of Practice, if they wanted to.

Twenty-five (15%) of the detainees claimed that they had not been advised of their legal rights by the Custody Officer, whose duty it is at the police station to advise detainees of their legal rights. The researchers' observations in the Custody Suite showed that not all detainees were handed the Notice to Detained Persons and many of those who were given the Notice claimed that they had not bothered to read it, or could not read it or understand it.

Results from Psychological Testing

The results from the psychological tests administered are shown in Table 3.2. The prorated IQ scores for the Verbal and Performance subscales produced a

Table 3.2. The mean and standard deviation scores from the psychological tests

Test	Mean	S.D.
IQ test:		
Full Scale IQ	82	14
Verbal IQ	83	14
Performance IQ	83	19
Reading test:		
Raw score	74	20
Suggestibility test:		
Immediate Recall	11.6	6.4
Delayed Recall	10.5	6.4
Yield	5.6	3.7
Shift	4.3	3.5
Total Suggestibility	10.0	6.0
Anxiety test:		
Trait Anxiety	42.9	12.0
State Anxiety	53.6	13.5

From Gudjonsson et al., 1993.

mean of 83, which is over one standard deviation below the mean of 100 for the general adult population. In fact, the mean scores fall at the bottom 15% of the general population. There was a wide range of scores, with prorated Full Scale IQ ranging from 61 to 131. Fourteen (9%) of the total sample had a Full Scale IQ below 70 (i.e. bottom 2% of the general population); about a third (34%) had an IQ of 75 or below (i.e. bottom 5% of the general population). Sixty-eight (42%) subjects had a Full Scale IQ that fell in the 'borderline' range (i.e. IQ between 70 and 79). The results indicate that a large number of detainees suffer from a significant intellectual impairment or fall in the borderline range of 'mental handicap'.

The mean score obtained on the Schonell Graded Word Reading Test was 74. This gives an average reading age of 11 years and 8 months. The scores extended across the full range, 0 to 100. Eleven (7%) of the detainees obtained a score below 43, which represents a reading age of below nine years and functional illiteracy.

In the study, reading ability correlated only modestly with prorated Verbal Scale IQ ($r = 0.40, p < 0.001$) and not at all significantly with prorated Performance IQ ($r = 0.16$, ns). In addition, only five (45%) of the 11 detainees with a reading age below nine years had a prorated Full Scale IQ of below 75 and only one (9%) below 70. Conversely, nine of the subjects with a reading age above nine years had a prorated Full Scale IQ of below 70. The findings suggest that reading ability is not a good indicator of an intellectual deficit. Reading ability is not a direct function of intellectual ability, although they are modestly correlated.

The immediate and delayed memory scores obtained on the GSS 2 are well below those found for the normal population, but they are consistent with the low IQ scores obtained and similar to those found for other forensic populations (Gudjonsson, 1997a). When the memory scores are compared with the norms for the general population, it is apparent that they fall approximately in the 10th percentile rank (i.e. more than one standard deviation below the mean for the general population). That is, they are still within normal limits, but at the lower end of the normal range for the general population. Since the detainees were being assessed under very stressful conditions (i.e. while waiting to be interviewed by the police), is this likely to have impaired their memory performance on the GSS 2? The conditions under which they were being assessed may have impaired the memory performance of some of them. Certainly, some of them appeared to have problems concentrating on the task. However, it is important to note in this context that the memory scores obtained are slightly higher than those obtained among defendants tested for court referral assessments (see Tables 5.7 and 5.8 in Gudjonsson, 1997a). Therefore, the scores obtained among the detainees may not have been significantly impaired as a result of the testing being conducted at a police station while they were waiting to be interviewed. Both groups may have been under stress during the testing and their scores consequently adversely affected. It is also likely that some detainees' memory performance would be more impaired by stress than those of others. No doubt, individual differences play an important part.

As far as suggestibility is concerned, the Yield, Shift and Total Suggestibility scores are shown in Table 3.2. The scores are very similar to the mean scores found for court referrals and fall approximately in the 70th percentile rank for persons in the general population (Gudjonsson, 1997a). This suggests that, as a group, detainees tested at police stations are somewhat more suggestible than persons in the general population (i.e. about 0.5 standard deviation above the mean). However, these fall well within normal limits and deviate less from the mean scores of persons in the general population than was found for their memory scores. This suggests that among police detainees, and the same holds for court referrals, the memory scores on the GSS 2 deviate more from those found in the general population than their suggestibility scores (i.e. just over one standard deviation for the memory scores in contrast to less than 0.5 standard deviation for the suggestibility scores). These findings do not support the notion, which is sometimes argued in court by defence counsel, that being detained at a police station for questioning is inherently so stressful that detainees' suggestibility is inevitably increased well above their normal level.

It is possible that the elevated suggestibility scores found are due to the detainees' impaired intellectual and memory functioning. However, the pro-rated Full Scale IQ correlated poorly with both Total Suggestibility ($r = -0.23$, $p < 0.05$) and immediate and delayed recall ($r = -0.36$, $p < 0.001$, for both analysed separately). The reason for the low relationship between suggestibility and cognitive functioning (IQ and memory) may have been due to the fact that there were several detainees of very low IQ who were far from being suggestible on testing; conversely, some intellectually able detainees were highly suggestible. Therefore, the level of suggestibility of detainees cannot be judged on the basis of their IQ alone, which is consistent with previous studies involving different groups of subjects (Gudjonsson, 1992a).

Table 3.3. Differences in mean scores on the WAIS-R, STAI and GSS 2 for the Caucasian and Afro-Caribbean detainees

	Caucasian			Afro-Caribbean			
Test	N	Mean	S.D.	N	Mean	S.D.	t-value
WAIS-R:							
FSIQ	116	83.0	12.4	40	81.0	12.1	0.9
STAI:							
State	116	54.0	13.5	40	51.2	13.5	1.1.
Trait	116	44.1	12.6	40	39.2	10.2	2.4*
GSS 2:							
IR	120	12.5	6.6	40	9.3	5.7	2.7**
DR	118	11.4	6.5	40	8.4	5.6	2.6**
Yield 1	118	5.2	3.4	40	7.4	4.1	−3.3***
Yield 2	115	6.4	4.1	39	8.5	4.7	−2.6**
Shift	115	4.0	3.2	39	5.4	3.5	−2.3*
TSS	115	9.1	5.6	39	12.8	6.2	−3.5***

From Gudjonsson et al., 1995.
* $p < 0.05$;   ** $p < 0.01$;   *** $p < 0.001$ (all two tailed tests).
Analysis of covariance with I.Q. and DR controlled for:
Yield 1: $F = 6.7$ (df = 1, 155), $p = 0.010$.
Yield 2: $F = 3.3$ (df = 1, 151), $p = 0.071$.
Shift: $F = 3.1$ (df = 1, 151), $p = 0.082$.
TSS: $F = 7.6$ (df = 1, 151), $p = 0.007$.

The Royal Commission study revealed significant differences in suggestibility between the Caucasian and Afro-Caribbean detainees. The Afro-Caribbean detainees scored significantly higher than their Caucasian counterparts on all the GSS 2 measures. The analyses presented in the HMSO Report were extended in a subsequent publication to control for IQ and memory scores by the use of covariant analyses (Gudjonsson et al., 1995). The findings are presented in Table 3.3.

It is evident that there was no significant difference in prorated Full Scale IQ between the Caucasian and the Afro-Caribbean detainees, but the immediate and delayed memory scores on the GSS 2 were significantly higher among the Caucasian detainees. Controlling for IQ and delayed recall did alter the figures slightly in that the Yield 2 and Shift scores did not quite reach the conventional 0.05 level. What the figures do show is that even after controlling for differences in the IQ and memory scores, the Afro-Caribbean detainees remained significantly more suggestible than their Caucasian counterparts on Yield 1 and Total Suggestibility. For Yield 2 and Shift there were clear trends for significant differences on these subscales, which should be investigated in future research.

Trait and state anxiety were measured by the STAI. The state anxiety score was significantly higher than trait anxiety ($t = 9.1, p < 0.001$), as expected, indicating that being detained at the police station made suspects feel more stressed than usual. However, it is interesting that 25 (16%) of the subjects had lower state than trait anxiety scores, which implied that being at the police station was less stressful than how they normally felt in everyday circumstances. The reasons for this unexpected finding are uncertain, but part of the explanation may relate to the feelings of relief that some subjects seemed to experience after speaking with the researchers. For example, some of detainees told the researchers that the assessment took their mind off their current predicament and made them feel more relaxed, indicating that the assessment functioned as a temporary distractor and as a possible social support system.

The mean trait anxiety score of the detainees is similar to the mean of 44.6 found for prison inmates (Spielberger et al., 1970), whereas the state anxiety score differs significantly from that of prison inmates: 53.6 in the present study compared with 45.95 for prison inmates, $(t = 6.02, \mathrm{df} = 371, p < 0.001)$. Therefore, the mean state anxiety score in the present study is markedly higher than that found for prison inmates, in spite of a similar trait anxiety score. The likely explanation is that detainees were tested in a more stressful setting than the prison inmates were.

It is possible that the state anxiety scores of some of the detainees in the present study may have been artificially suppressed when the researchers assessed the detainees because of the apparently relaxing influence of the presence of the researcher for several of the detainees.

The individual state anxiety scores showed great variability across detainees. For example, 31 suspects (19%) obtained a state anxiety score of above 65, which falls in the 95th percentile rank for prison inmates (Spielberger et al., 1970). Therefore, when compared with prison inmates, almost a fifth of the police station detainees exhibited an abnormally high level of state anxiety. However, not all detainees rated being at the police station as unduly stressful. Six subjects (4%) obtained a state anxiety score of below 30, which falls in the sixth percentile rank for prison inmates (Spielberger et al., 1970).

Gudjonsson et al. (1995) investigated the relationship between anxiety and suggestibility among the detainees from the Royal Commission Study. Clear differences existed between the Caucasian and Afro-Caribbean detainees. The correlations between suggestibility and the anxiety scores were consistently higher among the Caucasian than Afro-Caribbean detainees. Among both groups, the correlations with suggestibility were consistently higher for trait anxiety than state anxiety, which is in contrast to what would have been expected from the Gudjonsson (1988a) study. What the findings suggest is that the relationship between state anxiety and suggestibility is complicated and anxiety may affect suggestibility in different ways, depending on situational factors and the circumstances of the individual case.

Discussion

The purpose of the study was to investigate the psychological characteristics of suspects prior to their being interviewed by the police. The characteristics studied were those that are considered relevant to the potential vulnerabilities of suspects to giving erroneous or misleading information to the police during interviewing (Gudjonsson, 1992a). They include their current mental state, their intellectual functioning, reading ability, state and trait anxiety and interrogative suggestibility. The detainees' understanding of their legal rights was also investigated. The impetus for the study came from the observational studies carried out by Irving (1980) and Irving and McKenzie (1989) at Brighton Police Station. It extended the previous studies by interviewing and assessing the detainees clinically before the police interviewed them.

The findings indicated that the majority (71%) of the detainees had previous convictions, which means the majority had familiarity with the police and their procedures. Between 80 and 90% of the suspects had a reasonable understanding of their basic legal rights and entitlements whilst being detained at the police station.

Probably the most important findings were the low IQ scores of many of the detainees and the difficulties with identifying intellectual deficits without formal testing. The average prorated Full Scale IQ of 82 is low. Almost 9% of the sample had an IQ below 70 and a further 42% had an IQ of between 70 and 79 (i.e. falling in the 'borderline' range). Taking an IQ of 75 or below as a significant intellectual impairment, this would classify about one-third of the total sample as being intellectually disadvantaged.

The average IQ obtained in the present study is probably an underestimate of the detainees' 'true' intellectual ability. Many detainees were very distressed at their arrest and confinement and had problems concentrating on the tests and, in addition, the testing had to be carried out under time pressure and without the psychologist being able to establish as good a rapport as would normally be the case in a clinical interview. However, taking into account the circumstances and context of the testing, the researchers believed it was unlikely that the average IQ of suspects detained in police custody is much above 85. This means that the police are interviewing many suspects of low intelligence, a sizeable proportion of whom would, on a comprehensive pre-trial assessment, be found to be suffering from a significant intellectual impairment. These findings have recently been replicated (Fenner, Gudjonsson & Clare, 2002).

Many of the suspects assessed were agitated and very distressed about their arrest and detention. For the majority of suspects, being at the police station was very stressful, even though there were a minority of detainees who were not unduly distressed. Over 20% of the suspects were suffering from an exceptionally high level of anxiety and distress. For some detainees, participating in the research made them feel much relieved and temporarily reduced their anxiety.

In spite of many detainees' low intelligence and high level of anxiety, they did not all prove to be unduly suggestible on testing. The detainees' susceptibility to suggestions and pressure varied greatly from one suspect to another, and it would be erroneous to assume that the majority of suspects who are to be interviewed by the police are necessarily unduly suggestible.

On the basis of a brief clinical interview, the researchers found that about a third (35%) of the detainees were in an abnormal mental state due to extreme distress or mental disorder, or that they were under the influence of drugs. Only one detainee appeared to be under the influence of alcohol, which is in marked contrast to the findings of Irving (1980). The few detainees who were very intoxicated when they arrived at the police station were left in a cell to sober up before the police interviewed them. It seems from our study that since the implementation of PACE far fewer detainees are interviewed by the police if they are obviously under the influence of alcohol.

Not every detainee who was found to be in an abnormal mental state required the presence of an appropriate adult in accordance with PACE. An appropriate adult is there to provide special assistance to detainees who are 'at risk' of providing an unreliable statement due to their impaired mental state or capacity (see Chapter 10). Taking into consideration those who were identified on the basis of the clinical interview alone as mentally disordered, illiterate or having language problems, a conservative estimate, according to the researchers, is that 15% of the total sample interviewed by the police fulfilled the PACE criteria for the presence of an appropriate adult (admittedly the criteria given in the PACE Codes of Practice are poorly defined operationally and the researchers were principally using their clinical judgement in line with PACE). This is obviously much higher than the 4% whom the police identified as needing an appropriate adult. Taking into account the findings from the psychological tests, in addition to the clinical interview evaluation, the instances of need for an appropriate adult rise considerably above the 15% figure and the true figure probably lies in the region of 25%.

A small minority (7%) of detainees were suffering from mental illness, such as severe depression or schizophrenia, and were sufficiently disabled to require the presence of an appropriate adult as recommended by the PACE Codes of Practice. Most were not identified by the police as being mentally ill. An appropriate adult was requested in only four (33%) out of the 12 cases where mental illness had been identified by the researchers. Most of the remaining suspects would not have been readily identified as mentally ill without a brief clinical interview. The detainees with a history of schizophrenia were most readily identified by the police. It was the depressed detainees, some of whom were actively suicidal at the time of their detention, whom the police most commonly failed to identify as vulnerable. In addition, the three suspects who had severe language problems did not have an appropriate adult or an interpreter present during the police interview, even though their difficulties would have been easy to identify.

On the basis of a clinical interview alone, only four (3%) suspects were judged by the researchers to be learning disabled. Two were identified by the police and an appropriate adult was requested in both cases. On the basis of the IQ scores obtained, having taken into account the circumstances and context of the testing, there is no doubt that by observation alone over a short period of time, proper identification of mild learning disability, even by trained clinicians, is a very difficult task. There are three main reasons for this. First, many persons with a significant intellectual impairment have reasonable social functioning which may disguise their intellectual limitation (i.e. on superficial acquaintance they appear normal). Deficient social functioning is much easier to identify than an intellectual deficit, although it is more difficult to formally assess than IQ. Second, some persons with learning disability see their handicap as private and would not tell the police about it and may even deliberately disguise it as far as they are able to. Third, even when social functioning is significantly impaired, it may not be easy to identify on brief acquaintance or during a brief clinical interview.

In spite of problems with identification, the brief clinical interview conducted by the researchers identified many more persons with learning disability than the studies by Irving (1980) and Irving and McKenzie (1989), where only one detainee out of a total of 196 (0.5%) was judged to be of low intelligence or suffering from 'mental handicap'. Therefore, the brief clinical evaluation seems to have added substantially to the identification of learning disability.

WHO CONFESSES?

Interview Tactics and Detainees' Reactions

Following the psychological assessment of the detainees at Peckham and Orpington Police Stations, copies of the police interview tapes were obtained and analysed (Pearse & Gudjonsson, 1996a). As far as the duration of the interviews is concerned, 80% were completed in less than 30 minutes and 95% were completed within one hour. The results indicate that the great majority of interviews are very short, which is consistent with the findings of Baldwin (1993) and Williamson (1990). Williamson reported that 99% of the interviews observed were completed within 45 minutes and Baldwin found in his study that only 7% of interviews lasted longer than one hour.

A specially constructed coding frame was devised by Pearse and Gudjonsson (1996a) in order to analyse objectively the nature of the police interview tactics used and the detainees' reactions to the questioning.

As far as the police interviews were concerned, open-ended questions occurred in 158 (98%) of the interviews. Leading questions were found in 118 (73%) of the sample. The most common techniques of persuasion were the introduction of allegations against the suspect, which was found in 119 (74%) of the interviews, and challenging a lie or an inconsistency, which was present in 32 (20%) interviews. Other types of challenge, emphasizing the seriousness of the offence, and psychological manipulation, were individually noted in less than 8% of cases. The findings suggest that the multiple repertoires of tactics and the common use of psychological manipulation identified by Irving (1980), prior to the introduction of the Police and Criminal Evidence Act in 1986, are no longer present. It is tempting to speculate that the new legislation, which introduced the mandatory use of tape recordings, has in a major way influenced the duration and nature of police interview tactics, at least in the general or 'run-of-the-mill' criminal cases. As will be shown in Chapter 4, in the most serious criminal cases, there is much pressure and psychological manipulation sometimes employed by interviewing officers to break down suspects' resistance.

As far as the detainees' reactions are concerned, the great majority were polite (97%), generally compliant (83%), and gave full answers (62%). It was very rare for detainees to react in an angry or suspicious manner (2%) and crying and sobbing was only noted in four (3%) cases.

As far as confessions are concerned, 93 (58%) of the suspects made a full confession or a self-incriminating admission (i.e. some admission of involvement in the offence, but minimizing intent or the part played). In 90 (97%) cases the confession or admission occurred in the first interview. Only three suspects (3%) confessed in a subsequent interview. These were the only cases where a suspect confessed after having made an initial denial. In all other cases the confession was made readily at the beginning of an interview. This is consistent with the findings of other studies (Baldwin, 1993; Moston, Stephenson & Williamson, 1992), which suggests that once suspects enter a police interview they have already decided whether or not to deny or admit the offence and persist with their initial denial, irrespective of the police interview techniques.

What Predicts a Confession?

The fact that just over half of all detainees made a confession during the police interviews makes it important to identify the factors that differentiate between those who make a confession and those who make a denial. Pearse *et al.* (1998) used a logistic regression analysis to identify the variables from the Royal Commission Study that successfully predicted a confession versus a denial. The data from psychological testing and clinical evaluation, as well as the detainees' criminal history, were, together with the analysis of the police interview tapes, used as the exploratory (independent) variables. A forward logistic regression procedure was used to identify and extract the most significant exploratory variables.

Pearse *et al.* (1998) provide details of the findings from the individual analyses. As predicted from the review of the literature, age did differentiate between the confessors and deniers. The mean ages for the confessors and deniers were 27 and 30, respectively. This difference was significant ($t = 1.72, p < 0.05$). However, once all interactions were taken into account only three variables predicted a confession or a denial. These are shown in Table 3.4. The table provides the odds ratio, a 95% confidence interval and the significance level for each variable. It can be seen that one variable, illicit drug taking, predicted suspects making a confession, and two variables, having access to a solicitor at the police station and having been to prison, were associated with suspects making a denial.

No significant pairwise interactions were found between these three variables. The odds of a suspect making a confession were more than three times

Table 3.4. The outcome of police interview: the likelihood of confession or denial

Variable	Odds ratio	CI (95%)	Significance
Illicit drugs	3.37	1.36–8.32	0.01
Prison experience	0.46	0.22–0.95	0.05
Solicitor present	0.26	0.12–0.54	0.001

From Pearse *et al.*, 1998.

greater if that suspect had reported using an illicit (non-prescribed) drug within 24 hours of his or her arrest, compared with a suspect who claimed that he or she had not taken any illicit substance during that period. This is an important finding. The most likely explanation is that suspects who are dependent on illicit drugs are motivated by factors that they perceive as expediting their release from custody. Making a confession during police detention may be perceived by suspects as a way of cooperating with the police and hence furthering their early release from custody. In this way they can minimize the discomfort of withdrawal symptoms associated with their lack of access to illicit drugs while detained at the police station.

The two factors associated with denial, having access to a solicitor and previous prison experience, are also of considerable theoretical and practical importance. According to the logistic regression model, the odds of suspects not confessing was four times greater for a suspect who had a legal representative present compared with one who did not have access to a lawyer. As far as previous prison experience is concerned, the likelihood of denial is twice as great in cases where the suspect has been to prison.

Why should the presence of a solicitor so markedly reduce the likelihood of suspects making a confession? There are at least two possibilities. Firstly, a legal representative may advise his or her client to exercise their rights to silence, particularly where the evidence against their client is in their view weak. Secondly, suspects who have decided prior to the police interview not to make a confession may be more inclined to request the presence of a solicitor.

It is interesting that prison experience, either on remand or having served a sentence, rather than the number of previous convictions *per se*, was predictive of suspects making a denial. It may be that suspects with experience of prison were more focused on the potential consequences of making a confession. Having been to prison may have reinforced their view of the long-term consequences of conviction and made them more reluctant to make a confession.

The greatest likelihood of suspects of making a confession occurred where there was no solicitor present and the suspect had consumed illicit drugs within 24 hours of arrest and had not previously been to prison. The likelihood of a confession occurring under those circumstances was 92%, in contrast to the average confession rate of 58% for the entire sample.

DETAINEES' LEGAL RIGHTS

Under the Police and Criminal Evidence Act (PACE; Home Office, 1985a, 1985b, 1995) detainees are orally informed of their legal rights and in addition provided with written information in the form of a 'leaflet', entitled the 'Notice to Detained Persons'. Their five basic rights are the following.

- They can remain silent.
- They have the right to obtain legal advice.
- They can have somebody informed of their arrest.

- They are entitled to consult the PACE Codes of Practice.
- They have the right to a copy of the Custody Record.

Detainees' understanding of their legal rights has important practical and legal implications. First, unless detainees are able to understand the information they are given by the police they are unlikely to be able to exercise their legal rights. Secondly, if it can be shown at trial that the detainee had not understood his legal rights then any statement he made to the police may be ruled inadmissible (see Chapter 10).

In the early 1990s I investigated the reading complexity of the Notice to Detained Persons, using a similar methodology to that of Grisso (1986) concerning the comprehension of the *Miranda* rights in the USA. I found that the information contained in the Notice to Detained Persons would be understood by fewer than one in four persons in the general population and that intellectually disadvantaged persons would be most seriously affected (Gudjonsson, 1990a, 1991a). Following this study, in April 1991 the Notice to Detained Persons was simplified by the Home Office (1991). We set out to compare the reading complexity of the revised Notice with that of the previous one (Gudjonsson, Clare & Cross, 1992). We found that while some sentences in the revised Notice were now easier to understand others still remained far too difficult and the overall understanding of the document was significantly related to intellectual functioning. As a consequence of this finding, Isabel Clare and I set out to devise and pilot a simplified version of the revised Notice to Detained Persons for the Royal Commission on Criminal Justice (Clare & Gudjonsson, 1992). We found that our 'experimental' version of the Notice to Detained Persons was a significant improvement on the newly revised Home Office version, but unfortunately it has not yet been adopted by the Home Office. Our findings concur with Hartley's (2000) view that when writing legal texts more attention should be paid to the reader's likely understanding of it.

Our second recommendation to the Royal Commission on Criminal Justice was that detainees should be specifically asked by the police if they required 'special help', because of reading or learning difficulties, previous attendance at a special school or mental health problems. In our research we found that 80% of persons with learning difficulties could be identified by this form of questioning. Our methodology and recommendation has now been adopted by the Metropolitan (London) Police Service.

In April 1995 (Home Office, 1995) detainees' right to silence was modified under sections 34 and 37 of the *Criminal Justice and Public Order Act 1994* (England & Wales; Wasik & Taylor, 1995). This meant a change to the wording of the police caution. The current caution reads as follows:

> You do not have to say anything. But it may harm your defence if you do not mention when questioned something which you later rely on in court. Anything you do say may be given in evidence (Home Office, 1995, p. 50).

The problem with the current caution is that it is far too complex for most persons in the general population and suspects to understand (Shepherd, Mortimer & Mobasheri, 1995; Clare, Gudjonsson & Harari, 1998; Fenner,

Gudjonsson & Clare, 2002). Even some police officers do not understand the current caution (Clare, Gudjonsson & Harari, 1998). Indeed, even when the caution is presented under ideal conditions, one sentence at a time, only 10% of police detainees and persons in the general population are able to demonstrate full understanding of its meaning (Fenner, Gudjonsson & Clare, 2002). In addition, 96% of the participants claimed to have understood the caution fully after it was read out to them, which demonstrates that detainees' claim that they understand the caution gives no accurate indication of their real understanding of it. It is the middle sentence, warning of possible adverse inferences, which creates the greatest problem. Apart from reverting to the original caution, or changing the wording of the current caution, the best way around this problem is for the police to do the following.

- Ensure they understand the caution themselves.
- Carefully explain each sentence to detainees.
- Check detainees' understanding of the caution by having them paraphrase or explain it.

GENERAL CONCLUSIONS

In this chapter our studies commissioned by the Royal Commissions on Criminal Justice into the psychological vulnerabilities of police detainees and the complexity of documents relating to detainees' legal rights have been reviewed. Our studies conducted at two Metropolitan police stations complement the work of Barrie Irving and Ian McKenzie in two respects. First, rather than relying only on the observation of suspects in order to identify psychological vulnerabilities, a formal psychological assessment was conducted on suspects at the police station prior to their being interviewed by the police. This was the first study to include a formal psychological assessment. It revealed important findings about the nature and extent of psychological vulnerabilities among detainees. Probably the most surprising findings were the low IQ scores of the detainees and the fact that many persons with intellectual deficits could not be identified as such from a brief clinical interview. The findings are consistent with the literature on offenders (Eysenck & Gudjonsson, 1989) and pre-trial assessments (Gudjonsson, 1990a).

The second unique contribution relates to a follow-up study to the Royal Commission study, where the psychological vulnerabilities of detainees identified on testing and from a brief mental state examination were subsequently analysed in relation to detainees' performance in a subsequent police interview. Of particular importance are the factors that are directly associated with whether or not suspects make a confession during questioning. None of the test findings predicted either a confession or a denial. The only mental state factor that predicted a confession was whether or not the suspect had consumed illicit drugs within 24 hours of arrest. The presence of a lawyer and a previous experience of imprisonment were highly predictive of suspects denying any involvement in the crime.

Our research into 'Devising and piloting an experimental version of the notice to detained persons' has assisted with identifying how persons at risk during police detention can be better identified by the police so that their legal rights are fully protected. Our recommendations to the Royal Commission that the police should routinely ask detainees specific questions to assist with identification of vulnerabilities has now been adopted by the Metropolitan (London) Police Service. This shows how research can influence police practice.

CHAPTER 4

The Identification and Measurement of 'Oppressive' Police Interviewing Tactics in Britain

John Pearse and Gisli H. Gudjonsson

One of the questions this chapter will seek to address is whether we can identify what it is that makes a resistant suspect confess to a crime that he (or she) has been denying. To assist us in this process we shall outline a unique framework that has succeeded in measuring and displaying the type of tactic employed by police officers to overcome the resistance of reluctant criminal suspects. *The Police Interviewing Analysis Framework* (PIAF) was developed as part of a Ph.D. thesis that examined a number of psychological and interrogative factors associated with a suspect's confession (Pearse, 1997). Essentially, 20 serious criminal cases were subjected to a detailed examination of all that was taking place within the police interview. The results of this microanalysis were then subjected to a statistical process that produced a number of salient interrogation and response factors that we have converted into a graphic presentation. It would not be practical to provide a complete review of the entire methodological and statistical procedures undertaken for the thesis within the confines of this chapter, but we hope to provide sufficient detail to allow the reader an insight into the development and application of the framework.

BACKGROUND TO THE RESEARCH

The main hypothesis underlying our research was that suspects who move from an initial denial to a confession do so because of the amount of pressure and psychological manipulation applied by the interviewing officers. Put another way, we sought to establish the extent to which the techniques recommended by Inbau, Reid and Buckley (1986) were employed by police officers to overcome a suspect's resistance in serious criminal cases in England and Wales. Despite the intuitive appeal of our hypothesis, this is not a straightforward matter and we cannot automatically assume that the hypothesis will be supported. For example, Baldwin's early research on police interviewing challenged a number of accepted norms in this field (1992a, 1992b, 1993, see Chapter 3) and he was also highly critical of the absence of any established legal ground rules for police officers interviewing suspects (Baldwin, 1994).

In the first instance, he showed that in many cases eliciting a confession from a suspect was not directly linked to the type of interviewing style adopted or the 'persuasive' dialogue employed by the police. In fact, in highlighting the inept manner in which most interviews were conducted he questioned the whole 'myth' of the gladiatorial nature of police interviewing, which would predict that the interviewing officers eventually succeed in breaking down the reluctant suspect. What research has shown is that the distinction needs to be drawn between general 'run-of-the-mill' cases, where typically little or no persuasive interaction is taking place (Baldwin 1992a, 1992b, 1993; Pearse & Gudjonsson, 1996a), and serious criminal offences. It is serious criminal cases that have been the subject of a number of miscarriage of justice proceedings (Corre, 1995; Gudjonsson, 1992a), and it is from this select group that the PIAF was developed. Our definition of a serious criminal offence was taken from section 116 of PACE (Home Office, 1985a). This includes murder, rape, arson, armed robbery and blackmail.

Secondly, Baldwin also challenged the lack of guidance in relation to what was, and what was not, acceptable police interviewing practice. He berated the Royal Commission on Criminal Procedure (1993) on this subject for not seizing the opportunity presented:

> ...one was struck by the bland, unexceptional and unimaginative character of the Commission's recommendations on police interviewing procedures (Baldwin, 1994, p. 68)

was how he summarized the 'superficial' nature of their discussions. According to Baldwin, what needed to be addressed was

> ...to determine what kind of pressures police interviewers can legitimately exert upon suspects detained in police custody (Baldwin, 1994, p. 71).

For example, lying to or threatening a suspect would be contrary to the Codes of Practice that accompany PACE (Home Office, 1995). On their own, however, such tactics may not inevitably render a confession inadmissible. What is important, in English law, is the entire context of the case (i.e. the surrounding circumstances—see Chapter 10).

Accordingly, in an attempt to illuminate this very grey area, another objective of the PIAF was to measure and display, in an objective and scientific manner, what was and what was not an acceptable level of pressure in the police–suspect interview situation. To assist us in this regard, our base line measure was to examine the relationship between the type and frequency of tactics and the subsequent admissibility and reliability of the interview according to the judgment of the courts. Following on from earlier chapters, it was anticipated that tactics that seek to maximize or exaggerate the strength of the evidence against the suspect, or that seek to minimize the suspect's responsibility or role in the offence, would be present. Thus, the more manipulative and coercive the tactics, the greater the likelihood that the accompanying confession would be ruled inadmissible by the court.

THE CASES ANALYSED

Assembling a suitable group of cases was not a simple matter as there were a number of key criteria that had to be present. All suspects had to initially deny the allegation against them, and then, on audiotape, change their mind and make a confession. It was not acceptable for the confession to be made following an extensive break in the interview procedure (e.g. after a night's rest or on the suspect's return from a visit to the scene). This condition ensured that it was possible to capture the actual confession process: in other words, identifying, in controlled conditions, what was taking place leading up to and immediately before a confession was made. This requirement proved very difficult to comply with as (contrary to public opinion) there are actually very few adequately recorded examples where suspects are persuaded to change their mind during the course of a police interview (Baldwin, 1993; Moston, Stephenson & Williamson, 1992; Pearse & Gudjonsson, 1996a). Therefore, the cases presented are rather rare, but importantly they do demonstrate the process whereby suspects break down during an interview rather than before or between interviews.

All the defendants had been assessed by a clinical psychologist prior to the study for the purposes of a Court Report and in some of the cases expert testimony had been given. Nineteen of the cases were from Gudjonsson's case files and one case was from a colleague's case file. A summary of the case details is provided in Table 4.1.

The mean interviewing time for all 20 cases was 2 hours 16 minutes, with a range of 22 minutes to 12 hours 42 minutes. These were much longer interviews than have been reported for general or 'run-of-the-mill' cases (Baldwin, 1993; Williamson, 1990) and considerably longer than the mean interviewing time of 22 minutes recorded in our Royal Commission study (Pearse & Gudjonsson, 1996a). There were a total of 46 officers present in an interviewing capacity. 43 (93%) were male and three (7%) were female. Of this number, 40 (87%) were detectives and six (13%) were uniformed officers. The proportion of detectives and the inclusion of a number of more senior officers are thought to reflect the serious nature of the crimes under investigation. Interestingly, there was only one case where an officer interviewed alone in our sample, whereas Leo (1996a) found that a single officer conducted 70% of interviews in his American sample. Given the resource implications for police forces everywhere, this is clearly an area that warrants additional field research.

To help us understand what is going on in a police interview it is important not to lose sight of the context of each case. This will include the nature of the allegation, the criminal experience (or lack of it) of the suspect and the presence or absence of other parties. Although we are primarily concerned with

Table 4.1. Twenty serious criminal cases

Suspect details	Nature and year of case	Interview details	Outcome of case
1. M (18)	Burglary (with intent to rape). 1994	66 min—Legal adviser present	Guilty—burglary. Hospital Order
2. M (19)	Attempted rape, indecent assault. 1994	72 min—legal adviser present	Found not guilty
3. M (15)	Rape. 1992	24 min—AA and legal adviser present	Not guilty, interview ruled oppressive
4. M (54)	Buggery. 1992.	62 min—legal adviser present	Plea of guilty. 8 years imprisonment
5. M (18)	Rape and indecent assault. 1991	2 h 29 min—no other party	Guilty—indecent assault. 3 years detention
6. M (32)	Buggery. 1992	74 min—legal adviser present	Guilty—indecent assault. 2 years imprisonment
7. M (55)	Incest. 1994	86 min—legal adviser present	Found guilty. 6.5 years imprisonment
8. M (22)	Arson. 1992	2 h 18 min—only AA present	Interview not reliable. Withdrawn
9. M (18)	Arson. 1991	30 min—no other party	Case dismissed. Interview oppressive
10. M (18)	Arson. 1993	47 min—legal adviser present	Interview not reliable. Withdrawn
11. M (24)	Arson. 1995	94 min—only AA present	Not guilty—jury verdict
12. F (26)	Attempt pervert course justice. 1992	1 h 49 min—only AA present	Plea of guilty. 2 years probation
13. M (23)	Armed robbery. 1992	86 min—legal adviser present	Case dismissed. Interview oppressive
14. M (38)	Armed robbery. 1992	66 min–2 days—no other party	Not guilty, interview inadmissible, no AA
15. M (18)	Robbery. 1996	35 min—no other party	Pleaded guilty. 3 years detention
16. M (24)	Blackmail. 1995	43 min—no other party	Bound over to keep the peace (£150)
17. F (18)	Murder. 1993	4 h 15–2 days—AA and legal adviser	Guilty—manslaughter. 3 years probation
18. M (20)	Murder. 1995	61 min—AA and legal adviser	Guilty—manslaughter. Hospital Order
19. M (23) (Heron)	Murder. 1992	7 h 48 min–3 days—legal adviser present	Not guilty, directions of trial judge. Interviews oppressive
20. M (22) (Miller)	Murder. 1988	12 h 42 min–5 days—legal adviser present	Appeal Court ruled interviews oppressive. Conviction quashed

the interviewing tactics adopted by police officers, it is therefore important to bear in mind the activities and contributions of all the parties present. Thus we need to ask what the impact was in a case where a legal adviser or a family member was present. To what extent did their presence influence the dynamics of the interaction and the outcome of interview?

In this sample, a legal adviser was present in 12 (60%) of the cases, but it was not always possible to determine the actual status of each individual. In England and Wales it was acceptable for 'unqualified legal advisers', who may be contracted to a firm of established solicitors, to attend a police station, provide legal advice and be present for all police interviews. For a number of years the credibility and status of these representatives was rarely known or challenged. However, as a result of a highly critical study conducted for the Royal Commission on Criminal Justice (McConville & Hodgson, 1993), all legal advisers at police stations (if not qualified solicitors) must now undertake a recognized training programme, administered and approved by the Law Society (Ede & Shepherd, 2000). One of the criticisms leveled at legal advisers was the 'passive' nature of their role (Baldwin, 1993; McConville & Hodgson, 1993). In this sample, there was evidence available in two-thirds of the cases where the legal adviser remained silent, when there appeared good reason for them to interject. Indeed, in the Miller case (case 20), the Court of Appeal judges were very critical of the passive performance of the solicitor, who sat in on all the interviews and did not intervene during highly oppressive interviewing (see Chapter 19 for details of the judgment).

Another party often present in police interviews is the 'Appropriate Adult' (AA). Formulated within the Codes of Practice (PACE), the origins of this post can be traced back to the infamous 'Confait' case and the subsequent Fisher Public Inquiry, which was highly critical of the detention and treatment of three juvenile murder suspects by police in the early 1970s (Fisher, 1977). In lay terms, an AA is a person who is independent of the police and who should provide an additional safeguard for 'vulnerable' suspects (such as juveniles, or suspects with learning disability or mental illness). In this sample an AA was present in six (30%) of the 20 cases, and in five out of the six cases (83%) their performance was not in accordance with published guidelines. There were two examples of passive behaviour (i.e. they remained silent when the situation demanded otherwise) but, more worryingly, in the three remaining cases it was actually an intervention, or prompt, from the AA that preceded a confession. Allowing for the small sample size, concern exists that in only one case did the AA act in accordance with the provisions of this important 'safeguard'.

METHODOLOGY

Our objective was to develop a full understanding of the context of each individual case (macro examination) and then produce a detailed analysis of what was taking place in the interview setting (micro examination). In the first instance, witness statements, summaries and other relevant papers were studied to gain an understanding of the circumstances and evidence in each case. As both the typed transcript and audiotape were available, the next stage entailed listening to the audiotape in order to check each transcript, inserting any alterations or amendments that were required, and each individual interview tape was divided into five minute sections. Occasionally, some police questioning was so verbose that it extended over a considerable number of pages, and in these cases the five minute marker was inserted at a natural pause. Thus, by reading the available evidence, listening to the tape and correcting the transcript, it was possible to acquire a valuable insight into the history, nature and circumstances of each case. The final product of interview tactics and response variables was then subjected to a number of statistical tests (principally factor analysis), which identified the dominant 'clusters' of tactics that formed identifiable factors.

The approach undertaken for this study was designed to discriminate amongst the range of possible techniques or tactics, including the extent of their use (frequency), timing and degree of use (intensity) as well as the relevant context (i.e. the accompanying tactics and suspects' reactions). Given the crucial importance of our categorization of the 'interview tactics' and 'suspect responses' to the development of the PIAF we intend to outline these areas in some depth (Pearse, 1997; Pearse & Gudjonsson, 1999).

INTERVIEW TACTICS

A number of typologies have been provided in the literature to help identify and categorize the range of possible interviewing tactics. Kalbfleisch (1994) for example, presents a 15-part typology, whilst Kassin and McNall (1991) provide a two-tier 'maximization' and 'minimization' approach (although this was specifically designed to interpret the Inbau–Reid–Buckley (1986) Model. A separate typology is presented here, based on an assessment by the first author that identified a total of 39 tactic variables. This typology is composed of three distinct categories.

1. Delivery.
2. Maximization.
3. Manipulation.

Delivery

This category concerns the type of question asked and 'how' the questions are put (i.e. the manner in which they are delivered or the context of that delivery). A total of 12 variables contributed to this category. This research confined the categorization of type of question to three: *open, closed* or *leading*. An open question is often an invitation for the suspect to provide his account of events ('Tell us what you were doing then, today?'). A closed question is one that can be answered in a few words ('How did you get there, did you walk or cycle?'). A leading question is one that is 'loaded' or implies the answer the interviewer wants to hear ('Yeah and you turned some of the drawers out as well didn't you?': Gudjonsson, 1992a; Richardson, Dohrenwend & Klein, 1965).

The context in which questions are put is very important. Dialogue may take place in *hushed or lowered tones* (as recommended by Inbau, Reid & Buckley, 1986, when dealing with emotional suspects) or at the other end of the spectrum, questioning may take place in a hostile and intimidating environment. For example, the officers may use a *raised or aggressive tone*, continually *interrupting* the suspect and refusing to listen to their answers, and perhaps *swearing* at the suspect.

This category also caters for *multiple questions* and *multiple officers*. The latter relates to both officers asking questions one after the other, without an opportunity for the suspect to reply, whilst in the former, one officer might introduce a particularly long sentence that contains *multiple questions* or *multiple assertions* (here multiple is defined as more than two). Some officers also tend to repeat a suspect's response or the last few words of the reply. In some instances this can act as a prompt for the suspect to continue, but mindless repetition of replies, or *echoing*, as it is known, is not recommended (CPTU, 1992a). Finally, this section includes the tactic *the use of silence*. According to the national guidelines for police interviewers

> ...silence can be a powerful tool to prompt an interviewee to speak. After a question has been put to a person who is reluctant to answer, or after receiving a reply which you want elaborating, consider remaining silent (CPTU, 1992a, p. 57).

This variable was taken as any period of silence that exceeded nine seconds in length.

Maximization

According to Kassin and McNall (1991), maximization represents

> ...a hard sell technique in which the interrogator tries to scare and intimidate the suspect into confessing by making false claims about evidence and exaggerating the seriousness and the magnitude of the charges (p. 234).

In this study the term is extended to include any technique which would tend to increase a suspect's internal anxiety (already accentuated as a result of failing to admit the allegation—Inbau, Reid & Buckley, 1986) and any form of intimidation or challenge directed at the suspect (such as the threat of continued detention). There were 14 such tactics identified in this sample.

Instances where the officers categorically emphasized the serious nature of the offence under investigation (e.g. murder) or the mental torment that denial would bring represented obvious examples of *maximizing the serious nature of the offence* and *maximizing anxiety*, respectively. Similarly, *threats*, direct or implied, were also categorized. The *accusatorial* or direct approach identified by Moston and Stephenson (1993) is included in this sample, where the suspect is *confronted at the outset with the allegation*. This was often followed up with the *introduction of evidence*, or, more indirectly, the introduction of *implied evidence*, where the officers declined to be specific about the extent or exact nature of the evidence. Exposure to such evidence was designed to overcome the futility of denial (Irving, 1980) and to increase the pressure and anxiety on the suspect (Inbau, Reid & Buckley, 1986). Such continued pressure was also maintained where the officer made a direct *appeal* to the suspect's conscience or perhaps his good character.

The largest group of tactics in this category fell under the heading of *challenges*. These included challenges in relation to the suspect's *previous convictions* ('But you stabbed a boy three, four years ago with a knife?'); possible *accomplices* ('That is not the story your friend is telling us'); *contradictions* in his story or in relation to *witness information*, ('So why would the woman from the shop phone the fire brigade if the fire brigade were already there?') or challenges that the suspect's replies were simply *not believable* ('I think you have told so many stories you don't know what the truth is anymore, do you?'). Instances where the officers called the suspect a *liar* would fall into this section. It was noticeable that on occasions a *pantomime* sequence would develop with the suspect content to deny every challenge (e.g. 'I wasn't in on Wednesday night–you were–I wasn't–I'm telling you now that you were–I wasn't in there Wednesday night–We have got several people–I wasn't in on Wednesday night–Between 9 and 10 you went in–I wasn't–We've got people...'). Three or more repetitions (on the same theme) represented a pantomime sequence.

Finally, it was evident from the judgments provided in *R. v. Heron* (1993, unreported, Leeds Crown Court), and *R. v. Paris, Abdullahi and Miller* ([1993] 97 Cr.App.R. 99) [cases 19 and 20, respectively] that the continued and persistent challenges and verbal assaults on the veracity of the suspects' replies had a marked and deleterious effect on the defendant's willpower and resistance. The judgments concluded that a relentless refusal to entertain the suspect's point of view was bound to undermine the most resolute of defendants and amounted to 'oppression'. To capture this latent technique a *continual dispute* variable was introduced to itemize every instance where the officers directly or indirectly challenged, contradicted or undermined the substance of the suspect's account.

Manipulation

The debilitating effect of physical isolation and confinement on a suspect's resolve, especially when coupled with aggressive and intimidating interviewing tactics, was recognized by Lord Chief Justice Taylor, in *R. v. Paris, Abdullahi and Miller* [1993] 97 Cr.App.R. 99, in relation to Miller. It was noticeable however, that these tactics did not, on their own, succeed in eliciting a confession. This was achieved in a subsequent interview by more 'insidious questioning' (*R. v. Paris et al.*, 1993, p. 104). In that case the officers persuaded the suspect to admit that it was possible he was at the scene, even if he could not remember it, and as the judgment noted 'Once he opened that chink, the officers kept up the questioning to open it further' (*R. v. Paris et al.*, 1993, p. 104). Such questioning involves creating possible *scenarios* or *themes* for the suspect to adopt, which might lull him into a false sense of security or get him to make a minor admission that can be built upon. This is a classic example of manipulation, and 13 variations were identified. The techniques used in the case of Miller are very reminiscent of those recommended by Inbau, Reid and Buckley (1986).

The tactic *manipulate details* involved officers embellishing a particular witness statement or ignoring significant details. *Manipulating self-esteem* was an attack on the person's emotional well-being or stature, for example 'What sort of man are you?'. Minimization techniques were also included in this category, where the officers *minimized the serious nature of the offence*, or the *suspect's responsibility* for it. In some circumstances the part played by the victim or a significant *third party* was emphasized, manipulated or abused; all established face-saving excuses (Inbau, Reid & Buckley, 1986). On some occasions the officers offered some form of help or *inducement* if the suspect confessed, and it was not uncommon for officers to resort to *flattery* or offers of *reassurance*. At other times they would impress upon the suspect their considerable *experience* to gain an admission or that elusive 'chink' in the suspect's story. The benefits that might befall a suspect who confessed were also mentioned as *interest to confess*. The remaining two tactics included references to *non-verbal behaviour* and *shame reduction*.

SUSPECTS' RESPONSES

The first indication of the impact of various interview tactics will often be the verbal responses of the interviewee, and the importance of such variables cannot be under-estimated. Inbau, Reid and Buckley (1986) elevate the importance of direct observation and the evaluation of behavioural symptoms throughout the interview process (this may well reflect the influence of the behaviourist approach that had been so dominant in the United States). However, Farr (1982) makes the important point that

> Psychologists, when they accepted behaviourism, came to value what they could see and measure over what they could hear. It was only too easy to overlook the significance of something as invisible to the human eye as speech (p. 190).

There were six response groups in this study and a total of 33 response variables were identified.

Positive Responses

The bulk of this category constituted remarks that *agreed with*, *accepted* or *acceded* to any question or suggestion made. In more general terms this category also included where the suspect was openly providing an *account* of events, perhaps an *alibi* or extensive *free narrative account*. In a few cases a suspect might agree to a question or suggestion but would then go on to *introduce a qualification* to that answer that might also introduce additional knowledge (e.g. 'Were you on coke?–Coke and weed'). A distinction between a *confession* and an *admission* was made. It was often the case that an admission (without the element of intent) could relate to being at a relevant location and would often be made prior to a confession.

Negative Responses

These related to *denials* by the suspect or instances where he or she *disputed* an account or *declined* to agree to a remark. This section also included a *challenging response* where the suspect identified or perceived an inference that was implied within the body of the question, and which he was not prepared to accept (e.g. 'You didn't hear me say that, and you are putting words into my mouth now'). The *right to silence* (full or part) was included, but was very rarely invoked in this sample. A more common response was for the suspect to volunteer that he *couldn't remember* and very occasionally a *no reply* was entered, where perhaps the suspect did not have time to answer, as opposed to exercising his right to silence. *Withdraws a confession* was also included in this category.

Information or Knowledge

During the course of an interview a suspect might seek *additional information* from the officer to clarify an issue or he might ask for specific information in relation to *early release* or the likely *disposal route* for his particular predicament. This category also included where the suspect asked the officer to *repeat* the question.

Rationalization

In this section the suspect might *minimize the offence* or his *responsibility* for it. This would also include where the suspect *accepted a scenario or theme* that might have been suggested by the officers or where the suspect *provides a motive or reason* for the offence.

Projection

These include references by the suspect who might apportion *blame* to some other party or the victim (Inbau, Reid & Buckley, 1986; see Chapter 1, where these processes are dealt with in more detail).

Emotional Responses

The suspect may sound *distressed* or *cry*, and complain of feeling *tired or low*. This may coincide with a period of *self-blame or remorse* and their speech pattern may give some indication that they are *confused*, perhaps they do not understand a straightforward question, or they show signs of a *lack of orientation*. They become *abusive or angry* and *raise their voice*, or they may *seek assistance*. A combination of some of these responses may be indicative of a *psychologically vulnerable* individual.

METHODOLOGICAL ISSUES

Given the unique nature of this framework it is thought appropriate to highlight a few of the methodological issues that arose. The availability of both the written transcript and the audiotape recording proved invaluable when carrying out an in depth analysis. An accurate transcript provided a stable foundation and most importantly the time and space to investigate and analyse each segment in detail. The audiotape, first of all, provided the means to authenticate the transcript and also provided a contemporaneous audio 'insight' into what actually took place in the police interview. The audiotape illuminated the pauses and silences between the parties. It also often made it possible to determine the stress or intonation placed on a question or answer, as well as reproducing the pace and climate of the interview, for example whether the interview was conducted in a hostile or intimidating manner with raised voices from the police officers, who might bombard the suspect with repeated questions and frequent interruptions. On the other hand, it also reflected the quiet or softer approach adopted in some instances. In very many cases such sequences, whether intimidating and aggressive or gentle and compassionate, could not be ascertained from the transcript alone. Similarly, the responses or emotions of the suspect (crying, sniffling, angry outbursts) or other idiosyncratic behaviour (stammer, inarticulate responses) would not be obvious from the transcript in isolation. In many respects the transcript provided in 'black and white' a limited account of events. It required the addition of the audiotape to inject dimension and 'colour' into the proceedings. The tapes of interview are a most valuable research commodity and it is regrettable that audio and video-tapes, in our experience, are rarely scrutinized in judicial proceedings, which concurs with the views of Williamson (1993), an experienced and senior police officer.

The simple expedient of checking the typed transcript with the audiotape recording cannot be overlooked, for, without exception, discrepancies were unearthed. In a number of the cases these were major errors, which if left unchallenged would represent a serious example of misrepresentation. One example may serve to illuminate this problem. In this case the suspect was being interviewed for rape. The original typed transcript from the case papers reads:

Officer	'The fact is that something clicks when she's in your company, you start interfering with her?'
Suspect	'No'
Officer	'Don't ya?'
Suspect	No.

The suspect actually responds 'Yeh', to both questions. In other words a confession has been overlooked and literally 'written off'. A little after this the typed transcript reads:

Officer	'Did you ever touch their private parts?'
Suspect	'Yes'.

To this allegation the suspect actually replied 'No'.

STATISTICAL PROCEDURES

Factor analysis is a recognized technique widely used in the social sciences that is often employed as a method of simplifying large and complex sets of data. It is particularly useful in describing and understanding complex phenomena such as social interaction. What factor analysis does is to try and make sense of a large data set by identifying what variables cluster together. To allow for an effective analysis the procedure dictates that there has to be a sufficient number of observations. Unfortunately, this requirement could not be fulfilled in all cases because of the brief duration of some of the interviews (see Table 4.1). Accordingly, data from cases 1–18 were combined, although there was sufficient data to analyse cases 19 and 20 independently. In this chapter the findings of the factor analysis of the combined group (tactics), and cases 19 (Heron) and 20 (Miller), tactics and responses, will be presented.

Utilizing the same statistical programme it was possible to present the factor scores in graph form. The time segments in each case are featured on the horizontal axis (*x*-axis) and the vertical axis (*y*-axis) represents the individual factor score, calibrated by the number of standard deviation (SD) points from the mean. Descriptive labels were also applied to the factor levels on the *y*-axis. Factor scores that did not extend beyond plus or minus one SD, for example, were referred to as *average* scores. Factors that extended up to three SD points were referred to as *moderate* scores, those extending from three to five SD scores were labelled *marked* and finally those that extended beyond five SD points were identified as *extreme* scores. These descriptive terms were arbitrarily applied prior to an examination of any of the cases in this sample.

The factor analysis employed in the combined group identified six tactic factors. Factor 1 we have described as an *intimidation* factor. It is noticeable that this primary factor contains a very broad range of tactics, and, with eight variables, it is much larger than the remainder. This factor appears to embody a standard approach to intimidating a suspect into making a confession. The tactics concerned are *emphasizing the serious nature of the offence, maximizing the suspect's anxiety, manipulative use or reference to others, highlighting the experience of the officers, manipulating self-esteem, manipulating details, multiple assertions* and *the use of silence*.

The second factor has been labeled *robust challenge*. This contains the challenges *that the suspect was lying*, and one that *highlighted inconsistencies*. Also present were *the use of interruptions* and the *continued dispute* tactic. Factor 3 has been described as a *manipulation* factor as it is made up of four purely manipulative tactics. These were *minimizing the serious nature of the offence, minimizing the suspect's responsibility, the offer of inducements* and *suggesting themes or scenarios*.

Factor 4 has been described as *questioning style*. This was made up of *leading questions, closed questions, echo* and *multiple questions*. Factor 5 is best described as an *appeal* factor and contains *appealing to the suspect's good character or to tell the truth, reassurance*, suggestions that it is in the *suspect's interest to confess* and the *use of silence*. Finally, factor 6 is best described as *soft challenge*. This factor related to challenging by *introducing the witness's version of events, low tone*, the *introduction of evidence* and tactics aimed at *shame reduction*.

APPLICATION OF THE FRAMEWORK TO INDIVIDUAL CASES

To provide as broad as possible an insight into the nature of police interviewing tactics we shall examine a range of offence categories, including arson, robbery and incest. We shall also reproduce the relevant analysis of tactics and responses for selected extracts of the Heron and Miller murder cases.

Arson Case

Figure 4.1 provides details of the predominant tactics employed in an allegation of arson, leading up to and including the point of confession. A single male detective interviewed the suspect, who was 18 years of age. There were no other persons present. This case serves as a good example of the major factors used to overcome resistance within a short space of time (22 minutes).

For the sake of clarity, two factors, soft challenge and manipulation, have been removed as they failed to extend beyond the *average* level (i.e. beyond + or − 1 SD). Tape 1 lasts for 20 minutes and tape 2 lasts for only five minutes, and the time of the confession was recorded as 22 minutes. This graph indicates that from the outset there is an uninterrupted use of the robust challenge factor to an *extreme* level. This is accompanied in the closing ten minutes of tape 1 by an increase in intimidation (to a *marked* level) and both questioning style and appeal increase in use to the upper limits of the *moderate* level.

The confession in this arson case was timed at 22 minutes, making it the briefest interview in our sample. Although the suspect was reminded of his right to legal advice, the officer did so in a curt and very controlled manner. The officer kept the reminder of legal advice very brief and led the suspect throughout. For example, at the very beginning, the transcript version reads:

> Officer   'You are happy to be interviewed without a solicitor being present at this stage?'
> Suspect   'Yes, fine yes.'

What can be heard from the audiotape, however, suggests that the officer in a very forceful manner actually said:

> You are happy to be interviewed without a solicitor being present at this stage, *yes*?

with considerable emphasis on the final 'yes'. To which the suspect rather meekly replied,

> 'Fine, yes.'

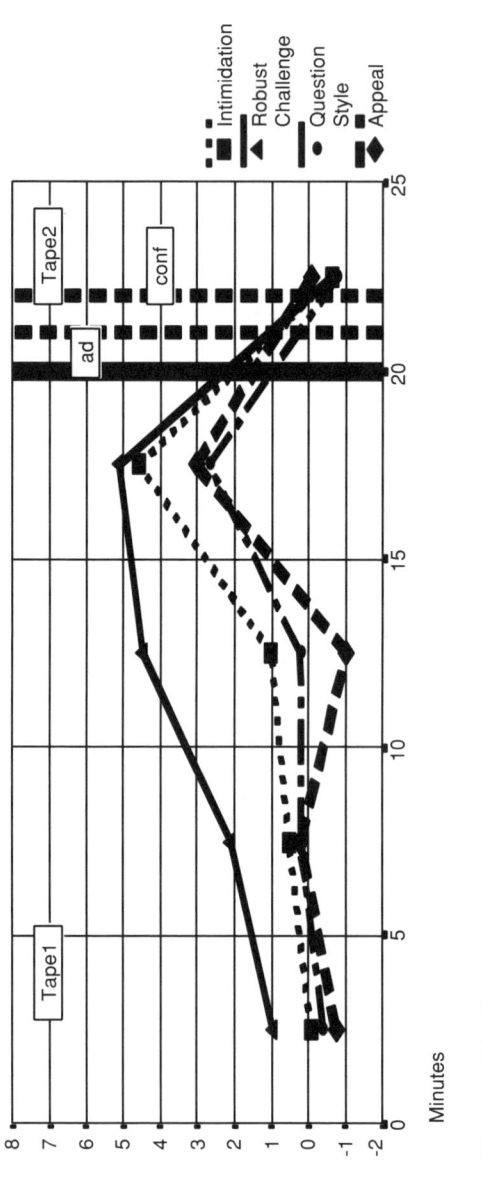

Figure 4.1. Arson case

The Identification and Measurement of 'Oppressive' Police Interviewing Tactics 89

There were a number of typographical errors and omissions on the transcript in this case, which failed to accurately convey the degree of control exercised by the officer (in this chapter, all quotations will be presented in the format provided to the courts; any alterations will be identified). From the outset this officer 'drove' the suspect and maintained a pressurized atmosphere throughout this brief interview. The robust challenge tactics included the officer repeatedly *interrupting* the suspect and often dismissing his replies; there were 52 *continual dispute* tactics from this officer in 22 minutes. The intimidation factor included introducing evidence from, and *using*, the suspect's girlfriend. It also included *maximization* and a blatant *manipulation* of detail, where the officer distorted what the suspect actually said to his own advantage (especially in relation to matches). The officer implied that it was the suspect who suggested that matches started the fire, which is a distortion of what was said, and he repeatedly accused the suspect of having some 'sort of problem'. The text has been reproduced according to the transcript. Early on the questions relate to the time the suspect was in the area with his girlfriend.

Det. Constable	'Because [name of girlfriend] says to me that you said to her, the fire must have started about three o'clock.'
Suspect	'Well I presumed because...' (he was interrupted by the officer and not allowed to complete his answer).
Det. Constable	'Why presume three o'clock?'
	The issue is not fully resolved before the officer changes his line of questioning,
Det. Constable	'You've got some sort of problem with the vicar haven't you...?'
Suspect	'No, I'm getting on well with him.'
Det. Constable	'That's not what I understand and that's not what [your girlfriend] is telling me.'
Suspect	'Well you know I'm getting on well with him I mean he's linked me up with my dad again.'
Det. Constable	'Yes but you've got a problem with your dad haven't you?'
Suspect	'Not like we used to have, against each other.'
Det. Constable	'Yes but you have got a problem with him haven't you?'
	Shortly afterwards,
Det. Constable	'You've obviously set fire to that church for some reason.'
Suspect	'I'm not guilty of...' (interrupted)
Det. Constable	'[name of suspect], you have got some sort of problem.'
Suspect	'...I just wouldn't set fire to a church.'
Det. Constable	'You've got some sort of problem and for some reason or other you are trying to get it out of your system.'
	A little later,
Det. Constable	'So do you associate that church with your problem?'
Suspect	'No.'
Det. Constable	'Because there is no doubt, without going in to lots of detail, you've had a chequered background in relation to your domestic problems with family, haven't you?'
Suspect	'Yeah, but I wouldn't link them with the church.'
Det. Constable	'Why?'
Suspect	'Not objective. Just wouldn't link them to the church. My problems are getting better now.'

Det. Constable	'They're not though are they because they're not resolving theirself, you've obviously got some sort of problem in relation to the church?'
	After repeated denials the emphasis moves towards the girlfriend, the time of the fire and how it was started.
Det. Constable	'You were there.'
Suspect	'I didn't set any fires.'
Det. Constable	'Why say to [girlfriend], the fire started at three o'clock then?'
Suspect	'I just presumed it was started at three o'clock, if it was alight?'
Det. Constable	'Why? Why? Why? Why three o'clock at quarter past four? Why not quarter past three? Why not half past three? Why not quarter past four?'
Suspect	'I don't know.' (reply not shown on transcript)
Det. Constable	'You said how the fire started at three o'clock. You told [your girlfriend] that and [she] told me that. [She's] told me that. I didn't dream three o'clock up. The reason you said the fire started at three o'clock was because you set it.'
Suspect	'I did not set any fire.'
Det. Constable	'There is no doubt whatsoever, at three o'clock ...'
Suspect	'I wasn't carrying any kind of matches or lighter on me at that time.'
Det. Constable	'It doesn't matter. You can get a match from anywhere. It's no hardship is it? Why should it be matches? I've not mentioned how the fire was started. I didn't say it was started with matches. You said that not me. So why should it be matches? Because you started it with matches.'
Suspect	'I didn't set any fire.'
Det. Constable	'You say it was started with matches. I've not said any of that, you said that. So how do you know that? There is only one way you could know that that fire started at three o'clock and that fire was started with matches and that is because you was there at three o'clock and you set fire with matches. There isn't no other way of knowing it. There isn't no other way of knowing it.'
Suspect	'Not at all any more. I didn't set no fire okay.'
Det. Constable	'You've got to, you've got to understand son, you've got some sort of problem. I'm only here trying to help. I'm a policeman, I'm trying to do my job.'
Suspect	'Well maybe, but I know in myself I didn't set that fire.'
Det. Constable	'Well why are you saying three o'clock and matches then?'
Suspect	'Because I presumed it started then ...'
	The officer interrupts the suspect and has raised his voice considerably,
Det. Constable	'Why, why presume? Why matches, why not a lighter, why not bloody petrol.'
Suspect	'I don't know, it's just an example isn't it.'
Det. Constable	'Why?'
Suspect	'Of a way of starting a fire.'
Det. Constable	'Why? I mean somebody could have gone in there and poured petrol all over the place and set fire to it. Couldn't they? Couldn't they, I mean it could have been started with petrol, diesel, anything, paraffin, a lump of rag, a pile of newspapers, and it could have started at any time that afternoon ... but you, out of the back of your mind you draw out the time three o'clock, started with matches. I never said it was started with

The Identification and Measurement of 'Oppressive' Police Interviewing Tactics 91

	matches. I never said it was started at three o'clock.... Did I, eh?'
Suspect	'No.'
Det. Constable	'No, but you did didn't you?'
Suspect	'I don't really know what time it started I just presumed the time.'
Det. Constable	'Why presume it? I mean...'
Suspect	'I just guessed.'
Det. Constable	'So why say the fire started at three o'clock? Half of you wants to admit it and the other half don't, why? What's your problem?"
Suspect	'The truth is I don't know what time it really started. I just, I just...'
Det. Constable	'You have obviously got some sort of problem [name of suspect]. You have obviously got some sort of problem. I'll help you all I can, but I can't help you until I know exactly what's gone on. I'll do what I can to help you, I mean I'm a policeman, I've got a job to do but I'll do what I can to help you. It's no good just sitting there keep saying "I never started it, I never..." (the suspect attempts to say something but is interrupted), and think that's going to be the end of it. It's not the truth. I mean I can... I've been a policeman a long time. I can see when somebody's sitting here lying to me. It's written across your face you're lying. It's written across your face that you're lying, you're not telling the truth. Now why are you not telling the truth? For what reason [name of suspect]? Eh?'
Suspect	'I don't know what the damn reason is, I just didn't do nothing wrong...'
	The suspect has started to cry, although there is no record of this on the transcript, and after some lengthy silences the first interview is terminated.

After a very short interval (less than five minutes) the interview resumed and the suspect made an admission and a confession within two minutes. This short case contained many of the recommended features found in police interrogation manuals (e.g. Inbau, Reid & Buckley, 1986). At court the tactics adopted by the officer were found to be oppressive and, as there was no other evidence against the suspect, the case was dismissed. In the short term therefore, the tactics might be considered successful, but in the long term the implications of such activity only serve to undermine the due process of the law. They also bring discredit on any police service and can cause lasting resentment amongst those who have been forced into making a confession.

Leo (1996a) sought to identify examples of coercive interrogation from a range of variables and he included examples of 'interrogation extending beyond six hours'. This 22 minute case brings into sharp focus the speed with which a person's resolve may crumble and it reinforces the importance of examining the context of each individual case.

Armed Robbery Case

Figure 4.2 provides an example of an armed robbery case from which the factors robust challenge, question style and soft challenge have been removed (again

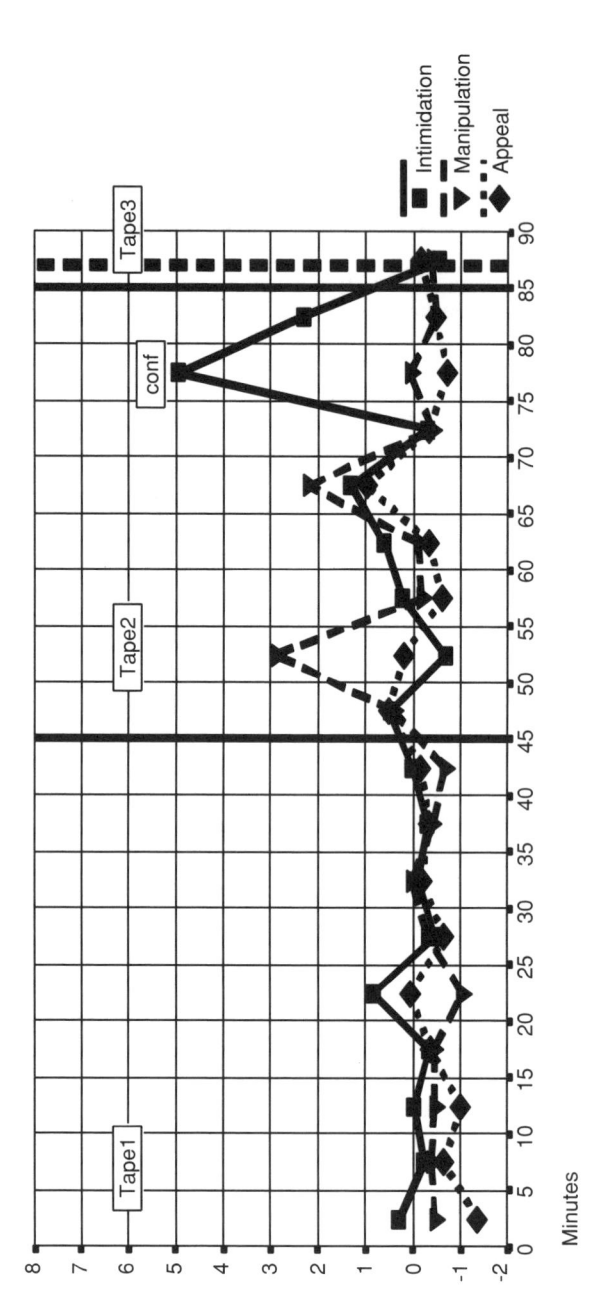

Figure 4.2. Armed robbery case

because of their limited presence). The suspect in this case was interviewed in relation to two allegations of armed robbery. At the time of the interview he was 23 years of age and two detective constables conducted the interviews. A legal adviser was present throughout.

The opening sequence is composed of mainly closed questions, taken from witness statements. The officers make selected use of this witness information and embellish some of the detail. In tape 2 manipulation and intimidation are the most popular tactics employed, with the latter almost reaching *extreme* proportions. The manipulation tactics included inducements that the suspect could have matters taken into consideration (TIC) by the courts which would be advantageous to him—'Now, that deal is on the table to you. ...You know there's other things we can go into. ...the more charges you have, the more punishment you get. ...Do you want charges or TIC's?' The officers also speculate on the effect of the suspect's behaviour to his wife and to his girlfriend. A long intimidating sequence from both officers brings the tape to a close, in which the suspect is constantly reminded of his family, the offer of TIC's and the extent of the fear and disruption caused to the victims of the robbery. As the use of tactics increase in tape 2, the suspect can be heard sniffing and after a consultation with his legal adviser he makes a confession.

One notable feature of this case was the presence of a number of very long questioning sequences. In some instances the 'question' would extend well beyond the five minute segment. This relentless onslaught (accompanied by raised voices) may have been responsible for the deterioration in the suspect's disposition, evident towards the end of the second tape when he began to cry and had '... gone past caring'. The officers who continued talking (*multiple officers, multiple questions*) displayed very poor listening skills and it is evident that they were convinced of this person's guilt. This was a very manipulative and very intimidating interview. Two psychologists (defence and prosecution) were in full agreement that the police in this case had resorted to the use of considerable pressure and psychological manipulation, which distressed the suspect greatly and seriously undermined the reliability of the confession. The interview was ruled inadmissible and the defendant was acquitted.

One reason this interview has been illustrated is because (towards the end of tape 2) the officers resort to nearly all the tactics that make up the factor intimidation: indeed it was the degree and extent of this activity that led to the title intimidation. Some selected extracts may help to demonstrate the point:

> Both the women in your life wonder if they are both being used by you...I've offered you a deal. Offered you an incentive...are you going to take the risk of lots and lots of charges?

> All of a sudden, he [the victim] is confronted with three men. Two carrying knives and one with a hammer. One holds a knife to his throat. Imagine the terror that would be. Some people would shit themselves when that happens. Imagine the absolute terror that must inflict on somebody...What about the guilt you must feel for that?...There has got to be some shame in that, en't there? Not you, sat here feeling sorry for yourself just because your Missus has made a statement against you.

That's just selfish...

Let's face up to facts. Accept responsibility.
You couldn't accept responsibility for your missus and kid.

There are people who go out and break into offices... don't do anybody harm,... but there are those that go in and cause terror and that's what you have done. And I wonder whether you are responsible for [the other suspects] being in their situation.

Am I getting through to you? Am I making you understand? I thought I could talk to you... but when I heard some of those things you had done, I was horrified... But why have you become the motivator? Why have you become so aggressive? Why have you had to sink to the depths of violence and force that you have on people?

You got some shame and boy, you should have.

Incest Case

Figure 4.3 provides an example of an incest case where three factors (intimidation, robust challenge and question style) have been removed. This was the only allegation of incest in the sample. The father, aged 55, was accused of raping his daughter on a number of occasions until she reached puberty. A male and a female officer conducted the interview and a solicitor was present throughout.

In the absence of the two 'overbearing' factors this interview opens with a *moderate* use of soft challenge. There are no obvious peaks immediately before an admission; rather, a succession of minor admissions was achieved as a result of the sustained effect of this one factor, that reaches *extreme* and *marked* levels in tape 2 (the only example of the *extreme* use of soft challenge in the entire sample).

This represents a striking example of the type of tactic recommended for offences of this nature: tactics that are concerned with reassurance and shame reduction, often delivered in a low tone yet firmly emphasizing the evidence in the case (Gudjonsson, 1992a). Examples of reassurance and shame reduction include:

> Erm before we go into that I'll just reassure you that myself and my colleague erm are used to dealing with these sorts of offences erm that's our every day job.
>
> Erm I know it's difficult to talk about these things, it's embarrassing and everything else but just be assured that you won't embarrass my colleague and me.
>
> Right look we'll just switch the tapes off, I'll just say to you before we do, myself and my colleague, we're not here to judge you okay?
>
> I mean we said before that the department where we work in deal with these sort of things all the time and we understand how these things can build up and happen.
>
> You know and I think we've gone perhaps beyond what could be explained away by accidental touching or any other reason so why why don't you try and sort of come to terms with the fact that this has been sexual attraction even though it is your own daughter and there's nobody saying that you don't love your daughter that this is something that can happen to people that love their children. It don't mean to say that you don't love them its another situation isn't it? Okay it shouldn't of happened.

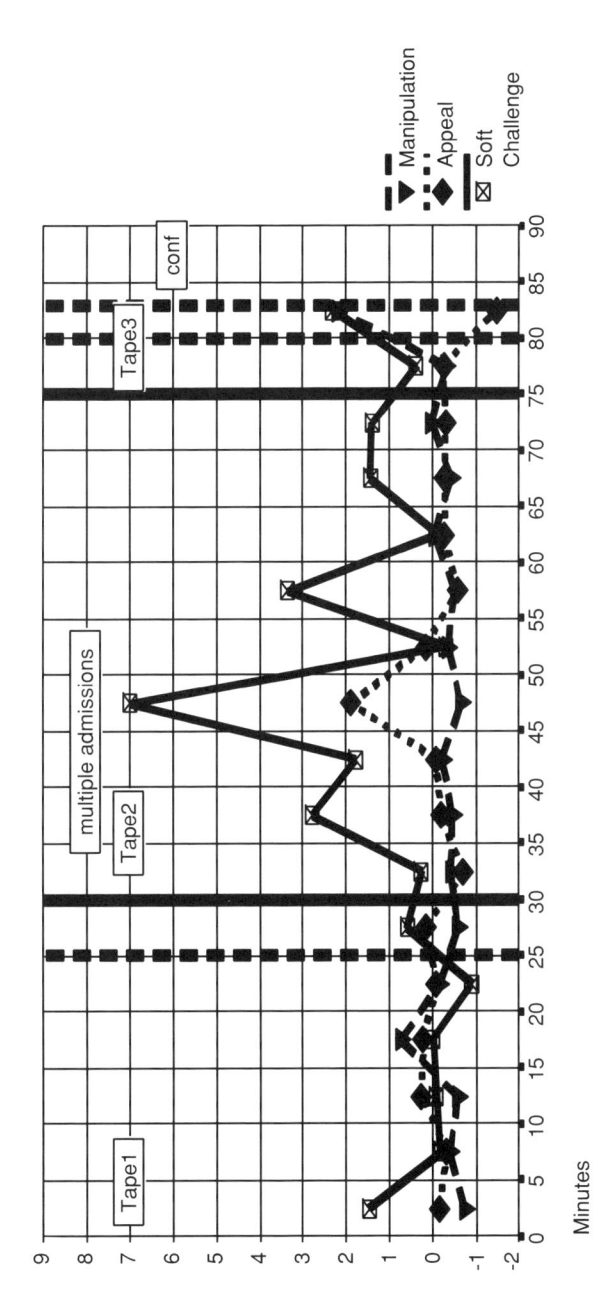

Figure 4.3. Incest case

The main approach adopted by the officers was to emphasize, in some detail and quite persistently, the legitimate evidence provided by the victim. It is true to say, however, that a more coherent structure was introduced to the interview process following an intervention from the suspect's solicitor, who recommended the officers '... put specific allegations to him from now on so that he can address his mind to them.' Such allegations included:

> Can you remember saying that you wouldn't hurt her and that it would be all right?
>
> Can you remember reassuring her?
>
> [she] goes into quite some detail don't she about all the things that she can remember?
>
> I can also remember one afternoon it must have been a weekend because I know it wasn't a school day, I was up in the bedroom tidying up and putting my clean clothes away, my dad came into the bedroom and said I got a surprise for you...

The officers referred to statements made by witnesses and, where necessary, read out a verbatim account, often timed to refute the denials of the suspect. It was noticeable also that this was an excellent example of the use of 'projection' by the suspect, who coped with the increasing amount of evidence by apportioning blame on the victim. For example,

> ...she come out of the toilet stark naked...and she said it's alright she said, I've seen you and she forced me hand on to her, down there and I pulled away...
>
> ...she was more or less asking me to touch her, do something.
>
> What happened. I'm not mistaken I think she said one day she was asking how they get babies and I said well I said a man got to make something and its got to go inside her—...

In this case the tactics were allowed in evidence and a jury at the conclusion of a contested hearing found the defendant guilty.

THE HERON MURDER CASE

Moving on to the Heron case, as it lasted almost eight hours it was possible to conduct a separate factor analysis. The case involved the murder of a seven-year-old girl in October 1992. Heron, who was 23 years of age at the time and had no previous convictions, became a suspect after resembling a person seen in the vicinity of a public house where the victim was last seen. Heron was first interviewed as a witness and was subsequently arrested and subjected to lengthy custodial interrogation. He had a legal adviser present during all interviews as a suspect.

The resultant factors share a number of similarities with the combined group, discussed above, except that the Heron factors are all intrinsically 'overbearing' in nature. One reason may be that the legal judgment highlighted the oppressive and persistent nature of the coercive tactics employed by the police. In this respect, it is encouraging that the factors developed within the framework have remained faithful to this legal determination, and appear to accurately reflect the particular nuances of this case. The same is also true of the Miller case (Pearse, 1997).

One reason for presenting details of the Heron case is to emphasize the potential importance of extending the analysis beyond that when the confession is made in interview. In such circumstances, it allows the reader to follow the nature and extent of tactics (and responses) post-admission, which according to Ofshe and Leo (1997a) may be the only objective and reliable test to assess a person's innocence or guilt.

Dividing the police interview in two stages, the pre-admission phase and the post-admission narrative, Ofshe and Leo suggest that

> Although indicators of a suspect's true state of innocence or guilt can be identified in the suspect's conduct in response to the interrogator's tactics, the differences between the guilty and the innocent *only become reliably and objectively observable* after each has made the decision to confess. The differences ... can only be detected with substantial confidence by analyzing the *contents* of their respective confession statements—... (Ofshe & Leo, 1997b, p. 197, original emphasis).

The forthright nature of their hypothesis warrants investigation and we shall examine the post-admission stage in some detail.

The factor analysis employed in the Heron murder investigation (case 19) produced four tactic factors and five response factors.

Tactics

Factor 1 is best described as *browbeating* and contained seven variables. *Challenging the suspect that he is lying*, the use of *raised voices* and *multiple assertions*, a *pantomime* style approach to questioning, *implying that evidence exists* and making an *appeal to the suspect to tell the truth*. Finally, a negative correlation was present in relation to the use of *closed questions*, which suggests that they tended not to be used in conjunction with the other variables.

Factor 2 is described as a *manipulation* factor. This included the *use or exploitation of others, minimizing the suspect's responsibility for the offence, manipulating self-esteem, offering reassurance* and *maximizing the suspect's anxiety*. Factor 3 has been described as a *persistent pressure* factor. This contained five variables—*multiple officers, multiple questions, the use of silence, echo* and *suggesting scenario or theme*. Factor 4 is best described as *exaggerating the evidence* and has three variables, *introducing evidence, manipulating detail* and *pantomime style*.

Responses

Factor 1 is best described as a *resistance* factor. There were four variables that loaded saliently on this factor—the *use of denials, challenges to the officers' account, not providing an account* and *not accepting what the officer was saying*. Factor 2 is an *admission* factor and has two variables, *admission* and *accepting a theme or scenario*.

Factor 3 has been described as a *poor memory* factor with two variables, *cannot or unable to remember* and *providing an alibi*. Factor 4 represents a *seeks information* factor. Again there are two variables, *seeking information* and *introducing a qualification*. Factor 5, contains only one salient variable, *signs of distress* and has been called a *distress* factor.

Figures 4.4, 4.5 and 4.6 relate to the Heron murder case. The interviews in this case took place over three days and extend to almost eight hours of interaction. Under such circumstances it is not possible to include the entire interview and the graphs have been confined to key sections. The first witnesses the variation in tactics produced by the introduction of two new (senior) officers towards the end of day one, leading to the confession. The remaining graphs examine the interview tactics and responses on days two and three. It is relevant to note that on day one there were eight tapes of interview, lasting almost four hours, which started at 11:04 hours and concluded at 23:47 hours. This represented the most tapes used in one day in the sample and also the longest period of interview in one day.

The arrival of two senior officers to take over the questioning at the beginning of tape 5 has a dramatic impact on events and is associated with overbearing factors reaching *extreme* and *marked* proportions within the first fifteen minutes. Although this explosive start produced two further admissions, one of the criticisms of police by the trial judge was their interpretation and reliance on the strength of available witness evidence. This tactic had been evident from earlier tapes but this opening sequence represents a good example where the officers mislead the suspect in this regard. For example, '... we know that you George, were with her round about quarter to ten... we have a witness who saw you... we have other witnesses who can put you in the area...'. Such evidence was not forthcoming at the trial and it prompted the presiding judge, Mr Justice Mitchell, to comment:

> The temptation for the suspect to trim his account to accommodate such evidence could be considerable.

Indeed the suspect himself began to adopt what he was being told and his admissions amounted to acceptance of the detail contained in the questions. For example:

> Officer 'So can you remember going there that night to get cigarettes?'
> Heron   'I can't really remember it. But if *I was seen* in there I must have' (our emphasis).

In tape 6 there are two manipulation peaks at a *marked* level, the second of which almost reaches an *extreme* level. This manipulation was very persistent and extensive. It took the following form.

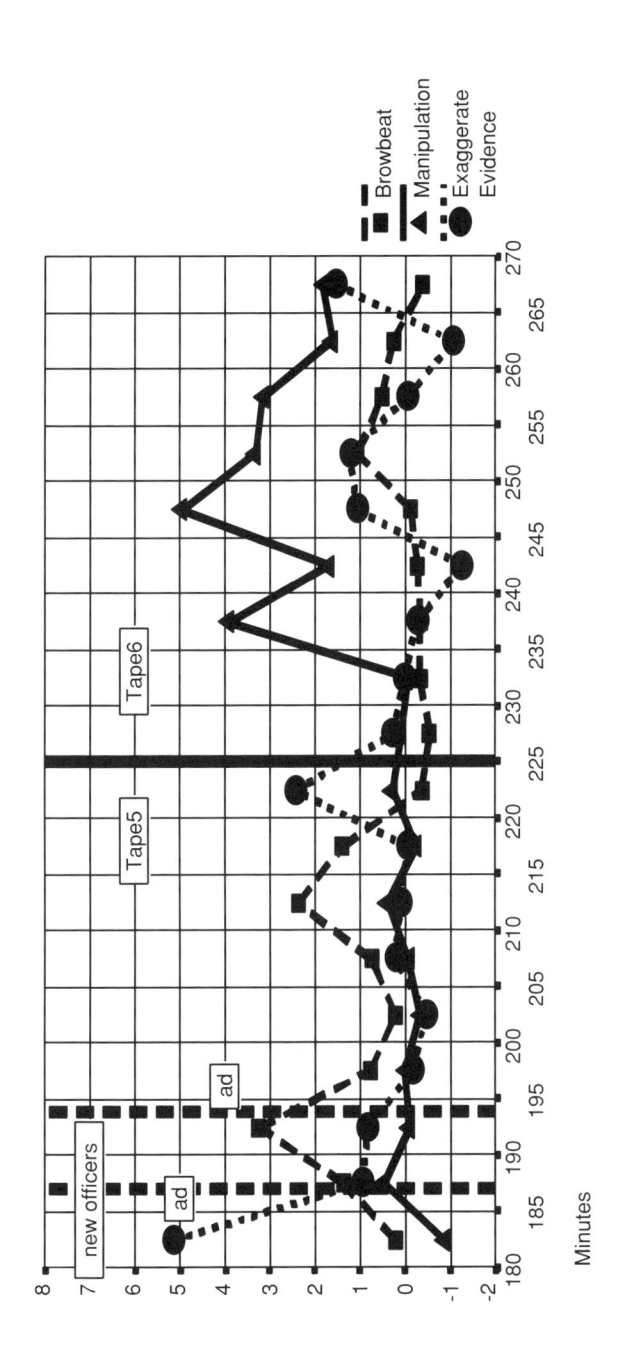

Figure 4.4. Heron murder case (arrival of two senior officers)

1. Attacking self-esteem (exploiting lack of sex life).
2. Using others (tender age and fondness for victim, 'It was an evil act, it was a despicable act on a little seven-year-old girl'. At one stage 13 consecutive questions were asked concerning the victim).
3. Reassurance ('there is nobody trying to stress you').
4. Maximizing anxiety ('now how much does it prey on your mind').
5. Minimizing responsibility ('now we are men of the world...and when it happens...perhaps there is a reason for them doing it').

This was an extremely manipulative period and to provide some indication of the impact on Heron, the response graph records two distress peaks that mirror the psychologically manipulative tactics (Pearse, 1997). One of the distress peaks is at an *extreme* level. In the following tape manipulation and browbeating continued unabated, culminating in a confession. The main difference was that the tactics were now delivered with raised voices and the tension in the atmosphere really was quite palpable leading up to the confession.

This period serves as a very real example where only listening to the tapes succeeds in removing you from the sterility of the written text, and provides the passion, intensity and 'colour' that we discussed earlier. That said, this framework cannot portray the whole process. It cannot illuminate the impact of detention (for one or more days) in a police station; it cannot cater for the thoughts or fears of an individual who may be incarcerated for the first time, and who, in an alien environment, is trying to consider the consequences of his predicament. One insight that is provided in this regard often emerges from the responses of the detainee, and in this final section we shall examine how Heron dealt with the questioning in the post-confession stage.

Post-Admission—Tactics and Responses

Figure 4.5 provides details of the tactics employed on the second and third days of interview (browbeat and manipulation have been removed). The same interviewing officers, a detective chief inspector and a detective inspector, that finished day one are present, together with the legal adviser.

These four tapes of interview take place over two days and tend to be dominated by the factor persistent pressure, which reaches a *marked* level in both tape 9 and tape 10 and a *moderate* level in tape 12. In this final tape it is also joined by the factor exaggerate evidence, to a *moderate* level. The reason for the increase in this previously subdued tactic (*multiple officers, multiple questions* and *the use of silence*) is that the officers are keen to cement the confession with the disclosure of special knowledge that can only come from the perpetrator.

Figure 4.6 provides details of the responses elicited from Heron post-admission.

In tape 9 the apparent lack of responses reflects the numerous monosyllabic replies that the suspect delivered ('yes' and 'yeah'). In tape 10, however, there

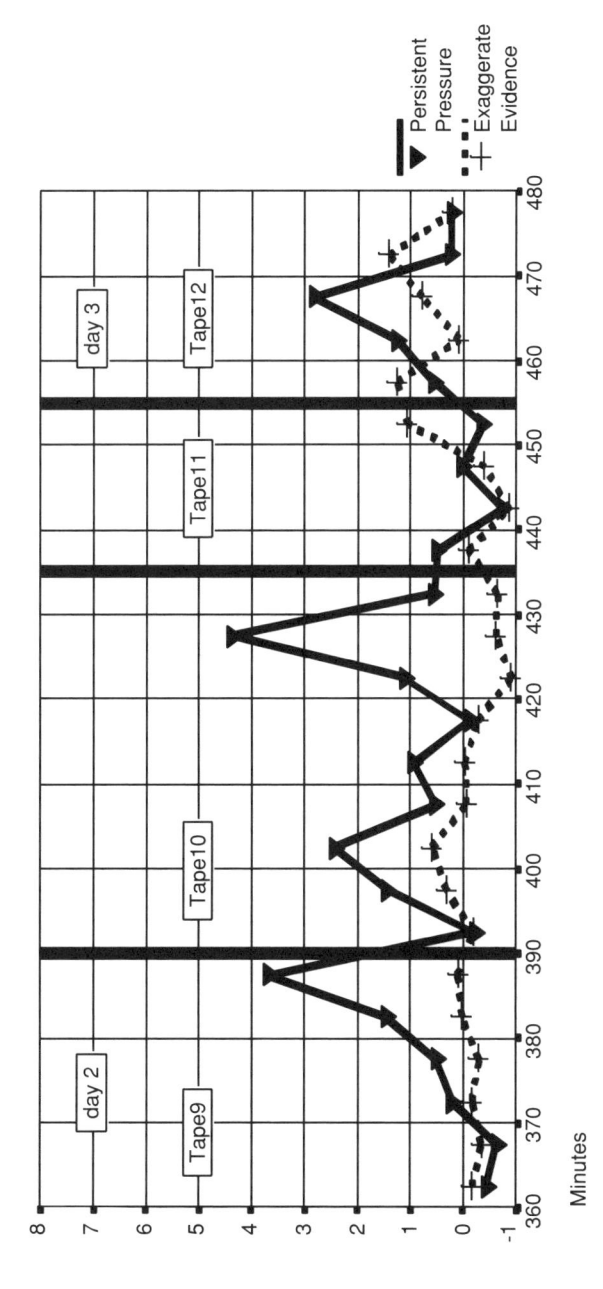

Figure 4.5. Heron murder case (post-admission tactics)

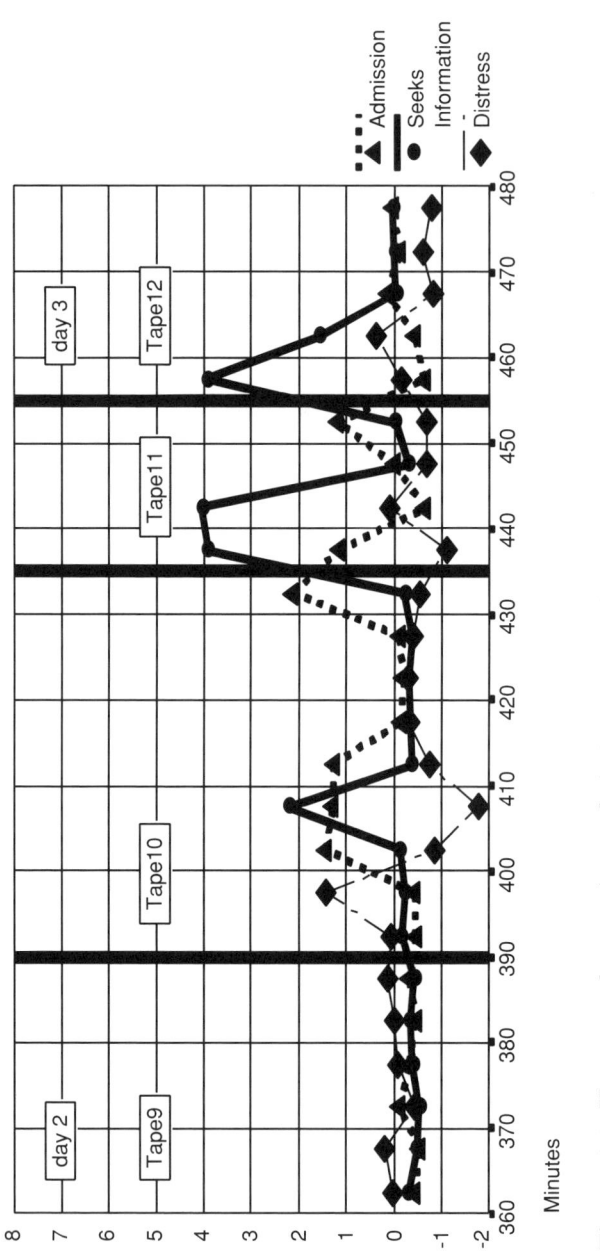

Figure 4.6. Heron murder case (post-admission responses)

is a *moderate* increase in distress, admission and seeks Information. This final factor then rises to a *marked* level in both tape 11 and tape 12 and appears to be in response to the continued use of the tactic persistent pressure.

Ever since the confession the officers have been leading the suspect through their understanding of what took place:

1st Officer	'Did that kill her George, with the brick? George it didn't did it, George?'
2nd Officer	'There is more isn't there?'

The suspect does not know and over these later tapes he is clearly guessing and introducing qualifications to his answers according to the prompts from the officers and what information he can glean from them. From the transcript it would appear that Heron was prompted and led in connection with almost every conceivable corroborative point. These included the point of entry to the disused building, the victim's clothing, the weapon or weapons, wounds (number and type), the position of the body and the route used inside the premises. It will not be possible to outline all of these points, but by concentrating on the discussions surrounding the weapons used and the type of wound inflicted it should be possible to portray an accurate synopsis of events. The impact of a close examination of these passages is immediate and profound. Indeed we would argue that it renders any commentary quite superfluous. The presentation (spelling, punctuation, etc.) is taken unaltered from the manuscript copy.

At the point of the confession, Heron states:

Heron	'Picked up the nearest thing and hit her with it.'
Officer	'And what was that?'
Heron	'A brick.'
Officer	'Where did you hit her George?'
Heron	'On the head.'
Officer	'How many times can you remember?'
Heron	'No.'
Officer	'How many times do you think?'
Heron	'I lost count.'

After talking about where this took place the first of many prompts is evident. Despite this tactic by the officers, Heron's responses remain ambiguous. One possible explanation could be that he might not know the actual answer, he is 'sitting on the fence' and waiting to feed off further cues or prompts.

Officer	'That is not all you did George is it? Howay you have told us the truth we are just about there George we are nearly finished alright. Did the Brick knock her out George?'
Heron	'There was blood.'
Officer	'Did that kill her George with the Brick? George it didn't did it, George?'
2nd Officer	'There is more isn't there George?'

1st Officer	'Howay you have told us there was blood all over the place what else did you do. George, we know what's happened, we know what's happened, so you know you are not holding anything back by not telling us, George what else did you do?'
1st Officer	'George howay son, just finish it off and tell us what else you did.'
1st Officer	'George.'
Heron	'Went to throttle her.'
Officer	'You went to throttle her, what with?'
Heron	'Me hands.'
Officer	'But you hit her with something else didn't you George?'
Heron	'Don't remember' (actually typed as 'probably I can't remember')
Officer	'George, think, I know its not very nice son, but just think what else did you hit her with. Eh George?'
Heron	'Fist.'
Officer	'What else? Howay George, you used something else didn't you? George, we know, howay, George what else did you do? Come on.'
Heron	'Piece of metal.'

After a change of tapes, the questioning continues.

Officer	'What did you do with it?'
Heron	'Hit her.'
Officer	'Hit her where?'
Heron	Unintelligible
Officer	'No you didn't George, tell us what you did with it... But you did something else to her didn't you, you say with a piece of metal, what did you do?... Now you did something with that piece of metal didn't you... the body has been examined George we know exactly what happened, if you're telling the truth just tell us what then happened.'
Heron	'Stuck it between her legs'
Officer	'Stuck what between her legs?'
Heron	'The metal pipe'
Officer	'And what did it do?'
Heron	'Blood.'
Officer	'Blood where?'
Heron	'On the floor on the pipe.'
Officer	'Where did the blood come from?'
Heron	'Nikki.'
Officer	'But where from? From her head?'
Heron	'From between her legs.'
Officer	'From between her legs? Howay George, look us in the eyes and tell me the truth... Well I'm saying to you that you did something else to her as well, didn't you eh?... what did you do?'
Heron	'Assaulted her.'
Officer	'What do you mean you assaulted her?'
Heron	'Sexually.'
Officer	'What did you do?'
Heron	'Tried to have sex with her.'
Officer	'How did you try to have sex with her? 'How did you try to have sex with her?'
Heron	'Same way everybody has sex.'
Officer	'... you didn't try to have sex with her, did you George?'
Heron	'No.'

The Identification and Measurement of 'Oppressive' Police Interviewing Tactics

The discussion changes to blood stained clothing, but returns to the type of weapon used.

Officer	'What did you use? Eh? Come on.'
Heron	'Metal.'
Officer	'A metal what?'
Heron	'Bar.'
Officer	'Bar!'
Heron	'Well, a piece of metal.'
Officer	'And what did you do with that piece of metal was it a knife, George?'
Heron	'It was sharp.'
Officer	'It was sharp, where did you get it from George, where did you get it from, did you have it with you?'
Heron	'No.'
Officer	'You must have had it with you.'
Heron	'I don't remember having it with me.'
Officer	' What did you do with (it)... are you going to tell us?'
Heron	'Can't.'
Officer	'What sort of metal?'
Heron	'Base metal.'

Thus far the weapons suggested by Heron have included brick, hands, metal, metal pipe, sharp metal and base metal. Eventually he was asked, was it a knife?

Heron is taken back over events and by tape 10 the questioning has focused on the actual assault:

Officer	'Hitting her, what with?'
Heron	'Something in me hand.'
Officer	'Now you've hit her with the brick, now she had another injury or injuries on her body. George.'
Heron	'Yes.'
Officer	'How did you do them?'
Heron	'Wounds.'
Officer	'Wounds, how did you cause the wounds?'
Heron	'Metal wounds.'
Officer	'... what sort of metal are we talking about?'
Heron	'Sharp.'
Officer	'Sharp metal.'
Heron	'Metal.'
Officer	'What are we talking about though, what was it, an object?'
Heron	'Small, sharp, metal.'
Officer	'Where did you get it from. Go on George. George do you want to tell us.'
Heron	'I am trying.'

The legal adviser (LA) now makes her first intervention:

LA	'You know when we were talking before George when the police officers weren't in the room, you said you wanted to tell them, these were the two police officers that you wanted to speak to. Once you have said it you have said it.'

Officer	'Can I ask you again George what it was. What was it George. What was this sharp metal object that you are talking about.'
Heron	'Knife.'
Officer	'Now what did you do to Nikki with the knife.... You've said wounds, you are saying you caused wounds to her with the knife?'
Heron	'Yes.'
Officer	'Whereabouts. Just where George.'
Heron	'Just remember wounds.'
Officer	'Where abouts George, come on? You say you are going to tell us the truth George, come on...Come on George we are nearly there...I know it is extremely painful but you said you would tell the truth. Where abouts come on, it's coming. Where abouts George...George you say you have used a knife to cause Nikki wounds, haven't you? Yeah.'
Heron	'Yeah.'
Officer	'So you have told us what you have done with the knife, haven't you, Yes. So we are just asking you whereabouts. 'George.'
Heron	'Torso.'
Officer	'The torso, is that the top of the torso, or the bottom of the torso, or the middle...Show me...about the middle, yeah, about the middle.'
LA	'I would say that is the middle.'
Officer	'...Do you know how many blows you would have rained on her with the knife? George? You are shaking your head, is that no?'
Heron	'No.'
Officer	'Was there a lot of blows. George.'
Heron	'Probably yes.'

A further interview, which attempted to discover why Heron had committed the murder (together with other important corroborative details) was conducted in the same leading fashion the following day. The temptation to continue to examine this post-admission dialogue is considerable, especially when one considers that we have only provided a small proportion of what is an extensive and intriguing record of events. However, it is reassuring to note that the developing framework has clearly identified the direction and nature of this interaction. It would of course be unwise to seek to support the hypothesis put forward by Ofshe and Leo (1997a) from just one case. Nevertheless, the case does illustrate the importance of carefully studying the post-admission narrative when determining the reliability of confession statements from electronically recorded interviews. Although the details provided here represent merely a 'snapshot' of the full proceedings, there must be cause for some concern over Heron's apparently very limited intimate knowledge of the murder and crime scene.

THE MILLER MURDER CASE

Originating in 1988, the Miller case was the oldest in our sample but in many respects the impact of this case on police interviewing tactics and procedure in the UK was monumental (for details of the case and the Court of Appeal judgment, see Chapter 19). The audio tape-recording of interviews was in its infancy and very few trials had enjoyed the benefit of a contemporaneous audio record of what had taken place in the confines of the police interview room. Miller, and his two co-accused Paris and Abdullahi, had been found guilty of the particularly gruesome murder of a prostitute in the dock area of Cardiff, in South Wales. There had been two Crown Court trials and the case went to appeal. The final judgment was delivered by the then Lord Chief Justice, Lord Taylor. A short example of what their Lordships thought of the officers' tactics is very revealing.

> The officers... were not questioning him so much as shouting at him what they wanted him to say. Short of physical violence, it is hard to conceive of a more hostile and intimidating approach by officers to a suspect. It is impossible to convey on the printed page the pace, force and menace of the officer's delivery (R. v. Paris, Abdullahi and Miller (1993) 97 Cr.App.R. 99, p. 103).

In some respects, the analysis and graphic presentation afforded by the PIAF represents our attempt 'to convey on the printed page the pace, force and menace of the officers' delivery'. The 19 tapes of interview in this case were spread over five days and lasted a total of 12 hours and 42 minutes. It was the longest interview process in the sample. The factor analysis produced five tactic factors and four response factors.

The primary factor for the officers' tactics is best described as a *Mr Nasty* factor. This contained the tactics *challenging the suspect's version of events as a lie or not believable, appealing to him to tell the truth, raised voices, the overarching tactic, continual dispute, the use of threats, the manipulative use of significant others* and *maximizing the suspect's anxiety*. Factor 2 has been described as a *Mr Nice* factor. In this factor the tactics used included *low tone, reassurance, multiple assertions* and *implying evidence*. Factor 3 is a *manipulation* factor containing *experienced officers, manipulating detail, minimizing responsibility for the offence* and *challenging the suspect with witness information*.

Factor 4 is as a *poor delivery* factor. It contained the *use of multiple questions, multiple assertions* and *echoing*. The final factor we have called *persistent pressure*. Its component parts were *multiple officers, maximization of the serious nature of the offence, use of inducements* and *not employing leading questions*.

In relation to the response factors, the leading factor is that of *angry denial*, with very high statistical loading for *the use of a raised voice, angry and/or suspicious, challenging accounts or events* and *denial*. The second fact has been titled *seeks information*. This contained *asks for the question to be repeated, seeks information* and *admission*. Factor 3 has been described as a *provide account* factor and includes *providing an account, agrees with or accepts what the officer is asking* and a negative correlation for *distress*. The final response factor was *accept scenario*. This included *accepting a theme, not remembering, introducing a qualification* and *signs of distress*.

Given the scale and dimension of this case it will not be possible to reproduce the full interview sequence. We shall limit the examination to what their Lordships referred to as the 'hostile and intimidating approach...' adopted by the officers in tape 7 and the responses it elicited.

In Figure 4.7 the tactic poor delivery has been removed. After about 15 minutes the interview has degenerated into one long shouting match, delivered in a fast and furious manner. In the middle section of the tape we recorded 109 examples of raised voices from the officers and, in the same period, 101 examples from the suspect.

In Figure 4.8 the response factor provide account has been removed and the admission shown in the first five minutes relates to an acceptance to living off immoral earnings. What is quite clear when the two graphs are viewed together is the symmetry found in relation to the *extreme* use of the tactic Mr Nasty and the response angry denial as both reach *extreme* levels.

In truth, it is not possible to reproduce on the printed page the fact that the interview had degenerated into a fast and furious confrontation with all participants shouting at one another. However the fact that we have recorded over a hundred examples each of the variable *raised voice*, for Miller and his interrogators, during just the middle phase of tape 7, amply demonstrates this feature. It may be more profitable to examine some of the other component variables in the principal tactic factor, *Mr Nasty*. Remaining in the key middle section of the tape we have identified 72 examples of the challenge *responses are lies or not believable*, and 94 examples of the *continual dispute* variable. Also present are six examples of *threats* and 13 examples of *maximizing anxiety*.

The threats took the form of the officers reminding Miller that they would continue to question him, regardless of the number of denials he persisted with (at his trial the defence team identified that Miller had denied involvement on more than 300 occasions during this interview). As an example, if Miller stated he had nothing to say the officers retorted:

> Cause I'm never gonna leave it at that...you know that. Cause I am still gonna keep going and I'm gonna put things into you everytime because I know the truth.

Other examples included:

> Now we're going to have the truth out of you one way or...you know.

> I'll keep digging and I'll keep digging because I believe you were there. I will keep digging.

It was during this crucial middle phase of tape 7 that the officers focused on the fact that Miller admitted he was stoned. As can be seen, this information opened up considerable opportunities for the officers, who pursued them relentlessly.

Miller	'Right. I don't know what I was doing. I was stoned.'
Officer	'Oh you're stoned now...'
Miller	'I was drinking...'
Officer	'We're going back...'
Miller	'I was drinking I told you that I was drinking and smoking.'
Officer	'You're stoned now are you?'
Miller	'Right, drinking and sm...'

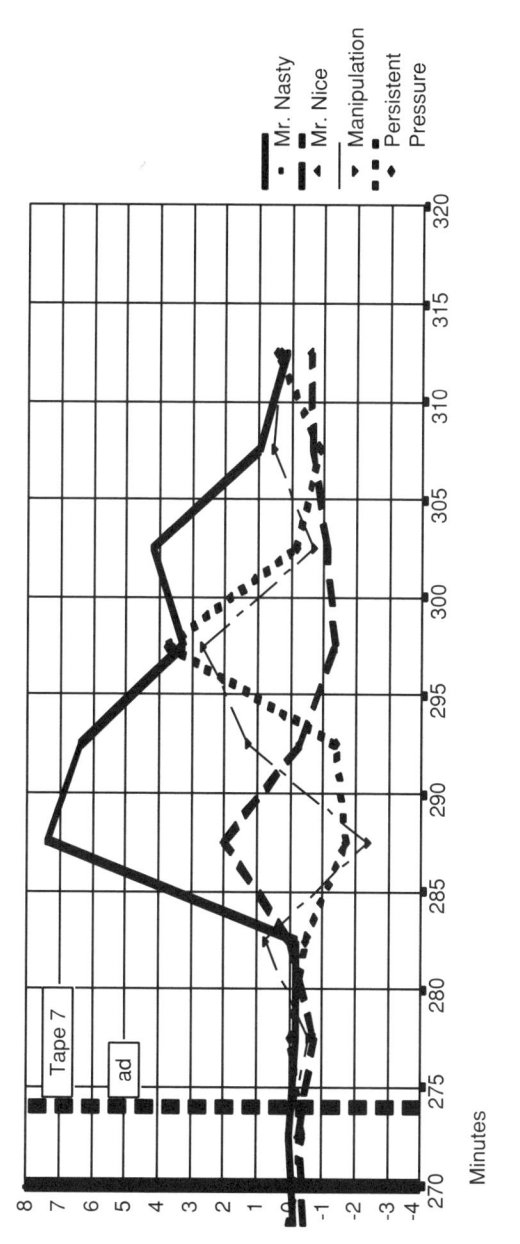

Figure 4.7. Miller murder case (tactics)

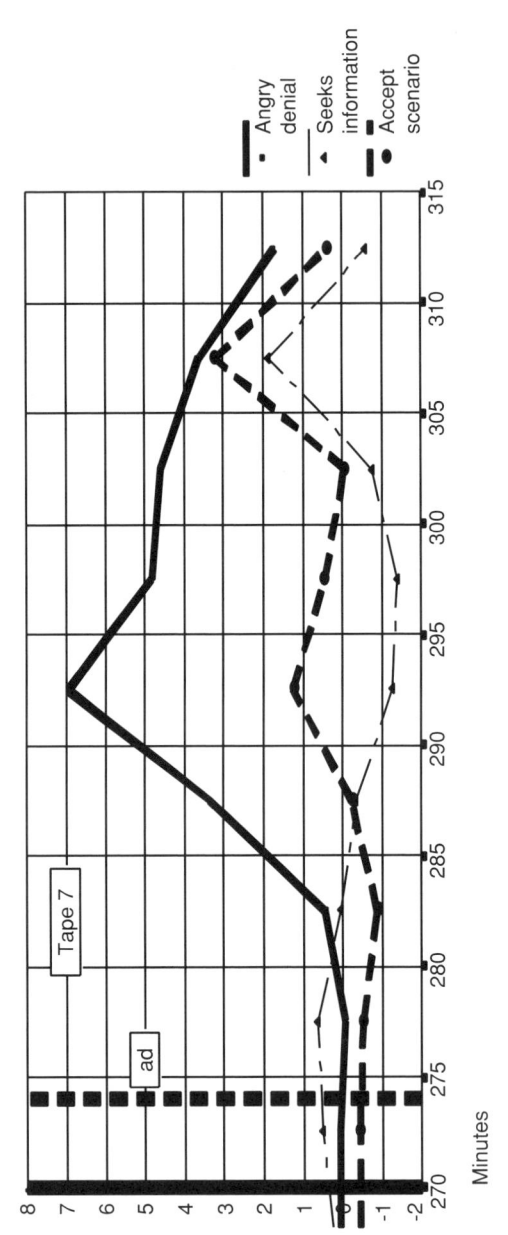

Figure 4.8. Miller murder case (responses)

The Identification and Measurement of 'Oppressive' Police Interviewing Tactics 111

Officer   'On the 13th?'
Miller   'Yeah I was uhh... smoking and drinking.'
Officer   'Right.'
Miller   'If you smoke and drink what d'you do? Are you still... are you still sober?'
Officer   'No you're not still sober no you're not.'
Miller   'Well then.'
Officer   'Okay.'
Miller   'Well then.'
Officer   'So did you... were you there on the night...'
Miller   'I wasn't.'
Officer   'Of the 13th...'
Miller   'No I wasn't.'
Officer   'So would you have known you were there?'
Miller   'What d'you mean would I have known I was there?'
Officer   'If you were stoned?'
Miller   'What d'you mean if I... I... knew I was there.'
Officer   'Would you have known...'
Miller   'I would have told you so that I was there.'
Officer   'Would you have known if you were stoned if you were in 7 James Street?'
Miller   'Stoned, stoned I don't mean stoned, stoned, stoned like your bollocks you know, I'm talking about stoned.'
Officer   'St...'
Miller   'You're in a nice buzz in a nice buzz.'
Officer   'Yeah, a nice buzz.'
Miller   'That's what I'm talking about.'
Officer   'Yeah, a nice buzz when you were stoned on drugs or whatever and you were stoned in the flat would you have known you were there. Would you have known you were at 7 James Street if you were stoned. Am I... gonna get an answer from you Stephen?'
Miller   'I told you already.'
Officer   'Come on.'
Miller   'I keep telling you over and over again right...'
Officer   'Would you have been...'
Miller   'I have not been there.'
Officer   'There if you were stoned?'
Miller   'I wouldn't know.'
Officer   'You wouldn't know. So you could have been there.'
Miller   'I wasn't there.'
Officer   'You could have been at...'
Miller   'I wasn't there.'
Officer   '7 James Street?'
Miller   'I wasn't there.'
Officer   'If you were stoned...'
Miller   'If... if... if you think...'
Officer   'You could have been at 7 James Street.'
Miller   'If you think you can... you can put things into my mouth...'
Officer   'I'm not putting things...'
Miller   'You are... you are...'

After further denials the conversation remains centred on the drugs issue:

Officer   'Would you have known if you were there?'
Miller   'I don't know.'

Officer	'You don't know?'
Miller	'Right.'
Officer	'You don't know?'
Miller	'I don't know.'
Officer	'So there's a possibility you could have been there?'
Miller	'Yeah, but I wasn't.'
Officer	'There's a possibility?'
Miller	'A possibility, right.'

Having accepted that there was a 'possibility' the officers stopped shouting at Miller and in tape 8 they lowered the tempo and tone of their questioning. Twenty minutes into tape 8 Miller provides a damning admission:

Miller	'I don't know, it... could do, it could have happened like that.'

The 'force and menace' of this style of questioning does not transfer onto the printed page and it remains important to remember the context of this interview. The defendant was not an intelligent individual, he had been detained for five days and subjected to a constant stream of relentless questioning, conducted by a number of officers who employed a variety of tactics. He did not provide a confession until the 18th tape of interview. When placed in the context of the entire case it is not surprising that their Lordships regarded this as an example of 'oppressive' police interviewing tactics.

In some respects, given the key role played by the availability of an audiotape record of this extensive interview session, we would have anticipated that much greater use would have been made of this modern contemporaneous record. It remains rather disappointing that so few tapes are reviewed in detail, by the prosecution and defence, and even less are played to the courts.

COURT OUTCOME

One immediate feature of the details presented in the case summary (see Table 4.1) is the large number of cases which were dismissed by the courts for the use of oppressive or coercive interviewing tactics. If the nine cases where a guilty plea was entered are removed, eight out of the remaining 11 cases (73%) were dismissed because of irregularities concerning the conduct of police interviewing tactics. This was so whether the interview took place on one day and lasted 22 minutes, or was spread over a number of days. Furthermore, in 17 out of the 20 cases (85%) a confession was elicited by tactics that reached at least the *marked* level. Allowing for the limitations of the small sample size, these findings support the main hypothesis that people may well break down in interview because of the application of police pressure and manipulation. This finding is in stark contrast to our Royal Commission research (Pearse & Gudjonsson, 1996a). Here the interviews were often short and conducted with suspects who tended to confess early on in the interview or, if they denied the allegation, were able to maintain their stance in the absence of any sustained pressure (see also Baldwin, 1993).

Table 4.2. Level of tactics used and outcome of interview

Allowed in evidence	Tactics up to a *marked* level	Tactics at an *extreme* level
Admissible	10 (50%)	2 (10%)
Not admissible*	2 (10%)	6 (30%)

* χ^2 $p = 0.0194$ (Fisher exact probability test).
From Pearse and Gudjonsson, 1999.

Table 4.2 provides details of the extent to which the PIAF was able to discriminate between the types of tactic used, and whether the interview evidence was admissible, according to the judgment of the court.

The present study has determined what types of individual police tactic cluster together, and it is encouraging to note the high level of conceptual clarity and discriminative power that has been achieved. For example, the factors identified distinguish between the 'overbearing' nature of some interviews (intimidation, robust challenge, browbeat, persistent pressure, exaggerate evidence and manipulation) and the more 'sensitive' style adopted, albeit to a lesser degree, in others (appeal and soft challenge).

In attempting to establish the validity of this framework this study relied on the judgment of the courts to determine what was, and what was not, an acceptable level of interviewing pressure, and a number of important findings have emerged. In the first instance, it is encouraging to note that a significant relationship was found between the use of all 'overbearing' factors at an *extreme* level and the likelihood that a court would rule such interviewing inadmissible ($p = 0.02$, Fisher exact, see Table 4.2). Allowing for the small sample size, a trend is beginning to emerge that suggests that the framework may be a suitable vehicle for measuring this complex social interaction and that there is merit in further research in this direction.

Secondly, out of the 20 cases, there were eight in which the factors reached an *extreme* level, and in only two of these did the factors relate to the less confrontational, more 'sensitive' tactics (appeal and soft challenge). In both of these cases, the interviews were allowed in evidence. This suggests that the framework has the potential to discriminate between what may be acceptable tactics and provide a measure in relation to those that the courts will not approve of, which was one of our original objectives. This has considerable implications for future police training and represents another important feature in the development of this framework.

In the Heron case the trial judge ruled the police interviews inadmissible and the defendant was acquitted. The judge was particularly critical of the interview tactics adopted in tapes 5–8 and ruled that they were oppressive. He concluded

> What occurred during that Friday night at that police station was an exercise in breaking the defendant's resolve to make no admissions. The means adopted to achieve that end meant, in effect, that regardless of the fact that his eventual confession may very well have been true, the prosecution were prevented from discharging the burden imposed upon them by the two limbs of Section 76(2) (this PACE Section will be discussed in Chapter 10).

The trial judge also considered it unfair that the police officers had misled Heron about the strength of the evidence against him.

CONCLUSIONS

This study has confirmed that in serious criminal cases, where there is an initial resistance to confess, British police officers have resorted to American style tactics (such as those recommended by Inbau, Reid & Buckley, 1986) to overcome resistance and secure a confession. Even though in these 20 cases the tactics were successful in terms of obtaining a confession, this was achieved at a considerable risk of the confession being rendered inadmissible by a court and the defendant acquitted. The PIAF has not only succeeded in analysing, measuring and displaying the nature and type of tactics employed, but it has also discriminated between overbearing and sensitive tactics, as determined by legal judgments.

The study also identified in all cases discrepancies between the official transcripts and the audiotapes. In some of the cases the inaccuracies were seriously misleading. We recommend that in serious criminal cases transcripts are carefully checked against the audiotapes and that tapes are played in court.

One limitation concerning the factor analytical approach adopted in this study was the amalgamation of cases in the combined group. This meant that the influence of potentially important variables, such as offence category, sex, duration and the presence of third parties, could not be controlled for. For example, the interviewing tactics of 37 officers (male and female) were combined to identify what type of tactic clustered together. To some extent this could be justified, as the overriding goal was to identify the nature of the tactics employed, and the results have been rather encouraging. In addition, the unique nature of this study dictates that this was very much an exploratory rather than a confirmatory exercise; amalgamation represented a logical option.

A further weakness relates to the small selective nature of the sample and the absence of a suitable control group, which reduce the opportunity to allow inferences to be drawn to a wider population. To some extent, though, we think that generalizing from the present work could be considered premature. This design is very much in its infancy and the coding remains rather subjective. The framework that has been created needs to be enlarged and refined in order that it may serve as a useful model against which other cases may be compared, to identify and measure oppressive interviewing tactics. However, these findings clearly have important implications for the judicial review of interviewing procedure and behaviour, and future police interview training.

It is hoped that the framework will also prove a useful vehicle to help researchers understand the legal and social complexities of the influential and highly enigmatic police–suspect interview.

CHAPTER 5

Why do Suspects Confess? Theories

Serious consequences normally follow from a self-incriminating admission or confession. The more serious the crime the more severe the consequences are likely to be for the offender concerned. Commonly, the offenders' self-esteem and integrity are adversely affected, their freedom and liberty are at stake and there may be financial or other penalties. Bearing in mind the potentially serious consequences of confessing to the police it is perhaps surprising to find that a substantial proportion of all suspects confess during custodial interrogation. The frequency with which suspects confess, and the empirical evidence relating to confessions, will be discussed in Chapter 6. The purpose of this chapter is to discuss the factors that inhibit suspects from confessing, and provide the reader with theoretical models that help to explain why people confess to crime either spontaneously, or for which they are being interrogated. It will become evident that there are varied reasons why suspects confess, and often a combination of factors needs to be considered. These relate to the circumstances and characteristics of the case, police behaviour and custodial factors and the attitude, personality and experiences of the suspect.

FACTORS INHIBITING CONFESSION

There are a number of factors that make it difficult for people to confess to crimes they have committed. This is not surprising when one considers the potential consequences of confessing for the offender and his family. Some of the most important potential consequences of confessing to a crime are as follows.

i. *Fear of legal sanctions*. All crimes carry the possibility of a certain penalty. The range of penalties and sentencing options varies considerably from one country to another, but in general the more serious the offence the greater the punishment is likely to be (Eysenck & Gudjonsson, 1989). Most criminal offences carry the possibility of a prison sentence, which means the loss of liberty for a certain amount of time. In many countries the most serious offences are subject to a mandatory prison sentence or even the death penalty. Another consequence of a criminal conviction, which may inhibit some first-time offenders from confessing, is the thought of having a criminal record. A criminal record may make it more difficult for the offender to obtain employment in the future.

ii. *Concern about one's reputation.* Some offenders are reluctant to confess because they are very concerned about what effect it may have upon their reputation in the community. The higher a person's standing in the community the more he perceives he has to lose, and the greater his reluctance to confess. It is, of course, the suspects' perceptions of their own standing in the community that is important in influencing their behaviour rather than the objective reality of the situation. In some instances a relatively minor offence, such as being apprehended for shoplifting or drunken driving, may be such a devastating experience for some people that they may become depressed and suicidal after being convicted. This reaction may be even more evident when the convicted person holds a senior position, or has led an otherwise exemplary life in the community.

iii. *Not wanting to admit to oneself what one has done.* After committing an offence people may 'suppress' the memory of the offence, because what they did is totally unacceptable to them (i.e. they push the memory out of conscious awareness). Being able to 'forget' what happened probably functions to protect the psychological well-being and self-esteem of the offender. As we saw in Chapter 2, the more reprehensible the offence, the more offenders are likely to exercise denial when being interviewed.

iv. *Not wanting one's family and friends to know about the crime.* Some offenders may be concerned that if their family and friends knew about the crime they had committed they might be adversely affected. In many cases the offender is undoubtedly right in thinking that his family and friends would be hurt, shocked and disappointed when learning about the crime. In reality, many families of suspects undoubtedly suffer from such tangible pain as adverse publicity via local newspapers, being shunned by neighbours and becoming the subject of much local gossip. Not wanting to hurt loved ones, and the possible fear of being rejected by them because of what one has done, are powerful emotions which may inhibit the willingness of the offender to confess.

v. *Fear of retaliation.* When an offender confesses to a crime he may implicate others and the fear of possible retaliation by them may act to inhibit confession. Indeed, the fear of retaliation may in some instances be much stronger than the fear of penal sanctions if convicted.

Reluctance to Confess: a Case Example

Sometimes the unwillingness or inability of people to confess to a crime they have committed can take extreme proportions. A case in point is that of Mrs R. She was a woman in her mid-fifties who was tried at the Central Criminal Court in London for the horrific murder of her best friend: a murder which she claimed to have no recollection of whatsoever.

Mrs R's friend had been bludgeoned to death in her own home with a heavy object during what appeared to be a frenzied attack. The murderer then tied a scarf around the deceased's neck and repeatedly stabbed and mutilated her body with a bread knife. At first sight the murder had many of the signs of a sexually motivated killing, which meant that the police would have been looking for a male suspect. As things turned out, the case was even more bizarre than it initially appeared.

Shortly after the discovery of the murdered woman's body, fingerprinting was carried out on friends and neighbours so that they could be excluded from the enquiry. Mrs R, who was the victim's closest friend, was discovered during fingerprinting to have lacerations on her hands. The police also noticed what looked like blood on her handbag. A search in her handbag revealed an even more surprising discovery, a piece of the established murder weapon! A conventional blood group analysis was carried out on the cross-matching of blood among the two women. The evidence suggested, but was not conclusive, that the victim's blood was on Mrs R's handbag and the rims of her glasses. Conversely, Mrs R's blood grouping was found on the dead woman's clothing and mixer taps within the victim's flat. Mrs R strongly denied any involvement in the murder and instructed her solicitor to have various blood specimens analysed by the newly developed DNA profiling technique so that she could once and for all prove her innocence. This was done and the results were conclusive. The blood on Mrs R's handbag and glasses did belong to the deceased woman and the blood found on the victim was that of Mrs R, who continued to insist that she had no recollection whatsoever of having killed her best friend. In fact, in spite of all the forensic evidence, which was clearly overwhelming, Mrs R could not contemplate the thought that she had murdered her friend in a most horrific way. In view of the forensic evidence, Mrs R pleaded guilty to manslaughter on the grounds of diminished responsibility, but she never 'admitted' that she could possibly have been responsible for the murder. In her own words, 'I could never have killed my closest and dearest friend no matter what the forensic evidence says'.

It is probable that the inability of Mrs R to 'admit' to the murder was primarily caused by the difficulties she had in accepting that she had committed a brutal and horrific act of violence against her best friend.

Psychological assessment showed Mrs R to be of average intelligence, but she had a strong tendency to deny painful and undesirable emotional experiences, particularly those relating to anger and hostility. She was a proud and strongly willed woman who found self-confrontation difficult.

Her psychological profile was that of an 'overcontrolled personality' (Megargee, 1966), that is, the type of person who has rigid inhibitions about the appropriate self-expressions of anger and frustration, and may suddenly lose control and act extremely explosively when provoked.

THEORETICAL MODELS OF CONFESSION

There are a number of theoretical models that have attempted to explain the mechanisms and processes that facilitate a confession during custodial interrogation. Five different models or theoretical orientations are reviewed in this chapter. Each model looks at confessions from a different perspective, and taken together the models provide an important insight into the reasons why suspects tend to confess during custodial interrogation.

This is not an exhaustive list of models. For example, Ofshe and Leo (1997a, 1997b) have developed their own classification of confessions, which they argue applies equally to true and false confessions. Their model is discussed in detail in Chapter 8 in relation to theories of false confessions, because it focuses primarily on false and coerced confessions. It builds on the work of Irving and Hilgendorf (1980), and extends the decision-making model in the rational choice tradition to false confessions.

The Reid Model of Confession

Jayne (1986) provides an informative model for understanding the process that results in a confession during interrogation. The model is based upon the 'nine steps' of interrogation discussed in detail in Chapter 1. Jayne refers to the model as the 'Reid Model', because it was developed by John E. Reid and Associates of Chicago. The model attempts to explain why the 'nine steps' of interrogation are successful in eliciting confessions.

The model construes interrogation as the psychological undoing of deception. Criminal deception is primarily motivated by avoidance behaviour; that is, avoiding the likely or possible consequences of being truthful. The two types of consequence of being caught in deception are labelled 'real' and 'personal'. *Real* consequences generally involve loss of freedom or financial penalties. *Personal* consequences involve lowered self-esteem and damaged integrity. Having to admit to criminal behaviour is embarrassing to most people and this makes it difficult for them to confess.

Successful deception is reinforced in accordance with operant conditioning principles. Thus, undetected lying is rewarding and increases the chances of further lying. However, successful socialization teaches people that it is wrong to lie and when lying occurs people may experience an internal conflict, which is comprised of feelings of frustration and anxiety. The increased level of anxiety associated with lying induces the person to confess. Least internal anxiety is generated by telling the truth. The level of anxiety is assumed to increase linearly from omission to evasion to blatant denial. As the level of anxiety increases, the person copes by the operation of defense mechanisms which function to reduce anxiety and restore self-esteem. The two main defense mechanisms relevant to interrogation are 'rationalization', which serves to help the offender by avoiding full responsibility for the offence (i.e. the offender somehow rationalizes the offence), and 'projection'. Projection means that the offender attributes blame for the offence to some external source (e.g. the victim). Both rationalization and projection serve to distort the account of what really happened.

According to the model, a suspect confesses (i.e. tells the truth) when the perceived consequences of a confession are more desirable than the anxiety generated by the deception (i.e. denial). The perceived consequences and perceived anxiety can be manipulated psychologically by the interrogator. Thus,

> (the) goal of the interrogation... is to decrease the suspect's perception of the consequences of confessing, while at the same time increasing the suspect's internal anxiety associated with his deception (Jayne, 1986, p. 332).

Jayne (1986) argues that there are three basic concepts relevant to the interrogator's manipulation of perceptions of consequences and anxiety. These are *expectancy*, *persuasion*, and *belief*. Expectancy refers to what is perceived by the suspects as desirable. At the beginning of an interrogation confessing is generally construed as highly undesirable. Persuasion is a way of changing the suspect's view of what is desirable ('expectancy' change) and his basic 'beliefs in the structure of internal messages that tend to support or refute an expectancy' (p. 333).

According to the model, there are four essential criteria for changing the suspect's expectancies and beliefs.

i. The information provided by the interrogator must be perceived as credible; this is made up of perceived sincerity and trust, which is communicated through subtle means to the suspect.
ii. The interrogator develops insight into the suspect's attitudes and weaknesses. It is particularly important to assess what consequences the suspect thinks he is avoiding by denial and what his propensity for anxiety tolerance is. Thus:

> The goal of the interrogation is to affect perceived consequences and anxiety, this information directs the selection of themes, the timing of alternatives, and the identification of the most appropriate anxiety-enhancement statements (p. 335).

iii. The suspect needs to internalize the interrogator's suggestions. This involves a three-stage process. First, the suspect must comprehend the interrogator's ideas (this is called 'relating'). Second, the suspect must accept the message communicated by the interrogator (called 'accepting'). Third, the suspect must internalize or believe the interrogator's suggestions. This points to the importance of suggestibility in the confession process: the more suggestible the suspect the easier it is, theoretically, to obtain a confession from him. The fundamental assumption inherent in the model is that the interrogator's suggestions are based on sound and well founded premises; in reality they are not and leading the suspect in this way may result in erroneous information being obtained.
iv. The interrogator must constantly observe whether or not the suspect is accepting the theme suggested, whether the suspect needs more anxiety-enhancement and whether the timing of presentation of an alternative is right. Persuasion is construed as a dynamic process that needs to be regulated according to the strengths and vulnerabilities of the suspect.

Jayne states that it is most difficult to elicit a confession from suspects with high tolerance for anxiety and guilt manipulation.

Jayne recommends a number of manipulative ploys that can be used by interrogators to reduce the perceived consequences of confessing during interrogation. This is mainly achieved by presenting the suspect with themes that increase self-deception and cognitive distortion through the use of two principal psychological mechanisms called 'rationalization' and 'projection'. These two 'defence mechanisms' enable the person to deal with threatening experiences by a form of self-deception of which he or she is unaware. In the case of interrogation either or both of these processes can reduce anxiety by altering the suspect's perceptions of the likely consequences of self-incriminating admissions. What the interrogator is doing is enhancing the natural tendency of offenders to employ defence mechanisms to justify their crimes and maintain their self-esteem.

Jayne states that in general rationalization and projection are most effective in reducing the perceptions concerning the *real* consequences for the criminal behaviour, whereas the ploy of using sympathy and compassion is relatively more effective in overcoming inhibitions about the perceptions of *personal* consequences.

Increasing perceived anxiety about persisting with denials is achieved through psychological manipulation that concentrates on making the suspect turn his anxiety inwards rather than outwards. Outwardly turned anxiety (e.g. suspiciousness, anger, hatred) inhibits confession-enhancing behaviours, whereas playing on the suspect's feelings of guilt and shame increases the kind of anxiety that commonly results in a confession.

According to the model, it seems that the success of the interrogation depends on the extent to which the interrogator is successful in identifying psychological vulnerabilities, exploiting them to alter the suspect's belief system and perceptions of the consequences of making self-incriminating admissions and persuading him to accept the interrogator's version of the 'truth'. This represents a potentially very powerful way of breaking down resistance during interrogation. According to Inbau *et al.* (2001), it results in an 80% success rate, although the authors provide no evidence for this claim.

A Decision-Making Model of Confession

Hilgendorf and Irving (1981) present an interesting conceptual model for understanding some of the factors that make suspects confess to the crime of which they are accused. The foundation for their model derives from an extensive review of the interrogation process, which was commissioned by the Royal Commission on Criminal Procedure (Irving & Hilgendorf, 1980). Hilgendorf and Irving argue that one of the main advantages of their model is that it is 'closely linked to the legal concepts of voluntariness and oppression' (p. 81).

The basic premise of the model is that when suspects are interrogated they become engaged in a complicated and demanding decision-making process. Some of the basic decisions that the suspect has to make relate to:

- whether to speak or remain silent,
- whether to make self-incriminating admissions or not,
- whether to tell the truth or not,
- whether to tell the whole truth or only part of the truth, and
- how to answer the questions asked by the police interrogator.

Applying the decision-making model of Luce (1967) to the police interrogation situation, Hilgendorf and Irving argue that decisions are determined by the following.

i. *Perceptions of the available courses of action.* The assumption here is that the suspect has more than one course of action open to him and he has to choose between them.
ii. *Perceptions concerning the probabilities of the likely occurrence of various consequences attached to these courses of action.* These are referred to as 'subjective probabilities'.
iii. *The utility values or gains attached to these courses of action.*

These factors indicate that suspects have to consider the kinds of option that are available to them. They have then to evaluate the likely consequences attached to these various options. For example, if they confess are they likely to be charged with the offence of which they are accused? If they insist on their innocence is the interrogation likely to continue?

The decision-making of the suspect is governed by the *subjective probabilities of occurrence of the perceived consequences.* In other words, decisions are not based on what is objectively, or even realistically, likely to happen. It is what the suspect *believes* at the time to be the likely consequences that influences his behaviour. This means that one cannot assume that the suspect objectively considers the serious legal consequences of making a self-incriminating confession. An innocent suspect may confess under the misguided belief that since he or she is innocent no court will bring in a guilty verdict and that the truth will eventually come out (Gudjonsson, 1989d).

The suspect has to balance the potential consequences against the perceived value ('utilities') of choosing a particular course of action. For example, would a confession inevitably lead to cessation of interrogation and would the suspect be allowed to go home? After confessing would visits from the family be allowed? Hilgendorf and Irving argue that threats and inducements, even when slight and implicit, can markedly influence the decision of the suspect to confess because of the perceived power the police have over the situation and the apparent credibility of their words.

Following the work of Janis (1959), Hilgendorf and Irving draw our attention to the important finding in the literature that decision-making is not just influenced by perceptions of utilitarian gains or losses; factors related to self- and social approval and disapproval can also be very important psychologically. Indeed, some authors, particularly those with psychoanalytic orientation (e.g. Reik, 1959; Rogge, 1975), emphasize the role of social and self-approval utilities in eliciting confessions. One illustration of the reasoning underlying the utilities of approval and disapproval is as follows. In general crime does not meet with social approval. Therefore confession involves the admission of a socially disapproved act. However, for the suspect not owning up to an offence allegedly committed by him can result in strong self- and social disapproval. Conversely, being able to 'get it off your chest', and accept punishment for what one has done, activates potential approval utilities.

Hilgendorf and Irving postulate that there are a number of *social*, *psychological* and *environmental* factors that can affect, or indeed seriously impair, the suspect's decision-making during police interrogation. On occasions these factors can undermine the reliability of the suspect's confession. The most salient factors are as follows.

i. The police can manipulate the social and self-approval utilities during interrogation in order to influence the decision-making of the suspect. In particular, the suspect's feelings of competence and his self-esteem are readily susceptible to manipulation. In view of the legitimate authority of police officers,

> ...the interrogation situation contains pressures on the suspect to give excessive emphasis in his decision-making to the approval or disapproval of the interrogator, and to be extremely sensitive to all communications both verbal and non-verbal which he receives from the interrogator (p. 81).

ii. The police interrogators can manipulate the suspect's perceptions of the likely outcome concerning a given course of action. One way of achieving this is by minimizing the seriousness of the alleged offence and by altering perceptions of the 'cost' associated with denial, resistance and deception.

iii. The police interrogators can impair the suspect's ability to cope with information processing and decision-making by various means. For example, they can, through social, psychological and environmental manipulation, increase the suspect's existing level of anxiety, fear and compliance. Personal threat is seen as an inherent part of any custodial interrogation and it can by itself raise levels of anxiety. Unfamiliarity and uncertainty are further anxiety-inducing factors. Social and physical isolation are seen as potentially powerful influences:

> The situation of physical confinement by the police supports and facilitates these pressures and the effect becomes more pronounced the longer the total period of detention in police custody (p. 81).

The Hilgendorf–Irving model relates to decision-making of suspects during custodial interrogation. It is not, strictly speaking, a model of false confession. However, the model highlights a number of important factors that can potentially render a confession unreliable.

Psychoanalytic Models of Confession

Various psychodynamic models of the 'need to confess' have been proposed. Such models rest upon the assumption that the feeling of guilt is the fundamental cause of confessions and false confessions. These psychoanalytic models are highly controversial as the theses upon which they are based have limited acceptance in the scientific community.

Undoubtedly, the most detailed formulation is that offered by Reik (1959), which is based on books and papers written in Germany in the 1920s. Reik's work attempts to show that the unconscious compulsion to confess plays an important part in religion, myths, art, language and other social activities, including crime.

Reik relies heavily on Freud's concepts of the id, ego and superego. Within this framework a confession is construed as 'an attempt at reconciliation that the superego undertakes in order to settle the quarrel between the ego and the id' (p. 216). Here the superego is seen to play a very important part in the need of the individual to confess. If the superego remains silent there develops a strong feeling of guilt and need for self-punishment. This may result in a 'compulsion' to confess, and on occasion false confession.

Freud's (1916) theory also suggests that some people may commit crime as a way of relieving 'an unconscious sense of guilt for which there seems no cause' (Van Velsen, 1999, p. 65). This includes making a false confession to the police, which is a crime in itself. There is also the likelihood that strong feelings of guilt may on occasions cause criminals to exaggerate the nature and extent of their crime.

The development of the feeling of guilt after transgression and the unconscious need for self-punishment are seen as universal characteristics of the individual and have an important impact upon his or her emotions and behaviour. It is only after the person has confessed that the ego begins to accept the emotional significance of the deed. For the criminal this is different to the intellectual acceptance of the deed, which always precedes its emotional acceptance. According to Reik's psychoanalytic model, emotional acceptance of the criminal act may take years to process. It is only after having confessed that the offender has made the first step back into society. A confession serves the function of relieving the person from the feeling of guilt.

Rogge (1975), like Reik, argues that confessions are based on feelings of guilt. He goes a step further and suggests that guilt feelings are made up of two components, which are fear of losing love and fear of retaliation:

> Those who are guilty of some criminal offense are under such anxiety lest they have lost love and lest there will be retaliation that they usually confess (p. 227).

Berggren (1975) presents a psychological model that highlights the need of the individual to confess to his or her transgression of social norms. People's knowledge of their transgression produces a sense of guilt, which is experienced as oppressive and depressing. The confession produces a sense of relief, which has important cathartic effects. For a satisfactory cathartic effect to occur the confession has to be to a person in authority, such as a priest or policeman.

Until recently, no empirical studies had looked at the role of feelings of guilt in facilitating a confession among criminals. A study carried out by myself into the electrodermal reactivity of Icelandic criminals, policemen and clergymen during a 'lie detection' experiment (Gudjonsson, 1979) indicates that there may be important group differences in relation to guilt following transgression. Criminals were found to be least physiologically responsive to deception and clergymen the most. This suggests that criminals, perhaps by virtue of early conditioning, or by habituation, no longer suffer the pangs of conscience following the commital of an offence. Psychoanalytic formulations seem to overlook the importance of individual and group differences in remorse following transgression.

In a small early study, Redlich, Ravitz and Dession (1951) found that people with a strong generalized feeling of guilt and anxiety were less able to resist interrogation whilst under the influence of sodium amytal. The authors argued that the findings supported Reik's formulation that guilt is a fundamental cause of confessions.

An Interaction Process Model of Confession

Moston Stephenson, and Williamson (1992) outlined a model that helps us explain how the background characteristics of the suspect and the case can influence the interrogator's style of questioning, which in turn affect the suspect's behaviour and the outcome of the interview. The model postulates that the suspect's initial response to an allegation, irrespective of his or her involvement in the crime under investigation, is influenced by the interaction of three main groups of factors:

- background characteristics of the suspect and the offence, e.g. type of offence, the severity of the offence, age and sex of suspect and the suspect's personality;
- contextual characteristics of the case, e.g. legal advice, the strength of the police evidence (a distinction is drawn between the suspect's initial reaction to the accusation and his or her subsequent responses) and
- the interviewer's questioning technique.

The model emphasizes the importance of looking at the interaction of a number of variables, rather than viewing them in isolation. Thus, the outcome of the interview is dependent upon an interaction process comprising a number of factors. One important implication of the model is that background characteristics of the suspect and the case, in conjunction with contextual factors, influence the interrogator's beliefs, attitudes and style of questioning, which in turn influences the suspect's behaviour. In addition, case characteristics may strongly influence the behaviour of *both* the suspect and the interrogator. The main limitation of the model is that it does not focus on the mental state and cognitive processes of the suspect.

A Cognitive–Behavioural Model of Confession

I have argued elsewhere (Gudjonsson, 1989d) that confessions are best construed as arising through the existence of a particular relationship between the suspect, the environment and significant others within that environment. The same applies to false confessions. In order to understand that relationship it is helpful to look closely at the *antecedents* and the *consequences* of confessing behaviour within the framework of behavioural analysis. The model brings together the essential elements of the other models and provides a social learning

Table 5.1. The antecedents and consequences of confessions

Antecedents	Consequences Immediate	Long-term
Social		
Isolation	Police approval, praise	Disapproval
Police pressure		
Emotional		
Distress	Feelings of relief	Feelings of guilt, shame
Cognitive		
'The police know I did it'	'It's good to get it off my chest'	'What is going to happen to me now?'
'The truth will come out in the end'	'My solicitor will sort it out'	'This is very serious'
'Perhaps I did do it, but I can't remember it'	'How could I have done such a dreadful thing'	'I'm now certain I had nothing to do with it'
Situational		
Nature of the arrest	Charged, allowed access to a solicitor	Judicial proceedings
Confinement?		
Solicitor present?		
Caution understood?		
Familiarity with police procedures?		
Physiological		
Aroused physical state, inhibitions reduced by alcohol or drugs; drug withdrawal	Arousal reduction	Arousal returns to base level

theory approach to confession. Table 5.1 shows typical antecedents to a confession and the immediate and long-term consequences.

'Antecedents' refers to the kinds of event that occur prior to interrogation. These are the factors that may trigger or facilitate the forthcoming confession. A large number of different factors may be relevant, such as fatigue, illness, deprivation of food and sleep, stress, social isolation, feelings of guilt and bereavement.

The are two major types of consequence, which are referred to in Table 5.1 as 'immediate' (or 'short-term') and 'long-term' consequences. The immediate or short-term consequences occur within minutes or hours of the suspects confessing to the alleged crime. The long-term consequences take place within days, weeks or years of the suspects confessing. The types of consequence, whether immediate or delayed, depend on the nature and circumstances of the case and the psychological characteristics of the individual concerned.

Antecedents and consequences are construed in terms of *social*, *emotional*, *cognitive*, *situational*, and *physiological* events. These types of event have been used to explain other types of behaviour, including delinquent behaviour (Stumphauzer, 1986).

Social Events

Table 5.1 gives two main types of social event that may trigger a confession. The first event refers to being isolated from one's family and friends. It was noted in Chapter 1 how much emphasis police manuals place on isolating the suspect from any external influence that may reduce a willingness to confess. The second type of social influence relates to the nature of the interrogation itself. The social process, as is so well illustrated by the Reid Model described earlier in this chapter, is an important factor in obtaining a confession from suspects.

The immediate consequence of confessing is social reinforcement by the police interrogators. The police may praise the suspect for owning up to what he has done. Visitors such as relatives may be allowed, and in some cases the suspect is allowed to go home. The long-term consequences commonly involve the defendant having to come to terms with social disapproval from the media and from the general public.

Emotional Events

Being arrested and brought to a police station is undoubtedly stressful for most suspects. Generally suspects can be expected to experience considerable levels of anxiety and distress. Some of the anxiety is caused by the uncertainty of the situation, the fear of what is going to happen at the police station, the fear of being locked in a police cell and the fear of the consequences regarding the alleged offence. A suspect who has committed a serious offence, possibly on impulse, may also be distressed by the nature of the conduct itself. Suspects who are experiencing bereavement at the time of their arrest are likely to be particularly vulnerable to emotional distress. For example, most suspects would find difficulty in coping with being interrogated in connection with the death of a close friend or family member.

There are two distinct emotional experiences that are particularly relevant to confessions: these are the feelings of *guilt* and *shame*. Within the context of confessions, shame is best viewed as a degrading and humiliating experience and it often accompanies a sense of exposure. In contrast, guilt is linked to the concept of conscience (i.e. it is associated with some real or imagined past transgression that is inconsistent with the person's internalized values and standards). There are marked motivational and behavioural differences between guilt and shame (Morrison & Gilbert, 2001; Tangney, 1990, 1996). Whereas a feeling of guilt motivates people towards reparative action (i.e. confessing, apologising, making amends), a feeling of shame has the reverse effect; it makes the person want to hide from others and not reveal what happened. Feelings of guilt are also important in the way offenders attribute blame for their criminal act (Gudjonsson, 1999a).

After confessing suspects may experience a sense of emotional relief as the immediate pressure is lifted and there is greater certainty about their immediate future (Irving, 1980). Guilty suspects may in addition experience relief from being able to talk about their offence. The police are often the first people suspects talk to about their crime. Before long, a feeling of shame sometimes sets in or becomes exacerbated, especially as the suspect may have to cope with unfavourable publicity about the case and begins to talk to friends and relatives about the crime.

Cognitive Events

Cognitive factors comprise the suspect's thoughts, interpretations, assumptions and perceived strategies of responding to a given situation. This kind of factor can very markedly influence behaviour. What is important to remember is that the suspects' behaviour during the interrogation is likely to be more influenced by their perceptions, interpretations and assumptions about what is happening than by the actual behaviour of the police. When the suspect perceives the evidence against him as being strong he is more likely to confess, believing that there is no point in denying the offence. Table 5.1 lists the kinds of self-statement that suspects may make during interrogation. Suspects who 'talk' themselves into believing that the interrogators are not going to give up until they have given a confession, or believe that the police have sufficient evidence to 'prove' that they committed the offence, may be greatly influenced by such thoughts and beliefs. For innocent people, the thought that the 'truth' will eventually come out even if they give in to persistent interrogation can facilitate a false confession. Similarly, innocent suspects who begin to doubt their own recollections of events because they are confused during interrogation may agree with the unfounded suggestions of the interrogator, and come to believe that they committed a crime of which they are in fact innocent. These are the so-called 'pressured–internalized' false confessions discussed in detail in Chapters 8, 18 and 23.

The immediate cognitive consequences may relate to thoughts associated with the easing of the pressure. For innocent suspects the thought (or hope) that their solicitor is going to sort everything out may predominate. Suspects who mistakenly come to believe that they have committed the offence of which they are accused may come to wonder how they could have committed such a terrible crime and have no recollection of it. Within days, after their confusional state has subsided, they may become fully convinced that they had nothing to do with it.

The most striking cognitive events associated with the potential long-term consequences of confession undoubtedly relate to thoughts about what is going to happen as the result of their self-incriminating confession. They begin to think about the seriousness of their predicament and this may make them inclined to retract their previously made confession.

Situational Events

Situational events are of many different kinds. The circumstance of the suspects' arrest (e.g. being arrested suddenly in the early hours of the morning) may affect the suspects' ability to cope with the subsequent interrogation, especially since this coincides with the nadir (i.e. lowest point) of the physiological cycle. Similarly, being locked up in a police cell for several hours or days may 'soften up' suspects (i.e. weaken their resistance) and make them more responsive to interrogation. On the other hand, familiarity with police procedures and interrogation is likely to provide suspects with knowledge and experience that make them more able to understand and assert their rights.

The immediate situational consequence commonly associated with a confession is that the suspect is charged with the alleged offence, after which he is allowed access to a solicitor when this has been previously denied. The long-term consequences relate to possible prosecution and judicial proceedings.

Physiological Events

The physiological antecedent to a confession is undoubtedly heightened arousal, which includes increased heart rate, blood pressure, rate and irregularity of respiration, and perspiration. These occur because suspects are commonly apprehensive, worried and frightened. Once the suspect has confessed there is likely to be sharp reduction in his level of physiological and subjective arousal because of greater certainty about the immediate future. Physiological arousal may then return to its normal level, although it should be noted that uncertainties about the pending court case and outcome may lead to an increased subjective and physiological state of arousal.

CONCLUSIONS

There are a number of reasons why it is difficult for people to confess to crimes they have committed. These are due to fear of legal sanctions, concern about one's reputation, not wanting to accept what one has done, not wanting friends and family to know and fear of retaliation. The reluctance to confess is not surprising when one considers the potential consequences of confessing for the offender and his family. In view of this it is perhaps surprising that a large proportion of suspects confess to the crime of which they are accused (i.e. in England over half make confessions; see Chapter 6). There are various models available to explain this phenomenon. Five different models or groups of model about confessions were discussed in this chapter. These are:

1. *the Reid model of confession*, where interrogation is construed as a psychological manipulation of overcoming resistance and deception;
2. *a decision-making model of confession*, where an attempt is made to draw attention to the kind of factors that influence the suspects' decision-making during interrogation;
3. *psychoanalytic models of confession*, where confessions are seen as arising from internal conflict and feelings of guilt;
4. *an interaction process model of confession*, where the outcome of interrogation is seen as resulting from the interaction of background variables and contextual characteristics, and
5. *a cognitive–behavioural model of confession*, where confessions are viewed in terms of their 'antecedents' and 'perceived consequences'.

Each of the models makes somewhat different assumptions about why suspects confess during custodial interrogation, although there is considerable overlap between some of the models. It is only recently that empirical studies have attempted to test out specific hypotheses generated by the models. A number of studies have been conducted so far and some general conclusions can be drawn about the reasons why suspects confess to crimes about which they are interrogated. These are discussed in the next chapter.

CHAPTER 6

Why do Suspects Confess? Empirical Findings

In this chapter the empirical studies that have been conducted into the importance, frequency and causes of confessions are reviewed. To what extent are the theories presented in Chapter 5 supported by the empirical evidence? This will also be addressed in this chapter.

Most of the studies into confessions during the past decades have been conducted in England. In contrast, most of the American studies date back to the 1960s, and these have largely focused on studying the effects of the *Miranda* ruling on the frequency with which suspects waive their rights and confess. There is currently a heated *Miranda* debate in the USA between Cassell (Cassell, 1996a, 1996b, 1998a, 1998b, 1999; Cassell & Fowles, 1998), who argues that the landmark ruling has resulted in many lost confessions and an enormous social cost, and others (e.g. Leo, 1996a, 1998; Leo & Ofshe, 1998b; 2001; Leo & White, 1999; Schulhofer, 1998; Thomas, 1998; Weisselberg, 1998), who dispute Cassell's claims and arguments.

HOW IMPORTANT ARE CONFESSIONS?

How important are confessions for solving a crime and in securing a conviction in a court of law? Zimbardo (1967) goes as far as to suggest that more than 80% of all crimes are solved by the suspect making a confession, and once a confession has been made defendants are seldom acquitted. Is Zimbardo's claim an exaggeration? The available evidence suggests that it is. However, the importance of confession evidence in securing a conviction should not be underestimated. In England defendants can, and sometimes are, convicted on the basis of confession evidence alone, even when the validity of the confession is disputed at trial. In England and Wales there is a general rule that the evidence of a single witness, including that from the suspect himself, is sufficient to prove the case (McConville, 1993; Royal Commission on Criminal Justice Report, 1993).

The importance of a confession to the police depends on the strength of the other evidence against the suspect (McConville, 1993). When the evidence against suspects is strong, then they are much more likely to confess (Irving &

McKenzie, 1989; McConville, 1993; Moston, Stephenson & Williamson, 1992; Softley, 1980), even though in such cases the confession may add little to the overall strength of the case. When the evidence against suspects is weak, then a confession may be the main evidence used at trial to convict them. In addition, when a confession is forthcoming, the post-admission statement (i.e. the details of the criminal act as provided by the suspect once he begins to confess) can be used to test out the validity of the confession and may provide important corroborative evidence. Does the suspect possess 'special knowledge' that was not in the public domain? The strongest corroboration is when the confession leads to the discovery of further incriminating evidence which was previously unknown to the police (e.g. discovery of the murder weapon, the victim's body, recovery of stolen goods). The extent to which the police attempt to corroborate pieces of information contained in the confession varies considerably. Inbau *et al.* (2001) strongly recommend that the validity of the confession be carefully investigated; their concern is about the large number of defendants who retract their confession and the risk of acquittal at trial without corroborative evidence. Obtaining a confession should not be seen as a substitute for a thorough criminal investigation. Indeed, McConville (1993) has noted a trend in England towards the acquisition of evidence independent of a confession. This is due to improved post-arrest investigative work.

The importance of confession evidence was recognized by the Royal Commission on Criminal Justice:

> Where a suspect has made a confession, whether at the moment of arrest, on the way to the police station, in the presence of the custody officer, or at a tape-recorded interview at the police station, it must normally constitute a persuasive indication of guilt, and it must in principle be desirable that, if a not guilty plea is entered in spite of it, the jury are given the opportunity of assessing its probative value for themselves. On the other hand, confessions which are later found to be false have led or contributed to serious miscarriage of justice (*Royal Commission on Criminal Justice Report*, 1993, p. 57).

What the Commission may not have fully appreciated is the potentially damaging impact that confession evidence can have on a jury. Kassin and Neumann (1997) have produced experimental evidence to show that confession evidence has a stronger impact on juror's decision making than any other type of probative evidence, including eyewitness and character evidence. This finding is very important. It helps to explain why confession evidence is found to be so common in cases of wrongful convictions.

One might expect that where there is a legal corroboration requirement, as in the United States of America and Scotland, detectives would be motivated to seek evidence to support the validity of the confession. According to Ayling (1984), this does not always appear to be the case. In other words,

> Contrary to the assumptions behind the corroboration rule, the rule does not motivate police to gather independent evidence (p. 1193).

Studies that have attempted to assess the importance of confession evidence as a part of the prosecution case are scarce. Inbau *et al.* (2001) make it clear that confession evidence is very important in a large number of cases in the USA and without it there would be no case against the defendant. Unfortunately, these authors do not give any figures in support of their claim. The critical research question is, in what proportion of cases do interrogations provide the police with substantial evidence against the suspect that would otherwise not have been available? The empirical findings on this point are somewhat contradictory, but suggest that confession evidence may be either crucial or important to the police in about 20% of cases. Furthermore, once a confession has been made, even if it is subsequently retracted, the defendant is convicted in the great majority of cases.

In a major English study, Baldwin and McConville (1980) analysed the committal papers among 1474 Crown Court cases. They found that confessions provided the single most important evidence against the suspect. In about 30% of cases the self-incriminating admission or confession was crucial to the prosecution case. Forensic evidence was only important in about five per cent of cases. Furthermore,

> No more than seven of the defendants who had made written confessions in London (5.2%) and 23 in Birmingham (2.4%) were eventually acquitted at trial. These figures thus provide striking confirmation for the hypothesis that to obtain a written confession from a suspect is tantamount to securing his conviction in court (p. 19).

Vennard (1980) found that 12% of cases rested heavily upon a confession. McConville and Baldwin (1981) found a similar figure, but this is dependent upon the type of crime investigated. Burglary and robbery cases were disproportionately represented in their reliance on confession evidence.

McConville (1993) found that in 13% of cases the only evidence brought before the court was the confession evidence. However, looking closely at his data, and estimating where corroboration would have been theoretically possible, McConville argues that the confessions are the only real prosecution evidence available in about 8% of cases. Therefore, he asserts, the introduction of a corroboration requirement in England, as laid down in *Baskerville* ([1916] 2 K.B. 658), would not result in a great many 'lost convictions'.

Three other English studies warrant a brief mention. Softley (1980), in an observational study in four police stations, found that detectives claimed that they would have dropped about 8% of the cases if a confession or an admission had not been forthcoming.

In two separate observational studies, Irving and McKenzie (1989) considered that the strength of evidence against suspects prior to interrogation was 'strong' in about 50% of cases and 'fair' in a further 30% of cases. This means that in about 20% of cases there was no tangible evidence against suspects prior to the interrogation.

Moston, Stephenson and Williamson (1992) analysed 1067 tape recorded police interviews and classified the strength of evidence against suspects prior to interrogation as either 'weak' (26%), 'moderate' (34%) or 'strong' (40%). The weaker the evidence against suspects, the less likely they were to confess.

In an important American observational study, conducted in New Haven, Wald et al. (1967) assessed the importance of confessions in solving crime, apprehending accomplices and clearing up other crimes. Having observed the interrogation of 127 suspects and interviewed the detectives involved, the authors found that interrogation was only necessary for solving the crime in about 17% of cases (Wald *et al.*, 1967; Table F-6, p. 1585). They concluded:

> Thus, even in a force as scientifically advanced as Los Angeles', there is strong evidence that confessions are of small importance, since arrests can be made only where the crime is for the most part already solved because such substantial evidence is available before interrogation (p. 1588).

In a more recent study, Leo (1996a) found that out of 182 cases observed, the strength of the evidence against the suspect prior to interrogation was weak in 33% of cases and is unlikely to have led to a charge without a confession. Leo concluded:

> *Suspects who provide incriminating information to detectives are significantly more likely to be treated differently at every subsequent stage of the criminal process than those suspects who do not provide incriminating information during interrogation* (p. 298, original author's italics).

Leo found that suspects who incriminated themselves during interrogation were 20% more likely to be charged by prosecutors, 24% less likely to have their case dismissed, 25% more likely to have their cases resolved by plea bargaining and 26% more likely to be found guilty and convicted. In addition, those who had confessed received heavier sentences following conviction.

On the basis of the review the American literature, Cassell (1996a) *estimates* that confessions are necessary for a conviction in about 24% of cases.

HOW COMMONLY DO SUSPECTS CONFESS?

Research shows that many suspects interrogated at police stations confess to the crime of which they are accused. A further proportion of suspects make self-incriminating admissions that fall short of a full confession. In 'run-of-the-mill' criminal cases in England a confession or an admission typically occurs at the beginning of an interview and the suspect typically sticks to his chosen position throughout the interview irrespective of the technique used (Baldwin, 1993; Evans, 1993; Irving & McKenzie, 1989; Moston, Stephenson & Williamson, 1992; Pearse and Gudjonsson, 1996a; Pearse *et al.*, 1998). This strongly indicates that once the suspect enters the interview he has already decided whether or not to make an admission or a full confession. Inbau *et al.* (2001) claim the contrary in the USA. Their argument is that the great majority of suspects initially deny their involvement in the offence, and with the assistance of the Reid Technique of interrogation about 80% of the denials change to a confession (see Chapter 1).

There is no empirical evidence to support these most extraordinary claims. The statement is presumably used to impress upon the readers the high success rate of the Reid Technique.

The admission or confession may be obtained orally ('verbal confessions'), in writing ('written confessions') or both orally and verbally. As we saw in Chapter 2 police interrogations in England are now tape recorded.

'Verbal confessions' which are not accompanied by written confessions can be problematic, unless they are tape recorded, because understandably suspects more readily retract such confessions, sometimes denying that they ever made them in the first place. The police, by knowledge of the previous record of the suspect, and by their perception of the total circumstances of the case, which may not be admitted as evidence, could easily become convinced of the guilt of the suspect whilst appreciating the absence of hard evidence required to secure a conviction. In such cases, some officers may be tempted to secure what they regard as justice by 'fitting up' suspects; that is, augmenting the existing evidence by claiming that suspects made verbal admissions which they subsequently refused to put into writing (see e.g. Graef, 1990; Kirby, 1989).

Confessions may also consist of offenders confessing to 'unsolved' offences whilst being interrogated. For example, Phillips and Brown (1998) found that 11% of suspects arrested confessed to crimes additional to those for which they had been arrested. Sometimes such offences may be 'taken into consideration' (commonly referred to as 'TIC') when the suspect's case eventually goes to court. Police officers may encourage such confessions in order to improve their clear-up rate.

Most confessions occur during so-called 'custodial interrogation'. Here the suspect is formally in police custody and is deprived of his freedom of action in a significant way (this usually means that the suspect is under arrest and is not able to leave the police station until the police say so). The distinction between 'custodial' and 'non-custodial' interrogation is an important one legally, particularly in America, because during the latter no *Miranda* warning needs to be provided and suspects can be pressured and 'softened up' prior to the formal interrogation (Inbau *et al.*, 2001).

The reported frequencies with which suspects confess to crimes during interrogation vary from study to study, which is in part due to differences in methodology. There are a number of potential problems here. First, definitions of a 'confession' clearly vary across studies. For example, many self-incriminating admissions may fall short of a full-blown confession. In one study they may be pooled together with full confessions, while in another they may be kept separate. A full confession means that the suspect admits to all the elements in the crime (Leo, 1996a). When some of the elements are absent (e.g. denial of intent, or the suspect claims he was present but did not take an active part in the offence), then these are classified as self-incriminating admissions. Another complicating feature is that denials can also be used as incriminating evidence against people at trial (Cassell & Hayman, 1998; Gudjonsson, 1995c; Leo, 1996a). This happens when suspects tell implausible lies or denials that the police can prove are false (e.g. an alibi that can be proved to be false, denying having been out of his house on the day of the crime when there is reliable evidence to the contrary). In his study, Leo (1996a) included this kind of denial in his calculation of the outcome of the interrogation. Forty-one (23%) suspects fell into this group. The distinction here is between incriminating denials and incriminating admissions. Both can be used against the suspect at trial.

Second, another source of difference relates to the basis on which the suspects' confessions are classified. The best methodology is to make the judgement on the basis of typed transcripts that have been carefully checked for accuracy against audio-taped interviews (Pearse & Gudjonsson, 1999). In England tapes are not routinely transcribed and often only a summary is produced by the police for judicial purposes. What researchers have tended to do when tapes are available is to listen to the tapes and make a judgement on that basis (Baldwin, 1993; Moston, Stephenson & Williamson, 1992; Pearse & Gudjonsson, 1996a). Other researchers have been present during interviews and noted evidence of admissions and confessions (Irving, 1980; Irving & McKenzie, 1989; Leo, 1996a). The weakest methodology is to rely exclusively on the police records, because admissions, confessions, and denials are not always accurately recorded in the files (Evans, 1993).

Third, the rate of confession is higher in cases that reach court than those that do not (Cassell, 1996a; Pearse *et al.*, 1998; Phillips & Brown, 1998). Therefore, focusing only on cases where there is a guilty plea and those that reach court (see e.g. Baldwin & McConville, 1980; Bryan, 1997; Mitchell, 1983; Zander, 1979) undoubtedly gives a misleading and exaggerated picture of the overall confession or admission rates. This has to be taken into consideration when comparing confession rates across different studies.

Fourth, there are a number of other factors that can also make a difference to the confession figures, such as adding to the figures suspects who are not interviewed, which for obvious reasons deflates the confession rate figure. For example, Cassell and Hayman (1998) included in their study 46 suspects who were not interviewed by the police. This lowered the confession rate from 42 to 33%. The majority (61%) were not interviewed because they could not be found for interrogation and in further 27% of cases there was already an overwhelming case against the suspect. We do not know the likely confession rate for the former group but the latter group would probably have had a high confession rate due to the strength of the existing evidence against them. The only legitimate cases to include in the figures are those where suspects could not be interviewed because they invoked their *Miranda* rights at the beginning of the interrogation, or in English cases, where suspects exercise their right to silence.

There are important legal and cultural differences between America and England with regard to suspects invoking their legal rights. For the American police there are potentially serious consequences when suspects invoke their *Miranda* rights, and between 4 and 78% do so, depending on the study (Leo, 1998). These are potentially more serious than English suspects requesting legal advice and exercising their right to silence. When suspects invoke their *Miranda* rights they effectively decline to give the police permission to interview them and they are rarely interviewed subsequently (Cassell & Hayman, 1998;

Leo, 1996a). Cassell (1996a, 1998b) refers to this as *Miranda's* 'social costs', or the so-called 'lost cases', because of the implementation of the *Miranda* rules in 1966. The cost may be viewed in terms of two independent criteria: first, in terms of how many confessions are lost because of successful defence motions at trial to suppress the confession due to *Miranda* problems, or convictions being subsequently overturned on appeal. Reviewing the relevant studies, Cassell (1996a) admits that motions to exclude confessions under *Miranda* are very rarely successful (the rate is between 0.3 and 0.7%), and convictions are very rarely reversed on appeal. The second and more serious problem, Cassell argues, are the 'lost confessions' due to suspects invoking one or more of their *Miranda* rights. Once suspects invoke their legal rights it seems that few American attorneys would advise clients to answer questions, never mind allowing them to confess.

In contrast, in England suspects typically request legal advice prior to the interview and a lawyer is commonly present during the interview. In spite of this many still confess (Pearse *et al.*, 1998). If a suspect asks for a lawyer during the interview, it is immediately terminated and re-commences once the solicitor has arrived. If a suspect chooses to exercise his right to silence the police interview will still go ahead, because the police are entitled, within reason, to ask questions, irrespective of whether or not the suspect decides to answer them. The typical answer given by suspects who are exercising their right to silence is to say 'no comment' to each question. Not all suspects can continue to refuse to answer questions. These differences between the American and English legal systems and procedures are of fundamental importance in terms of potentially 'lost confessions'.

However, in spite of the difficulties involved in comparing confession rates across studies, it is useful to have some approximation of the frequency with which suspects 'confess', or make serious self-incriminating admissions, to crimes during interrogation. Table 6.1 gives the proportion of suspects who made confessions in different studies. Only three of the studies are from the United States of America (Cassell & Hayman, 1998; Leo, 1996a; Neubauer, 1974). Prior to these three studies there had been about a dozen studies in the late 1960s that had studied the impact of the *Miranda* decision in 1966 on the confession rate (so-called 'before-and-after studies'). These studies have been reviewed by Cassell (1996a), who argues that there was a substantial fall in the confession rate immediately following the *Miranda* decision, an average reported drop of 16% in the confession rate across 12 studies (only one study showed an increase in the confession rate). According to his calculation, the *Miranda* ruling in 1966 is responsible for the loss of 3.8% of convictions in serious criminal cases. These studies represented the immediate or short-term effects of the *Miranda* rules and they may give a misleading picture of the current impact on the confession rate. In addition, several authors disagree with Cassell's analysis and interpretation of the data (e.g. Leo & White, 1999; Schulhofer, 1998; Thomas, 1998; Weisselberg, 1998). For example, Schulhofer (1998) has provided a critique of Cassell's analysis and conducted his own analysis of the relevant studies. He identifies methodological problems with Cassell's

Table 6.1. The proportion of suspects who confess or make admissions during interrogation

Study	Country of Origin	Type of data	Sample size	Proportion giving confession/admission (%)	Proportion having legal advice (%)
Baldwin and McConville (1980)	England	Crown Court files	282	76	
Cassell and Hayman (1998)	USA	Survey	173	42[a]	
Irving (1980)	England	Observational	60	62	10
Irving and McKenzie (1989)	England	Observational	68 (1986 sample)	65	29
			68 (1987 sample)	46	31
Leo (1996a)	USA	Observational	182	42[b]	
Mitchell (1983)	England	Crown Court files	394	71	
Moston and Stephenson (1992)	England	Questionnaire	558	59	14
Moston, Stephenson and Williamson (1992)	England	Taped interviews	1067	42	41
Neubauer (1974)	USA	Case files	248	47	
Pearse, et al. (1998)	England	Taped interviews	161	58	56
Phillips and Brown (1998)	England	Police documents/ questionnaire	4250	55	33
Softley (1980)	England	Observational	187	61	9
Zander (1979)	England	Crown Court files	282	76	

[a] Cassell and Hayman (1998) also calculated the confession rate by adding 46 suspects who were not interrogated for various reasons (e.g. they could not be found, the evidence against the suspect was overwhelming, the suspect was intoxicated). This reduced the overall confession rate to 33%.
[b] In addition to the 42% confession/admission rate a further 23% made incriminating statements typically in the form of 'implausible or contradictory denials' (Leo, 1996a, p. 280).

analysis and with the necessary adjustments the estimated drop in the confession rate post-*Miranda* goes from 16 to 4%, which means that there is a loss of convictions in less than 1% of cases. Thomas (1998) reviews the Cassell–Hayman (1998) Salt Lake County study, criticizes its methodology and argues for a 'steady-state' theory, according to which the fewer suspects who decide not to talk to the police following *Miranda* are compensated by others who now see it as an advantage to give full and more detailed statements to the police. This 'offsetting effect' has left the confession rate post-*Miranda* unchanged, Thomas argues. Unfortunately, the *Miranda* effect debate cannot be easily resolved due to various methodological problems. What is striking is the absence of recent American empirical studies on confession rates. There is desperate need for more American studies in this area.

The studies by Neubauer (1974), Leo (1996a) and Cassell and Hayman (1998) give an admission rate of between 42 and 47%, which is consistent with Ayling's (1984) review almost 20 years ago, which suggested that between 40 and 50% of American suspects confess during custodial interrogation.

As far as evaluating the English findings in terms of whether there was either an admission or a confession, the highest rates are found in the Baldwin–McConville (1980), Mitchell (1983) and Zander (1979) studies. These studies undoubtedly give artificially inflated admission/confession rates, because they included only suspects who were subsequently charged and committed to the Crown Court for trial. The Mitchell study was concerned with cases heard at the Worcester Crown Court in 1978, Baldwin and McConville looked at Crown Court cases in London and Birmingham and Zander looked at a sample of cases heard at the Central Criminal Court ('The Old Bailey'). The lowest rates were in the studies by Irving and McKenzie (1989) and Moston, Stephenson and Williamson (1992). The data in these studies were collected in 1987 and 1989, respectively, or between one and three years after the implementation of PACE. As a result of these studies I concluded in *The Psychology of Interrogations, Confessions and Testimony*:

> These findings indicate that with the introduction of PACE, and the more recent use of tape recordings, somewhat fewer suspects are confessing. This change could be attributed to at least two different factors. Firstly, the implementation of PACE and the increased use of tape recordings could mean that police officers are more restricted in the type of interrogation techniques they use (Irving & McKenzie, 1989) and this in turn may influence the frequency with which suspects confess. Secondly, Moston, Stephenson and Williamson (1992) argued that there appears to be a general mistrust of police questioning which may reduce the number of suspects who make confessions. If true, this may be related to changes in social attitudes towards the police, which encourage protests about wrongful conviction and resistance to interrogation (Gudjonsson, 1992a, pp. 53–54).

Does the current evidence support my 1992 conclusions? No, it does not. As illustrated in Table 6.1, more recent post-PACE studies of police station data clearly show admission/confession rates of between 55 and 59%. The Phillips–Brown (1998) study is based on a sample of 4250 police detainees, not all of whom were interviewed by the police (It is not clear from the study how many were not interviewed and how including these suspects in the figures may have influenced the confession rate.) The data were collected at 10 police stations in England and Wales between September 1993 and March 1994. The police station where suspects were interviewed was a significant predictor of admissions, the admission rate being between 65 (Croydon) and 42% (Hackney). Whereas Croydon is an outer South London Police Station, Hackney is an inner London Police Station in East London. The authors of the report concluded:

> The reason why station was a strong predictor of admissions is not obvious, bearing in mind that the regression analysis controlled for offence and a range of other variables. One possibility is that the prevailing culture among criminals in some areas may make them less inclined than in others to assist the police by providing admissions, even where the evidence against them is clear (Phillips & Brown, 1998).

Looking at the data from this study it seems that another possible explanation for station differences in the admission rate relates to the access to legal advice. The stations with the highest admission rates were those that had the lowest level of requests for legal advice. In contrast, stations with low admission rates tended to have the greatest number of requests for legal advice.

Moston and Stephenson (1993) argue that the relatively low admission rates in the Irving and McKenzie (1989) and Moston, Stephenson and Williamson (1992) studies may have been an artefact of focusing on more serious cases (in the latter study only interviews conducted by detectives were included, and this may have biased the results). Surprisingly, Moston and Stephenson (1993) also state that the admission rate of 42% in the Moston, Stephenson and Williamson (1992, 1993) only included full confessions:

> These figures can be compared to those of the largest post-PACE study to date, carried out in 1989 by Moston, Stephenson and Williamson (1992), involving 1,067 suspects who were interviewed by Metropolitan detectives. This study found that 42% of suspects made confessions. In addition, to these suspects, a further 13% made some form of damaging admission (see Moston, Stephenson and Williamson, 1993), making a combined total of 55% (Moston & Stephenson, 1993, p. 103).

The 55% figure would make good sense and be consistent with more recent studies. However, I have read carefully the two relevant articles (Moston, Stephenson & Williamson, 1992, 1993), but there is no reference to the additional 13% figure in either article. Indeed, in both articles the 42% figure is referred to as 'admissions', where 41.8% of the suspects admitted committing an offence, 41.6% denied it and 16.6% made neither an admission or a denial. Therefore, on the basis of two original articles I am assuming that the 42% figure refers to both confessions and admissions and that Moston and Stephenson (1993) have made a mistake in their reference to their previous work.

It is evident from the most recent confession studies shown in Table 6.1 that the admission/confession rate is substantially lower in the USA than it is in England. The difference is in the region of about 15%. There could be a number of reasons for this difference. First, in view of the scarcity of recent studies in the USA, and the relatively low number of cases evaluated in each study, it may be unwise to generalize from the available data about the USA current confession rates. Second, differences between England and America in confession rates may relate to the greater impact of the *Miranda* rules on the confession rate than the restrictions imposed by PACE. Third, it may be that many English legal representatives at police stations are passive and ineffectual in their role (McConville & Hodgson, 1993; Pearse & Gudjonsson, 1996b). As a consequence arguments have been put forward for a more active defence (Ede & Shepherd, 2000). Fourth, differences across nations in the confession rate may be related to cultural factors influencing both police and suspects rather than to the impact of *Miranda* warnings *per se*.

FACTORS ASSOCIATED WITH ADMISSIONS AND DENIALS

It is to be expected from the five theoretical models discussed in Chapter 5 that suspects are likely to confess to the police for a number of different reasons. There are three different ways of trying to understand the reasons why suspects confess during custodial interrogation. First, one can investigate the factors that are associated with admissions and denials, and this will be the focus of this section. Second, offenders can be systematically asked questions about what made them confess to the police and these can be correlated with other measurements, including those associated with intelligence, attitudes, attribution of blame and other personality dimensions (see e.g. Gudjonsson & Sigurdsson, 1999). The third method is to analyse the social interaction between the interviewer and suspect from the tape recordings of real life interrogation, or by observation at the time of the interrogation. This method was used by Pearse *et al.* (1998) and was discussed in Chapter 4. These three methods complement one another in understanding the reasons why suspects confess to the crimes they have committed.

The purpose of this section is to review the evidence for the types of factor that predict a confession. The factors are classified into three groups: (i) background characteristics of the suspect; (ii) characteristics of the offence; (iii) contextual characteristics.

It is evident from this discussion that not all suspects interrogated by the police confess to the crimes of which they are accused. Undoubtedly, some do not confess because they are innocent of the alleged offence. Others, probably a very small minority, confess to crimes they did not commit. This small subgroup of suspects is discussed in detail in subsequent chapters.

It is the purpose of this section of the chapter to review the evidence for some of the most noticeable characteristics that separate those who confess during interrogation from those who are able to resist doing so.

Out of persons detained at police stations in England and Wales between 80 and 90% have been arrested on suspicion of committing an offence. For example, Phillips and Brown (1998) found that out of 4250 detainees, 87% had been arrested on the suspicion of committing an offence; 13% were detained for breach of bail, common law breach of the peace or were on transfer from prison for attendance in Court.

About 1.75 million people suspected of committing offences are arrested every year in England and Wales, although a sizeable proportion of these will not be interviewed for a variety of reasons (Phillips & Brown, 1998). The proportion of these who are juveniles (i.e. under the age of 17) is about 15%. Phillips and Brown (1998) found that out of 4250 detainees, 635 (15%) were juveniles. In a major study at all Metropolitan (London) Police Stations over a one month period in 1997 (73 charging stations in total), Medford, Gudjonsson and Pearse (2000) found that out of 26 835 custody records, 3514 (12.6%) concerned juveniles. Moston, Stephenson and Williamson (1992) found that out of 1067 suspects interviewed by CID officers, 164 (15.3%) were juveniles. These studies illustrate the important point that a sizeable number of arrested persons detained at police stations are juveniles, who by law are considered to require special safeguards in view of their immaturity.

Background Characteristics of the Suspect

Are certain types of suspect more likely to confess than others? There is evidence from various studies that this is indeed the case.

Age and Confessions

Age is often considered as an indirect measure of maturity, and as Neubauer (1974) points out more mature suspects would be expected to cope better with the unfamiliarity and demands of police interrogation than less mature suspects. Is there a relationship between age and the readiness to confess? Yes, there is some evidence that younger suspects are more likely to confess to the police during interrogation than older suspects, but this has not been found in all studies.

Leiken (1970) found in Colorado that 42.9% of suspects under the age of 25 had made confessions under police interrogation compared with 18.2% of older suspects. Softley (1980), in an English study, found that 53% of suspects over 21 years of age made admissions or confessions, compared with 68% of those below the age of 21. The difference was statistically significant. Most important, however, was the frequency with which juveniles confessed. Of 38 juveniles in the study, 30 (79%) made admissions or confessions. Phillips and Brown (1998) found that the admission rate for juveniles was 62% in contrast to 54% for adults. Leng, McConville and Sanders (1989) (cited by Evans, 1993) found that 60.7% of juveniles made a full confession and a further 20% made incriminating admissions, giving a total admission/confession rate of over 80%. The corresponding figures for adults were 42.2 and 27.7%, giving a total rate of 69.9%.

The clearest example of a negative linear relationship between frequency of confessions and age comes from the British study of Baldwin and McConville (1980). The study was carried out in two major English cities, London and Birmingham. The samples comprised Crown Court cases. It is clear from the figures given by Baldwin and McConville that there is a consistent and significant trend for suspects to make fewer confessions the older they are. This trend was the same in the two cities studied and for both verbal and written confessions. Pearse *et al.* (1998) found that the mean age for confessors was 27 years in contrast to 30 among deniers, a statistically significant difference. However, the age difference disappeared when it was entered with other variables into a logistic regression analysis.

What are the interpretations that can be drawn from these findings? First, the younger the suspect the easier it is to obtain a confession from him or her. Second, there appears to be no clear cut-off point with regard to age. That is, it is not the case that after a certain age (e.g. 21 years) suspects have reached their ceiling of resistance. In fact, they continue to become increasingly more resistant as they grow older. Presumably, there is an upper age limit after which suspects' ability to resist the pressures of interrogation begins to decline again.

What are the factors that make suspects become less likely to confess with age? A number of different factors could be responsible. One factor suggested by Leiken (1970) is that older suspects are better equipped psychologically to cope with the demand characteristics of the interrogative situation, because of greater life experience. This interpretation is consistent with the results of a study by Gudjonsson (1988a), who found a highly significant relationship between the type of coping strategy utilized by people and their ability to resist interrogative pressure.

Another explanation, provided by Baldwin and McConville (1980), is that older suspects are more likely to understand and assert their legal rights during interrogation. This could be investigated by looking at the differences between younger and older suspects in this respect. For example, younger suspects may be more likely to waive their right to have access to a solicitor than older suspects. There is some evidence for this. For example, Evans (1993) found that a legal representative was present in only about 10% of cases, and when they were present during interviews they rarely contributed to the proceedings. However, in a much larger and detailed study (Phillips & Brown, 1998), age was not found to be a significant predictor of request for legal advice in a logistic regression analysis.

Temperamental differences related to age may also be important. For example, such factors as neuroticism, impulsiveness and venturesomeness are negatively correlated with age (Eysenck & Eysenck, 1975, 1978; Gudjonsson & Adlam, 1983) and these are the types of factor that may make some suspects confess more readily. Another factor that is likely to be important is that adolescents find negative feedback and interrogative pressure by interrogators more difficult to resist than adults (Gudjonsson & Singh, 1984a; Richardson, Gudjonsson & Kelly, 1995; Singh & Gudjonsson, 1992a). This may make them more likely to confess during interrogation, particularly in the more serious cases where the pressure to confess is greatest (Evans, 1993). Moston, Stephenson and Williamson (1992) found that juveniles were more likely to deny the allegations when the evidence against them was 'strong'. The authors interpreted this finding as suggesting that juveniles use 'inappropriate "escape" strategies' when interviewed by the police.

There have been studies that have not found age to be a significant factor. Neubauer (1974) gathered data on 248 criminal defendants in Prairie City (California) and found no significant difference in confession rates between minors (between 16 and 20 years) and adults (21 years or older). The confession rates for the two age groups were 50 and 44%, respectively. Similarly, Wald *et al.* (1967) and Leo (1996a) did not find a significant relationship between age and frequency of confession. With regard to English studies, Mitchell (1983) found no significant variation in the confession rate for defendants up to the age of 50 years. After the age of 50 markedly fewer defendants confessed. More recently, Moston, Stephenson and Williamson (1992) did not find age to be a significant discriminator in their study between confessors and deniers. Evans (1993) did not find a significant difference in admission rate for the three age groups: 10–13, 14 and 15–16 years.

The differences between the studies with regard to age are difficult to interpret. Whether they are caused by differences in the measurement of 'confession' or sampling bias, as Neubauer (1974) speculates, remains to be seen. The findings of Moston, Stephenson and Williamson (1992) and Pearse et al. (1998) indicate that age should not be considered in isolation from other salient variables, which may act as important intervening variables in their association with confession.

Gender

Approximately 85% of persons arrested and detained at police stations in England are male (Gudjonsson et al., 1993; Moston, Stephenson & Williamson, 1992; Phillips & Brown, 1998). Moston, Stephenson and Williamson (1992) and Pearse et al. (1998) found no gender differences in their studies with regard to the rate of admissions or denials. However, in the large sample study by Phillips and Brown (1998) a significant gender difference was found, with females confessing more commonly than males (the admission rate of females was 73%, compared with 52% of males).

Ethnic Differences

Pearse et al. (1998) specifically analysed ethnic background and the confession rate. Out of a total sample of 160 detainees, 73% were Caucasian and 27% were from ethnic minorities, primarily Afro-Caribbean. The confession rate for the Caucasian detainees was 62%, in contrast to 49% for the ethnic minority detainees. This difference failed to reach statistical significance. However, among a much larger sample, Phillips and Brown (1998) found that the admission rates for whites, blacks and Asians were 58, 48 and 44%, respectively. The Caucasian detainees were significantly more likely to provide a confession than the black or Asian detainees. Interestingly, black and Asian detainees were significantly more likely than the whites to request legal advice. This may partly explain the difference in the confession rate, except that when this variable was entered into the logistic regression analysis along with other variables there still remained a significant difference between the black and white detainees in the confession rate. This is in spite of the fact that black detainees have been found to be more suggestible than white detainees on psychometric testing (Gudjonsson, Rutter & Clare, 1995). This lower confession rate may reflect ethnic differences in relation to attitudes towards the police and the greater use of legal advisers (Phillips & Brown, 1998). Interestingly, in the famous New Haven study (Wald et al., 1967), white suspects were no more likely to confess than African–American suspects.

Mental State and Psychological Factor

Only one study, based on a psychological evaluation of detainees, has assessed the role of mental state and psychological factors in relation to confessions and denials (Pearse *et al.*, 1998). This study was discussed in detail in Chapter 3. The only psychological/mental state factor that predicted a confession was when suspects admitted to having consumed an illicit drug 24 hours prior to their arrest. Phillips and Brown (1998) assessed mental state from the Custody Record and did not find a relationship with the rate of confession. They recognize the limitation of their data since no formal clinical evaluation had been carried out on the detainees.

Previous Convictions and Confessions

It would be expected that the more experience suspects have had of police interrogation the less likely they are to confess. In other words, suspects who have had several previous convictions would be:

- expected to be more likely to know and to assert their legal rights;
- expected to be more familiar with the probable consequences of making self-incriminating admissions;
- expected to be more familiar with the police environment and interrogations, which helps them cope with the custodial predicament.

Supporting the above expectancy, Neubauer (1974) found that suspects with previous convictions were less likely than first offenders to (i) sign the custody interview form advising them of their legal rights and (ii) confess to the alleged offence. This indicates that first offenders are more compliant at the police station than offenders with previous convictions.

Leo (1996a) found that suspects with a previous felony record were four times more likely to invoke their *Miranda* rights than suspects without previous convictions.

Further support for the effects of previous convictions arises from an important observational study in four English police stations. Softley (1980) found a significant difference in the rate of confession among suspects who had previous convictions at the time of the interrogation and those without previous convictions. Among suspects without previous convictions, 76% had made either a self-incriminating admission or a full confession, compared with only 59% of those suspects with a criminal record. Similarly, Evans (1993) found that the admission rate for juveniles without a previous conviction was 68%, in contrast to 53% of those with a previous conviction.

Moston, Stephenson and Williamson (1992) found a bi-variable interaction of the strength of evidence between previous convictions and confession, relating to both conviction number and evidential strength. That is, generally confessions rise steadily in accordance with the strength of evidence that the police have against the suspect, but the rate of increase in the frequency of confessions is related to previous convictions. For example, there was no overall difference in the rate of confession between those with and without previous convictions, yet when the evidence against the suspect was strong those without previous convictions were significantly more ready to confess (78%) than those with previous convictions (59%). It is difficult to interpret these findings. It may be that it is the fear of going to prison that deters some suspects from confessing rather than previous convictions *per se*. As seen in Chapter 3, Pearse *et al.* (1998) found that it was not whether or not suspects had a previous conviction, or the mean number of previous convictions, that was important in predicting a confession or a denial. It was a previous prison experience that was associated with a reduced confession rate.

One American and two English studies have found no significant relationship between previous convictions and the rate of confession among criminal suspects (Leiken, 1970; Phillips & Brown, 1998; Zander, 1979), and two English studies found an unexpected positive relationship between the rate of confession and previous convictions (Baldwin & McConville, 1980; Mitchell, 1983). In the Phillips–Brown (1998) study, previous convictions did predict the likelihood that suspects requested legal advice, but once these had been taken into account then there was no significant relationship found for confessions.

Baldwin and McConville (1980) found that suspects with previous convictions were more likely to make verbal or written confessions than suspects who had no previous convictions. This was particularly true in their London sample. Similarly, Mitchell (1983), in his Worcester study, found that suspects with previous experience of the criminal process tended to confess more readily than those without such experience.

What factors account for the discrepancy between these findings? Mitchell (1983) suggests two possible explanations for the positive relationship he found. First, he speculates that suspects with previous convictions may more readily appreciate the advantages of confessing. Secondly, suspects with previous convictions may be less equipped to cope with police interrogations.

With regard to the first point, Mitchell does not spell out what advantages he has in mind for those who confess. For most suspects it is unlikely to be in their own interest to confess, although this is not always the case (see Phillips & Brown, 1998, on this point). The second point Mitchell makes seems rather strange, because it is not at all clear why suspects with previous convictions should find it more difficult to cope with the demands of police interrogation. There are a number of possible reasons for this. They include the following.

- Suspects with previous convictions having been 'traumatized' by their previous interrogation experiences and subsequently give in more easily. (I have seen such cases, but it is doubtful that it holds for the majority of suspects.)
- Those suspects who persist in crime possess certain idiosyncratic characteristics (e.g. low intelligence) that make them generally less able to cope with interrogative pressure.
- Suspects with previous convictions believing it is futile to deny their involvement in crimes.
- Confessions may be easier to make after suspects have confessed once; e.g. first offenders may find it particularly inhibiting to confess because their

reputation is at stake and they do not wish to be labelled as a criminal. 'Labelling', of course, has been argued by Matza (1967) to be an important factor in the development of a criminal career. It could be applied to confessions in the sense that, once labelled as a criminal, the suspect has less to 'lose' in terms of his reputation than he did during his first interrogation.

An important factor raised by Firth (1975) is that the potential resistance effect of previous convictions may be offset by the greater persistence and determined interrogation of suspects with previous convictions.

If Firth's suggestion is correct then one might expect to find least confounding effects of previous convictions during interrogations that are under observation by researchers. The reason for this is that police officers may control their interrogation tactics and techniques more when their behaviour is being observed. This is likely to result in more uniform methods of interrogation, irrespective of the number of previous convictions. This is exactly what one finds. For example, the strongest negative relationship between previous convictions and confessions was found in the Softley (1980) study. One possible interpretation is that direct observation affects the behaviour of the interrogators, which prevents or inhibits them from placing relatively more pressure on suspects with previous convictions.

There are, of course, important methodological issues that need to be considered when evaluating the outcomes from different studies. For example, different interrogation techniques, the duration and intensity of the interrogation, the policies adopted at different police stations and the nature of the alleged offence may potentially confound the results from the various studies quoted above and lead to inconsistent results. The study of Moston, Stephenson and Williamson (1992) provides a beginning, and an important methodology, for addressing these issues in future studies.

Characteristics of the Offence

It would be expected that for various reasons some offences attract more confessions than others. For example, it would be expected that the highest rate being found for offences where the strength of the evidence against the suspect is typically the strongest (e.g. being stopped and found driving while intoxicated, being found in the possession of drugs, being caught shoplifting). There is some evidence for this (Sigurdsson & Gudjonsson, 1994). In addition, as the offence becomes more serious the stakes in terms of perceived and real punishment rise and this is likely to inhibit some suspects from confessing.

Type of Offence

Neubauer (1974) found that suspects interrogated about property offences (e.g. theft, burglary, forgery) confessed more often (56%) than those suspected of non-property offences (e.g. violent offences) (32%).

Mitchell (1983) found that suspects interrogated about sexual offences confessed most readily. With an overall confession rate of 70% in the study, the rate for suspected sexual offenders was 89.3%, in contrast to 52.5% for non-sexual offenders. Suspects also appeared to confess more readily to property offences (76%) than to violent offences (64%), which is consistent with the findings of Neubauer (1974).

Neubauer (1974) argues that the main reason for the greater number of confessions among alleged property offenders than other offenders relates to the nature of the evidence that the police have at the time of the interrogation. He states that with regard to property offences there is more often forensic evidence (e.g. fingerprints) to link the suspect with the alleged offence than in non-property offences. This means that during interrogation the police have more persuasive evidence to convince the suspect that denials are futile. The position may be somewhat different with regard to sexual offenders in that there could be special psychological reasons that facilitate their confession-making behaviour. This point will be taken up again later in this chapter when discussing the results from a recent Icelandic study into factors that may facilitate or inhibit confessing among criminals.

Sigurdsson and Gudjonsson (1994) found among Icelandic prison inmates the highest confession rate was obtained for traffic violators (95%) and drug offenders (94%), whereas the lowest rate was found for sex offenders (83%). The authors argued that these findings could be explained by the fact that in the first two categories the offenders are typically caught in the commission of the offence, whereas sexual offenders are very rarely apprehended at the time of committing the offence. In another Icelandic study, Gudjonsson and Sigurdsson (2000) compared the confession rate of violent offenders, rapists and child molesters. The highest rate was found for child molesters (83%) and lowest for rapists (61%). The confession rate of violent offenders fell in between the other two groups (77%). These findings confirm the findings of Nugent and Kroner (1996) that rapists confess less readily to their crime than child molesters.

The study by Moston, Stephenson and Williamson (1992) found no significant differences in confession rates between offence types (offences against the person versus property offences). These authors argue that the previous significant findings may be an artifact of the studies' faulty methodology, because they did not take into account possible inter-associations between case characteristics. This is undoubtedly a valid point and should be carefully considered in future research into confessions.

Seriousness of the Offence

A number of studies have shown that suspects confess less readily to serious than non-serious offences (Evans, 1993; Irving & McKenzie, 1989; Moston, Stephenson & Williamson, 1992; Phillips & Brown, 1998). For example, in the Phillips–Brown (1998) study suspects in the less serious cases confessed more often (72%) than those suspected of 'moderately' (49%) and 'very serious' (46%) offences. However, Phillips and Brown point out that this difference was accounted for by interactions with other variables, such as greater access to legal advice in serious cases and the improved strength of evidence against the suspect. The relative lack of incentive among suspects to confess to serious crimes may sometimes be compensated for by the fact that the more serious the crime, the longer suspects tend to be interrogated and the larger the number of interrogation tactics utilized (Leo, 1996a). This is consistent with the British case data presented in Chapter 4.

Contextual Characteristics

There are a number of contextual factors that may be related to the outcome of a police interview (Moston, Stephenson & Williamson, 1992). These include access to legal advice, the strength of the evidence against the suspect, the type of interrogation techniques used, time spent in custody, the number of police interviews and the location of the police station. Certainly access to legal advice and suspects exercising their right to silence vary greatly across different police stations and regions (Phillips & Brown, 1998) and these factors will undoubtedly indirectly influence the confession rate. The three most important contextual factors appear to be legal advice, the strength of the evidence against the suspect and the police interrogation techniques.

Access to Legal Advice

Marked hindrance by the police in allowing suspects access to a solicitor is reported by Walsh (1982), who conducted a study of arrests and interrogation practice in Northern Ireland. Fifty per cent of the sample studied reported that they had requested a solicitor. Of these, 76% claimed that they were refused access to a solicitor and the 12% who were eventually allowed to see a solicitor had to wait more than 48 hours. In other words, no suspect was allowed access to a solicitor within 48 hours of arrest. Similar findings are reported for the USA by Leiken (1970), who found, in a reasonably comprehensive study, that after the implementation of the *Miranda* warning (i.e. a formal warning against self-incrimination), 67% of suspects claimed to have requested a solicitor, but only 6% were allowed to have one. Leiken concluded that 'the police are able to somehow effectively frustrate the right to counsel, despite the suspects' knowledge of their rights and their attempts to assert them' (p. 27).

In recent years there has been increasing emphasis on informing suspects of their legal rights. The most important of these are the right to silence (i.e. suspects are not obliged to say anything to the police unless they wish to do so and therefore can refuse to answer a question put to them) and the right to legal advice prior to and during interrogation. Being informed of these rights does not mean that suspects necessarily understand them (Fenner, Gudjonsson & Clare, 2002; Grisso, 1980; Gudjonsson, 1991a), or even if they do understand them they may choose or be persuaded by the police to waive their legal rights (Leiken, 1970). The purpose of these legal rights is to protect the suspect against self-incrimination.

What proportion of suspects exercise their legal right to silence? According to Irving (1980),

> To remain silent in a police interview room in the face of determined questioning by an officer with legitimate authority to carry on this activity requires an abnormal exercise of will (p. 153).

It is perhaps for this reason that suspects have been traditionally reluctant or unable to exercise their right to silence.

Softley (1980), in an early observational study in four English Police Stations, found that out of 187 suspects interrogated, 12% exercised their right to silence to a certain extent. Four per cent refused to answer all salient questions pertaining to the alleged crime. Older suspects were significantly more likely to exercise their right to silence, although it is worth noting that the great majority of suspects in all age groups did not exercise their right to silence. Similarly, suspects with previous convictions more frequently exercised their legal right to silence than those without previous convictions.

Other early studies support the infrequent use of the right to silence prior to or during custodial interrogation. Zander (1979) found that 4% of his sample had used their right of silence. Baldwin and McConville (1980) found that about 5% of their two samples made no statements of any kind to the police. Mitchell (1983) found that less than 1% of their sample made no statement of any sort. There is evidence that following the implementation of PACE in 1986 suspects are increasingly exercising their right to silence. Moston, Stephenson and Williamson (1993) found that 16% of the subjects had used their right to silence. Of these, half refused to answer any questions and the remainder refused to answer some. Great variation was found between different police stations in the use of silence; e.g., in Holborn only 8% of suspects used their right to silence, in contrast to 25% in Uxbridge. The authors suggest that both police tactics and the behaviour of solicitors may vary from station to station and affect the extent to which suspects exercise their right to silence. Similarly, Phillips and Brown (1998) found that 10% of suspects refused to answer all questions and a further 13% refused to answer some questions. Moston, Stephenson and Williamson (1993) found that certain case and background variables predicted the use of the right to silence. The use of the right to silence was associated with the seriousness of the offence, previous convictions and access to legal advice, but it did not adversely affect the decision to prosecute or their plea of 'guilty' when the case went to court. Those who used their right to silence were more likely to be convicted than those who denied the offence during interrogation. The authors suggest that the use of silence may not necessarily be to the advantage of the suspect. Certainly, the changes to the right of silence in England and Wales under Section 34 of the *Criminal Justice and Public Order Act 1994* means suspects are placed under pressure not to exercise their right to silence (Morgan & Stephenson, 1994).

There is much evidence that suspects are increasingly requesting, and being allowed access to, legal advice prior to custodial interrogation. In England PACE markedly strengthens the suspect's right to legal advice during custodial interrogation (Irving & McKenzie, 1989). Irving and McKenzie, in their observational studies at an English police station in 1986 and 1987, found that, of the 136 suspects observed, about 30% had had legal advice prior to the interrogation. Unfortunately, in the original study at Brighton Police Station, Irving (1980) made no mention of the number of suspects who had legal advice prior to or during their custodial interrogation. It is surprising that such an important factor as legal advice played no part in the original study. A similar omission was made in the study conducted by Baldwin and McConville

(1980). One possible explanation for this omission, which is supported by other English studies (Mitchell, 1983; Softley, 1980; Zander, 1972), is that legal advice was infrequently requested or allowed, before the implementation of PACE in 1986. Indeed, Bottomley et al. (1991) found that the overall proportion of suspects who received legal advice in 1984 was only 9% but it increased to 18% in 1986 and to 22% in 1987. A study by Sanders and Bridges (1989) looked at the operation of the legal advice provisions of PACE. They found that about 25% of suspects actually requested legal advice prior to or during interrogation. Of those requests, about 80% were successful, which indicated that about 20% of the suspects in the study were actually not allowed access to a solicitor. According to the authors, their figures were very similar to those previously obtained in a Home Office survey. Even higher figures have been reported by the Pearse et al. (1998) study (56%), followed by the Moston, Stephenson and Williamson (1992) study (41%) and the Phillips–Brown (1998) study (33%). The reason for the high rate in the Pearse et al. (1998) study probably relates to the fact that each suspect had been assessed psychologically while at the police station (see Chapter 3). This may have encouraged some suspects to seek legal advice, or that they were encouraged to do so by the police who were aware of the study being conducted at their police station.

Does receiving legal advice influence the confession rate? There is evidence that it does, although it should be pointed out that this does not appear to have reduced the overall confession rate. In other words, even with a high proportion of suspects being provided with legal advice, as in the studies of Moston, Stephenson and Williamson (1992), Pearse et al. (1998) and Phillips and Brown (1998), suspects are still confessing in more than half of all cases.

However, the presence of a legal adviser is an important predictor as to whether or not the suspect will confess. For example, Moston, Stephenson and Williamson (1992) found that over 50% of those who had no legal advice confessed, in contrast with less than 30% of those who had had legal advice. These authors concluded, on the basis of their findings, that confessions fall by about 20% once suspects have contact with a legal representative. An alternative explanation is that the suspects who requested a solicitor were different in their personality, or in their experiences and attitudes, than those who did not request a solicitor, and would not have confessed even if they had not had access to legal advice. Therefore, we may need to look closely at the type of suspect who requests a solicitor. This may explain why, with the increased proportion of solicitors attending interviews, the confession rate has been maintained.

Pearse et al. (1998) found that the those suspects who had legal advice were more than or about four times less likely to confess than those who did not receive legal advice. Phillips and Brown (1998) found almost identical results. All these three studies are important in that they used sophisticated statistics to control for interactions among variables.

The Strength of the Evidence

The Moston, Stephenson and Williamson (1992) study provides the strongest support for the strength of the evidence predicting the likelihood of a confession.

Confessions were rare (i.e. less than 10% of cases) and denials common (i.e. 77% of cases) when the evidence against the suspect was weak. When, on the other hand, the evidence against the suspect was viewed by the police as strong, then confessions were common (i.e. 67% of cases) and denials infrequent (i.e. 16% of cases). Similar findings have been reported by Evans (1993) and Phillips and Brown (1998). The most likely explanation for the relationship between the strength of evidence and the confession rate is that when suspects perceive the evidence against them as being strong they view it as futile to deny the offence.

Interrogation Techniques

There is evidence that the more serious the offence the more the police use persuasive techniques to break down resistance (Evans, 1993; Irving & McKenzie, 1989; Leo, 1996a). As shown in Chapter 4, the type of technique used in serious cases appears to influence the outcome of the interview. Leo (1996a) found that some interrogation tactics were more effective in eliciting a confession than others. The four most significant tactics were as follows:

- Appealing to the suspect's conscience.
- Identifying and pointing out contradictions in the suspect's denial and story.
- Offering moral justification or psychological excuse for the crime.
- Using praise and flattery.

There was also a significant relationship between the length of the interrogation and the number of tactics used, on the one hand, and the number of confessions obtained, on the other. Therefore, the more time and effort the detective puts into the interrogation process, the greater the likelihood that a confession will be elicited.

The Characteristics of the Interrogator

The characteristics of the officer who performs the interviewing may influence the outcome. For example, there is some evidence that detectives are more likely to obtain a confession than patrol officers (Cassell & Hayman, 1998). Perhaps detectives are more experienced, skilful and confident in their interviewing, or use more persuasive methods of interviewing. In the Moston, Stephenson and Williamson (1992) study, only CID officers (i.e. detectives) were included, because they tend to interview suspects in the most serious cases. The context of the interrogation can also make a difference to the outcome of the interview.

SELF-REPORT STUDIES INTO WHY SUSPECTS CONFESS

Very few studies have actually researched the precise reasons why suspects confess to crimes they have committed. It is easy to understand that suspects would generally be resistant to confessing, considering the adverse consequences of doing so. Nevertheless, many guilty suspects eventually confess to the crime.

Some confess readily and without much external pressure, whereas others take a long time to confess or only confess when the evidence against them is overwhelming, if at all. In three separate studies about 70% of suspects claimed that they would definitely not have confessed to the police if they had not been suspected of the crime by the police (Gudjonsson & Bownes, 1992; Gudjonsson & Petursson, 1991; Sigurdsson & Gudjonsson, 1994). About a further 20% said they would have confessed even if the police had not suspected them of the offence, and an additional 10% remained uncertain about what they would have done. The consistency of the figures across two different countries—Iceland and Northern Ireland—is striking. Why should 20% of suspects be motivated to confess to crimes of which they were not suspected by the police? Guilty conscience perhaps? These figures seem counter-intuitive in view of the potentially serious consequences for the person involved. Indeed, Inbau, Reid and Buckley (1986) certainly view it as '...impractical to expect any but very few confessions to result from a guilty conscience unprovoked by an interrogation' (p. xvi). Nevertheless, I have come across a number of murder cases where people had the need to talk about what they done, which resulted in their volunteering a confession to a spouse, a friend or the police. Of course, there may be cultural differences in this respect.

With my psychiatrist colleague Hannes Petursson (Gudjonsson & Petursson, 1991), I investigated the reasons for confessing among 74 Icelandic prisoners. We looked at a number of factors that could be associated with the reasons for the confession, such as the type of offence committed, the offenders' intelligence, attitudes, personality and the way they attributed blame for the crime they had committed. This study was replicated in Northern Ireland (Gudjonsson & Bownes, 1992) and on a large Icelandic prison population with an extended confession questionnaire (Gudjonsson & Sigurdsson, 1999; Sigurdsson & Gudjonsson, 1994). A copy of the revised Gudjonsson Confession Questionnaire (Gudjonsson & Sigurdsson, 1999; GCQ-R) is given in Appendix 1.

In all the studies we hypothesized, on the basis of the Gudjonsson *Cognitive–Behavioural Model of Confession*, that confessions would be predominantly caused by three types of facilitative factor. These are the following.

1. *External pressure* to confess, which is associated with persuasive police interrogation techniques, police behaviour and fear of confinement.
2. *Internal pressure* to confess, where suspects experience a great deal of guilt about the crime they committed and consequently need to relieve themselves of the guilt by confessing.
3. *Perception of proof*, where suspects believe that there is no point in denying the offence because the police will eventually prove they did it.

We administered a specially designed 'Confession Questionnaire' to 74 Icelandic prisoners who had been convicted of various offences, which included violent, property and sexual offences. Factor analysis of the Confession Questionnaire revealed the three *facilitative* factors listed above and one additional *inhibitory* factor (i.e. fear of the consequences), which were replicated in our research of 80 prisoners serving sentences for violence, sex or property offences in Northern Ireland. Six items loaded on a factor labelled *external pressure*. The contents of this factor were associated with the police environment, for example, subjects indicated they had confessed because of the fear of being locked up and as a result of police persuasion during questioning. In terms of frequency, fear of being locked up was rated as having been a very important reason for the confession in over 20% of the cases. Fear of the police or threats of violence were only rated as important in 5% of cases. Having confessed due to police pressure and persuasion were rated as very important in about 20% of the cases. The data from the Northern Ireland study were different in that the reasons for suspects having confessed were attributed much more to police persuasion, fear of the police and the belief that they had been bullied into a confession. Fear of being locked up was almost identical in both studies, which means that the two studies differed mainly in relation to the amount of police pressure used during questioning, rather than threats of custody.

The second factor, *internal pressure*, comprised four items, which were related to feelings of guilt about the commission of the offence and the relief associated with the confession. Over 42% of the subjects said they had experienced considerable relief after confessing and 40% said they had confessed because of feeling guilty about the offence. The corresponding figures from the Northern Ireland study are 40 and 35%, respectively. The findings indicate that talking about the offence to a person in authority was important in many cases because people were distressed by what had happened and wanted to give their account of it. These findings appear to give some support for psychoanalytic models of confessions (see e.g. Reik, 1959).

The third facilitative factor, *perception of proof*, consisted of only two items, which were associated with the subjects seeing no point in denying the offence as the police would sooner or later prove their involvement in it. With regard to frequency, 55% of the subjects said that they had confessed because they strongly believed at the time that the police would be able to prove they had committed the crime (the corresponding figure for Northern Ireland was 60%). The principal conclusion that can be drawn from these results is that the most frequent and important reason why suspects confess is the strength of their belief in the evidence against them. This is undoubtedly why the 'maximization' component of the Reid Technique is effective in breaking down resistance. By exaggerating the evidence against the suspect he begins to believe that there is no point in denying it any more. Both internal and external (police) pressure are important in many cases where the police have little or no proof. Interestingly, 20% of the sample in the Icelandic study and 22% in the Northern Ireland study stated that they would have confessed to the police even if they had not been suspected of the offence. This may explain why offenders sometimes give themselves up to the police without being suspected of the crime in question.

We found that the reasons offenders give for having confessed to the police during interrogation are related to the type of offence committed. For example, sex offenders confessed more frequently than other offenders because of a strong internal need to confess. This was in spite of the finding that sex offenders were the most inhibited of all groups about confessing because of the potential 'real' or 'personal' consequences of so doing. These findings were noted in both the Icelandic and Northern Ireland studies. Undoubtedly, the most important reason why sex offenders report stronger internal need to confess than other offenders relates to the high level of self-reported guilt associated with sexual offences. In three separate studies (Gudjonsson & Bownes, 1991; Gudjonsson & Petursson, 1991; Gudjonsson & Singh, 1988) sex offenders reported a greater amount of guilt concerning their offence than other offender groups (Gudjonsson, 1999a). This is likely to make their internal need to confess stronger than that of most other offenders and is consistent with the findings of Gudjonsson and Petursson (1991).

In a recent study, Gudjonsson and Sigurdsson (2000) compared the GCQ-R scores of three types of offender: violent offenders, rapists and child molesters. Significant differences emerged between the three groups. Child molesters had the greatest internal need to confess, followed by rapists and violent offenders. There were also highly significant differences with regard to the perception of proof, with violent offenders perceiving the strongest evidence against them at the time of the interrogation, followed by rapists and child molesters. The finding that child molesters report the strongest need to confess, in spite of their having the lowest degree of perception of proof, has important implications for police interrogation: most importantly, it gives the police an advantage. If sensitively interviewed by the police their inhibition about confessing can be readily overcome. This appears to apply somewhat less to rapists than child molesters, although these factors are relevant to both groups. It may be that the combination of the need to confess and feelings of shame found among sex offenders explains why they tend to be reluctant to give a full account of their offences even after confessing quite readily (Birgisson, 1996; Salter, 1988). They probably reach a compromise by making a partial and limited confession, which satisfies their need to confess while at the same time minimizing their feelings of shame when describing the offence.

We have also looked at a number of variables that might be associated with the reasons why offenders confess (Gudjonsson & Petursson, 1991; Gudjonsson & Sigurdsson, 1999). These included intelligence, extraversion, neuroticism, psychoticism, compliance, age, coping abilities, the offenders' attitudes and how they attribute blame for their crime. The findings indicate that personality factors are associated with the reasons offenders give for having confessed to the police and their attitudes towards having made a confession.

Gudjonsson and Petursson (1991) found that a confession which resulted principally from external pressure was associated with a perceived inability to cope with the police interrogation. It is of interest to note that both external pressure to confess, and the inability to cope with it, were associated with anxiety proneness (i.e. trait anxiety), antisocial personality characteristics (as measured by the psychoticism scale of the EPQ and the Gough Socialisation Scale), age and intelligence. One possible explanation is that the brighter, older and more emotionally stable offenders are better able to cope with interrogative pressure than other offenders. In a much larger study (Gudjonsson & Sigurdsson, 1999), involving 411 prison inmates and 108 juvenile offenders, we investigated more extensively the role of personality using multiple regression analyses to identify the most salient variables that predicted the reasons given for having made a confession to the police. The findings are of both theoretical and practical significance.

We found that EPQ psychoticism was the single best personality predictor of the reporting of external (police) pressure during interrogation both among the prison inmates and juvenile offenders (Gudjonsson & Sigurdsson, 1999). This raises an important question. Why should offenders scoring high on psychoticism report more external pressure during interrogation than the less personality-disordered offenders? Gudjonsson and Sigurdsson (1999) put forward an interesting hypothesis, which is supported by their data. Offenders who are disordered in their personality are generally less cooperative with the police and put up more initial resistance during interrogation. As a result more pressure is required from the police to obtain a confession from such personalities. This illustrates how the personality of the offender interacts with the interrogation techniques used by the police.

Gudjonsson and Petursson (1991) and Gudjonsson and Sigurdsson (1999) found that the offenders who are most disordered in terms of their personality are also most resistant to confessing. This is consistent with the findings of an earlier study we carried out in Iceland (Gudjonsson & Petursson, 1982). We found that offenders with the diagnosis of 'personality disorder' in homicide cases had tried hardest to cover up their crime and to avoid detection. In contrast, it was uncommon for those who were mentally ill to try to avoid detection. The defendants who had no diagnosable abnormality fell in between the other two groups in terms of avoidance of detection.

In the Gudjonsson–Petursson (1991) study, internal pressure correlated most strongly with feelings of remorse concerning the offence committed and the perception that the offence had resulted from mental causes, such as sudden loss of self-control rather than criminal disposition. The main implication is that if the crime is seen as being inconsistent with the persons' views about themselves (i.e. it is 'out of character'), then they are more likely to have an internal need to confess. The findings from the Gudjonsson–Sigurdsson (1999) study found that both among prison inmates and juvenile offenders, EPQ neuroticism and compliance, as measured by the GCS, were the two best predictors of the internal need to confess. In terms of their personality, offenders who are prone to anxiety and who are compliant in their temperament have the greatest need to confess due to internal pressure. This is probably due to their greater proneness towards feelings of guilt after transgression and the accompanied need to 'get it off their chest' (Gudjonsson, 1999a).

There were clear indications from all the studies that the offenders' views and attitudes about their confession were related to the reasons they gave for the confession. Confessions that resulted primarily from external pressure were associated with the greatest amount of dissatisfaction and regret. The subjects in this group considered retrospectively that they had confessed far too readily at the time of the interrogation and they had not fully appreciated the consequences of their confession. They subsequently began to regret bitterly having made the confession.

In marked contrast, the stronger the perceived proof and internal pressure to confess at the time of the police interrogation, the happier the offenders remained about having confessed. Offenders who remain bitter and dissatisfied because their confession resulted from police pressure may be less able to come to terms with the 'real' and 'personal' consequences of their crime than other offenders.

Another important finding from the Gudjonsson–Petursson (1991) study is the importance of the role of lawyers. Very few of the inmates in the study had a solicitor present during the interrogations, and 25% of the sample stated that they would definitely not have confessed if they had had access to a solicitor.

When there are co-defendants also being interrogated this complicates the situation. Sigurdsson and Gudjonsson (1994) and Gudjonsson and Sigurdsson (1999) found that where there are co-defendants, which in their study was most commonly found among drug related offenders, this places additional pressure on suspects to confess before their co-defendants do. Initial resistance may be overcome by the police playing one suspect off against another, as is indeed typically recommended in interrogation manuals.

CONCLUSIONS

From the evidence presented in this chapter, almost 60% of suspects in England make self-incriminating admissions or confessions during custodial interrogation. Contrary to my previous prediction (Gudjonsson, 1992a), the rate has not fallen following the implementation of the Police and Criminal Evidence Act (PACE). This finding is particularly important in that following PACE there has been a dramatic increase in the use of legal advisers at police stations, an increase that has grown from less than 10% in the mid-1980s to over 30% in the mid-1990s. In one study (Pearse et al., 1998) there was an admission/confession rate of 58% even though over half (56%) of the suspects had access to legal advice. How can this be explained when the presence of a legal advisor is a significant predictor of a denial?

It is evident that the admission/confession rate is substantially lower in the USA than it is in England. The difference is in the region of about 15%. One of the reasons for this difference may relate to the greater impact of the *Miranda* rules on the confession rate than the restrictions imposed by PACE. In England the presence of a legal advisor, or suspects exercising their right of silence, does not prevent the police from interviewing them and putting questions to them. This is different to the position in America, where suspects are rarely interviewed after they invoke their *Miranda* rights. In England many suspects make self-incriminating admissions or confessions in the presence of a lawyer. American lawyers may more forcefully advise their client against self-incrimination and curtail any attempt by the police to interview the suspect. If this is correct the confession rate in America may indeed fall if more suspects were to invoke their *Miranda* rights.

There are three different ways of trying to understand why suspects confess during custodial interrogation. First, one can investigate the factors that are associated with admissions and denials. Second, offenders can be systematically asked questions about what made them confess to the police and these can be correlated with other measurements, including those associated with intelligence, attitudes, attribution of blame and other personality dimensions (see e.g. Gudjonsson & Sigurdsson, 1999). The third method is to analyse the social interaction between the interviewer and suspect from the tape recordings of real life interrogation, or by observation at the time of the interrogation. This method was used by Pearse and Gudjonsson (1999) and was discussed extensively in Chapters 3 and 4. These three methods complement one another in understanding the reasons why suspects confess to the crimes they have committed.

Factors such as age and previous convictions appear to be related to readiness to confess, but these variables should be studied in conjunction with other variables, such as the seriousness of the offence, the strength of the evidence against the suspect, and access to legal advice. Research at the University of Kent indicates that many case and background variables are inter-related and studying these in isolation may give potentially misleading results.

The available evidence indicates that suspects confess due to a combination of factors, rather than to one factor alone. Three general factors appear to be relevant, in varying degree, to most suspects. These relate to an *internal* pressure (e.g. feelings of remorse, the need to talk about the offence), *external* pressure (e.g. fear of confinement, police persuasiveness), and perception of *proof* (e.g. the suspects' perceptions of the strength of evidence against them). The single strongest incentive to confess relates to the strength of the evidence against suspects. Furthermore, those who confess because of strong evidence against them, and where there is an internal need to confess, appear to be subsequently most content about their confession. Confessions that result from police persuasiveness and pressure seem to leave suspects disgruntled, even years afterwards.

CHAPTER 7

Miscarriages of Justice and False Confessions

In this chapter the literature and review studies into false confession are discussed within the broader framework of the miscarriage of justice, to which false confessions sometimes lead. The main purpose is to identify the reasons for wrongful convictions. It will be argued that wrongful convictions are typically caused by a combination of factors, rather than by one factor acting exclusively. Important case illustrations will be given of two notorious British cases of wrongful conviction resulting from false confessions.

MISCARRIAGES OF JUSTICE

It is difficult to think of a judicial system that is likely to be free of miscarriages of justice. Indeed, all judicial systems, whether adversarial or inquisitorial, are inherently fallible. The basic recognition of the inherent fallibility of judicial systems is essential if miscarriages of justice are to be properly identified and dealt with. Unfortunately, as Woffinden (1989) so rightly points out, too often people have a misguided faith in the infallibility of the criminal justice system. The situation is very serious in that people who are wrongly convicted may spend many years in prison before their conviction is quashed or they are pardoned. Woffinden goes as far as to suggest that the great majority of miscarriages of justice are never put right.

In its broadest sense, four different ways in which justice has miscarried can be identified.

1. It may occur because the defendant did not receive a fair trial, even though he may have committed the offence in question. Therefore, the defendant may be *legally innocent*, but *factually guilty*. For example, a defendant who is convicted on the basis of fabricated evidence, even though he committed the offence, is innocent in law as the use of unfair means and violation of due legal process convicted him.
2. There are cases of defendants who were only marginally involved in the case but were convicted of a more serious charge.

3. There are cases where the wrong person may be convicted for the offence committed.
4. On some occasions the miscarriage of justice arises when the alleged crime for which the defendant was convicted was never committed. In other words, the *actus reus* of the alleged offence has not been correctly established.

As we shall see later, there have been a number of cases where the alleged murder victim turned up very much alive after the defendant has been convicted or even executed. Generally speaking, research into miscarriages of justice has tended to focus on innocent people wrongly convicted rather than on those only technically innocent because of an error in due process.

Most countries have some kind of a mechanism for reviewing potentially wrongful convictions. Typically, this consists of some kind of an 'appeal hearing', which in Britain is referred to as the Court of Appeal (Criminal Division). The Court of Appeal confines itself to questions of law and the evaluation of 'new' evidence if this is available; it does not directly deal with questions related to guilt or innocence.

What are the main reasons for wrongful convictions? This question is best answered by reviewing the studies of wrongful convictions that have been carried out.

STUDIES OF MISCARRIAGES OF JUSTICE

A number of books have been written about cases where there has been an alleged or proven miscarriage of justice (e.g. Bedau, 1964; Borchard, 1932; Connery & Styron, 1996; Hill, Young & Sargant, 1985; Huff, Rattner & Sagarin, 1986, 1996; Kallio, 1999; Mansfield, 1993; Radelet, Bedau & Putman, 1992; Radelet, Lofquist & Bedau, 1996; Radin, 1964; Scheck, Neufeld & Dwyer, 2000; Victory, 2002; Walker & Starmer, 1999; Woffinden, 1989; Yant, 1991). These have generally given anecdotal and descriptive accounts rather than being based on rigorous scientific study. Considering the serious implications and consequences of miscarriages of justice it is perhaps surprising that so few empirical and scientific studies have been carried out. However, following the important study of Borchard (1932), which was the first systematic study conducted into wrongful convictions, a great deal has been learned about the types of error that result in innocent people being wrongfully convicted. It is to these that we now turn.

Borchard looked at 62 American and three British cases (Adolf Beck, William Habron & Oscar Slater) where defendants had been wrongfully convicted in the early part of the twentieth century. Twenty-nine (45%) of the cases involved defendants convicted of murder and a further 23 (35%) comprised offences of robbery and theft. The innocence of these defendants was principally established by the following.

1. The discovery of the alleged murder victim being alive.
2. Subsequent apprehension of the real culprit.
3. Discovery of some other new evidence that 'proved' the defendant's innocence.

In a total of 13 cases (20%), it was eventually established that no crime had actually been committed.

Borchard found that the most common causes of error were mistaken identification, relying unduly on circumstantial evidence, perjury by witnesses, self-incriminating confessions and unreliability of 'expert' evidence. Mistaken person identification was responsible for 29 (45%) of the convictions. In only two cases did the defendant bear a striking resemblance to the real culprit, which highlights the potential unreliability of person identification. The importance of the behaviour of police officers and prosecuting officials in potentially causing miscarriages of justice is evident from Borchard's study:

> In a very considerable number, the zealousness of the police or private detectives, or the gross negligence of the police in overlooking or even suppressing evidence of innocence, or the prosecution's overzealousness was an operative factor in causing the erroneous conviction (p. xv).

Another important finding in this study relates to the importance of deception by innocent defendants. Innocent defendants do sometimes resort to deception (e.g. lying about an alibi) in order to strengthen their case. The detection of such deception may be very damaging to the case as Borchard points out:

> Proof that an alibi or collateral testimony offered by the accused was false, was extremely prejudicial, if not fatal, in several cases (pp. xx–xxi).

Borchard points out that in several cases false confession resulted from police pressure. However, there were confessions that appeared to have been elicited more by internal psychological factors than by clearly coercive police tactics or techniques. Borchard states with regard to such confessions:

> The influence of a stronger mind upon the weaker often produces, by persuasion or suggestion, the desired result (p. xviii).

Borchard speculates that defendants' low intelligence may be an important factor in many false confessions.

Radin (1964) attempted to look at the reasons for wrongful convictions in 25 American States and the District of Columbia, without duplicating the cases discussed by Borchard. He looked at some 300 cases and highlighted different causes by illustrations of over 70 individual cases. Radin listed the various causes for wrongful conviction under different headings, such as 'The police', 'The prosecutor', 'The witnesses', 'The record' and 'Hue and cry'. He considered that the most shocking miscarriage was caused by Public Prosecutors deliberately abusing their power because of their overriding ambitions. This includes deliberately withholding evidence favourable to the defendant, smearing by innuendo the reputation of defence witnesses and covering up deficiencies that existed among prosecution witnesses.

One important cause of wrongful convictions that is often overlooked is 'Hue and cry'. This involves being a victim of gossip or public outcry due to the viciousness of the crime. Such an outcry may make the police act hastily in their attempts to respond to public pressure, which could result in their jumping to conclusions rather than carefully following the facts. Once a much needed suspect is identified an inept police investigation may follow, where facts supporting the suspect's innocence are ignored and overlooked.

Another important work into miscarriages of justice is the study by Brandon and Davies (1973). These authors looked at 70 British cases of 'wrongful imprisonment' where errors had been corrected either by the Home Secretary or the Court of Appeal between 1950 and 1970. These did not include defendants released because of some legal technicality. In the view of Brandon and Davies, all the cases they included in their study involved defendants who were considered innocent of the crime for which they were convicted. The defendants had either been given free pardon (52 cases) or their conviction had been quashed by the Court of Appeal (18 cases). The authors cogently argue that the cases they looked at comprised only 'the tip of a much larger iceberg' (p. 20) of wrongful convictions.

Brandon and Davies found that after mistaken identification, self-incriminating confessions were the most common cause of wrongful imprisonment. They categorized the defendants who had made false confessions as follows.

1. There were a number of mentally handicapped defendants, including the well publicized case of Timothy Evans, which is discussed later in this chapter. Many were also illiterate. Brandon and Davies state that they came across several other cases, in which the defendants had not been formally tested intellectually, but it was concluded from their behaviour that these individuals were probably mentally handicapped.
2. Many of the defendants who were pardoned were juveniles.
3. There were a number of defendants who were apparently of normal intelligence but were psychologically vulnerable or disturbed in some way.

Brandon and Davies concluded from their findings that people who confessed to crimes, for which they were subsequently pardoned or exonerated, were typically psychologically 'inadequate' in some way, because of low intelligence, psychological disturbance or youth. They speculated that what the three groups of 'inadequates' had in common was abnormal susceptibility to suggestion.

Rattner (1988) recently reviewed the American literature concerning cases of allegedly innocent people who were wrongfully convicted. He looked at 205 cases gathered from books, documents or newspaper articles. Murder (43%), robbery (29%) and forcible rape (12%) were the most common offences for which convictions had occurred. Twenty-one (10%) of the defendants had been sentenced to death.

The types of error that resulted in wrongful conviction were varied, but mistaken eyewitness identification was by far the most common cause (49%). 'Coerced confession' had been the cause of wrongful confession in 16 cases (8%).

Huff, Rattner and Sagarin (1986) looked at the frequency and major causes of wrongful convictions from their database of almost 500 cases, survey of criminal justice officials and a review of the literature.

On the basis of their findings, the authors estimated, conservatively in their view, that almost 1% of defendants in serious criminal cases are wrongfully convicted, with much higher rates for lesser charges.

As far as the causes of wrongful conviction are concerned, Huff, Rattner and Sagarin found that there was generally more than one factor involved in each case, although eyewitness identification was the single most important reason (i.e. almost 60% of the the cases involved such an error). The authors point out the increased risk of wrongful conviction in cases where the crime has resulted in a public outcry. Finally, the authors outline policy implications and recommendations for prevention, identification, exoneration and compensation.

The largest number of wrongful convictions has been studied by Bedau and his colleagues in the USA (Bedau & Radelet, 1987; Radelet, Bedau & Putman, 1992, 1996). Bedau and Radelet (1987) presented 350 cases where allegedly innocent defendants were in the 20th century wrongfully convicted of capital or potentially capital crimes in the USA. The sample consisted of 326 (93%) homicide and 24 (7%) rape cases. Of the sample, 139 (40%) were sentenced to death and 23 (7%) were executed before their 'innocence' was established.

Bedau and Radlet identified four groups of errors that were causes of the wrongful convictions. These were as follows.

1. *Errors caused by police investigation prior to trial*: these kinds of error were present in 23% of the sample. The largest source of error in this category was false confession, which was present in 49 (14%) cases. This typically involved the police 'coercing' confessions out of suspects by subjecting them to rigorous interrogation techniques and tactics. However, there were cases of voluntary confession. In one case an innocent man confessed to murder in order to 'impress' his girlfriend. In another case, a woman confessed and pleaded guilty to a murder she had not committed in an attempt to hide the fact that at the time of the murder she was having sexual intercourse. Other police errors involved negligence and over-zealous police work. There were also cases where the police had secured a conviction of an innocent defendant by threatening witnesses who were prepared to testify in his favour.

2. *Errors caused by the prosecution prior to or during the trial*: this was evident in 50 (14%) cases and the most common type of error was the suppression of exculpatory evidence (35 cases).

3. *Errors caused by prosecution witnesses*: this type of error comprised perjury (117 cases) and mistaken person identification (56 cases).

4. *Miscellaneous sources of error*: these included misleading circumstantial evidence (9%), insufficient consideration of alibi evidence (13%), incompetence of defence counsel (3%) and public demand and outrage (20%). The fact that in 70 cases public outrage and pressure appeared to have seriously influenced the trials' outcome highlights the difficulties involved in trying notorious cases.

This study indicates that in most cases wrongful convictions are caused by a combination of factors, rather than by any one factor acting exclusively.

How was the miscarriage of justice discovered in the 350 cases? There were a number of ways in which the defendants' 'innocence' was proven. In 20 (6%)

cases it was eventually discovered that no crime had been committed at all. There were 47 (13%) cases where the real culprit eventually confessed, sometimes after being apprehended for another crime. In addition, a number of real culprits confessed on their deathbeds.

What is very striking from this study is that the defendants themselves could do very little to have their cases re-opened. Almost without exception, the defendants were dependant upon the goodwill of others in proving their innocence. Almost one-third of the cases were re-opened because of the persistence and hard work of people who believed in their innocence. These comprised defence solicitors (16%), journalists or authors (11%) and other well disposed citizens, including the defendants' loyal friends and relatives.

This study clearly shows that the criminal justice system itself is deficient in discovering, admitting to and doing something about errors which they make. Once defendants have been convicted they can attempt to be vindicated by appealing against their conviction, but this can only happen when there appears to have been some procedural error at the trial, or there has been some newly discovered substantive evidence. As Bedau and Radelet (1987) point out, 'This leaves most erroneously convicted defendants with no place to turn to for vindication' (p. 71).

The studies reviewed above appear to have used reasonably stringent criteria when defining innocence for selection of cases in their study. What is striking about these cases is that so many of the defendants were proven innocent by sheer luck and good fortune. All the authors recognize that they were only dealing with a small proportion of all cases of wrongful conviction. There can be no doubt that for every proven case of wrongful conviction there are many more that remain unproven. However, proving a convicted person's innocence with absolute certainty is impossible in the great majority of cases of miscarriage of justice, although this task is becoming easier with improved DNA technology (Scheck, Neufeld & Dwyer, 2000). This raises the question, what degree of certainty should be required in the determination of innocence? Considering how difficult it is for people to prove their innocence once convicted, a criterion based on 'beyond reasonable doubt' is far too stringent for use in the kind of study cited above and a lower standard should be acceptable in the inclusion criteria. The following factors need to be taken into consideration when determining innocence.

1. What information is relied upon to determine innocence?
2. Is the information from original or secondary sources?
3. How reliable is the information?
4. How is the 'weight' of the evidence determined?
5. Who determines the 'weight' of the evidence?
6. What threshold of certainty is used?

Markman and Cassell (1988) argue that there are a number of methodological problems with the determination of innocence in the Bedau–Radelet study. Principally, they point to the largely subjective nature of the classification and the failure of these authors to consider allegedly compelling physical evidence of guilt at trial. Bedau and Radelet (1988), in their reply to the critique, point to the over-reliance of Markman and Cassell on the prosecution evidence and the validity of the original trial outcome, and misinterpretation or misrepresentation of the original Bedau–Radelet data.

Interestingly, an independent analysis of eight New York cases from the Bedau–Radelet study where allegedly innocent people were convicted and executed (Acker *et al.*, 1998), supported the conclusions by Bedau and Radelet of their factual innocence.

In a recent book, Radelet, Bedau and Putman (1992) extended the original 350 cases of miscarriages of justice to 416 and provide a brief inventory of the cases. The added 66 cases were wrongful convictions in homicide cases. The authors state that they relied on two kinds of evidence to determine a miscarriage of justice: first, 'official judgments of error', such as the reversal of a conviction on appeal or a pardon (90% of their cases fall into this category). The evidence for the second category of cases included is referred to as 'unofficial judgments' with new evidence or material suggesting innocence without a judicial action being instigated. The authors concluded, on the basis of their analysis of the 416 cases as they did in their previous study, that miscarriages of justice are caused by a number of different errors, often in combination, but the two most common errors were perjury by prosecution witnesses and mistaken eyewitness testimony. False confessions were also important in a number of the cases. In a follow-up study to the book, Radelet, Lofquist and Bedau (1996) studied 68 cases of death row inmates who were released between 1970 and 1995 because of doubts about their guilt. Thirty-one (46%) were not included in their previous publications. The main conclusion drawn was:

> ...the details of these 68 cases strengthen our belief that the risk of executing the innocent is not only inescapable, but also disturbingly high. This conclusion is supported by an examination of the role of pure luck in exonerating the defendants in our sample (p. 919).

As far as miscarriages of justice in Britain are concerned, these have recently been discussed extensively in a book edited by Walker and Starmer (1999).

Matthews (1995) recommends that scientists apply probabilistic (Bayesian) reasoning to judicial issues concerning DNA and confession evidence as a way of reducing the risk of a miscarriage of justice:

> As we now show, a Bayesian analysis of confessional evidence supports those who adopt the sceptical view. A potentially dangerous counter-intuitive situation can arise unless confessional evidence is assessed by a jury in the appropriate way (p. 3).

THE LEO–OFSHE STUDY

Leo and Ofshe (1998a) have carried out a study of 60 cases of alleged police coerced false confessions in the USA in the post-*Miranda* era (i.e. cases include the period 1973 to 1996). In 29 (48%) of the cases defendants were 'wrongfully convicted'. Twenty-four (83%) of the defendants received long prison sentences and four (14%) were sentenced to death, one of whom had already been executed at the time of the study. Out of the remaining 31 cases, the case was either not proceeded with (16%), it was dismissed prior to trial (58%) or the defendant was acquitted at trial (26%).

This is an important and authoritative empirical study, which addresses a number of issues related to coerced confession, wrongful convictions, the criminal justice process and the damage caused by coerced false confessions. The study is unique in that it focuses specially on miscarriages of justice allegedly caused by police-induced false confessions. The authors used four criteria for inclusion of cases.

- The police coerced the confession.
- The state's case at trial relied predominantly on the confession statement 'I did it'.
- The confession was not supported by physical or reliable inculpatory evidence.
- Other evidence proved or strongly supported the defendant's innocence.

The 60 cases were subsequently classified into three groups on the basis of the strength of the evidence against the person.

1. Proven false confession ($N = 34$). This included scientific evidence exonerating the defendant, the real perpetrator was apprehended or it was established that no crime had been committed.
2. Highly probable false confession ($N = 18$). Here there was overwhelming evidence that the confession was false (i.e. 'beyond a reasonable doubt'), there was no credible evidence to support the confession and the confession lacked 'internal reliability'.
3. Probable false confession ($N = 8$). In this group there was a preponderance of evidence to support the conclusion that the confession was false.

Leo and Ofshe (1998a) rightly point out that there is a possibility that one or more of the 60 'false confessors' may have committed the offence. This relates to the fact that the 'ground truth' (what actually happened) is difficult to establish retrospectively with complete certainty.

The methodology used in this study is a great improvement on that used in the studies cited in the previous section. Importantly, for each case the authors identify the sources on which their analysis is based. The following highlights the inevitable limitation with this kind of research:

> The amount of information on these cases varies. The analysis of some cases was based on access to virtually the entire case file, while the analysis of other cases was limited to journalists' accounts or published appellate court opinions (Leo & Ofshe, 1998a, p. 436).

Replying on secondary sources of information, such as the media's account of case material, is obviously a disadvantage when evaluating the evidence pertaining to a case. Ideally, all primary evidence should be thoroughly evaluated, but this is not always possible. On occasions material obtained from secondary sources, such as media and journalistic reports, may be selective and biased, giving a misleading picture of a case.

Cassell (1999) is critical of the methodology in the Leo and Ofshe (1998a) study used to determine innocence.

> ...like the Bedau and Radelet survey, the problem remains that Leo and Ofshe's judgment as to who is innocent is highly subjective and, in more than a few cases, demonstrably wrong (p. 538).

Cassell then discusses nine of alleged wrongful conviction and argues that

> Based on a more thorough description of the cases than Leo and Ofshe provide, the reader can readily see that this claim is untrue and that substantial evidence supported the guilt of each of these defendants (p. 538).

Cassell may of course be right that some of the nine cases that he discussed involved guilty defendants. However, Cassell's account of the evidence in these cases appears to rely very much on a prosecution perspective and police statements, which in my experience is not always objective and unbiased. Several times in his article he presents prosecutors' belief about a defendant's guilt as evidence that the confession is true (e.g. 'Prosecutors continue to believe that Earl Washington was guilty of rape and murder', p. 582—in view of Cassell's comment, it is of interest to note that in February 2001 Mr Washington was pardoned by the Governor of Virginia, Jim Gilmore, and released from prison after serving 17 years because new DNA evidence proved that Washington was wrongfully convicted on the basis of a false confession).

Leo and Ofshe (2001) provide a reply to Cassell's (1999) critique. They convincingly challenge Cassell's accusations by completing a detailed case-to-case analysis of the nine cases that Cassell reviewed. They argue that there are serious flaws in Cassell's arguments and critique, including a misrepresentation and exaggeration of the extent to which Leo and Ofshe relied on secondary sources of evidence, Cassell's over-reliance on a prosecution perspective and court outcome, failure to recognize the prejudicial effects of the false confession, failure to acknowledge exculpatory evidence and bias in the interpretation and presentation of the evidence.

SOME NOTORIOUS BRITISH CASES

There are a number of well publicized British cases of false confession. One of the earliest cases reported dates back to the year 1660 (Ayling, 1984). The case involves the confession of John Perry to the murder of William Harrison. During extensive interrogation by the Justice of the Peace, Perry implicated himself, his brother and mother. All three were publicly executed on the basis of Perry's confession. There was some circumstantial evidence to link Perry with Harrison's disappearance, in that Perry had failed to return home after being sent out to look for his master (Harrison). Two years after the execution of the Perrys the alleged murder victim reappeared alive. He had been kidnapped and held as a slave in Turkey.

Perry's case resulted in legal re-evaluation of uncorroborated confessions in England, although a 'corroboration requirement was never universally accepted and was not applied to prosecutions other than murder' (Ayling, 1984, p. 1126).

In more modern times there have been four highly publicized alleged false confession cases that all resulted in a public inquiry. These are the Timothy Evans case (Kennedy, 1988), the Confait case (Price & Caplan, 1977), the Cyprus spy trial (Calcutt, 1986) and the 'Guildford Four' (Kee, 1989; McKee & Franey, 1988). The 'Guildford Four' case is most recent and in view of its complexity and significance it will be discussed with the 'Birmingham Six' in Chapter 17. The case of the 'Birmingham Six', as seen in Chapter 3, resulted in the setting up of the Royal Commission on Criminal Justice (1993). The Timothy Evans and Confait cases will be discussed briefly in this chapter.

Timothy Evans

On 30 November 1949, Timothy Evans, who was 25 years of age at the time, walked into Merthyr Police Station in South Wales and voluntarily confessed to having disposed of his wife's body down a drain outside his home at 10 Rillington Place, North London. He made two statements to the police in Wales. The first statement consisted of his telling the police that his wife was pregnant and had died after he had given her some abortion pills that he had obtained from a stranger in a cafe in East Anglia. The Welsh police telephoned the Notting Hill Police in North London about Evans' statement. They went around to 10 Rillington Place, inspected the drain and found no body there. Being confronted with this, and the fact that it took three policemen to lift the manhole cover, Evans was interviewed again and made a further statement. He then implicated his landlord, Christie, who had allegedly performed an abortion on his wife and told Evans that she had died as a result of medical complications. Evans said that Christie had told him that he had disposed of the body in one of the drains. Evans told the police that after his wife's death Christie had arranged for their baby daughter Geraldine to be looked after by a couple in East Anglia. Unknown to Evans was the fact that Christie had strangled to death both his wife and his baby daughter about three weeks earlier.

After a subsequent search at 10 Rillington Place, the police found the bodies of Evans' wife and daughter in a wash-house. Evans was brought to London and interrogated. He made two detailed statements on 2 and 3 December and in both he confessed to the murder of his wife and daughter. After his appearance in a Magistrates' Court Evans was remanded in custody and taken to Brixton Prison, South London, where on admission he confessed again to the Principal Medical Officer. The following day, during a visit by his mother, Evans retracted his confession after his mother asked him why he had committed the murders.

> I didn't do it, Mum. Christie done it. Ask him to come and see me. He's the only one who can help me now (Kennedy, 1988, p. 141).

Unfortunately, for Evans, Christie and his wife became prosecution witnesses at Evans' trial and gave evidence against him.

Evans' case opened at the Central Criminal Court on 11 January 1950. Evans' defence was that Christie and not himself had murdered his wife and daughter. The defence relied on Evans' second statement in Wales as being reliable. The complicating factor was that at the time it was not known or suspected that Christie's abortion story was a lie to possess Mrs Evans and subsequently explain her death to Evans. In other words, Evans second statement did not provide the real insight into why Christie would have had the motive to murder Mrs Evans. There was medical evidence that Mrs Evans had been sexually penetrated, probably after her death, but this evidence, which provided an important insight into the possibility of a third party involvement (e.g. Christie), was not used by the defence at Evans' trial. Furthermore, a forensic examination of the spermatazoa found in Mrs Evans' vagina, which was never analysed, could possibly have cleared Evans. It seems that whereas Christie was remarkably lucky not to be implicated in the murders, Evans had no evidence in his favour at all.

Evans was found guilty by the jury of murdering his daughter (the jury were not asked by the judge to reach a verdict on Mrs Evans' death). He was sentenced to death and executed on 9 March 1950. He had persisted in maintaining his innocence to the end. Subsequent events were to show that Christie was indeed a murderer, as Evans had claimed. Three or four years prior to the murders of Evans' wife and daughter, he had murdered two women who he had lured to his home. Both had been murdered by strangulation. In December 1952, Christie murdered his wife by strangulation. Three more women were to die before Christie was finally apprehended at the end of March in 1953. Christie confessed to killing seven women, including Mrs Evans. He denied having murdered Evans' daughter. Kennedy gives two reasons why it might have been in Christie's interest to deny the child's murder; the fact that it meant he had been responsible for sending an innocent man, Evans, to his death, and secondly, unlike the other killings, which Christie tried to justify, he could see no possible justification for killing a baby. Christie was tried at the Central Criminal Court, convicted and sentenced to death. He was hanged on 15 July 1953.

Kennedy provides a very convincing case for Evans' innocence and gives five main reasons for his wrongful conviction.

1. Evans did not report his wife's death to the police immediately after discovering her body when he returned home from work.
2. The police blindly believed in Evans' guilt in spite of evidence from workmen that cast serious doubts on the validity of Evans' confession. In fact, the police suppressed this important evidence from the defence lawyers and an important time-sheet curiously went missing whilst in the possession of the police.
3. The defence lawyers appear to have believed in Evans' guilt and failed to appreciate and obtain evidence pointing to Evans' innocence.
4. The biased and inadequate summing-up by the judge at Evans' trial.
5. The incriminating evidence of Christie against Evans. Whereas Christie appears to have been a man of good intellect, and a former Special Constable,

Evans was of low intelligence (he was said to have an IQ of no more than 75) and had a reputation as a pathological liar. It is easy to see how the jury believed Christie and not Evans.

Kennedy has made an interesting analysis of Evans' confession, which focuses on the circumstances in which they were obtained and on Evans' vulnerabilities. First, he points to the discrepancy between the police and Evans in the timing of the two statements made. The Notting Hill police officers alleged that the confession was voluntary and spontaneous and without any prompting or prior questioning. Evans claimed that he was kept up and questioned for hours into the night until he confessed. Second, some of the vocabulary and phraseology seems to have been more consistent with that of police officers, rather than of Evans who was uneducated and illiterate. Svartvik (1968) analysed some of the linguistic features of Evans' statements and concluded that the linguistic discrepancies observed supported Kennedy's standpoint.

According to Kennedy, Evans was under considerable stress when he confessed to the police, much of which was self-induced. Following his wife's death he became increasingly upset and concerned about what had happened, which resulted in his going to the police station in Wales. Once arrested he was kept in custody (which largely consisted of solitary confinement) for over two days before being handed over to the London police. He had not been informed about what was happening, except that he knew that his wife's body had not been found in the drain as expected. This resulted in uncertainty and confusion. Once he arrived at Notting Hill police station he was shown his wife's and daughter's clothing, in addition to the ligature that was used to murder his daughter. He began to feel very guilty about not having done more to prevent their deaths, which Kennedy considers to have been an important contributory factor to his confession. The realization that his daughter had also been murdered must have been an enormous shock to him.

It is not clear from Kennedy's detailed account of the case whether Evans ever came to believe that he might have done the killings himself (i.e. a coerced–internalized false confession). Kennedy argues that Evans went through a 'period of conversion' (p. 140) and hints that he may temporarily have come to believe in his confession. However, the evidence that Evans' confession had become internalized is extremely weak and speculative. Kennedy's inferences about the nature of Evans' confession appear to have been heavily influenced by Sargant's (1957) book *Battle for the Mind*, which deals with interrogations among the Chinese Communists discussed in Chapter 8. Kennedy appears to have been unaware of the subtle distinction between the coerced and compliant type of false confession. My view is that it is more likely that Evans' confession was of the coerced–compliant type, but nobody will ever know as no detailed statement was ever taken from Evans about his beliefs at the time of the interrogation.

Irving and McKenzie (1989) have made an interesting analysis of the Evans case by attempting to see to what extent improved legislation in England (PACE) would hypothetically have made a difference in preventing a miscarriage of justice had it been in existence at the time. The conclusion is that the new legislation might have given Evans more legal protection than that available at the time, but even so there is no guarantee that he would not have been convicted.

There were two official inquiries into the case of Timothy Evans, following Christie's confession about Mrs Evans' murder. The first inquiry, conducted in 1953 by Mr J. Scott Henderson, QC, came to the conclusion that no miscarriage of justice had taken place. That is, the case against Evans was seen as overwhelming, he was considered responsible for both his wife's and daughter's death, and Christie's confession about having murdered Mrs Evans was rejected. Not surprisingly, in view of the Inquiry's ill founded conclusions, it was severely criticized in the House of Commons (Kennedy, 1988). The second inquiry into the case was conducted in 1965–1966 by Sir Daniel Brabin, a High Court Judge (Brabin, 1966). Evans was again considered guilty, but with a difference. Brabin thought that Evans probably had not killed his daughter (for which he was hanged), but thought he had murdered his wife (for which crime he was never tried).

On 18 October 1966, 16 years after his public execution, Evans was granted a free pardon by the Queen, on the recommendation of the Home Secretary, Mr Roy Jenkins. Evans' innocence had at last been officially recognized.

The Confait Case

In the early hours on 22 April 1972, firemen and police attended a fire at 27 Doggett Road, South London. The body of a 26-year-old man, Maxwell Confait, was discovered. According to the pathologist who attended the scene, death was caused by strangulation with a ligature. Two days later three youths, Colin Lattimore, Ronald Leighton and Ahmet Salih, were arrested following some fires. The three boys were detained from about 5.30 p.m. and within two and half hours they made verbal confessions regarding Confait's murder. By 11 p.m. that same evening all three boys had signed confession statements in the presence of their parents. No solicitors or third parties were present during the critical interviews. The three boys subsequently retracted their confessions but were nevertheless convicted.

Lattimore was 18 years of age at the time of his arrest. He was mentally handicapped (IQ = 66) and illiterate. Leighton, aged 15, was of borderline intelligence (IQ = 75) and near illiterate. Salih, of Turkish Cypriot background, was the youngest of the three boys. He was only 14 at the time of his arrest and appears to have been of normal intelligence, although it is worth pointing out that no intelligence testing appears to have been carried out in his case. He spoke English as a second language.

On 24 November 1972, Lattimore was found guilty of manslaughter on the grounds of diminished responsibility, Leighton was found guilty of murder, and all three boys were found guilty of arson at Confait's home.

There was a Court of Appeal hearing in October 1975 where the convictions of the three boys were quashed on the basis that they were 'unsafe and unsatisfactory'. The boys were freed after having spent three years in prison. There was a subsequent inquiry, conducted by Sir Henry Fisher (1977). The *Fisher*

Report found that there had been three breaches of the existing legislation, which was the Judges' Rules and Administrative Directions. These were that

1. two of the boys (Lattimore and Leighton) had been interviewed without their parents being present;
2. none of the boys had been informed of their rights to a solicitor and their entitlement to communicate with any other person and
3. the police questioning of Lattimore was leading. The police were at the time aware of Lattimore's mental handicap, but chose to ignore it.

However, in spite of the report's criticisms of the police, it concluded, erroneously as it turned out, that the confessions of the three boys could not have been made unless at least one of the boys had been involved in the murder of Confait. The main basis for this conclusion is that the boys seemed to know so much about the murder. This according to Fisher, indicated that they had to have been involved in Confait's murder. Fisher did not consider the other possibility that the police had unwittingly communicated details about the murder to the boys. Two years after the *Fisher Report* was published all three boys were exonerated after two other people confessed to the murder and provided information that showed the three boys to be innocent.

As in the Evans case, Irving and McKenzie (1989) have placed the information available on the Confait case into the hypothetical context of PACE. Would the interrogation and confessions of the three young men have been different if PACE had been in operation at the time? Irving and McKenzie attempted to answer this question by reviewing the case under five headings: 'the arrest', 'the duration of detention', 'the record of custody', 'interrogation tactics and records' and 'the presence of third parties and the questions of vulnerability'. Their conclusion is that there would have been no important differences with regard to the arrest and detention. However, a detailed recording of what went on during custody and interrogation would have been required under the new legislation. In fact, PACE and its accompanying codes of practice require a detailed 'custody record' to be kept for every detainee and this would have made it easier to establish in retrospect what the circumstances of the interrogations and confessions were.

Two further safeguards would have been important if PACE had been available in 1972. First, a senior interrogator stated in the presence of a junior officer, during the critical phase of the interrogation, that the boys would be allowed to go home after the interviews were over. Irving and McKenzie believe that this kind of inducement would constitute a breach under PACE. Second, and possibly most importantly, it is more likely under the current legislation that the boys would have been allowed access to a solicitor and a third party at the beginning of their interrogation. Whether or not the three boys would have confessed in spite of these added safeguards is impossible to predict, but they might have reduced the likelihood of the subsequent miscarriage of justice that resulted from their confessions. However, the irregularities that occurred in the interrogation of the three youths might still occur under the PACE codes of practice.

CONCLUSIONS

The literature on cases of miscarriage of justice has been briefly reviewed. Wrongful convictions are typically caused by a combination of factors, rather than by one factor acting exclusively. The most common causes are mistaken identification, perjury by prosecution witnesses, over-reliance on defendants' confession statements, over-zealousness on the part of the police, suppression of exculpatory evidence and undue reliance on circumstantial evidence. High profile cases, involving a public outcry ('Hue and cry'), carry an increased risk of wrongful conviction. Where false confessions were instrumental in leading to wrongful conviction, these were typically caused by such factors as police pressure (e.g. coercive interrogation techniques), psychological vulnerabilities (e.g. poor intellectual functioning, high suggestibility) and the fulfilment of a psychological need (e.g. a sense of a notoriety to enhance self-esteem). The defendants' innocence was often discovered by chance. This included the discovery that no crime had been committed in the first place, new forensic evidence (e.g. DNA) and the confession and apprehension of the real culprit. Reviewing the literature, one is left with the impression that once defendants are convicted, the criminal justice system is not good at discovering, admitting to and correcting the errors made.

CHAPTER 8

The Psychology of False Confession: Research and Theoretical Issues

Confessions and denials can be categorized into four groups: true confessions, false confessions, true denials and false denials. In determining the proportion of suspects who fall into each group we are faced with one major problem, which is best described as a *base rate* problem. At the most basic level, we do not know the proportion of suspects interrogated at police stations who are genuinely guilty of the offence of which they are accused. If the base rate of guilty suspects interrogated were very high (i.e. 95% or higher) then the risk of false confessions occurring would be very low, even if the police regularly coerced the confessions. Conversely, where there is a low base rate of guilty suspects (e.g. less than 50%) there would be greatly increased risk of false confessions. Therefore, the rate of false confessions in a given population is dependent, to a certain extent, on the base rate of guilty suspects interrogated. In serious and notorious cases, including homicide and terrorist offences, sometimes many suspects are subjected to lengthy and pressured interrogation and this increases the risk of false confessions occurring (Matthews, 1995).

The frequency with which false confessions occur in a given country is impossible to estimate. What we do know from anecdotal case histories and miscarriages of justice research is that false confessions do sometimes occur for a variety of reasons. Such confessions are subsequently commonly retracted, but once a confession has been given to the police the likelihood of a conviction when the case goes to court is greatly enhanced, even if the confession is disputed at the trial.

Why do people confess to crimes they have not committed, which is clearly against their self-interest? The reason is typically due to a combination of factors that are associated with the circumstances and nature of the custodial confinement and interrogation, and the accused's psychological vulnerabilities (Gudjonsson, 1992e).

Various types of false confession, differing in their psychological implications, have been described in the literature and these are reviewed in detail in this chapter. A detailed theoretical appraisal of the different types of false confession is given. This chapter serves as the theoretical foundation for other chapters, where case examples are given of the different types of disputed or false confession.

DEFINITIONS OF FALSE CONFESSION

Ayling (1984) suggests two ways of defining 'false confession'. First, there are those who are totally innocent of the crime they are alleged to have committed, and according to Ayling they are probably few in number. Secondly, there are those who were involved in the alleged offence, but they overstated their involvement during custodial interrogation. Ayling suggests that overstating one's involvement in a crime is much more common than confessing to a crime one has had nothing to do with, although he provides no data to substantiate his claim.

Ofshe (1989) gives an interesting definition of false confession. He states:

> A confession is considered false if it is elicited in response to a demand for a confession and is either intentionally fabricated or is not based on actual knowledge of the facts that form its content (p. 13).

This definition implies that a false confession can, theoretically, be induced from both innocent and guilty suspects. Thus, within Ofshe's definition, it is possible that a guilty suspect who has no recollection of having committed the alleged crime is considered to be a 'false confessor' when he is manipulated into confessing to the details of something of which he has no memory. In a recent publication Ofshe and Leo (1997b) define a false confession

> ...as detailed admission to a criminal act that the confessor either did not commit or is, in fact, ignorant of having committed (p. 240).

The most stringent criterion for defining a false confession is that the person confesses to a crime of which he or she is completely innocent.

Self-incriminating admissions, not amounting to the suspect accepting responsibility for the crime and giving a detailed account of his actions, can result in a wrongful conviction. For example, a parent may admit to shaking an infant who subsequently died without his or her being responsible for the death. A suspect may falsely admit to having been in the vicinity of the crime or even claim to have witnessed it. Such false admissions may be highly incriminating, but they must be distinguished from false confessions. The comment 'I did it', without a detailed explanation, should be treated as an admission and not as a confession.

THE FREQUENCY OF FALSE CONFESSIONS

When trying to estimate the frequency with which false confessions occur, it is important to be specific about the context one is referring to. For example, as discussed in the previous chapter, false confessions were apparently common during the 'show' trials and public confessions in Stalin's Russia (Hinkle & Wolff, 1956) and among American Military personnel and Western Civilians coerced by Chinese communists during the Korean War (Schein, Schneier &

Barker, 1961). Furthermore, even when one is specific about the context, such as false confessions within custodial interrogation, one cannot ignore cultural factors and fundamental differences in legal systems. For example, Israel's interrogation of Palestinians from the occupied territories differs markedly from custodial interrogation in the UK and USA. With a conviction rate of 96.8% by Israeli's military courts, and the main evidence against the defendant being a signed confession statement, the risk of a false confession should not be underestimated, particularly when

> In fact, the extraction of confessions under duress, and the acceptance into evidence of such confessions by the military courts, form the backbone of Israel's military justice system (Human Rights Watch/Middle East, 1994, p. 2).

Similarly, Morton (2001) gives a vivid description of the Japanese criminal justice system where there is no jury system and the conviction rate is over 99%.

Under such extreme circumstances, the proportion of false confessions versus true confessions is likely to be higher than in countries such as England, where coercive questioning is rapidly declining due to improved police procedures and training. With regard to the frequency of false confessions there are two crucial questions that remain unanswered.

1. What proportion of all confessions obtained during custodial interrogation is false?
2. How many false confessions lead to wrongful convictions?

Ofshe and Leo (1997a) state that there are three sources of information which suggest that false confessions 'occur regularly' in America.

- *Case studies.* They cite a number of American books and articles written by scholars and journalists on 'false confessions'.
- *Laboratory research.* They cite the experimental work of Kassin and McNall (1991) as evidence that commonly used interrogation techniques have a coercive impact, which can result in false confession.
- *Their own work on a large number of 'probable or confirmed' cases of false confession.* The basis of this work relates first to Ofshe's detailed analysis of interrogation transcripts, case files, sworn testimony concerning interrogations and interviews with police officers and suspects, and second to Leo's observations of police interrogations.

Ofshe and Leo rightly point out that the known and publicized cases of false confession may only represent 'the tip of the iceberg' of the real number of cases. We do not know what proportion of confessions is false. What we do know is that false confessions do happen on occasions and not all are brought to the attention of the authorities.

Richardson (1991), as a part of his M.Sc. Dissertation, asked 60 juveniles living in a residential home whether they had ever made a false confession to the police. Fourteen (23%) claimed to have made a false confession to the police. The main reason they gave for having given a false confession was to protect a peer or a friend. This figure seems very high and it does not tell us what proportion of police interrogations lead to false confessions. Another problem is that a person's claim to have made a false confession cannot be taken at face value, because people's perceptions and definition of what it is vary considerably (e.g. many might view exaggerating their role in an offence as a false confession). For this reason the researcher has to question the person in detail about the nature of the claimed false confession to ensure that it falls within an acceptable definition (Sigurdsson, 1998).

Two studies in Iceland have investigated, among prison inmates, the rate of false confessions obtained during police interrogation. Both are based on self-report and this should be borne in mind when interpreting the findings. In the first study (Gudjonsson & Sigurdsson, 1994), 95% of all inmates admitted to prisons in Iceland over a one-year period (August 1991–July 1992) agreed to be interviewed and were psychologically assessed. As a part of that assessment, one of the questions they were asked related to false confessions. There were 229 prisoners in total, and out of these 27 (12%) claimed to have made a false confession to the police sometime in the past. Included in this study were only those inmates who claimed not to have been involved at all in the offence to which they had falsely confessed. None of them said they had made a false confession with regard to the offence for which they were serving a prison sentence. Most of the false confessions were to property offences (67%) and serious traffic violations (18%). The reasons given for making the false confessions were protecting a significant other (52%) and police pressure and avoidance of custody (48%).

In a further study using the same methodology, Sigurdsson and Gudjonsson (1996) investigated the frequency of false confessions among 509 prison inmates in Iceland, and 108 juvenile offenders, aged 15–23 years, who had been given a sentence of conditional discharge after a guilty plea. None of the 108 juvenile offenders claimed to have made a false confession to the police. Out of the 509 prison inmates, 62 (12%) claimed to have made false confession to the police on one or more occasions, which is identical to the figure found in the Gudjonsson–Sigurdsson (1994) study. Only five (<1%) inmates claimed to have made a false confession to the offence for which they were currently serving a prison sentence. The confession rate for Icelandic prison inmates is about 92% (Sigurdsson & Gudjonsson, 1994), and the fact that so few claim to have made a false confession to their current offence suggests that, even among habitual offenders, the rate of false confession is a fairly rare event among prisoners in Iceland when viewed in the context of the overall number of interrogations conducted. On the basis of the findings in this study, it seems that the rate of false confession per interrogation is certainly below 1% in Iceland and approximately half are police-induced (coerced) false confession. It remains to be seen how far one can generalize from these findings cross-culturally, which is a point discussed at some length by Ofshe and Leo (1997a, 1997b).

The types of offence falsely confessed to included property offences (59%), serious traffic violations (20%), violent offences (7%) and drug related offences (5%). One of the violent offences involved a false confession to murder. This false confessor was subsequently convicted of wasting police time (see case Mr E in Chapter 9).

The majority (64%) of the false confessors claimed to have made the false confession when under the age of 21, with the peak (51%) being in the age group 16–20. This suggests that factors associated with youth make people particularly vulnerable to making false confessions. Two suggestions can be put forward to explain this finding. First, false confessions are most commonly made as a way of protecting someone else and this is a phenomenon that is particularly likely to occur in adolescence. Peer loyalty, and on occasions pressure from peers, may be particularly powerful in motivating juveniles to make a false confession. Secondly, as is the case with true confessions (see Chapter 6), false confessions are probably easier to elicit from young persons due to their relative inexperience of life.

With regard to the reasons for making a false confession, half (50%) claimed to have confessed falsely in order to protect somebody else, 48% blamed police pressure and 42% were wanting to avoid police detention. There were overlaps between the three reasons given, particularly between police pressure and avoidance of detention.

There were some sex differences with regard to the false confessions. Female inmates more commonly claimed to have made false confessions than male inmates. They were significantly more likely to report having falsely confessed in order to protect someone else, and none reported having falsely confessed in order to avoid police detention, compared with 48% of the males. This suggests that females cope better with police detention than males, but their vulnerability lies in their greater tendency to wish to protect others. Another interesting finding emerged: whereas males were most likely to be protecting a friend or a peer, females were more commonly protecting a fiancée or a spouse.

False confessions to protect someone else are not all necessarily voluntary, even when there is no police coercion. For example, in the Sigurdsson–Gudjonsson (1996) study, two of the false confessions resulted from the real culprit coercing the person to 'take on the case'.

Less than one-third (30%) of the false confessors claimed to have retracted their confession prior to their trial, claiming that they did not see the point in doing so as they were trying to protect somebody else, or that they believed they would be convicted because of their confession. This suggests that whether or not defendants retract their confession depends on their perception of the likely outcome at trial. The more defendants believe their false confession will be believed, and that they may be acquitted if they retract it, the greater the likelihood that it will be retracted and disputed at trial. For similar reasons, defendants who make genuine confessions may also be tempted to dispute the confession at trial when the confession is the principal evidence against them and seek medical evidence to support their case (Gudjonsson & MacKeith, 1997).

How many false confessions lead to wrongful convictions? The simple answer is that we do not know. In the Sigurdsson–Gudjonsson (1996) study, over two-thirds (72%) of the false confessors *claimed* that they were convicted of the offence (see Sigurdsson, 1998). Cases where the false confession is not subsequently retracted and the person pleads guilty to the offence are most likely to result in a wrongful conviction. In some cases the police themselves are able to identify that the confession is false, as in case Mr R (Chapter 9), and no miscarriage of justice occurs. This is most likely to happen when people volunteer a confession to a crime of which they appear to have little knowledge. However, sometimes the ability and willingness of police officers to look critically at the possibility that they may have coerced a false confession are seriously lacking, and even if they did suspect it they may not be prepared to do anything about it. This kind of behaviour may be interpreted in terms of an interrogation bias (Trankell, 1972), Festinger's (1957) theory of *cognitive dissonance*, faulty reasoning and erroneous beliefs (Gilovich, 1991) and poor police training and negligence (Ofshe & Leo, 1997a).

Leo and Ofshe (1998a) argue that there are three main reasons why it is impossible to estimate the number of police coerced confessions in the USA, or the proportion of wrongful convictions they cause. These are the following.

- American police officers do not typically record confessions in their entirety, making it impossible to determine what exactly happened during the interrogation.
- There is no official record kept of the number of interrogations conducted annually and how many result in true or false confessions.
- Most false confessions are not reported in the media and therefore go unnoticed by researchers.

In terms of the consequences of false confessions, Leo and Ofshe (1998b) make an important distinction between those cases that result in

1. deprivation of liberty prior to trial (e.g. after being detained in custody and interrogated the suspects may not be charged, because the police accept that the confession is false, if they are charged then the case may be dismissed prior to trial, or defendants may be eventually acquitted in court) and
2. wrongful convictions (e.g. an innocent person is convicted and may serve many years in prison, or even be executed).

In their review of 60 cases of alleged false confessions, Leo and Ofshe (1998b) found that 29 (48%) had resulted in wrongful conviction (This study is reviewed in more detail later in this chapter.)

FALSE, RETRACTED AND DISPUTED CONFESSIONS

Gudjonsson and MacKeith (1988) draw a distinction between the following concepts.

1. Proven false confessions.
2. Retracted confessions.
3. Disputed confessions.

Once an apparently credible false confession is given to the police it is often difficult, if not impossible, for the individual concerned to subsequently prove his innocence. This is particularly the case if the confession contains a detailed post-admission narrative account with apparent special knowledge (i.e. knowledge that should only be known to those who are familiar with the crime and the crime scene). Such special knowledge in the case of innocent persons arises through contamination (e.g. the case details were communicated by the police or obtained through some other sources, such as from the media or the real culprit).

The Post-Admission Narrative

Ofshe and Leo (1997a) and Leo and Ofshe (1998a) have emphasized the importance of thoroughly analysing the *post-admission narrative* account given by the suspect after he or she has uttered the words 'I did it'. If the detailed description of the confession fits the crime then the confession can be judged as reliable, assuming of course that the special knowledge is not due to *contamination* (i.e. the suspect having learned about the case from sources other than direct involvement in the crime). In contrast, a poor fit between the special knowledge and the crime may cast doubt on the reliability of the confession. Leo and Ofshe argue that there are at least three ways to determine the reliability of the confession.

1. Does the confession statement lead to the discovery of evidence that is unknown to the police (e.g. a location of a missing murder weapon, or stolen property)?
2. Does it include highly unusual features of the crime that have not been made public (e.g. special mutilation of the body, unusual method of killing or sexual act)?
3. Does the suspect provide accurate descriptions of the mundane crime scene detail, which have not been made public (e.g. the type of clothing the victim was wearing, presence of certain pieces of furniture at the crime scene)?

If one or more of the three criteria are met then this lends support for the view that the confession is reliable. Ofshe and Leo (1997a) and Leo and Ofshe (1998a) do mention the importance of non-contamination, which is something that Cassell (1999) fails to acknowledge in his critique of the work of Leo and Ofshe (1998a). Instead, Cassell emphasizes his view that

> ...even those who are guilty of crimes will frequently give a confession that is inconsistent with the known facts of the case. This presents a problem for Leo and Ofshe's proposal to suppress confessions whose post-admission narrative fails to closely track the facts of the case (pp. 577–578).

Cassell is presumably basing his view on the conclusion he has reached in his article that nine of the cases of alleged false confession presented by Leo and Ofshe are truly guilty individuals. If Cassell is wrong about the assumption he makes about the true guilt of these individuals then his argument about inconsistent details of innocent defendants has no basis.

A confession that contains an apparently detailed special knowledge may prove to be false (see, for example, Chapter 20). Special knowledge about a crime can be obtained and contaminated through a variety of sources, including the following.

1. The media.
2. The police.
3. Crime scene visits.
4. Crime scene material, such as photographs.
5. A third party (i.e. being told about it by the real perpetrator).

Any of the above modes of communication can contaminate the original knowledge the person had about the crime, making it appear as if he is providing knowledge that only the real perpetrator should possess. The best special knowledge is that which is only known to the real perpetrator (e.g. where an undiscovered body or murder weapon has been hidden). Once the police are in possession of that special knowledge, the possibility of it being communicated to the suspect during custodial confinement and interrogation may be difficult to rule out. Audio or video recording of all interrogations can be important to rule out such contamination, although even this procedure may not be foolproof.

As will be shown in Chapter 18, even if the suspect reveals no special knowledge, and appears to be unfamiliar with the crime, he may still be convicted on the basis of that confession alone (see the case of Peter Fell in Chapter 18).

The Discovery of a False Confession

When a false confession occurs, it may be discovered by different means, including one or more of the following.

1. Discovery that no crime was committed (e.g. an alleged murder victim turns up alive—see for example, Leo & Ofshe, 1998a; The Earl of Birkenhead, 1938).
2. New forensic evidence, including improved DNA testing capabilities (Gudjonsson & MacKeith, 1994; Scheck, Neufeld & Dwyer, 2000; Wambaugh, 1989).
3. New alibi evidence (see Chapter 17 with reference to Gerry Conlan).
4. Newly discovered medical evidence, which would have made it impossible for the person to have committed the crime (see e.g. Rose, Panter & Wilkinson, 1998). There may also be evidence that proves that the defendant could not have committed the crime, because he was in police custody or prison at the time of the offence (Leo & Ofshe, 1998a).
5. Somebody else confesses and is convicted of the offence (Cassell, 1999; Gudjonsson & MacKeith, 1990; Leo & Ofshe, 1998a).
6. Psychological and psychiatric evidence that casts serious doubts on the veracity of the confession (Gudjonsson, 1995d; Gudjonsson, Kopelman & MacKeith; 1999; Gudjonsson & Lebegue, 1989;).

7. A careful analysis of the post-admission statement, which reveals striking errors and omissions, rendering the confession unconvincing and inherently improbable. (See, for example, the case of David MacKenzie, Chapter 18; Leo & Ofshe, 1998a.)

A retracted confession consists of the suspect or defendant declaring that the self-incriminating admission or confession he made is false (i.e. the confession is recanted). As a result the confession may be disputed at the defendant's forthcoming trial. This does not necessarily mean that the confession is false, because guilty people as well as innocent people do retract their confession before the case goes to court.

In some circumstances a confession may be disputed at the trial even when the suspect has not formally retracted it. This probably happens more often in adversarial proceedings where the onus is on the prosecution to prove their case rather than establishing guilt or innocence by inquisitorial means. In such a case the confession may be ruled inadmissible in court because of legal technicality (e.g. breaches of existing codes of practice). With the English Courts becoming more receptive to expert psychological evidence, there appears to be a growing trend for lawyers to dispute confession evidence even when the defendant is not claiming he made a false or coerced confession (Gudjonsson, 1999b). This is where the legal profession can misuse expert testimony by trying to get the client acquitted on the basis of mental problems, which are not always relevant or salient to the credibility of the confession (Gudjonsson & MacKeith, 1997).

A suspect or defendant may also dispute that he actually made the confession in the first place. He or she may allege that the police fabricated the confession. In such instances the police may allege that the defendant made the confession but refused to sign it (Graef, 1990). Even if the suspect signs the self-incriminating statement he may allege that the police officers made the statement up and he just signed it.

Oral confessions, or so-called 'verbals', pose great problems. These consist of the police alleging that the suspect stated orally that he or she had committed the crime or implying that he or she was somehow involved. Many instances of such 'verbals' have been shown to be fabricated by the police. In the words of one British police officer,

> There are lots of side steps in the police. They rarely stick to testimony. The classic case is verbals. One of the magistrates actually said, 'Well, it's very hard for this court to believe that the PCs, Sergeants, the Inspectors all collaborated to produce this evidence'. Of course this is precisely what they'd bloody done (Graef, 1990, p. 278).

Verbal confessions to people other than the police can be allowed in evidence and require no corroboration in English law. A good illustration of this is what happened in a trial concerning the attempted murder of the well known English boxing promoter Frank Warren. Terry Marsh, a former world boxing champion, was charged with the attempted murder of Mr Warren. Marsh was alleged to have made a verbal confession about the attempted murder to another prisoner whilst on remand in prison. In the summing up the judge, Mr Justice Fennell, stated with regard to the prisoner's evidence about Marsh's confession:

As a matter of strict law, his evidence does not require corroboration. But, in my judgment and my direction to you, it would be very wise indeed to look for independent support before you proceeded to act on the basis of his evidence (*The Times*, 1990).

The Timing of the Retraction

The time of the retraction may vary greatly. Some suspects declare their innocence at the first opportunity (e.g. immediately the pressure is off, when a relative or a solicitor visits), while others retract days, weeks or even years afterwards. In some circumstances the suspect may never withdraw the confession, even though it is false, particularly if the purpose of making the confession is to protect somebody else (Gudjonsson & Sigurdsson, 1994). If a suspect actually makes a false confession that does not involve protecting someone else, then a delay in retracting it at the earliest opportunity requires an explanation. Two main possibilities exist:

1. The confession is of the internalized kind and the false belief by the defendant that he committed the offence may in some cases last for several months.
2. The defendant knows or believes that he is innocent of the offence, but nevertheless fails to retract the confession due to fear of repercussions, a need for notoriety or for some instrumental gain (e.g. wanting to go to hospital).

It is worth bearing in mind that it is very unlikely that all genuine false confessions are eventually retracted. There are a number of reasons for this as follows.

1. The suspect falsely confessed to protect somebody else.
2. The suspect believes there is no point in retracting the confession.
3. The suspect wants to be punished for the crime he confessed to, even though he did not commit it.
4. Having confessed to the crime the suspect prefers to plead guilty to the charge rather than dispute it, even though he is innocent.
5. The person believes that he has committed the offence even though he has no memory of having carried out the act.
6. Maintaining the confession fulfils a psychological need, such as providing a sense of notoriety and status among peers.
7. The suspect, or a prisoner serving a prison sentence, 'confesses' to further offences in order to assist the police in improving their crime figures (Graef, 1990). Such confessions are referred to in England as offences 'taken into consideration'.

How Commonly are Confessions Retracted?

This may vary considerably internationally or even within the same country. Inbau *et al.* (2001) go as far as to suggest that *many* guilty suspects subsequently retract their confessions.

They state:

> Many confessed criminal offenders will subsequently deny their guilt and allege that they either did not confess or else were forced or induced to do so by physical abuse, threats, or promise of leniency. Occasionally, the defendant in a criminal case will even go so far as to say that he was compelled to sign a written confession without reading it or having had it read to him, or that he was forced to place his signature on a blank sheet of paper and all that appears above it was inserted later (p. 375).

In the third edition of the book, Inbau, Reid and Buckley (1986) used the words 'Most confessed criminal offenders...' (p. 176). In the fourth edition the word 'most' has been replaced with the word 'many'. The reason for this change is not explained. The most likely explanation is that Inbau, Reid and Buckley (1986) overstated or exaggerated the position and this was corrected in the later edition. It is important to note that no empirical evidence is provided in either edition of the book for the claims made about retractions; it is undoubtedly based on the authors' impressions rather than empirical data. Support for this comes from the following statement:

> In our experience, the vast majority of retracted confessions are, in fact, trustworthy statements coming from the person who committed the crime (p. 437).

Inbau, Reid and Buckley (1986) do not consider the possibility that anybody who retracts a previously made confession could possibly be innocent. They work on the misguided assumption that their recommended tactics and techniques *never* induce an innocent person to falsely confess. There are sufficient numbers of proven cases of innocent persons retracting false confessions to demonstrate that this belief of Inbau, Reid and Buckley is unfounded. What their statement does highlight is the fact that criminal suspects very commonly retract their previously made confession to the police and give various excuses for having done so. Inbau, Reid and Buckley are wrong to assume that *all* such retractions involve guilty people claiming to be innocent.

In the more recent edition of their book, Inbau *et al.* (2001) do accept that false confessions occur:

> There is no question that interrogations have resulted in false confessions from innocent suspects (p. 411).

However, when citing a case involving a false confession, Inbau *et al.* do not cite a case involving police coercion. Instead, they cite a case of a 16-year-old youth who had been persuaded by his father to confess to a murder the father had committed. This suggests that Inbau *et al.* are still reluctant to accept that false confession may occur as a result of interrogation relying on the Reid Technique.

The process of denial may continue to operate after people have been convicted. Kennedy and Grubin (1992) found that convicted sex offenders who pleaded guilty to their offence at the time of their trial begin to deny their offence once they are in prison. This process of denial may serve some important psychological functions (Salter, 1988) and is also undoubtedly related to the hard time that sex offenders are given in prison by other inmates (Thornton, 1987).

There is indication from the outcomes in Crown Court Trials that defendants commonly dispute their confession, particularly in a large city such as London. For example, in the study by Baldwin and McConville (1980), which was quoted in some detail Chapter 2, about 10% of the defendants assessed in Birmingham and 24% of those in the London sample pleaded 'not guilty' at their trial after having provided the police with a written confession. Taking into account both verbal and written confessions, over 25% of those who pleaded not guilty at their trial in the two cities had verbal and written confessions recorded against them. Not surprisingly, verbal confessions were much more frequently disputed at the trial than written confessions. Kalven and Zeisel (1966), in an American study, found that about 20% of confessions are disputed when cases go to court.

Although not pleading guilty cannot be directly equated with a retraction of the confession, these results support the argument that a sizeable proportion of defendants in criminal trials retract their previously made confessions. There may be significant differences between cities and countries in the extent to which defendants do this. The implications of the differences in the figures between London and Birmingham are not discussed by Baldwin and McConville. There may also be changes over time. My impression is that, with the courts in England more commonly admitting psychological evidence, confessions are increasingly being disputed (Gudjonsson, 1999a).

THE INNOCENT PLEADING GUILTY

It would be expected that suspects who falsely confess would retract their confession before their case went to trial. However, there is evidence that some defendants in criminal trials may plead guilty to offences they did not commit (Bottoms & McClean, 1976; Dell, 1971; Leo & Ofshe, 2001). How often this happens is not known but the results from Dell's (1971) important survey of female prisoners in Holloway Prison indicates that 'inconsistent pleading' was a major problem in the lower courts in the early 1970s.

Dell (1971) found that of 527 women tried at Magistrates' Courts, 106 (20%) had claimed to the researchers that they were innocent of the offence with which they were charged. Of these 106 women 56 (53%) pleaded guilty in court. Dell refers to these women as 'inconsistent pleaders'. She compared them with a control group of 47 women who claimed to be innocent and pleaded not guilty. The 'inconsistent pleaders' were found to be younger than the other women, but both groups had similar social and medical backgrounds. Four further differences between the two groups emerged.

1. Inconsistent pleaders were more commonly charged with offences related to public disorder, such as soliciting and drunkenness, than the control group.
2. They were less commonly legally represented at court.

3. Inconsistent pleaders were less likely than the controls to be remanded in custody prior to their trial.
4. A large number of the inconsistent pleaders had no previous convictions.

What reasons did the inconsistent pleaders give for their inconsistency? According to Dell, the most common reasons given by the women were the following:

1. Police pressure and persuasion.
2. They saw no point in denying the allegation as it would be just their word against that of the police.
3. They wanted to avoid being remanded in custody.
4. They thought they might get a heavier sentence if they pleaded 'not guilty'.

Dell concluded that 'inconsistent pleading' stems from a number of factors, which include lack of legal advice and police persuasion. She suggests that one way of reducing 'inconsistent pleading' is to ensure that every accused person is allowed to speak to a solicitor before entering a plea. This is what seems to happen in the Crown court, where 'inconsistent pleading' was not found to be a problem.

A study by Bottoms and McClean (1976) also indicated that some defendants may plead guilty to offences of which they are innocent, for some instrumental gain (e.g. the probability of a lower sentence). The young and socially disadvantaged were most likely to plead guilty. Eighteen per cent of defendants were suspected of having pleaded guilty to an offence of which they were innocent. Bottoms and McClean recommended that the court should carefully examine guilty pleas before accepting them.

There have, of course, been many changes within the British judicial system since the Dell and Bottoms–McClean studies. Perhaps most importantly, legal representation in the Magistrates' Court is now commonplace and more detainees are being interviewed in the presence of a solicitor. However, this does not mean that some defendants do not still plead guilty in the Magistrates' Court to offences they have not committed. In fact, solicitors may advise their clients to plead guilty to certain offences where they are likely to be found guilty in any case, irrespective of their guilt or innocence, as a guilty plea typically results in a less severe sentence. Furthermore, some innocent defendants may plead guilty to charges as a way of avoiding being remanded in custody or having their case delayed.

Finally, on a related theme, plea-bargaining, a procedure that is more common and formalized in the USA than it is in England, encourages defendants to plead guilty to offences in exchange for a lesser penalty (Bordens & Bassett, 1985). Leo and Ofshe (2001) provide some evidence that innocent defendants may plead guilty to very serious charges, such as murder or manslaughter, in order to escape the likelihood of a harsher sentence (e.g. the death penalty). Jayne and Buckley (1998) naively use the practice of plea-bargaining in the USA as evidence that a promise of leniency during interrogation does not result in false confessions.

THE BROADER CONTEXT OF FALSE CONFESSIONS

It is important to be aware of the broader context in which false confessions occur. In fact, false confessions may arise in a variety of social, religious and political contexts (see e.g. Berggren, 1975; Hepworth & Turner, 1980; Sargant, 1957). They can also occur in the context of memories of childhood abuse recovered in adulthood (see e.g. Gudjonsson, 1997b; Ofshe & Watters, 1994; Leo, 1997; Ost, Costall & Bull, 2001).

Two specialized contexts are particularly theoretically relevant to this book, because of the types of psychological coercion utilized by the interrogators in order to extract a confession. These are the 'show' trials and public confessions in Stalin's Russia (Beck & Godin, 1951; Hinkle & Wolff, 1956; Leites & Bernaut, 1954) and the 'coercive persuasion' of American Military personnel and Western Civilians by Chinese communists (Hunter, 1951, 1956; Lifton, 1956, 1961; Orwell, 1951; Schein, 1956; Schein, Schneier & Barker, 1961).

The importance of the interrogation techniques of the Chinese Communists in eliciting false confessions is well expressed by Hinkle and Wolff (1956):

> The Communists are skilled in the extraction of information from prisoners and in making prisoners do their bidding. It has appeared that they can force men to confess to crimes which they have not committed, and then, apparently, to believe in the truth of their confessions and express sympathy and gratitude toward those who have imprisoned them (p. 116).

Beck and Godin (1951), whose book *Russian Purge and the Extraction of Confession* is based on their personal experiences of victimization during the Yezhov period, estimate that between 5 and 10% of the Soviet population was arrested between 1936 and 1939. The reasons for these arrests were political and served to overcome any opposition to the existing political regime. The extraction of confessions functioned to justify these arrests and was intended to reassure the public of these persons' guilt. The interrogation techniques applied were individualized according to the characteristics and resistance of the arrested person. Interrogations were typically carried out at night and combined beatings, extensive sleep-deprivation, deprivation of social contact, physical discomfort, threats and intimidation.

The book by Beck and Godin emphasizes the psychological aspects of these interrogations. *In many instances beatings were not required. Nevertheless, almost everybody confessed*:

> Years of experience had enabled the NKVD to develop a technique of protracted interrogation which practically no one was able to resist (p. 53).

One of the authors of the book, who was a history professor at the time of his arrest, had been prepared for his arrest and was determined not to confess. After 50 days of interrogation he eventually broke down and confessed falsely to armed revolt and acts of terrorism:

I had now found out why those involved in 'show' trials so readily admitted every accusation, and the comparison with the medieval witch-trials no longer seemed to me to be amusing. There are circumstances in which a human being will confess to anything (p. 161).

Hinkle and Wolff (1956) and Lifton (1956, 1961) use the term 'thought reform' to describe the process of indoctrination by the Communists. Similarly, Schein, Schneier and Barker (1961) use the term 'coercive persuasion'.

The critical features of these kinds of programme involve the extreme degree of social control imposed, the sustained attack on the person's self-concept, and environmental and social manipulation utilized to maintain and reinforce the behavioural and attitude change achieved (Lifton, 1961).

Cunningham (1973), who worked as a psychologist with the British military, interviewed many of the 900 British prisoners who were repatriated from Korea. What was most striking about them was the finding that about 80% had been interrogated so subtly by the Chinese that they did not even realize that they had been interrogated! Cunningham argues that the Chinese used a combination of intelligence briefings and subtle interrogation techniques with intensive group pressure for change.

What were the main differences between the methods of the Russians and Chinese interrogators? Hinkle and Wolff (1956) and Lifton (1956) argue that the experience and practice of the Russian State Police influenced the Chinese methods of extracting confessions, but there were clear differences.

1. The Russian confessions associated with the purge formed a part of 'the ritual of liquidation' (i.e. a way of fighting political opposition), whereas in China they were 'more the vehicle of individual reform' (Lifton, 1956). Both were intended to facilitate or uphold certain Governmental regimes.
2. The Chinese utilized extensive group re-education programmes in conjunction with confession extraction, a practice that had not been utilized previously by the Russians.
3. The Chinese utilized social and emotional isolation of prisoners more selectively than the Russians. In fact, Schein, Schneier and Barker (1961) argue that whereas Russian interrogators relied on *under-stimulation* (i.e. they tended to keep prisoners in social isolation) the Chinese interrogators tended to *over-stimulate* their prisoners (i.e. they prevented any privacy).
4. Unlike the Russians, the Chinese were using confession extraction as a vehicle for much more extensive and lasting 'thought reform' changes and indoctrination, where considerable emphasis was placed upon changing the prisoner's permanent values, attitudes and beliefs.
5. The Chinese used more subtle and manipulative strategies and tactics than the Russians, where the emphasis was on exploiting human interactions and psychological vulnerabilities rather than using physical violence. However, both the Russians and the Chinese exploited human vulnerabilities and weaknesses that had been induced or exacerbated by fatigue, sleep deprivation, insufficient or inadequate diet, uncertainty, pain and general physical discomfort.
6. Hinkle and Wolff (1956) argue that the procedures used by the Chinese were much less standardized than those employed by the Russians.

The 'Resisters' and 'Cooperators' of the Communist Regimes

Not all prisoners of the Chinese Communists made self-incriminating admissions and those who did, did so for different reasons. Schein (1956) gives a reasonably detailed description of the 'resisters' and the 'cooperators'. There were different types of resister, but the majority seemed to have been 'well-integrated resistance leaders', whose principal characteristics were their ability to form sound judgements in ambiguous or poorly defined situations and to handle the reactions of the Chinese and the other prisoners. Other types of resister included those men who had a long history of rebellious resistance to all forms of authority and those whose religious faith demanded total non-cooperation with the Chinese.

The 'cooperators' were of different types. There were those, labelled 'the weaklings', who were unable to withstand any physical or psychological discomfort. They were highly susceptible to suggestions when placed under pressure. The prisoners who were most vulnerable 'ideologically' were those who had poor standing in the social community prior to their arrest. These were labelled 'the low status persons' and tended to be young and unintelligent. Then there were the 'bored or curious intellectuals', who seldom became ideologically confused or converted, but who nevertheless cooperated with the Chinese for stimulation and instrumental gains (i.e. in order to gain a reward or avoid punishment).

Hinkle and Wolff (1956), in their discussion of the Russian and Chinese interrogation techniques, argue that the people most vulnerable to making false confession were those of high moral standing because of their guilt proneness. Possession of such a trait made them susceptible to self-criticism, which could easily be exploited by the interrogators. Conversely, some psychopathic individuals were seen as vulnerable in the sense that their behaviour could be easily influenced by rewards and immediate instrumental gain, rather than by self-criticism and guilt.

Theoretical Aspects of Communist Indoctrination

The most detailed model presently available on coercive persuasion in the context of Communist indoctrination is that of Schein, Schneier and Barker (1961). The basis of their model has its origin in Lewin's (1947) dynamic theory of groups and organizations, where it is assumed that beliefs, attitudes and values are closely integrated with one another around people's self-concept or self-image. The integration is dynamic rather than static and there are constant internal (e.g. needs and motives) and external (requests, demands) 'forces' acting upon people, which push them in different directions. People are assumed to be principally motivated to maintain stable self-esteem and to reduce uncertainty in their environment. These two factors determine the extent to which people's beliefs, attitudes, values and behaviour can be influenced by psychological manipulation.

The process of change or influence gradually takes place over a period of time and consists of three basic stages, labelled as *'unfreezing'*, *'changing'* and *'refreezing'* (Schein, Schneier & Barker, 1961, pp. 117–139). 'Unfreezing' refers to the process whereby the forces pushing people towards confessing are strengthened (e.g. persuading people that it is in their own interest to confess, that there is substantial evidence to link them to the crime) whilst forces maintaining resistance are weakened (e.g. by tiredness, lack of sleep, exhaustion, emotional distress). Unfreezing is seen as an essential prerequisite for any change to occur.

Whereas 'unfreezing' is construed as being principally influenced by the needs and motives of the prisoner, 'changing' is viewed by Schein, Schneier and Barker as being more cognitively determined. That is, it involves an active decision-making process, which includes clear ideas about the direction in which prisoners are required to change. The basic mechanism involves the *'identification'* of the prisoner, in order to establish a new identity or frame of reference, with the person (i.e. interrogator, cellmate) who constitutes the sources of influence.

'Refreezing' refers to the new information or belief being integrated into the prisoner's self-concept and value system. In order for this to be achieved successfully, the new beliefs, attitudes, values and behaviours need to be reinforced, at least temporarily, by significant others in the prisoner's environment. Ofshe and Leo (1997a, 1997b) draw attention to the extent to which the maintenance of such changes in attitudes in cases of false confessions tend to be environmentally dependent rather than enduring and stable. That is, once people are removed from the social support system that reinforces the attitude change, then they are likely to revert to their original beliefs.

In summary, for influence or change to take place, there has to be an incentive or a motive to change, the prisoner must have some indication or an idea about the direction in which he is to change, and change needs to be rewarded and reinforced for it to be sustained.

Schein, Schneier and Barker consider that the main difference between coercive persuasion and other kinds of influence is the extent to which the prisoner is confined involuntarily or coerced into remaining for exposure to 'unfreezing pressures' from which there is no escape and no alternative sources of influence (p. 139). The authors point to many parallels between coercive persuasion in Communist China and that found in non-Communist settings, such as prisons, hospitals and the military. The principal components involve placing subjects in a situation from which there is no escape, whilst weakening their resistance to influence, bombarding them with 'new' ideas and information and isolating them from outside influence that could counteract the impact of the change.

Although Schein, Schneier and Barker do not specifically discuss the parallels between false confessions extracted by Communist interrogators and interrogators in Europe and the United States of America, theories about the former have important implications about the psychology of false confessions in general. Coercive persuasion is a sociopsychological phenomenon involving a social process that can take place in a variety of contexts. Understanding the basic mechanisms and processes involved in Communist interrogations and indoctrination help to further our knowledge about some general principles that are applicable to a variety of interrogative situations.

Theoretically, the processes leading to attitude change and confession, respectively, may be independent, but Schein, Schneier and Barker found that the two processes were closely related; that is, making a confession facilitates an attitude change and vice versa. These findings are consistent with the more experimental results of Bem (1966, 1967), where it was found that making a 'false confession' subsequently resulted in subjects believing in the truthfulness of the confession. In other words, saying may become believing.

Schein, Schneier and Barker provide an excellent review of different theoretical explanations for coercive persuasion within the context of communist indoctrination. They review four major theoretical orientations, which fall under the following general headings: 'Psycho-physiological theories', 'Learning theories', 'Psychoanalytic theories', and 'Socio-psychological theories'. The authors argue that each theoretical orientation provides an important contribution to the understanding of the 'unfreezing', 'changing' and 'refreezing' of the prisoners' beliefs, attitudes, values and behaviour during the indoctrination process. However, no one theory, or a group of theories with similar orientation, can satisfactorily explain all the mechanisms and processes involved. Nevertheless, each theory contributes in unique ways, and taken together the various theories provide a good understanding of the overall processes involved.

The most noteworthy psychophysiological theories, according to Schein, Schneier and Barker, are those of Hinkle and Wolff (1956), Hunter (1951, 1956) and Sargant (1957). The theory of Hinkle and Wolff is perhaps the most impressive. Here the psychological changes taking place in the prisoners are seen as the result of mental and physical exhaustion, brought about by a combination of psychological and physiological stress over a long period of time. The sources of the psychological stress included isolation, dependency, uncertainty and induction of guilt. Physiological stress resulted from fatigue, deprivation of sleep, hunger, pain and low room temperature. The mental and physical exhaustion made prisoners more receptive to influence because they were confused, their thinking had become uncritical and they were in a state of heightened suggestibility. Hinkle and Wolff argued that once the immediate pressure was relieved (i.e. the prisoner was released and free of the communist environment), then the effect of the conversion disappeared in a matter of weeks. However, they recognized that some prisoners' attitudes and behaviour appeared to be permanently changed.

Sargant (1957) relies heavily on Pavlov's experimental induction of neuroses in dogs as the basis for his explanation of coercive persuasion. Severe stress is viewed as producing cortical inhibition and emotional breakdown, which result in heightened susceptibility to suggestion. According to Sargant, similar outcome may arise in the case of other stressors, such as those associated with some therapeutic treatments (e.g. psychotherapy, drug treatment).

Hunter (1951, 1956) gives less formulated theoretical reasoning for the effects of coercive persuasion than Hinkle and Wolff and Sargant, but his theory, like those of the other authors, emphasizes the importance of the deleterious effects of mental and physical stress, which result in a state of confusion so that the prisoner is unable to distinguish between 'what is true and what is untrue' (Hunter, 1956, p. 67).

According to Schein, Schneier and Barker, the three theories discussed above emphasize, in terms of a basic mechanism, the enhanced suggestibility and uncritical thinking that commonly result from mental and physical stress and exhaustion. Furthermore, the three theories imply that the 'new' beliefs, attitudes, values and behaviour co-exist with the previous ones rather than becoming fully integrated into the personality of the prisoner. This has important implications because it suggests that attempts at indoctrination have no long-lasting or permanent psychological changes upon the prisoner once he is repatriated.

Schein, Schneier and Barker disagree that psycho–physiological stress necessarily produces a state of uncritical thinking and high suggestibility. They prefer to argue that severe stress facilitates 'unfreezing' and is an incentive to change. The problem with the Chinese interrogators, according to Schein, Schneier and Barker, was that they were not very clear or explicit about the ways in which the prisoners should change. In other words, there were no explicit or implicit suggestions given by the interrogators, although the prisoners were all subjected to immense pressure to change. They had to work out, by trial and error it seems, how precisely they were to change. It is possible that by not describing the ways in which prisoners should change the interrogators were ensuring that each prisoner chose the outcome most acceptable to him personally. Alternatively, the Chinese interrogators were deliberately trying to confuse and disorientate the prisoners.

Schein, Schneier and Barker argue that the psychophysiological theories help explain how 'unfreezing' was facilitated by severe stress and how resistance was weakened over time, but they do not at all address the processes of 'changing' and 'refreezing'. For these important processes we need to look at learning, psychoanalytic and sociopsychological theories.

The Schein, Schneier and Barker review of *learning theories* identifies three main approaches, all of which rely in varying degrees on Pavlovian conditioning. First, Meerloo (1954) presents a rather loosely defined and poorly argued theory about Chinese interrogators, where the behaviour of prisoners is said to be controlled by 'negative and positive stimuli' (p. 810). Negative stimuli included physical and mental pressure, fatigue and hunger, which resulted in mental submission. Positive stimuli for desired behaviour included food and verbal praise. Second, there is Sargant's (1957) extension of Pavlov's experimental theory of neuroses, which was discussed in relation to psycho–physiological theories of stress. Third, there is the work of Farber, Harlow and West (1957) and Santucci and Winokur (1955). Here the principles of Pavlovian and instrumental conditioning are combined and this is the learning approach favoured by Schein, Schneier and Barker. The argument is that anxiety and guilt are conditioned by threats and punishments and this eventually results in compliant behaviour as a way of reducing conflict. Once compliant behaviour occurs then it is selectively reinforced by the interrogators.

Schein, Schneier and Barker argue that *psychoanalytic* formulations of confessions obtained by Communists point to the importance of an authoritarian superego, in conjunction with a relatively weak ego, as a predisposition and proneness to being influenced easily by people in authority. Similarly, Meerloo's psychoanalytic formulations (1951, 1954) emphasize the importance of guilt. External pressures weaken the ego's ability to fight and cope with pressure, whilst dependency needs and childhood hostilities are re-activated by the prison environment and produce guilt, which acts as an internal pressure to confess.

Cunningham (1973) gives an excellent illustration of how unresolved childhood conflicts were identified and exploited by the Chinese. Each prisoner was required to write out a detailed autobiography of his or her childhood, from which psychological weaknesses and vulnerabilities were identified. These were subsequently used by the Chinese to create stress and induce feelings of guilt.

Schein, Schneier and Barker discuss a number of theories relevant to persuasive interrogation, which they believe fall under the general heading of *'sociopsychological theories'*. These include theories that focus on the self-concept and identity (Lifton, 1956), cognitive dissonance (Festinger, 1957), group pressure (Asch, 1951, 1952) and differences between 'internalization', 'identification' and 'compliance' (Kelman, 1958).

According to Schein, Schneier and Barker, changes in self-concept and identity are central to explaining 'the breaking point' and why prisoners' beliefs and values changed, but theories relying on this explanation (see e.g. Lifton, 1956) fail to specify how the change comes about. 'Breaking point' is viewed by Schein, Schneier and Barker as a psychological phenomenon in which self-concept is central and where prisoners can be trained to resist interrogative pressure (p. 233).

Festinger's (1957) theory of dissonance has implications for confessions because it postulates that it is the behavioural commitment of the confession that produces dissonance (i.e. a special type of conflict), which is in turn reduced by change in belief and attitudes. Schein, Schneier and Barker point out several limitations of dissonance theory when it is applied to coercive persuasion. For example, they view the theory as oversimplifying the thinking process, because changes in attitudes and beliefs may precede as well as follow a confession.

Early workers in the field of social influence did not make a clear conceptual or theoretical distinction between private acceptance of information and compliance (McCauley, 1989). The experimental work of Kelman (1958) indicated three distinct processes of social influence, which he labelled 'compliance', 'identification', and 'internalization'. Compliance was said to occur when people agreed with propositions without private acceptance for some instrumental gain (i.e. in order to gain a reward or avoid punishment). Internalization implied that people privately accepted the proposition offered and it became integrated into their belief system. Identification occurred when people accepted influence because they desired to emulate the agent of influence.

Schein, Schneier and Barker consider Kelman's work to be an important contribution to the understanding of coercive persuasion. Its main contribution is to highlight different mechanisms of change that lead to different types of outcome. The main problem seems to be that one does not know to what extent the three distinct processes may overlap or interact. For example, it is possible that compliance may lead to identification or internalization? Similarly, identification may lead to internalization or compliance.

THE CAUSES OF FALSE CONFESSIONS

What are the principal causes of false confession? According to Munsterberg (1908), who was the first psychologist to write on the topic, a false confession can be elicited when emotional shock distorts people's memory during interrogation. Munsterberg viewed a false confession very much as a normal phenomenon that was triggered by unusual circumstances.

Undoubtedly, there are a number of different causes, or indeed different combinations of factors, which depend upon the individual case (Gudjonsson, 1992b). However, Kennedy (1986) considers that 'over-zealousness' on the part of the police officer is the single most common cause. The process involves the police having some circumstantial piece of evidence connecting a person to the alleged crime. Being highly motivated to obtain results the police

> ...allow their suspicions to harden into certainty. Believing they are serving the best interests of justice, they then:
>
> 1. Try to browbeat the suspect into a confession.
> 2. Pressurize witnesses to say what they want them to say.
> 3. Suppress or ignore the evidence of other witnesses whose evidence is favourable to the accused.
> 4. 'Lose' documents such as timesheets that support the accused's alibi.

Kennedy's observation summarizes well the kinds of police procedural factor that can lead to wrongful conviction. These are consistent with the results from the descriptive studies discussed above with regard to miscarriages of justice.

Kennedy gives an excellent illustration of how the above process led to the wrongful conviction and subsequent imprisonment of Noel Fellows. Fellows was a former policeman who was working as a taxi-driver when he was arrested in 1970 for the murder of a 67-year-old debt-collector. Unfortunately for Fellows, his mother-in-law's name had been discovered in the dead man's collection book and a witness alleged that he had seen the victim get into a taxi on the day of his murder.

With these two flimsy pieces of evidence the police became convinced that Fellows was the murderer. He was subjected to intensive police interrogation for about six hours, during which he made no self-incriminating admissions. The police then 'persuaded' witnesses that Fellows had a grudge against the victim, whom Fellows had never met. The police then suppressed evidence that was favourable to Fellows and the taxi firm's records, which showed where Fellows was working at the time of the alleged murder, went 'missing'. As a result, it was not possible to corroborate Fellows' alibi.

Fellows was subsequently convicted of manslaughter and received a seven year prison sentence. He was released on parole after serving four years in prison for a crime he had never committed. Several years later the real murderer was apprehended and in July 1985 Fellows' conviction was quashed by the Court of Appeal.

What Kennedy's elegant framework does not broach are the kinds of psychological factor that can make some individuals susceptible to making a false confession. Although Fellows never confessed to the murder of the debt-collector, extracts from his book (Fellows, 1986) give an important illustration of the types of interrogation technique and psychological factor that can result in a false confession in vulnerable individuals.

> By this time, the adrenalin was flowing and I could feel the sensation of fear creeping upon me. *What on earth is happening?* I thought to myself. *They wouldn't invent things like this* (p. 15).
> The fear grew as Mounsey started to say things like, 'We know you've done it, lad. Why don't you get it off your chest? We know you didn't really mean to kill him.' As I continued to plead my innocence, he became more determined. He started shouting and banging his fist upon the table. By this time fear had totally engulfed me and I just broke down. I could not control my emotions. As I tried to fight the tears back, they just kept on flowing. Deep shock set in and I was inwardly fighting to get words out of my mouth (p. 15).
> Six hours of intense questioning and still they didn't believe a word I said. All I repeated throughout that time was that I had never met the man and that I had absolutely nothing to do with the offence. By now signs of tiredness and frustration appeared in both their faces and voices. The tension mounted and they became more irate. We had gone full circle and were back to the more aggressive style of injecting fear by shouting accusations and desk-banging with clenched fists. This approach certainly worked to raise the level of fear within me, but if you are innocent, how can you confess to something you haven't done (p. 18).

Undoubtedly, there are a number of different psychological reasons why people confess to crimes they have not committed. Based on observations of anecdotal cases reported in the literature, and psychological theories of attitude change, Kassin and Wrightsman (1985) and Wrightsman and Kassin (1993) suggest three psychologically distinct types of false confession. These they call the 'voluntary', the 'coerced–compliant' and the 'coerced–internalized' types respectively. Kassin and Wrightsman discuss these types as if they are mutually exclusive. As will be discussed below, I shall argue that in some cases there may be a certain overlap between two or more of these psychological types.

Voluntary False Confessions

Voluntary false confessions are offered by individuals without any external pressure from the police. Commonly these individuals go voluntarily to the police station and inform the police that they have committed the crime in question. They may have read about the crime in a newspaper or seen it reported on television. Alternatively, no crime may have been committed and the individual may be deliberately misleading the police, or believe mistakenly that he or she has committed a crime.

Kassin and Wrightsman (1985) give the following reasons why people voluntarily give a false confession.

1. *A morbid desire for notoriety*. That is, the individual has a pathological need to become infamous, even if it means having to face the prospect of punishment, including imprisonment. Kassin and Wrightsman use the fact that over 200 people confessed falsely to the famous Lindbergh kidnapping

as a good example of voluntary false confessions being the result of desire for notoriety.

2. *An unconscious need to expiate guilt over previous transgressions via self-punishment.* In my view, the guilt over previous transgression can relate to some imagined act as well as a real one. Furthermore, there is no reason to believe that the 'guilt' has invariably to be linked to some previous identifiable transgression. In fact, the feeling of guilt may be generalized rather than caused by specific transgression. For example, Gudjonsson and Roberts (1983) found, in their study of 'secondary psychopaths', that the subjects' poor self-concept and high trait anxiety were reflected in a constant feeling of guilt, regardless of whether or not they were reporting a dishonest act. In contrast, normal subjects only rated themselves as feeling guilty after they had violated some specific norms of behaviour. One implication of the findings is that some individuals have a high level of generalized guilt, which is not related to a specific transgression, and this may influence a range of their behaviours, including their need to volunteer a false confession.

3. *Inability to distinguish facts from fantasy.* Here people give a voluntary false confession because they are unable to differentiate between real events (i.e. events actually experienced) and events that originate in their thinking, imagination or planning. This may be associated with a breakdown in 'reality monitoring' (Johnson & Raye, 1981), which is normally associated with major psychiatric illness, such as schizophrenia, but it may be found in a mild form in normal every day behaviour (Cohen, Eysenck & Levoi, 1986).

4. *A desire to aid and protect the real criminal.* This is an important reason why people may volunteer a false confession. It is, in my view, most likely to occur in minor cases, but in rare instances it may also be found in major criminal cases, such as homicide. As pointed out by McCann (1998), confessions can by coerced by people other than police officers. Therefore, a false confession given to protect the real offender may not always be freely given (i.e. voluntary).

5. *The hope for a recommendation of leniency.* This motive for giving a voluntary false confession is not explained by Kassin and Wrightsman, and it seems illogical and improbable.

I would add a sixth category, a false confession given to take revenge on another person (see the case of Mr E in Chapter 9 and the case of Henry Lee Lucas, Chapter 21, in relation to false robbery confessions).

It is not known how often voluntary false confessions occur or how easily they are recognized by police officers. It is likely that the voluntary type of false confession is more easily recognized and discounted by police officers than confessions that arise from police coercion.

Coerced–Compliant False Confessions

The coerced–compliant type of false confession results from the pressures or coerciveness of the interrogation process. The suspect does not confess voluntarily, but comes to give in to the demands and pressures of the interrogators for some immediate instrumental gain. Kassin and Wrightsman (1985) define compliance in the context of this type of false confession

> ... as an overt, public acquiescence to a social influence attempt in order to achieve some immediate instrumental gain (p. 77).

In my experience, the perceived instrumental gain may include the following:

1. Being allowed to go home after confessing.
2. Bringing the interview to an end.
3. A means of coping with the demand characteristics, including the perceived pressure, of the situation
4. Avoidance of being locked up in police custody. This is likely to be particularly important in cases where people are severely phobic about being locked up in a police station, often in a small cell, and in cases of drug addicts who are motivated to expedite their release from custody to feed their drug habit.

The suspect's perceived immediate instrumental gain of confessing has mainly to do with an escape from a stressful or an intolerable situation. The suspect may be vaguely or fully aware of the potential consequences of making the self-incriminating confession, but the perceived immediate gains outweigh the perceived and uncertain long-term consequences. In addition, making a false self-incriminating admission or confession is perceived as more desirable in the short-term than the perceived 'punishment' of continued silence or denial. Suspects may naively believe that somehow the truth will come out later, or that their solicitor will be able to sort out their false confession.

Coerced–Internalized False Confessions

Coerced–internalized false confessions occur when suspects come to believe during police interviewing that they have committed the crime they are accused of, even though they have no actual memory of having committed the crime. Gudjonsson and MacKeith (1982) argue that this kind of false confession results from a 'memory distrust syndrome' (MDS), which can be defined as

> a condition where people develop profound distrust of their memory recollections, as a result of which they are particularly susceptible to relying on external cues and suggestions.

The MDS is associated with two kinds of distinct condition.

The first kind is where the suspect has no memory of the alleged offence, even if he or she committed it. This may be due to amnesia or alcohol induced memory problems (Gudjonsson, 1992a; Santtila, Alkiora, Ekholm & Niemi, 1999). In cases where suspects did not commit the crime they are accused of, they may have no clear memory of not having done so. In other words, these people have no clear recollection of what they were doing at the time the alleged offence was committed and come to believe that they must have committed the offence.

The second type of memory distrust syndrome relates to suspects who at the beginning of the police interview have clear recollection of not having committed the alleged offence, but because of subtle manipulative influences by the interrogator they gradually begin to distrust their own recollections and beliefs.

As recognized by Ofshe and Leo (1997a), the above conceptual framework makes two main distinctions. First, whether the false confession is initiated by the persons or elicited by the police (voluntary versus coerced). Second, whether the police pressure leads the suspect to confess for instrumental reasons or causes a change in the suspect's belief about his guilt or innocence (compliance versus internalization).

THEORETICAL IMPLICATIONS OF THE DIFFERENT TYPES OF FALSE CONFESSION

Several conclusions can be drawn about the nature and implications of voluntary false confessions. First, voluntary confessions, which are given because of 'morbid desire for notoriety', are probably best construed as a pathological attempt to enhance self-esteem. The basic assumption here is that these individuals are experiencing marked feelings of inadequacy and have a strong need for recognition, even if it means being identified and labelled as a 'criminal' and being punished for something they did not do. The most likely psychiatric diagnosis is personality disorder. In a related disorder, in one case study the voluntary false confessions in a 19-year-old woman were linked to a Munchausen syndrome and pseudologia fantastica (Abed, 1995).

People who confess in order to aid or protect the real criminal are undoubtedly least psychologically disturbed of all the voluntary confessors. The motive, in general, is unlikely to arise from mental illness or pathological feelings of inadequacy. Rather the person makes a decision, which indeed may be quite a rational decision, to volunteer a confession so that somebody else is spared the potential penal consequences of the crime committed (e.g. in the case of juveniles the younger ones may falsely confess to protect older ones from prosecution). This type of false confession does not always have to be given voluntarily. It can arise out of police interrogation where the person is a suspect in the case, but he or she realizes that unless a confession is made the real offender, who may be somebody close to them, is likely to be apprehended. Being faced with two undesirable alternatives the person chooses to make a false self-incriminating confession rather than chance the apprehension of the real offender.

A false confession which is given in an attempt to relieve guilt, whether generalized or concerned with some specific previous transgression, would be most likely to be associated with depressive symptoms or illness. However, a very small proportion of all depressed people appear to actually volunteer a confession to the police concerning a crime they have not committed. Probably important mediating variables, which will be illustrated by case reports in Chapter 9, are related to the depressed person's personality.

False voluntary confessions that arise because the person is unable to distinguish between fantasy and reality are most likely to arise in cases of mental illness, such as schizophrenia. Here the person's perceptions of reality are distorted and their thought processes are adversely affected. These people's false confessions result from a false belief without there necessarily being a strong feeling of guilt attached to the perceived criminal act. This type of false confession can occur without the presence of a major mental illness, as it did in the case of Andrew Evans (see Chapter 18).

Kassin and Wrightsman (1985) highlight two potentially important implications concerning differences between coerced–compliant and coerced–internalized false confessions. The first refers to the timing of the suspect's subsequent retraction of the confession. The other relates to the types of interrogation technique that are most likely to elicit compliant and internalized false confessions.

Coerced–compliant false confessors are likely to retract or withdraw their false confession as soon as the immediate pressures are over (e.g. when seen by a solicitor or a relative after being charged). Coerced–internalized false confessors, on the other hand, will typically only retract after they themselves have become convinced, or suspect, that they are innocent of the crime they are accused of. How long this takes depends on the individual case. In a case reported by Ofshe (1992), it took months before the defendant realized that he had not committed the crime of which he was accused. The critical issue is to what extent, if at all, the suspect's original memory for events becomes permanently distorted as the result of coercive and manipulative police interviewing.

Kassin and Wrightsman (1985) state that what is most concerning about coerced–internalized false confessions

> ... is that the suspect's memory of his or her own actions may be altered, making its original contents potentially irretrievable (p. 78).

If the internalized false confessor's memory is potentially permanently altered during police interrogation, as Kassin and Wrightsman argue, then the implications are very serious. That is, innocent people potentially remain permanently convinced that they have committed a crime of which in fact they are innocent. Gudjonsson and Lebegue (1989) provide some evidence that the original memory may not necessarily be as permanently distorted as Kassin and Wrightsman suggest. This is supported by the evidence of a number of cases discussed later in this book.

Ofshe (1989) also reports cases in which suspects were induced to make coerced–internalized false confessions that were repudiated as soon as the social environment that supported them was disturbed. The limited empirical evidence that is available suggests that coerced–internalized false confessions are believed when they are made but, like other externally generated perceptions, are highly unstable (Ofshe & Leo, 1997a, 1997b).

Kassin and Wrightsman discuss two separate processes whereby coerced–internalized false confessions can occur. One type of process involves 'a trance-like state of heightened suggestibility', similar to that found in hypnosis (Foster, 1969), whereas the other proposed process results from changes in 'self-perception' and relates to the classic work of Bem (1966) and Lepper (1982).

The precise factors that determine whether or not a false confession is going to become internalized are not fully understood. One powerful determining factor is probably the type of interrogation technique utilized by the interviewer.

Kassin and Wrightsman argue, on the basis of 'self-perception' theory (Lepper, 1982), that coerced–compliant false confessions are most likely to occur when 'powerful and highly salient techniques of social control' are utilized, whereas 'internalization is best achieved through more subtle, less coercive methods' (p. 77). Similar arguments have been put forward by Bem (1967) in relation to false confession.

Ofshe (1989) attempted to explore the process whereby people come to falsely believe, as the result of interrogation, that they have committed a serious crime for which they have no memory. He looked closely at four cases of coerced–internalized false confessors and stated:

> The four people whose interrogations are commented on here are victims of the unconscious use of the sorts of interrogation tactics commonly practised throughout the United States. All four displayed substantial belief change and, for varying periods of time, became convinced that they had committed the crimes of which they were accused. They each came to believe in their guilt and acted on this belief by confessing. They confessed despite having no memory of the crime that they had supposedly committed (p. 3).

Ofshe argues the primary mechanism consists of inducing sufficient self-doubt and confusion in the suspects' mind which permits the alteration in their perceptions of reality. This involves the interrogator successfully convincing the suspects of the following.

1. There is incontrovertible evidence that they committed the crime they are accused of, even though they have no recollection of it.
2. That there is a good and valid reason why they have no memory of having committed the crime.

The types of interrogation technique and tactic that appear to increase the likelihood of coerced–internalized false confessions are as follows.

1. The interrogator repeatedly states, with great confidence, his belief in the suspect's guilt.
2. The suspect is isolated from people who undermine or contradict the interrogator's premise of the suspect's guilt. In addition, information that contradicts the interrogator's premise is concealed from the suspect.
3. Typically there is lengthy interrogation and considerable emotional intensity.
4. The interrogator repeatedly claims that there is incontrovertible scientific proof of the suspect's guilt.
5. The suspect is repeatedly reminded about his or her previous memory problems or blackouts, when these exist. When these do not exist the

interrogator argues for the existence of a mental disorder that would explain the lack of memory for the crime (e.g. multiple personality, dissociation etc). These ploys tend to undermine the confidence that suspects have in their ability to accurately recall that they had not committed the alleged crime.
6. The interrogator demands that the suspect accepts his premises and explanations of the alleged crime.
7. The interrogator attempts to induce fear in the suspect's mind about the potential consequences of repeated denials. Ofshe maintains that the tactics of interrogation in which American interrogators are trained will render them able to produce the result without being aware that they are generating a false confession (Ofshe, 1989).

Not all of the above tactics and techniques are likely to be evident in every case of coerced–internalized false confession, but they are the types of factor that facilitate the process. What seems to happen is that these tactics and techniques make the suspect lose confidence in his memory, he or she becomes very confused about what is happening and as a result is unable critically and rationally to evaluate the predicament he or she is in.

The four individuals that comprise Ofshe's small study of coerced–internalized false confessors had all been assessed psychologically. None of them were considered mentally ill. Three personality factors were evident although not particularly extreme.

1. Good trust of people in authority.
2. Lack of self-confidence.
3. Heightened suggestibility.

Ofshe argues that these personality characteristics made the false confessors vulnerable to the influence of manipulative forms of interrogation. In his view, these vulnerabilities 'probably contributed most significantly to the speed with which the process of thought reform could be carried out' (p. 14). The implication is that suspects who are not in any significant way psychologically vulnerable at the beginning of the interrogation can make coerced–internalized confessions, provided they are interrogated for extensive periods of time and the 'relevant' techniques and tactics are used by interrogators.

My own experience of coerced–internalized false confessions supports Ofshe's findings, but I would add the following.

- It is specifically the lack of confidence in one's memory that is important. Even people with good memories may lack confidence in their memory, or the confidence that they have in their memory may be easily challenged and undermined by the interrogator.
- As far as suggestibility is concerned, it is having problems with *discrepancy detection* that is more important than *suggestibility per se*. It is the failure of people to differentiate between what is real memory and what is suggested to them that is important. In other words, they are unable to recognize when errors and misinformation are being introduced into their memory and belief system.

- It is important to distinguish between a *false belief* and a *false memory* in relation to internalized false confession (Gudjonsson, 1997b, 1997c). Internalized false confessors can be persuaded, or may have convinced themselves, that they have committed a crime without their developing a recollection of the offence. This is in my experience what typically happens and is supported by the work of Ofshe and Leo (1997a, 1997b).

Coerced–internalized false confessions are typically characterized by tentative expressions, such as 'I must have', 'I think I did', 'I probably committed this crime' (Ofshe & Leo, 1997a, 1997b).

Critique of the Kassin–Wrightsman Model

There is no doubt that the psychological model of Kassin and Wrightsman (1985) is very important in furthering our understanding of the nature of false confessions. I have also found the model helpful in forensic practice and research, in that it enables one to classify false confessions into meaningful psychological categories. The theoretical distinction between compliant and internalized false confessions is the single most important contribution of the model. The main problem that I have had with the model is that not all compliant and internalized false confessions are coerced. They may result from stress or pressure that does not involve coercion by the police. The term coercion is clearly over-inclusive in the model. The other problem is that those who make false confessions to protect someone else do not fit well into the model psychologically and should probably be classified into a separate group. The only way to overcome the former problem is to increase the number of categories of false confessions, as Ofshe and Leo (1997a) do, to change the term 'coercion' to a more appropriate term that encompasses most relevant types of false confession (e.g. 'pressured–internalized' and 'pressured–compliant' false confessions), or to leave out the word 'coerced' when there is no evidence of coercion. In forensic practice I use the Kassin–Wrightsman (1985) threefold typology, but leave out the word 'coerced' when there is no evidence of coercion.

McCann (1998) has developed a decision-making conceptual framework for identifying different types of confession, where confessions are defined according to different dimensions (e.g. retracted versus non-retracted, true versus false, voluntary versus coerced, legal culpability). McCann does not specifically criticize the Kassin–Wrightsman typology, but adds a third type of coerced confession, which he calls 'coerced–reactive false confessions'. This is defined as

> ....when an individual (who may or may not be a criminal suspect) confesses in order to avoid or escape some coercive action that arises out of a relationship with one or more individuals other than police (p. 449).

McCann gives as examples peer group pressure (e.g. threats of physical violence) and an actual case of a battered wife who was allegedly coerced into making a false confessions to the murder of her child as way of escaping violence from her husband.

Kassin (1998) is not in favour of McCann's suggestion of increasing the classification to incorporate the coerced–reactive false confession type. He recommends that that existing typology is maintained, but suggests the following options.

- That the threefold typology acknowledges that coercion can be exerted by non-custodial factors.
- An introduction of a bivariate scheme where a distinction is made between the *eliciting process* and the *source* of pressure (i.e. a 3 × 3 classification).

Davison and Forshaw (1993) have two main concerns about the Kassin–Wrightsman typology. First, they consider the distinction between voluntary and coerced confessions to be over-simplistic. For example, false confessions that result from an abnormal mental experience, such as delusions or hallucinations, cannot strictly speaking be considered to be fully voluntary and are very different from other voluntary false confessions, such as those who falsely confess to protect someone else, or because of the need for notoriety. Secondly, a person who has been persuaded to believe that he has committed a crime of which he is innocent is not necessarily being coerced into making a false confession. The police persuasion may be subtle and there may be no perception of threat. In addition, a compliant false confession may result from factors other than police coercion (e.g. the impaired rational decision-making of a heroin addict). In view of this argument, if one accepts the Kassin–Wrightsman typology, it would be necessary to broaden the meaning of the term 'coercion'.

Davison and Forshaw accept that there is a useful distinction to be made between false confessions that are believed by the confessor (i.e. internalized) and those not believed (i.e. compliant).

In view of the weaknesses in the conceptual framework of Wrightsman and Kassin, Davison and Forshaw present a philosophical model of confessions that focuses on three issues.

- The psychological processes involved (e.g. whether these relate to normal processes, such as owning up to what one has done, or abnormal ones, such as psychotic experiences, physical illness, or abnormal suggestibility and compliance).
- The degree of autonomy related to making the confession. Here the person must be able to make a rational decision. This involves having the mental capacity to formulate appropriate goals, establish priorities between goals and determine the best way of achieving them. The basic assumption in Ancient and Common Law is that a person who acts freely and rationally is unlikely to make self-damaging statements that are not true.
- The legal issue of admissibility. This relates to whether or not the circumstances surrounding making the confession were such 'that the individual lacked the capacity for autonomy' (p. 288), rendering the confession unreliable.

Davison and Forshaw (1993) argue that a suspect who fulfils the above criteria, but nevertheless makes a false confession (e.g. to protect someone else), is of little interest to psychiatrists. They are nevertheless an important group, which I believe is of interest to psychologists (Sigurdsson & Gudjonsson, 1996).

Ofshe and Leo (1997a, 1997b) express three main criticisms of the Kassin–Wrightsman typology.

1. True and false confessions involve similar underlying processes of the police interrogation. There is no need for a separate distinction between the processes involved.
2. The threefold typology fails to encompass the police-induced confessions that do not involve coercion (e.g. there may be no threats or inducements offered by the police). This criticism is similar to that identified by Davison and Forshaw (1993).
3. The classification misrepresents the concept of internalization. Internalization is a psychological process whereby people come to accept beliefs and values that are stable over time and across situations. Ofshe and Leo (1997b) argue that no such stability exists with regard to false confessions. In other words, the police persuasion is only *temporary* and the suspect is never fully convinced of the belief in his guilt. 'His inability to retrieve actual memories of the crime explains his inability to achieve complete certainty of his guilt. The tactic of claiming overwhelming evidence of culpability prevents him from remaining certain of his innocence' (p. 209).

In order to overcome the conceptual weaknesses in the threefold typology and build on it, Ofshe and Leo (1997a, 1997b) have developed their own classification of confessions, which they argue apply equally to true and false confessions.

THE OFSHE–LEO MODEL OF CONFESSIONS

The Ofshe–Leo classification of confessions is shown in Table 8.1. Here there are five levels of confessions, categorized into two groups: true or false. Each type of confession can be either true or false, depending on the circumstances of the individual case.

First, there are *voluntary* confessions. If true they are considered reliable, if false they are unreliable. Voluntary false confessions have already been extensively discussed in this chapter and it is difficult to see how they can be

Table 8.1. The Ofshe–Leo type of confession and its legal implications

Type of confession	True confession	False confession
1. Voluntary	Voluntary/reliable	Voluntary/unreliable
2. Stress–compliant	Involuntary/reliable	Involuntary/unreliable
3. Coerced–compliant	Involuntary/reliable	Involuntary/unreliable
4. Non-coerced–persuaded	Impossible	Voluntary/unreliable
5. Coerced–persuaded	Impossible	Involuntary/unreliable

conceptually combined in one group within the Ofshe–Leo (1997b) definition of voluntary confessions:

> Voluntary confessions arise either in the absence of accusatory interrogation or in response to the use of legally permissible interrogation tactics. When elicited in response to interrogation, the confession results from the manipulation of a suspect's perceptions of his situation and his desire to obtain a legally insignificant benefit (p. 210).

From the above definition it seems that Ofshe and Leo are referring to true voluntary confessions. Unfortunately, they do not give an indication of how the true and false voluntary confessions are distinguished psychologically; instead they go on to give reasons why people may give voluntary false confessions. It is confusing conceptually to classify voluntary true and voluntary false confessions into the same category. The same psychological process does not produce them.

Second, there are *stress–compliant* confessions, which again are either reliable or unreliable. These confessions are precipitated by excessive use of mental or physical stressors. This is distinct from 'classical coercion' (i.e. where there are usually threats and promises offered by the interviewer). The stress–compliant type of confession is defined as follows:

1. It 'is elicited in response to exceptionally strong use of the aversive stressors typically present in interrogations'.
2. It is given knowingly in order to escape from the intolerable pressure of the interrogation.

The above definition implies that the emphasis is on what the police intentionally do during interrogation to cause stress in the suspect in order to break down resistance. Ofshe and Leo argue that there are multiple stressors built into the custodial environment that exert pressure on the suspect to comply with the demands of the police for a confession. These include social isolation, perceptions of physical control by the police over the environment and the emotional intensity of the interrogation. During the interrogation the emphasis is on maximizing the suspect's level of stress by confronting him with 'incontrovertible' evidence of guilt, preventing the suspect from proclaiming his innocence, using leading questions and pointing out inconsistencies in his account of events. The style of interrogation is confrontational and overbearing. Psychologically vulnerable suspects (e.g. those who are suggestible, compliant, acquiescent and intellectually impaired) are thought to be least able to cope with this kind of pressure (see Clare & Gudjonsson, 1995).

The third group is labelled *coerced–compliant confessions*. Here the confession is elicited by classical coercive interrogation techniques that focus on threats and promises (i.e. the suspect makes a conscious decision to confess in order to avoid anticipated punishment and to gain some benefit). These interrogation techniques are used with the intention of overbearing the person's will. For this reason confessions that are identified as resulting from threats and promises are more likely to be excluded at trial than those used in the stress–compliant group.

Non-coerced persuaded confessions represent the fourth group. Here the suspect is *persuaded* by the police to believe that he has committed a crime of which he is innocent. The confession is likely to be

> temporary, unstable, situationally adaptive and endures only as long as the suspect accepts the interrogator's definition of the situation (Ofshe & Leo, 1997b, p. 215).

Ofshe and Leo argue that there are two kinds of persuasion.

- Those that are produced *solely* by psychological manipulation.
- Those that also involve a significant degree of coercion.

If only the former kind of persuasion is involved then it is classified as being of the *non-coerced–persuaded* type and it should be considered to be unreliable in spite of its being voluntary. If classical coercion is involved then the confession is classified as *coerced–persuaded* (this is the fifth group in Table 8.1).

In both types of persuasion case the mechanism involves a mental confusion, doubts in the suspect's memory and temporary persuasion of his guilt. This mental state, which amounts to a memory distrust syndrome, is achieved by the police officer repeatedly challenging and undermining the suspect's confidence in his memory and innocence, and providing a seemingly plausible explanation for the lack of memory.

Comments

Ofshe and Leo (1997b) provide a helpful case illustration of the different types of 'false confession', which provides a good insight into their social psychological decision-making model. The main advantage that Ofshe and Leo have over Kassin and Wrightsman is that they appear to have had more direct involvement in evaluating cases of disputed confessions before constructing the classification system. This has clearly influenced their conceptualization. The original Kassin–Wrightsman framework was principally developed from historical anecdotes and cases (Kassin, 1998). This work has now been complemented by experimental studies, which have furthered our understanding of police interrogations and false confessions (Kassin & Fong, 1999; Kassin & Kiechel, 1996; Kassin & McNall, 1991).

What are the strengths and weaknesses of the Ofshe–Leo model? The main strengths are twofold. First, the model highlights the unstable and temporary nature of the change in the suspect's belief system. This is important, because it is doubtful that the suspect's belief in his guilt is ever fully or properly 'internalized' in relation to police-induced confessions (i.e. the conviction is in my experience not held with complete conviction). The common pattern is for suspects to come to believe that they *may* or *probably* did commit the crime, but there always appears to be an element of doubt in their mind about their involvement in the crime. This will be illustrated by case examples in other chapters in this book. Whether this justifies changing the word 'internalized' to 'persuaded' is unclear. I remain unconvinced that it is necessary to change the term internalization to persuasion. The term persuasion can also be misleading, because it does not exclusively refer to a change in the person's belief system (Corsini, 1999). From an interrogator's perspective, the purpose of using persuasion is to move the suspect from a position of a denial to one of confession (Inbau et al., 2001). It does not necessarily imply that the suspect comes to believe that he committed the offence of which he is accused. Of course, he may at the time hold the belief that the only way out of his predicament is to make a false confession.

Secondly, Ofshe and Leo make an important distinction between coerced and non-coerced confessions, a distinction of which Kassin (1998) appears to approve as a refinement of his model with Wrightsman. Ofshe and Leo use the classical meaning of the term coercion as determined in American legal judgments, which makes the psychological classification of different types of confession directly applicable to legal practice. American expert witnesses will undoubtedly find this classification helpful. The terms coercion and voluntariness, as typically used legally in the USA, incorporate two main principal components: *threats* and *promises*. The former refers to threats of punishment of some kind unless there is a confession (e.g. of physical violence to the suspect or his family, or a harsher sentence, sometimes including a threat of the death penalty). Promises are used as inducements to obtain a confession. These may include a promise that bail will be granted, that there will be no prosecution, that the suspect will be allowed to go to hospital rather than prison if convicted or that there will be a more lenient sentence (Ofshe & Leo, 1997a, 1997b; Leo, 2001a).

Inbau et al. (2001) accept the importance of inducements in eliciting a confession, but differentiate between permissible and non-permissible inducements:

> The interrogation process must provide some incentive or motivation for these suspects to choose to tell the truth. There are legally permissible incentives to persuade a suspect to confess and others that are not permissible because they are apt to cause an innocent person to confess (p. 413).

The experimental work of Kassin and McNall (1991) demonstrates that interviewers may effectively communicate both threats and promises subtly and indirectly (i.e. by the use of 'pragmatic implication'). In other words, the threats and promises need not be direct or explicit to impact on the suspect's decision-making. This is what appears to have happened once police interrogation techniques moved away from the use of the 'third degree' in the 1940s to psychological manipulation and trickery (Ofshe & Leo, 1997a).

What are the limitations of the Ofshe–Leo classification and theoretical framework? First, it is important to recognize that the Ofshe–Leo model focuses on police interrogative pressure and police-induced confessions. Little attention is paid to the impact of the custodial environment itself (e.g. being locked up and detained), non-police coercion (e.g. being coerced by a spouse or a peer to confess) or psychological vulnerabilities. Police interrogative pressure, which is used to break down resistance, forms an inherent part of the *stress–compliant*, *coerced–compliant*, *non-coerced–persuaded*, and *coerced–persuaded* confession groups. As was discussed in Chapters 2–4, the great majority of confessions in Britain do not involve a shift from a denial to admission. By the time suspects enter the interrogation room most have probably already decided whether they are going make a confession or denial. It is not clear whether or not this position is different in the USA. This should be carefully studied in future research. This readiness to confess is undoubtedly facilitated by suspects' perception of the likely evidence against them, combined with their own internal need to confess, once they are at the police station. Within the Ofshe–Leo model this group must fall within the *voluntary* confession group. Similarly, a heroin addict who is withdrawing from drugs and wants to be released from custody, but is not pressured directly by the police during interrogation, is presumably giving a voluntary confession according to the Ofshe–Leo model.

The model is therefore of limited value in understanding confessions that are voluntarily given, where a confession results from custodial confinement rather than the interrogation pressure *per se*, or where the coercion to confess occurs outside a police context.

There are some conceptual issues that need to be addressed. There appear to be problems with the ways in which the terms 'coercion', 'voluntary' and 'reliable' are used. In particular, the terms 'voluntary' and 'reliable' are not clearly defined and the relationship between the three terms, and the ways in which they differ and overlap, are not discussed. This could be improved in future work and incorporated into the Ofshe–Leo model.

From a psychological perspective Ofshe and Leo are restrictive in their use of the term coercion and more or less restrict it to evidence of threats and promises. They make a reference to 'other classically coercive interrogation techniques' (1997b, p. 219), but do not specify what these are. This is undoubtedly due to their desire to avoid the over-inclusive use of the term, as found in the Kassin–Wrightsman threefold typology, and their need to follow the necessary legal usage of the term as documented in American legal judgments. It appears as if the Ofshe–Leo social–psychological model has been forced into a convenient legal framework stipulated by American case law.

It could be argued that coercion can occur without the presence of threats and promises. Indeed, from a psychological perspective, coercion refers to a situation where a person is *compelled* or *forced* to perform acts (e.g. make a confession), which are against his will or wishes. Intimidation, relentless pressure (including repeated robust challenges) and psychological manipulation are overbearing techniques, which when extreme are highly coercive in nature (Pearse & Gudjonsson, 1999).

In their article, Ofshe and Leo (1997b) appear to use the term 'voluntary' in two different ways, seemingly psychologically and legally respectively. As seen in Table 8.1, it first relates to the type of confession (i.e. whether or not it was elicited by the police or volunteered by somebody who may not necessarily have been a suspect—a psychological classification), and second in terms of whether or not the confession was coerced (a legal classification). This leads to a further confusion. Why is a non-coerced–persuaded false confession classified as being 'voluntary/unreliable', whereas a stress–compliant false confession is rated as 'involuntary/unreliable'? Although these two different types of false confession are probably elicited by somewhat different interrogation techniques and psychological vulnerabilities, both are similar in that intimidation, robust challenges and psychological manipulation may have been involved.

Ofshe and Leo argue strongly for keeping true and false confessions within the same decision-making model. I am not convinced by their argument. I think the conceptualization of the two types of confession should be kept apart under their fivefold typology, because combining them into one model is simplistic. For example, how could voluntary true and false confessions, respectively, be construed within the same conceptual framework considering the Ofshe–Leo definition of voluntary confessions? The number of models of true confessions discussed in Chapter 5 illustrates the complexity of the factors and processes involved. The psychological processes involved in making true and false confessions are undoubtedly different and require a different model of understanding. The only way that true and false confessions can be incorporated into one model is to focus specifically on the antecedents (social, emotional, cognitive, situational and physiological) and consequences (immediate and long-term) associated with the confession, as I have done in my cognitive–behavioural model of confessions (see Chapter 5). An example of how my model can be applied to a real life case of proven false confession is provided by Gudjonsson and MacKeith (1994).

If Ofshe and Leo were to focus exclusively on police-induced confessions and the process of the interrogation, then their model would be helpful in explaining the techniques and processes that break down suspects' resistance and move them from a position of a denial to a confession. One limitation is that the model is only helpful in distinguishing between true and false confessions after the post-admission statement is made. A mere admission, 'Yes I did it', would be insufficient for validating the confession. True and false confessions are construed as arising out of similar psychological processes. Ofshe and Leo recognize that there are important differences between guilty and innocent suspects in their perceptions and thinking about the immediate situation, in their knowledge about the offence and in decision-making. However, they argue that there is no reliable difference in the demeanour of the two groups and

> Although indicators of a suspect's true state of innocence or guilt can be identified in the suspect's conduct in response to the interrogator's tactics, the difference between the guilty and the innocent *only becomes reliably and objectively observable* after each has made the decision to confess. The differences between the suspect's true state of guilt or innocence can only be detected with substantial confidence by analysing the *contents* of their respective confession statements—the statement which follows the person's admission of involvement (Ofshe & Leo, 1997b, p. 197).

DIFFERENCES BETWEEN TRUE AND FALSE CONFESSIONS

How can true confessions be differentiated from false confessions? In the absence of good forensic, eyewitness or alibi evidence, or a solid confession from somebody else, which essentially proves or disproves the veracity of the confession, it is typically very difficult to establish the ground or historical truth of the confession. In Part II I shall discuss in detail the psychological evaluation of cases of disputed confession and how confession evidence is applied to legal cases in England and the USA. This is followed up in Parts III and IV with the presentation of actual cases. It will be shown that the focus of the psychological evaluation is typically on the reliability and voluntariness of the confession rather than its truthfulness. The only exception to this rule was the unusual mandate in the Norwegian case discussed in Chapter 23.

The psychological evaluation of a given case is normally based on a comprehensive assessment of the defendant and the identification of relevant strengths and vulnerabilities, the circumstances and nature of the relevant custodial factors involved, the tactics and techniques used during the interrogation and the content of the post-admission statement. No psychological technique is available that will demonstrate with complete certainty the truthfulness of the confession. What the psychological evaluation is sometimes able to do is to identify psychological vulnerabilities or mental health problems, which, when placed in the context of the totality of the circumstances in the case, cast serious doubts on the reliability or trustworthiness of the confession. Each case must be considered on its own merit.

The use of the polygraph in eliciting and evaluating the truthfulness of a confession was discussed in detail in the *Psychology of Interrogations, Confessions and Testimony* (Gudjonsson, 1992a) and will not be discussed further in this book.

Whereas Inbau, Reid and Buckley (1986) ignored the phenomenon of false confession, in the fourth edition of the book Inbau *et al.* (2001) provide a chapter on how to distinguish between true and false confessions. This chapter provides some valuable information and is a step in the right direction, although these authors' familiarity with the literature on false confession appears limited, and the understanding of the psychological processes involved in false confessions is in parts not sophisticated. The main limitation of their discussion is the reluctance to accept that false confessions can and do occur without overt physical abuse by police officers and in the absence of serious mental disorder. The general impression one is left with after reading their chapter is that the authors reluctantly accept that false confessions do occur and then minimize the frequency with which they occur and the important role of police manipulation in eliciting such confessions. The most valuable points that Inbau *et al.* make in their chapter on false confessions are as follows.

- Confessions of people who voluntarily attend the police station and turn themselves in should be viewed with caution. The motive and reasoning given for confessing without being suspected of the crime will need to be assessed. When there is good corroboration for the details given in the confession, and when the person had previously confessed to the crime to relative or a friend, this supports the validity of the confession. As discussed earlier in this chapter, people do sometimes go the police station to confess in order to protect the real culprit or if they are under pressure from the real culprit to 'take the case'. Nevertheless, such voluntary confessions may well be true and this possibility should not be overlooked. I have come across genuine cases of truthful confessions to serious offences, such as murder, where the offender needed to 'get the offence off his chest' by confessing to it, even several years afterwards.
- The confession should be viewed with caution when it lacks essential details and corroboration, but it will need to be considered within the context of the

suspect's likely motivation. Is it a reflection of lack of genuine knowledge about the offence or a lack of motivation or ability to reveal information?
- Denial of certain parts of the offence is common and should not be regarded as evidence that the confession is false. It could be due to genuine memory problems or reluctance of the suspect to reveal the full details of the offence.
- The timing of the retraction is important; late retractions are viewed with suspicion (this is a complex issue, which is addressed in detail in Chapter 12).
- The defendant's explanation for having allegedly made a false confession is an important factor in determining the confession's validity. The reasons given need to be carefully evaluated, although Inbau et al. do not provide an objective basis for doing this.

Ofshe and Leo (1997a, 1997b) rightly place a great deal of importance on the content of the post-admission statement as a way of discriminating between true and false confessions. Unfortunately, as discussed earlier in this chapter, there are various sources of potential contamination that may not be identified unless all the police interviews were properly recorded. In many cases involving false confession, the record of interviews is too incomplete to properly analyse the significance of the post-admission statement. A proper record is essential for this to be a valuable method of analysis.

Only one study has investigated empirically the differences between true and false confessions using a within-subject design. Using the revised Gudjonsson Confession Questionnaire (GCQ-R), Sigurdsson and Gudjonsson (1996) compared among 51 prison inmates the factor scores relating to a false confession and a true confession that they had made to the police. The findings indicated that when making the false confession suspects had experienced far more police pressure and less internal pressure to confess than when making a confession to a crime they had committed. The implication is that making a false confession is largely associated with police pressure and the greater the pressure the more likely suspects are to make a false confession, but this does also depend on the nature of the false confession.

The reporting of police pressure was lowest where suspects were falsely confessing in order to protect somebody else. They also reported less regret about having made the false confession and offered less resistance during the interrogation than with other types of false confession. The argument put forward by Ofshe and Leo that the quality of the post-admission statement is the best discriminator between true and false confessions is problematic with these kinds of false confession, because the confessor often had good knowledge about the crime from their peer or friend.

Two significant differences on the GCQ-R emerged between compliant and internalized false confessors. First, internalized false confessors reported experiencing greater *internal pressure* to confess during the interrogation than compliant false confessors, including experiencing a greater feeling of guilt about the offence. This appears to relate to their coming to believe during the interrogation that they had committed the offence of which they were accused.

Secondly, the internalized false confessors scored higher than the compliant false confessors on a *drug intoxication* factor. This suggests that being under the influence of alcohol or drugs at the time of the alleged offence, or during the police interrogation, makes suspects more susceptible to believing that they have committed an offence of which they are innocent. This has important theoretical and practical implications.

A PROPOSED MODIFIED FRAMEWORK

There are two ways of overcoming the Ofshe–Leo (1997a) criticism of the three-fold typology of Kassin and Wrightsman. One approach is to increase the number of categories, as done by Ofshe and Leo. The other approach is to change the word *coerced* to a broader terminology, such as *pressured*, or to delete its use altogether unless there is clear evidence of coercion. In practice, what I have done to overcome this problem is to delete the term coercion when it does not apply and refer to cases as falling either into *internalized* false confessions or *compliant* false confessions. My preference is to keep the threefold typology, and unless there is clear evidence of coercion to refer to cases as either *pressured–internalized* or *pressured–compliant*. The word *pressured* implies that there is some external pressure on the person to confess. This involves stress associated with the custodial confinement (e.g. fear of being detained in custody or in a small cell, inability to sleep while in police custody and excessive tiredness, social isolation, withdrawal symptoms from drugs or alcohol) and the nature of the interrogation techniques used (e.g. challenges, intimidation, psychological manipulation). Even when the confession results from external pressure there may also be an element of internal pressure to confess falsely. For example, a suspect who has been persuaded that he committed a criminal act of which had he is innocent and has no memory may experience feelings of remorse, which provides a partial explanation for the false confession (Sigurdsson & Gudjonsson, 1996).

The additional problem with the Kassin–Wrightsman model is that there is no classification as to the source of the pressure placed upon the person to make a false confession. I propose a slightly modified version of the Kassin–Wrightsman typology, along the lines recommend by Kassin (1998). This comprises a bivariate classification system that distinguishes between the three types of false confession (i.e. voluntary, pressured–compliant and pressured–internalized) and categorizes the source of pressure (i.e. internal, custodial, non-custodial). The modified model that I recommend is presented in Table 8.2, and it replaces the word coerced with the word pressured.

Table 8.2. Proposed framework for classifying false confessions

Type of false confession	Source of pressure
1. Voluntary	Internal
2. Pressured–internalized	Custodial–non-custodial
3. Pressured–compliant	Custodial–non-custodial

According to this model, there are three sources of pressure involved in false confessions, referred to as *internal, custodial* and *non-custodial*. Internal pressure refers to the person having a psychological need to confess falsely. This can be caused by the person having either a delusional or a mistaken belief that he has committed a crime of which he is innocent, the need for a sense of notoriety, as an attempt to gain relief for a misplaced feeling of guilt, the need to protect a significant other or the desire to take revenge on some other person.

Custodial pressure implies being interrogated by the police. Other governmental agencies also have powers of arrest and detention and interrogate people, including customs and immigration officials and the security services. Non-custodial pressure includes persons other than the police pressuring or coercing a confession from an innocent person (e.g. a peer, a spouse, a cell mate in prison and undercover police officers).

RECOVERED MEMORY AND FALSE CONFESSION

Much has been written in recent years about the phenomenon of 'recovered memories' of childhood sexual abuse (see e.g. Brandon, Boakes, Glaser & Green, 1998; Davies & Dalgleish, 2001; Gudjonsson 1997b, 1997c; Leo, 1997; Loftus & Ketcham, 1994; Ofshe & Watters, 1994; Pendergrast, 1995; Pope & Brown, 1996). According to Gudjonsson (1997b),

> A typical case involves a well-educated female in her thirties who has attended therapy for some psychological problem, such as depression or eating disorder. During therapy the patient reveals that she was sexually abused by her father many years previously, but the memory for the abuse was 'repressed' until it was 'recovered' during therapy (p. 4).

When recovered memories can be shown to be false they are linked to the term 'false memory syndrome' (Rivera, 1997).

The assumption that is commonly made about recovered memories is that they are caused, or at least facilitated, by suggestions from therapists (e.g. Leo, 1997; Ofshe & Watters, 1994). While accepting that this is probably often the case, I have come across recovered memory cases where the *belief* and *memory* concerning the abuse appeared to be internally motivated and generated rather than being the result of suggestion during therapy. There is empirical evidence to support this view (Ost, Costall & Bull, 2001). The belief of abuse may sometimes serve a psychological function, such as providing an apparent explanation for the accuser's psychological problems. It is also important to recognize that not everybody who develops a false belief of abuse will be able to recall any instances of abuse (Gudjonsson, 1997b, 1997c; Ost, Costall & Bull, 2001).

Gudjonsson (1997c) argues that a false belief may be an important precursor for the development of a false memory. A false belief and a false memory are probably elicited by different psychological mechanisms and processes. The development of a false belief does not depend greatly on memory ability and it is probably more related to lack of confidence in one's memory. In contrast, a false memory is highly dependent on the individual being able to create or retrieve misinformation.

Imagination plays an important role in producing a false belief and a false memory (Loftus, 2001). For example, Loftus and her colleagues have shown that asking people to imagine that they had experienced a made-up event increased significantly the likelihood that the person subsequently believed that the event had taken place. This increased confidence that an event had taken place after having been instructed to imagine the event has been named 'imagination inflation' (Garry, Manning, Loftus & Sherman, 1996). There is evidence that individual differences are important in imagination inflation. What are the factors that make people susceptible to imagination inflation? Two different factors have been proposed (Loftus, 2001). First, memory problems and difficulties with reality monitoring (Heaps & Nash, 1999; Paddock *et al.*, 1998). Second, ability to produce vivid imagery (Horselenberg, Merckelbach, Muris & Rassin, 2000).

On the basis of individual case studies (see for example Chapters 18 and 23), I propose a third factor: namely distrust of one's memory. As discussed earlier in this chapter, Gudjonsson and MacKeith (1982) proposed the term 'memory distrust syndrome' to explain this phenomenon. This group is not confined to persons with poor memories, although persons prone to memory problems would be particularly susceptible to this syndrome. Individuals with reasonable memories may lack confidence in their memory, or the confidence they have in their memory may be undermined when the recollection is challenged by others. Confidence in one's memory, although related to the complexity of the task attempted as well as memory skills, is very flexible and may deteriorate following demanding questioning (Saucier & Gaudette, 2000).

Most of the studies carried out into imagination inflation have shown a change in belief rather than episodic recollection (Loftus, 2001). In one experiment looking at both a false belief and a false memory concerning an event that allegedly took place before the age of three, in about half of the cases the altered belief was accompanied by 'memories' of the event (Mazzoni, Loftus, Seitz & Lynn, 1999). The factors that determine whether or not a 'memory' trace accompanies the altered belief are poorly understood. One possible factor seems to be the number of imaginations used in the experiment (Goff & Roediger, 1998); as the number of imaginations increased the likelihood was greater that the participants reported the actions suggested earlier in the experiment.

Recovered memories are by their nature potentially unreliable and the English courts are reluctant to accepted unsubstantiated allegations based on recovered memories (Gudjonsson, 1997d). Lewis and Mullis (1999) have reviewed the legal problems involved in the prosecution of these cases and provide important guidelines about how such evidence should be evaluated in court. Lewis and Mullis present four legal options, referred to as 'automatic exclusion' 'pre-trial or *voire dire* reliability assessment', 'the identification approach' and 'testimony admissible'. In view of the absence of scientific consensus about the reliability of recovered memories (see Davies & Dalgleish, 2001, for a detailed review of the issues and controversy), Lewis and Mullis conclude that the best approach is that analogous to identification cases, where there is a requirement for supporting evidence in order for a conviction to stand.

Several authors have compared recovered memories with the phenomena of false confession and suggested certain similarities between the two types of case (Brown, 1997; Gudjonsson, 1997b, 1997c; Kassin, 1997; Kopelman & Morton, 2001; Ost, 2000; Ost, Costall & Bull, 2001). Kassin (1997) argues that recovered memories of childhood sexual abuse are a 'close cousin' of internalized false confession. Both types of case share two characteristics. First, psychological vulnerability, that is, a person 'whose memory is malleable by virtue of his or her youth, naivety, lack of intelligence, stress, fatigue, alcohol, or drug use' (p. 301). Second, the presentation of false evidence by persons in a position of authority, with the police being the authority figure in cases of false confessions, and the therapist in cases of recovered memory.

Ost, Costall and Bull (2001) found that all three types of false confession—voluntary, coerced–compliant and coerced–internalized—were found among recovered memory retractors. It is easy to see how a breakdown in reality monitoring among some voluntary and coerced–internalized false confessors resemble recovered memory cases, but the analogy with the coerced–compliant type of false confession is theoretically unsound. It is likely that the three persons classified by Ost, Costall and Bull as 'coerced–compliant false confessors' involved cases where there had been pressure from a third party to admit to childhood sexual abuse without his or her genuinely believing that abuse had taken place. The basis on which three persons were classified as coerced–compliant false confessors is not clear from the article, but it seems to be based on respondents reporting 'retracting their claims as soon as they had escaped the immediate stressful context'.

How do recovered memory cases of childhood sexual abuse differ from false confession cases? They differ in a number of ways.

- *The context*. The context is different: whereas false confessions typically occur in the context of police interrogation, the reporting of abuse in recovered memory cases often occurs during therapy.
- *Perpetrator versus victim*. The nature of the offence reported in cases of false confession involves the person confessing to something he or she has done. In contrast, cases of childhood sexual abuse the memory recovered typically involves the person being presented as a victim rather than a perpetrator, although the victim may also be pressured into the latter role, for example, in cases of alleged satanic abuse (Gudjonsson, 1997b). Cases of recovered memories have also been reported among alleged perpetrators (e.g. Gudjonsson, Kopelman & MacKeith, 1999; Ofshe & Watters, 1994).
- *Belief versus memory*. It will become evident in subsequent chapters that with internalized false confessions the person typically only presents a belief of having committed the offence and is often unable to produce or visualize any memories of the offence. In cases of recovered memories the accuser is often able to produce a very vivid 'memory' of the alleged abuse. This may well be related to the extent to which the belief and memory are internally

generated rather than resulting from suggestion or pressure from external sources (e.g. the police, therapist, family members).
- *Internally versus externally generated beliefs and memories.* In cases of false confession it is often easy to trace the external pressure that resulted in the person making a false confession. In some cases of recovered memory of childhood sexual abuse the belief and memory concerning the abuse appear to have been internally generated (i.e. without external suggestion). Confabulation may be more important in relation to recovered memories than suggestibility (Gudjonsson, 1997c).
- *Psychological vulnerability.* The psychological vulnerabilities associated with recovered memories of childhood sexual abuse are likely to be different to those found in cases of false confessions. Cases of recovered memories, unlike the typical cases of false confessions, often involve people from a good educational background, whose intellectual and memory functioning are reasonable (Gudjonsson, 1997b, 1997e) and there is no evidence that they are unduly suggestible (Gudjonsson, 1997c; Leavitt, 1997). Interestingly, findings of good intelligence and memory, and low suggestibility, have been found among children who claim memories of previous life existence (see Chapter 14 for details of the findings in relation to suggestibility).

CONCLUSIONS

Theories derived from communist interrogation and indoctrination are relevant to false confessions within the context of police interrogation. The greatest relevance is to the understanding and process of internalized false confessions. Schein, Schneier and Barker classify the various theories of persuasive interrogation under the general heading of *sociopsychological theories*. The basic mechanism involves enhanced suggestibility and uncritical thinking, which results from the mental and physical stress associated with the interrogation and confinement. Most importantly, the indoctrination of 'new' beliefs co-exists with previous beliefs rather than resulting in permanent cognitive and personality changes.

Kassin and Wrightsman (1985) have identified three distinct types of false confession, which are referred to as 'voluntary', 'coerced–compliant' and 'coerced–internalized' false confessions. Each type has a distinctive set of antecedents, conditions and psychological consequences. Much of the early knowledge about the psychology of 'coerced' false confessions came from research into attitude change within the field of social psychology. Of particular importance is the extensive work that has been carried out into coercive persuasion among communist interrogators. This has provided valuable empirical findings, which have resulted in extensive theoretical formulations and developments.

Ofshe and Leo (1997b) have provided a detailed critical review of the Kassin–Wrightsman model of false confessions. They propose a modified five level model, which distinguishes between coerced and non-coerced compliant and persuaded confessions. The model, as presented by Ofshe and Leo, applies to both true and false confessions. This is a conceptual weakness in the model, particularly in relation to voluntary confessions. I have provided a detailed critique of the Ofshe–Leo model and propose a slightly refined version of the Kassin–Wrightsman original model. I recommend two changes. First, the term *coerced* should be substituted by the term *pressured*. This overcomes problems related to legal definitions and applications of the term coercion, which are not necessarily consistently used within or across countries. Secondly, as recommended by Kassin (1998), I propose a bivariate classification system that distinguishes between the three types of false confession (i.e. voluntary, compliant and internalized) and categorizes the source of pressure (i.e. internal, custodial and non-custodial).

CHAPTER 9

The Psychology of False Confession: Case Examples

In this chapter the different psychological types of false confession are discussed by giving case examples for each type. I shall be using the bivariate classification system I proposed in Chapter 8. It distinguishes between the three types of false confession (i.e. voluntary, pressured–compliant and pressured–internalized) and categorizes the source of pressure (i.e. internal, custodial, non-custodial).

Some of the cases provided were assessed in detail by my interviewing the people concerned. Other cases have been obtained from colleagues or from literature reviews. The cases chosen for inclusion represent examples of false confessions of different types. I have also assessed many other cases where there was serious doubt about the trustworthiness of the confession. These will be discussed in Parts III and IV of the book.

Some sceptical readers may believe that not all the cases presented in this chapter have been proven innocent. This is a perfectly reasonable position to take. The reality is that 100% proof for a defendant's innocence, in cases of retracted confession, is very rare and one is often dealing with cases where some 'new evidence' throws serious doubts on the defendant's guilt. It seems that many people believe that normal individuals would never confess to a serious crime during police interrogation, when it is so blatantly against their self-interest. The implicit assumption is that people always act in a self-serving way. In reality this is often not the case. For example, when placed under pressure, many individuals are more likely to serve their immediate self-interests than their long-term ones, even though the former may be to their eventual detriment. The fact is that some people who are not obviously mentally ill or learning disabled do confess falsely to serious crimes and are consequently wrongfully convicted. Greater awareness of this is an important step forward in achieving justice. Scepticism about retracted confessions is often justified, but when it is not evaluated with an open-minded attitude, as is often the case, then our system of justice is seriously undermined. The opposite position is equally undesirable. Accepting uncritically all those in prison who persistently insist that they are innocent would bring the criminal justice system to a halt.

VOLUNTARY FALSE CONFESSIONS

Four case illustrations are given about voluntary false confession. All resulted from internally generated pressure. These case illustrations are not intended to provide examples of all possible types of voluntary false confession. Rather they highlight important differences in the nature of false confessions between three clinical conditions: schizophrenia, depression and personality disorder. The case presented with regard to personality disorder is psychologically the most complicated one, because the false confessions made seemed to comprise three overlapping features, *loss of reality testing, an element of depression* and *a need for notoriety*.

It was mentioned in Chapter 8 that schizophrenic patients have been known to falsely confess to a crime as a consequence of their mental state, which involves a loss of reality-testing, and hence their inability to distinguish between reality and their own distorted thought processes. Another type of voluntary false confession comes from the nosological group of those suffering from psychotic depression. The late Professor Lionel Haward (personal communication) argued that false confessions made by schizophrenic and depressed people originate from very different processes of psychopathology, which lead to the following hypotheses.

1. Schizophrenic patients have their false confession evoked by external contemporary events while those of depressed patients are internally determined and emerge spontaneously.
2. The false confession of the depressed patient is precipitated by deep-seated and long-standing feelings of guilt. The guilt is generated by past events and experiences and is projected onto some external event, which becomes the focus for the patient's guilt.
3. The paranoid persecutions of the depressed patient differ from those of the paranoid schizophrenic by being accusatorial, that is, the delusions of the depressed patient interpret the imagined persecution as stemming from the patient's past behaviour towards the persecutors. The locus of guilt is thus kept firmly within the patient and normally prevents any aggression from being directed outwards against others. This may explain why depressed patients commonly attempt suicide (i.e. self-directed aggression) whereas the paranoid schizophrenic patient is more outwardly aggressive.

Professor Haward provided me with two cases to illustrate these salient differences between the false confession of the schizophrenic and depressed patients.

Miss S—Paranoid Schizophrenia

Miss S, a middle-aged spinster, had been diagnosed as suffering from paranoid schizophrenia. One day she was admitted to hospital following a number of disturbances of the peace in which the patient accused neighbours of conspiring against her. Her disturbed behaviour subsided under heavy sedation, and she was allowed out of the hospital grounds, but she continued to maintain the delusion that others were trying to harm her. Following publicity about a local murder, she confessed to a uniformed constable that she was the person responsible for the murder. After being taken to the police station and interviewed she was returned to the hospital, where the medical officer on duty provided an irrefutable alibi and an explanation of her behaviour. Paranoid schizophrenics not uncommonly assault innocent victims in what they believe is self-defence, under the delusion that the person concerned is a threat to their well-being. In the present case, the patient was not only confused from heavy medication, but had impaired reality testing, a characteristic of psychosis. In the context of constant ward conversation about the murder, and her own thoughts of doing so to protect herself, it was not difficult for the wish to be replaced by the deed in her thinking.

Mrs H—Depression

Mrs H was a 38-year-old woman who suffered from severe depression following the birth of her only child two years previously. She failed to improve despite a variety of treatments in three different hospitals, and suffered so intensely from delusions of persecution that psychosurgery was recommended by her doctor. Mrs H made false confessions to the police on two separate occasions. In both instances she did so in the expressed belief that if she confessed her misdeeds and was publicly punished, the imagined persecution would cease. Since the onset of her psychiatric illness she believed that she was wanted by the police, and sometimes took the most extreme steps to avoid arrest. For example, on one occasion her husband returned home one evening to find her and their two-year-old child concealed in a cupboard under the kitchen sink. They had crouched there all day without food after a police siren had been heard in the vicinity during the morning rush hour. Following this episode, and in attempt to convince his wife that she was not wanted by the police, Mr H took her to the police station by arrangement, where a sympathetic and patient police inspector spent some hours demonstrating her absence from the lists and photographs of various wanted persons. The police inspector also introduced Mrs H to colleagues who assured her that the police had nothing against her and gave her a guided tour of the police station. She remained unconvinced but was reassured by their manner. However, Mrs H returned to the police station later during the week and confessed to an imaginary offence. A statement was taken. The police officer judged her to be mentally disordered by her behaviour and the nature of the statement given. He pretended to take her statement seriously and told her that she was 'being let off this time'. Mrs H gained a few hours of transitory relief by her confession but her delusions returned within days and she returned to the police station and was interviewed by another police officer. He appeared to have less insight into her condition than the previous officer and it was several hours before Mrs H's psychiatric problems were realized.

There is little doubt that this pattern of confession would have continued had Mrs H not been threatened with a Hospital Order should her behaviour continue. Mrs H had suffered a puritanical up-bringing by elderly, rigid and repressive parents, such that the slightest peccadillo resulted in excessive guilt. It is the sheer intensity of the guilt experienced, which can readily lead to suicide, that provides both the motive and the drive to confess by the psychotically depressed patient.

Mr M—Personality Disorder

This case involves false confessions by a man (Mr M) in his mid-30s who confessed to having committed several unsolved murders between 1979 and 1985. He first confessed to a murder to the police in 1979 but he was not charged as the police had reason to believe that he was not the murderer. Mr M was subsequently arrested in 1986 for a suspected sexual offence and before long he had confessed voluntarily to eight publicized murders. The reason he gave for the confessions was that he felt guilty about what he had done and wanted the killings to stop. Mr M was finally only charged with two of the eight murders as the evidence did not support his involvement in the others. There was no forensic evidence to link Mr M with the two murders he was charged with, but in his confessions he provided the police with some information which was to a certain extent suggestive of his guilt (i.e. he gave information which was not public knowledge).

A major problem with all the confessions was the fact that even though Mr M claimed to feel very guilty about the murders he had committed he appeared to have no clear recollection of having actually carried them out. In many instances the information that Mr M provided about the killings was factually wrong. The police worked on the assumption that Mr M suffered from amnesia and they questioned him with this in mind. It was clear to the police that Mr M could not have committed all the murders he confessed to. For example, in the case of one of the murders he was actually in hospital at the time and very far away.

Whilst on remand for two of the murders Mr M confessed to further murders he could not possibly have done. One case involved claiming responsibility for a brutal murder someone else had committed for a financial reward. The real murderer, whom he met whilst in prison on remand, is alleged to have provided Mr M with intimate details about the murder that were not public knowledge, and offered him a large sum of money for confessing to it so that he himself would be freed. The police confronted Mr M with the confession when they realized that he could not possibly have committed the murder.

It was clear that Mr M did not confess to murders at random. Nor did he feel responsible for all murders he read about in the newspapers or saw on television. There was at least one murder that he was questioned about by the police to which he did not confess. The common characteristic about the murders to which Mr M confessed was the general location where they had occurred. The critical factor seemed to be whether Mr M himself had ever been to the general region where the murder had taken place. If he had been to that part of the country at some point in his life then this became a salient trigger for a chain of thoughts that gradually hardened into the belief that he was responsible for the murder.

I interviewed Mr M prior to his trial in 1987, where he was found unfit to plead, and again in 1990 when the case was taken up by the courts again. I gave evidence twice at Mr M's trial about his personality and readiness to confess to murders. One part of my evidence involved describing how I had subtly implanted in Mr M's mind a completely fictitious murder to which he subsequently confessed. I interviewed Mr M twice in prison after his conviction for the two murders where I gained further insight into his apparent compulsion to confess and the gratification he gained from it.

Mr M had a disturbed and turbulent childhood. He reported his family life as having been very unhappy, he truanted a great deal from school and before long he had long list of criminal convictions. The offences for which he was convicted dated back to the age of 14 years. These include burglaries, road traffic violations, acts of violence and sexual offences. Mr M performed poorly at school and was transferred to a special school. He appears to have been sexually disinhibited from early adolescence (i.e. there were frequent reports of indecent exposure) and continued to expose himself to women until his latest arrest. He had been drinking excessively since adolescence and there were several reported instances of suicide attempts as an adult. He appeared to have had some history in childhood of falsely confessing to the police. On one occasion his mother intervened as Mr M had been with her at the time of the alleged offence. Mr M reported having falsely confessed in childhood for the excitement of it and in order to raise his status in the eyes of his peers.

In various psychiatric reports Mr M was consistently diagnosed as 'severely personality disordered'. This diagnosis was consistent with the psychological findings which were obtained from extensive testing, conducted in 1987 by myself and repeated in 1990. Mr M proved to be of borderline intelligence (IQ = 76), and reported a severe degree of depressive symptomatology. He showed marked symptoms of anxiety and intrusive thoughts about the various murders he reported having committed. Mr M proved to be highly suggestible on the GSS 1 and GSS 2. The results from the various tests administered in 1990 were entirely consistent with the 1987 results, except that Mr M's free recall on the GSS narrative was considerably better in 1990 than it had been in 1987. This was strikingly so for the GSS 1 story and was undoubtedly related to one important experimental manipulation that was incorporated into the 1990 assessment. That is, I added one sentence to the end of the GSS 1 narrative. The story describes a woman being robbed whilst being on holiday in Spain. The added sentence read, 'A few months later the woman was sexually assaulted and stabbed to death whilst visiting a friend in South West London'. The reason for adding this sentence to the story, which was presented to Mr M as a memory task, was to see whether Mr M's tendency to confess to murders could be produced by experimental means about a completely fictitious murder. The big question was would Mr M take the bait?

I presented the GSS 1 story to Mr M as a memory task, as I did for the GSS 2 story, which was also administered during the same session, but unlike the GSS 1 it contained no added sentence to the standardized narrative. As both stories had previously been administered to Mr M three years previously, I asked him if he had ever heard of either story before. He said he did not think so. After reading out both the stories I made no further mention of the sentence added. I knew that within a few days Mr M was to be seen by a psychiatrist. I telephoned the psychiatrist and told him about what I had done and requested that he were to ask Mr M what he knew about the murder of Anna Thompson. In the meantime Mr M had time to let the idea of Anna Thompson's murder ferment in his mind.

A few days later the psychiatrist visited Mr M and carried out his own forensic assessment, during which time he casually asked about the murder of Anna Thompson. Mr M quickly took the cue and gave a detailed account of her murder, which included considerable confabulation in addition to accurate material contained in the story. According to the psychiatrist, Mr M's reaction to the story was quite remarkable. He seemed to genuinely believe that he was involved in the murder and remained completely unaware of its origin. The fictitious story seemed to have become a reality and subsequently came to feature in Mr M's mind similarly to the other murders he had confessed to.

About two months after the interview with the psychiatrist, and whilst Mr M was waiting to be transferred to a Maximum Security Hospital after being convicted for two murders, I interviewed him again and asked him to tell me about all the murders he 'felt' he had committed. Among the many murders there was the murder of Anna Thompson. His recollection of the GSS 1 story was excellent and there had been hardly any deterioration in his memory from the initial free recall over two months previously. In contrast, Mr M claimed to have no recollection whatsoever of the GSS 2 story, which had been administered at the same time. The most likely explanation is that the added sentence of Mrs Thompson's murder had focused Mr M's mind on the content of the story and helped with its consolidation and retrieval. Of course, there had been a certain amount of rehearsal as Mr M repeatedly went through the 'murder' in his mind.

On the basis of Mr M's own statements to the police, he was a very dangerous serial killer. His confessions were problematic because of their incompleteness, apparent unreliability and lack of supportive evidence. In his own evidence to the jury at his trial, Mr M said he felt as if he had committed the murders, but had no actual memory of having done so. The general impression Mr M gave was that even if he was not responsible for the two murders he was being tried for he was well capable of brutal murder and might do so at a future date. The jury learned that Mr M had a long history of fantasizing about murders, which he commonly incorporated into his sexual fantasies. The jury must have been left with the general impression that Mr M was a very dangerous man and needed long-term confinement. It therefore came as no surprise to me that they found him guilty of the two murders he was charged with.

In spite of the fact that Mr M was convicted of two murders, it is clear that he also made a number of confessions that were false. Indeed, he appears to have had a long history of falsely confessing to crimes. Although the reason for confessing to each crime may have varied, there appeared to be three main reasons for his confessions, which were generally elicited without external pressure.

First, Mr M told me that he found confessing to gruesome murders very exciting. He reported thoroughly enjoying the notoriety and the attention he received from the police. The more horrific the murder the more exciting he found it. Mr M described feeling very important when he featured significantly in a murder investigation. In other words, it appears to have markedly enhanced his self-esteem.

Secondly, Mr M reported a long history of masturbating to the thought of murdering people. He found the idea of murdering people very exciting and it stimulated him sexually. He reported on occasions having fantasized that it was he who had committed the murders reported by the media. He told me that he had noticed a gradual decrease over the years in his desire to masturbate to violent themes. I asked him why he thought this was the case. He said he had noticed it in the context of his sex drive being reduced as he became older. Although Mr M reported being sexually excited by the fantasies of murder, he said it also made him feel very bad and he tried 'to push the thoughts away'. With time the thoughts appeared to become more consolidated within his mind, which he reported finding most distressing. The way Mr M described the thoughts indicated that they may have had an intrusive component to them. Having interviewed Mr M on many occasions about his fantasies and about the murders he "felt" he had committed I was in no doubt that he was very distressed by them and wanted to talk about them. Confessing to the murders may therefore have given him a sense of temporary relief. His distress appeared to be at least partly due to the fact that he was having increasingly little control over the intrusive thoughts and had serious problems distinguishing factual material from fantasy.

Thirdly, some psychiatrists involved in the case argued that Mr M's false confessions originated from his inability to distinguish between facts and fantasies. In other words, his severe personality disorder interfered with his reality monitoring, without there being any evidence of clear psychotic illness. His faulty reality monitoring seemed mostly related to difficulties in distinguishing between what he had experienced or done and what he had fantasized about. In addition, for some reason Mr M seemed remarkably unable to identify the source of any knowledge concerning the murders. For example, he could not easily differentiate between events he had read or been told about and those he had actually experienced. Even the GSS 1 narrative he reported as a real-life event he had been personally involved in.

The three reasons given for Mr M's tendency to make false confessions can all be construed as having arisen from his severely disordered personality. The confessions fulfilled some important psychological needs, such as enhanced self-esteem, sexual gratification and emotional relief. It was argued by the prosecution at Mr M's trial that he may have been falsely confessing to crimes in order to confuse the issues and 'water down' the impact of his true confessions. This may of course have been the case and there was evidence that Mr M was capable of major manipulative behaviour for instrumental gains. I discussed this possibility with Mr M in detail after his conviction. My impression is that he was not falsely confessing to crime as a way of influencing the outcome of his trial. Most importantly perhaps, Mr M did have a history of falsely confessing to crimes prior to his arrest in 1986.

Mr E—Taking Revenge

In November 1979, the police arrested a 20-year-old man, Mr E, on suspicion of having stolen a chequebook and attempted to commit a fraud. The man was enjoying himself at a party when two police officers arrived late one evening, arrested him and placed him in a cell at the local police station. At the time of his arrest the police noted that the man was moderately intoxicated. Within one hour of being brought to the police station Mr E requested to speak to one of the officers who had arrested him. Mr E told the officer that he knew about the location of the bodies of two missing persons and said he would tell him 'in exchange for the present case'. There was no further discussion about this and the officer left the cell. About half an hour later Mr E requested to speak to the other officer who had arrested him. He told the officer in some detail how one year previously he had murdered a man and robbed him. While giving this confession Mr E was in a very emotional state; and according to the officer he cried profusely and said that the murder had caused him great anguish and he needed to get if off his chest. The officer told Mr E that he would discuss the case with him further in the morning. The following day Mr E was interviewed but retracted the confession he had made the previous evening. He requested a consultation with a solicitor and subsequently gave a statement. He explained that the motive for giving a false confession to the murder was that he was intoxicated, was angry towards the police for having arrested him, and wanted to take his revenge. After the interview Mr E was remanded in custody by the court while the veracity of his confession was investigated. Of concern to the court was the fact that Mr E appeared to have a reasonably detailed knowledge of an unresolved murder, which indeed had taken place.

The police investigated the confession and found it was untrue. Mr E was released from custody, but was subsequently convicted of wasting police time and received a prison sentence.

When interviewed by a psychologist several years later (Sigurdsson, 1998), Mr E claimed to have made the false confession in order to take revenge on the police, because he had been arrested when he was having a good time at the party. Psychological testing revealed a man of good average intelligence, who had a history of alcohol abuse and personality disorder.

PRESSURED–COMPLIANT FALSE CONFESSIONS

Four cases of the pressured–compliant type of false confession are discussed; all involve custodial interrogation. A case of pressured–compliant confession involving a non-custodial interrogation is discussed in Chapter 22.

Mr F—Absence of Mental Disorder

In 1987 two frail and elderly women were found battered to death in their home. The police thought that the murderer had entered the house through an unlocked rear door in the early hours of the morning. The women had been sexually assaulted either before or after their death. A few days after the murder a 17-year-old neighbour (Mr F) was arrested and interrogated about the murders. Apparently a statement he had previously given to the police during a routine door-to-door enquiry about his movements on the night of the murder was inconsistent with statements given by two of his neighbours.

Mr F was arrested early on a Saturday morning and was kept in custody for about three and half hours before his first formal interview commenced. The interviews lasted for nearly 14 hours with various breaks in between. The interview was contemporaneously recorded in accordance with PACE. Five police officers questioned him at different times, including a senior detective, who after questioning him about his sexual habits and alleged failure with girls, eventually elicited a confession to the murders and sexual assault. This confession later proved to be false.

At the beginning of the first interview the police officers repeatedly challenged Mr F's claim that he had been nowhere near the scene of the murders and continually accused him of being a liar. The police claimed that they had witnesses (two of Mr F's neighbours) who had seen Mr F near the scene of the murders around the material time. Many of the questions asked were leading and accusatory. After a while Mr F began to show signs of distress, including sobbing, shaking and crying. He gradually began to give in to the interrogators, at first admitting that he had been out at the material time and then that he had been near the victims' house. After being asked about his sexual habits and alleged failure with girls Mr F was asked the following, 'Now listen to me. When you were in the back entry late last night, early morning, and were having a wank, is that right?'. Answer, 'Yes'. Mr F then went on to say how angry and frustrated he had been at the time, which had previously been suggested to him by the interrogators as a motive for the murders. This was followed by detailed confession to the murders, sexual assault on the women and theft of money from their house.

The following day Mr F was interviewed again by the police, but this time in the presence of a solicitor. Early on in the interview Mr F attempted to retract the admissions he had made the previous day concerning the murders and his presence in the victims' house, explaining that he had falsely confessed because of persistent pressure by the interrogators. Mr F was then again subjected to persistent pressure by the same senior detective to confess again:

> I've been fair with you...
> I want you to tell me now properly with some of the remorse that you showed last night what went on... It's not going to be easy but do it... Come on... do it.
> Look at me..., some of the things that you told me would only be known by a person who was at the house that night.
> I've taken the trouble and interest in discussing your problems that you obviously have, and even listening about your pornographic magazines...
> I know that you've not had much success with girls... I know how frustrated you get. I know that you were reading that pornographic magazine on Saturday night... I know that in that magazine there were explicit sexual acts shown.

After some more questions about the explicit nature of the pornographic magazine and Mr F's alleged sexual frustration, he made a full and detailed confession again. Mr F subsequently made further incriminating admissions to prison staff and to another inmate whilst at the beginning of his remand. A few days after his original confession Mr F was interviewed in prison by the senior detective, in the presence of a different solicitor, concerning the self-incriminating admissions to the prison staff and an inmate. Mr F admitted having made the admissions but stated, 'The truth is that I have lied all the way along and I have never hurt or touched them' (meaning the two murder victims). The senior detective became impatient and commented, 'I do not propose to ask you any more questions because I am of the firm opinion that you are lying and wasting valuable police time in this enquiry'. From that time onwards Mr F persistently claimed to be innocent of the murders and the related offences. Undoubtedly, he would have been convicted if the real murderer had not been apprehended whilst Mr F was on remand awaiting trial for the two murders he had not committed.

Whilst on remand Mr F had been assessed by two psychiatrists and a psychologist. The two psychiatrists failed to identify his specific vulnerabilities. The psychologist, who had been instructed by the defence, identified two related vulnerabilities on psychological tests in spite of Mr F being of average intelligence: proneness to anxiety as measured by the Eysenck Personality Questionnaire (Eysenck & Eysenck, 1975) and an abnormal tendency to give in to interrogative pressure as measured by the Gudjonsson Suggestibility Scale (Gudjonsson, 1984a). The psychologist concluded on the basis of his findings, that Mr F... would be very likely to shift his evidence during interrogation if any pressure was exerted'.

Together with a psychiatrist colleague, Dr James MacKeith, I assessed Mr F on two occasions after he had been acquitted and released from prison and studied all the documents available to Mr F's solicitor (Gudjonsson & MacKeith, 1990). Mr F's parents were also interviewed and gave valuable information about how he had changed following his release from 11 months in custody. According to the parents, Mr F was no longer the unassertive and timid young man he had been prior to his arrest. His prison experience seemed to have hardened him, his self-confidence had markedly improved after his acquittal and he had learned to resist pressure rather than give in to it. These changes in Mr F's personality were clearly evident on psychological tests (Gudjonsson & MacKeith, 1990) and were causing his parents some concern because he had become more difficult to live with.

The above case fulfils the criteria of pressured–compliant false confession. Mr F never came to believe that he had murdered the two women, but falsely confessed to escape from the persistent and lengthy pressure placed upon him by the interrogating officers. It appeared to be particularly important that Mr F's self-esteem had been manipulated by playing on his feelings of sexual inadequacy and alleged failures with girls. It is evident that the police officers strongly believed that Mr F had committed the murders and tried very hard to obtain a confession from him. They mistakenly believed that he had knowledge that only the real murderer would possess, knowledge which Mr F alleged originated from newspaper articles and from the police (a similarly mistaken belief by the police is well illustrated by Kellam, 1980, in a case involving an alleged sexual offence).

Mr F's vulnerabilities when placed under pressure were again highlighted at the beginning of his remand, when he made false self-incriminating admissions in prison in order to escape from pressure. On the face of it, these further self-incriminating admissions appeared to support Mr F's guilt concerning the two murders.

Mr F claimed that during the police interviews he never thought about the potential long-term consequences of his confession, believing naively that his alibi witnesses, especially his parents, would prove his innocence. Sadly, he had placed too much hope in the ability of his parents to prove his innocence, a fact that he realized only too late.

Mr Z—Learning Disability

In 1991, Mr Z was arrested by the police on suspicion of having one week previously murdered a mother and her 5-year-old daughter at their home (see Gudjonsson and MacKeith, 1994, for detailed discussion of the case). Mr Z was in his 30s and had a history of mild learning disability. During a video-recorded police interview Mr Z confessed to a double murder and rape. He was charged with the offences and remanded in custody. He spent almost 10 weeks in prison before it was established through DNA evidence that Mr Z could not have been the person who sexually assaulted the murdered child. Soon afterwards the real murderer was apprehended and the forensic evidence was conclusive about his involvement in the crime. He made a detailed confession to both murders and sexual assault upon the child. If it had not been for the DNA evidence Mr Z's innocence might never have been established and he would probably have been convicted of the crimes. After all, his confession contained incriminating special knowledge, which must have been communicated to him by the police during unrecorded interviews and conversations. Interestingly, there were certain aspects of the murders that he was not able to explain (e.g. the use of a washing up bowl found at the scene of the crime). The real culprit, when apprehended and interviewed, was able to explain some of the more bizarre aspects of the murders, which had puzzled the police.

Mr Z had become a suspect because he had been a friend of the victims and was one of the last persons to see them alive. He was asked to go to the police station to give a witness statement. He gave two witness statements sometime between 18.15 and 23.00 hours. He made no self-incriminating admissions and was further interviewed over a period of about one hour without being cautioned. There was no recording of this 'off the record' interview. Mr Z later alleged that during this interview he was accused of murdering the two victims. He kept denying any involvement in the offence. There were to be five further interviews over the next two days, all of which were tape-recorded. The last interview was also video-recorded.

The first tape-recorded interview commenced at 9.15 the following morning. Mr Z had now been at the police station for 15 hours. No solicitor was present but a relative acted in the capacity of an appropriate adult. The interview lasted 40 minutes, during which time Mr Z falsely admitted to having found the bodies of the two victims after entering their house. He expressed remorse about having moved one of the bodies and agreed with the police suggestion that he had indecently assaulted the little girl. He denied having committed the murders. The interview was terminated shortly after Mr Z's solicitor telephoned the police station and insisted that the interview be stopped until he could attend the police station.

That same afternoon there was a second interview in the presence of a solicitor and an appropriate adult. Mr Z now retracted having entered the house and seen the dead bodies of the two victims, but continued to admit that he had once sexually assaulted the little girl. The police then confronted Mr Z with the apparent special knowledge he had of the position of the two bodies in the house. The police accused Mr Z of lying and suggested that he had murdered the woman after losing his temper. After a one-hour break the third interview commenced with the solicitor and appropriate adult also present. The following day there was a very brief fourth interview before Mr Z was taken to a Magistrates' Court. No further admissions were made.

The fifth interview was most crucial. Mr Z had just returned from the Magistrates' Court after his detention was extended. He had now been in custody for over two days. Mr Z had confessed to two police detectives in the car on the way back to the police station from the Magistrates' Court. When back at the police station he said he wanted to be interviewed in the absence of his solicitor and appropriate adult, but they were allowed to watch the interview through a video-link. The interview was video-recorded and the confession looked convincing (i.e. it appeared freely given, it contains apparent special knowledge, and Mr Z appeared distressed and remorseful about crimes he was confessing to). Immediately after this interview Mr Z told his solicitor in private that he was innocent of the murders and rape, but he did not retract the confession formally at the police station.

After Mr Z confessed to the murders during the fifth formal interview, one of the officers left the room to get Mr Z a drink. In the presence of the other officer Mr Z tells the officer twice that he that he did not mean to do it (i.e. commit the murder). The officer tries to reassure Mr Z, hugs and comforts him. The officer then tells him that he has to go through events of the murders once for the benefit of the officer. The following conversation then takes place:

Mr Z	'Yes, but does this mean I don't have to go down or nothing?'
Police	'You're OK, all right. You're going to be fine.'
Mr Z	'I'm not going to go to prison?'
Police	'You'll be all right, don't worry.'
Mr Z	'Yes but you promised me I wasn't going to go down.'
Police	'You'll be fine.'

There was also a conversation during the first taped recorded interview where Mr Z expressed anxieties about going to prison and the officer tries to reassure him:

No one is saying you are going to prison, OK. You may need a bit of help.

After Mr Z was released from prison and his innocence established, he agreed to meet with my colleague Dr MacKeith and me. I assessed him psychologically. We were allowed access to all the relevant papers in the case and taped interviews. Mr Z told us that the reason for his having confessed to the murders was that one of the officers had promised during the car journey from the Magistrates' Court that if he confessed to the murder he would be allowed to go home and receive medical help; if he did not confess he would go to prison. Mr Z said he had believed the police officer and decided to confess to the murders to avoid going to prison. The officer allegedly further suggested that it would be less embarrassing if he did not confess at the police station in front of his solicitor and appropriate adult. Mr Z agreed. He was interviewed with his solicitor, a social worker and the previous appropriate adult watching the interview through a video-link.

What is important is that taped-recorded interviews themselves did not fully reveal the amount of pressure that Mr Z was under to confess to the murders. On the face of it he appeared to have been interviewed carefully and compassionately. The questions asked were often quite leading, but in spite of this Mr Z did not agree with nearly all of the suggestions offered to him. He was not agreeing with everything the officer was suggesting to him, and persistently denied some of the sexual aspects of the crime put to him (e.g. that he had had an erection and ejaculated into the girl's vagina), whilst agreeing with other matters (e.g. he eventually accepted the officer's suggestion that he had put his finger into the girl's vagina). In spite of confessing to the murders and rape, Mr Z's mind was not completely overborne by the detention and questioning. This suggests that when a suspect makes denials after confessing to a serious crime this should not be used as an indicator that the confession is necessarily true.

A detailed psychological testing revealed a significant intellectual impairment (i.e. a Full Scale IQ score of 64), illiteracy and abnormal acquiescence, but a normal degree of suggestibility. Mr Z's older brother, who accompanied him for the assessment, rated his brother's compliance as 16 on the GCS, which falls outside normal limits. Mr Z had obtained a score of 14 on the GCS. The results suggested that Mr Z was a man of mild learning disability, who was both acquiescent and compliant, but not particularly suggestible.

In our published article on the case (Gudjonsson & MacKeith, 1994) we explain in detail Mr Z's false confession within my Cognitive–Behavioural Model of confessions (see Chapter 5 for a description of the model). The salient components of Mr Z's false confession were his enduring psychological vulnerabilities (i.e. mild learning disability and high compliance), an abnormal mental state (i.e. severe emotional distress over being accused of the murders, a bereavement reaction to the death of his friends, extreme fear at the prospect of going to prison), complete trust and faith in the police and inducement made by police. The confession was made for an immediate instrumental gain: to terminate the interviews, to avoid going to prison, and to be allowed to go home. Mr Z's mild learning disability was an important component in that it impaired his ability to critically evaluate the consequences of his confession and made him an easy target for psychological manipulation by the police. The police had discovered that his greatest fear was of going to prison. They played on this vulnerability in order to get a confession from him by manipulating Mr Z's perceptions of likely consequences of his denials (i.e. going to prison) and admissions (going home and receiving medical help). The case demonstrates how dangerous such psychological manipulation can be.

Mr P—Learning Disability

Mr P was a 21-year-old man with a history of learning disability. He had gone to a police station to report the theft of a cheque belonging to him. While at the police station the detective asked him questions about an attempted robbery which had taken place the week before. The reasons for the police officer's suspiciousness related to the fact that the young man had gone to the police station on a bicycle (the alleged assailant had been riding a bicycle) and he fitted the victim's description in that he looked untidy. Mr P was cautioned and interviewed by the detective constable. No other persons were present during the interview. The interview, which was allegedly contemporaneously recorded, lasted for nearly one and half hours, during which time Mr P made damaging admissions. Five days later he was interviewed in the presence of his mother. Mr P had told his mother that he had not committed the offence and the mother forwarded this comment to the police officer prior to the interview. The officer told her that her son had definitely done it and interviewed him in her presence. During the 20 minute interview that followed, Mr P reiterated his admissions from the previous interview. Even though the victim in the case had clearly stated that she would recognize the man who tried to rob her, there was no identification parade. The case was referred to me before the Crown Court Hearing. At court I asked the detective why there had been no identification parade. He said that in view of the confession it had not been considered necessary.

I conducted a pre-trial assessment on Mr P and found him to have a mild learning disability (IQ = 66). His comprehension and reasoning were particularly limited. He obtained abnormally high suggestibility scores on the GSS 1 and GSS 2, the total suggestibility scores being 17 and 16 on the two tests, respectively (i.e. above the 95th percentile rank for normal subjects). I assessed Mr P's understanding of his legal rights. He claimed to understand the police caution, but when I asked him to describe to me what it meant, he was unable to do so. Mr P claimed to be innocent of the robbery. The interview record showed few leading questions and he claimed to have falsely confessed because the detective 'kept going on and on' and he feared being locked up. Mr P appeared to have confessed quite readily after his initial denials. The two interviews, on the basis of the contemporaneous record, were not obviously coercive, although the detective had been somewhat persistent in his questioning.

The case went to the Crown Court and I was requested to attend to give evidence on Mr P's psychological vulnerabilities. While waiting outside the Court room for the case to commence the victim took a good look at her alleged assailant. She immediately notified the prosecution that the defendant was definitely not the man who had attacked her. The woman gave a detailed written statement to that effect and the charges against the defendant were dropped. A few minutes later I came across the detective questioning Mr P outside the Court room. The conversation went as follows: 'How come you knew so much about the offence? Did the person who did it tell you about it?'. Answer: 'Yes'. I stopped the questioning being taken any further and took Mr P to one side. I asked him what the police officer had been asking him. 'Something about the person who did it'. I said, 'Do you know who robbed the woman?'. He replied 'No'. 'Why did you tell the police officer you did know?' He replied 'I wanted to help'. Clearly Mr P had not learned from his previous mistakes.

The lesson to be learned from this case is that after obtaining a confession the police relied far too much on it. From the start the detective was certain that he had the assailant and he did not consider other possibilities. In other words, he approached the case with a closed mind after his suspicions were initially aroused. Most importantly, the police unwisely did not consider it necessary to conduct an identification parade even though the victim had taken a good look at her assailant and claimed that she would definitely recognize him again. Had they taken this logical step, it would undoubtedly have saved both the victim and alleged assailant unnecessary distress, not to mention the costs involved.

Mr R—Admitting to Death in Self-Defence

In 1985, Mr R was arrested on suspicion of murder and rape. He had become a suspect a few months after the murder, when another woman alleged that Mr R had raped her at knifepoint. He was subsequently interrogated about the murder and rape over a period of about nine hours; he initially denied any involvement in the offence. He eventually confessed to the murder of the woman, claiming he had acted in self-defence. At his trial Mr R testified that he had not had sexual intercourse with either woman and he denied the murder. He claimed that his statements to the police had been beaten out of him. The jury found Mr R guilty of murder and aggravated criminal sexual assault. The judge sentenced him to death. His case was appealed to the American Supreme Court on various procedural grounds. The Supreme Court held that his confession had been obtained freely and voluntarily and his convictions and sentence of death were affirmed.

In 1997, after new DNA analysis showed he was not the person who had sexually assaulted the victim immediately prior to her death, his conviction was quashed and re-trial ordered. It was at this stage that I was brought in as a potential expert witness in the case and went to the USA to assess Mr R. Shortly prior to my returning to the USA in 1999 to testify in the case, the prosecution dropped the charges against Mr R. With the new DNA evidence and my testimony, they probably did not think they would be able to obtain a conviction.

I was commissioned by Mr R's defence team to assess the voluntariness of his 1985 confession prior to a scheduled re-trial. I interviewed Mr R and administered a number of psychological tests, including the GSS 2, and GCS, the Gough Socialisation Scale and the Eysenck Personality Questionnaire (EPQ). The findings suggested possible personality disorder, as evident by a very low score on the Gough Socialisation Scale; there was a moderately high degree of compliance on the GCS (85th percentile rank) and abnormally high Yield 1 and Yield 2 on the GSS 2.

A neuropsychological assessment had been conducted three years previous to my involvement in the case, and was repeated after my visit to the USA by an American clinical psychologist. Mr R was overall of low average intelligence with a significant Verbal–Performance discrepancy in favour of the former. His history of extensive alcohol abuse prior to his arrest in 1985 and previous closed head injury raised the possibility of organic problems, but a MRI brain scan in 1998 failed to find any significant cerebral damage.

Mr R told me that after his arrest he was extensively interrogated by the police and accused of the murder. They claimed they had a witness and gave Mr R detailed information of the crime scene and the victim. The police told him that the victim had been a prostitute who 'hanged out on the street a lot'. After a while Mr R offered to take a polygraph test, because he thought this would prove that he nothing to do with the murder. A polygraph test was then arranged for him and he was told afterwards by one of he officers that he had failed the test. He thought the officer was lying about the outcome of the test. The interrogation then continued and Mr R kept denying the murder. An officer then suggested that Mr R be taken to the murder scene and this was done. After the visit the interrogation continued again; Mr R kept denying any involvement in the murder. The police then allegedly suggested that the killing had been unintentional and that if he admitted to it he would be out of the police station in a couple of hours. With the continued denials, one of the officers became frustrated and handcuffed him to a ring in the wall. He was then allegedly physically beaten in the face and stomach and claimed that he felt frightened for his life, because he did not know how far they would go to force a confession out of him. Mr R now decided that he had to tell them something to stop the beatings and the interrogation. He decided to make up a story based on what he had been previously told about the victim by the police: namely that she was prostitute (there was no evidence that the victim was a prostitute, in fact the evidence points to the contrary) and that he had not meant to kill her.

The confession Mr R gave, which was signed by him and later reiterated in front of a State Attorney, comprised an account where Mr R had murdered the woman in self-defence. He had met the woman on the night of the murder, she had offered him sex for $10, after which he refused to pay for her services. She then pulled out a knife, they fought and she got stabbed. Mr R thought this would satisfy the officer and that he would be released from police custody, because the confession constituted self-defence and not murder. He only realized the seriousness of his self-incriminating admissions when the police refused to release him from custody, but he still did not think he would be convicted of murder.

Although Mr R claimed that the beatings and the fear of physical danger while in custody were the main reasons for his falsely confessing to the involvement in the woman's death, it is likely that he was at the time psychologically vulnerable due to his history of alcoholism and likely susceptibility to suggestions. Furthermore, Mr R completely failed to appreciate the seriousness of the compromise he reached by admitting to causing the death of the victim in self-defence in his desperate attempt to find a way out of his predicament. The case highlights the potential dangers of interrogators using *theme development* (see

Chapter 1 for a discussion of this technique) to distort suspects' perceptions of the likely consequences of their self-incriminating admissions.

There is no doubt that if it had not been for the discovery of the DNA evidence Mr R would not have been able to prove his innocence and probably would have been executed. His claims that that police had beaten a confession out of him could not be proved; it was just his word against that of the police. Without the beatings his confession appeared to have been given voluntarily.

PRESSURED–INTERNALIZED FALSE CONFESSIONS

Five cases of pressured–internalized false confession are discussed; four resulted during custodial interrogation and one in a non-custodial setting (i.e. it was coerced by a spouse). Detailed descriptions of other pressured–internalized false confessions are presented in Parts III and IV of this book.

Mr R—a False Belief

Whilst serving as a police detective with the Reykjavik Criminal Investigation Police before becoming a clinical psychologist, I interviewed a man in his late 20s in connection with an alleged theft of a purse from a woman with whom he had been drinking the previous evening. The suspect (Mr R) had met the woman at a nightclub and had later gone to the woman's flat where they continued drinking. The following morning, and shortly after the man had gone, the woman found that her purse, which contained some money, was missing. She reported the alleged theft of her purse to the police. Her drinking partner from the previous evening became the immediate suspect, because the woman had noticed the purse whilst the man was in the flat and nobody else had entered the flat from the time she had last seen the purse and until she had discovered it was missing.

Mr R was asked to attend the police station for questioning and was presented with the allegation. He had several previous convictions for minor theft and alcohol-related offences. He explained that he could not remember much about the previous evening, but had some recollection about having gone to the woman's flat after the nightclub closed. He said he had no recollection of having actually taken the purse, but as he frequently had memory blackouts after heavy drinking he thought it was quite likely. When confronted with the woman's allegation that the purse had disappeared whilst he was in her flat, he said 'I do not remember doing it, but I must have done it'. He signed a statement to that effect.

A few days later the woman telephoned the police and said that she had found her purse; it appeared to have fallen behind her sofa where the couple had sat whilst drinking.

This case is a good example of the way in which the circumstances of a particular alleged offence can be the critical factor that elicits the false confession rather than the interrogation techniques utilized. The man was not interrogated, but was presented with the woman's allegation, which was sufficient because of his general distrust of his memory and his belief in the woman's honest reporting of the theft. What none of us knew at the time was that no crime had been committed in the first place.

Mr Peter Reilly

One of the most publicized cases of internalized false confession is that of Peter Reilly, who has been the subject of two books (Barthel, 1976; Connery, 1977). In 1973 Reilly was an easygoing and well liked 18-year-old youth. He lived in Canaan, Connecticut, with his 51-year-old mother. At 8 p.m. on 28 September he went to a Methodist Church for a Youth Centre meeting. He returned home around 9.50 p.m. to discover his mother's mutilated body. She had been brutally murdered minutes before Reilly arrived home. He immediately called for an ambulance and was clearly in a distressed state. Within hours he became the prime suspect for the murder and after intensive interrogation he made a self-incriminating confession, which resulted in his arrest and conviction for manslaughter.

Connery (1977) states:

> Suddenly an orphan, and still in his teens, with no close ties to relatives, Peter was subjected to four great shocks in a day's time: the murder of his mother, the realization that he was suspected of being the murderer, his own amazed agreement that he might be his mother's killer and his arrest. He was put behind bars and there he remained for 143 days before going to trial (p. 21).

As the police investigation commenced Reilly remained voluntarily in police custody for several hours. He was eager to help the police to apprehend the murderer and according to police sources was fully co-operative. There was insufficient evidence to arrest him and he declined to have a lawyer present during the subsequent interrogation. Three years later he explained why he had not exercised his right to a lawyer: 'Because I hadn't done anything wrong and this is America and that's the way I thought it was' (p. 42).

Reilly's interrogation commenced at about 6.30 a.m., nearly nine hours after he had found his mother dead. It was tape recorded. His interrogator noted that Reilly appeared very relaxed, well poised and exhibited no emotion. For the next two hours Reilly gave a general description of his movements on the day of the murder and his discovery of the body. He was asked questions about his mother's sex life and whether he had ever had a sexual relationship with her. Reilly was later to say that these personal questions upset him a great deal.

After a four-hour break Reilly was asked to take a polygraph test. He agreed because 'I was sure of my innocence. I just wanted to get all the police garbage out of the way so I could get some rest and be with my friends' (p. 57). Prior to the polygraph examination, the examiner told Reilly about the effectiveness of the instrument:

> 'The polygraph reads your brain for me.'
> 'Does it actually read my brain?' Reilly asks.
> 'Oh, definitely, definitely. And if you've told me the truth this is what your brain is going to tell me.'

After the polygraph examination Reilly was told that he had a deceptive outcome. This was followed by more than six hours of interrogation, during which time Reilly was subtly persuaded that he murdered his mother, even though he had no recollection of having done so.

Following the polygraph examination Reilly still insisted that he did not kill his mother. The interrogator, who was also the polygraph examiner, presented Reilly with different scenarios ('theme development') of what he thought might have happened on the night of the murder. His basic premise seemed to be that Reilly had mental problems and as a result he could not remember killing his mother. The 'theme development' (see Chapter 1) included such statements as 'what happened here was a mercy thing'... 'something happened between you and your mother last night and one thing led to another and some way you accidentally hurt her seriously'... 'your mother flew off the handle and went for you or something and you had to protect yourself' (pp. 65–67).

Reilly's confidence in his memory began to weaken: 'now there is doubt in my mind. Maybe I did do it' (p. 66). Reilly vacillated for a while, saying 'I believe I did it', then expressed doubts that he did do it. He then stated 'the polygraph thing didn't come out right. It looked like I've done it'. The interrogator asks 'Well, what's it look like now?'. Reilly answered 'It really looks like I did it'. The interrogator asked 'You did it?'. Reilly replied 'Yes'.

The interrogation continued with different themes and scenarios being presented to Reilly to assist with his recollections about specific details. Reilly eventually gave a confession statement, declaring himself as his mother's killer. The confession was written down by a police friend of his. In it he stated among other things 'I remember slashing once at my mother's throat with a straight razor I used for model airplanes. This was on the living room table. I also remember jumping on my mother's legs'. Reilly also stated that he thought he might have raped his mother, but this was discounted by the interrogator as there had been no physical evidence of rape.

Reilly told the police officer who was writing out the confession three times to make sure that he mentioned in the statement the fact that he was not really sure of what he is saying. The officer promised to do so, but did not keep his promise. The officer was subsequently to allege that Reilly had made a verbal admission (i.e. 'I killed her') immediately prior to his written confession statement. There was no record of this having been said from the tape recording of the interview, although the officer insisted in court that it had been said and tape recorded. There were some differences between what the officer had written down in the confession statement and what Reilly was trying to say.

What is evident from Reilly's interrogation is that he was never completely sure that he had murdered his mother. He clearly came to doubt his own recollection, largely, it seems, because of the persistence of the interrogators that the polygraph is infallible and that he had a temporary mental block about what had really happened on the night of the murder. Reilly seems to have become very confused by the polygraph results and by the interrogators' repeated and suggestive questioning, which made him very unsure about his own memory of events on the evening of the murder.

There was some evidence that he was generally very trusting of police officers and respected them. Indeed, had expressed an interest in becoming a police officer himself and had police officers as friends.

Before the trial there was a pre-trial hearing concerning the admissibility of Reilly's confession. As the confession was the only significant evidence against Reilly it was important for the defence to have the judge rule it inadmissible. The defence argued that the confession was caused by psychological coercion and was therefore not voluntary. Conversely, the prosecution argued that the interrogation had been conducted properly and that his confession was voluntary. The Judge decided in favour of the State, 'There may have been some repetitive, suggestive questioning, or the planting of ideas, by members of the State Police but not enough to deprive the defendant of due process' (p. 133).

The case went to trial and the prosecution argued that the evidence against Reilly was 'overwhelming'. In reality the only evidence against Reilly, except for some circumstantial evidence, was his self-incriminating confession. No forensic evidence was ever found to link him with the murder and the prosecution tried hard to explain how Reilly could have changed his blood-stained clothes after the murder in order to avoid detection. It was emphasized by the prosecuting counsel that Reilly had been informed of his legal rights four times. Furthermore, Reilly was 'an intelligent, articulate, calm and alert individual' and his alleged off-the-record comment 'I killed her' surely indicated his guilt (p. 248). Reilly repeated his confession to two police officers after the interrogation was terminated, which was used by the prosecution to further indicate his guilt.

Reilly testified at the trial. According to Connery (1977), he made a poor witness and came across as vague, defensive and evasive. The main problem seemed to be that his recollection of what had been said and done during the lengthy interrogation was poor and this left the jury and the judge with an unfavourable impression about his honesty and willingness to tell the truth. The jury found Reilly guilty of manslaughter in the first degree. He was sentenced in May 1974 to imprisonment 'for a term of not less than six nor more than sixteen years' (p. 267).

No psychological or psychiatric opinions were offered at the trial. Psychological testing had been arranged while the trial was in progress, but as the evidence was not entirely favourable it was not offered in evidence. On the Wechsler Adult Intelligence Scale (WAIS), Reilly obtained a Full Scale IQ of 115, which places his intellectual functioning in the 'bright normal' range. The psychologist argued that Reilly had poor self-esteem and was easily influenced by others. However, the psychological report seems to have included speculative comments suggesting that in spite of Reilly's compliance, he seemed crafty or cunning, and exhibited 'profound mistrust and vigilance' (p. 240).

After the trial Reilly was still claiming to be innocent of his mother's murder. Five new people came to his rescue and they were, according to Connery (1977), instrumental in providing new evidence to prove his innocence. These were a lawyer, an eminent playwright, a private detective, a psychiatrist and a forensic pathologist.

The psychiatrist, who testified at a new-trial hearing in 1976, found that Reilly had 'none of the personality attributes, none of the measurements, that you would expect of a person who would develop amnesia; two, that he was able to give an account of every time segment; and three, when he was given the chance to lie, he didn't lie. So I came to the conclusion that he didn't have amnesia and that he was telling the truth' (p. 293). The question the psychiatrist was trying to answer related to the possibility that Reilly might have suffered from amnesia after allegedly murdering his mother.

In evidence, the psychiatrist considered that Reilly had in 1973 uncritically accepted the police officers' unfounded premises because of confusion, poorly integrated identity and long-standing respect for police officers. Reilly's vagueness and uncertainties during the interrogation were considered to be the result of a confusional state, induced by the demand characteristics of the interrogative situation, rather than due to psychogenic amnesia.

Prior to the re-trial it was discovered that the prosecuting counsel had suppressed 'seven statements and seventeen pieces of evidence that the defense was entitled to' (p. 314). The most important statements were discovered after the death of the original prosecuting counsel in the case. The new State Attorney handed the statements over to the defense counsel, statements his predecessor had clearly deliberately suppressed because they contradicted his mistaken and obsessive belief that Reilly was guilty of his mother's murder. The statements were those of two witnesses who had seen Reilly drive in the direction of his home at 21.40 on the night of the murder. Reilly could therefore not have been at his home until 21.45 at the earliest, which gave him insufficient time to have committed the murder and changed his clothing. The outcome was that the State had no alternative but to drop its case against Reilly. The persistent fight for proving Reilly's innocence had paid off. He was at long last a free man.

Sergeant E

Sergeant E was a 27-year-old Serviceman with the American Air Force and was stationed in England (see Gudjonsson & Lebegue, 1989, for a detailed account of the case). He was charged with murdering his best friend on their last evening out together before his friend returned to America. At around midnight on a clear winter's night the two friends had gone for a walk along some cliffs after having consumed a quantity of alcoholic drinks. Shortly afterwards Sergeant E telephoned the local police and told them that his friend had had an 'accident'. He explained that he had asked his friend to lie by his side at the cliff edge to look at the sea and the moon, but his friend suddenly fell over the cliff, which resulted in his death. The friend's alcohol level at the time of his death was 212 mg/100 ml. Sergeant E was also similarly intoxicated, having consumed about seven pints of beer over the five hours prior to his friend's death.

According to the British police, the friend's death was accidental. The case was handed over to the American Office of Special Investigation (OSI) and

Sergeant E was required to take a polygraph test in order to clear himself of any suspicion concerning his friend's death. Unfortunately for Sergeant E, he 'failed' the polygraph test (i.e. the test produced a deceptive outcome) and three further tests were administered on other occasions, all of which he 'failed'. In conjunction with the polygraph tests, Sergeant E was interrogated extensively by OSI special agents for a total of 24 hours over three days. Towards the end of the lengthy interrogation Sergeant E signed a self-incriminating confession, implicating himself in the death of his friend. In fact, he had become persuaded by the agents that he had murdered his friend, even though he had no memory of having done so. As a consequence of the confession, Sergeant E was charged with his premeditated murder.

Sergeant's E's confession resulted from extensive interrogation by the special agents, who employed the theme development technique described in Chapter 1. The special agents testified at the military hearing that they had 100% faith in the outcome of the polygraph and had tried to persuade Sergeant E that he had to have been involved in his friend's death as the polygraph 'never lies'. They admitted having deliberately played on Sergeant E's feelings of guilt and distress about what had happened to his friend, in an attempt to obtain a confession from him. Most importantly, as Sergeant E began to become confused by the questioning, the agents presented him with different scenarios about what they thought had happened and refused to allow him to talk about his own account of an accidental fall. They repeatedly suggested a scenario in which E struggled with his friend, and eventually Sergeant E accepted that the agents' scenario could be correct, but he claimed to have no recollection of it having happened that way.

Sergeant E was assessed psychologically by the present author, who testified at the military hearing (Gudjonsson & Lebegue, 1989) as to the unreliability of his confession. Sergeant E was of low average intelligence. On psychological testing he proved to be a compliant and a suggestible individual, who was emotionally labile and prone to strong feelings of guilt. He stated that he had trusted the special agents and tried hard to co-operate with them. He was puzzled at his failure in the polygraph tests, believing what the special agents had told him about the 100% accuracy of the polygraph. He said he had at the time of the interrogation felt very guilty about his friend's death, which he believed he should have been able to prevent. As the special agents repeatedly told him with marked confidence that he must have caused his friend's death (after all the polygraph 'never lies'), he become confused and began to distrust his own memory of what had happened. Although he accepted the special agent's scenario of having pushed his friend over the cliff, this scenario appears to have co-existed with his pre-existing 'true' memories rather than permanently contaminating or distorting them.

Within a couple of days of signing the incriminating confession, Sergeant E became fully convinced that his initial account of what had happened on the cliff was correct and that the agents' scenario was not what had happened. This appears to have coincided with Sergeant E's confusional state resolving when the pressure of the interrogation was over and he had time to think logically through what had really happened on the night of the tragedy. After becoming completely convinced of his innocence, Sergeant E was faced with the difficult task of proving his innocence before a court martial.

There was never any evidence to link Sergeant E with his friend's death, except for his confession, which the defence successfully argued had been obtained by psychological coercion. The case was heard by a military judge who dismissed the case after the prosecutor for the government announced, on the 11th day of the trial, that he would not continue to proceed with the case. Sergeant E was a free man and resigned from the US Air Force.

Mr J—Eagerness to Please

This case, which was discussed in detail by Gudjonsson (1995d), involved the confessions of a voluntary part-time fireman to setting fire to six caravans between 1989 and 1992. Prior to his interrogation he had been interviewed as a witness and given statements. It was not clear why he had been arrested and interrogated about the fires. There were four taped-recorded interviews that evening where Mr J confessed to setting the fires and making hoax telephone calls. There was no solicitor or appropriate adult present during the interviews. He was charged with the offences. The only evidence against him was his confession.

Early the following morning Mr J was visited by his mother and girlfriend, and when asked if he had set the fires he replied:

> I must have, that's what they say. They say I do it in drink and that I sleepwalk and can't remember anything afterwards.

Prior to his trial, I was commissioned by his defence team. I interviewed Mr J and his girlfriend, carried out psychometric testing of Mr J, read all the relevant documents in the case and listened to the four tape-recorded interviews. A careful analysis of the taped police interviews indicated that a conversation had taken place about fire-setting prior to the first taped interview (there was no proper recording of this conversation), Mr J appeared to have very poor recollection of what he was meant to have done, he commonly used such phrases as 'I might have', 'I think I did', his accounts of events were vague, confused and contradictory and the officers repeatedly encouraged him to give definite answers, which he then readily did. There was evidence that Mr J was very eager to please the police.

Mr J told me that, prior to the tape-recorded interviews, the police had been persuaded that he had committed the offences but had blocked out the memory of doing it. The police claimed to have witnesses to his setting fire to a caravan (no witnesses were ever identified), told him that he 'had done it in drink', and that they were there to help him. He had no memory of committing any of the offences, but came to believe that he had. He then with the help of the police tried to figure out what exactly he had done and made up what he thought he had done. He said he was trying hard to please the officers and assist them with their enquiries into the fires. After speaking to his mother and girlfriend further that morning Mr J said he realized he had not set the fires and retracted his confessions when visited shortly afterwards by his solicitor.

After my assessment the Crown Prosecution Service commissioned their own report from a clinical psychologist. Her findings were in agreement with mine and, in view of the fact that there was no evidence against Mr J apart from his confession, the charges against him were dropped.

Psychological testing showed that Mr J was of borderline intelligence (Full Scale IQ scores on the WAIS-R were 74 and 74, respectively, when tested by myself and later by a Crown expert). His compliance score on the two occasions fell outside normal limits, and the Yield scores on the GSS 1 and GSS 2 were moderately elevated.

In the context of the case, Mr J's most relevant psychological vulnerabilities were as follows.

- His eagerness to assist the police with their enquiries.
- Great respect, trust and faith in the police.
- Lack of confidence in his memory.
- High compliance and suggestibility.

I believe Mr J made a pressured–internalized false confession to setting the fires and making hoax telephone calls. Evidence for this came from considerable inconsistencies between what he was saying in his confessions and the forensic evidence from the crime scenes, the types of answer he gave to the police during his interrogation, conversations he had with his mother and girlfriend the day after making the confessions and his description to me of what went through his mind during the police questioning.

The case demonstrates the dangers involved in 'off the record' conversations between a suspect and police prior to a formal and properly recorded interview, and how eagerness to please and complete trust in the police can cause a person to confess to crimes of which he has no memory. A good description of Mr J's character is evident from a police statement showing that on the day of his arrest, when he was asked to go back to the police station to go through the witness statement he had given earlier in the day, he replied:

'I'll help you boys as much as I can.'

Mr J certainly kept his word.

Mr K—Non-Custodial Confession

This case involved a 40-year-old Englishman, Russell Key, who had a history of paranoid schizophrenia (*Cutting Edge*, 2001). He had been well looked after by his mother prior to her death and had held a responsible employment position. In the autumn of 1997 he responded to a lonely heart advertisement from an American woman, Dominique, who was in her late 50s. She was looking for a friendship and possible marriage. They corresponded and

Dominique arrived in England about the end of January 1998. They married on 14 February 1998 and lived in London until May when they moved to Stroud, where Mrs Key's grown-up daughter from a previous relationship lived.

After their honeymoon the relationship between the couple deteriorated. Mrs Key was to claim that her husband had talked in his sleep about murders he had committed. She began to question him and bully him into admitting that he had murdered several women. On 18 June 2001 Mrs Key had a tape-recorded telephone conversation with her husband. Mrs Key dominated the conversation and tried to browbeat her husband into accepting that he had killed several women. He explains that he is not sure if he had murdered anybody and claimed to have 'no conscious memories of it'. Mrs Key became angry and kept shouting at him things like 'You are a liar', 'You are a fucking murderer'. Mr Key said he could not confess to something he did not know for sure he had done. She told him she knew for certain he had killed these women and kept bullying him into accepting her scenarios. She pushed her husband for memories of the murders. Mr Key began to admit to the murders and gave very vague and tentative descriptions. He thought it had happened before 1989 in the north of England, possibly Blackpool. She suggested he strangled the women; he then agreed with this. She then took him through each of the killings. That same evening Mr Key gave himself up to the police and was admitted to hospital for a psychiatric assessment.

On 25 June Mr Key was arrested and interviewed by the Lancashire police. I have listened to the tape-recorded interview and the tapes of conversations between Mr Key and his wife in June and July 2001. In his interview with the Lancashire police on 26 June 2001, Mr Key sounds like an articulate and intelligent man. He was carefully and properly interviewed by the police in the presence of a solicitor. He explained that in 1989 he had been in hospital for two weeks and treated for paranoid delusions. He was suffering from paranoid schizophrenia and had been on medication since that time. He told the police how his wife says he has been talking in his sleep about having murdered five women and was allegedly threatening her. He had no recollection of having committed any murders, but tried hard to imagine how he might have done it. Mr Key wanted to know from the police if he had killed anybody. He expressed doubts about whether he had murdered anybody. The police investigated the case and found no evidence that Mr Key had murdered anybody. He was released from police custody. There was evidence that he had a history of making a false confession. Several years previously he had persuaded himself that he had murdered nine people on a motorway and confessed to it. This proved to be a false confession (*Cutting Edge*, 2001).

At the end of June Mrs Key left England and went to Phoenix, Arizona. Two weeks later Mr Key followed his wife to the USA. They both stayed with an old friend of Mrs Key. Mrs Key interviewed her husband further on tape about the murders in England, apparently in order to sell their story to the national press. Now, for the first time, Mr Key described his murder victims as having been foreign women (two Russian, a New Zealander, a French woman, and a Portuguese). The motive for the murders is that he wanted to get out of England, so he finds foreign women to get citizenship abroad. He said he invited the women to come to England, where he murdered them and buried them in shallow graves in Lancaster.

On 21 July 1998, within a week of Mr Key arriving in Arizona, Mr Key was shot dead by his wife. On the day of the murder she had purchased a powerful handgun, having shortly before had her and her husband's story of him being a British serial killer being turned down by a newspaper. Mrs Keys was charged with the murder of her husband. Her defence was that she had acted in self-defence. She alleged that she had shot her husband after he tried to strangle her. She viewed him as a serial killer and was convinced he was going to kill her. The police found no evidence of attempted strangulation and were of the view that Mrs Key had planned to murder her husband in order to sell her story to the media (*Cutting Edge*, 2001). She told the police that her case would be supported by tape-recorded conversations between them where her husband had confessed to being a serial killer. The police initially found the tapes supporting her case, but soon discovered that they were only "practice tapes" of Mr Key's confession to five murders. Left behind in England were tapes that showed how Mrs Keys had bullied her husband into confessing to the murders. These tapes were used at her trial in Phoenix to convict her. She was convicted of first degree, premeditated murder, and is serving a life sentence.

Was Mr Key a serial killer? The English police investigated the case and found no evidence that he was. They found no bodies in shallow graves as described by Mr Key. The Phoenix police did not believe the confessions either (*Cutting Edge*, 2001). The language of the confession had all the hallmarks of a pressured–internalized false confession, although I think it is likely that Mr Key was also going along with his wife in order to please her (i.e. a compliant type of a false confession), never being fully convinced that he was a serial killer. Mr Key's history of mental illness, and the apparent deterioration in his mental state during his marriage to Mrs Key, probably made him vulnerable to breakdowns in reality monitoring. He also appears to have been emotionally dependent upon his wife and was eager to please her. She seemed certain that he was a serial killer and tried hard to persuade him to provide her with a detailed confession, which she would then tape-record, for whatever motive.

CONCLUSIONS

In this chapter case examples have been provided to illustrate some of the critical components of the different psychological types of false confession that were discussed in Chapter 8. The cases demonstrate the importance of having a good conceptual framework for understanding the process and mechanisms of false confession. The different types of false confession should not be viewed as exclusive categories, because there may be an overlap between the different groups. For example, suspects may be partly persuaded by the police that they were involved in the alleged crime, but nevertheless confess mainly for instrumental gain (i.e. in spite of partly believing the police's account of events, they confess in order to escape from an intolerable situation).

There appear to be different critical factors operating in several of the cases reviewed. Specific vulnerabilities, such as low intelligence, mental illness, proneness to anxiety, high suggestibility, strong tendency to comply with people in authority, eagerness to please, may all contribute in varying degrees to the way the accused copes with his or her predicament. However, the cases discussed clearly illustrate that false confessions are not confined to the learning disabled or the mentally ill. The view that apparently normal individuals would never seriously incriminate themselves when interrogated by the police is wrong and this should be recognized by the judiciary.

It is clear from the cases discussed that innocent suspects do sometimes give information to the police that, on the face of it, seems to have originated from the accused, whereas the information was probably unwittingly communicated to them by the police in the first place. Such apparently 'guilty knowledge', which often makes the confession look credible, is then used to substantiate the validity of the confession given. The lesson to be learned is that unless the information obtained was unknown to the police, or it actually results in evidence to corroborate it (e.g. the discovery of a body or murder weapon), then great caution should be exercised in the inferences that can be drawn from it about the accused's guilt. Police officers will undoubtedly find it difficult to believe that they could inadvertently communicate salient information to suspects in this way. They may gain some comfort from the fact that the possibility of unconscious transmission of evidence, even by qualified psychologists, alerted the British Society of Experimental and Clinical Hypnosis to recommend that psychologists called in by the police to hypnotize witnesses should be kept ignorant of all details of the crime in order not to transmit such knowledge unwittingly during hypnotic interrogation.

PART II
LEGAL AND PSYCHOLOGICAL ASPECTS

CHAPTER 10

The English Law on Confessions

When assessing a case of retracted or disputed confession the clinical psychologist needs to be familiar with the relevant law, legal procedures and practice, and know what protection there is in law for suspects with mental problems. The reason is twofold. First, without some basic understanding of the legal issues the assessment may not cover the crucial areas of concern. For example, certain safeguards are provided for mentally ill persons and those suffering from learning disability, and without knowing what these are the expert witness may fail to assess the relevant disabilities or psychological vulnerabilities. Secondly, the expert witness's findings have to be placed in the context of the relevant legal questions. For example, what is the relevance of the psychological findings for the court's evaluation in relation to such terms as 'coercion', 'voluntariness', 'oppression', 'reliability' and 'fairness'? Of central importance is an understanding of the suspects' legal rights during custodial interrogation, the Police and Criminal Evidence Act 1984 (PACE) and the accompanying Codes of Practice, and the relevant 'exclusionary rules' (Gudjonsson, 1992, 1997f). In this chapter, the basic legal issue background is given for the psychological and psychiatric assessment of disputed confessions in England, Wales and Northern Ireland.

The law in Northern Ireland regarding interrogations and confessions is similar to that found in England and Wales. It is governed by the Police and Criminal Evidence (Northern Ireland) Order Act 1989 and is based almost entirely on the English and Welsh Police and Criminal Evidence Act 1984 and its accompanying Codes of Practice (PACE; Home Office, 1985a, 1995; Bevan & Lidstone, 1985; Corre, 1995). However, it should be noted that some important differences exist in law in relation to anti-terrorist legislation between England and Wales on the one hand, and Northern Ireland on the other. For example, in Northern Ireland, unlike the case in England and Wales, there is no entitlement for a solicitor to be present during police interviews with terrorist suspects, such interviews are not required to be tape-recorded and there are no jury trials for such cases (Dickson, 1999). The Republic of Ireland (Walsh, 1999) and Scotland (Walker, 1999a) have their own laws governing confession evidence, and these differ markedly from the law and legal procedures in England, Wales and Northern Ireland.

As an introduction to this chapter, the following general points should be borne in mind.

1. PACE and the Codes of Practice regulate the procedures surrounding detention, police interviews and the taking of confessions (e.g. the permissible length of detention, conditions of interview, right of access to solicitor, right to be cautioned and right to have the interview tape-recorded). There is special protection for vulnerable suspects, such as juveniles and those with mental problems. Nevertheless, the current protection afforded by the law may in some instances be inadequate.
2. PACE sets out the circumstances under which a confession may not be used against the defendant at trial; the court *must* exclude the confession if it finds it was obtained by 'oppression' or under circumstances likely to render it 'unreliable'. In addition, the court *may* exclude the confession if its admission is likely to have an adverse effect on the fairness of the proceedings.
3. Court decisions and case studies show how courts actually interpret legal concepts and what needs to be shown to argue that a confession should not be admitted. Decisions holding a confession inadmissible are generally based on a combination of *external factors* (police pressure, denial of procedural rights) and *internal factors* (the detainee's particular psychological or mental vulnerability).
4. The rules regulating the admissibility of expert testimony in cases of disputed confessions are based on legal judgments in the appellant court, which provide the lower courts with general principles to follow. As a result of some important High Court judgments in recent years, the courts are becoming more flexible about the admissibility of expert testimony in cases of disputed confessions.

THE ADMISSIBILITY AND RELIABILITY OF CONFESSION EVIDENCE

In English law, defendants can be convicted on the basis of uncorroborated confessions (McConville, 1993; Richardson, 2001), and in practice they often are. In Scottish law, on the other hand, there must be some evidence from an independent source that can corroborate or substantiate the confession (McConville, 1993; Walker, 1999b).

The central legal issues regarding confessions in England are the 'confession' and 'exclusion' issues (Mirfield, 1985). The 'confession' issue deals with claims by the defence that the alleged confession was never made in the first place. This is particularly likely with verbal admissions that have not been written down and signed. The 'exclusion' issue is the one more commonly raised in court. Here the defendant admits to having made the confession that is alleged by the prosecution, but claims that it was made under coercion and duress, or by hope of some advantage (e.g. being free to go home). In other words, the confession is said to have been made under such circumstances as to make it either involuntary or unreliable, or both.

Prior to the implementation of PACE the *Judges' Rules and Home Office Administrative Directions* assisted the police in administering justice (Home Office, 1978). The new legislation superseded the provisions in the *Judges' Rules* as well as introducing new material and safeguards. The *Judges' Rules* stated that the fundamental condition for the determination of admissibility is that the self-incriminating statement

> ... shall have been voluntary, in the sense that it has not been obtained from him by fear of prejudice or hope of advantage, exercised or held out by a person in authority, or by oppression.

Administrative Directions supplemented the *Judges' Rules* and specified the conditions under which a suspect was to be questioned. One of the conditions most relevant to psychology was that police officers should apply special care when interviewing people with learning disability (also known as mental handicap, mental impairment and mental retardation). Breaches of the *Judges' Rules and Administrative Directions* by police officers could result in judges rendering the confession inadmissible, either because it was not considered voluntary or had been the product of oppressive questioning. However, the legal safeguards contained in the *Judges' Rules and Administrative Directions* were in fact commonly ignored without the confession being rendered inadmissible at the defendant's trial (Irving, 1990).

PACE and the Codes of Practice

The legal significance of confession evidence in England and Wales is regulated by the Police and Criminal Evidence Act 1984 (PACE; Home Office, 1985a), which was implemented in January 1986. The Act is supplemented by five Codes of Practice, referred to as Codes A (on stop and search), B (entry and searches of premises), C (detention and questioning of suspects), D (on identification parades) and E (tape-recording of interviews). The Codes act as guidance to police officers about procedures and the appropriate treatment of suspects. Code C is particularly relevant to the present book in that it focuses specifically on the guidance 'on practice for the detention, treatment and questioning of persons by police officers' (Home Office, 1995, p. 25).

The most important interview procedures set out in PACE and its Codes of Practice are as follows.

1. A person suspected of a criminal offence must be cautioned before being questioned about it. The caution shall be read in the following terms:

   > You do not have to say anything. But it may harm your defence if you do not mention when questioned something which you later rely on in court. Anything you say may be given in evidence (Home Office, 1995, p. 50).

2. Persons detained at a police station must be informed of their legal rights; this includes that they are entitled to free legal advice at any time, that they can have somebody notified of their detention and that they have the right to consult the Codes of Practice. Under Section 58 of PACE, a detainee has an absolute right to legal advice; he or she is upon request entitled to consult with a solicitor at any time. The custody officer must give the detained person a written notice setting out the above legal rights, including the police caution.
3. Police can detain suspects for 24 hours without a charge (Section 41 of PACE). Officers of the rank of superintendent or above can authorize a continued detention of up to 36 hours (Section 42 of PACE). On an application on oath before a Magistrate, detention can be extended to a maximum of 96 hours (Section 44 of PACE).
4. In any 24 hour period the detainee must be allowed a continuous period of rest of least eight hours. There should be a break from questioning for at least 15 minutes every two hours. Meal breaks should normally last for at least 45 minutes.
5. There are special provisions for detainees who are vulnerable in terms of their age or mental problems relating to access to a responsible adult (known as an 'appropriate adult').
6. All interviews shall be tape-recorded (there are some exceptional circumstances when tape-recording is not required, as in the case of terrorist offences).

The Codes only have legislative power in as far as breaches may result in evidence, including confession evidence, being ruled inadmissible by a trial judge during a *voire dire*. Serious breach may lead to a disciplinary action against police officers, although this happens very infrequently (Zander, 1996).

There have been some changes made to the original Codes of Practice; one revision came into force on 1 April 1991 (Home Office, 1991) and another in April 1995 (Home Office, 1995). Corre (1995) has provided a guide to the 1995 revisions to the PACE Codes of Practice. The most significant change relates to a revised police caution of detainees, which warns of the adverse inferences that can be drawn from the accused's silence in Sections 34 to 39 of the Criminal Justice and Public Order Act 1994.

Leng (1993), Morgan and Stephenson (1994) and Starmer and Woolf (1999) provide comprehensive reviews of the background to the amendment of the right of silence in criminal trials and the surrounding legal controversy. Bucke and Brown (1997) and Bucke, Street and Brown (2000) review the impact of the amended right of silence.

Bucke and Brown (1997) have researched the impact of the changes to the 1995 revised Codes of Practice. The main findings are of a further increase in the use of legal advice by detainees. There has been a significant fall in the use of the right of silence by detainees, undoubtedly due to the adverse inferences that can be drawn from silence. There has been no change in the rate of confession. The study also found that detained juveniles are now more likely to be charged than before.

Definition of a Confession in PACE

PACE attempts to provide a working definition of the word 'confession'. It is construed in Section 82 (1) as including

> ... any statement wholly or partly adverse to the person who made it, whether made to a person in authority or not and whether made in words or otherwise (Home Office, 1985a, p. 75).

The terminology used in the Act to define a confession is very broad and implies that self-incriminating admissions, which fall short of a full confession, are also classified under the heading of a confession. Since under certain circumstances exculpatory statements, such as denials, can be construed as *adverse* and may even be used against defendants as evidence of deliberate lying and guilt (Gudjonsson, 1995c), this would also appear to fall under the above definition of a 'confession'. However, incriminating denials cannot meaningfully be described as a 'confession' and ought to be dealt with under Section 78 of PACE (Gudjonsson, 1993a). This is recognized in the leading legal authority *Archbold* (Richardson, 2001):

> The approach in *R. v. Sat-Bhambra, ante*, that exculpatory statements are not to be treated as confessions for the purposes of Section 76 simply because they are used against the defendant at trial as false or inconsistent statements, was confirmed in *R. v. Park*, 99 Cr.App.R. 270, CA. *Aliter*, in the case of remarks which, whilst not amounting to a confession of guilt, would only be made by a guilty person: see *R. v. Cox*, 96 Cr.App.R. 464 at 474, CA (p. 1482).

However, it is suggested in *Archbold* that

> The definition in section 82(1) is not exhaustive: the expression 'made in words or otherwise' may include, it is submitted, a defendant's failure to respond to questioning from which an adverse inference may be drawn under sections 34, 36 or 37 of the Criminal Justice and Public Order Act 1994 (Richardson, 2001, p. 1482).

It seems extraordinary to be suggesting that a defendant, who is exercising his right of silence by declining to answer questions, may be construed as making an expression that falls under the heading of a 'confession'. This can be attributed to the vagueness and broad nature of the definition in Section 82(1) and illustrates how important interpretations are in relation to legal concepts.

Challenges to Admissibility

As far as the admissibility of confession evidence is concerned, this may be challenged in one or more of four ways (Richardson, 2001). The first two tests relate to Section 76(2)(a) and (2)(b) of PACE and other tests invoke Sections 78(1) and 82(3). Section 76 states:

> If, in any proceedings where the prosecution proposes to give in evidence a confession made by an accused person, it is represented to the court that the confession was or may have been obtained—

(a) by oppression of the person who made it; or
(b) in consequence of anything said or done which was likely, in the circumstances existing at the time, to render unreliable any confession which might be made by him in consequence thereof, the court shall not allow the confession to be given in evidence against him except in so far as the prosecution proves to the court beyond reasonable doubt that the confession (notwithstanding that it may be true) was obtained as aforesaid (Home Office, 1985a, p. 73).

The concept of 'voluntariness', which was used in the *Judges' Rules*, has been replaced by the concept of 'reliability'. This means that confessions are excluded when it can be shown that they were obtained by such means or in conditions which are likely to render them *unreliable*. The concept of 'oppression' is retained in the new Act and

...includes torture, inhuman or degrading treatment, and the use of threat of violence (whether or not amounting to torture) (Home Office, 1985a, p. 73).

The English courts tend to restrict the use of the term 'oppression' to its ordinary dictionary meaning as defined in *Fulling* ([1987], 85 Cr.App.R. 136).

Unlike 'oppression', the term 'reliability' is not defined in PACE. The term 'anything said or done' potentially broadens the criteria for determining unreliability beyond threats or inducements (Mirfield, 1985).

Beside Section 76(2), two further sections are relevant to possible exclusion of confession evidence. These are Sections 78(1) and 82(3). The former deals with the 'exclusion of unfair evidence', whilst the latter leaves some room for exclusion, for whatever reason, at the judge's discretion. Section 78(1) states:

In any proceedings the court may refuse to allow evidence on which the prosecution proposes to rely to be given if it appears to the court that, having regard to all the circumstances, including the circumstances in which the evidence was obtained, the admission of the evidence would have such an adverse effect on the fairness of the proceedings that the court ought not to admit it (p. 73).

Section 82(3) states:

Nothing in this Part of this Act shall prejudice any power of a court to exclude evidence (whether by preventing questions from being put or otherwise) at its discretion (p. 76).

Birch (1989) describes the legal 'tests' as comprising a number of 'hurdles', where each hurdle needs to be completed before the next one can be attempted. The first hurdle relates to Section 76. Here the burden of proof lies with the prosecution. That is, they have to show that the confession was beyond reasonable doubt not obtained by oppression or in a manner that is likely to render it unreliable. The second hurdle relates to Section 78(1). Here the burden of proof is not made explicit in the Act, but it is commonly assumed that it rests with the defence. This means that the defence has to present evidence to indicate that all the circumstances of the case are such that it would be unfair if the proceedings were to use the confession. Here it is the fairness of the proceedings that is crucial rather than any arguments about police impropriety, although impropriety can also be relevant to the legal arguments (Feldman, 1990).

The final hurdle, if the other two have failed, lies with Section 82(3). The full discretionary powers of the judge to exclude evidence under this section are not made clear in the Act, but they cover the exclusion of evidence when the prejudicial effect outweighs its probative value. According to Birch (1989),

> In the context of confessions this would mean evidence the reliability of which is more apparent than real, for example the confession of an unusually suggestible defendant (p. 97).

The two most important sections with regard to confession evidence are undoubtedly Sections 76 and 78 (Birch, 1989; Cho, 1999). There are a number of differences between these two sections, one of which, as already stated, relates to where the onus of the burden of proof lies. Perhaps the most fundamental difference, however, relates to discretionary powers. That is, Section 76 involves 'proof of facts', whereas Section 78 involves 'the exercise of judgment by the court' (Birch, 1989, p. 96). In other words, these sections set out the circumstances under which a confession may not be used against the defendant at trial; the court *must* exclude the confession if it finds it was obtained by 'oppression' or under circumstances likely to render it 'unreliable' (Section 76). In contrast, the court *may* exclude the confession if its admission is likely to have an adverse effect on the fairness of the proceedings (Section 78).

Another difference is the emphasis in Section 76 on police behaviour and the reluctance of judges to include under this provision unreliability due solely to internal factors (e.g. drug withdrawal, disturbed mental state). There is generally the need to establish some kind of police impropriety or misconduct with regard to Section 76; that is, it would be unlikely to succeed in cases of ordinary and proper police questioning. This is particularly important in relation to Section 76(2)(a), which necessarily involves impropriety, whereas a confession may be ruled inadmissible under Section 76(2)(b) without any impropriety (Richardson, 2001). With regard to Section 76,

> Hostile and aggressive questioning which puts pressure on a defendant will not necessarily render the confession unreliable. The length of the interviews and the nature of the questioning are the important considerations: *R. v. L.* [1994] Crim.L.R. 839, CA (Richardson, 2001, p. 1483).

Emphasis on the characteristics of the individual when interpreting psychological coercion is recognized by some judges. For example, in the judgment of *R. v. Priestley* ([1966], 50, Cr.App.R. 183) it was stated:

> What may be oppressive as regards a child, an invalid or an old man or somebody inexperienced in the ways of the world may turn out not to be oppressive when one finds that the accused is of tough character and an experienced man of the world (cited by Bevan & Lidstone, 1985, p. 299).

The case of Stephen Miller, one of the 'Cardiff Three' (*R. v. Paris, Abdullahi & Miller* [1993], 97 Cr.App.R, 99), provides an important judgment in relation to oppressive interviewing. The police interrogated Miller for about 13 hours in total. He confessed towards the end of the interrogation period and was convicted along with two other defendants, neither of whom made confessions. He denied involvement in the murder on over 300 occasions. According to their Lordships on appeal, two of the officers were 'tough and confrontational' and Miller was 'bullied and hectored.' A detailed analysis of Miller's interrogation was discussed in Chapter 4, whereas the psychological and legal aspects of the case are discussed in Chapter 19.

The words 'said or done' in Section 76(2)(b) do not include anything that is said or done by the person making the confession (Richardson, 2001). It was held in *R. v. Goldenberg* (88 Cr.App.R. 285) that this has to be something external to the person making the confession and is something likely to have influenced him or her to confess. Goldenberg was a heroin addict who was arrested and charged with conspiracy to supply diamorphine. After being in custody for five days, he requested an interview with the police and confessed to the offence. The defence argued at trial that the confession should be ruled inadmissible under Section 76(2)b because the defendant would have been inclined to 'say or do anything' to obtain bail. The judge rejected the defence submission and the defendant was convicted. On appeal the conviction was upheld:

> In the circumstances of the present case the Court was satisfied that on the proper construction of Section 76(2)(b) the judge's ruling as to the admissibility of the evidence of the police interview was correct; further, the judge was right to rule against a submission that the prejudicial effect of the evidence outweighed its probative value (p. 285).

This case is commonly used to indicate that a confession resulting from a disturbed mental state without proof of impropriety by the police may not necessarily be excluded under Section 76(b). The implication is that self-induced or inherent factors that undermine unreliability have to be dealt with under Sections 78 and 82 and at the discretion of the judge.

In the case of *Harvey* ([1988], Crim.L.R. 241), Section 76(2)(b) was successfully invoked for a personality disordered woman of low intelligence who confessed, allegedly in order to protect her lesbian lover from prosecution after hearing her confessing to murder. The confession was the only evidence against her. This case, which was heard at the Central Criminal Court, is interesting because there was no inducement to confess and a 'person in authority' did not elicit the confession (i.e. it was given voluntarily to a police officer). Nevertheless, the judge held that

> ...he was not satisfied beyond reasonable doubt that the confession was not obtained as a result of hearing the lover's confession (p. 242).

The jury was directed to acquit.

In another case (*R. v. Moss*, Court of Appeal, March 9, 1990), the Court of Appeal held that the confession of a man with borderline IQ should not have gone before the jury. The crucial confession was elicited after the man had been in custody for several days and was interviewed without a solicitor being present. He was convicted of an indecent assault exclusively on the basis of his confession and was sentenced to five years' imprisonment. His conviction was successfully appealed against on the basis of Sections 76 and 78.

Breaches of PACE or the Codes or Practice may result in evidence being excluded by the trial judge, either under Section 76, or more typically under Section 78, or under the common law (Richardson, 2001). Judges sometimes use the term 'significant and substantial' to refer to serious breaches (*Keenan* [1990], 2 Q.B. 54; *Walsh* [1990], 91 Cr.App.R. 161). Even if the breach is found to be 'significant and substantial' evidence will not be automatically excluded. It is at the judge's discretion and the judge will have

> ... to consider whether there would be adverse effect on the fairness of the proceedings, but such an adverse effect that justice requires the evidence to be excluded (*R. v. Walsh* [1990], 91 Cr.App.R. 161, p. 163).

Similarly, in *R. v. Delaney* ([1989], 88 Cr.App.R. 338), Lord Chief Justice Lane ruled:

> But the mere fact that there had been a breach of the Code does not of itself mean that evidence had to be rejected. It was no part of the duty of the court to rule a statement inadmissible simply to punish the police for failure to observe the provisions of the Codes of Practice (p. 341).

Section 78 may be violated with or without any impropriety on the part of the police. The kinds of impropriety that may lead to invoking Section 78 include deliberate deceit and deception, such as lying to the suspect and his solicitor that his fingerprints were found at the scene of the crime (e.g. *R. v. Mason* [1987], 3 All E.R. 481), denying a suspect access to a solicitor on inadequate grounds (e.g. *R. v. Alladice* [1988], 87 Cr.App.R. 380), a failure to caution a suspect (*R. v. Hunt* [1992], Crim.L.R. 582), or failure to call an appropriate adult (*R. v. Aspinall* [1999], Crim.L.R. 741). For evidence to be excluded, the breach does not require the presence of bad faith on the part of the police and may simply constitute a breach of an important right (Choo & Nash, 1999). Acting in good faith does not excuse police officers committing serious breaches and acting in bad faith will usually result in exclusion of the evidence (Richardson, 2001; *R. v. Alladice* [1988], 87 Cr.App.R. 380).

Choo and Nash (1999) provide a detailed review of application of Section 78 to the admissibility of evidence, including confession evidence. They are critical of the approaches recently taken by the Court of Appeal in apparently moving away from the kinds of landmark approach taken in early confession cases (e.g. *Mason* [1987], 3 All E.R. 481; *Keenan* [1990], 2 Q.B. 54; *Walsh* [1990], 91 Cr.App.R. 161), where the focus was on the *nature of the breach* rather than the *nature of the evidence*. In recent cases (e.g. *Cook, Chalkley* [1998], 2 All E.R. 155), improperly obtained evidence that was considered reliable was not excluded, because the issue of reliability was the main concern rather than police impropriety. The reliability of the confession is often itself an issue and for this reason in such cases evidence may be easier to exclude than in some non-confession cases, where the reliability of the evidence itself is not in dispute (e.g. where reliable evidence was obtained by improper or illegal means).

As far as police trickery and deceit is concerned,

> The general approach of the courts to evidence obtained by trickery is to say that deceit which simply provides defendants with an opportunity to confess to the offence, as opposed to trickery that positively induces a confession, will not result in a confession being excluded (Richardson, 2001, p. 1535).

The importance of Section 78 in recognizing the legal significance of internal psychological factors, in the absence of police impropriety, is provided in the case of *Brine* ([1992], Crim.L.R. 122). During interrogation a defendant had confessed to indecently assaulting an eight-year-old girl. At trial, during a *voire dire*, a clinical psychologist testified that the defendant had when he made the admissions

> ...been suffering from a relatively mild form of paranoid psychosis, the effect of which was that, under stress of questioning, he would have felt very threatened, been likely to tell lies and, make untrue admissions (p. 123).

The psychologist testified during the *voire dire* that, as a result of the defendant's mental state during police questioning, his confession was unreliable. The Crown called no evidence in rebuttal. The judge stated that he had found the psychological evidence impressive and had accepted it, but nevertheless ruled the confession statement admissible, because he did not think Section 78 applied to the case. The case was appealed, and the Court of Appeal decided that the trial judge, having accepted the psychological evidence, had failed to exercise his statutory discretion to rule the defendant's confession inadmissible. He had misconstrued Section 78 by assuming that in addition to internal factors some misconduct on part of the police was required. The conviction was accordingly quashed on appeal.

McEwan (1991) argues that PACE is simply not designed to deal with the problem of self-induced unreliability. She recommends greater judicial acceptance of psychological evidence (e.g. personality characteristics that make people susceptible to unreliable testimony without mental illness or learning disability). As will be evident later in this chapter and in Part III of this book, the Appeal Courts in England and Northern Ireland are becoming increasingly receptive to psychological evidence that does not necessarily involve mental disorder.

The Truthfulness of the Confession

According to *Archbold*,

> The truth of the confession is immaterial. If the judge concludes that what was said and done was likely to render any resulting confession unreliable and the prosecution fail to prove that the confession was not obtained in consequence thereof, he has no discretion: *R. v. Kenny* [1994] Crim.LR. 284, CA. See also *R. v. Paris*, 97 Cr.App.R. 99 at 103, CA (Richardson, 2001, p. 1484).

What is of crucial importance is 'how the confession was obtained, not whether or not it may have been true' (*R. v. Paris*, 97 Cr.App.R. 99 at 103, CA). The emphasis is clearly on circumstances under which the confession may be rendered unreliable. The cases of *R. v. Cox* ([1990], Crim.L.R. 276) and *R. v. McGovern* (92 Cr.App.R. 233) demonstrate this point with regard to Section 76. Cox had an IQ of 58 and was described as abnormally suggestible, but he was nevertheless interviewed by the police in the absence of an 'appropriate adult', which was a breach of the Codes of Practice (Code C: 13.1). His appeal against conviction was successful because the trial judge had wrongly focused on the likely truthfulness of the confession rather than its reliability.

McGovern was one of three people convicted of murdering a woman in November 1987 by pushing glue into the victim's nostrils and mouth and pulling a rope round her neck, causing the victim to die of asphyxia. McGovern and her brother were arrested the day after the murder. McGovern was interviewed twice by the police. She was 19 years of age at the time and pregnant. During both interviews, and during the latter interview in the presence of a solicitor, she made a confession as to her complicity in the homicide. She gave a reasonably coherent account of the murder, particularly during the second interview, which was properly recorded. There was virtually no other evidence against McGovern. When she arrived at the police station she had requested to see a solicitor, but the police refused this. During the first interview she was questioned without a solicitor. At trial defence counsel submitted during a *voire dire* that the first interview should be excluded from the jury, because of a breach of Section 58 of the Police and Criminal Evidence Act 1984 (PACE) relating to the refusal of the police to allow her access to a solicitor. In addition, the officers had failed to contemporaneously record the first interview as required by law.

Pre-trial, I was commissioned by McGovern's solicitor to evaluate her psychological functioning. She was of borderline intelligence (Full Scale IQ of 73), with particularly poor verbal and non-verbal comprehension. She also proved to be abnormally suggestible, acquiescent and compliant on testing. I was concerned that she did not appear to have understood the police caution when interviewed by the police. This was to become an important point at trial and the subsequent appeal.

At trial I testified twice. First, I testified during the *voire dire* about McGovern's inability to have understood the police caution, which was evident from the record of the interviews. The trial judge, having heard my evidence and looking at the defendant's own statement, described her as 'streetwise' and admitted the first interview statement into evidence. A week later I gave evidence again, but this time in front of the jury. McGovern was not called to give evidence.

McGovern was convicted of manslaughter on the basis of diminished responsibility. She received a 10 year sentence and was to be detained in a young offender's institution.

The defence appealed against the conviction on the basis that the trial judge should have excluded the first interview. The case was heard in the Court of Appeal (London) in May 1990 before Lord Justice Farquharson, and Justices

Tudor, Evans and Brooke. The appeal was successful in spite of the fact that McGovern's involvement in the murders was not disputed:

> Having considered these conflicting arguments and submissions, this Court is clearly of the view that even if the confession given at the first interview was true, as it was later admitted to be, it was made in the consequence of her being denied access to a solicitor and is for that reason in the circumstances likely to be unreliable. It follows that the prosecution has not in our judgment proved otherwise. We think Mr Clegg is right, that if a solicitor had been present at the time this mentally backward and emotionally upset young woman was being questioned, the interview would have been halted on the very basis that her responses would be unreliable. It seems that the interview was held quickly and without the formalities prescribed by the Code of Conduct because the police were anxious to discover the missing girl, but this heightened the risk of the confession being unreliable (92 Cr.App.R., p. 233).

Their Lordships ruled the confession inadmissible under Section 76(2)(b) of PACE and quashed the conviction. McGovern was released from prison.

This case is an example of circumstances likely to make a confession unreliable; McGovern was denied her important right to a solicitor (external circumstances) *and* she was mentally backward (internal circumstances). There might therefore have been reason to doubt the truth of any statement she made, even though, in fact, the statement turned out to be true. The court might not have found either one of those factors sufficient without the other.

THE VOIRE DIRE

In order to decide on the question of admissibility the judge conducts 'a trial within a trial', which is known as the *voire dire*. The purpose of the *voire dire* 'is to enable the judge to determine an issue of fact, namely whether the alleged confession was, or may have been, obtained by oppression or in circumstances making it likely to be unreliable' (Rowe, 1986, p. 226).

The *voire dire*, post-PACE, takes place in the absence of the jury in accordance with the exclusionary rules, which are designed for the protection of the defendant. The jury are asked to withdraw whilst the questions of law are being discussed by the legal advocates. After both sides have made their submissions and the judge has made his ruling, the jury is invited back. If the confession evidence is made admissible, then the jury is allowed to hear it. If the judge rules it inadmissible, the jury will hear nothing of it, in which case the trial may proceed on the basis of other evidence, or the prosecution decides to 'offer no evidence'.

In a case where the only evidence against the defendant is his or her confession, the inadmissibility of that evidence means that the prosecution case collapses.

How much time is spent on challenging the reliability or accuracy of police interrogation evidence? According to Barnes and Webster (1980), about 5% of the Crown Court's trial time is taken up with this kind of dispute. Similar findings have been reported by Vennard (1984). In both studies infrequent use was made of the *voire dire*. Vennard found that a *voire dire* took place in only 7% of contested Crown Court cases, whereas Barnes and Webster reported a figure of 11%. Overall, in only about 13% of contested cases in the Crown Court and six per cent in the Magistrates' Courts are the issues of statement unreliability raised, either during the *voire dire* and/or the trial proper (Vennard, 1984).

How effective is the *voire dire* for excluding confession evidence? In the great majority of cases the submission to exclude confession evidence fails. According to Vennard's (1984) findings, only about 15% of *voire dire* cases in the Crown Courts succeed.

These studies are very out of date and the figures may not give an accurate picture of the current situation.

ISSUES AFFECTING VULNERABLE DEFENDANTS

Psychological (Mental) Vulnerability

There is no mention of mental disorder, apart from 'mental handicap', in PACE. However, in the Codes of Practice, mental disorder is discussed in relation to the need for an 'appropriate adult':

> The generic term 'mental disorder' is used throughout this code. 'Mental disorder' is defined in Section 1(2) of the Mental Health Act 1983 as 'mental illness, arrested or incomplete development of mind, psychopathic disorder and any other disorder or disability of mind'. It should be noted that 'mental disorder' is different from 'mental handicap' although the two are dealt with similarly throughout this code. Where the custody officer has any doubt as to the mental state or capacity of a person detained an appropriate adult should be called (Home Office, 1995, p. 29).

Section 77(1) of PACE deals with confessions obtained from persons with a 'mental handicap'. It states that in such cases the court shall warn the jury

> ...that there is a special need for caution before convicting the accused in reliance on the confession.

The warning is contingent on that:

(a) the case against the accused depends wholly or substantially on a confession by him; and
(b) the court is satisfied—
  (i) that he is mentally handicapped; and
  (ii) that the confession was not made in the presence of an independent person.

Section 77(3) of the Act defines a person with 'mental handicap' as the one who 'is in a state of arrested or incomplete development of mind which includes significant impairment of intelligence and social functioning' (p. 73). PACE gives greater protection to persons with mental handicap than the *Judges' Rules*, apparently as a result of the adverse publicity following the Confait case (see Chapter 7; Bevan & Lidstone, 1985). No mention is made in the PACE Act about a similar protection for the mentally ill, but this is covered in the accompanying

Codes of Practice, where it falls under the heading of 'mental disorder' (Home Office, 1995).

Code C has important provisions for the detention and interviewing of 'special groups', such as juveniles (i.e. persons under the age of 17), foreigners who do not speak much English, the deaf and persons who are mentally ill or handicapped. Where communicating in English is a problem an interpreter must be called to assist. The relevant legal provision for other 'special groups' includes the following.

> A juvenile or a person who is mentally disordered or handicapped, whether suspected or not, must not be interviewed or asked to provide or sign a written statement in the absence of the appropriate adult (Home Office, 1995, p. 55).

> If an officer has any suspicion, or is told in good faith, that a person of any age may be mentally disordered or mentally handicapped, or mentally incapable of understanding the significance of questions put to him or his replies, then that person shall be treated as mentally disordered or mentally handicapped for the purposes of this code (Home Office, 1995, p. 75).

The reasoning for the special protection of the mentally ill or handicapped relates to their being considered disadvantaged during police interviewing (i.e. they are considered to be 'vulnerable' suspects). More specifically,

> It is important to bear in mind that although mentally disordered or mentally handicapped people are often capable of providing reliable evidence, they may, without knowing or wishing to do so, be particularly prone in certain circumstances to provide information which is unreliable, misleading or self-incriminating. Special care should therefore always be exercised in questioning such a person, and the appropriate adult involved, if there is any doubt about a person's mental state or capacity. Because of the risk of unreliable evidence, it is important to obtain corroboration of any facts admitted whenever possible (pp. 77–78).

Gudjonsson (1993a) identified two main problems with PACE and the Codes of Practice in relation to the use of the generic term mental disorder. First, there is an absence of an operational definition for police officers, who are expected to identify the relevant psychiatric conditions without any formal training. Secondly, it is not specified how certain conditions, such as mental illness and mental handicap, place suspects 'at risk':

> The implicit assumption appears to be that mental disorder places these persons 'at risk' in the sense that they may unwittingly provide the police with unreliable testimony, including a false confession, because they may not fully understand the significance of the questions put to them or the implications of their answers, or that they are unduly influenced by short-term gains (e.g. being allowed to go home) and by interviewers' suggestions (Gudjonsson, 1993a, p. 121).

Appropriate Adults

There are five potentially important questions at trial with regard to the use of appropriate adults.

1. Was the detainee entitled to the services of an appropriate adult, even if the police did not recognize this at the time?

2. Did the police identify the detainee as vulnerable or 'at risk' but fail to obtain an appropriate adult as required by the Codes of Practice?
3. If the police obtained the services of an appropriate adult, was that person suitable and had the ability to fulfil the necessary role and functions?
4. Did the person acting in the capacity of an appropriate adult understand the nature of his or her role?
5. What was the impact or consequence if there was no suitable appropriate adult when one should have been present?

The special protection afforded to juveniles, and the mentally ill and handicapped, during custodial interrogation relates to their mandatory access to an appropriate adult. The person chosen to fulfil this role may be a defendant's relative or guardian, or in the case of mentally disordered detainees

> ...someone who has experience of dealing with mentally disordered or mentally handicapped people but is not a police officer or employed by the police (Home Office, 1995, p. 27).

In Code C, a distinction is made between juveniles (persons under the age of 17) and mentally disordered adults in relation to who should ideally act as an appropriate adult. In the case of juveniles, parents, guardians or social workers should normally act as an appropriate adult, whereas in the case of adults, a relative, guardian or a mental health professional is recommended. In the case of adults, the role of an appropriate adult is usually fulfilled by social workers and only occasionally by psychologists and psychiatrists. The requirement for an appropriate adult is that without such a provision these vulnerable individuals could make confessions which are inherently unreliable. The basic requirement for acting as an appropriate adult is that the person has to be over the age of 18 and is not a police officer or employed by the police. In addition

> A solicitor or a lay visitor who is present at the station in that capacity may not act as an appropriate adult (Home Office, 1995, p. 85).

According to the Codes of Practice, the police should inform the appropriate adult that he or she is not acting simply as an observer and that

> ...the purposes of his presence are, first, to advise the person being questioned and to observe whether or not the interview is being conducted properly and fairly, and secondly, to facilitate communication with the person being interviewed (Home Office, 1995, p. 76).

However, the role of the appropriate adult as set out in the Codes of Practice is brief and there are no specific guidelines as to what kind of advice the appropriate adult should provide, how and when communication should be facilitated or how the fairness of the interview should be evaluated by the appropriate adult (Bean & Nemitz, 1994; Hodgson, 1997; Palmer, 1996; Williams, 2000). If appropriate adults do not fully understand their role, as Hodgson argues, then they may not act in the best interests of the detainee. Indeed, on occasions appropriate adults may completely misconstrue their role and take on the role of an interrogator (Pearse & Gudjonsson, 1996c, 1996d). Importantly, Robertson, Pearson and Gibb (1996a) suggest that there has been a general failure in the Codes of Practice to distinguish between the needs and requirements of juveniles and vulnerable adults.

In a recent study, Bucke and Brown (1997) found that there is still an inadequate level of guidance given to appropriate adults about their role by custody officers. Parents often take the role of passive observers and do not intervene appropriately. Similar findings have been found by other researchers (Evans, 1993; Palmer & Hart, 1996). Rather than remaining overly passive, appropriate adults may also side with the police and taken on an interrogative role (Pearse & Gudjonsson, 1996c). Bean and Nemitz (1994) found when appropriate adults do intervene in an interview they may face disapproval by the police.

Hodgson (1997) and Pearse and Gudjonsson (1996d) have also raised concern that the mere presence of an appropriate adult during an interview may add a degree of legitimacy and credibility to the interview process at court.

The appropriate adult can consult with the detainee privately at any time (Code C: 3.12). This is an important provision, but it may cause problems and serious ethical issues when a detainee wishes to make a confession to the appropriate adult (Littlechild, 1996). In order to overcome this risk, Littlechild recommends that appropriate adults meet with detainees in private before a police interview and explain the boundaries of their role, including advising them not to make admissions to the appropriate adult, and explaining the possible consequences of making such admissions.

To a certain extent, a solicitor and an appropriate adult have overlapping functions (*R. v. Lewis (Martin)* [1996], Crim.L.R. 260), such as ensuring that a detainee understands his legal rights, understands the questions asked and is able to give coherent answers, and to ensure that the interview is conducted properly and fairly. Interestingly, police surgeons, psychiatrists, lawyers and police officers also view the roles of appropriate adults and solicitors as overlapping considerably, and generally see no need for both (Gudjonsson, Hayes & Rowlands, 2000). Out of the four professions, lawyers had the least faith in the use of an appropriate adult and police officers the most. The finding that police officers had faith in the services of appropriate adults is positive, since they are responsible for identifying the need for such persons and seeking their services.

However, in spite of overlapping roles (Pearse & Gudjonsson, 1997), there are some important differences between the functions of appropriate adults and those of solicitors, which must not be overlooked. For example, mental health professionals who fulfil the role of appropriate adults should have greater insight into problems associated with mental disorders than solicitors. In contrast, solicitors should have greater knowledge of the police caution and relevant legal issues to give sound legal advice compared with appropriate adults (Ede & Shepherd, 2000). My main concern is that with the problem of comprehension associated with the new police caution (Clare, Gudjonsson & Harari, 1998; Fenner, Gudjonsson & Clare, 2002; Gudjonsson, 1994a; Shepherd, Mortimer & Mobasheri, 1995), it is unrealistic to expect appropriate adults to deal satisfactorily with this important area (Gudjonsson, Hayes & Rowlands, 2000). Indeed, in one study (Fenner, Gudjonsson & Clare, 2002), we found that none of the police detainees fully understood the police caution when it was read out in its entirety, as happens in practice, although, when asked, 90% claimed to have understood it. In another study (Clare, Gudjonsson & Harari, 1998), some police officers were not able to articulate a proper understanding of the police caution themselves. Similar problems with comprehension have been identified with the Scottish caution (Cooke & Philip, 1998). These findings emphasize the importance of suspects having proper legal advice whilst being detained at the police station. In view of this, when appropriate adults are in attendance, they should ensure that detainees also seek the services of a solicitor. It is interesting that the complexity of the current police caution is recognized in Section 58 of the *Youth Justice and Criminal Evidence Act 1999*, where it is no longer permissible for the courts to draw adverse inferences from silence in cases where the detainee did not have access to legal advice.

Medford, Gudjonsson and Pearse (2000) found, in their study of 26 835 custody records at all Metropolitan Police Stations over a one month period in 1997, that the majority of psychologically vulnerable adult detainees, as evidenced from entries in the custody record, were not provided with the services of an appropriate adult or a solicitor. Therefore, even when there were clear indications in the custody record that the person was psychologically vulnerable (e.g. a documented history of mental illness or learning disability), the police often failed to act on this information by calling in an appropriate adult. The researchers also found that there was no well organized national training for appropriate adults, although in some areas there are voluntary appropriate adult training schemes available.

There are other important problems with the use of appropriate adults, including problems with initial identification. The great majority of vulnerable detainees are not identified as such by the police and are therefore not provided with their legal entitlement to the presence of an appropriate adult (Gudjonsson *et al.*, 1993). This situation has been improved by the Metropolitan Police adopting our recommendation to the Royal Commission on Criminal Justice, that detainees should routinely be asked searching questions relating to self-identification of vulnerabilities (Clare & Gudjonsson, 1992). This procedure was introduced by the Metropolitan Police in 1998 and is referred to as Form 57M. Future studies will be able to demonstrate the effectiveness Form 57M has on improved identification of vulnerable detainees.

In cases where there has been a breach with regard to the failure of the police to call in an appropriate adult, the courts may exclude the police interview from the jury (e.g. *R. v. Fogah* [1989], Crim.L.R. 141; *Maloney and Doherty* [1988], Crim.L.R. 523). However,

> The absence of an appropriate adult from an interview, at which the defendant's solicitor is present, is unlikely by itself to be a reason to exclude the interview: *R. v. Law-Thompson* [1997] Crim.L.R. 674, CA. There is no rule that a confession obtained from a mentally handicapped person in the absence of a solicitor and an 'appropriate adult' should automatically lead to exclusion under Section 78: *R. v. Ali* [1999] 2 *Archbold News* 2, CA (98 04160 X2) (Richardson, 2001, p. 1525).

In the case of *D.P.P. v. Cornish* (1997, *The Times*, 27 January), the Court of Appeal decided that a confession made in a police interview without an appropriate adult could still be admissible, even though due to learning disability one should have been present. It held that in determining whether a confession was unreliable due to the absence of an appropriate adult, the court should hear evidence as to who was present and what happened during the interview. The court would then be able to form an impression of the effect that the absence of an appropriate adult had in relation to Section 76(2)(b).

The ruling in *R. v. Aspinall* ([1999], Crim.L.R. 741) is particularly important in relation to the appropriate adult safeguard requirement for mentally ill defendants. The defendant had a history of schizophrenia and his condition was stabilized by medication. He was apparently lucid and well oriented in time and space. The police knew about his diagnosis prior to the interview, but decided to interview him in the absence of an appropriate adult. The defendant had declined an offer to consult with a solicitor, and commented, 'I want to get home to my missus and kids' (p. 742). The trial judge had rejected a defence submission that the interview should be excluded under Section 78 of PACE. The defendant was convicted and appealed.

The Court of Appeal held in allowing the appeal:

> ... there was a clear breach of the Code because A should have had an appropriate adult with him when being interviewed. The unfairness arising was compounded by the lack of a solicitor. There was also a breach of Article 6 of the European Convention on Human Rights from the delay in access to legal advice (the duty solicitor was not available at the time). This was particularly so in the case of a vulnerable person such as A who should have had an 'appropriate adult' present. The judge asked himself the wrong questions, whether A's condition obviated the need for an appropriate adult, rather than whether the admission of the evidence would have such adverse effect upon the fairness of the proceedings that it should be excluded: one aspect of unfairness was that admitting the interview might make A appear normal to the jury. The judge failed to have regard to the purpose for which an appropriate adult was required ... (p. 742).

The suitability of the appropriate adult is of great importance, because the person acting in that capacity must be able to discharge their duty (Pearse & Gudjonsson, 1996c). Technically, a failure to use a suitable person as an appropriate adult can render an interview statement inadmissible either under Sections 76 or 78. For example, in *R. v. Morse and Others* ([1991], Crim.L.R. 195) it was found that a juvenile's father was not a suitable appropriate adult because he suffered from a significantly impaired intelligence. This meant that 'the Prosecution had not discharged the burden of proving that the confession was not unreliable under Section 76(2)(b)' (p. 196).

However, usually there have to be some surrounding circumstances that cast doubts upon the reliability of the interview statement. For example, in *R. v. W and another* ([1994], Crim.L.R. 131), a 13-year-old girl was interviewed by the police in the presence of her mother who was mentally disordered (i.e. suffering from a psychotic illness and learning disability). If interviewed by the police herself as a suspect, the mother would have required an appropriate adult. In spite of this the trial judge ruled that the mother had been capable of fulfilling the role of an appropriate adult at the time of her daughter's interview with the police. He also considered that if the mother had not been capable of fulfilling the role of an appropriate adult, it had to be taken into consideration that the interview had been conducted properly and fairly, it had not been excessively long, there was no obvious police pressure, and there was nothing in the interview or in the circumstances of the case to render the daughter's answers unreliable, or to indicate an unfairness upon the proceedings. The case was appealed. The Court of Appeal dismissed the appeal.

Fitness for Interview

It is evident from the above discussion that when the police interview mentally disordered persons there are special legal provisions which help ensure that their statements to the police are reliable and obtained fairly. Even when all legal provisions are adhered to, a judge may on occasion consider it unsafe and unfair to allow the statement to go before the jury. In such cases, the crucial issue may be whether or not the defendant is considered by the judge to have been 'fit' mentally when he or she was interviewed by the police (Gudjonsson, 1995c). In contrast to issues concerning 'fitness to plead' and 'fitness to stand trial', where clear operational criteria exist (Grisso, 1986; Grubin, 1996; Gudjonsson & Haward, 1998), until recently there were no established criteria for determining 'fitness for interview' that could be applied by forensic medical examiners (FMEs, also known as police surgeons) and psychiatrists when assessing suspects at police stations. Indeed, 'fitness for interview' is not a phrase that appears anywhere within PACE or the Codes of Practice.

Robertson (1992) discusses in detail the role of forensic medical examiners in his report for the Royal Commission on Criminal Justice. Prior to the implementation of PACE, FMEs commonly addressed issues relevant to 'fitness for detention' (i.e. whether the suspect was physically or mentally well enough to be detained). In recent years they increasingly also specifically assess 'fitness for interview' and the need for an appropriate adult, although great regional variations have been found in England (Robertson, 1992). 'Fitness for detention' is undoubtedly easier to assess and determine than 'fitness for interview'. The former relies principally on physical signs and symptoms and possible referral to hospital, whereas the latter is typically concerned with the effects of mental factors on the suspect's functioning whilst in police custody, and these are not always easy to detect on the basis of a short interview.

Gudjonsson (1995c) discussed a conceptual framework for assessing 'fitness for interview' when mentally disordered suspects are detained in police custody. The framework was developed from a court case involving a mentally disordered man who had been arrested on suspicion of murder and interviewed by the police in the presence of a solicitor and an appropriate adult. Even though all legal provisions in accordance with PACE were adhered to in the case by the police and the interviews were conducted in 'an impeccably fair and considerate way' the interviews were ruled inadmissible by the trial judge. This judgment was given in spite of the fact that two doctors, both of whom testified at the trial during a *voire dire*, had found the detainee fit to be interviewed by the police.

The case illustrates the legal, psychiatric and psychological issues involved and provides a conceptual framework for assessing fitness for interview in cases of mental disorder. Following this case, improved criteria for evaluating fitness for interview have been developed for FMEs (Gall & Freckelton, 1999; Gudjonsson, Hayes & Rowlands, 2000; Home Office, 2001; Norfolk, 1997a, 1997b, 1999, 2001; Rix, 1997). Gall and Freckelton (1999) discuss fitness for interview in Australia, present empirical data and review the relevant legal cases and judgments. This article is important, because little work has been done on fitness for interview outside England. In Australia important safeguards have been developed and implemented for persons detained for interviews at police stations.

A Conceptual Framework for Fitness for Interview: a Case Study

Mr S was a 34-year-old man with a long history of schizophrenia. He left school at the age of 16 and worked as a hairdresser for three years and subsequently as a night security officer. In his early 20s he became increasingly withdrawn and was dismissed from his job because of mental illness. He was diagnosed as having schizophrenia. His main symptoms were extreme social and emotional withdrawal. He also complained of voices insulting him. He had four separate admissions to a psychiatric hospital, after which he was discharged from hospital and his care was transferred to a general practitioner. Mr S's intelligence was measured during his first admission to hospital. His Full Scale IQ score was 83, his Verbal and Performance scores being 89 and 78, respectively.

A few years after his discharge from hospital, Mr S was arrested on the suspicion of having battered a woman to death. The murder weapon was thought to be a champagne bottle, which had been found in the vicinity of the murder victim. Mr S's fingerprint was on the bottle and there was a small trace of blood found on the bottle that could have come from the victim, although this was not conclusive. Mr S had no previous criminal convictions.

Prior to being interviewed, the police knew that Mr S had a psychiatric history and through a local appropriate adult scheme they contacted a psychiatric social worker. He attended the police station and acted as an appropriate adult. After arriving at the police station, Mr S was seen by a forensic medical examiner, who considered that he was 'fit to be interviewed', but in view of the seriousness of the case and concerns raised by the solicitor he recommended that Mr S was assessed by a psychiatrist. Mr S was assessed by a consultant psychiatrist, who concluded

> He is calm and coherent; he has no overt psychotic symptoms but some evidence of thought block. He seems to understand why he has been brought to the police station. In my opinion he is fit to be interviewed.

The appropriate adult was also of the view that Mr S was fit to be interviewed.

The police interviewed Mr S on five occasions over a 36-hour period. The interviews were all fairly short. The longest interview lasted 40 minutes and the five interviews lasted in total less than two hours. A solicitor and an appropriate adult were present during all the interviews. It was evident from the audio-tape recording of the interviews that Mr S was interviewed very carefully by the police officers, who asked him simple and non-leading questions and avoided placing him under pressure.

Mr S made no confession to the murder during any of the interviews. However, he made certain incriminating comments that were used against him at his trial. First, he had made certain apparently untrue denials (e.g. not having been out of his house for three weeks, which was contradicted by witnesses), which the prosecution were relying on as indication of a sense of guilt. Secondly, there was, according to the prosecution, an indication of special knowledge, which involved his acknowledging during the third interview that the woman had been hit on the head with a bottle (i.e. 'I didn't hit her over the head at all with it. Well she was hit over the head by the bottle, was she?'). This reply was in response to the officer telling him 'I have a bottle and on that bottle is the blood of Miss... and also on it is your fingerprint. Can you tell me how that can be?'.

Prior to trial I was commissioned by the defence to evaluate whether or not Mr S had been 'fit for interview' whilst in police detention. This involved my focusing on his mental state at the time and the content of his answers to police questioning during the five interviews with a view to assessing their reliability. All the police interviews had been recorded on audio-tapes and transcripts made. I listened to the tapes of these interviews and read the transcripts.

Mr S was difficult to assess, because he was very agitated and seemed totally absorbed in his immediate needs (i.e. smoking his cigarettes, wanting to go and watch television). An intellectual assessment indicated an IQ of 62, which was very much lower than the score of 83 that he had obtained when assessed during his first admission in hospital 10 years previously. His memory and concentration also proved extremely poor on testing. It did not prove possible to have meaningful conversation with him and his answers were very concrete.

An inspection of the Custody Record indicated that Mr S's solicitor had been unsuccessful in explaining the 'old' police caution to him (he was arrested and interviewed prior to the introduction of the new caution in 1995). The solicitor told the Custody Officer that he did not think that his client was 'fit for interview'. The police were not obliged to accept the solicitor's views and continued to interview Mr S. They had the benefit of the opinion of two doctors and a psychiatric social worker, all of whom had considered at the time that Mr S was 'fit for interview'.

Mr S's answers and comments during the police interviews were of considerable interest, because they indicated that Mr S was not functioning well mentally. For example, at the beginning of the second interview Mr S said he could not recall anything about the previous interview that had been conducted a few hours previously. Second, the taped interviews showed that Mr S was preoccupied with being released from custody. Third, some of Mr S's statements were incoherent (referred to as 'gibberish' by the trial judge). Fourth, there was an indication from two of the tapes that Mr S confused the identity of his solicitor and the appropriate adult with the police officers (e.g. at one point he turned to his solicitor and said 'Are you the Chief Inspector?'). Fifth, during the fourth taped interview, Mr S became confused when the police asked him to think back six days.

An example of Mr S's concrete thinking is well illustrated during the fourth interview when he was asked what a lie is, as shown by the following conversation with a police officer.

Police	'Do you know what a lie is?'
Mr S	'What do you mean?'
Police	'Can you tell me what a lie is?'
Mr S	'What lie?'
Police	'Do you know the difference between truth and a lie?'
Mr S	'What lie?'
Police	'Any lie.'
Mr S	'What do you mean?'

The main conclusion from the psychological assessment was that Mr S had not been functioning well mentally during the police interviews and it was unsafe to rely on his answers. My view was that Mr S had not been 'fit for interview', which was highlighted by his confusion, disorientation and concrete thinking during the police interviews.

At Mr S's trial, the first legal issue addressed was his fitness to plead. He was found unfit to plead by a jury empanelled for that purpose. A second jury was then sworn in to try the issue of whether he had committed the criminal act he was charged with (i.e. murder or manslaughter). Prior to the actual trial, there was an application by the defence under PACE to exclude the five police interviews. The basis for the submission was Mr S's mental state at the time of the police interviews. That is, the defence argued that he had been unfit to be interviewed by the police and it would therefore be *unfair*, in accordance with Section 78 of PACE, to allow his statements to go before the jury.

The prosecution called the two medical witnesses who assessed him at the police station prior to the interviews. They gave evidence during the *voire dire*.

The forensic medical examiner testified that

> ...his views were that the question that he had to ask himself in the context were whether or not when he asked general questions about how he came to be there, and what he had been doing, and matters of that kind by way of general discussion, if his answers were given rationally and no incongruity was found...he regarded him as fit for interview.

The consultant psychiatrist testified that Mr S had been fit to be interviewed by the police.

I testified on behalf of Mr S's defence and argued on the basis of the psychological assessment that Mr S had not been fit to be interviewed whilst in police custody. I based my arguments on Mr S's poor mental functioning whilst in police custody and his answers and comments during the police interviews.

The judge ruled that the police interview statements were inadmissible under Section 78 of PACE:

> ...it would be unfair, and that the fair conduct of these proceedings would be adversely affected by the admission of these interviews.

This judgment was in spite of the fact that the judge clearly thought that the police had dealt with Mr S 'in an impeccably fair and considerate way'. Thus

> In the course of the interviews these officers were, in my judgment, extremely careful to avoid long, oppressive, complicated, or leading questions and they, as far as I can tell, did their utmost to avoid asking questions which were suggestive of the answers that they wished to be heard.

The main basis of the judge's ruling was as follows.

1. The two doctors, at the time of their assessment, had failed to approach 'the question of fitness on the basis of considering whether or not any answers given by Mr S... to any questions asked of him by the police officers were necessarily reliable'. Instead, the two doctors had 'considered that the ordeal and stress and strain of being interviewed, particularly on such a serious charge as this, was something that in their judgment the suspect could sustain without suffering any consequential harm to either his physical or mental health'.
2. The judge discussed the psychological evidence in detail and it formed the basis on which the judge ruled the police interview statements inadmissible (see Gudjonsson, 1995c, for details).
3. The judge accepted that Mr S was incapable of appreciating or understanding the full impact of the caution properly administered at the outset and beginning of each interview.
4. The judge concluded that the jury would find it impossible, even if they had the benefit of expert evidence and the appropriate warning that he would otherwise have given, to make sense of Mr S's comments in the interviews.

The case raised a number of important issues. Most importantly, the case provides a potential conceptual framework for the assessment of 'fitness for interview'. Prior to PACE, doctors attending police stations tended to focus on 'fitness for detention' and paid insufficient attention to 'fitness for interview'. This has now changed. The trial judge rightly pointed out that the term 'fitness for interview' does not appear in PACE and there are no standard criteria by which to assess it. This is a serious omission, which should be amended by the Home Office in their revision of PACE and the current Codes of Practice. Interestingly, fitness for interview was not an issue that was specifically addressed by the Royal Commission on Criminal Justice (Runciman, 1993), but recently a Working Group was set up by the Home Office to address this issue (Home Office, 2001).

The present case suggests that the criteria used by judges in the future to determine fitness for interview are likely to be very stringent. The trial judge came to the firm conclusion that the term does not mean that 'a person must be shown to be capable of understanding or dealing properly and accurately with questions put to him', because this is adequately dealt with by various provisions within PACE and its Codes of Practice for special groups considered to be vulnerable or 'at risk' during interviewing. This includes the presence of an appropriate adult during interviews and a warning to the jury by the judge about the defendant's vulnerabilities.

The additional vulnerabilities considered important by the trial judge for unfitness for interview are mental factors that *substantially impair the detainee's ability to*

- understand his or her basic legal rights such as the police caution and
- give a reliable statement to the police during questioning.

Using the present case as a yardstick, there appear to be at least three broad criteria for fitness for interview, although all three may not necessarily be required in every case.

First, does the detainee understand the police caution after it has been carefully explained to him or her? If, for example, a solicitor finds it impossible to explain the police caution to his client after making several attempts, this would be a strong sign that the detainee may be unfit for interview. This was the case with Mr S. It is of interest that since this case was dismissed a new and far more complicated police caution has been introduced and implemented (Clare, Gudjonsson & Harari, 1998; Home Office, 1995).

Second, is the detainee fully orientated in time, place and person and does he or she recognize the key persons present during the police interview (e.g. can he or she differentiate between the police, the solicitor and the appropriate adult)? In the case of Mr S, he confused both the solicitor and the appropriate adult with the police. This suggests a serious mental disturbance.

Third, is the detainee likely to give answers that can be misconstrued by the court? In the case of Mr S, the normal assumption that lies during a police interview indicate a sense of criminal guilt was possibly unfounded, because of his obsession with his immediate needs, concrete thinking and inability to foresee the likely consequences of his answers. In exceptional cases involving confessions, detainees may be so mentally disturbed that they will incriminate themselves in order to fulfil their immediate needs (e.g. being released from custody, going to hospital).

The three basic criteria proposed above involve the *functional abilities* of the detainees and it therefore requires a functional assessment (i.e. an assessment that directly addresses the relevant areas of the detainee's functioning, such as his or her understanding of what is happening).

Within the conceptual framework provided above, and based on the findings of the studies by Gudjonsson *et al.* (1993) and Gudjonsson, Clare and Rutter (1994), it is rare for suspects detained at a police station to be found to fulfil the criteria set out above as being unfit for interview. However, the case clearly indicates a worrying possibility of this happening, even if rare, and forensic medical examiners must learn to address issues relevant to *reliability* rather than focusing principally or exclusively on factors that relate to possible consequential harm from the interview to the detainee's physical and mental health.

Recent Developments with Regard to Fitness for Interview

The Report of the Home Office Working Group on Police Surgeons (Home Office, 2001) provides an important review of the current situation in England with regard to fitness for interview. The Group's recommendation is that any judgement about fitness for interview requires the consideration of the following three factors.

1. *The assessment of the person to be interviewed.* Here the FME will need to consider the physical and mental state of the detainee. The emphasis is on the functional ability of the detainee rather than relying on a medical diagnosis. Norfolk (2001) recommends that during the assessment process the FME should consider the detainee's personality as well as mental and physical health. The three personality factors that Norfolk considers to be central are suggestibility, compliance and acquiescence. I agree that personality factors need to be considered, but the emphasis should be on abnormal mental states rather than attempting to evaluate personality traits such as suggestibility, compliance and acquiescence, which are difficult to assess without formal testing (Gudjonsson, Hayes & Rowlands, 2000). Indeed, even if a detainee is found to be abnormally suggestible or compliant, this will not render him or her unfit for interview, nor will it necessarily require the presence of an appropriate adult (Gudjonsson, 1997g).
2. *The likely demand characteristics of the police interview.* Long, intellectually and emotionally demanding interviews require a greater physical and mental capacity than short and straightforward interviews.
3. *The impact of the physical or mental disorder on the interview process and the reliability of any statements made.* Here the FME will need to consider all the relevant factors and circumstances in the case, including the nature of the arrest, detention and police interview. The essential question relates to how the physical or mental condition will affect the capacity of the detainee to function in the police interview. The presence of mental illness *per se*, even when severe, does not automatically render a detainee unfit for interview. It is the effects of the mental illness on cognitive and emotional processes that are relevant and important, not the illness *per se*. Conversely, a detainee who is disorientated, has severe concentration problems, is very fatigued or is intoxicated or withdrawing from illicit substances while in police custody, but not mentally ill, is likely to be considered temporarily unfit for interview. In this instance, the impaired physical and mental condition may well be considered temporary and the FME will probably re-examine the detainee after a certain period of time to ascertain whether he or she is now fit for interview.

The Home Office Working Group advised that a detained person may be unfit for interview: in the following cases.

1. If the interview could to a significant degree worsen the physical or mental illness that is present.
2. When what the detainee says or does may be considered unreliable in subsequent court proceedings, because of the impaired physical or mental condition.

According to the Home Office Guidelines, the FME will need to quantify the risk of such unreliability into one of four categories.

- *Definite risk*. Here the detainee is unlikely to be fit for interview at any stage.
- *Major risk*. The detainee is unfit for interview at the time of the assessment, but a further evaluation is required at a later time.
- *Some risk*. Here precautions are advised, which may include a recommendation for the presence of an appropriate adult or a referral to other medical or psychiatric advice.
- *No discernible risk*. The interview can proceed without the presence of an appropriate adult or a further medical or psychiatric intervention.

Hopefully, the new guidelines will reduce the inconsistency previously found among FMEs in different police forces in determining fitness for interview and the need for an appropriate adult. Robertson (1992) found significant differences in the working practice of doctors in the Metropolitan Police and other forces. For example, in relation to cases referred to FMEs for an assessment of mental disorder, only 1% were found unfit for interview in the Metropolitan Police in contrast to 12% in other police forces. Conversely, FMEs in the Metropolitan Police were significantly more likely to recommend the need for an appropriate adult than doctors in other forces; 23 in contrast to 1%. Therefore, advice about appropriate adults was rarely given in police forces outside London. The explanation given by the FMEs for their failure to give advice about the need for an appropriate adult was that this was entirely a matter for the police. This view, although technically correct, may have serious consequences, because if the mentally disordered detainee is seen by an FME and there is no specific recommendation for an appropriate adult even if one is needed, the police tend not to seek one (Medford, Gudjonsson & Pearse, 2000). In other words, custody officers tend to abrogate to the FME their responsibility of deciding whether an appropriate adult is necessary.

So far I have only dealt with questions related to fitness for interview in connection with mental disorder. Whilst being detained at a police station there are other important issues to be addressed, such as fitness for detention, charge, transfer or release and detainees being able to give informed consent about the provision of intimate samples (e.g. blood specimen) and attending identification parades. In addition, assessing mental disorder among suspects represents less than 10% of the consultation time of forensic medical examiners (Robertson, 1992). Associated with the mental health of detainees is the growing problem of 'substance misuse', which was discussed in detail in Chapter 15.

Adverse Inferences

The Criminal Justice and Public Order Act 1994 (Wasik & Taylor, 1995) makes it possible for the court to draw adverse inferences from an accused's silence. This relates to the failure to mention facts when questioned under caution or when charged (Section 34), from failure to give evidence at trial (Section 35), from failure or refusal to account for objects, substances or marks (Section 36) and failure or refusal to account for one's presence at a particular place (Section 37). Section 38 provides definitions and interpretations of relevance to

Sections 34 to 37. Section 39 provides the authority to apply Sections 34 to 38 to the armed services.

One of the main impacts of changes to the right of silence is to place detainees under increasing pressure to answer questions (Bucke & Brown, 1997; Hodgson, 1997). The complexity of the new caution and the fact that the great majority of detainees do not fully understand it (Fenner, Gudjonsson & Clare, 2002) are additional problems.

Legal advice to a suspect to remain silent when interviewed by the police does not prevent an adverse inference being drawn under Section 34 when the case goes to court (Richardson, 2001). This was made clear by the ruling in *Condron and Condron* ([1997], Cr.App.R. 185). However, in view of a ruling by the European Court of Human Rights in Condron v. U.K., domestic courts will need to give 'appropriate weight' to mitigating circumstances because there may be good reasons for such legal advice (Richardson, 2001, p. 1503).

Section 58 of the Youth Justice and Criminal Evidence Act 1999 amends Section 34 of Criminal Justice and Public Order Act so that no adverse inferences can be drawn from silence, or failure to provide an explanation, whilst the suspect is detained at a police station, unless he or she has been provided with the opportunity to consult with a solicitor.

As far as Sections 34 and 35 are concerned there are some fundamental differences between these two sections (*R. v. Doldur* [2000], Crim.L.R. 178). With regard to Section 34 the issue is whether the explanation relied upon by the defendant at trial is suspicious due to it not having been provided earlier (e.g. at the time of the police interview or when charged). In their deliberation, the jury would usually be directed to consider both the prosecution and defence evidence. In contrast, Section 35 direction is confined to the prosecution evidence and the jury can only draw adverse inferences if they found the Crown's case required an answer. In other words, there has to be a *prima facie* case before the jury can draw adverse inferences. According to the decision and standard directions formulated in *Cowan, Gayle and Ricciardi* ([1996], Crim.App.R. 1) pursuant to Section 35, there are four essential requirements of the judge in terms of instructions to the jury. First, the judge has to make it clear that burden of proof remains with the prosecution throughout, and to specify what the required standard is. Second, the defendant has the legal right to exercise his right of silence. Third, an inference from failure to testify cannot on its own prove guilt. Fourth, the judge has to ensure that the jury knows that they must find a case to answer (i.e. a *prima facie* case) on the prosecution evidence before they draw any inferences from silence. A judge's failure to provide this direction may risk the jury drawing adverse inferences from silence before it considers whether there is a *prima facie* case. As recognized in *R. v. Birchall* ([1999], Crim.L.R. 311), an omission by a trial judge to give full standard directions to the jury resulted in the Court of Appeal quashing a murder conviction:

> ...standard directions were devised to serve the ends of justice and the Court must be astute to ensure that these ends were not jeopardised by failure to give directions where they were called for. The drawing of inferences from silence was a particularly sensitive area and many respected authorities had voiced the fear

that Section 35 and its sister sections may lead to wrongful convictions. The Court was of the view that it seemed very possible that the application of these provisions could lead to decisions adverse to the United Kingdom at Strasbourg under Article 6(1) and (2) of the European Convention on Human Rights unless the provisions were the subject of very carefully framed directions to juries (p. 312).

In the present case the omission to give full directions rendered the conviction unsafe because after consideration of new evidence the Court did not consider the Crown's case called for an answer from the appellant. The Court was left in doubt as to the appellant's guilt and accordingly quashed his conviction (pp. 312–313).

Section 35 applies to defendants who are 14 years or older. However, according to Subsection 1(b) no adverse inferences should be drawn if

...it appears to the court that the physical or mental condition of the accused makes it undesirable for him to give evidence.

The leading case with regard to the issue of undesirability due to mental factors is that of *R. v. Billy-Joe Friend* ([1997], Cr.App.R. 231). The case involved a 15-year-old youth who was charged with murder. Shortly prior to trial, I had assessed the defendant for the defence and found him to have an IQ score of 63. He did not prove to be suggestible on testing. I testified at the Central Criminal Court during a *voire dire* and stated that in spite of his low intelligence the appellant could give a clear account in an interview if allowed time to express himself and if care was taken that he understood, but his performance in the witness box might be a different matter due to the increased stress. The defence counsel submitted that on the basis of my evidence the jury should not be invited to draw an adverse inference from his failure to give evidence

...because his mental condition made it undesirable to do so in light of Section 35(1)(b). The judge declined so to rule and referred to the fact that children as young as eight years old gave evidence in Crown Court trials. In his summing-up he directed the jury that it was open to them to draw an adverse inference from the appellant's failure to give evidence. The appellant was convicted of murder (p. 231).

The judge's decision was appealed; the Court of Appeal delivered a detailed judgment concerning the weight of the psychological evidence and stated:

As envisaged in *Cowan* there was some evidential basis before the judge. Dr Gudjonsson had written a comprehensive report and gave evidence. This evidence, impressive as it undoubtedly was, was not conclusive of the issue. The judge was fully entitled to consider the rest of the evidence in the case including, in our view, the conduct before and after the offence was committed and the answers he gave to the police at interview (p. 241).

The case highlighted the fact that there are no formal guidelines as to how to exercise their discretion under Section 35. There are no specific tests that can be routinely applied to cases when construing the meaning of the word 'undesirable'. The court concluded that

> ...it will only be in very rare cases that a judge will have to consider whether it is undesirable for an accused to give evidence on account of his mental condition (p. 239). In the majority of cases there will be evidence that he is 'unfit to plead' (p. 240).

The word 'undesirable' means something less than 'unfit to plead' (*R. v. Barry George*, Central Criminal Court, 15 June 2001). Interestingly, in the well publicized Jill Dando murder case, the defendant Barry George, who had a history of epilepsy and significant neuropsychological deficits, was considered fit to plead and stand trial by three defence expert witnesses (Professor Gisli Gudjonsson, Professor Michael Kopelman & Dr Susan Young). Nevertheless, the defence experts considered that certain problems might arise during his testimony, which made it potentially undesirable for him to go into the witness box. The judge agreed and advised the jury that no adverse inferences should be drawn about Mr George's failure to go into the witness box.

Another important aspect of the Jill Dando case, which set precedent, was that at the beginning of the 10 week trial, the judge ruled that a social worker would stay with Mr George in the dock to provide him with emotional and practical support, and, in addition to this, a clinical psychologist, Dr Susan Young, was commissioned by the judge to sit in court throughout the trial, observe Mr George's demeanour and provide him in the breaks with the clinical psychology service required to help him cope with the trial. It was only by this provision that Mr George was fit to stand trial and the case could precede without any further problems and delays. During legal arguments, at the beginning of the trial, Mr George had developed a psychogenic blindness, which lasted five days and was overcome by my successfully providing him with a brief session of hypnosis.

THE ADMISSIBILITY OF EXPERT EVIDENCE

The question of admissibility can arise with regard to any evidence, including expert testimony. When lawyers seek to introduce the expert opinion or findings of psychologists or psychiatrists, then the judge has to decide on the admissibility of the evidence. The judge hears submissions and legal arguments by the defence and prosecution in the absence of the jury. The fundamental criteria for the admissibility of expert testimony were stated by Lord Justice Lawton in the case of *R. v. Turner* ([1975], 60 Cr.App.R. 80, C.A.). These are:

> An expert's opinion is admissible to furnish the court with scientific information which is likely to be outside the experience and knowledge of a judge or jury (Richardson, 2001, p. 439).

According to the *Turner* principle, it is not permitted for experts, whether psychiatrists or psychologists, to give evidence about how an ordinary person is likely to react to stressful situations. Neither can experts give evidence about matters directly related to the likely veracity of witnesses or defendants, although in 'very exceptional circumstances' this may happen (Richardson,

2001, p. 439). This means that English law has a rather restrictive approach to the admissibility of evidence from expert witnesses (Coleman & Mackey, 1995; Fitzgerald, 1987; Gudjonsson, 1992c; Mackey & Coleman, 1991). Mackey and Coleman (1991) argue that there are more problems with the admissibility of psychological than psychiatric evidence, because the science of psychology focuses more on normal behaviour; in contrast psychiatry is mainly devoted to the diagnosis and treatment of mental disorder. Psychologists are not allowed to give evidence on such matters as eyewitness testimony, unlike their counterparts in America (Davies, 1983), although in practice there have been exceptions to this rule (Gudjonsson & Haward, 1998). Generally, however, the evidence of psychologists, like that of psychiatrists, has to deal with the presence of mental abnormality. When this involves mental illness or learning disability the evidence is readily admissible.

Problems can arise when dealing with diagnosis of 'personality disorder' rather than mental illness or learning disability. For example, in the case of *R. v. Mackinney and Pinfold* ([1981], 72 Cr.App.R. 78) a social psychologist was not allowed to testify as to the likely unreliability of the testimony of a 'psychopathic' prosecution 'supergrass' whom he had observed in court but never formally interviewed. The decision to exclude the psychologist's evidence was upheld by the Court of Appeal. It was decided that

> Whether or not a witness in a criminal trial is capable of giving reliable evidence is a question of fact for the jury (Mitchell and Richardson, 1985, p. 420).

The principal set out in *Turner* has caused some difficulties. For example, in *R. v. Strudwick and Merry* ([1994], 99 Cr.App.R. 326) it was decided that

> The admissibility of expert psychiatric evidence is a question of fact in the particular circumstances of the case. The law is in a state of development in this area. There may well be mental conditions other than mental illness about which a jury might require expert assistance in order to understand and evaluate their effect on the issues of the case (p. 439).

The judgments in the Court of Appeal cases discussed in Part III illustrate well how in recent years the law has changed in relation to the admissibility of psychological and psychiatric evidence in the absence of mental illness. For example, psychological and psychiatric evidence has been admitted in cases of personality disorder, following the landmark case of *Judith Ward* ([1992], 96 Cr.App.R. 1; see Chapter 18 for a detailed discussion of the case and subsequent legal developments). A formal diagnosis of personality disorder is not even required for the admissibility of such evidence, as clearly ruled in *R. v. O'Brien, Hall and Sherewood* (*The Times*, 16 February 2000):

> ...for expert evidence as to some abnormality to be admissible in respect of the reliability of a defendant's confession it is neither necessary nor sufficient that the abnormality should fit into some recognised category; what is necessary is that the disorder must be of a type which might render a confession or evidence unreliable and it must represent a significant deviation from the norm (Richardson, 2001, p. 440; see Chapter 18 for details of the case and the ruling).

Another important case that is relevant to the admissibility of expert testimony concerning the reliability of testimony is that of *Toohey v. Commissioner of Metropolitan Police* ([1965], A.C. 595, H.L.). Here the Court of Appeal held that the trial judge had been wrong in not admitting the evidence of a police surgeon to the effect that, soon after alleging an assault, a prosecution witness had been in such a state of hysteria, which had been exacerbated by alcohol, that anything he said at the time was likely to be unreliable.

Relevant expert evidence is admitted when there is evidence of mental illness or learning disability. According to the judgment in the case of *Masih* ([1986], Crim.L.R. 395), an IQ of 69 or below is required for a defendant to be formally classified as mentally handicapped and here the expert evidence would be admissible, whenever it was considered relevant. In the *Masih* case the defendant's IQ was 72, which falls at the lower end of the 'borderline range' (i.e. bottom 3% of the population). Lord Lane's view was that expert testimony in a borderline case will not as a rule be necessary and should therefore be excluded.

However, in spite of Lord Lane's ruling in *Masih*, there have subsequently been many examples of judges allowing psychologists' evidence when the defendant's IQ was above 70, including *R. v. Delany* ([1989], 88 Cr.App.R. 338), where Lord Lane himself quashed a conviction under Section 76(2)(b) of PACE in part because of psychological evidence presented at the original trial:

> There was evidence before the court from an educational psychologist that the appellant had an IQ of 80 and his emotional arousal was such that he might wish to rid himself of an interview as rapidly as possible (p. 339)... Had the learned judge paid the attention which we think he should have paid to the long term expectations of the appellant rather than to the prospects of immediate release, and had he paid attention to the fact that the breaches of the Code deprived the court of the knowledge which should have been available to it, namely of precisely what was said by these officers in the vital interview, the judge would, and we think should, have ruled against the admission of these confessions, particularly against the background of the appellant's age, his subnormal mentality and the behaviour of the police and what they had admitted to him (p. 343).

Beaumont (1987) gives two examples. I have personally given evidence in a large number of cases in Britain where the defendants' IQ was in the borderline range or above. About 20% of defendants referred to me for a psychological assessment in cases of retracted confession have IQs below 70, and a further two-thirds have IQs that fall in the borderline range (i.e. 70–79; Gudjonsson, 1990a). My personal experience is that judges are generally reluctant to exclude psychological evidence when it seems relevant, even though within the rigid guidance from the Appeal Court the evidence should perhaps have been ruled inadmissible.

There are in practice some notable exceptions. In one case, heard at the Central Criminal Court, a defendant's IQ was 70, which is one point above the 'magic' figure of 69. The judge read my report and listened to legal submissions. He disallowed my evidence as the IQ was 70 and not 69 or below. However, during his summing up the judge referred to some of my findings without specifically stating that he did so. The first I learned about it was when the results of my assessment were mentioned on the radio. In the view of the barrister involved in the case, 'The judge gave your evidence for you'. There have been other similar cases where judges have disallowed the psychological evidence, but have themselves come to the same conclusion as expressed in the expert's report.

The landmark judgment in the case of Engin Raghip (*R. v. Silcott, Braithwaite, Raghip*; *The Times*, 9 December 1991) broadened and clarified the criteria for the admissibility of psychological evidence in cases of disputed confessions (Gudjonsson, 1992c; see Chapter 18 in this book for a detailed discussion of the case). It no longer became necessary to rely on an arbitrary IQ score of 69 as the cut-off point for defining 'mental handicap' under Section 77 of PACE; in addition, the concept of interrogative suggestibility, its measurement, validity and relevance were approved by the Court of Appeal, and the Court warned that high suggestibility and intellectual deficits could not satisfactorily be detected by observations of the defendant's performance in the witness box. As far as disputed confessions are concerned, this was the first and most groundbreaking judgment for the admissibility and role of expert psychological evidence.

Expert psychological evidence of a significant impairment in intellectual functioning is now routinely accepted, but until recently problems did sometimes arise when dealing with abnormal personality traits, such as suggestibility and compliance. Fortunately, as illustrated in Part III, clearer guidelines are being provided in the recent Court of Appeal judgments.

The reverse proposition is never put forward by the prosecution, that is, the argument that a person of superior intellect and abnormally low suggestibility is less susceptible than the average person to pressure, manipulation or coercion. Such evidence would not be admissible in English courts. Similarly, even if it can be shown that the suspect fully understood his legal rights unaided, a failure to read him his rights prior to custodial interrogation would normally, but not inevitably, be considered a breach. For example, in *Alladice* ([1988], 87 Cr.App.R. 380) a suspect had been arrested so often that it was assumed that he knew his rights already and he stated in evidence that this was indeed the case; therefore the refusal to have access to a solicitor was not a sufficiently serious breach to demand exclusion, as he did not need the advice:

> Had the solicitor been present, his advice would have added nothing to the knowledge of his rights which the appellant already had. The police, as the judge found, had acted with propriety at the interviews and therefore the solicitor's presence would not have improved the appellant's case in that respect. This is therefore a case where a clear breach of Section 58 nevertheless does not require the Court to rule inadmissible subsequent statements made by the defendant (p. 387).

Of course, the prosecution can use certain positive characteristics to support their case during rebuttal (i.e. when cross-examining the defence experts). For example, there are cases where defendants have been shown to suffer from learning disability, which makes the expert evidence admissible, but personality testing showed them to be exceptionally resistant to interrogative pressure. The defence would place emphasis on the low IQ with regard to the defendant's disputed confession, but the prosecution may use the personality findings (e.g. low suggestibility) to argue that in spite of low intellectual abilities the defendant is able to stand up to interrogation. Two cases illustrate this point. The third case shows that even if there is no evidence of deliberate police malpractice or internal vulnerability the confession may still be excluded on simply the basis of the words used by the police.

Mr F

Mr F was a 27-year-old man who was charged with armed robbery. He had several previous convictions for similar offences. The psychological assessment revealed that Mr F was of borderline intelligence (Full Scale IQ of 74), but he did not prove to be unduly suggestible or compliant on testing. A copy of my report was given to the prosecution before I gave my evidence at the Central Criminal Court during a *voire dire*. The judge stated in court that he would allow my evidence during this part of the proceedings but he might not if the confession went before the jury. During my evidence the defence concentrated on Mr F's borderline IQ and how that could have disadvantaged him during interrogation. In rebuttal, the prosecution noticed the reference in my report to the modest suggestibility and compliance scores and used it to support their argument that Mr F was well able to cope with the interrogation that resulted in his confession. The judge allowed the confession to go before the jury. Mr F was convicted and sentenced to prison.

Mr G

Mr G was a 25-year-old man with learning disability. He had been charged with murdering an elderly lady in her own home, which he had broken into. A psychiatrist and a psychologist for the defence had assessed him. Mr G had been interviewed for 45 minutes in the presence of a solicitor and an appropriate adult. During the interview Mr G made a confession to the murder and to having set fire to the room in which the woman had been murdered. Mr G subsequently retracted his confession, claiming that he had been frightened of the police and that they had put pressure on him to confess. Mr G's solicitors had succeeded, during a previous trial for arson, to have his confession excluded on the basis of his learning disability. The police had then interviewed him without an appropriate adult. Subsequently, following his arrest on suspicion of the murder, the police had interviewed him conscientiously and had ensured that both a solicitor and an appropriate adult were present. Nevertheless, at Mr G's trial the defence sought to have the confession excluded. I had assessed Mr G on behalf of the prosecution. I found him to have an IQ of 60, which was identical to that found when he had been previously tested by the defence psychologist. However, Mr G obtained low scores on the GSS 1 and GSS 2, where he had been tested on two separate occasions. I concluded that Mr G was a person with a learning disability, but in spite of this I found no evidence to indicate that he was unusually suggestible and vulnerable to interpersonal pressure. Indeed, considering his learning disability, he seemed overall less suggestible than most persons with learning disabilities whom I had tested in similar circumstances.

During Mr G's trial I gave evidence twice in rebuttal of the defence experts, first during the *voire dire* and again in front of the jury. On both occasions I was asked to comment on the tests I had used and on the interviewing technique used by the police. The defence had assumed Mr G was suggestible and susceptible to erroneous evidence because of his learning disability. My evidence showed that, in spite of learning disability, he appeared well able to cope with interrogative pressure. Furthermore, in my view, the police had carefully interviewed Mr G with the minimum number of leading questions.

The judge, at Maidstone Crown Court, allowed Mr G's confession to go before the jury who convicted him of manslaughter on the grounds of diminished responsibility.

Mr S

Confession evidence can be excluded on the basis of police misconduct or because of idiosyncratic vulnerability (e.g. low IQ, high suggestibility), or a combination of both. Even when no misconduct has taken place, the inadvertent use of the wrong words or phrases by the police may be sufficient to have the confession excluded. The following case illustrates the point.

Mr S was a 37-year-old man of average intelligence. He was charged with gross indecency concerning his teenage daughter. I assessed the man psychologically, but there were no specific vulnerabilities that were likely to assist the defence. However, the contemporaneous record of the police interview revealed a conversation which supported inadmissibility according to Section 76(2)(b). The relevant record was as follows.

> Q. 'Did you touch her private parts whilst she was in bed?'
> A. 'As a deliberate movement no.'
> Q. 'Did you take her into your bedroom whilst your wife was out working during the evening?'
> A. 'I did not take her into the bedroom.'
> Q. 'Tell me what happened.'
> A. 'You are asking me to say something I don't want to.'
> Q. 'You've got to, let's clear the air and get it over and done with.'
> A. 'It just disgusts me.' (The suspect then went on to describe in great detail what is alleged to have happened.)

The judge in this case, in Lewes Crown Court, ruled the confession inadmissible, because of the words used by the police officer. From the police point of view the remark may have been quite innocent and spontaneous, but it had serious consequences with regard to the exclusion of a detailed self-incriminating confession from being heard from the jury. Mr S was acquitted by the jury after it heard the evidence of the daughter.

CONCLUSIONS

It is a fundamental assumption in English law that the greatest reliance can be placed on a confession that is given freely and voluntarily. As a matter of law, confessions deemed to be involuntary and coerced are excluded. There is also a discretionary exclusion for unfairness, which is commonly used successfully. Confession evidence can be excluded on the basis of police misconduct or because of some idiosyncratic vulnerability (e.g. youth, low IQ, high suggestibility or compliance) or, indeed, the combination of both. Even when no deliberate police misconduct has taken place, the use of the wrong words or phrases during the interrogation may be sufficient to have the confession excluded.

In this chapter, the English law and legal practice in relation to confession evidence and the admissibility of expert psychological and psychiatric evidence have been reviewed. The introduction of the Police and Criminal Evidence Act 1984 (PACE) in England and Wales has had an impact in deterring police misconduct and in protecting the legal rights of suspects. However, English legal provisions only apply to *custodial interrogation*. They provide insufficient protection for suspects who are questioned whilst not under arrest (e.g. they may initially be interviewed informally and 'softened up' prior to the formal interrogation). Although this undoubtedly sometimes happens in England (Moston & Stephenson, 1992), it is less of a problem in England than it is in America (see Chapter 11).

The introduction of the Criminal Justice and Public Order Act 1994, which came into effect in April 1995, abolished the right to silence. This means that the judge and jury can draw adverse inferences of guilt against a defendant who exercised his right to silence or failed to mention a relevant fact during police questioning, or failed to take the witness stand. Another problem associated with the abolishment of the right to silence is that the accompanying change in the wording of the police caution has greatly increased its complexity, thus placing vulnerable detainees at a disadvantage in terms of not fully understanding the meaning of the new police caution.

Strictly speaking, expert psychiatric or psychological testimony is only admissible in the English courts when it deals with some mental abnormality, particularly in relation to mental illness and learning disability. However, in spite of the traditionally restrictive approach of the Court of Appeal to expert testimony, trial judges often seem reluctant to exclude psychological evidence when it is relevant to the legal issues, even when there is no evidence of mental illness or learning disability. Of particular importance is evidence that relates to certain personality traits (e.g. suggestibility and compliance). Such evidence is often relevant to the legal issues in cases of retracted confessions. English judges are more reluctant to admit this kind of evidence than evidence of significantly impaired intellectual abilities, but they are increasingly recognising its importance and are often allowing it, during the *voire dire* and the trial proper, particularly since the ruling in *Raghip* (see Chapter 18). Once the psychological evidence has been allowed in evidence it may help the judge to decide on issues related to confession admissibility, or if presented in front of the jury it may help them to deliberate on the weight and reliability of the confession.

This chapter shows that during the past decade there has been an unprecedented change in the attitude of the Court of Appeal to the admissibility and significance of psychological evidence. Psychological evidence is increasingly being admitted into evidence in the Court of Appeal, even in the absence of a diagnosis of mental disorder. Furthermore, it has been influential in identifying unreliable confessions, resulting in the quashing of wrongful convictions. This unique development is discussed in detail in Part III.

CHAPTER 11

The American Law on Confessions

GISLI H. GUDJONSSON AND LORCA MORELLO

This chapter presents an overview of United States law on confession evidence, which differs in significant ways from that of England. In evaluating a confession in an American case, it is essential to know what criteria the courts apply in determining whether it can be used as evidence against the accused. It is also necessary to know how American courts determine whether expert testimony on the subject of false confessions is admissible. The first section will discuss the basic principles of American confession law, particularly the requirement that a confession be 'voluntary'. The second section discusses how the law treats the particular problems of evaluating the voluntariness of confessions of mentally disabled suspects. The third section outlines the procedures of challenging the voluntariness or reliability of a confession in court and discusses recent cases relating to the admissibility of expert testimony. In the fourth section we discuss some of the significant differences between American and British confession law. It is of course impossible to offer a comprehensive view of American law within a single chapter, particularly since there are important variations among the states and between state and federal law. Nevertheless this chapter will attempt to provide a foundation for anyone faced with evaluating and seeking to introduce expert evidence about a confession in an American case.

THE BASIC LAW OF CONFESSIONS

The basis of American law is the United States Constitution as interpreted by the decisions of the US Supreme Court. The Constitution defines the basic protections that all state and federal courts must give criminal defendants. Supreme Court decisions set the minimum standards of protection that may not be curtailed by any law or court decision. The state courts or legislatures may, however, accord persons greater rights than the minimum required by the Supreme Court. For example, although the Supreme Court requires that the government prove a defendant's confession voluntary only 'by a preponderance of the evidence', i.e. that the confession is more likely than not to be voluntary, some states have passed laws holding the government to a higher standard of proof, requiring a showing that the confession is voluntary beyond a reasonable doubt. On the other hand, when Congress passed a law intended to reduce the protection afforded to suspects by the Supreme Court's decision in *Miranda*, the Court struck down the statute, holding that 'Congress may not legislatively supersede our decisions interpreting and applying the Constitution'.[1]

Supreme Court decisions frequently include opinions by individual justices who dissent from the majority opinion. These dissents, while obviously not authoritative as law, can influence how the law is actually applied in lower courts and how the Supreme Court itself decides subsequent cases.

When the prosecution seeks to introduce a defendant's confession into evidence, the defendant is entitled to a pre-trial hearing before a judge where the prosecution has to prove that the confession was voluntarily made and not coerced.[2] These hearings are called by different names according to the jurisdiction, but the generic name is a suppression hearing. If the prosecution cannot prove the confession's voluntariness, it will be suppressed, i.e. not admitted into evidence, without regard to the question of its reliability. The prohibition against using a defendant's involuntarily made confession against him derives from two sections of the Constitution: the Due Process Clause of the 14th Amendment, which provides that the government 'shall not deprive any person of life, liberty or property without due process of law', and the Fifth Amendment provision that no person 'shall be compelled in any criminal case to be a witness against himself'.[3] The latter is the basis of the well known *Miranda* warnings that must precede any police interrogation of a suspect in custody.

What Makes a Confession Involuntary? The Due Process Voluntariness Test

Clearly, in deciding the admissibility of a confession, much depends on how courts interpret the word 'involuntary'. The earliest American courts, applying the common law of England, equated involuntariness with unreliability, reasoning that a coerced confession induced by threats and promises was inherently untrustworthy.[4] Later Supreme Court decisions shifted from a focus on whether the confession was reliable to a concern that it be the product of free and rational choice, and not of police conduct that was 'such as to overbear the suspect's will'.[5] Thus, a confession extracted by force, threats of force, promises of protection from force or excessively lengthy interrogation is involuntary and therefore inadmissible, regardless of whether or not the confession is likely to be true.

---

[1] *Dickerson v. United States*, 530 US 428, 437 (2000) (reaffirming *Miranda v. Arizona*, 384 US 438 (1966), which required police to obtain from suspects a waiver of their right to silence).
[2] *Jackson v. Denno*, 378 US 368, 377 (1964).
[3] US Const. Amends. V, XIV.
[4] *See Dickerson v. United States*, 530 US 428, 432–433 (2000).
[5] *Rogers v. Richmond*, 365 US 534, 544 (1961). For a discussion of how the voluntariness test shifted from concern for the confession's reliability to the aim of deterring police misconduct, see White (1998) and Wrightsman and Kassin (1993).

Voluntariness was apparently completely severed from the question of reliability when the Supreme Court held in *Colorado v. Connelly* that 'free and rational choice' means only the absence of intimidation, coercion or deception by the police or other government actor.[6] Thus, a confession by a man suffering from psychotic delusions, although clearly of dubious reliability and not the product of any rational choice, was nevertheless held admissible because no police misconduct had been involved. The reliability of a confession, according to *Connelly*, is a matter of evidentiary law and a separate question from voluntariness.[7]

To decide whether a confession is voluntary, a court looks at the 'totality of the circumstances' surrounding the interrogation. The court will consider a combination of factors, such as the characteristics of the accused, the conditions of the interrogation and the conduct of the police.[8] 'The determination depends upon a weighing of the circumstances of pressure against the power of resistance of the person confessing.'[9] Under this test, the court must consider any particular vulnerabilities of the suspect such as youth, mental retardation or mental illness, in addition to such factors as the length of the questioning, whether food or breaks were allowed and whether the police made improper threats or promises. These factors are discussed in detail by Brophy and Huang (2000), Florian (1999), Mcguire (2000), Meyer (1999), White (1998).

Voluntariness Under Miranda

Undoubtedly, the most important and controversial decision in American law with regard to confessions was *Miranda v. Arizona*,[10] which attempted to create a 'bright line' test of voluntariness by requiring the police to inform suspects in custody prior to interrogation that they had a constitutional right not to answer questions about the crime and a right to have a lawyer present. According to Stuntz, the Supreme Court intended to achieve two objectives by its decision in *Miranda*: deterring police misconduct, and providing suspects in custody with the opportunity to make informed and rational decisions about whether to incriminate themselves (Stuntz, 1989). *Miranda*, citing numerous documented instances of brutal methods used by the police to extract confessions, observed that these examples 'are undoubtedly the exception now, but they are sufficiently widespread to be the object of concern'.[11] The Court went on to criticize psychological techniques capable of overbearing the suspect's will, quoting extensively from police interrogation manuals, including Inbau and Reid, about such deceptive techniques as 'Mutt and Jeff' described in Chapter 1, or staging a line-up where fictitious witnesses or victims would identify the suspect with unrelated crimes to make him 'desperate' enough to confess to the crime under

---

[6] *Colorado v. Connelly*, 479 US 157 (1986).
[7] *Colorado v. Connelly*, 479 US at 167.
[8] *Shneckloth v. Bustamonte*, 412 US 218 (1973).
[9] *Dickerson v. United States*, 530 US 428, 434 (2000) (citing *Stein v. New York*, 346 US 156).
[10] *Miranda v. Arizona*, 384 US 436 (1966).
[11] *Miranda v. Arizona*, 384 US at 447.

investigation to escape from false accusations.[12] The Court cited passages from the police manuals recommending various psychological ploys designed to isolate and dominate the suspect, concluding:

> It is obvious that such an interrogation environment is created for no purpose other than to subjugate the individual to the will of his examiner. This atmosphere carries its own badge of intimidation. To be sure, this is not physical intimidation, but is equally destructive of human dignity.[13]

Miranda held that the police are required to inform the suspect that:

1. he has the right to remain silent,
2. any statements can be used against him at trial,
3. he has the right to have an attorney present during questioning, and
4. if he cannot afford an attorney, one will be provided. A suspect may assert his right to silence at any time, even if he has begun answering questions.

These rights have to be actively *waived* 'voluntarily, knowingly and intelligently' by the accused before interrogation can commence, otherwise the resulting confession will be inadmissible (Frumkin, 2000; Grisso, 1986, 1998a, 1998b; Hourihan, 1995).[14] The voluntariness of the waiver is determined by the totality of the circumstances. 'Any evidence that the accused was threatened, tricked or cajoled into a waiver will, of course, show that the defendant did not voluntarily waive the privilege.'[15]

The *Miranda* decision was highly controversial when it was decided, and several of the Supreme Court justices strongly dissented from the majority opinion, arguing that such a rule would discourage confessions altogether, hinder the legitimate aims of law enforcement and allow guilty suspects to go free.[16] After more than 30 years, the actual effect of *Miranda* on law enforcement remains the subject of heated, if inconclusive, debate (Cassell & Fowles, 1998; DeFilippo 2001; Leo, 2001b; Leo & White, 1999; Weisselberg, 1998). Although both the majority and dissent assumed that most suspects, once informed of their rights, would naturally assert them, this has not been the case: most suspects waive their rights (DeFilippo, 2001; Rosenberg & Rosenberg, 1989; White, 2001).

Subsequent Supreme Court decisions limited *Miranda* in a number of ways, for example, by making the requirements for invocation of rights stricter and the requirements for waiver more lenient; and by creating a vaguely defined 'public safety exception' (Rosenberg & Rosenberg, 1989). Statements taken in violation of *Miranda* may be admissible as impeachment if the defendant testifies at trial.[17] Leo and White describe a standard interrogation technique of 'questioning outside *Miranda*', whereby a suspect who has asserted his rights may nevertheless be persuaded to speak 'off the record', mistakenly believing

---

[12] *Miranda v. Arizona*, 384 US at 453.
[13] *Miranda v. Arizona*, 384 US at 458.
[14] *Miranda v. Arizona*, 384 US at 479.
[15] *Miranda v. Arizona*, 384 US at 476.
[16] *Miranda v. Arizona*, 384 US at 541 (White, J., dissenting).
[17] *Harris v. New York*, 401 US 222 (1971).

that these statements cannot be used against him in any form (DeFilippo, 2001; Leo & White, 1999).

Additionally, since *Miranda* warnings are only required for the situation of 'custodial interrogation', courts have interpreted the terms 'custodial' and 'interrogation' so narrowly that police may circumvent its requirements by claiming that the suspect was in the police station 'voluntarily' or that the questioning was merely 'investigatory'. Moreover, notwithstanding *Miranda*'s disapproval of deception by the police, courts have found only the most egregious tactics sufficient to render a waiver or a confession involuntary (Roppe, 1994). Similarly, inducements or implied promises of leniency will not necessarily render a waiver invalid; they are only a factor in the 'totality of the circumstances' test (Leo & White, 1999).

Nevertheless, the Supreme Court recently declined to overrule *Miranda*, reaffirming in *Dickerson v. United States* that custodial confessions not preceded by *Miranda* warnings may not be used as evidence in the prosecution's direct case. *Dickerson* reiterated the rationale of *Miranda*:

> Because custodial police interrogation, by its very nature, isolates and pressures the individual, we stated that even without employing brutality, the 'third degree' or other specific stratagems, custodial interrogation exacts a heavy toll on individual liberty and trades on the weakness of individuals. We concluded that the coercion inherent in custodial interrogation blurs the line between voluntary and involuntary statements, and thus heightens the risk that an individual will not be accorded his privilege under the Fifth Amendment not to be compelled to incriminate himself.[18]

While recognizing that the 'disadvantage' of *Miranda* is that mere failure to administer the warnings could result in the suppression of an otherwise voluntary statement, thus permitting a guilty defendant to go free, the Court concluded that it provided more effective guidance for police and courts than the due process voluntariness test standing alone.[19]

The Due Process Voluntariness Test After Miranda

Dickerson also noted that the waiver of *Miranda* rights does not necessarily dispense with the due process voluntariness test.[20] This is significant because courts often automatically find that, so long as the warnings have been given, any ensuing confession must be voluntary (White, 2001, p. 1220). This is obviously incorrect, since, as one New York court observed, a confession beaten out of a suspect does not become voluntary just because he waived his *Miranda* rights.[21]

White argues that given the growing body of empirical data showing that false confessions occur frequently enough to be a societal problem, neither

---

[18] *Dickerson v. United States*, 530 US 428, 435 (2000) (citations and internal quotation marks omitted).
[19] *Dickerson v. United States*, 530 US at 444.
[20] *Dickerson v. United States*, 530 US at 444.
[21] *People v. Leonard*, 59 A.D.2d 1, 12 (NY App.Div. 1977).

Miranda nor the due process voluntariness test, as presently applied, provides adequate protection to suspects against making coerced or unreliable confessions (White, 1998, 2001). The traditional due process voluntariness test, which finds coercion only under the most extreme circumstances, was formulated without the benefit of contemporary research showing that some of the standard techniques commonly used by interrogators are likely to produce an unreliable confession (White, 2001). However, the Due Process Clause guarantees fair and reliable procedures to criminal defendants at every stage. Thus, even if after *Connelly*, 'the due process voluntariness test is not concerned with reliability of particular confessions, it may properly be concerned with regulating government interrogation techniques likely to lead to untrustworthy confessions' (White, 1997, p. 138). Accordingly, the Supreme Court should revisit the traditional due process standard to take account of the empirical data about the existence and causes of false or untrustworthy confessions (White, 2001).

VOLUNTARINESS AND MENTALLY VULNERABLE SUSPECTS

The Supreme Court's decision in *Colorado v. Connelly*, finding a mentally ill defendant's statement 'voluntary', merely because no police impropriety was involved, has serious implications for accused persons who are particularly at risk of giving false confessions by reason of their youth, mental illness or mental retardation (Frumkin, 2000; Hourihan, 1995).

Francis Connelly had approached a police officer on the street in Denver, Colorado, saying that he wanted to confess to a murder. The police, unaware that he was suffering from a mental illness, read him his *Miranda* rights and took his statement. The following morning, Connelly became disoriented and confused, saying that 'voices' had told him to go from Boston to Denver (a distance of several thousand miles) and confess to a murder. At the suppression hearing a psychiatrist testified that Connolly was suffering from chronic schizophrenia and was in a psychotic state when he left Boston for Denver at the command of the 'voice of God', which allegedly told him either to confess to the murder or commit suicide. According to the psychiatrist, Connelly was at the time of making the confessions experiencing 'command hallucinations'. This psychotic condition interfered with his 'volitional abilities; that is, his ability to make free and rational choices'.[22] The psychiatrist further testified that Connelly had understood his legal rights and admitted that the 'voices' could in reality be Connelly's interpretation of his own guilt. However, in his opinion it was Connelly's psychosis that motivated him to make a confession.

On the basis of the psychiatric evidence, the trial court suppressed all of Connelly's statements, finding that both his initial statement to the police officer and his subsequent waiver of his *Miranda* rights were 'involuntary' as not being the product of a rational intellect and free will. The trial court reasoned that although the police had acted properly and there was no coercion in securing his confession, Connelly's illness destroyed his volition and compelled

---

[22] *Colorado v. Connelly*, 479 US at 161–162.

him to confess.[23] The Supreme Court of Colorado affirmed the decision, holding that 'the absence of police coercion or duress does not foreclose a finding of involuntariness. One's capacity for rational judgement and free choice may be overborne as much by certain forms of severe mental illness as by external pressure'.[24]

The US Supreme Court reversed the judgment, holding that because there was no police impropriety, neither Connolly's confession nor his waiver of his *Miranda* rights was involuntary within the meaning of the Due Process Clause or the Fifth Amendment. Nevertheless, two of the justices dissented, pointing out that Connelly had been denied 'his fundamental right to make a vital choice with a sane mind, involving a determination that the State could deprive him of liberty or even life', and that 'a most basic sense of justice is affronted by the spectacle of incarcerating a human being upon the basis of a statement he made while insane'.[25]

Hourihan (1995) provides an appraisal of the effects of *Connelly*. In Hourihan's view,

> Concerns for reliability and preservation of 'free will' fell by the wayside as, in the interests of administrative ease and consistency, courts were removed from the business of looking into a defendant's mind in order to determine the voluntariness of his or her confession (p. 1503).

The implications for suspects suffering from mental illness and learning disability (the term mental retardation is used in the USA) are far reaching and serious. At the most basic level, without police impropriety, as legally defined and construed, no psychologically vulnerable suspect could make an involuntary confession. This is clearly a very unsatisfactory situation since psychological vulnerabilities, as will be seen in later chapters of this book, are sometimes crucial in producing unreliable confessions with or without police coercion.

As an example of the dangers and unfairness involved following *Connelly*, Hourihan describes in detail the case of Earl Washington, arguing that the case raises serious questions about whether the Fifth and 14th Amendment protections are sufficient to prevent a miscarriage of justice in cases of mentally retarded defendants (Hourihan, 1995; White, 1997).

Earl Washington was a mentally retarded man who was convicted and sentenced to death for murder and rape. He recanted his confession and appealed on the grounds that he had not voluntarily confessed or waived his *Miranda* rights knowingly or intelligently. The Virginia Supreme Court supported the decision of the trial judge and ruled that Washington had made knowing and intelligent waivers and that his admissions were obtained voluntarily. The evidence produced to support the view that Washington had properly waived his *Miranda* rights related to his giving 'yes, sir' responses when asked if he knew he was waiving his constitutional rights.

---

[23] *Colorado v. Connelly*, 479 US at 162.
[24] *Colorado v. Connelly*, 479 US at 162.
[25] *Colorado v. Connelly*, 479 US 157, 174 (1986) (Brennan, J., dissenting) (citing *Blackburn v. Alabama*, 361 US 199 (1960).

Hourihan shows from the trial record how it is apparent that Washington did not understand the legal implications of his waiver. In this case the trial judge and the Virginia Supreme Court uncritically accepted Washington's affirmative ('Yes, sir') answers and failed to take a close and meaningful look at his answers when asked to explain the meaning of the legal concepts. As discussed in detail in Chapter 10, recent research in England into suspects' understanding of their legal rights shows that their claim that they understand the 'police caution' is a very poor indicator of their genuine understanding of it (Fenner, Gudjonsson & Clare, 2002). Undoubtedly, the same applies to suspects' claims that they understand their *Miranda* rights, as highlighted by the work of Grisso (1998a, 1998b). White, citing the President's Panel on Mental Retardation, notes that some retarded persons, wishing to please authority and not understanding the consequences of making a confession, will 'cheat to lose', accepting blame for things they have not done so that the authority figure will not be angry with them. Thus, mentally retarded suspects such as Earl Washington may admit to the crimes suggested to them, 'simply because they think they are being friends and they're helping out the police' (White, 1997, p. 123).

After Washington had spent ten years on death row, the Virginia Attorney General ordered a DNA test, which showed that the sperm found in the victim's body did not come from Washington. Since it was undisputed that the rapist–murderer had acted alone, this should have exonerated Washington. In spite of this new and powerful evidence, however, the Attorney General refused to accept that Washington might have been wrongfully convicted. Following a public outcry, on his last day as Governor of Virginia, Douglas Wilder 'offered Washington a Hobson's choice with a two-hour deadline: accept commutation to a life sentence and end this appeal, or remain on death row and hope that the Virginia legislature would pass a new law allowing motions to set aside the verdict based on newly discovered evidence in capital cases after the otherwise applicable twenty-one day deadline' (Hourihan, 1995, p. 1472). Washington chose to live and accepted the Governor's offer. Fortunately, in the summer of 2000, another Governor ordered a more sophisticated DNA test and a further investigation into Washington's case. On 2 October 2000, Washington was finally pardoned after the new tests found no trace of his DNA from the crime scene. After nearly 18 years in prison, Washington was freed on 12 February 2001.

As Hourihan (1995) points out, some courts, albeit a minority, have declined to interpret *Connelly* as foreclosing consideration of the mental state of suspects who make confessions. *Connelly* did not do away with the due process requirement that a court consider the defendant's individual characteristics as part of the 'totality of the circumstances' when assessing the voluntariness of his confession or waiver of *Miranda* rights. It can therefore be argued that *Connelly* stands for 'the limited proposition that a defendant's mental condition is not *in itself* sufficient to make a confession involuntary'.[26]

Thus, while many courts have reduced the holding of *Connelly* into a mechanical two-step test—first look for police coercion, and if none is readily apparent, the inquiry stops there—other courts have applied *Connelly* from

---

[26] *State v. Rettenberger*, 984 P.2d 1009, 1114 (Utah, 1999).

a larger perspective, recognizing that what is not coercive for the general population may well be coercive for a mentally disabled person. For example, one court found that when a suspect exhibited 'a continuing pattern of mental instability',

> an interrogation that would not be coercive to a mentally stable person could be found coercive with regard to him.[27]

In another post-*Connelly* case, a court found a mentally retarded suspect's confession involuntary when methods used by the police were shown to be a 'type of subtle coercion that can have an extraordinary effect on one of low mental capabilities'.[28]

Finally, although *Connolly* commented that a court should not be required to conduct 'sweeping inquiries into the state of mind of a criminal defendant who has confessed', the decision itself makes clear that a suspect's mental limitations *are* relevant when the police have reason to be aware of them and can be shown to have exploited them in obtaining a confession or a waiver of his *Miranda* rights.[29]

The trial court's opinion in *United States v. Zerbo*[30] illustrates an unusually nuanced application of the totality of the circumstances test, concluding that police questioning of a 53-year-old mentally disabled man was 'unconstitutionally coercive in the light of his disabilities'.

Anthony Zerbo had been continuously treated for schizophrenia, polysubstance abuse and heart failure for several years as an outpatient in a government veteran's hospital where he also worked as a volunteer. Law enforcement agents from the hospital went to his sister's home, where Zerbo lived, wanting to question him about an alleged act of sodomy with a resident patient. The agents questioned Zerbo for an hour and a half without permitting his sister to be present and without giving *Miranda* warnings or telling him that he was being investigated for a crime. Indeed, they assured Zerbo and his sister that they were only there to 'help'. When Zerbo's sister asked if he was in trouble, the officer assured her that they were only looking for information.

Two days later, seven officers descended on the house as the family was sitting down to dinner and arrested Zerbo. Zerbo's sister gave his medication to the supervisor, telling him that Zerbo 'was a sick boy' and needed to take it several times a day. The officers put Zerbo in a holding cell for about 25 minutes and brought him out to be interviewed at about 9 p.m. They read him his *Miranda* rights and he signed a waiver form. He was questioned until 10.30 p.m. and not given any food or his medication. Zerbo had not eaten for about ten hours.

At the suppression hearing, the court heard testimony from Zerbo, his sister and the arresting officers. The court also considered three psychiatric reports, submitted on behalf of the prosecution, the defence and in response to a court

---

[27] *Smith v. Duckworth*, 910 F.2d 1492, 1497 (7th Cir. 1990).
[28] *Commonwealth of the Northern Mariana Islands v. Mendiola*, 976 F.2d 475, 485 (9th Cir. 1992).
[29] *Connelly v. Colorado*, 479 US at 165–167.
[30] *United States v. Zerbo*, 1999 WL 804129 (S.D.N.Y. 1999).

order, respectively, which detailed Zerbo's extensive history of mental illness and his IQ of 80.

As to the interview in Zerbo's home, the court first considered whether he was 'in custody'. Applying the test that a suspect is not in custody 'if a reasonable person in the suspect's position would have felt free to terminate the interrogation and leave', the court concluded that although Zerbo, because of his mental limitations, did not feel free to terminate the interview, a reasonable person would have known that he could have done so. Thus, the court found that custody was determined by what a 'reasonable person' would have felt, regardless of the suspect's actual characteristics. Accordingly, Zerbo was not 'in custody', and therefore not entitled to receive *Miranda* warnings.[31]

The court's second test was whether the statement was voluntary, taking into account Zerbo's characteristics, the conditions of the interrogation and the officers' conduct. Citing extensively from the three psychiatric reports, together with its own observations of Zerbo's testimony and demeanour, the court concluded that Zerbo was 'exceedingly submissive, highly suggestible and easily confused'. The court then found that the conditions of the interrogation—his isolation from his sister and the officers' assurances that they were there on his behalf, rather than to investigate a crime, 'improperly distorted Zerbo's view of the proceedings and interfered with his already tenuous capacity to make rational choices'.[32]

Regarding the officers' conduct, the court did not credit their claim that it was merely an investigatory conversation, since they had already determined that Zerbo had committed the alleged crime when they went to his house. Accordingly, their purpose was 'not to "investigate" or discover Zerbo's version of events, but to elicit a confession from a prime suspect'.[33] The court concluded that, under the totality of circumstances, the statements that Zerbo made in his home were the product of an overborne will and must be suppressed.

As to Zerbo's statements after his arrest two days later, the court found that, given his low intelligence, his testimony that he had not understood the *Miranda* warnings and the experts' assessment of his mental state, he could not have knowingly or intelligently waived his rights after his arrest.[34] Nor was his waiver voluntary given the following factors:

1. given Zerbo's average size and compliant attitude at the previous interview, sending seven officers to arrest him in his home indicated a desire to intimidate him, rather than legitimate law enforcement concerns;
2. the deprivation of food and medication, in conjunction with Zerbo's mental illness and diminished intelligence, made it impossible for him to 'voluntarily' relinquish his *Miranda* rights and
3. the court did not credit the officers' claim that they knew nothing of Zerbo's history of mental illness, since they knew, at the very least, that he was an outpatient at the same hospital where they worked, and had investigated his history there before going to his home.

---

[31] *United States v. Zerbo* at *8.
[32] *United States v. Zerbo* at *10.
[33] *United States v. Zerbo* at *11.
[34] *United States v. Zerbo* at *12.

The court commented, 'Requiring law enforcement officials engaged in criminal investigations at mental hospitals to take extra steps to protect the rights of patients with mental disabilities does not create an unnecessary burden'.[35] The court's unusually detailed analysis of the totality of circumstances illustrates how mental disability and police conduct may combine to make a confession involuntary.

CHALLENGING A CONFESSION IN COURT

The Legal Procedures

As already noted, when the prosecution proposes to use a defendant's confession against him at trial, the defendant is entitled to a pre-trial suppression hearing before a judge where the prosecution must show that the defendant made a knowing, intelligent and voluntary waiver of his *Miranda* rights and that neither the waiver nor the confession itself was extracted by coercion. In contrast to a trial, the issue before the suppression court is limited to the voluntariness, not the reliability of the confession. Thus, a finding that *Miranda* rights were not properly given should result in the suppression of the resulting confession, without consideration of the defendant's guilt or innocence.

At the suppression hearing, the defendant may argue that the *Miranda* rights were not properly administered, that he did not understand them, that his attempts to assert his rights were ignored or that he was induced to waive them by improper means, such as threats, promises or lengthy interrogation without food or sleep. The interrogating officers, on the other hand, will usually testify that the defendant's rights were honored in every respect, or that the defendant was neither 'in custody' nor being 'interrogated' when he made the incriminating statement. In practice, a suppression hearing often amounts to a swearing contest between the two sides because it is impossible to prove police impropriety where in most states interrogations are not mandatorily audio or video recorded (McMahon, 1993). In several of the American cases one of us (GHG) has worked on, the interrogations were not contemporaneously recorded throughout and an audio or video recording was only obtained after the suspect's resistance had been broken down during a previous interrogation. Therefore, even if the police had acted coercively in any of these cases it would have been impossible to prove in court.

If the confession is suppressed, the prosecution may not use it in its direct case and if it is the only evidence connecting the defendant to the crime, the prosecution's case will collapse. The prosecution may, however, appeal the hearing court's decision to suppress. On the other hand, if suppression is denied, the defendant cannot appeal until after he has been convicted. If the appellate court finds that the confession was improperly admitted, the court will apply the 'harmless error rule'. This means that the conviction will be struck down unless the prosecution can show that the error was harmless beyond a reasonable

---

[35] *United States v. Zerbo* at *13.

doubt, i.e. that there was no reasonable possibility that the confession could have contributed to the conviction.[36]

At trial, the defence will generally attack the reliability, rather than the voluntariness, of the confession. Nevertheless, the Supreme Court has held that, as part of the Sixth Amendment right to present a defence, a defendant cannot be prohibited from offering evidence about 'the physical and psychological environment that yielded the confession', because the jury will naturally want to know why, if he is innocent, he previously admitted guilt.[37]

Admissibility of Expert Testimony

It is clear that psychological assessment is potentially of great importance in determining the voluntariness or reliability of a confession. An intellectual assessment revealing significant mental retardation, for example, may show that the defendant could not have understood his *Miranda* rights and therefore could not have waived them 'knowingly'. Additionally, the tests devised by Grisso (1998b) can be used for this purpose. Findings of unusual levels of suggestibility or compliance may support an argument that the police conduct was coercive in relation to that defendant. An argument that the confession is false or untrustworthy is, of course, immensely strengthened by expert testimony on the phenomenon of false confessions and psychological vulnerability.

In seeking to introduce at trial the findings of an expert to demonstrate that a confession is involuntary or unreliable, the defence must satisfy the evidentiary requirements of admissibility. Although there are two distinct standards that American courts apply to specialized expert testimony, depending on the jurisdiction, all courts require a showing that the proffered evidence is relevant, the expert qualified and the findings not based on 'junk science'. American courts have traditionally distrusted expert testimony as invading the province of the jury by assessing the credibility of witnesses, usurping the court's function by offering a legal conclusion, or claiming an 'aura of special reliability' in matters that a jury could determine from its own experience.[38] These arguments are frequently brought against the admissibility of false confession testimony. Although there is not yet a large body of case law about its admissibility, Agar (1999), Imwinkelried (1999) and Shuman and Sales (1999) provide an overview of some of the recent appellate cases.

The *Frye* Standard

Until fairly recently, most courts have admitted novel scientific evidence only if it could be demonstrated to be based on a theory 'sufficiently established to have gained general acceptance in the particular field to which it belongs'.[39] This test, known as the *Frye* standard, is still used by several major jurisdictions including

---

[36] *Arizona v. Fulminante*, 499 US 279 (1991).
[37] *Crane v. Kentucky*, 476 US 688, 689 (1986).
[38] Weinstein on Evidence §§702.02, 704.04 [2][c] West 1998.
[39] *Frye v. United States*, 293 F. 1013, 1014 (D.C. Cir. 1923).

the state courts of New York, California, Massachusetts and Florida. The *Frye* test has been applied to a range of scientific evidence, including polygraph tests, voice print analysis, fingerprint evidence, hypnosis, rape trauma syndrome and psychological evidence related to witness perception and memory. Various criticisms have been made of the *Frye* standard by courts and academics (Burke, 1995). These fall into four groups:

1. the Frye standard is thought to be unnecessarily restrictive of the reliable evidence (i.e. scientific evidence may be reliable without being generally accepted);
2. it is not clear who make up the 'scientific community' relied upon for general acceptance (e.g. only those who use the technique or does it include related fields?);
3. it is not clear how 'general acceptance' should be defined (e.g. does it mean a simple minority of experts, a near universal acceptance among experts, or somewhere in between?);
4. it is not clear whether the standard should be applied to 'soft' scientific evidence, such as psychiatric and psychological evidence, in the same way as 'hard' scientific evidence. Goodman-Delahunty (1997) argues that in the past confusion has arisen when determining the admissibility of expert psychological evidence, because psychology as a discipline displays a combination of both physical ('hard') and social ('soft') sciences. A particular difficulty has been expressed in relation to the evidence presented by clinical psychologists. How far can such evidence be classified as 'scientific'? Views clearly differ on this point. In practice, trial courts often determine 'general acceptance' of a theory by how often it has been found admissible by other courts.

Cases Evaluating Admissibility of Expert Testimony Under the *Frye* Standard

Clearly, to get testimony admitted under the 'general acceptance' standard the proponent must be well informed about the existing literature. This is illustrated by a recent decision by a New York State trial court rejecting testimony about interrogative suggestibility under the *Frye* standard, on the grounds that the defendant 'has not shown any specific scientific tests, recognized procedures or findings' to show reliability.[40] This finding could not have been based on accurate information, since there is clearly an extensive body of literature detailing reliable tests and findings on the subject. The Gudjonsson Suggestibility Scales (GSSs) were rejected in a Massachusetts court, who found that the defence had presented 'no evidence' as to whether it was accepted in the scientific community.[41] Not surprisingly, a Florida court rejected the Grisso test when the defence expert who based his findings on it told the court that it 'was not a commonly used, nationally recognized test', and that it was 'very unusual' to use

---

[40] *People v. Philips*, 180 Misc.2d 934 (N.Y. Sup.Ct. 1999).
[41] *Commonwealth v. Soares*, 51 Mass.App.Ct. 273, 281 (App.Ct. Mass. 2001).

this test to argue that the defendant did not comprehend his *Miranda* rights.[42] In contrast, in *T.S.D. v. State*, another Florida court admitted the Grisso test where a better informed defense expert testified that the Grisso tests 'are highly regarded by people who do *Miranda* rights evaluations'.[43]

It is also essential that the expert be prepared to show precisely how the test findings are applicable to the issues in the case. In *Soares*, because the proffering expert was unable to explain to the trial court why the results of a GSS test were applicable to a custodial situation, the appellate court upheld the judge's decision to exclude it as unreliable.[44] In *Beltran v. State*, an intermediate Florida state court rejected proffered testimony about false confessions by a neuropsychologist who cited only a literature search on the Internet and the experimental study on college students by Kassin (1997). The court opined:

> The expert's testimony in this case provided no methodology or factors for the trial court to rely on in determining whether appellant's confession was a false confession. We cannot understand how the trier of fact should relate a study of college students signing a confession about an act of negligence in hitting the wrong key on a computer in the determination of whether a confession to a capital sexual battery was false.[45]

In contrast, *T.S.D.* found the Grisso test relevant where the defence was able to show specifically how the defendant's test answers demonstrated that he had not understood his right to have an attorney present during questioning.[46]

Moreover, even if a court finds a particular test not admissible under the 'general acceptance' test, this does not foreclose the defence from presenting expert testimony based on other tests whose credentials are undisputed if it can be shown that these tests are relevant to the assessment of the confession. Thus, in *Carter*, where the appellate court upheld the trial court's rejection of the Grisso test, the appellate court also found that the same expert's testimony about his findings based on IQ and other well recognized tests should have been admitted, since the defendant's mental capacities were a relevant factor in determining his comprehension of his *Miranda* rights.[47] Similarly, a Massachusetts appellate court found that the trial court should have allowed expert testimony about battered woman syndrome and substance abuse to support the defendant's claim that her confession was involuntary. The trial judge had excluded the testimony both at the suppression hearing and at trial, saying that he did not need any expert to make a voluntariness determination and neither did the jury, because it was 'something that the ordinary person can determine on all the evidence in this case'. The appellate court, noting that

---

[42] *Carter v. State*, 697 So.2d 529, 533 (Dist.Ct.App. Fla. 1997).
[43] *T.S.D. v. State*, 742 So.2d 536, 537 n.2. (Dist.Ct.App. Fla. 1999) (Sorondo, J. dissenting).
[44] *Commonwealth v. Soares*, 51 Mass.App. 273, 281 (App.Ct. Mass. 2001).
[45] *Beltran v. State*, 700 So.2d 132, 134 (Dist.Ct.App. Fla. 1997).
[46] *T.S.D. v. State*, 741 So.2d 1142 (Dist.Ct.App. Fla. 1999).
[47] *Carter v. State*, 697 So.2d 529, 534 (Dist.Ct.App. Fla. 1999).

battered woman syndrome testimony is admissible under the *Frye* standard, found that it was directly relevant to the question of whether the police questioning had been coercive and not within the common experience of the ordinary juror.[48]

Indeed, one of the earliest American cases dealing with expert testimony about false confessions pre-dated most of the current empirical research (Agar, 1999). In a murder trial that took place in the late 1980s, a California court admitted testimony under the *Frye* standard where the defence proffered Elliot Aronson, a professor of social psychology and an expert in 'persuasion and conformity'.[49] Having listened to tapes containing the defendant's interrogation and statement, Aronson identified certain characteristics of the interrogation that might have caused the resulting confession to be false. He described several social science experiments including the famous Milgram experiment (Milgram, 1974) where subjects were persuaded to administer what they believed to be possibly fatal electric shocks, to illustrate that people greatly overestimate their ability to resist pressure from an authority figure. He tied this experiment to the reliability of Page's confession by observing that 'we say to ourselves, "My God, I would never confess to this if it weren't true." But in my opinion, that's exactly what people say when we present them with this Milgram experiment. And yet we know that somewhere between 60 and 70 percent of the entire population would go all the way' [in administering electric shocks to test subjects when told to do so].[50] Aronson's testimony did not persuade the jury, however, and Page was convicted.

These cases suggest that the admissibility of expert testimony to challenge a confession does not necessarily stand or fall on the general acceptance of a particular test under the *Frye* standard. However, if a test is offered, the expert should obviously be prepared to testify about its general acceptance and to make a strong showing to the trial court about its specific relevance to an issue in the case.

The *Daubert* Standard

The federal courts and many state courts apply a more liberalized standard based on the Federal Rules of Evidence (FRE) and their interpretation by the recent Supreme Court cases, *Daubert v. Merrell Dow Pharmaceuticals*[51] and *Kumho Tire Co., Ltd. v. Carmichael*.[52] FRE 702 reads:

> If scientific, technical, or other specialized knowledge will assist the trier of fact to understand the evidence or to determine a fact in issue, a witness qualified as an expert by knowledge, skill, experience, training, or education, may testify thereto in the form of an opinion or otherwise, if (1) the testimony is based on sufficient

---

[48] *Commonwealth v. Crawford*, 429 Mass. 60 (1999).
[49] *People v. Page*, 2 Cal.App.4th 161 (1991).
[50] *People v. Page*, 2 Cal.App.4th at 183.
[51] 509 US 579 (1993).
[52] 526 US 139 (1999).

facts or data, (2) the testimony is the product of reliable principles and methods, and (3) the witness has applied the principles and methods reliably to the facts of the case.

Daubert set out a checklist for courts to use in assessing the reliability of scientific expert testimony, emphasizing that these factors were neither exclusive nor dispositive, while *Kumho* subsequently clarified that these factors might also be applicable to non-scientific expert testimony. The *Daubert* factors are:

1. whether the expert's technique or theory can be or has been tested—that is, whether the expert's theory can be challenged in some objective sense, or whether it is instead simply a subjective, conclusory approach that cannot be assessed for reliability,
2. whether the technique or theory has been subject to peer review and publication,
3. the known or potential rate of error of the technique or theory when applied,
4. the existence and maintenance of standards and controls, and
5. whether the technique or theory has been generally accepted in the scientific community.

Thus, in contrast to the *Frye* standard, 'general acceptance' is only one of several factors for the court to consider in determining admissibility.

Daubert emphasized that a 'reliability assessment does not require, although it does permit, explicit identification of a relevant scientific community and an express determination of a particular degree of acceptance within that community'.

The Advisory Committee Notes point out that Rule 702 'does not alter the venerable practice of using expert testimony to educate the factfinder on general principles'. The only requirement is that (1) the expert be qualified, (2) the testimony address a subject matter on which the factfinder can be assisted by an expert, (3) the testimony be reliable and (4) the testimony 'fit' the facts of the case.[53]

The Notes also explain that Rule 702 'expressly contemplates' that experience alone, or experience in conjunction with other knowledge, training or skill, may be a sufficient foundation for expert testimony, since in certain fields 'experience is the predominant, if not sole, basis for a great deal of reliable expert testimony'.[54]

Goodman-Delahunty (1997) argues that the application of the Federal Rules of Evidence to expert testimony 'should preclude some of the sources of variability, ambiguity, and confusion' (p. 125) that existed with the *Frye* standard. She discusses in detail the implications for forensic psychology and argues that the *Daubert* standard 'may offer more predictability and flexibility than pre-existing standards, facilitating more effective professional interactions between the courts and forensic psychologists in the future' (p. 137). A number of other authors have discussed the application of the *Daubert* standards to

---

[53] FRE Rule 702, 28 USC.A. Advisory Committee Notes (hereinafter 'Notes') at 36629.
[54] Notes at 36630.

psychological tests (Agar, 1999; Frumkin, 2000; Goodman-Delahunty, 1997; Grisso, 1998b; Reed, 1996; Rogers, Salekin & Sewell (1999).

Cases Applying *Daubert* to Expert False Confession Testimony

One of the most cogent and detailed applications of the *Daubert* principles to expert testimony in the area of false confessions is found in *United States v. Hall*.[55] This is an important case in relation to disputed confessions and the admissibility of expert psychological testimony under *Daubert*. The nature of the expert's evidence and the way the trial and appellate courts ruled on his testimony provide an important insight into expanding boundaries of psychological evidence in cases of alleged coerced confessions in the USA.

Larry Hall was arrested in connection with the disappearance and death of 15-year-old Jessica Roach. There was no evidence connecting Hall to the crime, but suspicion focused on him because of his history of 'stalking or following teenaged girls'.[56]

The first police officers to interview Hall realized that he had mental health problems and recommended him for treatment at a local facility. The police repeatedly called him in for questioning over a period of several weeks and at one point, when Hall continued to deny his involvement, the police officer became upset with him, moved closer, and started suggesting the 'right' responses. Hall began crying, asking what was expected of him and if he was allowed to leave. However, the subsequent interview lasted from 10.00 a.m. until 3.25 a.m. the following morning. When this was followed by a two-hour questioning by an FBI agent, Hall began to make admissions about his involvement. No notes were taken by the officers and there was no audio or tape recording of the interrogation or the admissions. The FBI agent wrote out a statement in a narrative format and asked Hall to sign it. Hall was charged with kidnapping Jessica Roach for the purposes of sexual gratification and was tried in federal court.[57]

At trial the defence argument was that 'due to a personality disorder that makes him susceptible to suggestion and pathologically eager to please, he "confessed" to a crime that he did not really commit, in order to gain approval from the law enforcement officers who were interrogating him; even the police had characterized him as a "wannabe"'.[58] The court permitted Arthur Traugott, a psychiatrist who had examined Hall, to testify about his mental and emotional problems. However, the court sharply limited Dr Traugott to testimony about Hall's mental condition (e.g. his attention-seeking behaviour and susceptibility to suggestions) and to offering his opinion that, because Hall was easily led, interrogators would experience difficulties obtaining reliable answers from him. The court would not allow Dr Traugott to testify about the nature of the interrogation techniques used by the police officers in the case, the number of suggestions put to Hall during questioning or the potential capacity of Hall to

---

[55] 93 F.3d 1337 (7th Cir. 1996) ('Hall I'); 974 F.Supp. 1198 (C.D. Ill. 1997) ('Hall II').
[56] Hall I at 1339.
[57] Hall I at 1340.
[58] Hall I at 1341.

confess to a crime he had not committed. The court 'found that the jury could appreciate whether police interrogation techniques were suggestive by themselves and that Dr Traugott's testimony would invade the prerogative of the jury to assess [the officers'] credibility'.[59]

Importantly the trial court had excluded altogether the testimony of Dr Richard Ofshe, who was offered as a social psychologist expert in the field of coercive police investigation techniques and the phenomenon of false or coerced confessions. The trial court opined that the testimony would amount to a judgment of the interrogating officers' credibility about what happened during the interrogation and that it 'would add nothing to what the jury would know from common experience'.[60]

After Hall was convicted, the appellate court reversed the judgment, finding that the trial court had not applied the correct standards under *Daubert*, and that this error was not harmless where 'Dr Ofshe's testimony went to the heart of Hall's defence'.[61]

The trial court had rejected or limited the expert testimony using the traditional criteria of whether the testimony would 'usurp' the jury's function of judging the witness's credibility, and whether it would add to what the jury knew from common experience. The appellate court pointed out that, under the broader standards of *Daubert* and the Federal Rules of Evidence, expert evidence need only be helpful to the jury and relevant to an issue in the case. Thus, there was 'no categorical reason to exclude expert testimony that bears on truthfulness', if, under the facts of a particular case, the testimony could give the jury 'a reason to reject the common sense evaluation of the facts that they would otherwise be entitled to use'.[62] Furthermore, expert testimony need not be excluded just because the subject matter was within the jury's own knowledge, particularly if the testimony challenged the jury's common-sense beliefs:

> This ruling overlooked the utility of valid social science. Even though the jury may have had beliefs about the subject, the question is whether those beliefs are correct. Properly conducted social science research often shows that commonly held beliefs are in error. Dr Ofshe's testimony, assuming its scientific validity, would have let the jury know that a phenomenon known as false confessions exists, how to recognize it, and how to decide whether it fits the facts of the case (p. 13).

The appellate court accordingly remanded Hall's case to the trial court for a new trial to be preceded by a new hearing applying the *Daubert* factors to determine whether Dr Ofshe's evidence was admissible.[63] Although *Kumho Tire* had not yet been decided at the time, the hearing court held that the framework of *Daubert* was applicable to the social sciences, even if these disciplines 'rely primarily on real-world experience', including systematic observation and analysis, rather than controlled experimentation to arrive at their conclusions.[64] The

---

[59] Hall I at 1341.
[60] Hall I at 1341.
[61] Hall I at 1345.
[62] Hall I at 1344 (citing *United States v. Shay*, 57 F.3d 126 (1st Cir. 1995)).
[63] Hall II at 1199.
[64] Hall II at 1202.

court found that Dr Ofshe could show that the use of coercive techniques in police interrogation was an established topic within the field of social psychology which 'involves the systematic study of real-world interrogation' and has an extensive peer-reviewed literature.[65] Dr Ofshe's recognition of the limitations of the field—that it was not based on empirical experiment, nor did it claim to offer a method of scientifically determining whether any given confession was false—increased the court's opinion of the testimony's reliability.[66]

Thus, the court ruled that Dr Ofshe would be permitted to testify that false confessions exist, that they are associated with certain interrogation techniques and that certain of these techniques were used in Hall's interrogation. However, he would not be permitted to say whether the interrogation methods used in this case caused Hall to falsely confess, because 'without experimental verification, such testimony would be speculative and prejudicial. Dr Ofshe will simply provide the framework which the jury can use to arrive at its own conclusions'.[67]

Similarly, although Dr Ofshe could talk about the general method of analysing a post-confession narrative for inconsistencies between the statement and the evidence as one of the signs that the confession is false, it must be left to the jury to actually apply this method to Hall's confession. The court's analysis thus answers the argument often raised against false confession testimony that it 'invades the province of the jury' by offering an expert opinion about a witness's credibility.

The court also addressed the objection that the subject matter is within the ordinary experience of the jury and does not require an expert. The Federal Rules of Evidence rejected the traditional rule that expert testimony is only admissible if the subject matter is beyond the ken of the jury. Under FRE 702, it only needs to be shown that such testimony would be helpful to them in understanding the evidence or determining a factual issue. The findings of social science about human behaviour are particularly helpful when they demonstrate that common-sense notions are inaccurate. Here, it was helpful for the jury to hear that studies of interrogations contradicted the widely held misperception that no one would confess to a crime unless he was, in fact, guilty.[68] However, Dr Ofshe could not testify about the account that Hall gave his lawyer about the coercive techniques used in his interrogation, which was inadmissible evidence, as not having been made under oath or subjected to cross examination. As is nearly always the case in America, the interrogation was not properly recorded, so the only way the defendant can offer his version is by testifying on the stand.

The court also found that Dr Traugott should have been permitted to testify about Hall's susceptibility to various interrogation techniques and his propensity to give a false confession, because this evidence was necessary 'to link the condition Dr Ofshe identified to Hall himself, and Dr Traugott was prepared to do this, based on his personal examination of Hall'.[69] Although such testimony

---

[65] Hall II at 1203.
[66] Hall II at 1205.
[67] Hall II at 1205.
[68] Hall II at 1205–1206. Despite Dr Ofshe's testimony, Hall was convicted again at his second trial.
[69] Hall I at 1345.

about Hall's propensity touched on a key issue in the case, the FRE permits experts to offer an opinion on the ultimate issue in a case:

> The fact that there was a dispute between Hall and the interrogating officers about the questioning itself provides no reason to exclude the expert testimony; it is a rare case where everything is agreed except the subject matter for which the expert is presented. It is enough if the expert makes clear what his opinion is, based on the different possible factual scenarios that might have taken place.[70]

The contrast between *Beltran* (see above) and *Hall* is interesting. The Florida court in *Beltran* compared the proffered expert testimony based on the Kassin study unfavourably with the kind of evidence proffered in *Hall*, saying that the latter 'would have let the jury know that a phenomenon known as false confessions exists, *how to recognize it, and how to decide whether it fit the facts of the case being tried*, while the former had failed to show the relevance'.[71] It is apparent that the court in *Beltran* was critical of the lack of ecological validity of Kassin's (1997) experimental study and its applicability and relevance to real life false confession involving serious crimes. It seems that proposed expert testimony in this case was too narrowly focused on a single experimental study of college students. The advantage of Ofshe's testimony in *Hall* is that he provided the court with a comprehensive and meaningful understanding of the phenomenon of false confessions in a real life scenario.

Other courts have determined the admissibility of expert testimony in the area of false confessions on a variety of grounds. The highest state court of North Carolina reversed a murder conviction where the trial court had excluded psychiatric testimony that the defendant's psychological characteristics made him 'likely to fabricate stories to reduce the stress demands of confrontation with authority', and therefore prone to make a false confession in police interrogation.[72] The appellate court found that, contrary to the trial court's opinion, this was not inadmissible 'character evidence', but relevant testimony about the defendant's mental condition affecting the circumstances surrounding his confession. Thus, the evidence was admissible as crucial to the defendant's claim that his confession had been coerced.

In contrast, the Supreme Court of Minnesota rejected a similar argument, concluding that:

> The trial court was well within its discretion in ruling that the jury, without the testimony of the psychological expert, was fully capable of observing and understanding [the defendant's] propensity to please authority figures, and taking those observations and that understanding into account in evaluating his confession.[73]

It is apparently a recurring notion among judges that the jury is capable of making a fully adequate psychological assessment of a defendant based on his

---

[70] *Hall I* at 1345–1346.
[71] *Beltran v. State*, 700 So.2d 132, 133–134 (1997) (emphasis in original) (citing *United States v. Hall*, 93 F.3d 1337, 1345 (1996)).
[72] *State v. Baldwin*, 125 N.C.App. 530 (1997).
[73] *Bixler v. State*, 582 N.W.2d 252, 256 (Sup.Ct.Minn. 1998).

or her performance on the witness stand. This notion changed in England with the landmark case of Engin Raghip (see Chapter 18).

As far as the Gudjonsson Suggestibility Scales (GSS) are concerned, in 1998 a New York federal court ruled that the expert testimony based on the GSS met the *Daubert* standard.[74] At the suppression hearing, Dr Sanford Drob, a clinical psychologist, testified extensively about Raposo's low-average IQ, opining that this usually correlates with a tendency to be more suggestible and less equipped to resist pressure. Further tests showed that Raposo, who had signed a written statement admitting to arson, had a 'self-defeating' personality, which tends to be isolated, manipulated by others and willing to be taken advantage of. The GSS showed that Raposo tended to fill in information he did not know, but that he did not display a tendency to shift his answers in response to negative feedback.

The hearing court, viewing the totality of circumstances, concluded that although the defendant's psychological condition might make him suggestible, the circumstances of the interrogation were not so onerous that his will was overborne. Accordingly, the confession was found to be admissible.

At trial, the defence sought to introduce Dr Drob's testimony that the defendant's psychological characteristics might render him more prone to making a false confession than the general population. The government did not dispute that the tests Dr Drob had used were generally accepted in the scientific community and had been administered according to the appropriate standards. It nevertheless sought to exclude the testimony, arguing that the defence had failed to show that these test results correlated with the likelihood of making a false confession, nor had their relevance to voluntariness been established. The Government further argued that Dr Drob was being offered as a 'human lie detector, who will purport to establish scientifically what is properly in the province of the jury'.[75]

The court disagreed, saying that Dr Drob's hearing testimony had gone into considerable detail on how the traits measured by each particular test related to the defendant's psychological state during the custodial interrogation. The testimony would therefore be 'helpful to the jury in understanding that an individual with a certain psychological profile could be more susceptible than other members of the general population to making a false confession'. The court found the government's 'human lie detector' concerns to be 'exaggerated', since Dr Drob would not be telling the jury whether the confession was false or voluntary. He would merely be providing information on the defendant's psychological condition to aid the jury's determination of those questions.[76] The testimony was accordingly ruled admissible.

Raposo illustrates that, even where the reliability of the GSS is undisputed by the prosecution, the defence still must make a strong and specific showing as to how its results are relevant to the issues before the court. Thus, a Wisconsin state court, while not disputing the reliability of the GSS, nevertheless rejected

---

[74] *United States v. Raposo*, 1998 WL 879723 (S.D.N.Y. 1998).
[75] *United States v. Raposo* at *5–*6.
[76] *United States v. Raposo*, at *6.

expert testimony based on it, finding the expert's proffer 'vague' and 'insufficiently detailed' as to how it would assist the jury in assessing the truth of the defendant's confession.[77]

Because the empirical study of false confessions is relatively recent, there is not yet a large body of case law dealing specifically with its admissibility. It is apparent from the cases cited here and by Agar (1999) that there is a great variety among courts in how they treat this evidence. Whether offered under the *Frye* standard or *Daubert*, probably the single most important factor in getting it admitted is the quality of the proffer, specifically the expert's knowledge about the field and the ability of the defence to address the standard objections, such as that the expert is posing as 'a human lie detector' or otherwise replacing the jury as the judge of the witness's credibility. It should also be noted that because the admission of evidence in a particular case is considered a matter for the trial court's discretion, appellate courts usually uphold the trial court's decision unless it can be shown that it was a complete failure to follow the applicable law. Therefore, an appellate decision upholding the exclusion of expert testimony in a particular case does not necessarily *require* its exclusion in future cases.

Additionally, a court's decision as to whether to admit expert testimony of any kind is often affected by the other evidence in the case. Hoeffel argues that courts have applied the *Daubert* factors far more flexibly to expert testimony about battered woman syndrome and rape trauma syndrome than to equally reliable testimony about false confessions or eyewitness identification, noting that the former is generally proffered on behalf of a more sympathetic class of persons, i.e. victimized women, than the latter, i.e. ordinary criminal defendants.[78] Hoeffel notes that the court's decision in *Hall* emphasizes the evidence indicating that Hall might be innocent: another person had confessed to the murder, Hall had been subjected to an 18 hour interrogation even though the police had reason to know of his mental disabilities, and his confession, at least at his first trial, was the only evidence connecting him to the crime (Hoeffel at 68). Whether or not Hoeffel's conclusion is warranted that courts are biased in their application of the *Daubert* factors, it is certain that anyone seeking to proffer false confession testimony must take account of all the particular facts and issues of the case.

DIFFERENCES BETWEEN ENGLISH AND AMERICAN LAW AND PRACTICE

There are important differences between English and American law and practice with regard to both the *admissibility of a confession*, decided at a suppression hearing, and the *admissibility of expert testimony*. We shall discuss each of these in relation to admissibility.

---

[77] *State v. Summers*, 630 N.W.2d 277 (Ct.App. Wisc. 2001) (unpublished opinion).
[78] Janet C. Hoeffel, *The Gender Gap: Revealing Inequities in Admission of Social Science Evidence in Criminal Cases* 24 U. Ark. Little Rock L. Rev. 41 (2001).

Admissibility of Confession Evidence

In England there is more protection available for suspects detained for questioning than there is in the USA. This includes, the use of a detailed Custody Record, mandatory tape or video recording of police interviews with suspects, frequent use of breaks and rest between interviews, the common use of forensic medical examiners (police surgeons) where there are physical or mental problems apparent and, the use of 'appropriate adults' when suspects are identified to be psychologically vulnerable or 'at risk' of giving erroneous accounts of events during questioning. This provides a detailed knowledge of what happens to suspects in police custody, the available material and tapes of interviews are subsequently open to close scrutiny by experts and the courts, suspects who are identified as having mental problems are provided with special assistance and if the police are in breach of their Codes of Practice (Home Office, 1995) a confession may be ruled inadmissible and without other corroborating evidence there is no case to answer.

A major problem with working on many American cases is that the questions and answers obtained during the interrogation are often not fully recorded and it is impossible to verify what exactly was said and done, or if and when things happened. For example, suspects may claim that the *Miranda* warning was given after they had been persuaded by the police to confess, whereas the police claim it was issued prior to the interrogation. It is not possible to verify the matter one way or the other without independent corroboration. A tape recording of the entire interrogation process is invaluable in such cases. Without this, it is all a question of who is to be believed and the courts will typically accept the police officer's version of events.

The English Courts are far less tolerant than American Courts of police impropriety, such as police officers lying to suspects about the strength of the evidence against them and using coercive interrogation tactics. PACE and the Codes of Practice of English police officers provide an important control and influence over their behaviour in relation to the arrest, detention and interrogation of suspects.

American trial judges appear to be much more reluctant than English judges to suppress confession statements provided suspects have been given their legal rights and they were considered by the Court to be competent to waive their legal rights. As far as voluntariness is concerned, the American Courts, unlike the English Courts, have great difficulties with suppressing confession evidence when in their view there is absence of police coercion. Indeed, as discussed earlier in the case of *Colorado v. Connelly* (1986), the Supreme Court held that coercive police activity is a necessary pre-requisite to finding that a confession is not voluntary. As discussed in Chapter 10, the English Courts sometimes exclude confession evidence in cases of psychologically vulnerable suspects even where there is no evidence of police coercion. In addition, in recent years there have been a number of convictions overturned by the English appellate courts in high profile murder cases on the basis of psychological and psychiatric testimonies (see Part III). In contrast, as seen in this chapter, the America appellant courts are far more reluctant to find defendants wrongfully convicted. The other difference is that when convictions are overturned in England appellants are often afforded a high level of compensation.

Admissibility of Expert Testimony

There are different standards for the admissibility of expert testimony in England than there are in the American courts. There are no parallel English tests to the *Frye* and *Daubert* standards and exclusionary rules. In England, scientists, including psychologists and psychiatrists, automatically qualify as experts provided they are testifying on the subject of their expertise. The English courts do not generally look closely at the reliability and validity of the expert evidence presented and its general acceptance in the scientific community. Indeed, the scientific merit of the evidence presented is often taken for granted and not challenged. In the USA there is more emphasis on properly and formally qualifying experts and closely scrutinizing the scientific foundation for their opinions before allowing them to testify. In England, traditionally the primary questions are whether or not the expert evidence is relevant and outside the experience of the ordinary juror (e.g. a mental abnormality or a disorder). The American courts are not so restricted to issues of mental disorder when determining the admissibility of expert psychological testimony.

CONCLUSIONS

Under English and American law the courts are confronted with certain practical problems with regard to assessing the probative weight of confessions (Zuckerman, 1989). These relate to the fact that police interrogations are conducted without outside supervision, so that police officers are motivated to suppress evidence of impropriety whilst defendants who regret making a confession have a motive to fabricate allegations of police malpractice. Adopting mandatory audio or video recording of all police custodial interrogations, as is currently the practice in England, will make it easier to identify police coercion and impropriety, while at the same time it will protect the police from false allegations by defendants. The courts have a duty to protect the constitutional rights of citizens against police coercion, but this has to be balanced against the police having sufficient power to carry out their investigations effectively and efficiently. Due process standards do fluctuate over time, but since the ruling in *Colorado v. Connelly* (1986) the American courts have shifted away from considering the reliability of confession evidence and mental state factors as being relevant to due process voluntariness determination towards relying exclusively on police coercion *per se*. Mental state factors and capacities, including intellectual functioning, are clearly relevant and important when determining the validity of a *Miranda* waiver and the reliability of confession evidence. In future the American courts may shift back towards taking more account of mental factors in producing involuntary confessions when considering the issues of coercion. With the *Daubert* standard superseding the *Frye* test of expert evidence, the scope for introducing psychological evidence relevant to coerced and unreliable confessions will increase.

There is a great variety among American courts in how they treat expert evidence. Whether offered under the *Frye* standard or *Daubert*, probably the single most important factor in getting it admitted is the quality of the expert witness and the ability of the defence to address the standard prosecution objections.

CHAPTER 12

The Psychological Assessment

Until the early 1980s, clinicians had no satisfactory conceptual framework for the assessment of disputed confession cases. To illustrate the point, a psychiatrist (Coid, 1981), in his assessment of a retracted confession case, devised six criteria for assessing suggestibility.

1. That the defendant can be made to change his story as a result of persuasion.
2. That the defendant could be made to believe false information that would be obvious to most people of normal intelligence.
3. That the defendant is unable to understand the implications of his or her predicament.
4. That the defendant is unable to understand the words and concepts used in the incriminating statement.
5. That the defendant has a tendency to confabulate or exhibits pseudologica fantastica (i.e. pathological lying).
6. That the defendant is unable to understand the concept of truth.

Coid applied his 'suggestibility criteria' to a homicide case where the major evidence against the defendant was his confession. The defendant proved not to be suggestible according to the six criteria.

Coid's 'suggestibility criteria' were poorly conceptualized, and crudely 'estimated' on the basis of a clinical judgement. No psychological instruments were used to measure the six 'criteria'. Like his colleagues at the time, Coid was faced with the lack of standardized assessment procedures and techniques. Extensive developments in recent years have markedly improved the knowledge and techniques available to clinicians who are preparing court reports in cases of disputed confession. Gudjonsson and MacKeith (1988) provided the first detailed conceptual framework for the assessment of disputed confession cases. I expanded and further developed this framework in my previous book on interrogation (Gudjonsson, 1992a) and provided detailed case studies illustrating the variety of assessment techniques and procedures that were available. In this chapter I shall build upon and expand our earlier work in this field and expand it considerably.

THE ASSESSMENT FRAMEWORK

Psychologists are increasingly being referred court cases directly from solicitors (Gudjonsson & Haward, 1998). Their contribution to the assessment of cases involving disputed or retracted confessions is growing rapidly (Fitzgerald, 1987; Gudjonsson & Haward, 1998). There appear to be four principal reasons for this increased demand.

First, there is a growing awareness among the legal profession that psychologists have a unique contribution to make. Psychiatrists originally provided the assessment of disputed confessions. My impression in the early 1980s was that these cases were only occasionally referred for evaluation to psychiatrists or psychologists, and when they were, the question of mental illness or learning disability was typically raised. In recent years it has become evident that in the majority of these cases the critical questions are psychological rather than psychiatric. Psychologists now have greater knowledge and more techniques available for the assessment of disputed confession cases.

Second, there appears to be increased legal acceptance of the psychologist's evidence. In 1985 I was commissioned by the British Psychological Society to study the involvement of psychologists as expert witnesses in the British courts (Gudjonsson, 1985). The results indicated that the demand for psychological services was on the increase and the majority of the psychologists involved stated that the courts were favourable towards accepting their evidence. This survey was repeated in 1995 with similarly positive results (Gudjonsson, 1996b). The survey also indicated that in civil cases, mainly involving the assessment of post-traumatic stress disorder and neuropsychological status, psychologists only had to testify orally in about two per cent of cases. In contrast, in criminal cases, including those involving disputed confessions, psychologists had to testify orally in about 20% of cases. In addition, during the past 10 years psychologists have increasingly been allowed to testify in the appellant courts. As an example, since 1991 I have testified orally in 10 high profile British murder cases in the Court of Appeal. These cases, among many others, are discussed in detail in Part III of the book.

Third, new legal provisions since 1986 have focused on regulating the behaviour of police officers during custodial interrogation and on improving the rights of detainees. The focus is now more on identifying inherent psychological vulnerabilities that may have a bearing on the legal issues. Prior to this, the emphasis at trial was very much on police behaviour and impropriety.

Fourth, my previous book on interrogations and confessions raised the profile of false confessions internationally and identified more clearly the role of psychologists as expert witnesses in cases of disputed confession (see e.g. Adams, 1993; Blinkhorn, 1993; Corre, 1995; Delaune, 1995; Fisher, 1993; Heaton-Armstrong, 1992; Perkins, 1993; *The Lancet*, 1994).

Basic Requirements for Assessment

The principal purpose of expert psychological evidence is to *inform* the court about psychological matters that are outside their knowledge so that the judge and jury can be assisted in their decision-making. In the process of doing this, the psychologist has to be able to identify the core issues and factors that are relevant to explaining the confession. This generally requires that there is both breadth and depth to the assessment.

When conducting the evaluation, it is useful to conceptualize it as falling into three distinct stages:

- the collection of relevant material;
- the psychological assessment and
- the presentation of the findings in written or oral form.

What are the most critical aspects of the assessment of disputed confessions? There are five basic prerequisites for a complete assessment, which are equally true whether the case is being referred by the defence or the prosecution. These are discussed in detail by Gudjonsson and Haward (1998), whose book *Forensic Psychology. A Guide to Practice* should be read in conjunction with this book in relation to the forensic assessment and testimony.

1. The lawyer who refers the case must properly instruct the psychologist. This includes receiving clear instructions about the issues to be addressed in the expert's report. Referral letters are often vague and a telephone conversation with the lawyer concerned may be necessary before the assessment can be undertaken. Often solicitors do not specify the legal issues to be addressed in the report. They may ask for 'intelligence and suggestibility to be assessed', which are straightforward instructions. However, during the assessment the psychologist may discover other relevant factors that need to be assessed, such as alcohol and drug abuse or specific anxiety problems. The broadest type of assessment, which is the common instruction in American cases but not in England, involves assessing voluntariness, psychological coercion and reliability of self-incriminating admissions. The assessment of cases in England is more restricted because traditionally the courts have been reluctant to allow psychologists to comment on the ultimate question of reliability. Generally speaking, experts have had to limit their comments on the results of their assessment to psychological vulnerability (e.g. low intelligence, literacy problems, suggestibility, compliance and mental health problems). However in court, psychologists are often asked questions about their observations on the relevant police interviews and in recent years psychologists are increasingly being allowed to comment on issues pertaining to the reliability of confessions. This will be evident in later chapters, particularly in relation to recent Court of Appeal judgments). The issue of reliability is, of course, ultimately a legal issue, on which the court must decide.
2. Psychologists must have access to all relevant documents and papers in the case, which include witness statements, records of police interviews, the custody record, the defendant's statements to his solicitors ('Proof of Evidence' and comments on the prosecution papers), medical reports, previous

psychological reports and school reports. These should be carefully studied before the defendant is interviewed and the psychologist should make a note of the questions that need to be asked of the defendant with regard to these. Tape-recorded police interviews should be listened to before interviewing the defendant. Even when interviews have been transcribed the tapes should always be listened to. *Psychologists should never rely on transcribed records when tape-recordings of the interviews are available.* I have often come across important errors or omissions in the transcription of tapes that were critical to the case. In addition, listening to interview tapes may give important further information about the way the interview was conducted and how the defendant coped during it. Informants may need to be interviewed for further information or as a way of corroborating information provided by the defendant. *Proper preparation is essential for the assessment, and when testifying in court.*

Psychologists should be aware that they may not be presented with all the evidence in the case by the referral agent because of the adversarial nature of the proceedings (Gudjonsson & Haward, 1998). This could be important when psychologists are attempting to interpret their findings within the broader context of the case. An assessment that is very narrowly focused (e.g. relying exclusively on IQ or suggestibility scores) can be seriously misleading.

3. Psychologists should be familiar with the literature on false and disputed confessions and the relevant legal framework and judgments. They should also know about the basic assessment tools, including the validation data for the tests used. Furthermore, the psychologist needs to be able to relate the findings of the assessment to the particular circumstances of the case. This is the most difficult part of the assessment and requires considerable experience. For example, if a defendant is found to be suggestible on testing, then its relevance and weight will need to be considered within the context of the case.

4. Psychologists should be objective and honest in their work, whichever side they are appearing for. They should confine themselves to the objective findings of the assessment and avoid being speculative and partisan. I always find it helpful to avoid prejudging guilt or innocence in cases of retracted confessions. One should approach the assessment with an open-minded attitude, but without being gullible.

The Factors to be Assessed

The psychological assessment, when dealing with issues relevant to voluntariness and reliability of self-incriminating statements, may require an evaluation of six groups of factors, which can be labelled as follows.

1. The circumstances of the arrest and custody.
2. Characteristics of the defendant.
3. Mental and physical state during custody.

4. Interrogative factors.
5. An explanation for the alleged false confession.
6. The retraction.

It is important to discuss briefly each of these in turn.

The Circumstances of the Arrest and Custody

The circumstances surrounding each case and their importance to the accused vary immensely. A person who is woken up in the early hours of the morning by armed police officers breaking into his home is likely to be in a different frame of mind than the one who goes to the police station as a witness and subsequently becomes a suspect. The more sudden and violent the arrest, the more likely the person is to be in a state of shock when taken to the police station for questioning. The timing of the interrogation may also be important. For example, interrogation late at night, when the accused would normally be asleep, places them at their lowest level of resistance and resilience.

As discussed in Chapter 7, high profile cases, and those involving 'hue and cry', often place enormous pressure on the police to solve the case. Once a much needed suspect is identified an inept police investigation may follow, which may involve coercive interrogation and refusal to provide the suspect with their legal entitlements. These broader circumstances of a case should not be ignored during the psychological assessment. The cases arising out of the 'Tottenham Riots', which are discussed in Chapter 18, illustrate this problem well.

The duration of custody will also need to be evaluated. Generally the longer suspects are detained in custody the greater the pressure on them to confess.

Characteristics of the Defendant

There are a number of characteristics associated with the defendant that can make him or her especially vulnerable to erroneous testimony during interrogation. These fall into four groups.

(a) *Physical characteristics, such as age, gender and race.* It is generally accepted that the very young and very old are least able to cope with the demands of the police interrogation. The importance of gender and race are not known.
(b) *Lack of life experience, unfamiliarity with police procedures and failure to understand their legal rights and entitlements* may place some defendants at a disadvantage during interrogation.
(c) *The psychological characteristics of the defendant.* This includes his or her cognitive skills (e.g. intelligence, reading ability, attentional deficits, memory capacity), personality (e.g. suggestibility, compliance, assertiveness, self-esteem, tendency to confabulate, anxiety proneness), specific anxiety problems (e.g. claustrophobia, fear of being isolated from significant others, extreme fear of police dogs), mental illness (e.g. depressive illness, psychosis) and personality disorder. A mental state examination should give

an indication of any current mental problems that the defendant has, which serves as an important baseline for inferences to be drawn about his or her mental state whilst in police custody.

(d) *Reactions to the interrogation and reasons for the confession.* It is often helpful to use a standard questionnaire, such as the Gudjonsson Confession Questionnaire (Gudjonsson & Sigurdsson, 1999), to monitor and evaluate the defendant's subjective experiences of the interrogation and confinement and the reasons given for having made the confession.

Psychologists should be aware that even when mental illness, learning disability or abnormal personality traits (e.g. suggestibility, compliance) are present, this does not necessarily mean that the defendant falsely confessed even when this is alleged to be the case. The specific abnormalities and vulnerabilities detected may very well be relevant to the possible unreliability and involuntariness of the self-incriminating confession, but they should not be viewed in isolation from the surrounding circumstances of the case.

Mental and Physical State During Custody

The mental and physical state of the accused whilst in police custody can affect the reliability of any statement, self-incriminating or otherwise, that he or she makes to the police. The work of Irving and his colleagues at the Brighton Police Station (Chapter 2) and our own work for the Royal Commission on Criminal Justice (Chapter 3) illustrate that many suspects are not in a normal physical or mental state whilst being interviewed by the police. This may be caused by the stress associated with their arrest and confinement, or by factors associated with alcohol intoxication and drug abuse.

Physical illness and disease are also important factors that may need to be assessed. When people are physically ill they are more vulnerable when having to cope with a stressful situation, such as interrogation. In cases of heart disease and diabetes, fear of not being able to obtain medication or medical care may be additional stressors that make people focus excessively on the short-term or immediate consequences of their behaviour (e.g. making a self-incriminating statement) at the expense of the long-term consequences (e.g. being prosecuted, convicted and sentenced).

Suspects who are accused of murdering someone close to them, such as a spouse, their offspring or a close friend, are often specially vulnerable during interrogation. This is irrespective of their guilt or innocence and relates to the fact that such a loss results in grief and bereavement (Bluglass, 1990; Curle, 1989; Gudjonsson 1992a; Parkes, 1986).

A reconstruction of the suspect's mental and physical state whilst in police custody needs to be carried out. If there are medical or psychiatric issues to be considered, then the psychologist should normally recommend to the solicitor that the case be referred to an appropriate medical person for a further report. In my experience, almost all cases involving alleged false confession involve psychological issues that are best addressed by psychologists. In some cases medical and psychiatric issues need to be considered as well. I have worked jointly on many cases with psychiatrists and often our individual contributions have complemented one another's very well indeed.

Three sources of information are potentially useful for the reconstruction of the defendant's mental state at the time of the police interrogation. First, the Custody Record needs to be scrutinized for information such as visits by relatives, a forensic medical examiner or police officers. Refusal to accept food or an inability to consume it may be noted in the Custody Record. In addition, note should be made of recorded sleep disturbance, which may include police officers going into the suspect's cell late at night or general sleeplessness. The less the suspect has been able to sleep, whether due to interruptions or sleeplessness, the less rested he or she is going to be when subsequently interrogated.

The second source of information is the accused. A detailed interview will give an insight into his or her mental and physical state at the time of confinement and interrogation. The reporting of various mental symptoms, including lack of appetite, disturbed sleep, nightmares, severe anxiety, a disturbed mood, specific phobic symptoms and hallucinations, may be important in terms of evaluating the reliability of self-incriminating admissions. Physical pain or discomfort may be similarly important.

I have come across two cases where the stress of confinement resulted in apparent hallucinations. In both cases the accused felt that the doors, the walls or the ceiling in the cell were moving in on them. In one of the cases, the accused reported the cell door moving like rubber and this caused him great distress.

The third source of potential information are people who visit the accused at the police station before or after interrogation. Relatives, friends or doctors, just to mention a few potential informants, are often able to give useful information about the likely physical and mental state of the accused. The role of forensic medical examiners is particularly important, although they do not have psychiatric training and would generally not be in a position to carry out a detailed mental state examination on the accused. Wood and Guly (1991) have drawn our attention to the potential dangers of failing to scrutinize the reliability of unsubstantiated confessions among mentally disordered patients.

On occasion, police officers may provide an important insight into the mental and physical state of the accused. For example, in one case a police officer reported that the accused had physically collapsed and fainted, on the way to a detention room, after being told that he was suspected of being involved in his mother's death. This corroborated the account the accused gave me about the distress he experienced at the accusation that he had murdered his mother. His distress was further augmented during subsequent interrogations when he was repeatedly accused by the interrogators of having neglected and badly treated his mother whilst she was alive. Following the accusations the son admitted to having suffocated his mother to death. At his trial the judge refused to allow the confession statements in evidence and accused the two police officers concerned of having bullied a murder confession out of him.

Any information obtained from the accused must, whenever possible, be supported or corroborated by other evidence, because it is essentially self-serving. Irrespective of whether people are guilty or innocent of the crime they are accused of, they may deliberately lie or misrepresent the facts as a way of improving their chances of acquittal. Sometimes the information they give is contradicted by the other evidence in the case. For example, in one murder case the accused told me that the police officers had gone to his cell on several occasions to question him in between formal interviews. This was one of the reasons he gave for having falsely confessed. There was no evidence from the Custody Record to support this claim that the police officers had gone to his cell to question him. During his evidence in court the accused conceded that he had lied to me about it. Not surprisingly, in view of the detrimental effects on the defence when defendants are shown during their testimony to have lied (Bedau & Radelet, 1987; Shaffer, 1985), the accused in the present case was convicted of the murder.

Interrogative Factors

Interrogative factors cover a range of verbal and non-verbal communication associated with the interrogation itself. Video recording of the interrogation provides the most informative account of what was said and done, and the manner in which the interrogation was conducted. Tape recordings give less overall information, but they are a formidable improvement on written notes. Not only is the recording more accurate than note taking; often certain attitudes and signs of distress are evident. Interrogators' bias and style of questioning may be observed as well as the techniques utilized. When leading questions have been asked by the interrogators and persuasive manipulation and pressure employed, then these have to be related to the accused's personality and mental state, as well as to the circumstances of the situation. Occasionally police officers are found to play on suspects' weaknesses, which in vulnerable suspects can result in a false confession. The manipulation of feelings of guilt, particularly in suspects who are accused of murdering loved ones, can markedly increase the likelihood of an unreliable statement.

An Explanation for the Alleged False Confession

When defendants claim that they have made a false confession to the police then it is important to obtain from them a detailed account of the factual and subjective experiences pertaining to the interrogation and confession. This includes providing, if they can, coherent reasons for having made a false confession. These explanations can then be used to test relevant hypotheses. For example, if a defendant claims that he was merely giving in to leading questions or that he did not understand the nature of the questions during the interrogation, then this could possibly be confirmed or refuted by psychological assessment and by carefully studying the record of the police interview. In some cases defendants provide explanations for the confession that can be borne out by the psychological evaluation, or at least on the face of it they appear to be credible. Do the explanations given by the defendant make sense on the basis of the psychological evaluation? For example, in one case of a proven false confession to double murder (see Chapter 9), a man suffering from learning disability told me that the primary reason for his having confessed falsely to the police was that he had been told unless he confessed he would go to prison; on the other hand, if he confessed he would go home and receive medical help. The police had allegedly induced a false confession by offering a combination of a threat and inducement. The man had expressed his fear of going to prison to the interrogator, who then used it to play on his vulnerability in order to obtain a confession. The interrogator succeeded in coercing a false confession. When I watched the videotape of the confession it transpired that after making the confession to the double murder, the suspect asked the officer 'Does the offer still hold?'. This supported his claim that there had been an inducement offered, which had clearly been crucial in making him give a false confession. In another case, a defendant claimed that during a tape-recorded interview the interrogator had at a crucial time scribbled on a piece of paper 'Say you are sorry'. Carefully listening to the tape of the relevant interview supported his claim. I testified about this and the trial judge dismissed the case after listening to the officer and his improbable explanation for the scribbling noise heard on tape (i.e. when confronted with my evidence and the scribbling sound from the tape he claimed he had been writing audio-tape labels).

The Retraction

As discussed in Chapter 8, not all false confessions are retracted, and a retraction by itself does not lend authenticity to the defendant's claim that the confession is false. However, it is important to establish whether the confession has been retracted and how soon after the confession it was retracted. An inordinately long delay in retracting a confession requires an explanation from the defendant. As a general principle, once the pressure of the interrogation is over an innocent defendant would be expected to retract the confession at the earliest opportunity, depending of course on the type of false confession it is. A confession that is first retracted several weeks after it has been made, and following a visit to a solicitor, is suspicious and will inevitably be treated with scepticism by the court unless there is a satisfactory explanation for the delay. However, in some cases the defendant may not retract the confession for several years, but still succeeds on appeal (see the cases of Judith Ward & Darren Hall in Chapter 18).

PSYCHOLOGICAL VULNERABILITIES

As far as the police interviewing of suspects is concerned, 'psychological vulnerabilities' refer to 'psychological characteristics or mental states which render a suspect prone, in certain circumstances, to providing information which is inaccurate, unreliable (or invalid) or misleading' Gudjonsson (1999b). This implies that test scores and interview data should not be interpreted in isolation from the circumstances of the case.

The assessment of psychological vulnerabilities can be categorized into four main groups:

Table 12.1. The psychological vulnerability of people with mental illness, learning disability and personality disorder

Mental illness	Learning disability	Personality disorder
Faulty reality monitoring.	Impaired intellectual capacity.	Lies readily.
Distorted perceptions and beliefs.	Poor memory capacity.	Manipulative.
	Poor understanding of legal rights.	Poor self-esteem.
Proneness to feelings of guilt.	Heightened suggestibility and acquiescence.	Need for notoriety.
		Tendency towards confabulation.
	Failure to appreciate the implications and consequences of answers given.	Lack of concern about consequences of giving an untrue statement.

- mental disorder;
- abnormal mental state;
- cognitive functioning and
- personality traits.

Each type of mental disorder is associated with different kinds of psychological vulnerability as shown in Table 12.1. These are relevant irrespective of whether the person is interviewed as a witness, victim or a suspect.

Mental Disorder

The term 'mental disorder' means that the person suffers from a diagnosable psychiatric problem, including mental illness (e.g. schizophrenia, depressive illness), learning disability or personality disorder.

Where there is mental illness, perceptions, cognitions, emotions, judgement and self-control may be adversely affected, and these may result in misleading information being provided to the police during an interview. Breakdown in 'reality monitoring' is an important symptom of mental illness and when present it impairs the patient's ability to differentiate facts from fantasy. In some circumstances this can result in people believing that they have committed crimes of which they are totally innocent (see Chapter 9). Breakdown in reality monitoring does not require the presence of mental illness (see Chapter 18). It occurs in everyday life in relation to the memory of thoughts, feelings and events (e.g. it is common for people to not be able to differentiate between what one intended to do and what one has done). However, mental illness makes the breakdown in reality monitoring more extensive and frequent (Bentall, Baker & Havers, 1991).

Depressive illness does cause some people to ruminate and implicate themselves falsely in criminal activity as a way of relieving strong feelings of free-floating guilt (Gudjonsson, 1999a). As discussed in Chapter 8 such attempts only relieve the feelings of guilt temporarily.

Police officers do sometimes experience problems when interviewing people who suffer from learning disability and some are so disabled that they are not fit to be interviewed (Gudjonsson, Murphy & Clare, 2000). This problem arises because their condition may impair their ability to give a detailed and coherent account of events to the police. They may have problems with remembering the material event, become confused when questioned, have problems understanding the questions and articulating their answers, not fully appreciating the implications and consequences of their answers (Clare & Gudjonsson, 1995; Gudjonsson, 1999b). They may also feel easily intimidated when questioned by people in authority (Gudjonsson, 1995d; Gudjonsson & MacKeith, 1994), often they do not understand their legal rights (Clare, Gudjonsson & Harari, 1998; Fenner, Gudjonsson & Clare, 2002), and they tend to be acquiescent and suggestible (Clare & Gudjonsson, 1995). In view of the potential importance of learning disability in relation to custodial interrogation and confession, a detailed review of the relevant issues and material is given below.

Bull and Cullen (1992, 1993) and Kebbell and Hatton (1999) have written important papers on how to identify witnesses with learning disability and on how to improve their performance during police interviewing and court attendence. Clare and Gudjonsson (1993), Dent (1986), Henry and Gudjonsson (1999, submitted), Perlman, Ericson, Esses and Isaacs (1994) and Tully and Cahill (1984) have all shown the kinds of problem that persons with learning disability have with reporting events by free recall and the extent to which they can be influenced by leading questions. Clare and Gudjonsson (1993) showed that persons with learning disability are particularly susceptible to yielding to leading questions and they are more prone to confabulate with regard to verbal memory recall.

'Cognitive interview' techniques developed and refined by Fisher and Geiselman (1992) can enhance the recall of witness, victims and cooperative suspects (Memon, 1999). Milne, Clare and Bull (1999) provide evidence that the cognitive interview techniques can be effectively used in cases of children and adults with learning disability. This is an area where psychological research has had an important impact on police practice (Milne, 1999).

The concept of personality disorder is an important psychiatric diagnosis in connection with a number of cases of disputed confessions since the case of Judith Ward (see Chapter 18). Personality disorder may represent an important psychological vulnerability among some witnesses and suspects in that they appear to have an enhanced tendency to confabulate in their memory recall (Smith & Gudjonsson, 1995a, 1995b) and more readily make false confessions as a part of their criminal lifestyle and (Sigurdsson & Gudjonsson, 1997).

Abnormal Mental State

Suspects may suffer from an abnormal mental state, which may adversely influence the reliability of their testimony, without their having had a history of mental disorder. Apart from feelings of extreme anxiety, detainees may experience specific phobic symptoms, such as claustrophobia (i.e. an irrational fear of being locked up in a confined space such as a police cell) or panic attacks (e.g. drug addicts panicking when they are withdrawing from drugs). In the

Royal Commission study (Gudjonsson et al., 1993), extreme fear of being locked up in a police cell was uncommon (i.e. only one case out of 171), although many detainees complained that they were distressed about being locked up at the police station. The most common anxiety was in relation to uncertainties over their current predicament. Detainees expressed concern over what was going to happen to them, kept asking the researchers for information about their detention and wanted to know when they were likely to be interviewed by the police.

Occasionally, detainees are in a state of bereavement when interviewed by the police due their having lost a loved one, such as a spouse or a child. This may make them vulnerable to giving unreliable statements because of feelings of guilt and subjective distress that typically accompanies the condition.

Drug and alcohol intoxication and withdrawal sometimes occur during interviewing and the effects of this are discussed in detail in Chapter 15.

Medical complaints (e.g. cardiovascular problems, epilepsy, diabetes) can result in a disturbed or abnormal mental state while the person is interviewed by the police. This may adversely influence the accuracy and reliability of their account and the ability to function in a stressful situation.

Intellectual Abilities

Limited intellectual abilities, not amounting to learning disability, can influence the ability of witnesses and suspects to understand questions, articulate their answers and appreciate the implications of their answers. As shown in Chapter 3, many detainees interviewed at police stations are of low intelligence (Gudjonsson et al., 1993). Nine per cent of the sample in the Royal Commission study had a prorated IQ score below 70, compared with about 2% of the general population; one-third (34%) had a prorated IQ score of 75 or below (i.e. bottom 5% of the general population). The findings indicate that the police commonly interview suspects of low intellectual abilities. It is of interest to note that the majority of appellants whose convictions have been overturned on the basis of unreliable confessions have been of borderline or low average intelligence, similar to those of the average police detainee (Chapter 18).

Personality Characteristics

There are a number of personality characteristics that may be relevant and important when evaluating the reliability of confession statements. The three most extensively researched variables are suggestibility, compliance and acquiescence (Clare & Gudjonsson, 1993; Gudjonsson, 1992a).

More recently confabulation has been investigated in relation to the reliability of verbal accounts given by witnesses (Clare & Gudjonsson, 1993; Sigurdsson, Gudjonsson, Kolbeinsson & Petursson, 1994). Extreme confabulation has been found in some cases of personality disorder, which was evident in the cases of Judith Ward, Joe Giarratano and John Wille (see Chapters 18 and 21). Persons with mental disorder, such as learning disability and severe depression, have impaired memory recall for events, but the accuracy of their accounts is not undermined by a heightened tendency to confabulate (Clare & Gudjonsson, 1993; Sigurdsson et al., 1994).

LEARNING DISABILITY AS A VULNERABILITY

The British Psychological Society (2001) has recently published a report from the Working Group on Learning Disability. The report provides important guidelines to clinical psychologists when assessing adults with learning disability in mental health and legal contexts. The term 'learning disability' is the current term used in the United Kingdom and it has replaced the term 'mental handicap'. In North America the term 'mental retardation' is in common usage. Throughout this book I shall use the term 'learning disability', unless I am referring to a specific legislation (e.g. Police and Criminal Evidence Act, PACE), where the term 'mental handicap' is used.

There are three core criteria for defining learning disability.

- Significant impairment of intellectual functioning.
- Significant impairment of adaptive/social functioning.
- Age of onset before adulthood (i.e. before the age of 18).

According to the BPS Working Group, all three criteria must be present for a diagnosis of learning disability to be made. Psychometric testing generally forms the basis for determining intellectual functioning, although there is a trend to move away from over-reliance on IQ scores and to take into consideration the individual needs of the person and the kind of support required. Adaptive or social functioning relates to the ability of the person to look after his or her practical day-to-day needs (i.e. 'personal life survival skills') and to adapt satisfactorily within the social community:

> The individual requires significant assistance to provide for his/her own survival (eating and drinking needs and to keep himself/herself clean, warm and clothed), and/or with his/her social/community adaptation (e.g. social problem solving, and social reasoning) (p. 6).

Social functioning is more difficult to assess objectively than intellectual skills. It is usually measured by direct observation and/or by information gathered from informants (e.g. a parent, a carer, a friend).

Learning disability is a developmental condition, due to either arrested or incomplete development, and it is generally accepted that it should have been evident prior to adulthood (i.e. before the age of 18 years). However, significant impairments in intellectual and social functioning may arise in adulthood due to cerebral trauma (e.g. head injury). This would normally be documented historically (e.g. from the person's medical records). Information about the early educational problems would be evident from school reports, if they are available. Irrespective of whether the impaired intellectual and social functioning is due to developmental or acquired factors, both groups should be considered to be psychologically vulnerable within the meaning of Section 77 of PACE and its Codes of Practice. In other words, an appropriate adult would be required in both instances.

Therefore, a proper definition of learning disability for legal and clinical purposes needs to take into consideration the suspect's social functioning as well as any intellectual deficits. There is empirical evidence from American studies that the majority of defendants with a history of learning disability do not receive a pre-trial evaluation of their disability (Brown, Courtless & Silber, 1970; McAfee & Gural, 1988). This means that only those with the most severe handicap will be identified (Allen, 1966; Denkowski & Denkowski, 1985). Those who are only mildly learning disabled are least likely to be identified, especially if their social functioning seems relatively satisfactory (Gudjonsson et al., 1993). At one extreme one may have an autistic individual, whose impaired social functioning is a key feature, but whose intellectual functioning may be relatively unimpaired (Happe, 1999). The police would probably identify the disability because of the social deficits and the necessary safeguards provided in law would be invoked. At the other extreme, which is undoubtedly much more common, the police interview suspects and witnesses who are significantly impaired intellectually but whose social functioning seems adequate and masks their true intellectual deficits. Of course, there are also those cases where both intellectual and social deficits are present, but the police nevertheless fail to identify or take appropriate action (Gudjonsson, 1992a; Medford, Gudjonsson & Pearse, 2000).

In my experience the police often fail to identify persons with learning disability and interview the suspect without an appropriate adult and a solicitor being present. When the case goes to court a later pre-trial assessment may reveal the disability and the self-incriminating confession may be ruled inadmissible by the judge (see Chapter 10). Therefore, the failure of the police to identify learning disability may prevent the suspect from exercising his or her full rights during custodial interrogation. If the disability is still not identified when the case goes to court then a miscarriage of justice may result. In other words, the learning disability of the defendant, which may have significant bearing on the reliability of the confession and the fairness of the proceedings, cannot be taken into consideration by the judge and jury unless it has been correctly identified. Therefore, identification of the disability during the early part of the police investigation is crucial, for the defendant and the police.

Possibly the most common reason for the failure of police officers to identify learning disability prior to or during custodial interrogation is that many mildly disabled adults function quite well socially (Richardson, 1978). This can disguise their more subtle disabilities. Another problem is that many police officers appear unaware of how to identify suspects with mild learning disability and why they may be vulnerable to giving unreliable information during interrogation (Williamson, 1990). Even when police officers are presented with unequivocal information about specific vulnerabilities (e.g. previous medical history), many fail to identify the suspect as being 'at risk' (Medford, Gudjonsson & Pearse, 2000; Pearse, 1991). In the Pearse (1991) study, the younger officers were much poorer at identification than the older officers, which indicates that maturity and experience are important for appreciating suspects' vulnerabilities.

It is very important to realize that it is not just the police who commonly fail to identify mild learning disability. I have come across numerous cases where Prison Medical Officers and psychiatrists have grossly overestimated the intellectual functioning of defendants: an error that could have resulted in miscarriages of justice. *Clinical impressions by mental health professionals about the defendant's intellectual strengths and weaknesses are often misleading.* In one case, a prison medical officer described a defendant in court as being of 'average intelligence'. It was only during the cross-examination of the doctor, at my instigation, that it transpired that his conclusion was based on a clinical impression from a very brief (5–10 minute) interview and certainly not on actual testing. I had tested the defendant and found him to have a Full Scale IQ of 69! This was the first case where I testified in a criminal trial in relation to a retracted confession. It was at the beginning of 1982. In addition to a significant intellectual impairment, I had found the defendant to have severe anxiety problems. The judge admitted the evidence in relation to the IQ, but refused to hear the evidence in relation to the defendant's anxiety problems. The judge then ruled the confession admissible and the defendant was convicted of murder.

There is evidence (Clare & Gudjonsson, 1991) that the majority of persons with a mild learning disability do not realize that they should inform the police of their disability if detained at a police station. Furthermore, 30% of the participants in the study stated that they would not tell the police about their learning disability, because they regarded the information as private and personal. This means that many persons with learning disability may deliberately try to cover up their deficits, including reading disability, which may inadvertently mislead the police.

Another problem with the identification of learning disability is that professional views on what should be the upper limit with regard to IQ vary immensely. Denkowski and Denkowski (1985) and Richard, Spencer and Spooner (1980) report that the cut-off scores for legal purposes range from 60 to 78. In the WAIS-R manual a score below 70 is considered to define learning disability (the same criterion applies to the WAIS-III). The cut-off point of 70 is quite arbitrary and was chosen on an historical rather than scientific basis. The convention seems to be not to unnecessarily label people, but keeping to such a low threshold runs the risk of intellectually impaired defendants not being properly provided with the assistance they need when interviewed by the police. There is now a trend not to rely rigidly on fixed IQ scores, but to judge each case on its own merit (British Psychological Society, 2001). In fact, an IQ of 75, which represents the bottom five per cent of the adult population, would be more in line with scientific thinking about a significant impairment and abnormality. An IQ of 70 represents the bottom two per cent of the general population and it is the figure that the Lord Chief Justice adopted in the case of *Masih* ([1986], Crim.L.R. 395). He considered an IQ of 69 or below as a definition of learning disability. The problems with this rigid legal definition are that no account is taken of social functioning and the 'standard error of measurement' of any given intelligence test. In certain cases, an assessment of social functioning is undoubtedly relevant to the deliberation of the judge and jury.

The 'standard error of measurement' of a given test has an important legal significance (Matarazzo, 1990), because it indicates the actual band of error around the obtained IQ score. This band of error is associated with variations in scores when people are tested on different occasions due to inherent unreliability of the test itself. Therefore, a score obtained from a single test administration, for example, an IQ of 69, is not a 'true' score as a certain margin of error would be expected due to the imperfection of the test. By a 'true' score we mean the average IQ score obtained from several administrations of the test. Therefore, if the person was tested on several separate occasions, several months apart with practice effect controlled for, the IQ scores could easily vary by a few points. The average 'standard error of measurement' of the WAIS-III Full Scale IQ is 2.3 (Wechsler, 1997), but there is some variability across different age bands. This means that the chances are 19 out of 20 (i.e. 95% probability) that the 'true' score lies within 4.6 IQ points of the score obtained during any one administration.

Legally, there appears to be a certain mystique associated with the scientific concept of IQ. The 'standard error of measurement' indicates that the IQ obtained during any given administration is not fixed; certain allowances must therefore be made for inherent weaknesses in any given test. Another factor that is often not appreciated by the courts is that IQ tests measure certain verbal and non-verbal skills rather than some 'fixed' overall ability. The precise IQ score obtained depends on the specific skills measured at a given time and the nature of the test used. The test most commonly used is the Wechsler Adult Intelligence Scale (WAIS-III, Wechsler, 1997). Some of the individual subtests used may have greater relevance to legal issues in a given case than others. For example, in cases of retracted confession it is, in my experience, often assumed by the courts that verbal skills (e.g. vocabulary, comprehension and reasoning) are more indicative of how able the accused was in handling police questioning than non-verbal intellectual skills. This is probably generally true, although I would hesitate to suggest that non-verbal skills are unimportant. In fact, one of the non-verbal subtests of WAIS-III, Picture Arrangement, appears to measure social awareness and participation (Schill, Kahn & Meuhleman, 1968), which could be relevant to the identification of learning disability. I have noticed that many of the defendants who appear strikingly good in their social functioning, even when their verbal abilities are significantly impaired, score relatively high on the Picture Arrangement subtest. This is interesting because it is the subtest that has the highest correlation with interrogative suggestibility (Gudjonsson, 1990b).

Persons who are detained at a police station have four basic rights, which need not be exercised immediately.

- They have the right to remain silent, which is a part of the police caution. The caution must be given before the suspect is asked any questions about the alleged offence.
- They have the right to consult a solicitor.
- They have the right to have somebody informed of their arrest and detention.
- They have the right to consult a copy of the Codes of Practice and the Custody Record.

After advising the detainee about these rights, the Custody Officer gives him or her a leaflet explaining their rights.

Research by Clare and Gudjonsson (1992) shows that the leaflet is so complicated to read and understand that the great majority of detainees would not understand it fully. Persons with learning disability are particularly disadvantaged in that they would understand very little of the leaflet. In fact, the majority of them do not fully understand the right to silence (Clare & Gudjonsson, 1991). Their limited intellectual functioning is highly relevant here, but so is their tendency to claim to have understood the caution when they did not. Here *acquiescence* is particularly relevant (Gudjonsson, 1990c). My standard practice when interviewing defendants of low intellectual ability is to read out the caution and ask if they understand it. Most say they understand it, but when I ask them to explain it, it is clear that many have no idea of what it means. Standard police practice in England is that officers read out the caution and say 'Do you understand?'. When suspects say 'Yes' it is not a reliable indication of their understanding of the caution (Fenner, Gudjonsson & Clare, 2002).

Clare and Gudjonsson (1991) found that even after having their rights read out to them from the Notice to Detained Persons, many persons with mild learning disability have problems with retaining the information. The most likely explanation is that the information contained in the document is so complicated that persons with mild learning disability fail to encode it. Persons with mental handicap have been found to have more limited ability to encode new information than persons of normal intelligence (Belmont & Butterfield, 1971). These problems are undoubtedly exacerbated when the material to be encoded, like the Notice to Detained Persons, is difficult to comprehend (Gudjonsson, 1991a).

Beaumont (1987) describes two defendants whose inability to understand the police caution, accompanied by an incidental breach of the Code of Practice in relation to having an 'appropriate adult' present during the police interviews, resulted in successful submission with regard to Section 76(b). I have been involved in several similar cases where persons with learning disability were interviewed without an 'appropriate adult' or a solicitor present.

Given that many people of low intellectual abilities may have little knowledge about their legal rights, it is also the case that they may be at a disadvantage in the sense that, even if they understand their rights, they are often less able to assert and implement them. For example, they might be easily persuaded by the police that they have no need to consult a solicitor.

It is commonly argued that people with learning disability are more suggestible than normal people (Brandon & Davies, 1973; Craft, 1984; Tully, 1980; Woolgrove, 1976). There is substantial empirical evidence to support this view (Tully & Cahill, 1984; Clare & Gudjonsson, 1991), but it is worth remembering that the relationship between suggestibility and intelligence is mediated by a number of factors, including previous interrogative experiences and convictions (Sharrock & Gudjonsson, 1993). However, I have assessed many persons with learning disability who were far from being suggestible or compliant. Therefore, one cannot assume that these persons are necessarily unduly suggestible, even though their condition increases the likelihood that they are. Conversely, there are many people of good intellectual ability who prove to be abnormally suggestible on testing. In other words, *suggestibility needs to be assessed directly rather than assumed on the basis of IQ scores*. Furthermore, when drawing inferences about an individual case, *possible situational sources of suggestibility must not be overlooked* (see Chapter 14).

Persons with learning disability are often considered to be prone to making false confessions because of their heightened suggestibility and eagerness to please people in authority (Brandon & Davies, 1973; Craft, 1984). Their understanding of questions and their ability to express themselves verbally in an interview situation is limited (Keane, 1972; Sigelman & Werder, 1975). A particular danger with regard to interviewing is to rely unduly on simple yes–no questions, because persons with learning disability are likely to answer such questions in the affirmative irrespective of content (Sigelman, Budd, Spanhel & Schoenrock, 1981). Dent (1986) suggests, on the basis of her empirical study, that the optimal interview technique for completeness and accuracy with children who have learning disability is one that uses general rather than specific questions. In contrast, normal children give the most reliable account when asked to give free recall without using general or specific questions (Dent & Stephenson, 1979). It seems, that when interviewing persons with learning disability, exclusive reliance on free recall results in incomplete accounts. Therefore, a certain amount of prompting is required in order to build on the sparse details given in their initial free recall. However, because of the likelihood of high suggestibility and acquiescence, interviewers should avoid asking specific questions. Broad and general questions of a non-leading nature give the best results (e.g. 'What happened next?' rather than 'What did you do next?').

The social context of police interrogation requires a complicated decision-making process (Irving & Hilgendorf, 1980). It would be expected that suspects of low intellectual abilities would be disadvantaged because their decision-making would be principally directed towards immediate gratification (e.g. terminating the police questioning, being free to go home) rather than careful appreciation of the long-term consequences (e.g. prosecution and possibly conviction) of their actions (see e.g. Menninger, 1986). This could in certain circumstances result in their confessing to crimes they have not committed.

We do not know the number of persons with learning disability who are so disadvantaged during interrogation that they make a false confession. There is evidence that persons with learning disability tend to confess particularly readily during custodial interrogation (Brown, Courtless & Silber, 1970). However, little is known about the characteristics that make persons with learning disability likely to confess falsely during custodial interrogation as opposed to making a true confession. They would be expected, generally speaking, to have fewer intellectual and social resources to cope with the demand characteristics of the interrogation and confinement. However, the factors that make persons with learning disability likely to confess falsely vary from case to case. We have to look at the combination of factors rather than any one acting in isolation. What is required is to identify specific vulnerabilities that are potentially relevant and evaluate these in the context of the total circumstances of the case. Just because a defendant has learning disability, it does not necessarily mean that he or she is prone to making false confessions or erroneous statements during interrogation. Each case must be assessed and considered on its own unique merit.

There is evidence that people with significant intellectual impairment do not fully appreciate the legal consequences for suspects of making self-incriminating admissions during questioning. Therefore, their ability to make informed decisions during interrogation is impaired. Clare and Gudjonsson (1995) asked persons with significant intellectual impairment (mean IQ score of 68) and normal controls (mean IQ score of 102) to watch a videotape of a fictional interrogation where a confession was made to a burglary and murder. At certain intervals the film was stopped and the participant was asked questions, focusing on the perceived consequences of the confession for the suspect's continued detention, understanding of the importance of making a false confession and perceived need for legal advice.

Whereas 95% of the normal participants stated that the suspect would be remanded in custody until the trial, only 48% of those with intellectual disability believed this to be the case. The intellectually disabled participants were significantly more likely than the normal participants to believe the suspect would be allowed to go home after making a confession to murder. They were also more likely to state that the interrogator would believe the suspect if he retracted the confession (24% versus 5%). As far as the need for legal advice was concerned, 90% of the normal participants believed that the suspect was in need of legal advice, in contrast to 52% of those with intellectual disability. Most importantly, the participants with intellectual disability were particularly likely to say that no legal advice was needed if the suspect was innocent of the offence. In other words, only guilty suspects were seen as requiring legal advice. This is an interesting finding, because I have encountered many defendants of borderline or significantly impaired intelligence, who had failed to request legal advice while at the police station on the basis that they were innocent and therefore did not need legal advice.

What are the implications of these findings? The main implication is that persons with intellectual disability have an impaired capacity for rational decision-making concerning custodial interrogation and confessions. They are likely to fail to fully appreciate the consequences of their admissions and believe that if they are innocent then the system will somehow protect them from the impact of their own admissions. This increases their propensity, under certain circumstances, to make false confessions.

The Assessment of Social Functioning

The importance of social functioning in the definition of PACE is not clear. There have been several trials in England where the argument has been put forward by counsel that the sentence 'includes significant impairment of intelligence and social functioning' does not mean that *both* intelligence and social functioning necessarily need to be significantly impaired. From the point of view of the Mental Health Act definition *both* would be required to define learning disability (British Psychological Society, 2001). A similar requirement is recommended by the American Association on Mental Deficiency (Matarazzo, 1972).

There are scales available for measuring social functioning, such as the Vineland Social Maturity Scale (Doll, 1965) and the Adaptive Behavior

Scale (American Association of Mental Deficiency, 1974; Atkinson, 1990). These developmental scales, which are usually completed by people who know the person with learning disability very well, focus on evaluating the ability of the learning disabled to cope with practical and social demands. There are at least five problems with using these scales to define learning disability in cases of alleged false confession.

1. Since independent informants are required (e.g. parents, teachers, carers) they are commonly much more time-consuming and problematic to administer than a standard intelligence test.
2. The subjects tested are often quite old, which makes interpretations of their scores difficult.
3. The correlations between tests of intelligence and tests of social functioning are often low (Sparrow, Balla & Cicchetti, 1984).
4. The results from these scales are more subjective than the scores from intelligence tests.
5. It is not clear how well these relate to the legal issues. Their significance in disputed or retracted confession cases is less clear than that of IQ.

THE COURT REPORT AND ORAL EVIDENCE

The amount of work involved in the assessment of the defendant and the preparation of a court report varies immensely. Generally, there is an absolute minimum of two hours of testing and interviewing. Often it takes considerably longer and I sometimes spend over 10 hours with clients over several sessions. Ideally, in complicated cases the defendant should be assessed on more than one occasion but this is not always possible or practical. With the introduction of tape- recorded police interviews, time must be allocated to listen to those.

It is not uncommon in practice to find that the psychological assessment consists both of favourable and unfavourable findings. For example, a defendant may prove to have poor intellectual abilities, but score low on tests of suggestibility or compliance, which imply that he or she may be able to cope reasonably well with interrogation in spite of limited cognitive abilities. Similarly, although the test findings are favourable, he or she may be caught lying during the interview with the psychologist. In one case the defendant of borderline intelligence had told his girlfriend and his solicitor that he had obtained five 'A' levels. He told me the same lie, but when challenged about it he admitted that he had lied as he had wanted everybody, including the jury, to think that he was 'clever'. Since he had made some serious self-incriminating admissions to attempted murder, it was an advantage for the defence to be able to demonstrate that he was of low intelligence, as indeed he was. Another defendant lied to everybody about his age and other matters. I spotted the lie when I was confirming his age from school reports. The case was written up by Sharrock and Cresswell (1989) in an attempt to explore the relationship between pathological lying and suggestibility.

If the psychological findings are not favourable then the defendant's solicitors have four choices. They can serve the report on the prosecution, keep the report from the prosecution, instruct another psychologist for a report in the hope that it will be more favourable or ask the psychologist to delete the unfavourable findings from the report. With regard to the last option, there have been many instances where solicitors have asked my colleagues or myself to delete the unfavourable findings from the report. This I refuse to do and no psychologist should ever be tempted to comply with the solicitors' wishes to alter the report in such a way that it could mislead the court. Unfortunately, in clinical practice this sometimes happens (Gudjonsson, 1996b; Gudjonsson & Haward, 1998). In one major criminal case, the solicitors had my report re-typed, with the unfavourable findings deleted from it, returned it to me by a courier and asked me to sign it! I refused and the report was used in full in court. In another case, when I declined to alter my report at the request of a solicitor he replied, 'I'm not asking you, I'm telling you'. After telling the solicitor that I would be reporting him to his professional body, he apologized. Generally speaking, the only time a psychologist should alter the report is when something in the report is worded in such a way as to be potentially misleading or ambiguous. The report could then be clarified or expanded. Otherwise the psychologist runs the risk of misleading the court.

It is important that the psychologist's findings are presented clearly and succinctly. The conclusions drawn should be substantiated and made relevant to the issues addressed. When the findings are presented clearly, and are relevant to the legal issues, then the report may be accepted by the respective legal advocates without the psychologist having to give oral evidence. When giving evidence the psychologist can be asked probing and challenging questions by the various legal advocates. He or she should be fully prepared. *It must not be assumed that the psychologist will only be asked questions about his or her report.* Psychologists can be asked any question that arises out of their assessment, including going in detail through police interview records. Often the psychological findings are accepted, but having to place them within the context of the totality of the case during one's evidence in court can be a difficult task. Having carefully considered the wider implications of the psychological findings before giving oral evidence often helps.

Poor Psychological Evidence

When preparing court reports, errors can occur at three stages: during the collection of material, the psychological assessment, or when presenting the findings (Gudjonsson, 1993b). The failure to discover or obtain relevant background material can limit the interpretations that can be made from psychological assessment and on occasions result in the psychologist forming wrong or misleading conclusions. The psychological assessment has to focus on the relevant psychological and legal issues. Only reliable and valid tests should be used. Since the chief purpose of the assessment is to inform, the findings should be presented clearly and succinctly. In recent years, I have increasingly read other experts' reports and witnessed their giving testimony in court.

The quality of the work varies greatly. On occasions the assessment is fundamentally flawed. I have identified the following reasons for poor psychological evidence.

1. *Lack of knowledge, skill and experience.* Sometimes psychologists exceed their level of competence when providing court assessments. This is often due to their entering a new area of work for which they are ill prepared and unsupervised. With a rapidly expanding field there is a shortage of psychologists who are able to carry out forensic assessments (Gudjonsson, 1999b). Experience of over 20 years in the field of forensic psychology has taught me the importance of peer supervision. Psychologists who are commencing court work should ensure that their work is properly supervised by experienced forensic psychologists.

2. *Lack of preparation and thoroughness.* It is common to find that psychologists carry out a forensic assessment without reading all the relevant papers in the case and failing to listen to police interview tapes. Sometimes this is due to time pressure, but most commonly it has to do with the attitude or working practice of the psychologist. Another common finding is that some psychologists assess the reliability of confessions without even asking the client any questions about the police interview and why they had made the confession.

3. *Eagerness to please the referral agent.* Some psychologists appear to be overeager to please the referral agent and this can result in unethical behaviour, either because they unsolicited provide only favourable or biased findings, or they allow themselves to be manipulated and tricked by the referral agent to provide a partisan report (Gudjonsson & Haward, 1998).

4. *Inappropriate use of psychological tests or misinterpretation of the results.* It is common to find that psychological tests are not used properly or in a standardized way. For example, working for the prosecution I have seen a number of cases where my suggestibility scales were inappropriately used, wrongly administered or scored or the findings were misinterpreted. On occasions, psychologists make ridiculous claims based on psychological test findings, such as unequivocally equating a high suggestibility score with the claim that the defendant is innocent of the offence when in fact suggestibility is not even relevant to the case. Such inappropriate use of psychological tests undermines the credibility of the profession.

The consequences of conducting a poor psychological evaluation can be very serious, including guilty defendants being inappropriately acquitted or innocent ones wrongly convicted (Gudjonsson, 1993b; Gudjonsson & Haward, 1998).

Potential Abuse of Expert Testimony

The courts' increasing acceptance of psychological and psychiatric evidence is open to abuse by defence solicitors. For this reason cases of disputed confessions are increasingly being referred to psychologists for an evaluation, even when the defendant has not retracted the confession (Gudjonsson, 1999b). Here the defence solicitor is seeking evidence that the defendant possesses some psychological vulnerability, such as a significant intellectual impairment or high suggestibility, in order to persuade a trial judge to rule the confession inadmissible. Such cases present a dilemma for psychologists, because they are at risk of colluding with the defendant being acquitted on the basis of technicality. This raises a number of ethical and professional issues (Gudjonsson, 1994b; Gudjonsson & Haward, 1998). My approach to these cases is to ensure that the evaluation is not so narrowly focused that there is a risk of the court being misled by the psychological evidence. If the defendant is openly admitting the offence to the expert then this should be mentioned in the report (Gudjonsson, 1994b). I have come across a number of cases where experts, on the basis of test scores alone, conclude that the confession is unreliable, even when the defendant is fully admitting the offence to his solicitor and the psychologist, but they fail to mention this latter fact in their report. Expert witnesses should always include in the report everything that is relevant and pertinent to the issues being assessed, irrespective of whether or not it is favourable to the side which commissioned them.

Gudjonsson and MacKeith (1997) raise concern about the potential abuse of psychological and psychiatric evidence:

> In the UK there is growing reliance in the Courts on the use of expert testimony. This includes cases of disputed confessions. What needs to be considered is the extent to which this is beneficial to the administration of justice. One side of the argument, which is fashionable at present, is that expert psychological and psychiatric evidence provides the Courts with information which helps them reach informed decisions and prevents wrongful convictions. This is often a valid argument. The contrary argument is that reliance on expert evidence now places too much emphasis on the importance of psychological vulnerabilities and mental disorder. In other words, there is a temptation for the defence in the current climate to attempt to discover some kinds of psychological vulnerabilities and then over-generalize from the limited findings in order to provide a defence argument. This may result in a number of guilty defendants being acquitted by the Courts, who otherwise would have been properly convicted (pp. 17–18).

CONCLUSIONS

This Chapter provides a conceptual framework for psychologists who are instructed to conduct an assessment on the reliability of testimony. There are a number of different areas that may need to be included, depending on the individual case. Each case needs to be assessed on its own merit, because there are invariably different problems and issues that need to be considered. Some cases are very complicated and require extensive interviewing, testing and reviewing of documents. The psychologist should whenever possible carry out a comprehensive assessment so that any vulnerabilities or potentials that could be relevant to the case are identified. The psychological findings will generally need to be interpreted within the total circumstances of the case. The most difficult cases are typically those where the psychologist is asked to testify as to the reliability of the self-incriminating statements, because this involves a careful consideration of *all* the surrounding circumstances of the case.

The knowledge base for the psychological assessment of disputed confessions is growing. Assessment procedures and tests have been developed and these form an important part of the psychologist's armoury. However, it is simplistic to think that any one test or procedure will provide all the answers to an individual case. Human behaviour is complex and often a careful consideration of all the available material is required before firm conclusions can be drawn about the reliability of the self-incriminating statements.

Psychological tests, like those that measure intellectual skills and interrogative suggestibility, often provide important information about the strengths and vulnerabilities of particular individuals, but these have to be interpreted in conjunction with the other material available in the case. Considerable advance has been made in recent years about the psychological aspects of disputed confessions, but we still have a great deal more to learn.

CHAPTER 13

Suggestibility: Historical and Theoretical Aspects

My interest in 'interrogative suggestibility' began in 1980 when I took a post as a Lecturer in Psychology at the Institute of Psychiatry, University of London. I was commonly being asked by defence and prosecution counsels to prepare court reports involving the assessment of the reliability of evidence. These referrals generally related to two types of case:

1. where victims with learning disability were going to be called to give evidence but there was concern about the likely reliability of their evidence;
2. where defendants had retracted confessions made during police interviewing.

Cases of the former type were generally referred by the prosecution, and the latter by defence counsel. It soon became apparent that the legal advocates were particularly interested in the individual's level of suggestibility.

In a pioneering single case study, Professor John Gunn and I (Gudjonsson & Gunn, 1982) established a precedent at the Central Criminal Court in London (also known as the Old Bailey). The case involved a 22-year-old woman with learning disability, called Mary, who claimed that she had been sexually assaulted by a group of young men and women. The Director of Public Prosecutions requested an answer to three main questions.

1. Was Mary competent as a witness in a court of law?
2. If she was competent, was she reliable as a witness?
3. Was she severely subnormal as defined in the Mental Health Act 1959?

Being able to establish the likely reliability of Mary's statements was particularly important as her testimony was the main prosecution evidence against six defendants.

The psychological assessment, carried out by myself, focused on Mary's learning disability and the likely reliability of her evidence. The assessment was carried out during two sessions on the same day. Mary obtained a Full Scale IQ of 47 on the Wechsler Adult Intelligence Scale (WAIS). At the time of the assessment there was no standardized psychological test available that could be used to assess the reliability of Mary's testimony. For this reason I used (experimental) psychological procedures to assess Mary's general level of 'suggestibility'. These were as follows.

1. Did Mary have a tendency to claim perceptions that had no objective basis?
2. Did Mary have a tendency to answer questions with information that the interviewer suggested?

The first procedure related to possible distortions in Mary's *sensory* processing, whereas the latter was concerned with her *memory* processing.

Mary's suggestibility was tested in the afternoon, whereas the intellectual assessment had been completed in the morning. She was told that the purpose of the afternoon session was to establish how much she remembered about the morning session. During free recall Mary was able to give a reasonably accurate account of the morning session and even remembered several of the questions asked and tests administered. Subsequently an attempt was made to induce in Mary false perceptions, both olfactory (the smell of a cigar) and tactile (feeling a pencil she was holding becoming increasingly hot and reaching the point of burning her fingers). Mary uncritically accepted both suggestions and during the tactile experiment she suddenly dropped the pencil on the floor claiming that it had burned her finger.

With regard to interrogative suggestibility, a special test was constructed which consisted of leading questions. After each leading question I challenged her answer and asked her to provide a more accurate one. Mary proved highly suggestible in response to many, but not all, of the questions. She was particularly suggestible when confronted with sophisticated or abstract ideas and then readily gave observations which had no basis in her own observations. When uncertain about events, she tended to confabulate. However, she was able to resist attempts to alter her account of those events she had experienced and clearly remembered.

The main conclusions from the psychological assessment, which were presented to the jury in the case, were that Mary had limited mental capacity, but she was capable of distinguishing between facts and fantasy when facts were clear to her. Her ability to distinguish between the two diminished markedly when she was unsure of facts. Then she became highly suggestible. However, those of her statements that had no objective basis could be easily altered under pressure, whereas those answers that were correct could not be altered.

The psychological findings were presented to the jury in such a way as to provide them with some guidelines by which they could discriminate between the reliable and unreliable evidence as pertaining to the case being tried. Thus, although Mary was in general very suggestible, she was able to give reliable evidence about facts that she had witnessed and was certain about. It was suggested that the jury could differentiate between Mary's reliable and unreliable evidence on the basis of her answers to careful cross-examination; reliable evidence pertaining to simple and basic facts should not alter under cross-examination whereas unreliable evidence was likely to. Mary's evidence was subjected to this test. Although unable to identify any of the six defendants as being responsible for specific acts, she gave a general account of events which the jury found reliable. The outcome of the case was that five of the six defendants were convicted on at least one charge.

The most important lesson from this case is that persons with moderate learning disability may well be able to give reliable evidence pertaining to basic facts, even when they are generally highly suggestible and prone to confabulation. A detailed psychological assessment of the learning disabled person's strengths and limitations may be necessary in some cases in order to provide the jury with information which helps them evaluate the reliability of the person's testimony.

The present case provides a model of how this can be achieved. Davies, Flin and Baxter (1986) consider that an extension of the procedure pioneered in our case could provide a useful innovation in the case of children's testimonies.

There was an important legal distinction made in the present case between Mary's competence as a witness and the reliability of her evidence. The two were dealt with as separate issues. Competence was decided by the judge on the basis of Mary's understanding of the concepts of truth, God and contempt of court, whereas the issue of reliability, the judge decided, was for the jury to decide upon.

Mary's case provided a conceptual framework for assessing the reliability of evidence by way of psychological procedures. It resulted in the development of a standardized psychological test for measuring interrogative suggestibility (Gudjonsson, 1983, 1984a), which formed the basis for the theoretical model of Gudjonsson and Clark (1986).

In this chapter the theoretical work that has been carried out into interrogative suggestibility will be reviewed in some detail. I will argue that it is a special type of suggestibility and it bears little resemblance to traditional classifications of suggestibility, such as that commonly associated with hypnosis. I shall endeavour to explain how precisely it differs from other types of suggestibility and what the implications are. Until the early 1980s interrogative suggestibility had been a neglected area of research and much of the review literature into suggestion and suggestibility have failed to specifically mention this type of suggestibility.

THEORETICAL APPROACHES

The are two main theoretical approaches to interrogative suggestibility. Schooler and Loftus (1986, 1993) refer to these as the 'individual differences approach' and the 'experimental approach'. According to these authors, the first approach is best illustrated by my own work (Gudjonsson, 1983, 1984a), which was integrated into a detailed model (Gudjonsson & Clark (1986). The model has specific domains of applicability to police interrogation and views suggestibility as being dependent upon the coping strategies people can generate and implement when confronted with the *uncertainty* and *expectations* of the interrogative situation. The emphasis of the model is on explaining *individual differences* in interrogative suggestibility.

The 'experimental approach' is illustrated by the work of Loftus and her colleagues (Loftus, 1979a, 1979b; Loftus, Miller & Burns, 1978; Schooler & Loftus,

1986, 1993). Here the emphasis is on understanding the conditions under which leading questions are likely to affect the verbal accounts of witnesses. Individual differences do not feature prominently in this approach and interrogative suggestibility is viewed as being mediated by a central cognitive mechanism, labelled 'discrepancy detection'.

Schooler and Loftus (1993) make an important distinction between immediate acceptance of misleading information and later retrieval of the misinformation. These involve different processes. Schooler and Loftus link the former, which is commonly found in children and persons with learning disability, with acquiescent responding. Here memory ability is of relatively minor importance. In the case of children they may be particularly accepting of misinformation, because of their unwillingness to challenge authority figures (Ceci, Ross & Toglia, 1987). Delayed misinformation retrieval, in contrast, requires an activation of a memory process that is less developed in children than in adults. In other words, the person has to remember the misinformation in order to be able to retrieve it.

There is no doubt that the two approaches—the individual differences and the experimental—are complementary to each other and they will feature extensively in the rest of this chapter. The emphasis in this chapter is on *theoretical* aspects of suggestibility. The procedural implications of the two theoretical approaches and the empirical evidence will be discussed in Chapter 14.

SOME CHARACTERISTICS OF SUGGESTION AND SUGGESTIBILITY

There is an important distinction to be drawn between the concepts of 'suggestion' and 'suggestibility'. These two concepts, although clearly linked, have been poorly defined and differentiated in the literature. In fact, in the early literature there seems to have been no distinction made between suggestion and suggestibility (Gudjonsson, 1987c).

With regard to the concept of suggestion, Gheorghiu (1989a) refers to the early definition of McDougall (1908) as still being of great influence. McDougall defined suggestion as

> A process of communication resulting in the acceptance with conviction of the communicated proposition in the absence of logically adequate grounds for its acceptance (p. 100).

McDougall thought that his definition covered all 'varieties' of suggestion and suggestibility. There are two major problems with McDougall's definition.

First, it implies that a particular suggestion inevitably results in the acceptance of the suggestion. As Gheorghiu (1989a) points out, this is not necessarily the case. In fact, he argues elsewhere (Gheorghiu, 1972) that an essential prerequisite is that in every suggestible situation the person must have the alternative for a suggestible or a non-suggestible reaction; if there is no opportunity for an alternative response then the response elicited is forced or coerced rather than selected.

The second problem with McDougall's definition of suggestion is that it fails to draw a distinction between suggestion as a stimulus and the reaction of the individual to the suggestion. Rather than construing suggestion as a complicated process, as McDougall does, it is operationally much simpler to conceptualize it as a *stimulus* that provides an individual with a certain message to respond to. This message may be variously referred to as a hint, a cue or an idea. Viewing suggestion as a stimulus that has the potential to trigger or elicit a reaction makes it easier to separate it conceptually from the concept of suggestibility.

Suggestibility refers to the *tendency* of the individual to respond in a particular way to suggestions. Therefore, whereas suggestion refers to the properties contained in a stimulus, suggestibility refers to characteristics of the person who is being incited to respond. The suggestion only has the potential to elicit a reaction; whether it does or not depends on the susceptibility of the person, the nature and characteristics of the suggestion and the person offering it, and the context in which the suggestion occurs.

Gheorghiu (1989b) makes the important differentiation between *direct* and *indirect* suggestion procedures, a distinction he attributes to Sidis (1898). A *direct* procedure involves the subject being told openly and explicitly what is expected of him or her. In other words, the intention of the influence is *overt*. *Indirect* suggestion procedure is more subtle and implicit. The experimenter does not make it clear or obvious that he or she is attempting to influence the responses of the subject. This typically means that the subject is not informed of the actual purpose of the test or procedure.

Gheorghiu (1989a) argues that the effects of suggestions can sometimes become compulsive. He gives as an example people whose lives become unwittingly influenced by the prediction of a fortune-teller. Similarly, he argues, 'people can autosuggestively talk themselves into thoughts of suicide and then more or less compulsively surrender to them' (p. 101). The idea of autosuggestion implies that people can generate their own suggestions, that is, spontaneously suggest things to themselves.

Gheorghiu (1989b) has drawn attention to the lack of unitary definitions of the concepts of suggestion and suggestibility. He cogently argues that because of the complexity and varied nature of the phenomena, collective theoretical and empirical input from specialists of different disciplines is required.

BRIEF HISTORICAL BACKGROUND TO SUGGESTIBILITY

Coffin (1941) stated that the early principle and theory of suggestion came from hypnotists in the 19th century, although the phenomena of suggestion were recognized long before that time. Coffin quotes the work of Noizt, who pointed out in 1820 that the fundamental psychological law at work is that every idea might become an action (the phenomenon was later labelled as an 'ideo-motor' response). Thus, the suggested action is transformed into action because the idea of the action has reached the respondent's consciousness. This shows how the concept of suggestion was originally developed as a way of explaining hypnotic phenomena, and replaced the 'fluidistic' theories that were prevalent at the time, such as those relating to 'animal magnetism'. Those theories viewed hypnosis as arising from physical influences and the psychological forces at work were either not recognized or minimized at the time. According to Gheorghiu (1989b), the concept of suggestion began to play a significant part in hypnosis when early workers, such as Bertrand (1823) and Braid (1846) began to consider hypnosis from a more psychological perspective.

Bernheim (1910) expanded the meaning of the term suggestion and considered it to be a normal phenomenon that might take place in a waking state as well as during hypnosis. He described a range of phenomena which he considered were related to suggestion, such as the daily influence of one person upon another resulting in changes in beliefs and attitudes and the phenomena observed in hypnotized individuals. It is important to note that Bernheim provided no evidence that these different phenomena were fundamentally related. Indeed, they probably were not related at all.

Gheorghiu (1989b, p. 3) argues that Bernheim's (1888, reprinted in 1964) work was particularly important in drawing attention to the concept of suggestion as 'a fundamental principle for the explanation of hypnosis itself' rather than considering it only as 'a vehicle for the induction of hypnotic phenomena'. This extended interpretation of the concept of suggestion meant that suggestion was seen as an important feature of hypnosis, where hypnosis was itself characterized by heightened suggestibility. Thus, no longer was suggestion only seen as a medium for inducing hypnosis; people who had been successfully hypnotized were seen as optimally susceptible to suggestions.

Interest in individual differences and experimental psychology at the turn of the 19th century resulted in many tests of suggestibility being developed. Here the term suggestion was operationally defined in tests and experimental procedures. These were initially limited to producing simple motor and sensory reaction, but they gradually included more complex phenomena such as change in judgement, opinion and attitude. The tests and procedures used were not based on clear theoretical foundations and it is for this reason that the theoretical work on suggestion and suggestibility has greatly lagged behind the experimental and applied work.

Most of the early tests of suggestibility measured the influence of suggestion upon the sensory system (visual, tactile, auditory, olfactory etc). Commonly the procedure consisted of the subject being presented with a real sensory stimulus, which was then omitted without informing the subject, whose reactions were monitored. In one test a small electric current was passed into the subject's hand, which made it slightly warm. The procedure was subsequently repeated without the current being on but the subject was not informed about this. The subject was considered suggestible if he or she reported warmth the second time, and the faster the response was elicited the more suggestible the subject was considered to be. Similar tests were developed by Binet (1900), which dealt with suggestively produced illusions of change concerning progressive weights and lines. In all these tests the suggestions were presented *indirectly* in that the subject did not know that he or she was being influenced.

Several tests of motor suggestibility have been developed and these are generally construed as *direct* tests in the sense that the subject is told that he or she is being influenced. Examples of these tests are the 'hand rigidity' test of Aveling and Hargreaves (1921) and Hull's (1933) well known 'body sway' test. With regard to the former test the subject is told that his arm is gradually becoming rigid like a steel poker, whereas on the 'body sway' test the subject is told that he is falling forward or backward and the distance he slopes in the suggested direction is carefully monitored.

THE CLASSIFICATION OF SUGGESTIBILITY

Eysenck's early and influential work into the nature of suggestibility was to establish, by the use of factor analysis, to what extent the range of different suggestibility tests were functionally related (Eysenck, 1943; Eysenck & Furneaux, 1945). The result of these studies was to demonstrate that there are at least two independent types of suggestibility, labelled by Eysenck and Furneaux as 'primary' and 'secondary' suggestibility respectively. The primary type consisted of so-called 'ideo-motor' tests, whose phenomena are characterized by non-volitional movements following the experimenter's repetitive and monotonous suggestion. The best single test of primary suggestibility is the body sway test discussed earlier, which has been consistently shown to correlate highly with hypnotizability. Eysenck and Furneaux (1945) showed that primary suggestibility correlated significantly with neuroticism. Gibson (1962) subsequently looked closely at personality variables associated with susceptibility to hypnosis and suggested that it was more meaningful to look at the combination of personality scores rather than individual correlations.

The evidence for a stable factor of secondary suggestibility is less clear than for primary suggestibility. It seems to embrace much more varied and complex phenomena than primary suggestibility. Eysenck (1947) associates it with 'indirection' and 'gullibility' and defines it as

> The experience on the part of the subject of a sensation or perception consequent upon the direct or implied suggestion by the experimenter that such an experience will take place, in the absence of any objective basis for the sensation or perception (p. 167).

Eysenck gave the 'ink blot' and 'odour' tests as examples of the kinds of test measuring secondary suggestibility. Secondary suggestibility did not correlate with hypnotizability and there was a negative correlation with intelligence.

Eysenck and Furneaux (1945) raise the possibility of 'tertiary' suggestibility, which involves attitude change resulting from persuasive communication originating from a prestige figure. Evans (1967) argues that the empirical evidence for this type of suggestibility is lacking, but the idea was nevertheless found to be meaningful in the work of Gibson (1962). The 'tertiary' type of suggestibility bears some resemblance to interrogative suggestibility.

Evans (1967, 1989) argues that the traditional distinction between primary and secondary suggestibility has been made without sufficient empirical evidence. He suggests that three types of suggestibility are identifiable, which he refers to as 'primary' (passive motor), 'challenge' and 'imagery' (sensory) suggestibility respectively. A fourth factor was vaguely identified, which related to 'dissociative' behaviour, and this was not thought to be related to 'waking' suggestibility dimensions.

Evans (1967, 1989) recognizes that factor-analytic studies following the work of Eysenck and Furneaux (1945) have consistently confirmed the existence of primary suggestibility, but much less support has been found for a single factor of secondary suggestibility of the kind described by Eysenck and Furneaux.

Evans (1989) discusses two further findings that are important in relation to the classification of suggestibility. First, a placebo response, which has important implications for various therapies, has no relationship with suggestibility or hypnotizability. It seems to be directly related to expectancy variables, particularly those found in a doctor–patient relationship. Secondly, the ability to produce meaningful behavioural responses to suggestion during REM ('rapid eye movement') sleep is significantly correlated with hypnotizability and 'dissociative' phenomena.

It is interesting to note that the detailed work of Evans (1967, 1989) completely ignores any mention of a suggestibility factor relevant to interrogation, although Binet (1900) and Stern (1910, 1938, 1939) had produced interrogative procedures that could well have been included in factor analytical studies into the classification of suggestibility.

The only early work that does highlight the importance of interrogative suggestibility in the classification of suggestibility is that of Stukat (1958). He carried out a number of factor analytical studies with children and adults in Sweden as a classification device for generating hypotheses and understanding the nature of suggestibility. Unlike the previous research, Stukat included in his research tests intended to measure 'personal' and 'prestige' types of suggestibility, and two 'leading question' tests. The results of his factor analysis revealed a secondary suggestibility factor of rather wide scope, which was somewhat dissimilar to that of Eysenck and Furneaux and represents tests

> ... in which different subjective influences, such as set, expectations, and need for conformity, direct the individual's perceptions, memory, and judgement (p. 239).

The kinds of test that had the highest factor loadings on Stukat's secondary suggestibility factor were:

1. 'contradictory suggestion' tests (the examiner contradicts the subject's judgement in a discrimination task);
2. 'co-judge suggestion' tests (a tendency to be influenced by co-judge suggestion in making one's judgement in a discrimination task);
3. weight and line pairs tasks (the subject has to classify non-identical weights and lines after a suggestion that they are identical).

The two 'leading question' tests had rather low loadings on this factor and correlated poorly with the secondary suggestibility tests described above. Stukat thought that the contradictory and co-judge tests were most clearly characterized by personal influence and pressure from one individual upon another, so that the individual's need for conformity was the most significant functional determinant in the secondary suggestibility process. Results from group comparisons supported Stukat's theory. That is, groups thought to have the strongest need for conformity (e.g. young children, anxious people) were found to be most suggestible. The findings were interpreted as showing that 'functional determinants', such as needs, attitudes, values and differential reinforcement, influence perception, memory and judgement, particularly in an unstructured situation.

It is evident from the above discussion that there are several different types of suggestibility. According to Gheorghiu (1989a), suggestion procedures have traditionally been used to influence three unrelated processes—motor processes, sensory processes and memory processes. We have seen that motor processes are commonly associated with *primary* suggestibility, which in turn is related to hypnotizability. *Secondary* suggestibility is found to cover a range of different test phenomena, which are mostly but not exclusively associated with sensory processes and perceptual judgements. Unfortunately, the tests that seem to make up the secondary suggestibility factor are not always closely interrelated. A broad definition of secondary suggestibility seems to have some theoretical implications for interrogative suggestibility, but it is the influence upon memory processes which is clearly most relevant.

After reviewing the literature on suggestibility I concluded that there were good theoretical and empirical reasons for construing interrogative suggestibility as a distinct type of suggestibility (Gudjonsson, 1987c). This view has been reinforced by Gheorghiu (1989b) in his critical review of the development of research on suggestibility. Indeed, interrogative suggestibility bears little resemblance to traditional definitions of suggestibility, whether classified into 'primary' and 'secondary' phenomena as Eysenck proposes (Eysenck, 1943; Eysenck & Furneaux, 1945) or 'primary', 'challenge' and 'imagery' suggestibility, as argued by Evans (1967). In particular, on conceptual grounds no relationship would be expected between interrogative suggestibility and primary suggestibility.

THEORIES OF SUGGESTIBILITY

A number of theories have been put forward in order to explain primary and secondary suggestibility. These have been extensively reviewed by Stukat (1958). Primary suggestibility is most commonly explained in terms of an ideo-motor response, which is fundamentally related to theories of conditioning. These seem of no relevance to interrogative suggestibility and will not be discussed in detail.

Various theories have been proposed to explain phenomena relevant to the elusive entity of secondary suggestibility. For example, Binet's (1900) tests of progressive weights and lines, as well as his 'prestige' and 'interrogatory' tests, were assumed by him to include:

1. obedience to mental influence from another person,
2. the tendency to imitate,
3. influence of a preconceived idea that paralysed the individual's critical sense and
4. expectative attention.

Stukat (1958) found some support for Binet's theoretical formulation from his factorial studies, where the first two categories (1 and 2 above) were quite similar to Stukat's 'need for conformity' factors and the last two (3 and 4) corresponded to an 'expectative' factor.

McDougall (1908), whose definition of suggestion was given earlier, associates suggestibility with four distinct conditions:

1. abnormal states of the brain (e.g. as during hypnosis, sleep and fatigue);
2. deficiency and poor organization of knowledge regarding the subject matter being communicated;
3. the impressive character of the person communicating the suggestion (i.e. 'prestige' suggestion) and
4. the character and disposition of the subject.

McDougall thought of the relative strengths of 'instincts', 'assertion' and 'subjection' as the most crucial conditions determining the individual's level of suggestibility. For example, an individual with a strong impulse of self-assertion when communicating with others of lower status makes the former non-suggestible to the influence of the latter. McDougall also emphasized the importance of the person's knowledge, and confidence in his knowledge, as mediating variables in the susceptibility to suggestion. McDougall's emphasis on both *motivation* and *cognitive* factors in determining suggestibility is fundamental to the understanding of secondary suggestibility, including interrogative suggestibility.

Another theoretical model of relevance to secondary suggestibility is that of Sherif (1936). He argues that a stimulus is never reacted to in isolation. It is always experienced, perceived, judged and reacted to in relation to other stimuli, present or past, to which it is fundamentally related. Sherif used the term 'frame of reference' to denote these functionally related factors that influence perceptions and judgements,

Coffin (1941) has expanded Sherif's theory. He regards suggestion as a framework response, determined by internal factors (e.g. attitude) and external features of the stimulus situation. When a situation is 'well structured' in terms of either attitudinal or situational factors, only those suggestions which accord with the existing frame of reference are likely to be accepted. The advantage of the *cognitive* model of Sherif and Coffin is that it is conceptually simple and seems to explain many experimental findings. A possible weakness is the strong emphasis on the cognitive aspects of internal factors, because even though suggestions may well function as a frame of reference usually there are emotional and motivational factors involved in the suggestion process that 'drive' the subject towards accepting or rejecting the suggestion.

A similar cognitive emphasis is evident in the work of Asch and his colleagues on prestige suggestion (Asch, 1952; Asch, Block & Hertzman, 1938; Crutchfield, 1955; Krech, Crutchfield & Ballachey, 1962). In accordance with *Gestalt* psychology, Asch (1952) argues that subjects' reactions in 'prestige' experiments such as those of Bridge (1914) and Moore (1921) are reasonable and rational and quite different from the uncritical automatic reactions of hypnotized subjects. One of Asch's most important contributions to the suggestibility literature is to point to a distinct cognitive difference between hypnotic suggestion and 'prestige' suggestion on the basis of qualitative analysis. Within this theoretical framework man is seen as a rational creature who searches logically for meaning and coherence. The emphasis on the rational character of suggestible behaviour is in contrast to a more sociological view where the emphasis is placed upon the passive and uncritical nature of the reaction in social situations.

Milgram (1974) has researched the effects of authority, status and power on such behaviour as obedience. He defined obedience as the action of a subject 'who complies with authority' (p. 113). He investigated the extent to which subjects were prepared to obey the instructions of an experimenter when it involved behaviour ordinarily regarded as unreasonable and socially unacceptable (e.g. seemingly administering a strong electric shock to helpless victims). Milgram concluded that the extensive willingness of subjects to uncritically obey the experimenter was due to the special relationship that developed between the experimenter and the subject. Most subjects reported that they felt under strong pressure to obey the experimenter, believing that disobeying would ruin the experiment and upset the experimenter. This raises an important point about the extent to which the implicit etiquette in a particular situation can influence human behaviour. Milgram discusses this point within the framework of Goffman's (1959) influential book *The Presentation of Self in Everyday Life*.

Milgram makes four important distinctions between authority and conformity to peer group pressure as described by Asch (1951), as follows:

1. obedience, unlike conformity, occurs within a hierarchical structure;
2. conformity means that people imitate the behaviours and values of others. In contrast, obedience refers to compliance without imitating the source of influence;
3. the message that results in obedience is typically direct (i.e. an order or a command), whereas it is implicit or indirect in the case of conformity, and
4. in Milgram's obedience research subjects admitted that they were complying with a force external to themselves, whereas it is evident from conformity studies that the subjects are largely unaware of the pressure acting on them to conform.

Irving and Hilgendorf (1980) have applied Milgram's findings to police interrogation situations and point out that during interrogation some subjects may obey instructions that ordinarily they would resist.

It is important to realize that the studies of Asch and Crutchfield are concerned with influence in the context of group pressure, whereas obedience research focuses on how subjects react to pressure from a person in authority. However, the behaviour of the subject in each setting may be mediated by similar factors, such as a desire to be liked, eagerness to please, the need to maintain self-esteem, the need to fulfil role obligations and expectations and avoidance of conflict and confrontation.

The powerful influence of perceived authority on behaviour has not just been demonstrated by laboratory studies, such as those of Milgram. For example, Bickman (1974) studied the effects of uniform on people's compliance in a natural social setting. He found that when the experimenter was dressed in a guard's uniform 83% of pedestrians obeyed his instruction to give a confederate a 'dime' for a parking meter in contrast to 46% when he was dressed in civilian clothing.

Within the field of social psychology the term 'conformity' is used to refer to a change in behaviour or belief as a result of pressure, real or imagined, from a group or a person (Kiesler & Kiesler, 1970). According to Kiesler and Kiesler, there are basically two types of conformity, which correspond to the terms 'compliance' and 'private acceptance'. With regard to compliance, people behave as others wish them to behave but without their believing in what they are doing. Kiesler and Kiesler argue that obedience studies, like those of Milgram, give a good illustration of compliance without private acceptance. Private acceptance, on the other hand, is more commonly seen in studies into suggestibility.

REINFORCEMENT AND SUGGESTIBILITY

The effects of prior reinforcement upon suggestibility (see e.g. Kelman, 1950) has important implications for interrogative suggestibility. The general finding is that individuals who experience success in a task when they are first examined tend to be more resistant to subsequent suggestions than those who experience failure. Such findings can be interpreted both along *motivational* (e.g. strength of the anxiety drive) and *cognitive* (thought processes) lines. The work of Kelman is particularly supportive of motivational factors in that certain personality factors (e.g. traits of submissiveness, inferiority feelings, anxiety) seem to interact with differential reinforcement. Related to this is the work of Seligman and his colleagues on 'learned helplessness' (Abramson, Seligman & Teasdale, 1978).

SUGGESTIBILITY: A STATE OR A TRAIT?

There is a considerable disagreement in the literature about whether suggestibility should be viewed as a 'trait' or a 'state'. Implicit in the concept of suggestibility is the idea that it refers to some stable tendency of the individual to respond in a particular way to a given situation. Prideaux (1919) viewed suggestibility as a general trait of the individual. The work of Eysenck (1947) on different types of suggestibility very much relies on the trait hypothesis. Critical advocates of the trait hypothesis, such as Baxter (1990), Krech and Crutchfield (1948) and Moston (1990a) emphasize that suggestibility is greatly affected by situational factors. Indeed, Krech and Crutchfield reject the trait hypothesis and are pessimistic about developing individual measures of suggestibility. They construe suggestibility as being dependant upon the 'total psychological situation' (p. 337).

Krech and Crutchfield put forward two reasons for rejecting the trait hypothesis. First, they point to the poor correlations between different suggestibility tests, and between suggestibility and personality type. Hence, the specific nature of the test situation is assumed to be more important than a person's psychological make-up. Second, even if consistently high correlations were found between different suggestibility tests this does not necessarily give support for the trait hypothesis, because subjects may consistently accept or reject suggestions for very different reasons.

Stukat (1958) is critical of the reasons put forward by Krech and Crutchfield against the trait hypothesis, but concedes that

> No analysis of suggestion and suggestibility can omit the actual needs and attitudes of the subject, the personal relationship between experimenter and subject, or the characteristics of the stimulus situation (p. 32).

Stukat argues that Krech and Crutchfield go too far in their emphasis on situational factors by denying the existence of suggestibility as a trait. He provides evidence from his own extensive research to support the trait hypothesis and states:

> Therefore we conclude that in view of the fact that the situational variation was maximized in our investigations there have appeared suggestibility factors that were not situationally caused. It then seems reasonable to refer the factors to relatively constant tendencies in the individual to be more or less suggestible, irrespective of the situation p. 92).

DEFINITION OF INTERROGATIVE SUGGESTIBILITY

One of the earliest experiments conducted into human testimony is that of Cattell (1895). He asked college students a number of questions that were potentially misleading and they had to indicate their degree of confidence in each answer. However, the idea of interrogative suggestibility appears to have been first introduced at the turn of the century by Binet (1900, 1905), whose contribution to the understanding and measurement of the various types of suggestibility has been quite outstanding. Unfortunately, his book *La Suggestibilite* has never been translated into English and it is undoubtedly for this reason that his work has not been as influential as it should have been. Binet's procedure for measuring interrogative suggestibility involved asking leading questions concerning a picture that subjects had been shown previously. This kind of 'interrogatory' procedure, which is of relevance to the effects of questioning upon memory recall and testimony, was subsequently used by other workers, such as Stern. The classical experimental work of Stern (1910, 1938, 1939) demonstrated that leading questions can produce distorted responses because they are phrased in such a way as to suggest the wanted response whether correct or incorrect. Several subsequent studies have employed a similar or modified procedure to that of Stern in order to elicit this type of suggestibility (e.g. Burtt, 1948; Cohen & Harnick, 1980; Powers, Andriks & Loftus, 1979; Trankell, 1958).

Davies, Flin and Baxter (1986) make the interesting observation that both Binet and Stern used static pictures rather than simulated incidents as stimulus material, although Stern (1910) did call for 'event tests' (i.e. studies of incidents). Davies *et al.* argue that static pictures may limit the forensic relevance of the material. This problem was overcome by the early innovative British study of Pear and Wyatt (1914), who used a realistic simulated incident as stimulus material.

Not all authors agree on a definition of interrogative suggestibility. Powers, Andriks and Loftus (1979) define it as

> ...the extent to which they (people) come to accept a piece of post-event information and incorporate it into their recollection (p. 339).

This definition highlights the importance of *memory processing* as an integral part of interrogative suggestibility and it was for this reason that the fundamental processes of perception and memory were discussed in detail in my earlier book on interrogations and confessions (Gudjonsson, 1992a).

There are two main problems with the above definition of interrogative suggestibility. First, it has not been proven that people necessarily *incorporate* the suggested information into their recollection, although the information may be accepted by the individual (i.e. they may believe it and accept it, but not incorporate the information into memory—this will become an important issue in some of the cases discussed in later chapters). Secondly, the definition is too vague to provide the researcher with operationally testable hypotheses.

A more focused definition is provided by Gudjonsson and Clark (1986), who define interrogative suggestibility as

> *The extent to which, within a closed social interaction, people come to accept messages communicated during formal questioning, as the result of which their subsequent behavioural response is affected* (p. 84).

This definition comprises five interrelated components which form an integral part of the interrogative process:

1. a social interaction;
2. a questioning procedure;
3. a suggestive stimulus;
4. acceptance of the stimulus; and
5. a behavioural response.

The first component relates to the nature of the social interaction involved. Many of the social aspects of the police interview were discussed in Chapters 1 and 2. It is evident from that discussion that the police interview is a closed social interaction. For example, in his observation of police interviews with the Brighton CID, Barrie Irving noted:

> The interview is a closed social interaction: the room is closed, the participants close to each other, interruptions are avoided as far as possible (Irving, 1980, p. 122).

Similarly, Inbau et al. (2001) comment:

> The principal psychological factor contributing to a successful interrogation is privacy—being alone with the person during questioning (p. 51).

The second distinguishing component of the police interview is that it involves a questioning procedure. There may be two or more participants and the questions asked typically relate to some factual material that the interviewer wishes to obtain about what the person has heard, seen or done. Feelings and intentions may also be enquired about. In most instances the questions asked are concerned with past events and experiences. This means that the memory recollections of the respondent are particularly important. Anything that interferes with the memory process makes it more difficult for the interviewer to obtain valid information from the respondent.

The third component relates to the nature of the suggestive stimulus. Questions can be 'leading' because they contain certain premises and expectations, which may or may not be informed and well founded. It was also shown that questions can be leading because of the context in which they appear.

The fourth component makes it explicit that there must be some kind of *acceptance* of the suggestive stimulus. This does not necessarily mean that the person incorporates the suggestive information into his or her memory. Rather, the suggestion must be perceived by the respondent as being plausible and credible.

The final component states that the respondent must give some kind of behavioural response to the suggestive stimulus. It is not sufficient for the interviewer that the respondent believes or accepts the suggestion privately. The respondent must indicate, either verbally or non-verbally, whether or not he or she accepts the suggestion. On occasions the respondent may accept the suggestion offered by the interviewer but is reluctant to commit himself or herself to a definite answer.

The Gudjonsson–Clark (1986) definition of interrogative suggestibility provides the framework for a theoretical model that helps to further our understanding of the process and outcome of the police interview. It was mentioned earlier in this chapter that interrogative suggestibility bears little resemblance to other types of suggestibility. Elsewhere (Gudjonsson, 1989b), I take this argument further and show that from a conceptual point of view there are four main features of interrogative suggestibility that differentiate it from other types of suggestibility. These have been incorporated into the Gudjonsson–Clark (1986) theoretical model, which will be discussed in detail later, and comprise the following.

1. Interrogative suggestibility involves a questioning procedure within a closed social interaction.
2. The questions asked are mainly concerned with past experiences and events, recollections, and remembered states of knowledge. This makes it different from suggestibility of those types that are concerned with the motor and sensory experiences of the immediate situation.
3. Interrogative suggestibility contains a strong component of uncertainty, which is related to the cognitive processing capacity of the individual.
4. An important feature of interrogative suggestibility is that it commonly involves a highly stressful situation with important consequences for a witness, victim or suspect (there are, of course, also important consequences for the interviewer and the police investigation).

THE GUDJONSSON–CLARK THEORETICAL MODEL

There are two distinctive types of suggestibility important to police work (Gudjonsson, 1983). The first type relates to the pioneering work of people such as Binet (1900) and Stern (1910, 1939) into the reliability of human testimony. Here the emphasis is on the impact of leading or suggestive questioning on testimony. The second type of suggestibility relates to the extent to which interrogators are able to 'shift' unwanted but perhaps accurate answers by challenge and negative feedback. This aspect of the interrogation process is implicit in some of the theories of interrogation and confessions discussed in Part I of this book, but until my own work (Gudjonsson, 1983) it had never been formally or systematically studied. I argued that these two aspects of suggestibility are conceptually distinct, showing subsequently (Gudjonsson, 1984a, 1991d), by the use of factor analysis, that the two types of suggestibility are indeed reasonably independent of each other.

The importance of negative feedback during interrogation is described as follows.

> One type of instruction that may markedly distort individual responses is criticism or negative feedback. An interrogator who communicates negative feedback to a suspect, witness or victim, may through an interrogative pressure shift unwanted, but perhaps true, responses in favour of untrue or distorted ones. For example, repeating the same questions several times because the answers given are not acceptable to the interrogator may make the S adapt himself to the expectations reflected in the interrogator's manner and style of questioning (Gudjonsson, 1984a, p. 303).

The importance of the last sentence is to emphasize the fact that negative feedback may be *implicit* rather than explicit; that is, negative feedback need not necessarily be stated explicitly or openly. It can be implied, for example, by the interrogator repeating the same question several times. In other words, repeated questioning may act as a form of negative feedback when interviewees begin to believe that the interrogator is not accepting their previous answers.

I make the point that the two distinct types of suggestibility lead to different inferences and practical implications:

> Knowledge of the types of suggestive questions Ss are particularly susceptible to and the extent to which they can be misled by such questions, may give useful practical information about the potential reliability of witness testimony. Applications of critical feedback... represent relatively greater pressured suggestibility and may therefore be more linked with anxiety and coping processes (Gudjonsson, 1984a, p. 311).

A psychometric instrument for measuring these two types of suggestibility was developed (Gudjonsson, 1983, 1984a). The content of this scale, and the parallel form (Gudjonsson, 1987a), will be described in Chapter 14. The early work into the validity of the first scale helped refine and extend the earlier theoretical conceptualization of interrogative suggestibility.

The Gudjonsson–Clark (1986) theoretical model is shown in Figure 13.1. The model integrates the 'leading questions' and 'negative feedback' aspects of suggestibility discussed by Gudjonsson (1983, 1984a). It construes suggestibility as arising out of the way the individual interacts with others within the social and physical environment. The basic premise of the model is that interrogative suggestibility is dependent upon the coping strategies that people can generate and implement when faced with two important aspects of the interrogative situation—*uncertainty* and *expectations*. The model begins by defining the social situation and the participants involved. The general cognitive set of the interviewee is then defined and this results in the interviewee adopting a 'general cognitive strategy', which can facilitate either a *suggestible* or *resistant* response repertoire. The police then begin asking a question, which undergoes cognitive processing by the interviewee, who then employs one or more strategies of general coping. As can be seen from Figure 13.1, this process involves the interviewee having to deal with *uncertainty* and *interpersonal trust* on the one hand and certain *expectations* on the other. These three components are seen as essential prerequisites for the suggestibility process. The cognitive processing of the question results in 'cognitive appraisal', which in turn results in either a *suggestible* or a *resistant* behavioural response.

Uncertainty means that the interviewee does not know for certain the right answer to a question. This may occur, for example, when his memory for events is incomplete or non-existent. Sometimes interviewees may accept a suggestion contained in a leading question, knowing that it is wrong, because they are eager to please the interrogator or are reluctant to disagree with the suggestion openly. When this happens the interviewee should be considered to be *compliant* rather than *suggestible*. Interviewees can only be described to be truly suggestible when they privately accept the suggestion offered or at least believe it to be plausible. This is inherent in the definitions of interrogative suggestibility given earlier in this chapter.

Suggestibility: Historical and Theoretical Aspects

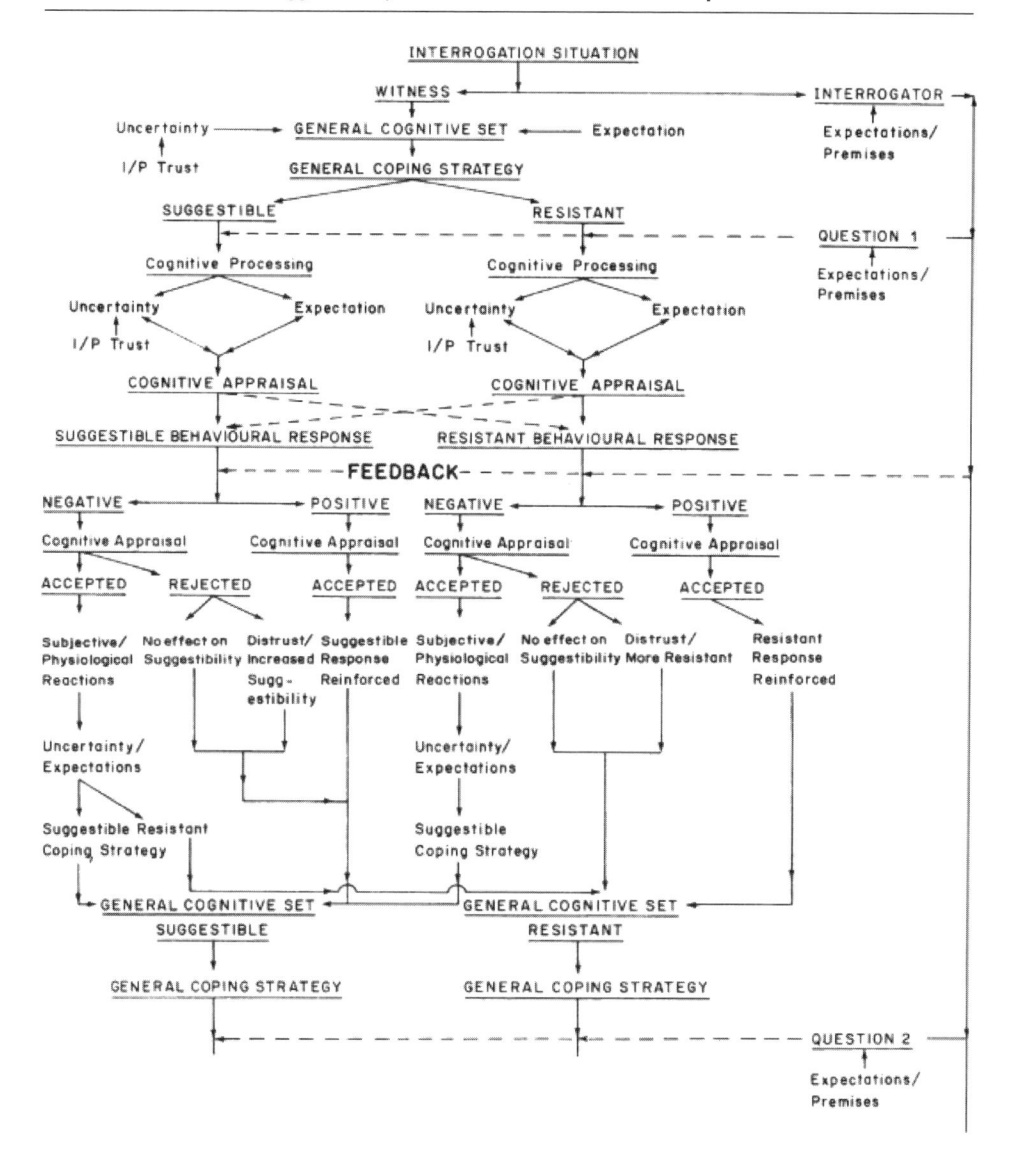

Figure 13.1. A theoretical model of interrogative suggestibility. I/P = interpersonal (reproduced by permission from Gudjonsson & Clark, 1986)

Interpersonal trust is another important prerequisite for yielding to suggestions. It means that the interviewee believes that the interrogator's intentions are genuine and that there is no trickery involved in the questioning. Interviewees who are suspicious of the interrogator's intentions will be reluctant to accept suggestions offered, even under conditions of increased uncertainty.

It is evident from the above discussion that uncertainty must be present in order for a response to suggestion to occur. In addition, leading questions must be sufficiently subtle that they are perceived as being plausible, believable and without trickery; otherwise, they are likely to be rejected. There is a link between uncertainty and interpersonal trust in that the latter may depend on the extent to which interviewees are able to detect that they are being misled. The better the interviewee's memory for events, the more readily he or she is likely to detect an attempt by the interrogator to mislead or influence the responses given.

Expectation of success is an essential prerequisite for a response to suggestion to occur. This is because uncertainty and interpersonal trust are necessary but not sufficient on their own to make people yield to suggestions. Indeed, if interviewees are uncertain about the correct answer to a particular question, then they can declare their uncertainty by giving a reply of 'I don't know', 'I am not sure' or 'I can't recall'. However, many people are reluctant to declare their uncertainty because they believe that:

1. they must provide a definite answer,
2. they should know the answer to the question, and
3. they are expected to know the answer and be able to give it.

The theory postulates that most people would be susceptible to suggestions if the necessary conditions of uncertainty, interpersonal trust and heightened expectations are present. The extent to which interviewees yield to suggestion is a function of their cognitive appraisal of the interrogative situation and the coping strategies they are able to adopt. A coping strategy that helps interviewees resist suggestions involves being able to look objectively and critically at the situation and not commit oneself to an answer unless one is absolutely sure of the facts. A coping strategy that is amenable to suggestion involves an unrealistic appraisal of the situation and the reluctance to admit the fallibility of one's memory when uncertain.

Figure 13.1 shows that *feedback* is an important part of interrogative suggestibility. This is conceptualized by Gudjonsson and Clark (1986) as

> ...a signal communicated by an interrogator to a witness, after he/she has responded to a question or a series of questions, intended to *strengthen* or *modify* subsequent responses of the witness (pp. 93–94).

The signal may be positive (i.e. reinforcing a previous response) or negative (i.e. tending to modify an unwanted answer). Feedback, whether positive or negative, may be communicated implicitly or explicitly. Repeated questioning is one example of implicit negative feedback. Implicit positive feedback may consist of providing interviewees with refreshments, praise or sympathy after they begin to give wanted answers. Explicit negative feedback consists of the interrogator openly stating that he or she thinks the interviewee has made a mistake or is lying. What is communicated is that the answer given is not acceptable and that a different one is required. Explicit positive feedback may consist of the interrogator reinforcing wanted or accepted answers by utilizing such utterances as 'good', 'that's right' or 'now we are getting somewhere'.

Gudjonsson and Clark argue that feedback, and particularly negative feedback, may have quite dramatic effects upon the subsequent behaviour of an interviewee. This is clearly illustrated by the work of Gudjonsson (1984a, 1984b), where negative feedback is shown to have two distinct effects: it (a) makes interviewees change or *shift* their previous answers and (b) heightens their responsiveness to further leading questions. The latter aspect of suggestibility is of greater theoretical relevance to the Gudjonsson–Clark model, but, as we shall see in later chapters, the *shift* aspect of suggestibility has important forensic implications.

During interrogation negative feedback may be given after each answer, when the answer is unacceptable to the interrogator, or at the end of a series of questions. Gudjonsson and Clark argue that negative feedback with regard to specific questions is easier for interviewees because they know precisely which questions require changing. Negative feedback after a series of questions is likely to affect the interviewee more because they may be unclear as to which answers they are required to change. For theoretical simplicity Figure 13.1 focuses on feedback, positive and negative, given question-by-question.

Following a behavioural response by the interviewee, which may be yielding or resistant, the interrogator provides either positive or negative feedback, which needs to be adequately processed and understood for it to have its proper effects. According to the model, the processing outcome of feedback is related to the previous behavioural responses of the interviewee, and these are differentiated as follows.

1. *Suggestible behavioural response followed by positive feedback*. Here previous yielding to suggestions is reinforced by the interrogator, which results in a general cognitive set that is more susceptible to suggestions during subsequent questioning.
2. *Resistant behavioural response followed by positive feedback*. Here positive feedback is accepted and reinforces the resistant behavioural response of the interviewee. This results in the general cognitive set of the interviewee becoming more resistant. This kind of positive feedback probably does not happen often during interrogation.
3. *Resistant behavioural response followed by negative feedback*. Gudjonsson and Clark consider this feedback aspect of the model to have the most important practical implications. Here negative feedback can be either 'accepted' or 'rejected'. Not all interviewees will 'accept' negative feedback. If negative feedback is rejected then it will have no major effects upon subsequent susceptibility to suggestions, but Gudjonsson and Clark point out that negative feedback can on occasions make some interviewees more resistant to subsequent suggestions. The reason for increased resistance is due to interviewees developing a suspicious cognitive set (e.g. thinking that they are being tricked) as the result of the negative feedback.

    When negative feedback is accepted it may result in strong emotional and physiological reactions which will further increase uncertainty. Self-esteem is most readily affected, followed by increased anxiety, both subjective and physiological. Lowered self-esteem results in debilitating thoughts and coping strategies, which means that interviewees are more likely to seek external cues rather than relying on their own judgement and internal frame of reference. The outcome of this process is assumed to influence the general cognitive set and coping strategies of the interviewee during subsequent questioning.

According to the model, negative feedback, if accepted by the interviewee, does not automatically lead to a suggestible general cognitive set, although this most commonly happens. For example, some interviewees may perceive negative feedback constructively as a form of challenge to improve, which as a result makes them take a more critical view of the situation.

4. *Suggestible behavioural response followed by negative feedback.* Gudjonsson and Clark argue that negative feedback is unlikely to be given after the interviewee has yielded to a suggestion, because it would confuse the person and serve no useful purpose for the interrogator. However, there are at least two circumstance where this situation may arise: first, where the interrogator has asked several questions and the interviewee has only yielded to some of them. The interrogator then attempts to elicit more yielding answers by giving negative feedback about the interviewee's overall performance. This approach is used with the administration of some suggestibility scales and will be discussed in the next chapter. Second, the interviewee may have yielded to a suggestion contained within a false alternative question (i.e. more than one alternative is suggested) and he or she fails to give the desired alternative because the question was not structured to explicitly indicate the wanted alternative answer. The model predicts that highly suggestible interviewees most readily respond to negative feedback by changing their answers to false alternative questions as opposed to closed yes–no answer questions because their response alternatives are more limited. The reason for this is that an individual who has yielded to nearly all of the yes–no type questions during interrogation is reaching a 'ceiling effect' in terms of suggestibility. Since false alternative questions give people more than one suggestible option it would be easier for them to alter their answers to these questions than yes–no type questions and still remain highly suggestible in terms of affirmative answers.

IMPLICATIONS OF THE MODEL AND HYPOTHESES

The best way of evaluating the merit of a theory is by finding out how well hypotheses derived from the theory are supported by empirical findings. A number of hypotheses can be predicted from the model and to what extent these have been supported will be discussed in the next chapter. Some of the main hypotheses derived from the model are as follows.

1. Implicit in the model is the assumption that interrogative suggestibility is a distinct type of suggestibility. In particular, it would not be expected to correlate with *primary* suggestibility as found in a hypnotic context.
2. The model views suggestibility as a dynamic process that is potentially *situation bound*. This is particularly true of negative feedback, whose impact is expected to vary according to the intensity, quality and nature of

the feedback, in addition to the interviewee's past experiences. However, the model recognizes that suggestibility can be reasonably stable over time because of the cognitive (e.g. memory, intelligence) and personality (e.g. self-esteem, method of coping with stress, anxiety proneness, dependence upon social approval) factors that mediate suggestibility. Therefore, stable individual differences in suggestibility can be measured reliably and these can predict how people are likely to cope with real life interrogation.

3. The three components of suggestibility—*uncertainty*, *interpersonal trust* and *expectation*—can be manipulated to a certain extent by an interrogator to alter the interviewee's susceptibility to suggestions.
4. Interviewees who enter the interrogation with a *suspicious* cognitive set are likely to be less suggestible than those with a trusting cognitive set.
5. The types of coping strategy people are able to use during interrogation affect their level of suggestibility. For example, avoidance coping is likely to facilitate acceptance of suggestions, whereby interviewees give answers that to them seem plausible and consistent with external clues provided, rather than only giving definite answers to questions they clearly remember. In contrast, a non-suggestible coping strategy involves a critical analysis of the situation and a facilitative problem-solving action.
6. Interviewees with poor memory recollections and those of low intelligence are generally more suggestible than those of higher cognitive abilities.
7. Suggestibility is related to certain personality variables, such as low self-esteem, anxiety proneness, lack of assertiveness and fear of negative evaluation.
8. Negative feedback can markedly affect interviewees' mood (e.g. self-esteem, anxiety) and heighten their acceptance of suggestions.
9. There are significant differences between the response alternatives of suggestible and non-suggestible individuals in response to negative feedback.

EXTERNAL EVALUATION OF THE MODEL

There have been two publications that give detailed external evaluation of the Gudjonsson–Clark theoretical model. The first critique was by Schooler and Loftus (1986) and the second by Irving (1987). The editor of the journal *Social Behaviour*, where the theoretical paper was published, invited the two distinguished scientists, Loftus and Irving, to provide an objective critique of the model. The work of Elizabeth Loftus in the field of eyewitness testimony (e.g. Loftus, 1979a) is well known internationally. Barrie Irving has been an influential figure within the British Criminal Justice System (Irving, 1990). These two distinguished scientists make somewhat different points and their critiques will therefore be discussed separately. The Schooler–Loftus critique is particularly important because it highlights certain differences and similarities between the 'individual differences' and 'experimental' approaches to interrogative suggestibility. These two approaches are clearly complementary to each other, as indeed Schooler and Loftus have pointed out, and taken together they further our understanding of interrogative suggestibility substantially.

Schooler and Loftus review in some detail the different components that make up the model and its theoretical implications. They conclude that the model

> ... represents a formidable attempt to make sense of a multi-faceted phenomenon. The emphasis on the role of individual differences in interrogative suggestibility complements the more experimental approach to the influence of post-event suggestions. For example, experimental studies of post-event suggestions have usually ignored the ways in which various personality variables may influence suggestibility... At the same time the individual differences approach is relatively devoid of detail regarding the precise cognitive mechanisms that may mediate the incorporation of post-event suggestions. Throughout their discussion, Gudjonsson and Clark hint at plausible mechanisms without explicitly describing them (p. 107).

Schooler and Loftus then proceed by discussing how Gudjonsson and Clark could enrich their model by considering some of the central cognitive mechanisms, such as 'discrepancy detection', that experimental research has identified as mediating suggestibility. The importance of the principle of discrepancy detection is that it helps to explain the process whereby people accept and integrate inconsistent information into their memory (see e.g. Tousignant, Hall & Loftus, 1986). According to this principle,

> Recollections are most likely to change if a person does not immediately detect discrepancies between post-event suggestions and memory for the original event (Schooler and Loftus, 1986, pp. 107–108).

Discrepancy detection is assumed to be affected by two factors: (i) 'the strength of the original information in memory' and (ii) 'the manner in which the post-event suggestion is influenced' (p. 108).

Studies providing evidence for the influence of memory on discrepancy detection have manipulated the interval between viewing the event and subsequent suggestions being offered (Hertel, Cosden & Johnson, 1980; Loftus, Miller & Burns, 1978). The results from these studies indicate that subjects are more likely to incorporate misleading suggestions into their recollection when there is a long interval between viewing the original event and the presentation of post-event suggestions. Schooler and Loftus argue that one interpretation is that the more memory deteriorates over time, the less subjects are able to detect discrepancies between what they observed and what is subsequently erroneously suggested to them. This implies that post-event suggestions are least likely to impair discrepancy detection when encountered very close to viewing the original event.

According to Schooler and Loftus, studies that have varied the sentence construction of misleading suggestions provide evidence that discrepancy detection is influenced by the manner in which the post-event suggestion is presented. For example, Loftus (1981) found that explicitly directing subjects' attention to the misleading information made them more willing or able to scrutinize their memories and detect discrepancies. Similarly, Greene, Flynn and Loftus (1982) advised subjects, prior to their reading a narrative containing misleading post-event information, to be on the look out for misleading information. This resulted in the subjects reading the passage more slowly and detecting more discrepancies between factual information and misleading post-event suggestions. Tousignant, Hall and Loftus (1986) found that just asking subjects to read post-event narratives slowly increases discrepancy detection of the material.

Schooler and Loftus conclude that incorporation of post-event suggestions is influenced by a number of factors, but they are all mediated by the general principle of discrepancy detection. These authors then go on to explore to what extent the various components of the Gudjonsson–Clark model can be explained in terms of discrepancy detection. They argue that several of the salient components can be explained by the principle of discrepancy detection. These are *uncertainty*, *interpersonal trust* and *negative feedback*.

According to Schooler and Loftus,

> Uncertainty facilities suggestibility by reducing the likelihood that a witness will experience a discrepancy between the original event and the subsequent suggestion (p. 107).

Applying the principle of discrepancy detection to individual differences in memory capacity these authors argue:

> ... presumably people who tend to be less certain as a result of poor memory abilities are less able to catch discrepancies between the original event and subsequent suggestions (p. 110).

With regard to interpersonal trust between a witness and an interrogator, Schooler and Loftus argue that a suspicious cognitive set makes witnesses scrutinize the interrogator's questions more closely and this helps them identify discrepancies between what they originally observed and what has been subsequently suggested to them. They cite the work of Dodd and Bradshaw (1980) as evidence for this phenomenon.

According to Schooler and Loftus, negative feedback can be interpreted in relation to discrepancy detection because:

1. negative feedback reduces subjects' confidence in their own memories and this makes them less likely to compare the suggestions of the interrogator with their own recollection and
2. increased anxiety caused by negative feedback may decrease the subjects' ability and/or motivation to adequately scrutinize the content of the interrogator's questions.

Schooler and Loftus acknowledge that positive feedback poses a problem for discrepancy detection. They state that people are most likely to incorporate inaccurate details into their recollection when 'they do not carefully attend to the inaccurate facts' (p. 109). Related to this is the tendency of people to be most influenced by 'unmemorable suggestions', that is, pieces of information that they do not take much notice of at the time they are suggested. Accordingly, blatant and obvious suggestions are less likely to influence people than subtle suggestions (Loftus, 1981). For positive reinforcement to work the suggestions have to be obvious so that people know what they are being reinforced for. This poses problems for the principle of discrepancy detection. Schooler and Loftus overcome this by suggesting two conditions where people may be influenced by obvious suggestions:

1. there may be situations where people do detect discrepancies between what they observed and what is suggested to them, but they nevertheless decide to *comply* with the interrogator;
2. obvious suggestions may be accepted and incorporated into recollections when people have little memory for the original detail. Where memory is very poor for a particular detail the suggestion may be quite obvious without the person detecting any kind of a discrepancy.

> Here, witnesses may recall having accepted a suggestion and may, in response to positive feedback, become increasingly suggestible in the future (p. 109).

Schooler and Loftus make no attempt to explain the *expectation* component of the Gudjonsson–Clark model in terms of discrepancy detection. The reason for this is undoubtedly that this component of the model cannot easily be explained by the principle of discrepancy detection. Indeed, the Gudjonsson–Clark model would predict that failure in discrepancy detection is a *necessary* but not a *sufficient* condition for people to yield to suggestions. This limitation or weakness of the discrepancy detection principle appears to be completely overlooked by Loftus and her colleagues. In other words, people may fail to detect discrepancies between what they observed and what is subsequently suggested to them, but this does not inevitably mean that they accept misleading information and incorporate it into their memory. After all, people can state that they do not know a particular answer after failing to detect a discrepancy.

In my view, the main advantage of the principle of discrepancy detection is that it highlights a central cognitive mechanism that has an important function in mediating suggestibility. However, as this discussion demonstrates, there is more to interrogative suggestibility than discrepancy detection. The implication of Schooler and Loftus that Gudjonsson and Clark could have been more economical in the description of their model is intuitively attractive, but in reality interrogative suggestibility is a more complex phenomenon that probably requires more than one model for complete understanding. It seems that by attempting to explain interrogative suggestibility comprehensively in terms of one cognitive mechanism, Schooler and Loftus are over-ambitious and overlook the complexity of the phenomenon. The main theoretical difference between the Gudjonsson–Clark model and the conceptual framework of Schooler and Loftus is that Gudjonsson and Clark postulate that suggestibility is mediated by a number of cognitive and personality variables, rather than relying on one central mechanism.

Irving (1987) describes his own approach to police interrogation as 'interrogation watching' (p. 19). This reflects his observational study of interrogation techniques at Brighton Police Station (Irving, 1980). His comments on the Gudjonsson–Clark model are therefore more empirical than theoretical, although his comments have theoretical implications.

Irving echoes the comments of Schooler and Loftus that the model could have been more simply described, but his reasoning is somewhat different. He states:

> ...would it not be more parsimonious to propose that the phenomenon which Gudjonsson and Clark want to label suggestibility, when it does occur, is merely an extreme form of a compliant reaction? All that is required to incorporate this suggestion into Gudjonsson and Clark's scheme is to postulate that at low levels of amplitude compliant responses (for example involving confabulation) do not obscure the original memory signal (i.e. are not sufficient to interfere with recall either at the time or after interrogation) but more extreme compliant reactions produce noise so intense that original memory signals (recall) are obscured (Irving, 1987, p. 20).

Irving continues:

> All the elements in Gudjonsson's model are reducible or functionally equivalent to the factors described as being pertinent to obtaining responses in suspects during interrogation (p. 21).

The strength of Irving's argument lies in highlighting the potential overlap between the concepts of 'suggestibility' and 'compliance', and this point will be dealt with in Chapter 14 in a discussion about the relationship between the two concepts, in terms of both theory and empirical findings.

The weakness of Irving's argument lies in his overlooking the main theoretical difference between the concepts of suggestibility and compliance. The difference relates to the *personal acceptance* of the information provided (see e.g. Wagstaff, 1981). Unlike suggestibility, compliance does not require personal acceptance of the information provided or request made. In other words, a compliant individual behaves as others wish him to behave without believing in what he is doing. In this respect, compliance is similar to Milgram's (1974) concept of obedience. Irving's comment concerning extreme compliant responses interfering with memory does not coincide with traditional definitions of compliance. In other words, it is not easy to see how extreme compliance, which Irving indeed relates to such work as that of Milgram (1974), can seriously affect memory. This does not mean that compliance cannot under certain circumstances affect memory. Indeed, the work of Bem (1966, 1967) indicates that 'saying can become believing', but this is more likely to occur at low levels of amplitude response rather than at extreme levels of compliance.

Irving makes the point that individual differences are likely to be of little importance during real-life police interrogation, because interrogators are able to neutralize their effects by applying various tactics and ploys. He then goes on to state, on the basis of his own observational studies, that tactics aimed at individual differences may be 'no more than the icing on the cake' (p. 25). The implication is that the reasons why people confess during custodial interrogation are have nothing to do with the personality of the suspect. To Irving's credit, he does not argue that individual characteristics are never relevant or important. In his view, personality characteristics, such as intelligence, are only important when extreme.

Irving draws our attention to the potential importance of the seriousness of the crime:

> In practice as long as the crime involved is relatively serious then *all* suspects, regardless of their individual proclivities, will tend to produce a level of attention sufficient to the task (Treisman, 1969), except where mental handicap or drug intoxication makes that impossible for them. Custodial interrogation does tend to focus the mind (p. 23).

Irving's bold assertion is based on an assumption rather than empirical facts. It is not clear why he refers to Treisman's (1969) article in support of his argument, because the article only deals with attention in the context of subjects being presented with more information than they can handle. The article does not deal with the critical components of attention which are relevant to police interrogation, such as vigilance, arousal and motivation.

CONCLUSIONS

The early experimental work of Cattell (1895) demonstrated the influence of suggestion upon human testimony. However, it appears to have been Binet (1900) who first introduced the idea of interrogative suggestibility and provided a conceptual framework for testing it. Before his work both French and German psychologists had known about the effects of suggestion upon sensation and perception, particularly in connection with hypnosis.

Many tests were developed to measure different types of suggestibility. Most of these appear to have had no clear theoretical base or rationale. Later workers factor analysed the results from these tests in an attempt to understand the nature of suggestibility. They discovered that there were at least two types of suggestibility, referred to by Eysenck and Furneaux (1945) as 'primary' and 'secondary'. 'Primary' suggestibility consisted of so-called 'ideo-motor' tests and correlated highly with hypnotizability. 'Secondary' suggestibility appeared to measure a much more varied and complex phenomena and was shown to be less stable and reliable. All the factor analytical studies, with the exception of those conducted by Stukat (1958), failed to include tests of interrogative suggestibility. This resulted in interrogative suggestibility being a neglected area of research.

Interrogative suggestibility is a special type of suggestibility and differs from other types of suggestibility in several important ways. Most significantly, it involves a questioning procedure that is typically concerned with past experiences and events, recollections and remembered states of knowledge. This makes it very different to suggestibility concerned with motor and sensory experiences of the immediate situation.

There are two main theoretical approaches to interrogative suggestibility. These are called the 'experimental' and 'individual differences' approaches.

The 'experimental' approach is principally concerned with the conditions under which leading questions are likely to affect the verbal accounts of witnesses. Here suggestibility is viewed as being mediated by a central cognitive mechanism, which is labelled 'discrepancy detection'. The 'individual differences' approach, on the other hand, views suggestibility as being mediated by a number of different cognitive and personality factors rather than by one central mechanism. This implies that witnesses and criminal suspects respond differently to interviewing and interrogation according to their cognitive abilities, mental state and personality.

The principal reason for the differences between the two approaches relates to the nature of the subjects studied, which formed the basis of the theoretical ideas behind the models. The 'experimental' approach has relied extensively on college students as experimental subjects, whereas the 'individual differences' approach is based on research with varied and heterogeneous samples, which include normal subjects, criminal subjects, prisoners and psychiatric patients. This chapter has highlighted the strengths and weaknesses of each approach and shows how the two radically different approaches complement each other in furthering our theoretical understanding of interrogative suggestibility.

CHAPTER 14

Interrogative Suggestibility: Empirical Findings

Until the development of the Gudjonsson Suggestibility Scale (GSS 1; Gudjonsson, 1983, 1984a) there were no measures of interrogative suggestibility available that could be used to assess an individual case. Certain laboratory procedures were available for measuring people's responses to leading questions, following the work of Loftus and her colleagues, but these were unsatisfactory and impractical for forensic application. I developed the GSS 1 because there was a need for such an instrument to assess pre-trial criminal cases involving retracted confessions. The purpose of this chapter is to look at the testing of interrogative suggestibility and its empirical aspects. Most of the early work was carried out on the GSS 1, but during the past 15 years a parallel form, the GSS 2, has also been extensively used in research. In addition to different measures of suggestibility (Yield 1, Yield 2, Shift and Total Suggestibility), both scales measure logical memory (immediate and delayed) and confabulation (distortions and fabrications). The norms for the different measures are similar but not identical on the two scales.

After the publication of the original articles in the 1980s, many clinicians and researchers contacted me and requested that I produce a manual with guidelines for the administration, scoring and statistical properties of the scales. The *Gudjonsson Suggestibility Scales Manual* has now been published and provides new and more extensive norms (Gudjonsson, 1997a). The manual should make it easier for clinicians and researchers to use the scales in a reliable way. The GSS 1 and GSS 2 are behavioural tests and therefore particular attention has to be paid to the careful administration of the instruments. In my experience, in clinical practice and research insufficient attention is commonly paid to the proper procedures and administration of the scales. This may undermine the validity of the test results obtained. For this reason I have been running training courses at the Institute of Psychiatry on how to administer, score and interpret the Gudjonsson Suggestibility Scales (GSS) and the Gudjonsson Compliance Scale (GCS).

Scullin and Ceci (2001) have recently developed a parallel test of the GSS 1 and GSS 2 for pre-school children, based on a video presentation of the stimulus material. This is an exciting development, because individual differences in suggestibility among children have long been overlooked in the literature. The results parallel those of the use of the GSS with adults in terms of Yield and Shift items loading on different factors.

Endres (1997) had developed the Bonn Test of Statement Suggestibility (BTSS) to measure individual differences in interrogative suggestibility in children aged 4–10 years. The test is partly based on the format of the GSS. The German version of the test has been translated into Dutch and validated (Candel, Merckelbach & Muris, 2000).

Can interrogative suggestibility be reliably measured? Is there empirical evidence that interrogative suggestibility differs from suggestibility described in a hypnotic context? How does suggestibility relate to the constructs of 'compliance' and 'acquiescence'? These are basic types of question that are addressed in this chapter before the more empirical findings are discussed in relation to the Gudjonsson–Clark model. Many of the theoretical questions raised in Chapter 13 are dealt with experimentally in this chapter.

The best way of testing the merit of a particular theory is on the basis of how well the various hypotheses derived from the theory can be supported by empirical findings. A number of hypotheses derived from the Gudjonsson–Clark model were listed in Chapter 13 and I now examine how well the theory has stood up to empirical investigations.

THE GUDJONSSON SUGGESTIBILITY SCALES

After laying the foundations for the theoretical work on interrogative suggestibility, which was discussed in detail in Chapter 13, the construction and early validation of a suggestibility scale were used to assess the individual's responses to 'leading questions' and 'negative feedback' instructions when being asked to report a factual event from recall. The scale, referred to as the Gudjonsson Suggestibility Scale (GSS 1), is particularly applicable to legal issues, such as police officers' questioning of witnesses to crime and interrogation of criminal suspects. It employs a narrative paragraph describing a fictitious robbery, which is read out to the subject. He or she is then asked to report all that can be recalled about the story. After the person has given free immediate and delayed recall to the story (the delay is generally about 50 minutes), he or she is asked 20 specific questions, 15 of which are subtly misleading. After answering the 20 questions the person is told that he or she has made a number of errors (even if no errors have been made), and it is therefore necessary to ask all the questions once more. The person is asked to be more accurate than before. Any change in the person's answers from the previous trial is noted as *Shift*. The extent to which people give in to the misleading questions is scored as *Yield 1*. Yield 1 and Shift are typically added together to make up *Total Suggestibility*.

Grisso (1986) reviewed the early validation studies on the GSS 1 and concluded:

> Construct validation research with the GSS has placed the forensic examiner in a good position to use GSS scores when considering questions of an examinee's decreased resistance to suggestion or subtle pressure in interrogations by law enforcement officers (p. 147).

Register and Kihlstrom (1988) argue, on the basis of their work on a modified version of GSS 1, that there are three possibly independent types of interrogative suggestibility:

1. responses to negative feedback;
2. responses to leading questions;
3. responses to repeated questions.

These authors found that, even when no negative feedback was given, their subjects would nevertheless alter some of their answers when re-interrogated on the GSS 1. Linton and Sheehan (1994) replicated this finding, using a modified version of the GSS 1. One probable reason for this finding is that repeated questioning or neutral feedback may act as a form of implicit negative feedback. That is, subjects assume that they have made errors and this is why they are being re-interrogated. Further work needs to be carried out in order to establish whether responses to repeated questions are independent of responses to negative feedback. Another possible explanation for the effects of repeated questioning is that some subjects may not recall how they responded to all the previous questions and therefore provide inconsistent answers.

The GSS 1 and GSS 2 were developed for two different purposes. First, the scales were intended to be used for research in order to further our understanding of interrogative suggestibility and its mediating variables and mechanisms. Second, the scales were intended for forensic and clinical applications. The primary application was to establish an instrument that could identify people who were particularly susceptible to erroneous testimony during questioning. In other words, the emphasis was on the measurement of individual differences.

Much of the early work on the GSS 1 was concerned with validating the scale and developing the theoretical basis for the Gudjonsson–Clark model. More recently, various experiments have been carried out to test the various hypotheses derived from the model using both the GSS 1 and GSS 2. As will be shown later in this chapter, many of the hypotheses derived from the Gudjonsson–Clark model have been tested and supported experimentally.

Types of Clinical Information Derived from the Scales

Most of the research with the GSS 1 and GSS 2 has been concerned with two types of information which can be readily derived from the scales. These correspond to Yield 1 and Shift. However, Yield 2, memory (immediate and delayed) and confabulation (distortions and fabrications) can also be measured for clinical and research purposes. Yield 2 is increasingly becoming an important measure in its own right.

1. *Immediate recall*. This measures immediate verbal recall on the GSS narrative and gives an indication of the subject's attention, concentration and memory capacity. The maximum number of 'ideas' that subjects can recall is 40. The mean score for people of average IQ on the GSS 1 is about 21, with a standard deviation of 7. A score of 8 falls at the fifth percentile rank for 'normal subjects' (i.e. it falls outside the normal range). Special groups,

such as forensic patients and court referrals, typically score more than one standard deviation below the mean for normal subjects (i.e. a score about 12 with a standard deviation of 7), even when their intellectual functioning is not known to be impaired.

2. *Delayed recall*. Delayed recall of the GSS narrative is usually obtained about 50 minutes after immediate recall. As with immediate recall, the maximum number of correct 'ideas' is 40. Memory on the GSS narratives typically deteriorates by about one or two points over a 50 minute period, which gives mean delayed memory scores of 19 and 10 for normal and forensic subjects, respectively. This means that verbal memory deteriorates about 10% within one hour. However, among normal subjects about 75% of the immediate recall is retained at one week follow-up (Singh & Gudjonsson, 1984; Tata & Gudjonsson, 1990) and about 40% is produced at four week follow-up (Sigurdsson et al., 1994).

Immediate and delayed recall on the GSS 1 and GSS 2 deteriorate with advanced age, particularly in old age where the deterioration is very marked (Sigurdsson et al., 1994).

3. *Yield 1*. Yield 1 refers to the number of suggestions the subject yields to on the GSS 1 and GSS 2 prior to negative feedback. The maximum score the subject can obtain is 15. The mean score on the GSS 1 for normal subjects is 4.6 with a standard deviation of 3. A Yield 1 score of 11 or above falls outside the normal range (i.e. the 95th percentile rank). Forensic patients, including court referrals, typically obtain a Yield 1 score of about 6, with a standard deviation of 3.5.

4. *Shift*. Shift refers to the number of times where there has been a distinct change in the subject's answers following negative feedback. The wording of the negative feedback, which is administered immediately after the 20 questions have been asked (Yield 1), is:

> You have made a number of errors. It is therefore necessary to go through the questions once more, and this time try to be more accurate.

This should be stated *firmly*, but not sternly. Subjects typically change some of their answers after they have been told that they have made a number of errors during the 20 questions. The direction of the change is irrelevant in the scoring of Shift. The highest possible Shift score on the GSS 1 and GSS 2 is 20 (i.e. all 20 questions are included in the scoring of Shift, unlike Yield 1 and Yield 2). The mean Shift score for normal subjects on the GSS 1 is about 2.9, with a standard deviation of 2.5. This means that a score of 8 or above falls outside the normal range. The mean score for forensic patients, including court referrals, is about 4 with a standard deviation of 3.

5. *Yield 2*. Yield 2 refers to the number of leading questions which the subject yields to after the negative feedback has been administered. Therefore, Yield 2 represents the number of suggestions accepted after interrogative pressure. Yield 2 indicates the type of change that has occurred as a result of the negative feedback. Usually, the change (i.e. Shift) is in the direction of *increased* suggestibility. That is, after negative feedback and repeated questioning subjects tend to yield more to the leading questions than they

did before (Gudjonsson, 1984a; Register & Kihlstrom, 1988). Typically Yield 2 is about one or two points higher than Yield 1; a score of 13 or above falls outside the normal range.

Yield 2 has been used in some of the more recent research with the GSS 1 and GSS 2. It provides additional information in that it tells the examiner precisely how interrogative pressure, which is administered in the form of negative feedback, affects the subsequent susceptibility of the subject to suggestive questions. Yield 2 is more highly correlated with Shift than Yield 1 among normal subjects, forensic cases and children (Gudjonsson, 1984a), which means that it gives a better indication than Yield 1 of the subjects' vulnerability to yielding to leading questions when placed under interrogative pressure.

6. *Total Suggestibility*. This is the sum of Yield 1 and Shift. This gives an indication of the subject's overall level of suggestibility. The mean Total Suggestibility score for normal subjects is 7.5 on the GSS 1, with a standard deviation of 4.6. This means that a score of 16 or above falls outside the normal range (i.e. 95th percentile rank). The mean score for forensic patients, which includes court referrals, is about 10 with a standard deviation of 6.

7. *Confabulation*. Confabulation is the most recently developed measure of the GSS. It refers to problems in memory processing where people replace gaps in their memory with imaginary experiences that they believe to be true. Confabulation can be measured on the memory part of the GSS 1 and GSS 2 stories. This includes major distortions in the story's content or that pieces of information have been added to the story. Clare, Gudjonsson, Rutter and Cross (1994) classified confabulations on the GSS 2 into two distinct groups:

- distortions, which represent a major change in the details of an existing 'idea' (e.g. house mentioned instead of a bungalow, one boy instead of two boys) and
- fabrications, where a new or novel element is added to the narrative (e.g. introducing a name of a person or place not mentioned in the story).

Distortions and fabrications are typically added to make up the total number of confabulations. For details about the scoring readers should read the *GSS Manual* (Gudjonsson, 1997a).

Reliability

The internal consistency of the 15 Yield 1 and 15 Shift items on the GSS 1 was measured by Cronbach's alpha for 195 subjects (Gudjonsson, 1984a). The coefficients were 0.77 and 0.67 for Yield 1 and Shift, respectively. Singh and Gudjonsson (1987) recommended some modifications in the scoring of Shift, which increased the internal reliability of the measure to 0.71. This consisted of slight modification in the scoring of Shift and increased the number of items from 15 to 20. This means that a distinct change in the answers given after 'negative feedback' applies to all the 20 items on the GSS 1, and not just to the 15 'leading' items, as had been used in the original work.

Following the early development of the GSS 1, and a comprehensive external review on the scale's validity by Grisso (1986), I constructed a parallel form, labelled GSS 2 (Gudjonsson, 1987a). The two scales are identical except for the content of the narrative paragraph and interrogative questions. The content of the GSS 1 reflected the forensic objectives of the instrument; that is, the narrative stimulus has a criminal content. However, since there is no reason to suppose that a criminal versus non-criminal narrative stimuli would affect the suggestibility scores (Grisso, 1986), the GSS 2 narrative has a non-criminal content. Correlating the scores obtained by subjects with the scores derived from the GSS 1 validated the GSS 2. The correlations between the two scales within the same session was 0.90 and 0.92 (Total Suggestibility) for normal and forensic subjects respectively (Gudjonsson, 1987a). For a group of forensic patients tested on two separate occasions the correlation was 0.81. In a separate study of 90 forensic cases, Gudjonsson (1997a) found that the correlation between the GSS 1 and GSS 2 Total Suggestibility scores, administered on two separate occasions, was 0.83. The correlations have been found to be consistently lower for Shift than Yield 1, which is consistent with the prediction from the Gudjonsson–Clark model. The findings give strong support for the test–retest reliability of interrogative suggestibility, even when people are tested many months apart. Therefore, interrogative suggestibility, as measured by the Gudjonsson Suggestibility Scales, appears to be reasonably stable over time when the testing conditions are similar.

The scoring of the Yield and Shift are highly non-discretionary in nature and one would therefore expect the inter-rater reliability to be high. Two studies have investigated the inter-rater reliability of the scales. Richardson and Smith (1993) studied the inter-rater reliability of Yield and Shift scores on the GSS 1 in a group of 57 juveniles. The correlation coefficients between two independent raters ranged between 0.949 for Shift and 0.993 for Total Suggestibility. In a similar study, Clare et al. (1994) investigated the Kappa coefficients across three independent raters among 101 subjects. The reliability coefficients ranged between 0.989 for Shift and 0.993 for Total Suggestibility. The inter-rater reliability for immediate and delayed recall was also very high (0.969 and 0.951 for immediate and delayed recall, respectively), Therefore, the GSS 1 and GSS 2 possess very high inter-rater reliability for both memory and suggestibility. Confabulation in memory recall is more difficult to score reliably compared to memory and suggestibility. The inter-rater reliability for confabulation on immediate and delayed recall is 0.803 and 0.724, respectively (Clare et al., 1994).

The GSS 1 and the GSS 2 have very similar norms (Gudjonsson, 1997a) and can be used interchangeably. The Cronbach alpha coefficients for the GSS 2 appear to be somewhat higher than for the GSS 1. In one study (Gudjonsson, 1992d), which comprised 129 subjects, the Cronbach alpha coefficients were 0.87 and 0.79 for Yield 1 and Shift, respectively. The coefficient for Yield 2 was 0.90. Factor analysis of the Yield 1 and Shift items on the GSS 2 indicated two factors, with Yield 1 items loading on the first factor and Shift items on the second factor. This finding is identical to that found for the GSS 1 (Gudjonsson, 1984a) and indicates that there are two reasonably independent types of interrogative suggestibility, which correspond to the extent to which people give in to misleading questions (Yield 1) and how they respond to interrogative pressure (Shift).

The content making up the GSS 2 narrative is somewhat simpler than that of the GSS 1. For this reason my colleagues and I preferred to use it for research with children and persons with mild to moderate learning disabilities (Henry & Gudjonsson, 1999; Gudjonsson, Murphy & Clare, 2000).

Wolfradt and Meyer (1998), using a German translation of the GSS 2, report Cronbach's alpha coefficents of 0.79, 0.78 and 0.81 for Yield 1, Yield 2 and Shift, respectively.

The finding that Yield 1 and Shift represent different types of suggestibility has recently been confirmed among 98 young children (3 to 5-year-olds), using a Video Suggestibility Scale based on the format and procedure of the GSS 1 and GSS 2 (Scullin and Ceci, 2001). Yield 1 and Shift items loaded on different factors as found previously for adults on GSS 1 and GSS 2. The Cronbach alpha coefficients for Yield 1 and Shift were 0.85 and 0.75, respectively, which is very similar to that found for adults.

Confabulation

The mean number of confabulations on the GSS 2 narrative for immediate and delayed (50 minutes) recall is typically between one and two (Clare & Gudjonsson, 1995). Four or more confabulations on either immediate or delayed recall will fall outside the normal range (Gudjonsson, 1997a). Similar norms have been obtained on the GSS 1 for Icelandic prisoners.

A number of studies have been carried out into confabulation using the GSS 1 and GSS 2 (Clare & Gudjonsson 1993; Clare *et al.*, 1994; Gudjonsson & Clare, 1995; Gudjonsson & Sigurdsson, 1995, 1996; Howells & Ward, 1994; Rassin, 2001; Register & Kihlstrom, 1988; Santtila *et al.*, 1999; Sigurdsson & Gudjonsson, 1996; Sigurdsson *et al.*, 1994; Smith & Gudjonsson, 1986, 1995a, 1995b; Tata & Gudjonsson, 1990).

What is emerging is that confabulation is a less reliable measure than memory and suggestibility both in terms of poorer inter-rater reliability (Clare *et al.*, 1994) and being less consistent over time (Tata & Gudjonsson, 1990; Smith & Gudjonsson, 1995a). In addition, the two types of confabulation—distortions and fabrications—are poorly correlated and appear to be associated with different psychological variables (Gudjonsson & Clare, 1995; Smith & Gudjonsson, 1995a; Gudjonsson & Sigurdsson, 1995, 1996). It is therefore probably sensible for research purposes to treat them as separate and independent measures.

The processes underlying confabulation are probably complex and multifactorial (Gudjonsson & Clare, 1995). Confabulation is most typically studied in relation to biological or organic conditions (see e.g. Dalla Barba, 1993) and pseudomemory associated with hypnosis (Laurence & Perry, 1983; Register & Kihlstrom, 1988; Sheehan, Green & Truesdale, 1992). Of particular interest to the present book is the suggestion of Berlyne (1972) that confabulation might be related to personality factors. In view of this, Gudjonsson and Sigurdsson (1995) investigated in a large group of prison inmates the relationship between confabulation, as measured by the GSS 1, and a number of personality tests as well as a test of intelligence. There was a poor relationship between confabulation and the other psychological variables. The only significant correlations were that confabulation correlated positively with GSS 1 Shift and negatively with intelligence as measured by Raven's Standard Progressive Matrices (Raven, Court & Raven, 1992). The study was replicated with 108 juvenile offenders and no significant findings emerged with regard to confabulation, although there was a significant correlation between fabrication and GSS 1 Yield 1, and a negative correlation between distortions and intelligence, as measured by Raven's Standard Progressive Matrices. Gudjonsson and Clare (1995) studied the relationship between confabulation (distortions and fabrications) and intellectual ability, memory, suggestibility and acquiescence in a reasonably large sample of subjects ($N = 145$ subjects). Distortions and fabrications did not correlate significantly with the scores from the other measures.

Smith and Gudjonsson (1995a, 1995b), who studied forensic in-patients, found that distortions and fabrications correlated with different psychological factors. Fabrication scores correlated significantly with the rate of memory decline over one week and with GSS 2 Shift and Yield 2, whereas distortion scores correlated significantly with state anxiety (Smith & Gudjonsson, 1995a). In order to test Johnson's (1991) hypothesis that confabulation is a memory disorder related to breakdown in reality monitoring, the patients completed the Reality Monitoring task of Bentall, Baker and Havers (1991) and were classified into hallucinators and non-hallucinators. Hallucinators did not confabulate significantly more than non-hallucinators (Smith & Gudjonsson, 1995b). Interestingly, a retrospective analysis based on psychiatric diagnosis found that fabrication scores were significantly higher among the personality disordered patients than the patients diagnosed with schizophrenia. This is an interesting finding, because it suggests that confabulation is more related to personality factors than breakdown in reality monitoring as seen in schizophrenia.

Confabulations at one week follow-up were studied by Tata and Gudjonsson (1990). The number of confabulations clearly increases as memory deteriorates over time, but factors such as the severity of negative feedback administered during the interrogation have a significant effect on the subsequent rate of confabulation (Tata & Gudjonsson, 1990). Normal subjects, who have not been subjected to negative feedback, typically have one or two confabulations after one week. The rate doubles when subjects have previously been given negative feedback during the interrogative part of the GSS 1. The type of negative feedback given in the Tata–Gudjonsson study was more severe than that given as part of the standard GSS 1 procedure. Even when no negative feedback is given, as in the Register–Kihlstrom (1988) study, repeated questioning and misleading interrogative questions significantly increase subsequent confabulations during free recall. No distinction was made in these studies between distortions and fabrications.

Depressed patients confabulate less than normal controls on the GSS 1 and once their depression is treated the level of confabulation resembles that of healthy people (Sigurdsson et al., 1994). The difference remained after immediate and delayed memory was controlled for by analysis of covariance. The interpretation put forward by the authors was that when people are depressed, they are less imaginative and creative, which impairs their normal tendency to confabulate.

SUGGESTIBILITY AND HYPNOTIC SUSCEPTIBILITY

I argued in Chapter 13 that the susceptibility to hypnosis is related to *primary* suggestibility, using Eysenck's conventional classification, whereas interrogative suggestibility is a special type of suggestibility that is unrelated to suggestibility of the primary type and only relates to the more elusive category of secondary suggestibility.

Evidence that interrogative suggestibility differs from susceptibility to hypnosis comes from six empirical studies. In the first study, Hardarson (1985) found no significant correlation ($r = 0.15$) between scores on the Harvard Group Scale of Hypnotic Susceptibility and interrogative suggestibility, as measured by the GSS 1, among 40 Icelandic University students.

In two different experiments, one comprising university students and one psychiatric patients, Young, Bentall, Slade and Dewey (1987) correlated the GSS 1 Total Suggestibility score with the Barber Suggestibility Scale (Barber & Calverley, 1964). The Barber Suggestibility Scale consists of eight test suggestions that are theoretically related to primary suggestibility. None of the three scores on the Barber Suggestibility Scale, which comprised the subjects' responses to suggestions, their rated subjective involvement in the tasks, and their verbalized resistance to the suggestions, correlated with interrogative suggestibility.

Register and Kihlstrom (1988) used a variant of the GSS 1 during an experiment into hypnosis. The subjects were 40 college students, who had all completed the Harvard Group Scale of Hypnotic Susceptibility and were interrogated after hypnotic induction. Negative feedback was not administered; instead the interrogation questions were repeated without any explicit negative feedback. No significant difference in interrogative suggestibility was found between hypnotizable and non-hypnotizable subjects. The authors concluded that the results

> ...support Gudjonsson's (1987) hypothesis that interrogative suggestibility is independent of suggestibility as measured in a hypnotic context (p. 556).

Gwynn and Spanos (1996) cite two studies where interrogative suggestibility, as measured by the GSS, was not found to be correlated with hypnotizability. In both studies hypnotizability was measured by the Carleton University Responsiveness to Suggestion Scale (CURSS). In the first study (Gwynn, Spanos, Nancoo & Chow, 1995, unpublished manuscript), 120 subjects who had previously completed the CURSS were administered the GSS. The CURSS score did not correlate significantly with Yield, Shift or Total Suggestibility. The second study (Gordon, Gwynn & Spanos, 1993) also involved 120 subjects, who had previously completed the CURSS. One half of the subjects were later tested on the GSS. No significant correlation was found between the hypnotizability score and the GSS scores.

The six studies quoted above all indicate that there is no correlation between interrogative suggestibility and hypnotic suggestibility.

However, Linton and Sheehan (1994) have replicated the Register–Kihlstrom (1988) study using a larger sample and improving the methodology. The Harvard Group Scale of Hypnotic Susceptibility (HGSHS:A) was administered to 920 psychology students. The 537 subjects who scored either low (0–4) or high (8–12) on Hypnotic Susceptibility were contacted. Of those contacted, 117 participated in an experiment where they were randomly assigned to conditions within a 2 (susceptibility: high versus low) × 2 (state: hypnosis versus waking) × 2 (feedback: neutral versus negative) design. All subjects were administered the GSS 1 with minor modifications to adapt the test to the Australian context. The standard negative feedback was given to about half the subjects, whereas the remaining subjects in the 'neutral condition' were told:

Let's just go through the questions once more (p. 58).

Analysis of variance tests revealed the following significant main effects.

- Hypnotic susceptibility was associated with elevated Yield 1, Yield 2 and Total Suggestibility scores. There was no affect on Shift.
- Negative feedback was more associated with elevated Yield 2, Shift and Total Suggestibility scores during the second trial of the interrogative questions (Yield 2) than neutral feedback.
- Hypnotic state did not influence any of the suggestibility scores.

The main implication of the findings is that subjects who are highly responsive to hypnosis are more likely than those who are very low to yield to leading questions. This finding contradicts those of the six previous studies cited above and suggests that there may, after all, be a significant relationship between susceptibility to hypnosis and yield type of interrogative suggestibility, although a formal hypnotic induction does not have any effect on interrogative suggestibility. Therefore, the fact that subjects are in a hypnotic state does not appear to influence their susceptibility to interrogative suggestibility. This conclusion is also supported by the findings of Register and Kihlstrom (1988) and Sheehan, Garnett and Robertson (1993).

What can explain the difference found between the studies with regard to hypnotizability? In the Linton–Sheehan (1994) study selected subjects were identified in a very large subject pool of psychology students, on the basis of extreme scores on hypnotizability rather than correlating the HGSHS and GSS 1 scores among an entire sample. This methodology will maximize any differences in interrogative suggestibility between the two groups. Using a similar methodology in a previous study, Sheehan, Garnett and Robertson (1993) also found that hypnotic susceptibility was significantly related to elevated Yield 1 and Total Suggestibility on the GSS 1, but not to Shift. These findings have potentially important theoretical implications about the nature of suggestibility. However, the problem with the findings is that the significant relationship between the Yield and the HGSHS scores may have to do with the nature of the hypnotic susceptibility scale and the personality of the individual, rather than the effects of a hypnotic induction or state on interrogative suggestibility. Without a clear relationship being found between interrogative suggestibility and a formal hypnotic induction the findings of a relationship between the two scales is of no forensic importance.

COMPLIANCE

In Chapter 13 I offered a theoretical distinction between suggestibility and compliance. The main difference, it was argued, was that suggestibility, unlike compliance, implies personal acceptance of the information provided or request made. In this chapter the concept of compliance, as it is relevant to interrogation, is explored in greater detail, particularly in relation to testing and empirical findings.

In its broadest sense, compliance refers to the tendency of the individual to go along with propositions, requests or instructions, for some immediate instrumental gain. The person concerned is fully aware that his or her responses are being influenced and an affirmative or a compliant response does not require personal acceptance of the proposition. In other words, people may disagree with the proposition or request made, but they nevertheless react in a compliant way. This is different to suggestibility, where there is personal acceptance of the proposition offered by the interrogator. This kind of distinction between suggestibility and compliance is also evident in the literature on suggestibility in relation to hypnosis (Wagstaff, 1981).

I have argued elsewhere (Gudjonsson, 1989c, 1997a) that compliance has two major components to it. First, there is an eagerness to please and the need of the person to protect his or her self-esteem when in the company of others. Second, there is avoidance of conflict and confrontation with people, and particularly those perceived as being in a position of some authority. These two components of compliant behaviour overlap extensively with Milgram's (1974) construct of 'obedience to authority'. Indeed, my compliance scale (GCS; Gudjonsson, 1989c, 1997a) is more closely associated with Milgram's work than that of Asch (1951, 1952), and it was Milgram's work that provided the conceptual basis for it. Milgram (1974) defined obedience as the action of a person 'who complies with authority' (p. 113). Within this framework highly compliant people appear fully aware of their difficulties in coping with pressure when in the company of people in authority, unlike the participants in Asch's experiments. As was mentioned in Chapter 13, the subjects in Asch's experiments were not aware that they were being influenced by the subtle suggestions introduced, and it therefore is more similar to the concept of suggestibility.

Compliance can be conceptualized in two different ways. It can be viewed either as a personality trait or as a behavioural response to a given situation (Gudjonsson, Sigurdsson, Brynjolfsdottir & Hreinsdottir, 2002). Irrespective of which conceptualization is preferred, there are two main ways of measuring compliance, which are based on behavioural observation and self-report procedures respectively.

Milgram's (1974) obedience experiments and the work of Asch (1952) into conformity were based on behavioural observation. Here experiments are conducted and the participant either agrees or disagrees with the source of influence (i.e. a request or a command by the experimenter, a peer group pressure). Conformity studies typically use count data such as the number of people who conform in a given condition or to a given suggestion. Other studies have used continuous measures such as a Likert scale, to assess the degree of conformity or changes in conformity (Beins & Porter, 1989). Unlike the measurement of suggestibility, compliance is difficult to measure psychometrically by the use of a behavioural observation for the purposes of research or a forensic evaluation. In addition, ethical issues arise regarding the extent to which people should be pressured to engage in activities they would rather not do. It is doubtful that ethical approval would be granted nowadays for research employing the famous Milgram obedience paradigm.

The second method for studying compliance is by way of a self-report inventory. I have constructed a 20 item compliance scale, which is relevant to police interrogation (GCS; Gudjonsson, 1989c, 1997a). The scale was intended to complement my work into interrogative suggestibility. It focuses on two different types of behaviour. First, when interviewed by the police, some individuals are prone to comply with requests and obey instructions that they would rather not do, for instrumental gain, such as termination of a police interview, release from custody, escaping from a conflict and confrontation or eagerness to please another person. Secondly, some individuals are susceptible to pressure from others to commit offences (i.e. they can be coerced into committing a crime).

The GCS is a paper and pencil test. It consists of 20 statements, which are answered as either 'true' or 'false'. Factor analysis of the scale revealed two main factors making up the scale. Statements loading significantly on the first factor indicated uneasiness or fear of people in authority and avoidance of conflict and confrontation (e.g. 'I tend to become easily alarmed and frightened when I am in the company of people in authority', 'I tend to give in to people who insist that they are right', 'I give in easily to people when I am pressured'). Statements loading on the second factor indicated an eagerness to please ('I try hard to do what is expected of me', 'I try to please others', 'I generally believe in doing as I am told').

The GCS requires people to rate their behaviour in terms of how they generally react to interpersonal pressure and demands from others. This overcomes difficulties with the measurement of compliance being potentially situation bound. Compliance, as measured by the GCS, is conceptualized as a personality trait.

In the manual (Gudjonsson, 1997a) I recommended that the GCS, unlike the GSS 1 and GSS 2, probably should not be used with young children and persons with IQ scores below 70, unless it is clear that they understand the content of the statements. Persons with learning disabilities do appear to have problems understanding some of the words and phrases (e.g. 'confrontation', 'obedient person'). If people are reasonably intellectually able, but have reading problems, then the items can be read out to them.

The GCS has satisfactory reliability (Gudjonsson, 1997a). The internal reliability of the scale, as measured by Cronbach's alpha coefficient, is 0.71, which is rather low. In two separate studies among Icelandic students (Gudjonsson & Sigurdsson, submitted; Gudjonsson et al., 2002b) and couples from the general population (Gudjonsson & Sigurdsson, in press) the Cronbach's alpha coefficient for the GCS ranged between 0.71 and 0.75. Test–retest reliability was measured by administering the scale twice, 1–3 months apart, to forensic patients. The test–retest reliability obtained was 0.88 (Gudjonsson, 1997a).

The GCS has been less extensively researched than the GSS 1 and the GSS 2, and, as emphasized by Cooke and Carlin (1998) in their review of the three scales, it is potentially a very important measure that requires more research. The research work that has been carried out so far gives support for the validity of the GCS. The construct validity of the GCS is supported by the fact that performance on the GCS has been found to correlate with other variables with which it should be theoretically related. The scale's validity has also been demonstrated in more naturalistic settings.

I found that compliance, as measured by the GCS (Gudjonsson, 1989c), correlated significantly ($r = 0.35$, df $= 123$, $p < 0.001$) with social desirability as measured by the Marlowe–Crowne Social Desirability Scale (Crowne & Marlowe, 1960). A low but significant correlation ($r = 0.27$, df $= 59$, $p < 0.05$) was found between compliance and Neuroticism as measured by the Eysenck Personality Questionnaire (EPQ; Eysenck & Eysenck, 1975). A moderately high correlation ($r = 0.54$, df $= 66$, $p < 0.001$) was found between compliance and the Social Conformity Scale of Pettigrew (1958).

Gudjonsson, Hannesdottir, Petursson and Bjornsson (2002) studied among university students four psychological factors, which are potentially related to compliance. These were self-esteem and anxiety (state and trait), on the one hand, and anger and paranoia on the other. Theoretically, low self-esteem and high anxiety should increase the tendency of the individual to exhibit compliant behaviour. Persons with poor self-esteem would be particularly likely to avoid conflict and confrontation with others, and would want to please them. High anxiety is a drive state, which motivates the person to avoid conflict and confrontation with others (Gudjonsson, 1992a). In contrast, feelings of paranoia and anger, according to Gudjonsson et al. (2002a), are likely to inhibit compliant behaviour. Theilgaard (1996) argues that people with paranoid tendencies are often difficult to engage in assessment and therapeutic activities and are very suspicious of others. This reasoning is consistent with the theory of interrogative suggestibility proposed by Gudjonsson and Clark (1986). Here a suspicious cognitive set makes people resistant to suggestions from others, primarily because of lack of interpersonal trust. Interpersonal trust, according to Gudjonsson and Clark, is one of the most important components of suggestibility. Similarly, anger makes people less receptive to the influence of others (Gudjonsson, 1989a). The tests used in the study were the State–Trait Anxiety Inventory (Spielberger, 1983), the Rosenberg Self-Esteem Scale (Rosenberg, 1965), the Novaco Anger Scale (Novaco, 1994) and the GCS. Gudjonsson et al. (2002a) hypothesized that similar inhibiting factors are likely to operate in relation to compliance. The findings were not entirely as expected.

State anxiety ($r = 0.16$, $p < 0.05$), trait anxiety ($r = 0.28$, $p < 0.001$), and low self-esteem ($r = 0.26$, $p < 0.001$), correlated positively with compliance, as measured by the GCS. In contrast to that predicted, Paranoia, as measured by the Paranoia/Suspiciousness Questionnaire (PSQ) was positively correlated with the GCS score ($r = 0.30$, $p < 0.001$), with the Interpersonal Suspiciousness/Hostility subscale having the highest correlation with compliance ($r = 0.37$, $p < 0.001$). The significant correlation of compliance with the PSQ is of interest. Paranoid thinking, and particularly the interpersonal suspiciousness and hostility part of paranoia, may act as a vulnerability to compliant behaviour. The reason may be that such individuals wish to avoid conflict and confrontation with others as a way of relieving distress. Their paranoia may activate avoidance behaviour and makes them focus on the immediate consequences of their behaviour as a way of relieving anxiety (e.g. terminating a police interview, getting out of a police station, giving in to peer pressure). They may comply with what is requested of them if they perceive that there is an immediate instrumental gain for doing so. The implication is that paranoid thinking, through an anxiety relieving mechanism, increases the susceptibility of people to engage in behaviours that they would rather not do. Another possible mechanism relates to the cognitive biases that typically accompany clinical and sub-clinical paranoia (Combs, Penn & Mathews, in press). People with paranoia are prone to make reasoning decisions based on insufficient information (Garety, Hemsley & Wessely, 1991) and they may fail to weigh up all relevant evidence in a given situation before making decisions (Combs, Penn & Mathews, in press). This may make them prone to comply uncritically with other persons' requests and demands.

Anger is made up of different components, including cognitive preoccupation, arousal and behavioural reactions to perceived provocation. Persons who are in the habit of acting out behaviourally their anger and frustration are not likely to comply readily to the requests of others when they do not wish to do so. Gudjonsson *et al.* (2002a) found that verbal and physical reactions to provocation are negatively associated with compliance. The acting out of anger during interrogation is likely to lead to uncooperative behaviour, which would need to be resolved before any interview could proceed satisfactorily (Gudjonsson, 1992a).

In another study, involving couples from the general population in Iceland, Gudjonsson and Sigurdsson (in press) studied the relationship of compliance with self-esteem and the strategies people use to cope with stress. The Self-Esteem Scale of Rosenberg (1965), the COPE Scale (Carver, Scheier & Weintraub, 1989) and GCS were administered to 212 males and 212 females. Again low self-esteem correlated significantly with compliance ($r = 0.41$, $p < 0.001$) and several of the COPE subscales correlated with compliance, with the highest correlations being with Denial Coping ($r = 0.39$, $p < 0.001$) and Behavioural Disengagement ($r = 0.30$, $p < 0.001$).

Therefore, high compliance is associated with an attempt by the individual to reject the reality of the stressful event and withdraw efforts from challenging the stressor and achieving their own goal. This suggests that compliant individuals avoid a proper appraisal of the stressful event, pretend that everything is fine, and withdraw effort from achieving their own goals or doing what they really want.

A multiple regression analysis showed that the two best predictors of compliance were low self-esteem and Denial Coping. Both added similarly to the variance in compliance and when combined accounted for 25% of the variance. This means that Denial Coping is related to compliance independently of self-esteem. This is important, because low self-esteem is significantly correlated with both compliance and dysfunctional coping.

Smith and Gudjonsson (1995a) failed to find a significant correlation between the GCS and the Rosenberg Self-Esteem Scale. The authors, in view of some of the reservations about the Rosenberg Scale raised by Wylie (1989), questioned the validity of the Self-Esteem Scale with a forensic inpatient population, where the patients' responses may have represented their ideal rather than actual self-esteem.

In a more naturalistic setting, the GCS has been shown to discriminate significantly between 'false confessors' and those suspects who are able to resist police pressure to confess (Gudjonsson, 1984b, 1991b; Sigurdsson & Gudjonsson, 1996). I looked at the normative GCS scores of different groups of subjects and hypothesized that alleged false confessors should score higher than, for example, those criminal suspects or defendants who had been able to resist confessing whilst being interrogated by the police. The results from the study clearly indicated that this was the case. This type of validation will be mentioned later in this chapter in relation to more recent studies of the GCS.

Birgisson (1996) used this classification when he studied the differences in the personality of convicted American sex offenders who admitted their offence and those who had denied it. The 70 'admitters' and 30 'deniers' completed the GCS and the Eysenck Personality Questionnaire (EPQ; Eysenck & Eysenck, 1975). The mean GCS scores were 10.0 and 7.9 for the admitters and deniers, respectively. This difference was highly significant ($p < 0.01$, one-tailed test). The admitters also had significantly higher Neuroticism score on the EPQ than the deniers ($p < 0.05$, one-tailed test) and a lower Lie score ($p < 0.05$, one-tailed test). The GCS score among the admitters correlated significantly with EPQ Psychoticism ($r = 30, p < 0.01$, one-tailed test) and Neuroticism ($r = 42$, $p < 0.001$, one-tailed test). None of the correlations were significant among the deniers. One possible reason for this is the high Lie, or social desirability score, among the deniers, which may have artificially lowered the Psychoticism and Neuroticism scores. Birgisson argues that the difference between the groups in the Lie score may reflect the greater defensiveness among the deniers. This is perhaps not surprising when considering the fact that the participants were all attending an outpatient clinic for court-ordered psychotherapy where denial concerning their offences would inevitably be challenged during therapy. Therefore, the defensiveness among the deniers may reflect the context in which they were tested. However, sex offenders, as a group, tend to have higher social desirability scores than violent offenders, which may reflect their level of defensiveness during psychological testing (Gudjonsson & Sigurdsson, 2000).

As discussed earlier in this chapter, one of the reasons for developing the GCS was to identify individuals who are susceptible to pressure from others to commit offences (i.e. they can be coerced into committing a crime). Gudjonsson and Sigurdsson (submitted) investigated this aspect of compliance among 305 university students and 320 secondary school students with regard to self-report offending. A 22-item Motivation Scale for offending was developed and the most serious offence reported was rated on the scale. Factor analysis of the Motivation Scale revealed five factors. The largest factor, comprised of seven items and accounting for 16.4% of the total variance, was labelled 'compliance'. The items with salient loadings on this factor were the following.

- To please my friend(s) (0.85).
- Giving in to pressure from peer(s) (0.85).
- Wanted to 'show off' to friend (s) (0.66).
- Asked by somebody to commit the offence (0.65).
- Was tricked into committing the crime (0.62).
- To show how brave and daring I was (0.61).
- Committed offence because my friends were doing it (0.59).

The GCS score correlated significantly with the compliance offence factor score among the secondary school ($r = 0.25, p < 0.001$) and university students ($r = 0.19, p < 0.05$), and hardly at all with any of the remaining four factors. Although the correlations are small, the findings support the view that compliance, as measured by the GCS, is significantly correlated with the reasons people give for having committed an offence. Compliance, as a personality trait, appears relevant in explaining why some people commit offences.

Situational Determinants of Compliance

The GCS, to a certain extent, overcomes problems with compliance being potentially situation bound, because the subject is rating how he or she generally reacts to interpersonal pressure rather than referring to any one particular situation. This does not, however, exclude the possibility that subjects may fill in the GCS differently according to their situational circumstances. For example, since many of the GCS items give a fair indication of what the scale is measuring, some criminal suspects, when this seems favourable to their case, may endorse items in such a way as to exaggerate their compliance scores. Similarly, it is possible that suspects who previously gave in to police pressure and confessed, when they did not really want to, have biased perceptions of their own compliance, which becomes reflected in their self-report scores. In other words, because the suspect gave in to the police pressure he thinks he must be compliant and fills in the scale accordingly.

A number of situational factors have been shown to influence compliance in a particular experimental setting. The types of factor that can increase compliance are happy mood state (Milberg & Clark, 1988), touch and gaze (Hornik, 1988; Kleinke, 1977, 1980), demand for eye contact (Hamlet, Axelrod & Kuerschner, 1984), the prestige of the communicator (Kelman & Holland, 1953), the perceived power of the experimenter (Bandura, Ross & Ross 1963), agreement with a smaller request previously (Freedman & Fraser, 1966), the gender of the experimenter (Heslin, Nguyen & Nguyen, 1983, Stier & Hall, 1984), the manipulation of self-esteem (Graf, 1971) and feelings of guilt (Carlsmith & Gross, 1969; Freedman, Wallington & Bless, 1967; Konoske, Staple & Graf, 1979).

The feeling of guilt is undoubtedly one of the most important factors that increase the individual's likelihood of complying with a request. Freedman, Wallington and Bless (1967) manipulated guilt feelings in two different ways in three studies. In all studies there was a marked increase in subsequent compliance. The authors put forward two possible mechanisms for this. Firstly, complying with a request after experimental guilt manipulation helps the individual expiate the guilt by doing something 'good' to compensate for what he or she had done 'wrong' previously. Konoske, Staple and Graf (1979) construe this as subjects' attempt to restore their lowered self-esteem. Secondly, compliance may be a way of punishing oneself for the action that caused the guilt feeling in the first place.

Another important finding in the Freedman–Wallington–Bless study is that guilt may strongly motivate people to avoid being confronted with the person they have allegedly harmed. Therefore, there appear to be two conflicting motivations as a result of guilt: people are motivated to engage in altruistic behaviour as a way of alleviating guilt feelings and restoring self-esteem, but there is a strong tendency towards avoidance behaviour when this means actually meeting the person allegedly harmed. The implication is that guilt feeling manipulation is most effective in increasing compliant behaviour when the subject does not subsequently have to be confronted with the victim. This is, however, unlikely to be a problem when the subject is already interacting with the victim. The most likely explanation is that subjects are too embarrassed to 'face' the victim. This highlights the importance of feelings of shame, as well as feelings of guilt, in influencing avoidance behaviour when being confronted with wrongdoings.

One of the most important findings with regard to guilt manipulation research, is that once guilt is induced in the subject, it can be directed into greater compliance with requests that are completely unrelated to the original source of guilt. This has important implications for police interrogation, because guilt induction is recommended in manuals on police interrogation.

Few studies have looked at the types of situational factor that reduce compliance. The most important one appears to be anger (Milberg & Clark, 1988), which will be discussed in detail later in this chapter.

The role of cultural factors has not been specifically studied in relation to suggestibility and compliance, but it has been shown to be relevant to conformity studies (Bond & Smith, 1996). In their meta-analysis study, Bond and Smith found that conformity was higher in collectivist than individualist cultures. In addition, differences in the degree of conformity may change over time within a culture, as demonstrated by the decline in conformity in the USA since Asch's conformity research began in the early 1950s (Bond & Smith, 1996).

ACQUIESCENCE

Acquiescence refers to the tendency of an individual to answer questions in the affirmative irrespective of the content (Cronbach, 1946). It shares with suggestibility the fact that both concepts are concerned with information obtained in response to questions or statements and when in doubt subjects may give affirmative answers. The main difference between the two concepts is that with regard to acquiescence the questions are not structured in such a way as to specifically suggest the wanted or expected answer, which is the case with suggestibility.

It is conceptually possible to break an acquiescent response into three stages (Gudjonsson, 1990b). First, the person has to read or listen to the question or statement. This links acquiescence with such factors as attention, interest, reading ease and powers of observation. Second, the person has to understand the words, concepts and meaning of the question. Here conceptual judgements, comprehension, general knowledge, vocabulary and concept formation are likely to play an important part. If the question asked is too difficult for the person to read or to understand then uncertainty or doubt is created, which is a prerequisite for an acquiescence response to occur (Gudjonsson, 1986). Third, when subjects are uncertain about how to answer the question they have three choices of action:

1. they can refuse to give simple yes–no or true–false answers;
2. they can give the answers they consider most plausible;
3. they can guess and give answers at random.

Out of the three available options, option two is most closely associated with an acquiescent response.

The above conceptual framework views acquiescence as resulting primarily from cognitive and motivational factors. Finlay and Lyons (in press) have argued that two additional factors should be added to this framework. First, uncertainty can arise when the person understands the question or statement but is uncertain about how to answer it. Second, interviewees may misperceive the question and respond in the way they perceive it, rather than feeling uncertain about the question.

Acquiescence can also be construed as a personality trait related to submissiveness and eagerness to please (Finlay & Lyons, 2001).

How can acquiescence be measured? Finlay and Lyons (2001) describe four different ways in which acquiescence can be measured: asking nonsense or absurd questions where the correct answer should be 'no', asking pairs of questions with opposite meaning (item-reversal techniques), using pairs of questions which ask the same questions in different formats, and comparing self-reports with those of informants. The best, and most common, way of measuring acquiescence is by way of an item-reversal technique (Sigelman *et al.*, 1981; Winkler, Kanouse & Ware, 1982). This consists of employing matched pairs of logically opposite items or statements. The degree of acquiescence is then measured by the number of items or statements where the person agrees affirmatively with both. For example, the statement 'I am happy most of the time' is logically opposite to the statement 'I am sad most of the time'. If the person answers both statements affirmatively then his response is acquiescent. If he answers both statements negatively then he is being *inconsistent* but not acquiescent.

CORRELATIONS BETWEEN SUGGESTIBILITY, COMPLIANCE AND ACQUIESCENCE

Do suggestibility, compliance and acquiescence scores correlate with one another? The evidence indicates that suggestibility and compliance are poorly correlated and that there is a weak, but significant, relationship between suggestibility and acquiescence. There is no significant relationship between acquiescence and compliance.

Three studies have investigated the relationship between GSS suggestibility and acquiescence. Two studies correlated GSS 1 scores with the acquiescence scale of Winkler, Kanouse and Ware (1982) and the third used the GSS 2. The first study (Gudjonsson, 1986) comprised a group of 30 male volunteers. A low but a significant correlation ($r = 0.33$, $p < 0.05$) was found between Total Suggestibility and acquiescence. The correlations with Yield 1 and Yield 2 were 0.32 and 0.42 ($p < 0.05$), respectively. No significant correlation was found with Shift. I suggested that a state of uncertainty and low self-esteem, which arises when subjects are in doubt about how to answer a question, produces an unpleasant feeling. This negative state motivates subjects to reduce uncertainty and to restore their self-esteem. Affirmative answers function to facilitate this process because they are seen as being more acceptable to the interviewer.

I subsequently failed to find a significant relationship ($r = 0.13$) between Total Suggestibility and acquiescence in a study comprising 60 forensic patients (Gudjonsson, 1990b). It seems that suggestibility does have some relationship with acquiescence but the relationship is very weak and may not be found in all studies. In the same study, acquiescence was not found to correlate significantly ($r = 0.11$) with compliance, as measured by the GCS.

In the third study, involving 145 participants of a wide range of abilities, Gudjonsson and Clare (1995) investigated the relationship of acquiescence with intellectual ability, verbal memory, confabulation and suggestibility. Acquiescence correlated negatively with IQ ($r = -0.52, p < 0.001$), GSS 2 Immediate and Delayed Recall ($r = -0.37$ and -0.40, $p < 0.001$, respectively), and with Yield 1 and Yield 2 ($r = 0.27$ and 0.21, $p < 0.01$, respectively). No significant correlation was found with Shift or confabulation.

There appears to be a certain overlap between the constructs of suggestibility and compliance. In fact, suggestibility and compliance may be mediated by similar factors, such as avoidance coping, eagerness to please and certain anxiety processes associated with how the individual copes with pressure. In one study (Gudjonsson, 1990b), I correlated the GSS 1 scores with the GCS score among 119 subjects. Yield 1, Shift and Total Suggestibility correlated significantly with compliance; the correlations were 0.40, 0.53 and 0.54 for the three suggestibility scores respectively ($p < 0.001$). The correlation between compliance and acquiescence among a subgroup of 57 subjects was 0.28 ($p < 0.05$).

On theoretical grounds compliance should be less correlated with intelligence than acquiescence and suggestibility (Gudjonsson, 1990b).

Studies have also found a significant correlation between acquiescence and acceptance of misleading information (similar to GSS Yield 1), using different instruments (Eisen, Morgan & Mickes, 2002).

Acquiescence is probably best construed as predominantly comprising intellectual and educational components rather than temperament or personality variables. This interpretation is consistent with the finding that highly acquiescent individuals tend to come from poorer educational backgrounds (Ware, 1978) and often have a history of learning disability (Sigelman et al., 1981). There is also evidence that acquiescence is related to a cognitive style rather than being a feature of personality (Knowles & Nathan, 1997).

Compliance, on the other hand, is best construed as a personality measure. Suggestibility probably falls in between the other two measures, but it is clearly more akin to compliance than acquiescence.

In one study (Gudjonsson, 1990b), comprising 55 subjects who had completed the GCS and the Wechsler Adult Intelligence Scale (WAIS-R), there was a small but significant negative correlation between compliance and Full Scale IQ ($r = -0.29$, $p < 0.05$). In contrast, both acquiescence and suggestibility have been found to have modest negative correlations with intelligence (the correlations with Full Scale IQ were -0.53 and -0.44, $p < 0.001$, respectively). Factor analysis (Varimax rotation) of the WAIS-R subtests, the GSS 1 Total Suggestibility score, the GCS score and acquiescence revealed three main factors. These factors are best construed as verbal intelligence, non-verbal intelligence and compliance. Acquiescence had clear loading on the first two factors, whereas suggestibility and compliance loaded highly on the third factor (-0.67 and -0.81 respectively). Compliance had particularly low loadings on the two intelligence factors.

SUGGESTIBILITY AND GENDER

With regard to the GSS 1, there seems to be some general tendency for females to score slightly higher on suggestibility than males, but the difference, which is about one point for Total Suggestibility, has not been found to be significant (Gudjonsson, 1984a; Gudjonsson & Lister, 1984). In one study employing the GSS 2 (Danielsdottir, Sigurgeirsdottir, Einarsdottir & Haraldsson, 1993), eight-year-old boys obtained significantly higher Shift scores than girls, but no significant difference was found for three other age groups (6, 10 and 12).

In an American doctorate dissertation, Redlich (1999) found that among young persons (12 to 26-year-olds), males were significantly more suggestible than females with regard to GSS Yield 1, Yield 2 and Total Suggestibility. Some of this gender difference may have been due to the significantly higher immediate recall scores of the female participants.

Powers, Andriks and Loftus (1979) found that female subjects were significantly more suggestible than male subjects. An interesting finding was that sex differences in accuracy were related to the type of information a question was aimed at. Women were significantly more accurate than men on questions dealing with female-oriented details (e.g. women's clothing and actions), whereas men were more accurate with regard to male-oriented details (e.g. the thief's appearance and offence's surroundings).

The authors conclude that males and females tend to be accurate on different items, which suggests that each sex pays more attention to those items which are of interest to them and most relevant to their own sex. One consequence of this is that there is a difference in the ease with which misleading information can be made to influence the subjects' memory and answers about specific items. The authors of the above study quote the work of Eagly (1978) in support of their conclusions. Eagly's study indicates that people's attitudes can be more readily influenced when they have little information about the subject area or regard it as trivial and unimportant.

SUGGESTIBILITY AND ETHNIC BACKGROUND

Only one study has investigated differences in suggestibility among people from different ethnic backgrounds. The study is discussed in detail in Chapter 3 and the findings have also been published elsewhere (Gudjonsson *et al.*, 1993; Gudjonsson, Rutter & Clare, 1995). The findings showed that Afro-Caribbean police detainees scored significantly higher than their Caucasian counterparts on all the GSS 2 suggestibility measures, after controlling for differences in verbal recall (there was no difference in IQ scores between the two groups).

SUGGESTIBILITY AND AGE

It seems that children of 12 years or older are able to provide as much free recall information as adults and they are no more likely to give in to leading questions than adults (Loftus, Greene & Doyle, 1990). For the purposes of this book I shall briefly mention the data available on the relationship between age and GSS and GCS scores.

No significant relationship has been found between GSS 1 and age for different groups of adult subjects (Gudjonsson, 1984a; Gudjonsson & Lister, 1984). Similarly, no significant correlation was found between age and compliance, as measured by the GCS, among 369 adult subjects (Gudjonsson, 1989d).

A number of studies have looked at GSS scores among normal children. In the first study, Warren, Hulse-Trotter and Tubbs (1991) administered a modified version of the GSS 1 to 30 7-year-olds, 30 12-year-olds and 39 adults. Each group was divided into 'experimental' and 'control' groups, where the former were warned that the questions were going to be 'tricky' and they should therefore only answer questions regarding what they 'really remembered'. The younger children yielded more to leading questions and shifted their answers more after negative feedback than the older children and adults. However, both groups of children shifted their answers significantly more after negative feedback than did adults. The warning that the questions were 'tricky' was successful among all three groups in reducing the Yield 1 score, but it had no effect on Shift.

Danielsdottir *et al.* (1993) administered the GSS 2 to 160 children, 6-, 8- and 12-year-olds with 20 boys and 20 girls in each group. Analysis of variance showed a significant effect of age on immediate recall, Yield 1 and Total Suggestibility for both boys and girls, but not for Shift. Multiple regression analyses showed that immediate recall on the GSS 2 explained most of the difference in the suggestibility scores. However, for the six-year-olds recall did not correlate with the suggestibility scores as it did for the other age groups. The authors concluded that for the youngest age group the children may have had problems in processing the story or providing free recall, or that suggestibility in that age group is not mediated by memory. Interestingly, overall the Shift suggestibility scores were higher among boys than girls; this difference was most marked among the eight-year-olds.

Three British studies have investigated the suggestibility scores of juvenile boys (between the ages of 11 and 16 in two of the studies and 10 to 17 in the third study). The results from all three studies indicate that youths are no more suggestible than adults, unless their answers are subjected to negative feedback (i.e. interrogative pressure). Then they become markedly more suggestible than adults. In the first study (Gudjonsson & Singh, 1984a) we compared the GSS 1 scores of 31 delinquent boys with those of 20 normal males (aged 16–29 years) who had similar memory scores on the GSS 1. No difference emerged between the two groups with regard to Yield 1, whereas the Shift scores were significantly higher among the youths. An identical pattern of GSS 1 scores has been found among 40 normal youths (Singh & Gudjonsson, 1992b) and 65 juvenile offenders who were in residential care (Richardson, Gudjonsson & Kelly, 1995).

Redlich (1999) found no significant differences in suggestibility among three groups of young persons, 12–13-year-olds, 15–16-year-olds and 18–26-year-olds. Interestingly, all the suggestibility scores were moderately elevated among all three groups.

In summary, the results of the above studies show that younger children are more suggestible than older children, in terms of giving in to both leading questions (Yield 1) and interrogative pressure (Shift). However, children who are 12 years of age or older perform similarly to adults with regard to memory and Yield 1. Nevertheless, adolescents are clearly more responsive to negative feedback than adults. This suggests that they do not cope as well with interrogative pressure as adults and it links this type of suggestibility with a social rather than an intellectual and memory process. This finding has an important implication for the police interviewing of children and juveniles. The research of Ceci and Bruck (1993, 1995) has demonstrated how children are often subjected to multiple interviews, during which questions are often repeated and this may function like implicit negative feedback.

SUGGESTIBILITY AND INTELLIGENCE

Gudjonsson and Clark (1986) suggested two reasons why there should be a negative relationship between intelligence and suggestibility. First, it is argued, suggestibility is related to uncertainty, which itself depends to a certain extent on the memory capacity of the individual. Memory in turn is to a significant extent correlated with intelligence. Second, suggestibility is considered to be influenced by the person's ability to cope with the uncertainty, expectations and pressure associated with interrogation. Persons of low intelligence would have more limited intellectual resources to assist them to cope with an unfamiliar task, such as interrogation.

There appears to be a significantly negative relationship between interrogative suggestibility and intellectual functioning, which has been demonstrated in a number of studies with different groups of subjects. However, there is strong evidence that the relationship between suggestibility and intelligence is significantly affected by range effects. That is, it is only studies utilizing subjects of average intelligence or below, or where a large range of IQ scores are used, that significant results emerge. An IQ range of average or above appears to have no significant correlation with suggestibility. That is, subjects with IQs above average are no less susceptible to suggestive influences than subjects of average IQ, but subjects with IQs well below average, such as those who are borderline or mentally handicapped, tend to be markedly more suggestible.

Two early studies suggested that there was a relationship between intelligence and the ability to give accurate recall. Howells (1938) found a small, but a positive correlation ($r = 0.27$) between accuracy during an eyewitness experiment and intelligence. In other words, there was a slight tendency for the more intelligent subjects to give more accurate accounts of events.

The second study is that by Burtt (1948). He found a correlation of -0.55 between intelligence and suggestibility, which indicated that subjects of lower intelligence tended to be more suggestible than those of higher intelligence.

In the first ever study on the GSS 1, I found that IQ, measured by the WAIS, correlated negatively with both Yield 1 and Shift (Gudjonsson, 1983). The correlation with Full Scale IQ was -0.55. Similar correlations were found for Verbal ($r = -0.47$) and Performance ($r = -0.50$) IQs.

Tully and Cahill (1984) found a correlation of -0.69 between intelligence, measured by Raven's Coloured Matrices and the Crighton Vocabulary Test, and suggestibility, which was measured by the GSS 1. The correlation is exceptionally high because the authors, unwisely in my view, pooled together for their analysis the scores of 15 normal control subjects and 30 learning disabled subjects. Some of the subjects in the learning disabled group had IQs of 50 or below, which is likely to have seriously skewed the distribution of IQ scores.

In one study I analysed the relationship between suggestibility and IQ among 60 normal subjects and 100 forensic patients (Gudjonsson, 1988b). The correlations with Full Scale IQ were -0.52 and -0.58 for the normal and forensic patients respectively. However, in spite of the highly significant negative correlations between IQ and suggestibility, the relationship between the two variables was dependant upon the range of IQ scores. That is, IQs above 100 in the two groups did not correlate significantly with suggestibility, whereas IQs below 100, as well as the entire IQ range, correlated significantly with suggestibility. These findings have important implications for studies that have relied on subjects whose IQs fall in the average range or above, such as college students.

In one study I looked at the types of intellectual skill that most highly correlated with suggestibility among 60 forensic referrals (Gudjonsson, 1990b). The subjects had all completed the WAIS-R (Wechsler, 1981). A negative correlation of -0.44 was found between Full Scale IQ and total suggestibility on the GSS 1. The subtests that had highest correlations with suggestibility were Picture Arrangement ($r = -0.48$), Similarities ($r = -0.43$) and Comprehension ($r = -0.40$). Lowest correlations were with Digit Span ($r = -0.24$) and Information ($r = -0.30$). Thus, I concluded that suggestibility is, as far as intelligence is concerned, most strongly associated with the capacity for logical reasoning, sequential thought, and social awareness and sophistication. In other words, people who can quickly size up a social situation are more able to critically evaluate the interrogative situation and adopt a facilitative problem-solving approach.

A number of other studies have also found a negative correlation between intellectual skills and suggestibility among children (Danielsdottir et al., 1993), adolescents (Singh & Gudjonsson, 1992a; Richardson & Kelly, 1995) and adults (Gudjonsson & Clare, 1995; Gudjonsson, Clare & Rutter, 1994; Sharrock & Gudjonsson, 1993). The trend among these studies is to find that intellectual skills correlate more strongly, in the negative direction, with Yield 1 than with Shift.

Sharrock and Gudjonsson (1993) argue that the relationship between intelligence and suggestibility among criminal suspects may be affected by their previous convictions. They suggest that previous convictions may act as a 'suppressor variable' in that they tend to reduce the correlation between intelligence and suggestibility. Therefore, certain types of experience may reduce the relationship between suggestibility and intellectual skills, which suggests that suggestibility is more than a simple cognitive variable.

Tata (1983) found no significant correlation between IQ, which was estimated from the National Adult Reading Test (Nelson, 1982), and suggestibility scores on the GSS 1. The mean IQ for the subjects in the study was 117, with the range of scores falling between 106 and 125.

Powers, Andriks and Loftus (1979) conducted an eyewitness experiment on 25 undergraduate students at the University of Washington. Suggestibility scores did not correlate significantly with nine intelligence-related subtests of the Washington Pre-College Test. The authors had expected a negative correlation between suggestibility and intelligence and explained the lack of a significant correlation on the basis of their subjects being of higher than average intelligence. They point to the possibility of range effects:

> It is entirely possible that an experiment conducted with subjects possessing a wider range of cognitive abilities would produce very different results (p. 344).

What are the main implications of the above findings concerning range effects? There are two broad implications. One implication relates to the nature of the subjects studied, and the other to the types of factor that facilitate a suggestible response.

Schooler and Loftus (1986) state in their review of the Gudjonsson–Clark (1986) model:

> It appears that individual differences in cognitive abilities may not always be as directly related to suggestibility as Gudjonsson and Clark would have us believe (p. 110).

The reason why Schooler and Loftus came to this conclusion is that American research has failed to find a significant relationship between suggestibility and cognitive variables associated with intelligence and memory. I have argued that the reason why American studies have failed to find the expected significant relationship is due to the homogeneous nature of their samples as far as cognitive abilities are concerned (Gudjonsson, 1987b).

The 'experimental approach' to suggestibility relies almost exclusively on college students as subjects, which seriously limits the type of inference that can be drawn about the cognitive variables that mediate suggestibility. The theory of 'discrepancy detection' was developed on the basis of studies utilizing American college students, where the range of intellectual functioning of the samples is typically very restricted. Therefore, generalizing the findings from such studies to some kind of general mechanism that is applicable to heterogeneous samples may not be warranted.

Intellectual functioning appears to affect the person's cognitive appraisal of the interrogative situation and the coping strategies that can be adopted. Adequate cognitive appraisal of the interrogative situation seems achievable by the majority of people at average level of intellectual functioning (Gudjonsson, 1988b). It is possible that with this minimum level of intellectual ability, other factors beside intelligence, such as anxiety, assertiveness and self-esteem, become more prominent. The advantage of this 'individual differences' approach is that it highlights the fact that suggestibility is undoubtedly mediated and affected by a range of factors, rather than one factor alone. Intellectual functioning is only one of several factors that are likely to mediate suggestibility and its overall influence may be comparatively modest.

SUGGESTIBILITY AND MEMORY

Suggestibility has been shown in a number of studies to correlate significantly with memory capacity. In other words, the poorer the subject's memory the more suggestible he or she is likely to be. Verbal recall on the GSS 1 and the GSS 2 has been found to correlate negatively with suggestibility as measured by these scales, but, as with IQ, the correlation is somewhat affected by range effects (Gudjonsson, 1988b). The size of the correlation between memory on the GSS and suggestibility is similar to that found for IQ (see Gudjonsson & Clare, 1995; Sharrock & Gudjonsson, 1993). Correlations of between -0.5 and -0.6 are typically found for normal subjects (Gudjonsson, 1983, 1988b). The correlations between memory and suggestibility are considerably lower among forensic patients than normal subjects (Gudjonsson, 1987b, 1988b).

Schooler and Loftus (1986) rightly point out that the significant correlation between memory and suggestibility on the GSS could be confounded by item similarities on the two within-scale measures. In other words, the significant relationship between the two variables could be an artefact due to the memory recall being based on the same items to which the misleading suggestions are later directed. This is an important point because one does not know whether it is memory capacity *per se* which makes subjects more susceptible to suggestions, or the fact that they have poor recall about the subject matter on which they are questioned.

I attempted to solve this issue by comparing the correlations between memory and suggestibility from independent tests as well as those from within a test (Gudjonsson, 1987b). I administered the GSS 1 and GSS 2 to three groups of subjects with the sequence of administration being counterbalanced. I then correlated memory and suggestibility both within and between tests. The correlations were very similar for the within and between measures, which indicates that the correlation between suggestibility and memory on the GSS is not markedly affected because of item similarities on the two measures. Furthermore, the findings indicate that suggestibility does correlate negatively with the memory capacity of the individual and with a similar magnitude as found between memory and IQ. These findings are consistent with those of Gudjonsson and Singh (1984a), who discovered that memory recall on the GSS 1 correlated negatively with observers' independent ratings of suggestibility.

Considering the moderate correlation between memory and intelligence, the question arises to what extent the two cognitive measures overlap in their relationship with suggestibility. The available evidence suggests that in spite of a considerable overlap in the variance explained, memory and intelligence also do contribute separately to the subject's susceptibility to suggestions. For example, I have found that both immediate and delayed recall on the GSS 1 add to the variance in suggestibility after IQ has been controlled for (Gudjonsson, 1983). Similarly, Sharrock and Gudjonsson (1993) found, by way of a 'path analysis', that both delayed memory and IQ contribute individually, as well as jointly, to the variance in suggestibility.

An interesting finding from the first study on the GSS 1 (Gudjonsson, 1983) is the importance of the rate at which memory deteriorates over time, as opposed to absolute memory levels. I found a highly significant negative correlation between suggestibility and the percentage of delayed versus immediate recall. In other words, the more rapidly memory deteriorated over a 40 or 50 minute period, the more suggestible normal subjects tended to be, irrespective of their absolute levels of memory. One possible explanation is that people whose memory deteriorates rapidly over time learn to distrust their own judgement and rely more on cues provided by others.

Sigurdsson *et al.* (1994) found that the memory scores on the GSS 1 and GSS 2 deteriorate significantly with age, particularly in old age, when the deterioration appears to be very marked. Therefore, when using elderly people as subjects in experiments, it is important that their memory scores are controlled for when studying the relationship between suggestibility and other variables.

SUGGESTIBILITY AND ANXIETY

Interrogative suggestibility appears to be significantly mediated by anxiety processes. Whether anxiety is generated through instructional manipulation or by other means may not be of critical importance. The general finding is that situational stress (i.e. 'state' anxiety) is more important than 'trait' anxiety, although one study, conducted among police detainees, found the reverse pattern (Gudjonsson, Rutter & Clare, 1995—this unexpected finding is discussed in detail in Chapter 3). Smith and Gudjonsson (1995a), studying forensic inpatients, found no significant relationship between any of the GSS 2 suggestibility scores and state anxiety at the time of the interrogation, but did so with regard to Yield 2, Shift and Total Suggestibility at one week follow-up. In the studies measuring 'state' and 'trait' anxiety the Spielberger State–Trait Anxiety Inventory (STAI, Spielberger, 1983) has been used.

The empirical evidence indicates that there is a poor relationship between suggestibility and trait anxiety as measured by self-report questionnaires. For example, Haraldsson (1985) found no significant correlation between GSS 1 suggestibility scores and neuroticism, which was measured by the Icelandic version of the Eysenck Personality Questionnaire (EPQ; Eysenck & Haraldsson, 1983). The sample consisted of 54 Icelandic University students.

In the first study on the GSS 1 (Gudjonsson, 1983), I found a low but significant correlation ($r = 0.28$, $p < 0.05$) between total suggestibility and Neuroticism as measured by the English version of the EPQ (Eysenck & Eysenck, 1975).

There is some evidence that suggestibility is more strongly associated with 'state' anxiety than 'trait' anxiety. The former is typically construed as a transitory emotional state that is characterized by subjective feelings of apprehension and heightened autonomic nervous system reactivity. Trait anxiety, on the other hand, refers to relatively stable individual differences in anxiety proneness.

In one study (Gudjonsson, 1988a), I set out to investigate the hypothesis that state anxiety is more strongly associated with suggestibility than is trait anxiety. I administered the Spielberger State Anxiety Inventory (STAI; Spielberger, 1983) twice to the subjects in the study. The subjects first completed the STAI prior to the GSS 1 interrogation and then after they had been interrogated and given the standard negative feedback. In contrast to studies utilizing trait anxiety, some highly significant correlations emerged. The correlations were consistently higher with the second administration of the STAI than the first. In addition, Shift and Yield 2 correlated significantly more highly with state anxiety, during both administrations of the STAI, than with Yield 1. The correlations with Shift were 0.42 and 0.69 for the two STAI tests respectively.

The findings from this study support the hypothesis that suggestibility is strongly associated with state anxiety. This indicates that it is how apprehensive subjects feel at the time of the interrogation that is more important than their more generalized anxiety proneness. In addition, state anxiety is clearly most strongly associated with how subjects react to interrogative pressure rather than to leading questions *per se*. This supports my theory (Gudjonsson, 1984a) that Yield 2 and Shift scores on the GSS are more linked to anxiety and coping processes than Yield 1. The findings complement those of Tata (1983), who found that negative feedback on the GSS 1 is accompanied by increased electrodermal reactivity as well as changes in mood as measured by the Multiple Affect Adjective Checklist (Zuckerman & Lubin, 1965).

In an early study (Gudjonsson & Singh, 1984a), we attempted to validate the GSS 1 by administering the scale to 31 delinquent and adolescent boys (ages 11–16 years) who had been independently rated by two teachers on measures of suggestibility and self-esteem. The teachers' behavioural ratings of suggestibility correlated highly significantly with the GSS 1 Shift score. Furthermore, one of the items from the Coopersmith Behaviour Rating Form (Coopersmith, 1967), which is a measure of self-esteem rated by independent informants, correlated highly significantly with the GSS 1 Shift score. The question asked was 'Does this child become alarmed and frightened easily?' (rated on a five-point Likert scale). This finding suggests that Shift is a measure of how readily the person becomes frightened when in the company of others.

Further evidence that Shift is related to how subjects cope with pressure emerges from a study (Gudjonsson, 1984c) where it was found that Shift correlated negatively ($r = -0.37$, df $= 48$, $p < 0.05$) with the Ego score as measured by the Arrow-Dot Test (Dombrose & Slobin, 1958). No significant correlation was found for Yield 1. The Arrow-Dot Test is a perceptual–motor task, which requires the solution of 23 simple graphic problems whilst subjects are placed under time pressure.

Studying anxiety from a different perspective, I investigated the relationship between suggestibility and social-evaluative anxiety (Gudjonsson, 1988a). The latter was measured by the Fear of Negative Evaluation (FNE) and Social Avoidance and Distress (SAD) scales of Watson and Friend (1969).

In view of the fact that people who score high on the FNE are prone to become apprehensive in evaluative situations and attempt to avoid social disapproval, it would be expected that they are more susceptible to suggestive influences than low FNE scorers. The theoretical reasoning for a relationship between the SAD and suggestibility is less clear, except that social distress may relate to how people respond to negative feedback.

It was found that the FNE scores correlated significantly with all the GSS 1 suggestibility scores, whereas no significant correlations were found for the SAD scale. The results support the view that interrogative suggestibility is more strongly associated with fear of negative evaluation than social distress.

Hansdottir, Thorsteinsson, Kristinsdottir and Ragnarsson (1990) attempted to study the effects of anxiety and instructional manipulation on suggestibility by a way of experimental manipulation. Forty subjects were divided into four experimental groups. At the beginning of the experiment half the subjects were instructed to imagine as vividly as they could a stress-provoking situation and immediately afterwards listened to Stravinsky's *Rite of Spring* to further their anxiety. The other half of the subjects listened to neutral music only. The 'anxious' and 'neutral' subjects were then divided into two further groups and given either a low or a high expectation about their performance on the GSS 1.

It was found that situational stress only had significant effect on suggestibility in the low expectation group. The authors point out that one explanation for this finding is that the high expectation instruction created performance anxiety in the subjects, which was similar to the anxiety generated by the anxiety manipulation. Administering the anxiety manipulation in addition to the high expectation instruction had no significant effect. Similarly, instructional manipulation did not significantly increase suggestibility among subjects who had been previously aroused by anxiety manipulation.

Wolfradt and Meyer (1998) used a German translation of the GSS 2 to test differences in suggestibility between 37 psychiatric patients suffering from anxiety disorders and 45 normal controls. Highly significant differences were found between the two groups on Yield 1, Shift and Total Suggestibility (no data were reported for Yield 2), with the patients being significantly more suggestible than the normal controls. The differences were more marked for Shift than Yield 1. These findings were in spite of there being no significant differences between the groups with regard to memory recall. The findings suggest that anxiety rather than memory process mediated the differences in suggestibility between the groups. Both groups had also completed the STAI and the patients were significantly more anxious than the normal controls. Interestingly, the state and trait anxiety scores did not correlate significantly with suggestibility for the two groups analysed separately, but did so when the two groups were combined. The authors confirmed the findings of Gudjonsson, Rutter and Clare (1995) that suggestibility cannot always be easily judged from self-reported anxiety scores such as those measured by the STAI.

The findings of Smith and Gudjonsson (1995a), using a forensic inpatient population, also highlight the potential problems with using the STAI reliably with certain populations. The authors found that state anxiety did not correlate with the suggestibility scores when administered immediately after GSS interrogative procedure, but it did correlate significantly with Yield 2, Shift and Total Suggestibility when the STAI was administered at one week follow-up.

One of the reasons for the apparent problems with using the STAI in the studies of Gudjonsson, Rutter and Clare (1995), Smith and Gudjonsson (1995a) and Wolfradt and Meyer (1998) could be that in all three studies the STAI was administered after immediate recall, but before the interrogation questions and negative feedback were administered. This may be significant in relation to state anxiety, because it is the anxiety that is generated by the interrogation that is of crucial importance. How anxious they felt prior to the interrogation may be less important. This is supported by the findings of Gudjonsson (1988a), where state anxiety was measured both before and after the interrogation. When state anxiety was rated in relation to how the subjects had felt during the interrogation, as opposed to how they had felt before, all the correlations become much more significant.

SUGGESTIBILITY AND IMPULSIVITY

One study has investigated the relationship between suggestibility and impulsivity. Gudjonsson (1984d) administered the GSS 1 and the Arrow-Dot Test (Dombrose & Slobin, 1958) to 50 normal subjects. None of the correlations were significant for Yield 1, but Shift correlated significantly with Id (impulsivity) and negatively with Ego strength. The correlations were 0.30 and −0.37 ($p < 0.05$), respectively. The findings suggest that impulsivity and poor ego control are associated with a tendency to give in to interrogative pressure.

SUGGESTIBILITY AND THE MMPI-2

Leavitt (1997) correlated the Total Suggestibility scores from the GSS 2 with the profile scores on the MMPI-2 (Hathaway & McKinley, 1991). There were two groups of psychiatric patients: those claiming recovered memories of childhood sexual abuse ($N = 44$) and a control group of other psychiatric patients ($N = 31$). One significant finding emerged for both groups. Total Suggestibility correlated negatively with the Psychopathic Deviate (Pd) Scale. The correlations were -0.42 ($p < 0.01$) and -0.55 ($p < 0.001$) for the recovered memories and control group, respectively. Leavitt contributed the lower suggestibility of the high Pd scorers to their general mistrust of people, which may act as a protection against suggestive influences.

SUGGESTIBILITY AND SLEEP DEPRIVATION

The effects of sleep deprivation on suggestibility have been studied extensively by Blagrove and his colleagues at the University of Swansea. Blagrove, Cole-Morgan and Lambe (1994) carried out two studies, employing 16 and 24 subjects, respectively. Half of the subjects in each group were deprived of sleep over one night and the other half were used as controls. All subjects were tested for baseline data using the GSS 1. They were tested again one day later using the GSS 2. By the time the sleep deprived subjects were re-tested with regard to suggestibility they had been deprived of sleep for 23–27 hours. In the first study only Yield 1 was measured, whereas in study 2 Yield 1 Yield 2, Shift and Total Suggestibility were measured. In both studies, sleep deprivation did not have significant effects on Yield 1. This was in spite of finding that sleep deprivation caused significant impairment in verbal recall on the GSS, increased score on a confusion scale and a poorer visual reaction time. In contrast, Study 2 showed significant effects on Shift, which suggests that the effect of sleep deprivation is to impair people's ability to cope with interrogative pressure.

In a further series of studies, Blagrove (1996) carried out studies on the effects of sleep deprivation on suggestibility. The first two studies involved one night (21 hours) of sleep loss and the third study two nights (43 hours) of sleep loss. In each of the three studies there was a control group. As before all groups of subjects completed the GSS 1 and GSS 2. The results showed that after loss of sleep all the suggestibility scores were adversely affected, the longer the sleep deprivation the greater the affects on suggestibility.

Blagrove and Akehurst (2000) studied, with sleep loss as a factor, the within- and between-subjects relationships between confidence ratings and susceptibility to leading questions both before (Yield 1) and after negative feedback (Yield 2) employing the GSS 1 and GSS 2. Sleep deprived subjects were divided into two groups according to length of sleep loss (29–35 and 47–50 hours, respectively). There were two control groups of subjects who had not been sleep deprived. All subjects were tested on day one in order to obtain baseline measures of their suggestibility, acquiescence, and cognitive functioning. The tests were repeated on day two (29–35 hour group) and day three (47–50 hour group). No significant differences in memory recall were found between conditions on either suggestibility scale. Nor did sleep loss significantly affect distortions and fabrications in relation to the verbal memory recall. As far as the suggestibility scores were concerned, Yield 1 was not affected by sleep loss, whereas Yield 2, Shift and Total Suggestibility all increased significantly with sleep loss. The effect sizes for Total Suggestibility were 0.49 and 0.75 for one and two nights of sleep deprivation, respectively.

The results of these studies show that sleep deprivation does increase suggestibility, particularly after negative feedback, and the longer the sleep deprivation the more suggestible people become. This has important implications for police interviewing.

SUGGESTIBILITY: DISSOCIATION AND FANTASY PRONENESS

Three studies have investigated the relationship between suggestibility and dissociation, using the Dissociation Experiences Scale (DES; Bernstein & Putnam, 1986). In the first study, Wolfradt and Meyer (1998) correlated the Yield 1, Shift and Total Suggestibility scores from the German translation of the GSS 2 with the overall DES score among 37 patients with anxiety disorders and 45 normal controls. The correlations were only significant among the normal subjects. Yield 1 correlated highly significantly ($r = 0.66$, $p < 0.001$) with dissociation, but no significant correlation was found for Shift ($r = -0.10$, ns). A small, but significant, correlation was found between Yield 1 and mental absorption ($r = 0.33$, $p < 0.05$), as measured by the Tellegen Absorption Scale (TAS; Tellegen & Atkinson, 1974). No correlations were reported between GSS 2 immediate recall and dissociation and absorption.

In a replication dissociation study, using the Dutch translation and validation of the GSS 1 (Merckelbach, Muris, Wessel & Van Koppen, 1998a), Merckelbach, Muris, Rassin and Horselenberg (2000) investigated the relationship of suggestibility with the DES, the Cognitive Failure Questionnaire (CFQ; Broadbent, Cooper, Fitzgerald & Parkes, 1982) and the Creative Experiences Questionnaire (CEQ; Merckelbach et al., 1998b). Fifty-six women undergraduate students completed all four tests. A significant correlation was found between the DES and Yield 1 ($r = 0.29$, $p < 0.05$), Total Suggestibility ($r = 0.37$, $p < 0.01$) and immediate recall ($r = -0.30$, $p < 0.05$). The CFQ correlated significantly with Shift ($r = 0.27$, $p < 0.05$) and Total Suggestibility ($r = 0.36$, $p < 0.01$). No significant correlations were found between suggestibility and fantasy proneness, as measured by the CFQ. Interestingly, the correlations between the GSS 1 and DES all became non-significant after the relationship with CFQ had been partialled out.

These two studies show that dissociation proneness is significantly correlated with Yield 1, but not with Shift. The finding that controlling for the influence of self-reported cognitive failures reduced the correlations between dissociation and Yield 1 and Total Suggestibility suggests that the relationship between suggestibility and dissociation is in part mediated by perceptions of memory failures in everyday life and lack of confidence in one's memory. Fantasy proneness was not found to correlate with suggestibility, but in future research it would be important to establish to what extent it may be related with confabulation (distortions and fabrications in GSS memory recall).

One study among psychiatric patients (Leavitt, 1997) failed to find a significant relationship between dissociation, as measured by the DES, and GSS 2 scores. Those patients who scored high on dissociation were not found to be more suggestible than the other patients. In view of the other two studies cited above, and the clinical literature where high suggestibility is assumed to be associated with dissociation (Leavitt, 1997), this is a surprising finding.

In one study (Rassin, 2001), thought suppression (i.e. a conscious attempt to avoid certain thoughts), applied to the GSS 1 narrative among 56 undergraduate students (i.e. participants were instructed not to think about or rehearse their memory of the narrative), resulted in fewer accurate details being recalled, but there was no effect on the Yield 1, Shift or Total Suggestibility scores.

SUGGESTIBILITY AND INSTRUCTIONAL MANIPULATION

The expectation component of the Gudjonsson–Clark (1986) model indicates that suggestibility can, to a certain extent, be influenced by the type of instruction given prior to interrogation. For example, telling subjects that they should be able to answer all the questions asked raises their expectation about performance and may increase their susceptibility to suggestions. Conversely, telling subjects that they are not expected to know all the answers to the questions asked makes them more cautious about guessing the answers.

Evidence that subjects' suggestibility can be affected by the type of instruction given prior to interrogation comes from four studies. In one study we administered the Yield 1 part of the GSS 1 to medical students (Gudjonsson & Hilton, 1989). One group of subjects were told that they should be able to remember most of the story read out to them and give definite answers to all the questions asked about it. The second group was given the standard GSS 1 instruction, which mentions no particular expectation about performance. The subjects are basically told to be as accurate as possible. The third group were told that they were not expected to be able to give a definite answer to all the questions asked. A one-way analysis of variance showed the difference between the three groups to be highly significant, and there was a significant linear trend across the three conditions as predicted. Tests on the mean scores indicated that it may be somewhat easier to lower than to raise suggestibility by giving instructions to manipulate expectations about performance.

The second study into the effects of instructional manipulation on suggestibility is that by Hansdottir *et al.* (1990), which was described earlier with regard to anxiety. This study was similar to that carried out by us except that there were only two instructional manipulation conditions, 'high' and 'low' expectations. The findings are consistent with those found in our study and give support for the theoretical model of Gudjonsson and Clark.

Warning subjects that the questions may be leading or 'tricky' reduces suggestibility. Warren, Hulse-Trotter and Tubbs (1991) found that warning children and adults that the questions were 'tricky' was successful in reducing the Yield 1 score, but it had no effect on Shift. In a more recent study, Boon and Baxter (2000) studied ways of minimizing interrogative suggestibility by giving warnings about the presence of misinformation prior to the interrogation phase of the GSS 2. The subjects were 60 undergraduate students. After the delayed recall of the GSS 2 narrative, the subjects were randomly allocated into one of three groups.

1. The 'Standard Group', where the normal GSS 2 procedure was given.
2. The 'Neutral Group', where the subjects were merely asked to be as accurate as possible. They were warned that the questions would be asked twice and no negative feedback was given.
3. The 'Warned Group', where subjects were told that the questions would be asked twice and that they might be misleading. They were told only to answer questions in accordance with what they actually remembered. Instead of negative feedback the subjects were merely told that the questions were going to be asked again and that they should be as accurate as possible. They were again warned about the possibility of misleading questions.

The warning had significant effect on Yield 1 and Yield 2, as predicted. The warning did not significantly affect the Shift scores. This means that the Standard Group and the Neutral Group, where no warning was given, were significantly more yielding to leading questions than the Warned Group. One-way ANOVAs showed that there were significant differences between the three groups with regard to Shift ($p = 0.0001$) and Total Suggestibility ($p = 0.0001$). Where the standard negative procedure was given, the mean Shift score was over three times higher than that found for the Warned and Neutral Groups. This demonstrates the importance of negative feedback on subsequent suggestibility.

SUGGESTIBILITY AND THE EXPERIMENTER EFFECT

Are the scores on a suggestibility test influenced by the characteristics of the experimenter? In one early paper I raised some concern about the consistency with which negative feedback could be administered on the GSS 1 and stated:

> It is generally more difficult to present pressured instructions in a systematic and uniform way than suggestive questions. The emphasis that is placed on the negative feedback may influence the response elicited. In addition, if Ss do very well on the first trial and make no or few errors then it can be embarrassing to inform them that they have made a number of errors. Such embarrassment may be unwittingly communicated to the S and affect subsequent responses (Gudjonsson, 1984a, p. 311).

There are two important points to consider with respect to the administration of the negative feedback. Firstly, it is imperative that the precise wording is used when one is relying on the existing normative data for interpretation of the results. I have come across clinicians and researchers who actually changed the wording, either because they had forgotten the actual wording or had found it too embarrassing to tell the subject that a number of errors had been made. Secondly, the negative feedback should be stated *firmly*, but not sternly or with an angry expression.

Evidence for an experimenter effect with regard to Shift comes from an Icelandic study which was conducted by six university students (Haraldsson, 1985). Whereas Yield 1 was not influenced by the experimenter, there was a trend, which was almost significant, for this to be the case with Shift. Haraldsson (1985) stated when interpreting this trend:

> Some of the experimenters commented that they had found it difficult and embarrassing to give negative feedback to Ss. Such an attitude may be communicated to the S and affect the resulting Shift scores (p. 766).

A similar trend to those found by Haraldsson was found in a study I conducted in 1984 (Gudjonsson & Lister, 1984). Here the male experimenter (myself) obtained higher Shift scores than the female experimenter (Lister). Although the difference between the experimenters was not quite significant in both of these studies they are worth reporting because they highlight potential problems with the measurement of Shift. Researchers and clinicians should be aware of the importance of paying careful attention to the way they administer negative feedback and ensure that they follow the proper instructions.

In an interesting study, Baxter and Boon (2000) investigated the effects on Yield 2 and Shift on differences in the way negative feedback is administered. Forty-five undergraduate students completed the GSS 2. The subjects were divided into three groups according to the manner in which the negative feedback was to be delivered. The demeanour adopted by the different experimenters was either *friendly*, *firm* or *stern*. There were 15 subjects in each group assessed by final year undergraduate interviewers. No significant differences were found between the three experimental conditions on immediate recall or on Yield 1. However, highly significant differences across conditions—friendly, firm or stern—were noted on Yield 2 and Shift. *Post hoc* testing only revealed significant differences between the two extreme demeanours—friendly versus stern. Interestingly, the suggestibility scores obtained during the firm demeanour condition closely resembled the GSS 2 norms for normal subjects (Gudjonsson, 1997a). In view of their findings the authors concluded:

> Generally, these results underline the importance of adhering to Gudjonsson's recommendation that interviewers should be 'firm' in delivering negative feedback if their results are to be comparable with established population norms for the scales (p. 761).

Baxter and Boon interpreted their findings in the following terms:

> In line with the argument of Gudjonsson and Lister (1984), this effect may be due to a linear increase in the psychological distance between the interviewer and the

interviewee, if increasing psychological distance is conceived as commensurate with a move from a positive, though a neutral, to a negative interviewer attitude toward the interviewee and a progressive decrease in the social support offered to the interviewee by the interviewer (p. 760).

Baxter and Boon also point out on the basis of their findings that Yield 2 is undoubtedly a very important measure of interviewees' vulnerability to interrogative pressure 'and may be a more important measure of witness vulnerability and reliability in its own right than has been acknowledged hitherto' (p. 760).

Bain and Baxter (2000) investigated the effects of the manner in which the GSS 1 was administered. Fifty-five first year undergraduate students were randomly allocated into one of two groups where the demeanour of the experimenter was either *friendly* or *abrupt* throughout the administration of the scale. It was hypothesized that the psychological distance between the interviewer and interviewee would be different in the two conditions, resulting in greater suggestibility during the abrupt condition. Out of the four suggestibility measures, one-way ANOVA tests showed that significant differences emerged with regard to Shift ($p = 0.02$) and Total Suggestibility ($p = 0.04$). No significant differences between conditions were found for immediate and delayed recall. The authors pointed out that their findings support my view that there are at least two distinct types of interrogative suggestibility, Yield 1 and Shift. The findings suggest that Yield 1 may be relatively independent of the interviewer's manner and demeanour, whereas Shift is clearly not:

> This finding may mean that initial responses to leading questions are mediated by more stable cognitive factors, perhaps involving a capacity for source monitoring or discrepancy detection, that are relatively unaffected by the manner of the interrogator, whereas the post-feedback GSS measures may be more sensitive to social aspects of suggestibility (Bain & Baxter, 2000, p. 131).

The finding that the effect of the abrupt manner was primarily on Shift rather than Yield 2 suggests that the subjects' level of uncertainty was increased regarding their performance and they consequently began to guess more of the answers after the negative feedback. In order to increase Yield 2 there may need to be more direct interpersonal pressure, as happened in the *stern* condition in the Baxter–Boon (2000) study discussed above.

SUGGESTIBILITY AND SOCIAL DESIRABILITY

Both suggestibility and compliance correlate with social desirability, but the correlation is small and may not prove to be significant in all studies. Social desirability is commonly associated with 'lie scales', such as those measured by the EPQ (Eysenck & Eysenck, 1975) and the Marlowe–Crowne scale (Crowne & Marlowe, 1960). A high 'lie' score is generally construed as an attempt by subjects to present themselves in a socially favourable light (Gudjonsson, 1990d).

In an early study (Gudjonsson, 1983), I found that the GSS 1 Total Suggestibility score correlated very modestly ($r = 0.34$, df $= 43$, $p < 0.01$) with social desirability as measured by the EPQ Lie Scale. Similarly low, but significant correlations, between GSS 1 suggestibility scores and social desirability have been reported by other authors (Tata, 1983; Haraldsson, 1985). In a large study of prison inmates, Gudjonsson and Sigurdsson (in preparation) found no significant relationship between the GSS 1 suggestibility scores and the scores on the Other and Self Deception Questionnaires of Sackeim and Gur (1979).

As far as compliance is concerned, I found a low but significant relationship with social desirability in one study (Gudjonsson, 1989c), but in other studies no relationship with social desirability has been found (Birgisson, 1996; Gudjonsson & Sigurdsson, in preparation).

SUGGESTIBILITY AND COPING STRATEGIES

The Gudjonsson–Clark (1986) model emphasizes the importance of coping strategies in the suggestion process. The findings from one study strongly support the view that suggestibility is significantly related to the coping strategies subjects can generate and implement when faced with the demands of the interrogative situation.

The study investigated the impact of coping on suggestibility among 30 normal subjects (Gudjonsson, 1988a). All subjects completed the GSS 1 and were afterwards asked about the coping strategies they had utilized during the GSS 1 interrogation. The subjects' descriptions of their coping strategies, both behavioural and cognitive, were classified according to the 'methods of coping' described by Billings and Moos (1981) and Moos and Billings (1982). These fell into three groups:

1. 'active–cognitive' methods (i.e. the subjects try actively to manage their thoughts and appraisal of the situation);
2. 'active-behavioural' methods (i.e. behavioural attempts by the subjects to deal directly and critically with the situation);
3. 'avoidance coping' (i.e. the subjects avoid a critical appraisal of the situation).

It was hypothesized that the 'avoidance coping' would be associated with heightened suggestibility, whereas 'active–cognitive' and 'active–behavioural' methods facilitate a critical analysis of, and coping with, the situation and therefore make the subject more resistant to suggestions.

A highly significant relationship between suggestibility and coping strategies was found. That is, subjects who reported having utilized 'avoidance coping' had much higher suggestibility scores (i.e. Yield 1, Yield 2 and Shift) than the subjects who had been able to use the active–cognitive/behavioural methods.

A typical coping strategy of a suggestible subject was to give answers that to them seemed plausible and consistent with the external cues provided rather than attempting to critically evaluate each question and only giving definitive (affirmative) answers to questions they could clearly remember. Typical self-statements of this group were 'I gave plausible answers', 'I didn't want to look stupid', 'It is always best to give a definite answer even if it is wrong' and 'I changed answers I wasn't sure about'.

Non-suggestible coping strategies involved a critical analysis of the situation and a facilitative problem-solving action. Common self-statements of this group were the following: *cognitive*, 'I can't be expected to know all the answers', 'Some of the questions were not in the story', 'I am sure I have done as well as anyone else'; *behavioural*, 'I tried to stick to what I remembered', 'I looked critically at each of my answers', 'I tried to look at the situation objectively'.

Howard & Hong (2002) investigated the relationship between coping style, using the COPE questionnaire (Carver, Scheier & Weintraub, 1989), and suggestibility, as measured by the GSS 1. Data were collected from 263 undergraduate students and on the basis of the extreme COPE scores, 51 participants were classified into problem-focused ($N = 25$) and emotion-focused ($N = 26$) copers. The emotion-focused copers scored significantly higher on Yield 1 and Total Suggestibility than the problem-focused copers. No significant differences between the two types of coper were found for Shift and immediate and delayed recall. These findings are consistent with the Gudjonsson and Clark model of interrogative suggestibility.

SUGGESTIBILITY AND ASSERTIVENESS

According to the Gudjonsson–Clark (1986) model, it would be expected that assertiveness correlated negatively with the GSS suggestibility scores. The reasoning for this is that unassertive individuals will find it difficult to implement facilitative coping strategies when faced with the uncertainty and expectations of the interrogative situation. One study, conducted by myself, has looked at this issue (Gudjonsson, 1988a).

The correlations between suggestibility, as measured by the GSS 1, and assertiveness, which was measured by the Rathus (1973) Assertiveness Scale were all significant. The correlations in a group of 30 normal subjects were as follows: Yield 1, $r = -0.42$; Yield 2, $r = -0.49$; Shift, $r = -0.40$; Total Suggestibility, $r = -0.46$.

I found a significant negative correlation (-0.53) between assertiveness and FNE. One possible explanation is that high fear of negative evaluation inhibits assertive behaviour (Lohr, Nix, Dunbar & Mosesso, 1984) as well as the coping strategies that subjects can implement during interrogation.

SUGGESTIBILITY AND SELF-ESTEEM

Three studies have found a negative relationship between self-esteem and suggestibility, which supports the theoretical model of Gudjonsson and Clark. The results indicate that feelings of powerlessness and incompetence are particularly effective in inducing suggestibility. Furthermore, the findings suggest that manipulating suspects' self-esteem during interrogation may markedly increase the risk of uncritical acceptance of misleading information.

In the first study (Gudjonsson & Singh, 1984a), we correlated the Yield 1 and Shift scores from the GSS 1 with self-esteem as measured by the Coopersmith Behavior Rating Form (BRF; Coopersmith, 1967). The subjects were 31 delinquent boys who were in an assessment centre. The BRF was filled in by members of staff who knew the boys well. Each boy was rated by two teachers and the average score was used for the statistical analysis. Self-esteem correlated negatively with Shift ($r = -0.40$, $df = 29$, $p < 0.05$), but no significant correlation was found for Yield 1 ($r = -0.14$).

Singh and Gudjonsson (1984) administered the GSS 1 to 30 subjects twice, one week apart. After each 'interrogation' the subjects completed a number of Semantic Differential Scales (Osgood, Suci & Tannebaum, 1957) related to self-concept. Three 'concepts' ('Myself as I am generally', 'Myself during the experiment', and 'The experimenter') were rated on 12 bipolar scales. Each bipolar scale consisted of a pair of bipolar adjectives. Factor analysis revealed three distinct factors in relation to each concept, which corresponded to Osgood's *Evaluative*, *Potency* and *Activity* dimensions.

The main findings of the study were that suggestibility (Yield 1 and Shift) correlated significantly with a low score on the Potency dimension but not with the other two dimensions. The correlations were significant with regard to the concepts 'Myself as I am generally' and 'Myself during the experiment'. The correlations between Potency and suggestibility were lower during the second interrogation than the first. Singh and Gudjonsson (1984) state:

> The implication of this is that the impact of self-esteem upon suggestibility is particularly likely to occur when Ss are unfamiliar with interrogative tasks and procedures. It also suggests that manipulation of self-esteem may be potentially more harmful to the reliability of testimony when naive and inexperienced Ss are employed who are unfamiliar with the nature of the task in hand (p. 208).

Lister and I (Gudjonsson & Lister, 1984) administered the GSS 1 to 25 males and 25 females and asked them afterwards to complete the Semantic Differential Scales used in the Singh–Gudjonsson study. The subjects also completed the Rotter (1966) Locus of Control Scale. The Semantic Differential concepts rated by the subjects were 'Myself during the experiment' and 'The experimenter'. Three factors emerged from factor analysis, which were called 'Potency', 'Competence' and 'Evaluative'. It was found that the greater the perceived distance between the self and the experimenter in terms of Potency and Competence the more suggestible the subjects were, both in terms of Yield 1 and Shift. The correlations were higher among the male subjects. The authors concluded from their findings that interrogation techniques aimed at manipulating confidence and self-esteem can increase subjects' susceptibility to suggestive influences.

In spite of the potential importance of self-esteem in mediating suggestibility, not all studies have found a positive relationship between the two psychological constructs. For example, Smith and Gudjonsson (1995a), using the Rosenberg Self-Esteem Scale in a forensic inpatient population, found no significant correlation between self-esteem and any of the GSS 2. Part of the problem may relate to poor reliability and validity of the Self-Esteem Scale when used with certain populations (Smith & Gudjonsson, 1995a).

SUGGESTIBILITY AND LOCUS OF CONTROL

There are theoretical and empirical grounds for expecting a relationship between suggestibility and the perception of control over the environment. Rotter (1966) describes a questionnaire which measures attribution style along the dimension of *internal–external* locus of control. People with a high internal locus of control attitude perceive reinforcement as being contingent on their own behaviour. Conversely, people high on external locus of control view reinforcement as being contingent on environmental factors, such as, fate and chance. One theoretical reason why locus of control would be expected to correlate with suggestibility is that people who perceive themselves as having strong control over environmental events (i.e. they have an internal locus of control) commonly describe themselves as potent and powerful (Hersch & Scheibe, 1967). From this perspective people with high external locus of control would be expected to be more suggestible than those with high internal locus of control.

In our study quoted above in relation to self-esteem (Gudjonsson & Lister, 1984), we found that Yield 1 and Total Suggestibility correlated significantly with external locus of control among the male subjects, but the correlation was not quite large enough to be significant for the female sample.

Liebman *et al.* (2002), studied the relationship between suggestibility, as measured by the GSS 2, and subscales of the Revised NEO Personality Inventory (NEO PI-R; Costa & McCrae, 1992), the Multidimensional Personality Questionnaire (MPQ; Tellegen, 1982), and four measures of perceived control (i.e. memory efficacy, general efficacy, locus of control and learned helplessness). The participants were 98 undergraduate psychology students. The main findings were as follows.

- Locus of control and memory efficacy correlated negatively with Yield 1, showing that people with an internal locus of control, and those who possess confidence in their memory, are more able to resist leading questions than those with an external locus of control and who lack confidence in their memory.
- On the NEO-PI R, the activity facet on the extraversion dimension correlated negatively with Yield 1 and Total Suggestibility, and the competence and self-discipline facets on the conscientiousness dimension correlated negatively with the Shift and Total Suggestibility measures, respectively. The findings suggest that people who are mentally and physically active give in less to leading questions than their less active counterparts, and those who have low opinions of their abilities are more prone to alter their answers in response to interpersonal pressure.
- Traditionalism on the MPQ correlated negatively with Yield 1 and Total Suggestibility, indicating that suggestible individuals are less able to challenge people in authority.

The findings from these studies are consistent with a number of other studies that have shown that people with an internal locus of control tend to be more resistant to influence and pressure than those with external locus of control (Biondo & MacDonald, 1971; Eisenberg, 1978; Ryckman, Rodda & Sherman, 1972).

Brehm and Brehm (1981) point out that the greatest effect of internal versus external locus of control is noted in those studies where there is greatest threat to the subject's freedom to choose or act. What differentiates external locus of control subjects most from those with an internal locus is the strong tendency of the latter to exhibit 'reactance' arousal when faced with threat. Reactance arousal is probably best construed as a counterforce, which motivates the subject to react forcefully to perceived threat or loss of freedom to act. If the task they are confronted with is perceived as having low threat value, then there appears to be much less difference between 'internals' and 'externals' in their reactions. The implication is that reactance arousal, which is generally activated when the individual's sense of freedom is threatened, is more readily activated in 'internals' than 'externals', which makes them particularly resistant to pressure under high threat conditions. This does not, however, exclude the possibility that the type of threat individuals are faced with may affect their reactance arousal in idiosyncratic ways.

I have used Brehm's (1966) 'reactance theory' to explain how people may become more assertive and less suggestible after negative feedback on the GSS and during real life interrogations when pressured excessively by the police (Gudjonsson, 1995b).

SUGGESTIBILITY AND FIELD DEPENDENCE

Two studies have investigated the relationship between suggestibility and field dependence. In the first study, on the basis of the Gudjonsson–Clark (1986) theoretical model of interrogative suggestibility, Singh and Gudjonsson (1992b) predicted that subjects scoring high on field dependence would be more suggestible than low scorers. The subjects were 40 youths, aged 11–16 years. The Embedded Figures Test (EFT; Witkin, Oltman, Raskin & Carps, 1971) was used to measure field dependence, and the GSS 1 was used to measure suggestibility. Field dependence correlated significantly with Yield 1 ($r = 0.36$, $p < 0.01$) and Total Suggestibility ($r = 0.32$, $p < 0.01$). Blagrove, Cole-Morgan and Lambe (1994) replicated the Singh–Gudjonsson study in two groups of university undergraduate students. The correlation between Yield 1 (no other suggestibility measure was used) and field dependence, using the Finding Embedded Figures Test (Thompson & Melancon, 1990), was significant for both samples (e.g. $r = 0.37$ and 0.42, respectively). Blagrove and his colleagues point to two possible theoretical mechanisms that may explain the relationships between Yield 1 suggestibility and field dependence. The first explanation relies on the cognitive analytical aspects of discrepancy detection (Tousignant, Hall & Loftus, 1986), or problems with critical analysis of the interrogation task by field dependent subjects (Singh & Gudjonsson, 1992b). The second explanation, focuses on increased receptivity to social cues of field dependent people (Melancon & Thompson, 1989). Both of these theoretical mechanisms may be relevant to explaining the relationship between suggestibility and field dependence.

SUSPICIOUSNESS AND ANGER

I suggested in Chapter 1 that interrogators are intuitively aware of the need to induce a positive mood in the suspect in order to built up rapport and trust. Without rapport and trust being successfully achieved, self-incriminating admissions will be less forthcoming. In particular, negative emotional states, such as suspiciousness and anger, are viewed as undesirable emotional states, which can potentially adversely affect the interrogative process and outcome.

Similarly, the Gudjonsson–Clark (1986) theoretical model indicates that *trust* is an essential component of the suggestion process. Lack of trust and suspiciousness are seen as seriously reducing the individual's receptiveness to suggestions. This is because the suspect or witness enters the police interview with a 'suspicious cognitive set', which seriously influences the way he or she copes with the demand characteristics of the situation. Anger is not specifically mentioned by Gudjonsson and Clark, but it can function to make the suspect more critical and suspicious of the interrogator and his motives.

What do empirical and experimental findings tell us about the effects of suspiciousness and anger upon suggestibility? There is growing evidence that the intuitive view of experienced interrogators about the effects of mood is well founded. What has been shown is that certain negative moods affect compliance and suggestibility in a rather predictable way and theoretical explanations can be put forward to explain such findings.

Loftus (1979b) found in her research into eyewitness testimony that if the questions asked are too blatantly misleading then subjects commonly react by subsequently becoming less receptive to suggestions. The reason seems to be that when subjects become suspicious of the experimenter then they will scrutinize the interrogator's questions more carefully and readily identify when they are being misled. Further evidence for this comes from a study by Dodd and Bradshaw (1980) into the effects of pragmatic conditions on the acceptance of misleading information. For example, subjects were more guarded about accepting accounts from informants who were not perceived as 'neutral'. In other words, if communicators appear to have something to gain from giving a particular account, then subjects become suspicious of the reliability of the information provided and less readily incorporate it into their memory.

I noted in my forensic work in some major criminal cases (Gudjonsson, 1989a) that on occasions defendants were highly inconsistent in their GSS suggestibility scores when tested on two separate occasions. As a standard clinical practice, I always keep detailed notes of the defendants' mood and mental state during testing, as well of their attitudes towards the tests administered and the clinician. Some interesting and striking observations were made with regard to the inconsistencies on the GSS. On the occasion when defendants proved highly suggestible their behaviour during testing was invariably associated with reasonable rapport and cooperation. In contrast, when these defendants were highly resistant to suggestions, there had been expressed indication of either suspiciousness and/or anger.

It can be tentatively suggested on the basis of these anecdotal observations, and some further cases, that in order for anger to encumber suggestibility it has to be directed *outwards* towards some third person or object rather than towards the self. The anger need not necessarily be felt towards the interrogator, but it will still seriously reduce the person's susceptibility to suggestions. In other words, an angry suspect is probably difficult to interrogate at the best of times even if the anger is not directed towards the interrogator. Suspiciousness, on the other hand, appears to have a more specific focus. It has to be directed either towards the experimenter or the tests themselves.

Stricker, Messick and Jackson (1967) discuss the implication of suspiciousness for conformity research. They found strong evidence that subjects' suspiciousness about the experiment they were participating in was related to lack of conformity and cooperation. In other words, those subjects who expressed ideas indicating suspiciousness about the testing procedure were much less conforming than those who expressed no such suspicions. The authors offered two possibilities for their findings. First, subjects' generalized suspicious cognitive set predisposes them to seek evidence of deception and makes them more able to identify it when it does occur. Second, when subjects, for whatever reason, happen to become suspicious during a particular experiment, they develop a resistant cognitive set, which helps them resist pressure and suggestions.

Singh and Gudjonsson (1992a) used institutionalized delinquent boys (aged 11–16 years) to examine the relationship between suggestibility, as measured by the GSS 1, and attitude towards authority and hostility, using the General Attitude to Institutional Authority Scale (Rigby, 1982) and the Buss–Durkee Hostility Inventory (Buss & Durkee, 1957), respectively. Neither attitude towards authority or hostility correlated significantly with the suggestibility scores. This is unexpected, because negative attitude and hostility would be expected to relate closely to suspicious cognitive set and distrust of others. Singh and Gudjonsson pointed out that the explanation for an absence of significant findings may relate to the fact that during the assessment the youths in the study were fully cooperative and did not display any suspiciousness or hostility. This suggests that it is the attitude towards the examiner and the testing which are more important in influencing suggestibility than the general level of hostility and attitude towards persons in authority. In other words, negative attitude towards people in authority and hostility need to be actively present at the time of testing to have any impact on suggestibility. The alternative explanation is that the concept of hostility and its measurement are complex and a significant relationship with suggestibility may not always be present. For example, in the study by Blagrove, Cole-Morgan and Lambe (1994) hostility ratings during baseline testing, when the GSS 1 was also administered, did not correlate significantly with the suggestibility scores.

Milberg and Clark (1988) examined the effects of different moods, which were experimentally induced, on compliant behaviour. Three different mood states were induced: happy, neutral mood and angry. Significant differences in compliance were noted according to mood. Subjects in the happy condition were subsequently significantly more compliant than subjects in the neutral condition. Furthermore, far less compliance was noted among the subjects in the angry than in the neutral condition.

The authors concluded that happiness not only increased compliance; in this experiment it was necessary in order for anybody to comply with a subsequent task request. Similarly, anger induction not only decreased compliance, but also resulted in significant changes taking place to the extent that subjects took an *opposite* view to that communicated by the experimenter. In other words, they reacted in quite an extreme way. The implication for real-life interrogation is that making suspects angry can badly backfire and result in a so-called 'boomerang' effect (Brehm, 1966; Brehm & Brehm, 1981). This principle is based on 'reactance theory', which is a counterforce that motivates people to assert themselves when their freedom to choose or act is threatened (Brehm & Brehm, 1981). I have discussed elsewhere (Gudjonsson, 1995b) how interrogative pressure may backfire and make suspects retract the confession they had previously made.

Another implication for real interrogations is that suspects who are interviewed by the police whilst in a negative emotional state, such as when suspicious or angry, need to be interviewed very carefully because they may be more likely to misinterpret interactional cues and attribute negative qualities to the interrogator and his or her messages. If this happens then the suspects are less likely to be forthcoming and open to suggestions, it will be more difficult to establish satisfactory rapport and the likelihood of reactive arousal will be greatly enhanced.

The studies reviewed indicate that mood does under certain circumstances influence susceptibility to suggestions. An individual who is in a positive mood is more likely to cooperate with requests and accept suggestions than a person who is in a negative mood. However, as Milberg and Clark (1988) rightly point out, when the mood of the subject is self-focused its effects on compliance may be quite different to those mentioned above. For example, a self-focused positive mood may make people feel more confident in their own judgement and abilities. This is likely to reduce their reliance on external cues when asked misleading questions or requested to do things they would rather not do. Indeed, earlier in this chapter it was shown how a sense of 'competence' and 'potency' in relation to perceptions of the self made subjects more resistant to misleading questions and interrogative pressure.

SUGGESTIBILITY AND TEST SETTING

Gudjonsson (1995e) investigated whether the setting where subjects were tested made a difference to the suggestibility scores on the GSS 1 and GSS 2. In this study, 353 subjects who were assessed for judicial purposes were classified into two groups according to where they were tested: prison versus hospital outpatients. No significant difference was found between the two groups with regard to any of the suggestibility scores. The mean suggestibility scores in this study were very similar to those found for subjects tested whilst detained at English police stations for questioning (Gudjonsson et al., 1993). The results suggest that the test setting does not influence the suggestibility scores.

SUGGESTIBILITY AND PREVIOUS CONVICTIONS

Gudjonsson and Singh (1984b) argue that there are at least two theoretical reasons why criminals with previous convictions should be less suggestible than those with no previous convictions. First, offenders with extensive experience of police interrogation may develop increased resistance to interpersonal pressure applied during interrogation. Second, criminal recidivists may be characteristically more prone to resist interpersonal pressure than less habitual offenders.

Two studies have found a negative relationship between suggestibility, as measured by the GSS 1, and previous convictions. Gudjonsson and Singh (1984b) correlated the number of previous convictions among 35 delinquent adolescent boys and their suggestibility scores obtained on the GSS 1. All but two of the boys had previous convictions and the mean number of previous convictions for the group as a whole was 3.2 (range 0–9). The correlations with the GSS 1 were -0.21, -0.36 ($p < 0.05$) and -0.38 ($p < 0.05$) for Yield 1, Shift and Total Suggestibility, respectively. The findings indicate that the extent to which delinquent boys resist interrogative pressure during interrogation is significantly correlated with their previous convictions.

Sharrock and Gudjonsson (1993) extended the study quoted above, by investigating the effect of previous convictions on suggestibility whilst controlling for memory and intelligence. The subjects were 108 defendants who had been assessed by the authors as part of a pre-trial assessment. The findings were very similar to those of Gudjonsson and Singh (1984b). Shift was more highly negatively correlated with previous convictions than Yield 1, although both were significant. The authors concluded that interrogative experience, which was assessed by the presence of previous convictions, had a causal bearing on both Yield 1 and Shift, independent of intelligence.

POLICE INTERVIEWING AND SUGGESTIBILITY

A study by Tully and Cahill (1984) suggests that the GSS 1 is able to predict, to a certain extent, the accuracy of witnesses' testimony during police interviewing. Forty-five subjects, 30 of whom can be loosely defined as having learning disability, took part in an experiment involving a staged scenario incident concerning the removal of some plants. The subjects were not aware at the time that one week later they were going to be asked questions about the incident. Prior to the staged scenario the subjects had completed a number of psychological tests, which included the GSS 1. One week later the subjects were all brought back to the testing centre and told that they were to be interviewed by police officers about the previous week's incident concerning the flower pots.

The subjects' interviews with the police were video-recorded and analysed for accuracy and details of information.

Tully and Cahill analysed the interview material in terms of the number of *accurate* and *erroneous* recollections given by the subjects. The authors did not correlate these with suggestibility as measured by the GSS 1, but as all the necessary raw scores are available in their book, such an analysis is possible. I have worked out these correlations. Suggestibility correlated negatively (-0.63, $p < 0.001$) with the number of items of accurate information provided by the subjects and positively with the amount of erroneous information given (0.39, $p < 0.01$). These results suggest that the more suggestible the subjects were, the less accurate information they gave, and the more errors they made when interviewed as witnesses by the police one week later. This indicates that interrogative suggestibility, as measured by the GSS 1, can to a certain extent predict the reliability of information given by witnesses when interviewed by the police.

The police officers who interviewed the subjects in this study had been asked to elicit 'accurate' information from the subjects and they knew that most of the subjects were learning disabled. In addition, they were aware that their interviews were being video-recorded. This means that they would probably have been trying not to lead or mislead their 'witnesses', although it is inevitable that they had to ask some specific questions in order to direct the focus of their questioning to the type of information they had been requested to obtain by the researchers.

Unfortunately, Tully and Cahill give no information about the police officers' interviewing techniques or the extent to which they may have been leading or misleading in their questioning. This is a major weakness in the study, especially since the authors had the data from the video-recorded interviews to study the effects of police interviewing styles on the reliability of the information obtained.

RESISTERS AND ALLEGED FALSE CONFESSORS

In 1988 my colleague Dr MacKeith and I reviewed the legal, psychological, and psychiatric aspects of alleged false confessions (Gudjonsson & MacKeith, 1988). We concluded that the two most relevant enduring psychological characteristics in the assessment of such cases were *interrogative suggestibility* and *compliance*. We further discussed the importance of these two psychological characteristics with reference to a proven case of false confession (Gudjonsson & MacKeith, 1990).

Three studies have compared the suggestibility scores of alleged false confessors and resisters in criminal trials. In 1984 I compared the GSS 1 scores of 12 alleged false confessors and eight resisters (Gudjonsson, 1984b). The resisters comprised a group of defendants who had all persistently denied any involvement in the crime they had been charged with in spite of forensic evidence against them. The alleged false confessors consisted of defendants who had retracted confessions they had previously made during police interrogation.

The resisters were found to be significantly more intelligent and less suggestible than the alleged false confessors. A particularly significant finding was the difference between the two groups in the type of suggestibility that related to the ability to resist interrogative pressure. These were the Shift and Yield 2 scores on the GSS 1.

I identified two limitations with the study. First, the number of subjects in each group was very small. Secondly, part of the difference in suggestibility between the two groups could have been influenced by the differences in IQ between the two groups. Sharrock (1988) goes further and states that the difference in the IQ between the two groups 'accounts for most of the difference in their suggestibility' (p. 220). Sharrock's bold statement seems to have been based on the erroneous assumption that, since there is a certain negative relationship between IQ and suggestibility, this is likely to have mediated the differences in suggestibility between the alleged false confessors and resisters. I take the view that suggestibility is mediated by a number of factors, intelligence being only one of them. However, Sharrock raised an important point, which warranted a study where the IQ of the two groups are controlled for.

In an attempt to investigate Sharrock's observation, I extended and replicated the 1984 study (Gudjonsson, 1991c). The resisters and alleged false confessors were different to those used in the 1984 study and the number of subjects in each group was much larger than in the previous study. Perhaps most importantly, however, the two groups of subjects were matched with respect to age, sex, intelligence and memory capacity. The study also had the advantage over the 1984 study in that the subjects had all completed both the GSS 1 and the GCS. Thus, both suggestibility and compliance were measured. It was hypothesized that, even with intelligence and memory capacity controlled for, the two groups would still show significant differences with regard to suggestibility and compliance, the main difference being related to the ability of subjects to resist interrogative pressure, as measured by the GCS and the Yield 2 and Shift parts of the GSS 1.

The most important finding was that highly significant differences emerged between alleged false confessors and resisters after their intelligence and memory capacity had been controlled for. This has important implications for the assessment of retracted confession cases. First, it demonstrates that the assessment of suggestibility and compliance, which are theoretically construed as overlapping characteristics (Gudjonsson, 1989c), contributes to discriminating between the two groups largely independently of the subjects' level of intelligence. In other words, intelligence may be an important factor in differentiating between alleged false confessors and retractors, but other factors, such as suggestibility and compliance, are also important and should not be underestimated. Secondly, the present findings are a clear warning to clinicians carrying out a forensic assessment. That is, even though suggestibility and intelligence are modestly correlated, it is erroneous to assume that differences in suggestibility and compliance are largely or necessarily mediated by differences in intelligence, as Sharrock (1988) postulated.

The mean suggestibility scores in this recent study are very similar to those found in the 1984 study for alleged false confessors and resisters. Furthermore, consistent with the previous findings, the most striking differences between the two groups is in relation to Yield 2 and Shift, which links confessing behaviour primarily with the suspect's ability to cope with pressure, rather than their tendency to give in to leading questions per se.

It is worth noting that whereas alleged false confessors as a group are markedly higher on suggestibility and compliance than the average male in the general population, the resisters are in contrast unusually resistant to suggestions and interrogative pressure. Having said that, it should be born in mind that we are dealing with group means and there are clear individual differences within the respective two groups. For example, not all of the alleged false confessors proved highly suggestible or compliant; similarly, but less striking, not all of the resisters were low on suggestibility and compliance. This raises an important point, which should always be carefully considered by the psychologist or psychiatrist when carrying out a forensic assessment in cases of alleged false confession. The suspect's ability to resist the police interviewer's suggestions and interrogative pressure, when these are present, is undoubtedly due to the combination of situational and interrogational factors on the one hand, and the suspect's mental state, motivation, personality and coping style on the other.

Figure 14.1 gives the suggestibility and compliance scores of three groups of subjects (Gudjonsson, 1991c). Here I compared the suggestibility and compliance scores of 76 alleged false confessors, 38 forensic patients who had not retracted their confession and still maintained their involvement in the crime and 15 criminal suspects or defendants who had been able to resist police interrogation in spite of other evidence against them on which they were

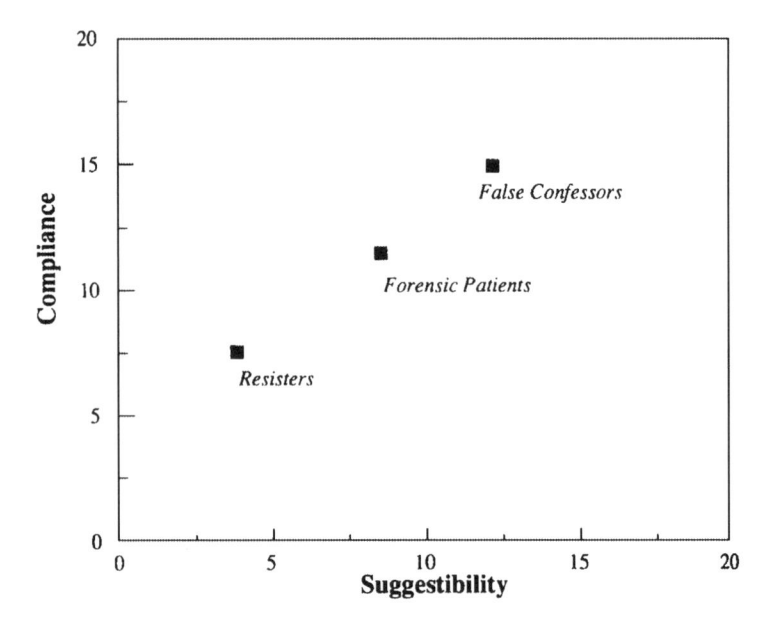

Figure 14.1. Mean suggestibility and compliance scores of 'false confessors', 'forensic patients' and 'resisters'

subsequently convicted. The subjects had all completed the GSS 1, the GCS and the WAIS-R. The three groups differed highly significantly in their suggestibility and compliance scores after IQ and memory recall on the GSS 1 had been controlled for by an analysis of covariance.

Figure 14.1 shows that there is a linear relationship between the three groups with regard to suggestibility (Total Score) and compliance. The alleged false confessors had the highest suggestibility and compliance scores and resisters the lowest. The other forensic cases obtained scores that fall in between the other two groups on the two measures. Therefore, suggestibility and compliance differentiate between 'false confessors', 'forensic patients' and 'resisters' in their own right and irrespective of differences in IQ. It is interesting to note in this study that differences between the three groups were more marked with regard to the suggestibility and compliance scores than intelligence. This suggests that personality, as measured by suggestibility and compliance, may be a better indicator of how people cope with police interrogation than intellectual functioning.

Irving (1987) makes the interesting point that whether or not defendants were able to cope with police interrogation may predict GSS 1 scores, but this does not necessarily mean that GSS 1 scores will predict prospectively how people will cope with police interrogation. This is a valid point to make, because it is only by implication that one can suggest from the above mentioned studies that the resisters' low suggestibility and compliance scores and the alleged false confessors' high scores influenced their behaviour at the time of the police interrogation.

No study has examined prospectively how low and high suggestibility and compliance scorers are able to cope with police interrogation. However, in one study (Pearse et al., 1998; see also Chapter 3), suggestibility was not found to predict whether or not suspects confessed. The main reasons appeared to be that detainees had decided prior to the interrogation about whether or not they were going to confess and there was very little pressure used in the interview to break down resistance (Pearse & Gudjonsson, 1996a).

SUGGESTIBILITY AND FALSE CONFESSIONS

Apart from individual case studies, which are presented in other parts of this book, is there empirical evidence that suggestibility is related to the making of false confessions? As discussed in Chapter 9, theoretically suggestibility should be particularly relevant to coerced–internalized false confessions. Only one study has investigated this issue. Sigurdsson and Gudjonsson (1996) compared the personality scores, including suggestibility and compliance, of 62 prison inmates who claimed to have made a false confession in the past to the police with the scores of other prison inmates. The false confessors were found to be more anxious and personality disordered than the other inmates and they had significantly higher mean GCS score (10.6 and 9.4, respectively), but did not differ significantly with regard to intelligence, verbal memory or suggestibility. A discriminant analysis performed on all the psychological tests administered (Sigurdsson & Gudjonsson, 2001) showed that the Gough Socialisation Scale and the Gudjonsson Compliance Scale (GCS) discriminated most significantly between the alleged false confessors and the other inmates (Wilks' lambda $= 0.8967; f(2,191) = 10.998$, $p < 0.001$).

When the false confessors were classified into type of false confession (coerced–internalized versus other) then significant differences emerged with regard to the scores on the GSS 1: the coerced–internalized false confessors scored higher on suggestibility than the other false confessors. Significant differences emerged with regard to Yield 1 ($Z = 1.97$, $p < 0.05$), Total Suggestibility ($Z = 2.21$, $p < 0.05$) and Confabulation ($Z = 2.01$, $p < 0.05$). All nine coerced–internalized false confessors gave convincing evidence of how during interrogation they had temporarily come to believe that they had committed the offence they were accused of, but later realized that they had nothing to do with the offence (see Sigurdsson, 1998, for details of the individual cases). The findings suggest that suggestibility and a tendency to confabulate with regard to memory recall are psychological factors that during interrogation make some people vulnerable to making a coerced–internalized false confession. What is particularly interesting is that the two groups did not differ with regard to GSS 1 immediate verbal recall or non-verbal IQ or on the EPQ (Eysenck & Eysenck, 1975), the Gough Socialisation Scale (Gough, 1960), the GCS and the Other and Self Deception Questionnaires (Sackeim & Gur, 1979).

Compliance, as measured by the GCS, appears to have a broader application to false confessions than suggestibility. This is due to the fact that false confessions are caused by a variety of factors, which are mainly associated with avoidance of pressure associated with interrogation and custodial confinement. Suggestibility, in contrast to compliance, is principally related to uncertainty in memory and changes in belief systems. The types of interrogation technique recommended by Inbau, Reid and Buckley (1986) tap into both suggestibility and compliance. There is considerable emphasis on psychological manipulation related to changes in suspects' beliefs concerning the strength of the evidence against them, what is allegedly in their best interest, and their perceptions about their involvement in the offence.

Redlich (1999), in a doctoral dissertation, studied the relationship between false confession and suggestibility among young persons, using a slightly modified (Americanized) version of the GSS 1. The false confession paradigm used was based on that developed by Kassin and Kiechel (1996). The study's two main aims were to investigate the relationship between false confession and two different types of vulnerability factor: (a) age and (b) psychological variables (suggestibility, free recall, errors in memory recall and maturity). The participants were accused of pressing the wrong key on a computer keyboard during a reaction time experiment and causing the computer to crash. This was used to elicit a signed false confession statement. There were three groups of participants, 32 in each group, as follows.

- 12 and 13-year-olds.
- 15 and 16-year-olds.
- College students, aged between 18 and 26.

After being administered the GSS 1 the participants entered the reaction time experiment where the attempt was made to induce a false confession. In relation to the false confession there were three measures of the effects of social influence: *compliance*, *internalization* and *confabulation*. Compliance refers to the number of participants who signed the false confession statement, which read 'I hit the ALT key and caused the computer to crash. Data were lost'. Internalization refers to participants telling another experimenter (i.e. the one who administered the GSS 1 and the maturity measures) that they had hit the wrong key and ruined the program. Confabulation was measured by asking the participants to retrace their steps and it was scored when the participant claimed to recall specific details, such as hitting the ALT key.

Half of the participants were after the experiment presented with a faked computer print-out 'showing that they had pressed the ALT key, which they had specifically been warned not to touch'. The purpose of this manipulation was to test the impact of the presentation of false evidence. The main findings were as follows.

- 69% of the participants signed a confession statement accepting responsibility for pressing the wrong key, when in reality none had pressed the wrong key. Of these 30% internalized the false confession and 19% confabulated.
- Age, gender and suggestibility were significantly related to at least one of the three dependent measures; there was no effect for maturity levels.
- The younger the participants the more likely they were to make a false confession (the percentages were 78%, 72% and 59% for the three age groups in ascending order of age).
- Age was not significantly related to internalization and confabulation. This finding suggests that younger persons are more compliant with authority even without questioning (i.e. mere confrontation and accusation was sufficient).
- In contrast to the findings by Kassin and Kiechel (1996), where no gender differences were noted, in the present experiment females were significantly less likely than males to sign a false confession statement. The explanation put forward by the researcher was that the person who asked for the signed confession was always a male. Interestingly though, the male participants scored significantly higher than the females on Yield 1, Yield 2 and Total Suggestibility.
- There was a significant relationship between Yield 1, Yield 2 and Total Suggestibility and making a false confession, even after controlling for age differences in the confession rate. Internalization was significantly related to Yield 1. There was no significant effect for Shift or free memory recall. Confabulation on the GSS 1 was related to internalization and confabulation in relation to the false confession.
- The presentation of the faked evidence (i.e. the computer print-out) resulted in significantly more internalized false confessions.

This study supports the importance of suggestibility as a vulnerability factor for making a false confession and the relationship between internalization of the false confession and GSS 1 confabulation is consistent with the findings of Sigurdsson and Gudjonsson (1996) in a real-life interrogation context. The findings also emphasize the importance of age as a vulnerability factor for making a false confession.

SUGGESTIBILITY AND EYEWITNESS TESTIMONY

Cardone and Dent (1996) have argued, on the basis of their research with adults who have learning disabilities (IQ range 53–74), that the GSS may have limited applicability to eyewitness testimony. The basis of their argument is that most eyewitness testimony is based on visually perceived material and the GSS presents only verbal information. They found in their research that the presentation of the GSS material visually as well as verbally resulted in improved immediate and delayed recall and lower Yield 1 suggestibility scores. The Shift scores were not affected by the modality of presentation. The finding that the mean Yield score was lower with the combined visual and verbal presentation of material is not surprising, and this can be interpreted both in terms of the *uncertainty* component of the Gudjonsson–Clark (1986) model and *discrepancy detection* theory (Schooler & Loftus, 1986). Thus, as the strength of the original information is improved by the dual modality of presentation, the more people are able to resist leading questions. This may be particularly important in cases of adults with learning disabilities, because the Yield 1 score is particularly elevated in contrast to a modest Shift score (Clare & Gudjonsson, 1993, 1995; Gudjonsson, Murphy & Clare, 2000). The impact of the optimum combination of visual and verbal presentation of material may be less in normal adults where the strength of the original information is so much better. Finally, the fact that eyewitness testimony is based largely on visually perceived material does not mean that suggestibility scales relying on verbally presented material are not transferable across modalities in terms of suggestibility. Indeed, the early work of Tully and Cahill (1984) supports the use of the GSS 1 in predicting the eyewitness accuracy of witnesses to a visually staged scenario.

Henry and Gudjonsson (1999) found that whereas GSS 2 Yield 1 suggestibility did correlate significantly with several of the eyewitness performance measures among children with learning disabilities (aged 11–12 years) and younger normal children (aged 8–9 years), the correlations failed to reach significance among normal 11 to 12-year-olds. This may have been partly due to the small sample size of the last group ($N = 19$), because several of the correlations were approaching significance and in the predicted direction. Interestingly, IQ performed even worse than the GSS 2; it was only related to one aspect of eyewitness performance, namely closed misleading questions, and only in the learning disabilities group.

Henry and Gudjonsson (submitted) studied further eyewitness memory and suggestibility among three groups of children.

- 47 children, 11 to 12-year-olds, who had a history of learning disabilities (Learning Disabilities Group, LD).
- 25 children, 11 to 12-year-olds, without a history of learning disability and with average IQ (Chronological Age Control Group, CA).

- 28 children, without learning disability and of average IQ, aged 5–8 (Mental Age Comparable Group, MA).

All the children completed the GSS 2 and also participated in an eyewitness memory task. With regard to immediate recall on the GSS 2, the LD and MA groups had similar mean scores, whereas the CA Group had over twice as much memory recall as the other two groups. The LD and MA groups also had similar Yield 1 scores, which were significantly higher than those found for the CA Group. Interestingly, the LD Group had significantly higher Shift scores than the other two groups. This means that when mental age is controlled for, children with learning disabilities are susceptible to shifting their answers after negative feedback. This suggests that Shift in children with learning disabilities may be more mediated by social than cognitive (memory and intelligence) factors. This last finding is interesting, because adults with learning disabilities score particularly high on Yield 1 and tend only to have a modest Shift score (Clare & Gudjonsson, 1993; Gudjonsson, Murphy & Clare, 2000).

SUGGESTIBILITY AND RECOVERED MEMORY

Much has been written about the recovered memory in adulthood of childhood sexual abuse (Gudjonsson, 1997b; Loftus, 1993; Ofshe & Watters, 1994). Brown (1995) suggests that when false memories occur in psychotherapy they 'probably have much more to do with interrogatory suggestion that with hypnotic or postevent suggestion per se' (p. 11). Brown identifies four primary risk factors.

- High hypnotizability.
- Uncertainty about past events.
- Evidence of 'interrogatory suggestive influence'.
- Social influences from people outside the psychotherapy context (e.g. peer, family, self-help groups).

According to Brown's theory, persons who score high on interrogative suggestibility should be particularly vulnerable to produce false memories related to childhood sexual abuse. I have argued elsewhere that this does appear to be the case (Gudjonsson, 1997c). Recovered memory cases I had come across in clinical practice appeared to involve people who were reasonably bright, had good memories and were not unduly suggestible. Similarly, in a study of 23 children claiming previous-life memories, which has some parallels to the false memory phenomenon, Haraldsson (1995) found these children to have better verbal memory and to perform better academically than a control group of their contemporaries. Haraldsson used the GSS 2 and found no significant differences between the two groups in terms of interrogative suggestibility.

Leavitt (1997) has provided data to show that 44 female psychiatric patients who claimed to have experienced recovered memories were less suggestible on the GSS 2 than other comparable psychiatric patients ($N = 31$). The immediate and delayed memory scores of the two groups were similar, but significant differences were found between the groups on Yield 1, Shift and Total Suggestibility.

The findings call into question the assumptions that interrogative suggestibility is a key factor in facilitating or creating false memories of childhood sexual abuse during psychotherapy.

I have argued elsewhere (Gudjonsson, 1997c) that of greater importance than interrogative suggestibility in cases of false memories, whether memories of childhood sexual abuse or previous-life experiences, may be the ability of children and adults to respond 'imaginatively' to stress and psychological problems. Haraldsson found that the previous-life memory children had more disturbed relationships with their parents than the controls. I found among the British False Memory Society members that relationship problems were the most common stressor precipitating the accusations (Gudjonsson, 1997b). False beliefs and memories of childhood sexual abuse may be largely internally generated, even if they are triggered and facilitated by outside stimuli (e.g. media, discussions with others), rather than being the result of heightened interrogative suggestibility.

CONCLUSIONS

In this chapter I have reviewed the psychometric and testing aspects of interrogative suggestibility and compliance, and validation data. The evidence presented indicates that interrogative suggestibility can be reliably and validly measured. The GSS 1 and GSS 2 are based on a theoretically sound suggestibility construct and the scoring can be objectively quantified. The advantage of these tests is that they involve the person being subjected to 'interrogation' under experimental conditions and the answers are recorded in a standardized way. This overcomes self-report bias, which may be a problem when we have to rely exclusively on suspects' own account of their behaviour (Cooke & Carlin, 1998).

The scales have conceptual roots in both the legal notions of reliability of testimony and psychological notions of individual differences in susceptibility to suggestions. Both scales have satisfactory internal consistency and correlate highly with each other. They are parallel scales and can be used interchangeably. Extensive research has now been carried out on both the GSS 1 and GSS 2. Research into compliance, using the GCS, has been less extensive than the research into suggestibility, but evidence for the GCS's validity and the nature of its psychological components are growing. The most noticeable change during the past ten years in the research has been the growing number of researchers internationally who have used the GSS 1 and GSS 2 in their research. My colleagues and I carried out almost all the early work into the scales. This has now changed considerably, which is evident from the research reviewed in this chapter. One of the greatest impacts of the work has been the increased recognition of suggestibility as an individual difference variable (Schooler & Loftus, 1993).

There is now substantial evidence that there are at least two kinds of interrogative suggestibility, which are only modestly correlated. These are referred to in the chapter as Yield 1 and Shift respectively. Yield 1 measures the extent to which people give in to misleading questions, whereas Shift is more a measure of how people respond to interrogative pressure, which links it particularly to anxiety and coping processes. Shift seems more akin to the concept of compliance than Yield 1, because people are making a conscious decision to alter their answers in an attempt to improve their performance. Shift is less stable as a measure than Yield 1 and it is more susceptible to an experimenter effect. However, both Yield 1 and Shift have been shown to be fairly stable over time and are valid measures of interrogative suggestibility. Yield 2 is emerging, in its own right, as an important measure of psychological vulnerability. It should be incorporated routinely into the clinical, forensic and research applications of the scales. The most impressive findings relate to the ability of the scales to differentiate between defendants who allege that they made a false confession and those who made no self-incriminating admissions during police interrogation, and the finding that the GSS 1 differentiated successfully between coerced–internalized and other type of false confessor.

The GSS 1 and the GSS 2 have been used to test a number of hypotheses raised by the Gudjonsson–Clark (1986) theoretical model of interrogative suggestibility. A number of studies have supported hypotheses derived from the model. Interrogative suggestibility is apparently distinct from that found in a hypnotic context, although there is some recent evidence to suggest a certain overlap between the two types of suggestibility. Interrogative suggestibility correlates with a number of cognitive and personality measures, including those measuring intellectual functioning, memory, self-esteem, anxiety, assertiveness, locus of control and field dependence. Of particular importance seems to be the ability of the person to cope with the demands, expectations and pressures of the interrogative situation.

Yield 1 and Shift are distinct and reasonably independent types of suggestibility. They are both mediated by similar factors, such as cognitive variables (memory, intelligence), anxiety, social factors and coping skills. However, there is growing evidence that Yield 1 is *relatively* more related to cognitive variables, whereas Shift is *relatively* more related to interpersonal and social factors. Yield 2 is best construed as combination of Yield 1 and Shift and may therefore *at times* give the best overall picture of vulnerability. However, there are problems with the measurement of Yield 2 when subjects score at the top of the scale on Yield 1 (i.e. due to ceiling effect), as commonly happens with adults with learning disabilities.

Suggestibility is, to a certain extent, influenced by situational factors and experience. Mood variables, such as anger and suspiciousness, have been shown to markedly reduce peoples' susceptibility to suggestions and their willingness to comply with requests. Sleep deprivation is associated with increased suggestibility, particularly Shift. The type and nature of instructions given prior to the interrogation, such as those related to expectations about performance, can also influence suggestibility in a given situation. Warning people prior to testing that the questions may be misleading does reduce the tendency of people to give in to leading questions. The manner in which the scales are administered, and particularly how the negative feedback procedure is carried out, does influence the scores. For these reasons it is important that the scales are administered in accordance with the instructions given in the manual. The GCS is much less of a problem with regard to administration, because it functions like a straightforward questionnaire.

Of the three measures—suggestibility, compliance and acquiescence—compliance is least related to intellectual skills and acquiescence the most. Suggestibility is clearly principally related to memory and information processing, personality and situational factors. In contrast, compliance is clearly mediated by personality factors, such as social conformity, anxiety proneness, low self-esteem and denial coping strategies. The concept and measurement of compliance are highly relevant to coerced–compliant types of confession.

One of the most difficult questions with regard to suggestibility relates to the extent to which one can generalize from a GSS test score to a trait concept of interrogative suggestibility. This is not a new issue, but nevertheless is a very important one, and will be taken up in the final chapter of this book, when all the evidence, theoretical, empirical and anecdotal, has been assessed.

CHAPTER 15

The Effects of Drugs and Alcohol upon the Reliability of Testimony

Suspects may be interviewed by the police while under the influence of alcohol or drugs, or when they are experiencing severe withdrawal symptoms from these substances while in custody. What is not known is how common a problem this is and what effects it may have on the reliability of statements obtained during interviews in police custody. What we do know is that defence counsels sometimes challenge the validity of confessions obtained while suspects are intoxicated or withdrawing from alcohol or drugs (Clark, 1991; Davison & Forshaw, 1993; Davison & Gossop, 1996, 1999). This could be on the basis that drug addicts, particularly those withdrawing from heroin, are not fit for interview while in that state, or even if they were technically fit for interview, it is either unfair or unsafe to rely on their answers (Gudjonsson, Hayes & Rowlands, 2000).

There are good grounds for raising concerns about the effects of drug withdrawal on the validity of answers given by drug addicts when questioned in custody. For example, in Chapter 3 it was shown how police detainees' claims of having consumed illicit substances during the 24 hours preceding their arrest was the single best psychological variable that predicted the likelihood of a confession being made in interview. Although we do not know whether any of these confessions were false confessions, the research highlights the importance of drug withdrawal as a factor that motivates some drug addicts to make a confession. One way of interpreting such findings is that drug withdrawal leads to mental states that limit the drug addict's ability for rational thinking and autonomy (Davison & Forshaw, 1993). Under such circumstances their confession will need to be treated with caution. Less has been written about the possible effects of alcohol withdrawal symptoms on the validity of suspects' accounts during interviewing. Some new research findings will be presented, which also raise concerns about some alcoholics' ability to cope with interrogative pressure while withdrawing from alcohol.

The main focus of this chapter is on two important questions in relation to confession evidence. First, how commonly are intoxication and withdrawal symptoms from drugs or alcohol found among persons detained in police custody? Second, what effects do drugs and alcohol intoxication and withdrawal have on the reliability of answers given during questioning? The research that has been carried out in this area has relied largely on studying the effects of drugs and alcohol on interrogative suggestibility. The tests used have been the GSS 1 and the GSS 2.

Even though the focus in this chapter is on suspects, much of what will be discussed is also relevant to reliability of statements made by witnesses and victims.

THE EXTENT OF THE PROBLEM

The extent to which witnesses, victims and suspects are interviewed by the police while under the influence of drugs or alcohol, or whilst withdrawing from such substances, is not known. Undoubtedly, great variability exists across different countries as well as between regions within a given country. A small number of studies have been conducted in this area and these will be reviewed before discussing the likely effects of drugs and/or alcohol intoxication on the validity of suspects' accounts of events.

Robertson (1992), on behalf of the Royal Commission on Criminal Justice, examined the role of 'police surgeons' (more recently referred to as forensic medical examiners or FMEs). He found that the majority of the work of FMEs involves attending to physical illness and injury (59%), followed by drunkenness (10%), drugs (9%) and mental illness (9%). Interestingly, drunkenness was far by the most common reason for finding suspects unfit for interview and comprised 61% of all decisions concerning unfitness. The advice most commonly given by the FME was that the suspect should be left to sober up for between four and six hours before an interview was commenced. No discussion or recommendations were offered in relation to alcohol withdrawal symptoms. In this study, one in six (17%) of detainees referred to the FME for drug related problems were considered to be unfit for interview, but, unlike the case with alcohol, no specific recommendations were given by the FMEs as to when the drug addict might be fit for interview. Taking a cautious approach, Robertson commented:

> It is considered that the validity of statements by drug addicts will *always* be open to question simply by virtue of the fact of their addiction (p. 39).

In a further but similar study, Robertson, Gibb and Pearson (1995) observed all detainees at seven London police stations. None of the detainees were interviewed by the researchers. There was a continuous 24 hour cover at each police station over a period of three weeks. The data collection took a total of six months. This research is important because it focused on detainees' drunkenness on arrival at the police station, their mental state and their behaviour at the police station. There were a total of 2947 custody records opened during the period of the study, which represented 2617 individuals. The detainees were divided into four groups according to level of impaired consciousness due to intoxication at the time of their arrival at the police station:

- group 1, 'not drunk';
- group 2, 'not fully alert' (i.e. diagnosed as drunk but showed little disturbance in their level of alertness);
- group 3, 'definite impairment' (e.g. slurred speech);
- group 4, 'major impairment' (i.e. needed help with walking).

Out of a total of 2708 detainees observed where a diagnosis of intoxication could be made, 590 (22%) arrived at the police station intoxicated. One-third and one-fifth of these fell into groups 3 and 4 as exhibiting 'definite impairment' and 'major impairment', respectively. These findings suggest that overall about 5% of the number of detainees are suffering from a 'major impairment' when they arrive at the police station and a further 8% exhibit a 'definite impairment', giving a total of 13%. The great majority (88%) of those in group 4 had been arrested for a drunkenness offence alone and these persons were rarely interviewed by the police or charged with an offence.

Drunkenness on reception was found to be significantly related with expressions of hostility and physical violence in the custody area, to the ethnicity of the detainee (i.e. Caucasians of Scottish or Irish background were over-represented), to drunkenness and public disorder offences, dirty physical appearance, premature aging, age of the detainee (i.e. the drunk detainees tended to be older than the other detainees) and the length of time it took for the detainee to be interviewed (i.e. being intoxicated delayed the time it took for them to be interviewed by the police).

As far as the police interviews were concerned, only 818 (30%) were interviewed by the police. The remaining 70% of detainees were either at the police station because of their bail conditions or they were not interviewed in view of the nature of their offence (not all suspects arrested by the police for criminal offences are interviewed by the police). Out of the 818 detainees, only 49 (6%) were considered to have been drunk on reception at the police station. Furthermore, only 16 (2%) were considered to have been moderately or very drunk. This negative relationship between arriving at the police station intoxicated and not being interviewed was due to the large number of intoxicated people who had been arrested for drunkenness alone and were never interviewed by the police (i.e. they were almost always cautioned rather than charged). What the study tells us is that, as far as seven London police stations are concerned, it is very rare for detainees who arrive drunk at the police station to be interviewed in connection with a criminal offence.

Do these findings suggest that we do not have to have to be concerned about alcohol intoxication and withdrawal symptoms? There are at least three reasons for concern. First, alcohol intoxication (including the inhalation of vomit by drunk detainees) and drug poisoning are the single most common causes of death in police custody (Johnson, 1982). Second, the data from the seven London police stations may not be representative of police stations in other areas or other countries. Third, even if suspects who arrive heavily intoxicated at the police station are not commonly interviewed, when they are interviewed they may be disadvantaged in terms of their being able to cope satisfactorily with police questioning (Clark, 1991). Clark suggests that intoxicated detainees should not be interviewed if the blood alcohol level exceeds that set by the state as the legal limit for driving, which in England is 80 milligrams of alcohol in 100 millilitres of blood. If the detainee is very heavily intoxicated it may take more than 24 hours for the blood alcohol level to drop below the legal limit for driving.

The issue of alcohol withdrawal symptoms of alcoholics is a particular concern as will become evident later in this chapter. The Robertson–Gibb–Pearson (1995) study does not make any mention of withdrawal symptoms associated with alcohol. This is an area that is much neglected in the literature on police interviewing.

In the Royal Commission study by Gudjonsson et al. (1993) reported in Chapter 3, it was found that 22% of suspects detained in custody for interviewing admitted to having taken illicit drugs within 24 hours of arrest. Unfortunately, the type of illicit drug was not known.

A study by Payne-James, Dean and Keys (1994) found that about 11% of individuals seen by two forensic medical examiners (FMEs) at 11 police stations in Central and East London between 10 June and 25 September 1992 were drug addicts. Of the 11% of drug addicts in the study, 73% stated that they were registered drug addicts and 32% were being prescribed drugs (e.g. methadone) by their general practitioner or a drug agency. Heroin was the main drug used and was reported in 77% of the cases of drug addicts. Thirty per cent used both heroin and cocaine regularly. Crack cocaine, amphetamines and ecstasy were rarely used.

Pearson, Robertson and Gibb (2000), as an extension of their previous study (Robertson, Gibb & Pearson, 1995), investigated the proportion of police detainees who were identified as opiate users. Out of 2832 police detainees, only 115 (4%) were identified as opiate users, but the authors suggested that the actual number was likely to be much higher. Fewer than half (47%) disclosed their drug habit on reception at the seven police stations in the study. Seventy-five (65%) of the identified opiate users were seen by a forensic medical examiner and 14 were prescribed medication due to drug withdrawal. The authors stated:

> In relation to opiate users the main concerns are the reliability of confessions given in a withdrawal state or, to a lesser extent, by a prisoner under the influence of drugs. A detainee may fear further detention will lead to a subsequent withdrawal state and thus be more vulnerable to false confession in the belief that confession will lead to earlier release. There may be concerns that treatment given to relieve withdrawal may itself affect a detainee's ability to undergo questioning (p. 311).

THEORETICAL PERSPECTIVES

In recent years there have been important review articles published on the influence of drugs upon the reliability of answers given during police questioning and fitness for interview (Davison & Forshaw, 1993; Davison & Gossop, 1999; Gossop & Davison, 2000; Lader, 1999; Stark, 1994). The focus of these articles is primarily on the adverse effects of opiates and opiate withdrawal symptoms on the validity of detainees' accounts during questioning by the police and on the management of opiate addicts in police custody. These articles provide a useful conceptual framework for assessing the difficulties that can arise when opiate addicts are interviewed in custody.

Lader (1999) also provides a useful review article on the varied effects of drugs on the behaviour of potential witnesses. The focus in his article is on prescribed drugs, although the effects of illicit drugs and alcohol are also discussed. The limitations of this article are that it does not provide a good review of studies directly relevant to the management of drug addicts in police custody, and there is no discussion on the effects of withdrawal symptoms on the validity of witnesses' accounts.

According to Lader (1999), generally speaking, drugs will either increase nervous activity in the brain or decrease it. However, drugs, including alcohol and other sedatives, may produce a 'biphasic' response depending upon the dose consumed. For example, at low doses alcohol and tranquillizers will decrease inhibitory activity of the highest functions of the brain, which has the effect of increasing general brain activity, whereas at higher doses, the excitation of the brain is directly reduced and the person may become withdrawn and less active (e.g. alcohol consumption may initially make the person more open and talkative, but with increased intake of alcohol he or she may become withdrawn).

Lader (1999) lists the types of drug that he considers are relevant to the validity of testimony as follows.

- Drugs prescribed to treat psychiatric disorders. These include tranquillizers, sleeping tablets, antidepressants and antipsychotics.
- Drugs used to treat neurological disorders that have psychological side-effects (e.g. anticonvulsants and antiparkinsonian drugs).
- Drugs used to treat non-nervous disorders that in some cases may have psychological side-effects.
- Illicit drugs, which are used by drug addicts in non-medical contexts.
- Alcohol, which has sedative effects similar to that of tranquillizers.

According to Lader, the main drug-induced states that are relevant to testimony are *sedation, disinhibition, paradoxical reactions* and alterations in *concentration, memory* and *learning*. Paradoxical reactions do sometimes occur with drugs (i.e. these are reactions that are opposite to those normally expected). This includes, for example, increased anxiety, anger and violent outbursts, which is sometimes seen during alcohol intoxication. There is no mention by Lader of how alcohol and/or drugs may influence the person's suggestibility during interviewing.

Tranquillizers and other sedatives, except at the lowest doses, will impair cognitive functions, such as concentration, memory and learning, in normal individuals. Among highly anxious persons these cognitive functions are often already impaired due to the high level of anxiety, and a low to moderate dose of a sedative may reduce the level of anxiety to the extent that cognitive functions are improved. However, at high doses it is likely that the anxiety-relieving properties of the drug will not outweigh its direct depressant effects, thus leaving the person's cognitive impairment no better than it was, or even exacerbating it.

The other problem with some sedatives is that at a high dose they can produce a major memory distortion, including fantasy and false memory. For example, Dundee (1990) has discussed how some women heavily sedated with benzodiazepines, given intravenously, report false allegations of sexual assault. The study involved 41 incidents where women reported fantasies during sedation. Of these, 27 (66%) contained sexual elements, including allegations of sexual assault. Seven of the 41 cases led to litigation against the anaesthetist. All the women were certain of the authenticity of their accusations and their experiences were apparently vividly recalled. According to Dundee (1990), in many of these cases the assault could not have happened (e.g. others were present at the time, the assault as stated was not physically possible). Most happened during dental procedures, followed by oral endoscopy and induction of anaesthesia. A relationship has been found between the dosage of drug administered and frequency of complaints (Dundee, 1990). The main implication of this paper is that fantasies of sexual nature do occur during heavy sedation of benzodiazepines given intravenously, albeit infrequently.

The effects of prescribed drugs on the validity of answers given during interviewing has not been specifically studied. The effects of illicit drug intoxication have been investigated and the relevant studies will be reviewed in this chapter. There are a large number of different kinds of illicit drug. These include cannabis, LSD (lysergic acid diethylamine), heroin, cocaine, amphetamines, magic mushrooms and ecstasy. In addition, the inhaling of solvents sold in shops, such as glue, cleaning fluid and lighter fuel, can lead to dependence and brain damage. Concerns about the effects on the validity of statements obtained during questioning have mainly focused on heroin. It is highly addictive and causes severe withdrawal symptoms, including extreme physical discomfort and pain, irritability, anxiety and fear. Opiate withdrawal symptoms commence within 4–12 hours, peak at 48 hours and are alleviated after one week (Jones, 1997). Other illicit drugs may cause problems, such as anxiety, memory impairment, feelings of paranoia and withdrawal symptoms.

Davison and Forshaw (1993) argue that a confession obtained in the circumstances of opiate withdrawal may be open to doubt, because 'the associated mental states may prohibit rational behaviour' (p. 285). From this conceptual perspective, which was based on one case study, the emphasis is on how drugs adversely influence mental states, which in turn reduces the capacity of the individual for autonomy. Here the emphasis is not on impaired concentration and memory. Rather, the physical and emotional distress associated with the opiate withdrawal impairs the drug addict's ability to formulate and prioritize goals. The drug addict is preoccupied by the immediate short-term goal of stopping any further distress and is unable to consider the long-term consequences of his or her actions. This may involve their trying to expedite their release from custody by making ill considered self-incriminating admissions, which on occasions may be false. Davison and Forshaw argue that under such circumstances the drug addict lacks the capacity for autonomy and the confession he or she makes is likely to be unreliable unless the withdrawal symptoms are medically treated. This raises an important point. When drug addicts and alcoholics are experiencing severe withdrawal symptoms while in police custody, is it better for the validity of their answers during questioning that they are medically treated prior to their being interviewed? This would, of course, depend on the nature and severity of their withdrawal symptoms and the type and amount of prescribed medication. In cases of opiate dependence methadone would most commonly be used, and in the cases of alcohol dependence benzodiazepines (e.g. librium) may be used to alleviate anxiety and distress. If the withdrawal symptoms are severe then medication may assist the addict with coping with the police interview. However, some prescribed drugs in high doses do themselves impair cognitive functions such as concentration and memory, albeit reducing anxiety and distress (Lader, 1999). If the person is over-medicated then the beneficial effects of the medication may not outweigh the deleterious effects of the withdrawal symptoms.

THE EFFECTS OF INTOXICATION AND WITHDRAWAL

A small number of studies have been carried out into the effects of alcohol and drugs on the validity of answers given during questioning. While one of the studies (Sigurdsson & Gudjonsson, 1994) focused on prisoners' self-report of how alcohol and drugs affected them during police interviewing, the other five studies used experimental measures, including the GSS 1 or GSS 2, to measure psychological vulnerability during interviewing.

A Study of Prison Inmates

Sigurdsson and Gudjonsson (1994) investigated the effects of alcohol, drug intoxication and withdrawal symptoms on the mental state of criminal suspects and the nature of their confession. The study focused on 344 sentenced prisoners in Iceland. They all completed a revised version of the Gudjonsson Confession Questionnaire (GCQ), which asked them various questions about their confession and their mental state at the time of making the confession. There were also questions related to the influence of drugs and alcohol at the time of committing the crime and at the time of the police interview. A description of the revised GCQ is given in Chapter 6 and the questionnaire is provided in full in Appendix 1. The questions were answered on a seven point Likert scale. The lower end of the scale is labelled 'not at all' (scores 1 and 2) and the upper end as 'very much so' (scores 6 and 7). The label 'somewhat' indicated a range in between the other scores (scores 3, 4 and 5).

Table 15.1 shows the five questions from the questionnaire that focused specifically on the use of drugs and alcohol during the commission of the offence or when they were interviewed by the police. The answers were classified into the three groups given above (i.e. 'not at all', 'somewhat', 'very much so'). It is probably most meaningful to focus on the most extreme scores ('very much so'). Over half (51%) of the inmates claimed to have been very intoxicated at the time of committing the offence and 26% said they had been under the influence of other intoxicating substances. Here the type of offence is important. Property

Table 15.1. The percentage of offenders who reported being under the influence of alcohol or drugs while committing the offence and during the police interview ($N = 344$)

Question	'Not at all' %	'Somewhat' %	'Very much so' %
Were you under the influence of alcohol when you committed the offence?	36	13	51
Were you under the influence of other intoxicating substances during the offence?	67	7	26
Were you under the influence of alcohol during the police interview?	64	20	16
Were you under the influence of other intoxicating substances during the police interview?	78	10	12
Did you experience withdrawal symptoms during the police interview?	61	19	20

Adapted from Sigurdsson and Gudjonsson (1994).

and drug offenders were most commonly under the influence of drugs while committing the offences, while violent offenders and traffic violators (mainly drunk drivers) were more commonly intoxicated by alcohol.

As far as the police interviews are concerned, 36% of the inmates claimed to have been under the influence of alcohol during the police interview, with 16% claiming that this was 'very much so'. The corresponding figures for other intoxicating substances were 22 and 12%, respectively. The figures were even higher with regard to withdrawal symptoms during the police interview. A total of 39% claimed to have experienced some symptoms, and 20% stated that this was 'very much so'.

These figures suggest that, among this group of Icelandic offenders, many of them claimed to have been under the influence of drugs or alcohol when interviewed by the police, or were experiencing withdrawal symptoms. This being the case it is important to understand how these factors may have affected them during the police interviews. This was achieved by examining the factor structure of the GCQ (see Sigurdsson & Gudjonsson, 1994). One of the findings from the study was that alcohol intoxication, drug intoxication and withdrawal symptoms are associated with suspects feeling confused during interrogation, but they do not appear to be associated with anxiety or difficulties in coping with police interview. The same findings were found in an extension to the 1994 study (Gudjonsson & Sigurdsson, 1999). The main implication of these findings is that drugs and alcohol may impair suspects' ability to think clearly and may impair their capacity for rational decision making. Not being able to think clearly may make it difficult for some suspects to fully understand their legal rights and the questions asked, as well as not being able to articulate a coherent answer and appreciate the consequences of answers provided. The effects appeared to be similar for alcohol and illicit drugs. The authors concluded that it was not possible to say from their findings to what extent different drugs may have differential effects on suspects' mental state and the validity of their confession. The different effects according to the type of drug is an area that has recently been investigated by Brignall (1998), and her study will be reviewed later in this chapter.

It is important to be aware of the limitations of the study. First, the data were collected retrospectively and typically several months after the police interview. This was a subjective rating of their thoughts, feelings and behaviours at the time of the police interview. Since memory deteriorates over time it may affect the reliability of the findings, although the GCQ factors are reliably recorded over time (Gudjonsson & Sigurdsson, 1999). The second limitation is that very few of the inmates reported the use of opiates or other hard drugs. The most common drugs taken were cannabis and cocaine. Thirdly, a factor not investigated in the study, but was shown in Chapter 3 to be important in the decision to confess, is the desire and motivation of drug addicts to expedite their release from custody. Their desire to obtain more drugs to avoid the distress of drug withdrawal is undoubtedly a powerful motive to get out of the police station as quickly as possible, which results in their focusing exclusively on the short-term consequences of their behaviour (i.e. being released from custody).

Studies into the Effects of Opiates

Two studies have specifically examined the effects of opiates on suggestibility and compliance. In both studies opiate-dependent in-patients from drug dependency units were used as subjects. Whereas the first study (Davison & Gossop, 1996) makes a within-group comparison, the second study (Murakami, Edelman & Davis, 1996), involves a between-group comparison.

Davison and Gossop (1996) employed as subjects consecutive patients admitted to the in-patient Drug Dependency Unit at the Bethlem Royal Hospital for detoxification between the period October 1991 and March 1992. This was the first study to examine the suggestibility and compliance of opiate addicts while under the influence of psychoactive drugs, during withdrawal and when drug free. The patients were assessed at three time periods: (a) while on opiates and before detoxification during a three day initial Unit assessment; (b) during detoxification and at the height of opiate withdrawal (i.e. between 10 and 14 days of the onset of withdrawal) and (c) after the drug withdrawal symptoms had abated and the subject was drug free (about 28 days after the first day of withdrawal). The subjects completed the GSS 1 during the first and third interview, and the GSS 2 during the second interview. All subjects completed the GCS, the Spielberger State Anxiety Inventory and a Withdrawal Problems Scale during each of the three interviews. All the patients were dependent on opiates and of these 20 were also benzodiazepine dependent. In order to help the patients cope with the withdrawal symptoms they were prescribed methadone. The patients were subsequently gradually detoxified from methadone over 10 days.

It was hypothesized that during drug withdrawal the patients would show increased anxiety and impaired ability to cope with pressure, both of which would be reflected in increased suggestibility.

Forty-three subjects completed the first interview, 29 (67%) of these the second and 19 (44%) the final interview. No significant differences were found on the three occasions between any of the suggestibility or compliance scores. The total suggestibility scores on the three occasions tested were 8.2, 8.2 and 6.5, respectively. The immediate recall scores on the GSS 1 were 17.2, 16.1 and 22.7, for the three time periods, respectively. The reason for the high score on the third testing undoubtedly relates to the GSS 1 having been administered about 28 days previously during the first interview and some residual memory may have existed from the previous testing Since only two forms of the GSS were available, the GSS 1 had to be administered on two occasions (i.e. during interviews 1 and 3). The GSS 2 was used during the second interview.

When the subjects in the study were divided into two groups on the basis of their median total suggestibility score (i.e. below 7 and equal to or greater than 8) on first testing, a significant difference emerged. Those drug addicts who were high on suggestibility during first testing, when still under the influence of opiates, were significantly less suggestible when tested drug free at the third interview. In contrast, those drug addicts who scored low on suggestibility on first testing showed no significant change in suggestibility when drug free. These findings suggest that there may be at least two different effects of opiates on interrogative suggestibility. This points to the importance of individual differences in drug addicts' reactions to opiates.

Davison and Gossop (1996) pointed out that their findings were consistent with those of Sigurdsson and Gudjonsson (1994) in suggesting that drug and alcohol intoxication or withdrawal did not cause participants to be unduly anxious, nor impair their ability to cope with the police interview. The main limitations of this study include the high drop-out rate, the possible contamination of the treatment medication (i.e. methadone), familiarity with the suggestibility procedure on subsequent testing and the long delay (10–14 days) between the first and second testing sessions. The reason for the 10–14 days withdrawal period, according to the authors, was that it is when methadone withdrawal symptoms are most severe. This suggests that there may have been possible contamination between opiate and methadone withdrawal during the second testing session. Since untreated opiate withdrawal symptoms peak at 48 hours (Jones, 1997), this study may not give a clear idea of how vulnerable suspects are within the first 48 hours in custody. It also raises important issues, as it did in the cases of Carol Richardson (see Chapter 17), about the effects of methadone on suspects' vulnerabilities while in police custody.

Murakami, Edelman and Davis (1996) also studied interrogative suggestibility among opiate users admitted for a methadone detoxification programme in a psychiatric facility. Two patient groups were compared. The first group consisted of 21 patients (14 males and seven females) who were actively withdrawing from opiates (i.e. on the second day of admission and before they had become stabilized on methadone). The second group consisted of 19 patients (13 males and six females) who were in the early stages of rehabilitation from opiate dependence. At the time of testing they had not taken opiates or other illicit drugs for at least two weeks. They were not currently suffering from acute withdrawal symptoms. The two groups were referred to as the 'detox' and 'rehab' groups, respectively. They were matched for IQ and a number of drug-related demographic variables. During the study all subjects completed the GSS 1, the GCS, the Hudson Index of Self-Esteem (Hudson, 1982) and the Spielberger State–Trait Anxiety Inventory (Spielberger, 1983). It was hypothesized that 'due to increased anxiety, compliance, lower self-esteem and other physical disturbance associated with opiate withdrawal syndrome, suggestibility would be higher during active withdrawal than when the person is abstinent' (p. 1367).

The data were analysed using t-tests for independent samples. The 'detox' group had a significantly higher total suggestibility score than the 'rehab' group, the mean scores being 12.2 and 9.1, respectively. State anxiety was also higher among the 'detox' group, which may explain the differences in the suggestibility scores between the two groups. The possible interaction between suggestibility and anxiety was not tested in the study. The immediate and delayed recall scores on the GSS 1 were very similar for the two groups, which suggests that acute withdrawal symptoms from opiates do not impair memory recall. A similar finding was noted in the Davison–Gossop (1996) study.

No significant differences were found for compliance. The GCS scores for the 'detox' and 'rehab' groups were 10.2 and 9.8, respectively. Again, this is consistent with the findings from the Davison–Gossop study and demonstrates that the GCS, unlike the GSS 1 and GSS 2, is not a good instrument for measuring transitory changes in behaviour.

There are important differences between the two studies discussed in this section. Probably the most crucial difference is that in the Davison–Gossop study testing took place at the peak of methadone withdrawal (i.e. between 10 and 14 days after the onset of withdrawal from opiates), whereas in the Murakami–Edelman–Davis (1996) study the GSS 1 was administered prior to the patients being stabilized on methadone. The Murakami–Edelman–Davis study may therefore give a clearer picture of the direct effects of acute opiate withdrawal on suggestibility than was obtained in the Davison–Gossop study and, as the authors argue, is more akin to that found in police custody.

The main advantage with the Davison–Gossop study is that it involved a within-group comparison in contrast to a between-group comparison. It is possible that the 'rehab' group in the Murakami–Edelman–Davis study was not an ideal control group. For example, they had a longer history of opiate abuse than the 'detox' group and were more actively involved in criminal activities. We do not know how important these factors were in influencing differences between the two groups of subjects in terms of suggestibility. The problem with this kind of research is the large number of patients who drop out of treatment. A good control group is therefore probably impossible to obtain. The high drop-out rate was also noted in the Davison–Gossop study.

The Differential Effects of Drugs on Interrogative Suggestibility

Different drugs may have differential effects on suggestibility, but empirical research in this area is lacking. In an undergraduate project at University College, London, Brignall (1998) compared the acute and residual effects of amphetamine and MDMA (ecstasy) on mood, memory and interrogative suggestibility using the GSS (only Yield 1 was measured). The participants were recruited in a nightclub setting and tested in a small quiet room away from the dance floor. Four days later the participants were re-tested at their home.

The data was analysed by the use of repeated analysis measures of variance (ANOVA) on all the psychological variables, with day (1 or 5) as the within subjects factor, and group (ecstasy, amphetamine or control) as a between subjects factor. As far as the GSS scores are concerned there were two significant findings. First, the memory scores differed significantly between the three groups, with the amphetamine group having by far the lowest memory scores on both occasions they were tested. The author explains this finding by the fact that the three groups differed markedly in their level of education, with only about one-quarter of the amphetamine group having attended university, in contrast to 86% of ecstasy users. This is an interesting finding in itself, because it suggests that different educational backgrounds are associated with the types of illicit drug taken as well as the abstinence from taking illicit drugs.

The second significant finding with regard to the GSS was that, whereas the mean Yield 1 suggestibility score was decreased on repeated testing for the ecstasy group, the reverse pattern was found for the amphetamine group. In other words, the participants who were under the influence of amphetamine on day one were less suggestible on that day than they were on day five, whereas participants who had consumed ecstasy were more suggestible on day one than on day five. This is an interesting finding and suggests possible differential effects of individual drugs on suggestibility.

When interpreting the findings it is important to consider the conditions under which the participants were tested. All participants were tested in one of two nightclubs. This has the advantage of being an environment in which both ecstasy and amphetamine are commonly taken, but there were two potential problems identified by the author about this setting. These relate to the fact the participants may have been tired when tested, and the participants, apart from one in the control group, had also taken cannabis that night. As far as alcohol was concerned over 60% of the participants in each group admitted to having consumed up to six units of alcohol more than four hours prior to the testing. According to the author, none of the participants were considered to be intoxicated at the time of testing. All participants reported similar and regular (most weekends or more often) use of cannabis and alcohol. Nevertheless, the potentially contaminating effects of cannabis and alcohol on the findings cannot be ruled out. The effects of cannabis on suggestibility are not known and await further research. Alcohol, as we shall see, has been found to reduce people's susceptibility to Yield 1 on the GSS (Santtila, Ekholm & Niemi, 1999).

The Effects of Alcohol Intoxication on Interrogative Suggestibility

The effects of alcohol on interrogative suggestibility have been investigated by Santtila and his colleagues in Finland (Santtila, Ekholm & Niemi, 1998, 1999; Santtila Alkiora, Ekholm & Neimi, 1999). They set out to investigate the effects of alcohol on interrogative suggestibility and to identify the mediating processes that underlined the effects observed. Considering the fact that many offenders commit offences when intoxicated and may be interviewed by the police while in an intoxicated state, these are important research objectives. Two competing hypotheses were formulated (Santtila, Ekholm & Niemi, 1999). First, it argued that alcohol would reduce anxiety and in turn increase resistance to leading questions and interrogative pressure (hypothesis 1). This hypothesis was formulated on the basis of two previous areas of work: (a) Gudjonsson (1988a) had found that anxiety is associated with increased suggestibility, therefore reducing anxiety would result in less suggestibility on testing, and (b) the Attention-Allocation Model (Steele & Josephs, 1988), suggested that alcohol reduces the level of anxiety in the individual concerned. The competing hypothesis was that alcohol has detrimental effects on cognitive abilities, and this in turn would impair discrepancy detection and increase suggestibility (hypothesis 2).

The study was experimental. Participants were given alcohol or a placebo and the effects were measured objectively on various psychological measures, including the GSS 2, the STAI (Spielberger, 1983), a shortened version of the Fear of Negative Evaluation (FNE; Watson & Friend, 1969), the Differential Emotions Scale (DES-IV; Izard, Libero, Putman & Haynes, 1993), an acquiescence scale (Winkler, Kanouse & Ware, 1982) and the Profile of Mood States (POMS: Lorr & McNair, 1980). All the instruments were translated into Finnish.

There were 51 participants (39 males and 12 females), who divided into four groups according to the amount of alcohol consumed. These were referred to as having 'high', 'medium' and 'low' levels of alcohol in the blood. The respective alcohol level in each of the three groups was 1.32, 0.66 and 0.132 ml of 95% alcohol per kilogram of body weight. There were 13 participants in the first two groups and 12 in the 'low' group. The control group consisted of 12 participants, who received a placebo drink containing no alcohol. The participants consumed the drink over a 20 minute period after the GSS 2 narrative had been read out to them.

The study shows that those who had consumed a 'low' level of alcohol or no alcohol were least suggestible. A MANOVA with the suggestibility variables revealed a significant main effect. Subsequent univariate analyses showed that high doses of alcohol were significantly associated with decreased Yield 1, Yield 2 and Total Suggestibility, whereas Shift was not significantly affected. State Anxiety and Clearheaded–Confused mood mediated the effects of alcohol on Yield 2. No other significant mediating effects were found. These findings supported hypothesis 1, although neither mood states nor anxiety explained all the mediating effects of the suggestibility scores (Santtila, Ekholm & Niemi, 1999).

In a separate article on the same data, Santtila, Ekholm and Niemi (1998) investigated whether emotional experiences and personality variables moderated the suggestibility-decreasing effect of alcohol. The subjects' scores on the acquiescence test, Fear of Negative Evaluation, Trait Anxiety and three subscales of the Differential Emotions Scale (DES-IV) were divided into two groups ('high' and 'low') by using the respective mean scores. Correlations were then provided between alcohol dose and the suggestibility scores separately for subjects with high and low values on the personality and emotional experience variables. The findings were in some respects difficult to interpret, but the most interesting finding was that alcohol led to significant decreases in suggestibility only in subjects scoring high on feelings of Anger and Guilt on the DES. The implication is that alcohol has greater effects on reducing suggestibility among persons who are prone to strong feelings of anger and guilt. Alcohol was also associated with decreases in suggestibility for subjects who scored low on Social Evaluative Anxiety and Trait Anxiety.

THE EFFECTS OF ALCOHOL WITHDRAWAL ON INTERROGATIVE SUGGESTIBILITY

The finding that alcohol intoxication decreases suggestibility is an interesting finding. However, not much is known about the effects of alcohol withdrawal on suggestibility and compliance. It would be expected that during severe alcohol withdrawal people would have problems coping with interrogation. This has been investigated recently in two studies of Icelandic alcoholics by Gudjonsson, Hannesdottir, Petursson and Tyrfingson (2000) and Gudjonsson, Hannesdottir, Petursson and Bjornsson (2002). In the first study Gudjonsson et al. (2000) attempted to test the hypothesis that alcoholics withdrawing from alcohol are more suggestible at the beginning of their alcohol withdrawal than towards the end of it. A group of 75 patients admitted as in-patients to a detoxification centre in Iceland completed measurements of Mini-Mental State Examination (MMSE), state and trait anxiety, suggestibility, memory, confabulation and compliance. The patients were randomly assigned to one of two groups: first, patients to be tested psychologically on the second or third day of their admission to hospital; second, patients who were to be assessed towards the end of their 10 day stay in hospital (i.e. after six or more days). Significant differences emerged between the two groups with regard to impaired cognitive abilities and heightened anxiety symptoms, but no differences were found for suggestibility, confabulation of compliance. However, a significantly larger Shift score on the Gudjonsson Suggestibility Scale was observed on the third day as an in-patient, as compared with that obtained on the second day of admission and for patients in group 2. The implication is that on the third day of detoxification patients become significantly less able to cope with interrogative pressure. This obviously has practical implications for police interviewing. Gudjonsson et al. (2000) suggested that an experimental study was needed to investigate the effects of alcohol withdrawal during the first week of hospital admission.

Gudjonsson et al. (2002a) extended the previous study in two ways. First, 127 admissions to the detoxification centre were tested psychologically from the second to the eighth day of admission. There were between 10 and 28 patients tested on each of the seven days, giving data for seven independent groups. Secondly, the psychological vulnerabilities of alcoholics who had stopped drinking were compared with those of the in-patients. These consisted of two control groups, which included 20 of the in-patients being re-assessed after they had been alcohol free for several months, and 27 ex-alcoholics who were attending groups run by Alcoholic Anonymous (AA). The same tests were used as

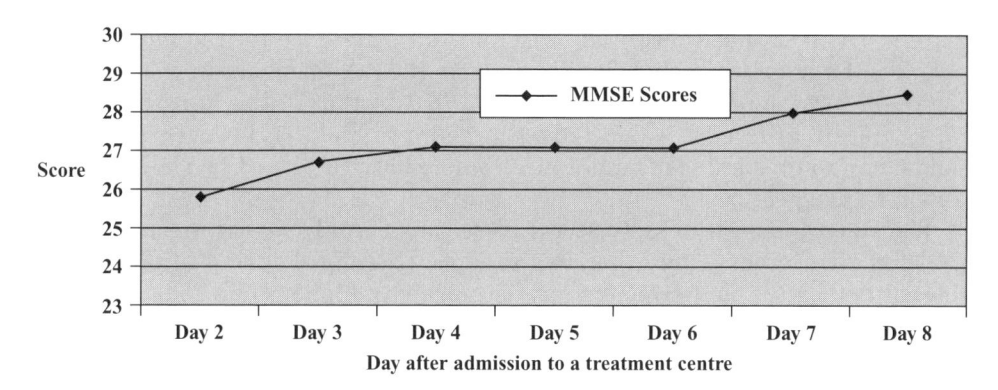

[Figure 15.1 chart: MMSE Scores by Day 2 through Day 8]

Figure 15.1. The Mini Mental State (MMSE) scores of the patients according to day after admission to a treatment centre

before, except that for the follow-up patients the GSS 2 was used since they had previously completed the GSS 1. Analysis of Variance (ANOVA) tests were performed on the scores for each test across the seven days. No significant differences emerged except on the Mini Mental State Examination Test (MMSE). On this test cognitive abilities improved steadily over the seven-day period (see Figure 15.1). The MMSE scores for the three groups indicated that the in-patients were cognitively impaired during their in-patient treatment. The scores for the follow-up patients and AA members are almost identical (28.9 and 28.8, respectively), whereas the score of the in-patients (27.0) is significantly lower than that of the other two groups. Therefore, during alcohol withdrawal cognitive abilities, including concentration, memory and new learning, are significantly impaired.

Figure 15.2 gives the Yield 1, Shift and Total Suggestibility scores for the 127 in-patients, 20 follow-up patients and 27 AA members. For the follow-up patients, all the suggestibility scores were significantly lower at follow-up in

[Figure 15.2 bar chart: Yield 1, Shift, Total Suggestibility scores — Inpatients: 4.8, 5.4, 10.2; Follow-up Patients: 3.0, 2.9, 5.9; AA Members: 4.6, 2.9, 7.5]

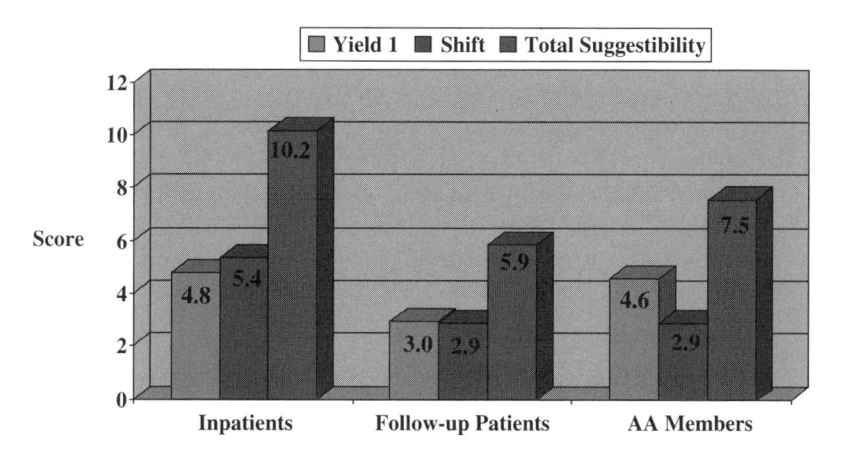

Figure 15.2. Suggestibility scores of in-patients, follow-up patients and AA members

spite of the fact that there was no significant difference in free memory recall. The findings were slightly different for the AA members in that the AA members have superior memory on the GSS 1 to that of the in-patients and no significant difference was noted with regard to Yield 1. However, as for the follow-up group, significant differences emerged with regard to Yield 2, Shift and Total Suggestibility.

The state and trait anxiety scores were considerably higher among the in-patients than among the other two groups. Therefore, during alcohol withdrawal both state and trait anxiety is markedly higher than it is once the individual has managed to stop drinking for a few months. This strongly suggests that alcohol withdrawal is associated with increased anxiety symptoms. Interestingly, both the state and trait anxiety scores are affected.

What can we make of these findings? The findings clearly indicate that persons who are in a state of alcohol withdrawal are psychologically vulnerable in that they are significantly cognitively impaired, their ability to cope with interrogative pressure is impaired and their state and trait anxiety scores are significantly elevated. There are of course marked individual differences, with the great majority of the participants having suggestibility scores that fell within normal limits (Gudjonsson et al., 2002a). What we do not know is how long after withdrawing from alcohol suggestibility returns to normal. The follow-up patients were re-tested between 7 and 14 months after their discharge from hospital, and the time the AA members had last consumed alcohol ranged between 4 and 17 months. By the time they were tested their level of suggestibility was well within normal limits. Indeed, the suggestibility scores of the follow-up patients and the AA members are similar to the British norms for the GSS 1 and GSS 2, whereas the scores obtained during alcohol withdrawal are highly elevated when compared with the British norms for the general population. For example, among the 127 in-patients in the Gudjonsson et al. (in press) study, 38 (30%) patients had a Shift score that exceeded 8, which falls in the fifth percentile rank for persons in the general population. In contrast, the Yield 1 score was very similar to that found in the British norms, and 13% of the in-patients had a Yield 2 score that exceeded the 95th percentile rank. What these findings tell us is that alcohol withdrawal most significantly impairs the ability of people to cope with interrogative pressure. When pressured during questioning almost one-third become abnormally suggestible with regard to Shift. This finding has implications for police interviewing. Are patients who are at the peak of their alcohol withdrawal fit to be interviewed by the police? Certainly, the findings suggest that many are potentially 'at risk' of giving misleading accounts to the police if pressured during questioning. However, issues about fitness to be interviewed and the 'reliability of testimony' are complicated and were discussed in Chapter 10.

FALSE CONFESSIONS TO MURDER BY A HEROIN ADDICT

In Chapter 3 it was shown that having taken illicit drugs 24 hours prior to being detained in custody was the single most important psychological variable which predicted the likelihood of a confession. Although the research did not suggest that these were false confessions, there is no doubt that, under certain circumstances, withdrawing from drugs or alcohol can result in suspects making a false confession to a serious crime, such as murder. The following case shows how this can happen. The case involved the murder of two elderly women who were living together at the time of their death, a false confession to the murders by a heroin addict, referred to as Mr D in this chapter, the apprehension of the real culprit after he murdered again and the subsequent withdrawal of the charges against Mr D.

At the time of his arrest, Mr D was in his early 20s and was living in a hostel. He had a history of learning disability and after leaving school he began to take illicit drugs. At first he only smoked cannabis, but later went on to consume heroin, which he had taken intravenously two or three times a day for about one year prior to his arrest. His normal routine was to obtain drugs after he got up every morning, which he financed by thieving. On the day of his arrest, which was several months after the murders of the two women, he had just got up and was getting ready to go out to obtain more heroin when the police arrived. He had last taken heroin early the previous evening (i.e. about 12 hours previously). Later that morning he was interviewed informally at a police station for over two hours. Mr D initially claimed that he could not remember his whereabouts on the day of the murder and blamed his poor memory on his drug taking at the time. At the end of the morning interview he was reported as becoming anxious and shaky, at which point he broke down, cried and confessed to the murders of the two women. After making a confession he was arrested and formally interviewed for over one hour during the early afternoon, an interview that was video-recorded. By this time Mr D had been without heroin for about 20 hours. Two hours after this interview terminated, Mr D was visited by a doctor at his own request, who prescribed him medication (methadone) for his withdrawal symptoms. According to the custody record, this medication was not given to Mr D until three hours later, during which time he was interviewed again, but this was not audio or video-recorded, and he gave a much more detailed confession than he had done during the video-recorded interview. Why should Mr D give a more detailed confession during the second formal interview? There are two alternative explanations for this. First, his memory of the murders had began to come back to him as he thought and talked about the offences. Second, Mr D had nothing to do with the murders and was able to use information communicated to him by the police to make the confession more detailed and apparently also more convincing. We now know that the second explanation is likely to be the correct one.

During the video-recorded interview he came across as being passive, acquiescent and compliant. The interview was quite leading and numerous suggestions and prompts were put to Mr D. He readily agreed with suggestions put to him and seemed vague and hesitant when asked open-ended questions. The impression he gave was that he did not have detailed knowledge about the murders and was just agreeing with what the police were suggesting to him.

A few weeks after Mr D's arrest another man was arrested in connection with other murders. He volunteered detailed admissions of the murders of the two elderly women in the presence of his solicitor. This included a great deal of special knowledge about the murders, which was more convincing than that obtained in Mr D's confessions. After spending several further months in custody, the charges against Mr D were withdrawn by the prosecution.

Why should Mr D have made a false confession to the police? I conducted a detailed psychological evaluation while Mr D was on remand, but before the charges against him were withdrawn. Mr D was significantly intellectually impaired (bottom 2% of the general population), was abnormally suggestible (98th percentile rank) on the GSS 2, his compliance score was highly elevated (90th percentile rank) and he had a strong tendency towards addiction and criminality (98th percentile rank) as measured by the Eysenck Personality Questionnaire (EPQ-R). His Psychoticism score on the EPQ-R was also highly elevated (90th percentile rank) and suggested personality problems. Therefore, in terms of his personality, Mr D was a vulnerable individual during questioning. In addition, his addiction to heroin, and the withdrawal symptoms he experienced during police detention, are of crucial importance in explaining his false confession. Mr D's own explanation to me for confessing falsely to the two murders was as follows.

- During the morning of informal questioning he was experiencing increased withdrawal symptoms. These included his feeling physically sick, his body was aching all over and he was experiencing shakes and a cold sweat.
- He was preoccupied with getting out of the police station so that he could get more heroin.
- The police told him that the sooner he confessed the sooner he would be allowed to leave the police station, even though he was not formally arrested until he had made the confession in the early afternoon of the day he was taken to the police station.
- He did not think about the long-term consequences of his making a confession to the murders.
- The police withheld his prescribed medication of methadone until after he had confessed during the video-recorded interview (Mr D alleged that he was seen by the doctor much earlier than is recorded on the custody record).
- The police fed him with information about the case and showed him a photograph of one of the dead women.

This case provides an insight into how a drug addict might make a serious false confession to the police. Perhaps the most striking feature of the case was Mr D's total preoccupation about the short-term consequences of his action (i.e. to terminate the withdrawal symptoms by obtaining more drugs), his impaired capacity for rational thinking (i.e. the belief that the police would release him if he confessed and the complete failure to consider the long-term consequences of his confession), his apparent belief in what the police were telling him and an inability to cope with the drug withdrawal and the pressure of police questioning.

CONCLUSIONS

Suspects are sometimes interviewed by the police while under the influence of alcohol and illicit drugs or while withdrawing from such substances. How often this happens undoubtedly varies across countries and between police stations. In England, suspects are commonly arrested and detained by the police while under the influence of alcohol and drugs. In such cases, forensic medical examiners (FMEs) are often called in to assess the detainee's fitness for interview. In cases of alcohol intoxication, the FME will normally recommend that the suspect be allowed to sober up for four to six hours before being interviewed. In cases of drugs, no such recommendation is usually made by the FME and the problems encountered when they are interviewed by the police are more likely to be in relation to drug withdrawal. Drug addicts are typically a more difficult group to assess than alcoholics, particularly with regard to intoxication.

Recent research has focused on the possible effects of alcohol and drugs on the validity of statements given by persons in police custody. In terms of its effects, a distinction must be made between *intoxication* and *withdrawal* from alcohol and drugs. It is also evident that there may be differential effects according to the type of drug consumed or being withdrawn from. For example, there is evidence that alcohol intoxication decreases suggestibility, at least with regard to being able to resist giving in to leading questions, whereas severe alcohol withdrawal leads to increased suggestibility, particularly with regard to impaired ability to cope with interrogative pressure. The main general effects of alcohol and drugs during interviewing appears to be related to the suspects' impaired ability to think clearly. The capacity for rational decision making may also be affected. The effects of prescribed drugs on the validity of answers given during interviewing has not been specifically studied. Tranquillizers and other sedatives, except at the lowest doses, will impair cognitive functions, such as concentration, memory and learning, in normal individuals.

As far as court cases are concerned, defence counsels are becoming increasingly aware that confessions made by opiate addicts while in police custody can be successfully challenged in court. The main concern of psychiatrists seems to be the apparently impaired capacity of drug addicts to make rational decisions during severe drug withdrawal (Davison & Forshaw, 1993). A case is presented that shows how a heroin addict made a false confession to two murders when interviewed during severe opiate withdrawal. Although each case must be considered on the basis of its merit, severe drug withdrawal from opiates should be viewed as a psychological vulnerability that does on occasions result in suspects making false confessions.

The effects of severe alcohol withdrawal symptoms may be similar to those of opiate withdrawal and caution should also be exercised when suspects are interviewed in such a state. As far as alcohol withdrawal is concerned, recent research indicates that there is an impaired ability to cope with interrogative pressure, which may under certain circumstances result in the person making a false confession. The limited current evidence is less clear with regard to drug withdrawal than alcohol withdrawal, although suggestibility does appear to be increased during opiate withdrawal, particularly among addicts who are already of a suggestible disposition.

PART III
BRITISH COURT OF APPEAL CASES

CHAPTER 16

The Court of Appeal

In England, Wales and Northern Ireland, after a trial has been completed there are 28 days in which the verdict can be appealed under Section 1 of the *Criminal Appeal Act 1968* (Walker, 1999c). There are two broad grounds for appeal (Taylor & Mansfield, 1999). First, it can be appealed on a point of law (i.e. that the judge made some procedural error, such as excluding evidence that should have been allowed), and second, on the basis of fresh evidence or argument. If the fresh evidence was available at the time of the trial then questions will be asked as to why it was not used. The explanations and reasons given may or may not be accepted. In other instances, and this applies to several of the cases included in following chapters, the fresh evidence was not available at the time of trial (e.g. new scientific developments). If the application for leave to appeal was not submitted within the 28 day period (occasionally applications 'out of time' are allowed), or if the appeal was not allowed or had failed, then, until 31 March 1997, applications in England and Wales had to be made to the Home Secretary and in Northern Ireland to the Secretary of State.

Since 31 March 1997, the functions of the Secretary of State in cases under appeal have been taken over by the Criminal Cases Review Commission (CCRC), which is an independent body investigating alleged miscarriages of justice in England, Wales and Northern Ireland (Leigh, 1997). It has no jurisdiction in Ireland, Scotland, the Channel Islands or the Isle of Man. The principal role of the Commission is to review the cases of people who claim that they were wrongly convicted or sentenced. The Commission can seek further information relating to a particular case and carry out its own inquiries or arrange for an investigation to be undertaken by others (e.g. a police force). In cases of disputed confession, the Commission may refer such cases to psychologists, psychiatrists and linguistic experts for advice or an assessment prior to deciding whether or not to refer the case to the Court of Appeal. The Commission refers a case to the Court of Appeal when it considers that there is a *real possibility* that the conviction or sentence will be considered unsafe on appeal.

James, Taylor and Walker (2000) provide a review of the work of the CCRC since its inauguration in April 1997. At the end of August 1999, over 2700 new applications had been received, of which 54 had been referred to the Court of Appeal. Out of 21 cases heard in the Court of Appeal, 14 (67%) were successful in terms of the conviction or sentenced being quashed, including the case of

Derek Bentley, whose conviction dating back to 1952 was quashed in July 1998 (*R. v. Bentley* [1999] Crim.L.R. 330). Interestingly, the Commission has the power, under Section 14 of the *Criminal Appeal Act 1995*, to investigate cases of miscarriages of justice without an application, but this has not happened yet (James, Taylor & Walker, 2000). The two main criticisms levelled against the Commission are shortages of resources to cope with the large number of cases and inability to finance their own independent investigations, and the subordinate role the Commission has to the Court of Appeal (James, Taylor & Walker, 2000; Taylor & Mansfield, 1999).

A Scottish Criminal Cases Review Commission was set up and commenced work in April 1999. It has more extensive powers than its English counterpart in terms of obtaining documents through an application to the court and being able to apply for warrants to compel people to give sworn statement before a sheriff (Duff, 2001). Recently the Scottish CCRC referred their first two disputed self-incriminating statement cases to the Court of Appeal, primarily because of fresh psychological evidence. These are the cases of George Beattie (Hill, Young & Sargant, 1985) and Raymond Gilmour (Walker, 1999a).

How many appeals against conviction are successful in the Court of Appeal? According to the figures given by Walker (1999b), for the 12 year period between 1985 and 1996, on average about 12% are successful in terms of convictions being quashed, the range being 9 to 16% for different years. The figure goes up to 13% if one takes into account the approximately 150 cases annually that are abandoned prior to appeal. Appeals against conviction from the Magistrates' Court, mainly to the Crown Court, are more successful, with 33% of cases in 1996 resulting in the conviction being quashed (Walker, 1999b).

In Table 16.1, I outline what I consider to be the leading cases of disputed confession appearing before the Court of Appeal in England and Northern Ireland since 1989, commencing with the landmark cases of the 'Guildford Four' and the 'Birmingham Six'. These are all murder cases, and some are also terrorist cases. All 22 cases involved an appeal against conviction. I am fortunate to have had the opportunity of being professionally involved, to a varying degree, in all the cases. In most of the cases I had assessed the appellants psychologically. In other cases my involvement was only minor. For example, in the case of Roberts I provided the clinical psychologist who had assessed the appellant with advice about how to interpret the GSS and GCS test scores and this is reflected in the judgment, and in the Carl Bridgewater case I provided the defence with a review for the appeal on scientific developments in relation to false confessions. In two of the cases (Kiszko & Darvell), I interviewed and assessed the appellants after their convictions had been overturned and they had been released.

I testified orally in the Court of Appeal in 10 of the 22 cases. In two further cases (Fletcher & Gordon) my reports were uncontested by the Crown and relied upon by the court in my absence. In the cases of MacKenzie and Miller I had testified at the original trial, but not at the appeal. In all but one of the 22 cases (95%) the convictions were quashed on appeal. The failed appeal of Donald Pendleton in 1999, and the subsequent quashing of the conviction by the House of Lords, is discussed in Chapter 20. There is one further recent case. On 15 January 2002, the conviction in 1974 of Stephen Downing for the murder of

Table 16.1. Some leading British court of appeal cases

	Name of case	Offence & year of conviction	Nature of relevant vulnerability	Year of appeal	Outcome
1.	'Guildford Four'	Terrorist offences, murder: 1975	See Chapter 17	1989	Conviction quashed; no retrial
2.	'Birmingham Six'	Terrorist offences, murder: 1975	See Chapter 17	1991	Conviction quashed; no retrial
3.	'Tottenham Three' (Engin Raghip)	Murder: 1987	Borderline IQ, suggestibility, compliance	1991	Conviction quashed; no retrial
4.	R. v. Kiszko	Murder: 1976	Hypogonadism, excessive fear of police, naivity, mental illness?	1992	Conviction quashed; no retrial
5.	R. v. Fletcher	Murder: 1988	Borderline IQ, undue feelings of guilt	1992	Conviction quashed; no retrial
6.	R. v. Ward	Terrorist offences, murder: 1974	Personality disorder, suggestibility, confabulation	1992	Conviction quashed; no retrial
7.	The Queen v Allen (Belfast)	Murder: 1986	Compliance	1992	Conviction quashed; no retrial
8.	R. v. MacKenzie	Manslaughter: 1990	Personality disorder, borderline IQ, suggestibility, compliance, serial confessor	1992	Conviction quashed; no retrial
9.	The Darvell Brothers	Murder: 1986	Borderline IQ, suggestibility	1992	Conviction quashed; no retrial
10.	R. v. Miller	Murder: 1990	Borderline IQ, suggestibility, compliance	1992	Conviction quashed; no retrial
11.	R. v. Ali	Murder: 1990	Borderline IQ, compliance, habitual lying	1994	Conviction quashed; retrial ordered
12.	R. v. Long	Murder: 1979	Depression	1995	Conviction quashed; no retrial
13.	The case of Carl Bridgewater	Murder: 1979	Not applicable (see Foot, 1998)	1997	Conviction quashed; no retrial
15.	The Queen v Kane (Belfast)	Murder: 1990	Borderline IQ, compliance, anxiety proneness	1997	Conviction quashed; no retrial
15.	R. v. Evans	Murder: 1973	Memory problems, confabulation, false internalized belief	1997	Conviction quashed; no retrial
16.	R. v. Bentley	Murder: 1952	Epilepsy, educational and behavioural problems	1998	Conviction quashed (posthumously)
17.	R. v. Roberts	Murder: 1983	Compliance	1998	Conviction quashed; no retrial
18.	R. v. King	Murder: 1986	Borderline IQ, suggestibility, compliance	1999	Conviction quashed; no retrial
19.	R. v. Hall	Murder: 1988	Personality disorder, compliance, impulsivity, habitual lying	1999	Conviction quashed; no retrial
20.	R. v. Pendleton	Murder: 1986	Suggestibility, compliance, acquiescence, anxiety proneness	2000	Appeal dismissed; convictions quashed by The House of Lords 13.12.2001
21.	The Queen v Gordon (Belfast)	Murder: 1953	Suggestibility, confabulation, sensitivity about sexuality	2000	Conviction quashed; no retrial
22.	R. v. Fell	Two counts of murder: 1985	Personality disorder, compliance, attention seeking	2001	Conviction quashed; no retrial

Wendy Sewell was quashed by the Court of Appeal in London. No reference was made to psychological or psychiatric evidence. It was the failure of the police to caution Mr Downing and provide him with a solicitor during eight hours of interrogation that was crucial in overturning his conviction (Boggan, 2002).

The English cases were all heard in the Royal Courts of Justice in the Strand, London, whereas the three Northern Ireland cases were heard in the Royal

Court of Justice in Belfast. There are no Scottish cases. The cases of the Guilford Four and the Birmingham Six, which were the groundbreaking cases in relation to coerced confession evidence, are discussed in Chapter 17. The cases that are of the greatest psychological and legal significance will be discussed in as much detail as is required to address all the relevant issues and implications. Other cases will only be discussed briefly. I have studied the legal judgments in all 22 cases and will provide extracts from the rulings as appropriate. The cases, and their most basic details, are provided in chronological order in Table 16.1.

In Chapters 17–20 most of the cases in Table 16.1 will be discussed. Cases are classified according to specific themes and presented in different chapters. The classification is principally based on the kinds of psychological issue that the cases raise (e.g. the psychological and psychiatric evidence in the cases of the Guildford Four & Birmingham Six; the admissibility of psychological evidence, its role and impact; the nature of internalized false confessions; problems with special knowledge and dangers associated with police misconduct and impropriety). There is an emphasis on the kinds of lesson that can be learned from the cases. The classification of cases into chapters is to a certain extent arbitrary in the sense that several of the cases involve more than one of the themes (e.g. several of the cases involve both psychological vulnerability and police impropriety).

THE BEGINNING OF EXPERT PSYCHOLOGICAL TESTIMONY

I first testified in a disputed confession case in January 1982 at the Central Criminal Court. Psychiatrists had been testifying in such cases prior to this (Gudjonsson & MacKeith, 1982) and other psychologists may also have done without my being aware of it. I subsequently testified increasingly in disputed confession cases at trial level, but this was mainly in relation to defendants with learning disability or IQ scores in the borderline range. The psychological evidence was generally heard during a *voire dire* in relation to the admissibility of the confession statement; gradually psychologists also began to testify before the jury with regard to psychological vulnerability when the confession statement had been ruled admissible. Here it was the weight of the confession statement and its reliability that the jury had to consider. In those early years judges were reluctant to accept evidence where there was no evidence of learning disability or mental illness. They appeared sceptical of psychological evidence and it was a hard fought battle over many years to overcome the resistance. During the mid- to late 1980s this gradually began to change. Important factors for this change in attitudes and practice were the development and publication of my original suggestibility scale in 1984, the research I was carrying out into false confessions with Dr MacKeith and lectures we gave on the topic to lawyers, and judges' increased understanding of psychological evidence and its role in challenging the reliability of confession statements. One important factor was undoubtedly the large number of cases arising out of the Tottenham riots in 1985, which were tried at the Central Criminal Court in 1986 and 1987. Many of the defendants were young and psychologically vulnerable individuals who had been subjected to great interrogative pressure by the police. As discussed in Chapter 18, my psychologist colleague Olive Tunstall and I testified in several of these cases. Testimony that addressed vulnerability in relation to personality (e.g. suggestibility, compliance, acquiescence) became accepted in the absence of learning disability and was presented before the jury. One of the Tottenham Riot defendants, Engin Raghip, appealed his conviction for the murder of a police officer. In 1988 the Court of Appeal refused Raghip and his two co-defendants leave to appeal and Lord Chief Justice Lane would not allow me to testify. In 1991 the Home Secretary referred the case back to the Court of Appeal and after listening to the psychological evidence Raghip's conviction was quashed, along with the convictions of his two co-defendants. No re-trial was ordered. The crucial evidence at the appeal was psychological evidence. The judgment in the case represented the most significant legal acceptance of psychological evidence and was to have far reaching consequences for the admissibility of expert psychological evidence in subsequent cases. The criteria for admitting psychological evidence were broadened, and for the first time the appellant court accepted personality factors, such as suggestibility, as being relevant to the legal issues in cases of disputed confessions. In view of the importance of the Tottenham Riot cases, and Raghip's case in particular, this development is discussed in detail in Chapter 18, after a discussion of the cases of the Guildford Four and Birmingham Six, which were landmark cases in their own right for different reasons.

CONCLUSIONS

Out of the 22 cases of disputed confession presented in Table 16.1, the convictions were overturned in 21 (95%) of them. Half of the cases were pre-PACE (i.e. the interrogation took place prior to January 1986). Two of the cases (Bentley & Gordon) date back to the early 1950s. The fact that half the cases were post-PACE demonstrates the fact that the introduction of PACE, with all its in-built protections for detainees, has still not entirely eliminated unreliable confessions and wrongful convictions. Perhaps the clearest example is the case of Miller (see Chapter 19), a psychologically vulnerable man whose denials and resistance were broken down by oppressive interrogation techniques in the presence of a solicitor.

As will become evident in the next four chapters, the importance of the psychological or psychiatric evaluation varied considerably across the cases. In the cases of the Guildford Four, and to a lesser extent in the Birmingham Six, the assessments that Dr MacKeith and I carried out assisted with getting the cases referred back to the Court of Appeal. Our assessments of the cases provided important insights into the confessions that eight of the appellants had made to the police in 1975. In one of the cases (Kiszko), no psychological or psychiatric evidence was presented at the appeal. It was the discovery of undisclosed scientific evidence relating to sperm heads that was crucial in establishing his innocence and overturning the conviction. Nevertheless, as shown in Chapter 20, the case is important in demonstrating the psychological factors that can result in a false confession being made. In the cases of Allen and Darvell, it was electrostatic detection apparatus (ESDA) evidence, which was the crucial evidence, although in the latter case psychological evidence was important in explaining to the Court of Appeal the reasons why Wayne Darvell had made a false confession. In 11 of the cases (Raghip, Ward, Ali, Long, Kane, Evans, Roberts, King, Hall, Gordon & Fell), the psychological or psychiatric evidence was the most important fresh evidence that resulted in the conviction being overturned. In the case of Bentley it was the testimony of a linguistic expert that the Court of Appeal found most helpful. In some of the remaining cases it was the combination of psychological and other evidence that contributed to the conviction being overturned.

The case of Evans is important, because it involved a voluntary confession of a man who had gradually convinced himself that he had committed a murder of a young girl he had seen in his sleep. No police coercion was involved. Psychogenic amnesia was subsequently misdiagnosed by doctors, and helped to convict Evans. The Court of Appeal accepted that the diagnosis of amnesia presented at trial was unsound, which implied that the confession was false and had resulted from a memory distrust syndrome, a condition first described by Gudjonsson and MacKeith (1982).

The cases of Raghip, Kiszko and King show that defendants' ability to resist suggestions in the witness box is sometimes used by the prosecution as evidence that they are not psychologically vulnerable. This seems an unfair testing ground in that if the defendant does not demonstrate evidence of suggestibility or compliance this can be used by the prosecution to undermine claims of his vulnerability during the police interviews; conversely, if the defendant is pressured in cross-examination and exhibits signs of suggestibility or compliance, this may result in self-incrimination, which may or may not be a true indication of guilt. I have seen a vulnerable defendant being pressured in the witness box by the prosecution, which resulted in his breaking down in the witness box and confessing to a murder. He had previously made a confession to the murder during police interrogation, which had been retracted. Under these circumstances a conviction seems inevitable, as indeed occurred in his case. Fifteen years later he is still proclaiming his innocence and is waiting for his case to be heard in the Court of Appeal in the near future.

The 'demand characteristics' and circumstances surrounding custodial interrogation and giving evidence in court and being cross-examined are not the same. Both are, of course, often highly stressful activities and require concentration and the ability to cope with pressure, but there are important differences and these may tap into different vulnerabilities. First, prior to giving evidence in court defendants have had time to think about their testimony, discuss it and prepare with their legal team and rehearse it in their mind. In spite of this they can, of course, make appalling witnesses and damage their own defence. Problems sometimes arise in court when defendants have little insight into their problems and make the mistake of appearing defensive, evasive, deceptive or arrogant. Second, at a police station suspects may be isolated from others who could provide them with social, emotional and moral support and it is more difficult to observe and control what goes on. Third, at the police station suspects experience considerable uncertainty, a situation that can cause them a great deal of stress (Gudjonsson et al., 1993).

There is no doubt from the judgments I have read in these 22 cases that post-admission details and apparent special knowledge often weigh very heavily against the accused at trial. An apparent intimate knowledge of the offence by suspects is very incriminating, and often rightly so. However, problems sometimes arise when too much emphasis is placed on pieces of special knowledge and it is assumed that only the real culprit could have possessed that knowledge, when in fact there could be a number of explanations for it apart from genuine guilt. The case of Mr Kiszko (Chapter 20) is a case in point. On the face of it, his apparent special knowledge was extremely convincing and incriminating, but we know now that it *must* have originated from the police. Even when there is absence of any knowledge about the offences and the confession is unconvincing, as it certainly was in the cases of MacKenzie and Fell, defendants are still convicted on the basis of their confession.

In several of the cases (e.g. MacKenzie, Kiszko, Darvell, Fell), the judges seem to have accepted the appellant's actual innocence and in other cases they were not satisfied of the appellant's actual innocence and expressed their reservations (Evans, King, Hall). Apparent special knowledge contained in the confession may have played an important part in their scepticism over the appellant's innocence.

The cases presented in this chapter have largely involved understanding the psychological vulnerabilities that cast doubts upon the reliability of the confession and the safety of the conviction. This has involved a psychological or psychiatric evaluation of the client, the findings of which have to be placed within the circumstances surrounding the confession, including the nature of the police interrogation, and the totality of the case. In the case of *Miller*, their Lordships found there to have been oppressive questioning, whereas in the remaining cases the legal issues centred on the reliability of the confession and the fairness of the interrogation and custodial detention (e.g. refusal to allow detainees to consult with a solicitor). In several of the cases there had been police impropriety, including falsifying records of the interview, failure to disclose crucial evidence favourable to the defence, failure to allow access to a solicitor, and coercive police interrogation tactics. What does the psychological assessment of appellants tell us about the characteristics of individuals whose convictions were quashed? Why did they make a confession that was not reliable and undoubtedly, in several of the cases, false?

In terms of psychological vulnerability, the cases presented in the following four chapters are potentially biased in that most of the appeals were successful because of the fact that the appellant had been found to be vulnerable to giving unreliable confessions. However, it is interesting to note that not all the appellants showed poor intellectual function. None of the appellants who had been tested had IQ scores that clearly fell in the learning disability range (i.e. an IQ score below 70). Therefore, their IQ scores alone do not seem to differentiate them greatly from police detainees. Nevertheless, according to the judgments, the borderline IQ score among several of the appellants was important in overturning a conviction, particularly when combined with other vulnerable qualities, such as high suggestibility and compliance. The single most common abnormal score on psychometric testing was compliance, as measured by the GCS, followed by suggestibility, measured either by the GSS 1 or GSS 2. Abnormally high compliance was found in 15 out of the 18 cases where it was measured. In the remaining three cases the compliance scores ranged from four (*Ward*) to 14 (*Gordon*). In the great majority of the cases it was the inability to cope with interrogative pressure or the custodial confinement that resulted in their making a confession to the police. This is consistent with the great majority of the confessions being of the pressured–compliant type. In the cases of *Evans* and *Gordon* the confessions were of the internalized type.

In terms of psychological vulnerabilities relating to the cases discussed in this chapter, it is important to remember that the confessions appear to have resulted from a combination of factors and reasons. Each case has a different story to tell and each case must be considered on its own merit. A major problem with fully understanding some of the cases and why the confession was made is that the assessment was often carried out several years after the confessions were made, during which time the mental state and personality of the individual may have markedly changed, as it undoubtedly did in the case of Long and probably also in some of the other cases. No direct assessment of Bentley could be carried out, as he was executed in 1953.

How important are threats and inducements in eliciting unreliable confessions? In most of the cases presented in the following chapters appellants made allegations that threats and/or inducements had been present during the custodial detention. The threats, which could be either explicit or implicit, were of physical violence, continued and lengthy interrogation, and custody. Inducements most commonly included an offer of bail, and suggestions that reduced responsibility for the crime. Whereas threats and inducements are clearly unacceptable on legal grounds, robust police questioning, including appropriate challenges and confrontation, does not necessarily undermine the reliability of a confession.

CHAPTER 17

The 'Guildford Four' and the 'Birmingham Six'

GISLI H. GUDJONSSON AND J. A. C. MACKEITH

The cases of the Guildford Four and the Birmingham Six have been described in newspapers as the worst miscarriages of justice in England last century. The two cases date back to 1975 when 10 individuals, nine Irish men and one English woman, were convicted and sentenced to life imprisonment for terrorist offences. Eight of the 10 individuals had made self-incriminating statements during custodial interrogation, which were subsequently retracted. All claimed to be innocent of the charges brought against them and more than a decade later their convictions were eventually quashed by the Court of Appeal. In this chapter we describe the background and circumstances to these cases, as well as some of the results of our own involvement in the medical, psychiatric and psychological assessment of the people concerned.

THE GUILDFORD FOUR

On 5 October 1974, members of the Irish Republican Army (IRA) planted bombs in two public houses in Guildford, Surrey: the Horse and Groom and the Seven Stars. No warning was given. The bomb in the Horse and Groom exploded at about 8.50 p.m. Five people were killed instantaneously and a further 57 were injured. At 9.25 p.m. there was a massive explosion at the Seven Stars. Fortunately, it had been evacuated by all customers following the explosion in the Horse and Groom. Some injuries were caused to the landlord and his bar staff, who had failed to find the bomb during a search of the premises. The explosions caused public outrage and some 150 detectives were drafted into Guildford to work on the case.

At 10.17 p.m. on 7 November 1974, almost five weeks after the Guildford explosions, an IRA bomb exploded at the King's Arms in Woolwich, South London. Unlike the two time bombs in Guildford, the bomb exploded after being thrown into the public house from outside. Two people died and a further 27 were injured. The Woolwich bomb was the sixth during that same autumn on mainland Britain and resulted in growing pressure on the police to apprehend the IRA Active Service Unit responsible (McKee & Franey, 1988; Victory, 2002).

On 28 November 1974, Paul Hill, a young Irishman, was arrested in Southampton. He was taken to Guildford Police Station and interviewed. Within 24 hours he had made a written confession about his involvement in the Guildford bombings and implicated his friend Gerry Conlon. Conlon was arrested in Belfast on 30 November and brought to Guildford for questioning. He confessed within two days and implicated a number of people, including Paddy Armstrong and Carole Richardson. Armstrong and Richardson were arrested on 3 December 1974, and within 48 hours they had also made serious self-incriminating admissions. A large number of other people were arrested in connection with the Guildford bombing case. Eight people were initially charged with the bombings. Of these, only four made confessions, Hill, Conlon, Armstrong and Richardson. All four had been denied any access to a solicitor for several days through the newly introduced Prevention of Terrorism Act. The charges against the remaining four defendants were dropped prior to the trial of the Guildford Four in September 1975.

On 16 September 1975, the trial of the Guildford Four opened at the Central Criminal Court. All four were charged with the Guildford bombings and five murders. Hill and Armstrong were in addition charged with the Woolwich bombing and the two murders arising from it. The prosecution argued that Hill, Conlon and Armstrong were all members of the IRA, but no evidence was ever produced to support this claim. Richardson was Armstrong's 17-year-old English girlfriend. There was no identification or forensic evidence ever produced to link them with the bombings. The prosecution relied almost exclusively on the confession statements that the four had made during the interrogation. There was highly circumstantial evidence produced at the trial in the case of Armstrong, which consisted of a Smith pocket-watch found in a flat where Armstrong had previously stayed for a fortnight and a testimony from a fellow squatter of Armstrong's (McKee & Franey, 1988).

The defence of the Four consisted of challenging the admissibility and reliability of the confession statements and alibi witnesses were produced to show that the defendants had all been elsewhere at the time of the bombings. The Four maintained that the confessions were not obtained voluntarily and were the result of pressure and coercion. The police completely denied impropriety of any kind. During the trial it was revealed that there were over 140 inconsistencies and inaccuracies between the statements of the four defendants. For example, Richardson said that she had been responsible for bombing both of Guildford's public houses. The police's own time plans showed that the persons who bombed the Horse and Groom could not have planted the bomb in the Seven Stars. Richardson also claimed to have thrown a bomb, which was incompatible with the prosecution case. The prosecution argued that the inconsistencies and inaccuracies in the statements were deliberate counter-interrogation ploys, the object being to confuse the police. It was a far-fetched speculation. The truth was that the inconsistencies and inaccuracies were caused by the lack of knowledge the defendants had about the bombings, because they were in no way involved.

The alibi evidence produced by the defendants was very mixed. Conlon's alibi was that he was in a hostel at Quex Road, London, on 5 October 1974. He named people whom he said could give evidence about his whereabouts on that day. The prosecution were in possession of one statement that amounted to verification of his alibi but failed to disclose it to the defence. Conlon was not implicated in relation to the Woolwich Bombing and therefore only had to provide an alibi for 5 October 1974.

Armstrong had an alibi that he was in a 'squat' on that night, during which time people were arrested by the police outside the squat. Witnesses testified to having observed that event, but no evidence was provided by the police to confirm that such an incident had taken place on 5 October 1974. Armstrong also had an alibi for 7 November 1974, the night of the Woolwich Bombing. That alibi was not seriously challenged in court because his confession to the police had only amounted to going on a reconnaissance trip on an unspecified date prior to the bombing. That made him a party to the bombing as a principal in the second degree, which was sufficient to attract a conviction.

Hill gave evidence for both the Guildford and Woolwich bombings. In relation to 5 October 1974, his alibi was that he was in Southampton with his girlfriend, Gina Clark. That alibi was discredited when Hill withdrew it in the presence of Gina Clark at the time he was being interrogated by the police, but it was subsequently reasserted by him at the trial. His alibi for 7 November 1974 was that at the time of the Woolwich Bombing he was visiting his aunt and uncle. There was an independent witness to his visit, which Hill had forgotten about. For some unknown reason, although present at the Old Bailey, she was not required to give evidence at the trial.

Richardson did not need to give any alibi for 7 November 1974. Her alibi evidence concerning the 5 October 1974 was by far the most compelling, because it was clearly established that between 7.30 and 8.30 on the evening of 5 October she was at the South Bank Polytechnic attending a 'Jack the Lad' concert. Indeed, there was a photograph available of her posing with the band. Stretching the crucial times to their limits, the prosecution maintained that Miss Richardson could have travelled from South West London to Guildford, which was almost 40 miles away, and planted the bomb there before returning to South London about 50 minutes later. A police driver, who ignored the speed limit, claimed to have made the journey in about 45 minutes. This was used by the prosecution to argue that Richardson might have just had enough time to have been to Guildford.

The all-male jury took 27 hours to reach their unanimous verdict of 'guilty' on all charges. All four were sentenced to life imprisonment with the following recommendations for the minimum sentence served: not less than 30 years for Conlon, not less than 35 years for Armstrong and Hill was never to be released. Because of her young age no minimum recommendation was made for Richardson.

At the end of October 1975 the Guildford Four began to serve their life sentences and were to remain in prison until 19 October 1989, when their convictions were quashed by the Court of Appeal. They were free at last, after spending more than 15 years in prison for crimes they did not commit.

The fight for the release of the Guildford Four began soon after their conviction in 1975. Their eventual release was due to the combined effort of many individuals. However, the four defendants would probably still be in prison had it not been for Alastair Logan, who from the beginning believed in their innocence and worked almost continuously on the case unpaid for over a decade. He was originally Paddy Armstrong's solicitor and for a while represented all four defendants. Later Hill and Conlon were to be represented by other solicitors. The two have told their own stories (Conlon, 1990; Hill & Bennett, 1990).

Following the so-called 'Balcombe Street Siege' in December 1975, where four IRA terrorists were arrested, two of them admitted to the police that they had carried out the Woolwich bombings and stated that Hill and Armstrong had nothing to do with it. The Director of Public Prosecutions was soon informed about this revelation but the solicitors of Hill and Armstrong were not informed and no official action was taken (McKee & Franey, 1988). The four defendants of the Balcombe Street Active Service Unit were tried at the Central Criminal Court in January 1977, but refused to plead on the basis that they had not been charged with the Guildford and Woolwich bombings, for which they claimed responsibility in addition to the other charges.

Before their conviction, Alastair Logan interviewed the four Balcombe Street defendants and another convicted terrorist and obtained testimony from four of them stating that they had carried out the Woolwich bombing. Two of them admitted to both the Guildford and Woolwich bombings. Furthermore, they stated that, to their knowledge, the four young people convicted of the bombings were totally innocent. This new evidence was presented at the appeal hearing of the Guildford Four in October 1977. The appeal failed and the convictions were upheld.

In 1987 a delegation lead by Cardinal Hume was pressing the Home Secretary to look at the case again, with particular reference to some new evidence concerning Carole Richardson's mental state at the time of her confession in 1974 (Victory, 2002). The delegation was supported by two former Home Secretaries and two distinguished law lords. On 16 January 1989, the Home Secretary announced in the House of Commons that the case of the Guildford Four was to be referred back to the Court of Appeal. The reasons given were related to new alibi evidence for two of the Guildford Four and questions over the mental state of Carole Richardson at the time of her interrogation in December 1974 (Ford & Tendler, 1989). A date for the Court of Appeal hearing was subsequently set for January 1990. That date was brought forward to 9 October 1989.

The Avon and Somerset Police, who were appointed by the Home Secretary in 1987 to look at the confessions of the Guildford Four, discovered from the archives at the Surrey Police Headquarters that crucial evidence concerning the confessions of Hill and Armstrong had been fabricated. The Director of Public Prosecutions responded by requesting that the convictions of the four be quashed by the Court of Appeal. Lord Chief Justice Lane and his two co-judges (Justices Glidewell & Farquharson) had no alternative but to concede that the police officers 'had lied' at the trial of the Guildford Four. The convictions of the Four were accordingly quashed.

Medical and Psychological Evidence

Except for the dubious circumstantial evidence in the case of Paddy Armstrong, the only evidence against the Guildford Four was their confessions. Alastair Logan soon realized that the reliability of the confessions had to be challenged. This led to employing experts, such as psychologists and psychiatrists. The first expert to become involved was Dr Tooley, a consultant psychiatrist at the London Hospital.

On 8 October 1975, after a day in court, Armstrong was given a barbiturate-aided interview by Dr Tooley. The intention was not to enhance Armstrong's recollection about events in 1974; the drug was used on the assumption that Armstrong would be more likely to tell the truth whilst under the influence of the drug. The information obtained confirmed Armstrong's previous accounts of the police interviews and his state of mind at the time.

The assumption that Armstrong could not have lied whilst under the influence of the drug, had he so wished, was ill founded in view of the poor validity of barbiturate-aided interviews as a 'truth drug' (see Chapter 8 in Gudjonsson, 1992a, for a detailed discussion on this point).

On 1 October 1977 Armstrong was interviewed in Wakefield Prison by Lionel Haward, a Professor in Clinical Psychology at the University of Surrey, Guildford. Professor Haward induced in Armstrong a light hypnotic trance and interviewed him about his involvement in the Guildford and Woolwich bombings. The purpose of the hypnosis-aided interview was similar to that of Dr Tooley. Haward asked Armstrong in detail about his experience and knowledge of firearms. Haward had previously been an armament instructor in the Royal Air Force (RAF) and concluded that Armstrong had no experience of firearms and that he was an unlikely IRA candidate. Furthermore, Professor Haward concluded from Armstrong's answers during the hypnosis that he had falsely confessed because of immense anxiety and fear of the police.

Before the appeal of the Guildford Four in 1977, Alastair Logan asked Barrie Irving, a social psychologist who had provided evidence at the inquiry into the Maxwell Confait Case, to comment on Armstrong's confession statements. He did not examine Armstrong but carefully examined the relevant documents in the case. Irving highlighted a number of concerns about Armstrong's confession, which related to his poor physical and mental state at the time of the interrogation, and concluded that Armstrong's confession should not have been accepted without corroboration.

What was the 'new' medical evidence that resulted in the Home Secretary re-opening the case in January 1988? This related to the mental state of Carole Richardson in December 1974 and questions over medication she was said to have received from a police surgeon who had been called to examine her prior to her confession. We had examined Richardson in April 1986 at Styal Prison at the request of the Prison Medical Service. A medical officer was very concerned about her welfare. He believed her to be innocent of the terrorist offences of which she was convicted and wanted an independent assessment conducted. The issue of false confession was relevant to his concern about appropriate psychiatric treatment of Richardson.

During our first interview with Richardson (there were to be further meetings) we spent about five hours with her. Richardson's demeanour was impressive. She looked pleased to see us when we arrived though she was not expecting us. During the next five hours she appeared to try hard to answer our questions. We kept firing difficult questions at her but all her answers were spontaneous and seemed unguarded. Her vulnerable qualities were also evident. She proved to be articulate and intelligent (her IQ score was above average). Although psychiatrically well at the time of our interview, she was very vulnerable to interrogative pressure and this was clearly evident on psychological testing. Further testing repeatedly demonstrated her tendency to avoid conflict and confrontation when faced with pressure. Our concern was also about Richardson's mental state whilst in police custody in 1974, which included her state of withdrawal from illicit barbiturates on which she was dependant. We expressed great concern about the reliability of Richardson's confession in our reports to the Prison Medical Service.

However, in spite of the firm conclusions we had reached in our reports, the Home Secretary made no mention of them in his address to Parliament in January 1987, when he decided to remit the case of the Birmingham Six back to the Court of Appeal but refused to do the same for the Guildford Four. There was some strong media coverage about our findings and in August 1987 we submitted fresh reports directly to the Home Office with the permission of Mr Logan by whom we were then instructed. Our revised reports were partly the basis on which the Home Secretary decided to re-open the case. An important development was that a social worker colleague of ours, Don Steuart-Pownall, had been able to trace the whereabouts of the police surgeon, Dr Makos, who had examined Miss Richardson in police custody in December 1974. One of us (MacKeith) interviewed Dr Makos in Belgium in August 1987; he stated that he had injected Richardson with pethidine shortly before her first confession to him on 4 December. Several months later, when interviewed by the police for the second time, the doctor withdrew his revelation to Dr MacKeith, which had been repeated to the police during their first interview with him. In fact, whether or not the police surgeon had administered pethidine to Richardson, which she incidentally had no recollection of, may actually have been of no great significance. Even if he had not done so, she would have been suffering from barbiturate withdrawal at the time of her confession.

In fact, Richardson had been abusing various drugs for several months preceding her arrest on 3 December 1974. On the day of her arrest she had been taking Tuinal barbiturate tablets, which were obtained two days prior to her arrest. She reported to us that taking drugs alleviated thoughts and feelings that made her unhappy. She had made attempts to come off drugs but experienced a period of tremulousness, depression, physical weakness and restlessness.

Richardson's Confession

Carole Richardson was arrested at about 7.00 p.m. on 3 December 1974. She claimed to have taken about 20 Tuinal capsules that day. Her interrogation began the following day; the time at which it commenced is disputed. The police were questioning her about her whereabouts on 5 October (the time of the Guildford bombing) and during the day she appears to have become increasingly distressed. A police surgeon, Dr Makos, was called in to examine Richardson at about 8.15 p.m. In his company, and in the presence of a woman police constable, Richardson is alleged to have admitted to having planted the bomb in Guildford with Armstrong. Richardson has no recollection of having made the admission to Dr Makos, and indeed disputes having done so.

Richardson was to make a total of four statements to the police. Three were in her handwriting. The four statements were dated 4, 5, 6 and 9 December 1974. Richardson alleged that after her arrest she was preoccupied about getting out of the police station, because for days she was not allowed to notify anybody of her arrest and found the police pressure very difficult to cope with. She said she confessed falsely mainly out of fear. Various matters were suggested to her by the police, and some of the statements were dictated by the police, whereas others she knowingly invented to satisfy the police. Part of the problem was that the intense questioning by the police made her confused and she began to doubt her own recollections (e.g. where she had been on the day of the Guildford bombing). She was not allowed to see a solicitor until 11 December and she then told him that she was innocent of the crimes she was accused of. On 12 December Richardson was interviewed at Guildford Police Station by two detectives from the Bomb Squad at New Scotland Yard. She again admitted her involvement in the Guildford bombings, although the interview appears not to have been in any way coercive. However, from Richardson's point of view, she did not want the police to re-interrogate her and went along with what she had told the police in her last statement.

Possibly the most interesting part of Richardson's reaction to the intense police interrogation relates to the extent to which she eventually began to believe that perhaps she had planted the bomb in Guildford without having any recollection of having done so. According to her own account to us, she initially confessed as a way of escaping from an intolerable situation. The police pressure was unbearable and she went along with the police interrogators, knowing that she had nothing to do with the explosions, or indeed with the IRA. After realizing that she was not going to be released, all she wanted was to be left alone, and this Richardson believed was the main reason for her false confession in conjunction with the fear she had of the police. It was not so much the interrogators' questions that bothered her but their attitude and apparent confidence about her involvement. After being allegedly hit by a police woman she realized that the police were in full control of the situation and that there was no point in resisting. At this point her confession was of the *pressured–compliant* type. That is, she knew she had nothing to do with the bombings but went along with the interrogators as a way of easing the pressure.

After several days in police custody Richardson began to believe that perhaps she had been involved in the Guildford bombing and was blocking it out from her memory. In other words, her alleged involvement in the Guildford bombings had become *internalized*. A decisive factor appears to have been the police officers' confidence in her involvement and the fact that she could not recall precisely where she had been on 5 October 1974. By this time she had become very confused; the 'memory distrust syndrome' had begun to set in. After having spent about two days in Brixton Prison on Remand, she felt the pressure easing off and she began to gain complete confidence in her own recollection of events, particularly with regard to her innocence.

Subsequent Developments

It was alleged in a *Panorama* programme in 1990 that at the trial of the Guildford Four in 1975 and at the appeal in 1977 the prosecution withheld from the defence crucial forensic and alibi evidence, which might very well have altered the outcome of the trial had it been known to the jury. The 'suppressed' forensic evidence linked the bombs that exploded in Guildford and Woolwich to several other bombs, which had exploded both before and after the Guildford and Woolwich bombs. It strongly indicated that all the bombs, 32 in total, had a 'common source of supply, information and expertise'. Furthermore, it pointed to the operation of a single IRA Unit operating on the mainland of Britain. Some of the members of this Unit were known to the police and had been identified through fingerprints that had been discovered on bombs that had failed to explode. These had no known associations with the Guildford Four. The remaining unidentified fingerprints were not those of the Guildford Four, nor were they ever questioned about the other bombings.

The other 'new' evidence allegedly suppressed by the prosecution relates to Gerry Conlon's alibi. He had always maintained that at the time of the Guildford bombings he was in a Roman Catholic hostel in Kilburn, London, which is over 30 miles away from Guildford. At his trial it was argued by the prosecution that Conlon's alibi lacked corroboration. In fact, according to the *Panorama* programme, two independent witnesses had corroborated his statements to the police, but crucial evidence from one witness was withheld from the defence by the prosecution.

THE BIRMINGHAM SIX

On 21 November 1974, two public houses in Birmingham were bombed by the IRA. Twenty-one people were killed. Later that same night four Irishmen (Gerry Hunter, Richard McIlkenny, William Power & John Walker) were stopped for questioning as they were boarding a ferry to Ireland. They were asked to accompany the police to Morecambe police station for forensic tests. They happened to mention that one of their friends (Patrick Hill) had been travelling with them. Hill, who had already boarded the ferry, was arrested. The five men were subjected to a Greiss test by Dr Frank Skuse, a Home Office scientist. The method, named after the chemist who discovered it, was at the time thought to be a foolproof way of detecting nitroglycerine, which is a substance commonly found on people's hands if they have been handling explosives. Nitroglycerine was allegedly found on the hands of two of the six men (Power & Hill). Dr Skuse told the police that he was 99% sure that two of the men had recently handled commercial explosives (Mullin, 1989). The five men were travelling together and they were all subjected to extreme pressure during the interrogations that were to follow (Mullin, 1989). The first to confess was Power. He signed a six-page confession, implicating himself and five of his friends in the Birmingham bombings. The sixth person, Hugh Callaghan, who was not travelling with the others at the time of their arrest, was arrested the following night at his home. Like McIlkenny, Power and Walker, Callaghan was to sign a confession to the Birmingham bombings. Two of the men (Hill & Hunter) did not write or sign any self-incriminating statements, but the police allege that they made some verbal admissions which both have always strongly denied that they ever made.

The six men were charged with the largest number of murders in British history and in June 1975 they were tried in Lancaster. The trial lasted 45 days. The evidence against the six men consisted of Dr Skuse's forensic evidence and the written confessions of four of the men. There was also circumstantial evidence about associations with known IRA people. The admissibility of the confessions was disputed by the defence on the basis that they had been beaten out of them. The judge allowed the confessions to go before the jury. All six defendants were convicted. As the Judge, Mr Justice Bridge, sentenced them to life imprisonment he stated

> You stand convicted on each of twenty-one counts, on the clearest and most overwhelming evidence I have ever heard, of the crime of murder (Mullin, 1989, p. 206).

As subsequent evidence indicated, the Birmingham Six defendants were wrongly convicted in 1975, in spite of the Judge's strong words about 'overwhelming evidence'. In the United Kingdom during the late 1980s new evidence was gathered and public feeling about the defendants' innocence grew. Various people argued for their innocence, including Christopher Mullin, a Member of Parliament. Sixteen years were to pass before the Appeal Court eventually quashed the convictions of the six men.

On 28 October 1985, *World in Action*, a Granada Television programme, presented evidence that seriously challenged, if not completely demolished, the validity of Dr Skuse's forensic science findings. The programme had commissioned two scientists to carry out a series of Greiss tests on a number of common substances, including nitrocellulose. The results showed that there are a number of common substances that will give a positive reaction on a Greiss test, including those that can be obtained from being in contact with playing cards. The five men who were tested for nitroglycerine had been playing cards shortly before their arrest, which could explain why two of them apparently had traces of nitroglycerine on their hands. In other words, the positive Greiss test reaction on the hands of two of the men could quite easily have been due to an innocent contamination.

Mullin (1989) claims to have traced and interviewed three of the men who are responsible for the Birmingham bombings. According to Mullin, they made it clear to him that none of the Birmingham Six were ever members of the Birmingham IRA, nor had they in any way been involved in the bombings for which they were convicted. The information that these people gave of the

Birmingham bombings suggested an apparent insightful knowledge about the explosions and supported the claim of the innocence of the six men convicted. In 1990 the Granada Television's *World In Action* programme named four men who were alleged to be the real bombers.

In October 1986 an ex-policeman, Tom Clarke, contacted Chris Mullin and told him that in 1974 he had been on night duty at Queen's Road police station during the two nights that the Birmingham Six were held there. Clarke (Mullin, 1989) gave an account of ill-treatment of the men during their period in custody, which included a dog handler encouraging a dog to bark throughout the night in an attempt to keep the six suspects awake.

In the autumn of 1987 the case of the Birmingham Six went to the Court of Appeal. The defence argued on two fronts: first, that the forensic evidence presented by Dr Skuse at the original trial was no longer valid; second, that the written confessions of the four men were unreliable and involuntary. Evidence to support this claim was given by Tom Clarke, the ex-police officer, and other witnesses. In January 1988, Lord Lane dismissed their appeal against conviction and stated:

> The longer this hearing has gone on, the more convinced this court has become that the verdict of the trial was correct.

On Thursday 14 March 1991, the Birmingham Six finally won their freedom. In March 1990 the Home Secretary had ordered a new enquiry into the case after representations from the men's solicitors where the forensic and police evidence was challenged. Following the Enquiry of Sir John May into the wrongful conviction in the Maguire Case (May, 1990), which was closely linked to the Guildford Four case, the credibility of the forensic science techniques used in the Birmingham Six case to test for traces of explosives was totally demolished. In August 1990 the Home Secretary referred the case back to the Court of Appeal after the police enquiry had quite independently found discrepancies in the police interview record of one of the men. It seemed, as in the Guildford Four case, that the police had fabricated documentary evidence against the six men. The Director of Public Prosecutions could no longer rely on either the forensic or the police evidence that convicted the six men in 1975. The appeal was heard by Lord Justices Lloyd, Mustill and Farquharson between 4 and 27 March 1991 and quashed the convictions of the six men (*R. v. McIlkenny, Hill, Power, Walker, Hunter and Callaghan*, [1991], 93 Cr.App.R 287).

Since their acquittal, two of the Birmingham Six have written their autobiographies (Callaghan & Mulready, 1993; Hill & Hunt, 1995).

The Psychological Findings

Considering that two of the six defendants did not make a written confession during the intensive interrogation in 1974, whereas four did, it would be interesting to look at their personality in terms of suggestibility and compliance. Thirteen years after their interrogation we had the opportunity in 1987 of assessing them, which included assessing their cognitive and personality

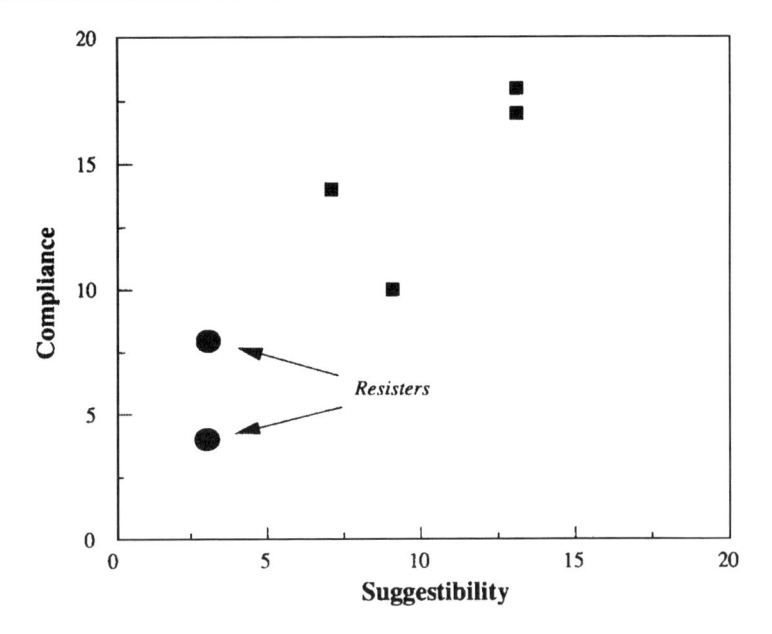

Figure 17.1. The suggestibility and compliance scores of the Birmingham appellants

functioning. The Gudjonsson Suggestibility Scales and the Gudjonsson Compliance Scale were administered to the six defendants whilst they were serving their sentence in prison. The GSS 1 and GCS scores are given in Figure 17.1.

It is clear from the graph that there is a great variability in the suggestibility and compliance scores among the six defendants. Two were very high on both measures and two scored very low. The remaining two defendants' scores fall in between the two pairs. In fact, their scores fall in the average range. It is of interest to note that the two defendants who scored lowest on the scales were the two defendants who did not confess. Hill's scores were particularly low.

The importance of the psychological findings is that they highlight immense variation in the suggestibility and compliance scores of the six prisoners, which appears to reflect whether or not they had made written confessions in 1974. The implications are that their relative suggestibility and compliance remained stable for over 13 years, and that their personality at the time influenced how they responded to the police interrogation 1974. Of course, nobody knows exactly what suggestibility and compliance scores they would have obtained had they been tested prior to their arrest in 1974. We had some behavioural ratings of compliance completed by relatives of the six men with regard to their behaviour prior to their arrest. The findings corresponded well with the men's self-report compliance scores.

The present analysis involves placing the men's psychological test scores retrospectively in the context of their behaviour in 1974. That is obviously different to being able to predict behaviour prospectively. One problem is the possibility that the behaviour itself (i.e. confessing) somehow influences how people subsequently perform on the psychological tests. This may be problematic, especially in the case of compliance as measured by the GCS, because it is a self-report inventory. Having previously given in to interrogative pressure (e.g. by confessing) this may itself alter their own perceptions of themselves. The change in their perception of themselves could then affect how they fill in the self-report scale. This is much less likely to be a problem on the Suggestibility Scales, because they measure how people respond *behaviourally* to a simulated interrogation and do not rely on self-report. However, this does not exclude the remote possibility that the shock of having confessed itself influences how they respond behaviourally to interrogation in the future.

The respective personality characteristics of the Birmingham Six were not considered relevant to the legal arguments in the Court of Appeal, because the emphasis was on the physical coerciveness of the police tactics used and on the unreliability of the forensic science evidence. The individual strengths and weaknesses of the six men are of interest because they possibly explain why four of the men confessed whilst two did not. It is also of interest to note that the IQ scores of the Birmingham Six were all within normal limits, the mean for the group being exactly 100.

CONCLUSIONS

Many people would argue that the cases of the Guildford Four and Birmingham Six represent the worst cases of miscarriage of justice in Britain last century. In the former case four defendants spent over 14 years in prison before having their convictions quashed by the Court of Appeal in October 1989. Almost one and a half years later the Birmingham Six had their convictions quashed, having spent about 16 years in prison.

There are certain similarities and differences between the cases of the Guildford Four and Birmingham Six. Both cases arose out of a devastating IRA bombing campaign on the mainland Britain in 1974. The police were under immense public pressure to apprehend the culprits and bring them to justice. Emergency laws were laid down in Parliament to deal with increased threats from terrorist activities, which allowed the police to detain people suspected of terrorist activities for extended periods without being charged. In both cases the police are alleged to have coerced the defendants to confess by subjecting them to psychological and physical pressure. Many years later, the police were discovered to have fabricated evidence concerning some of the defendants' interview records. Evidence favourable to the defence is alleged to have been suppressed by the prosecution when the cases went to court and at their appeal hearings.

All of the Guildford Four made written self-incriminating confessions, which they subsequently retracted and alleged that they were made under duress. Four of the Birmingham Six made written confessions; two did not. All of the Birmingham Six allege that they were extensively physically threatened and assaulted during their custodial interrogation in 1974; the Guildford Four have also made allegations of physical threats and assaults but of lesser severity than those reported by the Birmingham Six.

Whereas the 'Guildford Four' were convicted on the basis of uncorroborated confessions, there was forensic science evidence presented against two of the 'Birmingham Six': evidence that has subsequently been totally discredited.

In this chapter we have presented psychological data on one of the 'Guildford Four' (Richardson) and on all the 'Birmingham Six'. The most striking psychological finding regarding the 'Birmingham Six' is the difference in personality scores between the two defendants who did not confess and the four that did. Thirteen years after their interrogations, the two defendants who did not make written confessions scored exceptionally low on tests of suggestibility and compliance. We have argued that this may explain why they were able to resist extensive and coercive interrogations in 1974, whilst the remaining four, who were subjected to similarly intense questioning, confessed.

All of the ten defendants who made written self-incriminating confessions made confessions that are of the *pressured–compliant* type. However, there is some evidence provided from one of the 'Guildford Four' (Richardson) that 'saying may become believing', as Bem (1966) would describe it. That is, a *pressured–compliant* type of false confession may turn into a *pressured–internalized* type, given the right circumstances. The reason for this seems to be that after confessing for instrumental gains, the persistent questioning continues and the accused becomes increasingly confused and puzzled by the interrogators' apparent confidence in accused's guilt. In Richardson's case, she had problems recalling what she had been doing on the day of the Guildford bombing and kept asking for her diary, which had been left behind in the squat where she lived. It was only after the pressure of the police questioning ceased that she says she became totally convinced of her innocence. Conlon (1990) describes a similar, but less striking, example of having temporarily begun to doubt his innocence during the intense police interrogation.

CHAPTER 18

Psychological Vulnerability

In this chapter I shall focus on appellant cases that have had a significant bearing on the development of the criteria currently used for the admissibility of expert testimony in cases of disputed confessions. The 13 cases discussed in chronological order (Raghip, Fletcher, Ward, MacKenzie, Ali, Long, Kane, Evans, Roberts, King, Hall, Gordon & Fell) were all successfully appealed on the basis of psychological vulnerability.

It will be evident from reading this chapter that since the landmark decision in *Raghip*, there have been further legal developments that have set out more clearly the parameters and limits of expert psychological testimony. The general thrust of the criteria developed over the past 10 years has broadened the admissibility of expert testimony to include personality traits (e.g. suggestibility, compliance, anxiety proneness, poor self-esteem, impulsivity) that fall outside the normal range, but these must be of the type to render a confession potentially unreliable. Admissibility of expert testimony is no longer restricted to conditions of mental or psychiatric disorder, such as mental illness, learning disability or personality disorder.

ENGIN RAGHIP—THE BEGINNING: LANDMARK DECISION FOR PSYCHOLOGY

For the admissibility of psychological evidence in cases of disputed confessions, this is the single most important legal judgment. It broadened the criteria for the admissibility of psychological evidence and influenced subsequent court rulings. It will therefore be discussed in some detail and in the broader context of the 1985 'Tottenham riots'. In 1986 my psychology colleagues and I testified at the Central Criminal Court in several of the cases that arose out the 'Tottenham riots'. It was during these trials that psychological evidence came to be routinely admitted both during *voire dire* hearings and the trial proper. This was the beginning of psychological evidence being recognized and accepted in its own right in the lower courts. It was to be the build-up for a landmark decision in the case of Engin Raghip, one of three defendants convicted of murdering a police officer during the riots.

Background

On 6 October 1985, there was a major public disturbance on the Broadwater Farm Estate, Tottenham, North London. Several buildings and vehicles were damaged or destroyed by fire. Most tragically, a police officer, Keith Blakelock, was attacked by a mob of between 30 to 50 people and brutally murdered (*Burnham Report*, 1987). Several other police officers were injured. The riot was precipitated by the death, from a heart attack, of Mrs Cynthia Jarrett, after police officers entered her home in order to search it for stolen property following her son's arrest (Broadwater Farm Inquiry, 1986). About 100 people, mainly youngsters, gathered outside Tottenham Police Station to protest about Mrs Jarrett's death. The protest turned into a full-blown riot.

In the aftermath of the riot houses on the estate were raided by the police and many arrests were made. The police investigation was hampered by the fact that there was no forensic or other tangible evidence to assist in the Blakelock murder inquiry and the police began to rely on statements that were obtained from witnesses and suspects, many of whom were youths of limited education. There appears to have been a general feeling of antipathy towards the police and co-operation was not readily forthcoming from the people on the estate. This made the job of the police very difficult and the evidence that they were able to gather consisted almost entirely of uncorroborated confessions.

By May 1986, 359 people had been arrested in connection with the disturbance (Broadwater Farm Inquiry, 1986). Another ten people appear to have been arrested later, bringing the total figure up to 369. Seventy-one per cent were black and 25% were white. Eighteen per cent were juveniles (i.e. 17 or younger). Most detainees were denied access to a solicitor or their family, or waived their rights to a solicitor. Those detained were held 'incommunicado' and their family were not informed of where they were (Broadwater Farm Inquiry, 1986). One hundred and sixty-seven people (45%) were charged with offences arising out of the disturbance (Broadwater Farm Area Housing Committee, 1988). Of the 167 charged, 71 (43%) were charged with affray, riot, petrol bomb offences or murder. The remaining people were charged with such offences as looting, trespassing, burglary and handling stolen goods. Only three of the 71 defendants had a solicitor present at the time they made self-incriminating admissions. This is a very important finding, particularly in view of the fact that the Police and Criminal Evidence Act (PACE; Home Office, 1985a) was being introduced and implemented at the time. It illustrates how in high profile and difficult cases the police may actively discourage or prevent suspects from exercising their legal right to access to a solicitor.

According to the report produced by the Broadwater Farm Area Housing Committee (1988), out of the 71 most serious cases, 28% pleaded guilty. Of 49 defendants who pleaded not guilty (i.e. contested trials), 45% were convicted. Self-incriminating admissions or confessions were the *only* prosecution evidence presented in court in 76% of the disputed cases. This is an astonishingly high figure in comparison with findings from ordinary investigations (see Chapter 6). In the remaining cases some additional evidence was produced, such as witnesses and photographs. Therefore, one of the most striking features of the Tottenham riot trials was the reliance of the prosecution on confession evidence without any supportive evidence. The additional evidence produced by the prosecution was often very weak and appears to have had no significant effect upon the conviction rate.

As the police investigation into the riot was seriously hampered by lack of forensic or other tangible evidence, many arrests appear to have been made as a way of obtaining information and/or confessions. According to the police evidence in court (Broadwater Farm Area Housing Committee, 1988), every person arrested was a potential suspect to the murder of PC Blakelock and this, defence counsels argued in court, was used as a deliberate ploy by the police to enhance cooperation and compliance. It is not difficult to see how a potential murder charge could have softened up some suspects to the extent that they confessed to less serious crimes and implicated other people.

Certainly, any possible threat, whether explicit or implicit, of being charged with the murder of PC Blakelock is likely to have influenced the behaviour of many suspects during questioning. What we do not and never will know is how many of the cases involved untrue incrimination of self and others (i.e. there was also great pressure on suspects to implicate others). In the majority of cases (55%), the jury believed it was unsafe to convict on the evidence presented to the court. It is also of interest to note that, in every case involving affray, the judge refused a submission for a *voire dire* on the basis that it was for the jury to decide upon the weight of the confession evidence in these cases.

Psychological Evidence

At least 15 of the 71 defendants who faced the most serious charges out of the Tottenham riot were assessed psychologically. I personally assessed eight individuals for pre-trial defence court reports. I know of a further seven cases that were assessed by two other psychologists. One of the cases involved Engin Raghip, in whose case I was to become involved after his trial.

In two further cases mental illness had been diagnosed by psychiatrists. In all the eight cases that I assessed, the defendants alleged that they had been coerced into making a confession, believing that the interrogation would continue until they had confessed to something. According to the defendants' accounts, the confessions were all of the pressured–compliant type.

Out of the eight cases that I assessed for the defence, I gave oral evidence in four cases at the Central Criminal Court in front of the jury. All four defendants were charged with affray and were acquitted by a jury. Of the remaining cases, where I did not give oral evidence, three out of the four were convicted. It is tempting to speculate that the outcome of the eight cases is related to whether or not I testified in court. This is, of course, an indirect way of evaluating the impact of the psychological evidence before the jury, because in any one case there are a number of factors that determine the outcome, including the defendant's own testimony and any corroborating evidence that is available to support the prosecution or defence case.

In the cases where I testified, of what did the psychological evidence consist? The answer is that it varied in all four cases, but in all instances it was concerned with potentially challenging the reliability of the confession that the defendants had made during the police interrogation. It did not focus on the more technical issues such as the defendants' understanding of their legal rights (e.g. understanding of the police caution or the right to a solicitor).

The Full Scale IQs of the four defendants, as measured by the WAIS-R, were 65, 76, 78 and 93. Therefore, only one was functioning intellectually in the mental handicap (learning disability) range. Two were borderline. The defendant with the lowest IQ was the one who proved least suggestible and compliant on testing. The critical evidence in court was his low intellectual abilities, and this is what the defence focused on. The jury returned a not guilty verdict after four hours of deliberation. At the other extreme, the brightest defendant was most suggestible and compliant on testing. The prosecution objected to the admissibility of the psychological evidence because of the defendant's average intellectual functioning, but the judge nevertheless allowed it in evidence. The cross-examination of my evidence was most taxing in this case and lasted over three hours. Most of the cross-examination was spent on my going over the record of the police interviews. The defendant was acquitted by the jury in a matter of a few minutes. The remaining two cases, where the defendants were of borderline intellectual abilities, focused on their relatively low IQ and limited reading ability. In addition, high acquiescence and difficulties in understanding simple questions were focused on in one case; in the other it was the difficulty in coping with interrogative pressure (high 'Shift' on GSS 1 and GSS 2) that I was asked about in greatest detail.

The Murder Charges

Six defendants were charged with murder. Three were under the age of 17; that is, they were juveniles as far as the English judicial system is concerned. The charges against them with respect to murder were dismissed by the judge at their trial in January 1987. One of them had not confessed to the murder during interrogation; he was the only one of the six to be interviewed in the presence of a solicitor and also his father. The evidence against him was that of a witness who admitted in court during a *voire dire* that he had lied to the police. As a result the prosecution withdrew the charge of murder and the judge directed the jury to find him not guilty of murder. In the case of the second juvenile, the judge ruled during the trial that the police's behaviour during the interviews had been oppressive and the confession was unreliable. The jury was directed to find him not guilty. The third juvenile had his confession ruled inadmissible by the judge after a clinical psychologist (Olive Tunstall) found that he had not understood the police caution (Beaumont, 1987, 1988). The judge directed the jury, who had heard the expert evidence, to find the defendant not guilty.

The remaining three defendants, Winston Silcott, Mark Braithwaite and Engin Raghip, were tried and convicted of murder, riot and affray. Raghip's defence solicitors had instructed a clinical psychologist for a pre-trial report, but the psychologist did not trust the validity and reliability of his findings and the report was not used in court.

At the murder trial the case against Silcott was the weakest because he made no written or signed confession during the five interviews with the police in October, 1985, which were conducted over a period of two days. Furthermore, there was no evidence against him except for some alleged self-incriminating remarks, which he disputed were ever made. Nevertheless, Silcott was convicted and sentenced to life imprisonment, with the recommendation by the judge that he serve a minimum of 30 years.

Of the three, Braithwaite was the last one to be arrested. He was arrested on 4 February 1986. He was interviewed on 12 occasions and made self-incriminating admissions, which he subsequently retracted. No solicitor was present during the first eight interviews. During the sixth interview, which he had requested himself (apparently to relieve his feeling of claustrophobia when in the police cell), he admitted having hit a police officer twice with a bar, but did not think it was PC Blakelock. This was the most crucial admission. He was convicted because his admitted attack on a police officer, which the prosecution alleged was PC Blakelock, was seen as a joint or a common enterprise with a group of others, even if the blows given by Braithwaite did not kill the officer. Braithwaite was sentenced to life imprisonment with a recommendation that he serve a minimum of eight years. After his trial (in 1990) Braithwaite was interviewed and assessed psychologically by Dr Paul Salkovskis (now a Professor at the Institute of Psychiatry, King's College). Dr Salkovskis was satisfied that at the time of his police detention Braithwaite was suffering from a severe form of claustrophobia, accompanied by panic attacks, which rendered his self-incriminating admissions to the police unreliable (Rose, 1992). The striking feature in Braithwaite's interviews, similar to that seen in the case of Raghip, was the lack of recounted special knowledge relating to the murder of PC Blakelock.

For a detailed discussion of the murder of PC Blakelock and the trial of the three defendants, see Rose (1992).

The Case of Engin Raghip

Engin Raghip was one of the three people convicted of the murder of PC Blakelock. He was sentenced to life imprisonment, and like Braithwaite was given a recommended minimum of eight years to serve. He was arrested at his home at about 7.20 in the morning of 24 October 1985 and over the next five days he was interrogated on 10 separate occasions, which lasted a total of over 14 hours. On the third day of his detention Raghip was charged with affray and taken to a Magistrates' Court. He was remanded in custody for further interrogation, but the Magistrates ordered that he should be only interviewed further in the presence of a solicitor. This order was not followed by the police and Raghip subsequently made incriminating admissions concerning the murder. The case against Raghip on the murder charge rested entirely on contested evidence, which consisted of his admitting during interrogation that he had at the time of PC Blakelock's murder wanted to get close to the police officer so that he could hit him with a broom handle. He denied having had any intention of killing the police officer. In spite of Raghip never confessing to actually hitting the police officer he was convicted on the basis that the mob of which Raghip was part had a common purpose (i.e. to kill PC Blakelock).

Raghip was 19 years of age at the time of his arrest. His parents, who were Turkish, had come to England in 1955. Raghip was born and brought up in England. He had serious learning difficulties as child and remained illiterate. He was recommended for a special school but did not bother to attend regularly. At Raghip's trial in January 1987, two expert reports were available. One was a psychiatric report, where Raghip was described as being probably of average intelligence but dyslexic. The other report consisted of psychological testing, relating to Raghip's intelligence, reading ability and suggestibility. Raghip obtained a Full Scale IQ of 73 on the WAIS-R and had a reading age of six years and three months. He completed the GSS 1 and his scores were described as average. Neither the psychiatric or psychological reports were used at Raghip's original trial, because they were not entirely favourable to the defence. The psychologist appears to have played down the importance of Raghip's low IQ scores and expressed doubts about the validity of the scores. This appears to have been due to Raghip's average score on two of the Performance subtests. The psychologist concluded that Raghip suffered from limited educational experience rather than a true intellectual deficit.

After the trial and before an appeal was heard in December 1988, a new firm of solicitors represented Raghip. They referred the case to me because of my experience in assessing retracted confession cases. They requested an objective assessment of the reliability of Raghip's confession. I visited Raghip twice in Wormwood Scrubs Prison and carried out a comprehensive psychological assessment, which consisted of interviewing him in detail, in addition to testing his intelligence, reading ability, suggestibility, acquiescence, compliance, trait and state anxiety and self-esteem. I also interviewed Raghip's common-law wife, who was very helpful and insightful about her husband.

Whilst in prison Raghip had been tested on the WAIS-R by a prison psychologist. He obtained a Full Scale IQ of 74. The pattern of the scores was very similar to those obtained when Raghip was tested by the pre-trial defence psychologist eight months earlier.

The main results from my assessment were as follows: Raghip obtained a Verbal IQ of 74 and a Performance IQ of 76. His performance on one of the subtests (Picture Arrangement) fell in the 63rd percentile rank. The pattern of the subtest scores was remarkably similar to those found by the pre-trial and prison psychologists. He was also found to be illiterate. With regard to suggestibility, some interesting findings emerged on the GSS 1 and GSS 2, which were administered 11 days apart. On both tests Raghip scored low on Yield 1, but abnormally high on Yield 2 and Shift. In other words, his level of suggestibility was quite normal until he was placed under pressure, which was administered in the form of negative feedback. It was his inability to cope with interrogative pressure that was most striking. This pattern was consistent with a high (17) compliance score on the GCS. Raghip reported high trait and state anxiety, and in terms of self-esteem he rated himself as very timid and submissive.

There were three broad aspects to Raghip's case that I discussed in my report in relation to his retracted confession. First, there were the psychological findings, which highlighted some of his limitations and weaknesses. These included his borderline intellectual abilities, his marked literacy problems, his high level of anxiety and his marked responses to interrogative pressure.

Secondly, there were the circumstances of Raghip's arrest, interrogation and continued custody. Raghip was arrested by the police because a 'garrulous and silly friend' (his solicitor's phrase) mentioned his name whilst being interviewed by the police, after claiming to the *Daily Mirror* that he had seen PC Blakelock's murder. No other person mentioned Raghip's name, but he was nevertheless brought in for questioning. The intensity and duration of Raghip's interrogation, where he was interviewed without a solicitor or an 'appropriate adult' present, was undoubtedly very taxing. Indeed, on the third day, when Raghip was taken to the Magistrates' Court, he spoke briefly to a solicitor and told him that he could not cope with further interrogation. By this time he had already been charged with affray.

The solicitor has subsequently stated publicly that he found Raghip distressed and disorientated and did not think he was fit to be interviewed on the charge of murder. However, Raghip was to be further interviewed about being a party to the murder. After making self-incriminating admissions he was released on bail. He was re-arrested six weeks later and charged with the murder.

Thirdly, there was the question of Raghip's mental state at the time of the police interviews. For a few days prior to his arrest Raghip had been drinking heavily and smoking cannabis. He had not been sleeping well for several days, neither was he eating properly. Shortly before his arrest Raghip's common-law wife had left him, following an argument, and took with her their young baby. Raghip appeared to have been very upset about this. During Raghip's detention he complained of feeling ill and a police surgeon was called twice to examine him. The doctor found Raghip to have mild fever and enlarged neck glands. Raghip told the doctor that he was vomiting after meals. Therefore, at the time of his interrogation, Raghip was not physically or mentally well. These factors may well have exacerbated his existing vulnerabilities, such as his low IQ, high anxiety and difficulties in coping with interrogative pressure. It is also important that his self-incriminating admissions did not involve his having physically assaulted the officer. Raghip may therefore not have fully realized the potentially serious consequences of his admissions, particularly in view of his limited intellectual abilities (Clare & Gudjonsson, 1995).

Armed with the findings of my report, Raghip's solicitors asked for Leave to Appeal against his conviction. The case was heard in the Court of Appeal on 12 and 13 December 1988. The applications of Silcott and Braithwaite were heard at the same time. All three applications failed. At the hearing Lord Lane discussed my evidence in the context of the pre-trial defence reports, which were never used at the trial. The fact that the pre-trial psychologist had doubted the validity of his own findings was raised by Lord Lane. The psychologist's conclusion was:

> Unfortunately the very wide range of scaled scores from 3 to 10 scale score points, taken in context of Mr Raghip's personal and educational history, compels me to question the validity and reliability of the IQ figures obtained:

This in conjunction with the psychiatrist's opinion that Raghip was probably of average intelligence, but dyslexic, did not help Raghip's application for appeal.

The Appeal Court judges considered Raghip's IQ results in the context of the judgment in the case of *Masih*. As Raghip's IQ was above the 'magic' cut-off point of 69 the psychological evidence was not considered admissible. Furthermore, Lord Lane stated in his summing up:

> The jury had ample opportunity to gauge the degree of intelligence and susceptibility of Raghip when he gave evidence.

Another area of contention was the suggestibility scores of Raghip. The pre-trial psychologist had found Raghip's suggestibility to be average. When I tested him on two separate occasions, he was abnormally suggestible when placed under interrogative pressure. This raised a nagging question: 'What accounts for such marked discrepancies between the assessments?'. There was no indication in the pre-trial psychologist's report to indicate why this apparently suggestible young man had scored so low on the GSS 1 when he assessed him. As the psychologist had made no reference to the mental state of Raghip at the time of the assessment I contacted the psychologist and asked him to tell me about it. The psychologist replied 'He appeared angry and suspicious'.

Unfortunately, the psychologist had failed to mention this important observation in his report. Had he done so it would have been easy to explain the low suggestibility scores obtained, when placed in the context of existing work in this area (Gudjonsson, 1989a). There is no doubt that anger and suspiciousness reduces the ordinary person's susceptibility to suggestions.

In 1986 I was faced with an almost identical instance concerning another Tottenham riot defendant. He was very suspicious of me during the assessment, and proved non-suggestible on testing. Having recognized the importance of such negative mood on behaviour I gave him another appointment for the following week. His suspiciousness of me had gone by then and on this occasion he proved highly receptive to interrogative pressure, in an almost identical way to that of Raghip.

Following the dismissal of the application to appeal, Mr Raghip's solicitors sent a copy of my report to the pre-trial psychologist for his comments. He subsequently made a public statement on a television programme about the case. He was asked on the programme what he would be able to say if he was giving evidence in the case today. He replied:

> With the advantage of repeat intelligence testing, and with the suggestibility test done under a much more cooperative situation, one would now be in a position to say, one, that he was very suggestible, and secondly, that he is of very low intelligence.

In July 1990, the pre-trial psychologist wrote a report to confirm his current views on the case. The Home Secretary responded to the pre-trial psychologist's comments on my findings by referring the case back to the Court of Appeal (Tendler, 1990).

The Appeal

The appeal of the 'Tottenham Three' (Winston Silcott, Mark Braithwaite & Engin Raghip) was heard in the Court of Appeal (London) between 25 and 27 November 1991, before Lord Justice Farquharson, and Justices Alliott and Cresswell. Raghip's psychological vulnerabilities at the time of his interrogation in 1985 were central to the appeal. I was first to give evidence, followed by Mr Eric Ward, the original psychologist, who now agreed with my findings, and Mrs Olive Tunstall, who had made a special study of Raghip's social functioning. In cross-examination the prosecution was not able to challenge our professional conclusions. The prosecutor, Mr Roy Amlot, read out passages from the interview transcripts of Raghip to show that he 'managed perfectly well and was indeed quick-witted'. Mr Amlot also suggested to us 'that the jury could perfectly well make up their own minds about the reliability of the confessions despite the fact that the only deficit of which they were aware was his illiteracy'. We responded by arguing that Raghip's deficits and vulnerabilities were not immediately obvious without psychological testing and would not be noticeable to the jury from his appearance.

The judges ruled that the psychological evidence presented would have been admissible at trial upon submission under Section 76(2)(b) of PACE and if the trial judge had ruled the defendant's confession admissible before the jury then it was encumbent upon him to warn the jury, in accordance with Section 77 of PACE, that there was a special need for caution before convicting the defendant on the basis of his confession. In deciding whether the same psychological evidence would have been admissible before the jury the judges asked themselves the following question:

> Is the mental condition of the defendant such that the jury would be assisted by expert help in assessing it?

If the answer is yes, as appeal judges considered it was in the case of Raghip, then trial judges should admit such evidence before the jury. They concluded:

> The state of the psychological evidence before as outlined earlier in this judgment—in contradistinction to that which was available to the defence at Raghip's trial—is such as to demonstrate that the jury would have been assisted in assessing the mental condition of Raghip and the consequent reliability of the alleged confessions. Notwithstanding that Raghip's IQ was 74 just in the borderline range and a man chronologically aged 19 years 7 months at the date of interview with a level of functioning equivalent to that of a child of 9 years 9 months and the reading age of a child of 6 years 6 months cannot be said to be normal. It would be impossible for the layman to divine that data from Raghip's performance in the witness box still less the abnormal suggestibility of which Dr Gudjonsson spoke.

However, the appeal judges carefully differentiated between psychiatric or psychological evidence addressing a defendant's *mens rea* (guilty intent) and evidence going to the reliability of a confession. The question posed above by the judges about a defendant's mental condition should only be asked in relation to reliability of confession evidence.

Their ruling also broadened the criteria for defining 'mental handicap' under Section 77 of PACE. The judges were 'not attracted to the concept that the judicial approach to submissions under 76(2)(b) of PACE should be governed by which side of an arbitrary line, whether at 69/70 or elsewhere, the IQ falls'. This contradicted the 'judge for yourself' approach in respect of the jury outlined in *Masih* ([1986], Crim.L.R. 395), which read as follows:

> where the defendant however is within the scale of normality albeit as this man was, at the lower end of the scale, expert evidence in our judgment is not as a rule necessary and should be excluded.

At the end of the judgment the judges emphasized the need for solicitors to seek a further report if they believed the opinion of the previous expert was hostile or apparently defective. They concluded with regard to Raghip's case:

> At the date of trial in this case two medical experts had been consulted on behalf of Raghip and because of the content of their reports, neither was called to give evidence. Yet at a much later stage, after having seen Dr Gudjonsson's report both experts changed the opinions they had previously given. In these circumstances it is demonstrated that the need of a third opinion was necessary in the interests of justice.

The convictions of the two co-defendants, Silcott and Braithwaite, were also quashed, but not on psychological grounds. Braithwaite had been unlawfully refused access to a solicitor in breach of Section 58 of PACE and the relevant paragraph of the Code of Practice. The entire evidence against Silcott consisted of an alleged incriminating text in the last police interview, which police evidence said was contemporaneously recorded. Electrostatic detection apparatus (ESDA) clearly showed irregularities with regard to the recording of the interview. The ESDA technique examines the depression made on one page from the writing on another page which rests on it. It shows whether the records have been altered after the original statement was written.

Comments

What does Raghip's case teach us about the clinical assessment of retracted confession cases? There are two important lessons to be learned. Firstly, we cannot rely on clinical impressions of intellectual functioning. As was shown in Chapter 3, often such impressions are wrong. In all fairness to the psychiatrist involved, he did identify Raghip's reading problems and his poor vocabulary, and considered him susceptible to suggestion. Furthermore, most importantly, he did recommend that Raghip be tested by a psychologist. Unfortunately, a problem arose when the psychologist who assessed him did not believe that the IQ results obtained were reliable or valid.

The second lesson to be learned is that when we doubt the validity of our test results then we must, whenever possible, assess the defendant further so that erroneous inferences cannot be drawn from the assessment. For example, if faking is suspected with regard to cognitive functioning, then tests can be administered to substantiate or disprove this possibility (Gudjonsson & Shackleton, 1986; Gudjonsson & Haward, 1998). If the mental state of the defendant is such that it compromises the possible validity of the test results then this should be made clear in the report. Further testing may be required once the defendant's mental state has improved.

As far as the judgment in the case is concerned, the criteria for the admissibility of psychological evidence in cases of disputed confessions were broadened and clarified, and the concept of interrogative suggestibility, its measurement, validity and relevance were approved by the Court of Appeal. In addition, the court warned that high suggestibility and intellectual deficits could not satisfactorily be detected by observations of the defendant's performance in the witness box. These are subtle characteristics that require a comprehensive psychological evaluation. This is a very important point and it is easily overlooked in criminal trials.

JACQUELINE FLETCHER—UNIDENTIFIED BORDERLINE INTELLIGENCE

This case demonstrates the importance of borderline intelligence, accompanied by strong feelings of remorse for the sudden death of her baby, in producing an unreliable confession.

On 14 September 1988, in Birmingham Crown Court, Jacqueline Fletcher was convicted of the murder of her six-week-old infant son, Glen Richard Miles. He had died on 19 October 1984 and at post-mortem his death was certified as 'Sudden Infant Death Syndrome' (SIDS), also known as 'cot death'. In September 1987, Fletcher is alleged to have made a comment to her landlady that she had drowned her infant son Glen. At the time of the police interview Fletcher had just had another child, who was then three weeks old. The landlady notified the social services, who alerted the police (Campbell, 1992). Fletcher was interviewed by the police on 3 December 1987 in the presence of a legal representative. The legal representative advised her to answer each of the questions with the words 'no comment'. Miss Fletcher did not follow that advice and the interview proceeded for about two and a half hours, at which point a woman police constable, who had been present during the interview, suggested to Fletcher that the interview should proceed with just the two of them being present. Fletcher's legal representative immediately advised his client not to agree to this, but she disregarded it. The interview with the woman police constable lasted only 15 minutes, during which Fletcher confessed to having drowned her baby. This interview was not contemporaneously recorded, as required by law. The brief note of the interview read

> At Fletcher's request Mr Richardson (Sol.) and DI left the room. At this time Jackie Fletcher stated she had put the baby's head under the bath water until it died. She then dried the baby, clothed it in clean clothes and laid him in his cot. Shortly afterwards the postman arrived. The baby had been crying for most of the night. She was afraid of getting found out.

Fletcher then reiterated the confession in front of the legal representative and the Detective Inspector.

Slides of the baby's various organs had been sent to another pathologist, Dr Andrews, who concluded that the cause of death might have been drowning. Dr Andrews testified at trial and stated that he disagreed with the diagnosis of SIDS and suggested instead that the lungs might have been 'waterlogged', which supported the prosecution and the confession. Dr Andrews conclusions were not challenged at trial by other experts. In a letter dated 23 October 1991, four years after Fletcher's conviction, Dr Andrews stated that his use of the word 'waterlogged' had been unfortunate, because he had no evidence that the fluid in the infant's lungs was water. Another expert had carried out an experiment, using a similar bath to that allegedly used by Fletcher to drown the infant, and found it would have been extremely difficult to drown the baby in the way she had said in her confession.

I was commissioned by *Justice* in 1991 to assess Fletcher's intellectual abilities and suggestibility. Her Full Scale IQ fell in the second percentile rank, her verbal memory was significantly impaired and her total suggestibility scores on the GSS 1 and GSS 2 were in the average range for the general population. Fletcher denied having made the incriminating admissions to her lodger; she claimed to have made a false confession to the woman police officer in private, because she could not cope with the continued interrogation, felt pressured to speak, had been told that there was forensic evidence as to drowning and had allegedly been promised by her that she would not be locked up or go to prison if she confessed. Fletcher also stated that she had felt very guilty about the death of her son, because she thought she might have accidentally suffocated him whilst leaning on him on the settee. After my assessment, Fletcher was tested again intellectually by a Crown expert, Mr Paul Britton; his findings agreed with my findings. This was important, because a consultant forensic psychiatrist, Professor Robert Bluglass, appointed by the Crown, had categorically stated in his report that he did not accept the IQ scores from my assessment. He thought Fletcher was a great deal brighter than indicated by the borderline IQ score. He had been impressed by Fletcher's use of such words as 'traumatic' and 'custodial', and her satisfactory understanding of the term 'post natal depression'.

Leave to appeal was allowed in view of the psychological findings relating to Fletcher's borderline IQ score of 70. Her appeal was heard in February 1992 before Lord Chief Justice Lane and Justices Rose and Potts. I did not give evidence, but I was present during the appeal. With regard to the psychological evidence before the Court of Appeal, Lord Lane stated in the judgment:

> This appellant has been seen by a number of psychiatrists and perhaps the two most eminent members of that profession have had the opportunity of assessing her mental calibre. They are, one is glad to note, in agreement, that she is on the borderline of the mentally handicapped. She has an Intelligence Quotient which, if it had been one degree lower, would have put her within the category of the mentally handicapped. She is nevertheless, on the tests which these gentlemen conducted, not unduly susceptible to suggestions. In other words she does not readily accept propositions which are put to her, as is the case with some people of low mental calibre. Whether the tests of suggestibility could successfully mimic the sort of situation in which she found herself in Nuneaton Police Station is perhaps questionable, but there it is.

The Lordships concluded:

> What has concerned us, as we hope we have made clear, is first of all the circumstances of the confession to the police, and more particularly, these admittedly misleading remarks by Dr Andrews, made in all good faith be it said, which may very well have caused the jury to come to a conclusion contrary to the truth of the matter. In short we have come to the conclusion that this verdict is both unsafe and unsatisfactory. Accordingly the appeal will be allowed and the conviction quashed.

Comments

This case demonstrates the importance of psychometric testing of intellectual abilities. Fletcher superficially came across as being brighter than the IQ scores indicated and clinical impressions of intellectual functioning are often wrong, as was shown in Chapter 3. Whilst being interviewed by the police and at trial her intellectual limitations were not recognized. Had they been known, the outcome at the trial in 1988 might have been different. I do not think that Fletcher's low suggestibility was relevant in this case. I think she confessed, not because she was suggestible, but because she felt distressed about the death of her son, she found the police interview stressful and difficult to cope with and it brought back painful memories and emotions and she was looking for a way out of her predicament. If there was an inducement, as she claims, she is likely to have accepted it in order to avoid the pain of further questioning. Her limited intellectual abilities would have made her less able to evaluate satisfactorily the very real and likely consequences of her making such an incriminating confession.

JUDITH WARD—PERSONALITY DISORDER

Judith Ward was arrested in February 1974 and charged with three major terrorist offences, including the so-called M62 Coach Bombing, which resulted in the death of 12 passengers.

My psychiatrist colleague Dr James MacKeith and I were commissioned to work on the case in 1990 by Ward's solicitor. We interviewed her in Holloway

Prison and produced our reports. The main conclusions from the psychological test was that Ward was of average intellectual abilities, she was highly extraverted and sensation seeking in her character, confabulated abnormally on the GSS 2 delayed recall narrative, had a strong tendency to yield to leading questions and on the MMPI had an elevated score on the hysteria scale, suggesting that she might exhibit hysterical (dissociative) reactions when under stress.

Dr MacKeith agreed in court that Ward was suffering from personality disorder—hysterical type. Dr Bowden, a consultant forensic psychiatrist, was commissioned by the prosecution and concluded that Ward had 'exhibited evidence of mental disorder in the form of hysterical personality disorder since adolescence'. All three of us were to testify at the appeal hearing.

The appeal was heard in May 1992 before Lord Justices Glidewell, Nolan and Steyn. The judges were invited to hear the appeal in three parts. These involved non-disclosure of evidence by the police, scientists, a prison doctor and prosecution; the unreliability of Ward's admissions and confessions; and doubts about the validity of some of the scientific evidence presented at trial regarding Ward having been in contact with nitroglycerine.

The psychiatric and psychological evidence was heard first. The Lordships ruled:

> At the conclusion of the fresh evidence and submissions of this head of appeal, we have received persuasive and impressive evidence that in 1974 Miss Ward was suffering from a personality disorder of such a nature that no reliance could be placed on any statement of fact made by her. Thus we concluded that none of the admissions or confessions she made before her trial could be relied upon as the truth; since the admissions and confessions were the core of the prosecution's case, it follows on this ground alone that Miss Ward's conviction was unsafe and unsatisfactory.
>
> But we conclude on the authorities as they now stand that the expert evidence of a psychiatrist or a psychologist may properly be admitted if it is to the effect that a defendant is suffering from a condition not properly described as mental illness, but from a personality disorder so severe as properly to be categorized as mental disorder.

Ward's conviction was quashed by the appeal judges. She had spent over 18 years in prison and has written her autobiography (Ward, 1993).

Comments

The judgment in this case is important, because the diagnosis of personality disorder was ruled admissible in a case of disputed confession, and was clearly influential in overturning her conviction. Secondly, the judgment made it clear that psychologists, as well as psychiatrists, were entitled to give expert evidence on personality disorder.

This was, as the judges acknowledged, a most extraordinary case. For almost two years prior to her arrest, Ward had made others believe that she was actively involved in IRA terrorist activities, and after her arrest she apparently made voluntary confessions to three very serious terrorists acts. At trial she disputed the confessions, but they were supported by scientific evidence, which has now been discredited (Mansfield, 1993). After her conviction, Ward did not apply for leave to appeal against her conviction, and it was not until 1986, 11 years after her conviction, that she began to consistently deny her involvement in the offences (Gudjonsson & MacKeith, 1997). The reason why she did not deny her involvement in the offences earlier has not been established, but it may relate to her need for a sense of notoriety within the prison setting.

DAVID MACKENZIE—INABILITY TO DISTINGUISH FACTS FROM FANTASY

The background to this case and the psychological findings were discussed in detail in Chapter 9. In this chapter a brief summary of the case and the outcome of the Court of Appeal hearing will be presented.

At his trial in 1990 David MacKenzie was convicted of murdering two elderly women. He had confessed to both murders during police questioning. He had also confessed to 12 other murders, which the prosecution did not believe he had committed (*R. v. MacKenzie*, [1993], 96 Cr.App.R). At trial, first during a *voire dire* and then again in front of the jury, Dr Nigel Eastman and I testified on behalf of the defence. Dr Paul Bowden testified for the Crown. The trial judge had ruled the confessions to the two murders admissible, because they were not obtained by police pressure.

The appeal was heard in July 1992 before Lord Chief Justice Taylor, Mr Justice Simon Brown and Mr Justice Roch. The main ground of appeal was that the jury's verdicts were unsafe and unsatisfactory, having considered the unreliability of MacKenzie's confessions and the absence of other evidence of guilt. The prosecution argued, as they had done at trial, that the facts disclosed by MacKenzie in the confessions could only have been known by the murderer. Without this special knowledge the jury would not have been entitled to rely on the confessions. Therefore, at the appeal the principal issue was whether on close inspection Mr MacKenzie had revealed special knowledge in his confessions to the two murders. The appeal judges concluded:

> We have carefully reviewed the knowledge contained in the confessions, the errors contained therein and the omissions, some of which are striking. We also bear in mind the appellant's general credibility is diminished by his confessions to other killings, at least some of which he could not possibly have done, and by his motivation to say that which would ensure his confinement in Rampton (p. 110).

The judges also pointed to the surprising absence of any evidence against the appellant from other sources. There was also scientific evidence, not available at trial, that MacKenzie could not have committed a further much publicized murder, which the jury had been told he was suspected of and might be charged with. At appeal there was also evidence from a clinical psychologist, Mr John Hodge, that since the trial he had been able to assess MacKenzie and was of the opinion that his inability to recall significant details of the crimes was not due to his suffering from amnesia. At trial one of the hypotheses put forward by the Crown psychiatrist was that Mr MacKenzie's inability to recall much of the offences could have been due to amnesia for the offences.

The appeal judges concluded that the trial judge was entitled to admit the confessions into evidence before the jury:

> Nevertheless, applying the guidance given by this Court in *Galbraith* [1981] 73 Cr.App.R. 124, [1981] 2 ALL E.R. 1060, we consider that where (1) the prosecution case depends wholly upon confessions; (2) the defendant suffers from a significant degree of mental handicap; and (3) the confessions were unconvincing to a point where a jury properly directed could not properly convict upon them, then the judge, assuming he had not excluded the confessions, should withdraw the case from the jury. The confessions may be unconvincing, for example, because they lack the incriminating details to be expected of a guilty and willing confessor, or because they are inconsistent with other evidence, or because they are otherwise inherently improbable. Cases depending solely or mainly on confessions, like cases depending upon identification evidence, have given rise to miscarriages of justice. We are therefore of the opinion that when the three conditions tabulated above apply at any stage of the case, the judge should, in the interests of justice, take the initiative and withdraw the case from the jury (p. 108)

Comments

The judgment in this case set forward three criteria for determining the admissibility of confession evidence, which have been applied to other subsequent cases. The absence of credible special knowledge was clearly of importance, as well as MacKenzie's known tendency to make false confessions, which was seen to undermine his credibility in terms of self-incrimination in relation to the two murders of which he was convicted. Interestingly, MacKenzie was of borderline intelligence (IQ scores over time between 73 and 76) and his primary diagnosis was personality disorder, although he had been admitted to hospital in the past under a diagnosis of mental impairment. In the judgment it is not clear whether the term 'mental handicap' refers to his borderline IQ, a previous diagnosis relating to admission to hospital or encapsulates all of MacKenzie's mental (psychological) problems. There is no reference in the judgment to MacKenzie meeting the criteria for 'mental handicap' as set out in Section 77 of PACE, although this may have been argued at the appeal on MacKenzie's behalf by his counsel.

IDRIS ALI—PATHOLOGICAL LYING

This case involved the murder in 1981 or 1982 (a definite date of death was never established) of a teenage girl. The murder came to light in December 1989 while workmen were excavating an area at the back of a house in Cardiff. The case featured on a *Crimewatch* programme in February 1990, as a result of which Idris Ali came forward and identified the girl. He was interviewed extensively as a potential witness, but denied knowing anything about the murder. The officers did not believe him and Ali eventually admitted having been present during the murder and having a limited involvement in the girl's death. By this time he had been at the police station for 14 hours without any opportunity to rest. He was extensively interviewed as a suspect and during an interview in a police cell, which was not contemporaneously recorded, he said that he had been forced to strangle the girl at the request of another man. There were a total of 14 taped interviews. There were breaches of the police Codes of Practice and improper procedure, including delays in cautioning him, absence of contemporaneous records and insufficient time for rest. The defence argued, on the basis of the case of *R. v. McGovern*, that the trial judge should exclude the interviews following the improper procedures. The application failed. The interviews were admitted into evidence. Ali's confession was virtually the only evidence against him. He and his co-defendant were both convicted of murder and given life sentences. At the time of the murder, Ali was 16 years of age. His co-defendant was aged 21.

This case was heard by the Court of Appeal in October 1994, before Lord Justice Henry and Justices Rougier and Longmore. The appellant sought to call two clinical psychologists as witnesses. I was one of them. Mrs Olive Tunstall was the other. I had carried out an assessment of Ali's psychological functioning in January and February 1994. I had found Ali to suffer from a significant intellectual impairment and in my view he was of borderline learning disability. He proved to be abnormally compliant but not unduly suggestible or acquiescent on testing. My final paragraph, which is cited in the judgment, reads as follows:

> Mr Ali appears to have a long history of telling lies for instrumental and short term gains. I believe he was being truthful when he told me that lying comes easy to him and that he is in the habit of lying in order to get out of trouble or when he wants to make himself 'look big' in the eyes of others. His tendency to lie and not to consider the long term consequences of his lies, in conjunction with his low intelligence (particularly his very poor comprehension), makes it unwise to rely on his confessions to the police without corroboration.

Ali told me that he was present when his co-accused had murdered the girl, but had nothing to do with the murder. Indeed, he maintains that he tried to stop the other man from attacking the girl. His account to me about what happened was very similar to that which he gave before the jury at his trial and had also been supported by another young girl, who was also present during the murder.

Following my assessment, and shortly before the appeal hearing, Ali had been assessed by another clinical psychologist for the defence, Mrs Olive Tunstall. Mrs Tunstall found Ali to be significantly impaired both in terms of his intelligence and social functioning. The judges agreed to hear our evidence and concluded:

> Since the passing of PACE the Courts have frequently entertained expert psychological evidence as being admissible on questions relating to both the reliability and the admissibility of confessions. The early cases establishing this are

marshalled in the case of *R. v. Raghip & Others* (unreported, 5 December 1991). This expert evidence would clearly have been admissible on those issues.

Mrs Tunstall and I were thoroughly cross-examined on our evidence. I explained to the Court that outward appearance can be misleading and even doctors are not always able to identify intellectual deficits without formal testing. The judges accepted our evidence. In rebuttal the Crown had called their own clinical psychologist, who had not actually assessed Ali himself, but had commented in detail on my report.

The judges reviewed the fresh psychological evidence in terms of the three categories set out in *Stafford v DPP* ([1974] AC 878 at 907). These are the following.

1. This fresh evidence puts such an entirely new complexion on the case that we are sure that a verdict of guilty would not be safe. So we will quash the conviction and not order a new trial.
2. The fresh evidence though relevant and credible adds so little to the weight of the defence case as compared with the weight of the prosecution's case that a doubt induced by the fresh evidence would not be a reasonable doubt. So, we would leave the conviction standing.
3. We do not feel at this stage sure one way or the other. If this fresh evidence was given together with the original evidence and any further evidence which the Crown might adduce then it may be the jury—or we, if we constituted the jury—would return a verdict of guilty but on the other hand it might properly acquit. So we will order a re-trial.

The judges were of the view that Ali's case fell into this third category. They quashed the conviction and ordered a fresh indictment for a retrial. Six weeks later Mr Ali appeared at Cardiff Crown Court and pleaded guilty to manslaughter. A sentence of six years imprisonment was imposed. The nature of the plea was based on certain terms, including it being accepted that Ali suffered from a significant intellectual impairment, that the account given of his involvement by a witness who was present during the murder was accurate, and that the death of the woman might have remained a mystery if he had not come forward. This was accepted by the court and resulted in Ali being immediately released from prison after his guilty plea.

Comments

This is the only case discussed in this chapter where judges ordered a re-trial. There was no dispute that Mr Ali had been at the crime scene. The question was the extent of his involvement and whether he had been coerced to participate in the incident, which was no doubt instigated by his co-accused. Ali went voluntarily to the police after a *Crimewatch* programme revealing the discovery of the body, eight years after the murder. His downfall was that he was in the habit of lying as a way out of trouble, which had serious repercussions, when he was initially interviewed as a witness by the police. His tendency towards lying must have been apparent to the jury and undoubtedly made his testimony less credible, even if it were true.

GEORGE LONG—CLINICAL DEPRESSION

In July 1979, George Long, aged 20, was convicted at the Central Criminal Court of murdering and buggering a 14-year-old boy in Deptford, South London in 1978. He was convicted wholly on the basis of his confession and was sentenced to life imprisonment. It was not until July 1995, after Long had been in prison for 16 years, that the case was heard in the Court of Appeal before Lord Chief Justice Taylor and the conviction was quashed on the basis of fresh medical evidence.

Prior to his interrogation in 1979, Long was in the habit of telling fantastic tales about himself, including false military adventures while serving in the Army (he enlisted in the Army in July 1977 and was discharged due to mental problems in March 1978). In addition, he had boasted to his girlfriend and sister that on the day of the murder he had been confronted by a man wielding a knife, whom he had fought, whereupon the man had dropped the knife and run off. Long's sister subsequently happened to mention the knife incident to the police during a routine street enquiry. The police took a statement from Long about this on 1 December 1978.

On 25 January 1979, Long went, at the request of the police, to Dulwich police station, in order to give a further witness statement. He was detained overnight at the police station. During the following two days he was interviewed by the police on several occasions. At first he maintained his story about being attacked by the man with a knife. When the police pointed out to him that his story left an hour unaccounted for he stated:

Yes, it's a blank. I can't remember. I went missing, I must have.

At 5 p.m. on 26 January, Long admitted to the murder and added:

It is hazy. I had a blank until I got home.

During subsequent interviews Long gave a more detailed and incriminating account of the murder. The following morning Long reiterated the confession in the presence of his sister. At 3 p.m. that afternoon, Long had a 10 minute consultation with his solicitor in private and when further interviewed by the police in the presence of his solicitor, he again admitted to the killing, but he now introduced the admissions by the words 'I must have' rather than 'I did'. He also repeatedly complained of being 'confused'. At the end of this interview Long had a further consultation with his solicitor in private, after which he retracted his confession, now claiming that he had nothing to do with the murder and that the story he had told about the man wielding a knife was false.

He explained to the police the reasons for having falsely confessed to the murder and the knife incident:

All my life had been the same way. I am a coward and I want to be just locked up so that the world can't get to me. I never killed that boy. I never met him. I heard he was assaulted. Last night I was frightened, I thought that if I admitted it you would go easy on me because you were scaring me... I just wanted to be locked up. I've prayed for death many times but it never comes.

When asked to explain why he had been able to give details of the murder Mr Long stated:

All I can say is you said people have seen me with the boy and you told me the streets they had seen me in and things like the belt. I said I had because I wanted the officers to stop questioning me. I wanted you to put me away because I can't face the world. I can't live without lying and trying to be one of the boys. That's all I can say; that is the truth.

It was noted by the Court of Appeal that there were serious procedural shortcomings with regard to the case, including the facts that Long had not been advised about his right to legal advice, no contemporaneous record was made of the police interviews and after the initial admissions to the murder on 26 January no statement was taken immediately afterwards.

Importantly, in my view, the initial admissions suggested little familiarity with the crime (e.g. Long made no mention of a serious sexual assault that accompanied the murder, he was wrong about where the assault had taken place and where the boy had been stabbed and did not mention a broken belt with the word 'Elvis' on it found near the murder scene). The incriminating details were to come in subsequent interviews.

At the appeal hearing in 1995 the Crown sought to uphold the conviction on the basis that there were details revealed in the confessions that could only have been known by the murderer. The judges were not impressed by the prosecutor's arguments regarding special knowledge and concluded:

After considering severally and cumulatively the matters he relied upon we are not convinced that they could safely be relied upon to demonstrate knowledge in the appellant only available to the murderer.

Defence counsel argued that in view of the fresh medical evidence, if it had been available at trial a successful submission might well have been made for the judge to stop the trial at the end of the prosecution case. He cited the authority in the case of *MacKenzie* as the basis for his legal argument. The appeal judges accepted the first two points, namely that the prosecution case depended wholly upon confessions, and Long did, at the time of making the confessions suffer from a significant degree of 'mental handicap' (in the case of Long, the 'mental handicap' did not refer to learning disability, but depression). The judges did not accept that the confessions were so unconvincing as to meet the criterion set out in *MacKenzie*. Nevertheless, they were

... firmly of the view that his confessions cannot now be regarded as reliable.

I had interviewed and tested Long extensively in 1992 at the request of his solicitors. He told me that before his arrest he was very immature, was dependant on drugs and alcohol, felt very miserable and depressed most of the time and he had made a number of suicide attempts. He felt very inadequate and coped by telling people numerous lies about himself in an attempt to impress them. This temporarily appeared to raise his self-esteem and became a way of life over a period of many years.

Long claimed that whilst in prison he had greatly matured, he felt more confident in himself and had overcome his need to tell lies in order to impress people. He claimed not to have committed the offence of which he was convicted, even though he had confessed to the murder at the time. He claimed that at the time of the police interviews he was mentally unstable and could not cope with the police interviews. He had never been interviewed by the police before, was frightened of being beaten up by the police, wanted the interviews to stop and thought the police would send him to hospital if he confessed.

The conclusions from my assessment were as follows.

- Long was of High Average intelligence. He did not prove to be unduly suggestible, compliant or acquiescent on testing. I found no evidence of mental disorder during my interview with him. However, the results from the MMPI were consistent with a diagnosis of personality disorder, which by its nature must be of long standing.
- It seemed from the assessment that Long's mental state had improved markedly since his arrest in 1979. Following my interview with Long I formed the view that it was essential to assess, retrospectively, his mental state at the time of his arrest and police interviews, in order to be able to assess the reliability of his confession in 1979. His mental state and psychological functioning in 1992 was probably a poor indicator of his vulnerabilities when he was interviewed by the police in 1979. On the basis of my own assessment, I considered it probable that he had been suffering from clinical depression at the time of his arrest. This aspect of Long's case was being concurrently investigated by my psychiatrist colleague Dr MacKeith.

Dr MacKeith carried out a detailed and thorough assessment and found that Long had suffered from depression at the time of his interrogation in 1979. This finding was to become crucial at the appeal hearing in 1995 and the court heard the testimony of Dr MacKeith. There was also written evidence from Dr Bowden, another defence expert, which agreed with Dr MacKeith's diagnosis. A psychiatrist commissioned by the Crown, Dr Joseph, concluded that Mr Long suffered from a personality disorder. All three psychiatrists considered Mr Long's confessions to be unreliable.

The judges concluded:

> We simply do not know the impact the medical evidence might have had on the jury. It is sufficient to say that we were impressed by that evidence supported as it was by records of mental disorder well before the date of the murder.

Comments

This case is important in several respects. First, the current assessment of Long's psychological vulnerabilities suggested that his mental state and personality had changed very markedly since his interrogation in 1979. At the time of his interrogation he was a person with emotional, personality and self-esteem problems. These had markedly improved by the time he was assessed psychologically in 1992. The retrospective analysis performed by Dr MacKeith revealed contemporaneous evidence, including medical documentary evidence, that Long had been depressed at the time of his interrogation and this, under the circumstances, rendered his confession unreliable. Second, the criteria set out in *R. v. MacKenzie* were applied. His case met the first two criteria (i.e. there was no other evidence apart from the confession and he had a significant degree of 'mental handicap'), but failed on the third. In spite of Mr Long being of above average intellectual abilities, the 'mental handicap' condition in *MacKenzie* was successfully argued. This shows the importance of the legal and individual *interpretations* of medical concepts. In psychiatric terms, 'mental handicap' is normally used to refer to a condition of learning disability and this appears to be the way in which it was used in *MacKenzie*, although there were some ambiguities (see above in reference to the judgment). In the case of Long, the term was used in relation to a depressive condition. This has resulted in the term 'mental handicap' being used legally in a broad rather than in a more specialized way in relation to learning disability.

PATRICK KANE—ANXIETY AND COMPLIANCE

On 19 March 1988, a crowd of people attended the funeral in Belfast of Kevin Brady. He had been murdered three days previously while attending the funeral of IRA suspects shot dead by the British soldiers in Gibraltar. Mr Brady had been a taxi driver and the funeral cortege was led by a number of black taxis. Suddenly two British solders drove erratically towards the funeral procession. The crowd stopped the car, the soldiers were dragged out of it and taken into Casement Park, where they were beaten and stripped, before they were taken by taxi to a waste ground and shot dead. Many still photographs were taken at the funeral by the media as well as some television footage. The main events were recorded by the security services on video from a helicopter. The visual evidence was later used by the police to help identify the participants in the incident concerning the abduction and murder of the two soldiers.

Patrick Kane was one of the many persons arrested and interviewed about the murders. He was arrested on 12 December 1988, and was interviewed on five occasions that day and on one occasion the following day. None of the visual evidence identified him. During the first interview he admitted that he had been at the funeral but denied having taken part in the attack on the two corporals. The officers challenged Kane's account and told him that they had evidence which implicated him in the attack on the soldier's car. It was also put to him that he had attacked the car's windscreen by using a car-jack. These allegations were repeatedly put to Mr Kane during subsequent interviews. Both propositions were later proved to be false (McCollum, 1997). In the second interview, Kane began to incriminate himself by admitting that he had been inside the Casement Park at the material time. When asked what he had been wearing on the day he showed the police his green jacket. Later that same afternoon the police put it to Kane that video evidence showed two people in green jackets inside Casement Park, both of whom were allegedly involved in attacking the soldiers. Kane then admitted to being one of the persons involved and having kicked one of the soldiers and assisting with opening and closing the gates to Casement Park when the soldiers were being transported.

On 30 March 1990, at Belfast Crown Court, Mr Justice Carswell, who subsequently became Lord Chief Justice for Northern Ireland, sitting without a jury, convicted Kane and two other men of the murder of the two British soldiers. No application was made by the defence at the trial to exclude Kane's confession and no challenge was made to the admissibility of the confession. Instead the defence submitted that no weight should be given to Kane's confession, because he was illiterate, of low intelligence and had hearing problems. Kane gave evidence at the trial on Thursday and Friday, 22 and 23 February 1990. The previous Sunday (18 February). I had interviewed Kane in Belfast prison for the purposes of a psychological evaluation. The findings were highly favourable to the defence (Gudjonsson, 1999c), but were not offered to the court at the time or during a subsequent appeal hearing. This was apparently due to the fact that the defence team did not think the psychological findings would be allowed in evidence, because there was no evidence that Kane suffered from mental illness or learning disability, in spite of his being disadvantaged due to other psychological vulnerabilities.

In May 1997 the case was referred to the Court of Appeal by the Secretary of State for its opinion as to the admissibility in evidence of the psychological report prepared in 1990 by myself, and in the event that the court should decide that the evidence was admissible, the Secretary of State expressed a wish that the matter should be treated as a referral for hearing of my testimony. I testified in Belfast on 28 May 1997. No testimony was called on behalf of the prosecution.

At the time of the psychological assessment in 1990, Kane was a 31-year-old man of limited intelligence (Full Scale IQ of 78 on the WAIS-R). He was illiterate. Kane did not prove to be unduly suggestible on testing. However, I considered two features of Kane's personality as being particularly important in casting doubt on the reliability of his confession. These related to Kane's exceptionally high levels of anxiety and compliance, both of which were measured by psychometric tests when I assessed him in 1990 (for details of the assessment see Gudjonsson, 1999c). His high anxiety, which had been noticed during the clinical assessment and by the police officers interrogating him (i.e. he exhibited excessive shaking and sweating), indicated a man of a nervous disposition who would be at a considerable disadvantage when having to cope with an unfamiliar and demanding situation such as a police interrogation.

I argued in my testimony that the high compliance score, combined with his high level of anxiety, would have motivated him to escape from a stressful situation, such as the police interrogation, by agreeing with the officers' requests and demands for self-incriminating admissions. In a highly stressful situation, Kane would be likely to be focusing exclusively on the immediate consequences of his confessing behaviour, that is being allowed to go home, which in fact is what happened (Kane was allowed to go home after making the confession and was re-arrested and charged at a later date).

In their ruling, the judges quashed the conviction of Kane, concluding:

> We take the view that in the light of Doctor Gudjonsson's evidence a sufficient cloud is cast on the reliability of Kane's confession to create a situation of unfairness if it were to be admitted in evidence against him. We say this for two reasons. Firstly, Doctor Gudjonsson's evidence (which this court found to be authoritative and compelling) clearly demonstrated the disadvantages under which Kane laboured as an interviewee. The high level of anxiety which Doctor Gudjonsson considered Kane would have experienced in the interview setting predisposed him to produce explanations to please his interviewers rather than to give a truthful account. Secondly, it is clear that Kane was of limited intelligence (McCollum, 1997).

The judgment in this case shows the impact that the psychological evidence had on the judges' ruling. They clearly considered it to be highly relevant to the legal issues in the case and of sufficient weight and credibility to cast doubt on the safety of Kane's conviction.

Comments

This case was unusual in several respects. First, my report was not used at the trial in 1990, or at the first appeal hearing, because the defence team thought that, without a diagnosable mental disorder, the trial judge would not admit the psychological evidence. Previously the presence of mental disorder had typically been crucial in allowing psychological evidence to be admitted into evidence (Gudjonsson, 1992c). This all changed with the landmark case of *Raghip* in 1991. It took seven years before the psychological findings in Kane's case were brought before the Court of Appeal (Foster, 1998). In the absence of the ruling in *Raghip's* case in England, it is unlikely that the appeal in Northern Ireland would have been allowed.

The second interesting feature of this case is that the symptoms of anxiety on testing were extreme. I had to consider the possibility of faking or that Kane had not properly understood the tests, which had to be read out to him in view of his illiteracy. His severe anxiety during the assessment, which was evident by his excessive sweating and hand tremor, had also been noted by the police officers who interviewed Kane. This reinforced the view, noted on psychological testing, that Kane did have severe anxiety problems, although there was no indication from his self-report that he had ever had any formal mental disorder. Although Kane was of borderline intelligence, which was relevant to the legal issues in the case, it was his exceptionally high anxiety, combined with high compliance in an interrogative situation, that appeared to be more important in overturning the conviction. However, would Kane's conviction have been quashed if he had been of average intelligence? Possibly not, although there are a growing number of cases where persons of average intelligence have been shown to have made false confessions. The courts typically have to consider the impact of a combination of factors, which includes psychological vulnerabilities, the nature and circumstances of the interrogation, the surrounding circumstances of the case, other evidence that is available pointing to guilt or innocence and the effects of pressure groups and public opinion.

Third, the judges in Northern Ireland who presided over the appeal seemed well informed about psychological vulnerabilities in the context of police interrogation. They expressed interest and asked questions about the scientific basis of the assessment, including wanting to know about the research conducted into the validity of the compliance scale. Their questioning demonstrated the importance of the scientific foundation of the instruments used.

ANDREW EVANS—MISDIAGNOSED PSYCHOGENIC AMNESIA

On 7 June 1972, a 14-year-old girl, Judith Roberts, was battered to death in a field near Wiggington in Staffordshire. Her body was discovered three days later.

Andrew Evans was a Private in the Army between 24 April and 15 June 1972. He was discharged on medical grounds, because of asthma. Evans left the barracks on 8 June and was on terminal leave between 9 and 15 June. On 8 June he went to live with his grandmother in Longton, Stoke on Trent.

On 27 July 1972, Evans was visited by a police officer in order to complete a form regarding soldiers discharged from Whittington Barracks. He was asked about his whereabouts on 7 June. Evans stated that he had never left the barracks on that day.

At 2100 hours on Sunday 8 October 1972, two officers went back to see Evans and asked him questions concerning his previous statement. In his previous statement Mr Evans had given the names of three soldiers as having been with him on 7 June. According to witness statements two of the soldiers had left the barracks on 6 June and that was the last time they saw Evans. With regard to the third soldier, the officers told Evans that the man named by him as 'Horton' did not exist. They asked if he could remember what he was doing on 7 June and whom he was with. Mr Evans then looked for his discharge papers which he showed to the officers. He looked 'quite agitated' but calmed down after consuming a tablet from a bottle (this appears to have been from his prescription of Valium). The discharge papers indicated that Evans had left the barracks on 8 June and not 15 June as Mr Evans had told the officers. Evans commented 'I remember leaving the Army on the 8th. It was a Thursday. That paper came to me through the post'. When told that the 15th was also a Thursday Evans replied 'It may have been the 15th'. The officers told Evans that they would require some statement from him concerning his movements on 7 June. Evans said he would need to think about it and later that evening gave the statement to the officers. In that statement he said that as far as he could remember he was at the barracks all day on 7 June. He said he had been with some of his Army mates but could not recall exactly who they were.

According to Evans' grandmother, after the policemen left he looked worried and said he *might have done this murder*. The following morning he told his grandmother that he was going to the police station to look at the photograph of the murdered girl. She tried unsuccessfully to discourage him from doing so. Evans had never mentioned the murder to his grandmother prior to the officers' visit on the 8 October.

Evans arrived at Longton Police Station at 1500 hours on 9 October, apparently in a very nervous state (stuttering and shaking), and stated:

> I want to see a picture of the girl in the Tamworth murder, I am very nervous, I suffer from nerves, I keep dreaming about this girl, I have just come out of the Army.

A little while later Evans 'began crying and sobbing heavily and loudly'. When asked by another officer what he wanted, he replied:

> I want to see them two men who came last night. I want to see a photograph of the girl. I was in the Army. I don't remember where I was.

When asked if he had done the murder himself, he replied:

> I don't know whether I've done it or not. I know I was in the Army and I left on the Wednesday.

When asked about the time of the day when he left the Army Mr Evans appeared confused, at first stating that he left about mid-day and then commented:

> You see, I can't remember. This is how I am. I could have got home the next day. I don't know where I've been. *That is why I keep wondering if its me that's done this murder*. Can you show me a picture to see if I've ever met her.

This interview was concluded at 1530 hours and Evans is reported as having cried more or less continually throughout.

At 1615 hours the same day, Mr Evans was seen by two officers and was reported as being in a very distressed state. He said he wanted to see a photograph of the murdered girl and *said he thought he had killed her*. He said he kept seeing her face all the time and couldn't sleep. He said the girl had 'dark straightish hair, a full face, but not too big and dark eyes'. He further stated:

> She's wearing a dress. It's white with something like flowers on it. I must be going mad. I can see her all the time.

Evans stated that he had been in a bad mental state for a few weeks and was currently being treated for depression by his doctor. He said he was not happy with his job as a salesman and after explaining his medical discharge from the Army he began to cry bitterly. He was so distressed that he had to be assisted into another room and was having difficulties with his breathing. He stated several times '*I must have killed her*'.

There was then a discussion about Evans' bad memory and the discrepancies about his date of discharge from the Army and on which further enquiries were to be made.

When asked whether he had killed the girl, he replied:

> I think so. I must have because I can see a picture of her. I can see her lying near to a hedge. I can see her brown hair and she has got a mark on her face.

At 1825 hours Evans had his head in his hands and when asked what was the matter, replied:

> I keep seeing this girl. I can't get any sleep.

He explained that he kept seeing the girl's face and could see her lying down. He said he was all confused and asked for an aspirin, which the officer did not have. After a few minutes silence Mr Evans said:

> After I saw you, I was thinking. I don't know if I killed her or not. I keep seeing her.

Evans was then cautioned and asked what he could see. He replied 'This field'. He then drew a picture of the field.

At 1050 hours the following morning (10 October) Evans was seen in a police cell and said:

> I've not slept very well. I can't get it out of my mind.

The officers then left Evans after telling him they would come back and see him later, and in the meantime he was asked to try to remember what he could about the murder.

At 1130 hours the same officers spoke to Evans again and ask if he remembers anything else. He replied:

> I remember dragging her off her bike. I was in a field and saw her riding along the road towards me, I just grabbed her by the arm and shoulder, pulled her off and then we were rolling on the ground in the field. It was a very rough field.

After asking for a pen and paper to write things down Evans was told 'Anything you record may subsequently be used in evidence, do you understand?', to which he replied 'Yes, I want to remember. I'm sure I killed her. Do you think I did it?'.

Evans was then left again on his own to remember more. At 1520 hours an officer saw Evans at his request. As he walked into the cell Evans said:

> *I know now, I killed her.*

On 11 October at 1045 hours Evans was taken round the Whittington, Elford and Comberford areas. Between 1620 and 1750 hours on 11 October, Evans provided a 'Statement of Person Under Caution'. This statement was written down by a police officer and then typed. This statement was a confession to murder. He described how he went out of the barracks the day before he left the Army. It was in the afternoon and he got into a car. He then remembered standing in a field and seeing the girl. She had something dark on and a blue flowered dress. He pulled her off her bicycle, hit her in the face with a fist, and then dragged her across the field. She had a bruise on her face on the right hand side. He took her white knickers off, pulled off her brown blunt shoes, put her stockings inside the shoes and put the shoes inside the knickers. The girl had a gold coloured watch on with black figures. She had nothing on from the waist down, he hit her on the side of the face when she started to come round, then dragged her to the hedge. He put her clothes under the hedge, there was something lying across the body, he hit her with something which was so thick that he could only get three quarters of his hand around it. He said he did not have sex with her. She had a dark mark on the left of her face where he had struck her. He then pushed the bicycle into the hedge. The handles and seat were sticking out. He then went over some fields and climbed over a white fence.

At 1015 hours on 12 October Evans was seen in the police cell and after being cautioned he stated:

> I told you. I killed her, I don't want it to happen again. I'll help all I can, you must believe me now. I've told you what I did.

While in the police vehicle near the murder scene Mr Evans told an officer:

> I keep wondering why I did it.

When asked why he did it, Mr Evans replied:

> It must have been vengeance.

Mr Evans did not know against whom he had wanted vengeance, but thought it could be the Army.

At 1700 hours on 12 October Evans was visited by his mother. When his mother expressed scepticism about him having committed the murder Evans said:

> It's no good mum, I've done it, I have, I've told them all about it, I killed her.

This police account of a confession to Evans' mother was corroborated by her Witness Statement. He told his mother that he had killed the girl, after having dragged her off her bicycle. She described Evans as a lad who liked attention and he was always being bullied at school. He tended to be a daydreamer who was sometimes so engrossed in his thoughts that he was not aware of what was going on around him.

Evans was charged with the murder at 1815 hours on 12 October 1972, and replied:

Yes, I did it.

Evans was interviewed over a period of three days without the presence of a solicitor.

According to a Psychiatric Report dated 4 April 1973, on 30 March and 2 April 1973, Evans was given drugs intravenously in order to enhance his memory for events on 7 June 1972. During the first session Brietal was given and during the second session Brietal was given together with Methedrine. There was a third abreaction session on 7 April 1973. During the three abreaction sessions Evans denied murdering the girl. He reported standing by a gate and there was a hedge, he could hear a cry and a struggle going on. He then described a man with a darkish face who was bending over the body of a girl.

Evans was convicted of the murder on 13 April 1973, and remained in prison until 3 December 1997, when his conviction was quashed by the Court of Appeal in London.

Psychological Evaluation

According to the Medical Report dated 7 March 1973, Evans was assessed by a prison psychologist whilst on remand and obtained an IQ score of 100. The psychologist described Mr Evans as a person who has a 'predisposition toward neurotic–hysteric type reactions'. There were 'strong impressions of hysterical features'.

I became involved in the case in 1994 at the request of *Justice*. I interviewed Evans on three occasions in prison. The second and third interviews were conducted jointly with my psychiatrist colleague, Dr MacKeith, whom I had recommended to *Justice* after my first interview with Evans. The main findings from our evaluations were as follows.

Interviews

In interviews with me, Evans denied having had anything to do with the murder and claims to have confessed falsely to the police for a number of reasons.

- When the police officers came to his grandmother's house on 8 October 1972, they challenged his previous alibi accounts, which confused Evans. The fact that he had got his alibi wrong made him distrust his memory and he kept asking himself 'Why did I forget what I was doing on that day?', 'What else have I forgotten?'. At about 2230 hours that same night he went to bed and was still wondering why he had previously misled the police concerning his alibi. At about 0300 hours he woke up and saw a young girl's face staring at him. It was a reddish face and Evans became petrified. This made him think that it was the victim's face and that perhaps he had had something

to do with her murder. The following morning he told his grandmother about the nightmare and said he thought he might have done the murder. She told him not to be silly and later in the day he sneaked out while she was asleep. He went to the police station in order to see a photograph of the victim so that he could compare it with the face he had seen in his nightmare.
- After the police had come to his house on 8 October he in a way wished that he had witnessed the murder. For the first time in his life he was somebody, he felt important and wanted, and people were not ignoring him any more like they always had done in the past. Most importantly perhaps, he felt for first time in his life that he had something that somebody else wanted. Prior to having made the confessions to the police he had felt very low in his mood and a complete failure. Everything he had attempted he had failed at and the final shock was being medically discharged from the Army.
- Evans claimed that the police asked him many personal questions which upset him greatly. These included questions like 'Do you masturbate?', 'Do you like girls?', 'Do you think about girls?', 'Do you do things to them?'. Evans told us he that he was very embarrassed by these questions. He claimed that some of the answers he gave to the police concerning the murdered girl were related to memories of his sister (e.g. according to Evans his sister used to wear a dress with flowers on it).

Evans said that when he entered the police station on 9 October he had no firm belief or memory that he had committed the murder. While at the police station his belief that he had committed the murder gradually grew and when he woke up after the first night in custody he said to himself 'I've done this' and he wanted people, including the police, to think that he had done it. He then made up various details to fit in with what he thought might have happened and what the police wanted to hear. Evans claims that he was never completely convinced that he had committed the murder but rather thought that he might have done it and in a way wanted to believe that he had done it. *He claimed to have had various pictures and visions in his mind concerning the murder but had no clear memory of having committed it.* He tried to become totally absorbed in the case and used his imagination as best he could to create details. Even though he thought he had committed the murder, it was as though at another level he knew he had not done it. He claimed that it took him a long time to become convinced that he had had nothing to do with the murder.

Evans told us that as a child he often had nightmares and slept badly. He has suffered from asthma since infancy, which has been a serious physical handicap to him. He claimed to have been commonly bullied as a child; he was very fearful of physical aggression and was in the habit of exaggerating things. He had always had little confidence in his memory.

Prior to his going to the police station he had felt very low in mood since leaving the Army and had been prescribed Valium by his General Practitioner.

Psychometric Testing

Intellectually Evans was functioning in the average range, which was consistent with that found by the prison psychologist prior to his trial in 1973. The assessment indicated that Evans had serious problems with verbal memory recall. His memory performance on two suggestibility tests (GSS 1 and GSS 2) was abnormally poor and unusual for a person of his average intellectual ability. Evans had also been found to have poor memory when assessed during the pre-trial evaluation.

Evans proved on psychological testing to have an abnormal tendency to confabulate. Of course, we do not know what Evans' confabulatory responding was like in 1972, except in as far as knowing that he got many of the details of the murder wrong and one doctor in 1972 was of the opinion that Evans might be unwittingly producing distorted material.

Although Evans' suggestibility scores fell within normal limits they were somewhat elevated above average and his great vagueness in his replies to the questions on the GSS 1 and GSS 2 was unusual and suggests that Evans has problems with discrepancy detection (i.e. he was unable to identify when errors were being introduced into his memory) and lacked confidence in his memory.

Evans proved abnormally acquiescent on testing, which indicated that he was very prone to answering questions in the affirmative irrespective of content. His high acquiescence score was particularly unusual for a person of average intellectual abilities.

On a test of compliance Evans' scores fell outside normal limits. His scores on two occasions, 10 months apart, were identical. When Evans was asked to rate his compliance for the period prior to his arrest in 1972, his score was even higher.

In terms of his personality, Evans was an emotionally labile (anxious) extravert. The MMPI-2 clinical profile suggested a hysterical disorder and a tendency to develop a hysterical reaction when under stress. This is often associated with a strong need for attention and may be associated with memory problems. The personality profile was consistent with that found by the prison psychologist who assessed Evans prior to his trial in 1973.

The assessment indicated that Evans' self-esteem was very poor in 1972 and had markedly improved over the years. Witness statements from 1972 did corroborate Evans' self-report of his poor self-esteem at the time.

Many of the test findings were consistent with the personality of Evans in 1972 and 1973 as evident from the documentation provided for our evaluation. At the time of the psychological assessment in 1994 and 1995, he still possessed some personality characteristics that made him psychologically vulnerable during a police interview (i.e. poor memory, confabulatory tendencies, difficulties with discrepancy detection, high acquiescence, high compliance, anxiety proneness and possible hysterical reactions under stress). His self-esteem seemed to have markedly improved. I was in no doubt that at the time of his police interviews he had very poor feelings of self-worth. Prior to his arrest in 1972 he had experienced a number of failures, the main one being his medical discharge from the Army, which further exacerbated his already low self-esteem.

Psychological Formulation

From the evening of 8 October 1972, and until he was charged on 12 October, Evans was in an abnormal mental state. In addition to his clinical depression he was clearly suffering from an acute stress reaction, which, in conjunction with his enduring psychological vulnerabilities discussed above, made him susceptible to giving potentially misleading self-incriminating admissions. There is also the additional problem that Evans had been taking Valium for about 10 days prior to being interviewed by the police. It is known that Valium can have fantasy-inducing properties, which may result in false memories (Lader, 1999).

The circumstances of Evans' confessions are unusual. He began to doubt his own memory after being confronted by the police officers on 8 October 1972 about an alibi he had given to the police over two months previously. The visit appeared to have triggered off a 'memory distrust syndrome', which is quite distinct from psychogenic amnesia (Gudjonsson, 1992a). He then told his grandmother that he wondered whether he had done the murder. During the following night he had a vision or a dream where he saw the face of a young girl, then later in the day walked into Longton police station in order to see a photograph of the victim in case it happened to be the person he saw in his dream. He eventually gave a confession to the murder and apparently provided the police with 'special knowledge' (e.g. concerning the location of the body, injuries to the girl's face, the description of the girl's watch) while also getting many of the details wrong (e.g. the position of the bicycle, the colour of the girl's underwear and her clothing, the colour of the girl's hair and eyes).

Three doctors testified at trial with regard to Evans's trial. They made two fundamental assumptions.

- The doctors assumed Evans was genuinely amnesic for the offence (i.e., as the trial judges put it to the jury, Evans had 'forgotten certain painful facts'). The assumption was that Evans had either committed the murder himself or witnessed it, which had traumatized him to the extent that the memory of the event had been pushed out of consciousness awareness (i.e. 'repressed'). Interestingly, one of the three doctors did also seriously consider the possibility that Evans had a false memory.
- The doctors further assumed that Evans was wrong when he claimed not to have left the barracks on 7 June and must have been at the crime scene at the time of the girl's death.

These two assumptions played an important part in the doctors' testimony and in the judge's summing up. The doctors' evidence of the alleged psychogenic amnesia helped to link Mr Evans physically to the site of the murder. Without the doctor's evidence that crucial link would have been missing and the jury might have come to a different verdict.

The most salient psychological issue was whether or not the doctors were correct in their diagnosis of psychogenic amnesia (Gudjonsson, Kopelman & MacKeith, 1999). If Evans did not suffer from amnesia at all concerning 7 June 1972, but was experiencing 'normal' forgetting, which turned into a 'memory distrust syndrome', then his conviction was unsafe. Unless Evans suffered from psychogenic amnesia his original statement of 27 July, that he was at the barracks at the time of the murder, becomes credible.

There were good grounds for believing that Evans did not suffer from amnesia on 7 June 1972 and that the doctors misdiagnosed his condition. My reasons for believing this were as follows.

- The statements of Evans' Army colleagues concerning 7 June were no more detailed than his own statement to the police. Many of the statements were very vague and general. Evans' own statement gave no indication that he was amnesic for the material time (i.e. between 6 and 8 p.m. on 7 June 1972) when he was visited by the police on 27 July 1972. Prior to 8 October Evans had given no indication to anybody that he was suffering from amnesia for 7 June. This is important, because if Evans had been genuinely amnesic due to a major emotional trauma (i.e. by either witnessing or committing murder) he would have been expected to have been aware of it prior to 8 October. There is no evidence of any such awareness. The fact that the amnesia only appeared to emerge after the visit of the police officers on the 8 October made it very suspect and supported the view that he was suffering from 'memory distrust syndrome' rather than genuine psychogenic amnesia.
- Amnesia in cases of violence, particularly homicide, is common. Where amnesia occurs the victim is in the great majority of cases a close friend or a relative, the amnesia often takes place in the context of alcohol, there is usually evidence of mental illness and the offender tends to be older than other violent offenders (Taylor & Kopelman, 1984). Concerning the present case, Judith Roberts was not a close friend or a relative of Evans, he was apparently not intoxicated at the time of the offence and there was no history of prior alcohol abuse and he was very young (17 years) at the time of the offence. His depressive illness only emerged after he left the Army and was first diagnosed on 29 September 1972, or 10 days prior to his walking into Longton Police Station.
- A striking feature of Evans' alleged amnesia was that it did not appear to have followed the expected pattern of resolution. That is, once Evans' belief that he was the murderer developed and he appeared to develop some recollections then I would have expected his 'memory' of the murder to have become firmly established. (I am not convinced that his confessions represent clear memory images, and in any case they did not appear to have become fully or properly established in memory.) His 'memory' of the murder appears to have emerged and then disappeared again, which is unusual.
- Finally, the confession that Evans made to the police had the hallmarks of an internalized false confession (e.g. the way it was elicited and evolved, its vagueness, the language used by Evans and how the confessions changed over time and never became firmly established in memory). After the police visit on 8 October he appears to have developed a false belief that he might or could be the murderer, or that he had witnessed it. He found this exciting. This false belief appears to have developed into a kind of a 'false memory'

(I am not convinced it was a clear memory that he experienced—rather they appear to have been visual and perceptual experiences), which persisted intermittently during his prison sentence. Even when seen by Dr MacKeith and I, 23 years later, he seemed unsure about whether or not his 'memories' of the murder were real.

On the basis of our assessment in this case, Dr MacKeith and I believed that it was unsafe to rely on the confession as evidence of Evans having committed the murder of Judith Roberts.

The Appeal

Following the submission of my Psychological Report, and the Psychiatric Report of Dr MacKeith, *Justice* commissioned Professor Michael Kopelman, an expert on amnesia, to read all the papers in the case and provide a report. The prosecution later commissioned a psychiatrist, Dr Phil Joseph, to assess Evans and prepare a report. All four of us agreed that Evans' alleged amnesia had been misdiagnosed by the pre-trial doctors and that his confession was unreliable.

The appeal was heard in November 1997 before Lord Chief Justice Bingham, Mr Justice Jowitt and Mr Justice Douglas Brown. The judges pointed out that the prosecution case against Evans at trial rested entirely on his own confession. In their judgment they stated:

> We must also accept that the appellant's confessions were, as confessions, entirely unreliable. Such was the consensus among four very distinguished experts called to give evidence before us. While these experts did not enjoy the advantage enjoyed by the doctors who testified at the trial of examining the appellant within months of this offence, they were at one in regarding the diagnosis of amnesia as unsound.

Evans' conviction was quashed on 3 December 1997, and he was freed after spending 25 years in prison.

Comments

This is a most extraordinary case. As a result of his psychological problems at the time (e.g. low self-esteem), in 1972 Evans walked into a police station and gradually persuaded himself that he had committed the murder of Judith Roberts. His confession was voluntary and not coerced by the police. In fact, they were sceptical about it at first. The process of how this happened is well illustrated by the extracts presented from the police statements. The misdiagnoses of psychogenic amnesia by doctors and the subsequent use of pharmacological abreaction interviews were undoubtedly instrumental in Evans being convicted. Gudjonsson, Kopelman and MacKeith (1999) suggest that there were four main factors which facilitated the wrongful conviction in this case.

- The failure to call a police surgeon and solicitor at the police station.
- The failure to consider possibilities other than amnesia (e.g. a false memory) to explain the poor recollection for the offence.

- The misuse of pharmacological abreaction sessions in a legal setting.
- Psychiatrists assuming the defendant's guilt where there is a plea of 'not guilty'.

JOHN ROBERTS—ABNORMAL COMPLIANCE

In February 1983, John Roberts, aged 20, was convicted, along with a co-defendant, of a murder that took place in October 1980. In 1994 Roberts was seen by a clinical psychologist, Bryony Moore. She had found Roberts to be abnormally compliant on the GCS, but his suggestibility score was within normal limits. She concluded that his high compliance and the nature of the interrogation made his confession potentially unreliable. At least partly on the basis of her report, the Home Secretary referred the case to the Court of Appeal.

The case was heard in March 1998 before Lord Justice Henry and Justices Ognall and Toulson. The grounds for the appeal were that:

1. without his admissions and confessions to the police, there was no case against him to go before the jury,
2. the admissions and confessions were unreliable in view of Robert's vulnerable personality (i.e. exceptionally high compliance), and
3. denial of access to a solicitor.

At appeal two psychiatrists (Dr George & Dr Joseph) and two clinical psychologists (Miss Moore & Mr Bellamy) were available to give evidence. In the end, the court only heard from the two defence experts. The Crown experts were not called, because their evidence was in agreement with that of the defence experts. The Crown objected to the admissibility of the expert defence evidence on the basis that it did not meet the criterion set out in *R. v. Ward* that the personality disorder had to be 'so severe as properly to be categorized as a mental disorder'. The judges admitted the evidence, citing the judgment in *R. v. Long* that the importance was not the diagnostic label attached to the condition, 'but whether the confession might have been unreliable' (p. 19). The psychological evidence in Mr Richard's case 'went directly to the reliability of the confession, and in those circumstances the limitation suggested in Ward does not apply' (p. 19). Dr George stated in evidence that Mr Richard was a 'dependent personality' with passive and submissive features.

The court accepted Miss Moore as having 'expertise in the emerging field of science relating to the phenomenon of false confessions pioneered by Dr Gudjonsson' (p. 21). Miss Moore concluded that Robert's confession was of the coerced–compliant type. Mr Robert's high compliance score on the GCS was corroborated by the descriptions of professionals at the time of the trial in 1983.

With regard to the status of the psychological evidence, the judges stated:

> Additionally, since 1982 there has been much research and learning applied to the psychology of interrogation, and the phenomenon of false confessions. Particularly significant in that regard are the psychometric tests pioneered by Dr Gudjonsson, which the medical professions (and latterly the courts) today accept as capable of

providing a measure of the suggestibility and/or compliance of the accused such as might lead him to make a false and unreliable confession (p. 3).

In 1982 the distinction between suggestibility (involving the (usually temporary) acceptance of guilt by the suspect, who during interrogation becomes persuaded that he did commit the crime) tended not to be clinically distinguished from compliance (where the subject at all times believed himself to be not guilty of the offence but went along with the suggestion to relieve short-term pressure). This may have been because there existed no recognized method of measuring either. Dr Gudjonsson by his work then provided the tests now recognized as measuring each. In applying them retrospectively, in 1994, the tests did not show the appellant to be suggestible, but did show him to be considerably more compliant than either the figure that was average for prisoners, or the overall average for the population (p. 23).

The expert evidence is agreed as to the excessively compliant personality of this appellant, and his consequent vulnerability. He pre-eminently needed the attendance and support of a solicitor. There were no grounds for holding him 'incommunicado' (p. 30).

Had the new psychiatric and psychological evidence been before the court, the trial judge would have been bound to exclude the evidence of the confessions, and without that evidence there was no case to go before the jury (p. 31).

The court accordingly quashed Robert's conviction from 15 years previously. In their final paragraph the judges concluded:

Medical science and the law have moved a long way since 1982. We hope that the safeguards now in place will prevent others becoming victims of similar miscarriages of justice. The courts must ensure that lessons learnt are translated into more effective protections. Vigilance must be the watchword of the criminal justice system if public confidence is to be maintained.

Comments

The importance of the judgment is that the court recognized the pioneering scientific developments since 1982 that had taken place in relation to the assessment of psychological vulnerability and identifying false confessions. In particular, the court accepted the importance of experts being able to provide measurements of such psychological concepts such as suggestibility and compliance. It extended the ruling in *R. v. Raghip* in that high compliance on testing, supported by relevant background information, was a sufficient psychological vulnerability on its own, in the circumstances of this case, to overturn a conviction. There had been no formal psychiatric diagnosis of mental illness, personality disorder or learning disability. The Court also recognized the important distinction between the concepts of suggestibility and compliance.

ASHLEY KING—ABNORMAL SUGGESTIBILITY AND COMPLIANCE

Over a two-day period in November 1985, Ashley King was interviewed on 10 occasions by the police in connection with a woman, Mrs Greenwood, found murdered at her home. Eventually he confessed, and retracted the confession two days later after seeing a solicitor for the first time.

In June 1986 King was convicted of the murder. In 1993, King had been seen by a psychologist, Mrs Ann Scott Fordham. King was found to be of borderline IQ (Full Scale IQ of 77) and obtained an abnormally high Shift score on the GSS (the form used was not specified). Further and more detailed psychological testing was carried out by Mrs Olive Tunstall in September 1998. Again, King was found to be of borderline IQ (Full Scale IQ of 78) and scored abnormally high on Shift as measured by the GSS 2. He also proved to be abnormally compliant, as measured by the GCS. Mrs Tunstall concluded that during the police interviews in 1985 King would have been psychologically vulnerable, and his vulnerabilities would have been exacerbated by the absence of legal advice throughout his period of detention, the absence of an appropriate adult and physical and mental fatigue.

I was commissioned by the Crown Prosecution Service to evaluate Mrs Tunstall's report and conclusions. I produced a report and on the day of the appeal I had a conference with the prosecution team. In short, having studied the material provided, I agreed with Mrs Tunstall's conclusions. I had serious reservations about the reliability of the confession King had made to the police in 1985. I concluded:

> I think it is significant that when there was an appropriate adult present during the 6th interview, Mr King strongly retracted his confession and gave plausible reasons for the retraction. (There were also retractions in other interviews.) The explanation he gave to Mrs Tunstall for having made the retraction in 6th interview is credible. It is also of significance that in the 6th interview Mr King asked repeatedly to be allowed to go home. It suggests he was preoccupied about being released from custody and might make self-incriminating admissions if he perceived that this might result in his being released from custody more quickly.
>
> Even on the basis of the limited and poor transcripts of the police interviews, it is evident that Mr King was placed under considerable pressure by the police to confess and he was apparently not coping well with their questioning. In this context, his borderline intelligence, combined with abnormally high suggestibility and compliance, are relevant to evaluating the reliability of his confessions to the police.

The appeal was heard in December 1999 before Lord Bingham and Justices Morison and Nelson. Mrs Tunstall gave evidence, which was undisputed by myself, the appointed Crown expert. I was not required to give evidence, which was fortunate since I was giving evidence that same day in another Court of Appeal case (Darren Hall—see below). The judges found Mrs Tunstall's evidence was persuasive and stated with reference to the development of this kind of scientific testimony:

> There is, however, the additional finding that the appellant was suggestible and compliant to an abnormal degree. That was not a matter which could, practically speaking, have been tested, assessed or qualified in 1985 to 1986. Although there had been some published work on the subject, this was a new and embryonic science. Nor was the appellant's suggestibility and compliance a matter which it

would have been at all easy for a jury to judge because when they saw him in the witness box he was not accepting suggestions made by the prosecution and was not setting out to do what they wanted.

The prosecution argued that King had revealed special knowledge in some of his answers to the police questioning, 'which is inexplicable on any basis other than guilt'. Mr King responded by claiming that the interviewing officers had fed him with details about the crime.

The judges ruled that with the benefit of this expert evidence there would have been strong grounds for excluding the confession evidence under Sections 76 and 78 of PACE, and possibly also under Section 77. Had the jury heard the expert testimony they would have

> ... been very hesitant indeed to convict the appellant on the strength of his uncorroborated and retracted confessions, and rightly so. In light of this new evidence we feel bound to regard the appellant's conviction as unsafe and we accordingly quash it.

In response to the prosecution arguments, the judges pointed out that even though they were concerned about the safety of the conviction, it could not be said that actual innocence of the appellant was established.

Comments

The only evidence against Ashley King at trial was his confession. The Lorships commented that King's borderline IQ score would not by itself have been sufficient to cast doubt on the safety of his conviction. It was the additional evidence of King's abnormal suggestibility and compliance that was essential in overturning his conviction, in spite of the fact that during the trial King did not readily accept suggestions put to him by the prosecution when he was in the in the witness box. This case raised important issues about the cumulative effects of different kinds of vulnerability (e.g. low IQ, high suggestibility and compliance). The greater the number of vulnerabilities, assuming they are all individually relevant to the potential unreliability of the confession, the greater the likelihood of a false confession (see Sigurdsson & Gudjonsson, 2001). This case also illustrated how defendants' ability to resist suggestions in the witness box is still often used by the prosecution as evidence that they are not psychologically vulnerable.

DARREN HALL—DISORDER IN THE ABSENCE OF A PSYCHIATRIC DIAGNOSIS

This case relates to a murder in Cardiff in 1987 of a 52-year-old man called Mr Saunders, who owned a number of newspaper stands. The case is unusual, similar to the case of Judith Ward, in that Darren Hall did not retract the confession he had made to the police and proclaim his innocence until several years after conviction. In addition, he implicated two other people, who he had allegedly been with at the time of the offence, both of whom always proclaimed they were innocent. In interviews with the police he mainly claimed that he had not taken part in the murder, but had acted as 'look-out' man (he gave somewhat different versions of events) while his co-accused, Sherwood and O'Brien, had committed the murder and robbery. The only evidence against Hall at trial was his confession to the police and others afterwards. Hall's confession directly implicated Sherwood and O'Brien. There was no forensic evidence to link any of the three to the murder. Hall pleaded guilty to robbery and manslaughter. The three defendants were convicted of the murder in July 1988 by majority verdicts of 10 to 2. They were sentenced to life imprisonment. After conviction Hall gave substantially different versions of events concerning the murder.

1. In 1991 Hall began to claim that he had taken a more active role in the murder than he had previously admitted to.
2. During group therapy in prison in 1994 Hall claimed that he had committed the murder on his own.
3. In 1995 Hall wrote to his solicitors stating that he had hit Saunders on the head five times, while Sherwood had punched the victim and O'Brien stood some distance away.
4. In 1996 Hall retracted his confession and claimed that all three of them were completely innocent of the murder.

Shortly before his retraction in 1996, Hall had been interviewed in prison by Mrs Tunstall, who found him on testing to be of average intellectual abilities and verbal memory. In terms of his personality, as measured by the EPQ-R, he was an emotionally labile (anxious) extravert. He did not prove to be suggestible on the GSS 1 (a Total Suggestibility score of 6). In 1997, Mrs Tunstall produced a report at the request of the Criminal Cases Review Commission, where her findings were outlined. She raised concerns about the reliability of Hall's confession to the police and the case was referred to the Court of Appeal.

A few weeks prior to the hearing in December 1999, the defence solicitors referred the case to me and asked for a psychological evaluation. The solicitors were concerned that the psychological test findings in Mrs Tunstall's report might be insufficient for the expert testimony to be admissible. I agreed to take on the case, and interviewed Hall and carried out a number of psychological tests. The tests I administered included the MMPI-2, the Gough Socialisation Scale, the Gudjonsson Compliance Sale (GCS), tests of impulsivity, self-esteem and self and other deception. The findings were consistent with a diagnosis of anti-social personality disorder, poor self-esteem and an abnormally high level of compliance and impulsivity.

I asked Hall why he had made the confession to the police. He gave the following reasons.

- He was extensively pressured to confess by the police officers, and was allegedly threatened that unless he confessed and maintained his confession the police would harass him and his family. They kept bringing him up

from the police cell, interviewing him briefly and then taking him back to the cell. This went on for a long time. During the second arrest and set of interviews Hall was handcuffed to a very hot radiator during the interviews (there appears to be some independent support for this). There was no actual violence, only threats. Eventually he told the police what he thought they wanted to hear.
- He thought he was being clever and wanted to get 'one over on the police'.
- He wanted to be noticed and recognized. At the time of his arrest his life was very unhappy; he had been 'kicked out' by his parents, who did not want to have anything to do with him, he had few friends and he felt he had nothing worth living for. He was not worried about the prospect of going to prison or bothered about what would happen to him. He was tired of his life-style and was quite happy to go to prison.
- He did not think of the consequences of making a false confession, either to himself or to implicating his two co-accused. Nor did he think he would be convicted of murder and receive a life sentence.

Hall had not retracted the confession until 1996, eight years after making the confession. I asked him to explain why, if he was innocent, he had not retracted the confession at the earliest opportunity. He gave me an explanation that was identical to that given in his recent proofs to his solicitors. He emphasized that at the time of maintaining the confession he was doing what he thought was the best solution at the time, given the circumstances he was faced with. He claimed to have maintained his confession for eight years for three main reasons.

- Fear of potential repercussion from the police if he retracted the confession.
- He enjoyed the notoriety of his status as a murderer within the prison system.
- Prior to his arrest Hall had not enjoyed life on the outside. He found life in prison a great deal easier and he had no responsibilities. He had his bed and food provided. It was more than he had before going to prison.

The case was heard before Lord Justice Roch and Justices Keene and Astill on 9 December 1999. There were three expert witnesses for the defence, Professor Kopelman (a consultant psychiatrist), Mrs Tunstall (a clinical psychologist) and myself, and one for the Crown, Dr Brian Thomas-Peter (a clinical psychologist). Dr Thomas-Peter did not agree with the defence experts that Hall had an anti-social personality disorder. Instead, Dr Thomas-Peter accepted that Hall had 'a disordered personality', not amounting to a diagnosable personality disorder, due to such factors as his unusual upbringing and social disadvantage. This disagreement between the defence and Crown experts was potentially important in view of the ruling in *Ward*. If the court accepted the arguments of Dr Thomas-Peter, then the expert testimony could be ruled inadmissible. In addition, Dr Thomas-Peter did not accept that Hall was compliant to the influence of others in a way I had described on the basis on the GCS score. He had not formally tested Hall for compliance.

In my report I considered Hall's failure to retract his confession at the earliest opportunity after the interrogation sessions:

> On the face of it, perhaps the most logical explanation is that Mr Hall did not retract the confession for eight years, because he had been involved in the offence. How do we know that Mr Hall is not presenting us with just another convenient lie in order to further his need for notoriety? Simply, we do not know and this possibility cannot be disregarded completely. However, having studied this case in some detail, I am concerned that the Court considers carefully the alternative explanation, namely that Mr Hall may have made a false confession and did not retract it for a number of years due to his own peculiar needs and underlying psychopathology. This is certainly a possibility, which on the basis of my psychological evaluation has some merits. I have read the detailed explanation for the delayed retraction provided by Mrs Olive Tunstall in her report. I do agree with her views and arguments.

The judges carefully considered the expert testimony and concluded:

> Despite the differences between the views of the experts we heard, we are satisfied that Hall is and was a person having traits in his personality of the kind associated with those who make false confessions. Dr Gudjonsson gave evidence that Hall showed a very high level of compliance, to an extreme degree found in only about 2% of the population. All the experts were agreed that Hall was a man with low self-esteem but a high degree of impulsivity. The presence of these traits did not mean that the admissions Hall made and the evidence he gave were untrue; they rendered those admissions and evidence potentially unreliable.
>
> Despite what was said in the case of *Ward*, the test cannot, in our judgment, be whether the abnormality fits into some recognized category, such as anti-social personality disorder. That is neither necessary nor sufficient. It is not necessary, because as *R. v. Roberts* showed, the real criterion must simply be whether the abnormal disorder might render the confession or evidence unreliable. It is not sufficient because an anti social personality disorder does not necessarily mean that the defendant is a compulsive liar or fantasist or that his confession or evidence might be unreliable.
>
> The members of this Court, as were all counsel, who addressed us, are conscious of the need to have defined limits for the case in which expert evidence of this kind we have heard may be used. First the abnormal disorder must not only be of the type which might render a confession or evidence unreliable, there must also be a very significant deviation from the norm shown. In this case the abnormalities identified by the experts were of a very high level, Hall's test results falling within the top few percentiles of the population. Second, there should be a history predating the making of the admissions or the giving of evidence which is not based solely on a history given by the subject, which points to or explains the abnormality or abnormalities.
>
> If such evidence is admitted, the jury must be directed that they are not obliged to accept such evidence. They should consider it if they think it right to do so, as throwing light on the personality of the defendant and bringing to their attention aspects of that personality which they might otherwise have been unaware.
>
> The evidence, both factual and expert which has been placed before us has satisfied us that this is a case in which such evidence would now be admissible, and that a jury having heard such evidence may well have reached different verdicts.

Comments

This is an unusual case and in some respects resembles the case of Judith Ward. In both cases the confessions were not retracted for many years. Why should people who are wrongfully convicted for murder maintain their confession for several years if it is not true? A number of reasons can be put forward.

- They believe they were involved in the crime even if they are truly innocent (this is only likely to apply to internalized false confessions, or where the person is unable to distinguish fact from fantasy, as in the case of David MacKenzie).
- They think there is no chance of a successful appeal and the quickest way of being granted parole is to pretend that the confession is true. This is sometimes claimed by appellants with some justification, because without the confession the person is unable to comply with offence related work in prison which facilitates their release into the community (e.g. gaining insight into their offending, displaying feelings of remorse).
- They are frightened of repercussions if they retract the confession (e.g. that their families will be in danger, or that they will be re-interrogated by the police or in some way harassed).
- They want to keep up a notoriety status, for example by the need to appear hard and tough in the eyes of other prisoners.

The judgment builds upon the ruling in *Roberts*, but defines limits as to the admissibility of expert testimony. What is important is the *type* of vulnerability. The implication is that some vulnerabilities, even if they do not amount to a psychiatric disorder, are particularly relevant and important in rendering a confession unreliable. In the case of *Roberts* it was abnormally high compliance. In the case of *Hall* it was his abnormal personality (e.g. high compliance, low self-esteem, impulsivity) that rendered the confession unreliable. Second, these personality problems have to fall outside normal limits in terms of their severity (i.e. the degree to which they are present has to be very infrequent in the population). Third, it has to be established that these abnormal characteristics or traits were evident prior to the police interviews when the confession was made.

IAIN HAY GORDON—EXPLOITATION OF SEXUALITY

On 12 November 1952, Miss Patricia Curran, the 19-year-old daughter of a High Court Judge in Belfast, was murdered. She was last seen by witnesses at about 1720 when disembarking a bus near her home at Whiteabbey. Her body was found in the early hours (at about 2 a.m.) the following day by Mr Desmond Curran (her older brother and a member of a search party), in shrubbery off the private drive leading to her home at Glen House in Whiteabbey, a middle-class suburb of Belfast. It later emerged that she had been stabbed 37 times. A major murder inquiry was launched by the Royal Ulster Constabulary (RUC) and about 40 000 witness statements were taken. After the first weekend two detectives from Scotland Yard were called in to assist with the murder inquiry.

These were Detective Superintendent John Capstick and Detective Sergeant Denis Hawkins.

Iain Hay Gordon was soon to become a suspect in the case, because he had lied to the police about his alibi and he was acquainted with the Curran family. At the time of his arrest Gordon, a 20-year-old Scotsman, was doing his National Service with the Royal Air Force in Northern Ireland.

The Police Interviews

Gordon was first interviewed about the murder on the afternoon of 13 November 1952, about 13 hours after the discovery of the body. This was a part of a routine questioning of Royal Air Force (RAF) personnel at the Edenmore Camp where Gordon was stationed. Gordon said that between 2300 hours and midnight he had been in the billet (this was the initial time estimation of the victim's death). He was noted to have a black eye. (It later became apparent that Gordon had received the black eye when he had been hit by another airman three days previously.) Gordon volunteered that he knew the Curran family and had last been to the house about three weeks previously.

The following day Gordon was interviewed again and asked about his movements between 1700 and 1800 hours on 12 November 1952. This was because it had in the meantime become apparent that Miss Curran might have been murdered shortly after she returned home on the bus at 1720 and not about midnight as thought previously. Gordon said he had gone to the Whiteabbey post office at 1630 on the day of the murder and returned to the camp at 1700. He then had his evening meal in the dining hall. He then lied to the officer that he had walked out of the dining hall to the billet with Corporal Connor. This proved not to be the case. Gordon was later to claim that this had been at the suggestion of Corporal Connor, who also told the police that he and Gordon had been together. Later Mr Connor claimed that the lie about their alibi had been at the suggestion of Gordon. Both Gordon and Connor were later to be interviewed as suspects. Connor made no confessions to the murder during interrogation, but Gordon broke down on 15 January 1953 and confessed to the murder.

Gordon was again interviewed on 17 November 1952. He claimed that he had been alone in the camp all evening. He was also interviewed about his relationship with the Curran family and it was confirmed that he had met Miss Curran on a few occasions.

On 29 November, Gordon was interviewed again, but this time by Sergeant Denis Hawkins from Scotland Yard. Gordon was asked again to go over his movements between 1700 and 1800 hours on the day of the murder.

On 4 December, Gordon was interviewed for about 30 minutes by Sergeant Davidson of the RUC about his movements on 12 November 1952.

On 10 December, Gordon was interviewed for about one hour by Detective Superintendent John Capstick and County Inspector Albert Kennedy, a local officer who was responsible for the criminal investigation. Gordon was asked about his relationship with a local man, Wesley Courtenay. Known to the police was the fact that the two men had allegedly been involved in homosexual encounters.

Gordon was finally interviewed over a period of three days between 13 and 15 January 1953. The interviews commenced at 1000 a.m. on Tuesday 13 January and ended at 1835 in the evening. On Thursday 15 January 1953, after Gordon had signed a confession statement that afternoon, he was charged with the murder of Miss Curran. He was not legally represented during any of the interviews.

It is noteworthy that the confession statement produced at the end of the interrogation is quite vague and often tentative words are used, such as 'I believe', 'I think', 'I may have'. At one point Gordon states 'It was solely due to a blackout'.

The Trial

Gordon was tried before Lord Chief Justice, Lord McDermott, and a jury at Belfast Assizes in March 1953. The defence argued unsuccessfully against the admissibility of the signed confession statement of Gordon. The trial judge considered the confession to be obtained voluntarily. He had listened to the testimony of Detective Superintendent Capstick. It is evident from the transcript of the evidence of Capstick that he was closely cross-examined by defence counsel. It emerged that Gordon was questioned about matters other than the murder of Miss Curran. This included extensive questioning about Gordon's private (sex) life as early as 10 December 1952 and until Gordon began to make a confession on 15 January 1953.

It was alleged by the defence that the purpose of the extensive questioning of Gordon about his sex life was to break down his resistance and obtain a confession from him. Capstick said in his testimony that the purpose of asking Gordon about his sex life was 'to find out what type of boy this was, and what he was doing, and if he could tell the truth about matters like that, I could depend upon him to tell us other things, and he eventually did tell us the things he had been committing and he was speaking to us quite openly and freely, and not keeping things back'. (It is noteworthy that Detective Sergeant Hawkins and Head Constable Russell had on 13 January also focused their questions on Gordon's sex life, which suggests that there was considerable emphasis placed by different officers on Gordon's sex life.)

At the end of his testimony Detective Superintendent Capstick stated that during the time the confession statement was taken from Gordon (between 2.30 and 6.35 p.m. on 15 January 1953), there were no questions put to him by either himself or County Inspector Kennedy. Capstick had conducted the interview during the morning, up till lunchtime, without any other officer being present.

In his autobiography, *Given in Evidence*, Capstick (1960) discusses his interrogation of Gordon and his testimony under cross-examination about the way in which Gordon's confession statement was taken. He claims to have 'taken the only course open' to him:

> I had to make the boy tell me the truth about his private life and most secret thoughts. Only then could I begin to believe him when he began to tell the truth about the death of Patricia Curran. I hate to use what might well seem to some like ruthless measures. I was never sorrier for any criminal than for that unhappy, maladjusted youngster. But his mask had to be broken (pp. 332–333).

Once Lord Chief Justice, Lord McDermott, had ruled the confession admissible, the 0 defence shifted their efforts towards an insanity defence, because if convicted of murder Gordon would have received a mandatory death penalty sentence. After the jury had deliberated for about two hours in the evening of Saturday 7 March 1953, they returned a special verdict of guilty but insane under the Trial of Lunatics Act 1883, as a result of which Gordon was committed to a psychiatric hospital, where he was detained for seven years. No appeal was possible at the time against such a verdict of guilty but insane.

Dr Rossiter Lewis, a London-based psychiatrist, testified at the request of the defence. He had interviewed Gordon on 8 and 9 February 1953 and his examinations lasted for a total of about 11 hours. Dr Lewis assumed that Gordon had had distinct periods of memory loss concerning the murder and 'Having ascertained that he had a loss of memory, I decided to restore that memory by use of the thiopentone test'. The drug allegedly restored Gordon's 'memory for the early stages of the incidents, when Gordon was with the girl on the grass verge'. Dr Lewis stated that drug was not able to restore Gordon's memory for the actual stabbing.

Post-Trial

Gordon was admitted to the Holywell Hospital on 24 March 1953. The diagnosis on admission was 'Immature Personality'. No evidence of mental illness was ascertained, neither did Gordon ever receive treatment for a psychiatric disorder whilst in hospital.

Shortly after admission to the hospital Gordon was seen by Dr Smith and repeated the confession 'as it had appeared in the papers'. It appears that this was the last time Gordon reiterated his confession. Dr Smith described Gordon as 'definitely gullible and suggestible, not a chap to stand up for himself'.

In April 1957, Gordon was interviewed by a psychiatrist, Dr D. Curran (no relation to the victim's family). His report was detailed and informative. He found Gordon to be 'almost excessively polite' and with regard to his confession on 15 January 1953 'He claimed it was pointed out to him things would go badly for him if he did not admit to the murder, that he felt sleepy and had difficulty in concentrating after tea and at lunch on the third day and that he finally half believed that he might have had a lapse of memory and committed the crime'. Gordon 'said he periodically wondered if he had done it for six months after admission to mental hospital. It had been put to him that his only possible defence would be on medical grounds, and he said that Dr Rossiter Lewis's technique had been very similar to that of Capstick. He claimed that the statement was entirely Capstick's production on his answers to Capstick's questions with the exception of the statement of regret. "I added that myself. He had convinced me that I had killed Miss Curran and I thought it was the proper thing to say"'. Dr Curran's impression of Gordon was that he 'is a very suggestible, gullible subject'.

On 4 April 1953, Mr Gordon wrote a letter to his parents, in which he was beginning to express serious doubts about his involvement in the murder:

> I just cannot believe that I was there and was responsible. I have not any recollection of leaving Edenmore after I returned from the Post Office on November 12th

nor of any of the things I am supposed to have done. I never harmed anybody in my life and least of all a girl and I have never done a thing like what I am supposed to have done... The weekend preceding my arrest was the happiest in my whole life, I had no thought of admitting to it or even considered myself guilty—till the RUC and Scotland Yard kept at me till I was so tired and fed up that I was ready to say anything to be rid of them.

This strongly suggests that Gordon was persuaded during questioning that he had committed the murder, even though he had no previous memory of having done so. It also suggests that by 4 April 1953 he was having serious reservations about his involvement in the murder and no longer had the belief that he had committed the murder.

Gordon was finally released, after persistent petitioning of the Stormont administration by his parents, from Holywell Hospital in September 1960 to reside with his parents in Glasgow. Gordon's father died in 1980 and his mother in 1984. His parents bankrupted themselves trying to clear his name (Walker, 2000). He worked for 33 years as a stockroom assistant for a group of publishers and retired in 1993 due to bad health. After his retirement he began to campaign to clear his name. Gordon and his lawyer, Margot Harvey, had tried very hard to have the case referred to the Court of Appeal by the Criminal Cases Review Commission. A journalist, Mr John Linklater, had worked on the case for a number of years and gathered new evidence, which was to assist with the appeal.

In 1998, Mr Gordon made an application to the Criminal Cases Review Commission (CCRC), but in view of the nature of the special verdict Gordon received, the Commission did not have the powers to refer the case to the Court of Appeal. Such a referral became possible after Parliament amended the law by enactment of the Criminal Cases Review (Insanity) Act 1999. Gordon's efforts to clear his name were to become a reality.

Psychological Evaluation

I was commissioned to work on the case by the defence. In July 1999, Gordon travelled from Scotland to see me at the Institute of Psychiatry. At the time he was 67 years of age and looked frail. In spite of this he was able to give me a clear and coherent account of his interrogation with Detective Superintendent Capstick 46 years previously. Gordon told me that he had not committed the murder of Miss Curran. He said he had not left the RAF camp that evening after returning from going to the post office. He was in his room reading and writing, but went to the Registry to do some typing before going to bed. During the evening many people from the camp had been attending a dance in Belfast, but Gordon did not go and preferred to stay in the billet. He told me that during interrogation by Capstick he had come to believe that perhaps he had committed the murder, although he had no actual memory of doing so. This belief continued on and off for a few months, but he was never completely convinced of his guilt and deep down did not think he had committed the murder. (In November 1958 Gordon wrote a very detailed account of his background, himself, the police interviews and the confession. I found his written account most helpful in understanding his perspective on the police interviews and the nature of his confession. His account is entirely consistent with a pressured–internalized false confession.)

During the psychological assessment, Gordon completed a number of psychological tests including the WAIS-R, the GSS 2, the GCS and the EPQ-R. The findings were that Gordon was of average intellectual abilities, but he was abnormally suggestible on the GSS 2 (a Yield 1 score of 12 and a Shift score of 11, giving a Total Suggestibility score of 23) and confabulated abnormally with regard to immediate and delayed free recall on the test. His GCS (compliance) score was moderately elevated (14) and the social desirability score on the EPQ-R fell outside normal limits. Having had the opportunity of interviewing and testing Gordon, as well as having studied in detail all the relevant documents in the case, I concluded:

> I am of the view that this case has all the hallmarks of a coerced-internalized false confession and I have serious doubts about the reliability of the confession and the self-incriminating admissions made by Mr Gordon during interrogation and afterwards.

The basis of my conclusions can be seen from the following extracts taken from the conclusions in my Psychological Report, dated 26 February 2000:

> The confession Mr Gordon made to the police on 15 January 1953 is very vague, lacks much specific detail, and descriptions are prefaced by indefinite remarks suggesting that Mr Gordon was not confessing to an event of which he had a clear recollection. The content of the confession is consistent with a false confession of the 'coerced–internalized' type. The confession reads as if it was elicited by questioning rather than being a free narrative account, which contradicts the testimony of Detective Superintendent Capstick during the trial. In addition, Mr Gordon was clearly placed under considerable pressure during lengthy police questioning and I think it is very probable that the extensive questioning about Mr Gordon's sex life was instrumental in getting him to confess to the murder of Miss Curran. I am in no doubt that this method of questioning would have placed him under considerable additional pressure, irrespective of whether or not it was intended. Questioning young suspects about their sexuality can act as extreme pressure and result in a false confession (Gudjonsson & MacKeith, 1990).
>
> The present assessment indicates that Mr Gordon possesses strong psychological vulnerabilities which make him susceptible, under certain circumstances, to making an internalized false confession. These include a highly abnormal degree of suggestibility, including the inability to cope with interrogative pressure, and a tendency towards confabulatory responding. Of course, Mr Gordon was not tested psychologically prior to his trial in 1953 and we do not know for certain what his scores would have been on the tests at that time. However, there are strong grounds for inferring from colleagues and from reports that in 1953 Mr Gordon was an unassertive individual, who would have been open to suggestion and unable to cope with interrogative pressure. My other concerns are that at the time of his interviews with the police he was in a particularly difficult predicament, because he had been deceptive about his alibi and he was sensitive about his sexuality, and his alleged homosexual experiences in particular. Taken together, all these factors would have made him psychologically vulnerable to giving potentially unreliable self-incriminating admissions under pressure. It would have been quite possible for the police to persuade Mr Gordon that he had committed the murder, even if he had no memory of doing so. Once he had begun to believe that he might have

committed the murder he would then have tried to reconstruct in his own mind, perhaps with the assistance of the police interviewers, what could have happened.

The fact that Mr Gordon continued to make self-incriminating admissions after he was charged and convicted is not surprising in view of: (a) his psychological vulnerabilities; (b) the nature of the interrogation; and (c) the likely type of false confession that we are dealing with (i.e. coerced–internalized). I have come across other similar cases, including the recent case reported by Gudjonsson, Kopelman and MacKeith (1999).

The pharmacological abreaction sessions administered by Dr Lewis has had two potentially serious consequences for Mr Gordon's case. Firstly, Dr Lewis' testimony to the jury sounds as if the abreaction test resulted in Mr Gordon being able to recover some of his lost memory of the murder and that the drug had assisted in getting Mr Gordon to tell the truth. This must have been very damaging to the defence. In reality, such abreaction tests are highly unreliable and do not establish the 'truth' (Gudjonsson, 1992). Therefore, the jury may have been misled by Dr Lewis' testimony. Secondly, it is quite possible, if not likely, that the abreaction sessions contaminated Mr Gordon's memory and made it more difficult for him to differentiate real from false memories. This may have been part of the reason why it took Mr Gordon such a long time to be fully convinced of his innocence (see Gudjonsson, Kopelman and MacKeith, 1999, for a description of a similar case).

Outcome in the Court of Appeal

My psychological report was forwarded by the defence team to the Criminal Cases Review Commission, who had to take a view as to its significance. They commissioned a report of their own from Professor Michael Kopelman, a neuropsychiatrist, with whom I had worked closely on other cases of disputed confessions, including that of Andrew Evans.

Professor Kopelman focused mainly on the use by Dr Lewis of sodium thiopentone and concluded:

> In summary, I do not think that the diagnoses of schizophrenia, inadequate psychopath, or spontaneous hypoglycaemia, put forward at the original trial, are now acceptable: the evidence put forward in their support would not fulfil modern diagnostic criteria. Secondly, the use of sodium thiopentone in a medico-legal setting is extremely hazardous, as recent literature on false confession has indicated, because erroneous memories are likely to arise and the subject is vulnerable to suggestion unless the interview is very carefully conducted. Details and transcripts concerning the interview under sodium thiopentone do not seem to have been given to the Court, and Dr Lewis certainly did not provide any caution to the Court about the interpretation of his findings from this interview. I concur with Professor Gudjonsson that such interviews are highly unreliable, and, in this case, the interview may even have inculcated false memories into Mr Gordon's mind. In this connection, it is notable that Mr Gordon's confession is replete with qualification words, as if he were not at all confident about what he was recounting. In light of this, I agree with Professor Gudjonsson's opinion that the confession appears to be unreliable.

The Criminal Cases Review Commission subsequently referred the case back to the Court of Appeal in Belfast. The Director of Public Prosecutions sought the services of a clinical psychologist, Mr Hanley, who did not interview Mr Gordon himself, but agreed that, at the time of his interrogation in 1953, Mr Gordon was psychologically vulnerable to making a coerced–internalized false confession.

The appeal was heard in Belfast in December 2000, before the Lord Chief Justice of Northern Ireland, Sir Robert Carswell, Lord Campbell and Mr Justice Kerr. No live witnesses were called. As far as the psychological and psychiatric evidence was concerned, this was discussed in detail in the course of arguments at the appeal and in the judgment and our views concerning the unreliability of Gordon's confession were accepted by the court. There were also available to the court reports from two linguistic experts, Professor Coulthard and Dr French, both of whom, like myself, had cast doubt on the police account that Mr Gordon's confession had been taken by dictation rather than questions and answers.

The conviction from 1953 was quashed and no retrial was ordered. Gordon had finally succeeded in clearing his name, almost 48 years after his conviction (Walker, 2000). Importantly, the court adopted the standards set by Lord Chief Justice, Lord Bingham, in *R. v. Bently* ([1999], Crim.L.R. 330) by which the conduct of the trial, the admission of the confession, the direction to the jury and the safety of conviction should be judged. This involved applying current standards to decisions relating to procedure made in 1953.

Comments

This case gives an excellent illustration of a pressured–internalized false confession. It involved a famous Scotland Yard detective who felt justified to play on Gordon's most intimate sexual feelings and experiences in order to break down his resistance. At the time Gordon was a highly vulnerable individual and came to believe that he had committed the murder, although he denies ever having any memory of committing the offence. The psychological evidence was clearly crucial in persuading the Court of Appeal in Belfast to overturn the conviction and was accepted without any fresh live expert evidence.

PETER FELL—POOR SELF-ESTEEM

This case is unique in that it involved a combination of voluntary, internalized and compliant false confessions.

This case involves the murder by multiple stabbing of two women in May 1982, who were walking their dogs on common land on the outskirts of Aldershot. In October 1983 Peter Fell was charged with the two murders and in August 1985 he was convicted by a majority of the jurors (10–2) of both murders. The main evidence against him at trial was self-incriminating admissions he had made to the police during a series of telephone conversations in 1982 and 1983 and subsequent admissions during lengthy custodial interrogation. The admissibility of the admissions was disputed by the defence and after a *voire dire* the judge ruled the admissions were voluntary and the interviews were admitted into evidence. Fell was refused leave to appeal against his conviction in November 1985.

Fell, who was 22 years of age at the time of his interrogation, appears to have become a suspect in the case for two reasons. First, the day after the murders Fell, late at night and after his girlfriend had left him, telephoned the police twice and anonymously directed the police to himself as the murderer. Over a year later, after Fell had moved to Bournemouth, he made a series of telephone calls to the police when plainly intoxicated. He referred to the double murder and again anonymously identified himself as the murderer and gave the police his address in Bournemouth. His wife had left him the previous day and this seems to have precipitated the phone calls, as it did previously when his girlfriend had left him in Aldershot. A month later Fell was arrested by the police and questioned. The second reason why Fell became a suspect relates to his resemblance to a photofit of the suspect seen on the common at the material time. The police emphasized this resemblance during the subsequent interviews and used it to challenge Fell's repeated and persistent denials. Out of 157 calls to the police identifying persons resembling the picture, five identified Fell and 152 identified various other people.

Fell was extensively interviewed on seven occasions over a period of three days without access to a solicitor. The interviews were mostly tape recorded, although the quality of some of the tapes was very poor. During his period of detention, Fell was twice taken to the common where the murders had taken place. The first visit was on the afternoon of the second day in custody, following the fourth interview where it was repeatedly put to him in no uncertain terms that he had been to the common and that he was the murderer.

After returning from the visit to the common Fell was interviewed again (fifth interview). He was placed under considerable pressure to admit that he was on the common at the time of the murders. He now admitted that he might have been on the common, but remains unsure ('might have', 'must have', 'not sure if there at all', 'I was there'). Once Fell conceded that he might have been on the Common previously the officers used this as an additional pressure to obtain a confession from him to the murders. During this interview Fell sounded very distressed.

The following morning Fell was taken back to the common and he claims that prior to the sixth interview there was a discussion about the difference between murder and manslaughter. During the sixth interview, and after having been in custody for over 52 hours and denied guilt of the murders on 116 occasions, Fell broke down and made incriminating admissions to the murders, which did not quite amount to a full confession to both killings. During this period he was unable to consume any food, undoubtedly due to the stress of his predicament. About three hours after the confession interview was terminated, Fell requested to see the senior officer in the case and then retracted the confession in quite an assertive and determined way ('I didn't kill anyone, I didn't see those women, I don't even think I was on the Common'). He explained to the officer on tape during the seventh interview the reasons why he had made a false confession. This involved his fear at the time that he could not prove his innocence, the officers were not prepared to listen to his denial, he thought that he was about to be charged with the murders and would eventually be convicted of either murder or manslaughter. He decided to reach for a compromise and make a confession that would reduce the charge to manslaughter, but after having time to think about the confession in the police cell, decided to retract it. The content of the confession had all the hallmarks of a person who is trying to appear mentally disarranged, including claiming that he could hear the trees on the common talking to him and that one of the women had reminded him of his mother whom he hated. His post-admission statement to the police was also unconvincing in that some of the details he gave did not coincide with the known facts (e.g. he claimed to have hit the women, whereas they were stabbed to death). Within half an hour of the retraction interview terminating Fell was able to eat properly for the first time since his arrest.

Interestingly, in spite of Fell making a confession to the murders, he was able to resist repeated pressure from the police to get him to admit that he had had owned a double-edged knife and a green jacket as claimed by witnesses. He never admitted to these matters and has always claimed that he did not own double-edged knife or a green jacket. This suggests that when Fell broke down and confessed in the sixth interview he was not just agreeing with everything the police had suggested to him. In other words, his mind was not completely overborne by the pressure of the interrogation. This is something I have noted in other cases of false confession and it was discussed in Chapter 9.

The police interviews were conducted 14 months after the murders. The questioning during the interviews was persistent, determined and relentless. This included the officers repeatedly presenting their view that Fell was the man who had been seen at the material time on the common where the murders had taken place and that they had a large number of witnesses who had allegedly identified him from a photofit. He repeatedly requested to see a solicitor, but the officers completely ignored his requests and continued to interview him. A careful analysis of the interviews indicated that the techniques used to break down Fell's resistance were similar to the Inbau, Reid and Buckely (1986) type techniques found by Pearse and Gudjonsson (1999). They comprised 'Intimidation' (i.e. maximization of anxiety associated with denial, multiple assertions, gross exaggeration of the evidence, including false claims that Fell had been identified on the common, the use of his girlfriend to incriminate him and at times raised voices by the officers and rapid questioning), 'Robust Challenge' (i.e. repeatedly challenging Fell's denials) and 'Psychological Manipulation' (i.e. minimizing the seriousness of admitting to being on the common and then exaggerating its importance once he had admitted that he 'might' have been there, suggesting that he had committed the offence whilst drunk and had forgotten about it, inducements to admit to manslaughter). It is also evident that there were a number of unrecorded conversations with Fell in the police cell.

In September 1999, the Criminal Cases Review Commission referred the case to the Court of Appeal mainly on the grounds of new evidence concerning material non-disclosure and fresh psychological evidence concerning Fell's vulnerabilities during the interrogation and the effects of these on the reliability of the admissions he had made to the police in 1984. The defence sought to add further grounds for appeal, including the absence of a solicitor during the police interviews.

I had first become involved in this case in 1988 after being commissioned by Fell's solicitors. I interviewed Fell and on testing found him to be of low average intelligence, but abnormally compliant; he also possessed extremely poor self-esteem, and was an emotionally labile (anxious) introvert. He proved to be only moderately suggestible on the GSS 1. The very low score on the Gough Socialisation Scale, combined with a high Psychoticism (P) score on the Eysenck Personality Questionnaire (EPQ-R), suggested that Fell's personality profile was consistent with a diagnosis of personality disorder. I again interviewed Fell in 1993 at the request of his solicitors, and provided a detailed report, which included further psychometric testing, which supported my previous findings, but found that Fell's self-esteem had improved somewhat over time. Background statements from informants supported the psychometric finding of low self-esteem.

In 1998, I was asked by the CCRC to provide a further report and answer questions relating to possible false memory, psychogenic amnesia and inducements by the police. I concluded that there was no evidence of false memory or psychogenic amnesia relating to the offences, but there appeared to have been an inducement relating to a case for manslaughter as opposed to a conviction for murder.

Following my report, the CCRC commissioned a psychiatric report from Professor Michael Kopelman, a neuropsychiatrist with an interest in amnesia and false confessions. He did not interview Fell, but reviewed all the relevant papers in the case, including the police interview transcripts and my two psychological reports. His conclusions corroborated my own findings. The Crown commissioned a psychiatric report from Dr Philip Joseph, who interviewed Fell and produced a report, which also cast doubts on the reliability of Fell's confession. Dr Joseph concluded that it was Fell's personality disorder, accompanied by poor self-esteem and attention seeking behaviour, which made him vulnerable to making a false confession when interviewed by the police in 1983.

With regard to the expert evidence, the Court of Appeal judges stated:

> So far as the psychological evidence was concerned statements had been provided by Dr Gudjonsson and Professor Kopelman. These were before the commission. The Crown obtained evidence from Dr Joseph. His conclusions were to the same effect as those of Dr Gudjonsson and Professor Kopleman that the admissions were unreliable.

As a result of the conclusions of the three experts Mr Fell applied for bail on 1 December 2000. The court granted the appellant bail and also gave leave, unopposed by the Crown, for calling fresh expert evidence before the court. The case was heard at the beginning of March 2001. Dr Joseph and I testified on 1 March. Our evidence was supported by the testimony of Dr Robin Illbert, a prison doctor who had seen Mr Fell on a number of occasions after he was remanded in custody at Winchester prison in 1983. At the time of seeing Mr Fell in custody Dr Illbert viewed him as a 'pathological confessor' and experienced anxieties about the reliability of his confession. Mr Fell had a documented history of boasting and telling lies (e.g. he was known during his brief period in the Army for making up stories; he also boasted of fighting in the Falklands and claimed to be a boxing champion—he had a photograph taken of himself with a boxing trophy, which he had had engraved). About two months prior to the murders Mr Fell had been dishonourably discharged from the Army. He had served in the Army between May 1978 and March 1982. Whilst in the Army he drank excessively and received treatment for alcohol problems. Nine days after the Aldershot murders, Mr Fell had been interviewed at home by the homicide team. During the interview he volunteered that he had been dismissed from the Army because of committing an offence of Grievous Bodily Harm, which was not true. It seems that he made a false confession to the police prior to his arrest as a way of enhancing his self-esteem (he wanted to 'look big').

The Judgment stated:

> In the context of the above evidence the features of the telephone calls and the interviews which were no doubt stressed both at trial and on behalf of the appellant and on the application for leave to appeal, take on a different complexion. The starting point seems to us to be that if the above evidence had been before the jury their approach to the telephone calls would have been very different. Furthermore, their approach to the interviews would have been very different. With the benefit of that evidence we would say that all the indications are that the telephone calls were the appellant seeking to draw attention to himself and not calls made by the murderer. Our reasons depend to some extent on the view we take of the interviews, in relation to which we again would say, with the benefit of the experience of other cases and of the evidence called, bear the hallmarks of being false. They bear out paragraph 5 of Dr Gudjonsson's second report quoted above.

The paragraph from my second report referred to by their Lordships reads as follows:

> I believe there is evidence that would tend to support the argument that the admissions made by Mr Fell were the result of an inducement which may have been made to him. I think it is quite possible, if not likely, that his confession to the murders of Margaret Johnson and Ann Lee was made because of the officers' persistent and determined implication throughout the interviews that Mr Fell was the murderer, Mr Fell's failed efforts at effectively challenging the officers' assertions, the failure of the police to take any notice of his repeated and determined efforts to seek legal advice (which is likely to have exacerbated his low self-esteem and a sense of helplessness), and seeing the confession as a desperate compromise to reduce the charge to manslaughter. The content of the confession interview supports the view that Mr Fell was attempting to present a case which supported a manslaughter charge as opposed to murder.

Interestingly, the appeal judges did not listen to the tapes of the interviews, but they had read all the transcripts. They did not wish to comment specifically on the police interviews and concluded:

> The evidence we admitted showed that experts with an experience which the judge and the jury, and indeed the previous Court of Appeal would not have, were of the view that the admissions were unreliable. There would have been a danger in allowing the admissions to go before the jury if the judge was clearly of the view that it would be unsafe to act on them. It seems to us that the evidence we have heard would have added significantly to a submission that there was a need for someone such as the appellant to have a solicitor present before reliance could be placed on any admission he was making. A simple listening to the tapes might well indicate the absence of bullying or oppression in that sense, but the evidence would also add force to the submission that the sheer length of the interviews, without food, and the method of interrogation without protection of a solicitor, would be likely to lead to an unreliable and indeed a false confession.

The above extract suggests that their Lordships were careful in not unduly criticizing the methods of interrogation apart from duration of the length of the interviews and the absence of a solicitor. This may have been due to the fact that the trial judge and the previous Court of Appeal had listened to the police interview tapes and found them to be voluntary.

> As regards other allegations made against the police, the trial judge listened to the tapes, as did the previous Court of Appeal. We have not. We have of course read all the interviews. We do not think it right to make findings of 'oppression' in the sense of misconduct by the police, or of 'tricks', insofar as that imputes bad faith on the police who conducted these interviews.

With regard to the police refusal to allow Mr Fell access to a solicitor their Lordships concluded:

> They were, as we have said, quite wrong not to allow this appellant a solicitor. They allowed their quest for a conviction to override their responsibilities to an accused, and particularly to a vulnerable accused. If that fundamental right had not been denied this appellant a false confession would not have been made. We do not however make any other finding of misconduct against the police in this case.

The testimony of Dr Illbert, Dr Joseph and myself at the appeal focused on Fell's psychological vulnerabilities at the time of his making the telephone calls and when interviewed by the police. Dr Illbert and Dr Joseph had not listened to the police interviews and did not specifically comment on the police tactics used to break down Mr Fell's resistance.

I was allowed to comment briefly on the police interviews and emphasized the pressure that Fell was placed under by the interviewing officers. As the officers persisted in denying him access to a solicitor, Fell became increasingly desperate and frustrated, reaching a point where he perceived himself as having no choice but to make a confession to relieve the pressure in interview and to avoid being charged with a double murder. Once he had confessed, his generally reactive behaviour noted in the sixth interview quickly discontinued, resulting in sudden activation of strategic coping and assertive behaviour. The most likely explanation for such a change was a strong sense of injustice and/or feelings of anger, which was sufficient to cause a sudden activation of critical thinking, focused mental energy and assertive behaviour. In spite of his retraction, and insistence on his innocence ever since, he was convicted of the murders and had one unsuccessful appeal. He remained in prison for 17 years before the Court of Appeal finally accepted his innocence. The judgment is unusual in that the judges went as far as to state that Mr Fell was actually innocent of the murders.

Comments

The confession that Fell made was clearly of the pressured–compliant type, although I believe it was preceded by Fell being temporarily persuaded by the officers that he 'might' have been on the common on the day of the murder (i.e. an internalized belief). His implicating himself during the anonymous telephone calls was clearly voluntary and undoubtedly functioned at the time to enhance his sense of excitement and self-importance. Fell's poor self-esteem, which was clearly evident on psychometric testing and was corroborated by background information, and his personality disorder, are undoubtedly important in explaining his attention seeking behaviour.

CONCLUSIONS

In relation to disputed confession cases, the attitude of High Court judges to expert psychological evidence and their level of sophistication in evaluating it has greatly improved since 1988, when Lord Lane refused to hear my evidence in the case of Engin Raghip. The successful subsequent appeal of Raghip in 1991, and their Lordships' ruling regarding the admissibility of expert psychological evidence, was a landmark decision. The ruling has had an enormous impact on the admissibility of psychological evidence in the lower courts as well as on more recent Court of Appeal decisions. The next significant development was the decision in *Ward* in 1992, which had implications for the admissibility of both psychiatric and psychological evidence. Here a diagnosis of personality disorder was influential in overturning a conviction in relation to terrorist offences and 12 counts of murder.

In the appeal of David MacKenzie, their Lordships set three criteria for determining the admissibility of confession evidence:

1. the prosecution case depends wholly upon confessions;
2. the defendant suffers from a significant degree of mental handicap;
3. the confessions were unconvincing to a point where a jury properly directed could not properly convict upon them, then the judge, assuming he had not excluded the confessions, should withdraw the case from the jury.

The judgment did not make it clear whether the term 'mental handicap' referred to his borderline IQ, a previous diagnosis relating to admission to hospital or encapsulates all of MacKenzie's mental (psychological) problems. This is where the interpretation of the law and legal judgments becomes so important. It is not just a matter of what the law says, or what is said in the judgment of cases, it is really a question of how these are interpreted. In the case of *Long*, this interpretation became important. Their Lordships applied the criteria set out in *MacKenzie*. Long's case met the first two criteria, but not the third. His meeting the criteria for 'mental handicap' is particularly interesting, because in psychiatry and psychology this term is normally used to refer to learning disability, but in the case of Mr Long it was applied to a condition relating to depression. Mr Long was of average intellectual abilities, but at the time of the police interrogation he had suffered from depression.

In the case of *Kane*, in the Royal Court of Justice in Belfast, their Lordships ruled that expert testimony regarding a high level of anxiety proneness, which did not amount to a psychiatric disorder, combined with an abnormally high level of compliance and borderline IQ, was admissible and cast doubts on the safety of *Kane's* conviction.

The case of *Roberts* is important in that the Court of Appeal accepted 'the emerging field of science relating to the phenomenon of false confessions', which included the psychometric measurement of suggestibility and compliance. The principle set forward in this case is that when deciding issues of reliability and the safety of a conviction the court *'must take into account'* all that is known about the phenomenon of false confessions as well as expert evidence as to the 'mental condition' of the appellant. The ruling extends that decided in *Ward,* namely that there is now no need for a recognized diagnostic category, such as personality disorder, in determining a relevant mental condition. The abnormal results from relevant psychometric tests relating to personality, such as the Gudjonsson Compliance Scale or Gudjonsson Suggestibility Scale, are sufficient for determining a mental condition that has a bearing upon determining the safety of the conviction.

The principles developed in *Roberts* were subsequently applied and extended in the case of *Hall*. Here it was ruled that a recognized psychiatric diagnostic category is neither necessary nor sufficient in determining the admissibility and reliability of a confession. Their Lordships defined the limits for the cases in which psychological and psychiatric experts in cases of disputed confessions should be heard. These involve the following criteria.

- The mental condition or disorder must be of the type to render a confession potentially unreliable.
- There must be a very significant deviation from normal.
- There should be a history of the condition or disorder predating the making of the confession, which provides an explanation for its existence.

In the case of *King*, the borderline intelligence would not have been sufficient on its own to cast doubt on the safety of the conviction; it was the combination of borderline intelligence and abnormally high suggestibility and compliance that were the overriding factors in their Lordships view. This was in spite of the fact that Mr King appeared to cope well with the cross-examination when he was in the witness box.

The 13 cases presented in this chapter clearly show that it is wrong to assume that only persons with learning disability or those who are mentally ill make unreliable or false confessions. I have had access to the IQ score of 12 (92%) of the appellants discussed in this chapter. In one of the cases (Roberts) the IQ score was not given in the judgment, but he was described as being of 'below average intelligence', which means that his IQ score was probably in the low average or borderline range. His 'below average intelligence' was not raised as a significant factor at the appeal. The mean IQ score of the 12 appellants where the IQ score was known was 86 (range 70–112). Six (50%) had an IQ score that fell in the borderline range (70–79); the remaining IQ scores all fell in the low average range or above. The cases demonstrate the importance of personality factors in potentially rendering a confession unreliable.

CHAPTER 19

Police Impropriety

In Chapter 7, I discussed how police impropriety might on occasions cause a miscarriage of justice. This impropriety can take different forms, such as coercive or oppressive interviewing, fabrication of evidence, alteration of interview records that misleads the court, suppression of exculpatory evidence and perjury. In several of the cases discussed in the book so far there was evidence of police impropriety, which was influential at trial in causing a wrongful conviction. The cases of the 'Guildford Four', the 'Birmingham Six', the 'Tottenham Three', Stefan Kiszko and the Darvell brothers, are a few examples of such malpractice. In this chapter I shall discuss four further cases where the Court of Appeal identified police malpractice (Stephen Miller, Alfred Allen, the Carl Bridgewater case and Derek Bentley). In terms of oppressive police interviewing the case of Stephen Miller, whose interrogation tactics were analysed and discussed in detail in Chapter 4, is a landmark case and has had a significant effect on police training. In the case of Alfred Allen, one of the 'UDR Four', three of the four appellants were freed on appeal in 1992 after evidence emerged by the use of electrostatic detection apparatus (ESDA) tests that the police had improperly interfered with the notes of interrogations. According to Paisley (1992), this case became a unique challenge to the British criminal justice system. The case of Carl Bridgewater has been described as one of the worst miscarriages of justice during the 20th century (Foot, 1998). In 1978 the police had faked a confession from a co-accused (Vincent Hickey) and lied about it in order to extract a written confession statement from another suspect (Patrick Molloy). Molloy's confession resulted in four persons being implicated in the murder of a 13-year-old boy. The case of Derek Bentley, dating back to 1952, is well known (Corre, 1998). He was executed in January 1953 for the murder of police constable Sidney Miles, while his co-defendant, Christopher Craig, who fired the shot that killed PC Miles, escaped the death sentence due to his youth. Bentley's conviction was quashed posthumously in July 1998 on the grounds of irregularities at trial. Although most of the criticisms were directed at the trial judge, their Lordships were satisfied that Bentley's statement to the police had not been obtained in the way claimed by the police at trial (i.e. the implication is that the police officers had perjured themselves in their testimony).

STEPHEN MILLER

This case relates to a murder of a prostitute, Miss White, in Cardiff on Valentine's Day, February 1988. Miss White had been stabbed more than 50 times at her home, where she entertained her clients. Her head and one breast were almost severed. Ten months after her murder five men were arrested, having been implicated by two of Miss White's colleagues, who claimed to have witnessed the murder and been forced to participate in mutilating the body. In spite of a great deal of forensic evidence at the crime scene none of it matched any of the five defendants (Rose & Bhatti, 1991). In October 1989 the trial began. The preceding judge was Mr Justice McNeal, who refused to hear my evidence of Stephen Miller's psychological vulnerabilities during a *voire dire*. The trial before this judge lasted almost six months, but as the judge began the summing up he died of a heart attack. A re-trial was to commence three months later.

In August 1989 I had been commissioned by the defence to assess Miller and study the police interview tapes. My main conclusions were as follows.

- Mr Miller obtained a Full Scale IQ of 75, falling at the bottom 5% of the general population.
- Mr Miller proved to be abnormally suggestible on the GSS 1 and GSS 2, administered three weeks apart (the Total Suggestibility Scores were 18 and 20, respectively).
- Mr Miller was prone to symptoms of high anxiety.
- During the interrogation Mr Miller's self-esteem was severely manipulated by the officers, he was subjected to immense pressure to provide detailed accounts that agreed with the police officers' premises and expectations and the form and type of questioning was very leading. He showed clear evidence of distress at various times during the interviews.

In the final paragraph of my psychological report, I concluded:

> In view of Mr Miller's marked psychological vulnerabilities he would have been ill-prepared at the time of the interviews to cope psychologically with the pressure and demand characteristics of the situation. There is no doubt in my mind that bearing in mind the type, intensity and duration of the police pressure during the interviews and his psychological vulnerabilities, the reliability of the interviews must be considered to be unsafe and unsatisfactory.

Miller had been interviewed by the police on 19 occasions between 7 and 11 December 1988, comprising 14 hours of tape-recorded interviews over a 90 hour period. There was a solicitor present during all the interviews, but in spite of the oppressive nature of the questioning he failed to intervene appropriately. Miller's confession was crucial in implicating him and his co-defendants. Therefore, it was crucial for the Crown that Miller's interviews were allowed before the jury.

A second trial commenced in May 1990 under Mr. Justice Leonard, and ended approximately six months later. I was allowed by this judge to give evidence during a *voire dire* on 18 May, which took place at the beginning of the trial. My testimony in chief involved outlining the psychometric findings, particularly Miller's borderline intelligence and high suggestibility. The cross-examination focused predominantly on the police interviews and how Mr Miller had been able to resist suggestions and pressure. The judge ruled the interviews admissible. It is evident from the judge's ruling that he was impressed by Miller's apparent ability to resist suggestions during the police interviews and considered this far more important than the psychological test findings. The judge firmly rejected the idea that there was any evidence of oppression or that anything was said or done by the police to render the confession unreliable.

I gave evidence before the jury on 10 September 1990. Again, I was only required by the defence to state the psychological findings. Defence counsel did not ask me any questions about the police interviews or their unreliability. This appeared to have been a deliberate decision, which was very unwise. As it happened, the prosecutor did not ask me questions about the test findings, but focused again in great detail on the police interviews, trying to demonstrate how Miller was not suggestible, and asking a large number of questions, many of which were hypothetical, arising from the police interviews (e.g. why had I not asked Miller about this and that in my interview with him). The cross-examination also involved the prosecutor placing in front of me in the witness box photographs of White's mutilated body, the purpose allegedly being to see how Miller's description of the crime scene matched that given in his interviews. In re-examination by the defence, I was not asked how my overall assessment of the case cast doubts on Miller's confession.

In his summing up before the jury, the judge appears to have marginalized my testimony by pointing out how well Miller coped with the police interviews and in the witness box during the trial. The prosecutor clearly implied before the jury that Miller was functioning much better than the test findings indicated, a view which appears to have been shared by the trial judge and presented to the jury. However, there were many instances during the police interviews when Miller clearly did not cope well and exhibited signs of very high suggestibility. These do not appear to have been sufficiently communicated to the jury.

After their conviction in 1989, the 'Cardiff Three'—Stephen Miller, Tony Parris and Yusef Abdullahi—fought hard to get their convictions overturned. Miller was fortunate to find himself two outstanding lawyers to fight his case, solicitor Gareth Peirce and Michael Mansfield QC, a formidable team indeed.

The appeal was heard before Lord Chief Justice Taylor and Justices Popplewell and Laws in December 1992 ([1993], 97 Cr.App.R.). Lord Taylor in his judgment concluded:

> Having considered the tenor and length of these interviews as a whole we are of the opinion that they would have been oppressive and confessions obtained in consequence of them would have been unreliable, even with a suspect of normal mental capacity. In fact, there was evidence on the *voire dire* from Dr Gudjonsson, called on behalf of Miller, that he was on the borderline of mental handicap with an IQ of 75, a mental age of 11 and a reading age of eight (p. 105).

It is fair to the learned judge to say that, although he was invited to listen in part to tape 7, it was played only up to page 17 of the transcript. The bullying and shouting was from page 20 onwards. Why this most important part was not played to the learned judge has not been explained to us. Had he heard the rest of it, as we did, we do not believe he would have ruled as he did.

The judges were very critical of the techniques of interrogation adopted by the police in the case and considered them

> wholly contrary to the spirit and in many instances the letter of the code laid down under the Act. In our view, those responsible for police training and discipline must take all necessary steps to see that guidelines are followed (p. 110).

The judges were also very critical of the solicitor who was present during all 19 interviews and failed to intervene when he should have done.

The judges raised the important point that the proper recording of the interviews in accordance with PACE enabled them to listen to the interrogation and review the problems that emerged.

The final words in the judgment were:

> At the conclusion, we now direct the learned registrar to send copies of tape 7 to the Chief Inspector of Constabulary, to the Director of Prosecution and to the Chairman of the Royal Commission on Criminal Justice (p. 110).

Comments

The post-PACE case of Stephen Miller demonstrates the fact that the introduction of PACE, with all its in-built protections for detainees, has still not entirely eliminated unreliable confessions and wrongful convictions. Miller, a psychologically vulnerable man, was broken down by oppressive interrogation techniques in the presence of a solicitor.

Fortunately, all the police interviews were tape recorded, which made it possible to capture the nature and intensity of the techniques used by the police to break him down to obtain a confession. Without these crucial tapes the extent of the oppressive questioning would never have been properly revealed and his appeal would probably have failed.

ALFRED ALLEN (THE 'UDR FOUR')

Mr Adrian Carroll, a member of a Republican family, was shot at approximately 4.30 p.m. on 8 November 1983, outside his home in the centre of Armagh, after returning home from work. He was 24 years of age. He was shot three times from a revolver or pistol and died in hospital at 7.20 p.m. that same evening without regaining consciousness. Four UDR (Ulster Defence Regiment) soldiers based in Armagh, Alfred Winston Allen, Noel Bell, Neil Fraser Latimer, and James Irwin Hegan, were arrested, interrogated, and convicted on 1 July 1986 of the murder. The trial had proceeded as a Diplock Court (in the absence of a jury) before Lord Chief Justice Kelly. All four defendants were sentenced to life imprisonment (see Paisley, 1992, for a detailed background to the case). As far as Latimer was concerned, the Crown case at trial was that he was the gunman who shot Carroll and the other defendants acted as accomplices. The evidence against Allen, Bell and Hegan consisted entirely of their oral and written confessions. With regard to Latimer there was identification evidence from a Witness A.

All four appealed twice against their convictions. The first appeal was heard in 1988 and failed. The court held that the confessions were true and not obtained by oppression or police impropriety. A second appeal was allowed in 1992 in view of fresh ESDA evidence, which showed that the notes of police interviews with four appellants had in parts been re-written by the police. The appeal was heard before Lord Chief Justice Hutton. The Court of Appeal held that the ESDA evidence alone was sufficient to quash the convictions of Allen, Bell and Hegan, because the only evidence against them was their confessions. They all alleged maltreatment by the police. Latimer's appeal was not allowed in view of identification corroborating his confession evidence. His case has been referred to the Court of Appeal in Northern Ireland by the Criminal Cases Review Commission.

Prior to the second appeal, Dr James MacKeith and I had been commissioned by Allen's solicitor to assess him and provide reports. This assessment was conducted in March 1992. On 4 June 1992, Dr MacKeith and I gave evidence at the appeal hearing in Belfast. The prosecution objected to the admissibility of our evidence. With regard to our testimony, the Court concluded:

> Dr Gudjonsson and Dr MacKeith were called on behalf of Allen and gave evidence that he had a personality which made him susceptible to accepting suggestions put to him by interviewing police officers and to making unreliable confessions. However, we have reached our conclusion that the conviction of Allen is unsafe and unsatisfactory without having to weigh and assess the evidence of Dr Gudjonsson and Dr MacKeith. Therefore it is unnecessary for us to express any opinion on the validity, in the particular circumstances of this case, of the suggestibility tests which Dr Gudjonsson applied to Allen.

Comments

The psychological assessment showed that Alfred Allen was abnormally yielding to leading questions, in spite of his normal intelligence, and he lacked confidence in himself. During his lengthy and persistent interrogation in 1983, his accounts of events were repeatedly rejected by the police, he was accused of lying, the officers pretended that they had all the facts in the case and a large number of suggestions were put to him. It appears that he began to uncritically accept the suggestions put to him, doubting his own recollections of events. There were signs of great distress, lack of confidence in his own recollections and mental confusion. However, it was police impropriety in terms of re-writing the notes of the police interviews with the four appellants, and not the psychological and psychiatric evidence, that resulted in the convictions of three of the appellants being overturned on appeal in 1992.

THE CARL BRIDGEWATER CASE

This case was discussed in detail by Foot (1998) and in the Court of Appeal Judgment (The Royal Courts of Justice, 30 July 1997). Only a brief summary of the case will be provided here. The case involved the conviction in November 1979 of four men, Michael Hickey, Vincent Hickey, James Robinson and Patrick Molloy, for the murder by shooting on 19 September 1978 of a 13-year-old newspaper delivery boy, Carl Bridgewater, at Yew Tree Farm, Wordsley, West Midlands. Of crucial importance to the case was the confession of Patrick Molloy made on 10 December 1978, where he implicated himself and the other three co-accused in robbery and murder. Molloy did not take the witness stand during the trial, which meant that he had not officially denied his confession in court. Nevertheless, until his death in June 1981 he had always insisted to his lawyers that the confession statement was false and had been given to the police for at least two reasons (Foot, 1998). First, he claimed to have confessed after the police had shown him a signed confession statement from Vincent Hickey, implicating him in the murder. The police always denied the existence of any such statement. Second, Molloy had wanted to take his revenge on Vincent Hickey for implicating him in the case.

In December 1981, the other three remaining appellants were refused leave to appeal against their convictions. In October 1987 the Home Secretary referred the case to the Court of Appeal as a result of retractions of evidence given at trial and fresh alibi evidence. The appeal was dismissed in March 1989. In July 1996 the Home Secretary referred the case again to the Court of Appeal. There were two grounds for appeal. First, in 1994 evidence had come to the attention of the defence that two unidentified fingerprints found on the murdered boy's bicycle, which had not previously been disclosed by the prosecution, could not be matched to the appellants. Second, there appeared to have been breaches of the Judges Rules in relation to the interrogation and detention of Patrick Molloy.

On 21 February 1997 Michael Hickey, Vincent Hickey and James Robinson were released on unconditional bail by the Court of Appeal, pending a full court hearing. They had been in prison since their arrest 18 years previously. In view of the fresh evidence concerning Molloy's confession, the prosecution did not oppose the appeal. The appeal took place in July 1997 before Lord Justice Roch and Justices Hidden and Mitchell. The judgment is extremely detailed and informative about the case. The convictions of the four men were quashed and no re-trial was ordered.

Comments

This is an extreme case of police impropriety. If the jury had known about the fabricated confession they would undoubtedly have become suspicious of the remaining the police evidence. In addition, Molloy's confession statement, and the subsequent confessions he made, would have been ruled inadmissible by the trial judge, because the police deceit would have rendered the confession oppressive and involuntary (see transcript of the judgment).

Even though there was no psychological evidence presented at the appeal, considerable credit must go to Dr Eric Shepherd, a forensic psychologist, who had worked extensively and impressively on Molloy's interrogations and confessions, initially at the request of the police. He had raised serious concerns about the reliability of Molloy's confessions and about the integrity of the police officers involved in the case (Foot, 1998). Partly due to Shepherd's work the Home Office released the custody records concerning Molloy's detention. They showed that Staffordshire police officers had gone into Molloy's cell for interviews on 14 occasions; none of these interviews had been disclosed to the defence. In addition, linguistics experts were able to demonstrate that the confession could not have been given verbatim by Molloy, as the police had claimed.

DEREK BENTLEY

This case dates back to 2 November 1952. It involved the shooting and murder of Police Constable Sidney Miles, by Christopher Craig, aged 16, while on the roof of a warehouse in Croydon, Surrey. With Christopher Craig on the roof was a 19-year-old youth, Derek William Bentley, who had a history of educational and behavioural problems. At the trial, which took place at the Central Criminal Court between 9 and 11 December 1952, it was argued by the prosecution that Bentley would have known that Craig was armed and indeed incited him to shoot the officer by allegedly using the famous words:

Let him have it, Chris.

At the time of allegedly uttering these words, Bentley was under arrest on the roof and in the custody of another officer.

On 3 November 1952, Bentley is alleged to have dictated a statement voluntarily and without any assistance or questions from the interviewing officers. The statement contained some incriminating comments suggesting that he knew Craig had a gun.

Bentley's defence at trial was that he had not known that Craig was armed with a gun until they were on the roof and the first shot was fired. Bentley denied having uttered the incriminating words 'Let him have it, Chris' (Craig has also denied that these words were said), and claimed that his signed statement had been produced in response to questions rather than being a free narrative account, as claimed by the officers.

Both men were found guilty of murdering the police officer. Bentley was sentenced to death, whereas Craig, who was too young to be sentenced to death, was sentenced to be detained at Her Majesty's pleasure. Bentley was executed on 28 January 1953. On 29 July 1993, Her Majesty the Queen granted a pardon limited to the sentence of death. The conviction still stood.

The Criminal Cases Review Commission (CCRC) referred the conviction of Bentley to the Court of Appeal under Section 9 of the Criminal Appeal Act 1995. The appeal took place in July 1998 before Lord Chief Justice Bingham and two Justices. Two experts gave evidence. I gave evidence as to Bentley's mental capacity, having reviewed all the relevant material that existed prior to Bentley's execution. In addition to my testimony and two psychological reports, there were fresh reports available to the Court from Dr Peter Fenwick (Consultant Neuropsychiatrist) and Dr Phillip Joseph (Consultant Forensic Psychiatrist). Dr Joseph was instructed by the Crown. Neither Dr Fenwick or Dr Joseph were called to testify. After my testimony, the court heard from a linguistic expert, Professor Malcolm Coulthard, concerning the language used in the signed statement of Bentley. He had analysed Bentley's signed statement and found some of the phrases used suggestive of police language, the most important one being the use of frequent post-positioning of the word 'then' (Coulthard, 1999), which suggested that the police officer had been encouraging Mr Bentley to tell what happened next.

The judges decided that the fresh psychological and psychiatric reports contributed nothing of significance from a legal point of view to material that was available at the time of trial, although the material had not been used at trial. The court rejected the submission on behalf of the appellant that the prosecution had failed to disclose to the defence relevant medical and educational material. However,

> With reference to the psychiatric reports and the psychological evidence given by Dr Gisli Gudjonsson from the witness box, the Court of Appeal found clear evidence that Bentley suffered from serious educational and behavioural problems and from an impairment of his intellectual and cognitive functioning. This would have affected his understanding, his judgment and his memory (Corre, 1998, p. 777).

In contrast to the psychological evidence, their Lordships decided that the linguistic evidence of Professor Coulthard, and the written report of his colleague Dr French, constituted the type of evidence that had not been available at the time of trial in 1952. They therefore allowed that evidence, which provided additional support for the conclusion that Bentley's conviction was unsafe. The main grounds on which the conviction was quashed, and these grounds were sufficient on their own, were

> ...the failure of the trial judge to direct the jury on the standard and burden of proof, the prejudicial comments made about the defendants and their defences, the assertion that the police officers' evidence was more worthy of belief than that of the defendants, and an insufficient direction on the law of joint enterprise (Corre, 1998).

Their Lordships were also concerned about how Bentley's Statement under Caution had been obtained by the police:

> The statement is quite short. In transcript it is only one page long, and it is not well structured, but in the light of the psychiatric and psychological evidence which we have received, coupled with the difficulty most people have in dictating a succinct and relevant narrative, we find it difficult to accept that it was obtained in the way the officers described.

Comments

Their Lordships viewed the safety of the conviction in accordance with standards which would currently apply in any other appeal, and not by the standards that existed at the time. This has important implications for future cases. Although the linguistic evidence, of the kind and quality produced by Professor Coulthard and Dr French, would according to their Lordships probably not have been sufficient on its own to alter the verdict of the jury in this case, this kind of expert evidence is important in disputed cases where there is no audio or video recording of the police interview.

CONCLUSIONS

Apart from demonstrating the use of oppressive interviewing in the case of Stephen Miller, the other cases show that police officers sometimes mislead the courts by fabricating evidence or improperly interfering with their records of suspects' statements. The Carl Bridgewater case is particularly serious in that the police fabricated a confession, which was used to coerce a confession from a co-accused, and then lied about it. Four defendants were as a result wrongfully convicted. Molloy's allegations against the police were repeatedly ridiculed by the authorities, but were eventually proved right (Foot, 1998).

CHAPTER 20

Misleading Special Knowledge

In this chapter I discuss three cases that highlight the dangers of relying on special knowledge of the crime as proof of guilt. In the first two cases, those of Stefan Kiszko and Wayne Darvell, apparent special knowledge about certain details of the crime scene was used at trial to convince the jury of the men's guilt. In both cases the special knowledge, taken at face value, was extremely convincing. Many years later evidence emerged to persuade the Court of Appeal of the men's innocence. The special knowledge, which the prosecution argued must have come from the appellants, must in fact have come from the police and resulted in a miscarriage of justice. In the third case, involving the unsuccessful appeal in the year 2000 of Donald Pendleton, the prosecution convincingly argued for special knowledge to uphold a conviction for murder. A careful analysis of the special knowledge in the case casts doubt on its value as probative evidence.

STEFAN KISZKO

On 5 October 1975, an 11-year-old girl, Lesley Molseed, was sent by her mother to a local shop to buy bread. She never returned. Three days later her body was discovered on moorland several miles from her home. She had been stabbed 12 times on the upper part of the body. She was fully clothed and her private parts had not been interfered with. However, semen stains found on her knickers and skirt showed that the perpetrator had ejaculated over her (an excellent discussion of the case is provided by Rose, Panter & Wilkinson, 1998).

In August 1975 Stefan Kiszko had gone to his general practitioner complaining of tiredness. He was referred to a consultant physician and was admitted to hospital until 15 September when he was discharged. Kiszko was found to be suffering from severe anaemia. The doctors also discovered that he suffered from a condition called hypogonadism, which resulted in his being unable to produce sex hormones. His testicles and penis were underdeveloped, his sex drive was poor and he had problems with ejaculation. His condition was treated with the injection of a male hormone. He received his first injection on 11 September 1975 and the second one on 3 October, two days before Lesley Molseed's murder. The timing of the injections, and Kiszko's comments to a police surgeon on 22 December that his sex drive had now improved and that he was masturbating frequently and able to ejaculate, were to have crucial consequences for him. The doctor considered it essential to obtain a semen sample from Kiszko and compare it with the semen found on Lesley Molseed's clothing. The results from subsequent analyses, which clearly proved that Mr Kiszko was not the murderer, were suppressed at trial by the police and resulted in a wrongful conviction. The suppression of this crucial evidence was discovered by police officers who re-investigated the case in 1990–1991, following an application to the Home Secretary by a new defence team (Rose, Panter & Wilkinson, 1998).

The Police Interviews

Kiszko was initially questioned on 5 November 1975 in connection with a complaint concerning indecent exposure that occurred on 4 October 1975, and about his whereabouts at the beginning of October. These officers were not to interview Kiszko again. Instead, the detectives investigating the murder of Lesley Molseed were informed about Kiszko and the complaint of indecent exposure relating to 4 October (Rose, Panter & Wilkinson, 1998).

Kiszko was later to be interviewed again at his home on 7 and 10 November by homicide detectives regarding his whereabouts on the first weekend in October. He gave varied accounts of his activities and whereabouts, which made the police suspicious about his motive for doing so and he was challenged about this. It seems from reading the relevant statements that Kiszko was unsure about the precise date when he returned home from hospital.

At approximately 10.30 a.m. on Sunday 21 December 1975, Kiszko went voluntarily with the police to Rochdale Police Station (he was not arrested until the following day). He was to be extensively interviewed over a period of three days. He was 23 years of age. At the time he was employed as a clerk with the Inland Revenue. He was an only child and lived with his mother and aunt.

During the first interview, which occurred shortly after Kiszko arrived at the police station on the Sunday morning, he is asked about his whereabouts since the beginning of October 1975 and the indecent exposure allegation. It is pointed out to him that the police had information that contradicted his previous statements to the police that he had been in hospital at the time of the murder. Kiszko then admits that he had previously made a mistake about when he was discharged from hospital; he now states that he was discharged from hospital on 15 September, but he insists that he never left his home between 15 September and 12 October. He was also confronted with witness accounts that he had been out on Bonfire Night on 5 November, a date on which Kiszko claimed he had been at home. He then admitted that he might have gone out on 5 November, but had not got out of his car. He blamed his inconsistent and hazy memory account on his injections. According to Rose, Panter and Wilkinson (1998):

> Whilst Kiszko had been shown to be a liar, and there was little doubt that those lies had been told to conceal guilt of one or more offences of indecent exposure, there was now a strand of suspicion, linking his lies to the murder, and that his last answer as to his 'damned injections' added strength to the link (p. 102).

At 2.35 p.m. Kiszko is interviewed again. He states that he does not 'fancy girls', but mentions that before the murder he had received injections from his doctor to help him bring on his sex drive. This had obvious implications for Kiszko as a suspect.

The officers then searched his car and discovered magazines depicting nude women under the carpet in the boot of his car. When confronted with this and his previous claim that he had no interest in girls, according to the police his reactions were as follows:

> 'At this point Kiszko started to tremble violently and started to bite his nails. He said 'It's those damned injections. I never did anything like this before'.

In the glove compartment of the car the officers found two small pieces of paper with car registration numbers written on them. One of the numbers, ADK 539 L, which Kiszko had problems explaining, became linked to a car driven in the vicinity of the crime scene around the time of the murder. The implication was that Kiszko had been at the scene of the crime. Another finding was that carpet fibres found on the girl's body matched those found in the carpet in Kiszko's car.

At the end of this interview Kiszko admitted to the indecent exposure on 4 October, that he had been out on 5 November, and that the injections had stimulated his sexual interest in girls and made him masturbate in public.

The interrogation was now taken over by Detective Superintendent Holland. Kiszko now retracted the admission of indecent exposure and claimed that his trouser zip had been accidentally knocked down by a carpet he was carrying. When confronted Kiszko reverted back to the admission about the indecent exposure incident on 4 October, but denied the allegation of another incident dating back to 3 October. Kiszko was interviewed again that evening after officers had examined his car again.

The following night, at 1.45 in the morning, Kiszko was interviewed again, after which he was allowed to sleep. At 11.30 a.m. the officers returned to interview Kiszko. He was still not under arrest. He is asked about the registration number ADK 539 L, which was linking him to the crime scene. After Detective Superintendent Holland left the room, stating that he has to make some further enquiries, Kiszko asked the remaining officer whether he could now go home. The officer, according to his witness statement, responded by repeating what officer Holland had said, that is, further enquiries into the matter would need to be made. Kiszko is then reported to have confessed to stabbing Lesley Molseed to death. He blamed the murder on 'those damned injections'. The officer was then joined by Detective Superintendent Holland and Chief Inspector Steele and Kiszko repeated his confession to the murder.

At 5.35 p.m. on 22 December Kiszko completed making a statement, where he confessed to indecently exposing himself to two girls and to the murder of Lesley Molseed. The crucial part of the confession related to his statement that

> I laid down by her, side by side, and held her with one hand and used my left hand to wank with. She was laid facing me and I was laid on my right side. I shot between her legs over her knickers. I did not remove her knickers. I had a knife in my pocket and I took it out and stabbed her in the throat she was still crying I got a hazy feeling and I can't remember where or how I stabbed her.

Between 6.20 and 7.25 p.m. that same day, Kiszko made another statement, this time in the presence of his solicitor, where he retracted his previous confession.

He now denied having indecently exposed himself to the girls. He also retracted his confession to the murder of Lesley Molseed. The explanation he gave to the police for having made a false confession was:

> I thought if I made a statement like the other one I would get home tonight.

Later that night, at the request of Detective Superintendent Dibb who was in charge of the murder investigation, Kiszko was examined by the police surgeon, Dr Tierney.

In the afternoon of 23 December Kiszko was interviewed in the cell area by Detective Superintendent Holland, who allegedly asked him only one question:

> From your first statement you have described the effects of the drugs if you were hazy and can't remember how do you know that what you told me in the first statement is untrue?

Kiszko allegedly replied:

> I am all of a blue. I have told you the truth. I remember the girl by the shop in Broad Lane and taking her to the moors. I must have stabbed her. That's how I showed you the handled knife. (Out of the several knives in Kiszko's possession, the one he identified in his confession as the murder weapon did have traces of blood on it.)

This indicates that Kiszko was now reiterating the confession, although in less detailed and definite terms. The content of these two sentences suggested that after Kiszko made his retraction the previous evening, there had been a discussion with him about the case and he was claiming not having any memory of committing the murder. In addition, if Kiszko had genuinely remembered murdering the girl the previous day, then there would be no reason for him not being able to recall it a day later.

At 10.15 p.m. on 23 December 1975, Kiszko was taken to the crime scene and is reported to shake and hold his hands in a praying position, stating:

> I can hear noises can't you?

Kiszko was charged with the murder at 11.50 p.m. that same evening. He made no reply.

The Trial

Kiszko was convicted of Lesley Molseed's murder on 21 July 1976 by a 10–2 majority verdict at Leeds Crown Court. He was sentenced to life imprisonment.

In his direction to the jury, the judge stated:

> Well ladies and gentlemen, this defendant held up well in cross-examination by a skilled prosecutor in the middle of a murder trial, so how can he say he could not cope with the two policemen in an interview room? (Rose, Panter & Wilkinson, 1998, p. 179).

The trial judge was clearly implicitly telling the jury that he believed Kiszko to be unlikely to give in to the pressure of a police interview, and by implication that the confession to the murder was reliable.

The trial judge was also sceptical about Kiszko's claim that he had been ill treated at the police station and had made a false confession, because after making his confession Kiszko had had the opportunity to make a complaint to a police officer in the presence of his solicitor, but did not do so.

In May 1978 he was refused leave to appeal against his conviction.

The Final Appeal

Following the defence team's petition to the Home Secretary in 1990, and the outcome of the re-investigation by the West Yorkshire Police in 1991 which demonstrated suppression at trial of crucial scientific evidence supporting Kiszko's claims of innocence, the case was referred by the Home Secretary to the Court of Appeal. The crucial 'new' evidence related to the fact that Kiszko's semen was void of sperm heads (spermatazoa) and it therefore did not match that found on Lesley Molseed's clothing. This fact was known to the police and the forensic science service, which carried out the tests, at the time of Kiszko's trial.

The case was heard on 17 and 18 February 1992 before Lord Chief Justice Lane and Justices Rose and Potts.

In his Judgment, Lord Lane stated that on the facts presented by the prosecution at trial, the case against Mr Kiszko 'was extremely strong'. Not only was there a confession to the murder, there was an admission to indecent exposure. Perhaps the most important supportive evidence was that Mr Kiszko provided in his confession detailed descriptions of the murder, which the police and prosecution argued could only have come from somebody who was present during the killing. On the face of it, the intimate post-admission special knowledge was very incriminating and included the following.

- Detailed description of the circumstances of the murder and the place where it had taken place.
- Knowledge that the victim had been left fully dressed (this knowledge had been kept away from the public—Rose, Panter & Wilkinson, 1998).
- Seminal stains on the girl's knickers and skirt, which coincided almost exactly with Kiszko's description of how he held the girl and masturbated over her (the information had been withheld from the public and at the trial the superintendent in charge of the case testified 'that only five members of the enquiry team, none below the rank of chief inspector, knew that the killer had ejaculated over Lesley's body' (Rose, Panter & Wilkinson, 1998). The implication was that the special knowledge about the semen had to have come from the murderer: that is, Kiszko.
- Of the several knives Kiszko possessed the one he identified as the murder weapon had traces of blood on it (it was not possible to establish whether the blood was human or not).

However, in view of the fresh evidence the Court of Appeal had no alternative but to overturn the conviction, because it clearly proved Kiszko's innocence:

> The result is that it has been shown that this man cannot produce sperm. This man therefore cannot have been the person responsible for ejaculating over the little girl's knickers and shirt, and consequently cannot have been the murderer.

For those reasons, which we have endeavoured to express as concisely as possible, this appeal must be allowed and the conviction quashed as being unsafe and unsatisfactory.

Psychological Evaluation

In August 1992, with the consent of his solicitor Mr Campbell Malone, Dr MacKeith and I visited Kiszko at his home in Lancaster. The purpose of the visit was to interview Kiszko about the police interviews and his confessions in 1975 in order to try to understand what had made him falsely confess to the murder of Lesley Molseed. The main findings from the psychological testing were as follows.

- Kiszko was of low average intelligence, which is consistent with previous test results.
- His suggestibility, compliance and acquiescence scores were all moderately elevated, but fell within normal limits (70–80th percentile rank).
- The Social Desirability score on the Eysenck Personality Questionnaire fell well outside normal limits (98th percentile rank).
- On Semantic Differential Scales (Gudjonsson & Lister, 1984), Kiszko rated himself, as he had been at the time of his arrest, as very weak, tense, passive, timid and submissive, and viewed himself as being very kind, good and intelligent. His present self in 1992 was rated very differently with regard to the weak–strong and tense–relaxed dimensions. In great contrast to his position in 1975, he saw himself at that time as being very strong and relaxed.

With regard to having made the false confession to the murder, Kiszko told us that the following factors were of great importance.

- He strongly believed that if he did not confess, the police officers would beat him up. He described this fear of the police as being the single most important reason for his making a false confession. He alleges that during the first interview one of the detectives poked a finger into his shoulder and shouted 'I'll get the fucking truth out of you one way or another'.
- The officers kept asking him the same questions over and over again and Kiszko 'couldn't stand it any more' and began to give in to the pressure they placed him under as a way of escaping from the pressure.
- He felt very much on his own and did not know how to cope with his predicament. He retracted his confession once he saw his solicitor and did not think he would have confessed to the murder if a solicitor had been present throughout all the interviews. He saw a way out of his predicament when the solicitor arrived after his confession on the afternoon of 22 December.
- The police questioning made him feel confused.
- He thought that if he confessed he would be allowed to go home. It was approaching Christmas and Kiszko was keen to be home at Christmas. At the time he seemed to be rather over-dependent on his mother and had difficulty coping without her.

- He was embarrassed by the sex magazines found by the police in the boot of his car.

During his early imprisonment, concerns were raised about Kiszko's mental health, which resulted in his being recommended for hospital transfer in 1984. He was diagnosed as schizophrenic, the primary symptoms being auditory hallucinations and grandiose and persecutory beliefs. Dr MacKeith and I thought there were at least three factors which suggested that Kiszko may well have suffered from an undiagnosed psychiatric illness prior to his arrest, including his comment at the crime scene 'I can hear noises, can't you' and the fact that about nine months prior to his arrest he had made a very strange complaint to the police that vehicles were trying to force him off the road, which was not supported by subsequent police evidence. This strongly suggested delusional thinking. If indeed there was a psychotic process present prior to and at the time of Kiszko's interrogation in 1975, then it may have had adverse effects on Kiszko's mental state while at the police station and his ability to cope with his predicament.

Kiszko denied to us that he had committed the indecent exposure he was accused of but never prosecuted for. It is now evident that the alleged indecent exposure on 3 October did not take place at all; it was fabricated by the alleged victims (Rose, Panter & Wilkinson, 1998), which means that Kiszko made a false confession to that offence.

The leading prosecuting counsel in the case at trial, Mr Peter Taylor, became the Lord Chief Justice of England and Wales in 1992 around the time of the appeal. About a year before the appeal, the defence counsel, Mr David Waddington, became Home Secretary.

Comments

There is no doubt that the confession Kiszko gave to the police on 22 December 1975 was false. This was recognized by their Lordships who quashed his conviction. It was a confession of the pressured–compliant type, which was precipitated by Kiszko's fear of the police, inability to cope with the pressure of the police interviews, sexual and emotional naivety and allegedly intimidating interviewing tactics. Kiszko's account of new experiences of his sexuality, following his hormonal treatment for hypogonadism, paralleled that of teenage defendants and made him vulnerable to interrogation tactics that focused on the embarrassing aspects of his sexuality (e.g. being found in possession of pornographic magazines, masturbation). In this respect the case is similar to that reported by Gudjonsson and MacKeith (1990).

So how did Kiszko acquire such intimate special knowledge of the murder, which the police and prosecution argued could only have come from the murderer? What is crucial is that Kiszko did not give any details about the killing that would not have been known to the police, apart from perhaps the knife that contained traces of blood, human or otherwise. The details about the murder, where it took place and the seminal stains must have been communicated to Mr Kiszko by the police, as was always claimed by him, either deliberately or inadvertently. The police, of course, denied any such transferred special knowledge. This case highlights the dangers of relying unduly on apparent special knowledge, even when it is supported by the confident and convincing testimony of senior police officers. If it had not been for the discovery of the scientific evidence suppressed by the West Yorkshire Police then it is very unlikely that his conviction would ever have been overturned. Undoubtedly, at appeal the Crown would have successfully used Mr Kiszko's apparent special knowledge as evidence of the safety of his conviction. The police have now launched another inquiry into the murder (Herbert, 2001).

This is another case which highlights the dangers of relying on defendants' demeanor and performance in the witness box as evidence of his or her ability to resist pressure in a police interview, where the circumstances and demand characteristics of the situation are generally very different. Some vulnerable defendants may cope reasonably well with the cross-examination when properly prepared by their legal team. In addition, the types of vulnerability that are relevant to suspects making a false confession are very varied and some (e.g. giving in to threats or inducements because of inability to cope with the situation) would not be present when giving their testimony in court. In other words, the cross-examination may not necessarily tap into the vulnerabilities that were relevant at the time of the interrogation.

The case also demonstrates how dangerous it is to run the two defences concurrently—claims of innocence on the one hand, and diminished responsibility on the other, in the event of the jury considering him guilty of the offence. A defence psychiatrist colluded with this dangerous strategy and appears to have done more harm than good by testifying about Kiszko's long-standing hypogonadism, testosterone deficiency and emergent sexual interests and ejaculatory capacity shortly prior to the murder (Rose, Panter & Wilkinson, 1998). This appears to have provided the court with a possible motive for the murder.

On the positive side, Kiszko's innocence was eventually established and his conviction was quashed due to the hard work of his new legal team and the integrity and thoroughness of the police officers who re-investigated the case in 1990–1991. Sadly, on the evening of 21 December 1993, exactly 18 years to the day since he accompanied the officers to the Rochdale Police Station, Kiszko died from heart failure.

THE DARVELL BROTHERS

On 19 June 1986 at Swansea Crown Court, (Phillip) Wayne Darvell and Paul Darvell, two brothers, were convicted of murder on a 10–2 majority verdict. The victim of the murder was a 30-year-old woman, Mrs Sandra Phillips, who worked as a manageress of a sex shop in Swansea. The evidence at trial against the Darvell brothers related to sightings of them in the area of the murder at the relevant time, evidence of purchase of petrol, alleged discovery of an earring in the police car used to transport Wayne Darvell, confessions to the police of Wayne Darvell and alleged lies by Paul Darvell concerning his whereabouts (i.e. his persistent denials that he had been in Dillwyn Street on the day of the murder in spite of police evidence to the contrary). It was conceded by the Crown that the 'sighting evidence was weak'.

Wayne Darvell was arrested on 15 June 1985 and interviewed six times that day. He began to make admissions in the third interview. Up to the point of his admissions no contemporaneous recording was kept of the interrogation. Each interview was allegedly recorded in a police pocket book before the next interview began. In his admissions, Wayne Darvell minimized his own involvement in the murder and blamed it on his brother, who did not break down and make a confession to the murder. He claimed to have been present at the time of the murder and 'stood guard.' No solicitor or legal representative was present during these interviews. Wayne retracted his confession four days after his arrest at the earliest opportunity after meeting his solicitor. At the time of the police interviews, Wayne was 23 years of age. His brother Paul was 25. Both had a history of attending a special school because of learning disability.

At trial there was a *voire dire* regarding the admissibility of Wayne Darvell's admissions. A consultant psychiatrist, Dr Alexander Kellam, gave evidence regarding Wayne's borderline mental handicap, disordered personality and high suggestibility on the GSS 1 (Yield 1 = 11, Shift = 9, Total Suggestibility = 20). A psychiatrist called on behalf of the Crown, Dr Anna Thomas, argued that Wayne was of low average intelligence, because at age 16 he allegedly had obtained an IQ of 82, in spite of his having attended a school for the educationally subnormal. The trial judge, Mr Justice Leonard, ruled Wayne's admissions were admissible; his case did not fall within Section 77 of PACE, there had been no oppression and no leading questions asked by the police. Dr Kellam and Dr Thomas gave evidence again in front of the jury.

In his summing-up before the jury Mr Justice Leonard emphasized the special knowledge that Wayne apparently had about the murder:

> It is not a matter of one version being preferred to another version, it is a matter of a lot of detail coming out in those interviews, much of which, say the Crown, could not be known to the defendant and some of which could not really, at that stage, even be fully understood by the police, but you have to consider the position.

In November 1987 the Court of Appeal refused leave to appeal after hearing legal arguments about the case. Lord Justice Watkins, sitting with Justices Rose and Roch, concluded that there was nothing 'unsafe or unsatisfactory' about the jury's verdict. Indeed, Lord Justice Watkins concluded that Wayne's statement to the police contained known facts that only the two brothers could have known. The judges were critical of the fact that Paul had not gone into the witness box to refute the allegations made against him in his brother's statement.

The Final Appeal

After the brothers' conviction in 1986, concerns about the safety of the conviction in a BBC television programme, *Rough Justice*, and the organization *Justice*, which is supported by many distinguished English lawyers, petitioned to the Home Office to look into the case. The Home Secretary requested that the Devon and Cornwall Police conduct an investigation into the case. The outcome of this investigation cast grave doubts on the prosecution case. During the re-investigation of the case by the police, electrostatic detection apparatus (ESDA) was used by a forensic scientist to determine the authenticity and integrity of the written record of the police interviews. The analysis showed that a number of pages concerning Wayne's interviews with the police had been re-written with different content. Some of the amendments showed that leading questions had been re-written to make them appear non-leading. This suggested that, contrary to what the trial judge had emphasized to the jury, there had been a number of leading questions. The re-investigation also cast doubts on the discovery of the earring in a police car used to transport Wayne Darvell, on the police evidence of the brothers being seen on Dillwyn Street at 11.45 a.m. on the day of the murder, and on the non-disclosure of a blood-stained palm print at the crime scene, which did not belong to either of the Darvell brothers.

As a result of the ESDA and other findings from the re-investigation, the Home Secretary referred the case to the Court of Appeal. The appeal was heard in July 1992 by Lord Chief Justice Taylor and Justices Thomas and Judge. At the appeal the Crown, in view of the severe criticism levelled against the Swansea police, did not seek to uphold the conviction. The appeal judges stated that the ESDA findings and palm print evidence alone would have been sufficient to destroy the prosecution case. The other findings, including further psychological evidence from Dr Julian Fuller and Dr Gillian Grebler, reinforced the pre-trial defence view that Wayne Darvell was a vulnerable person who was suggestible, submissive and naive. Having read a number of witness statements, the judges stated:

> ...Wayne has been recognized for years to be unreliable, suggestible, desirous of ingratiating himself with those in authority, given to making false confessions of all kinds of offences and false attributions of criminal behaviour to his brother Paul.

The judges concluded that the psychological evidence, and background evidence supporting Wayne's vulnerabilities, provided an explanation as to why he had gone along with the police suggestions and made a false confession.

Comments

I was not directly involved in this case. However, I have had access to all the relevant papers in the case and in March 1994 I interviewed Wayne Darvell in connection with his false confession to the murder of Mrs Sandra Phillips. I am satisfied that the confession Wayne made to the police was of the coerced–compliant type. At no time was Wayne persuaded by the police that he had committed the murder. He claims that he falsely confessed because the police threatened to beat him up if he did not confess, he was asked leading questions and pressured to confess by the police, he wanted to get out of the police station and thought he would get bail and not be charged and he was in the habit of blaming his brother for things in order to get himself out of trouble. From the content of his confession it is evident that he was distancing himself from the offence by blaming it on his brother. For him this was undoubtedly an easy way out of a situation he was finding it difficult to cope with and represented a compromise between a continued denial and full confession.

During my assessment, Wayne proved to be abnormally compliant on the GCS, whereas he rated his brother Paul on the same scale as being very low on compliance. As was commented on by the trial judge in his summing-up to the jury, Paul appeared to be far more 'dominant' than Wayne, which was supported by my own assessment. It may be partly for this reason that Paul was able to resist the interrogation, whereas Wayne broke down and confessed, while placing most of the blame for the murder on his brother. Interestingly, unlike the results from the GSS 1 when tested by Dr Kellan in 1986, when I tested Wayne on the GSS 2 in 1994 he scored at the bottom of the test and demonstrated great critical faculty and resistance to leading questions and interrogative pressure. Why should this difference exist? One explanation is that, since his conviction, Wayne had become more critical in his thinking and less trusting of people, which is something that he told me he had experienced since his conviction. A similar change in personality was noted in another case of a false confession of the coerced–compliant type (Gudjonsson & MacKeith, 1990).

Finally, the emphasis by the Crown, trial judge and first Court of Appeal hearing on the apparent special knowledge that Wayne is supposed to have possessed about the murder is interesting, and if it had not been for the ESDA and fresh palm print evidence the conviction would probably not have been overturned.

DONALD PENDLETON

This case involves the failed appeal in June 2000 of Donald Pendleton. I had become involved in the case as a result of referral from the Criminal Cases Review Commission (CCRC). The case involved a murder in Bradford dating back to June 1971. At his trial at Leeds Crown Court in 1986, Pendleton and his co-defendant, Thorpe, were both convicted of murder. Pendleton did not give evidence at trial. In 1987 he was refused leave to appeal.

Pendleton was arrested in the early morning of 23 March 1985 and he was extensively interviewed and detained for three days without the presence of a solicitor. He was introduced to his solicitor on the evening of the third day. During the interviews he was placed under great pressure and eventually confessed exhibiting a great deal of distress during the interviews. On the afternoon of the second day Pendleton was taken to the crime scene, after which he provided the most incriminating details. The interviews were very leading, with Pendleton apparently having great problems with recalling what he had been doing 14 years previously. After the visit to the crime scene his memory about the murder improved considerably and this was commented upon by one of the officers. Pendleton explained his improved memory as follows:

Well it helped seeing the place again this afternoon.

Subsequently Pendleton has maintained that he made a false confession to the police due to the pressure he was placed under and his disturbed mental state at the time.

I interviewed Pendleton in October 1998 and produced a comprehensive report. In spite of his being of normal intelligence (upper end of the low average range), I had serious reservations about the reliability of his confession to the police:

> As far as the police interviews and Mr Pendleton's self-incriminating admission are concerned, I am of the view that in 1985 he was a psychologically vulnerable individual. He was an extremely anxious individual who was finding it difficult to cope with life (his medical records confirm this). The record of the police interviews gives an indication of his immense distress and agitation concerning his arrest and questioning, which appear to have been accompanied by a lack of concern or thought about the consequences of his admissions. His anxiety proneness seems less pronounced now than it was in 1985, but in spite of this he proved to be abnormally suggestible, compliant and acquiescent. These vulnerabilities are likely to have been present, and possibly more marked, in 1985. Finally, it is evident from the transcripts of the police interviews that Mr Pendleton was subjected to considerable pressure to confess, pressure he was clearly having difficulties coping with. Having considered this case carefully I have serious reservations about the reliability of the self-incriminating admissions Mr Pendleton made to the police in 1985.

As a result of my conclusions the CCRC referred the case to the Court of Appeal. The case was heard in June 2000 at the Royal Court of Justice before Lord Justice Pill and Justices Sachs and Steel. I testified and in rebuttal the Crown called a consultant psychiatrist, Dr Richard Badcock, who had interviewed Pendleton prior to his trial in 1986. Dr Badcock agreed with my conclusions that at the time of the interrogation in 1985 Pendleton had been psychologically vulnerable. However, in his testimony Dr Badcock was hesitant about challenging the reliability of Pendleton's confession. He appears to have provided the judges with grounds for rejecting the appeal when he stated that from his reading of the record of the police interview the confession, elicited after the crime scene visit, had a 'spontaneous and authentic flow'. This comment appeared to have an immediate effect on the view of the judges, who made use of it in their judgment. In their comments on the police interviews, the judges ruled:

> Professor Gudjonsson's evidence that the appellant was vulnerable in the manner described is unchallenged but the Court must make an assessment whether that vulnerability did, or may have, led the appellant, in the interview and statements given, to have made false admissions. Professor Gudjonsson could not definitively answer that question, as he frankly and fairly admitted. He expressed his open-mindedness as to whether the accounts given were true or guesswork. Dr Badcock's 'niggle' about the truth of the appellant's accounts was narrowly expressed and followed by evidence that the appellant's accounts appeared informed, natural and genuine. We bear in mind Professor Gudjonsson's analysis, and that of Dr Badcock, along with submissions made by counsel on each side and the other material.

> Given the accounts of the appellant's statements to the police, and the manner in which they were elicited, we have no doubts as to the reliability of the admissions made by the appellant as to his presence at the scene of the murder. None of the vulnerabilities described by Gudjonsson can, upon consideration of the interviews as a whole, put a flavour of falsity upon the admissions made. We find it inconceivable that his accounts were imagined or invented. Unless there is material,

extraneous to the interviews and the issues surrounding them, which otherwise casts doubt upon the admissions, they provide a sound and sufficient basis for the safety of the conviction.

Comments

The case makes an important ruling regarding the psychological testimony. That is, even when relevant psychological vulnerabilities can be demonstrated, and they are undisputed by the Crown, these will need to be interpreted within the totality of the evidence in the case and its surrounding circumstances. This is an important principle, which I fully support. Vulnerabilities are rarely sufficient by themselves to render a conviction unsafe. Indeed, the vulnerabilities identified may not be sufficient in the judges' view, even if in the opinion of the expert they cast doubts on the reliability of a confession, for the conviction to be quashed. Conversely, confessions can be unreliable when no vulnerabilities are identified by the psychological or psychiatric evaluation. Their Lordships have the ultimate say in the outcome of an appeal, and should of course be guided rather than ruled by expert witnesses. What is important is that judges consider the expert psychological evidence dispassionately, fairly and objectively.

However, having carefully considered the case of Pendleton, observed the appeal and having had time to reflect on it, I still have serious reservations about the reliability of Pendleton's confession to the police. Their Lordships appeared to be impressed by Pendleton's apparent special knowledge about the murder, which was skilfully argued by the Crown at the appeal. On the face of it, *after the crime scene visit* on the second day of custodial detention, Pendleton seemed to provide some incriminating detail about the victim (e.g. that the victim had been kicked, had rolled over, and that the victim might have been urinating when he was attacked). It is interesting that none of this informative detail was elicited during the six previous interviews at the police station. The last point concerning the urination was emphasized mostly strongly by the Crown, because the victim's flies were apparently found to be partly open when his body was discovered. With regard to this special knowledge, at the crime scene Pendleton is reported to have said to the officers:

> I seem to recall the guy was having a piss.

When interviewed later that evening, one of the officers says at the beginning of the interview:

> Now you said earlier that you had a recollection of the man having a piss.

Mr Pendleton replied:

> Like I say I think he was just having a piss and we were in high spirits.

None of the interviews were tape-recorded and we do not know what special knowledge information may have been communicated to Pendleton while he was in police custody over a three day period, or indeed what he may have successfully invented or guessed himself. The case illustrates how powerful one or two pieces of apparent special knowledge can be in terms of assumptions that are made about somebody's guilt. Of course, all that is required legally is that the appellant's guilt is the most reasonable explanation for his being in possession of the special knowledge information.

From reading the judgment, I was concerned that their Lordships might only have considered the impact of Pendleton's 'personality' on the reliability of the police interviews and not his vulnerable mental state at the time. Pendleton was under a great deal of stress at the time of his arrest and during the police interviews, in addition to being vulnerable in terms of his personality. Another observation relates to their Lordships' comment regarding the fact that I would not definitively state whether or not Pendleton had made a false confession. My reluctance to state that Pendleton had made a false confession relates to a scientific reality. It is extremely rare that a psychologist or a psychiatrist could categorically state, merely on the basis of a psychological evaluation, that a disputed confession is definitively false.

Postscript

In December 2001, five Law Lords in the House of Lords heard the case. The appeal was allowed and conviction was quashed (13 December 2001, UKHL 66). Pendleton was free after having spent 15 years in prison (Verkaik, 2001). Mr Michael Mansfield QC had successfully argued on behalf of Mr Pendleton that the Court of Appeal judges had taken upon themselves

> ... the task of assessing the fresh psychological evidence and so trespassing on the exclusive domain of the jury. The Court of Appeal was in effect undertaking the retrial of a case (p. 18 of The House of Lords Judgment).

Lord Bingham, who delivered the judgment, stated

> No one can now be sure what would have happened had the evidence of Professor Gudjonsson been available at the time of the trial. But the defence might in at least three respects have been conducted differently:

1. The appellant might have been called to give evidence on his own behalf.
2. There would have been more searching questions asked about the appellant's mental state during the police interviews.
3. It seems likely that there would have been more detailed enquiries into the unrecorded discussions and interactions between the appellant and the police.

> In light of these uncertainties and this fresh psychological evidence it is impossible to be sure that this conviction is safe, and that is so whether the members of the House ask whether they themselves have reason to doubt the safety of the conviction or whether they ask whether the jury might have reached a different conclusion (p. 22).

CONCLUSIONS

There is no doubt that post-admission details and apparent special knowledge often weigh very heavily against the accused at trial. An apparent intimate knowledge of the offence by suspects is very incriminating, and often rightly so. However, problems sometimes arise when too much emphasis is placed on pieces of special knowledge and it is assumed that only the real culprit could have possessed that knowledge, when in fact there could be a number of explanations for it apart from genuine guilt. The case of Kiszko is a case in point. On the face of it, his apparent special knowledge was extremely convincing and incriminating, but we know now that it *must* have originated from the police. Even when there is absence of any knowledge about the offences and the confession is unconvincing, as it certainly was in the cases of *MacKenzie* and *Fell*, defendants are still convicted on the basis of their confession.

PART IV

FOREIGN CASES OF DISPUTED CONFESSIONS

CHAPTER 21

Four High Profile American Cases

In this chapter I discuss four high profile American murder cases involving disputed confessions. In all four cases I had been commissioned by defence attorneys to assess their clients and study the relevant papers in the case. The first case concerns the confessions of Waneta Hoyt to the murder of her five children. My findings were on balance unfavourable to the defence and I was not required to testify. Nevertheless, the case is of great psychological, medical and legal interest. The second case discussed is that of Joe Giarratano. Dr James MacKeith and I assessed Giarratano in 1990 and considered his 1979 confession to double murder to be unreliable. Giarratano's death sentence was commuted to life imprisonment two days before his execution date in February 1991. The third case involves Henry Lee Lucas, who was estimated to have made over 600 confessions to murder in the 1980s. My assessment was important in understanding his psychopathology. In June 1998, four days before Mr Lucas's execution date, the Governor of Texas, George W. Bush, granted clemency and commuted Mr Lucas's death sentence to life imprisonment. The third case is that of John Wille and his partner Judith Walters, who confessed to several murders during custodial interrogation in 1985. Wille received a death penalty sentence and Walters life imprisonment. Both are still fighting to prove their innocence.

WANETA HOYT

Much has been written about this case in the national newspapers in the USA and two books have been devoted to the case (Firstman & Talan, 1997; Hickey, Lighty & O'Brien, 1996). In England, the case featured on a BBC 2 *Horizon* programme on 25 February 1999. The case involved a 48-year-old woman who in 1995 was convicted of murdering five of her infant children between 24 and 30 years previously. An influential publication in a medical journal in 1972 about the case eventually led to Waneta Hoyt's arrest. The article proposed a controversial theory of Sudden Infant Death Syndrome (SIDS), which according to the *Horizon* programme had set back cot-death research for a generation.

I became involved in the case shortly before the trial in 1995 and carried out a psychological evaluation at the request of the defence attorneys. There has been much speculation about what my findings had been in the light of my not being called to testify at the trial (Firstman & Talan, 1997; Hickey, Lighty & O'Brien, 1996). The main conclusion drawn by these authors was that I had found Hoyt not to be suggestible on the GSS. In this chapter I briefly describe the case and the main psychological findings, and explain why I was not called to testify. I shall show that Hoyt's low suggestibility scores were only a part of the explanation of why I was not called to testify. There were other aspects of the case that were intriguing and devastating to Hoyt's defence.

Brief Background to the Case

On 23 March 1994, Waneta Hoyt confessed to the police that she had murdered her five natural children, who died between 1965 and 1971. She was subsequently charged with their murders. The prosecution argued that Hoyt had smothered her babies to death. The first to die was Eric, who was three months and ten days old at the time of his death in 1965 (he allegedly bled from the mouth and died suddenly). Next was Julie, who died in 1968 at the age of one month and 18 days (she allegedly choked on rice cereal). Three weeks after Julie's death, James died (he allegedly bled from the nose and mouth and died suddenly). He was two years and four months of age (in view of his age it was difficult to construe his death as SIDS). Then Molly died. She died in 1970, aged two months and 18 days (she died the day she was discharged from hospital). The last to die was Noah, who died aged two months and 19 days in 1971 (he died the day after he was discharged from hospital). In terms of age, James was considerably older when he died than the other four children, all of whom died in early infancy. All the children had died on weekdays and during working hours. Apart from Eric, who died at 1.30 in the afternoon, the other four deaths had occurred between 8.30 and 10.00 a.m. Hoyt was alone with each of the children at the time of their death.

The last two babies, Molly and Noah, had since soon after birth been under close observation by Dr Alfred Steinschneider and his medical team at Upstate Medical Center, Syracuse, New York. This included being observed on an apnoea monitor. Molly was the first baby in the world to be provided with an apnoea monitor at home. In spite of this, both babies died within 48 hours of being discharged from hospital to their mother. Steinschneider (1972) wrote a landmark article on the relationship between prolonged apnoea (of 15 or more seconds) and SIDS. In the article he described his continued observations of Molly and Noah and how they subsequently died from SIDS. Steinschneider made a reference to the three previous deaths of Hoyt's babies and suggested that a hidden cardio-respiratory abnormality was responsible for multiple deaths of SIDS in a single family. Steinschneider became the father of the notion that SIDS deaths can occur repeatedly in the same family. The idea of a constitutional or genetic abnormality in cases of SIDS was subsequently used as a successful defence in many cases of suspected homicidal smothering of infants by their parents, with Steinschneider's article being produced as the supporting evidence (Firstman & Talan, 1997). In addition, as a result of the article home apnoea monitoring became advocated by many professionals in the 1970s and 1980s as a method of preventing SIDS and became a huge business enterprise. With the 1972 article he had built up an enormous reputation in the field of SIDS, but his apnoea theory has remained scientifically unproven and misleading. The validity of Steinschneider's theory became a critical issue at the trial of Hoyt in 1995.

How did Hoyt come to be arrested and charged with the murder of her infants more than two decades after their death? There is no doubt that it was Steinschneider's 1972 article, and the attention it received within the scientific community, that was to be the impetus for Hoyt's downfall. In 1986, during the prosecution of another multiple SIDS case, Bill Fitzpatrick, a prosecuting attorney in Onondaga County, hired a medical expert, Dr Linda Norton, a forensic pathologist in Dallas, to assist with the case. During a pre-trial conference with the prosecutors, Norton drew attention to Steinschneider's 1972 article and commented 'You may have a serial killer right here in Syracuse' (Firstman & Talan, 1997, p. 63), referring to the case of Hoyt's five dead infants. Fitzpatrick then began a process of identifying the Hoyt family from Steinschneider's 1972 article. Fitzpatrick allegedly had a grand jury secretly subpoena Noah Hoyt's medical records from the Upstate Medical Center, Syracuse (Hickey, Lighty & O'Brien, 1996, p. 184). His investigation eventually discovered the identity of Mr and Mrs Hoyt, who were living in Tioga County, where Fitzpatrick had no jurisdiction. Although two of the babies had been treated in Syracuse, all five children had died at their parents' home in Newark Valley, Tioga County, which is 70 miles south of Syracuse.

In 1992, Fitzpatrick, now a newly appointed district attorney for Onondaga County, contacted his counterpart in Tioga County, Bob Simpson, who took on the case 15 months later. The police investigation was allocated to Robert Courtwright, the State Senior Investigator. He carried out a discreet investigation in order not to alert Mr and Mrs Hoyt to the investigation. He discovered that Mr and Mrs Hoyt had lived in the county all their lives, they had no criminal record, they had a 17-year-old adopted son, Jay, there was no record of child abuse recorded against them, they had always been poor financially and they did not socialize much. In the summer of 1976 Mr and Mrs Hoyt adopted Jay through a private agency in Ithaca.

Chief Investigator Courtwright discovered that all the children had died when alone at home in the company of their mother. Mr and Mrs Hoyt had adopted Jay when he was about two and a half months old and there was no evidence that Mrs Hoyt had ever made an attempt to suffocate him or injure him in any way.

Simpson commissioned two pathologists to review the medical records in the case. They were Dr Michael Baden, a former New York medical examiner (Baden & Hennessee, 1992), and Dr Janice Ophoven, a paediatric forensic pathologist. Both pathologists concluded that in their opinion the five babies had been murdered and had not died from SIDS. The likely motive, they suggested, involved Mrs Hoyt suffering from a condition called 'Munchausen syndrome by proxy' (MBP). This condition, first labelled by Meadow (1977), involved people, nearly always women, to fake or cause illness in their children in order to gain attention and sympathy. Mothers are said to be the perpetrators in 98% of cases and in one study 9% of the children had died (Feldman, Ford & Reinhold, 1994).

The Confession to the Murders

On the morning of 23 March 1994, Hoyt drove her husband to work. She then stopped at the local post office to pick up the mail. At the post office she met a state trooper, Bobby Bleck, whom she knew well as a local policeman. Bleck asked her to meet somebody who was interested in discussing her deceased children in relation to SIDS research (the police denied at trial that she was tricked into thinking that she was discussing a research project). Hoyt agreed and was introduced to Susan Mulvey, who in fact was a police investigator. She agreed to accompany the officers to the state police barracks, but stated that she would first have to go home and take her teenaged son Jay to school. The officers agreed with this. While Jay was getting ready for school Hoyt showed the two officers her family photo album containing photographs of her deceased children, which she took with her to the police barracks.

Hoyt arrived at the police barracks between 10.30 and 10.45 in the morning. Investigator Courtwright was waiting there for them. Hoyt was then read her *Miranda* rights. Officer Mulvey then began to talk to her about her family, including the background to the deaths of her five infants. At about 11.30 there was a break and when the interview re-commenced shortly afterwards, Mulvey allegedly told Hoyt that they had proof that she had suffocated all of her babies while she and Officer Bleck comforted her physically by stroking her hands and placing an arm around her shoulder, respectively. She eventually broke down, began to cry and admitted to having murdered her five babies. At about 13.50 a written statement was taken from her, but she refused to sign it without the presence of her husband (Hoyt told me that the reason for this refusal was that she was in the habit of always signing important documents in the presence of her husband). Undoubtedly, the police were concerned that if they waited for her husband she might change her mind about signing the statement, or that her husband might advise her not to sign it. To overcome the risk of this happening, the police interviewed her again in the presence of a qualified shorthand court stenographer, who wrote down contemporaneously the questions and answers. This was then used as Hoyt's 'Sworn Statement'. The recording of this statement commenced at 2.30 in the afternoon. Present were the three officers, Courtwright, Mulvey and Bleck, all of whom asked some questions or made comments during the interview.

In this Sworn Statement Hoyt makes a full confession to the murder of her five babies by means of suffocation. The motive, she alleged, was her inability to cope with their crying or screaming. Regarding the death of her oldest child Jamie, she explained when asked to tell what had happened:

> I was getting dressed in the bathroom, and he wanted to come in, and I didn't want him to. I told him to wait out in the hall until I was done, and he kept yelling, mommy, mommy and screaming. And I took a towel and went out in the living room, and I put the towel over his face to get him to quiet down, and he struggled. And once he finally got quiet, he was gone.

At 15.43, after Hoyt's husband, Timothy, had arrived at the police barracks, Mrs Hoyt signed the original handwritten statement. Her signature was witnessed by her husband. A few minutes later she wished to add a few things to her previous statement. These consisted of her explaining that she had in the past unsuccessfully tried to seek psychiatric help from doctors, that she had acted alone, and felt great remorse for having murdered her children:

> ... I was seeking their help because I knew that something was wrong with me. I feel that if I got help from them, it would have prevented me from killing the rest of my children. I feel that I am a good person, but I know that I did wrong. I loved my children. I love my son Jay and my husband. I feel the burden I have carried by keeping the secret of killing my children has been a tremendous punishment. I most definitely feel remorse and regret my actions. I cannot go back and undo the wrong that I have done. My husband, Tim, had no part in any of the children's deaths and I was always alone.

When visited by her son Jay later that afternoon, Hoyt told her adopted son that she had murdered his brothers and sisters. He was clearly devastated by this revelation and began to cry (Firstman & Talan, 1997).

No lawyer was present during the police interviews. Hoyt was provided with a lawyer that same afternoon. When he arrived at the police barracks, he saw Hoyt, her husband and son. Jay Hoyt was crying. Officer Mulvey was still holding Hoyt's hand, presumably in order to comfort her. She had already extracted a confession from her. That same evening the lawyer handed the case over to Bob Miller, a public defender in Tioga County. He contacted another lawyer, Ray Urbanski, a colleague of his from Elmira. The following morning, Urbanski went to see Hoyt in prison. She told him that she was innocent of the murders, but had been forced by the police to make a false confession. Hoyt has proclaimed her innocence ever since. Miller and Urbanski were to represent and defend Hoyt at her trial in 1995.

There was a 'Suppression Hearing' in the Tiogo County Courthouse in Owego in September 1994. The defence motion to exclude Hoyt's confession statements was unsuccessful. It was now for a jury to consider what weight could be placed upon the reliability of those confession statements, which were going to be disputed at trial.

The Psychological Evaluation

On 11 March 1995, I travelled to Elmira, where I was met by Ray Urbanski. I studied the papers in the case and interviewed and tested Hoyt. I administered a large number of psychometric tests to Hoyt, which included an assessment of her intellectual abilities, memory, suggestibility, compliance, personality and mental state. I also interviewed her husband Timothy, and their adopted son Jay. After my interviews with Hoyt and her family, Urbanski and I went to Buffalo to meet Dr Charles Ewing. Dr Ewing, who was licensed both as a psychologist and an attorney, had examined Hoyt on four occasions in 1994 at the request of the defence team. In addition to lengthy interviews with Hoyt, Dr Ewing had administered one psychological test, the MMPI-2. He was well informed about the case and the relevant legal issues. I agreed with his view that Hoyt's confession appeared to have been induced by psychological manipulation and trickery by the police. Of course, this does not necessarily mean that the confession was false. True as well as false confessions can result from police pressure. Had Hoyt made a false confession to the murder of her children? Before addressing this question, it is important to recognize the importance of the confession in convicting her and how it came about in psychological terms. What was the process that made Hoyt confess to the murders of her children, after she had initially denied the offences?

The police must have known that they would not get a conviction without a confession. The fact that five children in one family had died was not sufficient by itself to obtain a conviction. In addition, there was no salient physical or medical evidence that Hoyt's five children had been murdered. All the police had was that Hoyt had the opportunity of murdering her children and she would have had the means to do it. The police carefully planned the best way of extracting a confession from Hoyt (Firstman & Talan, 1997; Hickey, Lighty & O'Brien, 1996). Having studied the case in detail, it seems the police employed the following tactics to break down Hoyt's resistance.

- They used a local police officer whom Hoyt liked and trusted to get her to cooperate with the police without her being aware of the dangers that lay ahead. Hoyt was tricked into a false sense of security and once her defences were down the police moved in to persuade and pressure her to confess to the murder of her five children.
- Hoyt was isolated from her husband as a way of making it easier to extract a confession from her. She was undoubtedly highly dependent on her husband for emotional support. His presence was undoubtedly seen by the police as a likely hindrance to the psychological manipulation and trickery that had already been planned in great detail.
- Hoyt consistently claimed that the police tricked her into believing that they were interested in talking to her about the death of her children and SIDS in connection with research. If this is true it was very misleading, dishonest and unethical. Although the police denied in their testimony that this account was true, I think it is quite possible that they employed such a strategy. Considering the importance of the 'sting' operation and the detailed planning involved, the police would not have risked being open and honest with Hoyt that she was suspected of murdering her children and that they were planning to interrogate her at the police barracks. The fact that Hoyt took her family photograph album with her to the police barracks (she told me this was at the suggestion of the police) supports the view that she thought she was assisting with research. I am satisfied, as undoubtedly the police were, that Hoyt would not have gone voluntarily to the police barracks if she had had any suspicion that they had wanted to interrogate her.
- Hoyt consistently claimed that the police underplayed the reading of the *Miranda* warning and made her believe that it was just a trivial routine that they had to follow. I found Hoyt's description of this to me credible and this is the kind of strategy the American police would probably employ in a situation like this (Macdonald & Michaud, 1992).

- Having a female interviewer actually physically touch Hoyt during the interrogation was undoubtedly a strategy aimed to break down her resistance (Hoyt also alleged that Officer Bleck had physically comforted her as well).
- I am in no doubt that Hoyt felt a great deal of guilt for the death of her children, irrespective of whether or not she had murdered them. The police either deliberately or unwittingly played on Hoyt's feelings of guilt by asking her to describe her children in detail and the moment of their death. This is likely to have been important in causing her emotional distress and breaking down her resistance during the interrogation.
- Hoyt claims that after a short break between the first and second interrogation sessions, the police officers repeatedly accused her of having murdered her children by smothering them and told her that they had the medical evidence to prove it. I found her explanation of this credible and I do not believe that she would have confessed to the police without such direct confrontation.
- The police allegedly used inducements, such as stating they would get her help if she confessed, that it was good for her to get the truth 'off her chest', that her family would not hate her for having murdered the children and after confessing she could get on with her life. Hoyt told me that she had not realized the seriousness of her having made a confession and thought she would be allowed to go home after making the confession (there is some support from this in her Sworn Statement when at the end of the interview she asks 'Just let me know if I can be at home until this is over, be with my family').

Analysing the above process of breaking down Hoyt's resistance, it seems that the strategy that the police used is consistent with that recommended by Inbau, Reid and Buckley (1986), which included ensuring her trust and faith in the police views and behaviours, playing on her emotional vulnerabilities (e.g. her feelings of guilt concerning her deceased children and poor self-esteem), isolating her from others who might interfere with her making a confession (i.e. her husband and a lawyer), exaggerating the evidence the police had against her, minimizing the seriousness of the situation and persuading her that it was in her interest to confess to the smothering of her children.

What did the psychometric assessment reveal about Hoyt's psychological strengths and weaknesses? Intellectually, Hoyt was functioning well within normal limits. Her memory scores on the GSS 1 and GSS 2 were consistent with her intellectual abilities. Hoyt proved to be quite resistant to both leading questions and interrogative pressure. These findings concurred with my clinical impression of her during our lengthy interviews. She did not come across as a suggestible individual. Her low susceptibility to suggestions would have been a strength in terms of her ability to cope with the police interviews and was, in my view, evident in the way she coped with the questioning during the Sworn Statement interrogation. Indeed, her low suggestibility, and the apparently accompanied critical faculty under questioning, may have been responsible for one of the most critical and incriminating aspects of her confession: her tendency during the questioning of not fully accepting the police suggestions and adding her own details to the answers. This is an interesting scenario, where her low susceptibility to suggestions probably resulted in her confession appearing more authentic and incriminating than it would otherwise have been.

So what were the findings with regard to psychological vulnerabilities? First, the MMPI-2 profile that was obtained when I assessed her was very similar to that found when she had been tested previously by Dr Ewing, although the scores on the elevated scales became more extreme. This was undoubtedly due to the increased distress as the trial date approached (I assessed her about two weeks before her trial commenced). The profile suggested a depressed and anxious individual who suffered from a pre-occupation with somatic symptoms. There was evidence of marked social introversion, which had increased since she had been assessed by Dr Ewing the previous year. This profile suggested a highly anxious and introverted person. The score obtained on the Gudjonsson Compliance Scale was very high (98th percentile rank), which suggested that Hoyt was very eager to please and tended to avoid conflict and confrontation with people. There was strong evidence on testing of poor self-esteem. There was no evidence of antisocial personality disorder from the score obtained on the Gough Socialisation Scale.

In terms of her personality and mental state, Hoyt's greatest vulnerabilities during interrogation were her high level of anxiety and compliance, which were accompanied by low self-esteem and strong feelings of guilt relating to the death of her children. I am in no doubt that with such a profile, even when the person is not found to be suggestible, psychological manipulation by the police and moderate pressure can result in a false confession. High anxiety and compliance were found to be crucial in overturning the conviction of the appellant in the IRA Funeral Murder Case and also in an English murder case (see Chapter 18). I am in no doubt that Hoyt's psychological vulnerabilities were exploited by the police to maximum effect and this made her confess to the killings of her five children. She would not otherwise have confessed so quickly (she seems to have broken down within about two hours of her arriving at the police barracks). If Hoyt was psychologically vulnerable during the interrogation and was subjected to police impropriety, why did I not testify in the case when it went for trial in March 1995? The answer is that the psychological test findings needed to be considered in the context of other factors in the case. The most damaging evidence against Hoyt was her Sworn Statement to the police. On the face of it, the confession it contained was overwhelmingly convincing and, unless its reliability could be seriously challenged, Hoyt would be convicted. I explained this to her two defence attorneys. During the taking of this statement, Hoyt seemed in good control over what she was saying, she was apparently not suggestible, and she even made various highly incriminating corrections when she felt the police were misleading her. In other words, she appeared to be giving an account in a way she wanted it to be told. She was not simply agreeing with the police. This was her story and I knew that it would have a devastating effect upon a jury.

There was another interesting and unusual aspect to this case. It is evident from reading about the case that many people developed great sympathy for Hoyt. She had a large number of 'believers'. After being convicted many people cried in court, including some jurors, and even the trial judge was overcome by emotions (Firstman & Talan, 1997). Hoyt had a remarkable skill in touching people's emotions and gaining their sympathy. I noticed this skill during my sessions with her. There were times when her descriptions of her past misfortunes touched my emotions. It was easy to feel sorry for her and believe in her innocence. Of course, this does not rule out her being innocent of the crimes of which she was convicted. We simply do not know with complete certainty that Hoyt's children were murdered, nor will we ever know. If they were murdered then she was certainly the culprit.

The Trial

The trial commenced in Tioga County Court on Monday 27 March 1995 with jury selection, just over one year after Hoyt had confessed to murdering her five children. The prosecution medical experts argued that Hoyt's children had all died from suffocation and that Hoyt had given a truthful confession. In contrast, the defence strategy was to persuade the jury that Hoyt's five children had all died of natural causes and that she had been tricked and coerced by the police into giving a false confession. Dr Steinschneider testified on behalf of Hoyt and defended his SIDS theory. Hoyt testified and denied having suffocated her children. She appeared to be reasonably calm and matter-of-fact under cross-examination, and even became defiant under pressure (Firstman & Talan, 1997; Hickey, Lighty & O'Brien, 1996).

The only psychological evidence presented at trial was the testimony of Dr Ewing. The defence strategy was to spring Dr Ewing's testimony on the prosecution as a surprise during the trial so that they would have little chance of producing their own evidence in rebuttal (i.e. it was an ambush defence, and Dr Ewing's psychological report from October 1994 had apparently not been disclosed to the prosecution). Dr Ewing was the last defence witness. The defence attorneys were hoping that Dr Ewing's testimony would be sufficiently strong to persuade the jury that she should not be convicted. According to the defence attorneys, Dr Ewing was an impressive witness. He argued that Hoyt had two types of long-standing personality disorder, Dependent Personality Disorder and Avoidant Personality Disorder. Her personality disorders made her vulnerable to the psychological manipulation she was subjected to on 23 March 1994. As a result, 'her statement to the police on that day was not made knowingly and it was not made voluntarily' (Firstman & Talan, 1997, p. 558). During the cross-examination the prosecutor accused Dr Ewing of believing Hoyt's story because he had been paid $150 per hour for his assessment (this is a common prosecution strategy in American courts). He pushed Dr Ewing to admit that Hoyt had either lied to the police or to him during his psychological evaluation and it implied that she was a liar (Firstman & Talan, 1997, p. 560). By doing this he made a serious mistake by inadvertently inviting Dr Ewing to state to the jury his belief that Hoyt was innocent of murdering her five children.

Mr Sampson	'And that indicates to me that she's a liar. Now what does it indicate to you?'
Dr Ewing	'It indicates to me that she was coerced into making a false statement to the Police.'

The prosecution called Dr David John Barry, a psychiatrist, to the witness stand in rebuttal. He argued that Hoyt did not suffer from dependent and avoidant personality disorders.

On 12 April 1995, Hoyt was found guilty by the jury. She was later sentenced to 15 years to life for each child, which was the minimum sentence for each child's death. At first sight this appeared to be a reasonable outcome for Mrs Hoyt, but there was a sting in the tail. The five sentences were to run consecutively, which meant that the total sentence would be seventy-five years to life. Hoyt was doomed to die in prison.

Conclusions

Sadly, Mrs Hoyt died in jail on 9 August 1998. She was 52 years of age and had served only three years of her prison sentence. Her confession, the trial and the long prison sentence undoubtedly caused her immense distress and resulted in her untimely death. What lessons are to be learned from the case? First, there remains a serious ethical issue about the ways in which the prosecution and the police pursued her so many years after the death of her children, and then used trickery and deceit to obtain a confession. Mrs Hoyt may well have given a true confession, but was it fully voluntary and obtained by fair means? I doubt it. I think it was obtained by psychological manipulation and coercion. Do the ends justify the means? No doubt the prosecution thought so. After all they achieved a conviction. No doubt the readers of this book will vary considerably in their views on this point.

The second issue relates to the emotional intensity of the case. Hoyt had many supporters who believed in her innocence, including the defence psychologist Dr Ewing. It is easy to take such a strong position when one becomes involved in a case like this. Hoyt had a remarkable capacity to generate sympathy and compassion in others. Conversely, there were those on the prosecution case who had no doubts about her guilt. Undoubtedly, this view was principally based on the fact that they did not believe that five children in one family could die from some genetic or constitutional abnormality. Recently, the issue concerning a gene for increased risk of 'cot death' has been raised in another case (Mahendra, 2001). From their point of view, it had to be murder. That was the only possible explanation they could consider. The two extreme positions taken in this case by the two 'camps' show us how a strong emotional investment could make it difficult to approach a case with an open mind.

JOE GIARRATANO

On 5 February 1979, Barbara Kline and her 15-year-old daughter, Michelle, were murdered in their apartment in Norfolk, Virginia. Barbara Kline had been stabbed to death whereas her daughter had been strangled and apparently raped. The two women had been sharing the apartment with a 21-year-old man, Joe Giarratano. The first the police learned about Giarratano as a potential suspect was when he walked up to a police officer at a Greyhound bus station in Jacksonville, Florida, at 3.20 a.m. on 6 February, and said 'I killed two people in Norfolk, Virginia, and I want to give myself up'.

Giarratano's original confession to the Jacksonville police alleged that he had killed Barbara Kline in an argument over money. Michelle was then killed to remove her as a witness. Here there was no mention of a sexual assault. This appears to have been a spontaneous account and no knowledge about the crime could possibly have been communicated to Giarratano by the Jacksonville officers as they had no details about the crime before the confession statements were made. Two days later Giarratano gave a totally different account to the Norfolk detectives. He now claimed to have raped Michelle before murdering her, and then killed her mother to cover up the crime. This account was consistent with what the Norfolk detectives had told Giarratano, prior to interviewing him, about their knowledge of the murders. Whilst in a State Psychiatric Hospital for a pre-trial examination Giarratano reverted back into the original version. At his trial the second version was accepted as it seemed to correspond better with the medical examiner's report and the police assumptions about the murders. Everybody at the trial, including Giarratano, accepted that he had murdered the two women and the reliability of the Norfolk confessions was never disputed, in spite of the fact that it was in several respects inconsistent with the physical and crime scene evidence. Giarratano's trial only lasted half a day. Nobody, including the defence, appeared to have looked long and hard at the serious flaws in the evidence that was to send Giarratano to Death Row. Apart from the confessions, the remaining evidence against him was mostly circumstantial. No independent evidence has ever emerged that clearly links Giarratano to the two murders (for a detailed discussion of the evidence see Leo & Ofshe, 1998a, 2001).

There is considerable evidence that Giarratano genuinely believed that he had been responsible for the women's deaths, even though he never appears to have had any clear recollection of having committed the crime. He claims to have woken up in the apartment where he lived with the two women and found them murdered. He *assumed* he had committed the murders and felt very guilty about what he thought he had done. As a result, he desperately wanted to die. This is evident from his suicide attempts whilst on remand and after being convicted and his expressed wish to be executed by the state for his deeds (Giarratano refused to accept plea bargaining to save his life and declined appeals after being convicted).

In 1983 Giarratano began to be seen in prison by a paralegal, Marie Deans, who was giving support and legal advice to prisoners on Death Row. For the first time in his life he was able to talk about his horrific childhood. Marie Deans discovered that Giarratano had no recollection of having killed the two women, but he still assumed that he had done so. With her extensive help over several years Giarratano began to question his own involvement in their death. He no longer wanted to die and began to fight for his life. By 1990 all appeals had been exhausted and Giarratano's time was running out.

The Psychological Assessment

In 1990, Dr MacKeith and I spent several days in Virginia working on the case, which included speaking to several independent informants, including one of the police officers from Jacksonville who had interviewed Giarratano before he made the most damaging confession to the Norfolk detectives. We watched two video-recorded interviews with a psychiatrist who had interviewed him at length in 1979 and 1989. We interviewed Giarratano for 12 hours at the Mecklenburg Correctional Facility. The main purpose of our assessment was to evaluate the likely reliability of the self-incriminating admissions made by Giarratano to the police on 6 and 8 February 1979. There were both psychological and psychiatric aspects to the case, as in the case of Carole Richardson, which meant that Dr MacKeith and I could fruitfully utilize our complementary approaches and expertise. Of particular medical importance were the effects of extensive drug and alcohol abuse on Giarratano's mental state, as well as probable depressive symptoms, whilst he was interrogated by the police in February 1979. Giarratano's psychological strengths and weaknesses were assessed and these were interpreted with references to the likely reliability of his confessions. The purpose of our assessment was not to attempt to establish whether Giarratano had committed the crimes of which he was convicted. All we were attempting to address was the reliability of his confessions, irrespective of whether or not he had killed the two women.

The aims of our interview with Giarratano were twofold: first, to interview him about the circumstances of the confessions, his background and substance abuse, his relationship with the two victims and his mental state in 1979 and afterwards; second, to assess his present mental state and personality, which included Giarratano completing a number of psychological tests. The psychological tests I administered fell into four groups according to their purpose:

1. tests designed to give a general profile of Giarratano's personality;
2. tests that focused on his current mental state, including possible anxiety, depressive, psychotic and phobic symptoms;
3. tests directly relevant to how Giarratano handled questioning and interrogative pressure;
4. rating scales of how Giarratano perceived himself and the police officers who interviewed him in 1979. No intellectual assessment was conducted as this had been carried out in 1986 by an American neuropsychologist. At that time, Giarratano was found to be of average intellectual ability, but a detailed neuropsychological assessment revealed certain significant deficits in mental processing, which were thought to reflect the residual effects of alcohol and drug abuse, and from head injuries sustained in fights and falls prior to his arrest.

What were the main findings from the current psychological assessment? They were as follows. There had been a very marked change in Mr Giarratano's emotional and mental functioning since 1979. He now came across as an assertive and articulate man. He was able to talk freely and openly about his feelings and thoughts. He showed none of the retarded and expressionless verbal and non-verbal responses that he did in 1979, which were strikingly evident from a video-recorded interview with a psychiatrist. His self-esteem appeared to have improved very markedly and there was no evidence of depressive symptoms.

In spite of Mr Giarratano's improvement since 1979, which seemed to be related to regular meetings with Marie Deans since 1983 and abstinence from drugs and alcohol, he was still left with a *marked* residual deficit in his memory processing, which related to a strong tendency to confabulate. This was noted on the free recall part of the GSS 1 and GSS 2. This deficit was subtle and possibly not immediately apparent without specific testing, although it is worth pointing out that a prosecution psychiatrist had made a reference to Giarratano's confabulation tendency at his trial in 1979. However, because everybody assumed Giarratano's confession to the Norfolk detectives was reliable the importance of his vulnerability was not recognized.

Giarratano's clearest vulnerability when I tested him related to his *abnormal* tendency to fill gaps in his memory with confabulated material, that is, imaginary experiences that he believed to be true. Even for material that he had reasonable memory about, he confabulated. In my view, this was a problem that related to how Giarratano had in the past learned to cope with gaps in his memory. It was not possible to say whether or not his tendency to confabulate resulted from his extensive substance abuse, but if it existed before that then the substance abuse is likely to have exacerbated the condition very markedly. Abstinence from substance abuse over a period of several years is likely to have made him less prone to confabulation, even though he is still left with a very substantial vulnerability, of which he and his lawyers appeared totally unaware.

A related problem to the confabulation was Mr Giarratano's tendency to incorporate post-event information into his memory recollection. In particular, being asked specific questions, which he said helped him focus his mind and improve his memory, markedly distorted his subsequent recollection without his apparently being aware of it. On the surface, Giarratano appeared quite resistant to suggestions. However, his resistance to suggestions was superficial and he was far more suggestible than is immediately apparent. His susceptibility to suggestions was probably mediated by his marked inability to detect discrepancies between what he observes and what is suggested to him.

Did the findings of confabulation and suggestibility have any bearing on the likely reliability or unreliability of the self-incriminating confessions Giarratano made to the police in 1979? There was no doubt in my mind that Giarratano's confabulation and suggestibility tendencies seriously challenged the reliability of the confessions he made to the police in 1979. As far as I was concerned, the question of unreliability centred around Giarratano's impaired memory and specific vulnerabilities at the time of the police interviews. In 1979 his tendency to confabulate and his level of suggestibility were undoubtedly much more marked than they are at present because of his extensive substance abuse, distressed mental state and apparently very low self-esteem.

It was evident that sometime before the first police interview at about 3 a.m. on Tuesday 6 February 1979 Giarratano had some knowledge about the two murders. He certainly knew that the two women had been murdered. How he obtained that basic information was not known. He told us that he woke up in the flat and discovered the two women murdered, but claimed to have no recollection of having actually committed the murders. Even the 'memory' of having seen the bodies of the two women in the flat, which seemed very clear and definite in his mind, one had to be cautious about because the specific details he remembers do not entirely fit in with all the known facts. A major problem was that Mr Giarratano had seen the police video of the scene and the photographs, and bearing in mind his tendency to incorporate post-event information into his recollection I did not think it is safe to rely on what he believed he observed at the time. As far as the police interviews were concerned, the statement to the Norfolk detectives on 8 February was particularly worrying because by that time Giarratano had been asked many specific questions by the police and may have been presented with different scenarios that seemed to fit the known facts at the time.

My final conclusion was that, in view of Giarratano's idiosyncratic vulnerabilities and the circumstances of the confessions, I considered it unsafe to rely on the self-incriminating confessions he had made to the police on 6 and 8 February 1979. Dr MacKeith, looking at the reliability of the confessions from a psychiatric perspective, came to a similar conclusion. We submitted our reports to the defence attorneys and they were made available to the Governor of Virginia.

Outcome

The day for Giarratano's execution was set for Friday 22 February 1991. His lawyers petitioned the Governor of Virginia, Lawrence Douglas Wilder, for a conditional pardon. All other appeal procedures had failed and the execution had been ordered by His Honour Thomas R. McNamara, Judge of the Circuit Court of the City of Norfolk. Two days before Giarratano's execution Governor Wilder, in view of the circumstances of the case and the 'new' evidence presented by the defence, invoked his clemency powers and commuted the death sentence to life imprisonment and made him eligible for parole after he had served a minimum of 25 years in prison. The Governor left the possibility of a re-trial at the discretion of the Attorney General of Virginia, who had issued a public statement that she does not intend to initiate further legal proceedings. Giarratano's life has been spared. He remains in prison and continues to fight for a re-trial so that all the new evidence in the case, including the psychological and psychiatric evidence, can be considered by a jury.

HENRY LEE LUCAS

Henry Lee Lucas, who in the early 1980s confessed to hundreds of unsolved murders in the USA, is undoubtedly the most prolific serial confessor in world history. Much can be learned from a detailed analysis of his case. I interviewed Lucas in 1996 and conducted a detailed psychological evaluation at the request of his defence team. At the time he was on Death Row in Texas, awaiting his execution (Gudjonsson, 1999d).

Brief Background

Lucas was 46 years of age when he was arrested on 11 June 1983 by Texas law enforcement officers on a firearms offence. At the time he was suspected of having murdered two women in North Texas, an elderly acquaintance (Kate Rich) and a 15-year-old girlfriend (Frieda Powell). After being held 'incommunicado' for four days he began to make confessions to murders. Initially he confessed to the murders of his girlfriend and the elderly acquaintance. He then added a confession to 60 other unspecified murders.

During the following 18 months, while in the custody of the Texas Rangers, he confessed to hundreds of murders across the USA. Nobody knows the precise number. One estimate was over 600 murders (Mattox, 1986). A special task force was set up by the Texas Rangers to investigate and assist officers from other jurisdictions around the country. It was called the 'Lucas Task Force'. Officers from all over the USA came to interview Mr Lucas at the invitation of the Task Force. The cases mainly involved homicides where there were no clear leads or suspects and the cases were unlikely to be ever solved. No forensic evidence was found to link Lucas with any of these murders. It is interesting that Lucas was not satisfied with just confessing to cases offered to him by the police. He also fabricated his own confessions. For example, he volunteered a confession to the murder of Jimmy Hoffa (former US union leader), confessed to having delivered poison to Reverend Jim Jones' Peoples Temple in Guyana and claimed to have been paid to stalk and assassinate President Jimmy Carter.

Had Lucas committed any of the murders he confessed to? What we do know is that in May 1960 Lucas was convicted of the murder of his mother, for which he received a term of imprisonment. He was released on parole from prison in August 1975. With regard to the murders of his 15-year-old girlfriend and the elderly acquaintance he pleaded guilty to one and was tried and found guilty of the other and received a life sentence. There was some corroborative evidence detailed in Lucas's confessions to link him to these two murders. His girlfriend, Frieda Powell, was last seen alive on 23 August 1982. On 16 September 1982 Kate Rich disappeared and was murdered. As a result of Lucas's confessions, articles belonging to Rich were found and also the apparent remains of Powell's body (it was assumed, but never proven, that the remains recovered were those of Powell).

A special investigation by the Attorney General of Texas (Mattox, 1986) into Lucas's confessions concluded that Lucas was probably only responsible for three murders (his mother in 1960, Powell and Rich in 1982) and his apparent 'special knowledge' of the other murders had been obtained from the police officers themselves.

In many of the other cases about which Lucas was interviewed, it was claimed by the police that he had special knowledge, which corroborated his confessions. The problem here is that several witnesses testified in court that they had witnessed Lucas being given salient case details by the Texas Rangers, and in some instances complete case files, prior to interrogation. This ensured that he had detailed knowledge about cases, which helped to convince officers from other jurisdictions, who were apparently ignorant of this procedure and were acting in good faith, about Lucas's guilt when they interviewed him. The Texas Rangers were undoubtedly concerned about the lack of detail shown by Lucas concerning the murders to which he confessed and decided to assist his memory by having him study the case files, details of which Lucas seemed well able to memorize prior to interrogations.

In April 1984 Mr Lucas was convicted, solely on the basis of his confession, of the murder of an unidentified female in Williamson County, Texas. The murder took place in 1979 and is known as the 'Orange Socks' murder due to the victim wearing orange socks at the time that her body was discovered. Lucas confessed to this murder during a series of interviews with Sherrif Jim Boutwell, whose jail in Williamson County served as the Command Centre for the Lucas Task Force. Lucas also confessed to having raped the woman, which resulted in him being convicted of a capital offence in spite of the fact that there was no physical evidence of rape. This was the only murder for which he received a death sentence. There was no forensic or circumstantial evidence to corroborate Lucas's confession. He did apparently have a good alibi, which consisted of work records showing him as being over 1300 miles away on the day of the murder (a round-trip of about 2700 miles) and the following day there was a record of his signing a cheque near his place of work.

In January 1996 Lucas sought federal habeas corpus relief against his death penalty by asserting actual innocence of the Orange Socks murder. The defence introduced two types of evidence:

1. alibi evidence showing that Lucas was in Jacksonville, Florida, when the offence occurred in Texas and could not have made the long car journey;
2. expert evidence from myself concerning Mr Lucas's Orange Socks confession.

On 7 February 1996, the federal district court denied relief on the defence petition and ordered that the stay of execution be lifted. In the judgment no reference was made to the expert psychological testimony, even though it had formed an important part of the defence case.

At the time of his arrest in June 1983 Texas Ranger Phil Ryan, who was the first police officer to interview Lucas after his arrest in June 1983, knew about Lucas's propensity to make false confessions. On 17 October 1982 Lucas had been arrested on suspicion of having murdered Rich and Powell and remained in custody until 2 November 1982. He was given a polygraph test, which indicated deception with regard to the death of the two women, and was interrogated. He made no confessions to the murders, but instead confessed to committing aggravated robberies in California and implicated Rich's son-in-law in the robberies. Texas Ranger Ryan told me that he had investigated the confessions to the robberies and found them to be fabricated by Lucas. The motive, so Lucas told me in January 1996, was to have Texas Ranger Ryan bring Rich's son-in-law back from California, so that he could be interrogated in connection with the disappearance of Rich.

The Psychological Assessment

In early January 1996, at the request of the defence, I went to Texas and spent 13 hours assessing Lucas. In addition, I read several thousand pages of documents and listened to tape recordings of the Orange Socks confessions and interviewed Texas Ranger Phil Ryan.

I wrote a detailed report and was formally cross-examined on my findings by Texas Assistant Attorney General, Austen. The judge received the psychological testimony by way of two lengthy depositions.

After having carefully considered the content and context of the Orange Socks confessions, in conjunction with the psychological evaluation of Lucas, I testified that it was 'totally unsafe' to rely on Mr Lucas's confessions to the crime as being a true indication of his guilt. Indeed, I believed, and still do, that the Orange Socks confessions were false. It is highly likely that Lucas has made more false confessions to murder than any other criminal suspect. In an interview with myself Lucas estimated that he had made over 3000 false confessions to murder, which is five times higher than the estimate of 600 by Mattox (1986). Lucas has consistently given this figure to different people over the years (Brad Shellady, private investigator, personal communication). This may, of course, be a grossly exaggerated figure, but in view of the massive number of records sent from hundreds of jurisdictions around the USA to the Lucas Task Force its claim cannot be completely discarded.

I asked Lucas in 1996 how he felt about his large number of confessions and the fact that he might be executed for the Orange Socks confession. Lucas told me that he had no regrets about the confessions, in spite of the fact that he might be executed as a result. His reasoning for this view was that prior to his arrest in 1983 he was 'nobody'; that is, he had no friends and nobody listened to him or took an interest in him. Once he began to make false confessions all that changed and he has thoroughly enjoyed his 'celebrity' (or notoriety) status and now had many friends.

In 1996 Lucas completed a number of psychological tests. The actual scores have been described in detail elsewhere (Gudjonsson, 1999d). Lucas was of low average intelligence (he had a Full Scale IQ score of 89), which suggested that he had no intellectual problems that could explain his serial confessions. He was not particularly suggestible on the GSS 1 or GSS 2, and his memory scores on the GSS 1 were within normal limits (45th percentile), whereas his memory scores on the GSS 2 were considerably poorer (10th percentile rank for immediate recall). The confabulation scores on both the suggestibility tests were outside normal limits (10 and 7 on delayed recall for the GSS 1 and GSS 2, respectively). Lucas proved to be highly acquiescent and compliant on testing. The EPQ indicated a personality profile of an unstable (emotionally labile) introvert, whose very high Psychoticism (P) score, accompanied by a very low score on the Gough Socialisation Scale, were strongly indicative of personality problems. The scores on the MMPI-2 validity scales fell well within normal limits, with the exception of the F scale, which was highly elevated ($T = 92$). Such a high F score often raises concern about the validity of the clinical profile due to exaggeration or malingering of psychological symptoms. However, such a high F score may suggest the presence of psychopathology rather than malingering (Pope, Butcher & Sleen, 1993). This is the interpretation that I favoured in the case and I do not consider Lucas's clinical profile to be invalid. As far as the clinical scales were concerned, there were elevations of scales 4 ('Psychopathic deviate') and 6 ('Paranoia'). This suggests a person who is immature, narcissistic and self-indulgent.

The Confessions

Lucas began making confessions to murders after being left in jail on his own over a period of four days. During his period of detention between 11 and 15 June 1983, he was not interviewed at all by the police and told me that he had been completely deprived of coffee and cigarettes, to both of which he was addicted. He also alleged that he was placed in a cell without clothes, with the air conditioning left on continuously, and this made him feel cold and shivery. The jailer refused him access to the telephone and his attorney, and Sheriff Conway threatened to keep him in the cell until he confessed to the murder of Mrs Rich.

On 15 June, four days after his arrest, he confessed to a jailer, who then passed a written confession to the murders of the juvenile girlfriend and the elderly acquaintance and 60 other unspecified murders to Sheriff Conway. Lucas told me that he had broken down and confessed because he was feeling so uncomfortable and distressed in the cell and thought at the time that it was the only way.

Lucas told me that he had added the 60 unspecified murders to the confession in order take out his revenge on the police for having arrested him on a made-up firearm charge and kept him in custody. He also stated, unprompted in court, that he had killed about 100 people. Unknown to him there were news reporters in court, which resulted in immense media attention and a further increase in the number of his confessions to homicide. I asked Lucas why he had increased the numbers to 100 when he appeared in court. Lucas replied that he had done this to impress the judge. Apparently the judge had not taken much notice of his previous claim of having committed 60 murders. Lucas therefore decided to increase the number to a more impressive figure.

Lucas claimed that prior to or during the police interviews he would be shown photographs of the victims and also in many instances crime scene photographs. In some cases he had access to the entire crime file in order that he could study the case before confessing to it. His strategy was to try to find out who the victim was and what the police wanted to hear. He would then try to piece the case together when giving a plausible confession to it. Lucas claimed that the medication (Thorazine) he was given while in jail (the prison medical records confirmed that he was prescribed Thorazine) impaired his ability to function effectively and was partly responsible for his false confessions (Texas Ranger Ryan noticed that for about three days after being prescribed Thorazine his behaviour changed temporarily—he became more disoriented and confused and did not seem to care about anything. Lucas then settled down to his normal self again).

Lucas told me that as he confessed to an increasing number of murders his mental processes changed. He became much better able to visualize the murder scenes and they became much more vivid and reached a point in early to mid-1984 when he could see in his mind the murders being committed, although he could not see the identity of the murderer (this is corroborated by Texas Ranger Ryan, who told me that Mr Lucas would sometimes give the appearance of being totally absorbed in the murders to which he was confessing to the point of describing them in the present tense as if hypnotized).

Lucas told me that he would not 'take' every case offered to him by the police or agree with everything put to him. 'If it didn't sound right I wouldn't go along with it'. He said he was reluctant to 'take' murder cases involving child victims. He tried to make each of the murder cases look more frightening and gruesome than they appeared to be from the information he had been given about them. 'I would put final little touches to it', he claimed.

Lucas told me that he never thought about the long term consequences of his confessions. He claims that what actually stopped him making false confessions were his contacts with the families of the victims and his relationship with a prison visitor, 'Sister Clemmie'.

Lucas described his confessions to the murders in positive terms, although he stated that he knew it was wrong to confess to crimes he had not actually committed. He told me that he genuinely believed that he was providing the police with useful insight into the murders and told me that he was able to provide the police with details, including burial sites, that only the police knew (he sounded boastful when describing to me how helpful he had been to the police). The other positive consequences were all the privileges he was provided with by the police (he claims the police gave him everything he asked for), all the attention he got and the fact that he has made more friends than he ever had before. He claims that if it had not been for the Orange Socks case and Sheriff Boutwell he would not have met Sister Clemmie (Lucas spoke affectionately of Sheriff Boutwell, treated him as a friend and expressed considerable admiration for him).

Lucas told me that in the eyes of the media he became the biggest monster alive and it made him feel good. He spoke proudly about going on television and warning women against hitchhiking. Everybody was paying attention to him whereas before making his confessions nobody took any notice of him.

As far as the Orange Socks murder is concerned, Lucas did not confess to this murder when briefly questioned about it by Texas Ranger Ryan from the Crime Analysis Bulletin around 17 June 1983, even though he was confessing to many other murders. Lucas first confessed to the Orange Socks murder when interviewed by Sheriff Boutwell on 22 June 1983. He claims that he set out to kill himself (i.e. to commit 'legal suicide'), although he claims this was not the primary reason why he initially confessed to the Orange Socks murder. At the time things were not going well for him and he felt he had nothing to live for. He made four failed attempts to kill himself in jail and thought he might as well get the state to execute him. He claims he had nothing to do with the Orange Socks murder but initially confessed to it in order to please Sheriff Boutwell. He claims that Sheriff Boutwell showed him photographs and discussed the case with him before the formal tape recorded interview commenced on 22 June 1983, which included a discussion of the victim having a period and wearing a 'towel' (Lucas labelled this a 'Kotex'). Once his trial approached in 1984 he no longer wanted to 'commit legal suicide' (i.e. let the State execute him for murder), because discussions with Sister Clemmie made him want to live. By this time he said he had become fearful of Sheriff Boutwell and did not want to upset him by fighting his case (including his fear that Sheriff Boutwell would stop Sister Clemmie from visiting him if he stopped cooperating with the police—at this point Clemmie had become very important to him). He claims that it was his fear of Sheriff Boutwell that resulted in his refusal to testify at his trial.

Police officers involved in his case appear to have achieved cooperation from Lucas by playing on his poor self-esteem and by shaping his behaviours with positive reinforcement. For example, according to Texas Ranger Ryan (personal communication), the strategy he used when interviewing Lucas was to tell him that he (Ryan) was not very bright and needed Lucas's help to solve the murders (he reportedly told Lucas 'I'm not very bright I guess and I need your help'). Similarly, in the first Orange Socks confession on 22 June 1983, Sheriff Boutwell comments at the beginning of the interview 'Henry, I'm, of course, told that you have been cooperating with these other officers, and I appreciate it'. Lucas's cooperation with producing confessions was therefore from the beginning reinforced by comments of social approval. This was probably the first time in Lucas's life that he was given social approval by people in authority, which probably enhanced his sense of self-importance. Later on the positive reinforcement for making confessions became much more extensive and Lucas was provided with various privileges within the jail (e.g. plenty of social contact, travel, coffee, cigarettes, cable television, immense attention, notoriety status).

At the time of making the Orange Socks confessions I am satisfied that Lucas was vulnerable to making a false confession due to a combination of the following factors.

1. Persons with personality disorder have been shown to be particularly susceptible to making false confessions to the police during custodial interrogation (Sigurdsson & Gudjonsson, 1996). They seem relatively unperturbed by the fact that they are lying to the police and interfering with the course of justice. In this research study three personality factors significantly differentiated the 'false confessors' from the other offenders: a low score on the Gough Socialisation Scale and elevated scores on the Gudjonsson Compliance Scale and EPQ Neuroticism scale. Lucas's scores on all three tests are in that predicted direction and suggested a vulnerability to making a false confession. The finding that he did not prove unduly suggestible is not of primary importance in view of the nature of the confessions he made (i.e. they were apparently not of the coerced–internalized type where suggestibility is of particular importance).

2. Lucas had already begun making a large number of confessions, some of which were to fictitious murders invented by Texas Ranger Ryan, who had become sceptical about Mr Lucas's confessions and attempted to test their reliability. Texas Ranger Ryan told me that the 60 original confessions were not verified and appeared to have been made up by Lucas. By the time he was interviewed by Sheriff Boutwell about the Orange Socks murder, Lucas had learned the powerful *immediate* effects of making confessions (i.e. the officers were interested in him, paid attention to him, expressed a need for his help, moved him to more comfortable surroundings). *This placed him in a confession mode*, irrespective of whether or not the confessions were true or false. There is evidence from the false confessions that Lucas made to

robberies in 1982 that he was capable of making false confessions to serious crimes for the purpose of short-term instrumental gain.
3. Lucas was undoubtedly a very inadequate man, who in 1983 was suffering from low self-esteem. Prior to his arrest, nobody paid much attention to him, even though he tried hard to achieve things (e.g. he appears to have been an ambitious and hard working man). The attention he obtained from making confessions was highly reinforcing for him and no doubt temporarily enhanced his feelings of self-worth. I was in no doubt that the notoriety aspect of the confessions was appealing to him and fed into his psychopathology. The fact that the number of confessions he made grew fairly rapidly over time provides support for the reinforcing effects of his confessions. His vulnerability was his need for attention and recognition.
4. The psychological assessment indicated that Lucas was eager to please and impress people. He would say and do things for immediate gain, attention and reaction. This vulnerability undoubtedly existed in 1983 and 1984 and was noted very early on by Texas Ranger Ryan (personal communication).
5. Lucas showed total disregard for the long term consequences of his confessions. He clearly did not seem to care about the future consequences of his behaviour. He was dominated by the immediate positive consequences without consideration of the long term effects.
6. Lucas had a very strong tendency to confabulate (i.e. produce imagined material from memory), which was noticeable during psychological testing. I believe that he produced this without being aware of it. It was particularly strong with regard to a crime-related story he was asked to memorize. One possibility is that Lucas was hyper-vigilant to crime-related material and had a strong imaginative capacity, which could result in grossly inaccurate recall. This tendency may have been exacerbated when combined with a strong internal need to be helpful (e.g. recalling fictitious murder scenes). Since his memory recall capacity for crime-related material was excellent for a person of his low average intelligence, he was able to collate successfully the information he gathered from interviewing officers with the fictitious material that had been internally generated.
7. I believe that Lucas had a strong need, related to his psychopathology, to convince the police that he was able to assist them with their murder enquiries. By portraying himself as the perpetrator of these crimes he was seeking to establish himself as an interesting, productive, not to say notorious, witness. He was using skills of collation and interpretation from information and cues given to him in interview situations.

The Unreliability of the Orange Socks Murder

An inspection of the content of the Orange Socks confessions revealed signs of unreliability, including unfamiliarity with salient aspects of the murder; use of language when making his confession; the inconsistencies in his accounts and the way he was led by Sheriff Boutwell.

I was in no doubt that it was unsafe to rely on Lucas's confessions to the Orange Socks murder. There was no corroborative physical (forensic) or other independent evidence concerning this murder. The only form of corroboration relates to Lucas apparently having some 'special knowledge' about the case (i.e. knowing that the victim was having a period, the presence of a matchbook from the Holiday Inn in Oklahoma, that he could not have full sexual satisfaction because of the presence of a sanitary towel, pointing out the crime scene from Sheriff Boutwell's car). However, none of this 'special knowledge' is truly independent. By truly *independent* evidence I mean evidence that was not known to the police at the time the suspect made the confession.

Conclusions

What made Lucas such a prolific serial false confessor? Undoubtedly, his confessions resulted from a combination of factors, but the nature of his personality was of crucial importance. There was evidence of personality disorder, which included difficulties in forming and maintaining interpersonal relationships, poor self-esteem, self-centredness, impulsivity, anti-social tendencies and total disregard for the consequences of his behaviour to himself and others. He was also emotionally labile, compliant and acquiescent and had an abnormal tendency to confabulate on memory testing, particularly in relation to crime-related material. Interestingly, he did not prove to be unduly suggestible on testing. I am in no doubt that of crucial importance were Lucas's need for notoriety, his eagerness to please the police officers, the immediate reinforcement he received for his confessions (people taking an interest in him, making him feel he had something valuable to offer and giving him special privileges within the jail) and his total disregard for the long term consequences of his behaviour.

The psychological assessment provided an important insight into Lucas's personality problems, which helped to explain his unusual, if not bizarre, behaviour prior to, during, and after the Orange Socks murder case. It raised questions as to his capacity to rationally assist his attorneys in the case at trial. The main advantage of the psychological findings was to help explain his Orange Socks confession in terms of his own needs and psychopathology.

I believe that the police made a serious mistake by their uncritical willingness to accept Lucas's confessions, most of which appeared to have been offered by Lucas voluntarily and determinedly, and their belief that Lucas's lack of knowledge about the murders for which he was confessing was due to his having committed so many murders that he had problems remembering individual details. As a result, the police tried to assist Lucas's memory recall by showing him crime scene photographs and other salient information before or while interviewing him. It is therefore not surprising that Lucas eventually appeared to have special knowledge about the murders for which he was being interviewed. This special knowledge was then unwisely viewed by the police as evidence of his guilt. The Lucas case provides a fascinating and a unique insight into some of the factors that make a serial false confessor. The fact that Lucas could well have been executed for his Orange Socks confessions shows how reluctant judges in the USA are to accept that false confessions can and do on occasions occur. No doubt Lucas's confessions were an embarrassment to law enforcement agencies in the USA, and the case should make police officers more cautious about accepting uncorroborated confessions and providing suspects with 'special knowledge' material prior to or while interviewing them.

Outcome

Lucas's execution was set for 1801 hours in Huntsville, Texas, on Tuesday 30 June 1998. The previous February Karla Faye Tucker had become the first woman to be executed in the State of Texas since the Civil War. On 26 June, four days before Lucas's execution, the Governor of Texas, George W. Bush, granted clemency and reduced Lucas's death sentence to life imprisonment. Announcing that he was commuting the sentence to life, Governor Bush stated:

> I believe that there is enough doubt about this particular crime that the State of Texas should not impose its ultimate penalty (Usborne, 1998, p. 21).

The day before the State Board of Pardons and Paroles had apparently reached the same conclusion and recommended to the governor that he commute the death sentence to a life term imprisonment.

This was the first time that Texas had commuted a death penalty since execution was reintroduced in 1976 (Usborne, 1998). Lucas's life was spared, but this was not a complete victory, because he was not fully vindicated on this charge. At the time of the clemency the case was pending before the United States Supreme Court for Certiorari. Mr Lucas died of a heart failure on 12 March 2001.

JOHN WILLE

In 1985 John Wille, his girlfriend Judith Walters and Walters's 14-year-old daughter Sheila confessed to their involvement in the murders of Nichole Lopatta, aged 8 years, and Billy Phillips, a schizophrenic and a hemiplegic (he had a pronounced limp and a reduced use of an arm). Wille and Walters were extensively interviewed by the police over a period of three weeks in August 1985. During their interrogation, they both made confessions to several murders. Several of the interviews were tape-recorded. Sheila Walters was interviewed extensively by FBI agents on 3 September, after being isolated from her grandmother, and implicated the other two in the murders of Lopatta and Phillips. The interview was in two parts. There is only a tape-recording of the second half of the interview. There were clearly important conversations between Sheila Walters and the FBI prior to the taped interview, which had apparently not been recorded. Several other police officers were present during these interviews. All three people subsequently retracted their confessions and have proclaimed their innocence ever since. In 2000, Dr MacKeith and I testified at a trial level court hearing in Louisiana. The case is still pending.

Nichole Lopatta had been abducted, raped and murdered at the beginning of June 1985. She was last seen on 2 June. The alleged sequence of events by the prosecution was that Wille, accompanied by his girlfriend and her daughter Sheila, drove from Florida to Louisiana. After entering Louisiana Wille picked up Billy Phillips, who was hitchhiking on the highway. Phillips and Wille were drinking alcohol in the car as they drove into New Orleans. Phillips said he wanted to pick up a young girl and take her for a ride in the car. He directed Wille where to go and they picked up Lopatta. The girl, according to Wille's confession, was then sexually assaulted and murdered. Wille allegedly subsequently murdered Phillips by stabbing him to death. Judith and Sheila Walters, in their confessions, described their role and activities at the crime scene. As the confessions of the three progressed they became increasingly sexually explicit, pornographic and bizarre. At one point Sheila Walters described how five people, including the hemiplegic Phillips, were having sexual intercourse in the back of Wille's car. From the confessions of Wille and Walters, Wille was allegedly able to achieve several sexual orgasms at the crime scene, and engaged in necrophilia with both of the victims.

The bodies of Lopatta and Phillips were discovered on 6 June, at separate locations. Lopatta had been strangled, had a broken jaw, and there was tearing of the vagina and rectum. Phillips body had been stabbed 80 times and his hand and arm were severed.

Wille was arrested on 6 August 1985, because he was suspected of trying to set fire to a trailer. He was interviewed extensively on many occasions until 27 August. According to Wille after the attempted arson incident he had an argument with Walters. She overdosed on Elavil (an antidepressant medication) and was admitted to hospital. The following day (7 August), while still in hospital recovering from her overdose, she was interviewed by the police in connection with setting fire to the trailer. She was subsequently taken into police custody and interviewed extensively on many occasions until 28 August.

Wille had a history of bragging about violence and murder. For example, he boasted to people that he had murdered a former neighbour, Ida Boudreaux, by setting fire to her house. The house had burned down during a thunderstorm. There was nothing to indicate that Wille had murdered the woman and the fire service's report provided evidence to the contrary. Soon after his arrest for the arson of the trailer, Wille admitted to the offence, but he also made voluntary confessions to murders. He confessed to the murder of Boudreaux and to several other murders. He claimed to have run over a man, Frank Powe, on a Florida highway and killed him. He then confessed to drowning a man in a lake, and running down another man in Lafayette. He boasted to one police officer (Larry Pearson) that he had murdered 20 people and buried their bodies down a hole. The police found no evidence to substantiate any of these confessions. Indeed, in the case of Powe, several witnesses reported seeing the man's body being struck by cars in the interstate. It was a local case and had been reported in the newspapers. The car which, according to Wille, he used in the murder of Powe was examined by the Florida police and the FBI in Quantico. No evidence was found to link Wille to Powe's death.

Unlike the confessions to the other murders, Wille did not volunteer a confession to the murder of Lopatta or Phillips. When these murders were broached in the early interviews he did not seem to have any knowledge of them. Indeed, he denied several times having had anything to do with those murders. He confessed to these murders almost three weeks after his arrest, and only after Judith Walters had implicated him in the rape and murder of Lopatta and Phillips.

Five days after his arrest Wille told a prosecutor that he had lied to the police and made false confessions in order to

> ... get everybody off my ass.

The following day, at the end of the interrogation with the police on that day, he claimed that he had not murdered anybody.

On 22 August Wille told a prison doctor that he had never committed any murders and that that he was just 'a bullshitter'.

Wille did not confess to the murders of Lopatta and Phillips until 27 August, on the final day of his interrogation. At the beginning of the interview on that day he told the officers that he had never killed anybody and that he did not know anything about the murders of Lopatta and Phillips. Later in the same interview he confessed to the murders. An FBI document states that on that day agents placed three photographs of Lopatta in front of Wille. This included a photograph of her body as it appeared on the autopsy table, and a large colour autopsy photograph depicting Lopatta's lower torso, including her vagina and rectum.

The entire case relied almost exclusively on confession evidence. There was no forensic evidence to link any of the three persons to the murders, which was surprising if the descriptions of the three persons in their confessions about sex and violence in the back of the car were correct. There was possible corroborative evidence, but this was very weak. There was identification testimony of a fast-food restaurant employee that Wille had on the night of the murder gone to the restaurant and asked for two empty bags, and a hair found on Nichole Lopatta's body which could have come from Wille. The fast-food restaurant employee had made identification to the police, after pictures of Wille had appeared on the television and newspapers. The employee testified at trial, but was not required to make an in-court identification. At trial regarding these two murders, Wille had been denied effective assistance of counsel; unknown to him, his defence counsel, who had no experience with homicide or capital cases, had been ordered to represent Wille as a punishment for a felony conviction.

Wille was sentenced to death in 1986 for the murder of Lopatta; he was never tried for the murder of Phillips, although the facts were before the jury in the Lopatta case. He had previously pleaded guilty to another murder (the interstate incident involving Powe), allegedly as a way of protecting Walters from being charged with the offence (there is evidence in the record of the confession that he extracted a promise that Walters would not be charged with the offence, and she never was). Walters was sentenced to life imprisonment for the two murders of Lopatta and Phillips. Sheila Walters was not prosecuted, but the prosecution called her to testify at the sentencing phase of Wille's case (i.e. when the jury decided whether aggravating factors outweigh mitigating factors in determining whether sentence should be death). She refused to testify, invoking her privilege against self-incrimination (*State v. Wille*, 559 So.2nd 1321, La 1990).

Psychological and Psychiatric Evaluation

In 1993 my psychiatrist colleague Dr MacKeith and I travelled to Louisiana to assess Wille, Walters and Sheila Walters. We carried out detailed assessments, which were tape-recorded and later transcribed. We produced interim reports, where we requested access to more material, including copies of all tape-recorded interviews with the three accused. We had serious doubts about the reliability of the confessions of Wille, Walters and Sheila Walters. We considered that for different reasons all three individuals had been psychologically vulnerable to giving unreliable confessions.

During our assessment, all three individuals denied having had anything to do with the murders, nor did they witness them. Wille claimed to have confessed to the murders as a way of coping with suggestions and pressure from the police, and he also wanted to protect his girlfriend, Walters. He told us he pleaded guilty to the murder of Powe as a deal to prevent Walters being prosecuted for the offence.

Walters claimed to have been heavily drugged during the interrogation sessions, and alleges that she was coerced into making false confessions to murders by intimidation, threats, physical abuse and inducements. She told us that knowledge and details about the murders came from the police, and she was so confused and distressed that she began to believe that perhaps she had been involved in the murders, even though she had no memory of it.

Sheila Waters told us that the details of the murders concerning Lopatta and Phillips during the tape-recorded interview came from the police when she had been interviewed in the presence of a large number of officers earlier that day. At that time she had been deliberately separated by the police from her grandmother, who remained outside the room. The police officers allegedly showed her distressing photographs depicting the bodies of the two victims. She was pressured to confess to having witnessed and participated in the murders. She said she had been told that if she did not confess her mother would be electrocuted. She kept making persistent denials, which were disregarded by the police and the FBI. After a while she began to wonder whether any of these things had happened, but she had no memory of any of it happening.

With regard to the murders of Lopatta and Phillips, on the basis of what the three individuals told us, it appeared that Wille had made a coerced–compliant type of false confession, subsequent to several voluntary false confessions, whereas the confessions of Walters and Sheila Walters were of the coerced–internalized type. There is convincing corroborative evidence from medical records that at the time of her custodial interrogation in August 1985 Walters began to distrust her own memory and developed a memory distrust syndrome (see Chapter 8 about the nature of this syndrome).

Extracts from Judith Walters' Medical Records

It was evident from the Santa Rose County Medical Records that after her arrest in early August 1985 Walters was in a very disturbed mental state. She was referred to the Mental Health Clinic in mid-August, because of severe anxiety, headaches, depression and insomnia. She had a history of alcohol abuse and she appeared to have suffered from alcohol withdrawal symptoms following her arrest. On admission there was

> No significant thought disorder though delusional guilt system where she feels to blame for John's crimes.

It seems from this entry that after about one week of interrogation she had a belief that Wille had committed the murders and she was blaming herself for his crimes.

Walters was very heavily medicated during her stay at the Santa Rose County Jail to help her deal with her symptoms of physical pain, anxiety and depression (e.g. she was prescribed Lortab, Phenergan, Placidyl & Elavil). There was some evidence that she developed tolerance and dependence on these drugs while in the jail. On 18 December Walters was discharged to a jail in Louisiana to face charges pending there. Walters made at least one false confession to murder when interviewed by the police in August 1985. This involved the murder of a man named Michael Faulk, whom she claimed to have met in a bar and had sexual intercourse with. In her confession, Walters provided the police with salient details about the murder. The prosecuting attorney, Curtis Golden, dismissed the case against Walters. He was concerned that an investigator had suggested details about the murder to her. Subsequently others, unknown to Walters or Wille, were convicted of the murder.

Extracts from a counsellor's notes of her sessions with Walters while in custody provides a fascinating insight into her confessions and mental state at the time.

28 August

> Tearful periodically... Stated repeatedly there was a discrepancy between what she 'knew' and what she 'believed' re: the case... Feels strongly that her recurring nightmares re: killing are result of the information she has been confronted with during her various lengthy interrogations. Confused about sequence of events and is angered by her sense that what she tells the investigators is disregarded. Believes they are fabricating stories to get her to admit to events she did not, in fact, witness nor participate in. Feels highly manipulated and victimised.

It is evident from this entry that Walters had by now developed a 'memory distrust syndrome'. She was confused and did not trust her own memory of events. The police were disregarding her version of events, they were allegedly feeding her with information about cases and trying to coerce a confession from her. She clearly did not fully trust the police and believed they were presenting her with fabricated stories.

4 September

> ... Again quite tearful when discussing frustration and anger with newspaper coverage in interrogation sessions. She experiences these as largely false allegations

designed to make others look good, get promotions... Discussed daughter, Sheila, and history of daughter's tendency to tell lies as a form of revenge toward her and her father... Judy is reluctantly stating she might be involved somehow in the various murders. 'I don't know. I just wish they'd given me that truth serum so I could find out for sure and get it over with'.

Walters is expressing considerable uncertainty about whether or not she had been involved in the various murders of which she was accused. She appears motivated to find out whether she has been involved.

11 September

...Quite incensed after talking with 14-year-old daughter by phone re: investigation. Says daughter admitted she had lied under duress and threats that if she didn't admit to helping her mother commit various crimes, etc., her mother would be sent to the electric chair and she, daughter, would be put in prison, At this point Judy feels her mind is clear and memory much better; she believes she allowed her interrogators to intimidate her to the point where she began to doubt her sanity and the truth as she remembers it... John has written to her telling her a number of false allegations his questioners have stated she made against him. These were untrue per Judy and match what they've told her he has said about her. Judy is beginning to feel indignant about the tactics and lies she feels her investigators have used to coerce her into giving them the story she thinks they want from her.

This telephone conversation with her daughter appears to have been important in making Walters come to realize that she had been manipulated and tricked by the interrogators to confess to murders of which she had no memory. Her memory distrust syndrome was now beginning to be resolved and her faith in her own memory was returning. The counsellor's entry also indicates how the interrogators were using the one person against the other as a way of coercing a confession out of them and telling each one lies about the other.

18 September

...She displayed little affective change, but later became tearful... She is thoroughly convinced at this point that she is being manipulated by the authorities into admitting to a number of crimes she did not commit or, in any way, witnessed... An important element here is Judy's sense of support from mother, 14-year-old daughter and other family members.

This entry indicates that by now Walters's memory distrust syndrome was completely resolved. Of great importance appears to have been the social support she received from her family. This demonstrates the importance of social support as a way of people gaining confidence in their recollections after having been in a confusional state. Walters did not appear to have developed a memory of having witnessed or being involved in the murders. The interrogators undermined her confidence in her memory, her belief system had been altered, but she apparently never experienced any actual memory of witnessing or participating in the murders.

4 December

> Discussed her anger toward her boyfriend, John Wille re: his signed admission to various charges. She states he did this to protect her and as a means to get leniency for her. She sees this as a betrayal and playing into the hands of those investigating the various allegations. She adamantly denies that she or John Wille had anything to do with the individuals they supposedly killed.

There is evidence that Wille tried to protect Walters from prosecution regarding the murders. For example, a record of a conversation Wille had with a prosecutor on 11 August, five days after his arrest, shows that he sought a promise for Walters not to be prosecuted.

11 December

> Talked about her decision to hold firm to her story and refuse an offer of immunity for admission of John's guilt as well as her knowledge. She continues to deny any such knowledge or complicity or charges. Found out this a.m. that John had pleaded guilty to manslaughter charges stating he had witnessed Judy and her daughter committing crimes and had tried to get them to stop without success. She now feels betrayed, frightened and resigned to possibility of 30 years in prison for 1st degree murder, arson plus charges of murder.

The Appeal

I heard nothing for several years. In the year 2000 Wille was allowed to appeal against his death sentence and at the time of completing this book the case is still being heard in the 40th Judicial District Court, State of Louisiana. A hearing was granted to bring in new evidence at trial court level by a different judge to the original trial judge. When the case is eventually decided there, a review will be sought in the Louisiana Supreme Court.

In September 2000, Dr MacKeith and I travelled to New Orleans. We testified as to our qualifications and qualified as experts. The following day Dr MacKeith gave his testimony. He testified as to the vulnerabilities of the three accused persons at the time of their interrogations, the problems associated with the absence of complete contemporaneous records of the interrogations, the importance of the medical records of Walters during her stay at Santa Rose County Jail and the unreliability of the confessions made by Wille, Walters and Sheila Walters. I testified the following November.

The Psychological Testimony

My testimony, which lasted most of one day, was broadly in four parts.

1. *Scientific developments of the instruments and techniques.* I provided the court with a conceptual framework for the assessment (i.e. focusing on custodial, interrogation and vulnerability factors), background information about the development of assessment instruments and outlining the psychological processes and factors that break down resistance during interrogation.

2. *Method of assessment.* This outlined how I had conducted the assessment, which consisted of studying all relevant documents, listening to available police interviewing tapes, interviewing and testing Wille, Walters and Sheila Walters and interviewing informants.
3. *General concerns I had about the case.* The general concern I had about the case included the poor recording of the interviews (there were references to interviews not recorded, and some had apparently been recorded but were no longer available), the transcripts and tapes of interviews that existed were of poor quality, the three accused had not been independently interviewed and there was evidence of contamination, the lack of forensic and other evidence to corroborate the confessions, the improbability of some of the actions alleged to have taken place at the crime scene, major inconsistencies in the accounts given (internally for all three over time, between the three persons and with the forensic evidence), and the fact that Wille and Walters made false confessions to other murders to their interrogators.
4. *The assessment and findings concerning Wille, Walters and Sheila Walters.* Wille was severely personality disordered, he was a confabulator and abnormally suggestible, had a history of bragging about murder and violence and had made voluntary false confessions to the police prior to admitting to the Lopatta and Phillips murders. At the time of her arrest Walters was recovering from a drug overdose, she was an alcoholic with severe emotional problems and she was suffering from severe anxiety and depression during the three-week period of her interrogation, which was accompanied by sleeplessness and tiredness. At the time of psychological testing in 1993, she was abnormally compliant and moderately suggestible. Her high level of anxiety, tiredness and sleeplessness in August 1985 would undoubtedly have made her particularly susceptible to suggestion. There was evidence that, at the time of making her confessions, Walters was suffering from a memory distrust syndrome. At the time of their interrogations in August 1985, Wille and Walters were clearly very emotionally dependent on each other, which would have made it easier for the police to play one against the other. Sheila Walters was at the time an emotionally disturbed adolescent, who had very poor self-esteem, and was likely to have been suggestible and compliant, particularly to people in authority, such as agents of the FBI.

Conclusions

This is a most worrying case. I am very concerned about the lengthy, intensive and contaminated nature of the interrogations of Wille, Walters and Sheila Walters, all of whom were, for different reasons, psychologically vulnerable at the time of making the confessions. There are also other serious grounds for concern: the bizarre content of the confessions, the serious inconsistencies contained within and across the confessions of the three individuals, the fact that Wille and Walters made false confessions to other murders during their interrogations in August 1985 and the absence of any forensic evidence or other salient corroborative evidence linking them to the murders. Having looked into this case in considerable depth, I have serious reservations about the reliability of the confessions of the individuals concerned. This case raises an extremely important question. Should confessions, which are demonstrably fundamentally flawed, ever be used as the sole basis for convicting defendants of homicide? I do not think so. If the present appeal fails, their defence attorneys will undoubtedly go to the federal court to petition for a writ of habeas corpus.

Similarities in the Personalities of Lucas and Wille

Lucas and Wille both made a number of voluntary false confessions to the police. What is it that makes people *repeatedly* voluntarily confess to murders they did not commit? In Chapter 9, I discussed the different types of voluntary false confession. Seeking attention or notoriety and inability to distinguish facts from fantasy were two important motives. What about people who falsely confess to a number of different murders? The personalities of Lucas and Wille were similar in some respects. Both involved severely personality disordered individuals who did not have a history of mental illness, and they were falsely confessing to crimes they knew they had not committed. The principal motive in both cases was the need for attention and notoriety. The MMPI profiles of both men were almost identical, although Wille had completed the MMPI and Lucas the MMPI-2. The high F score among both men is interesting and rather than invalidating the profile it may reflect their extreme psychopathology, including a tendency towards exaggeration and a plea for help. The profile of both men can be interpreted as follows:

> Persons with the '46/64' code are immature, narcissistic, and self-indulgent. They are passive–dependent individuals who make excessive demands on others for attention and sympathy, but they are resentful of even the most mild demands made on them by others (Graham, 1987, p. 107).

Wille and Lucas scored low on the Gough Socialisation Scale (scores 17 and 22, respectively), reinforcing the MMPI profile that they were prone to

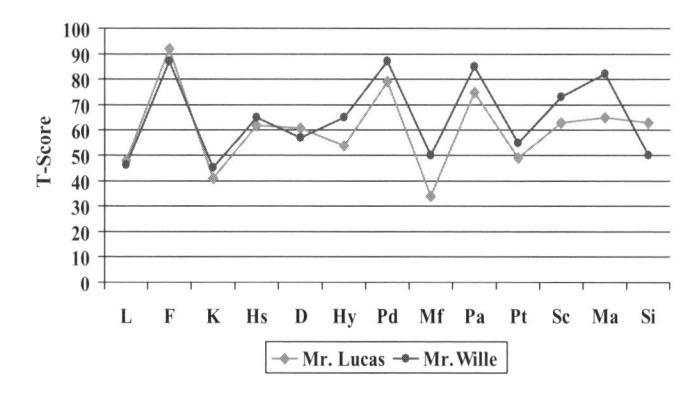

Figure 21.1. The MMPI profiles of Lucas and Wille.

antisocial behaviour. Both were of low average intelligence, they had average verbal memory recall on the GSS 1 and both confabulated abnormally on the GSS 1 and GSS 2 narratives.

What does the personality profile of these two men tell us about serial false confessors? It is of course unwise to generalize from two cases, but it may be speculated on the basis of the cases of Lucas and Wille that personality disorder, comprised of difficulties in interpersonal relationships, low self-esteem, excessive need for attention, dependency, tendencies towards exaggeration, proneness to confabulate and disregard for the consequences of their behaviour, is probably crucial in explaining repeated voluntary false confessions to murders.

GENERAL CONCLUSIONS

Waneta Hoyt was assessed for a pre-trial evaluation. In spite of some relevant psychological vulnerabilities (i.e. high compliance and anxiety), and the likelihood that the confession to murdering her five children was elicited by coercive questioning, the overall conclusions of my findings were not favourable to the defence. This case demonstrates how psychological strengths and weaknesses have to be interpreted within the context of the total circumstances in a case. Interpreting test scores in isolation can be misleading. The remaining three individuals, Joe Giarratano, Henry Lee Lucas and John Wille, had all been on Death Row for many years when the psychological assessment was conducted at the request of their attorneys. In all three cases, the psychological assessment cast serious doubts on the reliability of the confessions that resulted in their death sentence. The death sentences of Giarratano and Lucas were subsequently commuted to life imprisonment. The case of John Wille is still before the courts. All three individuals were of normal intelligence and scored abnormally low on the Gough Socialisation Scale (suggestive of proneness to antisocial behaviour), and on testing they all had an abnormal tendency to confabulate in their memory recollections. The case of Giarratano was different to that of Lucas and Wille in that at the time of the interrogations he appeared to have convinced himself that he had murdered two people. This is probably the reason why he did not retract the confession for several years, irrespective of whether this was a true or a false belief. In contrast, the crucial confessions of Lucas (the Orange Socks murder) and Wille (the Lapotta and Phillips murders) had no such internalized belief. In addition to these crucial confessions, Lucas and Wille had given volunteered false confessions to other murders. The motive was notoriety and attention seeking. The similarities in the personalities of Lucas and Wille provide a tentative insight into the psychological factors that are important in cases of serial false confessors.

CHAPTER 22

Canadian and Israeli Cases

The cases discussed so far in this book almost exclusively fall within the context of police custodial interrogation. Interrogations do take place in other settings and may involve different agencies, including undercover police officers and the security services. The two cases presented in this chapter involve confessions being coerced in specialized settings; first, during a lengthy police undercover operation by the Canadian Police, and second, by the Israeli General Security Service (GSS) in their fight against terrorism. The techniques used are different to those typically found during custodial interrogation, and as we shall see, concerns have been raised about their legality. The two cases highlight problems with the use of the term 'voluntariness' to decide on the admissibility of confession evidence obtained outside custodial interrogation.

A CANADIAN CASE OF NON-CUSTODIAL INTERROGATION

When the police anticipate problems in obtaining confessions during custodial interrogation they may resort to undercover activities, which may take different forms. Undercover officers may pose as a suspect or criminal and be placed in a prison cell with the accused (*Rothman v. The Queen* [1981] 59 C.C.C. (2d) 30 (S.C.C.)), portray themselves as members of a criminal organization (*R. v. French* [1998] 98 B.C.A.C.265 (B.C.C.A.)) or violent criminals (*R. v. Roberts* [1997] 90 B.C.A.C.213 (B.C.C.A.)) or use a promise of sex and a loving relationship as an inducement to confess (*R. v. Stagg*, Central Criminal Court; 14 September 1994).

The Canadian rules that apply to in- and out-of-custody situations are so markedly different as to give rise to what some think are anomalous consequences. It has traditionally been the rule in Britain and Canada that custody interrogations were covered by the *Ibrahim* rule (*Ibrahim v The Queen* [1914] A.C. 599), assuming that the police were identifiable as police officers. In Canada, undercover officers may pose as a suspect or criminal, although the Canadian Constitution puts certain limitations upon what the police may do. Once a person has asserted that he or she wishes to contact counsel, the police are prohibited from using the accused's custodial status, coupled with an undercover agent, to subvert the person's expressed right to remain silent

(*R. v. Herbert* [1990] 57 C.C.C. (3d) 1 (S.C.C)). Undercover agents in cells may observe such a person, but not actively elicit information by subterfuge.

The case discussed raises some important issues related to the use of undercover operators to elicit confessions from resistant suspects.

Brief Background

The case involved the murder in Canada of two German tourists, a young couple, who were visiting friends and relatives. They were last seen at the end of September 1983. Their bodies were discovered on 6 October 1983, in a wooded area 32 kilometres west of the village Chetwynd. Both victims had been shot in the head.

On 7 October a pair of blue jean trousers, size 34, were found in a refuse container just over one kilometre from the area where the bodies had been found. An examination of the jeans revealed that they had been exposed to high velocity spraying of blood. The trousers were heavily blood stained, particularly below the knees. The blood on the jeans was consistent with that of the victims. Five of the victims' travellers' cheques were cashed at petrol stations on 4 and 5 October. There was a bloodlike substance under the fingernails of the female victim.

Andrew Rose was convicted of the two murders at his first trial in 1991. He successfully appealed against his conviction in 1992, because of misdirection to the jury by the trial judge. A second trial commenced in April 1994. He was again convicted of two counts of second-degree murder. At both trials, the main witness against Rose was Madonna Kelly, who was a friend of Rose's at the time of the murders. There was no other evidence against him. During the summer of 1983 they had both worked on a farm near Chetwynd. Ms Kelly did not inculpate Rose until August 1989. Her alleged conversation with Rose in 1983 came to light because she had mentioned the conversation to a drug dealer who was staying with her in 1989.

Kelly's story was that in the early morning of 3 or 4 October 1983, Rose came to her trailer and told her he had killed two people. He was allegedly wearing blood stained jeans. Kelly's evidence was crucial in convicting Rose; without it there was no case to answer. After reporting the alleged conversation with Rose to the police in 1989, Kelly at the request of the police had a one hour telephone conversation with Rose on 7 September 1989 where she tried to get him to confess to the murder. Rose persistently insisted that he had not killed anybody and denied having confessed to her in 1983. However, he admitted that one night he had had a fight outside a bar. He forcefully challenged Kelly and claimed that he would not have had access to a gun.

The circumstantial evidence was largely in Rose's favour. He did not own a car, he had no access to firearms, he did not cash the five travellers cheques belonging to the victims, and none of the forensic evidence found at the crime scene implicated him. What did appear to match is that Rose wore size 34 jeans, but those linked to the murder could not be proven to be his. Subsequent to the second trial, Rose voluntarily provided the police with a blood sample for further DNA testing of the bloody jeans and the fingernail clippings from the female victim. The DNA analysis excluded Rose as a source of the DNA from the two exhibits.

The circumstances associated with Mr Rose's second appeal in 1998 and the pending third trial were that new evidence had come forward from Californian witnesses that someone else had confessed to the murder, an American man called Vance Hill.

Hill was an American construction worker and lived in Western Canada between 1967 and 1983. He lived there with his wife and children. He had a history of chronic alcoholism. In April 1983 his wife left Canada and moved back with the children to California. Hill remained behind in Prince George. In November 1983, at the age of 55, Hill returned to his family in California 'in a hurry'. Within months of returning to California he disclosed to his wife that he had murdered two hitchhikers whom he had met in a bar in Chetwynd and gave a detailed account of what had happened. She did not believe the story at the time and thought it one of his 'drunken fantasies'. Shortly after telling his wife about the murders Hill left his wife a suicide note, stating that he was going to kill himself because he 'wouldn't go to jail'. He did not kill himself at that time.

On 28 July 1985 Mr Hill killed himself by placing a gun barrel in his mouth and pulling the trigger. Mrs Hill told her children about the confession to the murders of the hitchhikers. Many years later she told the story to her nephew, who was bothered by it and contacted the police in September 1997. As a result, Rose was given bail in 1998 and a re-trial was ordered. Hill's surviving wife and their daughter were to testify at the forthcoming trial.

The Canadian police were undoubtedly concerned that in view of the fresh evidence from the Californian witnesses, Rose might not be convicted again. In order to ensure a conviction they set out to trick Rose into a confession through an undercover operation, which was to last between October 1998 and July 1999, which included early on setting up surveillance at Rose's home. The main undercover operator was a man named 'Fred'. His primary task was to build up Rose's trust and the credibility of the boss of the criminal organization, 'Al'. Fred first met Rose in January 1999 and established a cover story (i.e. that he was looking for a particular girl and needed Rose's assistance, for which he was offered $50). Within two weeks Rose told Fred that he had been wrongly convicted twice of murder. He told Fred that he was innocent of the murders and was confident in view of the fresh evidence from California that he would not be convicted again. The two men then met regularly over the next few months, during which the undercover officers got Rose involved in alleged criminal activities, mainly to do with drug dealing, but it also involved Rose being made to be in breach of his own bail conditions. Rose was being provided with regular payments for his assistance with the organization, which to him were large sums of money. He was told that he could make a great deal of money from his work with the organization. A big and profitable job was coming up, but in the meantime a meeting was to be organized for Rose to meet the big boss, Al, who would allegedly help him with his 'problems' (i.e. the murder charges). Three meetings took place on 16 and 17 July 1999 in a hotel room. They were surreptitiously video-recorded. Rose was to confess to the murders during the second and third taped interviews.

The Canadian Law on Voluntariness

The law in Canada concerning voluntariness, which is the same as that existing in the Britain before the introduction of the Police and Criminal Evidence Act 1984, is found in *Ibrahim v The Queen*, [1914] A.C. 599. In essence, if a suspect gives a statement to a person in authority while in custody or detained by the police then the prosecution has to prove beyond a reasonable doubt that the statement was obtained voluntarily (i.e. without fear of prejudice or hope of advantage as a consequence of anything said or done by the police). In Canadian law, the voluntariness rule does not apply if the accused person is speaking to a police officer whom he does not know is a police officer. The reason for this principle is that unless the accused knows that he is speaking to a police officer there could be no fear of prejudice or hope of advantage regarding the prosecution against him. This means that threats or inducements made by undercover police officers in order to obtain a confession are sanctioned legally, the weight of which is for the jury to decide upon (e.g. *Rothman v. The Queen* [1981], 59 C.C.C. (2d) 30 (S.C.C.); *R. v. Roberts* [1997] 90 B.C.A.C.213 (B.C.C.A.); *R. v. French* [1998] 98 B.C.A.C.265 (B.C.C.A.); *R. v. McCreery* [1999] 8 W.W.R. 699 (B.C.C.A.)). Therefore, if the confession is not made to persons who the accused understands to be persons in authority, there is no obligation on the Crown to prove it was obtained voluntarily. If the person is in custody then the traditional rules mostly apply (*R. v. Herbert* [1990], 57 C.C.C. (3d) 1 (S.C.C)).

Rose's third trial was to commence in June 2000. It began with legal arguments during the *voire dire*. The main legal argument was the admissibility of my expert psychological evidence. Two days before the trial started I had interviewed Mr Rose when I met him in Vancouver and conducted a psychological assessment.

The Psychological Evaluation

In addition to interviewing and testing Rose, I read through the various papers and documents in the case, which included transcripts of the telephone conversation that Rose had with Kelly on 7 September 1989, and the transcripts of Rose's three interviews with the undercover officers on 16 and 17 July 2000. I had also listened to the audiotape of the telephone conversation and watched the three videotapes of the undercover interviews. I had come to the conclusion that the confessions to the undercover officers were unreliable and indeed unsafe to rely on. The reasons for my views were as follows.

Psychological Vulnerabilities

During my assessment Mr Rose proved very resistant to suggestions on the GSS 2, but he was abnormally compliant on the GCS. On the EPQ-R his profile was that of a somewhat anxious introvert. He scored very low on the Gough Socialisation Scale, suggesting problems with role taking ability and personality problems. A Canadian Clinical Psychologist assessed Rose on the WAIS-III. Mr Rose proved to be of high average intelligence. In terms of his enduring personality, it was the combination of his high compliance and poor role taking ability that made him vulnerable to giving into pressure during the undercover interrogation. The poor role taking ability suggested problems in interpersonal relationships, which undoubtedly made him more dependent on the criminal organization for emotional, social and financial support.

Surrounding Circumstances

There were a number of situational factors that made Rose vulnerable to making a false confession during the undercover operation. These were the following.

i. Rose had been convicted twice before on the same charge. He served seven years in prison before he was given bail pending the current trial. He would have had little faith that he might not be convicted again. Undoubtedly, the Californian witnesses gave him new hopes that he might not be reconvicted.
ii. He had the forthcoming court case with its uncertain outcome preoccupying him. He was trying to save money to enable himself and his brother to stay in Vancouver during the trial.
iii. The role of the undercover officer, 'Fred', over an eight-month (January–September) period, was to build up a good friendship with Mr Rose. According to Fred's testimony at the *voire dire* in June 2000, he had to work hard at Rose's 'trust level'. Rose had problems with trusting people. This took some time. Rose told Fred about one week after their meeting that he needed $2000 for his Court case in Vancouver during the forthcoming May. This was to enable him to afford to stay in Vancouver for a month.
iv. Fred told him that in the past he had committed a murder and had a murder charge hanging over him. His boss, Al, had conveniently taken care of the problem and Fred had narrowly escaped a conviction for the murder. Al was presented to Rose as having much money, power and influence. Fred's task was to build up Al's credibility as a person who can make murder charges go away and to make Rose believe that without the assistance of the organization, he would be convicted. It was evident that Rose completely trusted Fred and at one point said to him 'I love you'.
v. Rose became dependent on the organization. There was a good potential for making money, he appeared to be interested in the work, he valued his friendship with Fred, and the organization could ensure that he was not going to be convicted of the murders for a third time.
vi. Rose was subtly made to believe that the organization could help him with this forthcoming court case, but the murder charge and court case could ruin his future prospects with the organization. His problem had to be sorted out before he was accepted by the organization. The organization could help him make the court case fall apart, but there was a condition: Rose had to tell all the details of the murder, otherwise the organization would not help him.

vii. The day before the video-recorded interviews with the undercover officers, Al told him that, without their help, Rose would go back to prison: he had been set up to be in desperate need of help from the organization.

The Undercover Interrogation Sessions

During the sessions there was relentless pressure, abusive language, threats, inducements, robust challenges and psychological manipulation. For most of the time there were three undercover officers in the room, 'Fred', 'Al' and 'Street'. The process went as follows.

Al repeatedly told Rose that there was 'this evidence' and that he was 'going back to jail'. He was also told that Al had information that the police had been interfering with the Californian witnesses. His hope of an acquittal was repeatedly challenged. Rose's confidence in his possible acquittal was seriously undermined.

It was made clear to him that Al could sort out his problem. Al could guarantee acquittal, but it required a confession and a disclosure of details. It was made clear to Rose that unless he confessed to the murders the organization could not assist him.

Rose tried extremely hard to persuade Al that he did not commit the murders and that he was completely innocent. He repeatedly stated that he could not and would not confess to something he did not do. Al responded firmly that Rose was lying (e.g. 'And don't fucking lie to me').

There were continued threats and inducements. During the first interview alone, Rose was told 24 times that if he did not confess to the murders he would go back to jail. If he confessed, his problems would be taken care of by the organization (Al—'I know I can help there is no doubt about that', 'If I fucking help you, you would be guaranteed not to be found guilty', 'You won't even go to another trial. But, I gotta be sure you need my help').

Al stated repeatedly that he did not care whether Rose had committed the murders (e.g. 'I don't give a fuck', was repeated several times).

As Rose continued to deny the murders, Street became very abusive and aggressive towards him (e.g. 'Just shut the fuck up', 'Think then fucking talk'). When Rose tried to explain his position Street shouted at him 'Did I say talk yet?'.

Al told Rose that the police had been interfering with the Californian witnesses ('The police have been fucking soft-shoeing her big time'). Rose expresses surprise; 'Really? Now you're telling me some news right?'.

As the first interview progressed Rose became increasingly desperate:

Can you help me?
I need your help.
I want your help.
Help me, please (at this point he was begging for help).

At the end of the first interview his perceptions of the chances of an acquittal were shattered. He then looked totally helpless. During this interview Rose was sitting next to Al on a settee. Two other undercover officers, including Fred, were also in the room. Rose was cornered, with the exit being blocked by a table and one officer's outstretched feet. There was then a break for almost two hours where Rose spent time in the bar with Fred drinking beer. When they returned to the hotel room for a further interview, Rose sat at the end of the settee, and leant away from Al (he was clearly trying to distance himself physically and psychologically from Al). His manner looked different. He looked defeated. At the beginning of the second interview he expressed his despair, included his begging for help:

> I need your help.
> Can I get your help please.
> I seriously need your help.
> Help, help me.
> Christ I need it (help).

The pressure and incentive for confessing was by this time extremely strong. He kept denying the offences, but eventually realized that it was not getting him anywhere. Al told him that he has been lying and when Rose asks what he has lied about Al states:

> Well, I'm convinced you did these two people.
> Rose now makes a compromise and replies
> Nope. Well, we'll go with I did okay?
> When further pressured he eventually states
> Okay, I did 'em.

Rose then made numerous attempts to retract the confession, which were met with more pressure from the undercover officers, including an angry outburst by his friend Fred. He was not allowed to retract the confession and confessed again. The following morning Rose retracted the confession again and said he could not confess to something he had not done. He was firmly challenged on his retractions and told that he was talking 'bullshit'. He then confessed again.

When the undercover officers ask for details he should know if he were the murderer he was unable to provide any apart from what is already known. For example, in the final interview Rose was pressured to tell where he got the gun from. He apparently could not think of a good answer and replied:

> Oh I had it, I had it.

The Final Trial

Crown counsel, Gil McKinnon QC, representing Her Majesty, argued that the reliability, or weight, of the confession statement was for the trier of fact to determine and no question of admissibility need to be decided at a *voire dire*. In contrast, defence counsel, Ian Donaldson QC sought to persuade the trial judge to hold a *voire dire* concerning the admissibility of the confession Mr Rose gave on videotape to the undercover officers. This was not an easy objective to achieve for the defence, because previous Canadian legal judgments ('authorities') predominantly argued that this was really a matter of weight, and not admissibility. In other words, without an admissibility issue there was no right to a *voire dire* and the jury would have to consider the weight of confession evidence. Fortunately for the defence, Mr Donaldson was able to persuade the judge to hold a *voire dire* concerning the admissibility of the videotaped confession. The defence was going to argue that ruling the confession statements admissible would have brought the administration of justice into disrepute. In addition, this was a perfect case in which the residual discretion to exclude a confession statement ought to be exercised. The defence said that the cases constituted an abuse of the judicial process. Rose had been convicted twice before for the same offence, he was on bail because fresh evidence had surfaced to indicate that he was innocent and the undercover agents had falsely made him believe that the police were interfering with the exculpatory witnesses who were going to be testifying at his trial.

The defence sought to qualify me as an expert at a *voire dire* to give evidence with regard to the 'putative reliability' of Rose's confession statement, pursuant to the decision on *R. v. Hodgson* [1998], 127 C.C.C. (3d) 449 (S.C.C.), and *R. v. Moham* [1994], 114 D.L.R. (4th) 419 (S.C.C.). The main issues with which I was going to be assisting the Court were the following.

- The scientific literature relating to false and coerced confessions.
- The nature of coercive police interrogation techniques.
- The similarities between the non-custodial interrogation conducted in Rose's case and techniques used by the police in custodial interrogations.
- The nature of the techniques used to break down Rose's denials, and the extent of coerciveness used by the undercover officers.
- Factors in the case that were consistent with those typically found in cases of false confessions.
- The results of the psychological evaluation of Rose and his psychological vulnerabilities at the time the statements were obtained by the undercover officers.
- The 'putative reliability' of the confession statements.

The main overall purpose of my testifying was to assist the trier of fact (the judge during the *voire dire*, and the jury during the trial proper, if the confession statements were ruled admissible) with an understanding of why and how an innocent man might confess falsely.

The first few days of the *voire dire* were spent on legal arguments, the undercover officers testified, and the two Californian witnesses gave their testimony. Mrs Hill, aged 72, seemed very clear in her testimony regarding her husband's confession. Her testimony was entirely credible. Her husband's confession had been detailed and was very convincing, which including a motive for the murders. The only thing that did not go in Rose's favour was that her husband did not wear jeans, and wore trousers size 40–42, whereas Rose wore size 34.

Towards the end of the first week I testified regarding my qualifications. I spent most of the day in the witness box. The Crown was going to challenge the scientific foundation of my evidence. They requested two days to cross-examine me on my qualifications. I returned to England and it was agreed that the cross-examination could take place through a video link. In the meantime the Crown requested, with Rose's consent, that DNA testing was carried out on the blood stained jeans found near the crime scene. The Crown was undoubtedly concerned, and rightly so, about the lack of physical evidence linking Rose to the murders and the testimony of the California witnesses, and my testimony, if allowed in by the trial judge, would have further undermined the Crown's case.

Outcome

In January 2001 the prosecution announced that they were not going to proceed with the case against Rose. Further DNA testing revealed that non-deceased DNA found on the inside pocket of the bloody jeans did not come from Rose, whereas Hill could not be eliminated as a contributor to some of the non-deceased DNA which was found. In view of the DNA testing results, the defence had succeeded in Rose being released by the trial judge shortly before Christmas 2000.

Conclusions

I am in no doubt that this case was of a pressured–compliant type of confession. It is highly probable that the confession was false. It was coerced by the undercover police officers who portrayed themselves as members of a criminal organization. They encouraged Rose to participate in apparent criminal activities of that organization, psychologically manipulated his perception of the likely outcome in his forthcoming trial, played on his vulnerabilities and distress concerning his case and used threats and inducements to break down his persistent claims of innocence. The immense pressure that Rose was placed under, and the extreme distress he displayed during the three videotaped interviews, raises important ethical issues about the use of non-custodial interrogations in a case like this. No doubt there are good reasons why the police sometimes resort to undercover interrogations. Unfortunately, such operations are open to abuse, because police in Canada know from legal judgments that normal procedural standards relevant to custodial interrogations do not apply and that the courts almost invariably rule confessions so obtained as admissible. The argument typically put forward by the Crown, and accepted by the court, is that since the accused does not know that the lies and pressure are exercised by persons in authority there can be no threats and inducements which would be influential in determining the outcome of the prosecution.

In the present case, the defence argued that the police had exceeded their professional and ethical boundaries, and potentially brought the administration of justice into disrepute, when they told Rose that the police were interfering with the Californian witnesses, who were at the time his greatest chance of an acquittal. This clearly influenced his perception of the likely outcome in his case and made him desperate to accept the assistance of the bogus criminal organization. The type and intensity of the threats and inducements clearly amounted to oppressive questioning. Admitting confessions coerced in this way into evidence, and letting the jury determine their weight, is worrying, because the risk of such confessions being false is considerable if an innocent person is coerced in this way. It is possible to argue that the risk of a false confession being obtained under such conditions *may on occasions* be even greater than during custodial interrogation. The reason is that during undercover operations accused persons are unlikely to fully appreciate the adverse consequences of making the confession. They may confess merely as a way of compromising between agreeing to something they did not do (i.e. telling lies about the involvement in the offence) and fear of the consequences if they do not confess (i.e. perceived certainty of a conviction, upsetting the members of the organization with whom they have developed a relationship and being rejected by the criminal organization).

What is interesting about Rose is that on psychometric tests he scored very low with regard to suggestibility, but very high with regard to compliance. How did this combination of scores influence the outcome of the undercover interrogation? Certainly, the low level of suggestibility indicates that he did have a critical faculty, which up to a point assisted him in resisting the pressure in the police interview. His determined and frequent attempts to retract the confession suggest that he was able at times to temporarily discontinue his reactive responding and instigate strategic coping. Here his low level of suggestibility is likely to have facilitated that process (Gudjonsson, 1995b). Unfortunately, Rose's high level of compliance, which was also evident on occasions during the video-recorded undercover interrogations (e.g. towards the end of the third and final interrogation he commented at one point, 'Whatever you say, I'll do'), meant that he would have been very eager to please his interrogators and that he was susceptible to avoidance coping (e.g. avoiding upsetting his interrogators, pretending everything was going to be alright).

AN ISRAELI TERRORIST CASE

Shortly after the occupation of the West Bank and Gaza in 1967 the Israeli authorities established military courts, which were empowered to try Palestinians for security or public order offences (Human Rights Watch/Middle East, 1994). Every year between 4000 and 6000 Palestinians are interrogated by the two security agencies, the Israeli General Security Service (GSS) and the Israel Defense Force (IDF). Numerous allegations have been made that these two agencies have used torture against Palestinian prisoners in order to obtain confessions from them (Cohen & Golan, 1991, 1992; Human Rights Watch/Middle East, 1994).

In a historic legal ruling in 1986, the Israeli Supreme Court overturned the conviction of an Israeli army officer who had been wrongly convicted of espionage on the basis of a confession coerced by the GSS. This led to the Government setting up a Commission, under the Chairmanship of Justice Landau, to investigate the interrogation methods of the GSS and form legal conclusions concerning them. The Commission reported in 1987, and it is referred to as the 'Landau Report' (Gur-Arye, 1989). The Israel Law Review published an English translation of Part One of the Report (Landau Commission Report, 1989). It reviewed the activities of the GSS and justified the use of psychological and 'moderate physical pressure' to obtain confessions. The report acknowledged that since 1971 GSS agents routinely obtained confessions by the use of physical and psychological pressure and then lied to the courts by claiming that such confessions were given voluntarily. The Commission recommended that agents who lied in court should not be prosecuted for it. The Commission Report revealed that almost half of all interrogations result in no charge being brought against detainees (i.e. they were released without charge unless they had confessed).

The detailed content of Part Two of the Report has not been made public. It outlined the interrogation techniques used by the GSS and gave agents operational guidelines about the use of psychological and physical pressure to obtain confessions. The Landau Report legalized the use of 'moderate physical pressure' to break down resistance from resistant suspects and made it unnecessary for GSS agents to continue to lie about their methods of extracting confessions. The reasoning behind the legal decision to allow 'moderate physical pressure' and psychological manipulation in order to extract confessions from Palestinians was that, unlike ordinary criminals, terrorists are highly motivated to conceal information from the interrogators as a result of ideological indoctrination and the fear of reprisals from terrorist organizations.

About a month after the Landau Commission made its report in 1987, there was a major Palestinian uprising ('intifada'), which resulted in mass arrests. Frequently there was insufficient evidence to justify detention and subsequent court proceedings. In order to be able to successfully prosecute detainees the GSS needed more confessions and began to use increasingly coercive methods of extracting them, including torture (Cohen & Golan, 1991).

According to Cohen and Golan (1991), the GSS is responsible for security and counter-intelligence within Israel and the occupied territories. It is accountable directly to the Prime Minister. One of its functions is to apprehend and interview people who are suspected of being involved in activities that endanger the security of the State of Israel. A person arrested can be detained, in the first instance, for up to 18 days without appearing before a court. A judge can authorize a further extension. Detainees can be kept in isolation from their family and solicitor for a period of two weeks, during which time they are usually interviewed intensively. Many confess and subsequently make plea bargains.

Once a confession is extracted by the GSS they are handed over to police officers who formally record the confession in accordance with the law and present it to the court. If the detainee attempts to retract the confession made to the GSS agents, he or she is sent back to the GSS for further interrogation. GSS agents generally do not testify in court but if they do, they do so behind a screen and use code names so that they cannot be identified. Prior to 1971 GSS interrogators were not required to give evidence in court. However, in 1971 a fundamental change occurred with regard to the legal admissibility of confession statements because they began to become increasingly disputed by defence lawyers. As a result GSS interrogators began to appear as prosecution witnesses in a 'trial within a trial' (Landau Commission Report, 1989), also known as a 'mini-trial' (Human Rights Watch/Middle East, 1994).

Detainees who confess almost invariably accept a plea bargain to reduce the likely length of their sentence, because their confession, even when it is disputed, will inevitably result in a conviction (Human Rights Watch/Middle East, 1994). Confession evidence can be disputed during a 'mini-trial' (Cohen & Golan, 1991; Landau Commission Report, 1989), where the judge will consider the admissibility of the confession after hearing evidence about the method, process and circumstances of the interviews. Unlike the situation in England, where confessions can be disputed on the basis of psychological vulnerability alone, a disputed confession in Israel invariably implies some impropriety on behalf of the GSS agents and therefore reflects on their integrity.

During a 'mini-trial' the prosecutor has to prove that the defendant's confession was voluntary (i.e. given by his own 'free will'). The legal guidelines concerning admissibility follow the English Judges' Rules, which were incorporated into Israeli law by way of Supreme Court rulings (Landau Commission Report, 1989). This means that a breach due to impropriety by the police could technically result in a confession being ruled inadmissible by a trial judge. However, the

> Supreme Court has occasionally observed that the Police would do well to act in accordance with the Judges' Rules, but things have never reached the stage where a confession was thrown out because of a violation of the Rules. Instead, emphasis has always been placed on the condition that the confession must be given 'of free will' (Landau Commission Report, 1989, p. 166).

As discussed in Chapter 8, the conviction rate by the Israeli's military courts is extremely high (96.8%), and the main evidence against the defendant is typically a signed confession statement. In order to illustrate the techniques used by the GSS to extract a confession from suspects and the legal issues involved, a case will be presented. The case is of particular interest because the GSS agents, during their 'mini-trial' testimony, admitted in court that they used coercive tactics, including sleep deprivation, to extract confessions. The background to the case is extensively discussed in the book *Israel's Interrogation of Palestinians from the Occupied Territories* (Human Rights Watch/Middle East, 1994). Gudjonsson (1995b) has discussed the psychological aspects of the case in detail and an abbreviated version is presented here.

Brief Background

In June 1992, a 27-year-old Palestinian, Mr A, from the West Bank of Jerusalem was arrested on suspicion of aiding two Palestinian men who planned to carry out terrorist explosions against the State of Israel. He was sent to a holding facility in the Bethlehem military headquarters, where he spent three days before being transferred to the GSS interrogation centre at Hebron where he was detained and interrogated for 16 days.

On the seventh day of GSS detention, Mr A confessed to the GSS agents that he was a member of the outlawed Islamic Resistance Movement 'Hamas', which is a relatively minor offence if no other charges are proved. The following morning, Mr A was found to suffer from facial injuries, which the agents said had been self-inflicted that same morning. According to the agents, Mr A had been able to untie himself whilst in a period of 'waiting' and repeatedly banged his head against the rough surface of the room's wall. Mr A's account, in contrast, was that a GSS agent had slammed his head repeatedly against the wall whilst he sat shackled to a small chair in order to extract a more damaging confession from him than he had given the previous day. About 24 hours later a doctor, who described him as being in a 'hysterical state', examined him. Mr A was given a sedative and re-interrogated four days later.

On the 16th day of his detention, Mr A signed a confession in which he admitted to having driven in his minicab two activists of Hamas. The terrorists were carrying explosives and intended to use them to attack the Israeli military forces.

A 'log book' had been kept by the interrogators of the periods of interrogation, and where Mr A was transferred to after the interrogation sessions. After interrogation, there were three possible options, referred to as 'waiting', 'cell' and 'rest'. Each period appears to have a special function as part of a method of breaking down the detainee's resistance (Human Rights Watch/Middle East, 1994).

Mr A's GSS interrogators were summoned to give evidence about the nature and circumstances of his interrogation and confinement. The agents' identity remained secret, but they testified in public.

According to the agents' testimony, the term 'waiting' is deliberately used to denote confinement in a painful body position, together with hooding and sleep deprivation. Whilst in 'waiting', detainees are invariably unable to obtain any sleep, except for very brief moments. They can sleep when they are in their cell.

According to the agents' testimony, the 'cell' is located outside the interrogation wing and is administered by the Israeli Prison Service. According to the 'log book', during his 16-day confinement, Mr A was sent to a cell on only three separate occasions. The first period was between 12 June and the morning of 14 June. The second period was between late afternoon on 18 June (after his face injury was discovered) and 23 June in the afternoon. The third period was in the afternoon on 25 June, after he had signed his second, and more damaging, confession.

According to the 'log book', Mr A was sent on several occasions to the 'rest' option for two or three hours at a time, where he was allowed to rest on a mattress. A part of the rest period involved Mr A being taken to the lavatory, where he had to have his meals.

The agents testified that they had used various methods during 'waiting' in order to extract a confession from Mr A. These included the following.

1. *Sleep deprivation.* The agents had deliberately deprived Mr A of sleep as a way of extracting a confession from him. According to their evidence, there were three major periods of sleep deprivation, the longest one being over four and a half days. One agent admitted that agents commonly made sleep contingent upon detainees' willingness to talk to the interrogators.
2. *Painful bodily position.* Mr A had been handcuffed and tied to a small chair in a closet or corridor near the interrogation room, with a sack over his head.

Mr A was shackled to a small child's chair and to pipes or rings embedded in the wall. The detainees cannot move about at all, although they can move their legs a little. Various uncomfortable positions are used to cause the maximum amount of pain and discomfort (Human Rights Watch/Middle East, 1994). Mr A remained in this uncomfortable position of 'waiting' over periods of several days.

The Psychological Assessment

The Medical Foundation for the Care of Victims of Torture referred the case to me in 1993. The reason given for the psychological assessment was to evaluate whether or not Mr A's 'free will' had been overborne by the GSS agents' methods of interrogation to the extent that his confessions were involuntary.

The psychological assessment consisted of an interview with Mr A, the studying of court file material that had been translated into English, and discussions with the defendant's solicitor.

I interviewed Mr A for approximately two and a half hours at Hebron Prison. The assessment was difficult, because my questions had to be translated by one interpreter into Hebrew and by another into Arabic and there was little privacy during the assessment (i.e. prison staff were walking in and out of the office and sometimes appeared to be listening to the interview).

Mr A was a Palestinian in his late twenties. At the time of his arrest, Mr A was married and had a two-year-old daughter. At the age of 14, he left school and studied metal work for three years. He then worked in his brother's hardware shop and did some part time, unofficial, mini-cab driving.

Mr A had no history of psychiatric problems. He said he performed rather poorly at school and had some problems with reading and writing although he was literate. He complained that he had always had a bad memory, but he appeared to have a reasonable memory of the interrogation by the GSS agents and his conditions of confinement.

Mr A told me that he was not a member of Hamas and he claimed to be innocent of the two charges brought against him.

Mr A said he had not confessed to the GSS agents of his own free will and claimed that his confessions were coerced. As a result of the very uncomfortable physical posture he was kept in during long periods of 'waiting', he had developed severe back pain that grew progressively worse during his 16 day confinement. He reported having become very tired and sleepy. He claimed to have been physically threatened and that there was loud music being played, which gave him a headache. Consequently, he desperately wanted to be allowed to rest. He alleged that the agents told him that if he made a confession he could be allowed to see a doctor to attend to his back pain and have a proper rest. These, Mr A claimed, were the main reasons for his making the first confession. However, he was able to continue to deny the more serious allegations that he had willingly transported terrorists to plant explosives.

The reasons he gave for having made the second, and more damaging confession, were similar, but by this time he felt in a worse physical and mental state. He reported feeling as if his brain had 'dried up' and that his life was over.

These were feelings and beliefs that he had not experienced before. It seemed that at the time he made his second confession, on the 16th day of his confinement, and without any legal advice or social support, he had completely given up. That is, his free will had become totally overborne by the GSS agents.

The Legal Issues

The case was heard in the Hebron military court, which is used exclusively for alleged crimes by Arabs against Israeli soldiers or settlers (Helm, 1994; Human Rights Watch/Middle East, 1994). The main legal issues in the present case involved the voluntariness of Mr A's two confessions to the GSS agents as well as their subsequent reiteration to the police.

After hearing evidence of Mr A's hooding, abusive body posture and sleep deprivation, the trial judge commented 'Well, some of these methods are authorized, you know'. This response suggests that the Israeli military judicial system does not regard these techniques as likely to render a confession statement involuntary and hence unreliable, even though such techniques are consistent with definitions of torture (Haward, 1974). The legal criteria for determining voluntariness in an Israeli military court are clearly very stringent and bear no relationship to the psychological meaning of the term (Gudjonsson, 1995a).

I testified in a small, crowded and noisy room inside the fortified barracks that contains the court. I had been informed by Mr A's solicitor that no defendants are ever acquitted. They invariably admit the charges in order to be able to plea bargain for the best possible sentence, knowing that they have no realistic prospect of an acquittal. This view is shared by other lawyers who practice in Hebron (Helm, 1994).

I testified for well over two hours. I argued that at the time of Mr A's second confession his free will had been completely overborne by the methods of interrogation and confinement. I could not argue the same regarding the first confession, although psychologically there was no doubt that the confession had been made against his free will, even if this did not fulfil the legal criteria according to Israeli military law. Mr A's facial injuries on 18 June and the 'hysterical state' he was reported to have been in when visited by a doctor the following day were important in demonstrating the deleterious effects that the confinement and interrogation were having on his mental state and his ability to give a voluntary confession. The GSS agent's explanations of Mr A's facial injuries were unconvincing and I expressed my reservations in my evidence. I pointed out that if the injuries had been self-inflicted as the agent maintained then it was clear that Mr A had been in a very disturbed mental state during the latter part of his GSS detention and when giving his second confession. Mr A had no previous history of mental problems and his alleged self-injurious behaviour the day after he had made his first confession, accompanied by a very disturbed mental state when seen by a doctor 24 hours later, meant that by the time he gave the second confession he would not have been mentally capable of giving a voluntary confession. This was corroborated by Mr A's account to me that at the time of giving the second confession he was no longer capable of resisting the pressure placed upon him by the GSS agents.

After being released from GSS custody, Mr A reiterated his confessions to the police, who took down a statement from him to that effect. This was a standard procedure since the GSS have no legal authority to formally take down confession statements. In cross-examination I was asked why Mr A, if he had genuinely given involuntary confessions to the GSS, had not refused to incriminate himself to the police once he had been released from GSS confinement. The answer was simple. If Mr A had refused to reiterate his confessions to the police he would have been sent back to the GSS for further interrogation. The police allegedly made this very clear to him. Therefore, it is evident that Mr A's loss of free will during the final confession with the GSS carried over into the subsequent session with the police when they took a formal statement from him, even thought he had been allowed to rest in the meantime.

Outcome

The judge did not decide on the admissibility of my evidence, because the case ended in a plea bargain. According to the attorney acting for the defendant, my evidence carried enough weight to persuade the prosecution to drop the major charge, namely, being an accomplice in placing explosives. This was important because it reduced their prior request for a seven-year sentence to one of two years. By this time the defendant had already served well over one year in prison and preferred to accept a plea bargain rather than requesting a judicial decision that could prolong the procedure for many more months. In addition, even though my expert evidence had undermined the prosecution case, the defence solicitor did not trust the judge's freedom to make an independent decision in favour of the defendant.

Conclusions

The case shows that the special status of the GSS allows their agents to use psychological and physical pressure without clear legal authority with which to operate. There is no proper recording of what they do, nor do they have any public accountability. Once the confession has been extracted by the agents the case is referred to the police, who take a statement of what the detainee told the agents; if detainees wish to retract or alter the confession then they are sent back, or threatened to be sent back, to the GSS for further interrogations.

The methods used by the GSS to extract confessions from suspected Palestinian terrorists are similar to those used in Northern Ireland over 20 years ago (Landau Commission Report, 1989; Shallice, 1974). These methods have now long been outlawed in Northern Ireland, although in exceptional circumstances the police may resort to extracting confessions by the use of torture (Collins, 1997). No doubt, these and other similar methods are used and legally sanctioned in many countries throughout the world. They do not constitute humane treatment of detainees and are clearly akin to torture, where the primary aim is to deliberately inflict psychological and physical pain for the instrumental purpose of breaking down detainees' will to resist interrogative pressure. In their defence, the GSS considers such techniques to be necessary and effective in the fight against terrorism (Izenberg, 1995). It has been argued that Israel is under constant threat of terrorism and fighting terrorism is a matter of the nation's survival (Kellerman, Siehr & Einhorn, 1998).

In September 1999, the High Court of Justice in Israel, comprised of nine justices, ordered GSS interrogators to stop using physical pressure to extract confessions from suspects (Izenberg, 1999a, 1999b).

GENERAL CONCLUSIONS

The two cases discussed in this chapter raise important issues about the admissibility of confession statements and the risk of a false confession. Most important, the concept of voluntariness, as used in law, has primarily to do with the type and intensity of psychological and physical pressure that is legally sanctioned to break down detainees' resistance and their free will during interrogation. Therefore, what is legally allowed may not permit the exercise of free will and freedom of choice, because the criteria used are adjusted to suit the purpose of a given legal system. In the two cases, the pressure exerted upon the suspects was extreme and considerably greater than would typically be seen during police custodial interrogation. In each of the two countries, the law provided the interrogators with considerable authority to exercise powerful and coercive tactics, which could lead to false as well as true confessions. Does the end justify the means? Are such tactics ever morally justified? No doubt, the views of members of the public, police, judges and legislators in different countries will vary immensely. What is particularly important is that interrogators, prosecutors and judges are aware of the potentially deleterious consequences of applying such tactics to suspects and exercise caution in their practice and judgement.

CHAPTER 23

Murder in Norway: a False Belief Leading to a False Confession

This case provides a fascinating insight into the nature of a pressured–internalized false confession and how it was elicited and maintained over a period of several months. The case involved the conviction in November 1997 of a 20-year-old man for the murder of his 17-year-old cousin. It shows how a highly intelligent young man without any mental problems was psychologically manipulated during interrogation, and his confidence in his own recollection devastatingly undermined, to the extent that he came to believe that he had murdered his cousin, although he never developed any 'memory' of the murder. His confession was the only salient evidence against him at trial in 1997 and DNA evidence supported his claim of innocence. In spite of this he was convicted. Such was the faith of the court in the police and confession evidence. I became involved in the case in 1998 as a court-appointed expert by the Gulating High (Appeal) Court in Bergen, after a re-trial had been ordered. The re-trial was set for May 1998, and I testified in Stavanger, along with a Swedish police psychiatrist who claimed that the confession was 'true'. The psychiatrist had assisted the police with the investigation of the case from January 1997, had provided a psychological profile of the suspect, and subsequently became an independent court-appointed expert in the case. The jury acquitted the young man and he was released from prison. Subsequently evidence has emerged that further supports the accused man's innocence.

BACKGROUND TO THE CASE

In the early hours of the morning of 6 May 1995, a 17-year-old girl, Miss T, was found dead by a land owner near a public road on Karmoy island, in Norway. There were crushing injuries to the head and a 23 kilogram bloodstained stone was found beside the deceased's head. There had been about 10 blunt blows to the head. There was also evidence of strangulation and suffocation. There appeared to have been sexual interference, although no trace of semen was found. Death was estimated to have occurred around 0100 hours. The victim was last seen in Kopervik around 0010 hours. The distance between Kopervik centre and the crime scene was about 4000 metres (2.5 miles) depending on the route taken.

The local police were provided with assistance from Kripos, the Norwegian National Bureau of Crime Investigation, which is based in Oslo. Crime scene analysts from Kripos arrived and conducted their investigations. The investigation focused on two avenues of evidence, a 'car avenue' and a 'hair avenue'.

The car avenue aspect of the investigation was based on the theory that the victim could have left Kopervik centre by car and probably in the company of the perpetrator. There were a number of sightings of identified cars on the night of the murder. One of the cars was reported as racing in the direction of the murder scene at about 0030 hours on the night of the murder. Neither the car nor the driver were identified by the police.

The hair avenue focused on a number of hairs found at the crime scene, including two identical hairs, one found in the victim's clenched fist, and the other on her underwear. These hairs did not establish the identity of the murderer and were discarded by the police and prosecution.

As far as the car and hair avenues were concerned they did not assist the police with solving the case. As a result, the police were considering closing the investigation. However, in January 1997 a decision was made to review once again all the material in the case. Detectives working on the case were convinced that the perpetrator was already somewhere in the case pile and there were several suspects who had not been satisfactorily 'checked out'; among them was Mr A, the victim's 17-year-old cousin. He was to be re-interviewed, arrested, subjected to custodial confinement and interrogation, and ultimately convicted of the murder.

The Interviews of Mr A as a Witness

The police interviewed Mr A, originally as a witness on 10 and 11 May 1995. It appears that at the time he had became a suspect after a previous headmaster had notified the police, shortly after the offence, that Mr A had a history of sexually inappropriate behaviour with girls.

Mr A lived close to the victim's home. It appears that at the time he had been a prime suspect, but he strenuously denied any involvement in the murder. He claimed that on the night of the murder he had gone to the cinema with some friends in a nearby town, Kopervik. The film ended at approximately 2230 hours. He then visited a discotheque and spent some time in Kopervik's pedestrian street before returning home on his bicycle shortly after midnight. His parents confirmed to the police his arrival home about midnight.

Prior to Mr A being re-interviewed in January 1997, it was clear that he was a prime suspect. A careful and detailed preparation took place prior to Mr A being re-interviewed to plan how to break down his resistance and elicit a confession. The police officers in the case seemed sure of his guilt and focused all their efforts on proving his involvement in the murder. Two police officers from Kripos were to play a central role in the investigation: officer E, who became the principal interrogator, and officer F, who was in overall charge of the investigation (i.e. the 'team leader'). They were assisted by a local police officer,

officer G. Officers E and G kept notebooks from the beginning of their involvement in the case. Unknown to them at the time, these notebooks were to provide crucial evidence in the case during the re-trial and provided an excellent insight into the thinking of the officers and their plans and use of psychological manipulation and trickery to persuade Mr A of his guilt and elicit a confession.

Officer E interviewed Mr A extensively as a witness on 29 and 30 January 1997. Officer E's notebook describes Mr A as being 'nice and cooperative'. He kept denying his involvement in the murder. No self-incriminating admissions were made, but there were certain discrepancies between his current account and the account he had given two years previously, which will be discussed later.

Furthermore, in his enthusiasm to support his claim of innocence, Mr A had made one crucial mistake during the 1995 witness interviews that was later to have serious consequences. In order to assist the police at the time he was trying hard to think of people who might have seen him cycling home on the evening when the murder was committed. He recalled that on his way through Kopervik he had seen a girl he recognized from school but he could not recall her name at the time of the police interviews. However, in the week after the two witness interviews in May 1995, he thought he recognized the girl after meeting her in Kopervik, stopped her, asked for her name and whether she had seen him riding by on the night of the murder. She said she remembered him riding past her by a little bridge ('Litlabru'). Mr A told her she should go to the police with this new information. The girl did this and was interviewed by the police. Unfortunately for Mr A, the girl (witness H) timed his cycling by Litlabru later than that reported by Mr A, or at 0145 hours, which suggested that he had been out later than reported in his witness statements and he could therefore technically have had time to commit the murder. This was later to be used in court against Mr A. The defence argument was that the girl had either estimated the time wrongly or was unwittingly referring to another day.

The Arrest

Mr A was arrested in Stavanger on 8 February 1997, and remanded in custody two days later by the court for a period of four weeks. He was isolated from all social contacts, but was allowed to speak with his advocate and a psychiatric nurse who looked after him in the local prison. There was a ban on all correspondence. The psychiatric nurse became an important independent informant during my psychological evaluation. Mr A was held in custody at a Regional Prison and the interrogations were conducted at a Police Station.

The main thrust of the interrogation of Mr A was to get him to explain the discrepancy in the timing of his movements between him and the girl (witness H) who had allegedly seen him close to the Litlabru bridge in Kopervik at 0145 on the morning of the murder. Mr A, by finding witness H himself and informing the police, had unwittingly given the police a very strong weapon with which they could break down his confidence in his memory and insistence that he had been home by midnight and could therefore not have committed the murder. The challenge presented to Mr A by the police was to remember what he had been doing during the missing period between 0005 and 0200. This challenge was to prove fatal to his ability to resist the interrogation.

Between 10 February and 19 March 1997, Mr A was interviewed for well over 100 hours by officer E. The defence solicitor was in telephone contact with the accused and was available for consultations if required. He was not present during the interrogation. When he became involved in the case officer E had already spent many hours with Mr A, and officer E appears to have soon established excellent rapport with Mr A. The solicitor's advice to his client was for him not to give a statement, but Mr A ignored this advice. He wanted to assist the police and erroneously believed that he could convince officer E of his innocence.

There were no formal notes made of the interviews, apart from three interviews dated 25 February, and 1 and 19 March, when self-incriminating admissions were made in the form of Mr A admitting that he was responsible for the murder while claiming to have no memory of actually being involved in the murder. The interviewing officer apparently persuaded Mr A that he had committed the murder and had 'repressed' the memory. He spent many hours assisting Mr A in bringing back the repressed memories, but without success. Mr A was highly motivated to bring out the 'memories', but his belief that he had committed the murder apparently never progressed to the development of having a memory of committing the murder.

On 21 February 1997, Mr A handed a note to his solicitor where he had written 'I killed B. T.'. The solicitor asked him 'Do you actually remember having done it?'. Mr A replied 'No I don't remember it, but it must have been me because everyone says so'. The solicitor then took the note from him and told him that he should not confess to something he could not remember. Mr A told officer E, in whom he had apparently developed complete trust, about the note to his lawyer. However, he declared that he could not actually recall committing the murder, but during the interrogation and confinement had developed the belief that he had done so. In view of the absence of detail the police were not satisfied with Mr A's confession and continued to interview him. When Mr A insisted that he could not remember committing the murder the police officer asked him to make up a film script of what he thought might have happened. This he did with the assistance of the officer, but he kept stating that this was only a theory. In all his statements to the police Mr A did not explicitly admit to having an actual memory of being involved in the murder. To the contrary, he kept saying that he had no memory of having committed the offence. He gave the same story to the prison psychiatric nurse, who saw him regularly in the evenings in prison after the interrogations. Her observations of Mr A in prison custody were very important and I therefore requested a meeting with her prior to completing my psychological report. This proved invaluable.

The Retraction

The first indication of a retraction came on the 18 April 1997, almost two months after the self-incriminating admission. The psychiatric nurse telephoned the police and said that Mr A was now wondering whether he had admitted to something he had not done. Mr A was reported to be looking for things that would convince him that he was the murderer, but he had failed to find any evidence to satisfy him that this was the case. Shortly afterwards Mr A was transferred to Bergen Prison. He now told his solicitor that he wanted evidence to show that he had committed the offence, because he was very concerned that he could not remember anything about it. He asked the solicitor not to inform the police about his actually not remembering the murder, because he was afraid that it might result in his being placed back in isolation. He appeared terrified of being placed back in isolation.

On 18 May 1997, Mr A retracted his confession to his father. On 7 June, the solicitor, without his client's consent but with the agreement of his parents, informed the police that Mr A had retracted the confession.

In a police statement on 12 August, Mr A formally retracted his confession. On 6 September, Mr A, on his own initiative, took a polygraph ('lie detector') test, administered by a Norwegian polygraph examiner. The outcome was that Mr A was classified as being 'truthful' concerning his denial of the murder. This appears to have been very important in finally convincing Mr A that he was innocent of the murder of his cousin.

PRE-TRIAL (1997) PSYCHOLOGICAL EVALUATION

After being transferred to Bergen Prison, Mr A was seen on 15 occasions by a clinical psychologist. At first Mr A complained of amnesia and wanted help to remember what happened after he left the cinema in Kopervik on the evening of the murder and until he arrived home that night. The psychologist had the impression that Mr A very much wanted to remember that 'lost period', but he was completely unable to do so. Mr A claimed to have no memory of having committed the murder or being involved in any way. He told the psychologist that during the custodial interrogation he had felt isolated and under pressure to confess. He expressed concern that he was not experiencing any feelings of remorse, nightmares or sleep problems. Officer E had told him that it was common for people who had committed murder to experience such reactions. He felt unsure as to whether or not he had committed the murder. At first he said that he would be relieved if there was forensic or technical evidence to implicate him in the murder, but over the next few weeks he appeared to become increasingly convinced that he had nothing to do with the offence. On 16 June, Mr A told the psychologist that he felt under pressure to stand by his earlier police testimony, which he believed was unwittingly invented. For the first time he expressed a wish to take a polygraph test in order to find out the truth.

On 14 July 1997, Mr A completed psychological tests, including the Norwegian translation of the Minnesota Multiphasic Personality Inventory

(MMPI; Hathaway & McKinley, 1991). The MMPI profile obtained during the testing indicated a highly abnormal mental state. This will be discussed later in this chapter when a comparison is made with the findings on the same test completed on 16 May 1998.

When seen by the psychologist on 18 August, Mr A was in good form and reported that he believed that he could not be found guilty of the offence. It was clear to the psychologist that Mr A was gradually believing himself to be innocent and was counting on acquittal at his forthcoming trial. During the last session on 13 October, Mr A was expressing a great deal of bitterness towards the police about having 'brain-washed' him and 'enticed' him into confessing to the murder. Mr A now seemed completely convinced that he was innocent of the offence. This has remained his position since.

THE FIRST TRIAL

The case was heard in Haugesund, between 20 October and 19 November 1997. The court heard 84 witnesses to fact and five expert witnesses. Mr A testified before the court and denied any involvement in the murder. His parents testified and confirmed his alibi that he had arrived home at about midnight. Mr A was convicted of murder and rape on 27 November 1997, and sentenced to 14 years imprisonment. He had already served 283 days while on remand. In addition, Mr A was ordered to pay, within two weeks, Nkr 100 000 (approximately £10 000) to the victim's parents. The victim's parents had filed for compensation under the Norwegian Injury Compensation Act and the case of the civil claim ran concurrently with the criminal case, in the same court.

Undoubtedly of importance was the fact that the Swedish psychiatrist who had been assisting the Norwegian police from January 1997 in 'profiling' Mr A and advising them about the case testified at the trial that Mr A's confession was 'true'. The psychiatrist had not interviewed Mr A and based his conclusions on studying the prosecution papers in the case and talking with the police officers. The psychiatrist was later offered the opportunity of interviewing Mr A in order to obtain a more balanced picture of the case. He refused, apparently without any good reason.

It is evident from the transcript of the first court judgment that the court placed much emphasis on Mr A's apparent special knowledge, especially about the sexual assault. From officer E's notebook it is evident that he visited the crime scene on 28 January 1997, and he was present during the remand hearing where the details of the case were discussed. He must have known a great deal about the crime details, which could easily have been communicated and discussed with Mr A during the lengthy interviews. It is also evident from his notebook that officer E was in very frequent contact with officer F, who was in possession of all the relevant details, and it would be very surprising if they did not discuss various aspects of the case. Therefore, the special knowledge attributed to Mr A should under no circumstances have been relied upon as evidence of his guilt.

THE PSYCHOLOGICAL EVALUATION PRIOR TO THE APPEAL

In April 1998 Dr Barrie Irving, a British Social Psychologist, and I were appointed as expert witnesses by the Gulating High (Appeal) Court in Bergen

> ...in order to be able to give an account of whether a false confession or real repression had been made.

This is an extreme mandate to be addressed by an expert and it would not be allowed within the British or American adversarial systems. The mandate was close to broaching issues concerning 'guilt' or 'innocence', which in Britain would not be within the province of an expert witness. Prior to commencing my assessment of Mr A I raised my concern about the nature of the mandate in a meeting with the defence and prosecution. The prosecution insisted that I should work in accordance with the mandate specified in my letter from the Gulating High Court outlining my terms of reference.

The Framework for the Assessment

The framework adopted for the assessment consisted of the following.

- Studying all the relevant background and case material, including witness statements, confession statements, the notebooks of two police officers, police reports, previous psychological and psychiatric reports and a copy of the judgment from the District Court in Haugesund.
- Interviewing Mr A for a period of 13 hours on three separate occasions, during which clinical interviews were conducted and psychometric tests were administered.
- Visiting the crime scene and the route that may have been taken by the victim when travelling from Kopervik to Gamle Sundsvei Road on Karmoy, where she was found murdered.
- Interviewing informants, including the two main police officers from Kripos, officers E and F, Mr A's original solicitor, the psychiatric nurse who saw Mr A regularly after the interrogation sessions and the clinical (prison) psychologist who interviewed Mr A in Bergen Prison.

A government authorized translator was present throughout the assessment of Mr A, but the interviews were conducted in English and when appropriate the translator interpreted or explained questions and answers. Mr A's command of English was good and he could be interviewed in English without any difficulties. All tests, apart from one (the Norwegian version of the MMPI), were administered in English.

I studied all the relevant papers, which had been translated into English. I produced a detailed report, which served as the foundation to my subsequent testimony. Whereas my assessment focused on the validity of Mr A's self-incriminating admissions to the police, Dr Irving's report focused specifically on the custodial interrogation of Mr A. The conclusions in Dr Irving's report were read out to the jury and judges during the trial, but he was not required to testify. This was a decision that was made at the beginning of the appeal by the presiding judge.

Brief Background to Mr A

At time of the murder Mr A was less than two weeks short of his 18th birthday. At the time of my assessment he was 21 years of age. His parents were in their mid-40s and Mr A was the second of four siblings. The victim was his cousin on his mother's side (i.e. his mother and the victim's father were siblings). The two families lived close to each other and were on good terms, until Mr A's arrest. Since then the good relationship between the two families has been destroyed.

Mr A left college at the age of 19. In January 1997, shortly before his arrest, he went to Stavanger to serve the initial year of his compulsory military service. He was academically good at school and showed great interest in sports. He was an excellent handball player. While in custody he took university entrance exams with good results. At the time of my assessment Mr A was doing a foundation course in history at the University of Bergen.

Mr A had no history of mental or developmental problems. He was physically healthy during his upbringing. He described his childhood as being happy. He got on well with his parents and always found them supportive. It appears that his parents set firm boundaries and limits during childhood and adolescence. There was no history of alcohol abuse or illicit drug use.

In the autumn of 1993, when aged 15, he exposed his genitals to girls of his age in the cloakroom in a sports facility. The act did not appear to have been planned, there was no erection, and the incident was not reported to the police. One year later, Mr A was reported to the police for touching on the breast a girl with whom he was exercising in a training room. Mr A was not charged with the offence, but Mr A became hypersensitive about the incident. He felt stigmatized and began to believe that people were talking about it behind his back. This vulnerability appeared to play an important part in his reactions to the police interviews. During the trial in Haugesund the prosecution tried to prove this offence by calling the girl and other witnesses to testify. They did not repeat this during the second trial.

Test Results

The results of the psychological tests completed by Mr A during the evaluation prior to his appeal in 1998 are presented below. These aimed at identifying his personality and psychological vulnerabilities that may have been present when he was interviewed by the Norwegian police in 1997.

Mr A obtained a score of 58 on the Raven Standard Progressive Matrices (Raven, Court & Raven, 1992), which indicated that his non-verbal intellectual abilities fell at least in the upper 90th percentile rank of the general population (there are some difficulties with arriving at a precise IQ score on the matrices: see Gudjonsson, 1995f).

The GSS 1 and the GSS 2 were both administered. The memory scores fell well within normal limits. The scores fell approximately in the 50th percentile rank for persons in the general population in England. Considering the fact that the test was administered in English, the results indicate that Mr A has had least average verbal memory capacity. He would be expected to do somewhat better if tested in his own language. It is noteworthy that Mr A retained his overall memory performance very well over a two week period (i.e. he retained almost 80% of the material on both tests). The confabulation scores on immediate recall and delayed recall after approximately one hour fell within normal limits. However, there was an unusually large increase in Mr A's confabulatory responses after a two week period, even though his memory for the material had deteriorated only slightly. This indicates that time delay has marked effects upon his producing confabulations. Although confabulations on the scales do increase over time as memory of the story deteriorates (see Chapter 12), the increase in confabulation noted in Mr A's case was unusually large, particularly with regard to the GSS 2 (i.e. there were 11 items of confabulation).

In spite of the general absence of undue susceptibility to suggestions (the suggestibility scores on both scales fell in the average range—50th percentile rank), it is noteworthy that the answers given by Mr A to the 20 specific questions tended to be very vague, and he was hesitant and kept changing his answers (e.g. 'I don't remember, probably, can't remember that'; 'maybe traffic lights, don't know, yes'). This suggested that Mr A lacked confidence in his memory and found it difficult to discriminate between true recollections and erroneous material. This tendency of his to be so hesitant in his answers was very unusual for somebody who has a good intellectual and memory capacity.

Figure 23.1 shows the *T*-scores obtained on the Minnesota Multiphasic Personality Inventory (MMPI; Hathaway & McKinley, 1991) on two separate occasions, 10 months apart. The MMPI was first administered to Mr A by the clinical (prison) psychologist, on 14 July 1997. The psychologist provided me with a copy of the MMPI in Norwegian, which was completed by Mr A during my assessment in May 1998. The reason for administering this test was to see whether there had been any change in his mental state since the previous testing, on the same test. On the previous testing a number of the clinical scales

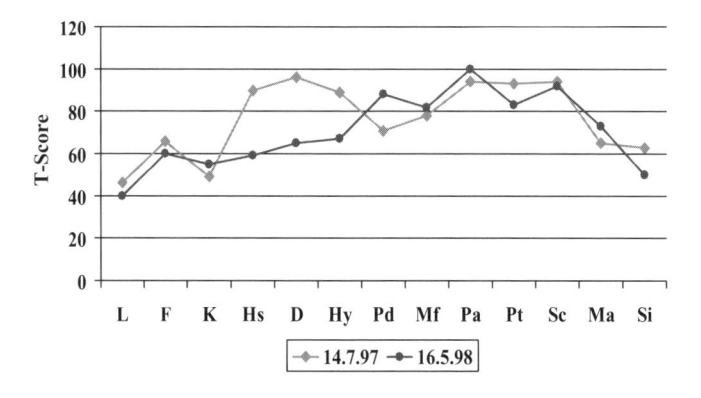

Figure 23.1. The MMPI profile scores of Mr A during (14 July 1997) and after (16 May 1998) a confusional state

were highly elevated and suggested major problems with Mr A's mental state at the time. At the time of the assessment conducted in 1997 it was not possible to say whether the clinical symptoms noted on the MMPI testing were temporary or enduring.

I made a careful comparison between the T-scores on the two MMPI tests (see Figure 23.1). The scores obtained on the three validity scales were almost identical to those obtained on the previous assessment. Again, all the validity scales were well within normal limits, indicating a valid clinical profile. It appeared that Mr A had made a continued effort to follow instructions and read the items carefully. He appeared to be open, consistent and truthful in his answers.

A number of the clinical scales were highly elevated in a very similar way to the previous assessment. The 1998 MMPI profile, like that from the previous year, indicated a strong feeling of persecution and maltreatment, poor social judgement, stubbornness, over-sensitivity, preoccupation with abstract and theoretical concepts, excessive fantasy proneness and restlessness. These symptoms appear to be persistent and enduring. The extremely strong feeling of persecution and maltreatment may be largely a result of Mr A's perception of his present predicament concerning his conviction for the murder of his cousin.

Three of the clinical scales (1, 2 and 3), which were highly abnormal in 1997, were now within normal limits. These were *hypochondriasis* (i.e. preoccupation with somatic and bodily complaints), *depressive symptoms* (i.e. extreme worrying, feelings of indecisiveness, inadequacy and self-depreciation) and *hysteria* (i.e. strong dependency needs, social and emotional immaturity and stress communicated through the development of physical symptoms). These three broad categories of symptoms were undoubtedly related to the severe anxiety and confusional state Mr A experienced at the time. With his confusional state being resolved these symptoms were markedly reduced and were no longer outside normal limits.

The other tests administered were the Eysenck Personality Questionnaire—Revised (EPQ-R; Eysenck & Eysenck, 1975), the GCS and the Other-Deception and Self-Deception Questionnaires (ODQ, SDQ; Sackeim & Gur, 1979).

All the scores fell within normal limits. The very low scores on the EPQ-R Lie scale and ODQ indicate that during the assessment Mr A was not attempting to present himself in a socially desirable fashion. The SDQ score obtained fell in the average range and indicates only a modest rate of self-deception. Mr A did not prove to be unduly compliant in terms of his temperament. His score was average for persons in the general population. Mr A was somewhat anxiety prone as suggested by his moderately high EPQ-R neuroticism score (i.e. just over one standard deviation above the mean for his English contemporaries), and the low psychoticism score suggests an absence of antisocial personality characteristics. The EPQ-R profile is that of a rather anxious (emotionally labile) extravert.

Interview with Mr A

During the lengthy interviews I had with Mr A he appeared forthcoming, honest and spontaneous in his answers. There were no indications of defensiveness or evasiveness. I interviewed him in detail about his background, the police interrogation and confinement and the confession. Here I shall only present briefly the pertinent findings that I consider relevant to understanding his 'confession'.

At the time of the assessment Mr A said that he was completely convinced that he did not commit the murder. He denied ever having had any memory of having performed the murder or being involved in his cousin's death in any way. When asked how he explained the confession he replied '*I was in a serious confusion*'. He explained that he was shocked by the fact that he was arrested on 8 February 1997, and was determined to help the police to 'sort out this misunderstanding'. Officer E allegedly kept telling him that he had evidence against him and that sometimes people commit serious crimes without being able to remember it. Prior to his interrogation he had always had a clear memory of the night of the murder and had been home just after midnight. He said that he had not seen the victim that night. During the very lengthy and detailed interviews with officer E, he gradually came to believe that he had committed the murder, but without having had any memory of doing so. He claimed that at no point was he absolutely sure that he had been involved in the murder, but he believed he probably had. The officer seemed so sure of his involvement and allegedly told him that the confession did not really matter because he would have to prove his involvement in the murder independent of the confession. Once he came to believe that he had possibly or probably committed the murder, but he had no memory of it, the officer suggested different ways of retrieving the 'repressed' memory, which included him telling it and writing it down as if it were a script for a film. Mr A claims that all he was doing was using his imagination to create a theory of what he thought may have happened. The scenarios were his but the officer allegedly discussed these in detail and helped him to make amendments to make it consistent with the evidence.

Mr A told me that the first question he asked his solicitor, after his arrest on 8 February, was 'Do they convict innocent people?'. The solicitor replied 'No' (the solicitor has confirmed this conversation in my interview with him), which greatly reassured Mr A and appears to have given him a false sense of security (i.e. it appears to have made him feel safe and free to 'open up' completely to the officer, whom he, at the time, liked and trusted).

I asked Mr A to explain from where he obtained the crime details. He said that much was common knowledge in the neighbourhood, but salient details were given at his remand hearing and officer E was also present at the hearing. This indicated that both Mr A and the officer had detailed knowledge about the case and the technical evidence two weeks before Mr A gave his first detailed confession on 25 February. Mr A claimed to have discussed in detail the technical and crime related details with officer E during their lengthy interviews.

Mr A was allegedly told by officer E during the police interviews that two things would happen. First, his memory for the murder would in due course come back. Secondly, he would experience nightmares. Neither happened, and this surprised Mr A, and gradually over time he began to 'slide backwards', that is, doubt that he had anything to do with the murder. For this reason he spoke to a psychiatric nurse in the prison. She advised him to tell his solicitor and the police, which Mr A was very reluctant to do for two reasons. First, he did not want to 'look like a clown in court' (i.e. make a fool of himself). Secondly, he did not want to risk being kept in solitary confinement as he had been before he began to confess to the police (once he had given his confession he was no longer kept in solitary confinement).

After Mr A was transferred to Bergen Central Prison he began to see the prison psychologist, and gradually he became increasingly convinced that he had not committed the murder. By the end of August he was more or less convinced he was totally innocent. This belief was confirmed and strengthened after Mr A passed a polygraph test in September 1997. Since that time he has not at any time believed that he committed the murder (this was confirmed in his account to others, including his solicitor and family).

I asked Mr A what he considered to be the most salient factors in making him confess to the murder. He identified the following, but they are not in order of significance (Mr A had problems with identifying which of the factors below were most important, and pointed out that it was 'no one thing', rather the combination of factors).

1. *Total trust and confidence in the interviewing officer.* After the indecent exposure incident in 1995, Mr A became extremely sensitive about people talking about him behind his back, and this appears to have reached paranoid proportions. He felt very ashamed and embarrassed about the incident but had nobody to talk to about it. He tried on several occasions to tell his girlfriend, but was never able to. The officer seemed interested in the incident and began to talk to him about it and Mr A found this very helpful, even therapeutic. This made him feel very close to the officer and he preferred talking to him rather than being locked up in a bare police cell. At the time he thought the officer was a 'good listener'. Mr A said that after the indecent exposure incident he 'dreamed of being a normal guy again'. At the time of the assessment he viewed his indecent behaviours as being a form of juvenile experimentation.

2. *His determination to cooperate with the police.* Mr A said he was determined to cooperate with the police and clear the 'misunderstanding'. Once he came to believe that he had committed the murder he tried very hard to 'force the memories out'. Indeed, he appeared to have made a very determined effort to do so. He claims that the officer went into immense detail about everything and kept telling him that he had to prove his innocence. Mr A thought of different ways of achieving this, including asking for the use of hypnosis, requesting to see a psychologist and taking a lie detector test.

3. *Academic curiosity about memory.* Mr A said that in some respects he found the idea of 'repressed' memories exciting. He has a general curiosity about learning new things and was fascinated about the officer's theories of memory loss. He liked to develop theories and speculate about what might have happened to the victim, his cousin. He said that when he was at school his teachers praised him on his ability to tell stories and make them realistic. He claims to have a capacity to 'merge' himself into things and use his imagination very effectively. When making up the scenarios of what might have happened to his cousin it always felt like a theory and not like a reality, but

he was prepared to go along with it. The officer gave him homework to do, where he had to write down what he thought could have happened to the victim.

4. *Social isolation.* Mr A said that after his arrest on 8 February, he had a great need to speak to his family, and particularly his girlfriend. He explained that he needed their reassurance and support but this was not possible and it upset him a great deal (he seemed distressed when discussing this). According to Mr A., another problem with the isolation was that he could not exercise physically. For many years he had been very keen on sports, and fitness and exercise were very important to him. The deprivation of exercise was, he said, distressing to him. Speaking to the officer was in his view much better than staying in the cell on his own.

5. *Increased confusion.* Mr A claimed that as the police interviews progressed he became increasingly confused about his movements and whereabouts on the night of the murder. The officer would spend day after day asking him to explain the missing 'two hours'. He told me he had even become confused about an alleged aggressive incident at Kopervik School, which was mentioned at his remand hearing. The headmaster had mistakenly accused him of an incident that he had nothing to do with, but at the time of the police interviews he falsely believed that he had done it even though he had no memory of the incident.

6. *Somatic symptoms.* Mr A claimed that during the police interviews he had bad headaches, which he was not used to. He thought the headaches were caused by officer's extensive smoking, although he recognized that the stress of the interrogations may also have had something to do with it. During the first day of custodial interviews the officer had asked Mr A if he minded his smoking. Mr A did not want to upset the officer and agreed to his smoking, but later regretted it when he realized how much the officer smoked and the inordinate length of the interviews.

7. *Fear of the officer in charge.* Mr A claimed to have been frightened of officer F, but at the same time respected him and thought he might be able to 'frighten the memories out of the brain'. He did not claim that officer F was in any way aggressive towards him, but viewed him as a person in authority whose 'voice went up and down'.

INTERVIEWS WITH INFORMANTS

Officer E

I interviewed officer E for approximately three hours in May 1998. The interview took place at Stavanger Police Station. The interpreter was present throughout the interview. It proved difficult to interview officer E. He appeared to be very anxious and defensive. His command of the English language seemed quite good, but he commonly reverted back to Norwegian. When I asked him questions about his behaviour during the interviews of Mr A, he was in the habit of looking for the reply in his notebook rather than giving a spontaneous answer.

Officer E told me that he had no formal training in police interviewing techniques, nor had he had any training in psychology. He was adamant that there was never any pressure on him from anybody to obtain a confession from Mr A, not even from officer F, who was his superior officer at the time. This was contradicted by a comment in his notebook dated 24 February 1997, which said 'Talked to F... during lunch time. *I have a deadline until Monday to get a confession*', which was in one week's time. The following day Mr A made a full confession to the murder of his cousin.

Officer E denied having in any way manipulated or tricked Mr A in order to extract a confession from him. He did not think he placed Mr A under any pressure at all and thought he had been very fair to him. He said that at the time he viewed Mr A as an intelligent person, who had a strong personality. He explained that the purpose of the lengthy interviews with Mr A was to find out what he was doing on the night of the murder and not specifically to obtain a confession. The focus was on giving Mr A the opportunity of proving his innocence. The officer told me that when suspects are resistant during the interrogation he always gives them the opportunity to prove their innocence. Indeed, officer E said he sometimes spent days giving suspects the opportunity of proving their innocence.

As far as the present case was concerned, from early on during the interviews Mr A had major problems talking about his previous indecent exposure and officer E thought it would be helpful if he wrote down his thoughts and ideas between the interviews. He also suggested it might help if he described the accounts (scripts) in the third person. Mr A agreed to do this. According to the officer, Mr A had 'problems putting into words his sexuality' and it was important to get over his sexual embarrassment in case the murder of his cousin was sexually motivated. Officer E recognized how important it was to get the suspect to trust the interviewer and he tried to establish good rapport and trust between the two of them.

Officer F

I interviewed officer F shortly after completing my interview with officer E. The interview lasted just over an hour. Officer F seemed confident, comfortable and forthcoming during the interview. The interview was conducted in English. Officer F was fluent in English.

Officer F told me that he had disagreed with officer E about the interviewing strategy used with Mr A. He wanted a more direct approach. Mr A was his prime suspect and at the time he firmly believed in his guilt, and at the time of my interview with him he said he still firmly believed in Mr A's guilt. Officer E was specially chosen for the interrogation, because of his patience and good temperament. He thought Mr A had memory problems and needed assistance with remembering what had happened. Mr A never told him that he remembered having committed the murder, only that he believed that he had done so.

Officer F came across as a very persuasive individual, and it would have been easy for him to persuade others, including the prosecutor, the judges, the jury and the victim's family, that Mr A was the murderer. Officer F was probably the strongest prosecution witness, followed by the Swedish psychiatrist.

The Clinical (Prison) Psychologist

After interviewing the two officers, I met the prison psychologist and interviewed him for over an hour. He told me that during the 15 meetings he had with the accused in Bergen Prison, Mr A always maintained that he had no actual memory of committing the murder, but at first expressed the thought that he 'must have done it'. He gradually expressed the view with increased conviction that he was innocent. It was the lack of technical evidence against him and the favourable outcome of the polygraph test that seemed to make a difference to his confidence in his innocence. The psychologist's view was that Mr A did not cope well with stress, although superficially he seemed to give the impression of doing so.

The Psychiatric Nurse

I interviewed the psychiatric nurse who had been in regular contact with Mr A during his period of solitary confinement. The nurse used to meet him in the evenings in order to give him support and counselling. There were several occasions when she was not able to see him on the set days, because he was delayed returning from the police station (she worked between 4 and 10 p.m.), because the police interviews were often prolonged late into the evenings. On the Tuesday before he was transferred to Bergen Prison Mr A told her he wanted to bring up something very difficult. He told her that for some time he had been in doubt about his involvement in the murder of his cousin. It was obvious to her that he had been thinking seriously about this for some time, but was very reluctant for his lawyer and the police to be informed. Mr A seemed to find solitary confinement difficult and appeared distressed by the restrictions on his liberty. It was wearing him down not having contact with his family. He was sometimes tearful during their sessions together. Once he had confessed the restrictions were lifted and he appeared much happier.

Mr A made it clear to the nurse that he had no memory of having committed the murder, but thought he suffered from the defence mechanism 'repression'. He told her that officer E had given him homework to do, which consisted of his writing a story of how the murderer had killed his cousin. He seemed to regard officer E as a friend and trusted him. He told her if he cooperated well enough he would be released from prison. He told her that he was upset about officer E's heavy smoking during the interviews but did not want to upset him by objecting to his smoking. Mr A seemed fascinated by psychology and the idea of a repression mechanism.

Mr A's First Solicitor

I interviewed the solicitor Mr A had representing him while he was detained in police custody. He had not sat in on the police interviews with Mr A, because being a criminal case his 'presence gives the approval of what the police are doing'. At the time he was readily available on the telephone and would regularly speak to Mr A in the evenings. He would spend the time with his client going through the documents in the case. Unfortunately, the police failed to provide him with many documents favourable to the defence case. About five months after Mr A made the confession to the police the solicitor discovered about 1300 witness statements that the police had failed to disclose to the defence. On 20 February 1997, Mr A handed a note to his solicitor stating that he had killed his cousin, but when asked whether he actually remembered doing it he replied 'No'. The solicitor told Mr A that such a confession was not valid. He had to give an account and an explanation and this was required.

The solicitor told me that Mr A's behaviour changed greatly after he was transferred from Haugesund to Bergen Prison. While in Haugesund he seemed very confused, unassertive and un-challenging of everything. While in Bergen Prison his uncertainties were gradually resolved and he became more confident and assertive.

MR A'S STRENGTHS AND VULNERABILITIES

The psychological assessment I conducted indicated that Mr A was a person of above average intellectual abilities. In addition, he had good memory and learning capacity. He was not particularly suggestible or compliant in his temperament and is in a general sense able to stand up for himself. He appeared able to assert himself appropriately. His academic background indicated that he was able to utilize his abilities very successfully. He also had the capacity and motivation for working hard at what is of interest to him. He was not mentally ill at the time of the assessment.

What were Mr A's enduring psychological vulnerabilities at the time of the assessment?

Psychological testing indicated that he was still over-sensitive in his temperament and he experienced an unusually strong feeling of persecution, which did not appear to have changed since he was assessed on the same test (MMPI) in July 1997. He was quite emotionally labile (a person who is prone to worry and experienced symptoms of anxiety), which may not be obvious to others.

Two further current psychological vulnerabilities were noted on psychological testing. First, when Mr A was asked specific questions where subtle errors were introduced his answers were unusual in that he was very hesitant and uncertain in his answers. This suggested that he had problems with discrepancy detection (i.e. he had difficulties identifying when errors we being introduced into his memory) and the confidence in his memory was easily undermined when he was placed under pressure. Secondly, even though Mr A's memory after two weeks was very good, with time his tendency to confabulate increased rapidly. This may have been related to his capacity for imaginative thinking.

It is likely that his poor discrepancy detection and proneness to producing confabulatory responses placed him in a vulnerable position when he was interrogated by officer E. There was considerable evidence that at the time of making the confession to officer E, and for several months afterwards, Mr A was suffering from a memory distrust syndrome and had a grossly impaired capacity to distinguish facts from fantasy (i.e. there was a breakdown in reality monitoring). The results of psychological testing conducted in July 1997 strongly supported the view that Mr A was depressed and in a state of confusion at the time. This confusional psychological state explains why it took him such a long time to be finally convinced of his innocence.

THE INTERROGATION AND CONFINEMENT

The effects of the custodial isolation that Mr A was subjected to should not be underestimated. There was ample evidence that he was very distressed by the fact that he was not allowed to see or communicate with his girlfriend and family, and this was clearly evident to the police officers. It is likely that the isolation had significant deleterious effects on his mental state and ability to cope with the interrogation. I had serious reservations about the legitimacy of the extreme restrictions associated with the custodial confinement. It is very likely that the intended purpose was to place pressure on Mr A to confess. It was oppressive in its effects upon Mr A.

Mr A was interviewed very extensively after he was arrested on 8 February 1997. The interviews appeared to have been particularly intense after the remand hearing on 10 February, after which Mr A began giving self-incriminating statements on 25 February. The interviews he was subjected to were inordinately long, there were insufficient breaks and the total number of hours of interviews was exceptionally long, at least by English standards.

Unfortunately, there was no contemporaneous recording of the content of the interviews and no audio- or video-recording was conducted. It is therefore impossible to know what exactly was said and done by Mr A and the two principal officers, officer E and officer F. The failure of officer E to properly record the sessions was a serious omission and indicated poor practice.

The notebooks of officers E and G gave an insight into the nature of the interview techniques applied and the involvement and the role of officer F in directing and shaping the interview process. Both the notebooks indicate that Mr A was subjected to persistent, deliberate and intense pressure and psychological manipulation. Is also appears from the two notebooks that officer F encouraged, if not insisted on, pressure being placed on Mr A in order to break down his resistance. There is also a reference in officer G's notebook, dated 25 February, on the day of the first confession statement, that officer F had been in contact with the Swedish psychiatrist, who had recommended that more pressure should be applied on Mr A in order to break down his resistance.

One of the most fundamental mistakes in this case, as far as the police interviews are concerned, is that Mr A was subjected to pressure and psychological manipulation by police officers with a strong 'confirmatory bias'. In this context a 'confirmatory bias' is characterized by the interviewers' (officers E and F) prior firm belief that Mr A was the perpetrator of the murder, as a result of which they focused in the interviews exclusively on eliciting statements from

Mr A that were consistent with these prior beliefs. The hallmark of their bias was their single-minded and persistent attempt to gather only confirmatory evidence and to avoid all avenues of enquiry that might have produced contradictory evidence. It is evident that the interview techniques and pressure applied to break down Mr A's resistance were driven and directed by this strong confirmatory bias.

Some of the psychological strategies used to extract a confession from Mr A, which were evident from the notebooks of officers E and G, included the following.

1. *Isolating him from friends and family.* I believe this was deliberately used as a form of pressure and the potential lifting of the restrictions was implicitly used as a form of inducement to confess.
2. *Exaggerating and overstating the strength of the evidence against Mr A.*
3. *Creating an atmosphere that would facilitate a confession* (e.g. officer E developing good rapport and trust and showing an understanding of how things might have gone wrong rather than the murder being deliberate and malicious; telling Mr A that his friends and family stood by him in spite of what he had done; offering to get professional help for him).
4. *Repeatedly challenging and undermining Mr A's own recollection concerning his alibi* (it appears that a great deal of the interviews centred around the so-called 'missing' two hours). When Mr A began to believe, falsely in my view, that he had a memory loss for the 'missing two hours', the memory loss or supposed psychogenic amnesia was not acceptable to the officers (indeed, officer F is quoted in officer G's notebook as stating 'Him not remembering was not acceptable, we wouldn't buy that', dated 19 February 1977).
5. Creating anxieties in Mr A about his maintaining his innocence (e.g. telling him that his talking about 'what had really happened' would increase his credibility with the court; that unless he talked about 'what he had done' he would not be able to sleep).
6. There are indications from officer E's own notebook that he coached Mr A on salient details concerning the crime scene. There are likely to be many other instances of coaching and leading questioning we do not know about, because they were not recorded.
7. Officer E utilized a number of different techniques for assisting Mr A with recovering his 'repressed memories'. This included asking him to write down what he thought could have happened, telling the story in the third person and utilizing a film script to tell the story. Mr A repeatedly stated that he could not remember anything, but officer E totally ignored this and encouraged him to give a story. In fact, officer E encouraged Mr A to produce a hypothetical and speculative account as the first step towards extracting a full confession. It seems from officer E's notebook that the idea of obtaining Mr A's account in the third person came from the Swedish psychiatrist, who was later to become an independent court-appointed expert.
8. Emphasizing the seriousness of the charges and the likely sentence he would receive if he did not cooperate (officer E's diary, 'there is no minimum sentence in this case because we still don't have anything other than

the result of what happened up there that night—the implication here is that if Mr A confessed and gave an account the sentence would be less, which amounts to an inducement consistent with pragmatic implications in the Kassin–Neumann (1997) model.

Mr A's legal advocate failed to provide him with the support that he needed during the interrogation sessions. In fact, there are a number of entries in the officers' notebooks that indicate that the solicitor colluded with the police in extracting a confession from his client. This appears to have been due to the solicitor being persuaded by the police that his client was guilty of the murder and their failure to provide him with essential documents in the case.

REPRESSION AND PSYCHOGENIC AMNESIA

It appears from officer E's notebook that he thought Mr A had repressed the memory for the murder and needed assistance to bring it into consciousness.

During the police interviews in 1995 and in January 1997, Mr A appeared firm in his belief about his movements on 6 May 1995. He claimed to have arrived home shortly after midnight, and this was confirmed by his parents. There was no evidence to indicate that immediately after the murder Mr A had a memory loss for the material time (i.e. around the time the murder was committed). During the inordinately long police interviews in February 1997 Mr A appeared to have gradually developed memory problems and uncertainties concerning his alibi, which are fundamental in understanding his confession to the murder of his cousin.

There are three possibilities concerning Mr A's apparent memory problems for the events on 6 May 1995, when the murder took place. First, Mr A fully remembered committing the murder, but he was unwilling or unable to admit to it until being assisted to do so by officer E. In other words, he was faking amnesia. There was no evidence to support this and it is an extremely unlikely scenario.

The second possibility is that Mr A had genuine amnesia for the murder due to a mechanism of repression, which slowly recovered over time during his conversations and interviews with the police. This was clearly the police view. This is based on the unlikely assumption that Mr A had 'recovered memories' of the murder during his interviews with officer E, which might have been either true or false memories of events. The problem here is that his apparent amnesia did not follow all of the characteristics typically found for psychogenic amnesias (Kopelman, 1995). That is, Mr A was apparently not psychotic and delusional at the time of the murder and he was not intoxicated with alcohol (in a study of amnesia and major crime in Iceland alcohol intoxication was a very important variable; see Gudjonsson, Petursson, Skulason & Sigurdardottir, 1989).

Mr A did fulfil one of the features commonly associated with psychogenic amnesia in that he did know the victim, although this does not appear to have been a close emotional relationship. In addition, there was never any suggestion of Mr A having amnesia about the murder until he had been extensively interviewed by the police, when his own alibi was apparently repeatedly challenged and he was trying hard to prove his whereabouts on the night of the murder.

It is extremely unlikely that Mr A suffered massive ('robust') repression about the murder without having some awareness of it (Brandon et al., 1998). All the evidence in the case suggested that he had no such awareness.

The third possibility is that Mr A's confession had resulted from a memory distrust syndrome. This was the position I took in my testimony. As discussed in Chapter 8, this condition is characterized by a confusional state where the person's confidence in his memory is seriously undermined and his susceptibility to developing a false belief and a false memory are greatly enhanced. Mr A, while in a vulnerable mental state and having problems with discrepancy detection, was subjected to psychological manipulation and pressure during long police interviews, which resulted in his making a false confession.

THE APPEAL

The appeal, which was a re-trial of the entire case, was heard by a jury of 10 persons and three judges. The trial lasted seven weeks, between 4 May and 17 June 1998. There was a civil case run concurrently with the criminal case involving compensation to the victim's family. This was a matter for the three judges to determine and not for the jury. During the second trial there was evidence from two British scientists concerning DNA found on two individual hairs from the crime scene; one was found in the dead victim's clenched fist. The hairs did not match those of the victim or Mr A. This evidence supported the defence case that Mr A was not the murderer. The prosecution claimed there had to have been some laboratory error in the analysis, such was their confidence in Mr A's confession and his guilt. There was no evidence ever found of a laboratory error.

During the appeal the appellant was the first person to give evidence. I listened to him give evidence. He was rigorously cross-examined by the presiding judge. Both the prosecutor and the presiding judge focused heavily on the incident of indecent exposure that had occurred when Mr A was aged 15. He was never charged with that offence, but it clearly became an important part of the evidence against Mr A in the murder and suspected rape of his cousin. He had remained embarrassed about the incident. It became public knowledge in the small community where he lived. His previous history of indecent exposure appears to have made him a prime suspect in the murder of his cousin, especially after a psychiatrist, commissioned by the police, visited the crime scene and spent two days with the police before Mr A was arrested. Apart from the dubious confession there was no evidence against Mr A.

I returned to Norway five weeks after the trial started to give my evidence. I testified on 8 and 9 June, immediately after the court had heard the testimony of a Swedish police psychiatrist, who now gave evidence as an independent court-appointed expert. His testimony lasted for almost a day and a half. I listened to the psychiatrist's evidence. He explained to the court his view that

Mr A had made a 'true' confession to the police. This view was based on his studying the documents in the case, which included the confession statements. When forming his opinion, he seemed to rely very much on the precise wording contained in the confession statements, even though the confessions had not been contemporaneously recorded. In addition, we do not know how contaminated the words and sentences attributed to Mr A had been due to the apparent absence of memory for the murder, the inordinately lengthy questioning and undoubtedly leading questioning.

The psychiatrist testified that on 21 January 1997 he had given a two hour lecture to the police in the case about offender profiling. Officer E attended the lecture. The psychiatrist had not interviewed Mr A and had refused the defence invitation to do so. He had not testified in a case of a disputed false confession before and had not made a study of false confessions.

After the psychiatrist had completed his testimony on the afternoon of 8 June, I went into the witness box and stated in accordance with my mandate that I considered the confession to be 'false'. I had extreme reservations about the validity of the confession and considered it unsafe to rely on it. The confession, I stated, had all the hallmarks of a false confession. In my testimony I outlined my assessment of Mr A, his psychological vulnerabilities during the custodial interrogation, the nature and content of the confession and the type of manipulation and police pressure that had resulted in the confession. The presiding judge hurried me through my evidence and made me shorten it considerably. Interestingly, the psychiatrist spent about twice as long in the witness box as I, telling the court that Mr A had made a 'true' confession. The judges appeared to allow him all the time he wanted to express his view that the confession was 'true' (i.e. at no point did I notice that he was he hurried through his evidence by the judges as I was). The main features of my evidence were as follows.

On the basis of the present psychological evaluation, I was satisfied, beyond any reasonable doubt, that Mr A had made a false confession to the police in February 1997. His false confession was of the coerced–internalized type.

One fundamental problem with the self-incriminating admissions Mr A made to the police related to his apparently confessing in detail to a crime of which he has no memory. It is clear that Mr A developed, during lengthy interviews with Officer E the *belief* that he had committed the murder and sexual assault. This belief was first documented on 20 February 1997. I obtained no satisfactory evidence that Mr A had ever had a recollection, either true or false, of having committed the murder. In this sense he made a totally unsatisfactory confession to murder, which should have had no legal standing. I had no doubt that Mr A tried very hard to bring out memories he believed were there, but this was apparently without success. This is a case of a false belief, which resulted from a *memory distrust syndrome*.

On 17 June the jury reached their verdict after nine hours of deliberation. They found Mr A not guilty of the murder of his cousin and he was released from prison. The following day the judges gave their verdict on the civil matter of compensation to the victim's family. In spite of the acquittal on the criminal charges, the judges considered that, on the balance of probabilities, Mr A had murdered his cousin and was ordered to pay Nkr 100 000 (approximately £10 000) to the victim's parents. The reason given by the presiding judge was Mr A's confession to the police. Apparently, my testimony that the confession was fundamentally flawed and 'false' was not accepted by the judges.

CONCLUSIONS

Guilt or Innocence?

Did Mr A commit the murder? Of course, there is no way of telling at present with 100% certainty whether or not he committed the murder. As far as I am concerned, I have found no evidence whatsoever to satisfy me, or to raise any serious suspicions, that he committed the murder. Indeed, I consider it highly probable that Mr A is totally innocent of murdering his cousin. The only evidence against him was the alleged confession, which probably did not amount to a confession at all. All Mr A confessed to was his belief that he had committed the murder: a belief that had been subtly implanted in his mind by the interviewing officer, officer E, who was absolutely certain of his guilt and made a patient and determined effort to elicit a confession from him, and succeeded in doing so. The nature of the confession ultimately obtained from Mr A falls into the category of false confession that Richard Ofshe (1989) describes in his influential article on internalized false confessions. There was also the DNA evidence, which by itself would normally have cast serious doubts on Mr A's guilt. The prosecution tried to discredit this evidence, undoubtedly because it did not support their prosecution case against Mr A. Basically, it seems, the prosecution and the judges would not accept that there had been a miscarriage of justice. They appeared to have had blind faith or sentimental trust in the police and confession evidence, or were incapable of accepting publicly that an error had occurred during the investigation with regard to the confession evidence.

On the basis of my knowledge of the case, I am satisfied that the content provided by Mr A in the confession statements was not based on his actual memory or knowledge of the murder. Nor did I think that Mr A had some 'robust suppression' after the offence, which enabled him to be totally unaware of his having killed his cousin.

The Swedish psychiatrist and I were both criticized in court by another court-appointed expert, a Norwegian psychiatrist, for taking extreme positions with regard to whether or not the confession was 'true' or 'false'. There are three things that I think justify my apparently 'extreme' position. First, I was answering a question dictated by the mandate given to me by the court. I did question the extreme nature of the mandate at the first meeting with the prosecution and defence team. I was instructed to act in accordance with the mandate. Of course, if I had been unable to come to an opinion regarding whether the confession was 'true' or 'false' I could have stated that I simply did not know. Second, the Swedish psychiatrist had already come to his, extreme, position that the confession was 'true'. Any reservations I had about the validity of the confession would inevitably place me in opposition to his views. Third, the nature and content of the confession, and the way it was elicited, gave me great concern about the validity of the confession. The confession was fundamentally flawed and I was in no doubt that it was unwise and unsafe to place any reliance on it.

This was indeed a very unusual case. The court's resistance in acknowledging the inherent problems with the confession highlights an attitude that needs to change.

Solitary Confinement

One of the lessons from the present case is the danger of using solitary confinement for suspects remanded in custody. During a visit to Norway in 1993 the European Committee for the Prevention of Torture and Inhuman or Degrading Treatment or Punishment (Council of Europe, 1997) noted and criticized the common practice by the Norwegian police of keeping suspects in solitary confinement over a prolonged period, and in some instances for up to a month, which is the maximum allowed by a court. The Committee stressed that it would not be acceptable for such measures to be applied with the aim of exerting psychological pressure on a detained person (Council of Europe, 1997). In the case of Mr A, there were strong indications, to say the least, that his solitary confinement was a way of exerting pressure on him to confess.

During the period 17–21 March 1997, the Committee again visited prisons in Bergen and Oslo. The prison in Bergen was the one to which Mr A was transferred to less than two weeks after his solitary confinement in Haugesund Regional Prison. Although Mr A was not kept in solitary confinement in Bergen Prison, it is of interest to note the comments of the Council of Europe with regard to the complaints of inmates in Bergen Prison who had been subjected to restrictions:

> Although they were interviewed separately, many of the detainees described suffering from similar experiences, when commenting on the effects of solitary confinement: fatigue, insomnia, loss of appetite, nausea, headaches, crying fits and bouts of depression becoming more acute as the solitary confinement continued. Some detainees mentioned suicidal thoughts; almost all referred to the distress consequent upon not being allowed contacts with families and friends. Foreign detainees who could not speak Norwegian or English were disturbed by the fact that their communication problems exacerbated their difficulties. The detainees' complaints were corroborated by both the prison staff with whom they were in daily contact and by social workers and medical staff (p. 13).

Therefore, the symptoms and problems reported by Mr A as a consequence of solitary confinement were not unique. His headaches, distress and low mood are probably largely attributable to the solitary confinement. However, his problems were undoubtedly exacerbated by the extensive and psychologically manipulative interrogation he was subjected to by officer E, which appeared, in conjunction with the solitary confinement, to have resulted in the confusional state that took many months to resolve. Fortunately, for Mr A, his memory was not permanently contaminated by the experience.

False Belief Versus False Memory

An interesting aspect of this case relates to Mr A's inability to create memories associated with the murder of his cousin. This is in great contrast to the case of Mr Evans, which was discussed in a previous chapter. On all accounts, Mr A tried very hard to 'force out' the memories after having been persuaded by the police that he had committed the murder. What were the protective factors which prevented his being able to create false memories of his involvement in the murder? Mr A seems to have believed that the memories of having committed the murder, and the details of the murder, would emerge from his 'unconscious' and 'repressed' mind. If it is true, as he says, that he was trying hard to 'get out' the repressed memories, what prevented him from being able to do so? Being able to understand the process involved is of great scientific importance.

Manipulation of Sexuality

An important aspect to this case was Mr A's sensitivity about his previous sexual misbehaviour. This was important to the outcome of the police interviews for three reasons. First, it made Mr A a prime suspect from very early on in the police investigation and diverted the police inquiry away from other, perhaps more noteworthy, suspects. Second, it made him vulnerable to psychological manipulation and trickery, which was the essence of officer E's interviewing strategy. Third, Mr A's previous sexual misbehaviour was used as evidence against him at the trial, not only by the prosecutor, but also by the presiding judge.

This case indicates a fundamental flaw and bias in his interviewing strategy, which is something commonly seen in cases of miscarriage of justice. Not approaching interviews with an open mind can have serious consequences on the outcome of interviews, as highlighted by Williamson (1994).

Postscript

Mr A appealed against the Gulating Court of Appeal's decision to pay the victim's family compensation for non-pecuniary damages. The case was heard in the Supreme Court of Norway on 24 September 1999 and the decision of the Court of Appeal was upheld (Case No. 63/1999). The case will be heard in the future in the European Court of Human Rights. In the meantime, two further developments have occurred. First, in May 2001, Mr A and his parents were awarded compensation for his wrongful conviction, but the sum awarded was substantially less than that claimed. The court ruled that on the balance of probability Mr A was innocent of the criminal charges brought against him, but it did not think his innocence was proven beyond a reasonable doubt. This decision has been appealed and will be heard in the Supreme Court in Oslo towards the end of the year 2002. The defence is hoping that by that time Mr A's innocence can be proved beyond a reasonable doubt. The Appeal Court has agreed to my testifying with regard to the confession.

The second important development is that the private detective in the case, Mr Harald Olsen, has discovered serious flaws in the original criminal investigation, where important evidence was not analysed or followed up and other good suspects were not properly investigated. This new evidence includes forensic evidence found at the crime scene, and a man who is now known to have been in the vicinity of the crime scene at the material time and shortly afterwards was seen covered in blood and very distraught. He subsequently committed suicide. The Norwegian police have not followed up these new lines of enquiry. However, on 6 February 2002, the Attorney General in Norway ordered an investigation into the new forensic evidence in the case. A crime scene DNA specimen was sent to Austria for analysis. At the beginning of September 2002 the results were announced. None of the DNA material matched Mr. A and a new murder enquiry is to commence. Hopefully the real murderer will be apprehended before long.

Conclusions

GENERAL COMMENTS AND CONCLUSIONS

I have discussed in detail the theoretical and empirical aspects of police interrogations and confessions and highlighted specific issues throughout the book by giving extensive case illustrations and research findings. I agree with Davies (1991) that it is only by creatively integrating theory and practice that interviewing can move closer to a science than to an art. We are getting closer to a full 'creative synthesis' of theory and practice. Indeed, as noted by Fisher (1993), important advances have been made in elevating the status of investigative interviewing from art to science. Since the publication of *The Psychology of Interrogations, Confessions and Testimony* in 1992, many further advances have been made in terms of understanding the psychological aspects of interrogations and confessions, and the factors that make people susceptible to making false confessions (i.e. the area of psychological vulnerability).

The amount of research conducted internationally in the field during the past two decades has been unprecedented. This has been accompanied by a number of High Court judgments in England and Northern Ireland, where convictions based chiefly on confession evidence in high profile murder and terrorist cases have been quashed on appeal. The impact of psychological research and expert testimony on law and procedure, police practice and legal judgments is a development unparalleled in the rest of the world. It demonstrates the crucial relationship between research and practice. In this book I have traced the relevant cases and scientific advances that have occurred and demonstrated their legal and psychological significance.

What has facilitated the legal changes, in addition to the impact of research, has been the willingness of the British Government, the judiciary and the police to accept that serious mistakes have been made and that something needed to be done about it. Valuable lessons have been learned as a result, which should encourage other nations to review their own practice.

The changes began with the Fisher Inquiry (1977) into the wrongful convictions of three youths who had made confessions to the police to the murder of Maxwell Confait. This was followed by the Royal Commission on Criminal Procedure (1981), research that emerged from the Commission, and significant changes in legal provisions with the introduction of the Police and Criminal

Evidence Act (PACE) 1984. Importantly, this involved the introduction of mandatory tape recording of police interviews with suspects and offered special safeguards for those who were deemed mentally disordered or 'at risk'. In October 1989 and March 1991, respectively, the convictions of the 'Guildford Four' and 'Birmingham Six' were quashed. The freeing of the 'Birmingham Six' resulted in the setting up of the Royal Commission on Criminal Justice (1993), with extensive research being commissioned into police interrogations, confessions, psychological vulnerability and the legal process.

In addition to the research emerging from the two Royal Commissions, a substantial amount of research had been carried out in Britain into false confessions and psychological vulnerability during interrogation. In the late 1980s and early 1990s this research was accompanied by increased recognition by the judiciary that wrongful convictions can occur from false confessions and psychological vulnerability. Not only did the Court of Appeal recognize the importance of expert evidence in cases of learning disability and mental illness, it came to recognize the concepts of 'interrogative suggestibility', 'compliance' and 'personality disorder' as factors that may render a confession unreliable. The single most important and influential legal judgement for psychologists was the case of Engin Raghip (one of the Tottenham Three), which was heard in the Court of Appeal in December 1991. Here the criteria for the admissibility of psychological evidence in cases of disputed confessions was substantially broadened to include borderline intelligence and personality factors such as suggestibility.

Since the landmark ruling in *Raghip*, there have been a number of other leading judgments in high profile murder or terrorist cases where convictions have been quashed on appeal. Out of the 22 appeal cases reviewed in detail in Part III of this book it was in half of these (*Raghip, Ward, Ali, Long, Kane, Evans, Roberts, King, Hall, Gordon* and *Fell*), that the psychological or psychiatric evidence was the most important new evidence that resulted in the conviction being overturned. In addition, *Pendleton*, whose appeal failed in June 2000, took his case to the House of Lords, where his conviction was quashed due to 'uncertainties and fresh psychological evidence'. The House of Lords ruled that the Court of Appeal had exceeded its authority in the case by intruding into the territory of the jury and upholding the conviction.

In relation to disputed confession cases, the attitude of High Court judges to expert psychological evidence, and their level of sophistication in evaluating it, have greatly improved since the late 1980s. The cases reviewed show that it is wrong to assume that only persons with learning disability or those who are mentally ill make unreliable or false confessions. The cases demonstrate the importance of personality factors in potentially rendering a confession unreliable. The focus of the English and Northern Ireland cases has largely been on psychological vulnerability rather than on custodial factors (e.g. interrogation techniques), although these two sets of factors are often reviewed jointly in the psychological evaluation. It is essential that the vulnerabilities identified by the psychologist or psychiatrist are relevant to the case, that they are measured reliably and corroborated as far as possible, and placed appropriately in the context of the totality of evidence in the case, including the nature of the interrogation.

Outside England and Northern Ireland there are still large battles to be fought in convincing the judiciary that miscarriages of justice can be occasioned by false confessions and psychological vulnerability. Judiciaries are typically very protective of the police and the integrity of the establishment. There is commonly a failure to recognize and accept mistakes, and when mistakes have occurred there is often poor motivation to learn from them and implement the necessary changes to prevent future miscarriages of justice. Institutions such as the police and the judiciary must approach cases with an open mind and be receptive to new ideas and scientific advances. Psychological evidence is often viewed as 'soft science', but with the advancement in assessment techniques and theory in relation to disputed confessions the scientific basis of such evidence is greatly improving. There is no doubt that many judges, including some British judges, believe that psychological vulnerabilities in the absence of diagnosed mental disorder (i.e. either learning disability or mental illness) should not be admitted into evidence. The fear seems to be the following.

1. Such evidence will infringe on the province of the jury. Personality traits such as suggestibility and compliance are seen by some judges as falling within the experience of members of the jury.
2. What emerges from the psychological evaluation is seen as being largely based on self-serving material from defendants, whose account is inherently unreliable.
3. A risk that opening the floodgates to legal submissions undermines the responsibility an individual must take for his or her actions.

I am of the view that judges should treat psychological evidence objectively and fairly. Psychological evidence clearly does not fall into the same category as DNA evidence in terms of its validity and scientific status, but a comprehensive evaluation carried out by an experienced and competent clinical psychologist can often provide valuable insights into the defendant's likely reactions to the interrogation and confinement, which will assist the jury in their deliberation. Abnormal traits of suggestibility and compliance, and their impact during interrogation, are not within the experience of the ordinary juror any more than are intellectual impairment and the most common types of mental illness. With regard to the second point of concern, there are various ways of corroborating what defendants say to reduce the potentially unreliable nature of self-serving statements. The third point represents a genuine fear and has been expressed in relation to other types of innovative psychological evidence (Gudjonsson & Sartory, 1983). I have noticed that in Britain defence lawyers are increasingly referring cases for psychological evaluation in the hope that it will reveal a vulnerability that will assist in ruling a confession statement inadmissible, even in cases where defendants fully admit their role in the offence to their lawyer (Gudjonsson, 1999b). Each case must of course be considered on its own merit. One way around this problem is for the prosecution to seek expert evidence in rebuttal and ensure the integrity and relevance of the expert defence assessment and conclusions. This is already happening in Britain and in recent years I have acted as an expert for defence and prosecution in about an equal proportion of cases.

Having evaluated many other experts' reports, my two greatest concerns regarding expert testimony are the poor quality of some of the assessments and the way in which psychological and psychiatric evidence can be misrepresented and abused by experts and legal advocates. The psychological evaluation of cases involving disputed confessions is complicated. It requires considerable knowledge, experience and expertise in the fields of forensic psychology, interrogations and confessions, psychometric testing and clinical evaluation. Poor psychological testimony falls into two overlapping categories: first, evidence that fails to inform the court of the relevant information; and second, evidence that misleads the court. The main reasons for poor psychological evidence are poor preparation, lack of knowledge, experience and thoroughness, inappropriate use or misinterpretation of test results, failure to place test results appropriately in the context of the case and bias (Gudjonsson & Haward, 1998). In addition, with the courts becoming more receptive to psychological evidence, defence lawyers may on occasions abuse such evidence in order to secure acquittals (Gudjonsson & MacKeith, 1997). Colluding with such practice undermines the integrity of the expert and the profession as a whole. As Florian (1999) so elegantly put it,

> A delicate balance must be struck between protecting all citizens from involuntarily making self incriminating statements while at the same time not allowing mental illness to serve as a shield against the consequences of a truly voluntary confession (p. 292).

The focus in this book is on two different legal systems: the law and practice in England (and Wales) and North America, respectively. There are important differences between these two legal systems with regard to both the *admissibility of a confession*, decided at a suppression (*voire dire*) hearing, and the *admissibility of expert testimony*. In England there is more protection available for suspects detained for questioning than there is in the USA. A major problem with American cases is that the questions and answers obtained during the interrogation are often not fully recorded and it is impossible to verify what exactly was said and done. It is the defendant's word against that of the police, which almost invariably goes in the favour of the police. A tape recording of the entire interrogation process is invaluable and offers the single most important protection for detainees, and for the integrity of the police. Of course, mandatory tape-recording is not a foolproof procedure, because some officers compensate by shifting suggestions and pressure from the formal police interview to other parts of the investigative process (e.g. informal conversations and suspects being placed under pressure prior to or between interviews).

The English courts are less tolerant than American courts of police impropriety. PACE and the Codes of Practice for English police officers provide an important control and influence over their behaviour in relation to the arrest, detention and interrogation of suspects. The most important components in relation to detention and interrogation are the following.

- Mandatory tape recording of suspect interviews.
- Improved access to solicitors.

- Regular use of forensic medical examiners and appropriate adults in cases of suspected medical problems and psychological vulnerability.
- The recognition of the need of suspects for appropriate breaks and rest.
- The creation of the role of a Custody Officer.

PACE also introduced new standards for determining the admissibility of suspect interviews at trial, which allows the courts to exclude evidence both on the basis of police impropriety and psychological vulnerability.

American trial judges are more reluctant than English judges to suppress confession statements, provided suspects have been given their legal rights or were considered by the court to be competent to waive their legal rights. The American courts, unlike the English courts, have great difficulties with suppressing confession evidence when in their view there is absence of police coercion (i.e. the focus is almost exclusively on the behaviour of the police rather than on the vulnerability of the suspect).

There are different standards for the admissibility of expert testimony in England than there are in the American courts. There are no parallel English tests to the *Frye* and *Daubert* standards and exclusionary rules. In England, scientists, including psychologists and psychiatrists, automatically qualify as experts provided they are testifying on the subject of their expertise.

INTERROGATION

The term 'investigative interviewing' is now commonly used in England to refer to both suspect and witness interviews. The term accompanied the introduction of new police training manuals and national training courses on interviewing, where there was a general move away from interviewing suspects primarily for obtaining a confession to obtaining complete and reliable information, using techniques based on the cognitive interview approach (Fisher & Geiselman, 1992). This represents a more ethical and scientific approach to interviewing and should result in fewer wrongful convictions in the future.

An important development since 1992 has been that English police officers now routinely receive basic training in interviewing techniques and a recent review of the effectiveness of training has produced some positive results. Nevertheless, there is scope for further improvements, particularly in relation to officers integrating their training more effectively into practice. There also needs to be better supervision of interviews and more constructive feedback provided to interviewers. There are greater problems in relation to the interviewing of witnesses where the quality of the interviewing appears to be inferior to that of suspect interviews. Ideally, all such interviews, at least in serious cases, should also be tape-recorded and greater care needs to be taken to ensure that witnesses are not led or pressured by interviewers. Serious problems do sometimes arise where witnesses are subsequently interviewed as suspects and there is an unsatisfactory record of what was said and done during those prior interviews.

With the implementation of the Police and Criminal Evidence Act (PACE) in January 1986, and the accompanying Codes of Practice, research has shown that the manipulative tactics of the past have been largely eliminated. The review presented in this book has revealed that there is an important interaction between the seriousness of the offence and the nature of the pressure applied by officers to break down resistance. As demonstrated in Chapter 4, in serious criminal cases where there is an initial resistance to confess, English police officers still sometimes resort to American-style tactics to overcome resistance and secure a confession. This is undertaken even when there is a considerable risk of the confession being rendered inadmissible by a court and the defendant acquitted. The newly developed *Police Interviewing Analysis Framework* (PIAF) objectively analyses, measures and displays the nature and type of tactics employed by the British police to break down resistance.

Nevertheless, in general the persuasive interrogation style of the past has been replaced in England by questioning that is less manipulative in nature and is not dependent on lying to suspects. Interestingly, this change in approach does not appear to have had detrimental effects on the confession rate (see below).

The style and culture of interviewing is very different in the USA than it is in England. Influential interrogation manuals, such as that of Inbau *et al.* (2001), typically recommend trickery, deceit and psychological manipulation as a way of breaking down the suspect's resistance during interviews and the American courts are tolerant of this approach. There is undoubtedly a fear among the American judiciary and some academics that if the police were not able to exert pressure and trickery during interrogation there would be a significant reduction in the confession rate and an enormous social cost. How realistic this fear is remains to be seen. Based on the English experience, assuming there would be parallel outcomes, which may of course not necessarily be the case, this fear may be overstated.

The tactics and techniques recommended by Inbau and his colleagues are undoubtedly effective in overcoming resistance in some cases and eliciting confessions, although there is no empirical evidence available to prove their effectiveness. In my view, some of the tactics recommended in order to obtain a confession (e.g. police officers implying to suspects that they themselves have committed, or thought of committing, similar offences) are unethical. Furthermore, the statement by the authors of these techniques that they do not result in a false confession is naïve: simply, we do not know how often such techniques result in a false confession or other types of erroneous testimony. The procedure recommended by Inbau *et al.* (2001) of 'softening up' suspects in an informal pre-interrogation interview, which does not require suspects to be advised of their legal rights, and then tricking them into making a confession during a formal interrogation, is also a potentially dangerous procedure. It seems that in practice the distinction between informal and formal interviews is sometimes quite blurred and is abused by officers. To prevent possible miscarriages of justice, informal interviews should ideally be tape-recorded along with any subsequent interrogation. What is needed is more research into the effectiveness and pitfalls of different methods of interviewing suspects and witnesses.

The focus in this book has been on custodial interrogation, where suspects are technically in the custody of police, have been advised of their legal rights and are formally interviewed. As discussed in Chapter 22, self-incriminating admissions and confessions that are obtained by undercover officers can present serious problems, and it is this area of activity that requires greater attention from research.

PSYCHOLOGICAL VULNERABILITY

There is no doubt that there are large individual differences in the ways in which suspects cope with police interviews and custodial confinement. This ranges from those detainees who are so mentally disturbed that they are not 'fit for interview' to those who are 'at risk', under certain circumstances, of giving misleading statements to the police because of some psychological vulnerability (e.g. low intellectual functioning, high suggestibility and compliance, psychotic symptoms, anxiety and phobic problems, and personality disorder). Research into the psychological vulnerabilities of detainees dates back to the early 1980s (Irving, 1980). However, prior to 1993 only three English studies had investigated the psychological vulnerabilities of persons detained at police stations. The main weakness of the studies was that the evaluation was based on observations only (i.e. no formal interview or psychometric testing was conducted). Gudjonsson *et al.* (1993) conducted the first study where detainees were formally assessed psychologically at the police station prior to their being interviewed by the police. It revealed important findings about the nature and extent of psychological vulnerabilities among detainees, which were discussed in detail in Chapter 3. Among the most important findings were the low IQ score of many detainees and the fact that many persons with intellectual deficits could not be identified as such from a brief clinical interview. Similarly, other potentially relevant psychological vulnerabilities, such as suggestibility, compliance, acquiescence, mild depression and specific anxiety problems, are difficult to identify without a formal clinical evaluation.

In addition to the vulnerability study, our research into *Devising and Piloting an Experimental Version of the Notice to Detained Persons* (Clare & Gudjonsson, 1992) has assisted with identifying how persons at risk during police detention can be better identified by the police so that their legal rights are fully protected. Our recommendations to the Royal Commission that the police should routinely ask detainees specific questions to assist with identification of vulnerabilities has now been adopted by the Metropolitan (London) Police Service and incorporated into the Custody Record. This demonstrates how research can influence police practice.

An important factor in this research development has been the 'partnership' formed between the Institute of Psychiatry and the Metropolitan Police, which has stimulated collaborative research and improved police practice (Fenner, Gudjonsson & Clare, 2002; Gudjonsson *et al.*, 1993; Medford, Gudjonsson & Pearse, 2000).

TRUE CONFESSIONS

There are many reasons why people would be reluctant to confess to crimes they have committed. These include fear of legal sanctions, concern about one's reputation, not wanting to accept what one has done, not wanting friends and family to know and fear of retaliation. In view of this it is perhaps surprising to find that almost 60% of suspects in England make self-incriminating admissions or confessions during custodial interrogation. Contrary to my previous prediction (Gudjonsson, 1992a), the rate has not fallen following the implementation of PACE. This finding is particularly important in that following PACE there has been a dramatic increase in the use of legal advisers at police stations, a practice that has grown from less than 10% in the mid-1980s to over one-third in the mid-1990s. How can this be explained when the presence of a legal advisor is a significant predictor of a denial? One possible explanation is that it is not the presence of a lawyer itself that is of significance in 'run-of-the-mill' cases; rather it is characteristics of those suspects who elect to have legal advice that is of importance. It is evident from English research reviewed in this book that most suspects enter the police interview having already decided whether or not to confess and they stick to that position: only in the more serious cases where the interviews tend to be longer and more pressured is resistance likely to be broken down.

A number of models about confessions have been reviewed. Each of the models makes somewhat different assumptions about why suspects confess during custodial interrogation, although there is considerable overlap between some of the models. It is only recently that empirical studies have attempted to test out specific hypotheses generated by the models. A number of studies have been conducted so far and some general conclusions can be drawn about the reasons why suspects confess to crimes about which they are interrogated. Factors such as age and previous convictions appear to be related to readiness to confess, but these variables should be studied in conjunction with other variables, such as the seriousness of the offence, the strength of the evidence against the suspect, and access to legal advice. There is evidence that suspects confess due to a combination of factors, rather than to one factor alone. Three general factors appear to be relevant, in varying degrees, to most suspects. These include *internal* pressure (e.g. feelings of remorse, the need to talk about the offence), *external* pressure (e.g. fear of confinement, police persuasiveness) and perception of *proof* (e.g. the suspects' perceptions of the strength of evidence against them). The single strongest incentive to confess relates to the strength of the evidence against suspects. Furthermore, those who confess because of strong evidence against them, and where there is an internal need to confess, appear to be subsequently most content about their confession. Confessions that result from police persuasiveness and pressure are likely to be retracted and seem to leave suspects disgruntled and resentful.

In a follow-up study to our Royal Commission study (Gudjonsson *et al.*, 1993), we investigated the relationship between psychological variables assessed immediately prior to interrogation and the likelihood of detainees' subsequently confessing to the police (Pearse *et al.*, 1998). None of the tests predicted either confession or denial. This finding is probably due to the fact that the police interviews were generally very short and without any obvious interrogative pressure and, as a consequence, specific psychological vulnerabilities were of less importance. Once the pressure in interviews becomes more evident then psychological vulnerabilities are likely to play a more prominent role in the suspects' abilities to resist suggestions and pressure (Gudjonsson, 1999b). The only mental state factor in the study that predicted a confession was whether or not the suspect had consumed illicit drugs within 24 hours of arrest. The most likely explanation of this is that suspects addicted to drugs confessed more readily than other detainees, because they wanted to expedite their release from custody (we do not know whether any of these suspects made a false confession; for the purpose of this book I am assuming the confessions were all true). As illustrated in this book, on occasion, drug withdrawal in custody can result in a false confession to a serious crime. In the study, the presence of a lawyer and a previous experience of imprisonment were highly predictive of suspects denying any involvement in the crime.

How important confessions are in solving crimes depends primarily upon the strength of the alternative evidence against suspects. Where the alternative evidence is strong a confession may add little or nothing to the prosecution case, although in some cases it does provide important additional information about motive and intent. It seems from the available studies that confession evidence is crucial to a significant proportion of criminal cases. Once a suspect has confessed, even where there is little or no corroborative evidence, the chances of a conviction are substantial.

It seems that the admission/confession rate is substantially lower in the USA than it is in England. The difference is in the region of about 15%, although this figure should be interpreted with caution due to the scarcity of recent American studies into confession rates. One possible reason for the difference in the confession rates may relate to the greater impact of the *Miranda* rules on the confession rate than the restrictions imposed by PACE. Unlike the case in America, in England the presence of a legal advisor, or suspects exercising their right of silence, does not prevent the police from interviewing them and putting questions to them, which sometimes results in a confession being obtained. Other factors, including cultural and attitudinal ones, the base rate of guilty suspects arrested and interrogated and the nature of interrogation and custodial environment are also undoubtedly important in explaining cross-cultural differences in confession rates.

RETRACTED AND FALSE CONFESSIONS

It is important to distinguish between proven false confessions, retracted confessions and disputed confessions that have not been retracted. Confessions are commonly disputed at trial when there is absence of good independent corroboration. What proportion of these disputed cases represent genuinely false confessions is not possible to estimate, but it is likely to be in a minority of cases. On the other hand, once an apparently credible false confession is given to the police it is often impossible for the individual concerned to subsequently prove his innocence. This is particularly the case if the confession contains a detailed post-admission narrative account with apparent special knowledge of the crime scene. Such special knowledge in the case of innocent persons arises through contamination (e.g. the case details were communicated by the police or obtained through some other sources, such as from the media or the real culprit). Recent improvements in forensic science, particularly DNA technology, have greatly assisted in proving actual innocence. This situation has improved considerably in England with the independence of the Forensic Science Service from the police. However, there are still worrying tendencies for some police forces to resist investigating available evidence that might exonerate an accused or convicted person, or for crucial forensic evidence to become lost while in the possession of and under the control of the police.

It is not known how frequently false confessions to the police happen and there is likely to be considerable variability across countries due to cultural factors and differences in police practice. There are methodological difficulties in establishing reliable data due to inherent problems in establishing the 'ground truth' (i.e. the factual basis of the confession). In cases where the confession is the main evidence against defendants, a retraction prior to trial is essentially self-serving and must accordingly be treated with caution. Nevertheless, there are many documented cases where defendants have made false confessions, and a retraction of a confession where there is no solid independent corroborative evidence should always be investigated with an open mind. In addition, not all false confessions are retracted and two recent studies conducted among Icelandic prison inmates have highlighted the frequency with which people make false confessions to the police as a way of protecting a significant other (i.e. a peer, friend or relative). This group of false confessors has been neglected in research, because they do not readily come to the attention of researchers and other professionals.

False confession is undoubtedly a universal phenomenon, but considerable cross-cultural variability is likely to exist. The higher the base rate of innocent suspects interrogated, which is not uncommonly seen in terrorist cases and some notorious murder cases where the police trawl in a large number of people for interrogation, the greater the proportion of false confessions that are likely to occur. In such cases there is often a great deal of pressure on the police to solve the case and this often influences their methods of extracting confessions from suspects.

Innocent suspects do sometimes give incriminating information to the police that, on the face of it, seems to have originated from the perpetrator. Such apparently 'guilty knowledge', which often makes the confession look credible, is then used to substantiate the validity of the confession given. The lesson to be learned from cases presented in this book is that unless the information obtained was unknown to the police, or actually produces further evidence to corroborate it (e.g. the discovery of a body or murder weapon), then great caution should be exercised in the inferences that should be drawn from it about the suspect's guilt. Police officers will undoubtedly find it difficult to believe that they could inadvertently communicate salient information to suspects in this way, but it happens.

The reasons why people make false confessions to the police are numerous and vary from case to case. The reasons may include the following: a desire for notoriety, a wish to be released from custody, not being able to cope with the pressure of the police interview, not being able to distinguish facts from fantasy, wanting to protect someone else and taking revenge on the police or someone else (e.g. by implicating others). The cases reviewed in this book demonstrate the importance of having a good conceptual framework for understanding the process and mechanisms of false confession.

Kassin and Wrightsman (1985) identified three distinct types of false confession, which are referred to as 'voluntary', 'coerced–compliant' and 'coerced–internalized' false confessions. Each type has a distinctive set of antecedents, conditions and psychological consequences, but should not be viewed as necessarily exclusive categories, because they may on occasions overlap between the different groups (e.g. a 'coerced–compliant' false confession changing into a 'coerced–internalized' false confession). In spite of the importance and influence of the Kassin and Wrightsman model, some weaknesses have been identified. In order to overcome these, I propose a slightly refined version of the Kassin and Wrightsman original model and recommend two changes. First, the term *coerced* should be substituted by the term *pressured*. This overcomes problems related to legal definitions and applications of the term coercion. Secondly, I propose a bivariate classification system that distinguishes between the three types of false confession (i.e. voluntary, compliant and internalized) and categorizes the source of pressure (i.e. internal, custodial or non-custodial).

How can true confessions be differentiated from false confessions? In the absence of good forensic, eyewitness or alibi evidence, or a solid confession from somebody else, it is typically very difficult to establish the ground or historical truth of the confession. The focus of the psychological evaluation is typically on the reliability or voluntariness of the confession rather than its historical truthfulness.

The psychological evaluation is normally based on a comprehensive assessment of the defendant and the identification of relevant strengths and vulnerabilities, the circumstances and nature of the relevant custodial factors involved, the tactics and techniques used during the interrogation, the content of the post-admission statement and the timing and nature of the retraction. No psychological technique is available that will demonstrate with complete certainty the truthfulness of a confession. What the psychological evaluation is sometimes able to do is to identify psychological vulnerabilities or mental health problems that, when placed in the context of the totality of the circumstances in the case, cast serious doubts on the reliability or trustworthiness of the confession. Each case must be considered on its own merit. Of crucial importance is to have a good overview of the entire case and its total surrounding circumstances, and to formulate a good psychological understanding of the processes involved that resulted in the confession. There are different factors operating in individual cases and generalizing from one case to another can be helpful but should be done with caution. The expert's work typically involves evaluating the interaction between the interrogation and custodial environment on the one hand, and psychological vulnerabilities and mental health factors on the other. Specific vulnerabilities, such as low intelligence, mental illness, proneness to anxiety, high suggestibility, a strong tendency to comply with people in authority, drug addiction and eagerness to please, may all contribute in varying degrees to a fuller understanding of cases. Cases reviewed in this book show that false confessions are not confined to the mentally ill and those with learning disability (also known as mental handicap and mental retardation). The view that apparently normal individuals would not seriously incriminate themselves when interrogated by the police is wrong and this point should be recognized by the judiciary.

I have discussed the clinical assessment of retracted confession cases in detail. This is a highly specialized area of forensic psychology and often requires considerable knowledge, skill, experience and intuition. In recent years the conceptual framework for assessing such cases, the development of psychological tests for assessing individual vulnerabilities and greater understanding of the factors that break down resistance during interrogation have advanced immensely. One important development has been the construction and standardization of scales for assessing interrogative suggestibility and compliance. One of the most difficult questions with regard to such concepts as 'suggestibility' and 'compliance' relates to the extent to which one can generalize from test scores to trait concepts and from test scores retrospectively to a real life interrogation, which in some cases happened many years previously. A psychological evaluation of individuals many years, and in some cases decades, after the interrogation is problematic, but I have shown in this book that such an evaluation is possible and can often be effectively undertaken.

I have argued and shown that different types of false confession are associated with different psychological factors. As a general rule, internalized false confessions are easier to identify on psychological grounds than compliant false confessions, because of the tentative language often used by suspects making such confessions, the nature of the interrogation that produces a false confession in such cases, and the prominent psychological vulnerabilities present at the time (i.e. distrust of one's memory, problems with discrepancy detection, susceptibility to suggestions, good imagination and tendency towards confabulation). Interestingly, the internalized false confessors reviewed in this book were intellectually normal, and on the whole they were brighter than the pressured–compliant false confessors.

As far as pressured–internalized false confessions are concerned, these are typically accompanied by unstable changes in a belief system, but occasionally a false memory is also generated. Imagination plays an important role in producing a false belief and a false memory. Future research should focus on understanding why in some cases a false belief is accompanied by a false memory, while in others there is only false belief, even when the person tries very hard to 'recall' what allegedly happed in the commission of the crime. A false memory is more likely to accompany a false belief when there is an internal pressure and motivation to believe in one's involvement in the crime or victim abuse (e.g. as sometimes seen in cases of a false memory of childhood sexual abuse), rather than when there is only an external pressure to remember (e.g. police suggestions and pressure).

Only one study has investigated empirically the differences between true and false confessions using a within-subject design (Sigurdsson & Gudjonsson, 1996). The findings indicated that when making the false confession suspects had experienced far more police pressure and less internal pressure to confess than when making a confession to a crime they had committed. The implication is that making a false confession is largely associated with police pressure and the greater the pressure the more likely suspects are to make a false confession, but this does also depend on the nature of the false confession. The second finding was that being under the influence of alcohol or drugs at the time of the alleged offence, or during the police interrogation, makes suspects more susceptible to believing that they have committed an offence of which they are innocent. This has important theoretical and practical implications and requires further research.

Finally, investigative interviewing forms a crucial part of most police investigations. A well and fairly conducted interview of victims, witnesses and suspects is in the interests of justice. There is an inherent and inevitable pressure on suspects to incriminate themselves during custodial interrogation. The pressure may be due to custodial and interrogative factors, psychological vulnerability or most typically a combination of factors. There is a fine line between *legitimate* and *excessive* custodial and interrogative pressure. This book has shown the strengths and potential pitfalls of interrogation and confessions. Many important lessons have been learned and are documented in this book. Unprecedented scientific and legal advances have been made in Britain in recent years. This has been a painful transition, but an invaluable learning process, where many weaknesses throughout the criminal system have been exposed in public. What one is left with is a more open, more accountable and fairer system. It is now time for all judicial systems to review their procedures and practice, learn from the new developments and have the courage and willingness to implement the necessary changes.

APPENDIX

The Gudjonsson Confession Questionnaire—Revised (GCQ-R)*

Below are a number of questions concerning why some people confess to the offences that they have committed. Please read each question carefully and circle the number which applies best to your confession.

	Not at all		Somewhat		Very much	
1. Did you think that after confessing you would be allowed to go home?	1 2	3	4	5	6	7
2. Did you confess because you felt guilty about the offence?	1 2	3	4	5	6	7
3. Did you believe that there was no point in denying it?	1 2	3	4	5	6	7
4. Did you feel you wanted to get it off your chest?	1 2	3	4	5	6	7
5. Did you think that you might get a lighter sentence if you confessed?	1 2	3	4	5	6	7
6. Did you think the police would eventually prove you did it?	1 2	3	4	5	6	7
7. Did you confess because of police pressure during the interview?	1 2	3	4	5	6	7
8. Would you have confessed to the police if they had not suspected you of the offence?	1 2	3	4	5	6	7
9. Did you think it was in your own interest to confess?	1 2	3	4	5	6	7
10. Did you confess because you believed that your co-defendant(s) would implicate you? (Please ignore this question if there were no co-defendants.)	1 2	3	4	5	6	7
11. Did you confess to protect somebody else?	1 2	3	4	5	6	7
12. Are you now pleased that you confessed?	1 2	3	4	5	6	7
13. Do you think you would have confessed if at the time you had fully realised the consequences of doing so?	1 2	3	4	5	6	7
14. Did you experience a sense of relief after confessing?	1 2	3	4	5	6	7

		Not at all			Somewhat		Very much	
15.	Did you confess because you were afraid about what would happen if you did not confess?	1	2	3	4	5	6	7
16.	Were you initially very unwilling to confess?	1	2	3	4	5	6	7
17.	Do you think you confessed too readily or hastily?	1	2	3	4	5	6	7
18.	Do you feel the police bullied you into confessing?	1	2	3	4	5	6	7
19.	Did you feel tense or nervous whilst being interviewed by the police?	1	2	3	4	5	6	7
20.	Were your rights explained to you?	1	2	3	4	5	6	7
21.	Did you at the time understand what your rights were?	1	2	3	4	5	6	7
22.	Did you understand the Police Caution?	1	2	3	4	5	6	7
23.	Did you confess because you were frightened of being locked up?	1	2	3	4	5	6	7
24.	Did you become confused during the police interviews?	1	2	3	4	5	6	7
25.	Did you feel you confessed because you did not cope well with the police interviews?	1	2	3	4	5	6	7
26.	Did thoughts (or talks with) your family and friends make it more difficult for you to confess?	1	2	3	4	5	6	7
27.	Do you now regret having confessed?	1	2	3	4	5	6	7
28.	Did you at first deny having committed the offence?	1	2	3	4	5	6	7
29.	Did the thought that you might be viewed by others as a 'criminal' make you less willing to confess?	1	2	3	4	5	6	7
30.	Did you confess because you had the need to talk to somebody?	1	2	3	4	5	6	7
31.	Did you confess because at the time you felt you needed help?	1	2	3	4	5	6	7
32.	Did you find it difficult to confess because you did not want others to know what you had done?	1	2	3	4	5	6	7
33.	Did you find it difficult to confess because you did not want to accept what you had done?	1	2	3	4	5	6	7
34.	Did you confess because the police persuaded you it was the right thing to do?	1	2	3	4	5	6	7
35.	Did you confess because you were frightened of the police?	1	2	3	4	5	6	7
36.	Did you confess because you saw no point in denying at the time?	1	2	3	4	5	6	7
37.	Did you confess because at the time you believed the police would beat you up if you did not confess?	1	2	3	4	5	6	7

38.	Would you have confessed if a solicitor had been present during the interrogation? (Please ignore this question if a solicitor was present during the interrogation.)	1	2	3	4	5	6	7
39.	Did you exaggerate your involvement in the offence?	1	2	3	4	5	6	7
40.	Did you find it difficult to confess because you were ashamed about having committed the offence?	1	2	3	4	5	6	7
41.	Did you confess because you felt isolated from your family and friends?	1	2	3	4	5	6	7
42.	Did you find it difficult to confess because you wanted to avoid the consequences (e.g. be sentenced, go to prison)?	1	2	3	4	5	6	7
43.	Did you minimise your involvement in the offence when interviewed by the police?	1	2	3	4	5	6	7
44.	Did you confess because you were apprehended committing the offence?	1	2	3	4	5	6	7
45.	Did you confess because it was obvious that you had committed the offence?	1	2	3	4	5	6	7
46.	Did you find it difficult to confess because you wanted to cover up the offence in order to protect a co-defendant?	1	2	3	4	5	6	7
47.	Did you confess because your co-defendant implicated you?	1	2	3	4	5	6	7
48.	Were you under the influence of alcohol during the police interview?	1	2	3	4	5	6	7
49.	Were you under the influence of other intoxicating substances during the police interview?	1	2	3	4	5	6	7
50.	Did you experience withdrawal symptoms during the police interview?	1	2	3	4	5	6	7
51.	Were you under the influence of alcohol when you committed the offence?	1	2	3	4	5	6	7
52.	Were you under the influence of other intoxicating substances during the offence?	1	2	3	4	5	6	7

* Gudjonsson and Sigurdsson (1999)

References

Abed, R.T. (1995). Voluntary false confessions in a Munchausen patient: a new variant of the syndrome. *Irish Journal of Psychological Medicine*, **12**, 24–26.
Abramson, L.Y., Seligman, M.E.P. & Teasdale, J.D. (1978). Learned helplessness in humans: critique and reformulations. *Journal of Abnormal Psychology*, **87**, 49–74.
Acker, J., Cunningham, E., Donovan, P., Fitzgerald, A., Flexon, J., Lombard, J., Ryn, B. & Stodghill, B. (1998). *Gone but not forgotten: investigating cases of eight New Yorkers (1914–1939)*. Paper presented at the Annual Meeting of the American Society of Criminology, Washington, DC, USA.
Action for Justice (2001). Achieving Best Evidence in Criminal Proceedings: Guidance for Vulnerable or Intimidated Witnesses, including Children. London: Home Office Communication Directorate.
Adams, C.H. (1993). The psychology of interrogations, confessions and testimony. A book review. *British Journal of Criminology*, **33**, 581–582.
Agar, J.R. (1999). The admissibility of false confession expert testimony. *Army Lawyer*, August, 26–43.
Allen, R.C. (1966). Toward an exceptional offender's court. *Mental Retardation*, **4**, 3–7.
American Association of Mental Deficiency (1974). *Adaptive Behavior Scale manual*. Washington, DC: American Association of Mental Deficiency.
Asch, S.E. (1951). Effects of group pressure upon the modification and distortion of judgments. In H. Guetzkow (Ed.), *Groups, leadership, and men*. Pittsburgh, PA: Carnegie.
Asch, S.E. (1952). *Social psychology*. New York: Prentice-Hall.
Asch, S.E., Block, H. & Hertzman, M. (1938). Studies in the principles of judgements and attitudes: two basic principles of judgement. *Journal of Psychology*, **5**, 219–251.
Atkinson L. (1990). Intellectual and adaptive functioning: some tables for interpreting the Vineland in combination with intelligence tests. *American Journal of Mental Retardation*, **95**, 198–203.
Aveling, F. & Hargreaves, H. (1921). Suggestibility with and without prestige in children. *British Journal of Psychology*, **11**, 53–75.
Ayling, C.J. (1984). Corroborating confessions: an empirical analysis of legal safeguards against false confessions. *Wisconsin Law Review*, **4**, 1121–1204.
Baden, M. & Hennessee, J.A. (1992). *Unnatural death. Confessions of a forensic pathologist*. London: Warners.
Bain, S.A. & Baxter, J.S. (2000). Interrogative suggestibility: the role of interviewer behaviour. *Legal and Criminological Psychology*, **5**, 123–133.
Baldwin, J. (1992a). *Video taping police interviews with suspects: a national evaluation. Police Research Series Paper 1*. London: Home Office Police Department.
Baldwin, J. (1992b). *The role of legal representatives at the police station. Royal Commission on Criminal Justice Research Study No. 2*. London: HMSO.
Baldwin, J. (1993). Police interviewing techniques. Establishing truth or proof? *The British Journal of Criminology*, **33**, 325–352.

Baldwin, J. (1994). Police interrogation: what are the rules of the game? In D. Morgan and G.M. Stephenson (Eds), *Suspicion and silence. The right to silence in criminal investigation*. London: Blackstone, 66–76.

Baldwin, J. & McConville, M. (1980). *Confessions in Crown Court trials. Royal Commission on Criminal Procedure Research Study No. 5*. London: HMSO.

Bandura, A., Ross, D. & Ross, S.A. (1963). A comparative test of the status envy, social power, and secondary reinforcement theories of identificatory learning. *Journal of Abnormal Social Psychology*, **67**, 527–534.

Barber, T.X. & Calverley, D.S. (1964).'Hypnotic-like' suggestibility in children and adults. *Journal of Abnormal Social Psychology*, **66**, 589–597.

Barnes, J.A. & Webster, N. (1980). *Police interrogation: tape recording. Royal Commission on Criminal Procedure Research Study No. 8*. London: HMSO.

Barthel, J. (1976). *A death in Canaan*. New York: Congdon.

Basoglu, M., Paker, M., Paker, O., Oezmen, E. et al. (1994). Psychological effects of torture: a comparison of tortured with nontortured political activists in Turkey. *American Journal of Psychiatry*, **151**(1), 76–81.

Baxter, J.S. (1990). The suggestibility of child witnesses: a review. *Applied Cognitive Psychology*, **3**, 393–407.

Baxter, J.S. & Boon, J.C.W. (2000). Interrogative suggestibility: the importance of being earnest. *Personality and Individual Differences*, **28**, 753–762.

Bean, P. & Nemitz, T. (1994). *Out of depth and out of sight*. London: MENCAP.

Beaumont, M. (1987). Confession, cautions, experts and the sub-normal after R. v. Silcottt and others. *New Law Journal*, 28 August, 807–814.

Beaumont, M. (1988). Psychiatric evidence: over-rationalising the abnormal. *Criminal Law Review*, 290–294.

Beck, F. & Godin, W. (1951). *Russian purge and the extraction of confession*. London: Hurst and Blackett.

Bedau, H.A. (1964). *The death penalty in America: an anthology*. Garden City, NY: (Ed.) Anchor/Doubleday.

Bedau, H.A. & Radelet, M.L. (1987). Miscarriages of justice in potentially capital cases. *Stanford Law Review*, **40**, 21–179.

Bedau, H.A. & Radelet, M.L. (1988). The myth of infallibility: a reply to Markman and Cassell. *Stanford Law Review*, **41**, 161–170.

Beins, B.C. & Porter, J.W. (1989). A ratio scale measurement of conformity. *Educational and Psychological Measurement*, **49**, 75–80.

Belmont, J.M. & Butterfield, E.C. (1971). Learning strategies as determinants of memory deficiencies. *Cognitive Psychology*, **2**, 411–420.

Bem, D.J. (1966). Inducing belief in false confessions. *Journal of Personality and Social Psychology*, **3**, 707–710.

Bem, D.J. (1967). When saying is believing. *Psychology Today*, **1**, 21–25.

Bennett Committee (1979). *Report of the Committee Inquiry into Police Interrogation Procedures in Northern Ireland*. Cmnd 7497. London, TSO Ltd.

Bentall, R.P., Baker, G.A. & Havers, S. (1991). Reality monitoring and psychotic hallucinations. *British Journal of Clinical Psychology*, **30**(3), 213–222.

Berggren, E. (1975). *The Psychology of Confessions*. Leiden: Brill.

Berlyne, N. (1972). Confabulation. *British Journal of Psychiatry*, **120**, 31–39.

Bernheim, H. (1888). *Hypnosis and suggestion in psychotherapy*. Reprinted by University Books, New York, 1964.

Bernheim, H. (1910). *Hypnotisme et suggestion*. Paris: Doin.

Bernstein, E.M. & Putnam, F.W. (1986). Development, reliability, and validity of a dissociation scale. *Journal of Nervous and Mental Disease*, **174**, 727–735.

Bertrand, A. (1823). *Traite due somnambulisme*. Paris: Dentu.

Bevan, V. & Lidstone, K. (1985). *A guide to the Police and Criminal Evidence Act 1985*. London: Butterworths.

Bickman, L. (1974). Social roles and uniforms; clothes make the person. *Psychology Today*, April, 49–51.

Billings, A.G. & Moos, R.H. (1981). The role of coping responses and social measures in attenuating to stress of life events. *Journal of Behavioral Medicine*, **4**, 139–157.
Binet, A. (1900). *La suggestibilite*. Paris: Doin.
Binet, A. (1905). La science du temoignage. *Annee Psychologique*, **11**, 128–136.
Biondo, J. & MacDonald, A.P. (1971). Internal–external locus of control and response to influence attempt. *Journal of Personality*, **39**, 407–419.
Birch, D. (1989). The pace hots up: confessions and confusions under the 1984 Act. *Criminal Law Review*, 95–116.
Birgisson, G.H. (1996). Differences of personality, defensiveness, and compliance between admitting and denying male sex offenders. *Journal of Interpersonal Violence*, **11**(1), 118–125.
Blagrove, M. (1996). Effects of length of sleep deprivation on interrogative suggestibility. *Journal of Experimental Psychology:* Applied, **2**(1), 48–59.
Blagrove, M. & Akehurst, L. (2000). Effects of sleep loss on confidence–accuracy relationships for reasoning and eyewitness memory. *Journal of Experimental Psychology: Applied*, **6**, 59–73.
Blagrove, M., Cole-Morgan, D. & Lambe, H. (1994). Interrogative suggestibility: the effects of sleep deprivation and relationship with field dependence. *Applied Cognitive Psychology*, **8**, 169–179.
Blinkhorn, S. (1993). Unfair cops? The psychology of interrogations, confessions and testimony. A book review. *Nature*, **362**, 655.
Bluglass, K. (1990). Bereavement and loss. In R. Bluglass and P. Bowden (Eds), *Principles and practice of forensic psychiatry*. London: Churchill Livingstone, 587–596.
Boggan, S. (2002). Downing is cleared of cemetery murder, 28 years later. *The Independent*, 16 January, 6.
Bond, R. & Smith, P.B. (1996). Culture and conformity: a meta-analysis of studies using Asch's (1952b, 1956) line judgment task. *Psychological Bulletin*, **119**, 111–137.
Boon, J.C.W. & Baxter, J.S. (2000). Minimizing interrogative suggestibility. *Legal and Criminological Psychology*, **5**, 273–284.
Borchard, E.M. (1932). *Convicting the innocent: sixty-five actual errors of criminal justice*. Garden City, NY: Doubleday.
Bordens, K.S. & Bassett, J. (1985). The plea-bargaining process from the defendant's perspective: a field investigation. *Basic and Applied Social Psychology*, **6**, 93–110.
Bottomley, K., Coleman, C., Dixon, D., Gill, M. & Wall, D. (1991). The detention of suspects in police custody. *British Journal of Criminology*, **31**, 347–364.
Bottoms, A.E. & McClean, J.D. (1976). *Defendants in the criminal process*. London: Routledge and Kegan Paul.
Brabin, D. (1966). *The case of Timothy John Evans. Report of an inquiry by the Hon. Mr. Justice Brabin*. London: HMSO.
Braid, J. (1846). *The powers of the mind over the body*. London: Churchill.
Brandon, R. & Davies, C. (1973). *Wrongful imprisonment*. London: Allen and Unwin.
Brandon, S., Boakes, J., Glaser, D. & Green, R. (1998). Recovered memories of childhood sexual abuse. Implications for clinical practice. *British Journal of Psychiatry*, **172**, 296–307.
Brehm, J.W. (1966). *A theory of psychological reactance*. New York: Academic.
Brehm, S.S. & Brehm, J.W. (1981). *Psychological reactance: a theory of freedom and control*. New York: Academic.
Bridge, J.W. (1914). An experimental study of decision types and their mental correlates. *Psychological Monographs*, **17**(1).
Brignall, C. (1998). *A comparison of the mood and cognitive effects of recreational drugs—methylenedioxymethamphetamine (MDMA) and amphetamine*. Unpublished B.Sc. Thesis, University College, London.
British Psychological Society (2001). *Learning disability: definitions and contexts*. Leicester: British Psychological Society.

Britton, P. (1997). *The jigsaw man*. London: Bantam.
Broadbent, D.E., Cooper, P.F., Fitzgerald, P. & Parkes, L.R. (1982). The Cognitive Failures Questionnaire (CFQ) and its correlates. *British Journal of Clinical Psychology*, **21**, 1–16.
Broadwater Farm Area Housing Committee (1988). *The operation of the criminal justice system as applied to the Broadwater Farm investigation*. London: London Borough of Haringey Broadwater Farm Area Housing Committee.
Broadwater Farm Inquiry (1986). *Report of the Independent Inquiry into Disturbance of October 1985 at the Broadwater Farm Estate, Tottenham*. Chaired by Lord Gifford, QC. London: Karia.
Brophy, E.E. & Huang, W.W. (2000). Twenty-ninth annual review of criminal procedure. I. Investigation and police practices. Custodial interrogations. *Georgetown Law Journal*, **88**, 1021–1043.
Brougham, C.G. (1992). Nonverbal communication: can what they don't say give them away? *FBI Law Enforcement Bulletin*, July, 15–18.
Brown, D. (1995). Pseudomemories: the standard science and the standard care in trauma treatment. *American Journal of Clinical Hypnosis*, **37**, 1–24.
Brown, D. (1997). *PACE ten years on: a review of the research. Home Office Research Study No. 155*. London: HMSO.
Brown, B.S., Courtless, T.F. & Silber, D.E. (1970). Fantasy and force: a study of the dynamics of the mentally retarded offender. *Journal of Criminal Law, Criminology and Police Science*, **61**, 71–77.
Bryan, I. (1997). *Interrogation and Confession. A study of progress, process and practice*. Dartmouth: Ashgate.
Bucke, T. & Brown, D. (1997). *In police custody: police powers and suspects' rights under the revised PACE Codes of Practice*. London: Home Office.
Bucke, T., Street, R. & Brown, D. (2000). *The right of silence: the impact of the Criminal Justice and Public Order Act 1994. Home Office Research Study 199*. London: Home Office.
Bull, R. (1999). Police investigative interviewing. In A. Memon and R. Bull (Eds), *Handbook of the psychology of interviewing*. Chichester: Wiley, 279–292.
Bull, R. & Cullen, C. (1992). *Witnesses who have mental handicaps*. Edinburgh: Crown Office.
Bull, R. & Cullen, C. (1993). Interviewing the mentally handicapped. *Policing*, **9**, 88–100.
Bull, R. & Davies, G. (1996). Child witness research in England. In B. Bottoms and G. Goodman (Eds), *International perspectives on child abuse and children's testimony*. Thousand Oaks, CA: Sage.
Burke, B.W. (1995). The admissibility of novel scientific evidence in New York State: has New York been left out to Frye? *Pace Law Review*, **15**, 539–574.
Burnham Report (1987). *Report of findings of international jurists in respect of Broadwater Farm trials*. London: Broadwater Farm Defence Campaign.
Burtt, H.E. (1948). *Applied psychology*. New York: Prentice-Hall.
Buss, A.H. & Durkee, A. (1957). An inventory for assessing different kinds of hostility. *Journal of Consulting Psychology*, **21**, 343–349.
Butcher, J.N. (1996). *International adaptations of the MMPI-2. Research and clinical applications*. Minneapolis, MN: University of Minnesota Press.
Callaghan, H. & Mulready, S. (1993). *Cruel fate. One man's triumph over justice*. Dublin: Poolberg.
Calcutt, D. (1986). *Report by David Calcutt QC on his inquiry into the investigations carried out by the service police in Cyprus in February and March 1984*. London: HMSO.
Campbell, D. (1992). Mother serving life freed. The Guardian, 29 February, 1.
Candel, I., Merckelbach, H. & Muris, P. (2000). Measuring interrogative suggestibility in children: reliability and validity of the Bonn Test of statement suggestibility. *Psychology, Crime and Law*, **6**(1), 61–70.
Capstick, J. (1960). *Given in evidence*. London: Long.

Cardone, D. & Dent, H. (1996). Memory and interrogative suggestibility: the effects of modality of information presentation and retrieval conditions upon the suggestibility scores of people with learning disabilities. *Legal and Criminological Psychology*, **1** (Part 2), 165–177.

Carlsmith, J.M. & Gross, A.E. (1969). Some effects of guilt on compliance. *Journal of Personality and Social Psychology*, **11**, 232–239.

Carver, C.S., Scheier, M.F. & Weintraub, J.K. (1989). Assessing coping strategies: a theoretically based approach. *Journal of Personality and Social Psychology*, **56**(2), 267–283.

Cassell, P.G. (1996a). Miranda's social costs: an empirical reassessment. *Northwestern University Law Review*, **90**, 387–499.

Cassell, P.G. (1996b). All benefits, no costs: the grand illusion of Miranda's defenders. *Northwestern University Law Review*, **90**, 1084–1124.

Cassell, P.G. (1998a). The statue that time forgot: 18 U.S.C. 3501 and the overhauling of Miranda. *Iowa Law Review*, **85**, 175–259.

Cassell, P.G. (1998b). Protecting the innocent from false confessions and lost confessions—and from Miranda. *Journal of Criminal Law and Criminology*, **88**, 497–556.

Cassell, P.G. (1999). The guilty and the 'innocent': an examination of alleged cases of wrongful conviction from false confessions. *Harvard Journal of Law and Public Policy*, **22**, 523–603.

Cassell, P.G. & Fowles, R. (1998). Handcuffing the cops? A thirty-year perspective on Miranda's harmful effects on law enforcement. *Stanford Law Review*, **50**, 1055–1145.

Cassell, P.G. & Hayman, B.S. (1998). Police interrogation in the 1990s: an empirical study of the effects of Miranda. In R.A. Leo and G.C. Thomas III (Eds), *The Miranda debate, justice and policing*. Boston: Northeastern University Press, 222–235.

Cattell, J.M. (1895). Measurements of the accuracy of recollection. *Science*, **2**, 761–766.

Ceci, S.J. & Bruck, M. (1993). Suggestibility of the child witness: a historical review and synthesis. *Psychological Bulletin*, **113**, 403–439.

Ceci, S.J. & Bruck, M. (1995). *Jeopardy in the courtroom: a scientific analysis of children's testimony*. Washington, DC: American Psychological Association.

Ceci, S.J., Ross, D.F. & Toglia, M.P. (1987). Age differences in suggestibility: narrowing the uncertainties. In S.J. Ceci, M.P. Toglia and D.F. Ross (Eds), *Children's eyewitness memory*. New York: Springer, 79–91.

Cho, K. (1999). Reconstruction of the English criminal justice system and its reinvigorated exclusionary rules. *Loyola of Los Angeles International and Comparative Law Journal*, **21**, 259–312.

Choo, A.L.-T. & Nash, S. (1999). What's the matter with Section 78? *Criminal Law Review*, December, 927–1006.

Cialdini, R.B. (1993). *Influence. The psychology of persuasion*. New York: Quill William Morrow.

Clare, I.C.H. & Gudjonsson, G.H. (1991). Recall and understanding of the caution and rights in police detention amongst persons of average intellectual ability and persons with a mental handicap. *Issues in Criminological and Legal Psychology*, 1(17), 34–42.

Clare, I.C.H. & Gudjonsson, G.H. (1992). *Devising and piloting a new 'notice to detained persons'*. Royal Commission on Criminal Justice. London: HMSO.

Clare, I.C.H. & Gudjonsson, G.H. (1993). Interrogative suggestibility, confabulation, and acquiescence in people with mild learning disabilities (mental handicap): implications for reliability during police interrogations. *British Journal of Clinical Psychology*, **32**(3), 295–301.

Clare, I.C.H. & Gudjonsson, G.H. (1995). The vulnerability of suspects with intellectual disabilities during police interviews: a review and experimental study of decision making. *Mental Handicap Research*, **8**, 110–128.

Clare, I.C.H, Gudjonsson, G.H. & Harari, P.M. (1998). Understanding of the current police caution (England and Wales). *Journal of Community and Applied Social Psychology*, **8**(5), 323–329.

Clare, I.C.H., Gudjonsson, G.H., Rutter, S.C. & Cross, P. (1994). The inter-rater reliability of the Gudjonsson Suggestibility Scale (Form 2). *British Journal of Clinical Psychology*, **33**, 357–365.

Clark, M.D.B. (1991). Fit for interview? *The Police Surgeon*, **40**, 15–18.

Clarke, C. & Milne, R. (2001). *National evaluation of the PEACE investigative interviewing course. Police Research Award Scheme. Report No. PRAS/149*. Institute of Criminal Justice Studies, University of Portsmouth.

Coffin, T.E. (1941). Some conditions of suggestion and suggestibility: a study of certain attitudinal and situational factors influencing the process of suggestion. *Psychological Monographs*, **53**, 1–121.

Cohen, G., Eysenck, M.W. & Levoi, M.E. (1986). *Memory: a cognitive approach*. Milton Keynes: Open University Press.

Cohen, R.L. & Harnick, M.A. (1980). The susceptibility of child witnesses to suggestion. *Law and Human Behavior*, **4**, 201–210.

Cohen, S. & Golan, D. (1991). *The interrogation of Palestinians during the intifada: ill-treatment, 'moderate physical pressure' or torture?* Jerusalem: The Israeli Information Center for Human Rights in the Occupied Territories.

Cohen, S. & Golan, D. (1992). *The interrogation of Palestinians during the intifada: follow-up to March 1991 B'TSELEM Report*. Jerusalem: The Israeli Information Center for Human Rights in the Occupied Territories.

Coid, J. (1981). Suggestibility, low intelligence and a confession to crime. *British Journal of Psychiatry*, **139**, 436–438.

Coleman, A.M. & Mackey, E.D. (1995). Psychological evidence in court. Legal developments in England and the United States. *Psychology, Crime and Law*, **1**, 261–268.

Collins, E. (1997). *Killing rage*. London: Granta.

Combs, D.R., Penn, D.L. & Mathews, R.C. (in press). Implicit learning and sub-clinical paranoia. Does content matter? Personality and Individual Differences.

Conlon, G. (1990). *Proved innocent. The story of Gerry Conlon of the Guildford Four*. London: Hamish Hamilton.

Connery, D.S. (1977). *Guilty until proven innocent*. New York: Putnam.

Connery, D.S. & Styron, W. (1996). *Convicting the innocent. The story of a murder, a false confession, and the struggle to free a wrong man*. Cambridge, MA: Brookline.

Conroy, J. (2000). *Unspeakable acts. Ordinary people. The dynamics of torture*. New York: Knopf.

Cooke, D.J. & Carlin, M.T. (1998). Gudjonsson Suggestibility Scales manual. Book review. *Expert Evidence*, **6**, 62–68.

Cooke, D.J. & Philip, L. (1998). Comprehending the Scottish caution: do offenders understand their right to remain silence? *Legal and Criminological Psychology*, **3**, 13–27.

Coopersmith, S. (1967). *The antecedents of self-esteem*. San Francisco: Freeman.

Corre, N. (1995). *A guide to the 1995 revisions to the PACE Codes of Practice*. London: Callow.

Corre, N. (1998). Could Bentley have been convicted now? *Justice of the Peace*, **162**, 776–162.

Corsini, R.J. (1999). *The dictionary of psychology*. Philadelphia, PA: Brunner/Mazel.

Costa, P.T. Jr. & McCrae, R.R. (1992). *Revised NEO Personality Inventory (NEO PI-R) and NEO Five-Factor Inventory*. Odessa, Florida. FL: Psychological Assessment Resources.

Coulthard, M. (1999). Forensic application of linguistic analysis. In D. Canter and L. Alison (Eds), *Interviewing and deception*. Aldershot: Dartmouth, 105–123.

Council of Europe (1997). *Report to the Norwegian Government on the visit to Norway carried out by the European Committee for the Prevention of Torture and Inhuman or Degrading Treatment or Punishment (CPT)*. Strasbourg: Council of Europe.

CPTU (1992a). *The interviewer's rule book*. London: Home Office, The Central Planning and Training Unit.

CPTU (1992b). *A guide to interviewing*. London: Home Office, The Central Planning and Training Unit.

Craft, M. (1984). Low intelligence, mental handicap and criminality. In M. Craft and A. Craft (Eds), *Mentally abnormal offenders*. London: Bailliere, 177–185.
Criminal Justice and Public Order Act (1984). Chapter 33. London: HMSO.
Cronbach, L.J. (1946). Response sets and test validity. *Educational and Psychological Measurement*, **6**, 475–494.
Crowne, D.P. & Marlowe, D. (1960). A new scale of social desirability independent of psychopathology. *Journal of Consulting Psychology*, **24**, 349–354.
Crutchfield, R.S. (1955). Conformity and character. *American Psychologist*, **10**, 191–198.
Cunningham, C. (1973). Interrogation. *The Medico-Legal Journal*, **41**, 49–62.
Curle, C.E. (1989). *An investigation of reaction to having killed amongst male homicide patients resident in a maximum security hospital*. Unpublished Ph.D. Thesis, University of London.
Cutting Edge (2001). The strange case of Russell Key (Broadcast 22 May 2001). London: Channel Four Television.
Dalla Barba, G. (1993). Different patterns of confabulation. *Cortex*, **29**, 567–581.
Daly, R.J. (1980). Compensation and rehabilitation of victims of torture. *Danish Medical Bulletin*, **27**, 245–248.
Danielsdottir, G., Sigurgeirsdottir, S., Einarsdottir, H.R. & Haraldsson, E. (1993). Interrogative suggestibility in children and its relationship with memory and vocabulary. *Personality and Individual Differences*, **14**, 499–502.
Davies, G. (1983). The legal importance of psychological research in eyewitness testimony. British and American experiences. *Journal of the Forensic Science Society*, **24**, 165–175.
Davies, G. (1991). Research on children's testimony: implications for interviewing practice. In C.R. Hollin and K. Howells (Eds), *Clinical approaches to sex offenders and their victims*. Chichester: Wiley, 93–115.
Davies, G. (2001). Is it possible to discriminate true from false memories. In G.M. Davies and T. Dalgleish (Eds), *Recovered memories. Seeking the middle ground*. Chichester: Wiley, 153–174.
Davies, G.M. & Dalgleish, T. (Eds) (2001). *Recovered memories. Seeking the middle ground*. Chichester: Wiley.
Davies, G., Flin, R. & Baxter, J. (1986). The child witness. *The Howard Journal of Criminal Justice*, **25**, 81–99.
Davison, S.E. & Forshaw, D.M. (1993). Retracted confessions: through opiate withdrawal to a new conceptual framework. Medicine, *Science and the Law*, **33**, 285–290.
Davison, S.E. & Gossop, M. (1996). The problem of interviewing drug addicts in custody: a study of interrogative suggestibility and compliance. *Psychology, Crime and Law*, **2**, 185–195.
Davison, S.E. & Gossop, M. (1999). The management of opiate addicts in police custody. *Medicine, Science and the Law*, **39**, 153–160.
DeFilippo, M. (2001). You have the right to better safeguards: looking beyond Miranda in the new millennium. *John Marshall Law Journal*, **34**, 637–712.
Delaune, P.L. (1995). Fact or fiction? The psychology of disputed confessions and witness veracity. The psychology of interrogations, confessions and testimony. A book review. *American Journal of Criminal Law*, **22**, 547–552.
Dell, S, (1971). *Silent in court, Occasional Papers on Social Administration No. 42*. London: The Social Administration Trust.
Denkowski, G.C. & Denkowski, K.M. (1985). The mentally retarded offender in the state prison system: identification, prevalence, adjustment and rehabilitation. *Criminal Justice and Behavior*, **12**, 55–70.
Dent, H. (1986). An experimental study of the effectiveness of different techniques of questioning mentally handicapped child witnesses. *British Journal of Clinical Psychology*, **25**, 13–17.
Dent, H. & Stephenson, G.M. (1979). An experimental study of the effectiveness of different techniques of questioning child witnesses. *British Journal of Clinical Psychology*, **18**, 41–51.

Dickson, B. (1999). Miscarriages of justice in Northern Ireland. In C. Walker and K. Starmer (Eds), *Miscarriages of justice. A review of justice in error*. London: Blackstone, 287–303.

Dixon, D., Bottomley, K., Cole, C., Gill, M. & Wall, D. (1990). Safeguarding the rights of suspects in police custody. *Policing and Society*, **1**, 115–140.

Dodd, D.H. & Bradshaw, J.M. (1980). Leading questions and memory: pragmatic constraints. *Journal of Verbal Learning and Verbal Behavior*, **19**, 695–704.

Doll, E.A. (1965). *Vineland Social Maturity Scale: manual of directions*. Minneapolis, MN: American Guidance Service.

Dombrose, L.A. & Slobin, M.S. (1958). The IES Test. *Perceptual and Motor Skills*, **8**, 347–389.

Driver, E.D. (1968). Confessions and the social psychology of coercion. *Harvard Law Review*, **82**, 42–61.

Duff, P. (2001). Criminal Cases Review Commissions and 'deference' to the courts: the evaluation of evidence and evidentiary rules. *Criminal Law Review*, 341–362.

Dundee, J.W. (1990). Fantasies during sedation with intravenous midazolam or diazepam. *Medico-Legal Journal*, **58**, 29–34.

Eagly, A.H. (1978). Sex differences in influenceability. *Psychological Bulletin*, **85**, 86–116.

Ede, R. & Shepherd, E. (2000). *Active defence. A lawyer's guide to police and defence investigation and prosecution and defence disclosure in criminal cases*. London: Law Society.

Eisen, M.L., Morgan, D.Y. & Mickes, L. (2002). Individual differences in eyewitness memory and suggestibility: examining relations between acquiescence, dissociation and resistance to misleading information. *Personality and Individual Differences*, **33**, 553–571.

Eisenberg, G.H. (1978). *The relationship of locus of control to social influence. A test of reactance theory*. Unpublished Masters Thesis, University of South Florida.

Ekman P. (1992). *Telling lies. Clues to deceit in the marketplace, politics, and marriage*. New York: Norton.

Endres, J. (1997). The suggestibility of the child witness: the role of individual differences and their assessment. *The Journal of Credibility Assessment and Witness Psychology*, **1**, 44–67.

English, J. & Card, R. (1999). *Butterworths police law*. 6th edn. London: Butterworths.

Evans, F.J. (1967). Suggestibility in the normal waking state. *Psychology Bulletin*, **67**, 114–129.

Evans, F.J. (1989). The independence of suggestibility, placebo response, and hypnotizability, In V.A. Gheorghiu, P. Netter, H.J. Eysenck and R. Rosenthal (Eds), *Suggestion and suggestibility. Theory and research*. London: Springer, 145–154.

Evans, R. (1993). *The conduct of police interviews with juveniles. Royal Commission on Criminal Justice Research Report No. 8*. London: HMSO.

Eysenck, H.J. (1943). Suggestibility and hysteria. *Journal of Neurological Psychiatry*, **6**, 22–31.

Eysenck, H. (1947). *Dimensions of personality*. London: Routledge and Kegan Paul.

Eysenck, H.J. & Eysenck, S.B.G. (1975). *Manual of the Eysenck Personality Questionnaire*. London: Hodder and Stoughton.

Eysenck, H.J. & Furneaux, W.D. (1945). Primary and secondary suggestibility: an experimental and statistical study. *Journal of Experimental Psychology*, **35**, 485–503.

Eysenck, H.J. & Gudjonsson, G.H. (1989). *The causes and cures of criminality*. New York: Plenum.

Eysenck, S.B.G. & Eysenck, H.J. (1978). Impulsiveness and venturesomeness: their position in a dimensional system of personality description. *Psychological Reports*, **43** (3, Part 2), 1247–1255.

Eysenck, S.B.G. & Haraldsson, E. (1983). National differences in personality: Iceland and England. *Psychological Reports*, **53**, 999–1003.

Farber, I.E., Harlow, H.F. & West, L.J. (1957). Brainwashing, conditioning and DDD. *Sociometry*, **20**, 271–285.

Farr, R.M. (1982). Interviewing: the social psychology of the inter-view. In C.L. Cooper and P. Makin (Eds), *Psychology for managers*. London: MacMillan, 182–200.

Feldman, D. (1990). Regulating treatment of suspects in police stations: judicial interpretations of detention provisions in the Police and Criminal Evidence Act 1984. *Criminal Law Review*, 452–471.

Feldman, M.D., Ford, C.V. & Reinhold, T. (1994). *Patient or pretender: inside the strange world of factitious disorders*. Chichester: Wiley.

Fellows, N. (1986). *Killing time*. Oxford: Lion.

Fenner, S., Gudjonsson, G.H. & Clare, I.C.H. (2002). Understanding of the current police caution (England & Wales) among suspects in police detention. *Journal of Community and Applied Social Psychology*, **12**, 83–93.

Festinger, L. (1957). *A theory of cognitive dissonance*. Evanston, IL: Row, Peterson.

Fielder, M. (1994). *Killer on the loose. The inside story of the Rachel Nickell murder investigation*. London: Blake.

Finlay, W.M.L. & Lyons, E. (2001). Methodological issues in interviewing and using self-report questionnaires with people with mental retardation. *Psychological Assessment*, **13**, 319–335.

Finlay, W.M.L. & Lyons, E. (in press). Acquiescence in interviews with people with mental retardation. Mental Retardation.

Firstman, R. & Talan, J. (1997). *The death of innocents*. Bantam: New York.

Firth, A. (1975). Interrogation. Police Review, No. 4324, 1507.

Fisher, H. (1977). *Report of an inquiry by the Hon. Sir Henry Fisher into the circumstances leading to the trial of three persons on charges arising out of the death of Maxwell Confait and the fire at 27 Doggett Road, London SE6*. London: HMSO.

Fisher, R. (1993). Police interrogation: from art to science. The psychology of interrogations, confessions and testimony. A book review. *Contemporary Psychology*, **38**, 1320–1321.

Fisher, R.P. & Geiselman, R.E. (1992). *Memory enhancing techniques for investigative interviewing: the cognitive interview*. Springfield, IL: Thomas.

Fitzgerald, E. (1987). Psychologists and the law of evidence: admissibility and confidentiality. In G.H. Gudjonsson and J. Drinkwater (Eds), *Psychological evidence in court. Issues in criminological and legal psychology, No. 11*. Leicester: British Psychological Society, 39–48.

Florian, A. St. (1999). Fifth amendment Miranda waiver and fourteenth amendment voluntariness. Doctrine in cases of mentally retarded and mentally ill criminal defendants. *Suffolk Journal of Trial and Appellate Advocacy*, **4**, 271–293.

Foot, P. (1998). *Murder at the farm. Who killed Carl Bridgewater?* London: Headline.

Forrest, D. (Ed) (1996). *A glimpse of hell. Reports on torture worldwide*. London: Amnesty International.

Foster, H.H. (1969). Confessions and the station house syndrome. *De Paul Law Review*, **18**, 683–701.

Foster, P. (1998). Psychological tests clear man pressed to confess murder. *The Times*, 20 March, 13.

Frank, M.G. & Ekman, P. (1997). The ability to detect deceit generalizes across different types of high-stake lies. *Journal of Personality and Social Psychology*, **72** (6), 1429–1439.

Freedman, J.L., & Fraser, S.C. (1966). Compliance without pressure: the food-in-the-door technique. *Journal of Personality and Social Psychology*, **4**, 195–202.

Freedman, J.L., Wallington, S.A. & Bless, E. (1967). Compliance without pressure: the effect of guilt. *Journal of Personality and Social Psychology*, **7**, 117–124.

Freud, S. (1916). Some character types met with in psychoanalytic work (iii) Criminals from a sense of guilt. In *Standard edition of the complete psychological work of Sigmund Freud*, Vol. XIV. London: Hogarth Institute of Psycho-Analysis, 332–333.

Frumkin, B. (2000). Competency to waive Miranda rights: clinical and legal issues. *Mental and Physical Disability Law Reporter*, **24**, 326–331.

Gall, J.A. & Freckelton, I. (1999). Fitness for interview: current trends, views and an approach to the assessment procedure. *Journal of Clinical Forensic Medicine*, **6**, 213–223.

Garety, P.A., Hemsley, D.R. & Wessely, S. (1991). Reasoning in deluded schizophrenic and paranoid patients. *Journal of Nervous and Mental Disease*, **179**, 194–201.

Garry, M., Manning, C.G., Loftus, E.F. & Sherman, S.J. (1996). Imagination inflation: imagining a childhood event inflates confidence that it occurred. *Psychonomic Bulletin and Review*, **3**, 208–214.

Geller, W.A. (1992). *Police videotaping of suspect interrogations and confessions*. Wilmette, IL: Police Executive Forum.

Gheorghiu, V.A. (1972). On suggestion and suggestibility. *Scientia*, **16**, 811–860.

Gheorghiu, V.A. (1989a). The difficulty in explaining suggestion: some conceivable solutions. In V.A. Gheorghiu, P. Netter, H.J. Eysenck and R. Rosenthal (Eds), *Suggestion and suggestibility: theory and research*. London: Springer, 99–112.

Gheorghiu, V.A. (1989b). The development of research on suggestibility: critical considerations. In V.A. Gheorghiu, P. Netter, H.J. Eysenck and R. Rosenthal (Eds), *Suggestion and suggestibility: theory and research*. London: Springer, 3–55.

Gibson, H.B. (1962). *An investigation of personality variables associated with susceptibility to hypnosis*. Unpublished Ph.D. Thesis, University of London.

Gilovich, T. (1991). *How we know what isn't so. The fallibility of human reason in everyday life*. New York: Free Press.

Goff, L.M. & Roediger, H.L.M. (1998). Imagination inflation. The effects of number of imaginings on recognition and source monitoring. *Memory and Cognition*, **26**, 20–33.

Goffman, E. (1959). *The presentation of self in everyday life*. New York: Doubleday/Anchor.

Gonsalves, C.J., Torres, T.A., Fischman, Y., Ross, J. & Vargas, M.O. (1993). The theory of torture and the treatment of its survivors. An intervention model. *Journal of Traumatic Stress*, **6**, 351–365.

Goodman-Delahunty, J. (1997). Forensic psychological expertise in the wake of Daubert. *Law and Human Behavior*, **21**, 121–140.

Gordon E., Gwynn, M.I. & Spanos, N.P. (1993). *Effects of hypnosis, suggestion and delay on interrogative suggestibility and confidence*. Unpublished Masters Thesis, Carleton University, Ottawa.

Gossop, M.R. & Davison, S.E. (2000). Arrest, interrogation, statements and confessions: The complications of drug dependence. *American Journal of Forensic Psychiatry*, **21**, 49–68.

Gough, H.G. (1960). Theory and measurement of socialization. *Journal of Consulting Psychology*, **24**, 23–30.

Graef, R. (1990). *Talking blues. The police in their own words*. London: Fontana.

Graf, R.G. (1971). Induced self-esteem as a determinant of behavior. *The Journal of Social Psychology*, **85**, 213–217.

Graham, J.R. (1987). *The MMPI. A practical guide*. 2nd edn. New York: Oxford University Press.

Grant, A. (1987). Videotaping police questioning: a Canadian experiment. *Criminal Law Review*, 375–383.

Greene, E., Flynn, M.S. & Loftus, E.F. (1982). Inducing resistance to misleading information. *Journal of Verbal Learning and Verbal Behavior*, **21**, 207–219.

Griffiths, J. & Ayres, R.E. (1967). A postscript to the Miranda project: interrogation of draft protesters. *Yale Law Journal*, **77**, 300–319.

Grisso, T. (1980). Juveniles' capacities to waive Miranda rights: an empirical analysis. *California Law Review*, **68**, 1134–1166.

Grisso, T. (1986). *Evaluating competencies. Forensic assessments and instruments*. New York: Plenum.

Grisso, T. (1998a). *Forensic evaluation of juveniles*. Sarasota, FL: Professional Resources.
Grisso, T. (1998b). *Instruments for assessing understanding and appreciation of Miranda rights*. Sarasota, FL: Professional Resources.
Grubin, D. (1996). *Fitness to plead in England and Wales*. Hove: Psychology.
Gudjonsson, G.H. (1979). Electrodermal responsivity in Icelandic criminals, clergymen and policemen. *British Journal of Social and Clinical Psychology*, **18**, 351–353.
Gudjonsson, G.H. (1983). Suggestibility, intelligence, memory recall and personality: an experimental study. *British Journal of Psychiatry*, **142**, 35–37.
Gudjonsson, G.H. (1984a). A new scale of interrogative suggestibility. *Personality and Individual Differences*, **5**, 303–314.
Gudjonsson, G.H. (1984b). Interrogative suggestibility: comparison between 'false confessors' and 'deniers' in criminal trials. *Medicine, Science and the Law*, **24**, 56–60.
Gudjonsson, G.H. (1984c). Interrogative suggestibility and perceptual motor performance. *Perceptual Motor Skills*, **58**, 671–672.
Gudjonsson, G.H. (1985). Psychological evidence in court: results from the BPS survey. *Bulletin of the British Psychological Society*, **38**, 327–330.
Gudjonsson, G.H. (1986). The relationship between interrogative suggestibility and acquiescence: empirical findings and theoretical implications. *Personality and Individual Differences*, **7**, 195–199.
Gudjonsson, G.H. (1987a). A parallel form of the Gudjonsson Suggestibility Scale. *British Journal of Clinical Psychology*, **26**, 215–221.
Gudjonsson, G.H. (1987b). The Relationship between memory and suggestibility. *Social Behaviour*, **2**, 29–3.
Gudjonsson, G.H. (1987c). Historical background to suggestibility: how interrogative suggestibility differs from other types of suggestibility. *Personality and Individual Differences*, **8**, 347–355.
Gudjonsson, G.H. (1988a). Interrogative suggestibility: its relationship with assertiveness, social-evaluative anxiety, state anxiety and method of coping. *British Journal of Clinical Psychology*, **27**, 159–166.
Gudjonsson, G.H. (1988b). The relationship of intelligence and memory to interrogative suggestibility: the importance of range effects. *British Journal of Clinical Psychology*, **27**, 185–187.
Gudjonsson, G.H. (1989a). The effects of suspiciousness and anger on suggestibility. *Medicine, Science and the Law*, **29**, 229–232.
Gudjonsson, G.H. (1989b). Theoretical and empirical aspects of interrogative suggestibility. In V.A. Gheorghiu, P. Netter, H.J. Eysenck and R. Rosenthal (Eds), *Suggestion and suggestibility*. London: Springer, 135–143.
Gudjonsson, G.H. (1989c). Compliance in an interrogation situation: a new scale. *Personality and Individual Differences*, **10**, 535–540.
Gudjonsson, G.H. (1989d). The psychology of false confessions. *The Medico-Legal Journal*, **57**, 93–110.
Gudjonsson, G.H. (1990a). One hundred alleged false confession cases: some normative data. *British Journal of Clinical Psychology*, **29**, 249–250.
Gudjonsson, G.H. (1990b). The relationship of intellectual skills to suggestibility, compliance and acquiescence. *Personality and Individual Differences*, **11**, 227–231.
Gudjonsson, G.H. (1990c). The response alternatives of suggestible and non-suggestible individuals. *Personality and Individual Differences*, **11**, 185–186.
Gudjonsson, G.H. (1990d). Self-deception and other-deception in forensic assessment. *Personality and Individual Differences*, **11**, 219–225.
Gudjonsson, G.H. (1991a). The 'Notice to Detained Persons', PACE Codes, and reading ease. *Applied Cognitive Psychology*, **5**, 89–95.
Gudjonsson, G.H. (1991b). Suggestibility and compliance among alleged false confessors and resisters in criminal trials. *Medicine, Science and the Law*, **31**, 147–151.
Gudjonsson, G.H. (1991c). The effects of intelligence and memory on group differences in suggestibility and compliance. *Personality and Individual Differences*, **12**, 503–505.

Gudjonsson, G.H. (1991d). The application of interrogative suggestibility to police interviewing, In J.F. Schumaker (Ed.), *Human suggestibility. Advances in theory, research, and application*. London: Routledge, 279–288.

Gudjonsson, G.H. (1992a). *The psychology of interrogations, confessions and testimony*. Chichester: Wiley.

Gudjonsson, G.H. (1992b). The psychology of false confession and ways to improve the system. *Expert Evidence*, **1**, 49–53.

Gudjonsson, G.H. (1992c). The admissibility of expert psychological and psychiatric evidence in England and Wales. *Criminal Behaviour and Mental Health*, **2**, 245–252.

Gudjonsson, G.H. (1992d). Interrogative suggestibility: factor analysis of the Gudjonsson Suggestibility Scale (GSS 2). *Personality and Individual Differences*, **13**, 479–481.

Gudjonsson, G.H. (1992e). The psychology of false confessions. *New Law Journal*, **142**, 1277–1278.

Gudjonsson, G.H. (1992f). Interrogation and false confessions: vulnerability factors. *British Journal of Hospital Medicine*, **47**, 597–599.

Gudjonsson, G.H. (1993a). Confession evidence, psychological vulnerability and expert testimony. *Journal of Community and Applied Social Psychology*, **3**, 117–129.

Gudjonsson, G.H. (1993b). The implications of poor psychological evidence in court. *Expert Evidence*, **2**, 120–124.

Gudjonsson, G.H. (1994a). Psychological vulnerability: suspects at risk. In D. Morgan and G. Stephenson (Eds), *Suspicion and silence. The right to silence in criminal investigation*. London: Blackstone, 91–106.

Gudjonsson, G.H. (1994b). Confessions made to the expert witness: some professional issues. *Journal of Forensic Psychiatry*, **5**, 237–247.

Gudjonsson, G.H. (1994c). Investigative interviewing: recent developments and some fundamental issues. *International Review of Psychiatry*, **6**, 237–245.

Gudjonsson, G.H. (1995a). Alleged false confession, voluntariness and 'free will': testifying against the Israeli General Security Service (GSS). *Criminal Behaviour and Mental Health*, **5**, 95–105.

Gudjonsson, G.H. (1995b). The effects of interrogative pressure on strategic coping. *Psychology, Crime and Law*, **1**, 309–318.

Gudjonsson, G.H. (1995c). 'Fitness for interview' during police detention: a conceptual framework for the forensic assessment. *Journal of Forensic Psychiatry*, **6**, 185–197.

Gudjonsson, G.H. (1995d). 'I'll help you boys as much as I can'—how eagerness to please can result in a false confession. *Journal of Forensic Psychiatry*, **6**, 333–342.

Gudjonsson, G.H. (1995e). Interrogative suggestibility: does the setting where subjects are tested make a difference to the scores on the GSS 1 and GSS 2? *Personality and Individual Differences*, **18**, 789–790.

Gudjonsson, G.H. (1995f). The Standard Progressive Matrices: methodological problems associated with the administration of the 1992 adult standardisation. *Personality and Individual Differences*, **18**, 441–442.

Gudjonsson, G.H. (1996a). Custodial confinement, interrogation and coerced confessions. In D. Forrest (Ed.), *A glimpse of hell. Reports on torture worldwide*. London: Amnesty International, 36–45.

Gudjonsson, G.H. (1996b). Results from the 1995 survey: psychological evidence in court. *The Psychologist*, **9**(5), 213–217.

Gudjonsson, G.H. (1997a). *The Gudjonsson Suggestibility Scales manual*. Hove: Psychology.

Gudjonsson, G.H. (1997b). Accusations by adults of childhood sexual abuse: a survey of the members of the British False Memory Society (BFMS). *Applied Cognitive Psychology*, **11**, 3–18.

Gudjonsson, G.H. (1997c). False memory syndrome and the retractors: methodological and theoretical issues. *Psychological Inquiry*, **8**, 296–299.

Gudjonsson, G.H. (1997d). Members of the British False Memory Society: the legal consequences of the accusations for the families. *Journal of Forensic Psychiatry*, **8**, 348–356.

Gudjonsson, G.H. (1997e). The members of the BFMS, the accusers and their siblings. *The Psychologist*, **10**, 111–115.

Gudjonsson, G.H. (1997f). The Police and Criminal Evidence Act (PACE) and confessions. *British Journal of Hospital Medicine*, **57**, 445–447.

Gudjonsson, G.H. (1997g). Interrogative suggestibility — can it be recognised in custody? In G.A. Norfolk (Ed.), *Fit to be interviewed by the police?* Harrogate: The Association of Police Surgeons, 12–14.

Gudjonsson, G.H. (1999a). Feelings of guilt and reparation for criminal acts. In M Cox (Ed.), *Remorse and reparation*. London: Kingsley, 83–94.

Gudjonsson, G.H. (1999b). Police interviewing and disputed confession. In A. Memon and R. Bull (Eds), *The psychology of interviewing*. Chichester: Wiley, 327–341.

Gudjonsson, G.H.(1999c). The IRA funeral murders: the confession of PK and the expert psychological testimony. *Legal and Criminological and Psychology*, **4**, 45–50.

Gudjonsson, G.H. (1999d). The making of a serial false confessor: the confessions of Henry Lee Lucas. *Journal of Forensic Psychiatry*, **10**(2), 416–426.

Gudjonsson, G.H. (2001). False confession. *The Psychologist*, **14**, 588–591.

Gudjonsson, G.H. & Adlam, K.R.C. (1983). Personality patterns of British police officers. *Personality and Individual Differences*, **4**, 507–512.

Gudjonsson, G.H. & Bownes, I. (1991). The attribution of blame and type of crime committed: data for Northern Ireland. *Journal of Forensic Psychiatry*, **2**, 337–341.

Gudjonsson, G.H. & Bownes, I. (1992). The reasons why suspects confess during custodial interrogation: data for Northern Ireland. *Medicine, Science and the Law*, **32**, 204–212.

Gudjonsson, G.H. & Clare, I.C.H. (1995). The relationship between confabulation and intellectual ability, memory, interrogative suggestibility and acquiescence. *Personality and Individual Differences*, **19**, 333–338.

Gudjonsson, G.H., Clare, I.C.H. & Cross, P. (1992). The revised PACE 'Notice to Detained Persons': how easy is it to understand? *Journal of the Forensic Science Society*, **32**, 289–299.

Gudjonsson, G.H., Clare, I.C.H. & Rutter, S. (1994). Psychological characteristics of subjects interviewed at police stations: a factor-analytic study. *Journal of Forensic Psychiatry*, **5**(3), 517–526.

Gudjonsson, G.H., Clare, I.C.H., Rutter, S. & Pearse, J. (1993). *Persons at risk during interviews in police custody: the identification of vulnerabilities. Royal Commission on Criminal Justice*. London: HMSO.

Gudjonsson, G.H. & Clark, N.K. (1986). Suggestibility in police interrogation: a social psychological model. *Social Behaviour*, **1**, 83–104.

Gudjonsson, G.H. & Gunn, J. (1982). The competence and reliability of a witness in a criminal court. *British Journal of Psychiatry*, **141**, 624–627.

Gudjonsson, G.H., Hannesdottir, K., Petursson, H. & Bjornsson, G. (2002a). The effects of alcohol withdrawal on mental state, interrogative suggestibility, and compliance: an experiment study. *The Journal of Forensic Psychiatry*, **13**, 53–67.

Gudjonsson, G.H., Hannesdottir, K., Petursson, H. & Tyrfingson, T. (2000). The effects of alcohol withdrawal on memory, confabulation, and suggestibility. *Nordic Journal of Psychiatry*, **54**, 213–220.

Gudjonsson, G.H. & Haward, L.R.C. (1998). *Forensic psychology: a guide to practice*. London: Routledge.

Gudjonsson, G.H., Hayes, G.D. & Rowlands, P. (2000). Fitness to be interviewed and psychological vulnerability: the view of doctors, lawyers and police officers. *Journal of Forensic Psychiatry*, **11**(No. 1), 74–92.

Gudjonsson, G.H. & Hilton, M. (1989). The effects of instructional manipulation on interrogative suggestibility. *Social Behaviour*, **4**, 189–193.

Gudjonsson, G.H., Kopelman, M.D. & MacKeith, J.A.C. (1999). Unreliable admissions to homicide: a case of misdiagnosis of amnesia and misuse of abreaction technique. *British Journal of Psychiatry*, **174**, 455–459.

Gudjonsson, G.H. & Lebegue, B. (1989). Psychological and psychiatric aspects of a coerced–internalized false confession. *Journal of the Forensic Science Society*, **29**, 261–269.

Gudjonsson, G.H. & Lister, S. (1984). Interrogative suggestibility and its relationship with perceptions of self-concept and control. *Journal of the Forensic Science Society*, **24**, 99–110.

Gudjonsson, G.H. & MacKeith, J.A.C. (1982). False confessions: psychological effects of interrogation. A discussion paper. In A. Trankell (Ed.), *Reconstructing the past: the role of psychologists in ciminal trials*. Deventer: Kluwer, 253–269.

Gudjonsson, G.H. & MacKeith, J.A.C. (1988). Retracted confessions: legal, psychological and psychiatric aspects. *Medicine, Science and the Law*, **28**, 187–194.

Gudjonsson, G.H. & MacKeith, J.A.C. (1990). A proven case of false confession: psychological aspects of the coerced–compliant type. *Medicine, Science and the Law*, **30**, 329–335.

Gudjonsson, G.H. & MacKeith, J.A.C. (1994). Learning disability and the Police and Criminal Evidence Act 1984. Protection during investigative interviewing: a video-recorded false confession to double murder. *Journal of Forensic Psychiatry*, **5**, 35–49.

Gudjonsson, G.H. & MacKeith, J.A.C. (1997). *Disputed confessions and the criminal justice system. Maudsley Discussion Paper No. 2*. London: Institute of Psychiatry.

Gudjonsson, G.H., Murphy, G.H. & Clare, I.C.H. (2000). Assessing the capacity of people with intellectual disabilities to be witnesses in court. *Psychological Medicine*, **30**, 307–314.

Gudjonsson, G.H., & Petursson, H. (1982). Some criminological and psychiatric aspects of homicide in Iceland. *Medicine, Science and the Law*, **22**, 91–98.

Gudjonsson, G.H., & Petursson, H. (1991). Custodial interrogation: why do suspects confess and how does it relate to their crime, attitude and personality? *Personality and Individual Differences*, **12**, 295–306.

Gudjonsson, G.H., Petursson, H., Skulason, S. & Sigurdardottir, H. (1989). Psychiatric evidence: a study of psychological issues. *Acta Psychiatrica Scandinavica*, **80**, 165–169.

Gudjonsson, G.H. & Roberts, J.C. (1983). Guilt and self-concept in 'secondary psychopaths'. *Personality and Individual Differences*, **4**, 141–146.

Gudjonsson, G.H., Rutter, S.C. & Clare, I.C.H. (1995). The relationship between suggestibility and anxiety among suspects detained at police stations. *Psychological Medicine*, **25**, 875–878.

Gudjonsson, G.H. & Sartory, G. (1983). Blood-injury phobia: a 'reasonable excuse' for failing to give a specimen in a case of suspected drunken driving. *Journal of the Forensic Science Society*, **23**, 197–201.

Gudjonsson, G.H. & Shackleton, H. (1986). The pattern of scores on Raven's Matrices during 'faking bad' and 'non-faking' performance. *British Journal of Clinical Psychology*, **25**, 35–41.

Gudjonsson, G.H. & Sigurdsson, J.F. (1994). How frequently do false confessions occur? An empirical study among prison inmates. *Psychology, Crime and Law*, **1**, 21–26.

Gudjonsson, G.H. & Sigurdsson, J.F. (1995). The relationship of confabulation to the memory, intelligence, suggestibility, and personality of juvenile offenders. *Nordic Journal of Psychiatry*, **49**(5), 373–378.

Gudjonsson, G.H. & Sigurdsson, J.F. (1996). The relationship of confabulation to the memory, intelligence, suggestibility and personality of prison inmates. *Applied Cognitive Psychology*, **10**(1), 85–92.

Gudjonsson, G.H. & Sigurdsson, J.F. (1999). The Gudjonsson Confession Questionnaire—Revised (GCQ-R): factor structure and its relationship with personality. *Personality and Individual Differences*, **27**(5), 953–968.

Gudjonsson, G.H. & Sigurdsson, J.F. (2000). Differences and similarities between violent offenders and sex offenders. *Child Abuse and Neglect*, **24**(3), 363–372.

Gudjonsson, G.H. & Sigurdsson, J.F. (submitted). Motivation for offending and personality.

Gudjonsson, G.H. & Sigurdsson, J.F. (in press). The relationship of compliance with coping strategies and self-esteem. *European Journal of Psychological Assessment*.

Gudjonsson, G.H. & Sigurdsson, J.F. (in preparation). The relationship of compliance and suggestibility with personality and social desirability among prison inmates.

Gudjonsson, G.H., Sigurdsson, J.F., Brynjolfsdottir, B. and Hreinsdottir, H. (2002). The relationship of compliance with anxiety, self-esteem, paranoid thinking and anger. *Psychology, Crime and Law*, **8**, 145–153.

Gudjonsson, G.H. & Singh, K.K. (1984a). Interrogative suggestibility and delinquent boys: an empirical validation study. *Personality and Individual Differences*, **5**, 425–430.

Gudjonsson, G.H. & Singh, K.K. (1984b). The relationship between criminal conviction and interrogative suggestibility among delinquent boys. *Journal of Adolescence*, **7**, 29–34.

Gur-Arye, M. (1989). Introduction. *Israel Law Review*, **23**, 141–145.

Gwynn, M.I. & Spanos, N.P. (1996). Hypnotic responsiveness, nonhypnotic suggestibility and responsiveness to social influence. In R.G. Kunzendorf, N.P. Spanos and B. Wallace (Eds), *Hypnosis and imagination*. Amityville, NY: Baywood, 147–175.

Gwynn, M.I., Spanos, N.P., Nancoo, S & Chow L (1995). Interrogative suggestibility, hypnotisability and persuasibility: are they related? Unpublished manuscript, Carleton University.

Hamlet, C.C., Axelrod, S. & Kuerschner, S. (1984). Eye contact as an antecedent to compliant behavior. *Journal of Applied Behavior Analysis*, **17**, 553–557.

Haney, C., Banks, C. & Zimbardo, P. (1973). Interpersonal dynamics in a simulated prison. *International Journal of Criminology and Penology*, **1**, 69–97.

Hansdottir, I., Thorsteinsson, H.S., Kristinsdottir, H. & Ragnarsson, R.S. (1990). The effects of instructions and anxiety on interrogative suggestibility. *Personality and Individual Differences*, **11**, 85–87.

Happe, F. (1999). *Autism. An introduction to psychological theory*. Hove: Psychology.

Haraldsson, E. (1985). Interrogative suggestibility and its relationship with personality, perceptual defensiveness and extraordinary beliefs. *Personality and Individual Differences*, **5**, 765–767.

Haraldsson, E. (1995). Personality and abilities of children claiming previous life memories. *Journal of Nervous and Mental Disorders*, **183**, 445–451.

Hardarson, R. (1985). *Samband Daleidslu-og Yfirheyrslusefnaemis og Fylgni; Vid Persenuleika og Namsarangur*. B.A. Thesis (No. 173) in Psychology, University of Iceland.

Hartley, J. (2000). Legal ease and 'legalese'. *Psychology, Crime and Law*, **6**, 1–20.

Hathaway, S.R. & McKinley, J.C. (1991). *The Minnesota Multiphasic Personality Inventory manual*. Minneapolis, MN: University of Minnesota Press.

Haward, L.R.C. (1974). Investigations of torture allegations by the forensic psychologist. *Journal of the Forensic Science Society*, **14**, 299–310.

Heaps, C. & Nash, M. (1999). Individual differences in imagination inflation. *Psychonomic Bulletin and Review*, **6**, 313–318.

Heaton-Armstrong, A. (1987). Police officers' notebooks: recent developments. *Criminal Law Review*, 470–472.

Heaton-Armstrong, A. (1992). The psychology of interrogations, confessions and testimony. A book review. *Criminal Law Review*, 683–684.

Helm, S. (1994). West Bank law loaded against Arabs. The Independent on Sunday, 29 March.

Henry, L.A. & Gudjonsson, G.H. (1999). Eyewitness memory and suggestibility in children with learning disabilities. *American Journal on Mental Retardation*, **104**, 491–508.

Henry, L.A. & Gudjonsson, G.H. (submitted). Eyewitness memory, suggestibility and repeated recall sessions in children with mild and moderate intellectual disabilities.

Hepworth, M., & Turner, B.S. (1980). *Confession. Studies in deviance and religion*. London: Routledge and Kegan Paul.

Herbert, I. (2001). Police to launch third inquiry into 1975 killing of schoolgirl. *The Independent*, 3 May, 6.
Hersch, P.D. & Scheibe, K.E. (1967). Reliability of internal–external control as a personality dimension. *Journal of Consulting Psychology*, **31**, 609–613.
Hertel, P.T., Cosden, M. & Johnson, P.J. (1980). Passage recall: schema change and cognitive flexibility. *Journal of Educational Psychology*, **72**, 133–140.
Heslin, R., Nguyen, T.D. & Nguyen, M.L. (1983). Meaning of touch: the case of touch from a stranger or same sex person. *Journal of Nonverbal Behavior*, **7**, 147–157.
Hickey, C., Lighty, T. & O'Brien, J. (1996). *Goodbye my little ones*. New York: Penguin.
Hilgendorf, E.L., & Irving, B. (1981). A decision-making model of confessions. In M.A. Lloyd-Bostock (Ed.), *Psychology in legal contexts. Applications and limitations*. London: MacMillan, 67–84.
Hill, P. & Bennett, R. (1990). *Stolen years. Before and after Guildford*. London: Doubleday.
Hill, P.J. & Hunt, G. (1995). *Forever lost, forever gone*. London: Bloomsbury.
Hill, P., Young, M. & Sargant, T. (1985). *More rough justice*. Harmondsworth: Penguin.
Hinkle, L.E. (1961). The physiological state of the interrogation subject as it affects brain function. In A.D. Biderman and H. Zimmer (Eds), *The manipulation of human behaviour*. New York: Wiley, 19–50.
Hinkle, L.E. & Wolff, H.G. (1956). Communist interrogation and indoctrination of 'enemies of the states'. *American Medical Association Archives of Neurology and Psychiatry*, **76**, 115–174.
Hodgson, J. (1997). Vulnerable suspects and the Appropriate Adult. *Criminal Law Review*, 763–844.
Home Office (1978). *Judges' rules and administrative directions to the police. Police Circular No. 89/1978*. London: Home Office.
Home Office (1985a). *Police and Criminal Evidence Act 1984*. London: HMSO.
Home Office (1985b). *Police and Criminal Evidence Act 1984 (S.66), Codes of Practice*. London: HMSO.
Home Office (1991). *Police and Criminal Evidence Act 1984. Codes of Practice*. Revised Edition. London: HMSO.
Home Office (1995). *Police and Criminal Evidence Act 1984. Codes of Practice*. Revised Edition. London: HMSO.
Home Office (2001). *Report of the Home Office Working Group on Police Surgeons*. Police Leadership and Powers Unit. London: Home Office.
Hornik, J. (1988). The effect of touch and gaze upon compliance and interest of interviewees. *Journal of Social Psychology*, **127**, 681–683.
Horselenberg, R., Merckelbach, H., Muris, P. & Rassin, (2000). Imagining fictitious childhood events. *Clinical Psychology and Psychotherapy*, **7**, 128–137.
Hourihan, P.T. (1995). Earl Washington's confession: mental retardation and the law of confessions. *Virginia Law Review*, **81**, 1471–1503.
Howard, R. & Hong N.S. (2002). Effects of metamotivational state and coping style on interrogative suggestibility. *Personality and Individual Differences*, **33**, 479–485.
Howells, K. & Ward, M. (1994). Intellectual impairment, memory impairment, suggestibility and voire dire proceedings: a case study. *Medicine, Science and the Law*, **34**, 176–180.
Huff, C.R., Rattner, A. & Sagarin, E. (1986). Guilty until proven innocent: wrongful conviction and public policy. *Crime and Delinquency*, **32**, 518–544.
Huff, C.R., Rattner, A. & Sagarin, E. (1996). *Convicted but innocent: wrongful convictions and public policy*. London: Sage.
Hull, C. (1933). *Hypnosis and suggestibility*. New York: Appleton–Century–Crofts.
Human Rights Watch/Middle East (1994). *Torture and ill-treatment. Israel's interrogation of Palestinians from the occupied territories*. New York: Human Rights Watch.

Hunter, E. (1951). *Brainwashing in Red China*. New York: Vanguard.
Hunter, E. (1956). *Brainwashing*. New York: Farrar, Strauss, and Cudahy.
Imwinkelried, E.J. (1999). The escape hatches from Fry and Daubert: sometimes you don't need to lay either foundation in order to introduce expert testimony. *American Journal of Trial Advocacy*, 23, 1–17.
Inbau, F.E. (1942). *Lie detection and criminal interrogation*. Baltimore, MD: Williams and Wilkins.
Inbau, F.E. (1948). *Lie detection and criminal interrogation*. 2nd edn. Baltimore, MD: Williams and Wilkins.
Inbau, F.E. & Reid, J.E. (1953). *Lie detection and criminal interrogation*. 3rd edn. Baltimore, MD: Williams and Wilkins.
Inbau, F.E. & Reid, J.E. (1962). *Criminal interrogation and confessions*. Baltimore, MD: Williams and Wilkins.
Inbau, F.E. & Reid, J.E. (1967). *Criminal interrogation and confessions*. 2nd edn. Baltimore, MD: Williams and Wilkins.
Inbau, F.E., Reid, J.E. & Buckley, J.P. (1986). *Criminal interrogation and confessions*. 3rd edn. Baltimore, MD: Williams and Wilkins.
Inbau, F.E., Reid, J.E., Buckley, J.P. & Jayne, B.C. (2001). *Criminal interrogation and confessions*. 4th edn. Gaithersberg, MD: Aspen.
Irving, B. (1980). *Police interrogation. A case study of current practice. Research Studies No. 2*. London: HMSO.
Irving, B. (1987). Interrogative suggestibility: a question of parsimony. *Social Behaviour*, 2, 19–28.
Irving, B. (1990). The Codes of Practice under the Police and Criminal Evidence Act 1984. In R. Bluglass and P. Bowden (Eds), *Principles and practice of forensic psychiatry*. London: Churchill Livingston, 151–159.
Irving, B. & Hilgendorf, L. (1980). *Police interrogation: the psychological approach. Research Studies No. 1*. London: HMSO.
Irving, B. & McKenzie, I. K. (1989). *Police interrogation: the effects of the Police and Criminal Evidence Act*. London: Police Foundation of Great Britain.
Izard, C.E., Libero, D.Z., Putman, P. & Haynes, O.M. (1993). Stability of emotion experiences and their relations to traits of personality. *Journal of Personality and Social Psychology*, 64, 847–860.
Izenberg, D. (1995). GSS defends use of 'torture'. Tells court harsh interrogation helps prevent torture. *The Jerusalem Post*, 19 May.
Izenberg, D. (1999a). Ten-year battle against brutality ends in victory. *The Jerusalem Post*, 10 September.
Izenberg, D. (1999b). Court orders GSS to stop using physical pressure. *The Jerusalem Post*, 7 September.
James, A., Taylor, N. & Walker, C. (2000). The Criminal Cases Review Commission: economy, effectiveness and justice. *Criminal Law Review*, March, 125–208.
Janis, I.L. (1959). Decisional conflicts: a theoretical analysis. *Journal of Conflict Resolution*, 3, 6–27.
Jayne, B.C. (1986). The psychological principles of criminal interrogation. An appendix. In F.E. Inbau, J.E. Reid and J.P. Buckley (Eds), *Criminal interrogation and confessions*. 3rd edn. Baltimore, MD: Williams and Williams, 327–347.
Jayne, B.C. & Buckley, J.P. (1991). Criminal interrogation techniques on trial. The Prosecutor. *The Journal of the National District Attorney's Association*, 25/2.
Jayne, B.C. & Buckley, J.P. (1998). Interrogation alert! Will your next confessions be suppressed? *The Investigator*. Special Edition.
Johnson, H.R.M. (1982). Deaths in police custody in England and Wales. *Forensic Science International*, 19, 231–236.
Johnson, M.K. (1991). Reality monitoring: evidence from confabulation in organic brain disease patients. In G.P. Prigatano and D.L. Schacter (Eds), *Awareness of deficit after brain injury: clinical and theoretical issues*. New York: Oxford University Press, 176–197.

Johnson, M.K. & Raye, C.L. (1981). Reality monitoring. *Psychological Review*, **88**, 67–85.

Jones, A. (1997). Substance misuse and fitness for interview. In G.A. Norfolk (Ed.), *Fit to be interviewed by the police*. Proceedings of a multidisciplinary symposium, Blackpool, UK.

Kalbfleisch, P.J. (1994). The language of detecting deceit. *Journal of Language and Social Psychology*, **13**, 459–496.

Kallio, L.E. (1999). *Confess or die. The case of William Heirens*. London: Minerva.

Kalven, H. & Zeisel, H. (1966). *The American jury*. Boston, MA: Little, Brown.

Kassin, S.M. (1997). False memories turned against the self. *Psychological Inquiry*, **8**, 300–302.

Kassin, S.M. (1998). More on the psychology of false confessions. *American Psychologist*, March, 320–321.

Kassin, S.M. & Fong, C.T. (1999). 'I'm innocent!' Effects of training on judgements of truth and deception in the interrogation room. *Law and Human Behavior*, **23**, 499–516.

Kassin, S.M. & Kiechel, K.L. (1996). The social psychology of false confessions. Compliance, internalisation, and confabulation. *Psychological Science*, **7**, 125–128.

Kassin, S.M. & McNall, K. (1991). Police interrogations and confessions. *Law and Human Behavior*, **15**, 233–251.

Kassin, S.M. & Neumann, K. (1997). On the power of confession evidence: an experimental test of the fundamental difference hypothesis. *Law and Human Behavior*, **21**, 469–484.

Kassin, S.M. & Wrightsman, L.S. (1985). Confession evidence. In S.M. Kassin and L.S. Wrightsman (Eds), *The psychology of evidence and trial procedures*. London: Sage, 67–94.

Keane, V.E. (1972). The incidence of speech and language problems in the mentally retarded. *Mental Retardation*, **10**, 3–8.

Kebbell, M.R. & Hatton, C. (1999). People with mental retardation as witnesses in court: a review. *Mental Retardation*, **37**, 179–187.

Kee, R. (1989). *Trial & error. The true events surrounding the convictions and trials of the Guildford Four and the Maguire Seven*. London: Penguin.

Kellam, A.M.P. (1980). A convincing false confession. *New Journal*, **10**, 29–33.

Kellerman, A.E., Siehr, K. & Einhorn, T. (1998). *Israel among nations. International and comparative law perspective on Israel's 50th anniversary*. London: Kluwer.

Kelman, H.C. (1950). The effects of success and failure on 'suggestibility' in the autokinetic situation. *Journal of Abnormal Social Psychology*, **46**, 267–285.

Kelman, H.C. (1958). Compliance, identification and internalization: three processes of opinion change. *Journal of Conflict Resolution*, **2**, 51–60.

Kelman, H.C. & Holland, C.I. (1953). 'Reinstatement' of the communicator in delayed measurement of opinion change. *Journal of Abnormal and Social Psychology*, **48**, 327–335.

Kennedy, H. (1992). *Eve was framed. Women and criminal justice*. London: Chatto and Windus.

Kennedy, H.G. & Grubin, D.H. (1992). Patterns of denial in sex offenders. *Psychological Medicine*, **22**(1), 191–196.

Kennedy, L. (1986). Foreword. In N. Fellows (Ed.), *Killing time*. Oxford: Lion, 6–8.

Kennedy, L. (1988). *10 Rillington Place*. London: Grafton.

Kiesler, C.A. & Kiesler, S.B. (1970). *Conformity*. Reading, MA: Addison-Wesley.

Kirby, T. (1989). New powers urged on DNA fingerprinting. *The Independent*, **27** September, 3.

Kleinke, C.L. (1977). Compliance to requests made by gazing and touching experimenter in field settings. *Journal of Experimental Social Psychology*, **13**, 218–232.

Kleinke, C.L. (1980). Interaction between gaze and legitimacy on requests on compliance in a field setting. *Journal of Nonverbal Behavior*, **5**, 3–12.

Knowles, E.S. & Nathan, K.T. (1997). Acquiescent responding in self-reports: cognitive style or social concern? *Journal of Research in Personality*, **5**, 293–301.

Konoske, P., Staple, S. & Graf, R.G. (1979). Compliant reactions to guilt: self-esteem or self-punishment. *Journal of Social Psychology*, **108**, 207–211.

Kopelman, M.D. (1995). The assessment of psychogenic amnesia. In A.D. Baddeley, B.A. Wilson and F.N. Watts (Eds), *Handbook of memory disorder*. Chichester: Wiley, 427–448.

Kopelman, M. & Morton, J. (2001). Psychogenic amnesias: functional memory loss. In G.M. Davies and T. Dalgleish (Eds), *Recovered memories. Seeking the middle ground*. Chichester: Wiley, 219–243.

Krech, D. & Crutchfield, R.S. (1948). *Theory and problems of social psychology*. New York: McGraw-Hill.

Krech, D., Crutchfield, R.S. & Ballachey, E.L. (1962). *Individual in society*. New York: McGraw-Hill.

Lader, M. (1999). The influence of drugs upon testimony. *Medicine, Science and the Law*, **39**, 99–105.

Landau Commission Report (1989). *Israel Law Review*, **23**, 146–188.

Lassiter, G.D. & Irvine, A.A. (1986). Videotaped confessions: the impact of camera point on view of judgements of coercion. *Journal of Applied Social Psychology*, **16**(3), 268–276.

Laurence, J.R. & Perry, C. (1983). Hypnotically created memories among highly hypnotizable subjects. *Science*, **222**, 523–524.

Leavitt, F. (1997). False attribution of suggestibility to explain recovered memory of childhood sexual abuse following extended amnesia. *Childhood Abuse and Neglect*, **21**, 265–271.

Leigh, L.H. (1997). The Criminal Cases Review Commission. *Archbold News*, **3**, 6–8.

Leiken, L.S. (1970). Police interrogation in Colorado: the implementation of Miranda. *Denver Law Journal*, **47**, 1–53.

Leites, N. & Bernaut, E. (1954). *Ritual of liquidation*. Glencoe, IL: Free Press.

Leng, R. (1993). *The right to silence in police interrogation: a study of some of the issues underlying the debate. The Royal Commission on Criminal Justice Research Study No. 10*. London: HMSO.

Leng, R., McConville, M. & Sanders, A. (1989). *Discretion to charge and prosecute. Report to the ESRC*.

Leo, R.A. (1992). From coercion to deception: the changing nature of police interrogation in America. *Crime, Law and Social Change: an International Journal*, **18**, 35–59.

Leo, R.A. (1994). *Police interrogation in America: a study of violence, civility and social change*. Unpublished Ph.D. Thesis, University of California at Berkeley.

Leo, R.A. (1996a). Inside the interrogation room. *Journal of Criminal Law and Criminology*, **86**, 266–303.

Leo, R.A. (1996b). Miranda's revenge: police interrogation as a confidence game. *Law and Society Review*, **30**, 259–288.

Leo, R.A. (1997). The social and legal construction of repressed memory. *Law and Social Inquiry*, **22**, 653–693.

Leo, R.A. (1998). Miranda and the problem of false confessions. In R.A. Leo and G.C. Thomas III (Eds), *The Miranda debate, justice and policing*. Boston, MA: Northeastern University Press, 271–282.

Leo, R.A. (2001a). False confessions. Causes, consequences and solutions. In S.A.Westervelt and J.A. Humphrey (Eds), *Wrongly convicted. Perspectives on failed justice*. London: Rutgers University Press, 36–54.

Leo. R.A. (2001b). Questioning the relevance of Miranda in the twenty-first century. *Michigan Law Review*, **99**, 1000–1028.

Leo, R.A. & Ofshe, R.J. (1998a). The consequences of false confessions: deprivations of liberty and miscarriages of justice in the age of psychological interrogation. *Journal of Criminal Law and Criminology*, **88**, 429–496.

Leo, R.A. & Ofshe, R.J. (1998b). Using the innocent to scapegoat Miranda: another reply to Paul Cassell. *Journal of Criminal Law and Criminology*, **88**, 557–578.

Leo, R.A. & Ofshe, R.J. (2001). The truth about false confessions and advocacy scholarship. *Criminal Law Bulletin*, **37**, 293–370.

Leo, R.A. & White, W.S. (1999). Adapting to Miranda: modern interrogators' strategies for dealing with the obstacles posed by Miranda. *Minnesota Law Review*, **84**, 397–472.

Lepper, M.R. (1982). Social control processes, attributions of motivation, and the internalizations of social values. In E.T. Higgins, D.N. Ruble and W.W. Hartup (Eds), *Social cognition and social behavior: a developmental perspective*. San Francisco: Jossey-Bass.

Lewin, K. (1947). Frontiers in group dynamics: concepts, method and reality in social science. *Human Relations*, **1**, 5–42.

Lewis, P. & Mullis, A. (1999). Delayed criminal prosecutions for childhood sexual abuse: ensuring a fair trial. *Law Quarterly Review*, **115**, 265–295.

Liebman, J.I., McKinley-Pace, M.J., Leonard, A.M., Sheesley, L.A., Gallant, C.L., Renkey, M.E. & Lehman, E.B. (2002). Cognitive and psychosocial correlates of adults' eyewitness accuracy and suggestibility. *Personality and Individual Differences*, **33**, 49–66.

Lifton, R.J. (1956). 'Thought reform' of Western civilians in Chinese prisons. *American Journal of Psychiatry*, **110**, 732–739.

Lifton, R.J. (1961). *Thought reform and the psychology of totalism*. New York: Norton.

Linton, C.P. & Sheehan, P.W. (1994). The relationship between interrogative suggestibility and susceptibility to hypnosis. *Australian Journal of Clinical and Experimental Hypnosis*, **22**(1), 53–64.

Littlechild, B. (1996). *The Police and Criminal Evidence Act 1984. The role of the Appropriate Adult*. Birmingham: British Association of Social Workers.

Loftus, E.F. (1979a). *Eyewitness testimony*. London: Harvard University Press.

Loftus, E.F. (1979b). Reactions to blatantly contradictory information. *Memory and Cognition*, **7**, 368–374.

Loftus, E.F. (1981). Metamorphosis: alterations in memory produced by mental bonding of new information to old. In J. Long and A. Baddeley (Eds), *Attention and performance* Vol. IX. Hillsdale, NJ: Erlbaum, 417–434.

Loftus, E.F. (1993). The reality of repressed memories. *American Psychologist*, **48**, 518–537.

Loftus, E F. (2001). Imagining the past. *The Psychologist*, **14**, 584–587.

Loftus, E.F., Greene, E.L. & Doyle, J.M. (1990). The psychology of eyewitness testimony. In D.C. Raskin (Ed.), *Psychological methods in criminal investigations and evidence*. New York: Springer, 3–45.

Loftus, E.F. & Ketcham, K. (1994). *The myth of repressed memory*. New York: St Martin's.

Loftus, E.F., Miller, D.G. & Burns, H.J. (1978). Semantic integration of verbal information into a visual memory. Journal of Experimental Psychology: *Human Learning and Memory*, **4**, 19–31.

Lohr, J.M., Nix, J., Dunbar, D. & Mosesso, L. (1984). The relationship of assertive behaviour in women and a validated measure of irrational beliefs. *Cognitive Therapy and Research*, **8**, 287–297.

Lorr, M. & McNair, D.M. (1980). *Profile of Mood States Bipolar Form (POMS-BI)*. San Diego, CA: Educational and Industrial Testing Service.

Luce, R.D. (1967). Psychological studies of risky decision making. In W. Edwards and A. Tversky (Eds), *Decision making*. London: Penguin, 334–352.

Macdonald, J.M. & Michaud, D.L. (1992). *Criminal interrogation*. Denver, CO: Apache.

Mackey, R.D. & Coleman, A.M. (1991). Excluding expert evidence: a tale of ordinary folk and common experience. *Criminal Law Review*, 797–864.

Mahendra, B. (2001). Science in the miscarriage of justice. *New Law Journal*, **99**, 1686–1687.

Mansfield, M. (1993). *Presumed guilty. The British legal system exposed*. London: Mandarin.

Markman, S.J. & Cassell, P.G. (1988). Protecting the innocent: a response to the Bedau–Radelet study. *Stanford Law Review*, **41**, 121–160.

Matarazzo, J.D. (1972). *Measurement and appraisal of adult intelligence*. Baltimore, MD: William and Wilkins.
Matarazzo, R.G. (1990). Psychological assessment versus psychometric testing. *American Psychologist*, **45**, 999–1017.
Matthews, R.A.J. (1995). The interrogator's fallacy. *The Institute of Mathematics and its Applications*, **31**, 3–5.
Mattox, J. (1986). *The Lucas Report*. Texas: Attorney General of Texas.
Matza, D. (1967). *Becoming deviant*. Englewood Cliffs, NJ: Prentice-Hall.
Mazzoni, G.A.L., Loftus, E.F., Seitz, A. & Lynn, S. (1999). Changing beliefs and memories through dream interpretation. *Applied Cognitive Psychology*, **13**, 125–144.
McAfee, J.K. & Gural, M. (1988). Individuals with mental retardation and the criminal justice system: the view from States' Attorneys General. *Mental Retardation*, **26**, 5–12.
McCann, J.T. (1998). A conceptual framework for identifying various types of confessions. *Behavioral Sciences and the Law*, **16**, 441–453.
McCauley, C. (1989). The nature of social influence in Groupthink: compliance and internalisation. *Journal of Personality and Social Psychology*, **57**(2), 250–260.
McCollum, Lord Justice (1997). *The Queen v. Patrick Gerard Kane*. In Her Majesty's Court of Appeal in Northern Ireland. Judgment delivered December 19.
McConville, M. (1992). Videotaping interrogations: police behaviour on and off camera. *Criminal Law Review*, 532–548.
McConville, M. (1993). *Corroboration and confessions. The impact of a rule requiring that no conviction can be sustained on the basis of confession evidence alone. The Royal Commission on Criminal Justice Research Study No. 36*. London: HMSO.
McConville, M. & Baldwin, J. (1981). *Courts prosecution and conviction*. Clarendon: Oxford.
McConville, M. & Hodgson, J. (1993). *Custodial legal advice and the right to silence. The Royal Commission on Criminal Justice Research Study No. 16*. London: HMSO.
McConville, M. & Morrell, P. (1983). Recording the interrogations: have the police got it taped? *Criminal Law Review*, 158–183.
McDonald, P. (1993). *Make 'em talk! Principles of military interrogation*. Bouldu, CO: Paladin.
McDougall, W. (1908). *An introduction to social psychology*. London: Methuen.
McEwan, J. (1991). *Evidence and the adversarial process: the modern law*. Oxford: Blackwell.
Mcguire, R.E. (2000). A proposal to strengthen juvenile Miranda rights: requiring parental presence in custodial interrogations. *Vanderbilt Law Review*, **53**, 1355–1387.
McGurk, B., Carr, M. & McGurk, D. (1993). *Investigative interviewing courses for police officers: an evaluation. Police Research Group Paper 4*. London: Home Office.
McKee, G. & Franey, R. (1988). *Time bomb*. London: Bloomsbury.
McKenzie, J. (1994). Regulating custodial interviews: a comparative study. *International Journal of Sociology and Law*, **22**, 239–259.
McMahon, M. (1993). A false confession of child sexual abuse on the Navajo reservation: the Gudjonsson Suggestibility Scale and expert testimony. *Issues in Child Abuse Accusations*, **5**, 211–219.
Meadow, R. (1977). Munchausen syndrome by proxy—the hitherland of child abuse. The Lancet, 8033, August 13.
Medford, S., Gudjonsson, G. H. & Pearse J. (2000). *The identification of persons at risk in police custody. The use of appropriate adults by the Metropolitan Police*. London: Institute of Psychiatry and Metropolitan Police.
Meerloo, J.A.M. (1951). The crime of menticide. *American Journal of Psychiatry*, **107**, 594–598.
Meerloo, J.A.M. (1954). Pavlovian strategy as a weapon in menticide. *American Journal of Psychiatry*, **110**, 809–813.
Megargee, E.I. (1966). Undercontrolled and overcontrolled personality types in extreme antisocial aggression. *Psychological Monographs*, **80**(611).

Memon, A. (1999). Interviewing witnesses: the cognitive interview. In A. Memon and R. Bull (Eds), *The psychology of interviewing*. Chichester: Wiley, 343–355.

Menninger, K.A. (1986). Mental retardation and criminal responsibility: some thoughts on the idiocy defence. *International Journal of Law and Psychiatry*, **8**, 343–357.

Merckelbach, H., Muris, P., Rassin, E. & Horselenberg, R. (2000). Dissociation experiences and interrogative suggestibility in college students. *Personality and Individual Differences*, **29**, 1133–1140.

Merckelbach, H., Muris, P., Wessel, I. & Van Koppen, P.J. (1998a). The Gudjonsson Suggestibility Scale (GSS): further data on its reliability, validity, and metacognition correlates. *Social Behavior and Personality*, **26**, 203–210.

Merckelbach, H., Muris, P., Schmidt, H., Rassin, E. & Horselenberg, R. (1998b). De Creatieve Ervaringen Vragenlijst als maat voor 'fantasy proneness' [The Creative Experiences Questionnaire (CEQ) as a measure of fantasy proneness]. *De Psycholoog*, **33**, 204–208.

Meyer, T. (1999). Testing the validity of confessions and waivers of the self-incrimination privilege in the juvenile court. *University of Kansas Law Review*, **47**, 1035–1078.

Mikulincer, M., Babkoff, H. & Caspy, T. (1989). The effects of 72 hours of sleep loss on psychological variables. *British Journal of Psychology*, **80**, 145–162.

Milberg, S. & Clark, M.S. (1988). Moods and compliance. *British Journal of Social Psychology*, **27**, 79–90.

Milgram, S. (1974). *Obedience to authority*. London: Tavistock.

Milne, R. (1999). Interviewing children with learning disabilities. In A. Memon and R. Bull (Eds), *The psychology of interviewing* Chichester: Wiley, 165–180.

Milne, R., Clare, I. & Bull, R. (1999). Using the cognitive interview with adults with mild learning disability. *Psychology, Crime and Law*, **5**, 81–99.

Milner, N.A. (1971). *The court and local law enforcement: the impact of Miranda*. Newbury Park, CA: Sage.

Mirfield, P. (1985). *Confessions*. London: Sweet and Maxwell.

Mitchell, B. (1983). Confessions and police interrogation of suspects. *Criminal Law Review*, September, 596–604.

Mitchell, S. & Richardson, P.J. (1985). *Archbold. Pleading, evidence and practice in criminal cases*. 42nd edn. London: Sweet and Maxwell.

Moore, H.T. (1921). The comparative influence of majority and expert opinion. *American Journal of Psychology*, **32**, 16–21.

Moos, R. & Billings, A.G. (1982). Conceptualizing and measuring coping resources and processes. In L. Goldberger and S. Brenznite (Eds), *Handbook of stress: theoretical and clinical aspects*. New York: Free Press.

Morgan, D. & Stephenson, G. (Eds) (1994) *Suspicion and silence. The right to silence in criminal investigation*. London: Blackstone.

Morrison, D. & Gilbert, P. (2001). Social rank, shame and anger in primary and secondary psychopaths. *Journal of Forensic Psychiatry*, **12**, 330–356.

Mortimer, A. (1994). *Cognitive process underlying police investigative interviewing*. Unpublished Ph.D. Thesis, University of Portsmouth.

Mortimer, A. & Shepherd, E. (1999). Frames of mind: schemata guiding cognition and conduct in the interviewing of suspected offenders. In A. Memon and R. Bull (Eds), *Handbook of the psychology of interviewing*. Chichester: Wiley, 293–315.

Morton, J. (2001). *Catching the killers. A definitive history of criminal detection*. London: Ebury.

Moston, S. (1990a). *The ever-so gentle art of police interrogation*. Paper presented at the British Psychological Society Annual Conference, Swansea University, UK.

Moston, S. (1990b). How children interpret and respond to questions: situation sources of suggestibility in eyewitness interviews. *Social Behaviour*, **5**, 155–167.

Moston, S. & Engelberg, T. (1993). Police questioning techniques in tape-recorded interviews with criminal suspects. *Policing and Society*, **6**, 61–75.

Moston, S. & Stephenson, G.M. (1993). *The questioning and interviewing of suspects outside the police station. The Royal Commission on Criminal Justice Research Study No. 22*. London: HMSO.

Moston, S.J. & Stephenson, G.M. (1992). Predictors of suspect and interviewer behaviour during police questioning. In F. Loesel, D. Bender and T. Bliesener (Eds), *Psychology and law: international perspectives*. Berlin: De Gruyter, 212–218.

Moston, S. & Stephenson, G.M. (1993). The changing face of police interrogation. *Journal of Community and Applied Social Psychology*, **3**, 101–115.

Moston, S., Stephenson, G.M. & Williamson, T.M. (1992). The effects of case characteristics on suspect behaviour during questioning. *British Journal of Criminology*, **32**, 23–40.

Moston, S., Stephenson, G.M. & Williamson, T.M. (1993). The incidence, antecedents and consequences of the use of the right to silence during police questioning. *Criminal Behaviour and Mental Health*, **3**(1), 30–47.

Mullin, C. (1989). *Error of judgement. The truth about the Birmingham bombings*. Dublin: Poolbeg.

Munsterberg, H. (1908). *On the witness stand*. Garden City, NY: Doubleday.

Murakami, A., Edelman, R.J. & Davis, P.E. (1996). Interrogative suggestibility in opiate users. *Addiction*, **91**, 1365–1373.

National Crime Faculty (1996). *Investigative interviewing: a practical guide*. Hook: Training and Development Unit, Bramshill Police College.

Nelson, H.E. (1982). *National Adult Reading Test*. Windsor: NFER.

Neubauer, D.W. (1974). Confessions in Prairie City: some causes and effects. *Journal of Criminal Law and Criminology*, **65**, 103–112.

Newburn, T. & Hayman, T. (2002). *Policing, surveillance and social control. CCTV and police monitoring of suspects*. Cullompton: Willan.

Norfolk, G.A. (1997a). Fit to be interviewed—a proposed scheme of examination. *Medicine, Science and the Law*, **37**, 228–234.

Norfolk, G.A. (1997b). Fit to be interviewed—a police surgeon's perspective. In G.A. Norfolk (Ed.), *Fit to be interviewed by the police*. Harrogate: Association of Police Surgeons.

Norfolk, G.A. (1999). Physiological illnesses and their potential for influencing testimony. *Medicine, Science and the Law*, **39**, 105–112.

Norfolk, G. (2001). Fit to be interviewed by the police—an aid to assessment. *Medicine, Science and the Law*, **41**, 5–12.

Novaco, R.W. (1994). Anger as a risk factor for violence among the mentally disordered. In J. Monahan and H. Steadman (Eds), *Violence and mental disorder: developments in risk assessment*. Chicago, IL: University of Chicago Press, 21–59.

Nugent, P.M. & Kroner, D.G. (1996). Denial, response styles, and admittance of offenses among child molesters and rapists. *Journal of Interpersonal Violence*, **11**(4), 475–486.

Ofshe, R. (1989). Coerced confessions: the logic of seemingly irrational action. *Cultic Studies Journal*, **6**, 1–15.

Ofshe, R, (1992). Inadvertent hypnosis during interrogation: false confessions due to dissociative state: misidentified multiple personality disorder and the satanic cult hypothesis. *Journal of Clinical and Experimental Hypnosis*, **40**, 125–156.

Ofshe, R.J. & Leo, R.A. (1997a). The decision to confess falsely: rational choice and irrational action. *Denver University Law Review*, **74**, 979–1122.

Ofshe, R.J. & Leo, R.A. (1997b). The social psychology of police interrogation. The theory and classification of true and false confessions. *Studies in Law, Politics and Society*, **16**, 189–251.

Ofshe, R. & Watters, E. (1994). *Making monsters. False memories, psychotherapy and sexual hysteria*. New York: Scribner.

Ord, B. & Shaw, G. (1999). *Investigative interviewing explained. The operational guide to practical interviewing skills*. Woking: New Police Bookshop.

Orwell, G. (1951). *Animal farm*. Harmondsworth: Penguin.

Osgood, C.E., Suci, G.J. & Tannebaum, P. (1957). *The measurement of meaning*. Urbana, IL: University of Illinois Press.

Ost, J. (2000). *Recovering memories: convergent approaches towards an understanding of the false memory debate*. Unpublished Ph.D. Thesis, University of Portsmouth.

Ost, J., Costall, A. & Bull, R. (2001). False confessions and false memories: a model for understanding retractor's experiences of making and repudiating claims of childhood sexual abuse. *Journal of Forensic Psychiatry*, **12**, 549–579.

Paddock, J.R., Joseph, A.L., Chan, F.M., Terranova, S., Manning, C. & Loftus, E.F. (1998). When guided visualization procedures may backfire: imagination inflation and predicting individual differences in suggestibility. *Applied Cognitive Psychology*, **12**, 63–75.

Paisley, I.J.R. (1992). *Reasonable doubt: the case for the UDR Four*. Dublin: Mercier.

Palmer, C. (1996). Still vulnerable after all these years. *Criminal Law Review*, 633–644.

Palmer, C. & Hart, M. (1996). *A PACE in the right direction? The effectiveness of safeguards in the Police and Criminal Evidence Act 1984 for mentally disordered and mentally handicapped suspects. A South Yorkshire study*. Sheffield: Institute for the Study of the Legal Profession.

Parkes, C.M. (1986). *Bereavement studies in grief in adult life*. 2nd edn. London: Tavistock.

Payne-James, J.J., Dean, P.J. & Keys D.W. (1994). Drug addicts in police custody: a prospective survey. *Journal of Royal Society of Medicine*, **87**, 13–14.

Pear, T.H. & Wyatt, S. (1914). The testimony of normal and mentally defective children. *British Journal of Psychology*, **3**, 388–419.

Pearse, J. (1991). *Police interviewing. Who is at risk?* Unpublished B.Sc. Thesis, London School of Economics.

Pearse, J.J. (1997). *Police interviewing: an examination of some of the psychological, interrogative and background factors that are associated with a suspect's confession*. Unpublished Ph.D. Thesis, University of London.

Pearse, J. & Gudjonsson, G.H. (1996a). Police interviewing techniques at two South London police stations. *Psychology, Crime and Law*, **3**, 63–74.

Pearse, J. & Gudjonsson, G.H. (1996b). A review of the role of the legal adviser in police stations. *Criminal Behaviour and Mental Health*, **6**, 231–239.

Pearse, J. & Gudjonsson, G.H. (1996c). Understanding the problems of the Appropriate Adult. *Expert Evidence*, **4**, 101–104.

Pearse, J. & Gudjonsson, G.H. (1996d). How appropriate are Appropriate Adults? *Journal of Forensic Psychiatry*, **7**, 570–580.

Pearse, J. & Gudjonsson, G.H. (1997). Police interviewing and mentally disordered offenders: changing the role of the legal adviser. *Expert Evidence*, **5.** 49–53.

Pearse, J. & Gudjonsson, G.H. (1999). Measuring influential police interviewing tactics: a factor analytic approach. *Legal and Criminological Psychology*, **4** (Part 2), 221–238.

Pearse, J., Gudjonsson, G.H., Clare, I.C.H. & Rutter, S. (1998). Police interviewing and psychological vulnerabilities: predicting the likelihood of a confession. *Journal of Community and Applied Social Psychology*, **8**(1), 1–21.

Pearson, R., Robertson, G. & Gibb, R. (2000). The identification and treatment of opiate users in police custody. *Medicine, Science and the Law*, **40**, 305–312.

Pendergrast, M. (1995). *Victims of memory*. London: Harper Collins.

Perkins, D. (1993). The psychology of interrogations, confessions and testimony. A book review. *Journal of Forensic Psychiatry*, **4**, 163–164.

Perlman, N.B., Ericson, K.I., Esses, V.M. & Isaacs, B.J. (1994). The developmentally handicapped witnesses. Competency as a function of question format. *Law and Human Behavior*, **18**, 171–187.

Pettigrew, T.F. (1958). Personality and sociocultural factors in intergroup attitudes: a cross-national comparison. *Conflict Resolution*, **11**, 29–42.

Phillips, C. & Brown, D. (1998). *Entry into the criminal justice system: a survey of police arrests and their outcomes*. London: Home Office.

Pope, K.S. & Brown, L.S. (1996). *Recovered memories of abuse. Assessment, therapy, forensics*. Washington, DC: American Psychological Association.

Pope, H.S., Butcher, J.N. & Sleen, J. (1993). *The MMPI-2 in court*. Washington, DC: American Psychological Association.

Powers, P.A., Andriks, J.L. & Loftus, E.F. (1979). Eyewitness account of females and males. *Journal of Applied Psychology*, **64**, 339–347.

Price, C. & Caplan, J. (1977). *The Confait confessions*. London: Boyars.

Prideaux, E. (1919). Suggestion and suggestibility. *British Journal of Psychology*, **10**, 228–241.

Rabon, D. (1992). *Interviewing and interrogation*. Durham, NC: Carolina.

Rabon, D. (1994). *Investigative discourse analysis*. Durham, NC: Carolina.

Radelet, M.L., Bedau, H.A. & Putman, C.E. (1992). *In spite of innocence. Erroneous convictions in capital cases*. Boston, MA: Northeastern University Press.

Radelet, M.L., Lofquist, W.S. & Bedau, H.A. (1996). Prisoners released from death rows since 1970 because of doubts about their guilt. *Thomas M. Cooley Law Review*, **13**, 907–966.

Radin, E.D. (1964). *The innocents*. New York: Morrow.

Rassin, E. (2001). Thought suppression, memory, and interrogative suggestibility. *Psychology, Crime and Law*, **7**, 45–55.

Rathus, S.A. (1973). A 30-item schedule for assessing assertive behavior. *Behavior Therapy*, **4**, 398–406.

Rattner, A. (1988). Convicted but innocent. Wrongful conviction and the criminal justice system. *Law Human Behavior*, **12**, 283–293.

Raven, J.C., Court, J.H. & Raven, J. (1992). *Standard Progressive Matrices*. 1992 edn. Oxford: Oxford Psychologists.

Redlich, A.D. (1999). *False confessions: the influence of age, suggestibility, and maturity*. Unpublished Ph.D. Thesis, University of California.

Redlich, F.C., Ravitz, L.J. & Dession, G.H. (1951). Narcoanalysis and truth. *American Journal of Psychiatry*, **107**, 586.

Reed, J.E. (1996). Fixed vs. flexible neuropsychological test batteries under the Daubert standard for admissibility of scientific evidence. *Behavioral Sciences and the Law*, **14**, 315–322.

Register, P.A. & Kihlstrom, J.F. (1988). Hypnosis and interrogative suggestibility. *Personality and Individual Differences*, **9**, 549–558.

Reik, T. (1959). *The compulsion to confess: on the psychoanalysis of crime and punishment*. New York: Farrar, Straus and Cudahy.

Richard, C.L., Spencer, J. & Spooner, F. (1980). The mentally retarded defendant–offender. *Journal of Special Education*, **14**, 113–119.

Richardson, G. (1991). *A study of interrogative suggestibility in an adolescent forensic population*. Unpublished M.Sc. Thesis, University of Newcastle.

Richardson, G., Gudjonsson, G.H. & Kelly, T.P. (1995). Interrogative suggestibility in an adolescent forensic population. *Journal of Adolescence*, **18**(2), 211–216.

Richardson, G. & Kelly, T.P. (1995). The relationship between intelligence, memory and interrogative suggestibility in young offenders. *Psychology, Crime and Law*, **1**, 283–290.

Richardson, G. & Smith, P. (1993). The inter-rater reliability of the Gudjonsson Suggestibility Scale. *Personality and Individual Differences*, **14**, 251–253.

Richardson, P.J. (2001). *Archbold. Criminal pleading, evidence and practice*. London: Sweet and Maxwell.

Richardson, S.A. (1978). Careers of mentally retarded young persons: services, jobs and interpersonal relations. *American Journal of Mental Deficiency*, **82**, 349–358.

Richardson, S.A., Dohrenwend, B.S., & Klein, D. (1965). *Inverviewing: its forms and functions*. London: Basic.

Rigby, K. (1982). A concise scale for the assessment of attitudes towards institutional authority. *Australian Journal of Psychology*, **34**, 195–204.

Rivera, J. (1997). The construction of false memory syndrome: the experience of retractors. *Psychological Inquiry*, **8**, 271–292.

Rix, K.J.B. (1997). Fit to be interviewed by the police? *Advances in Psychiatric Treatment*, **3**, 33–40.
Robbins, T. (2001). Acquittals by juries reach record levels. The Sunday Times, 28 January, News 1.3.
Robbins, T. (2002). Liverpool juries twice as likely to acquit as Old Bailey courts. The Times, 6 January.
Robertson, G. (1992). *The role of police. Royal Commission on Criminal Justice*. London: HMSO.
Robertson, G., Gibb, R. & Pearson, R. (1995). Drunkenness among police detainees. *Addiction*, **90**, 793–803.
Robertson, G., Pearson, R. & Gibb, R. (1996a). Police interviewing and the use of appropriate adults. *Journal of Forensic Psychiatry*, **7**, 297–309.
Robertson, G., Pearson, R. & Gibb, R. (1996b). The entry of mentally disordered people to the criminal justice system. *British Journal of Psychiatry*, **169**, 172–180.
Rogers, R., Salekin, R.T. & Sewell, K.W. (1999). Validation of the Millon Clinical Multiaxial Inventory for Axis II disorders: does it meet the Daubert standard? *Law and Human Behavior*, **23**, 425–443.
Rogge, O.J. (1975). *Why men confess*. New York: Da Capo.
Roppe, L.F. (1994). True blue Whether police should be allowed to use trickely and deception to extract confessions. *San Diego Law Review*, **31**, 729–773.
Rose, D. (1992). *A climate of fear. The murder of PC Blakelock and the case of the Tottenham Three*. London: Bloomsbury.
Rose, D. & Bhatti, H. (1991). Cardiff three 'innocent' of brutal murder. The Observer on Sunday, 3 February, 6.
Rose, J., Panter, S. & Wilkinson, T. (1998). *Innocents. How justice failed, Stefan Kiszko and Lesley Molseed*. London: Fourth Estate.
Rosenberg, I.M. & Rosenberg, Y.L. (1989). A modest proposal for the abolition of custodial confessions. *North Carolina Law Review*, **68**, 69–115.
Rosenberg, M. (1965). *Society and Adolescent Child*. Princeton, NJ: Princeton University Press.
Rotter, J.B. (1966). Generalized experiences for internal versus external control of reinforcement. *Psychological Monographs*, **80** (Whole No. 609).
Rowe, P (1986). The voire dire and the jury. *Criminal Law Review*, 226–232.
Royal Commission on Criminal Justice Report (1993). Cmnd. 2263. London: HMSO.
Royal Commission on Criminal Procedure Report (1981). Cmnd. 8092. London: HMSO.
Royal, R.F. & Schutte, S.R. (1976). *The gentle art of interviewing and interrogation. A professional manual and guide*. Englewood Cliffs, NJ: Prentice-Hall.
Runciman, Viscount W.G. (1993). *The Royal Commission on Criminal Justice*. Cmnd. 2263. London: HMSO.
Ryckman, R., Rodda, W. & Sherman, M. (1972). Locus of control and expertise relevance as determinants of changes in opinion about student activities. *Journal of Social Psychology*, **88**, 107–114.
Sackeim, H.M. & Gur, R.C. (1979). Self-deception, other-deception and self-reported psychopathology. *Journal of Consulting and Clinical Psychology*, **47**, 213–215.
Salter, A. (1988). *Treating child sex offenders and victims. A practical guide*. London: Sage.
Samuels, A. (1997). Custody time limits. *Criminal Law Review*, April, 245–304.
Sanders, A. & Bridges, L. (1989). The duty solicitor scheme: an unreliable safety net. *Law Society Gazette*, **44**, 12–14.
Sanders, A. & Bridges, L. (1999). The right to legal advice. In C. Walker and K. Starmer (Eds), *Miscarriages of justice. A review of justice in error*. London: Blackstone, 83–99.
Santtila, P., Alkiora, P., Ekholm, M. & Niemi, P. (1999). False confessions to robbery: the role of suggestability, anxiety, memory disturbance and withdrawal symptoms. *The Journal of Forensic Psychiatry*, **10**, 399–415.
Santtila, P., Ekholm, M. & Niemi, P. (1998). Factors moderating the effects of alcohol on interrogative suggestibility. *Psychology, Crime and Law*, **4**, 139–152.

Santtila, P., Ekholm, M. & Niemi, P. (1999). The effects of alcohol on interrogative suggestibility: the role of state-anxiety and mood states as mediating factors. *Legal and Criminological Psychology*, **4**, 1–13.
Santucci, P.S. & Winokur, G. (1955). Brainwashing as a factor in psychiatric illness. *A.M.A. Archives of Neurological Psychiatry*, **74**, 11–16.
Sargant, W. (1957). *Battle for the mind. A physiology of conversion and brainwashing*. London: Heinemann.
Saucier, D. & Gaudette, N. (2000). Actual memory ability significantly predicts self-evaluations of memory. *Expert Evidence*, **8**, 3–14.
Scheck, B., Neufeld, P. & Dwyer, J. (2000). *Actual innocence*. Garden City, NY: Doubleday.
Schein, E.H. (1956). The Chinese indoctrination program for prisoners of war. A study of attempted 'brainwashing'. *Psychiatry*, **19**, 149–172.
Schein, E.H., Schneier, I. & Barker, C.H. (1961). *Coercive persuasion. A socio-psychological analysis of the 'brainwashing' of American civilian prisoners by the Chinese Communists*. New York: Norton.
Schill, T., Kahn, & Meuhleman, T. (1968). WAIS PA performance participation in extracurricular activities. *Journal of Clinical Psychology*, **24**, 95–96.
Schonell, F.J. & Goodacre, E.J. (1974). *The psychology and teaching of reading*. 5th edn. Edinburgh: Oliver and Boyd, 216–217.
Schooler, J.W. & Loftus, E.F. (1986). Individual differences and experimentation: complementary approaches to interrogative suggestibility. *Social Behaviour*, **1**, 105–112.
Schooler, J.W. & Loftus, E.F. (1993). Multiple mechanisms mediating individual differences in eyewitness accuracy and suggestibility. In J.M. Puckett and H.W. Reese (Eds), *Mechanisms of everyday cognition*. London: Erlbaum, 177–203.
Schulhofer, S.J. (1998). Miranda's practical effects: substantial benefits and vanishingly small social costs. In R.A. Leo and G.C. Thomas III. (Eds), *The Miranda debate, justice and policing*. Boston: Northeastern University Press, 191–207.
Scullin, M.H. & Ceci, S.J. (2001). A suggestibility scale for children. *Personality and Individual Differences*, **30**, 843–856.
Sear, L. & Stephenson, G. (1997). Interviewing skills and individual characteristics of police interrogators. In G. Stephenson and N. Clark (Eds), *Procedures in criminal justice: contemporary issues*. Leicester: British Psychological Society 27–34.
Shaffer, D.F. (1985). The defendant's testimony. In S.M. Kassin and L.S. Wrightsman. (Eds), *The psychology of evidence and trial procedure*. London: Sage, 124–149.
Shallice, T. (1974). The Ulster depth interrogation techniques and their relation to sensory deprivation research. *Cognition*, **1**, 385–406.
Sharrock, R. (1988). Eyewitness testimony: some implications for clinical interviewing and forensic psychology practice. In F.N. Watts. (Ed.), *New developments in clinical psychology*. Vol. 2 New York: Wiley, 208–225.
Sharrock, R. & Cresswell, M. (1989). Pseudologia fantastica: a case study of a man charged with murder. *Medicine, Science and the Law*, **29**, 323–328.
Sharrock, R. & Gudjonsson, G.H. (1993). Intelligence, previous convictions and interrogative suggestibility: a path analysis of alleged false-confession case. *British Journal of Clinical Psychology*, **32**(2), 169–175.
Sheehan, P.W., Garnett, M. & Robertson R. (1993). The effects of cue level, hypnotizability and state instruction on responses to leading questions. *International Journal of Clinical and Experimental Hypnosis*, **41**, 287–304.
Sheehan, P.W., Green, V. & Truesdale, P. (1992). The influence of rapport on hypnotically induced pseudomemory, *Journal of Abnormal Psychology*, **101**, 690–700.
Shepherd, E.W., Mortimer, A.K. & Mobasheri, R. (1995). The police caution: comprehension and perceptions in the general population. *Expert Evidence*, **4**, 60–67.
Sherif, M (1936). *The psychology of social norms*. New York: Harper.
Shuman, D.W. & Sales, B.D. (1999). The impact of Daubert and its progeny on the admissibility of behavioural and social science evidence. *Psychology, Public Policy, and Law*, **5**, 194–202.

Shuy, R.W. (1998). *The language of confession, interrogation, and deception*. Thousand Oaks, CA: Sage.

Sidis, B. (1898). *The psychology of suggestion*. New York: Appleton.

Sigelman, C.K., Budd, E.C., Spanhel, C.L. & Schoenrock, C.J. (1981). When in doubt say yes: acquiescence in interviews with mentally retarded persons. *Mental Retardation*, **19**, 53–58.

Sigelman, C.K. & Werder, P.R. (1975). The communication skills of the mentally retarded: a new analysis. *Journal of Developmental Disabilities*, **1**, 19–26.

Sigurdsson, E., Gudjonsson, G.H., Kolbeinsson, H. & Petursson, H. (1994). The effects of ECT and depression on confabulation, memory processing, and suggestibility. *Nordic Journal of Psychiatry*, **48**, 443–451.

Sigurdsson J.F. (1998). *Alleged false confessions among Icelandic offenders: an examination of some psychological criminological and substance use factors that are associated with the reported false confessions*. Unpublished Ph.D. Thesis, University of London.

Sigurdsson, J.F. & Gudjonsson, G.H. (1994). Alcohol and drug intoxication during police interrogation and the reasons why suspects confess to the police. *Addiction*, **89**, 985–997.

Sigurdsson, J.F. & Gudjonsson, G.H. (1996). Psychological characteristics of 'false confessors': a study among Icelandic prison inmates and juvenile offenders. *Personality and Individual Differences*, **20**, 321–329.

Sigurdsson, J. & Gudjonsson, G.H. (1997). The criminal history of 'false confessors' and other prison inmates. *Journal of Forensic Psychiatry*, **8**, 447–455.

Sigurdsson, J. & Gudjonsson, G.H. (2001). False confessions: the relative importance of psychological, criminological and substance abuse variables. *Psychology, Crime and Law*, **7**, 275–289.

Singh, K.K. & Gudjonsson, G.H. (1984). Interrogative suggestibility, delayed memory and self-concept. *Personality and Individual Differences*, **5**, 203–209.

Singh, K.K. & Gudjonsson, G.H. (1987). The internal consistency of the 'shift' factor on the Gudjonsson Suggestibility Scale. *Personality and Individual Differences*, **8**, 265–266.

Singh, K.K. & Gudjonsson, G.H. (1992a). The vulnerability of adolescent boys to interrogative pressure: an experimental study. *Journal of Forensic Psychiatry*, **3**, 167–170.

Singh, K.K. & Gudjonsson, G.H. (1992b). Interrogative suggestibility among adolescent boys and its relationship with intelligence, memory, and cognitive set. *Journal of Adolescence*, **15**(2), 155–161.

Smith, K. & Gudjonsson, G.H. (1986). Investigation of the responses of 'fakers' and 'non-fakers' on the Gudjonsson Suggestibility Scale. *Medicine, Science and the Law*, **26**, 66–71.

Smith, P. & Gudjonsson, G.H. (1995a). Confabulation among forensic inpatients and its relationship with memory, suggestibility, compliance, anxiety and self-esteem. *Personality and Individual Differences*, **19**, 517–523.

Smith, P. & Gudjonsson, G.H. (1995b). The relationship of mental disorder to suggestibility and confabulation among forensic inpatients. *Journal of Forensic Psychiatry*, **6**, 499–515.

Softley, P. (1980). *Police interrogation. An observational study in four police stations. Home Office Research Study No. 61*. London: HMSO.

Sommer, R. (1969). *Personal space*. Englewood Cliffs, NJ: Prentice-Hall.

Sparrow, S.S., Balla, D.A. & Cicchetti, D.V. (1984). *Vineland Adaptive Behavior Scales. Interview edition. Expanded Form manual*. Circle Pines, MN: American Guidance Service.

Spielberger, C.D. (1983). *Manual for the State–Trait Anxiety Inventory (form Y)*. Palo Alto, CA: Consulting Psychologists Press.

Spielberger, C.D., Gorsuch, R. & Lushene, R.E. (1970). *State–Trait Anxiety Inventory manual*. Palo Alto, CA: Consulting Psychologists Press.

Stagg, C. & Kessler, D. (1999). *Who really killed Rachel?* London: Aspire.

Stark, M. (1994). Management of drug addicts in police custody. *Journal of the Royal Society of Medicine*, **87**, 584–587.

Starmer, K. & Woolf, M. (1999). The right to silence. In C. Walker and K. Starmer (Eds), *Miscarriages of justice. A review of justice in error*. London: Blackstone, 100–118.

Steele, C.M. & Josephs, R.A. (1988). Drinking your troubles away II: an attention-allocation model of alcohol's effect on psychological stress. *Journal of Abnormal Psychology*, **97**, 196–205.

Steinschneider, A. (1972). Prolonged apnea and the sudden infant death syndrome: clinical and laboratory observations. *Pediatrics*, **50**, 646–654.

Stern, W. (1910). Abstracts of lectures on the psychology of testimony and on the study of individuality. *American Journal of Psychology*, **21**, 273–282.

Stern, W. (1938). *General psychology: from the personalistic standpoint*. New York: Macmillan.

Stern, W. (1939). The psychology of testimony. *Journal of Abnormal and Social Psychology*, **34**, 3–20.

Stier, D.H. & Hall, J.A. (1984). Gender differences in touch: an empirical and theoretical review. *Journal of Personality and Social Psychology*, **47**, 440–459.

Stockdale, J. (1993). *Management and supervision of police interviews. Police Research Group Paper 4*. London: Home Office.

Stricker, L.J., Messick, S. & Jackson, D.N. (1967). Suspicion of deception: implication for conformity research. *Journal of Personality and Social Psychology*, **5**, 379–389.

Stubbs, C. & Newberry, J.J. (1998). *Analytic interviewing*. Queensland: Australian Institute of Analytic Interviewing.

Stukat, K.G. (1958). *Suggestibility: a factor and experimental analysis*. Stockholm: Almgvist & Wiksell.

Stuntz, W.J. (1989). The American exclusionary rule and defendants' charging rights. *Criminal Law Review*, 117–128.

Stumphauzer, J.S. (1986). Helping delinquents change: a treatment manual of social learning approaches. *Child and Youth Services*, **8**(1/2), 213.

Svartvik, J. (1968). The Evans statements. A case for forensic linguistics. Goethenburg: Almqvist & Wiksell.

Tangney, J.P. (1990). Assessing individual differences in proneness to shame and guilt: development of self-conscious affect and attribution inventory. *Journal of Personality and Social Psychology*, **59**, 102–111.

Tangney, J.P. (1996). Conceptual and methodological issues in the assessment of shame and guilt. *Behavioural Research and Therapy*, **34**, 741–754.

Tata, P. (1983). *Some effects of stress and feedback on interrogative suggestibility: an experimental study*. Unpublished M.Phil. Thesis, University of London.

Tata, P.R. & Gudjonsson, G.H. (1990). The effects of mood and verbal feedback on interrogative suggestibility. *Personality and Individual Differences*, **11**, 1079–1085.

Taylor, N. & Mansfield, M. (1999). Post-conviction procedures. In C. Walker and K. Starmer (Eds), *Miscarriages of justice. A review of justice in error*. London: Blackstone, 229–246.

Taylor, P.J. & Kopelman, M.D. (1984). Amnesia for criminal offences. *Psychological Medicine*, **14**, 581–588.

Tellegen, A. (1982). *Brief manual for the Differential Personality Questionnaire*. Unpublished manuscript, University of Minnesota Department of Psychology.

Tellegen, A. & Atkinson, G. (1974). Openness to absorbing and self-altering experiences ('absorption'), a trait related to hypnotic suggestibility. *Journal of Abnormal Psychology*, **83**, 268–277.

Tendler, S. (1990). Blakelock killing conviction referred back to appeal court. The Times, 5 December, 24.

The Earl of Birkenhead (1938). *More famous trials*. London: Hutchinson.

Theilgaard, A. (1996). A clinical psychological perspective. In C. Cordess and M. Cox (Eds), *Forensic psychotherapy, crime, psychodynamics and the offender patient*. London: Kingsley, 47–62.

The Lancet (1994). Editorial. Guilty innocents: the road to false confessions. *The Lancet*, **344**, 1447–1450.

The Times (1990). Judge urges care on Marsh 'confession'. The Times, 7 November, 3.

Thomas, G.C. (1998). Plain talk about the Miranda empirical debate: a 'steady-state' theory of confessions. In R.A. Leo and G.C. Thomas III (Eds), *The Miranda debate. Law, justice, and policing*. Boston: Northeastern University Press, 236–248.

Thompson, B. & Melancon, J. (1990) Measurement characteristics of the Finding Embedded Figures Test: a comparison across three samples and two response formats. *Educational and Psychological Measurement*, **50**, 333–342.

Thornton, D. (1987). Sex offenders segregated for their own protection under Rule 43. In B.J. McGurk, D. Thornton and M. Williams (Eds), *Applying psychology to imprisonment: theory and practice*. London: HMSO, 431–443.

Tousignant, J.P., Hall, D. & Loftus, E.F. (1986). Discrepancy detection and vulnerability to misleading post event information. *Memory and Cognition*, **14**, 329–338.

Trankell, A. (1958). Was Lars sexually assaulted? A study in the reliability of witnesses and of experts. *The Journal of Abnormal and Social Psychology*, **56**, 385–395.

Trankell, A. (1972). *Reliability of evidence*. Stockholm: Beckmans.

Treisman, A.M.(1969). Strategies and models of selective attention. *Psychological Review*, **76**, 282–299.

Tully, B. (1980). Interrogating mentally handicapped suspects. In *Law and the mentally retarded citizen*. Report of the Thirteenth Spring Conference of Mental Retardation, Exeter, UK. London: MENCAP.

Tully, B. & Cahill, D. (1984). *Police interviewing of mentally handicapped persons: an experimental study*. London: Police Foundation of Great Britain.

Underwager, R. & Wakefield, H. (1992). False confessions and police deception. *American Journal of Forensic Psychology*, **10**(3), 49–66.

Usborne, D. (1998). Southern justice in the dock. One-eyed murder sets a precedent in Texas: they let him live. Independent on Sunday, 28 June, 21.

Van Velsen, C. (1999). Freud and remorse. In M. Cox (Ed.), *Remorse and reparation*. London: Kingsley, 63–67.

Vennard, J. (1980). *Contested trials in magistrates' courts. Royal Commission on Criminal Procedure Research Study No. 6*. London: HMSO.

Vennard, J. (1984). Disputes within trials over the admissibility and accuracy of incriminating statements: some research evidence. *Criminal Law Review*, 15–24.

Verkaik, R. (2001). Man freed after law lords quash murder conviction. *The Independent*, 14 December.

Victory, P. (2002). *Justice and truth. The Guildford Four and the Maguire Seven*. London: Sinclair-Stevenson.

Vrij, A. (2000). *Detecting lies and deceit. The psychology of lying and the implications for professional practice*. Chichester: Wiley.

Vrij, A. (2001). Detecting the liars. *The Psychologist*, **14**, 596–598.

Wade, N. (1972). Technology in Ulster: rubber bullets hit home brainwashing backfires. *Science*, **176**, 1102–1105.

Wagstaff, G.F. (1981). *Hypnosis, compliance and belief*. Brighton: Harvester.

Wakefield, H. & Underwager, R. (1988). *Accusation of child sexual abuse*. Springfield, IL: Thomas.

Wakefield, H. & Underwager, R. (1998). *Coerced or nonvoluntary confessions*. Springfield, IL: Thomas.

Wald, M., Ayres, R., Hess, D.W., Schantz, M. & Whitebread, C. H. (1967). Interrogations in New Haven the impacts of Miranda. *Yale Law Journal*, **76**, 1519–1648.

Walker, C. (1999a). Miscarriages of justice in Scotland. In C. Walker and K. Starmer (Eds), *Miscarriages of justice. A review of justice in error*. London: Blackstone, 323–353.

Walker, C. (1999b). The judiciary. In C. Walker and K. Starmer. (Eds), *Miscarriages of justice. A review of justice in error*. London: Blackstone, 203–228.

Walker, C. (1999c). Miscarriages of justice in principle and practice. In C. Walker and K. Starmer (Eds), *Miscarriages of justice. A review of justice in error*. London: Blackstone, 31–62.
Walker C. (2000). Court clears 'killer' after 48 years. The Times, 21 December, 5.
Walker, C. & Starmer, K. (Eds) (1999). *Miscarriages of justice. A review of justice in error*. London: Blackstone.
Walkley, J. (1983). *Police interrogation: a study of the psychology, theory and practice of police interrogations and the implications for police training*. Unpublished M.Sc. Thesis, Cranfield Institute of Technology.
Walkley, J. (1987). *Police interrogation. A handbook for investigators*. London: Police Review Publication.
Walsh, D. (1999). Miscarriages of justice in the Republic of Ireland. In C. Walker and K. Starmer (Eds), *Miscarriages of justice. A review of justice in error*. London: Blackstone, 304–322.
Walsh, D.P.J. (1982). Arrest and interrogation: Northern Ireland 1981. *Journal of Law and Society*, **9**, 37–62.
Wambaugh, J. (1989). *The blooding*. London: Bantam.
Ward, J. (1993). *Ambushed. My story*. London: Vermilion.
Ware, J.W. (1978). Effects of acquiescent response set on patient satisfaction ratings. *Medical Care*, **16**, 327–336.
Warren, A., Hulse-Trotter, K. & Tubbs, E.C. (1991). Inducing resistance to suggestibility. *Children, Law and Human Behavior*, **15**, 273–285.
Wasik, M. & Taylor, R. (1995). *Blackstone's guide to the Criminal Justice and Public Order Act 1984*. London: Blackstone.
Watson, D. & Friend, R. (1969). Management and social evaluative anxiety. *Journal of Consulting and Clinical Psychology*, **33**, 448–457.
Wechsler, D. (1981). *WAIS-R manual*. New York: Psychological Corporation–Harcourt Brace Jovanovich.
Wechsler, D. (1997). *WAIS-III administration and scoring manual*. London: Psychological Corporation.
Weisselberg, C.D. (1998). Saving Miranda. *Cornell Law Review*, **84**, 109–192.
Westcott, H.L., Davies, G.M. & Bull, R.H.C. (Eds) (2002). *Children's testimony. A handbook of psychological research and forensic practice*. Chichester: Wiley.
White, W.S. (1996). False confessions and the constitution: safeguards against untrustworthy confessions. *Harvard Civil Rights–Civil Liberties Law Review*, **32**, 105–157.
White, W.S. (1997). False confessions and the constitution: safeguards against untrustworthy confessions. *Harvard Civil Rights–Civil Liberties Law Review*, **32**, 105–157.
White, W.S. (1998). What is an involuntary confession now? *Rutgers Law Review*, **50**, 2001–2057.
White, W.S. (2001). Miranda's failure to restrain pernicious interrogation practices. *Michigan Law Review*, **99**, 1211–1247.
Williams, J. (2000). The Crime and Disorder Act 1998: conflicting roles for the Appropriate Adult. *Criminal Law Review*, 877–934.
Williamson, T.M. (1990). *Strategic changes in police interrogation: an examination of police and suspect behaviour in the Metropolitan Police in order to determine the effects of new legislation, technology and organizational policies*. Unpublished Ph.D. Thesis, University of Kent.
Williamson, T.M. (1993). From interrogation to investigative interviewing. Strategic trends in the police questioning. *Journal of Community and Applied Social Psychology*, **3**, 89–99.
Williamson, T.M. (1994). Reflections on current police practice. In D. Morgan and G. Stephenson (Eds), *Suspicion and silence. The rights of silence in criminal investigations*. London: Blackstone, 107–116.
Willis, C.F., Macleod, J. & Naish, P. (1988). *The tape recording of police interviews with suspects: a second interim report. Home Office Research Study No. 97*. London: HMSO.

Winkler, J.D., Kanouse, D.E. & Ware, J.E. (1982). Controlling for acquiescence response set in score development. *Journal of Applied Psychology*, **67**, 555–561.

Witkin, H.A., Oltman, P.K., Raskin, E. & Carps, S.A. (1971). *A manual for the Embedded Figures Test*. Palo Alto, CA: Consulting Psychologists.

Woffinden, B. (1989). *Miscarriages of justice*. London: Hodder and Stoughton.

Wolchover, D. & Heaton-Armstrong, A. (1991). The questioning code revamped. *Criminal Law Review*, 232–251.

Wolfradt, U. & Meyer, T. (1998). Interrogative suggestibility, anxiety and dissociation among anxious patients and normal controls. *Personality and Individual Differences*, **25**, 425–432.

Wood, P.J.W. & Guly, O.C.R. (1991). Unfit to plead to murder: three case reports. *Medicine, Science and the Law*, **31**, 55–60.

Woolgrove, K. (1976). *The questioning of the mentally backward*. A report commissioned by the Religious Society of Friends.

Wrightsman, L.S. & Kassin, S.M. (1993). *Confessions in the courtroom*. London: Sage.

Wylie, R. (1989). *Measures of self-concepts*. NE: University of Nebraska Press.

Yant, M. (1991). *Presumed guilty. When innocent people are wrongly convicted*. Loughton: Prometheus.

Young, H.F., Bentall, R.P., Slade, P.D. & Dewey, M.E. (1987). The role of brief instructions and suggestibility in the elicitation of auditory and visual hallucinations in normal and psychiatric subjects. *Journal of Nervous and Mental Disease*, **175**, 41–48

Zander, M. (1972). Access to a solicitor in the police station. *Criminal Law Review*, 342–350.

Zander, M. (1979). The investigation of crime: a study of cases tried at the Old Bailey. *Criminal Law Review*, 203–219.

Zander, M. (1996). You have no right to remain silent: abolition of the privilege against self-incrimination in England. *Saint Louis University Law Journal*, **40**, 659–675.

Zimbardo, P.G. (1967). The psychology of police confessions. *Psychology Today*, **1**, 17–27.

Zuckerman, M. (1989). *The principles of criminal evidence*. Oxford: Clarendon.

Zuckerman, M. & Lubin, B. (1965). *Manual for the Multiple Affect Adjective Checklist*. Palo Alto, CA: Consulting Psychologists.

Author Index

Abed, R.T., 197
Abramson, L.Y., 343
Acker, J., 164
Adams, C.H., 309
Adlam, K.R.C., 142
Agar, J.R., 294, 297, 299, 304
Akehurst, L., 389
Alkiora, P., 196, 426
Allen, R.C., 321
Andriks, J.L., 345, 380, 383
Asch, S.E., 192, 342, 343, 370
Atkinson, G., 390
Atkinson, L., 327
Aveling, F., 338
Axelrod, S., 375
Ayling, C.J., 25, 131, 138, 166, 167, 174
Ayres, R., 27

Babkoff, H., 31
Baden, M., 543
Bain, S.A., 394
Baker, G.A., 317, 367
Baldwin, J., 22, 23, 38, 46, 48–9, 49–50, 54, 69, 70, 76, 77, 79, 112, 132, 133, 135, 137, 138, 141, 142, 145, 149, 184
Balla, D.A., 327
Ballachey, E.L., 342
Bandura, A., 375
Banks, C., 30
Barber, T.X., 368
Barker, C.H., 174–5, 186, 187, 188, 189, 190, 191, 192, 215
Barnes, J.A., 23, 258, 259
Barthel, J., 234
Basoglu, M., 35
Bassett, J., 185
Baxter, J.S., 334, 344, 345, 392, 393, 394
Bean, P., 261, 262
Beaumont, M., 277, 325, 461
Beck, F., 186
Bedau, H.A., 159, 162, 163, 164, 166, 315

Beins, B.C., 371
Belmont, J.M., 325
Bem, D.J., 190, 199, 357, 457
Bennett, R., 448
Bentall, R.P., 317, 367, 368
Berggren, E., 123, 186
Berlyne, N., 366
Bernaut, E., 186
Bernheim, H., 337
Bernstein, E.M., 390
Bertrand, A., 337
Bevan, V., 42, 247, 253, 259
Bhatti, H., 515
Bickman, L., 343
Billings, A.G., 395
Binet, A., 337, 339, 340, 341, 344, 345, 347, 358
Biondo, J., 399
Birch, D., 252, 253
Birgisson, G.H., 154, 374, 395
Bjornsson, G., 372, 428
Blagrove, M., 31, 389, 399, 401
Bless, E., 375, 376
Blinkhorn, S., 309
Block, H., 342
Bluglass, K., 313
Boakes, J., 212
Boggan, S., 439
Bond, R., 376
Boon, J.C.W., 392, 393, 394
Borchard, E.M., 159, 160
Bordens, K.S., 185
Bottomley, K., 24, 150
Bottoms, A.E., 184, 185
Bownes, I., 35, 152, 154
Brabin, D., 170
Bradshaw, J.M., 355, 400
Braid, J., 337
Brandon, R., 161, 212, 324, 325, 609
Brehm, J.W., 36, 399, 401
Brehm, S.S., 36, 399, 401

Author Index

Bridge, J.W., 342
Bridges, L., 150
Brignall, C., 423, 425
Britton, P., 8
Broadbent, D.E., 390
Brophy, E.E., 285
Brown, B.S., 321, 325
Brown, D., 46, 212, 214, 250, 262, 273, 411
Brown, L.S., 134, 135, 137, 138, 139, 140, 141, 142, 143, 144, 145, 147, 148, 149, 150, 151
Bruck, M., 381
Bryan, I., 55, 135
Brynjolfsdottir, B., 370
Bucke, T., 46, 250, 262, 273
Buckley, J.P., 7, 8, 9, 10, 11, 14, 25, 26, 33, 51, 52, 75, 81, 82, 83, 84, 91, 152, 183, 185, 209, 408, 508, 547
Budd, E.C., 325
Bull, R., 2, 52, 53, 54, 186, 212, 214, 318
Burke, B.W., 295
Burns, H.J., 334, 354
Burtt, H.E., 345, 382
Buss, A.S., 401
Butcher, J.N., 557
Butterfield, E.C., 325

Cahill, D., 318, 324, 382, 403–4, 410
Calcutt, D., 167
Callaghan, H., 454
Calverley, D.S., 368
Campbell, D., 468
Candel, I., 361
Caplan, J., 167
Card, R., 22
Cardone, D., 410
Carlin, M.T., 372, 412
Carlsmith, J.M., 375
Carps, S.A., 399
Carr, M., 54
Carver, C.S., 373, 396
Caspy, T., 31
Cassell, P.G., 130, 133, 134, 135, 136, 137, 138, 151, 163, 166, 179, 180, 286
Cattell, J.M., 344, 358
Ceci, S.J., 335, 360, 366, 381
Cho, K., 253
Choo, A.L.-T., 255
Chow, L., 368
Cialdini, R.B., 8
Cicchetti, D.V., 327
Clare, I.C.H., 22, 26, 27, 57, 67, 72, 73, 143, 148, 204, 262, 263, 270, 273, 290, 318, 319, 322, 324, 325, 326, 364, 365, 366, 367, 378, 380, 383, 384, 386, 388, 410, 411, 464, 621

Clark, M.D.B., 415, 417
Clark, M.S., 375, 376, 401, 402
Clark, N.K., 334, 345, 346, 347, 348, 349, 350, 351, 352, 353, 354, 355, 356, 357, 372, 381, 391, 395, 396, 399, 400, 410, 413
Clarke, C., 2, 54
Coffin, T.E., 336, 341
Cohen, G., 195
Cohen, R.L., 345
Cohen, S., 582, 583, 584
Coid, J., 308
Cole, C., 24
Coleman, A.M., 276
Cole-Morgan, D., 31, 389, 399, 401
Collins, E., 588
Combs, D.R., 373
Conlon, G., 448, 457
Connery, D.S., 159, 234, 236
Conroy, J., 34, 44
Cooke, D.J., 263, 372, 412
Cooper, P.F., 390
Coopersmith, S., 387, 397
Corre, N., 52, 247, 250, 309, 514, 521
Corsini, R.J., 206
Cosden, M., 354
Costa, P.T. Jr, 398
Costall, A., 186, 212, 214
Coulthard, M., 521
Court, J.H., 367, 597
Courtless, T.F., 321, 325
Craft, M., 324, 325
Cronbach, L.J., 376
Cross, P., 72, 364
Crowne, D.P., 372, 394
Crutchfield, R.S., 342, 343, 344
Cullen, C., 318
Cunningham, C., 187, 192
Curle, C.E., 313

Dalgleish, T., 212, 213
Dalla Barba, G., 366
Daly, R.J., 35
Danielsdottir, G., 379, 380, 383
Davies, C., 161, 324, 325
Davies, G.M., 2, 54, 212, 213, 276, 334, 345, 615
Davis, P.E., 423, 424, 425
Davison, S.E., 202, 203, 415, 418, 420, 423, 424, 425, 433
Dean, P.J., 418
DeFilippo, M., 286, 287
Delaune, P.L., 309
Dell, S., 184
Denkowski, G.C., 321, 322
Denkowski, K.M., 321, 322

Dent, H., 318, 325, 410
Dession, G.H., 124
Dewey, M.E., 368
Dickson, B., 247
Dixon, D., 24
Dodd, D.H., 355, 400
Dohrenwend, B.S., 81
Doll, E.A., 326
Dombrose, L.A., 387, 388
Dorkee, A., 401
Doyle, J.M., 380
Driver, E.D., 25
Duff, P., 438
Dunbar, D., 396
Dundee, J.W., 420
Dwyer, J., 159, 163, 180

Eagly, A.H., 380
Ede, R., 49, 79, 140, 262
Edelman, R.J., 423, 424, 425
Einarsdottir, H.R., 379
Einhorn, T., 589
Eisen, M.L., 378
Eisenberg, G.H., 399
Ekholm, M., 196, 426, 427
Ekman, P., 34
Endres, J., 361
Engelberg, T., 38, 45, 46
English, J., 22
Ericson, K.I., 318
Esses, V.M., 318
Evans, F.J., 338, 339, 340
Evans, R., 133, 135, 141, 142, 143, 144, 147, 151, 262
Eysenck, H.J., 73, 115, 142, 226, 338, 339, 340, 343, 358, 372, 374, 386, 394, 408, 599
Eysenck, M.W., 195
Eysenck, S.B.G., 142, 226, 372, 374, 386, 394, 408, 599

Farber, I.E., 191
Farr, R.M., 83
Feldman, D., 253
Feldman, M.D., 543
Fellows, N., 194
Fenner, S., 26, 67, 72, 73, 148, 262, 263, 273, 290, 318, 325
Festinger, L., 178, 192
Fielder, M., 8
Finlay, W.M.L., 377
Firstman, R., 541, 542, 543, 545, 546, 549
Firth, A., 146
Fischman, Y., 35
Fisher, Sir Henry, 39, 55, 79, 170
Fisher, R.P., 53, 309, 318, 619, 615

Fitzgerald, E., 276, 309
Fitzgerald, P., 390
Flin, R., 334, 345
Florian, A. St., 285, 618
Flynn, M.S., 354
Fong, C.T., 34, 205
Foot, P., 17, 514, 519, 520, 522
Ford, C.V., 543
Forrest, D., 35
Forshaw, D.M., 202, 203, 415, 418, 420, 433
Foster, H.H., 199
Foster, P., 481
Fowles, R., 130, 286
Franey, R., 167, 446, 448
Frank, M.G., 34
Fraser, S.C., 375
Freckelton, I., 266
Freedman, J.L., 375, 376
Freud, S., 12
Friend, R., 387, 427
Frumkin, B., 286, 288, 299
Furneaux, W.D., 338, 339, 340, 358

Gall, J.A., 266
Garety, P.A., 373
Garnett, M., 369
Garry, M., 213
Gaudette, N., 213
Geiselman, R.E., 53, 318, 619
Geller, W.A., 23
Gheorghiu, V.A., 335, 336, 337, 340
Gibb, R., 262, 416, 418
Gibson, H.B., 338
Gilbert, P., 126
Gill, M., 24
Gilovich, T., 178
Glaser, D., 212
Godin, W., 186
Goff, L.M., 213
Goffman, E., 342
Golan, D., 582, 583, 584
Gonsalves, C.J., 35
Goodacre, E.J., 60
Goodman-Delahunty, J., 295, 298, 299
Gordon, E., 368
Gorsuch, R., 60
Gossop, M., 415, 418, 423, 424, 425
Gough, H.G., 408
Graef, R., 134, 181, 182
Graf, R.G., 375, 376
Graham, J.R., 571
Grant, A., 23
Green, R., 212
Green, V., 366
Greene, E.L., 354, 380

Griffiths, J., 27
Grisso, T., 72, 148, 265, 286, 290, 294, 299, 361, 365
Gross, A.E., 375
Grubin, D., 265
Grubin, D.H., 183
Gudjonsson, G.H., 2, 3, 8, 9, 11, 12, 14, 17, 22, 26, 27, 28, 34, 35, 36, 38, 39, 44, 46, 51, 52, 54, 57, 58, 59, 60, 61, 63, 64, 65, 66, 67, 69, 72, 73, 76, 77, 80, 81, 94, 112, 113, 115, 121, 123, 124, 126, 133, 134, 135, 138, 140, 141, 142, 143, 146, 147, 148, 152, 154, 155, 156, 157, 173, 176, 177, 178, 180, 181, 182, 184, 186, 193, 195, 196, 198, 201, 203, 204, 207, 208, 209, 210, 211, 212, 213, 214, 215, 226, 229, 238, 239, 247, 251, 260, 262, 263, 264, 265, 266, 269, 270, 271, 272, 273, 276, 277, 278, 290, 308, 309, 310, 311, 313, 316, 317, 318, 319, 321, 322, 323, 324, 325, 326, 328, 329, 330, 332, 334, 335, 340, 345, 346, 347, 348, 349, 350, 351, 352, 353, 354, 355, 356, 357, 360, 363, 364, 365, 366, 367, 368, 370, 371, 372, 373, 374, 377, 378, 379, 380, 381, 382, 383, 384, 385, 386, 387, 388, 391, 392, 393, 394, 395, 396, 397, 398, 399, 400, 401, 403, 404, 405, 406, 407, 408, 409, 410, 411, 412, 413, 415, 418, 421, 422, 423, 424, 427, 428, 430, 440, 442, 443, 464, 465, 468, 472, 480, 481, 489, 491, 495, 504, 505, 508, 528, 529, 533, 554, 557, 560, 582, 584, 587, 597, 608, 617, 618, 621, 622, 623, 627
Guly, O.C.R., 314
Gunn, J., 332
Gur, R.C., 395, 408, 599
Gural, M., 321
Gur-Ayre, M., 582
Gwynn, M.I., 368

Hall, D., 354, 355, 399
Hall, J.A., 375
Hamlet, C.C., 375
Haney, C., 30
Hannesdottir, K., 372, 428
Hansdottir, I., 391
Happe, F., 321
Haraldsson, E., 379, 386, 393, 395, 411
Harari, P.M., 72, 73, 262, 263, 270, 318
Hardarson, R., 368
Hargreaves, H., 338
Harlow, H.F., 191
Harnick, M.A., 345
Hart, M., 262
Hartley, J., 72
Hathaway, S.R., 389, 595, 598

Hatton, C., 318
Havers, S., 317, 367
Haward, L.R.C., 8, 218, 265, 276, 309, 310, 311, 328, 329, 330, 468, 587, 618
Hayes, G.D., 262, 263, 266, 271, 415
Hayman, B.S., 134, 135, 136, 137, 138, 151
Hayman, T., 23
Haynes, O.M., 427
Heaps, C., 213
Heaton-Armstrong, A., 24, 309
Helm, S., 587
Hemsley, D.R., 373
Hennessee, J.A., 543
Henry, L.A., 318, 366, 410
Hepworth, M., 186
Herbert, I., 530
Hersch, P.D., 398
Hertel, P.T., 354
Hertzman, M., 342
Heslin, R., 375
Hess, D.W., 27
Hickey, C., 541, 542, 543, 546, 549
Hilgendorf, E.L., 120, 121, 122
Hilgendorf, L., 17, 26, 27, 38, 39, 118, 325, 342
Hill, P., 159, 438, 448, 454
Hilton, M., 391
Hinkle, L.E., 31, 35, 174, 186, 187, 188, 190
Hodgson, J., 79, 140, 261, 262, 273
Hoeffel, J.C., 304
Holland, C.I., 375
Hong, N.S., 396
Hornik, J., 375
Horselenberg, R., 213, 390
Hourihan, P.T., 286, 288, 289, 290
Howard, R., 396
Howells, K., 366, 382
Hreinsdottir, H., 370
Huang, W.W., 285
Huff, C.R., 159, 161, 162
Hull, C., 338
Hulse-Trotter, K., 380, 392
Hunt, G., 454
Hunter, E., 186, 190

Imwinkelried, E.J., 294
Inbau, F.E., 7, 8, 10, 11, 12, 14, 15, 16, 17, 18, 19, 20, 21, 22, 25, 28, 29, 30, 34, 35, 36, 37, 120, 131, 134, 182, 206, 346, 620
Irvine, A.A., 23
Irving, B., 17, 26, 27, 30, 38, 39–41, 42, 43, 46, 51, 58, 67, 69, 82, 118, 120, 121, 122, 126, 130, 131, 132, 133, 135, 137, 138, 139, 147, 148, 149, 151, 169, 171, 249, 325, 342, 346, 353, 356, 357, 358, 407, 621

Isaacs, B.J., 318
Izard, C.E., 427
Izenberg, D., 589

Jackson, D.N., 401
James, A., 437, 438
Janis, I.L., 121
Jayne, B.C., 7, 8, 10, 11, 118, 119–20, 185
Johnson, H.R.M., 417
Johnson, M.K., 195, 367
Johnson, P.J., 354
Jones, A., 420, 424
Josephs, R.A., 427

Kahn, 323
Kalbfleisch, P.J., 80
Kallio, L.E., 159
Kalven, H., 184
Kanouse, D.E., 377, 378, 427
Kassin, S.M., 9, 21, 34, 80, 81, 131, 175, 194, 196, 198, 199, 201–3, 205, 206, 211, 214, 215, 216, 296, 302, 408, 409, 608, 625
Keane, V.E., 325
Kebbell, M.R., 318
Kee, R., 167
Kellam, A.M.P., 226
Kellerman, A.E., 589
Kelly, T.P., 142, 381, 383
Kelman, H.C., 192, 343, 375
Kennedy, H, 52
Kennedy, H.G., 183
Kennedy, L., 167, 170, 193
Kessler, D., 8
Ketcham, K., 212
Keys, D.W., 418
Kiechel, K.L., 205, 408, 409
Kiesler, C.A., 343
Kiesler, S.B., 343
Kihlstrom, J.F., 362, 364, 366, 367, 368, 369
Kirby, T., 134
Klein, D., 81
Kleinke, C.L., 375
Knowles, E.S., 379
Kolbeinsson, H., 319
Konoske, P., 375, 376
Kopelman, M.D., 180, 214, 489, 490, 491, 505, 608
Krech, D., 342, 344
Kristindottir, H., 387
Kroner, D.G., 147
Kuerschner, S., 375

Lader, M., 418, 419, 421, 489
Lambe, H., 31, 389, 399, 401
Lassiter, G.D., 23

Laurence, J.R., 366
Leavitt, F., 215, 389, 391, 411
Lebegue, B., 180, 198, 238
Leigh, L.H., 437
Leiken, L.S., 27, 141, 142, 145, 148
Leites, N., 186
Leng, R., 141, 250
Leo, R.A., 7, 8, 9, 10, 23, 25, 27, 31, 32–4, 36, 77, 91, 97, 106, 118, 130, 133, 134, 135, 136, 137, 138, 142, 144, 148, 151, 164, 165, 166, 174, 175, 176, 178, 179, 180, 181, 184, 185, 186, 189, 197, 198, 201, 203, 204, 205, 206, 207, 208, 210, 211, 212, 215, 216, 286, 287, 551
Lepper, M.R., 199
Levoi, M.E., 195
Lewin, K., 188
Lewis, P., 213
Libero, D.Z., 427
Lidstone, K., 42, 247, 253, 259
Liebman, J.I., 398
Lifton, R.J., 186, 187, 192
Lighty, T., 541, 542, 543, 546, 549
Linton, C.P., 362, 369
Lister, S., 379, 380, 393, 397, 398, 528
Littlechild, B., 262
Lofquist, W.S., 159, 164
Loftus, E.F., 212, 213, 334, 335, 345, 353, 354, 355, 356, 357, 380, 383, 384, 399, 410, 411, 412
Lohr, J.M., 396
Lorr, M., 427
Lubin, B., 386
Luce, R.D., 121
Lushene, R.E., 60
Lynn, S., 213
Lyons, E., 377

MacDonald, A.P., 399
Macdonald, J.M., 8, 9, 546
MacKeith, J.A.C., 26, 35, 52, 177, 178, 180, 181, 196, 208, 213, 214, 226, 229, 308, 318, 330, 404, 440, 442, 472, 489, 491, 504, 505, 529, 533, 618
Mackey, E.D., 276
Macleod, J., 23
Mahendra, B., 550
Manning, C.G., 213
Mansfield, M., 159, 437, 438, 472
Markman, S.J., 163
Marlowe, D., 372, 394
Matarazzo, J.D., 322, 326
Mathews, R.C., 373
Matthews, R.A.J., 164, 173
Mattox, J., 555, 557
Matza, D., 146
Mazzoni, G.A.L., 213

McAfee, J.K., 321
McCann, J.T., 9, 195, 201–2
McCauley, C., 192
McClean, J.D., 184, 185
McCollum, Lord Justice, 480, 481
McConville, M., 22, 24, 79, 130, 131, 132, 135, 137, 138, 140, 141, 142, 145, 149, 184, 248
McCrae, R.R., 398
McDonald, P., 8
McDougall, W., 335, 336, 341
McEwan, J., 256
Mcguire, R.E., 285
McGurk, B., 54
McGurk, D., 54
McKee, G., 167, 446, 446, 448
McKenzie, I.K., 38, 39, 42, 43, 51, 58, 67, 69, 131, 132, 133, 135, 137, 138, 139, 147, 149, 151, 169, 171
McKenzie, J., 52
McKinley, J.C., 389, 595, 598
McMahon, M., 293
McNair, D.M., 427
McNall, K., 21, 80, 81, 175, 205, 206
Meadow, R., 543
Medford, S., 141, 263, 272, 321, 621
Meerloo, J.A.M., 191
Megargee, E.I., 117
Melancon, J., 399, 400
Memon, A., 318
Menninger, K.A., 325
Merckelbach, H., 213, 361, 390
Messick, S., 401
Meuhleman, T., 323
Meyer, T., 285, 366, 388, 390
Michaud, D.L., 8, 9, 546
Mickes, L., 378
Mikulincer, M., 31
Milberg, S., 375, 376, 401, 402
Milgram, S., 27, 297, 342, 343, 357, 370
Miller, D.G., 334, 354
Milne, R., 2, 54, 318
Milner, N.A., 31
Mirfield, P., 248, 252
Mitchell, P., 135, 137, 138, 143, 145, 146, 149, 150
Mitchell, S., 276
Mobasheri, R., 72, 262
Moore, H.T., 342
Moos, R.H., 395
Morgan, D., 46, 149, 250
Morgan, D.Y., 378
Morrell, P., 22
Morrison, D., 126
Mortimer, A., 46, 51, 52, 53, 54
Mortimer, A.K., 72, 262

Morton, J., 175, 214
Mosesso, L., 396
Moston, S., 24, 38, 44, 45, 46, 70, 77, 81, 124, 131, 132, 133, 135, 137, 138, 139, 141, 142, 143, 144, 146, 147, 149, 150, 151, 344
Mullin, C., 452, 453, 454
Mullis, A., 213
Mulready, S., 454
Munsterberg, H., 193
Murakami, A., 423, 424, 425
Muris, P., 213, 361, 390
Murphy, G.H., 318, 366, 410, 411

Naish, P., 23
Nancoo, S., 368
Nash, M., 213
Nash, S., 255
Nathan, K.T., 379
Neimi, P., 196, 426, 427
Nelson, H.E., 383
Nemitz, T., 261, 262
Neubauer, D.W., 136, 137, 138, 141, 142, 143, 144, 146, 147
Neufeld, P., 159, 163, 180
Neumann, K., 131, 608
Newberry, J.J., 8, 34
Newburn, T., 23
Nguyen, M.L., 375
Nguyen, T.D., 375
Nix, J., 396
Noizt, 336
Norfolk, G.A., 266, 271
Novaco, R.W., 372
Nugent, P.M., 147

O'Brien, J., 541, 542, 543, 546, 549
Ofshe, R.J., 9, 97, 106, 118, 130, 164, 165, 166, 174, 175, 176, 178, 179, 180, 181, 184, 185, 186, 189, 197, 198, 199, 200, 201, 203, 204, 205, 206, 207, 208, 210, 211, 212, 214, 215, 216, 411, 551, 611
Oltman, P.K., 399
Ord, B., 22, 49, 51, 54
Orwell, G., 186
Osgood, C.E., 397
Ost, J., 186, 212, 214

Paddock, J.R., 213
Paisley, I.J.R., 514, 518
Palmer, C., 261, 262
Panter, S., 180, 523, 524, 526, 527, 529, 530
Parkes, C.M., 313
Parkes, L.R., 390
Payne-James, J.J., 418

Pear, T.H., 345
Pearse J., 22, 27, 38, 39, 51, 57, 69, 70, 75, 76, 77, 80, 97, 100, 112, 113, 133, 135, 136, 137, 140, 141, 143, 144, 145, 150, 156, 157, 207, 262, 263, 264, 272, 321, 407, 508, 621, 622
Pearson, R., 262, 416, 418
Pendergrast, M., 212
Penn, D.L., 373
Perkins, D., 309
Perlman, N.B., 318
Perry, C., 366
Petursson, H., 35, 152, 154, 155, 156, 319, 372, 428, 608
Philip, L., 263
Phillips, C., 134, 135, 137, 138, 139, 140, 141, 142, 143, 144, 145, 147, 148, 149, 150, 151
Pope, H.S., 557
Pope, K.S., 212
Porter, J.W., 371
Powers, P.A., 345, 380, 383
Price, C., 167
Prideaux, E., 343
Putman, C.E., 159, 162, 164
Putman, P., 427
Putnam, F.W., 390

Rabon, D., 2, 8
Radelet, M.L., 159, 162, 163, 164, 166, 315
Radin, E.D., 159, 160
Ragnarsson, R.S., 387
Raskin, E., 399
Rassin, E., 213, 366, 390, 391
Rattner, A., 159, 161, 162
Raven, J.C., 367, 597
Ravitz, L.J., 124
Raye, C.L., 195
Redlich, F.C., 124, 379, 381, 408
Reed, J.E., 299
Register, P.A., 362, 364, 366, 367, 368, 369
Reid, J.E., 7, 8, 9, 10, 14, 25, 26, 33, 51, 52, 75, 81, 82, 83, 84, 91, 152, 183, 209, 408, 508, 547
Reik, T., 121, 122–3, 153
Reinhold, T., 543
Richard, C.L., 322
Richardson, G., 142, 175, 365, 381, 383
Richardson, P.J., 248, 251, 253, 254, 255, 256, 263, 273, 276
Richardson, S.A., 81, 321
Rigby, K., 401
Rivera, J., 212
Rix, K.J.B., 266
Robbins, T., 36
Roberts, J.C., 195

Robertson, G., 262, 265, 272, 416, 418
Robertson, R., 369
Rodda, W., 399
Roediger, H.L.M., 213
Rogers, R., 299
Rogge, O.J., 121, 123
Roppe, L.F., 287
Rose, D., 52, 462, 515
Rose, J., 180, 523, 524, 526, 527, 529, 530
Rosenberg, I.M., 286
Rosenberg, Y.L., 286
Ross, D., 375
Ross, D.F., 335
Ross, J., 35
Ross, S.A., 375
Rotter, J.B., 397, 398
Rowe, P., 258
Rowlands, P., 262, 263, 266, 271, 415
Royal, R.F., 8, 28
Runciman, Viscount W.G., 269
Rutter, S.C., 22, 27, 57, 143, 270, 362, 380, 383, 386, 388
Ryckman, R., 399

Sackeim, H.M., 395, 408, 599
Sagarin, E., 159, 161, 162
Salekin, R.T., 299
Sales, B.D., 294
Salter, A., 154, 184
Sanders, A., 141, 150
Santilla, P., 196, 366, 426, 427
Santucci, P.S., 191
Sargant, T., 159, 438
Sargant, W., 169, 186, 190, 191
Sartory, G., 617
Saucier, D., 213
Schantz, M., 27
Scheck, B., 159, 163, 180
Scheibe, K.E., 398
Scheier, M.F., 373, 396
Schein, E.H., 174–5, 186, 187, 188, 189, 190, 191, 192, 215
Schill, T., 323
Schneier, I., 174–5, 186, 187, 188, 189, 190, 191, 192, 215
Schoenrock, C.J., 325
Schonell, F.J., 60
Schooler, J.W., 334, 335, 353, 354, 355, 356, 357, 383, 384, 410, 412
Schulhofer, S.J., 130, 136
Schutte, S.R., 8, 28
Scullin, M.H., 360, 366
Sear, L., 38, 47
Seitz, A., 213
Seligman, M.E.P., 343
Sewell, K.W., 299

Shackleton, H., 468
Shaffer, D.F., 315
Shallice, T., 26, 31, 35, 44, 588
Sharrock, R., 324, 383, 384, 385, 403, 405
Shaw, G., 22, 49, 51, 54
Sheehan, P.W., 362, 366, 369
Shellady, Brad, 557
Shepherd, E., 49, 51, 52, 53, 54, 79, 140, 262
Shepherd, E.W., 72, 262
Sherif, M., 341
Sherman, M., 399
Sherman, S.J., 213
Shuman, D.W., 294
Shuy, R.W., 23
Sidis, B., 336
Siehr, K., 589
Sigelman, C.K., 325, 377, 379
Sigurdardottir, H., 608
Sigurdsson, J.F., 12, 14, 17, 35, 140, 146, 147, 152, 154, 155, 156, 157, 176, 177, 182, 203, 210, 211, 313, 318, 319, 363, 366, 367, 370, 371, 372, 373, 385, 395, 407, 408, 409, 421, 422, 423, 424, 495, 560, 627
Sigurgeirsdottir, S., 379
Silber, D.E., 321, 325
Singh, K.K., 142, 154, 363, 364, 381, 383, 385, 386, 397, 398, 399, 401, 403
Skulason, S., 608
Slade, P.D., 368
Sleen, J., 557
Slobin, M.S., 387, 388
Smith, P., 318, 365, 366, 367, 374, 386, 388, 397, 398
Smith, P.B., 376
Softley, P., 38, 43, 131, 132, 137, 141, 144, 146, 149, 150
Sommer, R., 27
Spanhel, C.L., 325
Spanos, N.P., 368
Sparrow, S.S., 327
Spencer, J., 322
Spielberger, C.D., 35, 60, 66, 372, 386, 425, 427
Spooner, F., 322
Stagg, C., 8
Staple, S., 375, 376
Stark, M., 418
Starmer, K., 159, 164, 250
Steele, C.M., 427
Steinschneider, A., 542, 543
Stephenson, G.M., 24, 38, 44, 46, 47, 70, 77, 81, 124, 131, 132, 133, 135, 137, 138, 139, 141, 142, 143, 144, 146, 147, 149, 150, 151, 250, 325

Stern, W., 339, 345, 347
Stier, D.H., 375
Stockdale, J., 54
Street, R., 250
Stricker, L.J., 401
Stubbs, C., 8, 34
Stukat, K.G., 339, 340, 341, 344, 358
Stumphauzer, J.S., 125
Stuntz, W.J., 285
Styron, W., 159
Suci, G.J., 397
Svartnik, J., 169

Talan, J., 541, 542, 543, 545, 546, 549
Tangney, J.P., 126
Tannebaum, P., 397
Tata, P.R., 363, 366, 367, 383, 386, 395
Taylor, N., 437, 438
Taylor, P.J., 490
Taylor, R., 46, 72, 272
Teasdale, J.D., 343
Tellegen, A., 390, 398
Tendler, S., 466
Theilgaard, A., 372
Thomas, G.C., 130, 136, 138
Thompson, B., 399, 400
Thornton, D., 184
Toglia, M.P., 335
Torres, T.A., 35
Tousignant, J.P., 354, 355, 399
Trankell, A., 178, 345
Treisman, A.M., 358
Truesdale, P., 366
Tubbs, E.C., 380, 392
Tully, B., 318, 324, 382, 403–4, 410
Turner, B.S., 186
Tyrfingson, T., 428

Underwager, R., 9
Usborne, D., 563

Van Koppen, P.J., 390
Van Velsen, C., 123
Vargas, M.O., 35
Vennard, J., 132, 258, 259
Victory, P., 159, 446, 448
Vrij, A., 34

Wade, N., 44
Wagstaff, G.F., 357, 370
Wakefield, H., 9
Wald, M., 27, 31, 43, 132, 133, 142, 143
Walker, C., 159, 164, 247, 248, 437, 438, 506
Walkley, J., 7, 8, 28, 51, 52
Wall, D., 24

Author Index

Wallington, S.A., 375, 376
Walsh, D., 38, 43–4, 148, 247
Wambaugh, J., 180
Ward, J., 52, 471
Ward, M., 366
Ware, J.E., 377, 378, 427
Ware, J.W., 379
Warren, A., 380, 392
Wasik, M., 46, 72, 272
Watson, D., 387, 427
Watters, E., 186, 212, 214, 411
Webster, N., 23, 258, 259
Wechsler, D., 60, 323, 382
Weintraub, J.K., 373, 396
Weisselberg, C.D., 130, 136, 286
Werder, P.R., 325
Wessel, I., 390
Wessely, S., 373
West, L.J., 191
Westcott, H.L., 2
White, W.S., 130, 136, 285, 286, 287, 288, 289, 290
Whitebread, C.H., 27
Wilkinson, T., 180, 523, 524, 526, 527, 529, 530
Williams, J., 261
Williamson, T.M., 2, 36, 38, 44, 46, 47, 51, 52, 53, 54, 56, 69, 70, 77, 85, 124, 131, 132, 133, 135, 137, 138, 139, 141, 142, 143, 144, 146, 147, 149, 150, 151, 321, 613
Willis, C.F., 23
Winkler, J.D., 377, 378, 427
Winokur, G., 191
Witkin, H.A., 399
Woffinden, B., 158, 159
Wolchover, D., 24
Wolff, H.G., 174, 186, 187, 188, 190
Wolfradt, U., 366, 388, 390
Wood, P.J.W., 314
Woolf, M., 250
Woolgrove, K., 324
Wrightsman, L.S., 9, 194, 196, 198, 199, 201–3, 205, 206, 207, 211, 215, 216, 625
Wyatt, S., 345
Wylie, R., 374

Yant, M., 159
Young, H.F., 368
Young, M., 159, 438

Zander, M., 135, 137, 138, 145, 149, 150, 250
Zeisel, H., 184
Zimbardo, P.G., 9, 30, 130
Zuckerman, M., 306, 386

Subject Index

Abdullahi, Yusef, 516
abusiveness, 84
accepting, 119
access to legal advice, confession and, 148–50
accomplices, 82
accusatorial approach, 45, 81–2
acquiescence, 376–7
  correlations between suggestibility, compliance and, 378–9
Adaptive Behavior Scale, 326–7
admissibility
  of a confession, 248–58, 304, 305–6, 618
  of evidence, 255
  of expert testimony, 294, 304, 306, 618
    case studies, 279–80
    English law, 275–80
admission, 83–4
  factors associated with, 140–51
age
  confession and, 141–3
  suggestibility and, 380–1
Agreeableness, 47
alcohol
  effects on interrogative suggestibility, 426–8
  interviewing under influence of, 67–8
  suggestibility and, 428–30
  reliability of testimony and, 415–33
  withdrawal, 40
  withdrawal, effects on interrogative suggestibility, 428–30
Ali, Idris, 442, 473–5
Allen, Alfred, 442, 514, 517–18
Alliott, Justice, 466
American Association on Mental Deficiency, 326
American law on confessions, 283–307
  basic law on confessions, 283–7
  challenging a confession in court, 293–304

admissibility of expert testimony, 294
applying *Daubert* to expert false confession testimony, 299–304
Daubert standard, 297–9, 304, 306, 307
evaluating admissibility of expert testimony under *Frye* standard, 295–7
Frye standard, 294–5, 304, 306, 307
legal procedures, 293–4
differences between English law and practice and, 304–6
  admissibility of a confession, 304, 305–6
  admissibility of expert testimony, 304, 306
Due Process Voluntariness Test, 284–5
  after *Miranda*, 287–8
  involuntary confession, 284–5
  voluntariness
    mentally vulnerable suspects and, 288–93
    under *Miranda*, 285–7
American research on interrogation, 31–4
Amlot, Roy, 466
amphetamines, 420
Andrews, Dr, 470
anger
  during interrogation, 84
  of interrogators, 28
  suggestibility and, 400–2
  of suspects, 28
animal magnetism, 337
antecedents of confession, 124–8
anxiety
  during interrogation, 25–8, 118, 119
  suggestibility and, 385–8
Appropriate Adult (AA), presence of, 79, 260–5
arbitrary control, 30
Archbold, 251, 256

Subject Index

Armstrong, Paddy, 446, 447, 448, 449
Astill, Justice, 497
assertiveness
  suggestibility and, 396
Attention–Allocation Model, 427
attributes of interrogator, desirable, 29–30
Austen, Texas Assistance Attorney general, 557
automatic exclusion, 213
avoidance, 46

Badcock, Dr Richard, 534
Baden, Dr Michael, 543
Balcombe Street Siege, 448
Baldwin's study, 46–50
  interview techniques, 48–9
  suspects' responses, 49–50
Barber Suggestibility Scale, 368
Barry, Dr David John, 550
Baskerville [1916], 132
Beattie, George, 438
Behavior Rating Form (BRF) (Coopersmith), 387, 397
belief, 119
Bell, Noel, 517, 518
Beltran v. State (1997), 296, 302
Bennett Committee, 44
Bentley, Derek, 438, 442, 444, 514, 520–2
benzodiazepines, 420, 421
bereavement, 319
Bingham, Lord Chief Justice, 491, 494, 506, 520, 536
Birmingham Six, 52, 55, 57, 167, 438, 440, 441, 452–6, 616
Blakelock, PC Keith, 459, 462
blame, 84
Bleck, Officer Bobby, 544, 544, 547
Bluglass, Professor Robert, 469
body sway test, 338
Bonn Test of Statement Suggestibility (BTSS), 361
boomerang effect, 36, 402
Boudreaux, Ida, 564
Boutwell, Sheriff Jim, 556, 559–60, 562
Bowden, Dr, 471
Brabin, Sir Daniel, 170
Brady, Kevin, 479
Braithwaite, Mark, 461, 462, 464, 466
breaking point, 192
Bridge, Mr Justice, 453
Bridgewater, Carl, murder of, 438, 514, 519–20
Brine [1992], 256
British training manuals, 51–5
Britton, Paul, 469

Brooke, Justice, 258
Brown, Mr Justice Douglas, 491
Brown, Mr Justice Simon, 472
Bush, George W., 563
business-like interrogation style, 47
Buss–Durkee Hostility Inventory, 401

Callaghan, Hugh, 453
Campbell, Lord, 506
Canadian case of non-custodial interrogation, 573–82
cannabis, 420
Capstick, Detective Superintendent John, 500, 501, 504
Cardiff Three, 52–3, 55, 253–4
Carleton University Responsiveness to Suggestion Scale (CURSS), 368
Carroll, Adrian, 517
Carswell, Mr Justice Robert, 480, 506
Carter, President Jimmy, 555
Carter v. State (1997), 296
Caucasian/Afro-Caribbean
  differences in suggestibility, 65, 66
  differences in trait/state anxiety, 65–6
cautions, 72–3
challenging response, 82, 84
changing, indoctrination of, 188, 190
child witnesses and victims, 54
Chinese, interrogation methods, 186–7, 188
Christie, 167–70
Clark, Gina, 447
Clarke, Tom, 454
claustrophobia, 40, 318
Clegg, Mr, 258
Clemmie, Sister, 559–60
closed circuit television (CCTV), 23
cocaine, 420
coerced–compliant confessions, 204, 205, 206, 215
coerced–compliant false confessions, 194, 195–6, 198–9, 625
coerced–internalized false confessions, 194, 196–7, 198, 199–200, 215, 625
coerced–persuaded confessions, 206
coerced–reactive false confessions, 201–2
coercion, 33–6
coerciveness, 25
cognitive–behavioural model of confession, 124–8, 128
cognitive dissonance, 178
cognitive events, confession and, 127
Cognitive Failure Questionnaire (CFQ), 390
cognitive interview techniques, 53, 318
co-judge suggestion tests, 339

collusive interrogation style, 47
Colorado v. Connelly (1986), 285, 288, 289, 290, 291, 305, 306
Communist regimes
  indoctrination, 188–92
    changing, 188, 190
    refreezing, 188, 189, 190
    unfreezing, 188–9, 190, 191
  'registers' and 'cooperators' of, 188
compliance, 192, 370–6, 626
  correlations between suggestibility, acquiescence and, 378–9
  situational determinants, 375–6
Condron and Condron [1997], 273
confabulation, 364, 366–8
Confait, Maxwell, 170–1, 449
  case, 39, 55, 79, 167, 170–1, 615
confession
  consequences, 124–8
  disputed, 178
  factors inhibiting, 115–17
  format and recording, 21–4
  importance of, 130–3
  interview tactics and detainees' reactions, 69–70
  prediction of, 70–1
  rate of, 133–40
  reasons for, 151–6
  theoretical models, 117–28
confidence game, 27–8
confrontation, 82
confusion, 84
Conlon, Gerry, 446, 447, 448, 452
Connelly, Francis, 288–9
conscience, appeal to, 82
conscientiousness, 47
contamination, 179
contextual factors
  confession and, 148–51
  of the interrogation, 24–31
continual dispute, 82
contradictions, 82
contradictory suggestion tests, 339
control, lack of, 26
Conversation Management, 53
Conway, Sheriff, 558
Cook, Chalkley [1998], 255
cooperation, 28
Coopersmith Behavior Rating Form (BRF), 387, 397
COPE Scale, 373
coping strategies, suggestibility and, 395–6
Coulthard, Professor Malcolm, 506, 521, 522

counselling interrogation style, 47
Court of Appeal (British), 437–44
Courtenay, Wesley, 500
Courtwright, Chief Investigator, 543, 544
Cowan, Gayle and Ricciardi [1996], 273, 274
crack cocaine, 418
Craig, Christopher, 514, 520
Creative Experiences Questionnaire (CEQ), 390
Cresswell, Justice, 466
Crighton Vocabulary Test, 382
Criminal Appeal Act
  1968, 437
  1995, 438
Criminal Cases Review Commission (CCRC), 437–8
Criminal Justice and Public Order Act (1994), 46, 72, 149, 272, 273, 281
Cronbach's alpha coefficient, 371–2
crying, 18, 84
Curran, Dr D. (psychiatrist), 502
Curran, Desmond, 499
Curran, Miss Patricia, 499, 500, 501, 503
Custody Officer, 25
Custody Record, 25, 314, 315, 621
custody, effects of, 40
Cyprus spy trial, 167

D.P.P. v. Cornish (1997), 264
Dando, Jill, 275
Darvell, Paul, 438, 530–3
Darvell, Wayne, 438, 442, 443, 530–3
Daubert standard, 297–9, 304, 306, 307, 619
  expert false confession testimony and, 299–304
Daubert v. Merrell Dow Pharmaceuticals, 297–9, 300, 303
Deans, Marie, 551, 553
deception/trickery, 7, 8–9, 37, 55, 335, 620
  PACE and, 256
decision-making model of confession, 120–2, 128
delayed recall, 363
denials, 84
  factors associated with, 140–51
dependency, 30
depression, 68, 317
  voluntary false confessions and, 219–20
Dibb, Detective Superintendent, 526
Dickerson v. United States, 287
direct accusation, 45
direct suggestion procedure, 336

Subject Index

discrepancy detection, 200, 335, 354–5, 359, 410
disputed confession, 178
disputes, 84
dissociation, suggestibility and, 390–1
Dissociation Experiences Scale (DES), 390, 391, 427
dissociative phenomena, 339
dissonance, theory of, 192
distress, 84
dominance, 47
dominant interrogation style, 47
Donaldson, Ian, QC, 579–80
downgrading, 46
Downing, Stephen, 438, 439
Drob, Dr Sanford, 303
drugs, reliability of testimony and, 415–33
  differential effects on interrogative suggestibility, 425–6
  drug withdrawal, 40
  effects of intoxication and withdrawal, 421–8
  extent of the problem, 416–18
  theoretical perspectives, 418–21
  see also alcohol
Due Process Voluntariness Test, 284–5
  after *Miranda*, 287–8
duration of interview, 68

eagerness to please, 239–40
echoing, 81
ecstasy, 418, 420, 426
ego, 123
electrostatic detection apparatus (ESDA), 442, 467, 514, 532
emasculation, 30
Embedded Figures Test, 399
emotional events, confession and, 126–7
emotional offenders, 13, 14–15
English Law on Confessions
  admissibility of expert evidence, 275–80
  adverse influences, 272–5
  appropriate adults, 260–5
  confession evidence, admissibility and reliability, 248–58
  fitness for interview, 265–6
  psychological (mental) vulnerability, 259–60
  truthfulness of the confession, 256–8
  voire dire, 250, 256, 258–9
  vulnerable defendants, 259–75
environment
  interrogation, 26
  physical, of interrogation, 30–1
  stress and, 26–7

ethnic background
  confession and, 143
  suggestibility and, 380
Evans, Andrew, 198, 442, 443, 444, 482–92
Evans, Geraldine, 167
Evans, Justice, 258
Evans, Timothy, 161, 167–70
Evans, Mrs Timothy, 167–8
evidence
  confession, admissibility and reliability, 248–58
  strategy, 45
  strength of, confession and, 150–1
Ewing, Dr Charles, 545, 548, 549, 550
expectancy, 119
expectation of success, 350, 353, 355
experimental approach to interrogative suggestibility, 334–5, 353
experimenter effect, suggestibility and, 392–4
expert testimony, 440–1, 618
  potential abuse of, 329–30
external pressure, confession and, 152–3, 157, 622
eyewitness testimony, suggestibility and, 410–11
Eysenck Personality Questionnaire (EPQ), 154, 155, 372, 374, 386, 394–5, 408
EPQ-R, 432

factor analysis, 86
false belief, 201, 233–4
false confession, 9, 37
  broader context, 186–92
  case examples, 217–43
  causes of, 193–7
  coerced–compliant types, 194, 195–6, 198–9
  coerced–internalized types, 194, 196–7, 198, 199–200
  critique of Kassin–Wrightsman model, 201–3, 211
  definitions, 174
  discovery of, 180–2
  due to coercion, 34
  frequency, 174–8
  by a heroin addict, 430–2
  innocent pleading guilty, 184–5
  pressured–compliant false confession, 224–33
    absence of mental disorder, 224–7
    admitting to death in self-defence, 231–3
    learning disability, 227–30, 230–1

false confession (cont.)
　pressured–internalized false
　　confession, 233–42
　　eagerness to please, 239–40
　　false belief, 233–4
　　non-custodial confession, 240–2
　　Peter Reilly, 234–7
　　Sergeant E, 237–9
　proven, 178
　rates of, 36
　recovered memory and, 212–15
　cf. retracted confessions, 623–7
　suggestibility and, 407–10
　true confession and, differences
　　between, 208–11
　types, theoretical implications,
　　197–203
　voluntary, 194–5, 218–24
false confessors, alleged, suggestibility
　and, 404–7
false evidence of guilt, 8–9
false memory syndrome, 201, 212–13
family, confession inhibition and, 116
fantasy proneness, suggestibility and,
　390–1
Farquharson, Lord Justice, 257, 448, 454,
　466
fatigue, 31
Faulk, Michael, 567
fear
　during interrogation, 25–8
　of legal sanctions, 115–16
　of retaliation, 116
Fear of Negative Evaluation (FNE) scale,
　387, 427
Federal Rules of Evidence (FRE), 297
Fell, Peter, 442, 443, 506–12
Fellows, Noel, 193–4
Fennell, Mr Justice, 181
Fenwick, Dr Peter, 521
Fisher, Sir Henry, 39
　Inquiry, 55, 79, 170–1, 615
field dependence, suggestibility and,
　399–400
fitness for interview, 265–6
　case study, 266–70
　recent developments, 270–2
Fitzpatrick, Bill, 543
flattery, 83
Fletcher, Glen Richard Miles, 468
Fletcher, Jacqueline, 468–70
Fordham, Mrs Ann Scott, 494
forensic evidence, 132
format of the confession, 21–4
French, Dr, 506, 521, 522
Freud, Sigmund, 123

'friendly–unfriendly' technique, 17–18
friends, confession inhibition and, 116
Frye standard, 294–5, 304, 306, 307, 619
　admissibility of expert testimony under,
　　295–7
Fuller, Dr Julian, 532
Fulling [1957], 252

Galbraith [1981], 473
gender
　confession and, 143
　false confession and, 177
　suggestibility and, 379–80
General Attitude to Institutional
　Authority Scale, 401
George, Barry, 275
Gestalt psychology, 342
Giarratano, Joe, 319, 550–4
Gilmore, Jim, 166
Gilmour, Raymond, 438
Glidewell, Justice, 448
Goldenberg, 254
Gordon, Iain Hay, 442, 499–506
Gough Socialisation Scale, 154, 408
Grebler, Dr Gillian, 532
Greenwood, Mrs, 493
Gudjonsson–Clark theoretical model of
　interrogative suggestibility, 347–52
　external evaluation of the model, 353–8
　model implications and hypotheses,
　　352–3
Gudjonsson Cognitive–Behavioural
　Model of Confession, 152
Gudjonsson Compliance Scale (GCS),
　155, 360, 371–5, 378, 379, 407, 408,
　455, 456
Gudjonsson Confession Questionnaire
　(GCQ), 421–3
　GCQ-R, 154, 210, 660–2
Gudjonsson Suggestibility Scales (GSSs),
　31, 60, 63–4, 295, 303, 361–70, 455
　confabulation, 366–8
　correlations between, compliance and
　　acquiescence and, 378–9
　GSS 1, 360, 361–8, 368–9, 378, 379, 391
　GSS 2, 360, 361–8, 378, 391
　reliability, 364–6
　types of clinical information derived
　　from, 362–4
　see also suggestibility
Guildford Four, 52, 55, 167, 438, 440, 441,
　445–52, 616
guilt, feelings of, 13, 123, 126
　compliance and, 375–6
　need to expiate, 195
gullibility, 338

Hall, Darren, 442, 443, 495–9
Hall, Larry, 299–302
hand rigidity test, 338
Hanley, Mr (clinical psychologist), 505
Harrison, William, 166
Harvard Group Scale of Hypnotic Susceptibility, 368, 369
Harvey [1988], 254
Harvey, Margot, 503
Haward, Lionel, 449
Hawkins, Detective Sergeant Denis, 500, 501
Hegan, James Irwin, 517, 518
Henderson, J. Scott, QC 170
Henry, Lord Justice, 474, 492
heroin, 418, 420
  false confessions to murder by an addict, 430–2
Heron murder case, 96–106
  post-admission, 100–6
  responses, 97–100
  tactics, 97
Hickey, Michael, 519
Hickey, Vincent, 514, 519
Hidden, Justice, 519
Hill, Patrick, 452
Hill, Paul, 446, 447, 448
Hill, Vance, 575, 580, 581
Hill, Mrs Vance, 580
HMSO Report 1993, 58
Hodge, John, 472
Hoffa, Jimmy, 555
Holland, Detective Superintendent, 525, 526
Home Office Circular 22/1992, 53
Home Office Circular 7/1993, 53
'hooding', 44
Hoyt, Jay, 543, 544, 545
Hoyt, Timothy, 543, 544–5
Hoyt, Waneta, 541–50
Hudson Index of Self-Esteem, 425
Hume, Cardinal, 448
hunger, 31
Hunter, Gerry, 452–6
hushed/lowered tones, 81
Hutton, Lord Chief Justice, 518
hypnosis, 337, 342
hypnotic susceptibility, suggestibility and, 368–70
hypnotizability, 338, 340

Ibrahim v. The Queen [1914], 573, 576
id, 123
identification, 192
ideo-motor response, 336, 338, 358
Illbert, Dr Robin, 509, 511

immediate recall, 362–3
impatience among interrogators, 28
implied evidence, 82
importance of confession, 130–3
impulsivity, suggestibility and, 388
inadmissible confessions, 34–5
Inbau–Reid–Buckley Model, 80
inconsistent pleaders, 184–5
indirect suggestion procedure, 336
indirection, 338
individual differences approach to interrogative suggestibility, 334–5, 353
indoctrination, 188–92
inducement, 83
inquisatorial strategies, 45
instructional manipulation, suggestibility and, 391–2
intelligence, 73, 277–8, 319, 320, 322–3, 324, 326, 443
  suggestibility and, 381–4
interaction process model of confession, 124, 128
interest to confess, 83
internal pressure, 210, 211, 622
  confession and, 152, 153, 157
  false confession and, 212
interpersonal trust, 348, 349–50, 353, 355
interrogation, definition, 1–2
interrogation techniques, confession and, 151
interrogative suggestibility, 52
interrogator characteristics
  confession and, 151
  desirable, 29–30
interrupting the suspect, 81
interview, definition, 1
interview tactics, confession and, 69–70
interviewing tactics in Britain, oppressive, 75–114
  application of framework to individual cases, 87–96
    armed robbery, 91–4
    arson, 87–91
    incest, 94–6
  cases analysed, 77–9
  court outcome, 112–14
  delivery, 80–1
  manipulation, 82–3
  maximization, 81–2
  methodology, 79–80, 85
  research background, 75–7
  suspects' responses, 83–4
    emotional responses, 84
    information or knowledge, 84
    negative, 84

interviewing tactics in Britain, (*cont.*)
   positive, 83–4
   projection, 84
   rationalization, 84
   statistical procedures, 86–7
investigative interviewing, definition, 2
involuntary confession, 284–5
IQ *see* intelligence
Irving, Dr Barrie, 73, 449, 596
   observational studies, 39–42
isolation, 44
Israeli terrorist case, 582–9

Jarrett, Mrs Cynthia, 459
Jenkins, Roy, 170
Johnson, Margaret, 510
Joseph, Dr Philip, 478, 491, 509, 511, 521
Jowitt, Mr Justice, 491
Judge, Justice, 532
Judges' Rules and Home Office Administrative Directions, 249
Judith Ward [1992], 276

Kane, Patrick, 442, 479–82, 512–13
Kassin–Wrightsman model of false confessions, 625
   critique of, 201–3, 211
Keenan [1990], 255
Keene, Justice, 497
Kellam, Dr Alexander, 531
Kelly, Lord Chief Justice, 518
Kelly, Madonna, 573, 576
Kennedy, County inspector Albert, 500, 501
Kerr, Mr Justice, 506
King, Ashley, 442, 443, 493–5, 513
Kiszko, Stefan, 438, 441, 443, 523–30
   final appeal, 527–8
   police interviews, 524–6
   psychological evaluation, 528–9
   trial, 526–7
Kline, Barbara, 550–1
Kline, Michelle, 550–1
Kopelman, Professor Michael, 275, 491, 497, 505, 509
Kumho Tire Co., Ltd. v. Carmichael (1999), 297–8, 300

labelling as a criminal, 146
lack of orientation, 84
Landau, Justice, 582
Landau Report, 582–3
Lane, Lord Chief Justice, 441, 448, 454, 464–5, 469, 470, 512, 527
language problems, 68

Latimer, Neil Fraser, 517, 518
Lattimore, Colin, 170
Laws, Justice, 516
Lawton, Lord Justice, 275
leading question tests, 339, 340
learning disability, 68–9, 72
   assessment of social functioning, 326–7
   false confession in, 227–30, 230–1
   fitness for interview, 318
   as a vulnerability, 320–7
learning theories, 190, 191
Lee, Ann, 510
legal advice prior to interrogation, confession rate and, 149–50
legal advisor, presence of
   criticism of, 79
   effect on rate of confession, 71, 73
legal rights of detainees, 71–3
Leighton, Ronald, 170
leniency, promises of, 11
Leonard, Mr Justice, 515, 531
Lewis, Dr Rossiter, 502, 505
lie detection, 123
Lindbergh kidnapping case, 194–5
Linklater, John, 503
Lloyd, Lord Justice, 454
Locus of Control Scale, 397
   suggestibility and, 398–9
Logan, Alastair, 448, 449, 450
logistic regression analysis, 70–1
Long, George, 442, 444, 476–9
Longmore, Justice, 474
Lopatta, Nichole, 563–4, 565, 570
LSD, 420
Lucas, Henry Lee, 554–63, 571–2

MacKenzie, David, 438, 443, 472–3, 499, 512
magic mushrooms, 420
Maguire case, 454
Makos, Dr, 450, 451
Malone, Campbell, 528
Maloney and Doherty [1988], 263
manipulative interrogation tactics, 41
Mansfield, Michael, QC 516, QC 536
Marlowe–Crowne Social Desirability Scale, 372, 394
Marsh, Terry, 181
Masih [1986], 277, 322, 465, 467
maximization, 21, 36, 80, 153
May, Sir John, 454
McDermott, Lord, 501, 502
McDonald, Patrick: *Make 'Em Talk!*, 8
McGovern, 257–8
McIlkenny, Richard, 452–6
McKenzie, Ian, 73

McKinnon, Gil, QC 579
McNamara, His Honour Thomas R., 554
McNeal, Mr Justice, 515
MDMA (ecstasy), 418, 420, 426
memory
　processing, 345
　suggestibility and, 384–5
　suppression, confession inhibition and, 116
memory distrust syndrome (MDS), 196–7, 213, 452, 490, 566, 567, 610
mental disorder, 317–18
mental handicap, 40
Mental Health Act, 326
mental illness, 40, 68
mental retardation *see* learning disability
mental state, 40–1
　abnormal, 318–19
　confession and, 144
methadone withdrawal, 424
Miles, Sidney, 514, 520
Miller, Bob, 545
Miller, Stephen, 253–4, 438, 443, 514, 515–17
Mini-Mental State Examination (MMSE), 428, 429
minimization, 21, 36, 80
mini-trial, 583–4
Miranda v. Arizona (1966), 25, 27, 32, 33, 130, 284, 285–7, 293, 294, 296, 306, 623
　confession rate and, 134–6, 138, 140
　rights, 72, 144, 156
　voluntariness under, 285–7
miscarriages of justice, 158–9
　Leo–Ofshe study, 164–6
　notorious British cases, 166–71
　studies, 159–64
Mitchell, Justice, 519
MMPI-2, suggestibility and, 389
Molloy, Patrick, 514, 519–20
Molseed, Lesley, 523, 524, 525–6, 527, 528
Moore, Bryony, 492
Morison, Justice, 494
Motivation Scale, 374–5
Mullin, Christopher, 453–4
Multidimensional Personality Questionnaire (MPQ), 398
Multiple Affect Adjective Checklist, 386
multiple assertions, 81
multiple officers, 81
multiple questions, 81
Mulvey, Officer Susan, 544, 545
Munchausen by proxy syndrome, 543
Munchausen syndrome, 197

Mustill, Lord Justice, 454
'Mutt and Jeff' technique, 17–18

National Adult Reading Test, 383
National Training Programme, 54, 56
Nelson, Justice, 494
NEO Personality Inventory – Revised (NEO-PI-R), 398
Neuroticism, 47
Nickell, Rachel, murder of, 8
Nine Steps of Interrogation (Inbau et al.), 51, 118
non-coerced persuaded confessions, 205, 206
non-custodial confession, 240–2
non-custodial interrogation, 134
non-custodial pressure, false confession and, 212
non-emotional offenders, 13, 15–17
non-verbal behaviour, 34, 83
Norton, Dr Linda, 543
Norway, murder in, 590–614
　appeal, 609–11
　background to the case, 590–4
　arrest, 592–3
　Mr A as a witness, 591–2
　retraction, 594
　false belief vs. false memory, 613
　guilt or innocence?, 611–12
　interrogation and confinement, 606–8
　interviews with informants, 602–5
　manipulation of sexuality, 613
　pre-trial psychological evaluation, 594–5
　psychological evaluation prior to appeal, 596–602
　interview with Mr A, 599–602
　repression and psychogenic amnesia, 608–9
　solitary confinement, 612
　strengths and vulnerabilities of Mr A, 605–6
　trial, 595
Notice to Detained Persons, 71–2, 324
notoriety, morbid desire for, 194–5, 197
Novaco Anger Scale, 372

obedience to authority, 370
O'Brien, 496
offence characteristics, confession and, 146–8
　seriousness of the offence, 147–8
　type of offence, 146–7
offence specific information gathering, 45
official judgments of error, 164
Ofshe, Dr Richard, 300–1, 302

Ofshe–Leo model of confessions, 203–8
  coerced–compliant confessions, 204, 205, 206, 215
  coerced–persuaded, 206
  non-coerced persuaded confessions, 205, 206
  stress–compliant confessions, 204, 206
  voluntary confessions, 203–4, 207, 215
Ognall, Justice, 492
Olsen, Harald, 614
Openness, 47
Ophoven, Dr Janice, 543
opiates, effects of, 423–5
oppression, 252
Orange Socks murder, 556, 557, 559–60, 561–2
Other and Self-deception Questionnaires, 408
over-stimulation, 187

pain, physical and emotional, 31
panic attacks, 318
pantomime sequence, 82
paradoxical reactions, 419
Paranoia/Suspiciousness Questionnaire (PSQ), 372–3
paranoid schizophrenia, voluntary false confessions and, 218–19
Parris, Tony, 516
PASCE Codes of practice, 620
Pavlovian conditioning, 191
PEACE model, 53–4
Pearson, Larry, 564
peer loyalty, false confession and, 177
Peirce, Gareth, 516
Pendleton, Donald, 438, 533–6, 616
perception of proof, confession and, 152, 153, 157, 622
Perry, John, 166–7
persistence, 46
personal consequences, 118
personal identity, loss of, 30
personal qualities of interrogators/interviewers, 29
personal space, invasion of, 27
personality characteristics, 319
personality disorder, 318
  admissibility of evidence and, 276
  confession and, 155
  false confession and, 197
  voluntary false confessions and, 220–3
persuasive interrogation tactics, 41, 119
Phillips, Billy, 563–4, 570
Phillips, Mrs Sandra, 530, 532
physical abuse, 44
physiological events, confession and, 128

Pill, Lord Justice, 534
plea-bargaining, 185
Police and Criminal Evidence Act 1984 (PACE) (England and Wales), 24, 42, 47, 50, 51, 55, 67–8, 69, 149–50, 156, 171, 615–16, 617–18
  challenges to admissibility, 251–6
  Codes of Practice, 25, 52, 54, 68, 79, 247, 248, 249–50
  confession rate and, 138–9, 140
  definition of a confession in, 251
  detainees' legal rights under, 71–3
Police and Criminal Evidence (Northern Ireland) Order Act (1989), 247
police impropriety, 514–22
police interviewing, suggestibility and, 403–4
Police Interviewing Analysis Framework (PIAF), 75, 76, 114, 620
police training manuals, 7–9
polygraph examination, 11
Popplewell, Justice, 516
post-admission narrative, 179–80
post-confession interviews, 12
post-traumatic stress disorder, coercion resulting in, 35
Potts, Justice, 469, 527
Powe, Frank, 564
Powell, Frieda, 555, 556
Power, William, 452–6
prediction of confession, 70–1
pressured–compliant coercion, 211, 457
pressured–compliant false confession, 224–33, 625
  absence of mental disorder, 224–7
  admitting to death in self-defence, 231–3
  learning disability, 227–30, 230–1
pressured–internalized coercion, 211, 216, 457
pressured–internalized false confession, 127, 233–42, 625, 626
  eagerness to please, 239–40
  false belief, 233–4
  non-custodial confession, 240–2
  Peter Reilly, 234–7
  Sergeant E, 237–9
pre-trial reliability assessment, 213
Prevention of Terrorism Act, 446
previous convictions, 82, 144–6
  effect on rate of confession, 71, 73
  suggestibility and, 403
prima facie case, 273
Profile of Mood States, 427
projection, 96, 118, 120
promises, 206

property offenders, confession and, 147
pseudologia fantastica, 197
psychoanalytic models of confession, 122–4, 128
psychoanalytic theories, 190
psychological assessment, 308–31
   assessment framework, 309–16
     basic requirements, 309–11
     characteristics of the defendant, 312–13
     circumstances of arrest and custody, 312
     explanation for the alleged false confession, 315–16
     factors to be assessed, 311–16
     interrogative factors, 315
     mental and physical state during custody, 313–15
     retraction, 316
   court report and oral evidence, 327–30
psychological factor, confession and, 144
psychological (mental) vulnerability, 259–60, 316–19, 458–513, 621
psycho-physiological theories, 190, 191
psychoticism, confession and, 155
public confidence, coercion undermining, 36

Queen v. Gordon [1953], 444
questioning
   closed, 80
   leading, 80
   multiple, 81
   open, 80

R. v. Ali [1999], 263
R. v. Alladice [1988], 255, 278
R. v. Aspinall [1999], 255, 264
R. v. Barry George [2001], 275
R. v. Bentley [1999], 438, 506
R. v. Billy-Joe Friend [1997], 274
R. v. Birchall [1999], 273
R. v. Cox [1996], 251, 257
R. v. Delaney [1989], 277
R. v. Doldur [2000], 273
R. v. Fogah [1989], 263
R. v. French [1998], 573, 576
R. v. Goldenberg [1988], 254
R. v. Herbert [1990], 574, 576
R. v. Heron [1993], 53, 82
R. v. Hodgson [1998], 580
R. v. Hunt [1992], 255
R. v. Kenny [1994], 256
R. v. Law-Thompson [1997], 263
R. v. Lewis (Martin) [1996], 262
R. v. Long [1995], 492, 512
R. v. MacKenzie [1993], 472, 477, 512
R. v. Mackinney and Pinfold [1981], 276
R. v. Mason [1987], 255
R. v. McCreery [1999], 576
R. v. McGovern [1992], 257, 474
R. v. McIlkenny, Hill, Power, Walker, Hunter and Callaghan [1991], 454
R. v. Moham [1994], 580
R. v. Morse and Others [1991], 264
R. v. Moss [1990], 254–5
R. v. O'Brien, Hall and Sherewood [2000], 276
R. v. Paris, Abdullah and Miller [1993], 53, 82, 106–12, 253, 256, 257
R. v. Park [1999], 251
R. v. Priestley [1966], 253
R. v. Raghip [1991], 52, 481, 493, 616
R. v. Roberts [1997], 498, 499, 513, 573, 576
R. v. Sat-Bhambra, ante, 251
R. v. Silcott, Braithwaite, Raghip [1991], 278, 281
R. v. Stagg [1994], 573
R. v. Strudwick and Merry [1994], 276
R. v. Turner [1975], 275, 276
R. v. W and another [1994], 264
R. v. Ward [1992], 444, 492, 512
Raghip, Engin, 278, 303, 441, 442, 458–68, 512
   appeal, 466–7
   background, 459–60
   case of, 462–6
   comments, 467–8
   murder charges, 461–2
   psychological evidence, 460–1
raised/aggressive tone, 81
rapid eye movement (REM) sleep, 339
Raposo, 303
rapport, 28
rate of confession, 133–40
rationalization, 46, 118, 120
Raven's Coloured Matrices, 382
Raven's Standard Progressive Matrices, 367
reactance theory, 36, 399, 402
real consequences, 118
reality
   distorted perceptions of, 194, 198, 317
   monitoring, 195
reassurance, 83
recording the confession, 21–4
recovered memory
   false confession and, 212–15
   suggestibility and, 411–12
refreezing, doctrination of, 188, 189, 190

Reid Technique, 10–21, 37, 118–20, 128, 153, 190
  assumptions, 11
  coercive nature, 33, 34
  disclaimer, 10
  rate of confession and, 133
  steps for effective interrogation, 12–21
    converting an oral confession into a written confession, 20
    direct positive confrontation, 13
    handling denials, 17–18
    handling suspect's passive mood, 18
    having suspect orally related various details of offense, 20
    overcoming objections, 18
    presenting an alternative question, 19–20
    procurement and retention of suspect's attention, 18
    theme development, 13–14
    themes for emotional suspects, 14–15
    themes for non-emotional suspects, 15–17
Reilly, Peter, 234–7
relating, 119
reliability of confession evidence, 248–58
remorse, 84
reputation, 146
  confession inhibition and, 116
resentment, coerced confessions resulting in, 35
resisters, suggestibility and, 404–7
retracted confessions, 84, 177, 178, 181, 316
  cf. false confessions, 623–7
  frequency, 182–4
  timing of retraction, 182
revenge, voluntary false confession as, 223–4
Rich, Kate, 555, 556
Rich, Mrs, 558
Richardson, Carole, 446, 447, 448, 449, 450–2
right to silence, 46, 72, 84, 148–9
Roach, Jessica, 299
Roberts, John, 442, 492–3
Roberts, Judith, 482, 490, 491
Robinson, James, 519
Roch, Lord Justice, 472, 497, 519, 531
Rose, Andrew, 574–82
Rose, Justice, 469, 527, 531
Rosenberg Self-Esteem Scale, 372, 373, 374, 397–8
Rothman v. The Queen [1981], 573, 576
Rougier, Justice, 474

Royal Commission on Criminal Justice, 57, 72
  1993 study, 58–69
    aims, 58–9
    detainees' mental state at the police station, 61, 67, 68
    general background, 60
    IQ scores, 62–3, 64, 67, 68
    knowledge of their legal rights, 62, 67
    mental state prior to arrest, 60–1, 66
    methodology, 59–60
    psychological evaluation, 59–60, 62–6
    use of an appropriate adult, 61–2, 68
Royal Commission on Criminal Procedure, 39, 55
Royal Ulster Constabulary (RUC), 43–4
Russell, Head Constable, 501
Russians, interrogation methods, 186–7, 188
Ryan, Phil, Texas Ranger, 556, 558, 559–60, 561

Sachs, Justice, 534
Salih, Ahmet, 170
Salkovskis, Dr Paul, 462
Saunders, Mr, murder of, 495
schizophrenia, 68, 198
  voluntary false confessions and, 218–19
Schneckloth v. Bustamonte, 25
Schonell Graded Word Reading Test, 60, 63
Scottish Criminal Cases Review Commission, 438
self-blame, 84
self-defence, false confession in, 231–3
self-esteem
  manipulating, 83
  suggestibility and, 396–8
Semantic Differential Scales, 397
sensory deprivation, 31, 44
Sewell, Wendy, 439
sex offenders
  cases, 14
  confession and, 147, 154
shame, 13, 126–7
  reduction, 83
Shepherd, Dr Eric, 520
Sherwood, 496
shift, 363
Silcott, Winston, 461, 462, 464, 466
silence, use of, 81
Simpson, Bob, 543
situational events, confession and, 127–8
Skuse, Dr Frank, 452, 453, 454

sleep
  deprivation, 31, 389–90
  rapid eye movement (REM), 339
Smith, Dr, 502
Social Avoidance and Distress (SAD) scale, 387
social desirability, suggestibility and, 394–5
social events, confession and, 126
social isolation, 31
social learning theory approach, 124–5
socio-psychological theories, 190, 192, 215
sodium amytal, 124
Softley, P., study by, 43
special knowledge, misleading, 523–37
Spielberger State Anxiety Inventory, 35, 423, 425
Stafford v. DPP [1974], 475
State v. Christoff [1997], 16
State–Trait Anxiety Inventory (STAI) (Spielberger), 60, 65–6, 372, 386, 388, 427
Steel, Justice, 534
Steele, Chief Inspector, 525
Steinschneider, Dr Alfred, 542–3, 549
Steuart-Pownall, Don, 450
stress–compliant confessions, 204, 206
stressors, classes of, 26
suggestibility, 64, 200, 626
  age and, 380–1
  alcohol and, 428–30
  anger and, 400–2
  anxiety and, 385–8
  assertiveness and, 396
  coping strategies and, 395–6
  criteria, 308
  dissociation and fantasy proneness, 390–1
  ethnic background and, 380
  experimenter effect, 392–4
  eyewitness testimony and, 410–11
  false confessions and, 407–10
  field dependence and, 399–400
  gender and, 379–80
  hypnotic susceptibility and, 368–70
  impulsivity and, 388
  instructional manipulation, 391–2
  intelligence and, 381–4
  locus of control, 398–9
  memory and, 384–5
  MMPI-2 and, 389
  police interviewing and, 403–4
  previous convictions, 403
  recovered memory and, 411–12
  resisters and alleged false confessors, 404–7
  self-esteem and, 396–8
  sleep deprivation and, 389–90
  social desirability and, 394–5
  test setting and, 402–3
  see also suggestibility, interrogative
suggestibility, interrogative, 332–59
  characteristics, 335–6
  classification, 338–40
  definition, 344–7
  Gudjonsson–Clark theoretical model, 347–52
  historical background, 336–8
  primary, 338–9, 340, 358
  reinforcement and, 343
  secondary, 338–9, 340, 358
  state v. trait, 343–4
  tertial, 338
  theoretical approaches, 334–5
    experimental approach, 334–5, 353
    individual differences approach, 334–5, 353
  theories of, 340–3
superego, 123
supported direct accusation, 45
suspiciousness, 28
  suggestibility and, 401
swearing at suspect, 81

tactics, classification, 41
taken into consideration (TIC), 93, 134
tape recording of interrogation, 21–4
Taylor, Lord Chief Justice, 82, 476, 516, 532
Taylor, Peter, 529
test setting
  suggestibility and, 402–3
Thomas, Justice, 532
Thomas-Peters, Dr Brian, 497
thought reform, 187
threats, 31, 81–2, 206
Tierney, Dr, 526
Toohey v. Commissioner of Metropolitan Police [1965], 277
Tooley, Dr, 449
torture, 44
total suggestibility, 364
Tottenham Riots, 312, 441
Tottenham Three, 52, 55, 466
Toulson, Justice, 492
training in interviewing techniques, 619
trait and state anxiety, 65–6, 67
tranquillizers, 419
Traugott, Arthur, 299–300, 301
trickery *see* deception/trickery

true confessions, 622–3
  false confession and, differences between, 208–11
trust, 28
truth drug, 449
truthfulness of the confession, 256–8
T.S.D. v. State, 296
Tucker, Karle Faye, 563
Tudor, Justice, 257–8
Tunstall, Mrs Olive, 461, 466, 474–5, 494, 496, 497

uncertainty, 26, 27, 348, 353, 355
under-arousal, 31, 40
undercover operations, 8
under-stimulation, 187
unethical behaviour, 46
unfreezing, doctrination of, 188–9, 190, 191
United States v. Hall, 302, 304, 513
United States v. Zerbo, 291
University of Kent, research at, 44–8
upgrading, 46
Urbanski, Ray, 545

verbal abuse, 44
verbal confession, 181, 134
video-recording of interrogation, 21–4
Vineland Social Maturity Scale, 326
voire dire, 250, 256, 258–9, 618
  pre-test reliability assessment, 213
voluntariness, 252
  Canadian law on, 576
  and mentally vulnerable suspects, 288–93
  under *Miranda*, 285–7

voluntary confessions, 203–4, 207, 215
voluntary false confessions, 194–5, 218–24, 625
voluntary types, 194
vulnerable defendants, 259–75

Walker, John, 452–6
Walkley, J.: *Police Interrogation., A Handbook for Investigators*, 7, 51–2
Walsh [1990], 255
Walsh, D. study by, 43–4
Walters, Judith, 563–4, 565, 566–9
Walters, Sheila, 563–4, 565, 566
Ward, Eric, 466
Ward, Judith, 319, 442, 470–2
Warren, Frank, 181
Washington, Earl, 166, 289–90
Watkins, Lord Justice, 531
Wechsler Adult Intelligence Scale Revised (WAIS-R), 60, 322, 322, 379, 382, 407
WAIS-III, 322, 323
weight and line pairs tasks, 339
White, Miss, murder of, 515, 516
Wilder, Lawrence Douglas, 290, 554
Wille, John, 319, 563–72
Withdrawal Problems Scale, 423
witness information, 82
written confessions, 134

Young, Dr Susan, 275
Youth Justice and Criminal Evidence Act 1999, 263, 273

Zerbo, Anthony, 291–2
Zimbardo, P.G., 9